ELIZABETHAN PLAYS

ELIZABETHAN PLAYS

EDITED BY

ARTHUR H. NETHERCOT

FRANKLYN BLISS SNYDER PROFESSOR
OF ENGLISH, EMERITUS
NORTHWESTERN UNIVERSITY

CHARLES R. BASKERVILL

LATE PROFESSOR OF ENGLISH
UNIVERSITY OF CHICAGO

VIRGIL B. HELTZEL

PROFESSOR OF ENGLISH, EMERITUS
NORTHWESTERN UNIVERSITY

REVISED BY

ARTHUR H. NETHERCOT

HOLT, RINEHART AND WINSTON, INC.
New York · Chicago · San Francisco · Atlanta · Dallas
Montreal · Toronto · London · Sydney

PREFACE

This collection of Elizabethan and Stuart plays exclusive of Shakespeare has the advantage of a larger compass than similar anthologies for students. It opens with such plays as *Roister Doister*, *Gammer Gurton's Needle*, and *Gorboduc*, in which, through imitation of the classics, English drama broke with medieval tradition as represented in the hybrid moralities, and it extends to the closing of the theaters in 1642, when the tone of the drama was already foreshadowing the Restoration period. Enough plays are included, moreover, to show the richness and variety of the great dramatic art of the era without neglecting the various phases of its historical development. It has been possible, for example, to print five plays and a masque as representative of Jonson's work, and at the same time to give specimens of popular romantic drama like *Mucedorus* or of a hitherto neglected form like the jig. All the significant types of drama in the period are illustrated here.

The plays have been arranged in two groups as Elizabethan and Stuart for the purpose of emphasizing what is distinctive in each period. In this way the Elizabethan group may more readily be studied in connection with medieval drama or Shakespeare, and the Stuart group as a background for Restoration drama. The division is useful even when the two eras are studied together. In Shakespeare's immediate predecessors and contemporaries, the Elizabethan characteristics of boldness of conception and execution are obvious, resulting in an imaginative and emotional power which is frequently accompanied by a disregard for restraint, structure, and form. This distinctive quality survives in the final work of Shakespeare and in the two great tragedies of Webster, so that *The Duchess of Malfi*, in spite of its late date, is included with the Elizabethan plays. Already, however, Jonson had written his chief works that represent the Stuart reaction in drama, following classical ideals of restraint and unity in design; and a change of attitude, with a more searching study of manners, resulted. The centering of interest on form and technique, even in romantic plays, gives a sufficiently distinct character to the plays of the Stuart period as a whole.

The text used as a basis of the editing is indicated in the introduction to each play. For about half the plays, original early editions, photostatic copies of them, reproductions in the Farmer Facsimile Texts, or facsimile reprints of the Malone Society have been used. The rest are based on standard modern editions, in most cases recent critical editions. These have also been checked with other modern editions, or where possible with Farmer Facsimiles or the Malone Society reproductions. In whatever affects the actual content of the play, including stage directions, the principle followed has been one of strict fidelity to the original. Emendations have been avoided when any logical interpretation of the reading given seemed possible, and those adopted are duly recorded in the footnotes. Added material has been enclosed in square brackets. When no source of an emendation is stated, it has been made on the authority of the basic text, except that in stage directions the bracketed material has usually been added by the present editors. Plays with no act and scene division have been divided simply into scenes, with bracketed numbers. Likewise few liberties have been taken with the verse arrangement found in the sixteenth and seventeenth century originals, unless by a simple change in the division of lines a whole passage could be made to fall into pattern. Footnotes call attention to such revision in the plays in which it occurs. In *George a Greene* and the additions to *The Spanish Tragedy*, there are so many doubtful cases or cases in which no satisfactory arrangement of the lines is possible that no attempt has been made to change the original arrangement even in the passages where the dramatist's intention seems fairly clear.

In matters of less fundamental importance, the editing has been done with a view to aiding the student who is interested primarily in the literary and dramatic qualities of the plays. Hence spelling, punctuation, and capitalization have been modernized.

Where differences in spelling, however, suggest significant differences in pronunciation resulting from the survival in Elizabethan times of variant forms now obsolete (as in *hunderd, renowm, accompt,* for example), the original has been followed, at times even in doubtful cases. On the other hand, in certain very common words where the vowel varies so frequently as to suggest that perhaps to an Elizabethan there was little distinction in sound, the modern spelling has been adopted. Examples include the use of *than* for *then* (in the modern sense of *than*), *whither* and *hither* for *whether* and *hether* (except in dialect or consciously archaic passages or for rime), *devil* for *divel, show* for *shew, ambassador* for *embassador,* and many *in-* combinations for *en-* combinations (for instance, *increase* for *encrease*). In such original forms as *marchant* and *clark,* -*er-* has regularly been substituted for -*ar-*. The spellings *dost* and *doth,* rather than *doest* and *doeth,* are regularly used for the words as auxiliaries. *Wive's* as a possessive singular is printed *wife's,* but in general such voicings have been retained whenever any modern justification for them could be found. Again, obvious misprints have been silently corrected throughout. Numerals also are written out, and a compound form like 24 is expanded into the common Elizabethan form *four-and-twenty*. In many of the plays, speech heads vary so irrationally that they have been frankly reduced to some consistency. The prevalent or the most logical form of each speaker's name, usually an abbreviation, has been adopted throughout a play, except that, where there are two or three different names for the same speaker, they are retained, with explanation in the notes. As the original speech heads in *Cambises* are printed in full consistently, however, they have been left unchanged. It is perhaps unnecessary to mention the omission of imprints, colophons, titles repeated at the head of the text proper, and running heads, or the occasional disregard of certain unusual arrangements of the material on the page of the original.

As an aid in the matter of meter, an accent has been placed over *e* in the verbal suffix -*ed* when it is pronounced as an additional syllable contrary to ordinary usage, and an apostrophe marks the omission of a vowel when a shortening in pronunciation seems to be indicated by the spelling of the original (as in *wav'ring,* for example). For the rest, it is felt that with a little attention to Elizabethan practice, the reader will quickly fall into the rhythm of the various dramatists, representing various periods. Especially after playwrights learned to give verse some of the flexibility of speech, blank verse was handled very freely. Occasionally the line is as short as one foot, or as long as six. The foot may have an extra syllable, or a syllable may be omitted, usually at the beginning of a line or after a pause. Inverted stress is frequent in the first foot and occasionally occurs elsewhere, especially after a pause. It is to be noted also that some Elizabethan words differ from modern usage in the position of the accent, and a much larger number seems to have been very flexible as to accent, at least in verse. *Academy, revénue, infámous, envý, cómplete, canónize, obdúrate, pórtray, déprive,* and *aspéct* are a few examples taken from the plays printed here. Another large group of words, especially those with endings in -*ion,* -*ian,* -*ia,* -*ience,* -*ier,* etc., are often to be scanned as having a syllable more than is normal in modern pronunciation (as in *motion, ocean, Christian, Persia, Delia, soldier, marriage*). Not infrequently, too, an extra syllable is developed, especially in connection with *l* and *r* (as in *fair, fire, hour, mild, sure, sworn*).

Webster's *Collegiate Dictionary* has been taken as the standard of what the reader might properly be expected to know in the matter of current vocabulary. Old forms that are not obvious, and words and phrases that are obsolete, or have shifted meaning, or for any other reason might not be understood, have been explained in the notes for each play, but as a rule only in the first occurrence in a given play.

The editors wish to thank Professor J. C. Murley, Professor J. G. Fucilla, and Dr. N. A. Bennetton for help in translating a few difficult or corrupt passages from Latin, Italian, and Spanish, and Professor F. H. Heidbrink, Professor M. E. Prior, Dr. L. S. Wright, and Dr. Z. S. Fink for help in proof-reading the second part.

PREFACE TO THE REVISED EDITION

Since the first publication of this anthology thirty-five years ago so many new articles and books on Elizabethan and Stuart drama and its biographical, intellectual, and artistic environment have appeared that it became obvious that a revised edition was called for to maintain the collection's appeal to the large body of students and teachers who have found it useful. In accordance with recent textbook-format trends and for ease in handling, it was decided to publish this edition in two volumes, one to be entitled *Elizabethan Plays* and the other *Stuart Plays*, rather than in the one bulky volume.

In undertaking this revision alone, since Professor Baskervill is dead and Professor Heltzel is unavailable for anything more than consultation because of his residence in Austria, I have completely rewritten and considerably expanded the introductions to the plays in order to take advantage of what I consider the most important of the new articles and books which have recently come out. To make these introductions more interesting to the student, I have given much more attention to the lives of the playwrights, in the hope that this approach will help to make the times in which they lived more vivid. While retaining the initial and elastic Elizabethan spelling and punctuation for direct quotations from documents, manuscripts, and original texts, in order to add authenticity and picturesqueness to the portrayal of Elizabethan life, I have kept the modernized spelling and punctuation of the plays themselves and the titles of the various works referred to.

For teachers I have endeavored to furnish concise digests of the most important of the published ideas and discoveries of their fellow-scholars. For the most part I have tried to present points of view impartially whenever controversies over interpretations, purposes, textual problems, datings, etc., have arisen. In this way I have attempted to raise discussion questions without giving answers, and have, I hope, cleared the ground of some bibliographical and biographical underbrush that might otherwise have to be disposed of through time-consuming lectures. The bibliographical paraphernalia which may seem to pockmark some of the pages have been inserted for the guidance and reassurance of the teacher, and may well be skimmed by the well-trained student who knows what is useful for his own purpose. In the case of books of a general nature, which deal with genres, ideas, influences, and movements, affecting many individual playwrights, I have given the imprint of publication only on their first citation. Knowing that our anthology offers a much wider range of plays to choose from than any other on the market and realizing that probably few instructors will be able to use all the plays and introductions, I suggest that when a new title turns up without an identifying imprint it may be found by looking back through earlier introductions.

The texts of the plays have remained essentially the same, since many users of the anthology have assured me that they have found them sound. I have, however, been able to correct inevitable typographical errors and to improve many footnotes and add new ones by taking advantage of the several excellent editions of individual plays that have recently been published. I take this opportunity of thanking their editors for their unwitting aid in making many of these glosses more helpful and meaningful than they might otherwise have been.

Only two changes have been made in the selection of plays to be included. In the first volume, *Elizabethan Plays*, the 1616 text of Marlowe's *Doctor Faustus* has been substituted for the former 1604 text, since the consensus of recent scholarship seems to have concluded that the later and longer version is closer to what Marlowe intended. In second volume, *Stuart Plays*, *The Revenger's Tragedy* has been added by popular demand. We had planned to use it in the 1934 edition, but it was forced out by lack of space. Because of the intense recent interest in the play (which I am listing as anonymous), it is now impossible to keep it out of any group of representative Jacobean dramas. I am also shifting Webster's *The Duchess of Malfi* from the first to the second volume, where it clearly belongs.

A.H.N.

January, 1971

ABBREVIATIONS

To save space, the following abbreviations of the names of periodicals and series have been used in the introductions:

AS	*Aberystwyth Studies*
AUL	*Annales de l'Université de Lyons*
BRMMLA	*Bulletin of the Rocky Mountain Modern Language Association*
BUW	*Bulletin of the University of Wisconsin*
CE	*College English*
DUJ	*Durham University Journal*
EA	*Études Anglaises*
ELH	*English Literary History*
E&S	*Essays and Studies*
ES	*English Studies*
F	*Folklore*
FUS	*Furman University Studies*
HLQ	*Huntington Library Quarterly*
HSNPL	*Harvard Studies and Notes in Philology and Literature*
HSE	*Harvard Studies in English*
JEGP	*Journal of English and Germanic Philology*
MLN	*Modern Language Notes*
MLQ	*Modern Language Quarterly*
MLR	*Modern Language Review*
MP	*Modern Philology*
NQ	*Notes and Queries*
PLPS	*Proceedings of the Leeds Philosophical Society*
PQ	*Philological Quarterly*
REL	*Review of English Literature*
RES	*Review of English Studies*
RLC	*Revue de la Littérature Comparée*
S	*Scrutiny*
SAB	*Shakespeare Association Bulletin*
SAS	*Stratford-upon-Avon Studies*
SJ	*Shakespeare Jahrbuch*
SP	*Studies in Philology*
TLS	*London Times Literary Supplement*
TRSC	*Transactions of the Royal Society of Canada*
UIS	*University of Illinois Studies*
UNS	*University of Nebraska Studies*
UTSE	*University of Texas Studies in English*
YSE	*Yale Studies in English*
YWES	*Year's Work in English Studies*

CONTENTS

ELIZABETHAN PLAYS

NICHOLAS UDALL

One day in the early nineteenth century the Reverend Thomas Briggs attended a public auction of books and came away with what has so far turned out to be a unique copy, in black letter, of *Roister Doister*, which shares with *Gammer Gurton's Needle* the somewhat misleading designation of "the first regular English comedy." "Regular" would seem to many historians of English drama to mean that it followed the established classical rules or principles.

Sometime between July 22, 1566, and July 22, 1567, the Register of the stationers, printers, and booksellers of London recorded a fee of fourpence as "Recevyd of Thomas hackett for his lycence for pryntinge of a play intituled Rauf Ruyster Duster, etc." Since Briggs's copy lacked either a title page or a colophon, it was fortunate that Thomas Wilson, an old Etonian pupil of Nicholas Udall's, in the third edition of *The Rule of Reason, Containing the Art of Logic* (1553), had printed, as an example of the vast difference punctuation can make in the meaning of a text, the garbled letter which Ralph Roister Doister had carelessly copied from his scrivener and sent to the object of his suit, Dame Christian Custance. Wilson had stated that this letter was "taken out of an entrelude made by Nicolas Vdal." (Udall had already written a few introductory lines for Wilson's *The Art of Rhetoric* in the same year.) *Roister Doister* then dropped out of sight until Thomas Tanner mentioned it in his *Bibliotheca Britannica-Hibernica* in 1748. Then it again disappeared until 1813, when Philip Bliss alluded to Tanner's reference in his re-edition of Anthony à Wood's *Athenae Oxonienses*. It remained for J. P. Collier in his 1825 *Select Collection of Old Plays* to put these fragments together and determine authorship. However, the play had already been printed in 1818 by its discoverer, Thomas Briggs, an old Etonian, who had then loyally deposited it in the Eton College library, where it still lies. The history of this playbook became so romantically famous that on April 22, 1922, a correspondent signing himself simply C. K. S. (Clement K. Shorter) wrote to *The Nation and Athenaeum* in London that a complete copy of the play, with the missing title page, had just been discovered behind a modern grate in a chimney corner by the unidentified owner of a country house; but a note in *Notes and Queries* as late as 1940 was unable to elicit any further information about this probably fictitious copy.

Nicholas Udall (the name also appears as Owdall, Owdale, Woodall, Wodale, Uvedale, Vuedale, and so on) was born in the parish of the Holy Rood, Southampton, about Christmastime in 1504, 1505, or 1506. (The records are incomplete and the references contradictory.) He got his early education at St. Mary's College (really a "school," according to today's terminology), Winchester. (Winchester's modern archivist, Herbert Chitty, has unearthed many new facts from the records of the school and town, made use of by G. Scheurweghs in his painstaking and elaborate edition of *Nicholas Udall's Roister Doister*, Vol. XVI of the Bang-DeVocht *Materials for the Study of the Old English Drama* (Louvain' 1939). Nicholas's father, or at least a close relative, may have been Thomas Wodale (or Owdal), a notary who from 1510 to 1525 resided in or owned a tenement in Kingsgate Street near the school. The boy was entered in St. Mary's register in 1517 and remained at least until January 15, 1520. Instead of going to New College, Oxford, as Winchester boys generally did, he was admitted to Corpus Christi by its founder, Richard Fox, Bishop of Winchester, on June 18, 1520, although he did not take up residence until 1521. After a time he was appointed lecturer for the younger students and received a small stipend for teaching in 1526–7 and 1528–9. Finally, after being elected a Fellow, he was given his B.A. degree in 1526, as "Nicolaus Woddallys." During his stay at the University he displayed the first sign of rebelliousness and unconventionality, for he got into trouble with the authorities because of his involvement with one Thomas Garet, who was suspected of Lutheranism, a dangerous persuasion during these early days leading to the Reformation. He left Oxford in 1529, but in 1534 declared that he had studied outside it for five years.

Sometime before May 1533, he got an appointment as a teacher in a London grammar school, possibly St. Anthony's. About Whitsuntide of that year he and his fellow-Oxonian John Leland, recently appointed King's Antiquary, composed verses and songs to be used in various pageants at Queen Anne Boleyn's coronation. Udall's first important literary and educational work, however, came in the next year: *Flowers for Latin Speaking, Selected and Gathered out of Terence, and the Same Translated into English*. Although this textbook was often reprinted during the sixteenth century, when Udall later "supplicated" for and received his M.A. in 1534, the University authorities for some unknown reason asked him not to translate any more Latin works into English. As might be expected, the independent young teacher paid no attention to this recommendation, and within a few years achieved a high reputation as a classical scholar and author.

In June 1534 he was made a "headmaster" at Eton College, which meant simply that he was engaged as a teacher of the humanities. Part of his job was to oversee the production of school plays, one of which was given before Thomas Cromwell himself, Cardinal Wolsey's favorite and the secretary of the Privy Council. Although Udall soon became noted for both his learning and his severity in punishment, he also revealed the kind of anomalous streak which marked so many Renaissance men of talent: his public and private lives were quite different things. He quickly fell into a morass of debts, and on November 25, 1538, was actually outlawed from the city of London until he paid them. Only after several court appearances and a final settlement (discussed by H. J. Byrom in "Some Lawsuits of Nicholas Udall" in *RES*, 1935) was he able to take advantage of the 1544 Act of General Pardon. In 1537 he was appointed Vicar of Braintree, London, although he never took holy orders or even resided there. It is suspected that he paid a curate to perform his parochial duties and pocketed the rest of this income. He kept this vicarage until December 1544, although in 1541 he, along with his servant and two late scholars at the college, was suspected of being involved in a theft of silver plate and other articles from the school. While apparently not guilty of the actual theft, he was committed to the Marshalsea prison for some months and dismissed from his job. Even a long and repentant letter to Sir Thomas Wriothesley of Titchfield, one of the Secretaries of State and a friend of his friend John Leland, was unsuccessful in regaining his position. In this letter, as Scheurweghs puts it, he "humbly owns that he has led up to then an unruly life, doing his work very carelessly, neglecting study and teaching, losing his time in laziness and indulging in riotous pleasure," including "buggery" with one of the students; and so on.

In spite of these misadventures, Udall continued his scholarly interests and in 1542 published his *Apophthegms*, a translation of Erasmus's *Apothegmata*. Although he was still heavily in debt, he lent money to his friends as well as borrowed it, and by 1545 even owned a "tenement" in the Greyfriars district in London, which he was fined for keeping in very bad repair. He was still in and out of the courts for his financial transactions, but had friends in high places and later received aid from Queen Catherine Parr. It was at her request that in 1545 he accepted the translation of Erasmus's paraphrase upon the gospel of Luke in his *Paraphrases* of the New Testament, and when in 1547 the Privy Council ordered that copies of Erasmus's work, in English, were to be set up in all the churches, the editing of the first volume, containing the Gospels and the Acts, was entrusted to Udall. In his preface to his translation of the Luke paraphrase he showed increasing allegiance to the Reformation in all its phases and informed the Queen of his desire to translate into English all the best Latin works conducive to the New Learning so that they could be brought within the range of the ordinary reader. Because of these intentions he was granted patent letters by the Lord Chancellor to print, in 1550, his translation of Peter Martyr's *Tractatio de Sacramento Eucharistiae* and other works. For these educational and cultural contributions he was highly praised by leaders such as John Bale (bishop, militant Protestant reformer, and author of several morality and mystery plays), and was commonly designated as "generosus," or "gentleman," in official documents.

Udall was still living in London in 1550. By June 1552 his income had considerably improved, but his financial troubles made him no stranger to the civil courts, whose records preserve a great deal of what is known of his private affairs. At the end of 1551 he was appointed a prebendary of the Royal Chapter of St. George within Windsor Castle and moved to Windsor, but apparently did not work too hard to earn his special stipend by preaching. Nevertheless, in March 1553 he was made rector of Calborne, Newport, on the Isle of Wight, but probably never went there. Back in London by the Easter Term of 1554, he was once more arrested for not paying for a ring he had acquired several years before. Yet on December 16, 1555, he was made a master at St. Peter's Grammar School (better known unofficially as Westminster School), which was affiliated with the Abbey. A "Nicholas Yevedale" was buried in St. Margaret's Church, Westminster, on December 23, 1556.

As an author Udall's interests were by no means confined to classical translations and religious works. Bishop Bale, in his important *Scriptorum Illustrium Majoris Britanniae . . . Catalogus*, or *Catalogue of Illustrious Writers of Great Britain* (1557), listed as one of the items in Udall's bibliography: "Comoedias plures, Lib. I." This volume of "Several Comedies" has never been discovered, but many traces of Udall's interest in the drama and in theatrical performances remain. He directed school plays at Eton and many scholars, such as Willi Bang, Leicester Bradner, Laurie Magnus, A. R. Moon, W. H. Williams, and E. K. Chambers, attribute to him many anonymous plays, such as *Placidas, Jacob and Esau, Jack Juggeler, Respublica*, and *Thersites*. Jules E. Bernard, Jr., in *The Prosody of the Tudor Interlude* (*YSE*, 1939), has found what he regards as metrical support for Udall's authorship of *Respublica* and *Jack Juggeler*, but not for *Thersites*. It is known, too, that Udall wrote a play entitled *Ezekias* (i.e., *Hezekiah*, obviously not a comedy) and that it was performed before Queen Elizabeth on her visit to Cambridge University in 1564. But the play is not extant. During the reign of the violently Roman Catholic Bloody Mary, with whom he managed to stay on friendly terms in spite of his Erasmian Protestantism (see William L. Edgerton, "The Apostasy of Nicholas Udall," *NQ*, 1950), Udall established a connection with the court theater. Payments for "certen plaies made by Nichols vdall" were made by the Clerk of the Revels between December 13, 1554, and January 6, 1555, and the Master of the Revels was ordered by the Queen to "delyuer or cause to be delyuered to the said vdall . . . soche apperel for his Auctors as he shall thinke necessarye and requisite for the furnishing and condigne setting forth of his Devises before vs and soche as may be semely to be shewid in our Royall presens," and to continue this coöperation "from tyme to tyme . . . ." Scheurweghs, however, thinks that these orders do not prove any permanent appointment with the court theater and certainly do not show any clear association with the court masques.

The only extant play, therefore, that can be confidently assigned to Udall is *Roister Doister*. This comedy in its simple, almost naive, indigenous English features might not at first seem to have emanated from a playwright with such a life and background. But classical and humanistic elements, clearly present, could easily have come from this quill. Although early students of the play assigned it to Udall's Eton period, it is now generally assigned to the last years of his life. From topical references in the play itself, Scheurweghs concludes that it must have been written between 1545 and 1552.

He prefers the later date because of the final prayer. He believes the prayer was originally addressed to Edward VI, but that pronouns were changed to fit Mary, during whose reign Udall died. (See also William Peery, "The Prayer for the Queen in *Roister Doister*," *UTSE*, 1948, and Edgerton, *op. cit.*) The play was apparently composed as a Christmas comedy for the boys at some London school. (Herbert T. Webster in *"Ralph Roister Doister* and the Little Eyases," *NQ*, 1951, discusses several episodes which "seem to be addressed to a childhood world which had been rarely invoked in Udall's time.")

For his plot Udall obviously drew on several classical comedies which would have been familiar to his audience, both youthful and adult: the general "braggart soldier" motif from Plautus's *Miles Gloriosus;* the story of Roister Doister's wooing from Terence's *Eunuchus;* and perhaps the idea of imagining oneself to be dead from Terence's *Phormio.* The parody of the burial service was probably suggested by the poem "On the Death of the Duke of Suffolk" on May 3, 1450, or perhaps some intermediate imitation of this poem by John Skelton, Alexander Barclay, or Erasmus. Edwin S. Miller discusses the liturgical aspects of the scene in "Roister Doister's Funeralls" (*SP*, 1946) and suggests that its satirical or nonsatirical tone would depend on the date; that is, on whether the Roman liturgy was or was not in favor. In *From "Mankind" to Marlowe: Growth of Structure in the Popular Drama of Tudor England* (Harvard, 1962), D. M. Bevington concludes that the recurrence of certain classical structural elements in early Tudor drama, including courtly and humanistic plays performed by schoolboys and college students as in *Roister Doister*, goes to prove that "the elite never lost contact with the native stage." Scheurweghs points out that, although the setting has the complete unity of place of classical comedy, the action covers almost three days and thus stretches the unity of time. He also believes that Udall did not intend his play to be divided into scenes because no regular principle of scene division seems to be followed. He attributes the present state of the text, with the two songs relegated to a sort of appendix, to the surmised fact that they existed in separate leaflet form and that the whole play had been handled freely in manuscript form by choirmasters, stage directors, and copyists before being finally turned over to a rather incompetent printer after Udall's death.

Aspects of the play which would give it an appeal to more mature and sophisticated audiences have also been noted. In "The Elizabethan Dramatic Parasite" (*SP*, 1935) E. P. Vandiver has maintained that the character type which began with Merrygreek was essentially a composite of the classical parasite, the Vice of the morality plays, the Italian parasite of the *commedia erudita* and the *commedia dell'arte*, and the parasite of the Teutonic school-drama, in which he was "regarded as a very opprobrious character." In "Satirical Parody in *Roister Doister:* A Reinterpretation" (*SP*, 1964) G. W. Plumstead has directed attention to another overlooked dimension of the play: its parody of the chivalric love ethic of humility, courtesy, and "gentilesse," which makes the principal characters much funnier than mere imitations of the stock braggart soldier, the mistress, and the parasite of Roman comedy. Finally, in *"Ralph Roister Doister:* Miles vs. Clericus" (*NQ*, 1960) Nan Cooke Carpenter has related the situation to the medieval debate, the play being a sort of dramatization of the question of who is the ideal lover— the soldier or the scholar—and deciding it in favor of neither, but giving the answer to a member of the rising wealthy merchant class.

Of the several modern reprints of the play, the text of Ewald Flügel in C. M. Gayley's *Representative English Comedies* has been generally followed, even to the extent of beginning a new line for each speech. In the original, however, the speeches, if short or irregular in length, were run along on the same line until a rhyming word was reached (the prosodic form), after starting with a limping rhyme royal, and becoming in general a rough Alexandrine or iambic hexameter.

ROISTER DOISTER

BY

NICHOLAS UDALL

[DRAMATIS PERSONÆ

RALPH ROISTER[1] DOISTER, *a braggart.*
MATTHEW MERRYGREEK,[2] *a parasite.*
GAWIN GOODLUCK, *betrothed to Dame Custance.*
TRISTRAM TRUSTY, *his friend.*
DOBINET DOUGHTY, *a boy* } *servants to Roister Doister.*
HARPAX[3] }
TOM TRUEPENNY, *a boy, servant to Dame Custance.*

SIM SURESBY, *servant to Goodluck.*
SCRIVENER.
MUSICIANS *and* OTHERS.

DAME CHRISTIAN CUSTANCE,[4] *a widow.*
MARGERY, *or* MADGE, MUMBLECRUST, *her old nurse.*

TIBET TALKAPACE } *her maids.*
ANNOT ALYFACE[5] }

SCENE: *The scene remains fixed throughout as a street, probably in London, with the house of Custance on one side and that of Roister Doister on the other.*

TIME: *Contemporary.*]

THE PROLOGUE

What creature is in health, either young or
    old,
  But some mirth with modesty will be
    glad to use,
As[6] we in this interlude shall now unfold,
  Wherein all scurrility we utterly refuse,
  Avoiding such mirth wherein is abuse,
Knowing nothing more commendable for a
    man's recreation
Than mirth which is used in an honest
    fashion?

For mirth prolongeth life and causeth
    health;
  Mirth recreates our spirits and voideth
    pensiveness;
  Mirth increaseth amity, not hind'ring our
    wealth;   10
  Mirth is to be used both of more and less,[7]

Being mixed with virtue in decent comeliness,
  As we trust no good nature can gainsay
    the same—
Which mirth we intend to use, avoiding
    all blame.

The wise poets long time heretofore,
  Under merry comedies secrets did declare,
Wherein was contained very virtuous lore,
  With mysteries and forewarnings very
    rare.
  Such to write neither Plautus nor Terence did spare,
Which among the learned at this day bears
    the bell;   20
These with such other therein did excel.

Our comedy or interlude which we intend
    to play
  Is named *Roister Doister* indeed,
Which against the vainglorious doth inveigh,
  Whose humor the roisting[8] sort continually doth feed.
  Thus by your patience we intend to
    proceed
In this our interlude by God's leave and
    grace,
And here I take my leave for a certain space.

[1] To roist was to bluster or bully. The meaning of most of the humors names in the cast is self-explanatory.
[2] A common expression for a boon companion. "Greek" also carried the implication of a sharper or cunning person.
[3] Rapacious (a slave in Plautus).
[4] Constance, or constancy.
[5] Beery face.   [6] Such as.
[7] By great and small.
[8] Blustering.

FINIS.

5

ACTUS I. SCENA i.

Matthew Merrygreek. He ent'reth singing.

[M. MERRY.] As long liveth the merry man,
  they say,
As doth the sorry man, and longer by a
  day.
Yet the grasshopper, for all his summer
  piping,
Starveth in winter with hungry griping;
Therefore another said saw[1] doth men
  advise
That they be together both merry and
  wise.
This lesson must I practice, or else ere
  long,
With me, Matthew Merrygreek, it will
  be wrong.
Indeed men so call me, for by Him that
  us bought,
Whatever chance betide, I can take no
  thought;   10
Yet wisdom would that I did myself
  bethink
Where to be provided this day of meat
  and drink;
For know ye that, for all this merry
  note of mine,
He might appose[2] me now that should
  ask where I dine.
My living lieth here and there, of God's
  grace:
Sometime with this good man, sometime
  in that place;
Sometime Lewis Loit'rer[3] biddeth me
  come near;
Somewhiles Watkin Waster maketh us
  good cheer;
Sometime Davy Diceplayer, when he
  hath well cast,
Keepeth revel rout as long as it will
  last;   20
Sometime Tom Titivile maketh us a
  feast;
Sometime with Sir Hugh Pie I am a
  bidden guest;
Sometime at Nichol Neverthrive's I get
  ·a sop;
Sometime I am feasted with Bryan
  Blinkinsop;

Sometime I hang on Hankin Hoddy-
  doddy's sleeve,
But this day on Ralph Roister Doister's
  by his leave.
For truly of all men he is my chief
  banker
Both for meat and money, and my chief
  shoot-anchor.[4]
For, sooth [5] Roister Doister in that he
  doth say,
And, require what ye will, ye shall have
  no nay.   30
But now of Roister Doister somewhat to
  express,
That ye may esteem him after his
  worthiness,
In these twenty towns and seek them
  throughout,
Is not the like stock, whereon to graff [6]
  a lout.
All the day long is he facing and craking [7]
Of his great acts in fighting and fray-
  making;
But when Roister Doister is put to his
  proof,
To keep the queen's peace is more for
  his behoof.
If any woman smile or cast on him an
  eye,
Up is he to the hard ears in love by-and-
  by,[8]   40
And in all the hot haste must she be his
  wife,
Else farewell his good days, and farewell
  his life.
Master Rafe [9] Roister Doister is but
  dead and gone
Except she on him take some compas-
  sion;
Then chief of counsel must be Matthew
  Merrygreek.
"What if I for marriage to such an one
  seek?"
Then must I sooth it, whatever it is;
For what he saith or doth cannot be
  amiss.
Hold up his yea and nay, be his nown
  white son,[10]
Praise and rouse him well, and ye have
  his heart won,   50

---

[1] Much repeated proverb.   [2] Nonplus.
[3] Most of these humors names are probably
from well-known mystery, miracle, and morality
plays and interludes.

[4] Sheet-anchor.   [8] Immediately.
[5] Soothe, support.   [9] Variant of *Ralph*.
[6] Graft.   [10] His own dear friend.
[7] Bullying and boasting.

For so well liketh he his own fond [1] fash-
ions
That he taketh pride of false commenda-
tions.
But such sport have I with him as I
would not leese,[2]
Though I should be bound to live with
bread and cheese.
For exalt him, and have him as ye lust [3]
indeed—
Yea, to hold his finger in a hole for a
need.
I can with a word make him fain or loath;
I can with as much make him pleased or
wroth;
I can when I will make him merry and
glad;
I can when me lust make him sorry and
sad;   60
I can set him in hope and eke in despair;
I can make him speak rough and make
him speak fair.
But I marvel I see him not all this same
day.
I will seek him out.—But lo, he cometh
this way!
I have yond espied him sadly coming,
And in love for twenty pound, by his
glomming.[4]

ACTUS I. SCENA ii.

Rafe Roister Doister, Matthew Merrygreek.

R. ROISTER. Come, death, when thou wilt!
I am weary of my life!
M. MERRY. [*Aside.*] I told you, I, we
should woo another wife.
R. ROISTER. Why did God make me such
a goodly person?
M. MERRY. [*Aside.*] He is in by the
week;[5] we shall have sport anon.[6]
R. ROISTER. And where is my trusty
friend, Matthew Merrygreek?
M. MERRY. [*Aside.*] I will make as I saw
him not; he doth me seek.
R. ROISTER. I have him espied, methink-
eth; yond is he.
Ho! Matthew Merrygreek, my friend,
a word with thee.
M. MERRY. [*Aside.*] I will not hear him,
but make as I had haste.—

[*To the audience.*] Farewell, all my good
friends; the time away doth waste. 10
And the tide, they say, tarrieth for no
man.
R. ROISTER. Thou must with thy good
counsel help me if thou can.
M. MERRY. God keep thee, worshipful
Master Roister Doister,
And fare well thee, lusty Master Roister
Doister.
R. ROISTER. I must needs speak with thee
a word or twain.
M. MERRY. Within a month or two I will
be here again.
Negligence in great affairs, ye know, may
mar all.
R. ROISTER. Attend upon me now, and
well reward thee I shall.
M. MERRY. I have take my leave, and the
tide is well spent.
R. ROISTER. I die except thou help; I pray
thee, be content. 20
Do thy part well now, and ask what thou
wilt,
For without thy aid my matter is all
spilt.
M. MERRY. Then to serve your turn I will
some pains take,
And let all mine own affairs alone for your
sake.
R. ROISTER. My whole hope and trust
resteth only in thee.
M. MERRY. Then can ye not do amiss,
whatever it be.
R. ROISTER. Gramercies, Merrygreek, most
bound to thee I am.
M. MERRY. But up with that heart, and
speak out like a ram.
Ye speak like a capon that had the cough
now.
Be of good cheer; anon ye shall do well
enow. 30
R. ROISTER. Upon thy comfort, I will all
things well handle.
M. MERRY. So, lo! that is a breast [7] to
blow out a candle!
But what is this great matter, I would
fain know?
We shall find remedy therefore, I trow.
Do ye lack money? Ye know mine old
offers;
Ye have always a key to my purse and
coffers.

[1] Foolish.
[2] Lose.
[3] Desire.
[4] Sullenness.
[5] Trapped.
[6] At once.
[7] Pair of lungs.

R. Roister. I thank thee. Had ever man
such a friend?

M. Merry. Ye give unto me; I must needs
to you lend.

R. Roister. Nay, I have money plenty
all things to discharge.

M. Merry. [*Aside.*] That knew I right
well when I made offer so large.   40

R. Roister. But it is no such matter.

M. Merry.   What is it then?
Are ye in danger of debt to any man?
If ye be, take no thought nor be not
afraid.
Let them hardly [1] take thought how they
shall be paid.

R. Roister. Tut, I owe naught.

M. Merry.   What
then? Fear ye imprisonment?

R. Roister. No.

M. Merry.   No, I wist [2] ye offend
not, so to be shent. [3]
But if ye had, the Tower could not you
so hold,
But to break out at all times ye would
be bold.
What is it? Hath any man threatened
you to beat?

R. Roister. What is he that durst have
put me in that heat?   50
He that beateth me, by His arms, shall
well find
That I will not be far from him nor run
behind.

M. Merry. That thing know all men ever
since ye overthrew
The fellow of the lion which Hercules
slew.
But what is it then?

R. Roister.   Of love I make my
moan.

M. Merry. Ah, this foolish a[h]-love, wilt
ne'er let us alone?
But, because ye were refused the last day,
Ye said ye would ne'er more be entangled
that way.
I would meddle no more, since I find all
so unkind.

R. Roister. Yea, but I cannot so put love
out of my mind.   60

M. Merry. But is your love, tell me first,
in any wise,
In the way of marriage, or of merchandise?

<hr>

[1] Assuredly.   [2] Knew.   [3] Shamed.

If it may otherwise than lawful be found,
Ye get none of my help for a hundred
pound.

R. Roister. No, by my troth, I would
have her to my wife.

M. Merry. Then are ye a good man, and
God save your life!
And what or who is she with whom ye
are in love?

R. Roister. A woman whom I know not
by what means to move.

M. Merry. Who is it?

R. Roister.   A woman yond.

M. Merry.   What is her name?

R. Roister. Her yonder.

M. Merry.   Whom?

R. Roister.   Mistress—ah—

M. Merry.   Fie, fie,
for shame!   70
Love ye, and know not whom but "her
yond," "a woman"?
We shall then get you a wife—I cannot
tell when.

R. Roister. The fair woman that supped
with us yesternight;
And I heard her name twice or thrice,
and had it right.

M. Merry. Yea, ye may see ye ne'er take
me to good cheer with you;
If ye had, I could have told you her name
now.

R. Roister. I was to blame indeed, but
the next time perchance—
And she dwelleth in this house.

M. Merry.   What,
Christian Custance?

R. Roister. Except I have her to my wife,
I shall run mad.

M. Merry. [*Aside.*] Nay, unwise perhaps,
but I warrant you for mad.   80

R. Roister. I am utterly dead unless I
have my desire.

M. Merry. Where be the bellows that
blew this sudden fire?

R. Roister. I hear she is worth a thousand pound and more.

M. Merry. Yea, but learn this one lesson
of me afore:
An hundred pound of marriage-money,
doubtless,
Is ever thirty pound sterling, or somewhat less,
So that her thousand pound, if she be
thrifty,

Is much near [1] about two hundred and fifty,
Howbeit wooers and widows are never poor.
R. ROISTER. Is she a widow? I love her better therefore. 90
M. MERRY. But I hear she hath made promise to another.
R. ROISTER. He shall go without her, and [2] he were my brother.
M. MERRY. I have heard say—I am right well advised—
That she hath to Gawin Goodluck promised.
R. ROISTER. What is that Gawin Goodluck?
M. MERRY.   A merchant man.
R. ROISTER. Shall he speed afore me? Nay, sir, by sweet Saint Anne.
Ah, sir, "'*Backare*,' [3] quod [4] Mortimer to his sow." [5]
I will have her mine own self, I make God avow.
For, I tell thee, she is worth a thousand pound.
M. MERRY. Yet a fitter wife for your ma'ship might be found: 100
Such a goodly man as you might get one with land,
Besides pounds of gold a thousand, and a thousand,
And a thousand, and a thousand, and a thousand,
And so to the sum of twenty hundred thousand.
Your most goodly personage is worthy of no less.
R. ROISTER. I am sorry God made me so comely, doubtless.
For that maketh me each where so highly favored,
And all women on me so enamored.
M. MERRY. "Enamored," quod you? Have ye spied out that?
Ah sir, marry, now I see you know what is what. 110
"Enamored," ka? [6] Marry, sir, say that again!
But I thought not ye had marked it so plain.
R. ROISTER. Yes, each where they gaze all upon me and stare.

M. MERRY. Yea, Malkin! [7] I warrant you as much as they dare!
And ye will not believe what they say in the street,
When your ma'ship passeth by, all such as I meet,
That sometimes I can scarce find what answer to make.
"Who is this?" saith one. "Sir Launcelot du Lake?"
"Who is this? Great Guy of Warwick?" saith another.
"No," say I, "it is the thirteenth Hercules' brother." 120
"Who is this? Noble Hector of Troy?" saith the third.
"No, but of the same nest," say I, "it is a bird."
"Who is this? Great Goliah, Sampson, or Colbrand?"
"No," say I, "but it is a Brute [8] of the Alie [9] land."
"Who is this? Great Alexander or Charles le Maigne?"
"No, it is the tenth Worthy," say I to them again.
I know not if I said well?
R. ROISTER.   Yes, for so I am.
M. MERRY. Yea, for there were but nine Worthies before ye came.
To some others, the third Cato I do you call. 129
And so, as well as I can, I answer them all.
"Sir, I pray you, what lord or great gentleman is this?"
"Master Ralph Roister Doister, dame," say I, "iwis." [10]
"O Lord," saith she then, "what a goodly man it is!
Would Christ I had such a husband as he is!"
"O Lord," say some, "that the sight of his face we lack!"
"It is enough for you," say I, "to see his back.
His face is for ladies of high and noble parages, [11]
With whom he hardly scapeth great marriages."—
With much more than this, and much otherwise.

[1] Nearer. [3] Keep back. [5] An old proverb.
[2] An, if. [4] Quoth, said. [6] Quoth he.
[7] Probably *by Malkin.*
[8] Brutus, the legendary great grandson of Aeneas and founder of the British kingdom.
[9] Holy(?) [10] Certainly. [11] Lineage.

R. ROISTER. I can thee thank that thou
　canst such answers devise;　　140
　But I perceive thou dost me throughly
　know.
M. MERRY. I mark your manners for mine
　own learning, I trow.
　But such is your beauty, and such are
　your acts,
　Such is your personage, and such are
　your facts,[1]
　That all women fair and foul, more and
　less,
　They eye you, they "lub you," they talk
　of you doubtless.
　Your p[l]easant look maketh them all
　merry,
　Ye pass not by, but they laugh till they
　be weary;
　Yea, and money could I have, the truth
　to tell,
　Of many, to bring you that way where
　they dwell.　　150
R. ROISTER. Merrygreek, for this thy re-
　porting well of me—
M. MERRY. What should I else, sir? It
　is my duty, pardee.[2]
R. ROISTER. I promise thou shalt not lack,
　while I have a groat.
M. MERRY. Faith, sir, and I ne'er had
　more need of a new coat.
R. ROISTER. Thou shalt have one to-
　morrow, and gold for to spend.
M. MERRY. Then I trust to bring the day
　to a good end.
　For, as for mine own part having money
　enow,
　I could live only with the remembrance
　of you.
　But now to your widow whom you love
　so hot.
R. ROISTER. By Cock,[3] thou sayest truth.
　I had almost forgot.　　160
M. MERRY. What if Christian Custance
　will not have you, what?
R. ROISTER. Have me? Yes, I warrant
　you, never doubt of that;
　I know she loveth me, but she dare not
　speak.
M. MERRY. Indeed, meet it were some-
　body should it break.[4]

R. ROISTER. She looked on me twenty
　times yesternight,
　And laughed so.
M. MERRY.　　That she could not sit
　upright.
R. ROISTER. No, faith, could she not.
M. MERRY.　　No, even
　such a thing I cast.[5]
R. ROISTER. But for wooing, thou know-
　est, women are shamefast.[6]
　But, and she knew my mind, I know
　she would be glad,
　And think it the best chance that ever
　she had.　　170
M. MERRY. To her then like a man, and
　be bold forth to start.
　Wooers never speed well that have a
　false heart.
R. ROISTER. What may I best do?
M. MERRY.　　Sir, re-
　main ye awhile [here].[7]
　Ere long one or other of her house will
　appear.
　Ye know my mind.
R. ROISTER.　　Yea, now hardly let
　me alone.
M. MERRY. In the meantime, sir, if you
　please, I will home,
　And call your musicians, for in this your
　case
　It would set you forth, and all your
　wooing grace.
　Ye may not lack your instruments to
　play and sing.
R. ROISTER. Thou knowest I can do that.
M. MERRY.　　As well as anything.　　180
　Shall I go call your folks, that ye may
　show a cast?[8]
R. ROISTER. Yea, run, I beseech thee, in
　all possible haste.
M. MERRY. I go.　　　　*Exeat*.[9]
R. ROISTER.　　Yea, for I love singing
　out of measure,
　It comforteth my spirits and doth me
　great pleasure.
　But who cometh forth yond from my
　sweetheart Custance?
　My matter frameth well; this is a lucky
　chance.

[1] Deeds.
[2] From *par Dieu* (by God), an oath that had
become innocuous.
[3] Corruption of *By God*.　　[4] Reveal.

[5] Forecast, expected.
[6] Shamefaced, bashful.
[7] Added by Cooper.
[8] Specimen.
[9] Let him go out.

ACTUS I. SCENA iii.

Madge Mumblecrust, spinning on the distaff.
Tibet Talkapace, sewing. Annot Aly-
face,¹ knitting. R[alph] Roister.

M. MUMBL. If this distaff were spun,
　Margery Mumblecrust—
TIB. TALK. Where good stale ale is, will
　drink no water, I trust.
M. MUMBL. Dame Custance hath prom-
　ised us good ale and white bread.
TIB. TALK. If she keep not promise, I will
　beshrew ² her head!
　But it will be stark night before I shall
　have done.
R. ROISTER. [*Aside.*] I will stand here
　awhile, and talk with them anon.
　I hear them speak of Custance, which
　doth my heart good.
　To hear her name spoken doth even
　comfort my blood.
M. MUMBL. Sit down to your work, Tibet,
　like a good girl.
TIB. TALK. Nurse, meddle you with your
　spindle and your whirl.³　　　　　10
　No haste but good, Madge Mumblecrust;
　for "Whip and whir," ⁴
　The old proverb doth say, "never made
　good fur."
M. MUMBL. Well, ye will sit down to your
　work anon, I trust.
TIB. TALK. "Soft fire maketh sweet malt,"
　good Madge Mumblecrust.
M. MUMBL. And sweet malt maketh jolly
　good ale for the nonce.
TIB. TALK. Which will slide down the lane
　without any bones.　　　　　*Cantet.*⁵
　Old brown bread crusts must have much
　good mumbling,
　But good ale down your throat hath
　good easy tumbling.
R. ROISTER. [*Aside.*] The jolliest wench
　that e'er I heard, little mouse!
　May I not rejoice that she shall dwell in
　my house?　　　　　20
TIB. TALK. So, sirrah, now this gear ⁶ be-
　ginneth for to frame.
M. MUMBL. Thanks to God, though your
　work stand still, your tongue is not
　lame.

TIB. TALK. And though your teeth be
　gone, both so sharp and so fine,
　Yet your tongue can renne on pattens ⁷
　as well as mine.
M. MUMBL. Ye were not for naught named
　Tib Talkapace.
TIB. TALK. Doth my talk grieve you?
　Alack, God save your grace.
M. MUMBL. I hold ⁸ a groat, ye will drink
　anon for this gear.
TIB. TALK. And I will pray you the stripes
　for me to bear.
M. MUMBL. I hold a penny, ye will drink⁹
　without a cup.
TIB. TALK. Whereinsoe'er ye drink, I wot¹⁰
　ye drink all up.　　　　　30

[Enter Annot.]

AN. ALYFACE. By Cock, and well sewed,
　my good Tibet Talkapace.
TIB. TALK. And e'en as well knit, my
　nown Annot Alyface.
R. ROISTER. [*Aside.*] See what a sort¹¹ she
　keepeth that must be my wife!
　Shall not I, when I have her, lead a merry
　life?
TIB. TALK. Welcome, my good wench, and
　sit here by me just.
AN. ALYFACE. And how doth our old bel-
　dame here, Madge Mumblecrust?
TIB. TALK. Chide, and find faults, and
　threaten to complain.
AN. ALYFACE. To make us poor girls shent,
　to her is small gain.
M. MUMBL. I did neither chide, nor com-
　plain, nor threaten.
R. ROISTER. [*Aside.*] It would grieve my
　heart to seen one of them beaten.　40
M. MUMBL. I did nothing but bid her
　work and hold her peace.
TIB. TALK. So would I, if you could your
　clattering cease;
　But the devil cannot make old trot¹² hold
　her tongue.
AN. ALYFACE. Let all these matters pass,
　and we three sing a song.
　So shall we pleasantly both the time
　beguile now,
　And eke despatch all our works ere we
　can tell how.

---

¹ Enters later.　　　　　⁴ Hurry.
² Curse.　　　　　⁵ Let her sing.
³ Small flywheel on the spindle.　⁶ Affair.
⁷ Run on wooden shoes.　　　　⁸ Wager.
⁹ Absorb punishment.
¹⁰ Know.　　¹¹ Company.　　¹² Hag.

TIB. TALK. I shrew [1] them that say nay,
and that shall not be I.

M. MUMBL. And I am well content.

TIB. TALK.   Sing on then by-and-by.

R. ROISTER. [*Aside.*] And I will not away,
but listen to their song.

Yet Merrygreek and my folks tarry very
long.   50

Tib[et], An[not], and Margery do sing here.
Pipe, merry Annot, etc.
Trilla, trilla, trillarie.
Work, Tibet; work, Annot; work, Margery.
Sew, Tibet; knit, Annot; spin, Margery.
Let us see who shall win the victory.

TIB. TALK. This sleeve is not willing to be
sewed, I trow.
A small thing might make me all in [2] the
ground to throw.

Then they sing again.
Pipe, merry Annot, etc.
Trilla, trilla, trillarie.
What, Tibet! what, Annot! what, Marg-
ery!   60
Ye sleep, but we do not; that shall we try.
Your fingers be numbed; our work will not
lie.

TIB. TALK. If ye do so again, well I would
advise you nay.
In good sooth, one stop [3] more, and I
make holiday.

They sing the third time.
Pipe, merry Annot, etc.
Trilla, trilla, trillarie.
Now, Tibet; now, Annot; now, Margery.
Now whippet [4] apace for the mast'ry;
But it will not be, our mouth is so dry.

TIB. TALK. Ah, each finger is a thumb
today, methink;   70
I care not to let all alone, choose it swim
or sink.

They sing the fourth time.
Pipe, merry Annot, etc.
Trilla, trilla, trillarie.
When,[5] Tibet! When, Annot! When, Mar-
gery!
I will not, I cannot, no more can I.
Then give we all over, and there let it lie.
Let her cast down her work.

TIB. TALK. There it lieth! The worst is
but a curried coat.[6]
Tut, I am used thereto; I care not a
groat.

AN. ALYFACE. Have we done singing since?
Then will I in again.
Here I found you. and here I leave both
twain.   *Exeat.* 80

M. MUMBL. And I will not be long after.
[*She sees Roister Doister*] Tib Talkapace!

TIB. TALK. What is the matter?

M. MUMBL.   Yond
stood a man all this space
And hath heard all that ever we spake
togither.

TIB. TALK. Marry, the more lout he for
his coming hither.
And the less good he can to listen maidens
talk.
I care not and I go bid him hence for to
walk.
It were well done to know what he maketh hereaway.

R. ROISTER. [*Aside.*] Now might I speak
to them, if I wist what to say.

M. MUMBL. Nay, we will go both off, and
see what he is.

R. ROISTER. One that hath heard all your
talk and singing, iwis.   90

TIB. TALK. The more to blame you; a good
thrifty husband [7]
Would elsewhere have had some better
matters in hand.

R. ROISTER. I did it for no harm, but for
good love I bear
To your dame, Mistress Custance, I did
your talk hear.
And, mistress nurse, I will kiss you for
acquaintance.

M. MUMBL. I come anon, sir.

TIB. TALK.   Faith, I
would our Dame Custance
Saw this gear.

M. MUMBL.   I must first wipe all
clean, yea, I must.

TIB. TALK. Ill chieve it, [8] doting fool, but
it must be cust.[9]
[*He kisses Madge Mumblecrust.*]

[5] A whipping.
[1] Beshrew, curse.   [2] On.   [3] Hindrance.
[4] Whip it (?) *i.e.*, move briskly.
[5] An exclamation of impatience.
[7] Manager of a household.
[8] Achieve, succeed.
[9] Kost, kissed.

M. MUMBL. God yeld [1] you, sir; chad not
so much, ichotte not when,
Ne'er since chwas bore, chwine, of such
a gay gentleman. [2]   100

R. ROISTER. I will kiss ye too, maiden,
for the good will I bear you.

TIB. TALK. No, forsooth, by your leave,
ye shall not kiss me.

R. ROISTER. Yes, be not afeard; I do not
disdain you a whit.

TIB. TALK. Why should I fear you? I have
not so little wit.
Ye are but a man, I know very well.

R. ROISTER.   Why then?

TIB. TALK. Forsooth, for I will not; I use
not to kiss men.

R. ROISTER. I would fain kiss you too,
good maiden, if I might.

TIB. TALK. What should that need?

R. ROISTER.   But to honor you,
by this light.
I use to kiss all them that I love, to God
I vow.

TIB. TALK. Yea, sir? I pray you, when
did ye last kiss your cow?   110

R. ROISTER. Ye might be proud to kiss
me, if ye were wise.

TIB. TALK. What promotion were therein?

R. ROISTER.   Nurse is not so nice. [3]

TIB. TALK. Well, I have not been taught
to kissing and licking.

R. ROISTER. Yet I thank you, mistress
nurse; ye made no sticking.

M. MUMBL. I will not stick for a koss [4]
with such a man as you.

TIB. TALK. They that lust. I will again to
my sewing now.

[Enter Annot Alyface.]

AN. ALYFACE. Tidings, ho! tidings! Dame
Custance greeteth you well.

R. ROISTER. Whom? me?

AN. ALYFACE.   You, sir? No,
sir! I do no such tale tell.

R. ROISTER. But, and she knew me here—

AN. ALYFACE.   Tibet Talkapace,
Your mistress, Custance, and mine must
speak with your grace.   120

TIB. TALK. With me?

AN. ALYFACE.   Ye must come in
to her, out of all doubts.

TIB. TALK. And my work not half done?
A mischief on all louts.
               Ex[eant] am[bæ].

R. ROISTER. Ah, good sweet nurse!

M. MUMBL.   A
good sweet gentleman.

R. ROISTER.   What?

M. MUMBL. Nay, I cannot tell, sir, but
what thing would you?

R. ROISTER. How doth sweet Custance,
my heart of gold, tell me how?

M. MUMBL. She doth very well, sir, and
command me to you.

R. ROISTER. To me?

M. MUMBL.   Yea, to you, sir.

R. ROISTER.   To me? Nurse,
tell me plain,
To me?

M. MUMBL.   Ye.

R. ROISTER.   That word maketh
me alive again.

M. MUMBL. She command me to one last
day, [6] whoe'er it was.

R. ROISTER. That was e'en to me and
none other, by the Mass.   130

M. MUMBL. I cannot tell you surely, but
one it was.

R. ROISTER. It was I and none other; this
cometh to good pass.
I promise thee, nurse, I favor her.

M. MUMBL.   E'en so, sir.

R. ROISTER. Bid her sue to me for marriage.

M. MUMBL.   E'en so, sir.

R. ROISTER. And surely for thy sake she
shall speed.

M. MUMBL.   E'en so, sir.

R. ROISTER. I shall be contented to take
her.

M. MUMBL.   E'en so, sir.

R. ROISTER. But at thy request and for
thy sake.

M. MUMBL.   E'en so, sir.

R. ROISTER. And, come, hark in thine ear
what to say.

M. MUMBL.   E'en so, sir.

*Here let him tell her a great long tale in
                      her ear.*

[1] Reward.
[2] Madge speaks an artificial Southern dialect,
regularly used by stage rustics. Chad = ich
had = I had; ichotte = ich wot = I know; chwas =
I was; chwine = I ween = I think; etc.
[3] Fastidious.   [4] Kiss.
[5] Let both go out.
[6] Yesterday.

Actus I. Scena iv.

*Matthew Merrygreek, Dobinet Doughty, Har-
pax, [Musicians,] Ralph Roister, Margery Mumblecrust.*

M. Merry. Come on, sirs, apace, and quit
yourselves like men.
Your pains shall be rewarded.

D. Dough.   But I
wot not when.

M. Merry. Do your master worship as ye
have done in time past.

D. Dough. Speak to them; of mine office
he shall have a cast.

M. Merry. Harpax, look that thou do
well too, and thy fellow.

Harpax. I warrant, if he will mine example follow.

M. Merry. Curtsy, whoresons, duck you
and crouch at every word.

D. Dough. Yes, whether our master speak
earnest or bord.[1]

M. Merry. For this lieth upon [2] his preferment, indeed.

D. Dough. Oft is he a wooer, but never
doth he speed.   10

M. Merry. But with whom is he now so
sadly rounding [3] yond?

D. Dough. With *Nobs nicebecetur mise-
rere* [4] fond.

[M.] Merry. God be at your wedding! Be
ye sped already?
                  [*Approaches Roister Doister.*]
I did not suppose that your love was so
greedy.
I perceive now ye have chose of devotion,
And joy have ye, lady, of your promotion.

R. Roister. Tush, fool, thou art deceived; this is not she.

M. Merry. Well, mock [5] much of her, and
keep her well, I vise [6] ye.
I will take no charge of such a fair piece
keeping.

M. Mumbl. What aileth this fellow? He
driveth me to weeping.   20

M. Merry. What, weep on the wedding
day? Be merry, woman.
Though I say it, ye have chose a good
gentleman.

R. Roister. Kock's nowns,[7] what meanest thou, man? Tut, a whistle!

[M. Merry.] [8] Ah, sir, be good to her; she
is but a gristle.[9]
Ah, sweet lamb and cony! [10]

R. Roister.   Tut, thou
art deceived.

M. Merry. Weep no more, lady; ye shall
be well received.—
[*To Musicians.*] Up with some merry
noise, sirs, to bring home the bride.

R. Roister. Gog's [11] arms, knave, art thou
mad? I tell thee thou art wide.

M. Merry. Then ye intend by night to
have her home brought.

R. Roister. I tell thee no.

M. Merry.   How then?

R. Roister.   'Tis neither
meant ne [12] thought.   30

M. Merry. What shall we then do with
her?

R. Roister.   Ah, foolish harebrain,
This is not she.

M. Merry.   No, is? Why then, unsaid
again!
And what young girl is this with your
ma'ship so bold?

R. Roister. A girl?

M. Merry.   Yea. I dare say,
scarce yet three score year old.

R. Roister. This same is the fair widow's
nurse, of whom ye wot.

M. Merry. Is she but a nurse of a house?
Hence home, old trot,
Hence at once!

R. Roister. No, no.

M. Merry.   What, an please
your ma'ship,
A nurse talk so homely [13] with one of your
worship?

R. Roister. I will have it so; it is my
pleasure and will.

M. Merry. Then I am content. Nurse,
come again; tarry still.   40

R. Roister. What! She will help forward
this my suit for her part.

M. Merry. Then is't mine own pigsnie,[14]
and blessing on my heart.

---

[1] Jest.   [2] Is necessary to.   [3] Whispering.
[4] Burlesque Latin for something like "darling
sweetheart, pity me."
[5] Hazlitt suggests *make*.   [6] Advise.

[7] God's wounds.
[8] This speech is assigned to Roister Doister
in the original.
[9] A delicate person; with a pun on the meaning
tough. [10] Rabbit, a term of endearment. [11] God's.
[12] Nor. [13] Familiarly. [14] Pig's eye, darling.

R. Roister. This is our best friend, man.

M. Merry. Then teach her what to say.

M. Mumbl. I am taught already.

M. Merry. Then go; make no delay.

R. Roister. Yet hark, one word in thine ear.

M. Merry. Back, sirs, from his tail.

R. Roister. Back, villains, will ye be privy of my counsel?

M. Merry. Back, sirs, so. I told you afore ye would be shent.

R. Roister. She shall have the first day a whole peck of argent.[1]

M. Mumbl. A peck? *Nomine patris*,[2] have ye so much spare?

R. Roister. Yea, and a cart-load thereto, or else were it bare, 50
Besides other movables, household stuff, and land.

M. Mumbl. Have ye lands too?

R. Roister. An hundred marks.

M. Merry. Yea, a thousand.

M. Mumbl. And have ye cattle too, and sheep too?

R. Roister. Yea, a few.

M. Merry. He is ashamed the number of them to shew.
E'en round about him, as many thousand sheep goes,
As he and thou, and I too, have fingers and toes.

M. Mumbl. And how many years old be you?

R. Roister. Forty at least.

M. Merry. Yea, and thrice forty to them.

R. Roister. Nay, now thou dost jest. I am not so old; thou misreckonest my years.

M. Merry. I know that; but my mind was on bullocks and steers. 60

M. Mumbl. And what shall I show her your mastership's name is?

R. Roister. Nay, she shall make suit ere she know that, iwis.

M. Mumbl. Yet let me somewhat know.

M. Merry. This is he, understand,
That killed the blue spider in Blanche-powder land.

M. Mumbl. Yea, Jesus! William! Zee, law! Did he zo? Law![3]

M. Merry. Yea, and the last elephant that ever he saw,
As the beast passed by, he start out of a busk,[4]
And e'en with pure strength of arms plucked out his great tusk.

M. Mumbl. Jesus, *nomine patris*, what a thing was that?

R. Roister. Yea, but, Merrygreek, one thing thou hast forgot.

M. Merry. What? 70

R. Roister. Of th' other elephant.

M. Merry. O, him that fled away.

R. Roister. Yea.

M. Merry. Yea, he knew that his match was in place that day.
Tut, he bet[5] the king of crickets on Christmas day,
That he crept in a hole, and not a word to say.

M. Mumbl. A sore[6] man, by zembletee.[7]

M. Merry. Why, he wrong[8] a club
Once in a fray out of the hand of Belzebub.

R. Roister. And how when Mumfision—

M. Merry. O, your coustreling[9]
Bore the lantern afield so before the gozeling[10]—
Nay, that is too long a matter now to be told.
Never ask his name, nurse; I warrant thee, be bold. 80
He conquered in one day from Rome to Naples,
And won towns, nurse, as fast as thou canst make apples.

M. Mumbl. O Lord, my heart quaketh for fear! He is too sore!

R. Roister. Thou makest her too much afeard, Merrygreek; no more.
This tale would fear my sweetheart Custance right evil.

M. Merry. Nay, let her take him, nurse, and fear not the devil.
But thus is our song dashed. [*To Musicians.*] Sirs, ye may home again.

R. Roister. No, shall they not. I charge you all here to remain.
The villain slaves, a whole day ere they can be found!

---

[1] Silver, money.
[2] In the name of the Father.
[3] Madge relapses into dialect.
[4] Bush.　　[5] Beat.　　[6] Terrible.
[7] Semblety, semblance—a rustic oath.
[8] Wrung.　　[9] Arms-bearer.
[10] Gosling, *i.e.*, a foolish person (?).

M. MERRY. Couch on your marybones,[1]
     whoresons, down to the ground! 90
Was it meet he should tarry so long in
     one place
Without harmony of music, or some
     solace?
Whoso hath such bees as your master in
     his head,
Had need to have his spirits with music
     to be fed.
By your mastership's license—
[*Picks something from Roister Doister's
               coat.*]
R. ROISTER.   What is that? A mote?
M. MERRY. No, it was a fool's[2] feather
     had light on your coat.
R. ROISTER. I was nigh no feathers since
     I came from my bed.
M. MERRY. No, sir, it was a hair that was
     fall from your head.
R. ROISTER. My men come when it please
     them.
M. MERRY.   By your leave—
R. ROISTER.   What is
     that?
M. MERRY. Your gown was foul spotted
     with the foot of a gnat.   100
R. ROISTER. Their master to offend they
     are nothing afeard.
What now?
M. MERRY.   A lousy hair from your
     mastership's beard.
OMNES FAMULÆ.[3] And, sir, for nurse's sake,
     pardon this one offense.
We shall not after this show the like
     negligence.
R. ROISTER. I pardon you this once, and
     come, sing ne'er the worse.
M. MERRY. How like you the goodness of
     this gentleman, nurse?
M. MUMBL. God save his mastership that
     so can his men forgive!
And I will hear them sing ere I go, by his
     leave.
R. ROISTER. Marry and thou shalt, wench.
     Come, we two will dance.
M. MUMBL. Nay, I will by mine own self
     foot the song perchance.   110
R. ROISTER. Go to it, sirs, lustily.

M. MUMBL.   Pipe up a
     merry note.
Let me hear it played; I will foot it for a
     groat.   *Cantent.*[4]
R. ROISTER. Now, nurse, take this same
     letter here to thy mistress;
And, as my trust is in thee, ply my busi-
     ness.
M. MUMBL. It shall be done.
M. MERRY.   Who made it?
R. ROISTER.   I wrote it each
     whit.
M. MERRY. Then needs it no mending.
R. ROISTER.   No. no.
M. MERRY.   No, I know
     your wit.
I warrant it well.
M. MUMBL.   It shall be delivered.
But, if ye speed, shall I be con-
     sidered?
M. MERRY. Whough! Dost thou doubt of
     that?
MADGE [MUMBL.] What shall I have? 120
M. MERRY. An hundred times more than
     thou canst devise to crave.
M. MUMBL. Shall I have some new gear?
     For my old is all spent.
M. MERRY. The worst kitchen wench shall
     go in ladies' raiment.
M. MUMBL. Yea?
M. MERRY.   And the worst drudge
     in the house shall go better
Than your mistress doth now.
MAR. [MUMBL.]   Then I trudge
     with your letter.   [*Exeat.*]
R. ROISTER. Now may I repose me. Cus-
     tance is mine own.
Let us sing and play homeward that it
     may be known.
M. MERRY. But are you sure that your
     letter is well enough?
R. ROISTER. I wrote it myself.
M. MERRY.   Then sing
     we to dinner.
     Here they sing, and go out singing.

ACTUS I. SCENA v.

Christian Custance, Margery Mumblecrust.

C. CUSTANCE. Who took[5] thee this letter,
     Margery Mumblecrust?

---

[1] Marrowbones.
[2] With a pun on *fowl's*.
[3] All the servants.

[4] Let them sing (probably "The Second Song,"
printed at the end of the play).   [5] Gave.

M. MUMBL. A lusty gay bachelor took it
  me of trust,
  And, if ye seek to him, he will low [1] your
  doing.
C. CUSTANCE. Yea, but where learned he
  that manner of wooing?
M. MUMBL. If to sue to him you will any
  pains take,
  He will have you to his wife, he saith,
  for my sake.
C. CUSTANCE. Some wise gentleman, belike. I am bespoken; [2]
  And I thought verily this had been some
  token
  From my dear spouse Gawin Goodluck,
  whom, when him please,
  God luckily send home to both our
  hearts' ease.   10
M. MUMBL. A joyly [3] man it is, I wot well
  by report,
  And would have you to him for marriage
  resort.
  Best open the writing, and see what it
  doth speak.
C. CUSTANCE. At this time, nurse, I will
  neither read ne break. [4]
M. MUMBL. He promised to give you a
  whole peck of gold.
C. CUSTANCE. Perchance, lack of a pint
  when it shall be all told.
M. MUMBL. I would take a gay rich husband, and I were you.
C. CUSTANCE. In good sooth, Madge, e'en
  so would I, if I were thou.
  But no more of this fond talk now; let
  us go in,
  And see thou no more move me folly to
  begin,   20
  Nor bring me no mo [5] letters for no man's
  pleasure,
  But thou know from whom.
M. MUMBL.   I warrant
  ye shall be sure.

ACTUS II. SCENA i.

Dobinet Doughty.

D. DOUGH. Where is the house I go to, before or behind?
  I know not where nor when nor how I
  shall it find.

If I had ten men's bodies and legs and
  strength,
This trotting that I have must needs
  lame me at length.
And now that my master is new set on
  wooing,
I trust there shall none of us find lack of
  doing.
Two pair of shoes a day will now be too
  little
To serve me, I must trot to and fro so
  mickle. [6]
"Go bear me this token!" "Carry me
  this letter!"
Now, "This is the best way;" now,
  "That way is better!"   10
"Up before day, sirs, I charge you, an
  hour or twain!"
"Trudge! Do me this message, and bring
  word quick again!"
If one miss but a minute, then, "His
  arms and wounds,
I would not have slacked for ten thou-
  sand pounds.
Nay, see, I beseech you, if my most
  trusty page
Go not now about to hinder my mar-
  riage."
So fervent hot wooing, and so far from
  wiving,
I trow, never was any creature living.
With every woman is he in some love's
  pang,
Then up to our lute at midnight, twangle-
  dom twang;   20
Then twang with our sonnets, and twang
  with our dumps, [7]
And heigh-ho from our heart, as heavy
  as lead lumps;
Then to our recorder [8] with toodle-
  loodle poop,
As the howlet out of an ivy bush should
  hoop. [9]
Anon to our gittern, thrumpledum,
  thrumpledum thrum,
Thrumpledum, thrumpledum, thrumple-
  dum, thrumpledum thrum.
Of songs and ballads also he is a maker,
And that can he as finely do as Jack
  Raker;
Yea, and extempore will he ditties com-
  pose—

---

[1] Allow, approve.
[2] Promised, betrothed.
[3] Jolie, jolly, pretty.
[4] Break the seal.
[5] More.
[6] Much.
[7] Melancholy music.
[8] Flute.
[9] Whoop.

Foolish Marsyas[1] ne'er made the like, I
  suppose.   30
Yet must we sing them; as good stuff, I
  undertake,
As for such a penman is well fitting to
  make.
"Ah, for these long nights! Heigh-ho!
  When will it be day?
I fear ere I come she will be wooed
  away."
Then when answer is made that it may
  not be,
"O death, why comest thou not?" by-
  and-by saith he.
But then, from his heart to put away
  sorrow,
He is as far in with some new love next
  morrow.
But in the mean season we trudge and
  we trot;
From dayspring to midnight I sit not
  nor rest not.   40
And now am I sent to Dame Christian
  Custance,
But I fear it will end with a mock for
  pastance.[2]
I bring her a ring, with a token in a
  clout[3]—
And by all guess this same is her house
  out of doubt.
I know it now perfect; I am in my right
  way.
And lo! yond the old nurse that was with
  us last day.

Actus II. Scena ii.

Madge Mumblecrust, Dobinet Doughty.

M. Mumbl. I was ne'er so shoke up[4] afore
  since I was born.
That our mistress could not have chid,
  I would have sworn;
And I pray God I die if I meant any
  harm,
But for my lifetime this shall be to me
  a charm.
D. Dough. God you save and see,[5] nurse,
  and how is it with you?
M. Mumbl. Marry, a great deal the worse
  it is for such as thou.

D. Dough. For me? Why so?
M Mumbl.   Why, were not thou
  one of them, say,
That song and played here with the
  gentleman last day?
D. Dough. Yes, and he would know if
  you have for him spoken.
And prays you to deliver this ring and
  token.   10
M. Mumbl. Now by the token that God
  tokened, brother,
I will deliver no token, one nor other.
I have once been so shent for your mas-
  ter's pleasure,
As I will not be again for all his trea-
  sure.
D. Dough. He will thank you, woman.
M. Mumbl.   I will none of his
  thank.   *Ex[eat]*.
D. Dough. I ween I am a prophet! This
  gear will prove blank.[6]
But what! should I home again without
  answer go?
It were better go to Rome on my head
  than so.
I will tarry here this month, but some of
  the house
Shall take it of me, and then I care not
  a louse.   20
But yonder cometh forth a wench or a
  lad;
If he have not one Lombard's[7] touch,
  my luck is bad.

Actus II. Scena iii.

*Truepenny, D[obinet] Dough[ty], Tibet T[alk-
  apace], Annot Al[yface]*[8]

Truepenny. I am clean lost for lack of
  merry company;
We gree[9] not half well within, our wenches
  and I.
They will command like mistresses; they
  will forbid;
If they be not served, Truepenny must
  be chid.
Let them be as merry now as ye can
  desire,
With turning of a hand, our mirth lieth
  in the mire.

---

[1] The Phrygian satyr who was cruelly killed
by Apollo for challenging him on the flute.
  [2] Pastime.   [4] Scolded.
  [3] Cloth.   [5] Watch over.

[6] Unsuccessful.
  [7] The Lombard was proverbially a money
changer. Here, one who likes to handle gold.
  [8] Last two enter later.   [9] Agree.

I cannot skill of [1] such changeable
  mettle;
There is nothing with them but "in
  dock, out nettle." [2]
D. Dough. Whether is it better that I
  speak to him first,
Or he first to me? It is good to cast the
  worst.   10
If I begin first, he will smell all my pur-
  pose;
Otherwise I shall not need anything to
  disclose.
Truepenny. What boy have we yonder?
  I will see what he is.
D. Dough. He cometh to me.—It is here-
  about, iwis.
Truepenny. Wouldest thou aught, friend,
  that thou lookest so about?
D. Dough. Yea, but whether ye can help
  me or no, I doubt.
I seek to one Mistress Custance' house,
  here dwelling.
Truepenny. It is my mistress ye seek to,
  by your telling.
D. Dough. Is there any of that name here
  but she?
Truepenny. Not one in all the whole
  town that I know, pardee.   20
D. Dough. A widow she is, I trow.
Truepenny.   And what
  and she be?
D. Dough. But insured to an husband.
Truepenny.   Yea, so think we.
D. Dough. And I dwell with her husband
  that trusteth to be.
Truepenny. In faith, then must thou
  needs be welcome to me.
Let us for acquaintance shake hands
  togither,
And whate'er thou be, heartily welcome
  hither.

[*Enter Tibet and Annot.*]

Tib. Talk. Well, Truepenny, never but
  flinging? [3]
An. Alyface.   And frisking?
Truepenny. Well, Tibet and Annot, still
  swinging and whisking?
Tib. Talk. But ye roil [4] abroad.

An. Alyface.   In the street
  everywhere.
Truepenny. Where are ye twain, in
  chambers when ye meet me there?   30
But come hither, fools; I have one now
  by the hand,
Servant to him that must be our mistress'
  husband.
Bid him welcome.
An. Alyface.   To me truly is he
  welcome.
Tib. Talk. Forsooth, and as I may say,
  heartily welcome.
D. Dough. I thank you, mistress maids.
An. Alyface.   I hope we shall
  better know.
Tib. Talk. And when will our new master
  come?
D. Dough.   Shortly, I trow.
Tib. Talk. I would it were tomorrow; for
  till he resort,
Our mistress, being a widow, hath small
  comfort,
And I heard our nurse speak of an hus-
  band today
Ready for our mistress, a rich man and
  a gay.   40
And we shall go in our French hoods
  every day,
In our silk cassocks, I warrant you,
  fresh and gay,
In our trick ferdegews [5] and billiments [6]
  of gold;
Brave [7] in our suits of change, seven
  double fold.
Then shall ye see Tibet, sirs, tread the
  moss so trim—
Nay, why said I tread? Ye shall see her
  glide and swim,
Not lumperdee clumperdee like our spaniel Rig.
Truepenny. Marry, then, prick-me-dain-
  ty,[8] come toast me a fig!
Who shall then know our Tib Talkapace,
  trow ye?
An. Alyface. And why not Annot Alyface as fine as she?   50
Truepenny. And what had Tom Truepenny, a father or none?
An. Alyface. Then our pretty new-come
  man will look to be one.

---

[1] Understand.
[2] Proverbial phrase for inconstancy, referring
to the curing of nettle stings by dock leaves.
[3] Running about.   [4] Gad.

[5] Neat farthingales.
[6] Habiliments, perhaps headdresses.
[7] Gay.   [8] Finical person.

TRUEPENNY. We four, I trust, shall be a joyly merry knot.

Shall we sing a fit [1] to welcome our friend, Annot?

AN. ALYFACE. Perchance he cannot sing.

D. DOUGH.   I am at all essays. [2]

TIB. TALK. By Cock, and the better welcome to us always.

Here they sing.

A thing very fit
For them that have wit
And are fellows knit,
    Servants in one house to be,   60
Is fast, fast for to sit,
And not oft to flit,
Nor vary a whit,
    But lovingly to agree.

No man complaining,
No other disdaining,
For loss or for gaining,
    But fellows or friends to be.
No grudge remaining,
No work refraining,   70
Nor help restraining,
    But lovingly to agree.

No man for despite,
By word or by write
His fellow to twite, [3]
    But further in honesty;
No good turns entwite, [3]
Nor old sores recite,
But let all go quite,
    And lovingly to agree.   80

After drudgery,
When they be weary,
Then to be merry,
    To laugh and sing they be free;
With chip [4] and cherry,
Heigh derry derry,
Trill on the bery, [5]
    And lovingly to agree.
          FINIS.

TIB. TALK. Will you now in with us unto our mistress go?

D. DOUGH. I have first for my master an errand or two.   90

But I have here from him a token and a ring;

They shall have most thank of her that first doth it bring.

---

[1] Song.   [4] Crust of bread.
[2] Ready for all contingencies.
[3] Twit, blame.   [5] Dance on the hill.

TIB. TALK. Marry, that will I.

TRUEPENNY.   See, and Tibet snatch not now!

TIB. TALK. And why may not I, sir, get thanks as well as you?   *Exeat.*

AN. ALYFACE. Yet get ye not all; we will go with you both

And have part of your thanks, be ye never so loath.

[Exeant all but Doughty.]

D. DOUGH. So my hands are rid of it; I care for no more.

I may now return home; so durst I not afore.   *Exeat.*

ACTUS II. SCENA iv.

C[hristian] Custance, Tibet, Annot Alyface, Truepenny.

C. CUSTANCE. Nay, come forth all three; and come hither, pretty maid.

Will not so many forewarnings make you afraid?

TIB. TALK. Yes, forsooth.

C. CUSTANCE.   But still be a runner up and down,

Still be a bringer of tidings and tokens to town?

TIB. TALK. No, forsooth, mistress.

C. CUSTANCE.   Is all your delight and joy

In whisking and ramping abroad like a tomboy?

TIB. TALK. Forsooth, these were there too, Annot and Truepenny.

TRUEPENNY. Yea, but ye alone took it, ye cannot deny.

AN. ALYFACE. Yea, that ye did.

TIB. TALK.   But if I had not, ye twain would.

C. CUSTANCE. You great calf, ye should have more wit, so ye should.   10

But why should any of you take such things in hand?

TIB. TALK. Because it came from him that must be your husband.

C. CUSTANCE. How do ye know that?

TIB. TALK.   Forsooth, the boy did say so.

C. CUSTANCE. What was his name?

AN. ALYFACE.   We asked not.

C. CUSTANCE.   No, did? [6]

---

[6] This word might be omitted for the sake of the rhyme.

AN. ALYFACE. He is not far gone, of likelihood.

TRUEPENNY. I will see.

C. CUSTANCE. If thou canst find him in
the street, bring him to me.

TRUEPENNY. Yes. *Exeat.*

C. CUSTANCE. Well, ye naughty girls,
if ever I perceive

That henceforth you do letters or tokens
receive,

To bring unto me from any person or
place,

Except ye first show me the party face
to face, 20

Either thou or thou, full truly aby [1] thou
shalt.

TIB. TALK. Pardon this, and the next time
powder me in salt.

C. CUSTANCE. I shall make all girls by
you twain to beware.

TIB. TALK. If ever I offend again, do not
me spare.

But if ever I see that false boy any more,

By your mistress-ship's license, I tell you
afore,

I will rather have my coat twenty times
swinged [2]

Than on the naughty wag not to be
avenged.

C. CUSTANCE. Good wenches would not so
ramp abroad idly,

But keep within doors, and ply their work
earnestly. 30

If one would speak with me that is a
man likely,

Ye shall have right good thank to bring
me word quickly.

But otherwise with messages to come in
post

From henceforth, I promise you, shall
be to your cost.

Get you in to your work.

TIB. [TALK.] }
AN. [ALYFACE.] } Yes, forsooth.

C. CUSTANCE. Hence, both twain.
And let me see you play me such a part
again! [*Exeant Tibet and Annot.*]

[*Enter Truepenny.*]

TRUEPENNY. Mistress, I have run past the
far end of the street,

Yet can I not yonder crafty boy see nor
meet.

[1] Pay the penalty.   [2] Beaten.

C. CUSTANCE. No?

TRUEPENNY. Yet I looked as far
beyond the people

As one may see out of the top of Paul's
steeple. 40

C. CUSTANCE. Hence, in at doors, and let
me no more be vexed.

TRUEPENNY. Forgive me this one fault,
and lay on for the next. [*Exeat.*]

C. CUSTANCE. Now will I in too, for I
think, so God me mend,

This will prove some foolish matter in
the end. *Exeat.*

ACTUS II[I]. SCENA i.

Matthew Merrygreek.

M. MERRY. Now say this again: he hath
somewhat to doing

Which followeth the trace of one that is
wooing,

Specially that hath no more wit in his
head

Than my cousin Roister Doister withal
is led.

I am sent in all haste to espy and to mark

How our letters and tokens are likely to
wark.[3]

Master Roister Doister must have answer
in haste,

For he loveth not to spend much labor
in waste.

Now as for Christian Custance, by this
light,

Though she had not her troth to Gawin
Goodluck plight, 10

Yet rather than with such a loutish dolt
to marry,

I dare say would live a poor life solitary.

But fain would I speak with Custance,
if I wist how,

To laugh at the matter.—Yond cometh
one forth now.

ACTUS III. SCENA ii.

*Tibet, M[atthew] Merrygreek, Christian Cus-
tance.*[4]

TIB. TALK. Ah, that I might but once in
my life have a sight

Of him that made us all so ill shent! By
this light,

He should never escape if I had him by
the ear,

[3] Work.   [4] Enters later.

But even from his head I would it bite or
    tear!
Yea, and if one of them were not enow,
I would bite them both off, I make God
    avow.[1]
M. MERRY. [*Aside.*] What is he whom
    this little mouse doth so threaten?
TIB. TALK. I would teach him, I trow, to
    make girls shent or beaten.
M. MERRY. [*Aside.*] I will call her.—Maid,
    with whom are ye so hasty?
TIB. TALK. Not with you, sir, but with a
    little wagpasty,[2]   10
A deceiver of folks by subtle craft and
    guile.
M. MERRY. [*Aside.*] I know where she is:[3]
Dobinet hath wrought some wile.
TIB. TALK. He brought a ring and token
    which he said was sent
From our dame's husband, but I wot
    well I was shent;
For it liked her as well, to tell you no lies,
As water in her ship, or salt cast in her
    eyes.
And yet whence it came neither we nor
    she can tell.
M. MERRY. [*Aside.*] We shall have sport
    anon; I like this very well.—
And dwell ye here with Mistress Cus-
    tance, fair maid?
TIB. TALK. Yea, marry, do I, sir. What
    would ye have said?   20
M. MERRY. A little message unto her by
    word of mouth.
TIB. TALK. No messages, by your leave,
    nor tokens forsooth.
M. MERRY. Then help me to speak with
    her.
TIB. TALK.   With a good will that.
Here she cometh forth. Now speak ye
    know best what.

[*Enter Custance.*]

C. CUSTANCE. None other life with you,
    maid, but abroad to skip?
TIB. TALK. Forsooth, here is one would
    speak with your mistress-ship.
C. CUSTANCE. Ah, have ye been learning
    of mo messages now?
TIB. TALK. I would not hear his mind, but
    bade him show it to you.

C. CUSTANCE. In at doors!
TIB. TALK.   I am gone.   *Ex[eat.]*
M. MERRY.   Dame Custance,
    God ye save.
C. CUSTANCE. Welcome, friend Merry-
    greek, and what thing would ye
    have?   30
M. MERRY. I am come to you a little
    matter to break.
C. CUSTANCE. But see it be honest; else
    better not to speak.
M. MERRY. How feel ye yourself affected
    here of late?
C. CUSTANCE. I feel no manner change but
    after the old rate.
But whereby do ye mean?
M. MERRY.   Concerning
    marriage.
Doth not love lade you?
C. CUSTANCE.   I feel no such
    carriage.[4]
M. MERRY. Do ye feel no pangs of dotage?
    Answer me right.
C. CUSTANCE. I dote so that I make but
    one sleep all the night.
But what need all these words?
M. MERRY.   O Jesus,
    will ye see
What dissembling creatures these same
    women be?   40
The gentleman ye wot of, whom ye do so
    love
That ye would fain marry him, if ye
    durst it move,
Among other rich widows, which are of
    him glad,
Lest ye for leesing of him perchance
    might run mad,
Is now contented that, upon your suit
    making,
Ye be as one in election of taking.
C. CUSTANCE. What a tale is this! That I
    wot of? Whom I love?
M. MERRY. Yea, and he is as loving a
    worm,[5] again, as a dove.
E'en of very pity he is willing you to take,
Because ye shall not destroy yourself for
    his sake.   50
C. CUSTANCE. Marry, God yeld his ma'-
    ship whatever he be.
It is gentmanly[6] spoken.

[1] An oath, a promise.   [2] Rogue.
[3] I know what's the matter with her.
[4] Burden.
[5] Little creature; a term of endearment.
[6] Colloquial for *gentlemanly.*

M. Merry.   Is it not,
trow ye?
If ye have the grace now to offer your-
self, ye speed.
C. Custance. As much as though I did,
this time it shall not need.
But what gentman is it, I pray you tell
me plain,
That wooeth so finely?
M. Merry.   Lo, where ye be
again,
As though ye knew him not.
C. Custance.   Tush, ye
speak in jest.
M. Merry. Nay, sure, the party is in
good knacking [1] earnest,
And have you he will, he saith, and have
you he must.
C. Custance. I am promised during my
life; that is just.   60
M. Merry. Marry, so thinketh he, unto
him alone.
C. Custance. No creature hath my faith
and troth but one—
That is Gawin Goodluck; and, if it be
not he,
He hath no title this way whatever he be,
Nor I know none to whom I have such
word spoken.
M. Merry. Yea, know him not you by his
letter and token?
C. Custance. Indeed, true it is that a
letter I have,
But I never read it yet, as God me
save.
M. Merry. Ye a woman, and your letter
so long unread?
C. Custance. Ye may thereby know what
haste I have to wed.   70
But now, who it is for my hand I know
by guess.
M. Merry. Ah, well I say.
C. Custance.   It is Roister
Doister, doubtless.
M. Merry. Will ye never leave this dis-
simulation?
Ye know him not?
C. Custance.   But by imagination,
For no man there is but a very dolt and
lout
That to woo a widow would so go about.
He shall never have me his wife while
he do live.

M. Merry. Then will he have you if he
may, so mote [2] I thrive,
And he biddeth you send him word by me,
That ye humbly beseech him, ye may his
wife be,   80
And that there shall be no let [3] in you
nor mistrust,
But to be wedded on Sunday next if he
lust,
And biddeth you to look for him.
C. Custance.   Doth
he bid so?
M. Merry. When he cometh, ask him
whether he did or no.
C. Custance. Go, say that I bid him keep
him warm at home,
For, if he come abroad, he shall cough
me a mome.[4]
My mind was vexed; I shrew his head,
sottish dolt!
M. Merry. He hath in his head—
C. Custance.   As much
brain as a burbolt.[5]
M. Merry. Well, Dame Custance, if he
hear you thus play choploge [6]—
C. Custance. What will he?
M. Merry.   Play the
devil in the horologe.[7]   90
C. Custance. I defy him, lout!
M. Merry.   Shall I
tell him what ye say?
C. Custance. Yea, and add whatsoever
thou canst, I thee pray,
And I will avouch it, whatsoever it be.
M. Merry. Then let me alone; we will
laugh well, ye shall see.
It will not be long ere he will hither resort.
C. Custance. Let him come when him
lust; I wish no better sport.
Fare ye well. I will in, and read my
great letter.
I shall to my wooer make answer the
better.   Exeat.

Actus III. Scena iii.

Matthew Merrygreek Roister Doister.

M. Merry. Now that the whole answer
in my devise doth rest,
I shall paint out our wooer in colors of
the best.

[1] Downright.

[2] May.   [3] Hindrance.
[4] Show what a blockhead he is.
[5] Birdbolt, sometimes carried by jesters;
hence, a fool.   [6] Choplogic.   [7] Clock, belfry.

And all that I say shall be on Custance's
　mouth;
She is author of all that I shall speak
　forsooth.
But yond cometh Roister Doister now
　in a trance.
R. Roister. Juno send me this day good
　luck and good chance.
I cannot but come see how Merrygreek
　doth speed.
M. Merry. [*Aside.*] I will not see him, but
　give him a jut [1] indeed.—
　　　　　　　　　　　　[*Runs into him.*]
I cry your mastership mercy!
R. Roister.　　　　　　　　　　　And
　whither now?
M. Merry. As fast as I could run, sir, in
　post against you.　　　　　　　　10
But why speak ye so faintly, or why are
　ye so sad?
R. Roister. Thou knowest the proverb—
　"Because I cannot be had."
Hast thou spoken with this woman?
M. Merry.　　　　Yea, that I have.
R. Roister. And what will this gear be?
M. Merry.　　　　No, so God me save.
R. Roister. Hast thou a flat answer?
M. Merry.　　　　　Nay, a sharp answer.
R. Roister.　　　　　　　　What?
M. Merry. Ye shall not, she saith, by her
　will, marry her cat.
Ye are such a calf, such an ass, such a
　block,
Such a lilburn,[2] such a hoball,[3] such a
　lobcock,[4]
And because ye should come to her at
　no season,
She despised your ma'ship out of all
　reason.　　　　　　　　　　　　20
"Bawawe [5] what ye say," ko [6] I, "of such
　a gentman!"
"Nay, I fear him not," ko she, "do the
　best he can.
He vaunteth himself for a man of prowess
　great,
Whereas a good gander, I dare say, may
　him beat.
And where he is louted [7] and laughed to
　scorn,
For the veriest dolt that ever was born,
And veriest lover,[8] sloven, and beast,

Living in this world from the west to the
　east,
Yet of himself hath he such opinion,
That in all the world is not the like
　minion.[9]　　　　　　　　　　30
He thinketh each woman to be brought
　in dotage
With the only sight of his goodly per-
　sonage;
Yet none that will have him. We do him
　lout and flock,[10]
And make him among us our common
　sporting stock,
And so would I now," ko she, "save only
　because—"
"Better nay," ko I; " I lust not meddle
　with daws.[11]
Ye are happy," ko I, "that ye are a
　woman;
This would cost you your life in case ye
　were a man."
R. Roister. Yea, an hundred thousand
　pound should not save her life.
M. Merry. No, but that ye woo her to
　have her to your wife.　　　　40
But I could not stop her mouth.
R. Roister.　　　　　　　　　Heigh-
　ho, alas!
M. Merry. Be of good cheer, man, and
　let the world pass.
R. Roister. What shall I do or say now
　that it will not be?
M. Merry. Ye shall have choice of a
　thousand as good as she,
And ye must pardon her; it is for lack of
　wit.
R. Roister. Yea, for were not I an hus-
　band for her fit?
Well, what should I now do?
M. Merry.　　　　　　　　In faith, I
　cannot tell.
R. Roister. I will go home and die.
M. Merry.　　　　　　　　Then shall
　I bid toll the bell?
R. Roister. No.
M. Merry.　　　　God have mercy on
　your soul! Ah, good gentleman,
That e'er ye should thus die for an un-
　kind woman!　　　　　　　　50
Will ye drink once ere ye go?
R. Roister.　　　　　　　　　No, no,
　I will none.

---

[1] Jolt.
[2] Dolt.
[3] Clodhopper.
[4] Lubber.
[5] Beware(?).
[6] Quoth, said.
[7] Ridiculed.
[8] Lubber(?).
[9] Darling, favorite.
[10] Treat contemptuously.
[11] Fools.

M. MERRY. How feel your soul to God? [1]
R. ROISTER.   I am nigh gone.
M. MERRY. And shall we hence straight?
R. ROISTER.   Yea.
M. MERRY.   *Placebo.*[2] *Dilexi.*[3]
Master Roister Doister will straight go
home and die.   *Ut infra.*[4]
R. ROISTER. Heigh-ho, alas, the pangs of
death my heart do break!
M. MERRY. Hold your peace! For shame,
sir, a dead man may not speak!
Nequando.[5] What mourners and what
torches shall we have?
R. ROISTER. None.
M. MERRY.   *Dirige.*[6] He will go
darkling to his grave—
Neque lux, neque crux, neque mourners,
neque clink.[7]
He will steal to heaven, unknowing to
God, I think.   60
A porta inferi.[8] Who shall your goods
possess?
R. ROISTER. Thou shalt be my sector,[9]
and have all, more and less.
M. MERRY. *Requiem æternam.*[10] Now, God
reward your mastership.
And I will cry halfpenny-dole for your
worship.
Come forth, sirs, hear the doleful news
I shall you tell. *Evocat servos militis.*[11]

[*Enter four Servants.*]

Our good master here will no longer with
us dwell.
But, in spite of Custance, which hath
him wearied,
Let us see his ma'ship solemnly buried.
And while some piece of his soul is yet
him within,   69
Some part of his funerals let us here begin.
Audivi vocem.[12] All men take heed by
this one gentleman,

How you set your love upon an unkind
woman.
For these women be all such mad peevish
elves,
They will not be won except it please
themselves.
But in faith, Custance, if ever ye come
in hell,
Master Roister Doister shall serve you
as well.
And will ye needs go from us thus in
very deed?
R. ROISTER. Yea, in good sadness.
M. MERRY.   Now,
Jesus Christ be your speed.
Good night, Roger, old knave; farewell,
Roger, old knave!
Good night, Roger, old knave; knave,
knap! [13]   *Ut infra.* 80
Pray for the late Master Roister Dois-
ter's soul,
And come forth, parish clerk, let the
passing bell toll.   *Ad servos militis.*[14]

[*Enter Parish Clerk.*]

Pray for your master, sirs, and for him
ring a peal.[15]
He was your right good master while he
was in heal.[16]
Qui Lazarum.[17]
R. ROISTER.   Heigh-ho!
M. MERRY.   Dead men go
not so fast
In paradisum.[18]
R. ROISTER.   Heigh-ho!
M. MERRY.   Soft, hear what
I have cast.
R. ROISTER. I will hear nothing; I am
past.
M. MERRY.   Whough, wellaway!
Ye may tarry one hour, and hear what
I shall say.
Ye were best, sir, for a while to revive
again,
And quite [19] them ere ye go.
R. ROISTER.   Trowest thou so?

---

[1] From the service for the visitation of the sick.
[2] I shall be acceptable(?). This word begins
a parody on the Catholic service for the dead.
[3] I have loved(?).
[4] As below. (See "Psalmody" at end of play.)
[5] Never.
[6] Direct [my way].
[7] Neither light nor cross nor mourners nor bell.
[8] From the gate of hell.
[9] Executor.
[10] Eternal rest.
[11] He calls the soldier's [Roister Doister's]
servants.
[12] I have heard a voice.

[13] This word may mean either *knave* or *nap* or
strike (the bell).
[14] To the servants of the soldier.
[15] See "Peal of Bells" at the end of play.
[16] Health.
[17] Thou who [didst raise] Lazarus.
[18] Into paradise.
[19] Requite, get even with.

M. Merry.   Yea, plain.   90

R. Roister. How may I revive, being now
so far past?

M. Merry. I will rub your temples, and
fet [1] you again at last.

R. Roister. It will not be possible.

M. Merry.   Yes,
for twenty pound.

R. Roister. Arms! [2] what dost thou?

M. Merry.   Fet
you again out of your sound. [3]

By this cross, ye were nigh gone indeed;
I might feel

Your soul departing within an inch of
your heel.

Now follow my counsel.

R. Roister.   What is it?

M. Merry.   If I were you,
Custance should eft [4] seek to me, ere I
would bow.

R. Roister. Well, as thou wilt have me,
even so will I do.

M. Merry. Then shall ye revive again for
an hour or two.   100

R. Roister. As thou wilt; I am content
for a little space.

M. Merry. "Good hap is not hasty;"
yet "In space com[e]th grace."

To speak with Custance yourself should
be very well;

What good thereof may come, nor I
nor you can tell.

But now the matter standeth upon your
marriage,

Ye must now take unto you a lusty courage;

Ye may not speak with a faint heart to
Custance,

But with a lusty breast and countenance,

That she may know she hath to answer
to a man.

R. Roister. Yes, I can do that as well
as any can.   110

M. Merry. Then because ye must Custance face to face woo,

Let us see how to behave yourself ye
can do.

Ye must have a portly brag after your
estate. [5]

R. Roister. Tush, I can handle that after
the best rate.

M. Merry. Well done! so, lo! up, man,
with your head and chin,

Up with that snout, man! so, lo! now ye
begin!

So, that is somewhat like! But, pranky-
coat, [6] nay, whan? [7]

That is a lusty brute; hands under your
side, man.

So, lo! now is it even as it should be;

That is somewhat like, for a man of your
degree.   120

Then must ye stately go, jetting [8] up
and down.

Tut, can ye no better shake the tail of
your gown?

There, lo, such a lusty brag it is ye must
make.

R. Roister. To come behind, and make
curtsy, thou must some pains take.

M. Merry. Else were I much to blame, I
thank your mastership.

The Lord one day all-to [9] begrime you
with worship.

"Back, sir sauce, let gentlefolks have
elbow room.

[Shoves imaginary persons out of the way.]

Void, [10] sirs, see ye not Master Roister
Doister come?

Make place, my masters."

[Jostles Roister Doister.]

R. Roister.   Thou justlest
now too nigh.   129

M. Merry. "Back, all rude louts!"

R. Roister.   Tush!

M. Merry.   I cry your ma'ship mercy!

Hoiday, if fair fine Mistress Custance
saw you now,

Ralph Roister Doister were her own, I
warrant you!

R. Roister. Ne'er an M [11] by your girdle? [12]

M. Merry.   Your good mastership's
Mastership were her own mistress-ship's
mistress-ship's! [13]

Ye were take up for hawks [14]— ye were
gone, ye were gone.

But now one other thing more yet I
think upon.

[1] Fetch.   [3] Swoon.
[2] By God's arms.   [4] Again.
[5] Pompous bearing befitting your rank.

[6] Frolicsome fellow.   [9] Completely.
[7] When.   [10] Make room.
[8] Strutting.
[11] Abbreviation for *master* or *mistress*.
[12] *I.e.*, Can't you speak respectfully—address
me as master?   [13] Supply *property, husband.*
[14] Farmer suggests: "You would be snapped
up for a husband like hawks' meat."

R. Roister. Show what it is.

M. Merry.   A wooer, be he never so poor,

Must play and sing before his best-belove's door;

How much more, then, you?

R. Roister.   Thou speakest well, out of doubt.

M. Merry. And perchance that would make her the sooner come out.   140

R. Roister. Go, call my musicians; bid them hie apace.

M. Merry. I will be here with them ere ye can say "trey ace."[1]   *Exeat.*

R. Roister. This was well said of Merry-greek; I low his wit.

Before my sweetheart's door we will have a fit,

That if my love come forth, that I may with her talk,

I doubt not but this gear shall on my side walk.

But lo, how well Merrygreek is returned sence.[2]

[*Enter Merrygreek with Musicians.*]

M. Merry. There hath grown no grass on my heel since I went hence;

Lo, here have I brought that shall make you pastance.

R. Roister. Come, sirs, let us sing to win my dear love Custance.   150

Cantent.[3]

M. Merry. Lo, where she cometh! Some countenance to her make,

And ye shall hear me be plain with her for your sake.

Actus III. Scena iv.

Custance, Merrygreek, Roister Doister.

C. Custance. What gauding[4] and fooling is this afore my door?

M. Merry. May not folks be honest, pray you, though they be poor?

C. Custance. As that thing may be true, so rich folks may be fools.

R. Roister. Her talk is as fine as she had learned in schools.

M. Merry. Look partly toward her, and draw a little near.

C. Custance. Get ye home, idle folks.

M. Merry.   Why may not we be here? Nay, and ye will ha's,[5] ha's; otherwise, I tell you plain,

And ye will not ha's, then give us our gear again.

C. Custance. Indeed, I have of yours much gay things, God save all.

R. Roister. Speak gently unto her, and let her take all.   10

M. Merry. You are too tender-hearted. Shall she make us daws?

Nay, dame, I will be plain with you in my friend's cause.

R. Roister. Let all this pass, sweetheart, and accept my service.

C. Custance. I will not be served with a fool in no wise;

When I choose an husband, I hope to take a man.

M. Merry. And where will ye find one which can do that he can?

Now this man toward you being so kind, You not to make him an answer some-what to his mind!

C. Custance. I sent him a full answer by you, did I not?

M. Merry. And I reported it.

C. Custance.   Nay, I must speak it again.   20

R. Roister. No, no, he told it all.

M. Merry.   Was I not metely[6] plain?

R. Roister. Yes.

M. Merry.   But I would not tell all; for faith, if I had,

With you, Dame Custance, ere this hour it had been bad,

And not without cause; for this goodly personage

Meant no less than to join with you in marriage.

C. Custance. Let him waste no more labor nor suit about me.

M. Merry. Ye know not where your preferment lieth, I see,

He sending you such a token, ring, and letter.

C. Custance. Marry, here it is; ye never saw a better.

M. Merry. Let us see your letter.

---

[1] A throw of dice.
[2] Since.
[3] Probably "The Fourth Song," printed at the end of the play.   [4] Jesting.
[5] Have us.   [6] Tolerably.

C. CUSTANCE. Hold,
read it if ye can. 30
And see what letter it is to win a woman.
M. MERRY. "To mine own dear cony,
bird, sweetheart, and pigsnie,
Good Mistress Custance, present these
by-and-by."
Of this superscription do ye blame the
style?
C. CUSTANCE. With the rest, as good stuff
as ye read a great while.
M. MERRY. "Sweet mistress, whereas I
love you nothing at all,
Regarding your substance and richesse
chief of all,
For your personage, beauty, demeanor,
and wit,
I commend me unto you never a whit;
Sorry to hear report of your good wel-
fare, 40
For, as I hear say, such your conditions
are,
That ye be worthy favor of no living
man;
To be abhorred of every honest man;
To be taken for a woman inclined to
vice;
Nothing at all to virtue giving her due
price.
Wherefore, concerning marriage, ye are
thought
Such a fine paragon as ne'er honest
man bought.
And now by these presents I do you
advertise
That I am minded to marry you in no
wise.
For your goods and substance, I could
be content 50
To take you as ye are. If ye mind to be
my wife,
Ye shall be assured for the time of my
life,
I will keep ye right well from good rai-
ment and fare;
Ye shall not be kept but in sorrow and
care.
Ye shall in no wise live at your own
liberty;
Do and say what ye lust, ye shall never
please me;
But, when ye are merry, I will be all
sad;
When ye are sorry, I will be very glad;

When ye seek your heart's ease, I will
be unkind.
At no time in me shall ye much gentleness find. 60
But all things contrary to your will and
mind
Shall be done; otherwise I will not be
behind
To speak. And, as for all them that
would do you wrong,
I will so help and maintain, ye shall not
live long.
Nor any foolish dolt shall cumber you
but I.
I, whoe'er say nay, will stick by you
till I die.
Thus, good Mistress Custance, the Lord
you save and keep
From me, Roister Doister, whether I
wake or sleep.
Who favoreth you no less (ye may be
bold)
Than this letter purporteth, which ye
have unfold." 70
C. CUSTANCE. How by this letter of love?
Is it not fine?
R. ROISTER. By the arms of Calais, it is
none of mine.
M. MERRY. Fie, you are foul to blame;
this is your own hand!
C. CUSTANCE. Might not a woman be
proud of such an husband?
M. MERRY. Ah, that ye would in a letter
show such despite!
R. ROISTER. O, I would I had him here,
the which did it indite.
M. MERRY. Why, ye made it yourself, ye
told me by this light.
R. ROISTER. Yea, I meant I wrote it mine
own self yesternight.
C. CUSTANCE. Iwis, sir, I would not have
sent you such a mock.
R. ROISTER. Ye may so take it, but I
meant it not so, by Cock. 80
M. MERRY. Who can blame this woman to
fume and fret and rage?
Tut, tut! yourself now have marred your
own marriage.
Well, yet, Mistress Custance, if ye can
this remit,
This gentleman otherwise may your love
requit.
C. CUSTANCE. No, God be with you both,
and seek no more to me. *Exeat.*

R. ROISTER. Wough! she is gone forever;
    I shall her no more see.
M. MERRY. What, weep? Fie, for shame!
    And blubber? For manhood's sake,
    Never let your foe so much pleasure of
    you take.
    Rather play the man's part, and do love
    refrain.[1]
    If she despise you, e'en despise ye her
    again.   90
R. ROISTER. By Goss,[2] and for thy sake I
    defy her indeed.
M. MERRY. Yea, and perchance that way
    ye shall much sooner speed,
    For one mad property these women have,
    in fay:[3]
    When ye will, they will not; will not ye,
    then will they.
    Ah, foolish woman! ah, most unlucky
    Custance!
    Ah, unfortunate woman! ah, peevish
    Custance!
    Art thou to thine harms so obstinately
    bent
    That thou canst not see where lieth thine
    high preferment?
    Canst thou not lub dis man, which could
    lub dee so well?
    Art thou so much thine own foe?
R. ROISTER.   Thou
    dost the truth tell.   100
M. MERRY. Well, I lament.
R. ROISTER.   So do I.
M. MERRY.   Wherefore?
R. ROISTER.   For this
    thing:
    Because she is gone.
M. MERRY.   I mourn for an-
    other thing.
R. ROISTER. What is it, Merrygreek, where-
    fore thou dost grief take?
M. MERRY. That I am not a woman my-
    self for your sake;
    I would have you myself—and a straw
    for yond Gill[4]—
    And mock[5] much of you though it were
    against my will.
    I would not, I warrant you, fall in such a
    rage[6]
    As so to refuse such a goodly person-
    age.

R. ROISTER. In faith, I heartily thank
    thee, Merrygreek.
M. MERRY. And I were a woman——
R. ROISTER.   Thou wouldest
    to me seek.   110
M. MERRY. For, though I say it, a goodly
    person ye be.
R. ROISTER. No, no.
M. MERRY.   Yes, a goodly man
    as e'er I did see.
R. ROISTER. No, I am a poor homely man,
    as God made me.
M. MERRY. By the faith that I owe to
    God, sir, but ye be.
    Would I might, for your sake, spend a
    thousand pound land.
R. ROISTER. I dare say thou wouldest have
    me to thy husband.
M. MERRY. Yea; and I were the fairest
    lady in the shire,
    And knew you as I know you, and see
    you now here—
    Well, I say no more.
R. ROISTER.   Gramercies, with
    all my heart.
M. MERRY. But since that cannot be, will
    ye play a wise part?   120
R. ROISTER. How should I?
M. MERRY.   Refrain from
    Custance a while now,
    And I warrant her soon right glad to seek
    to you.
    Ye shall see her anon come on her knees
    creeping,
    And pray you to be good to her, salt
    tears weeping.
R. ROISTER. But what and she come not?
M. MERRY.   In faith, then, farewell she.
    Or else, if ye be wroth, ye may avenged
    be.
R. ROISTER. By Cock's precious potstick,[7]
    and e'en so I shall.
    I will utterly destroy her, and house and
    all!
    But I would be avenged in the mean
    space
    On that vile scribbler that did my wooing
    disgrace.   130
M. MERRY. "Scribbler," ko you? Indeed,
    he is worthy no less.
    I will call him to you, and ye bid me
    doubtless.

[1] Desist from.
[2] By God (a mild oath).
[3] Faith.
[4] Wench.
[5] Make (?).
[6] Madness.
[7] Farmer suggests the stick used to extend the sponge to Christ on the cross.

R. Roister. Yes, for although he had as
    many lives
As a thousand widows, and a thousand
    wives,
As a thousand lions, and a thousand
    rats,
A thousand wolves, and a thousand
    cats,
A thousand bulls, and a thousand calves,
And a thousand legions divided in halves,
He shall never scape death on my sword's
    point,
Though I should be torn therefor joint
    by joint.   140
M. Merry. Nay, if ye will kill him, I will
    not fet him;
I will not in so much extremity set
    him.
He may yet amend, sir, and be an honest
    man;
Therefore pardon him, good soul, as
    much as ye can.
R. Roister. Well, for thy sake, this once
    with his life he shall pass,
But I will hew him all to pieces, by the
    Mass.
M. Merry. Nay, faith, ye shall promise
    that he shall no harm have,
Else I will not fet him.
R. Roister.   I shall, so God
    me save.
But I may chide him agood.[1]
M. Merry.   Yea, that
    do hardly.[2]
R. Roister. Go, then.
M. Merry.   I return, and bring
    him to you by-and-by.   *Ex[eat]*. 150

Actus III. Scena v.

*Roister Doister, Matthew Merrygreek, Scriv-
ener.*[3]

R. Roister. What is a gentleman but his
    word and his promise?
I must now save this villain's life in any
    wise,
And yet at him already my hands do
    tickle;
I shall uneath[4] hold them, they will be
    so fickle.
But lo, and Merrygreek have not brought
    him sence.

[1] In earnest.
[2] Hardily, boldly.
[3] Last two enter later.
[4] With difficulty.

[*Enter Merrygreek and Scrivener.*]

M. Merry. Nay, I would I had of my
    purse paid forty pence.
Scrivener. So would I too; but it needed
    not that stound.[5]
M. Merry. But the gentman had rather
    spent five thousand pound,
For it disgraced him at least five times
    so much.
Scrivener. He disgraced himself, his lout-
    ishness is such.   10
R. Roister. [*Aside.*] How long they stand
    prating!—Why com'st thou not away?
M. Merry. Come now to himself, and
    hark what he will say.
Scrivener. I am not afraid in his presence
    to appear.
R. Roister. Art thou come, fellow?
Scrivener.   How
    think you? Am I not here?
R. Roister. What hindrance hast thou
    done me, and what villainy!
Scrivener. It hath come of thyself, if
    thou hast had any.
R. Roister. All the stock thou comest of,
    later or rather,[6]
From thy first father's grandfather's
    father's father,
Nor all that shall come of thee to the
    world's end,
Though to threescore generations they
    descend,   20
Can be able to make me a just recom-
    pense
For this trespass of thine and this one
    offense.
Scrivener. Wherein?
R. Roister.   Did not you make
    me a letter, brother?
Scrivener. Pay the like hire, I will make
    you such another.
R. Roister. Nay, see and these whoreson [7]
    Pharisees and Scribes
Do not get their living by polling and
    bribes! [8]
If it were not for shame——
Scrivener.   Nay, hold
    thy hands still!
M. Merry. Why, did ye not promise that
    ye would not him spill? [9]

[5] Amazement; *i.e.*, the shock of the letter was
unnecessary (?).   [6] Sooner.   [7] Rascally.
   [8] Swindling and robbery.   [9] Destroy.

SCRIVENER. Let him not spare me.

R. ROISTER.   Why,
wilt thou strike me again?

SCRIVENER. Ye shall have as good as ye
bring of me, that is plain.   30

M. MERRY. I cannot blame him, sir,
though your blows would him grieve,
For he knoweth present death to ensue
of all ye give.

R. ROISTER. Well, this man for once hath
purchased thy pardon.

SCRIVENER. And what say ye to me? Or
else I will be gone.

R. ROISTER. I say the letter thou madest
me was not good.

SCRIVENER. Then did ye wrong copy it,
of likelihood.

R. ROISTER. Yes, out of thy copy word
for word I wrote.

SCRIVENER. Then was it as ye prayed to
have it, I wot,
But in reading and pointing [1] there was
made some fault.

R. ROISTER. I wot not, but it made all
my matter to halt.   40

SCRIVENER. How say you, is this mine
original or no?

R. ROISTER. The selfsame that I wrote
out of, so mote I go.[2]

SCRIVENER. Look you on your own fist,
and I will look on this,
And let this man be judge whether I
read amiss.
"To mine own dear cony, bird, sweetheart, and pigsnie,
Good Mistress Custance, present these
by-and-by."
How now? Doth not this superscription
agree?

R. ROISTER. Read that is within, and
there ye shall the fault see.

SCRIVENER. "Sweet mistress, whereas I
love you—nothing at all
Regarding your richesse and substance,
chief of all   50
For your personage, beauty, demeanor,
and wit—
I commend me unto you; never a whit
Sorry to hear report of your good welfare.
For, as I hear say, such your conditions
are
That ye be worthy favor; of no living
man

<hr />

[1] Punctuating.   [2] *I.e.*, so may I live.

To be abhorred; of every honest man
To be taken for a woman inclined to vice
Nothing at all; to virtue giving her due
price.
Wherefore concerning marriage, ye are
thought
Such a fine paragon as ne'er honest man
bought.   60
And now by these presents I do you
advertise
That I am minded to marry you—in no
wise
For your goods and substance. I can be
content
To take you as you are. If ye will be my
wife,
Ye shall be assured for the time of my
life,
I will keep you right well. From good
raiment and fare
Ye shall not be kept; but in sorrow and
care
Ye shall in no wise live; at your own
liberty
Do and say what ye lust. Ye shall never
please me
But when ye are merry; I will be all sad 70
When ye are sorry; I will be very glad
When ye seek your heart's ease; I will
be unkind
At no time; in me shall ye much gentle-
ness find.
But all things contrary to your will and
mind
Shall be done otherwise. I will not be
behind
To speak.   And as for all them that
would do you wrong
(I will so help and maintain ye) shall
not live long.
Nor any foolish dolt shall cumber you,
but I,
I, whoe'er say nay, will stick by you till
I die.
Thus, good Mistress Custance, the Lord
you save and keep.   80
From me, Roister Doister, whether I
wake or sleep,
Who favoreth you no less (ye may be
bold)
Than this letter purporteth, which ye
have unfold."
Now, sir, what default can ye find in this
letter?

R. ROISTER. Of truth, in my mind there
cannot be a better.
SCRIVENER. Then was the fault in reading,
and not in writing;
No, nor I dare say in the form of inditing.
But who read this letter, that it sounded
so naught?
M. MERRY. I read it, indeed.
SCRIVENER.   Ye read it
not as ye ought.
R. ROISTER. Why, thou wretched villain,
was all this same fault in thee?   90
M. MERRY. I knock your costard [1] if ye
offer to strike me.
R. ROISTER. Strikest thou, indeed, and I
offer but in jest?
M. MERRY. Yea, and rap you again ex-
cept ye can sit in rest.
And I will no longer tarry here, me be-
lieve.
R. ROISTER. What, wilt thou be angry,
and I do thee forgive?
Fare thou well, scribbler; I cry thee
mercy indeed.
SCRIVENER. Fare ye well, bibbler, and
worthily may ye speed.
R. ROISTER. If it were another but thou,
it were a knave.
M. MERRY. Ye are another yourself, sir,
the Lord us both save,
Albeit in this matter I must your pardon
crave.   100
Alas, would ye wish in me the wit that
ye have?
But as for my fault I can quickly amend;
I will show Custance it was I that did
offend.
R. ROISTER. By so doing her anger may
be reformed.
M. MERRY. But, if by no entreaty she will
be turned,
Then set light by her and be as testy as
she,
And do your force upon her with ex-
tremity.
R. ROISTER. Come on, therefore, let us go
home in sadness.
M. MERRY. That if force shall need, all
may be in a readiness.   109
And, as for this letter, hardly let all go.
We will know whe'er [2] she refuse you for
that or no.   *Exeant am[bo].*

[1] Apple, *i.e.*, head.   [2] Whether.

ACTUS IV. SCENA i.

Sim Suresby.

SIM SURE. Is there any man but I, Sim
Suresby alone,
That would have taken such an enter-
prise him upon,
In such an outrageous tempest as this
was,
Such a dangerous gulf of the sea to
pass?
I think, verily, Neptune's mighty god-
ship
Was angry with some that was in our
ship,
And, but for the honesty which in me
he found,
I think for the others' sake we had been
drowned.
But fie on that servant which for his
master's wealth [3]
Will stick for to hazard both his life and
his health.   10
My master, Gawin Goodluck, after me
a day,
Because of the weather, thought best his
ship to stay;
And now that I have the rough surges so
well passed,
God grant I may find all things safe here
at last.
Then will I think all my travail well
spent.
Now the first point wherefore my master
hath me sent
Is to salute Dame Christian Custance,
his wife
Espoused, whom he tend'reth no less
than his life.
I must see how it is with her, well or
wrong,
And whether for him she doth not now
think long.   20
Then to other friends I have a message
or tway, [4]
And then so to return and meet him on
the way.
Now will I go knock that I may despatch
with speed,
But lo, forth cometh herself happily, [5]
indeed.

[3] Welfare.
[4] Two.
[5] Fortunately.

ACTUS IV. SCENA ii.

Christian Custance, Sim Suresby.

C. CUSTANCE. [*Aside.*] I come to see if any
more stirring be here.
But what stranger is this which doth to
me appear?

SIM SURE. [*Aside.*] I will speak to her.—
Dame, the Lord you save and see.

C. CUSTANCE. What, friend Sim Suresby?
Forsooth, right welcome ye be!
How doth mine own Gawin Goodluck?
I pray thee tell.

SIM SURE. When he knoweth of your
health, he will be perfect well.

C. CUSTANCE. If he have perfect health,
I am as I would be.

SIM SURE. Such news will please him well;
this is as it should be.

C. CUSTANCE. I think now long for him.

SIM SURE.   And he as long for you.

C. CUSTANCE. When will he be at home?

SIM SURE.   His heart is here e'en now;
His body cometh after.

C. CUSTANCE.   I would see that
fain.   11

SIM SURE. As fast as wind and sail can
carry it amain.
But what two men are yond coming
hitherward?

C. CUSTANCE. Now I shrew their best
Christmas cheeks,[1] both togetherward!

ACTUS IV. SCENA iii.

*Christian Custance, Sim Suresby, Ralph
Roister, Matthew Merrygreek, Truepenny.*[2]

C. CUSTANCE. [*Aside.*] What mean these
lewd fellows thus to trouble me still?
Sim Suresby here perchance shall thereof
deem some ill,
And shall suspect in me some point of
naughtiness,
And [3] they come hitherward.

SIM SURE.   What is
their business?

C. CUSTANCE. I have naught to them, nor
they to me, in sadness.[4]

SIM SURE. Let us hearken them.—[*Aside.*]
Somewhat there is, I fear it.

R. ROISTER. I will speak out aloud best,
that she may hear it.

M. MERRY. Nay, alas, ye may so fear [5]
her out of her wit.

R. ROISTER. By the cross of my sword, I
will hurt her no whit.

M. MERRY. Will ye do no harm indeed?
Shall I trust your word?   10

R. ROISTER. By Roister Doister's faith, I
will speak but in bord.

SIM SURE. Let us hearken them.—[*Aside.*]
Somewhat there is, I fear it.

R. ROISTER. I will speak out aloud; I care
not who hear it.

[*Pretends to call to his servants within.*]
Sirs, see that my harness, my target,
and my shield
Be made as bright now as when I was
last in field,
As white as I should to war again to-
morrow;
For sick shall I be, but I work some folk
sorrow.
Therefore see that all shine as bright as
Saint George,
Or as doth a key newly come from the
smith's forge.
I would have my sword and harness to
shine so bright [6]   20
That I might therewith dim mine
enemies' sight.
I would have it cast beams as fast, I tell
you plain,
As doth the glittering grass after a shower
of rain.
And see that, in case I should need to
come to arming,
All things may be ready at a minute's
warning.
For such chance may chance in an hour—
do ye hear?

M. MERRY. As perchance shall not chance
again in seven year.

R. ROISTER. Now draw we near to her,
and hear what shall be said.

M. MERRY. But I would not have you
make her too much afraid.

R. ROISTER. Well found, sweet wife (I
trust), for all this your sour look.   30

C. CUSTANCE. Wife? Why call ye me
wife?

---

[1] A defiant curse (*N.E.D.*); *i.e.*, I curse their
unrestrained effrontery.
[2] Enters later.   [3] If.   [4] Seriousness.

[5] Frighten.
[6] This passage is based on Plautus, *Miles
gloriosus*, I, i.

SIM SURE. [*Aside*.]   Wife? This gear go'th acrook.

M. MERRY. Nay, Mistress Custance, I warrant you, our letter

Is not as we read e'en now, but much better,

And, where ye half stomached this gentleman afore,

For this same letter, ye will love him now therefor;

Nor it is not this letter, though ye were a queen,

That should break marriage between you twain, I ween.[1]

C. CUSTANCE. I did not refuse him for the letter's sake.

R. ROISTER. Then ye are content me for your husband to take.

C. CUSTANCE. You for my husband to take? Nothing less truly.   40

R. ROISTER. Yea, say so, sweet spouse, afore strangers hardly.

M. MERRY. And, though I have here his letter of love with me,

Yet his ring and tokens he sent, keep safe with ye.

C. CUSTANCE. A mischief take his tokens, and him and thee too.

But what prate I with fools? Have I nought else to do?

Come in with me, Sim Suresby, to take some repast.

SIM SURE. I must, ere I drink, by your leave, go in all haste

To a place or two with earnest letters of his.

C. CUSTANCE. Then come drink here with me.

SIM SURE.   I thank you!

C. CUSTANCE.   Do not miss.

You shall have a token to your master with you.   50

SIM SURE. No tokens this time, gramercies! God be with you.   *Exeat.*

C. CUSTANCE. Surely this fellow misdeemeth some ill in me—

Which thing, but God help, will go near to spill me.

R. ROISTER. Yea, farewell, fellow, and tell thy master Goodluck

That he cometh too late of this blossom to pluck.

Let him keep him there still, or at leastwise make no haste,

As for his labor hither he shall spend in waste.

His betters be in place now.

M. MERRY. [*Aside*.]   As long as it will hold.

C. CUSTANCE. I will be even with thee, thou beast, thou mayst be bold.[2]

R. ROISTER. Will ye have us then?

C. CUSTANCE.   I will never have thee.   60

R. ROISTER. Then will I have you!

C. CUSTANCE.   No, the devil shall have thee.

I have gotten this hour more shame and harm by thee

Than all thy life-days thou canst do me honesty.

M. MERRY. [*To Roister Doister*.] Why, now may ye see what it com'th to, in the end,

To make a deadly foe of your most loving friend.—

And iwis this letter, if ye would hear it now——

C. CUSTANCE. I will hear none of it.

M. MERRY.   In faith, would ravish you.

C. CUSTANCE. He hath stained my name forever, this is clear.

R. ROISTER. I can make all as well in an hour—

M. MERRY. [*Aside*.]   As ten year.—

How say ye, will ye have him?

C. CUSTANCE.   No.

M. MERRY.   Will ye take him? 70

C. CUSTANCE. I defy him.

M. MERRY.   At my word?

C. CUSTANCE.   A shame take him.

Waste no more wind, for it will never be.

M. MERRY. This one fault with twain shall be mended, ye shall see.

Gentle Mistress Custance now, good Mistress Custance!

Honey Mistress Custance now, sweet Mistress Custance!

Golden Mistress Custance now, white [3] Mistress Custance!

Silken Mistress Custance now, fair Mistress Custance!

---

[1] Imagine.

[2] Certain.

[3] Dear.

C. Custance. Faith, rather than to marry
with such a doltish lout
  I would match myself with a beggar, out
  of doubt.
M. Merry. Then I can say no more; to
speed we are not like,   80
  Except ye rap out a rag of your rhetoric.[1]
C. Custance. Speak not of winning me,
for it shall never be so.
R. Roister. Yes, dame, I will have you,
whether ye will or no.
  I command you to love me! Wherefore
  should ye not?
  Is not my love to you chafing and burning
  hot?
M. Merry. To her! That is well said!
R. Roister.   Shall I so break my brain
  To dote upon you, and ye not love us
  again?
M. Merry. Well said yet.
C. Custance.   Go to, you goose.
R. Roister.   I say, Kit Custance,
  In case ye will not ha's—well, better yes,
  perchance.
C. Custance. Avaunt, losel;[2] pick thee
hence![3]
M. Merry.   Well, sir, ye perceive,   90
  For all your kind offer, she will not you
  receive.
R. Roister. Then a straw for her, and a
straw for her again;
  She shall not be my wife, would she never
  so fain;
  No, and though she would be at ten
  thousand pound cost.
M. Merry. Lo, dame, ye may see what
an husband ye have lost.
C. Custance. Yea, no force;[4] a jewel
much better lost than found.
M. Merry. Ah, ye will not believe how
this doth my heart wound.
  How should a marriage between you be
  toward,
  If both parties draw back, and become
  so froward?
R. Roister. Nay, dame, I will fire thee
out of thy house,[5]   100
  And destroy thee and all thine, and that
  by-and-by.
M. Merry. Nay, for the passion of God,
sir, do not so.

R. Roister. Yes, except she will say yea
to that she said no.
C. Custance. And what! be there no
officers, trow we, in town
  To check idle loiterers, bragging up and
  down?
  Where be they by whom vacabunds[6]
  should be repressed,
  That poor silly[7] widows might live in
  peace and rest?
  Shall I never rid thee out of my company?
  I will call for help. What ho! come forth,
  Truepenny:
Truepenny. [Within.] Anon.[8]

[Enters.]
            What is your will, mistress?
  Did ye call me?   110
C. Custance. Yea; go run apace, and, as
fast as may be,
  Pray Tristram Trusty, my most assured
  friend,
  To be here by-and-by, that he may me
  defend.
Truepenny. That message so quickly
shall be done, by God's grace,
  That at my return ye shall say I went
  apace.   Exeat.
C. Custance. Then shall we see, I trow,
whether ye shall do me harm.
R. Roister. Yes, in faith, Kit, I shall
thee and thine so charm
  That all women incarnate by thee may
  beware.
C. Custance. Nay, as for charming me,
come hither if thou dare;
  I shall clout thee till thou stink, both
  thee and thy train,   120
  And coil thee[9] mine own hands, and
  send thee home again.
R. Roister. Yea, sayest thou me that,
dame? Dost thou me threaten?
  Go we; I still[10] see whether I shall be
  beaten.
M. Merry. Nay, for the pashe[11] of God,
let me now treat peace,
  For bloodshed will there be in case this
  strife increase.
  Ah, good Dame Custance, take better
  way with you.

---

[1] *I.e.*, unless you spout a bit of your rhetoric.
[2] Rascal. [3] Away with you! [4] No matter.
[5] Perhaps "stye" to rime.

[6] Vagabonds.   [9] Beat thee [with].
[7] Simple.   [10] Cooper suggests *will*.
[8] The usual answer of servants. [11] Passion.

C. Custance. Let him do his worst!

M. Merry.   Yield in time!

R. Roister.   Come hence,
thou!

    Exeant Roister et Merry[greek].

Actus IV. Scena iv.

*Christian Custance, Annot Alyface, Tibet
T[alkapace], M[adge] Mumblecrust.*[1]

C. Custance. So, sirrah, if I should not
with him take this way,
  I should not be rid of him, I think, till
doomsday.
  I will call forth my folks, that, without
any mocks,[2]
  If he come again, we may give him raps
and knocks.
  Madge Mumblecrust, come forth, and
Tibet Talkapace.
  Yea, and come forth too, Mistress Annot
Alyface.

    [Enter the three Maids.]

An. Alyface. I come.

Tib. Talk.   And I am here.

M. Mumbl.   And I am here too,
at length.

C. Custance. Like warriors, if need be,
ye must show your strength.
  The man that this day hath thus beguiled you,
  Is Ralph Roister Doister, whom ye know
well inowe,[3]   10
  The most lout and dastard that ever on
ground trod.

Tib. Talk. I see all folk mock him when
he go'th abroad.

C. Custance. What, pretty maid, will ye
talk when I speak?

Tib. Talk. No, forsooth, good mistress.

C. Custance.   Will ye my tale break?
  He threat'neth to come hither with all
his force to fight.
  I charge you, if he come, on him with all
your might!

M. Mumbl. I with my distaff will reach
him one rap!

Tib. Talk. And I with my new broom
will sweep him one swap,
  And then with our great club I will reach
him one rap!

An. Alyface. And I with our skimmer
will fling him one flap!   20

Tib. Talk. Then Truepenny's firefork[4]
will him shrewdly fray,[5]
  And you with the spit may drive him
quite away.

C. Custance. Go, make all ready, that
it may be e'en so.

Tib. Talk. For my part, I shrew them
that last about it go.   *Exeant.*

Actus IV. Scena v.

*Christian Custance, Truepenny, Tristram
Trusty.*[6]

C. Custance. Truepenny did promise me
to run a great pace,
  My friend Tristram Trusty to fet into
this place.
  Indeed he dwelleth hence a good start,[7]
I confess;
  But yet a quick messenger might twice
since, as I guess,
  Have gone and come again. Ah, yond
I spy him now.

*[Enter Truepenny, followed by Tristram
Trusty.]*

Truepenny. Ye are a slow goer, sir, I
make God avow.
  My mistress Custance will in me put all
the blame.
  Your legs be longer than mine; come
apace for shame.

C. Custance. I can thee thank, Truepenny; thou hast done right well.

Truepenny. Mistress, since I went, no
grass hath grown on my heel,   10
  But Master Tristram Trusty here maketh no speed.

C. Custance. That he came at all, I
thank him in very deed,
  For now have I need of the help of some
wise man.

T. Trusty. Then may I be gone again,
for none such I [a]m.

Truepenny. Ye may be, by your going,[8]
for no alderman
  Can go, I dare say, a sadder[9] pace than
ye can.

---

[1] The last three enter later.   [2] Pretenses.
[3] *I.e.*, enow. Emendation suggested by Cooper,
original reads *mowe*.

[4] Poker.   [7] Distance.
[5] Frighten.   [8] Gait.
[6] Last two enter later.   [9] Soberer.

C. CUSTANCE. Truepenny, get thee in; thou shalt among them know
How to use thyself like a proper man, I trow.
TRUEPENNY. I go.   [*Exeat.*]
C. CUSTANCE.   Now, Tristram Trusty, I thank you right much,
For, at my first sending, to come ye never grutch.[1]   20
T. TRUSTY. Dame Custance, God ye save, and while my life shall last,
For my friend Goodluck's sake ye shall not send in waste.
C. CUSTANCE. He shall give you thanks.
T. TRUSTY.   I will do much for his sake.
C. CUSTANCE. But, alack, I fear great displeasure shall be take.
T. TRUSTY. Wherefore?
C. CUSTANCE.   For a foolish matter.
T. TRUSTY.   What is your cause?
C. CUSTANCE. I am ill accumbered with a couple of daws.
T. TRUSTY. Nay, weep not, woman, but tell me what your cause is.
As concerning my friend, is anything amiss?
C. CUSTANCE. No, not on my part. But here was Sim Suresby—
T. TRUSTY. He was with me and told me so.
C. CUSTANCE.   And he stood by   30
While Ralph Roister Doister with help of Merrygreek
For promise of marriage did unto me seek.
T. TRUSTY. And had ye made any promise before them twain?
C. CUSTANCE. No, I had rather be torn in pieces and flain.[2]
No man hath my faith and troth but Gawin Goodluck,
And that before Suresby did I say, and there stuck.
But of certain letters there were such words spoken —
T. TRUSTY. He told me that too.
C. CUSTANCE.   And of a ring and token,
That Suresby, I spied, did more than half suspect
That I my faith to Gawin Goodluck did reject.   40
T. TRUSTY. But there was no such matter, Dame Custance, indeed?

C. CUSTANCE. If ever my head thought it, God send me ill speed.
Wherefore, I beseech you, with me to be a witness,
That in all my life I never intended thing less;
And what a brainsick fool Ralph Roister Doister is,
Yourself know well enough.
T. TRUSTY.   Ye say full true, iwis.
C. CUSTANCE. Because to be his wife I ne grant nor apply,[3]
Hither will he come, he sweareth, by-and-by,
To kill both me and mine, and beat down my house flat.
Therefore I pray your aid.
T. TRUSTY.   I warrant you that.   50
C. CUSTANCE. Have I so many years lived a sober life,
And showed myself honest, maid, widow, and wife,
And now to be abused in such a vile sort?
Ye see how poor widows live all void of comfort.
T. TRUSTY. I warrant him do you no harm nor wrong at all.
C. CUSTANCE. No, but Matthew Merrygreek doth me most appall,
That he would join himself with such a wretched lout.
T. TRUSTY. He doth it for a jest; I know him out of doubt.—
And here cometh Merrygreek.
C. CUSTANCE.   Then shall we hear his mind.

ACTUS IV. SCENA vi.

Merrygreek, Christian Custance, Trist[ram] Trusty.

M. MERRY. Custance and Trusty both, I do you here well find.
C. CUSTANCE. Ah, Matthew Merrygreek, ye have used me well:
M. MERRY. Now for altogether[4] ye must your answer tell.
Will ye have this man, woman, or else will ye not?
Else will he come never boar so brim[5] nor toast so hot.

---

[1] Grumble.   [2] Flayed.   [3] Incline.   [4] Once for all.   [5] Fierce.

Tris. and Cus. But why join ye with him?

T. Trusty.   For mirth?

C. Custance.   Or else in sadness?

M. Merry. The more fond of you! Both? Hardly! The matter guess!

T. Trusty. Lo, how say ye, dame?

M. Merry.   Why, do ye think, Dame Custance, That in this wooing I have meant aught but pastance?

C. Custance. Much things ye spake, I wot, to maintain his dotage.   10

M. Merry. But well might ye judge I spake it all in mockage. For why? Is Roister Doister a fit husband for you?

T. Trusty. I dare say ye never thought it.

M. Merry.   No, to God I vow. And did not I know afore of the insurance [1] Between Gawin Goodluck and Christian Custance? And did not I for the nonce, by my conveyance,[2] Read his letter in a wrong sense for dalliance, That, if you could have take it up at the first bound, We should thereat such a sport and pastime have found, That all the whole town should have been the merrier?   20

C. Custance. Ill ache your heads both! I was never wearier, Nor never more vexed since the first day I was born.

T. Trusty. But very well I wist he here did all in scorn.

C. Custance. But I feared thereof to take dishonesty.[3]

M. Merry. This should both have made sport and showed your honesty, And Goodluck, I dare swear, your wit therein would low.

T. Trusty. Yea, being no worse than we know it to be now.

M. Merry. And nothing yet too late; for when I come to him, Hither will he repair with a sheep's look full grim, By plain force and violence to drive you to yield.   30

C. Custance. If ye two bid me, we will with him pitch a field,[4] I and my maids together.

M. Merry.   Let us see; be bold.

C. Custance. Ye shall see women's war.

T. Trusty.   That fight will I behold.

M. Merry. If occasion serve, taking his part full brim, I will strike at you, but the rap shall light on him, When we first appear.

C. Custance.   Then will I run away As though I were afeard.

T. Trusty.   Do you that part well play And I will sue for peace.

M. Merry.   And I will set him on. Then will he look as fierce as a Cotswold lion.[5]

T. Trusty. But when goest thou for him?

M. Merry.   That do I very now.   40

C. Custance. Ye shall find us here.

M. Merry.   Well, God have mercy on you.   Ex[eat].

T. Trusty. There is no cause of fear; the least boy in the street——

C. Custance. Nay, the least girl I have will make him take his feet. But hark! methink they make preparation.

T. Trusty. No force, it will be a good recreation.

C. Custance. I will stand within, and step forth speedily, And so make as though I ran away dreadfully.[6]   [Exeaut.]

Actus IV. Scena vii.

R[alph] Roister, M[atthew] Merrygreek, C[hristian] Custance,[7] D[obinet] Doughty,[7] Harpax, Tristram Trusty.[7]

R. Roister. Now, sirs, keep your ray,[8] and see your hearts be stout. But where be these caitiffs? Methink they dare not rout.[9] How sayest thou, Merrygreek? What doth Kit Custance say?

Betrothal, promise.   [2] Trickery.   [3] Dishonor.

[4] Engage in a battle.   [7] Enters later.
[5] *I.e.*, a sheep.   [8] Array, due order.
[6] Full of fear.   [9] Assemble.

M. Merry. I am loath to tell you.

R. Roister.   Tush,
   speak, man: yea or nay?

M. Merry. Forsooth, sir, I have spoken
   for you all that I can.

But if ye win her, ye must e'en play the
   man;

E'en to fight it out, ye must a man's
   heart take.

R. Roister. Yes, they shall know, and
   thou knowest I have a stomach.[1]

[M. Merry.] "A stomach," quod you?
   Yea, as good as e'er man had.

R. Roister. I trow they shall find and
   feel that I am a lad.   10

M. Merry. By this cross, I have seen you
   eat your meat as well

As any that e'er I have seen of or heard
   tell.

"A stomach," quod you? He that will
   that deny

I know was never at dinner in your
   company.

R. Roister. Nay, the stomach of a man
   it is that I mean.

M. Merry. Nay, the stomach of a horse
   or a dog, I ween.

R. Roister. Nay, a man's stomach with a
   weapon, mean I.

M. Merry. Ten men can scarce match
   you with a spoon in a pie.

R. Roister. Nay, the stomach of a man
   to try in strife.

M. Merry. I never saw your stomach
   cloyed yet in my life.   20

R. Roister. Tush, I mean in strife or
   fighting to try.

M. Merry. We shall see how ye will
   strike now, being angry.

R. Roister. Have at thy pate then, and
   save thy head if thou may.
            [They strike at each other.]

M. Merry. Nay, then have at your pate
   again by this day.

R. Roister. Nay, thou mayst not strike
   at me again in no wise.

M. Merry. I cannot in fight make to you
   such warrantize;[2]

But as for your foes, here let them the
   bargain by.[3]

R. Roister. Nay, as for they, shall every
   mother's child die.

And in this my fume a little thing might
   make me

To beat down house and all, and else
   the devil take me.   30

M. Merry. If I were as ye be, by Gog's
   dear mother,

I would not leave one stone upon another,

Though she would redeem it with twenty
   thousand pounds.

R. Roister. It shall be even so, by His
   lily wounds.

M. Merry. Be not at one with her, upon
   any amends.

R. Roister. No, though she make to me
   never so many friends,

Nor if all the world for her would undertake, [4]

No, not God himself neither shall not her
   peace make.

On, therefore, march forward—soft, stay
   a while yet!

M. Merry. On!

R. Roister.   Tarry!

M. Merry.   Forth!

R. Roister.   Back!

M. Merry. On!

R. Roister.   Soft! Now forward
   set!   40

[Enter Custance.]

C. Custance. What business have we
   here? Out! alas, alas!   *[Exeat.]*

R. Roister. Ha, ha, ha, ha, ha!

Didst thou see that, Merrygreek, how
   afraid she was?

Didst thou see how she fled apace out of
   my sight?

Ah, good sweet Custance, I pity her, by
   this light.

M. Merry. That tender heart of yours
   will mar altogether;

Thus will ye be turned with wagging of
   a feather.

R. Roister. On, sirs, keep your ray!

M. Merry.   On,
   forth, while this gear is hot!

R. Roister. Soft, the arms of Calais! I
   have one thing forgot.

M. Merry. What lack we now?

R. Roister.   Retire,
   or else we be all slain.   50

---

[1] Courage.   [3] Aby, pay the penalty for.
[2] Guarantee.

[4] Assume responsibility.

M. MERRY. Back, for the pashe of God!
  Back, sirs, back again!
What is the great matter?
R. ROISTER.   This hasty
  forthgoing
Had almost brought us all to utter un-
  doing;
It made me forget a thing most necessary.
M. MERRY. Well remembered of a cap-
  tain, by Saint Mary.
R. ROISTER. It is a thing must be had.
M. MERRY.   Let us have it then.
R. ROISTER. But I wot not where nor how.
M. MERRY.   Then wot not I when.
But what is it?
R. ROISTER.   Of a chief thing I am to
  seek.
M. MERRY. Tut, so will ye be, when ye
  have studied a week.
But tell me what it is?
R. ROISTER.   I lack yet an
  headpiece.   60
M. MERRY. The kitchen collocavit,[1] the
  best hens to grease![2]
Run, fet it, Dobinet, and come at once
  withal,
And bring with thee my potgun,[3] hanging
  by the wall.   [*Exeat Dobinet.*]
I have seen your head with it full many
  a time
Covered as safe as it had been with a
  skrine;[4]
And I warrant it save your head from
  any stroke,
Except perchance to be amazed[5] with
  the smoke.
I warrant your head therewith, except
  for the mist,
As safe as if it were fast locked up in a
  chist.[6]
And lo, here our Dobinet cometh with it
  now.   70

[Enter Dobinet.]

D. DOUGH. It will cover me to the shoulders well enow.
M. MERRY. Let me see it on.
R. ROISTER.   In faith,
  it doth metely well.

M. MERRY. There can be no fitter thing.
  Now ye must us tell
What to do.
R. ROISTER.   Now forth in ray, sirs,
  and stop no more.
M. MERRY. Now, Saint George to bor-
  row,[7] drum dub-a-dub afore.

[Enter Trusty.]

T. TRUSTY. What mean you to do, sir,
  commit manslaughter?
R. ROISTER. To kill forty such is a matter
  of laughter.
T. TRUSTY. And who is it, sir, whom ye
  intend thus to spill?
R. ROISTER. Foolish Custance here forc-
  eth me against my will.
T. TRUSTY. And is there no mean your
  extreme wrath to slake?   80
She shall some amends unto your good
  ma'ship make.
R. ROISTER. I will none amends.
T. TRUSTY.   Is her
  offense so sore?
M. MERRY. And he were a lout, she could
  have done no more.
She hath called him fool, and dressed[8]
  him like a fool,
Mocked him like a fool, used him like a
  fool.
T. TRUSTY. Well, yet the sheriff, the jus-
  tice, or constable,
Her misdemeanor to punish might be able.
R. ROISTER. No, sir, I mine own self will,
  in this present cause,
Be sheriff, and justice, and whole judge
  of the laws;
This matter to amend, all officers be I
  shall,   90
Constable, bailiff, sergeant—
M. MERRY.   And hang-
  man and all.
T. TRUSTY. Yet a noble courage, and the
  heart of a man,
Should more honor win by bearing with
  a woman.
Therefore take the law, and let her
  answer thereto.
R. ROISTER. Merrygreek, the best way
  were even so to do.
What honor should it be with a woman to
  fight?

---

[1] Humorous latinization of *collock*, a large
kitchen pail.
[2] Or, punning, "the best hence to Greece."
[3] Popgun, pistol.   [5] Stupefied, bewildered.
[4] Box, chest.   [6] Chest.
[7] Saint George for a pledge; Saint George help
us.   [8] Addressed.

M. MERRY. And what then? Will ye thus
forgo and leese your right?

R. ROISTER. Nay, I will take the law on
her withouten grace.

T. TRUSTY. Or if your ma'ship could pardon this one trespace,[1]
I pray you forgive her.

R. ROISTER.   Hoh!

M. MERRY.   Tush,
tush, sir, do not.   100

[T. TRUSTY.] Be good, master, to her.

R. ROISTER.   Hoh!

M. MERRY.   Tush, I say, do not.
And what! shall your people here return
straight home?

T. TRUSTY.[2] Yea; levy the camp,[3] sirs, and
hence again each one.

R. ROISTER.[2] But be still in readiness, if I
hap to call;
I cannot tell what sudden chance may
befall.

M. MERRY. Do not off your harness, sirs,
I you advise,
At the least for this fortnight in no
manner wise.
Perchance in an hour when all ye think
least,
Our master's appetite to fight will be
best.
But soft, ere ye go, have once at Cus-
tance' house.   110

R. ROISTER. Soft, what wilt thou do?

M. MERRY.   Once discharge my harque-
bouse,   [Shoots the harquebus.]
And, for my heart's ease, have once more
with my potgun. [Shoots the popgun.]

R. ROISTER. Hold thy hands; else is all
our purpose clean fordone!

M. MERRY. And it cost me my life—

R. ROISTER.   I say,
thou shalt not.

M. MERRY. By the Matte,[4] but I will.
Have once more with hail shot.
I will have some pennyworth! I will not
leese all!

Actus IV. Scena viii.[5]

M[atthew] Merrygreek, C[hristian] Custance,
R[alph] Roister, Tib[et] T[alkapace],[6]
An[not] Alyface,[6] M[adge] Mumblecrust,[6]

Truepenny, Dobinet Doughty, Harpax,
two Drums[7] with their ensigns.

C. CUSTANCE. What caitiffs are those that
so shake my house wall?

M. MERRY. Ah, sirrah! now Custance, if
ye had so much wit,
I would see you ask pardon, and yourselves submit.

C. CUSTANCE. Have I still this ado with a
couple of fools?

M. MERRY. Hear ye what she saith?

C. CUSTANCE.   Maidens, come forth
with your tools.

[Enter Maids.]

R. ROISTER. In a ray!

M. MERRY.   Dubbadub, sirrah.

R. ROISTER.   In a ray!
They come suddenly on us.

M. MERRY.   Dubbadub.

R. ROISTER.   In a ray!
That ever I was born! We are taken
tardy![8]

M. MERRY. Now, sirs, quit ourselves like
tall men and hardy!

C. CUSTANCE. On afore, Truepenny! Hold
thine own, Annot!   10
On toward them, Tibet! for scape us
they cannot.
Come forth, Madge Mumblecrust! So
stand fast togither.

M. MERRY. God send us a fair day!

R. ROISTER.   See, they march on hither.

TIB. TALK. But, mistress——

C. CUSTANCE. What sayest you?

TIB. TALK.   Shall I go fet our goose?

C. CUSTANCE. What to do?

TIB. TALK.   To yonder
captain I will turn her loose.
And she gape and hiss at him, as she doth
at me,
I durst jeopard my hand she will make
him flee.

C. CUSTANCE. On! Forward!

R. ROISTER.   They come!

M. MERRY.   Stand!

R. ROISTER.   Hold!

R. ROISTER. Keep![9]

R. ROISTER.   There!

M. MERRY.   Strike!

R. ROISTER.   Take
heed!

---

[1] Trespass.   [3] Raise the siege.
[2] Speakers are reversed in original.   [4] Mass.
[5] For this scene cf. Plautus, Miles gloriosus, V.
[6] Enters later.
[7] I.e., drummers.   [8] Unprepared.   [9] Take care!

C. Custance. Well said, Truepenny!

Truepenny. 　　　　　Ah, whoresons!

C. Custance. 　　　　　Well done,
　indeed!　　　　　　　　　　　　　20

M. Merry. Hold thine own, Harpax;
　down with them, Dobinet!

C. Custance. Now, Madge! There, An-
　not! Now stick them, Tibet!

Tib. Talk. [*To Dobinet.*] All my chief
　quarrel is to this same little knave

That beguiled me last day; nothing shall
　him save.

D. Dough. Down with this little quean [1]
　that hath at me such spite;

Save you from her, master; it is a very
　sprite.

C. Custance. I myself will *mounsire
　graunde captaine* undertake.[2]

R. Roister. They win ground.

M. Merry. 　　　　　Save your-
　self, sir, for God's sake!

R. Roister. Out, alas! I am slain, help!

M. Merry. 　　　Save yourself!

R. Roister. 　　　　　　　Alas!

M. Merry. Nay, then, have at you, mis-
　tress!

R. Roister. 　Thou hittest me, alas! 30

M. Merry. I will strike at Custance
　here.

R. Roister. 　Thou hittest me!

M. Merry. [*Aside.*] 　　　　So I
　will. —

Nay, Mistress Custance!

R. Roister. 　　　　　Alas, thou
　hittest me still!

Hold!

M. Merry. 　Save yourself, sir!

R. Roister. 　　　　　　Help!
　Out, alas! I am slain!

M. Merry. Truce, hold your hands; truce
　for a pissing while or twain.

Nay, how say you, Custance? For saving
　of your life,

Will ye yield and grant to be this gent-
　man's wife?

C. Custance. Ye told me he loved me.
　Call ye this love?

M. Merry. He loved a while even like a
　turtledove.

C. Custance. Gay love, God save it!
　So soon hot, so soon cold!

M. Merry. I am sorry for you. He could
　love you yet, so he could.　　　40

[1] Wench.　　　　　　　[2] Engage with.

R. Roister. Nay, by Cock's precious,[3]
　she shall be none of mine.

M. Merry. Why so?

R. Roister. 　　　　Come away; by the
　Matte, she is mankine.[4]

I durst adventure the loss of my right
　hand,

If she did not slee [5] her other husband.

And see if she prepare not again to fight!

M. Merry. What then? Saint George to
　borrow, our Lady's knight!

R. Roister. Slee else whom she will, by
　Gog, she shall not slee me!

M. Merry. How then?

R. Roister. 　　　　Rather than to be
　slain, I will flee.

C. Custance. To it again, my knightesses;
　down with them all!

R. Roister. Away, away, away! She will
　else kill us all.　　　　　　　50

M. Merry. Nay, stick to it, like an hardy
　man and a tall.

R. Roister. O bones, thou hittest me!
　Away, or else die we shall!

M. Merry. Away, for the pashe of our
　sweet Lord Jesus Christ!

C. Custance. Away, lout and lubber, or
　I shall be thy priest!

*Exeant om[nes; i.e., Roister Doister and
　　　　　　　　　　　　his Men].*

So this field is ours; we have driven them
　all away.

Tib. Talk. Thanks to God, mistress, ye
　have had a fair day.

C. Custance. Well, now go ye in, and
　make yourself some good cheer.

Omnes pariter.[6] We go! [*Exeant Maids.*]

T. Trusty. 　　　　　Ah, sir, what a
　field we have had here!

C. Custance. Friend Tristram, I pray
　you be a witness with me.

T. Trusty. Dame Custance, I shall de-
　pose for your honesty.　　　　60

And now fare ye well, except something
　else ye would.

C. Custance. Not now, but when I need
　to send I will be bold.

　　　　　　　　　　　Exeat [Trusty].

I thank you for these pains. And now I
　will get me in.

Now Roister Doister will no more wooing
　begin.　　　　　　　　*Ex[eat].*

[3] By God's precious (blood, bones, etc.).
[4] Fierce, Amazonian.　[5] Slay.　[6] All together.

Actus V. Scena i.

Gawin Goodluck, Sim Suresby.

[G. Good.] Sim Suresby, my trusty man,
now advise thee well,
And see that no false surmises thou me
tell.
Was there such ado about Custance, of a
truth?
Sim Sure. To report that I heard and saw,
to me is ruth,
But both my duty and name and prop-
erty [1]
Warneth me to you to show fidelity.
It may be well enough, and I wish it so
to be;
She may herself discharge,[2] and try her
honesty.
Yet their claim to her methought was
very large,
For with letters, rings, and tokens, they
did her charge;   10
Which when I heard and saw I would
none [3] to you bring.
G. Good. No, by Saint Mary, I allow [4]
thee in that thing.
Ah, sirrah, now I see truth in the proverb
old,
"All things that shineth is not by-and-by
pure gold."
If any do live a woman of honesty,
I would have sworn Christian Custance
had been she.
Sim Sure. Sir, though I to you be a serv-
ant true and just,
Yet do not ye therefore your faithful
spouse mistrust,
But examine the matter, and, if ye shall
it find
To be all well, be not ye for my words
unkind.   20
G. Good. I shall do that is right, and as
I see cause why.
But here cometh Custance forth; we shall
know by-and-by.

Actus V. Scena ii.

*C[hristian] Custance, Gawin Goodluck, Sim
Suresby.*

C. Custance. I come forth to see and
hearken for news good,

For about this hour is the time of likeli-
hood
That Gawin Goodluck by the sayings of
Suresby
Would be at home, and lo, yond I see
him, I.
What! Gawin Goodluck, the only hope
of my life!
Welcome home, and kiss me, your true
espoused wife.
G. Good. Nay, soft, Dame Custance! I
must first, by your license,
See whether all things be clear in your
conscience.
I hear of your doings to me very strange.
C. Custance. What, fear ye that my faith
towards you should change?   10
G. Good. I must needs mistrust ye be
elsewhere entangled;
For I hear that certain men with you
have wrangled
About the promise of marriage by you
to them made.
C. Custance. Could any man's report
your mind therein persuade?
G. Good. Well, ye must therein declare
yourself to stand clear;
Else I and you, Dame Custance, may
not join this year.
C. Custance. Then would I were dead,
and fair laid in my grave.
Ah, Suresby, is this the honesty that ye
have,
To hurt me with your report, not know-
ing the thing?
Sim Sure. If ye be honest, my words can
hurt you nothing.   20
But what I heard and saw, I might not
but report.
C. Custance. Ah, Lord, help poor widows,
destitute of comfort!
Truly, most dear spouse, naught was
done but for pastance.
G. Good. But such kind of sporting is
homely [5] dalliance.
C. Custance. If ye knew the truth, ye
would take all in good part.
G. Good. By your leave, I am not half
well skilled in that art.
C. Custance. It was none but Roister
Doister, that foolish mome.
G. Good. Yea, Custance, better, they say,
a bad scuse than none.

C. CUSTANCE. Why, Tristram Trusty, sir, your true and faithful friend,
Was privy both to the beginning and the end. 30
Let him be the judge, and for me testify.
G. GOOD. I will the more credit that [1] he shall verify,
And because I will the truth know e'en as it is,
I will to him myself, and know all without miss.
Come on, Sim Suresby, that before my friend thou may
Avouch the same words which thou didst to me say. *Exeant.*

ACTUS V. SCENA iii.
Christian Custance.

C. CUSTANCE. O Lord! how necessary it is now-of-days
That each body live uprightly all manner ways;
For let never so little a gap be open,
And be sure of this—the worst shall be spoken.
How innocent stand I in this for deed or thought,
And yet see what mistrust towards me it hath wrought.
But thou, Lord, knowest all folks' thoughts and eke intents,
And thou art the deliverer of all innocents.
Thou didst help the advoutress,[2] that she might be amended;
Much more then help, Lord, that [3] never ill intended. 10
Thou didst help Susanna, wrongfully accused,
And no less dost thou see, Lord, how I am now abused.
Thou didst help Hester, when she should have died;
Help also, good Lord, that my truth may be tried.
Yet if Gawin Goodluck with Tristram Trusty speak,
I trust of ill report the force shall be but weak.
And lo, yond they come, sadly talking together.
I will abide, and not shrink for their coming hither.

[1] That which. [2] Adulteress. [3] One that.

ACTUS V. SCENA iv.
Gawin Goodluck, Tristram Trusty, C[hristian] Custance, Sim Suresby.

G. GOOD. And was it none other than ye to me report?
T. TRUSTY. No, and here were ye wished [4] to have seen the sport.
G. GOOD. Would I had, rather than half of that in my purse.
SIM SURE. And I do much rejoice the matter was no worse,
And like as to open it I was to you faithful,
So of Dame Custance' honest truth I am joyful.
For God forfend that I should hurt her by false report.
G. GOOD. Well, I will no longer hold her in discomfort.
C. CUSTANCE. Now come they hitherward; I trust all shall be well.
G. GOOD. Sweet Custance, neither heart can think nor tongue tell 10
How much I joy in your constant fidelity.
Come now, kiss me, the pearl of perfect honesty.
C. CUSTANCE. God let me no longer to continue in life
Than I shall towards you continue a true wife.
G. GOOD. Well, now to make you for this some part of amends,
I shall desire first you, and then such of our friends
As shall to you seem best, to sup at home with me,
Where at your fought field we shall laugh and merry be.
SIM SURE. And, mistress, I beseech you, take with me no grief.
I did a true man's part, not wishing you reprief.[5] 20
C. CUSTANCE. Though hasty reports through surmises growing
May of poor innocents be utter overthrowing,
Yet because to thy master thou hast a true heart,
And I know mine own truth, I forgive thee for my part.

[4] "By me" is understood. [5] Reproof, reproach.

G. Good. Go we all to my house, and of
this gear no more.
Go, prepare all things, Sim Suresby;
hence, run afore.
Sim Sure. I go.   *Ex[eat]*.
G. Good.   But who cometh yond,
M[aster] Merrygreek?
C. Custance. Roister Doister's cham-
pion, I shrew his best cheek.
T. Trusty. Roister Doister self, your
wooer, is with him too.
Surely something there is with us they
have to do.   30

ACTUS V. SCENA v.[1]

*M[atthew] Merrygreek, Ralph Roister, Gawin
Goodluck, Tristram Trusty, C[hristian]
Custance.*

M. Merry. Yond I see Gawin Goodluck,
to whom lieth my message.
I will first salute him after his long
voyage,
And then make all thing well concerning
your behalf.
R. Roister. Yea, for the pashe of God!
M. Merry.   Hence, out of sight, ye calf,
Till I have spoke with them, and then I
will you fet.
R. Roister. In God's name.   [*Exeat.*]
M. Merry.   What, Mas-
ter Gawin Goodluck, well met!
And from your long voyage I bid you
right welcome home.
G. Good. I thank you.
M. Merry.   I come to you
from an honest mome.
G. Good. Who is that?
M. Merry.   Roister Doister,
that doughty kite.
C. Custance. Fie! I can scarce abide ye
should his name recite.   10
M. Merry. Ye must take him to favor,
and pardon all past.—
He heareth of your return, and is full ill
aghast.
G. Good. I am right well content he have
with us some cheer.
C. Custance. Fie upon him, beast! Then
will not I be there.
G. Good. Why, Custance, do ye hate him
more than ye love me?

C. Custance. But for your mind,[2] sir,
where he were would I not be.
T. Trusty. He would make us all laugh.
M. Merry.   Ye ne'er had better sport.
G. Good. I pray you, sweet Custance, let
him to us resort.
C. Custance. To your will I assent.
M. Merry.   Why, such a fool it is,
As no man for good pastime would forgo
or miss.   20
G. Good. Fet him to go with us.
M. Merry.   He will
be a glad man.   *Ex[eat].*
T. Trusty. We must to make us mirth
maintain him all we can.
And lo, yond he cometh, and Merry-
greek with him.
C. Custance. At his first entrance ye
shall see I will him trim.
But first let us hearken the gentleman's
wise talk.
T. Trusty. I pray you, mark if ever ye
saw crane so stalk.

ACTUS V. SCENA vi.

*R[alph] Roister, M[atthew] Merrygreek,
C[hristian] Custance, G[awin] Goodluck,
T[ristram] Trusty, D[obinet] Doughty,
Harpax.[3]*

R. Roister. May I then be bold?
M. Merry.   I war-
rant you on my word,
They say they shall be sick but ye be at
their board.
R. Roister. They were not angry then?
M. Merry.   Yes, at first,
and made strange;[4]
But, when I said your anger to favor
should change,
And therewith had commended you ac-
cordingly,
They were all in love with your ma'ship
by-and-by,
And cried you mercy that they had done
you wrong.
R. Roister. Forwhy[5] no man, woman,
nor child can hate me long.
M. Merry. "We fear," quod they, "he
will be avenged one day;
Then for a penny give all our lives we
may!"   10
R. Roister. Said they so indeed?

M. Merry.   Did
they? Yea, even with one voice.
"He will forgive all," quod I. O, how
they did rejoice!
R. Roister. Ha, ha, ha!
M. Merry. "Go fet him," say they,
"while he is in good mood,
For have his anger who lust, we will not,
by the Rood."
R. Roister. I pray God that it be all
true, that thou hast me told,
And that she fight no more.
M. Merry.   I warrant
you, be bold.
To them, and salute them.
R. Roister. [*Advancing.*]   Sirs, I greet
you all well.
Omnes. Your mastership is welcome.
C. Custance.   Saving my quarrel,
For sure I will put you up into the
Exchequer.[1]   20
M. Merry. Why so? Better nay. Where-
fore?
C. Custance.   For an usurer.
R. Roister. I am no usurer, good mis-
tress, by His arms!
M. Merry. When took he gain of money
to any man's harms?
C. Custance. Yes, a foul usurer he is;
ye shall see; else [2]—
R. Roister. Didst not thou promise she
would pick no mo quarrels?
C. Custance. He will lend no blows but
he have in recompense
Fifteen for one, which is too much, of
conscience.[3]
R. Roister. Ah, dame, by the ancient
law of arms, a man
Hath no honor to foil [4] his hands on a
woman.
C. Custance. And where other usurers
take their gains yearly,   30
This man is angry but he have his by-
and-by.
G. Good. Sir, do not for her sake bear me
your displeasure.
M. Merry. Well, he shall with you talk
thereof more at leisure.
Upon your good usage, he will now shake
your hand.
R. Roister. And much heartily welcome
from a strange land.

M. Merry. Be not afeard, Gawin, to let
him shake your fist.
G. Good. O, the most honest gentleman
that e'er I wist.
I beseech your ma'ship to take pain to
sup with us.
M. Merry. He shall not say you nay,
and I too, by Jesus,
Because ye shall be friends, and let all
quarrels pass.   40
R. Roister. I will be as good friends with
them as ere I was.
M. Merry. Then let me fet your quire
that we may have a song.
R. Roister. Go.

[*Merrygreek beckons to the Musicians, who
enter.*]

G. Good.   I have heard no melody
all this year long.
M. Merry. Come on, sirs, quickly.
R. Roister.   Sing on,
sirs, for my friends' sake.
D. Dough. Call ye these your friends?
R. Roister.   Sing on,
and no mo words make.
                 Here they sing.[5]
G. Good. The Lord preserve our most
noble queen of renown,
And her virtues reward with the heavenly
crown.
C. Custance. The Lord strengthen her
most excellent majesty,
Long to reign over us in all prosperity.
T. Trusty. That her godly proceedings
the faith to defend,   50
He may stablish and maintain through
to the end.
M. Merry. God grant her, as she doth,
the Gospel to protect,
Learning and virtue to advance, and
vice to correct.
R. Roister. God grant her loving subjects
both the mind and grace,
Her most godly proceedings worthily to
embrace.
Harpax. Her highness' most worthy coun-
selors God prosper,
With honor and love of all men to min-
ister.

[1] Law court.   [3] A mild oath.
[2] Besides.   [4] Soil.

[5] This song seems to be missing, since the conventional final prayer for the queen, which follows, was usually spoken, not sung.

Omnes. God grant the nobility her to
  serve and love,
With all the whole commonty,[1] as doth
  them behove.

Amen.

Certain Songs to Be Song by Those
  Which Shall Use This Comedy or
  Interlude

The Second Song

Whoso to marry a minion wife
  Hath had good chance and hap,
Must love her and cherish her all his life,
  And dandle her in his lap.

If she will fare well, if she will go gay,
  A good husband ever still,
Whatever she lust to do or to say,
  Must let her have her own will.

About what affairs soever he go,
  He must show her all his mind.   10
None of his counsel she may be kept fro;[2]
  Else is he a man unkind.

The Fourth Song

I mun[3] be married a[4] Sunday;
I mun be married a Sunday;
Whosoever shall come that way,
  I mun be married a Sunday.

Roister Doister is my name;
Roister Doister is my name;
A lusty brute I am the same;
  I mun be married a Sunday.

Christian Custance have I found;
Christian Custance have I found;   10
A widow worth a thousand pound;
  I mun be married a Sunday.

Custance is as sweet as honey;
Custance is as sweet as honey;
I her lamb and she my cony;
  I mun be married a Sunday.

When we shall make our wedding feast,
When we shall make our wedding feast,
There shall be cheer for man and beast;
I mun be married a Sunday.   20
  I mun be married a Sunday, etc.

---

[1] Commons.   [2] From.   [3] Must.   [4] On.

The Psalmody

Placebo dilexi,
Master Roister Doister will straight go
  home and die;
Our Lord Jesus Christ his soul have mercy
  upon.
Thus you see today a man, tomorrow John.[5]
Yet saving for a woman's extreme cru-
  elty,
He might have lived yet a month or two
  or three,
But in spite of Custance, which hath him
  wearied,
His ma'ship shall be worshipfully buried.
And while some piece of his soul is yet
  him within,
Some part of his funerals let us here begin.
  Dirige. He will go darkling to his grave. 10
Neque lux, neque crux, nisi solum clink,[6]
Never gentman so went toward heaven, I
  think.
Yet, sirs, as ye will the bliss of heaven win,
When he cometh to the grave, lay him
  softly in,
And all men take heed by this one gentle-
  man,
How you set your love upon an unkind
  woman.
For these women be all such mad peevish
  elves,
They will not be won except it please
  themselves.
But in faith, Custance, if ever ye come in
  hell,
Master Roister Doister shall serve you as
  well.   20
Good night, Roger, old knave; farewell,
  Roger, old knave!
Good night, Roger, old knave; knave, nap!
  *Nequando. Audivi vocem. Requiem
  æternam.*

The Peal of Bells Rong by the Parish
  Clerk and Roister Doister's Four
  Men

The first bell a triple. When died he? When
  died he?
The second. We have him! We have him!
The third. Roister Doister! Roister Doister!
The fourth bell. He cometh! He cometh!
The great bell. Our own! Our own!

Finis.

---

[5] A funeral death's head; thus a corpse.
[6] Except only a bell.

"MR. S."

In 1563, according to the Stationers' Register, Thomas Colwell was granted a license to print a play entitled *Dyccon of Bedlam.* This was probably a provisional title for *Gammer Gurton's Needle,* the earliest extant edition of which was issued by him in 1575 with the following title: *A Right Pithy, Pleasant, and Merry Comedy Entitled Gammer Gurton's Needle, Played on Stage Not Long Ago in Christ's College in Cambridge. Made by Mr. S., Mr. of Art.*

The authorship of the play, in spite of a great deal of discussion, still remains a matter of dispute. As early as 1782 Isaac Reed attributed it to John Still, Bishop of Bath and Wells. Although the initials fit and although the only living M. A. of Christ's College with these initials that Reed could find was the bishop, "the character of Bishop Still," as Henry Bradley puts it in his edition of the play for Gayley's *Representative English Comedies* in 1903, "as it is known from the testimony of several of his personal friends, renders it incredible that he can ever have distinguished himself as a comic writer." In fact, there is "no evidence that he ever made a joke, that he ever wrote a line of verse, or that he had any interests other than those connected with his sacred calling."

In 1838 Joseph Hunter set forth the authorship claim of Dr. John Bridges, another churchman, on the basis of two passages in the famous "Martin Marprelate" tracts, the *Epistle* and the *Epitome,* both issued in 1588. In these the anonymous pamphleteer alludes to Bridges by name as the author of the play as if it were a well-known fact, although his description of the Dean of Salisbury is highly sarcastic: "You have bin a worthy writer, as they say, of a long time; your first book was a proper enterlude, called *Gammar Gurtons Needle.* But I think that this trifle, which sheweth the author to have had some witte and invention in him, was none of your doing, because your books seem to proceed from the braynes of a woodcocke, as having neither wit nor learning." In spite of the Martin tracts, the colloquial and sprightly literary style of the Dean in his identifiably published works makes this attribution of the authorship of a juvenile play quite feasible. But two facts cannot be reconciled by the theory: A "J. B." could not have been a "Mr. S.," and Bridges attended Pembroke rather than Christ's. Nevertheless, since Bridges, as Bradley puts it, "was resident at Cambridge in 1560 (having taken the degree of A.M. in that year), it is quite possible that he may have assisted William Stevenson in the composition or revision of the play."

As late as 1940 Charles W. Roberts ("The Authorship of *Gammer Gurton's Needle,*" *PQ*) attempted to identify "Mr. S." with Sebastian Westcote, Master of the Children of Paul's, who with his cathedral choirboys presented many plays between 1551 and 1582; but Roberts's suggestion, though attractive, is highly suppositional. However, in 1943 C. J. Sisson, though dubious of Roberts's theory, contributed a note to the *RES* calling attention to two contemporary references to Westcote.

Generally, however, ever since the appearance of Bradley's 1903 preface, William Stevenson has been accepted as the author. According to Bradley's discoveries, in the 1559–60 records at Christ's College there is an entry: "Spent at Mr. Stevenson's plaie, 5 *s.*" Since a William Stevenson was a Fellow of the College from 1559 to 1561, and was probably identical with a similarly named Fellow there from 1551 to 1554 whom the bursar's accounts name as the author of a play acted in 1553–54, the link with the facts stated on the title page of *Gammer Gurton's Needle* seems to be clear.

49

Whether *Gammer Gurton* was the first or the last of the plays mentioned as coming from Stevenson's pen will probably never be ascertained.   However, the ecclesiastical allusions in the play and the direct reference to the King in V, ii, 236, would seem to place it before the death of Edward VI in 1553, though this date would require that Colwell had held the manuscript for some time before printing it.   Bradley, assuming that the two William Stevensons are the same, speculates that he was deprived of his Fellowship under the Roman Catholic Mary and had it restored under the Protestant Elizabeth.   The other known facts about his life are that he was born in Hunwick in Durham, matriculated at Christ's as a sizar (an undergraduate who receives college aid for his maintenance) in November 1546, and proceeded B.A. in 1549–50, M.A. in 1553, and B.D. in 1560.   In 1552 he was ordained deacon in London, was appointed prebendary of Durham in January 1561, and died in the same year that saw the publication of *Gammer Gurton's Needle*.

Like *Roister Doister*, Stevenson's play, with its very earthy speech and its realistic picture of English village life, scarcely seems appropriate to an academic atmosphere; but both plays show that even the highly educated Englishman continued to maintain close contact with the soil.   But here, again, the influence of classical Latin comedy is to be seen in the five-act division with subdivision into scenes, the simple stage setting, and the narrow limitation of the time and place of the action.   In *Gammer Gurton's Needle*, however, the broadly farcical treatment follows a tradition reaching back through John Heywood to the *Secunda Pastorum* (*Second Shepherds' Play*), the mystery play of the Wakefield cycle, and to medieval farce in general.   As an intriguer and manipulator of the action, Diccon is a figure parallel to the tricky rascals of Roman comedy; but both as a joker and as a rogue and vagabond, he is more clearly a successor to the Vices of the morality play.   Above all, the characters and the life portrayed are far more distinctly English than in *Roister Doister*.   In the words of Bradley: "as the first known attempt to present a picture of contemporary rustic life in the form of a regular comedy, it may be admitted to represent a distinct advance in the development of English dramatic art."

Even prosodically the play marks an advance over *Roister Doister*.   Although the authors of both plays show a desire to experiment metrically, Stevenson's lines are more easily scannable by the modern reader.   Starting with an anapestic hexameter in the Prologue, Stevenson moves to iambic hexameters and septenaries, often rather rough, but he intersperses these with more varied patterns in his songs and in Diccon's incantation.

The language of the play is a somewhat inaccurate representation of the dialect of the southwestern counties of England, which was to be established as the conventional speech of the stage rustic.   In making the first attempt to modernize the play, the editors have sought to preserve all forms which may be regarded as dialectal variations from the normal speech of the period.

The text of the present edition is based upon the 1575 quarto as reprinted by H. F. Brett-Smith in the Percy Reprints (1920).

GAMMER¹ GURTON'S NEEDLE

BY
MR. S.

THE NAMES OF THE SPEAKERS IN THIS COMEDY

DICCON *the bedlam.*²
HODGE, *Gammer Gurton's servant.*
TIB, *Gammer Gurton's maid.*
GAMMER GURTON.
COCK,³ *Gammer Gurton's boy.*
DAME CHAT.

DOCTOR RAT, *the curate.*
MASTER BAILY.⁴
DOLL, *Dame Chat's maid.*
SCAPETHRIFT, *Mast[er] Baily's servant.*
MUTES.

[SCENE: *A village in England.*

TIME: *Contemporary.*]

GOD SAVE THE QUEEN!

THE PROLOGUE

As Gammer Gurton with many a wide stitch
Sat piecing and patching of Hodge her
    man's breech,
By chance or misfortune as she her gear⁵
    tossed,
In Hodge' leather breeches her needle she
    lost.
When Diccon the bedlam had heard by
    report
That good Gammer Gurton was robbed in
    this sort,
He quietly persuaded with her in that
    stound⁶
Dame Chat, her dear gossip,⁷ this needle
    had found.
Yet knew she no more of this matter, alas,
Than knoweth Tom, our clerk,⁸ what the
    priest saith at Mass!   10
Hereof there ensued so fearful a fray

Mas' Doctor was sent for, these gossips to
    stay,
Because he was curate, and esteemed full
    wise,
Who found that⁹ he sought not, by Dic-
    con's device.
When all things were tumbled and clean
    out of fashion,
Whether it were by fortune or some other
    constellation,
Suddenly the neele¹⁰ Hodge found by the
    pricking,
And drew it out of his buttock where he
    felt it sticking.
Their hearts then at rest with perfect
    security,
With a pot of good nale¹¹ they stroke¹² up
    their plaudity.¹³   20

THE I ACT. THE i SCENE.¹⁴

Diccon.

DICCON Many a mile have I walked, di-
    vers and sundry ways,
And many a good man's house have I
    been at in my days,

---

¹ Grandmother, old woman.
² A partially cured lunatic discharged from the Hospital of St. Mary of Bethlehem in London; he was licensed to make his living by begging.
³ Original reads *Docke.*
⁴ Bailiff.
⁵ *I.e.,* sewing materials.
⁶ Occasion.
⁷ Crony.
⁸ The original spelling, *clarke*, indicates the pronunciation.

⁹ That which.   ¹¹ Ale.   ¹³ Applause.
¹⁰ Needle.   ¹² Struck.
¹⁴ The scene for the entire play is a village street with Gammer Gurton's house on one side and Dame Chat's alehouse on the other.

Many a gossip's cup in my time have I
tasted,
And many a broach and spit have I both
turned and basted,
Many a piece of bacon have I had out of
their balks [1]
In running over the country with long
and weary walks;
Yet came my foot never within those
doorcheeks, [2]
To seek flesh, or fish, garlic, onions, or
leeks,
That ever I saw a sort [3] in such a plight
As here within this house appeareth to
my sight!   10
There is howling and scowling, all cast in
a dump,
With whewling and puling, as though
they had lost a trump; [4]
Sighing and sobbing they weep and they
wail.
I marvel in my mind what the devil they
ail.
The old trot [5] sits groaning, with "alas!"
and "alas!"
And Tib wrings her hands, and takes on in
worse case.
With poor Cock, their boy, they be driven
in such fits
I fear me the folks be not well in their
wits.
Ask them what they ail, or who brought
them in this stay, [6]
They answer not at all but "alack!" and
"welaway!"   20
When I saw it booted not, out at doors I
hied me,
And caught a slip of bacon, when I saw
that none spied me,
Which I intend not far hence, unless my
purpose fail,
Shall serve for a shoeing-horn to draw on
two pots of ale.

THE I ACT.   THE ii SCENE.

Hodge, Diccon.

HODGE. See!   So cham [7] arrayed with
dabbling in the dirt!

She that set me to ditching, ich wold [8] she
had the squirt! [9]
Was never poor soul that such a life had!
Gog's bones, [10] this vilthy glay [11] has
dressed me too bad!
God's soul, see how this stuff tears!
Ich were better to be a bearward and set
to keep bears!
By the Mass, here is a gash! A shameful
hole indeed!
And [12] one stitch tear furder, [13] a man may
thrust in his head.
DICCON. By my father's soul, Hodge, if I
shuld now be sworn,
I cannot choose but say thy breech is
foul be-torn!   10
But the next remedy in such a case and
hap
Is to planch [14] on a piece as broad as thy
cap.
HODGE. Gog's soul, man, 'tis not yet two
days fully ended
Since my Dame Gurton, cham sure, these
breeches amended!
But cham made such a drudge, to trudge
at every need,
Chwold rend it, though it were stitched
with sturdy packthread.
DICCON. Hodge, let thy breeches go, and
speak and tell me soon
What devil aileth Gammer Gurton and
Tib, her maid, to frown.
HODGE. Tush, man, th'art deceived! 'Tis
their daily look;
They cower so over the coals, their eyes
be bleared with smoke.   20
DICCON. Nay, by the Mass, I perfectly
perceived, as I came hether, [15]

[8] Both *wold* and *would, cold* and *could, shold*
or *shuld* and *should*, and these words, especially
would, in combination with *ch* for *ich* (*I*)—*chold*
and *chould* with a few other variants—occur in
the play. In part the variations in this series of
words are probably unintentional, but the shorter
forms predominate so decidedly in the aggregate
that they cannot be disregarded as a feature of
dialect. Hence it has seemed best to retain the
spelling of the original with its inconsistencies,
except for dropping the meaningless final *e* wherever it occurs.
[9] Diarrhea.
[10] By God's bones.
[11] In the rustic dialect, initial $v=f$, $g=c$, $z=s$.
[12] If.   [13] Further.   [14] Plank, clap.
[15] A common form for *hither*, which has been
retained in this play because of the dialect and
rime.

[1] Beams, rafters.   [3] Company.   [5] Hag.
[2] Doorjambs.   [4] A game of cards.   [6] State.
[7] I am.   For use and characteristics of this
conventional stage dialect for rustics, see *Roister
Doister* I, iii, 100, n.

That either Tib and her dame hath been
    by the ears together,
Or else as great a matter, as thou shalt
    shortly see.
HODGE. Now ich beseech our Lord they
    never better agree!
DICCON. By Gog's soul, there they sit as
    still as stones in the street,
As though they had been taken [1]
    with fairies, or else with some ill
    sprite.[2]
HODGE. Gog's heart, I durst have laid my
    cap to a crown
Chwould learn of some prancome [3] as
    soon as ich came to town!
DICCON. Why, Hodge, art thou inspired?
    Or didst thou thereof hear?
HODGE. Nay, but ich saw such a wonder
    as ich saw nat this seven year: 30
Tom Tankard's cow, by Gog's bones,
    she set me up her sail,
And flinging about his half-acre, fisking [4]
    with her tail,
As though there had been in her arse a
    swarm of bees,
And chad not cried, "Tphrowh, whore!"
    she'd leaped out of his leas. [5]
DICCON. Why, Hodge, lies the cunning [6]
    in Tom Tankard's cow's tail?
HODGE. Well, ich chave hard [7] some say
    such tokens do not fail.
But canst thou not tell, in faith, Diccon,
    why she frowns, or whereat?
Hath no man stolen her ducks or hens,
    or gelded Gib, her cat?
DICCON. What devil can I tell, man? I
    cold not have one word;
They gave no more heed to my talk than
    thou woldst to a lord.[8]   40
HODGE. Ich cannot still but muse what
    marvelous thing it is!
Chill in and know myself what matters
    are amiss.
DICCON. Then farewell, Hodge, awhile,
    since thou dost inward haste,
For I will into the Goodwife Chat's, to
    feel how the ale doth taste.   [*Exit.*]

[1] Bewitched.
[2] Probably pronounced *spreet.*
[3] Unusual incident, freak.
[4] Frisking.
[5] Pastures.
[6] *I.e.*, prophetic power.
[7] Heard.
[8] Armstrong suggests *tord, turd.*

THE I ACT. THE iii SCENE.

Hodge, Tib.

HODGE. [*To himself.*] Cham aghast, by the
    Mass! Ich wot [9] not what to do.
Chad need bless me well before ich go
    them to!
Perchance some felon sprite may haunt
    our house indeed,
And then chwere but a [10] noddy to ven-
    ter [11] where cha' [12] no need!
TIB. [*To herself.*] Cham worse than mad,
    by the Mass, to be at this stay!
Cham chid, cham blamed, and beaten all
    thours [13] on the day,
Lamed, and hunger-starved, pricked up
    all in jags,[14]
Having no patch to hide my back save a
    few rotten rags!
HODGE. I say, Tib—if thou be Tib, as
    I trow sure thou be—
What devil make-ado is this between our
    dame and thee?   10
TIB. Gog's bread, Hodge, thou had a good
    turn thou wert not here [this while!] [15]
It had been better for some of us to have
    been hence a mile!
My gammer is so out of course and fran-
    tic all at once
That Cock, our boy, and I, poor wench,
    have felt it on our bones.
HODGE. What is the matter—say on, Tib—
    whereat she taketh so on?
TIB. She is undone, she saith; alas, her
    joy and life is gone!
If she hear not of some comfort, she is,
    saith, but dead;
Shall never come within her lips one inch
    of meat ne [16] bread!
HODGE. By'r Lady, cham not very glad to
    see her in this dump.
Chold a noble [17] her stool hath fallen and
    she hath broke her rump!   20
TIB. Nay, and that were the worst, we
    wold not greatly care,

[9] Know.
[10] Original reads *at.*
[11] Venture.
[12] I have.
[13] The hours.
[14] Dressed in tatters.
[15] This line is partially cut away in copies of early edns., but is completed by Brett-Smith from 1661 quarto.
[16] Nor.
[17] I hold (*i.e.*, wager) a noble (*i.e.*, a piece of money). The form *ichold* also appears.

For bursting of her huckle bone,[1] or
breaking of her chair;
But greater, greater, is her grief, as,
Hodge, we shall all feel.
HODGE. Gog's wounds, Tib, my gammer
has never lost her—neele?
TIB. Her neele!
HODGE.   Her neele?
TIB.   Her neele!
By Him that made me, it is true, Hodge,
I tell thee.
HODGE. Gog's sacrament, I would she had
lost thart [2] out of her belly!
The devil, or else his dame, they ought [3]
her, sure, a shame!
How a murrion [4] came this chance—say,
Tib—unto our dame?
TIB. My gammer sat her down on
her pess,[5] and bade me reach thy
breeches;   30
And by-and-by [6]—a vengeance in it!—
or [7] she had take two stitches
To clap a clout [8] upon thine arse, by
chance aside she leers,
And Gib, our cat, in the milk pan she
spied over head and ears.
"Ah, whore! Out, thief!" she cried aloud,
and swapt [9] the breeches down.
Up went her staff, and out leaped Gib at
doors into the town,[10]
And since that time was never wight
cold set their eyes upon it.
Gog's malison chave Cock and I bid
twenty times light on it.
HODGE. And is not then my breeches
sewed up, tomorrow that I shuld
wear?
TIB. No, in faith, Hodge, thy breeches lie,
for all this, never the near.[11]
HODGE. Now a vengeance light on all the
sort, that better shold have kept
it—   40
The cat, the house, and Tib, our maid,
that better shold have swept it!
See where she cometh crawling! Come
on, in twenty devils' way!
Ye have made a fair day's work, have
you not? Pray you, say!

THE I ACT. THE iv SCENE.

Gammer, Hodge, Tib, Cock. [12]

GAMMER. Alas, Hodge, alas, I may well
curse and ban
This day, that ever I saw it, with Gib
and the milk pan!
For these and ill luck together, as knoweth Cock, my boy,
Have stack [13] away my dear neele, and
robbed me of my joy—
My fair, long, straight neele, that was
mine only treasure!
The first day of my sorrow is, and last
end of my pleasure!
HODGE. Might ha' kept it when ye had it,
but fools will be fools still!
Lose that is vast in your hands? Ye
need not, but ye will!
GAMMER. Go hie thee, Tib, and run, thou
whore, to th'end here of the town!
Didst carry out dust in thy lap. Seek
where thou pourest it down;   10
And, as thou sawest me roking [14] in the
ashes where I mourned,
So see in all the heap of dust thou leave
no straw unturned.
TIB. That chall, gammer, swith and
tight, [15] and soon be here again!
GAMMER. Tib, stoop and look down to
the ground to it, and take some
pain!   [*Exit Tib.*]
HODGE. Here is a pretty matter, to see
this gear [16] how it goes!
By Gog's soul, I think you wold lose
your arse and it were loose!
Your neele lost? It is pity you shold
lack care and endless sorrow.
Gog's death, how shall my breeches be
sewed? Shall I go thus tomorrow?
GAMMER. Ah, Hodge, Hodge, if that ich
cold find my neele, by the Reed,[17]
Chould sew thy breeches, ich promise
thee, with full good double thread,   20
And set a patch on either knee, shuld
last this moneths [18] twain.
Now God and good Saint Sith [19] I pray to
send it home again!
HODGE. Whereto served your hands and
eyes but this your neele to keep?

---

[1] Hip bone.   [7] Ere, before.
[2] The heart.   [8] Cloth, patch.
[3] Owed.   [9] Swept.
[4] Murrain, plague.   [10] Yard.
[5] Hassock.   [11] Nearer.
[6] At once.

[12] Enters later.   [15] Quickly and speedily.
[13] Stuck.   [16] Business.
[14] Raking, searching.   [17] Rood, Cross.
[18] Months.   [19] Bradley suggests St. Osyth.

What devil had you else to do? Ye kept,
ich wot, no sheep!
Cham fain abroad to dig and delve, in
water, mire, and clay,
Sossing [1] and possing [2] in the dirt still [3]
from day to day;
A hundred things that be abroad, cham
set to see them weal [4]—
And four of you sit idle at home, and
cannot keep a neele!
GAMMER. My neele, alas! Ich lost it,
Hodge, what time ich me uphasted
To save the milk set up for thee, which
Gib, our cat, hath wasted.   30
HODGE. The devil he burst both Gib and
Tib, with all the rest!
Cham always sure of the worst end,
whoever have the best!
Where ha' you been fidging [5] abroad
since you your neele lost?
GAMMER. Within the house, and at the
door, sitting by this same post,
Where I was looking a long hour before
these folks came here.
But, welaway! All was in vain; my neele
is never the near!
HODGE. Set me a candle; let me seek and
grope wherever it be.
Gog's heart, ye be so foolish, ich think
you know it not when you it see!
GAMMER. Come hether, Cock! What,
Cock, I say!

[Enter Cock.]

COCK.   How, gammer!
GAMMER.   Go hie thee soon,
And grope behind the old brass pan;
which thing when thou hast done,[6]
There shalt thou find an old shoe, where-
in, if thou look well,   41
Thou shalt find lying an inch of a white
tallow candle.
Light it, and bring it tight away.
COCK.   That shall be done anon.[7]
                    [Exit.]
GAMMER. Nay, tarry, Hodge, till thou
hast light, and then we'll seek each
one.

HODGE. Come away, ye whoreson [8] boy!
Are ye asleep? Ye must have a crier![9]
COCK. [*Within.*] Ich cannot get the candle
light; here is almost no fire.
HODGE. Chill hold thee a penny chill
make thee come if that ich may catch
thine ears!
Art deaf, thou whoreson boy? Cock, I
say, why canst not hear 's?
GAMMER. Beat him not, Hodge, but help
the boy, and come you two together.
                   [Exit Hodge.]

THE I ACT. THE V SCENE.

Gammer, Tib, Cock, Hodge.[10]

GAMMER. How now, Tib? Quick, let's hear
what news thou hast brought hether!

[Enter Tib.]

TIB. Chave tossed and tumbled yender [11]
heap over and over again,
And winnowed it through my fingers as
men wold winnow grain;
Not so much as a hen's turd but in
pieces I tare it,
Or whatsoever clod or clay I found, I
did not spare it,
Looking within, and eke without, to
find your neele, alas!
But all in vain, and without help—your
neele is where it was!
GAMMER. Alas, my neele! We shall never
meet! Adieu, adieu, for aye!
TIB. Not so, gammer; we might it find
if we knew where it lay.

[Enter Cock.]

COCK. Gog's Cross, gammer, if ye will
laugh, look in but at the door,   10
And see how Hodge lieth tumbling and
tossing amids the floor.
Raking there some fire to find among
the ashes dead,
Where there is not one spark so big as a
pin's head,
At last in a dark corner two sparks he
thought he sees,
Which were [12] indeed naught else but
Gib our cat's two eyes.
"Puff!" quod [13] Hodge, thinking thereby
to have fire without doubt;

---

[1] Sousing, making oneself muddy.
[2] Pushing, beating out.
[3] Continuously.   [4] Prosper.   [5] Fidgeting.
[6] Line division in this couplet made by Manly.
[7] At once.
[8] Rascally.   [10] Last three enter later.
[9] Town crier.   [11] Yonder.
[12] Original reads *where*.   [13] Quoth, said.

With that Gib shut her two eyes, and
    so the fire was out,
And by-and-by them opened, even as
    they were before;
With that the sparks appeared, even
    as they had done of yore.
And, even as Hodge blew the fire, as he
    did think,   20
Gib, as she felt the blast, straightway
    began to wink,[1]
Till Hodge fell of swearing, as came best
    to his turn,
The fire was sure bewitched, and there-
    fore wold not burn.
At last Gib up [2] the stairs among the
    old posts and pins;
And Hodge he hied him after till broke
    were both his shins—
Cursing and swearing oaths, were never
    of his making,
That Gib wold fire the house if that she
    were not taken.
GAMMER. See, here is all the thought that
    the foolish urchin taketh,
And Tib, methink, at his elbow almost
    as merry maketh!
This is all the wit ye have, when others
    make their moan.   30
Come down, Hodge! Where art thou?
    And let the cat alone!
HODGE. [*Within.*] Gog's heart, help and
    come up! Gib in her tail hath fire,
And is like to burn all if she get a little
    higher!
"Come down," quoth you? Nay, then
    you might count me a patch! [3]
The house cometh down on your heads
    if it take once the thatch.
GAMMER. It is the cat's eyes, fool, that
    shineth in the dark!
HODGE. [*Within.*] Hath the cat, do you
    think, in every eye a spark?
GAMMER. No, but they shine as like fire
    as ever man see.
HODGE. [*Within.*] By the Mass, and she
    burn all, you sh' bear the blame for
    me!
GAMMER. Come down, and help to seek
    here our neele, that it were found.   40
Down, Tib, on the knees, I say! Down,
    Cock, to the ground!

To God I make avow,[4] and so to good
    Saint Anne,
A candle shall they have apiece, get it
    where I can,
If I may my neele find in one place or in
    other.

[*Enter Hodge.*]

HODGE. Now a vengeance on Gib light,
    on Gib and Gib's mother,
And all the generation of cats both far
    and near!
Look on the ground, whoreson? Thinks
    then the neele is here?
COCK. By my troth, gammer, methought
    your neele here I saw,
But, when my fingers touched it, I felt
    it was a straw.
TIB. See, Hodge, what's t[h]is? May it
    not be within it?   50
HODGE. Break it, fool, with thy hand,
    and see and thou canst find it.
TIB. Nay, break it you, Hodge, accord-
    ing to your word.
HODGE. Gog's sides, fie, it stinks! It
    is a cat's turd!
It were well done to make thee eat it,
    by the Mass!
GAMMER. This matter amendeth not; my
    neele is still where it was.
Our candle is at an end; let us all in
    quite,
And come another time, when we have
    more light.   [*Exeunt.*]

THE II ACT.

First a song.

Back and side, go bare, go bare;
   Both foot and hand, go cold;
But, belly, God send thee good ale enough,
   Whether it be new or old!

I cannot eat but little meat,
   My stomach is not good;
But sure I think that I can drink
   With him that wears a hood.[5]
Though I go bare, take ye no care,
   I am nothing acold,   10
I stuff my skin so full within
   Of jolly good ale and old.

Back and side, go bare, go bare;
   Both foot and hand, go cold;
But, belly, God send thee good ale enough,
   Whether it be new or old!

---

[1] Close the eyes; not merely to blink.
[2] *I.e.*, ran up.
[3] Fool.
[4] Promise.   [5] *I.e.*, a friar.

I love no roast but a nut-brown toast [1]
  And a crab [2] laid in the fire;
A little bread shall do me stead,
  Much bread I not desire.   20
No frost nor snow, no wind, I trow,
  Can hurt me if I wold,
I am so wrapped and throughly lapped
  Of jolly good ale and old.

Back and side, go bare, etc.

And Tib, my wife, that as her life
  Loveth well good ale to seek,
Full oft drinks she till ye may see
  The tears run down her cheeks;
Then doth she troll [3] to me the bowl,
  Even as a maltworm [4] shuld,   30
And saith, "Sweetheart, I took my part
  Of this jolly good ale and old."

Back and side, go bare, etc.

Now let them drink till they nod and wink,
  Even as good fellows should do;
They shall not miss to have the bliss
  Good ale doth bring men to.
And all poor souls that have scoured [5] bowls
  Or have them lustily trolled,
God save the lives of them and their wives,
  Whether they be young or old!   40

Back and side, go bare, etc.[6]

THE i SCENE.

Diccon, Hodge. [7]

DICCON. Well done, by Gog's malt! Well
  sung, and well said!
Come on, Mother Chat, as thou art true
  maid;
One fresh pot of ale let's see, to make an
  end,
Against this cold weather my naked
  arms to defend!   [*Drinks.*]
This gear it warms the soul! Now, wind,
  blow on the worst,
And let us drink and swill till that our
  bellies burst!
Now were he a wise man, by cunning
  cold define

Which way my journey lieth, or where
  Diccon will dine.
But one good turn I have: be it by night
  or day,
South, east, north, or west, I am never
  out of my way!   10

[*Enter Hodge.*]

HODGE. Cham goodly rewarded, cham I
  not, do you think?
Chad a goodly dinner for all my sweat
  and swink! [8]
Neither butter, cheese, milk, onions,
  flesh, nor fish,
Save this poor piece of barley bread—
  'tis a pleasant, costly dish!
DICCON. Hail, fellow Hodge, and well [9] to
  fare with thy meat—if thou have
  any!
But by thy words, as I them smelled, thy
  daintrels [10] be not many.
HODGE. Daintrels, Diccon? Gog's soul,
  man, save this piece of dry horse-
  bread,
Cha' bit no bit this livelong day; no
  crumb come in my head;
My guts they yawl, [11] crawl, and all my
  belly rumbleth;
The puddings [12] cannot lie still; each one
  over other tumbleth.   20
By Gog's heart, cham so vexed and in my
  belly penned[13]
Chould one piece were at the spittle-
  house,[14] another at the Castle's End!
DICCON. Why, Hodge, was there none at
  home thy dinner for to set?
HODGE. Gog's bread, Diccon, ich came too
  late; was nothing there to get,
Gib—a foul fiend might on her light—
  licked the milk pan so clean!
See, Diccon, 'twas not so well washed
  this seven year, as ich ween!
A pestilence light on all ill luck! Chad
  thought yet, for all this,
Of a morsel of bacon behind the door at
  worst shuld not miss;
But when ich sought a slip to cut, as ich
  was wont to do,

---

[1] Toast soaked in ale.   [3] Pass around.
[2] Crab apple.   [4] Tippler.
[5] Emptied by drinking healths.
[6] This is a shortened version of an earlier
drinking song printed in Dyce's edn. of Skelton.
[7] Enters later.

[8] Labor.
[9] Emended by Dodsley. Original reads *will.*
[10] Delicacies.
[11] Howl.
[12] Entrails   [13] Pined, starved.
[14] Almshouse.

Gog's soul, Diccon, Gib, our cat, had eat
the bacon too! 30
Which bacon Diccon stole, as is declared before.
DICCON. Ill luck, quod he? Marry, swear
it, Hodge, this day, the truth to tell.
Thou rose not on thy right side, or else
blessed thee not well.
Thy milk slopped up, thy bacon filched—
that was too bad luck, Hodge!
HODGE. Nay, nay, there was a fouler fault:
my gammer ga' me the dodge![1]
Seest not how cham rent and torn—my
heels, my knees, and my breech?
Chad thought as ich sat by the fire, help
here and there a stitch;
But there ich was pooped[2] indeed!
DICCON. Why, Hodge?
HODGE. Boots not, man, to tell.
Cham so dressed[3] amongst a sort of fools,
chad better be in hell!
My gammer, cham ashamed to say, by
God, served me not weel![4]
DICCON. How so, Hodge?
HODGE. Has she not gone, trowest
now, and lost her neele? 40
DICCON. Her eel, Hodge? Who fished of
late? That was a dainty dish!
HODGE. Tush, tush, her neele! her neele!
her neele, man! 'Tis neither flesh nor
fish.
A little thing with an hole in the end, as
bright as any siller,[5]
Small, long, sharp at the point, and
straight as any pillar.
DICCON. I know not what a devil thou
meanest. Thou bring'st me more in
doubt.
HODGE. Knowest not with what Tom
Tailor's man sits broaching[6] through
a clout?
A neele! neele! a neele! My gammer's
neele is gone!
DICCON. Her neele, Hodge? Now I smell
thee! That was a chance alone![7]
By the Mass, thou hadst a shameful
loss, and it were but for thy breeches!
HODGE. Gog's soul, man, chould give a
crown chad it but three stitches! 50
DICCON. How sayest thou, Hodge? What
shuld he have, again thy neele got?

HODGE. Bem[8] vather's soul, and chad it,
chould give him a new groat!
DICCON. Canst thou keep counsel in this
case?
HODGE. Else chwold my tongue were
out.
DICCON. Do thou[9] but then by my advice,
and I will fetch it without doubt.
HODGE. Chill run, chill ride, chill dig,
chill delve, chill toil, chill trudge, shalt
see;
Chill hold, chill draw, chill pull, chill
pinch, chill kneel on my bare knee;
Chill scrape, chill scratch, chill sift, chill
seek, chill bow, chill bend, chill sweat,
Chill stoop, chill stir, chill cap,[10] chill
kneel, chill creep on hands and feet;
Chill be thy bondman, Diccon, ich swear
by sun and moon.
And channot somewhat to stop this gap,
cham utterly undone! 60
Pointing behind to his torn breeches.
DICCON. Why, is there any special cause
thou takest hereat such sorrow?
HODGE. Kirstian Clack, Tom Simson's
maid, by the Mass, comes hether to-
morrow!
Cham not able to say, between us what
may hap—
She smiled on me the last Sunday when
ich put off my cap.
DICCON. Well, Hodge, this is a matter of
weight, and must be kept close;
It might else turn to both our costs, as
the world now goes.
Shalt swear to be no blab, Hodge?
HODGE. Chill, Diccon!
DICCON. Then, go to!
Lay thine hand here; say after me as thou
shalt hear me do.
Hast no book?
HODGE. Cha' no book, I!
DICCON. Then needs must force
us both
Upon my breech to lay thine hand, and
there to take thine oath. 70
HODGE. [*Repeating after Diccon.*] I.
Hodge, breechless,
Swear to Diccon rechless,[11]
By the Cross that I shall kiss,

---

[1] Deceived me.
[2] Befooled.
[3] Mistreated.
[4] Well.
[5] Silver.
[6] Piercing.
[7] Unique mishap.
[8] By my.
[9] Emended by Dodsley. Original reads *than.*
[10] Doff the cap.
[11] Without reservation.

To keep his counsel close,
And always me to dispose
    To work that his pleasure is.
        Here he kisseth Diccon's breech.
Diccon. Now, Hodge, see thou take heed
And do as I thee bid,
    For so I judge it meet.
This needle again to win   80
There is no shift therein
    But conjure up a sprite.

Hodge. What, the great devil, Diccon, I
    say?
Diccon. Yea, in good faith, that is the
    way—
    Fet [1] with some pretty charm.
        [*Begins to draw a magic circle.*]
Hodge. Soft, Diccon! Be not too hasty
    yet,
By the Mass, for ich begin to sweat!
    Cham afraid of some harm!

Diccon. Come hether then, and stir thee
    not
One inch out of this circle plot,   90
    But stand as I thee teach.
Hodge. And shall ich be here safe from
    their claws?
Diccon. The master devil with his long
    paws
    Here to thee cannot reach.

Now will I settle me to this gear.
Hodge. I say, Diccon, hear me, hear!
    Go softly to this matter!
Diccon. What devil, man, art afraid of
    naught?
Hodge. Canst not tarry a little thought
    Till ich make a curtsy of water?   100

Diccon. Stand still to it! Why shuldest
    thou fear him?
Hodge. Gog's sides, Diccon, methink ich
    hear him!
    And tarry, chall mar all!
Diccon. The matter is no worse than I
    told it.
Hodge. By the Mass, cham able no longer
    to hold it!
    Too bad ich must bewray [2] the hall!
Diccon. Stand to it, Hodge' Stir not,
    you whoreson!

[1] Fetched. [2] Befoul. Above, Hodge needed
    only to "make water."

What devil, be thine arse-strings brus-
    ten? [3]
    Thyself awhile but stay;
The devil—I smell him—will be here
    anon.   110
Hodge. Hold him fast, Diccon! Cham
    gone! Cham gone!
    Chill not be at that fray!
        [*Exit, running.*]

The II Act. The ii Scene.

Diccon, Chat. [4]

Diccon. Fie, shitten knave, and out upon
    thee!
Above all other louts, fie on thee!
    Is not here a cleanly prank?
But [5] thy matter was no better,
Nor thy presence here no sweeter,
    To fly I can thee thank.

Here is a matter worthy glozing [6]
Of Gammer Gurton's needle losing,
    And a foul piece of wark! [7]
A man, I think, might make a play   10
And need no word to [8] this they say,
    Being but half a clerk.

Soft, let me alone! I will take the charge
This matter further to enlarge
    Within a time short.
If ye will mark my toys,[9] and note,
I will give ye leave to cut my throat
    If I make not good sport.

Dame Chat, I say, where be ye? Within?

[*Enter Dame Chat with cards in her hand.*]

Chat. Who have we there maketh such
    a din?   20
Diccon. Here is a good fellow, maketh
    no great danger.[10]
Chat. What, Diccon? Come near; ye
    be no stranger!
We be fast set at trump, man, hard by
    the fire.
Thou shalt set on the king, if thou come
    a little nigher.

[3] Burst, broken. [4] Enters later. [5] Because (?).
[6] Worth glossing, *i.e.*, commenting on.
[7] Work.   [9] Tricks, pranks.
[8] In addition to.   [10] Trouble.

DICCON. Nay, nay, there is no tarrying,
  I must be gone again.
But, first, for you, in counsel I have a
  word or twain.
CHAT. Come hether, Doll!

[Enter Doll.]

Doll, sit down and play this game,
And, as thou sawest me do, see thou do
  even the same.
There is five trumps beside the queen—
  the hindmost thou shalt find her.
Take heed of Sim Glover's wife; she hath
  an eye behind her!   *[Exit Doll.]* 30
Now, Diccon, say your will.
DICCON.   Nay, soft a little yet!
I wold nct tell it my sister, the matter
  is so great.
There I will have you swear by our dear
  Lady of Bullain,[1]
S[aint] Dunstan, and S[aint] Donnick,[2]
  three Kings of Kullain,[3]
That ye shall keep it secret.
CHAT.   Gog's bread, that will I do!
As secret as mine own thought, by God,
  and the devil too!
DICCON. Here is Gammer Gurton, your
  neighbor, a sad and heavy wight—
Her goodly fair red cock at home was
  stole this last night.
CHAT. Gog's soul! Her cock with the
  yellow legs, that nightly crowed so
  just?[4]
DICCON. That cock is stolen.
CHAT.   What, was he fet out of
  the hens' rust?[5]   40
DICCON. I cannot tell where the devil he
  was kept, under key or lock;
But Tib hath tickled[6] in gammer's
  ear that you should steal the cock.
CHAT. Have I? Strong whore! By bread
  and salt—
DICCON.   What, soft, I say! Be still!
Say not one word for all this gear.
CHAT.   By the Mass, that I will!
I will have the young whore by the head
  and the old trot by the throat!
DICCON. Not one word, Dame Chat, I
  say! Not one word, for my coat!
CHAT. Shall such a beggar's brawl[7] as
  that, thinkest thou, make me a thief?

The pox light on her whore's sides, a
  pestilence and a mischief!—
Come out, thou hungry, needy bitch!
  O, that my nails be short!   49
DICCON. Gog's bread, woman, hold your
  peace! This gear will else pass sport!
I wold not for an hundred pound this
  matter shuld be known,
That I am auctor[8] of this tale or have
  abroad it blown!
Did ye not swear ye wold be ruled, be-
  fore the tale I told?
I said ye must all secret keep, and ye
  said sure ye wold.
CHAT. Wold you suffer, yourself, Dic-
  con, such a sort to revile you,
With slanderous words to blot your
  name, and so to defile you?
DICCON. No, Goodwife Chat; I wold be
  loath such drabs shuld blot my
  name;
But yet ye must so order all that Diccon
  bear no blame.
CHAT. Go to, then! What is your rede?[9]
  Say on your mind; ye shall me rule
  herein.
DICCON. God-a-mercy[10] to Dame Chat!
  In faith, thou must the gear begin.   60
It is twenty pound to a goose turd, my
  gammer will not tarry,
But hetherward she comes as fast as her
  legs can her carry,
To brawl with you about her cock. For
  well I heard Tib say
The cock was roasted in your house to
  breakfast yesterday;
And, when ye had the carcass eaten, the
  feathers ye out flung;
And Doll, your maid, the legs she hid a
  foot deep in the dung.
CHAT. O gracious God, my heart it[11]
  bursts!
DICCON.   Well, rule yourself a space!
And Gammer Gurton when she cometh
  anon into this place—
Then to the quean! Let's see! Tell her
  your mind, and spare not,
So[12] shall Diccon blameless be; and then
  go to, I care not!   70
CHAT. Then, whore, beware her throat!
  I can abide no longer!

---

[1] Boulogne.   [2] Dominic.   [3] Cologne.
[4] Regularly.   [5] Roost.   [6] Whispered.   [7] Rrat.
[8] Author.   [9] Advice.   [10] Thanks.
[11] Emended by Dodsley. Original reads *is*.
[12] So long as.

In faith, old witch, it shall be seen which
 of us two be stronger!
And, Diccon, but at your request, I
 wold not stay one hour.
DICCON. Well, keep it in till she be here,
 and then—out let it pour!
In the meanwhile get you in, and make
 no words of this.
More of this matter within this hour
 to hear you shall not miss.
Because I know you are my friend, hide
 it I cold not, doubtless.
Ye know your harm; see ye be wise
 about your own business!
So fare ye well! [1]
CHAT.   Nay, soft, Diccon, and drink!
 What, Doll, I say!
Bring here a cup of the best ale; let's
 see! Come quickly away! [*Exeunt.*] 80

THE II ACT. THE iii SCENE.

Hodge,[2] *Diccon.*

DICCON. Ye see, masters, the one end
 tapped of this my short device!
Now must we broach tother[3] too, be-
 fore the smoke arise.
And, by the time they have awhile run,
 I trust ye need not crave it;
But look, what lieth in both their hearts,
 ye are like, sure, to have it.

[*Enter Hodge.*]

HODGE. Yea, Gog's soul, art alive yet?
 What, Diccon, dare ich come?
DICCON. A man is well hied[4] to trust to
 thee! I will say nothing but mum.
But, and ye come any nearer, I pray
 you see all be sweet!
HODGE. Tush, man! Is gammer's neele
 found? That chould gladly weet![5]
DICCON. She may thank thee it is not found,
 for, if thou had kept thy standing,
The devil he wold have fet it out, even,
 Hodge, at thy commanding. 10
HODGE. Gog's heart! And cold he tell noth-
 ing where the neele might be found?
DICCON. Ye foolish dolt, ye were to seek
 ere we had got our ground;
Therefore his tale so doubtful was that
 I cold not perceive it.

HODGE. Then ich see well something was
 said. Chope[6] one day yet to have it.
But, Diccon, Diccon, did not the devil
 cry "Ho, ho, ho"?
DICCON. If thou hadst tarried where thou
 stood'st, thou woldest have said so.
HODGE. Durst swear of[7] a book, chard[8]
 him roar, straight after ich was gone!
But tell me, Diccon, what said the
 knave? Let me hear it anon.
DICCON. The whoreson talked to me, I
 know not well of what:
One while his tongue it ran and paltered
 of a cat; 20
Another while he stammered still upon
 a rat;
Last of all, there was nothing but every
 word "Chat! Chat!"
But this I well perceived, before I wold
 him rid,
Between "Chat" and the "rat" and
 the "cat," the needle is hid.
Now, whether Gib, our cat, have eat it in
 her maw,
Or Doctor Rat, our curate, have found it
 in the straw,
Or this Dame Chat, your neighbor, have
 stolen it, God he knoweth!
But by the morrow at this time we shall
 learn how the matter goeth.
HODGE. Canst not learn tonight, man?
 Seest not what is here?
Pointing behind to his torn breeches.
DICCON. 'Tis not possible to make it
 sooner appear. 30
HODGE. Alas, Diccon, then chave no shift
 but, lest ich tarry too long,
Hie me to Sim Glover's shop, there to
 seek for a thong,
Therewith this breech to tatch[9] and tie
 as ich may.
DICCON. Tomorrow, Hodge, if we chance
 to meet, shalt see what I will say.
        [*Exit Hodge.*]

THE II ACT. THE iv SCENE.

Diccon, Gammer.[10]

DICCON. Now this gear must forward go,
 for here my gammer cometh.
Be still awhile, and say nothing; make
 here a little romth![11]

---

[1] Dodsley's reading. Original reads *will.*
[2] Enters later.   [4] Sped.
[3] That other.   [5] Know.

[6] I hope. [7] On. [8] I heard. [9] Attach, fasten.
[10] Enters later.   [11] Room.

[Enter Gammer.]

GAMMER. Good Lord, shall never be my
luck my neele again to spy?
Alas the while, 'tis past my help! Where
'tis, still it must lie!
DICCON. Now Jesus, Gammer Gurton,
what driveth you to this sadness?
I fear me, by my conscience, you will sure
fall to madness.
GAMMER. Who is that? What, Diccon?
Cham lost, man. Fie! fie!
DICCON. Marry, fie on them that be
worthy! But what shuld be your
trouble?
GAMMER. Alas, the more ich think on it,
my sorrow it waxeth double!
My goodly tossing [1] spurrier's neele,
chave lost, ich wot not where.   10
DICCON. Your neele! When?
GAMMER.   My neele! Alas, ich might
full ill it spare!
As God himself he knoweth, ne'er one
beside chave.
DICCON. If this be all, good gammer, I
warrant you all is save.
GAMMER. Why, know you any tidings
which way my neele is gone?
DICCON. Yea, that I do, doubtless, as ye
shall hear anon.
A [2] see a thing this matter toucheth,
within these twenty hours,
Even at this gate,[3] before my face, by a
neighbor of yours:
She stooped me down, and up she took a
needle or a pin.
I durst be sworn it was even yours, by all
my mother's kin.
GAMMER. It was my neele, Diccon, ich
wot; for here, even by this post,   20
Ich sat what time as ich upstart, and so
my neele it lost.
Who was it, lief [4] son? Speak, ich pray
thee, and quickly tell me that!
DICCON. A subtle quean as any in this
town, your neighbor here, Dame Chat.
GAMMER. Dame Chat, Diccon? Let me
be gone! Chill thither in posthaste.
DICCON. Take my counsel yet or ye go,
for fear ye walk in waste!
It is a murrion crafty drab, and froward
to be pleaséd;

And ye take not the better way, our
needle yet ye lose [5] it.
For, when she took it up, even here before your doors,
"What, soft, Dame Chat," quoth I,
"that same is none of yours!"
"Avaunt," quoth she, "sir knave! What
pratest thou of that I find?   30
I wold thou hadst kissed me I wot where"
(she meant, I know, behind).
And home she went as brag [6] as it had
been a bodylouse,
And I after as bold as it had been the
goodman of the house.
But there and ye had hard her how she
began to scold—
The tongue it went on pattens,[7] by Him
that Judas sold!
Each other word I was a knave, and you
a whore of whores,
Because I spake in your behalf and said
the neele was yours.
GAMMER. Gog's bread! And thinks the
callet [8] thus to keep my neele me
fro? [9]
DICCON. Let her alone, and she minds none
other but even to dress you so!
GAMMER. By the Mass, chill rather spend
the coat that is on my back!   40
Thinks the false quean by such a sleight [10]
that chill my neele lack?
DICCON. Slepe [11] not you[r] gear, I counsel you, but of this take good heed:
Let not be known I told you of it, how
well soever ye speed.
GAMMER. Chill in, Diccon, a clean apern [12]
to take and set before me;
And ich may my neele once see, chill sure
remember thee!   *[Exit.]*

THE II ACT. THE V SCENE.

Diccon.

DICCON. Here will the sport begin! If
these two once may meet,
Their cheer, durst lay money, will prove
scarcely sweet!
My gammer, sure, intends to be upon her
bones

[1] Brett-Smith suggests the movement of the
needle in sewing with a long thread.
[2] I.   [3] Door.   [4] Dear.
[5] Rime would require *leese*.   [6] Briskly.
[7] On wooden shoes, *i.e.*, noisily.
[8] Strumpet.   [9] From.
[10] Dodsley's reading. Original reads *slygh*.
[11] Slip, neglect.   [12] Apron.

With staves or with clubs or else with
    cobblestones.
Dame Chat, on the other side, if she be
    far behind,
I am right far deceived; she is given to it
    of kind.[1]
He that may tarry by it awhile, and that
    but short,
I warrant him—trust to it—he shall see
    all the sport.
Into the town will I, my friends to visit
    there,
And hether straight again to see th'end of
    this gear.—[*Turns to musicians.*]   10
In the meantime, fellows, pipe up your
    fiddles! I say, take them,
And let your friends hear such mirth as
    ye can make them!   [*Exit.*]

The III Act. The i Scene.

Hodge.

HODGE. Sim Glover, yet gramercy! Cham
    meetly well sped now.
Th'art even as good a fellow as ever
    kissed a cow!
Here is a thing[2] indeed; by the Mass,
    though ich speak it,
Tom Tankard's great bald curtal,[3] I
    think, could not break it!
And, when he spied my need to be so
    straight and hard,
Hais[4] lent me here his nawl[5] to set the
    jib forward.[6]
As for my gammer's neele, the flying
    fiend go weet![7]
Chill not now go to the door again with it
    to meet.
Could make shift good enough and chad
    a candle's end.
The chief hole in my breech with these
    two chill amend.   10

The III Act. The ii Scene.

Gammer, Hodge.

GAMMER. How, Hodge! mayst now be
    glad! Cha' news to tell thee.
Ich know who hais my neele; ich trust
    soon shalt it see.

HODGE. The devil thou does! Hast hard,
    gammer, indeed, or dost but jest?
GAMMER. 'Tis as true as steel, Hodge.
HODGE.   Why, knowest well where
    didst leese it?
GAMMER. Ich know who found it, and
    took it up; shalt see, or it be long.
HODGE. God's Mother dear, if that be
    true, farewell both nawl an' thong!
But who hais it, gammer? Say on!
    Chould fain hear it disclosed.
GAMMER. That false fixen,[8] that same
    Dame Chat, that counts herself so
    honest!
HODGE. Who told you so?
GAMMER.   That same did Diccon
    the bedlam, which saw it done.
HODGE. Diccon? It is a vengeable knave,
    gammer! 'Tis a bonable[9] whoreson! 10
Can do mo[10] things than that, else cham
    deceived evil.
By the Mass, ich saw him of late call up
    a great black devil!
O, the knave cried, "Ho! ho!" He roared,
    and he thundered.
And ye'd been here, cham sure you'ld
    murrainly ha' wondered!
GAMMER. Was not thou afraid, Hodge,
    to see him in this place?
HODGE. No! And chad come to me,
    chould have laid him on the face,
Chould have promised him!
GAMMER.   But, Hodge, had he no
    horns to push?
HODGE. As long as your two arms! Saw
    ye never Friar Rush[11]
Painted on a cloth, with a side[12] long
    cow's tail,
And crooked cloven feet, and many a
    hooked nail?   20
For all the world, if I shuld judge,
    chould reckon him his brother.
Look, even what face Friar Rush had,
    the devil had such another!
GAMMER. Now[13] Jesus' mercy, Hodge, did
    Diccon in him bring?
HODGE. Nay, gammer, hear me speak!
    Chill tell you a greater thing:

---

[1] By nature.
[2] *I.e.*, the thong he had gone for.
[3] Horse with a docked tail.
[6] *I.e.*, help things on.
[4] Has.
[5] Awl.
[7] Wi' it, with it.
[8] Vixen.
[9] Powerful; Hodge's mispronunciation of *abominable.*   [10] More.
[11] A name assumed by the devil in a popular German folk tale.
[12] Great (literally, *long*).
[13] Dodsley's reading. Early edns. read *new.*

The devil, when Diccon had him—ich
  hard him wondrous weel—
Said plainly, here before us, that Dame
  Chat had your neele.
GAMMER. Then let us go and ask her
  wherefore she minds to keep it!
Seeing we know so much, 'twere a mad-
  ness now to slepe it.
HODGE. Go to her, gammer.

[Enter Chat.]

See ye not where she stands in her doors?
Bid her give you the neele. 'Tis none
  of hers, but yours! 30

THE III ACT. THE iii SCENE.

Gammer, Chat, Hodge.

GAMMER. Dame Chat, chold pray thee
  fair, let me have that is mine!
Chill not this twenty years take one
  fart that is thine.
Therefore give me mine own, and let
  me live beside thee!
CHAT. Why art thou crept from home
  hether to mine own doors to chide me?
Hence, doting drab, avaunt, or I shall
  set thee further!
Intends thou and that knave me in my
  house to murther?
GAMMER. Tush, gape not so on [1] me,
  woman! Shalt not yet eat me!
Nor all the friends thou hast, in this
  shall not entreat me!
Mine own goods I will have, and ask
  thee on beleve.[2]
What, woman! Poor folks must have
  right, though the thing you aggrieve. 10
CHAT. Give thee thy right, and hang thee
  up, with all thy bagger's [3] brood!
What, wilt thou make me a thief, and
  say I stole thy good?
GAMMER. Chill say nothing, ich warrant
  thee, but that ich can prove it well.
Thou fet my good even from my door,
  cham able this to tell!
CHAT. Did I, old witch, steal oft [4] was
  thine? How should that thing be
  known?
GAMMER. Ich cannot tell; but up thou
  tookest it, as though it had been thine
  own.

CHAT. Marry, fie on thee, thou old gib,[5]
  with all my very heart!
GAMMER. Nay, fie on thee, thou ramp,[6]
  thou rig,[7] with all that take thy
  part!
CHAT. A vengeance on those lips that
  layeth such things to my charge!
GAMMER. A vengeance on those callet-
  ships whose conscience is so large! [8] 20
CHAT. Come out, Hodge!
GAMMER.   Come out, Hodge, and
  let me have [9] right!
CHAT. Thou arrant witch!
GAMMER.   Thou bawdy bitch, chill
  make thee curse this night!
CHAT. A bag and a wallet! [10]
GAMMER.   A cart for a callet! [11]
CHAT.   Why, weenest thou thus to
  prevail?
I hold thee a groat I shall patch thy
  coat!
GAMMER.   Thou wart [12] as good
  kiss my tail!
Thou slut, thou cut,[13] thou rakes,[14] thou
  jakes! [15] Will not shame make thee
  hide thee?
CHAT. Thou scald,[16] thou bald, thou rot-
  ten, thou glutton! I will no longer
  chide thee!
But I will teach thee to keep home.
GAMMER.   Wilt thou, drunken beast?
                        [They fight.]
HODGE. Stick to her, gammer! Take her by
  the head! Chill warrant you this feast!
Smite, I say, gammer! Bite, I say, gammer! I trow ye will be keen!
Where be your nails? Claw her by the
  jaws! Pull me out both her eyen! [17] 30
           [Chat throws Gammer down.]
Gog's bones, gammer, hold up your head!
CHAT.   I trow, drab, I shall dress thee.—
[To Hodge.] Tarry, thou knave! I hold
  thee a groat I shall make these hands
  bless thee!—

                      [Hodge retires.]

---

[1] Emended by Hazlitt. Original reads *no*.
[2] Belive, lively, at once.
[3] Beggar's (?).   [4] Aught.

[5] Cat.   [7] Wanton woman.
[6] Shameless woman.   [8] Liberal, easy.
[9] Manly's reading. Original reads *let have me*.
[10] Accouterments of a beggar.
[11] A drab was commonly punished by being
whipped at the tail of a cart as it was driven
through the streets.
[12] Wert.   [15] Privy.
[13] Docked horse or dog.   [16] Scabby person.
[14] Dissolute person.   [17] Old plural of *eye*.

Take thou this, old whore, for amends,
and learn thy tongue well to tame,
And say thou met at this bickering, not
thy fellow, but thy dame!

[Hodge returns with a club.]

HODGE. Where is the strong stewed
whore? Chill gear [1] a whore's mark!
Stand out one's way that ich kill none
in the dark!
Up, gammer, and ye be alive! Chill
fight now for us both.
Come no near me, thou scald callet! To
kill thee ich were loath.

CHAT. Art here again, thou hoddypeak! [2]
What, Doll, bring me out my spit!

HODGE. Chill broach thee with this!
Bim father soul, chill conjure that
foul sprite!—　　　　　40
Let door stand, Cock! Why comes indeed? Keep door, thou whoreson boy!

CHAT. Stand to it, thou dastard, for thine
ears! Ise [3] teach thee a sluttish toy!

HODGE. Gog's wounds, whore, chill make
thee avaunt! *[Flees into the house.]*
Take heed, Cock, pull in the latch!

CHAT. I' faith, sir loose-breech, had ye
tarried, ye shold have found your
match!

[Gammer attacks Chat from behind.]

GAMMER. Now ware thy throat, losel! [4]
Thouse [5] pay [6] for all!

[Throws Chat down.]

HODGE.　　　　Well said, gammer,
by my soul!
Hoise [7] her! Souse her! Bounce her!
Trounce her! Pull out her throatboll! [8]

CHAT. Com'st behind me, thou withered
witch? And I get once on foot,
Thouse pay for all, thou old tarleather! [9]
I'll teach thee what longs [10] to it!
Take thee this to make up thy mouth till
time thou come by more!

[Chat beats Gammer and goes out.]

HODGE. Up, gammer! Stand on your
feet. Where is the old whore?　　50
Faith, would chad her by the face!
Chould crack her callet crown!

GAMMER. Ah, Hodge, Hodge, where was
thy help, when fixen had me down?

HODGE. By the Mass, gammer, but for my
staff, Chat had gone nigh to spill you!
Ich think the harlot had not cared, and
chad not come, to kill you.
But shall we lose our neele thus?

GAMMER.　　　　No, Hodge, chwar [11] loath
do so.
Thinkest thou chill take that at her
hand? No, Hodge, ich tell thee, no!

HODGE. Chold yet this fray were well take
up, and our own neele at home.
'Twill be my chance else some to kill,
wherever it be, or whom!

GAMMER. We have a parson, Hodge, thou
knows, a man esteeméd wise,
Mast' Doctor Rat; chill for him send,
and let me hear his advice.　　60
He will her shrive for all this gear, and
give her penance straight;
Wese [12] have our neele, else Dame Chat
comes ne'er within heaven-gate!

HODGE. Yea, marry, gammer, that ich
think best. Will you now for him send?
The sooner Doctor Rat be here, the
sooner wese ha' an end.
And here, gammer! Diccon's devil, as
ich remember well,
Of cat, and Chat, and Doctor Rat a
felonious tale did tell.
Chold you forty pound that is the way
your neele to get again!

GAMMER. Chill ha' him straight! Call out
the boy: wese make him take the pain.

HODGE. What, Cock, I say! Come out!
What devil, canst not hear?

[Enter Cock.]

COCK. [13] How now, Hodge? How does
gammer? Is yet the weather clear?　70
What wold chave me to do?

GAMMER.　　　　Come hether, Cock, anon!
Hence swith to Doctor Rat! Hie thee
that thou were gone!
And pray him come speak with me; cham
not well at ease.
Shalt have him at his chamber, or [14] else
at Mother Bee's;
Else seek him at Hob Filcher's shop, for,
as chard it reported,
There is the best ale in all the town, and
now is most resorted.

---

[1] Gi' her, give her.
[2] Simpleton.
[3] I shall.
[4] Worthless person.
[5] Thou shalt.
[6] Emended by Dodsley. Original reads *pray*.
[7] Lift.
[8] Adam's apple.
[9] Strip of dried sheepskin.
[10] Belongs.
[11] Ich were, I were. Bradley's emendation for *chwarde*.
[12] We shall.
[13] Original assigns this speech to Gammer.
[14] Original reads *of*.

COCK. And shall ich bring him with me, gammer?

GAMMER. Yea, by-and-by, good Cock.

COCK. Shalt see that shall be here anon, else let me have on the dock! [1] [*Exit.*]

HODGE. Now, gammer, shall we two go in, and tarry for his coming?

What devil, woman, pluck up your heart, and leave off all this glumming! [2]   80

Though she were stronger at the first, as ich think ye did find her,

Yet there ye dressed the drunken sow, what time ye came behind her.

GAMMER. Nay, nay, cham sure she lost not all; for set th'end to the beginning,

And ich doubt not but she will make small boast of her winning.

[*They start to go in.*]

THE III ACT. THE iv SCENE.

Tib [with a cat], Hodge, Gammer, Cock. [3]

TIB. See, gammer, gammer, Gib, our cat! Cham afraid what she aileth!

She stands me gasping behind the door, as though her wind her faileth.

Now let ich doubt what Gib shuld mean, that now she doth so dote. [4]

HODGE. Hold hether! [5] Ichold twenty pound your neele is in her throat!

Grope [6] her, ich say! Methinks ich feel it. Does not prick your hand?

GAMMER. Ich can feel nothing.

HODGE.   No? Ich know thar's not within this land

A murrainer cat than Gib is, betwixt the Thames and Tyne;

Sh'as as much wit in her head almost as chave in mine!

TIB. Faith, sh'as eaten something that will not easily down.

Whether she gat it at home or abroad in the town   10

Ich cannot tell.

GAMMER.   Alas, ich fear it be some crooked pin!

And then, farewell Gib! She is undone and lost—all save the skin.

HODGE. Tib, your neele, woman, I say! Gog's soul, give me a knife,

And chill have it out of her maw, or else chall lose my life!

GAMMER. What! Nay, Hodge, fie! Kill not our cat! 'Tis all the cats we ha' now!

HODGE. By the Mass, Dame Chat hais me so moved ich care not what I kill, ma' [7] God avow!

Go to, then, Tib! To this gear! Hold up her tail, and take her!

Chill see what devil is in her guts! Chill take the pains to rake [8] her!

GAMMER. Rake a cat, Hodge? What woldst thou do?

HODGE.   What! Think'st that cham not able?

Did not Tom Tankard rake his curtal t'or [9] day, standing in the stable?   20

[*Enter Cock.*]

GAMMER. Soft, be content; let's hear what news Cock bringeth from Mast' Rat!

COCK. Gammer, chave been there as you bade, you wot well about what.

'Twill not be long before he come, ich durst swear of a book.

He bids you see ye be at home, and there for him to look.

GAMMER. Where didst thou find him, boy? Was he not where I told thee?

COCK. Yes, yes, even at Hob Filcher's house, by him that bought and sold me;

A cup of ale had in his hand, and a crab lay in the fire.

Chad much ado to go and come, all was so full of mire.

And, gammer, one thing I can tell: Hob Filcher's nawl was lost,

And Doctor Rat found it again, hard beside the doorpost.   30

Ichold a penny, can say something your neele again to fet.

GAMMER. Cham glad to hear so much, Cock; then trust he will not let [10]

To help us herein best he can; therefore, till time he come,

Let us go in. If there be aught to get, thou shalt have some.   [*Exeunt.*]

THE IV ACT. THE i SCENE [11]

Doctor Rat, Gammer Gurton.

D. RAT. [*To himself.*] A man were better twenty times be a bandog and bark,

Than here, among such a sort, be parish priest or clerk,

---

[1] Tail, *i.e.*, a beating.
[2] Sullenness.
[3] Enters later.
[4] Act foolishly.
[5] Give her to me!
[6] Feel.
[7] I make. [8] Clean. [9] Tother. [10] Forbear.
[11] Original reads *The II Act. The iv Scene.*

Where he shall never be at rest one
    pissing-while a day,
But he must trudge about the town, this
    way and that way,
Here to a drab, there to a thief, his shoes
    to tear and rent,
And, that which is worst of all, at every
    knave's commandment!
I had not sit the space to drink two pots
    of ale
But Gammer Gurton's sorry boy was
    straightway at my tail,
And she was sick, and I must come—to
    do I wot not what!
If once her finger's end but ache,
    "Trudge! Call for Doctor Rat!"   10
And, when I come not at their call, I only
    thereby lose;
For I am sure to lack therefore a tithe-
    pig or a goose.
I warrant you, when truth is known, and
    told they have their tale,
The matter whereabout I come is not
    worth a halfpennyworth of ale!
Yet must I talk so sage and smooth as
    though I were a glozier,[1]
Else, or the year come at an end, I shall
    be sure the loser.
            [*He spies Gammer Gurton working.*]
What work ye, Gammer Gurton! How,
    here is your friend M[aster] Rat!
GAMMER. Ah, good M[aster] Doctor, cha'
    troubled, cha' troubled you, chwot
    well that!
D. RAT. How do ye, woman? Be ye lusty,
    or be ye not well at ease?
GAMMER. By Gis,[2] master, cham not
    sick,[3] but yet chave a disease.[4]   20
Chad a foul turn now of late; chill tell it
    you, by Gigs!
D. RAT. Hath your brown cow cast her
    calf, or your sandy sow her pigs?
GAMMER. No, but chad been as good they
    had, as this, ich wot weel.
D. RAT. What is the matter?
GAMMER.   Alas! alas! cha' lost my good
    neele!
My neele, I say! And, wot ye what? A
    drab came by and spied it,
And, when I asked her for the same, the
    filth flatly denied it.

D. RAT. What was she that—
GAMMER.   A dame, ich warrant you!
    She began to scold and brawl—
Alas, alas! Come hether, Hodge! This
    wr[e]tch can tell you all.

THE IV ACT. THE ii SCENE.[5]

Hodge, Doctor Rat, Gammer, Diccon, Chat.[6]

HODGE. Good morrow, Gaffer Vicar!
D. RAT.   Come on, fellow; let us hear.
    Thy dame hath said to me, thou knowest
    of all this gear;
    Let's see what thou canst say.
HODGE.   Bym fay,[7] sir, that ye shall!
What matter soever here was done, ich
    can tell your ma'ship all.
My Gammer Gurton here, see now, sat
    her down at this door, see now;
And, as she began to stir her, see now, her
    neele fell in the floor, see now;
And, while her staff she took, see now, at
    Gib, her cat, to fling, see now,
Her neele was lost in the floor, see now.
    Is not this a wondrous thing, see now?
Then came the quean, Dame Chat, see
    now, to ask for her black cup, see
    now;
And even here at this gate, see now,
    she took that neele up, see now.   10
My gammer then she yeed,[8] see now,
    her neele again to bring, see now,
And was caught by the head, see now.
    Is not this a wondrous thing, see now?
She tare my gammer's coat, see now,
    and scratched her by the face, see
    now;
Chad thought sh'ad stopped her throat,
    see now. Is not this a wondrous case,
    see now?
When ich saw this, ich was wroth,[9] see
    now, and start between them twain,
    see now;
Else, ich durst take a book oath, see
    now, my gammer had been slain, see
    now.
GAMMER. This is even the whole matter,
    as Hodge has plainly told.
And chould fain be quiet, for my part,
    that chould.

[5] Hazlitt, Manly, and Adams begin a new
scene at l. 52 and again at l. 94.
[6] The last two enter later.
[7] By my faith.   [8] Went.
[9] Original misprints *worth*.

[1] Flatterer.   [2] Jesus.
[3] Emended by Dodsley. Original reads *sich*.
[4] Dis-ease, anxiety.

But help us, good master—beseech ye
  that ye do—
Else shall we both be beaten, and lose
  our neele too. 20
D. RAT. What wold ye have me to do?
  Tell me, that I were gone.
I will do the best that I can to set you
  both at one.
But be ye sure Dame Chat hath this
  your neele found?
GAMMER. Here comes the man that see
  her take it up of [1] the ground;
Ask him yourself, Master Rat, if ye be-
  lieve not me;
And help me to my neele, for God's sake
  and Saint Charity!

[Enter Diccon.]

D. RAT. Come near, Diccon, and let us
  hear what thou can express.
Wilt thou be sworn thou seest Dame
  Chat this woman's neele have?
DICCON. Nay, by S[aint] Benit,[2] will I not!
  Then might ye think me rave.[3]
GAMMER. Why, didst not thou tell me so
  even here? Canst thou for shame
  deny it? 30
DICCON. Ay, marry, gammer; but I said
  I wold not abide by it.
D. RAT. Will you say a thing, and not
  stick to it to try it?
DICCON. "Stick to it," quoth you, Master
  Rat? Marry, sir, I defy it!
Nay, there is many an honest man,
  when he such blasts hath blown
In his friend's ears, he would be loath
  the same by him were known.
If such a toy be uséd oft among the
  honesty,[4]
It may beseem a simple man of [5] your
  and my degree.
D. RAT. Then we be never the nearer,
  for all that you can tell?
DICCON. Yes, marry, sir, if ye will do by
  mine advice and counsel.
If Mother Chat see all us here, she know-
  eth how the matter goes; 40
Therefore I rede [6] you three go hence,
  and within keep close;
And I will into Dame Chat's house. and
  so the matter use

That, or you cold go twice to church, I
  warrant you hear news.
She shall look well about her, but, I
  durst lay a pledge,
Ye shall of gammer's neele have shortly
  better knowledge.
GAMMER. Now, gentle Diccon. do so; and,
  good sir, let us trudge.
D. RAT. By the Mass, I may not tarry so
  long to be your judge.
DICCON. 'Tis but a little while, man.
  What, take so much pain!
If I hear no news of it, I will come sooner
  again.
HODGE. Tarry so much, good Master
  Doctor, of your gentleness! 50
D. RAT. Then let us hie us inward; and,
  Diccon, speed thy business!
DICCON. Now, sirs, do you no more but
  keep my counsel just,
And Doctor Rat shall thus catch some
  good, I trust.—
    [Exeunt Hodge, Rat, and Gammer.
To himself.] But Mother Chat, my
  gossip, talk first withal I must,
For she must be chief captain to lay the
  Rat in the dust.

[Enter Dame Chat.]

God deven,[7] Dame Chat, in faith, and
  well met in this place!
CHAT. God deven, my friend Diccon.
  Whether [8] walk ye this pace?
DICCON. By my truth, even to you, to
  learn how the world goeth.
Hard ye no more of the other matter,
  say me now, by your troth?
CHAT. O, yes, Diccon. Here the old whore
  and Hodge, that great knave— 60
But, in faith, I would thou hadst seen!—
O Lord, I dressed them brave! [9]
She bare me two or three souses [10] be-
  hind in the nape of the neck,
Till I made her old wesen [11] to answer
  again, "keck"! [12]
And Hodge, that dirty dastard that at
  her elbow stands.
If one pair of legs had not been worth
  two pair of hands,

---

[1] Off.
[2] Benedict.
[3] To be mad.
[4] Persons of quality.
[5] Original reads if.
[6] Advise.
[7] God give you good even.
[8] Whither.
[9] Finely.
[10] Thwacks.
[11] Weasand, throat.
[12] Sound of vomiting.

He had had his beard shaven if my nails
    wold have served!
And not without a cause, for the knave
    it well deserved!
DICCON. By the Mass, I can thee thank,
    wench, thou didst so well acquit
    thee!
CHAT. And th'adst seen him, Diccon, it
    wold have made thee beshit thee
For laughter. The whoreson dolt at last
    caught up a club   70
As though he would have slain the
    master devil, Belsabub;
But I set him soon inward.
DICCON.   O Lord, there is the thing
    That Hodge is so offended, that makes
    him start and fling!
CHAT. Why, makes the knave any moil-
    ing,[1] as ye have seen or hard?
DICCON. Even now I saw him last. Like
    a madman he fared,
And sware by heaven and hell he would
    awreak [2] his sorrow,
And leave you never a hen on-live by
    eight of the clock tomorrow.
Therefore mark what I say, and my
    words see that ye trust:
Your hens be as good as dead if ye leave
    them on the rust!
CHAT. The knave dare as well go hang
    himself as go upon my ground!   80
DICCON. Well, yet take heed, I say! I
    must tell you my tale round.[3]
Have you not about your house, behind
    your furnace or lead,[4]
A hole where a crafty knave may creep
    in for need?
CHAT. Yes, by the Mass, a hole broke
    down even within these two days.
DICCON. Hodge he intends this same
    night to slip in thereaways.
CHAT. O Christ, that I were sure of it!
    In faith, he shuld have his meed!
DICCON. Watch well, for the knave will
    be there as sure as is your creed.
I wold spend myself a shilling to have
    him swingéd well.
CHAT. I am as glad as a woman can be of
    this thing to hear tell.
By Gog's bones, when he cometh, now
    that I know the matter,   90

He shall sure at the first skip to leap in
    scalding water—
With a worse turn besides! When he will,
    let him come!
DICCON. I tell you as my sister. You
    know what meaneth "mum"!—
                  [Exit Chat.]
Now lack I but my doctor to play his
    part again.
And lo, where he cometh towards—per-
    adventure to his pain!

           [Enter Rat.]

D. RAT. What good news, Diccon? Fel-
    low, is Mother Chat at home?
DICCON. She is, sir, and she is not, but it
    please her to whom.
Yet did I take her tardy,[5] as subtle as
    she was!
D. RAT. The thing that thou went'st for,
    hast thou brought it to pass?
DICCON. I have done that I have done,
    be it worse, be it better!   100
And Dame Chat at her wit's end I have
    almost set her.
D. RAT. Why, hast thou spied the neele?
    Quickly, I pray thee, tell!
DICCON. I have spied it, in faith, sir, I
    handled myself so well.
And yet the crafty quean had almost
    take my trump.
But, or all came to an end, I set her in
    a dump!
D. RAT. How so, I pray thee, Diccon?
DICCON.   Marry, sir, will ye hear?
She was clapped down on the back side,[6]
    by Cock's Mother dear,
And there she sat sewing a halter, or a band,
    With no other thing save gammer's
    needle in her hand.
As soon as any knock, if the filth be in
    doubt,   110
She needs but once puff, and her candle
    is out.
Now I, sir, knowing of every door the pin,
Came nicely,[7] and said no word till
    time I was within;
And there I saw the neele, even with
    these two eyes.
Whoever say the contrary, I will swear
    he lies!

[1] Worry, vexation.
[2] Avenge.
[3] Directly.
[4] Pot.
[5] Unaware.
[6] Seated in the back of the house.
[7] Stealthily.

D. RAT. O Diccon, that I was not there
then in thy stead!

DICCON. Well, if ye will be ordered and
do by my rede,

I will bring you to a place, as the house
stands,

Where ye shall take the drab with the
neele in her hands.

D. RAT. For God's sake, do so, Diccon,
and I will gage [1] my gown   120

To give thee a full pot of the best ale
in the town!

DICCON. Follow me but a little, and mark
what I will say.

Lay down your gown beside you. [*Rat
takes off his gown.*] ' Go to, come on
your way!

See ye not what is here? A hole wherein
ye may creep

Into the house, and suddenly unwares
among them leap.

There shall ye find the bitch fox and the
neele together.

Do as I bid you, man; come on your
ways hether!

D. RAT. Art thou sure, Diccon, the swill-
tub stands not hereabout?

DICCON. I was within myself, man, even
now, there is no doubt.

Go softly, make no noise. Give me your
foot, Sir John! [2]   130

Here will I wait upon you till you come
out anon.

[*Rat climbs through the hole and is beaten.*]

D. RAT. Help, Diccon! Out, alas! I
shall be slain among them!

DICCON. If they give you not the needle,
tell them that ye will hang them.

Ware that!—How, my wenches, have ye
caught the fox

That used to make revel among your
hens and cocks?

Save his life yet for his order, though he
sustain some pain.—

Gog's bread, I am afraid they will beat
out his brain!   [*Exit Diccon.*

Enter Rat.]

D. RAT. Woe worth the hour that I came
here!

And woe worth him that wrought this
gear!

---

[1] Pledge.   [2] Conventional name for a parson.

A sort of drabs and queans have me
blessed! [3]   140

Was ever creature half so evil dressed?

Whoever it wrought and first did invent
it,

He shall, I warrant him, ere long repent
it!

I will spend all I have, without [4] my skin,

But he shall be brought to the plight I
am in!

Master Baily, I trow, and he be worth his
ears,

Will snaffle these murderers and all that
them bears. [5]

I will surely neither bite nor sup

Till I fetch him hether, this matter to
take up.   [*Exit.*]

THE V ACT. THE i SCENE.

*Master Bailey, [attended by Scapethrift,] Doc-
tor Rat.*

BAILY. I can perceive none other, I speak
it from my heart,

But either ye are in all the fault, or else
in the greatest part.

D. RAT. If it be counted his fault, besides
all his grieves, [6]

When a poor man is spoiled and beaten
among thieves,

Then I confess my fault herein at this
season;

But I hope you will not judge so much
against reason.

BAILY. And methinks, by your own tale,
of all that ye name,

If any played the thief, you were the very
same.

The women they did nothing, as your
words make probation,

But stoutly withstood your forcible invasion.   10

If that a thief at your window to enter
should begin,

Wold you hold forth your hand and help
to pull him in?

Or you wold keep him out? I pray you,
answer me.

D. RAT. Marry, keep him out, and a good
cause why!

But I am no thief, sir, but an honest,
learned clerk.

---

[3] Wounded.   [4] Except.
[5] Everybody that supports them.   [6] Griefs.

BAILY. Yea, but who knoweth that when
he meets you in the dark?

I am sure your learning shines not out at
your nose.

Was it any marvel though the poor
woman arose

And start up, being afraid of that was in
her purse?

Methink you may be glad that you[r]
luck was no worse.   20

D. RAT. Is not this evil enough, I pray
you, as you think?

Showing his broken head.

BAILY. Yea, but a man in the dark, if [1]
chances do wink,

As soon he smites his father as any other
man,

Because for lack of light discern him he
ne can.

Might it not have been your luck with a
spit to have been slain?

D. RAT. I think I am little better—my
scalp is cloven to the brain!

If there be all the remedy, I know who
bears the k[n]ocks.

BAILY. By my troth, and well worthy besides to kiss the stocks!

To come in on the back side, when ye
might go about!

I know none such, unless they long to
have their brains knocked out.   30

D. RAT. Well, will you be so good, sir, as
talk with Dame Chat,

And know what she intended? I ask no
more but that.

BAILY. [*To Scapethrift.*]   Let her be
called, fellow, because of Master Doctor.   [*Exit Scapethrift.*]

I warrant in this case she will be her own
proctor;

She will tell her own tale, in meter or in
prose,

And bid you seek your remedy, and so go
wipe your nose!

THE V ACT. THE ii SCENE.

*M[aster] Baily, Chat, [led in by Scapethrift,]
D[octor] Rat, Gammer, Hodge, Diccon.* [2]

BAILY. Dame Chat, Master Doctor upon
you here complained

That you and your maids shuld him
much misorder,

And taketh many an oath that no word
he feigned,

Laying to your charge how you thought
him to murder;

And, on his part again, that same man
saith furder

He never offended you in word nor intent.

To hear you answer hereto, we have now
for you sent.

CHAT. That I wold have murdered him?
Fie on him, wretch!

And evil mought he thee [3] for it, our
Lord I beseech.

I will swear on all the books that opens
and shuts,   10

He feigneth this tale out of his own guts!

For this seven weeks with me, I am sure,
he sat not down.

Nay, ye have other minions, [4] in the other
end of the town,

Where ye were liker to catch such a blow

Than anywhere else, as far as I know!

BAILY. Belike then, Master Doctor, yon
stripe there ye got not?

D. RAT. Think you I am so mad that
where I was bet [5] I wot not?

Will ye believe this quean before she
hath tried [6] it?

It is not the first deed she hath done and
afterward denied it.

CHAT. What, man, will you say I broke
your head?   20

D. RAT. How canst thou prove the contrary?

CHAT. Nay, how provest thou that I did
the deed?

D. RAT. Too plainly, by S[aint] Mary!

This proof, I trow, may serve though I no
word spoke!

Showing his broken head.

CHAT. Because thy head is broken, was it
I that it broke?

I saw thee, Rat, I tell thee, not once
within this fortnight.

D. RAT. No, marry, thou sawest me not,
forwhy [7] thou hadst no light;

But I felt thee, for all the dark, beshrew
thy smooth cheeks!

And thou groped me[8]—this will declare,
any day this six weeks.

Showing his head.

---

[3] Ill may he thrive.   [5] Beaten.   [7] Because.
[4] Darlings.   [6] Proved.   [8] Gripped, handled.

---

[1] Original reads *of*.   [2] Last three enter later.

BAILY. Answer me to this, M[aster] Rat:
　when caught you this harm of yours? 30
D. RAT. A while ago, sir, God he know-
　eth; within less than these two hours.
BAILY. Dame Chat, was there none with
　you—confess, i'faith—about that sea-
　son?
　What, woman! Let it be what it will,
　'tis neither felony nor treason.
CHAT. Yes, by my faith, Master Baily,
　there was a knave not far
　Who caught one good fillip on the brow
　with a door bar,
　And well was he worthy, as it seemed to
　me.
　But what is that to this man, since this
　was not he?
BAILY. Who was it then? Let's hear!
D. RAT. 　　　　Alas, sir, ask you that?
　Is it not made plain enough by the own
　mouth of Dame Chat?
　The time agreeth, my head is broken, her
　tongue cannot lie; 　　　　40
　Only upon a bare "nay" she saith it was
　not I.
CHAT. No, marry, was it not, indeed. Ye
　shall hear by this one thing:
　This afternoon a friend of mine, for good
　will, gave me warning,
　And bade we [1] well look to my rust and
　all my capons' pens,
　For, if I took not better heed, a knave
　wold have my hens.
　Then I, to save my goods, took so much
　pains as him to watch;
　And, as good fortune served me, it was
　my chance him for to catch.
　What strokes he bare away, or other what
　was his gains,
　I wot not—but sure I am he had some-
　thing for his pains!
BAILY. Yet tells thou not who it was.
CHAT. 　　Who it was? A false thief, 50
　That came like a false fox my pullen [2] to
　kill and mischief!
BAILY. But knowest thou not his name?
CHAT. 　　I know it. But what than? [3]
　It was that crafty cullion, [4] Hodge, my
　Gammer Gurton's man.

[1] Me (?).
[2] Poultry.
[3] A common Elizabethan spelling of *then*, retained here for the rime.
[4] Rascal.

BAILY. Call me the knave hether. 　He
　shall sure kiss the stocks.
　I shall teach him a lesson for filching hens
　or cocks! 　　　　[*Exit Scapethrift.*]
D. RAT. I marvel, Master Baily, so
　bleared be your eyes!
　An egg is not so full of meat as she is full
　of lies.
　When she hath played this prank, to
　excuse all this gear
　She layeth the fault in such a one as I
　know was not there.
CHAT. Was he not there? Look on his
　pate! That shall be his witness! 　60
D. RAT. I wold my head were half so
　whole, I wold seek no redress!

　　　　[Enter Gammer.]

BAILY. God bless you, Gammer Gurton!
GAMMER. 　　God dyld you, [5] master mine!
BAILY. Thou hast a knave within thy
　house—Hodge, a servant of thine.
　They tell me that busy knave is such a
　filching one
　That hen, pig, goose, or capon thy neigh-
　bor can have none.
GAMMER. By God, cham much ameved [6]
　to hear any such report!
　Hodge was not wont, ich trow, to b'ave [7]
　him in that sort.
CHAT. A thievisher knave is not on-live,
　more filching nor more false!
　Many a truer man than he has hanged up
　by the hals. [8]
　And thou, his dame, of all his theft thou
　art the sole receiver. 　　　　70
　For Hodge to catch and thou to keep, I
　never knew none better.
GAMMER. Sir [9] reverence of your master-
　dom, and you were out-a-door,
　Chold be so bold, for all her brags, to call
　her arrant whore!
　And ich knew Hodge so bad as tow, [10] ich
　wish me endless sorrow
　And should not take the pains to hang
　him up before tomorrow!
CHAT. What have I stolen from thee or
　thine, thou ill-favored old trot?

[5] God yield you; God reward you.
[6] Moved, disturbed.
[7] Behave. 　　　　　　　　　　[8] Neck.
[9] Probably a contraction of *save your*.
[10] Thou.

GAMMER. A great deal more, by God's
  blessed,[1] than chever [2] by thee got!
That thou knowest well. I need not say it.
BAILY.   Stop there, I say!
  And tell me here, I pray you, this matter
  by the way:
  How chance Hodge is not here?   Him
  wold [3] I fain have had.   80
GAMMER. Alas, sir, he'll be here anon; ha'
  be handled too bad!
CHAT. Master Baily, sir, ye be not such a
  fool, well I know,
  But ye perceive by this lingering there
  is a pad [4] in the straw.
Thinking that Hodge his head was broke,
and that Gammer would not let him come
                    before them.
GAMMER. Chill show you his face, ich warrant thee.—Lo now, where he is!

[*Enter Hodge, led in by Scapethrift.*]

BAILY. Come on, fellow! It is told me
  thou art a shrew, iwis.[5]
  Thy neighbors' hens thou takest, and
  plays the two-legged fox;
  Their chickens and their capons too, and
  now and then their cocks.
HODGE. Ich defy them all that dare it say!
  Cham as true as the best!
BAILY. Wart not thou take within this
  hour in Dame Chat's hens' nest?
HODGE. Take there? No, master. Chold
  not do't for a house full of gold!   90
CHAT. Thou, or the devil in thy coat!
  Swear this, I dare be bold.
D. RAT. Swear me no swearing, quean!
  The devil he give thee sorrow!
  All is not worth a gnat thou canst swear
  till tomorrow.
  Where is the harm he hath? Show it, by
  God's bread!
  Ye beat him, with a witness, but the
  stripes light on my head!
HODGE. Bet me?   Gog's blessed body,
  chold first, ich trow, have burst thee.
  Ich think, and chad my hands loose, cal-
  let, chould have crust [6] thee!
CHAT. Thou shitten knave, I trow thou
  knowest the full weight of my fist!
  I am foully deceived unless thy head and
  my door bar kissed!

HODGE. Hold thy chat, whore!   Thou
  criest so loud, can no man else be
  hard.   100
CHAT. Well, knave, and I had thee alone, I
  wold surely rap thy costard! [7]
BAILY. Sir, answer me to this: is thy head
  whole or broken?
CHAT. Yea, Master Baily, blessed be every
  good token!
HODGE. Is my head whole? Ich warrant
  you 'tis neither scurvy nor scald!
  What, you foul beast, does think 'tis
  either pilled [8] or bald?
  Nay, ich thank God, chill not, for all that
  thou mayst spend,
  That chad one scab on my narse as
  broad as thy finger's end.
BAILY. Come nearer here!
HODGE.   Yes, that ich dare.
BAILY. [*Examining Hodge's head.*] By our
  Lady, here is no harm.
  Hodge's head is whole enough, for all
  Dame Chat's charm.[9]
CHAT. By Gog's blessed, however the
  thing he clocks or smolders,[10]   110
  I know the blows he bare away either
  with head or shoulders.
  Camest thou not, knave, within this
  hour creeping into my pens,
  And there was caught within my house
  groping among my hens?
HODGE. A plague both on thy hens and
  thee! A cart, whore, a cart!
  Chould I were hanged as high as a tree
  and chware as false as thou art!
  Give my gammer again her washical [11]
  thou stole away in thy lap!
GAMMER. Yea, Master Baily, there is a
  thing you know not on, mayhap:
  This drab she keeps away my good—the
  devil he might her snare!
  Ich pray you that ich might have a right
  action on her.
CHAT. Have I thy good, old filth, or any
  such, old sows? [12]   120
  I am as true, I wold thou knew, as skin
  between thy brows!
GAMMER. Many a truer hath been hanged,
  though you escape the danger!
CHAT. Thou shalt answer, by God's pity
  for this thy foul slander!

[1] *Cf.* l. 96.   [2] I ever.   [3] Original reads *wole.*
[4] Toad; a proverbial term for something hid-
den.   [5] Indeed.   [6] Crushed.

[7] Apple, head.   [10] Cloaks or smothers.
[8] Peeled, shorn.   [11] What-you-call-it.
[9] Chatter.   [12] Souse (?).

BAILY. Why, what can ye charge her
  withal? To say so, ye do not well.
GAMMER. Marry, a vengeance to her heart,
  that whore has stolen my neele!
CHAT. Thy needle, old witch? How so?
  It were alms thy skull to knock!
So didst thou say the other day that I
  had stolen thy cock,
And roasted him to my breakfast—which
  shall not be forgotten.
The devil pull out thy lying tongue and
  teeth that be so rotten!
GAMMER. Give me my neele! As for my
  Cock, chould be very loath   130
That chuld hear tell he shuld hang on
  thy false faith and troth.
BAILY. Your talk is such I can scarce
  learn who shuld be most in fault.
GAMMER. Yet shall ye find no other wight
  save she, by bread and salt!
BAILY. Keep ye content awhile; see that
  your tongues ye hold;
Methinks you shuld remember this is
  no place to scold.
How knowest thou, Gammer Gurton,
  Dame Chat thy needle had?
GAMMER. To name you, sir, the party,
  chould not be very glad.
BAILY. Yea, but we must needs hear it,
  and therefore say it boldly.
GAMMER. Such one as told the tale full
  soberly and coldly;
Even he that looked on—will swear on
  a book—   140
What time this drunken gossip my fair
  long neele up took:
Diccon, master, the bedlam. Cham very
  sure ye know him.
BAILY. A false knave, by God's pity! Ye
  were but a fool to trow [1] him.
I durst aventure well the price of my
  best cap
That when the end is known all will
  turn to a jape.[2]
Told he not you that, besides, she stole
  your cock that tide?[3]
GAMMER. No, master, no, indeed; for then
  he shuld have lied!
My cock is, I thank Christ, safe and well,
  a-fine.[4]
CHAT. Yea, but that ragged colt, that
  whore, that Tib of thine,

Said plainly thy cock was stolen and in
  my house was eaten.   150
That lying cut is lost that she is not
  swinged and beaten,
And yet for all my good name it were a
  small amends!
I pick not this gear, hear'st thou, out of
  my fingers' ends;
But he that hard it told me, who thou
  of late didst name:
Diccon, whom all men knows; it was
  the very same.
BAILY. This is the case: you lost your
  needle about the doors,
And she answers again she has no cock
  of yours;
Thus, in your talk and action, from that
  you do intend
She is whole five mile wide from that
  she doth defend.[5]
Will you say she hath your cock?
GAMMER.   No, marry, sir, that chill
  not!   160
BAILY. Will you confess her neele?
CHAT.   Will I? No, sir, will I not![6]
BAILY. Then there lieth all the matter.
GAMMER.   Soft, master, by the way!
Ye know she could do little and she cold
  not say nay.
BAILY. Yea, but he that made one lie
  about your cock-stealing,
Will not stick to make another what
  time lies be in dealing.
I ween the end will prove this brawl did
  first arise
Upon no other ground but only Diccon's
  lies.
CHAT. Though some be lies, as you belike
  have espied them,
Yet other some be true—by proof I
  have well tried them.
BAILY. What other thing beside this,
  Dame Chat?
CHAT.   Marry, sir, even this: 170
The tale I told before, the selfsame
  tale it was his;
He gave me, like a friend, warning
  against my loss,
Else had my hens be stolen, each one,
  by God's Cross!
He told me Hodge wold come, and in he
  came indeed;

[1] Believe, trust.
[2] Jest.
[3] Time.
[4] Finally.
[5] Deny.
[6] Rime would require "I will not."

But, as the matter chanced, with greater
   haste than speed.
This truth was said, and true was found,
   as truly I report.
BAILY. If Doctor Rat be not deceived, it
   was of another sort.
D. RAT. By God's Mother, thou and he
   be a couple of subtle foxes!
Between you and Hodge I bear away
   the boxes.[1]
Did not Diccon appoint the place where
   thou shuldst stand to meet him?   180
CHAT. Yes, by the Mass; and, if he came,
   bade me not stick to speet [2] him.
D. RAT. God's sacrament, the villain
   knave hath dressed us round about!
He is the cause of all this brawl, that
   dirty, shitten lout!
When Gammer Gurton here complained,
   and made a rueful moan,
I heard him swear that you had gotten
   her needle that was gone;
And this to try, he furder said, he was
   full loath; howbeit
He was content, with small ado, to
   bring me where to see it.
And where ye sat, he said full certain,
   if I wold follow his rede,
Into your house a privy way he wold me
   guide and lead,
And where ye had it in your hands,
   sewing about a clout;   190
And set me in the back hole, thereby to
   find you out.
And, whiles I sought a quietness, creeping upon my knees,
I found the weight of your door bar for
   my reward and fees.
Such is the luck that some men gets
   while they begin to mell [3]
In setting at one such as were out,
   minding to make all well.
HODGE. Was not well blessed, gammer, to
   scape that scour? [4] And chad been
   there,
Then chad been dressed, belike, as ill,
   by the Mass, as Gaffer Vicar.
BAILY. Marry, sir, here is a sport alone.
   I looked for such an end.
If Diccon had not played the knave,
   this had been soon amend.

My gammer here he made a fool, and
   dressed her as she was;   200
And Goodwife Chat he set to scole,[5]
   till both parts cried "alas";
And D[octor] Rat was not behind, whiles
   Chat his crown did pare;
I wold the knave had been stark blind,
   if Hodge had not his share!
HODGE. Cham meetly well sped already
   amongs;[6] cham dressed like a colt!
And chad not had the better wit, chad
   been made a dolt.
BAILY. [To Scapethrift.] Sir knave, make
   haste Diccon were here; fetch him
   wherever he be!   [Exit Scapethrift.]
CHAT. Fie on the villain, fie, fie, that
   makes us thus agree!
GAMMER. Fie on him, knave, with all my
   heart! Now fie! and fie again!
D. RAT. "Now fie on him!" may I best
   say, whom he hath almost slain.

[Enter Diccon, led in by Scapethrift.]

BAILY. Lo, where he cometh at hand.
   Belike he was not far!   210
Diccon, here be two or three thy com-
   pany cannot spare.
DICCON. God bless you—and you may
   be blessed, so many all at once!
CHAT. Come, knave, it were a good deed
   to geld thee, by Cock's bones!
Seest not thy handiwark? Sir Rat, can
   ye forbear[7] him?
              [Doctor Rat strikes Diccon.]
DICCON. A vengenance on those hands
   light, for my hands came not near
   him!
The whoreson priest hath lift the pot[8]
   in some of these alewives' chairs
That his head wold not serve him, belike, to come down the stairs.
BAILY. Nay, soft! Thou mayst not play
   the knave and have this language
   too!
If thou thy tongue bridle awhile, the
   better mayst thou do.
Confess the truth, as I shall ask, and
   cease awhile to fable;   220
And for thy fault, I promise thee, thy
   handling shall be reasonable.
Hast thou not made a lie or two to set
   these two by the ears?

[1] Blows.
[2] Spit, i.e., beat with a spit.
[3] Meddle.   [4] Scouring, beating.
[5] School.   [7] Tolerate, spare.   [8] Tankard.
[6] All this time.

DICCON. What if I have? Five hundred such have I seen within these seven years.

I am sorry for nothing else but that I see not the sport

Which was between them when they met, as they themselves report.

BAILY. The greatest thing—Master Rat! Ye see how he is dressed!

DICCON. What devil need he be groping so deep in Goodwife Chat's hens' nest?

BAILY. Yea, but it was thy drift to bring him into the briers.

DICCON. God's bread! hath not such an old fool wit to save his ears?

He showeth himself herein, ye see, so very a cox [1]　　　230

The cat was not so madly allured by the fox

To run into the snares was set for him, doubtless;

For he leaped in for mice, and this Sir John for madness.

D. RAT. Well, and ye shift no better, ye losel, lither [2] and lazy,

I will go near, for this, to make ye leap at a daisy. [3]

In the king's name, Master Baily, I charge you set him fast!

DICCON. What, fast at cards, or fast on sleep? It is the thing I did last.

D. RAT. Nay, fast in fetters, false varlet, according to thy deeds!

BAILY. Master Doctor, there is no remedy; I must entreat you, needs,

Some other kind of punishment.

D. RAT.　　　Nay, by All Hallows,　240 His punishment, if I may judge, shall be naught else but the gallows.

BAILY. That were too sore. A spiritual man to be so extreme!

D. RAT. Is he worthy any better, sir? How do ye judge and deem?

BAILY. I grant him worthy punishment, but in no wise so great.

GAMMER. It is a shame, ich tell you plain, for such false knaves entreat!

He has almost undone us all; that is as true as steel.

And yet for all this great ado cham never the near my neele!

[1] Fool.　　[2] Worthless, idle.　　[3] I.e., be hanged.

BAILY. Canst thou not say anything to that, Diccon, with least or most?

DICCON. Yea, marry, sir, thus much I can say well: the needle is lost!

BAILY. Nay, canst not thou tell which way that needle may be found?　250

DICCON. No, by my fay, sir, though I might have an hundred pound.

HODGE. Thou liar, lickdish, [4] didst not say the neele wold be gitten?

DICCON. No, Hodge, by the same token you were [6] that time beshitten

For fear of Hobgobling—you wot well what I mean;

As long as it is sence, [7] I fear me yet ye be scarce clean.

BAILY. Well, Master Rat, you must both learn and teach us to forgeve. [8]

Since Diccon hath confession made and is so clean shreve, [9]

If ye to me consent, to amend this heavy chance

I will enjoin him here some open kind of penance,

Of this condition. Where ye know my fee is twenty pence　260

For the bloodshed, [10] I am agreed with you here to dispense.

Ye shall go quite, [11] so that ye grant the matter now to run

To end with mirth among us all, even as it was begun.

CHAT. Say yea, Master Vicar, and he shall sure confess to be your debtor,

And all we that be here present will love you much the better.

D. RAT. My part is the worst; but, since you all hereon agree,

Go even to, [12] Master Baily—let it be so for me!

BAILY. How sayest thou, Diccon? Art content this shall on me depend?

DICCON. Go to, M[aster] Baily, say on your mind. I know ye are my friend.

BAILY. Then mark ye well to recompense this thy former action,　270

Because thou hast offended all, to make them satisfaction,

[4] Scullion.　　　　　　　　　　[5] Gotten.
[6] Dodsley's reading. Original reads *where*.
[7] Since, past.
[8] Forgive; a common spelling retained here for the rime.　　　　　[11] Quit, free.
[9] Shriven.　　　　　[12] Go ahead then.
[10] Case involving violence.

Before their faces here kneel down, and
as [1] I shall thee teach.
For thou shalt take an [2] oath of Hodge's
leather breech:
First, for Master Doctor, upon pain of
his curse,
Where he will pay for all, thou never
draw thy purse,
And when ye meet at one pot, he shall
have the first pull,
And thou shalt never offer him the cup
but it be full;
To Goodwife Chat thou shalt be sworn,
even on the same wise,
If she refuse thy money once, never to
offer it twice;
Thou shalt be bound by the same, here
as thou dost take it,   280
When thou mayst drink of free cost,
thou never forsake it;
For Gammer Gurton's sake, again sworn
shalt thou be,
To help her to her needle again, if it do
lie in thee;
And likewise be bound, by the virtue of
that,
To be of good abearing [3] to Gib, her
great cat;
Last of all, for Hodge, the oath to scan,
Thou shalt never take him for fine
gentleman.
HODGE. [*Stooping over.*] Come on, fellow
Diccon! Chall be even with thee now!
BAILY. Thou wilt not stick to do this,
Diccon, I trow?
DICCON. No, by my father's skin; my
hand down I lay it!   290
Look! As I have promised, I will not
denay [4] it.
But, Hodge, take good heed now thou
do not beshit me!
And gave him a good blow on the buttock.
HODGE. Gog's heart! Thou false villain,
dost thou bite me?
BAILY. What, Hodge, doth he hurt thee
or ever he begin?
HODGE. He thrust me into the buttock
with a bodkin or a pin!
                [*He draws out the needle.*]
I say, gammer! gammer!

GAMMER.   How now, Hodge? How
now?
HODGE. God's malt, Gammer Gurton!
GAMMER.   Thou art mad, ich trow!
HODGE. Will you see the devil, gam-
mer?
GAMMER.   The devil, son? God
bless us!
HODGE. Chould ich were hanged, gam-
mer!
GAMMER.   Marry, see, ye might
dress us—
HODGE. Chave it, by the Mass, gammer!
GAMMER.   What, not my neele,
Hodge?   300
HODGE. Your neele, gammer, your neele!
GAMMER.   No, fie, dost but dodge! [5]
HODGE. Cha' found your neele, gammer!
Here in my hand be it!
GAMMER. For all the loves on earth,
Hodge, let me see it!
HODGE. Soft, gammer!
GAMMER.   Good Hodge!
HODGE.   Soft, ich say; tarry awhile!
GAMMER. Nay, sweet Hodge, say truth,
and do not me beguile!
HODGE. Cham sure on it, ich warrant
you it goes no more astray.
GAMMER. Hodge, when I speak so fair,
wilt still say me nay?
HODGE. Go near the light, gammer.
This—well, in faith, good luck!—
Chwas almost undone, 'twas so far in
my buttock!
GAMMER. 'Tis mine own dear neele,
Hodge, sikerly [6] I wot!   310
HODGE. Cham I not a good son, gam-
mer, cham I not?
GAMMER. Christ's blessing light on thee!
Hast made me forever!
HODGE. Ich knew that ich must find it,
else choud 'a' [7] had it never!
CHAT. By my troth, Gossip Gurton, I
am even as glad
As though I mine own self as good a
turn had!
BAILY. And I, by my conscience, to see
it so come forth,
Rejoice so much at it as three needles
be worth!
D. RAT. I am no whit sorry to see you
so rejoice!

---

[1] In the manner that.
[2] Dodsley's reading. Original reads *on.*
[3] Bearing, behavior.
[4] Deny.

[5] Trick me.   [7] I would have.
[6] Truly.

DICCON. Nor I much the gladder for all this noise!

Yet say, "Gramercy, Diccon," for springing of the game.   320

GAMMER. Gramercy, Diccon, twenty times! O, how glad cham!

If that chould do so much, your masterdom to come hether,

Master Rat, Goodwife Chat, and Diccon, together—

Cha' but one halfpenny, as far as ich know it,

And chill not rest this night till ich bestow it.

If ever ye love me, let us go in and drink!

BAILY. I am content, if the rest think as I think.

Master Rat, it shall be best for you if we so do;

Then shall you warm you and dress yourself too.

DICCON. Soft, sirs, take us with you; the company shall be the more!   330

As proud comes behind, they say, as any goes before!— [*Addresses the audience.*]

But now, my good masters, since we must be gone

And leave you behind us here, all alone—

Since at our last ending thus merry we be,

For Gammer Gurton's needle sake let us have a plaudity!

FINIS, GURTON. PERUSED AND ALLOWED, ETC.

THOMAS PRESTON

Thomas Preston's *Cambises, King of Persia*, although almost totally devoid of any real literary merit, is one of the most interesting plays of mid-sixteenth century England. In the first place, it seems to have been the property of some small troupe of professional or semi-professional actors, perhaps strollers, whose personnel of eight men (the last two of whom are clearly boys) is indicated by "The Division into Parts" on the title page of the published version. The play was not divided into acts and scenes nor were stage directions used to indicate or describe the exact setting when the scene changed. A bare platform stage and limited stage properties were probably used. Second, the play was obviously intended to appeal to as wide a variety of tastes as possible, since its full title calls it "A Lamentable Tragedy, Mixed Full of Pleasant Mirth," and claims both its historicity and its value as a moral lesson. Finally, the play displays the still-continuing relationship of early Elizabethan and medieval drama, since the technique is clearly that of the late hybrid moralities, in a number of which historical and farcical material was freely mixed with allegory.

The story is carried on and explained chiefly by Ambidexter, a brilliant example of the morality Vice. The name immediately indicates that he "plays with both hands," and a lack of conscience or steadfastness on his part is constantly emphasized in his own speeches and comments throughout the play. But the abstractions of characters (or personifications) like Shame, Preparation, Common's Complaint, Murder, and so on, do not contend directly for the soul of the protagonist, as they would in the earlier morality play. In *Cambises*, they are simply minor characters who, as Irving Ribner has pointed out in *The English History Play in the Age of Shakespeare* (Princeton, 1957), would probably have been given names like "First Servant," "First Murderer," and so on, by later Elizabethan dramatists. The introduction of many scenes of crude horror on the stage shows the love of pure sensationalism in the audience. Coupled with the brutal character of the "hero," these scenes may reflect also an influence of events like the torturing of Christ or of the martyrs in the medieval drama. The structure is loose and episodic, seemingly more in the tradition of the miracle play than the morality, and the drama lacks any real tragic impact because the catastrophe does not develop logically from any preceding incidents. Preston, like most of his fellow-Elizabethans, undoubtedly believed that Cambises' ultimate death proved that God had been watching him all along, and finally intervened to punish him for his crimes against his subjects. The form of the play is also akin in spirit to the medieval type of narrative "tragedy" in the emphasis on the fall of a great figure at the height of his arrogant pride. Popular interest in this form was indicated at that time by the reprinting of John Lydgate's *The Fall of Princes* and the publication of *The Mirror for Magistrates*. A somewhat similar combination of elements had been found in Bishop John Bale's *King John*, about 1548, which was the first English play to deal with secular history in this fashion.

The source of the main story of the play goes back to the *Histories* of the Greek Herodotus, often called "The Father of History," in the fifth century B.C. As W. A. Armstrong has shown in "The Background and Sources of Preston's *Cambises*" (*ES*, 1950), there are two separate passages on Cambises in Herodotus: the first, in Book III, lists his crimes and attributes them to a combination of madness, passion, and drunkenness; and the second, in Book V, shows his one good deed, the punishment of

his magistrate, Sisamnes, for his corrupt actions.   But since Herodotus was not available in English translation until 1584, Preston must have had to go to some other account
of Cambises for his material.   In 1934 in *MLN*, Don C. Allen proposed as this source a
pocket history of the world by Johan Carion, first published in German in 1532 and
then translated into Latin as *Chronicorum Libri Tres* at Frankfort in 1550.   An English
translation by Gwalter Lynne was published in London in the same year.   In 1936
William Farnham in *The Medieval Heritage of Elizabethan Tragedy* (University of
California Press) suggested another English source relating similar episodes in Cambises' bloody career, but putting them in an order closer to that of the play.   This was
Richard Taverner's *The Garden of Wisdom*, a collection of moral anecdotes published
in 1539.   Taverner apparently drew on the original German version of Carion, but
Armstrong's evidence shows pretty clearly that Preston used only Taverner's book.
Like Preston, Taverner had brought the two aspects of Cambises' career together to
show the workings of providence both in the punishment of unjust rulers, and in the
performance of virtuous acts.
     Since *Cambises* is both a tragedy and a history play, this is the appropriate place to
call attention again to Ribner's *The English History Play in the Age of Shakespeare*,
which offers a valuable analysis of the backgrounds and purposes of the Elizabethans'
use of historical material for literary works.   The basic purposes of such historical
tragedies, says Ribner, may be ranged under two general headings, each broken down
into smaller categories:

> Those stemming from classical and humanist philosophies of history include (1) a
> nationalistic glorification of England; (2) an analysis of contemporary affairs, both
> national and foreign, so as to make clear the virtues and failings of contemporary states-
> men; (3) a use of past events as a guide to political behavior in the present; (4) a use of
> history as documentation for political theory; and (5) a study of past political disaster
> as an aid to Stoical fortitude in the present.   Those stemming from medieval Christian
> philosophy of history include: (6) illustration of the providence of God as the ruling force
> in human—and primarily political—affairs; and (7) exposition of a rational plan in
> human events which must affirm the wisdom and justice of God.

Consequently, Ribner excludes as true historical tragedies all plays based on genuine
factual matter which do not serve these ends, all plays based on legends which do not
place primary emphasis on political lessons, and all plays that use historical material
merely as a basis for romance.   He doubts that the Elizabethans themselves ever made
a real distinction between tragedy and history, since "A historical play . . . is, after
all, [only] an adaptation of drama to the purposes of history, and tragedy is merely one
form of drama."   As for the dramatic traditions of such plays, he concludes that they
fall into two groups, "the one embodying a dramatic structure stemming from the
[episodic] miracle play and the other stemming from the morality."
     The date when *Cambises* was written has been somewhat in dispute.   The play was
entered on the Stationers' Register in 1569/70 by John Allde.   The first edition,
undated, probably appeared simultaneously with the entry or soon afterward.   A
second edition, also undated, was issued not earlier than 1584 by Edward Allde, who
succeeded to his father's business in that year.   The play continued in popularity
for many years.   As late as 1598 the audience understood Falstaff's allusion perfectly
in *I Henry IV*, II, iv, when Shakespeare had Falstaff tell Prince Hal, when examining
him for his misdeeds in the assumed role of King Henry, that he "must speak in passion," and would do so "in King Cambises' vein."   M. Channing Linthicum, in "The
Date of *Cambyses*" (*PMLA*, 1934), stated his belief that the play was written "many
years before 1569"; and as early as 1923 E. K. Chambers in *The Elizabethan Stage*
(Oxford, 1923) had observed that on February 17, 1560/1, a play called *Huff, Suff, and
Ruff* had been given at court before the Queen.   These names are almost identical with
those of the three ruffianly soldiers in one of the slapstick scenes in *Cambises*, and may

have been derived from them. In 1924 Joseph Quincy Adams in his *Chief Pre-Shakespearean Dramas* had also opted for a date about 1560. Abraham Feldman in "King Cambises' Vein" (*NQ*, 1954) supported this view, although to do so he had to assume that the reference toward the end of the play to Bishop Edmund Bonner of London as a bloody tyrant (Bonner died in September 1569) was a later interpolation. On the other hand, Feldman suggests that the description of King Cambises' accidental death through being wounded by his own sword as he mounted his horse would have had a special meaning to an audience of 1559 or 1560 since in the spring of 1559 the anti-Protestant bigot, Henry II of France, had been killed accidentally by a lance-thrust in a friendly tilt.

There has been similar uncertainty about the identification of Thomas Preston as the author. Early students of the stage were inclined to identify him with the Thomas Preston who was born in 1537, was Fellow of King's College, Cambridge, where he took his B.A. and M.A.—the latter in 1561—and became Master of Trinity Hall in 1584 and Vice-Chancellor in 1587. He won Elizabeth's favor and a pension as her "scholar" in 1564 by disputing before her in Latin and acting in the Latin play, *Dido*. Other students, such as Chambers, J. M. Manly, and Adams, doubted that a man admired for his Latinity would write a play of such a popular and miscellaneous nature as *Cambises*, and conjectured that the author was the ballad-writer, two of whose ballads have at the end a subscription, much like that at the end of *Cambises*—"Finis, Quod Thomas Preston." In "The Authorship and Political Meaning of *Cambises*" (*ES*, 1955), W. A. Armstrong attempted to reconcile and combine these two attributions, maintaining that there was nothing inconsistent in the same man's writing both the play and the ballads. The style of much of the play, with the highly Latinized vocabulary of Cambises himself, along with the classical allusions in the Prologue to Agathon (the minor Athenian tragic poet of the fifth century B.C.), to Cicero (under the guise of Tully), and to Seneca (even though there is no trace of Seneca in either the form or the ideas of the play itself), as well as the references to such classical tales as the fall of Icarus and the "Sisters Three," could have been that of the Cambridge scholar in his youth. The colloquial language of Ambidexter and of Huf, Ruf, and Snuf, together with the country dialect of Hob and Lob, simply sets off the grandiloquent language of Cambises. Armstrong maintained that there is enough evidence to show that Preston was "a polemical writer who propagated a consistent body of doctrine concerning kingship, tyranny, and the duties of subjects" and showed how the play reflected loyal Anglican views on these matters, all of which gave it more ethical and polemical interest to a sixteenth century audience than it now has. Preston also seems to have had some interest in metrical experimentation, since different characters speak more or less consistently in different meters and rhymes. Moody E. Prior, in *The Language of Tragedy* (Columbia University Press, 1947), has discussed the use of "fourteeners" rather than blank verse in much of the play, particularly in the speeches of Cambises. He concluded that the author apparently felt that the verse form that was selected by translators of Seneca for *Seneca His Ten Tragedies* (Thomas Newton in 1581) was the proper form for an original English tragedy.

The present text is based on the second edition, reproduced photographically by John S. Farmer in his Tudor Facsimile Texts in 1910. Of the critical editions, that of J. M. Manly in his *Specimens of the Pre-Shaksperean Drama* (Boston, 1897) has been most helpful.

CAMBISES, KING OF PERSIA

BY
THOMAS PRESTON

[DRAMATIS PERSONÆ

CAMBISES, *King of Persia.*
SMIRDIS, *his brother.*
SISAMNES, *the judge.*
OTIAN, *his son.*
PRAXASPES, *a courtier.*
YOUNG CHILD, *his son.*
FIRST LORD ⎫
SECOND LORD ⎬ *attendants of the king.*
THIRD LORD ⎭

A LADY, *kinswoman of the king and later*
 QUEEN.
WAITING-MAID, *attending her.*
MOTHER *of Young Child and wife of Prax-*
 aspes.

HUF ⎫
RUF ⎬ *ruffianly soldiers.*
SNUF ⎭
MERETRIX, *a courtesan.*
HOB ⎫
LOB ⎬ *clownish countrymen.*
MARIAN-MAY-BE-GOOD, *Hob's wife.*

LORD.[2]
KNIGHT.[2]
COUNSEL.[2]

SHAME.
ATTENDANCE.
DILIGENCE.
PREPARATION.
SMALL HABILITY.[3]
COMMONS' CRY.
COMMONS' COMPLAINT.
TRIAL.
PROOF.
EXECUTION.
CRUELTY.
MURDER.

AMBIDEXTER, *the Vice.*

VENUS.
CUPID.

SCENE: *Persia.*
TIME: *Sixth century B.C.*]

THE DIVISION OF THE PARTS

COUNSEL ⎫
HUF ⎥
PRAXASPES ⎥
MURDER ⎬ *for one man.*
LOB ⎥
THE THIRD LORD ⎭

LORD ⎫
RUF ⎥
COMMONS' CRY ⎥
COMMONS' COMPLAINT ⎬ *for one man.*
LORD SMIRDIS ⎥
VENUS ⎭

KNIGHT ⎫
SNUF ⎥
SMALL HABILITY ⎥
PROOF ⎬ *for one man.*
EXECUTION ⎥
ATTENDANCE ⎥
SECOND LORD ⎭

[1] The complete title reads as follows: "A Lamentable Tragedy, Mixed Full of Pleasant Mirth, Containing the Life of Cambises, King of Persia, from the Beginning of His Kingdom unto His Death, His One Good Deed of Execution, after That Many Wicked Deeds and Tyrannous Murders Committed by and through Him, and Last of All, His Odious Death by God's Justice Appointed. Done in Such Order as Followeth." The running-title, however, reads: "A Comedy of King Cambises."

[2] The character is generic, representing the entire class. [3] Ability.

83

CAMBISES ⎫
EPILOGUS ⎬ *for one man.*

PROLOGUE ⎫
SISAMNES ⎪
DILIGENCE ⎪
CRUELTY ⎬ *for one man.*
HOB ⎪
PREPARATION ⎪
THE FIRST LORD ⎭

AMBIDEXTER ⎫
TRIAL ⎬ *for one man.*

MERETRIX ⎫
SHAME ⎪
OTIAN ⎪
MOTHER ⎬ *for one man.*
LADY ⎪
QUEEN ⎭

YOUNG CHILD ⎫
CUPID ⎬ *for one man.*

The Prologue entereth.

Agathon, he whose counsel wise to princes'
  weal [1] extended,
By good advice unto a prince three things
  he hath commended:
First is, that he hath government and rul-
  eth over men;
Secondly, to rule with laws, eke justice,
  saith he, then;
Thirdly, that he must well conceive he may
  not always reign.
Lo, thus the rule unto a prince Agathon
  squaréd plain.
Tully the wise, whose sapience in volumes
  great doth tell,
Who in wisdom in that time did many men
  excel,
"A prince," saith he, "is of himself a plain
  and speaking law;
The law, a schoolmaster divine"—this by
  his rule I draw.   10
The sage and witty Seneca his words
  thereto did frame:
"The honest exercise of kings, men will
  ensue [2] the same;
But, contrariwise, if that a king abuse his
  kingly seat,
His ignom'y and bitter shame in fine shall
  be more great."
In Persia there reigned a king, who Cyrus
  hight [3] by name,
Who did deserve, as I do read, the lasting
  blast of fame;
But he, when Sisters Three had wrought to
  shear his vital thread,
As heir due, to take the crown Cambises did
  proceed.

He in his youth was trainéd up by trace [4]
  of virtue's lore;
Yet, being king, did clean forget his perfect
  race before;   20
Then, cleaving more unto his will, such vice
  did imitate
As one of Icarus his kind; forewarning then
  did hate,
Thinking that none could him dismay, ne [5]
  none his fact [6] could see.
Yet at the last a fall he took, like Icarus to
  be;
Else,[7] as the fish, which oft had take the
  pleasant bait from hook,
In safe [8] did spring and pierce the streams
  when fisher fast [9] did look
To hoist up from the wat'ry waves unto
  the driéd land,
Then scaped, at last by subtle bait come to
  the fisher's hand:
Even so this King Cambises here, when he
  had wrought his will,
Taking delight the innocent his guiltless
  blood to spill,   30
Then mighty Jove would not permit to
  prosecute offense;
But, what measure the king did mete, the
  same did Jove commence,
To bring to end with shame his race—two
  years he did not reign.
His cruelty we will delate,[10] and make the
  matter plain.
Craving that this may suffice now your
  patience to win,
I take my way. Behold, I see the players
  coming in.   [*Exit.*]

FINIS.

---

[1] Welfare.
[2] Follow.
[3] Was called.

[4] Track, course.
[5] Nor.
[6] Deed.
[7] Or.

[8] Safety.
[9] Intently.
[10] Describe fully.

First enter [1] *Cambises the King, Knight,*
[*Lord,*] *and Counselor.* [2]

CAMBISES. My counsel grave and sapient,
  with lords of legal train,
Attentive ears towards me bend, and
  mark what shall be sain; [3]
So you likewise, my valiant knight, whose
  manly acts doth fly
By bruit of Fame, that sounding trump
  doth pierce the azure sky—
My sapient words, I say, perpend. [4] and
  so your skill delate!
You know that Mors [5] vanquishéd hath
  Cyrus, that king of state,
And I, by due inheritance, possess that
  princely crown,
Ruling by sword of mighty force in place
  of great renown.
You know, and often have heard tell, my
  father's worthy facts—
A manly Mars's heart he bare, appearing
  by his acts.   10
And what, shall I to ground let fall my
  father's golden praise?
No, no! I mean for to attempt this same
  more large to raise.
In that, that I, his son, succeed his
  kingly seat, as due,
Extend your counsel unto me in that I
  ask of you.
I am the King of Persia, a large and
  fertile soil;
The Egyptians against us repugn [6] as
  varlets slave and vile;
Therefore I mean with Mars's heart with
  wars them to frequent,
Them to subdue as captives mine—this
  is my heart's intent;
So shall I win honor's delight, and praise
  of me shall go.
My counsel, speak, and, lordings, eke:
  is it not best do so?   20
COUNSEL. O puissant king, your blissful
  words deserves abundant praise,
That you in this do go about your father's fame to raise.

O blissful day, that king so young such
  profit should conceive,
His father's praise and his to win from
  those that would deceive!
Sure, my true and sovereign king, I fall
  before you prest, [7]
Answer to give, as duty mine, in that
  your grace request.
If that your heart addicted be the Egyptians to convince, [8]
Through Mars's aid the conquest won,
  then deed of happy prince
Shall pierce the skies unto the throne of
  the supernal seat,
And merit there a just reward of Jupiter
  the Great.   30
But then your grace must not turn back
  from this pretenséd [9] will;
For to proceed in virtuous life employ
  endeavor still;
Extinguish vice, and in that cup to drink
  have no delight;
To martial feats and kingly sport fix all
  your whole delight.
KING. My counsel grave, a thousand
  thanks with heart I do you render,
That you my case so prosperous entirely
  do tender.
I will not swerve from those your steps
  whereto you would me train.
But now, my lord and valiant knight,
  with words give answer plain:
Are you content with me to go the
  Mars's games to try?
LORD. Yea, peerless prince! To aid your
  grace myself will live and die!   40
KNIGHT. And I, for my hability, for fear
  will not turn back,
But, as the ship against the rocks, sus-
  tain and bide the wrack.
KING. O willing hearts! A thousand
  thanks I render unto you!
Strike up your drums with courage great;
  we will march forth even now!
COUNSEL. Permit, O king, few words to
  hear—my duty serves no less.
Therefore give leave to counsel thine his
  mind for to express.
KING. Speak on, my counsel; what it be,
  you shall have favor mine.
COUNSEL. Then will I speak unto your
  grace as duty doth me bind.

[1] "As this play is not divided into acts and scenes, and as the events occur apparently in a place which is now a council-chamber, now a street, and now a garden, it seems improper to subdivide the play or to indicate changes of scene. When necessary for intelligibility, the location is announced in the text" (Manly).
[2] *I.e.,* Counsel.   [3] Said.   [4] Consider.
[5] Death.   [6] Oppose.

[7] Quickly.   [8] Overpower.   [9] Intended.

Your grace doth mean for to attempt of
  war the manly art;
Your grace therein may hap receive, with
  others, for your part,   50
The dent of death—in those affairs all
  persons are alike.
The heart courageous oftentimes his det-
  riment doth seek.
It's best therefore for to permit a ruler
  of your land
To sit and judge with equity when things
  of right are scanned.
KING. My grace doth yield to this your
  talk. To be thus now it shall.
My knight, therefore prepare yourself
  Sisamnes for to call.
A judge he is of prudent skill; even he
  shall bear the sway
In absence mine, when from the land I
  do depart my way.
KNIGHT. Your knight before your grace
  even here himself hath ready pressed
With willing heart for to fulfill as your
  grace made request.   *Exit.* 60
COUNSEL. Pleaseth your grace, I judge of
  him to be a man right fit;
For he is learned in the law, having the
  gift of wit.
In your grace's precinct I do not view for
  it a meeter man.
His learning is of good effect—bring
  proof thereof I can.
I do not know what is his life—his conscience hid from me;
I doubt not but the fear of God before
  his eyes to be.
LORD. Report declares he is a man that
  to himself is nigh,[1]
One that favoreth much the world and
  sets too much thereby.
But this I say of certainty: if he your
  grace succeed
In your absence but for a while, he will be
  warned indeed   70
No injustice for to frequent, no partial
  judge to prove,
But rule all things with equity, to win
  your grace's love.
KING. Of that he shall a warning have my
  hests [2] for to obey;
Great punishment for his offense against
  him will I lay.

[1] *I.e.,* self-seeking.
[2] Behests, commands.

[Enter Sisamnes.]

COUNSEL. Behold, I see him now aggress [3]
  and enter into place.
SISAMNES. O puissant prince and mighty
  king, the gods preserve your grace!
Your grace's message came to me, your
  will purporting forth;
With grateful mind I it received according to mine oath,
Erecting then myself with speed before
  your grace's eyes,
The tenor of your princely will from you
  for to agnize.[4]   80
KING. Sisamnes, this the whole effect the
  which for you I sent:
Our mind it is to elevate you to great
  preferment.
My grace, and gracious counsel eke,
  hath chose you for this cause;
In judgment you do office bear, which
  have the skill in laws.
We think that you accordingly by justice' rule will deal,
That for offense none shall have cause,
  of wrong you to appeal.[5]
SISAMNES. Abundant thanks unto your
  grace for this benignity!
To you, his counsel, in like case, with
  lords of clemency!
Whatso your grace to me permits, if I
  therein offend,
Such execution then commence (and use
  it to this end)   90
That all other, by that my deed, example
  so may take
To admonish them to flee the same by
  fear it may them make.
KING. Then, according to your words, if
  you therein offend,
I assure you, even from my breast correction shall extend.
From Persia I mean to go into the Egypt
  land,
Them to convince by force of arms and
  win the upper hand.
While I therefor absent shall be, I do
  you full permit,
As governor in this my right, in that
  estate to sit,
For to detect and eke correct those that
  abuse my grace.
This is the total of my will. Give answer
  in this case!   100

[3] Approach.   [4] Learn.   [5] Accuse.

SISAMNES. Unworthy much, O prince, am
I, and for this gift unfit;
But, sith [1] that it hath pleased your grace
that I in it must sit,
I do avouch, unto my death, according to
my skill,
With equity for to observe your grace's
mind and will,
And naught from it to swarve,[2] indeed,
but sincerely to stay;
Else let me taste the penalty, as I before
did say.
KING. Well then, of this authority I give
you full possession.
SISAMNES. And I will it fulfill also as I
have made profession.
KING. My counsel, then let us depart a
final stay to make;
To Egypt land now forth with speed my
voyage I will take. 110
Strike up your drums, us to rejoice to
hear the warlike sound.
Stay you here, Sisamnes, judge, and look
well to your bound! [3]
Exeunt King, Lord, and Counsel.
SISAMNES. Even now the king hath me
extolled, and set me up aloft.
Now may I wear the bordered guard,[4]
and lie in down-bed soft;
Now may I purchase house and land,
and have all at my will;
Now may I build a princely place, my
mind for to fulfill;
Now may I abrogate the law as I shall
think it good;
If anyone me now offend, I may demand
his blood.
According to the proverb old, my mouth
I will up-make.[5]
Now it doth lie all in my hand to leave,
or else to take, 120
To deal with justice to me bound, and
so to live in hope.
But oftentimes the birds be gone while
one for nest doth grope.
Do well or ill, I dare avouch some evil on
me will speak.
No, truly—yet I do not mean the king's
precepts to break;
To place I mean for to return my duty
to fulfill. *Exit.*

*Enter the Vice, with an old capcase [6] on his
head, an old pail about his hips for
harness,[7] a scummer [8] and a potlid by
his side, and a rake on his shoulder.*

AMBIDEXTER. Stand away, stand away, for
the passion of God!
Harnessed I am, prepared to the field!
I would have been content at home to
have bode,
But I am sent forth with my spear and
shield.
I am appointed to fight against a
snail, 130
And Wilkin Wren the ancient [9] shall
bear.
I doubt not but against him to prevail—
To be a man my deeds shall declare!
If I overcome him, then a butterfly
takes his part.
His weapon must be a blue-specked
hen;
But you shall see me overthrow him with
a fart.
So, without conquest, he shall go home
again.
If I overcome him, I must fight with a
fly,
And a black-pudding the fly's weapon
must be.
At the first blow on the ground he shall
lie; 140
I will be sure to thrust him through
the mouth to the knee.
To conquest these fellows the man I will
play.
Ha, ha, ha! now ye will make me to
smile.
. . . .[10]
To see if I can all men beguile.
Ha! my name? My name would ye so
fain know?
Yea, iwis,[11] shall ye, and that with all
speed!—
I have forgot it; therefore I cannot show.
Ah! ah! now I have it! I have it, in-
deed!
My name is Ambidexter. I signify
one 150
That with both hands finely can play:
Now with King Cambises, and by-and-
by [12] gone.

[1] Since.
[2] Swerve.
[3] Bond, contract.
[4] Trimming.
[5] Please my palate.
[6] Bandbox. [7] Armor. [8] Skimmer. [9] Ensign
[10] The rime indicates that a line is missing here
[11] Certainly. [12] Immediately.

Thus do I run this way and that way.
For while I mean with a soldier to be;
Then give I a leap to Sisamnes the judge.
I dare avouch you shall his destruction see!
To all kind of estates I mean for to trudge.
Ambidexter? Nay, he is a fellow, if ye knew all!
Cease for a while; hereafter hear more ye shall.

Enter three ruffians, Huf, Ruf, and Snuf, singing.

Huf. Gog's [1] flesh and His wounds, these wars rejoice my heart!   160
By His wounds, I hope to do well, for my part!
By Gog's heart, the world shall go hard if I do not shift;
At some old carl's budget [2] I mean for to lift.
Ruf. By His flesh, nose, eyes, and ears, I will venter,[3] void of all cares!
He is not a soldier that doth fear any doubt,
If that he would bring his purpose about.
Snuf. Fear that fear list,[4] it shall not be I.
By Gog's wounds, I will make some neck stand awry!
If I lose my share—I swear by Gog's heart—   170
Then let another take up my part!
Huf. Yet I hope to come the richest soldier away.
Ruf. If a man ask ye, ye may hap to say nay.
Snuf. Let all men get what they can; not to leese [5] I hope;
Wheresoever I go, in each corner I will grope.
Ambidexter. What and [6] ye run in the corner of some pretty maid?
Snuf. To grope there, good fellow, I will not be afraid.
Huf. Gog's wounds, what art thou that with us dost mell? [7]
Thou seemest to be a soldier, the truth to tell;

Thou seemest to be harnessed—I cannot tell how;   180
I think he came lately from riding some cow.
Such a deformed slave did I never see!
Ruf, dost thou know him? I pray thee, tell me.
Ruf. No, by my troth, fellow Huf, I never see him before.
Snuf. As for me, I care not if I never see him more.
Come, let us run his arse against the post!
Ambidexter. Ah, ye slaves! I will be with you at ost! [8]
          Here let him swinge them about.
Ah, ye knaves! I will teach ye how ye shall me deride!
Out of my sight! I can ye not abide!
Now, goodman pouchmouth, I am a slave with you?   190
Now have at ye afresh—again—even now!
Mine arse against the post you will run?
But I will make you from that saying to turn!
Huf. I beseech ye heartily to be content.
Ruf. I insure you, by mine honesty, no hurt we meant.
Beside that, again, we do not know what ye are.
Ye know that soldiers their stoutness will declare;
Therefore, if we have anything offended,
Pardon our rudeness, and it shall be amended.
Ambidexter. Yea, God's pity, begin ye to entreat me?   200
Have at ye once again! By the Mass, I will beat ye!   *Fight again.*
Huf. Gog's heart, let us kill him! Suffer no longer!   *Draw their swords.*
Snuf. Thou slave, we will see if thou be the stronger!
Ruf. Strike off his head at one blow!
That we be soldiers, Gog's heart, let him know!
Ambidexter. O the passion of God, I have done, by mine honesty!
I will take your part hereafter, verily.
All. Then come, let us agree!
Ambidexter. Shake hands with me—I shake hands with thee.

[1] God's.
[2] Countryman's wallet.
[3] Venture.
[4] Pleases.
[5] Lose.
[6] If.
[7] Meddle.
[8] Host; *i.e.*, be intimate with you.

Ye are full of courtesy; that is the best.
And you take great pain; ye are a man-
　　nerly guest.　　　　　　　　　　211
Why, masters, do you not know me?
　　The truth to me tell.
ALL. No, trust us, not very well.
AMBIDEXTER. Why, I am Ambidexter,
　　who [1] many soldiers do love.
HUF. Gog's heart, to have thy company
　　needs we must prove!
We must play with both hands, with our
　　hostess and host,
Play with both hands, and score on the
　　post; [2]
Now and then, with our captain, for
　　many a delay,
We will not stick with both hands to play.
AMBIDEXTER. The honester man, ye may
　　me trust!　　　　　　　　　　220

Enter Meretrix, with a staff on her shoulder.

MERETRIX. What! is there no lads here
　　that hath a lust
　　To have a passing trull to help at their
　　need?
HUF. Gog's heart, she is come, indeed!
What, Mistress Meretrix, by His wounds,
　　welcome to me!
MERETRIX. What will ye give me? I pray
　　you, let me see.
RUF. By His heart, she looks for gifts
　　by-and-by!
MERETRIX. What? Master Ruf? I cry
　　you mercy!
The last time I was with you I got a
　　broken head,
And lay in the street all night for want
　　of a bed.
SNUF. Gog's wounds, kiss me, my trull so
　　white! [3]　　　　　　　　　　230
In thee, I swear, is all my delight!
If thou shouldst have had a broken head
　　for my sake,
I would have made his head to ache.
MERETRIX. What? Master Ambidexter?
　　Who looked for you?
AMBIDEXTER. Mistress Meretrix, I thought
　　not to see you here now.
There is no remedy—at meeting I must
　　have a kiss!

MERETRIX. What, man, I will not stick
　　for that, by Gis! [4]　　　　*Kiss.*
AMBIDEXTER. So now, gramercy! I pray
　　thee be gone!
MERETRIX. Nay, soft, my friend; I mean
　　to have one!
Nay, soft! I swear, and if ye were my
　　brother,　　　　　　　　　　240
Before I let go, I will have another!
　　　　　　　　　　Kiss, kiss, kiss.
RUF. Gog's heart, the whore would not
　　kiss me yet!
MERETRIX. If I be a whore, thou art a
　　knave; then it is quit.
HUF. But hear'st thou, Meretrix? With
　　who this night wilt thou lie?
MERETRIX. With him that giveth the most
　　money.
HUF. Gog's heart, I have no money in
　　purse, ne yet in clout! [5]
MERETRIX. Then get thee hence and pack,
　　like a lout!
HUF. Adieu, like a whore!　　*Exit Huf.*
MERETRIX.　　　　　　Farewell, like
　　a knave! [6]
RUF. Gog's nails, Mistress Meretrix, now
　　he is gone,
A match ye shall make straight with
　　me:　　　　　　　　　　250
I will give thee sixpence to lie one night
　　with thee.
MERETRIX. Gog's heart, slave, dost think
　　I am a sixpenny Jug? [7]
No, wis [8] ye, Jack, I look a little more
　　smug!
SNUF. I will give her eighteenpence to
　　serve me first.
MERETRIX. Gramercy, Snuf, thou art not
　　the worst!
RUF. By Gog's heart, she were better be
　　hanged, to forsake me and take thee!
SNUF. Were she so? That shall we see!
RUF. By Gog's heart, my dagger into her
　　I will thrust!
SNUF. Ah, ye boy, ye would do it and ye
　　durst!
AMBIDEXTER. Peace, my masters; ye shall
　　not fight.　　　　　　　　　260
He that draws first, I will him smite.
RUF. Gog's wounds, Master Snuf, are ye
　　so lusty?

---

[1] Whom(?).
[2] *I.e.*, mark the reckonings on the tavern
doorposts.　　　　　　　　[3] Dear.

[4] Jesus.　　　　　　[5] In my clothes.
[6] " The rhyme seems to demand some such word
as *whoreson*" (Manly).　[7] Joan, a whore.　[8] Know.

SNUF. Gog's sides, Master Ruf, are ye so
  crusty?

RUF. You may happen to see!

SNUF. Do what thou darest to me!

Here draw and fight. Here she must lay on
  and coil [1] *them both; the Vice must run*
  his way for fear; Snuf fling down his
  sword and buckler and run his way.

MERETRIX. Gog's sides, knaves! Seeing to
  fight ye be so rough,

Defend yourselves, for I will give ye both
  enough!

I will teach ye how ye shall fall out for
  me!

Yea, thou slave, Snuf, no more blows wilt
  thou bide?

To take thy heels a time hast thou
  spied?   270

Thou villain, seeing Snuf has gone away,

A little better I mean thee to pay!

He falleth down; she falleth upon him, and
  beats him, and taketh away his weapons.

RUF. Alas, good Mistress Meretrix, no
  more!

My legs, sides, and arms with beating be
  sore!

MERETRIX. Thou a soldier, and lose thy
  weapon!

Go hence, sir boy; say a woman hath
  thee beaten!

RUF. Good Mistress Meretrix, my weapon
  let me have;

Take pity on me, mine honesty [2] to save.

If it be known this repulse I sustain,

It will redound to my ignomy and
  shame.   280

MERETRIX. If thou wilt be my man and
  wait upon me,

This sword and buckler I will give thee.

RUF. I will do all at your commandment;

As servant to you I will be obedient.

MERETRIX. Then let me see how before me
  you can go.

When I speak to you, you shall do so:

Off with your cap at place [3] and at
  board [4] —

"Forsooth, Mistress Meretrix," at every
  word.

Tut! tut! in the camp such soldiers there
  be,

One good woman would beat away two
  or three!   290

Well, I am sure customers tarry at home.

Mannerly before, and let us be gone!

                                Exeunt.

Enter Ambidexter.

[AMBIDEXTER.] O the passion of God! Be
  they here still or no?

I durst not abide to see her beat them so!

I may say to you, iwis, in such a flight, [5]

Body of me, I see the hair of my head
  stand upright!

When I saw her so hard upon them lay
  on,

"O the passion of God!" thought I, "she
  will be with me anon!"

I made no more [6] ado, but avoided the
  thrust,

And to my legs began for to trust,   300

And fell a-laughing to myself when I was
  once gone.

"It is wisdom," quoth I, "by the Mass,
  to save one!"

Then into this place I intended to trudge,

Thinking to meet Sisamnes the judge.

Behold where he cometh! I will him
  meet,

And like a gentleman I mean him to
  greet.

Enter Sisamnes.

SISAMNES. Since that the king's grace's
  majesty in office did me set,

What abundance of wealth to me might
  I get!

Now and then some vantage I achieve;
  much more yet may I take,

But that I fear unto the king that some
  complaint will make.   310

AMBIDEXTER. Jesu, Master Sisamnes, you
  are unwise!

SISAMNES. Why so? I pray thee, let me
  agnize.

What, Master Ambidexter, is it you?

Now welcome to me, I make God avow!

AMBIDEXTER. Jesu, Master Sisamnes, with
  me you are well acquainted.

By me rulers may be trimly painted. [7]

Ye are unwise if ye take not time while
  ye may;

If ye will not now, when ye would ye shall
  have nay.

[1] Beat.   [3] House.
[2] Honor.   [4] Table.

[5] Possibly a misprint for *fright.*
[6] Original reads *mare.*   [7] Cheated.

What is he that of you dare make ex-
clamation,
Of your wrong-dealing to make explica-
tion? 320
Can you not play with both hands, and
turn with the wind?
SISAMNES. Believe me, your words draw
deep in my mind.
In color wise unto this day,[1] to bribes I
have inclinéd;
More the same for to frequent, of truth
I am now minded.
Behold, even now unto me suitors do
proceed.

[*Enter Small Hability.*]

SMALL HABILITY. I beseech you here, good
Master Judge, a poor man's cause to
tender![2]
Condemn me not in wrongful wise that
never was offender.
You know right well my right it is. I
have not for to give.
You take away from me my due, that
should my corpse[3] relieve.
The commons of you do complain from
them you devocate;[4] 330
With anguish great and grievous words
their hearts do penetrate;
The right you sell unto the wrong, your
private gain to win;
You violate the simple man, and count it
for no sin.
SISAMNES. Hold thy tongue, thou prattling knave, and give to me reward;
Else, in this wise, I tell thee truth, thy
tale will not be heard.
Ambidexter, let us go hence, and let the
knave alone.
AMBIDEXTER. Farewell, Small Hability, for
help now get you none;
Bribes hath corrupt him good laws to
pollute.
Exeunt [*Sisamnes and Ambidexter*].
SMALL HABILITY. A naughty man, that
will not obey the king's constitute![5]
With heavy heart I will return, till God
redress my pain. *Exit.* 340

[1] Taking color from the practices of the day (?)
[2] Regard favorably.
[3] Body.
[4] Call away, take away.
[5] Law.

Enter Shame, with a trump, black.

SHAME. From among the grisly ghosts I
come, from tyrants' testy train.
Unseemly Shame, of sooth, I am, pro-
curéd to make plain
The odious facts and shameless deeds
that Cambises king doth use.
All piety and virtuous life he doth it
clean refuse;
Lechery and drunkenness he doth it
much frequent.
The tiger's kind[6] to imitate he hath
given full consent.
He naught esteems his Counsel grave ne
virtuous bringing-up,
But daily still receives the drink of
damned Vice's cup.
He can bide no instruction, he takes so
great delight
In working of iniquity for to frequent his
spite. 350
As Fame doth sound the royal trump of
worthy men and trim,
So Shame doth blow with strained blast
the trump of shame on him. *Exit.*

Enter the King, Lord, Praxaspes, and
Sisamnes.

KING. My judge, since my departure
hence, have you used judgment right?
If faithful steward I ye find, the same I
will requite.
SISAMNES. No doubt your grace shall not
once hear that I have done amiss.
PRAXASPES. I much rejoice to hear so good
news as this.

Enter Commons' Cry running in, speak this
verse, and go out again hastily.

COMMONS' CRY. Alas, alas, how are the
commons oppressed
By that vile judge, Sisamnes by name!
I do not know how it should be redressed.
To amend his life no whit he doth
frame. 360
We are undone and thrown out of door;
His damnable dealing doth us so tor-
ment;
At his hand we can find no relief nor suc-
cor.
God grant him grace for to repent!
Run away crying.

[6] Nature.

KING. What doleful cries be these, my
l[ord], that sound do in mine ear?
Intelligence if you can give, unto your
king declare.
To me it seemeth my commons all they
do lament and cry
Out of [1] Sisamnes, judge most chief, even
now standing us by.
PRAXASPES. Even so, O king, it seemed to
me, as you rehearsal made.
I doubt [2] the judge culpable be in some
respect or trade.[3]   370
SISAMNES. Redoubted king, have no mistrust! No whit your mind dismay!
There is not one that can me charge, or
aught against me lay.

Enter Commons' Complaint, with Proof and
Trial.

COMMONS' COMPLAINT. Commons' Complaint I represent, with thrall of doleful state.
My urgent cause erected forth my grief
for to dilate.
Unto the king I will prepare my misery
to tell,
To have relief of this my grief and fettered feet so fell.[4]
Redoubted prince and mighty king, myself I prostrate here.
Vouchsafe, O king, with me to bear for
this that I appear.
With humble suit I pardon crave of your
most royal grace
To give me leave my mind to break before you in this place.   380
KING. Commons' Complaint, keep nothing
back! Fear not thy tale to tell.
Whate'er he be within this land that
hath not used thee well,
As prince's mouth shall sentence give, he
shall receive the same.
Unfold the secrets of thy breast, for I
extinguish blame.
COMMONS' COMPLAINT. God preserve your
royal grace, and send you blissful days,
That all your deeds might still accord to
give the God the praise!
My complaint is, O mighty king, against
that judge you by,
Whose careless deeds, gain to receive,
hath made the commons cry.

He, by taking bribes and gifts, the poor
he doth oppress,
Taking relief from infants young, widows,
and fatherless.   390
KING. Untrustful traitor and corrupt
judge, how likest thou this complaint?
Forewarning I to thee did give of this to
make restraint;
And hast thou done this devilish deed
mine ire for to augment?
I sentence give, thou Judas judge. Thou
shalt thy deed repent!
SISAMNES. O pusant [5] prince, it is not so.
His complaint I deny.
COMMONS' COMPLAINT. If it be not so,
most mighty king, in place then let me
die.
Behold that I have brought with me both
Proof and Trial true,
To stand even here, and sentence give
what by him did ensue.
PROOF. I, Proof, do him in this appeal: he
did the commons wrong;
Unjustly he with them hath dealt, his
greedy [6] was so strong.   400
His heart did covet in to get, he caréd
not which way;
The poor did leese their due and right,
because they want [7] to pay
Unto him for bribes. Indeed, this was
his wonted use.
Whereas your grace good laws did make,
he did the same abuse.
TRIAL. I, Trial, here to verify what Proof
doth now unfold,
To stand against him in his wrong, as
now I dare be bold.
KING. How likest thou this, thou caitiff
vile? Canst thou the same deny?
SISAMNES. O noble king, forgive my fact!
I yield to thy mercy.
KING. Complaints and Proof, redress will
I all this your misery.
Depart with speed from whence you
came, and straight command by
me   410
The execution man to come before my
grace with haste.
ALL. For to fulfill this your request no
time we mean to waste.

Exeunt they three.

[1] On.
[2] Suspect.
[3] Course, practice.
[4] Cruel, cruelly treated.
[5] Puissant.
[6] Greediness(?); greed it(?).
[7] *I.e.*, lacked the wherewithal.

KING. My lord, before my grace go call
    Otian, this judge's son,
And he shall hear and also see what his
    father hath done.
The father he shall suffer death, the son
    his room succeed;
And, if that he no better prove, so like-
    wise shall he speed.
PRAXASPES. As your grace hath command-
    ment given, I mean for to fulfill.
            Step aside and fetch him.
KING. Accurséd judge, couldst thou con-
    sent to do this cursed ill?
According unto thy demand, thou shalt,
    for this thy guilt,
Receive thy death before mine eyes. Thy
    blood it shall be spilt.   420

      [Enter Praxaspes with Otian.]

PRAXASPES. Behold, O king, Sisamnes' son
    before you doth appear.
KING. Otian, this is my mind; therefore
    to me come near:
Thy father here for judgment wrong pro-
    curéd hath his death,
And thou, his son, shalt him succeed
    when he hath lost his breath;
And, if that thou dost once offend, as
    thou seest thy father have,
In like wise thou shalt suffer death. No
    mercy shall thee save!
OTIAN. O mighty king, vouchsafe your
    grace my father to remit.
Forgive his fault. His pardon I do ask
    of you as yet.
Alas, although my father hath your
    princely heart offended,
Amends for miss [1] he will now make, and
    faults shall be amended.   430
Instead of his requested life, pleaseth
    your grace take mine.
This offer I as tender child, so duty doth
    me bind.
KING. Do not entreat my grace no more,
    for he shall die the death!
Where is the execution man him to be-
    reave of breath?

      Enter Execution.

EXECUTION. At hand, and if it like your
    grace, my duty to despatch,
In hope that I, when deed is done, a good
    reward shall catch.

[1] Wrongdoing.

KING. Despatch with sword this judge's
    life; extinguish fear and cares.
So done, draw thou his curséd skin
    straight over both his ears.
I will see the office done, and that before
    mine eyes.
EXECUTION. To do the thing my king com-
    mands I give the enterprise. [2]   440
SISAMNES. Otian, my son, the king to
    death by law hath me condemned,
And you in room and office mine his
    grace's will hath placed;
Use justice, therefore, in this case, and
    yield unto no wrong,
[Lest thou do purchase the like death ere
    ever it be long.] [3]
OTIAN. O father dear, these words to hear
    —that you must die by force—
Bedews my cheeks with stilléd tears.
    The king hath no remorse.
The grievous griefs and strained sighs
    my heart doth break in twain,
And I deplore, most woeful child, that I
    should see you slain.
O false and fickle frowning dame, that
    turneth as the wind,
Is this the joy in father's age thou me
    assignest to find?   450
O doleful day, unhappy hour, that loving
    child should see
His father dear before his face thus put
    to death should be!
Yet, father, give me blessing thine, and
    let me once embrace
Thy comely corpse in folded arms, and
    kiss thy ancient face!
SISAMNES. O child, thou makes my eyes to
    run, as rivers do, by stream.
My leave I take of thee, my son. Be-
    ware of this my Beam! [4]
KING. Despatch even now, thou man of
    death; no longer seem to stay!
EXECUTION. Come, M[aster] Sisamnes,
    come on your way.
My office I must pay; forgive therefore
    my deed.
SISAMNES. I do forgive it thee, my friend;
    despatch therefore with speed!   460
Smite him in the neck with a sword to signify
                      his death.

[2] I readily undertake.
[3] Line supplied from first edn.
[4] Affliction, alluding to the Cross.

PRAXASPES. Behold, O king, how he doth bleed, being of life bereft!

KING. In this wise he shall not yet be left. Pull his skin over his eyes to make his death more vile.

A wretch he was, a cruel thief, my commons to beguile!

Flay him with a false skin.

OTIAN. What child [1] is he of nature's mold could bide the same to see—

His father flayed in this wise? O, how it grieveth me!

KING. Otian, thou seest thy father dead, and thou art in his room;

If thou beest proud, as he hath been, even thereto shalt thou come.

OTIAN. O king, to me this is a glass; with grief in it I view

Example that unto your grace I do not prove untrue.   470

PRAXASPES. Otian, convey your father hence to tomb where he shall lie.

OTIAN. And if it please your lordship, it shall be done by-and-by.

Good execution man, for need, help me with him away.

EXECUTION. I will fulfill, as you to me did say.   *They take him away.*

KING. My l[ord], now that my grace hath seen that finished is this deed,

To question mine give tentive [2] ear, and answer make with speed:

Have not I done a gracious deed, to redress my commons' woe?

PRAXASPES. Yea, truly, if it please your grace, you have indeed done so.

But now, O king, in friendly wise I counsel you in this:

Certain vices for to leave that in you placéd is—   480

The vice of drunkenness, O king, which doth you sore infect,

With other great abuses, which I wish you to detect.

KING. Peace, my lord! What needeth this? Of this I will not hear!

To palace now I will return, and thereto make good cheer.

God Bacchus he bestows his gifts—we have good store of wine—

And also that the ladies be both passing brave and fine.

[1] Suggested by Manly. Original reads *thilde.*
[2] Attentive.

But stay! I see a lord now come, and eke a valiant knight.

What news, my lord? To see you here my heart it doth delight.

Enter Lord and Knight to meet the King.

LORD. No news, O king; but of duty come to wait upon your grace.

KING. I thank you, my l[ord] and loving knight. I pray you with me trace. [3]   490

My lords and knight, I pray ye tell—I will not be offended—

Am I worthy of any crime once to be reprehended?

PRAXASPES. The Persians much do praise your grace, but one thing discommend,

In that to wine subject you be, wherein you do offend.

Sith that the might of wine's effect doth oft subdue your brain,

My counsel is, to please their hearts, from it you would refrain.

LORD. No, no, my lord, it is not so! For this of prince they tell,

For virtuous proof and princely facts Cyrus he doth excel.

By that his grace by conquest great the Egyptians did convince,

Of him report abroad doth pass to be a worthy prince.   500

KNIGHT. In person of Crœsus I answer make: we may not his grace compare

In whole respect for to be like Cyrus, the king's father,

Insomuch your grace hath yet no child as Cyrus left behind;

Even you I mean, Cambises King, in whom I favor find.

KING. Crœsus said well in saying so. But, Praxaspes, tell me why

That to my mouth in such a sort thou should avouch a lie,

Of drunkenness me thus to charge. But thou with speed shalt see

Whether that I a sober king or else a drunkard be.

I know thou hast a blissful babe, wherein thou dost delight;

Me to revenge of these thy words I will go wreak this spite.   510

When I the most have tasted wine, my bow it shall be bent.

[3] Walk.

At heart of him even then to shoot is
row my whole intent,
And, if that I his heart can hit, the king
no drunkard is;
If heart of his I do not kill, I yield to
thee in this.
Therefore, Praxaspes, fetch to me thy
youngest son with speed.
There is no way, I tell thee plain, but I
will do this deed.

PRAXASPES. Redoubted prince, spare my
sweet child. He is mine only joy!
I trust your grace to infant's heart no
such thing will employ.
If that his mother hear of this, she is so
nigh her flight,
In clay her corpse will soon be shrined
to pass from world's delight. 520

KING. No more ado! Go fetch me him.
It shall be as I say.
And if that I do speak the word, how
dare ye once say nay?

PRAXASPES. I will go fetch him to your
grace; but so, I trust, it shall not be!

KING. For fear of my displeasure great, go
fetch him unto me. [*Exit Praxaspes.*]
Is he gone? Now, by the gods, I will do
as I say!
My lord, therefore fill me some wine, I
heartily you pray;
For I must drink to make my brain
somewhat intoxicate.
When that the wine is in my head, O,
trimly I can prate!

LORD. Here is the cup, with fillèd wine,
thereof to take repast.

KING. Give it me to drink it off, and see
no wine be waste. *Drink.* 530
Once again enlarge this cup, for I must
taste it still. *Drink.*
By the gods, I think of pleasant wine I
cannot take my fill!
Now drink is in, give me my bow and
arrows from Sir Knight.
At heart of child I mean to shoot, hoping
to cleave it right.

KNIGHT. Behold, O king, where he doth
come, his infant young in hand.

[*Enter Praxaspes with the Child.*]

PRAXASPES. O mighty king, your grace'
behest with sorrow I have scanned,
And brought my child fro mother's knee
before you to appear,

And she thereof no whit doth know that
he in place is here.

KING. Set him up, my mark to be. I
will shoot at his heart.

PRAXASPES. I beseech your grace not so
to do! Set this pretense apart!— 540
Farewell, my dear and loving babe!
Come, kiss thy father dear!
A grievous sight to me it is to see thee
slain even here.
Is this the gain now from the king for
giving counsel good—
Before my face with such despite to spill
my son's heart-blood?
O heavy day to me this is, and mother
in like case!

YOUNG CHILD. O father, father, wipe your
face;
I see the tears run from your eye.
My mother is at home sewing of a band.
Alas, dear father, why do you cry?

KING. Before me as a mark now let him
stand. 550
I will shoot at him my mind to fulfill.

YOUNG CHILD. Alas, alas, father, will you
me kill?
Good Master King, do not shoot at me;
my mother loves me best of all. *Shoot.*

KING. I have despatched him! Down he
doth fall!
As right as a line his heart I have hit.
Nay, thou shalt see, Praxaspes, stranger
news yet.
My knight, with speed his heart cut out
and give it unto me.

KNIGHT. It shall be done, O mighty king,
with all celerity.

LORD. My Lord Praxaspes, this had not
been but your tongue must be walking.
To the king of correction you must needs
be talking. 560

PRAXASPES. No correction, my lord, but
counsel for the best.

KNIGHT. Here is the heart, according to
your grace's behest.

KING. Behold, Praxaspes, thy son's own
heart! O, how well the same was hit!
After this wine to do this deed I thought
it very fit.
Esteem thou mayst right well thereby
no drunkard is the king
That in the midst of all his cups could
do this valiant thing.

My lord and knight, on me attend. To
palace we will go,
And leave him here to take his son when
we are gone him fro.
ALL. With all our hearts we give consent
to wait upon your grace.
                      [*Exeunt all but Praxaspes.*]
PRAXASPES. A woeful man, O Lord, am I,
to see him in this case!   570
My days, I deem, desires their end. This
deed will help me hence.
To have the blossoms of my field destroyed by violence!

Enter Mother.

[MOTHER.] Alas, alas, I do hear tell the
king hath killed my son!
If it be so, woe worth the deed that ever
it was done!
It is even so! My lord I see, how by him
he doth weep.
What meant I that from hands of him
this child I did not keep?
Alas, husband and lord, what did you
mean to fetch this child away?
PRAXASPES. O lady wife, I little thought
for to have seen this day.
MOTHER. O blissful babe! O joy of womb!
Heart's comfort and delight!
For counsel given unto the king is this
thy just requite?   580
O heavy day and doleful time, these
mourning tunes to make!
With blubbered eyes, into mine arms
from earth I will thee take,
And wrap thee in mine apron white.
But, O my heavy heart!
The spiteful pangs that it sustains would
make it in two to part,
The death of this my son to see! O
heavy mother now,
That from thy sweet and sugared joy to
sorrow so shouldst bow!
What grief in womb did I retain before I
did thee see!
Yet at the last, when smart was gone,
what joy wert thou to me!
How tender was I of thy food, for to
preserve thy state!
How stilléd I thy tender heart at times
early and late!   590
With velvet paps I gave thee suck with
issue from my breast,

And dancéd thee upon my knee to bring
thee unto rest!
Is this the joy of thee I reap? O king of
tiger's brood!
O tiger's whelp, hadst thou the heart
to see this child's heart-blood?
Nature enforceth me, alas, in this wise
to deplore,
To wring my hands. O welaway, that I
should see this hour!
Thy mother yet will kiss thy lips, silk-
soft and pleasant white,
With wringing hands lamenting for to see
thee in this plight!
My lording dear, let us go home our
mourning to augment.
PRAXASPES. My lady dear, with heavy
heart to it I do consent,   600
Between us both the child to bear unto
our lordly place.   *Exeunt.*

Enter Ambidexter.

[AMBIDEXTER. (*To the audience.*)] Indeed, as
ye say, I have been absent a long space.
But is not my cousin Cutpurse with you
in the meantime?
To it, to it, cousin, and do your office
fine!
How like you Sisamnes for using of me?
He played with both hands, but he sped
ill-favoredly!
The king himself was godly uptrained;
He professed virtue—but I think it was
feigned.
He plays with both hands, good deeds
and ill;
But it was no good deed Praxaspes' son
for to kill.   610
As he for the good deed on the judge was
commended,
For all his deeds else he is reprehended.
The most evil-disposed person that ever
was
All the state of his life he would not let
pass,
Some [1] good deeds he will do, though they
be but few.
The like things this tyrant Cambises
doth shew.
No goodness from him to none is ex-
hibited,
But still malediction abroad is distrib-
uted;

[1] *I.e.*, but some.

And yet ye shall see in the rest of his race
What infamy he will work against his
own grace. 620
Whist! No more words! Here comes
the king's brother.

*Enter Lord Smirdis with Attendance and
Diligence.*

SMIRDIS. The king's brother by birth am
I, issued from Cyrus' loins;
A grief to me it is to hear of this the
king's repines.[1]
I like not well of those his deeds that he
doth still frequent;
I wish to God that other ways his mind
he could content.
Young I am, and next to him; no mo [2] of
us there be.
I would be glad a quiet realm in this his
reign to see.
ATTENDANCE. My lord, your good a[nd] [3]
willing heart the gods will recompense,
In that your mind so pensive is for those
his great offense.
My lord, his grace shall have a time to
pair [4] and to amend. 630
Happy is he that can escape and not his
grace offend.
DILIGENCE. If that wicked vice he could
refrain, from wasting wine forbear,
A moderate life he would frequent,
amending this his square.[5]
AMBIDEXTER. My lord, and if your honor
it shall please,
I can inform you what is best for your
ease:
Let him alone; of his deeds do not talk;
Then by his side ye may quietly walk.
After his death you shall be king;
Then may you reform each kind of thing.
In the meantime live quietly; do not
with him deal; 640
So shall it redound much to your weal.
SMIRDIS. Thou say'st true, my friend; that
is the best.
I know not whether he love me or do me
detest.
ATTENDANCE. Lean from his company all
that you may.
I, faithful Attendance, will your honor
obey;

[1] Dissatisfactions.
[2] More.
[3] Added by Manly.
[4] Repair.
[5] Regularity of conduct.

If against your honor he take any ire,
His grace is as like to kindle his fire
To your honor's destruction as otherwise.
DILIGENCE. Therefore, my lord, take good
advice,
And I, Diligence, your case will so
tender 650
That to his grace your honor shall be
none offender.
SMIRDIS. I thank you both, entire friends.
With my honor still remain.
AMBIDEXTER. Behold where the king doth
come with his train!

Enter King and a Lord.

KING. O lording dear and brother mine, I
joy your state to see,
Surmising much what is the cause you
absent thus from me.
SMIRDIS. Pleaseth your grace, no absence
I, but ready to fulfill,
At all assays, my prince and king, in that
your grace me will.
What I can do in true defense to you, my
prince, aright,
In readiness I always am to offer forth
my might.
KING. And I the like to you again do here
avouch the same. 660
ALL. For this your good agreement here,
now praised be God's name!
AMBIDEXTER. [*To Smirdis.*] But hear ye,
noble prince; hark in your ear:
It is best to do as I did declare.
KING. My lord and brother Smirdis, now
this is my mind and will:
That you to court of mine return, and
there to tarry still
Till my return within short space your
honor for to greet.
SMIRDIS. At your behest so will I do till
time again we meet.
My leave I take from you, O king; even
now I do depart.
Exeunt Smirdis, Attendance, and Diligence.
KING. Farewell, lord and brother mine!
farewell with all my heart!
My lord, my brother Smirdis is of youth
and manly might, 670
And in his sweet and pleasant face my
heart doth take delight.
LORD. Yea, noble prince, if that your
grace before his honor die,

He will succeed, a virtuous king, and rule
with equity.

KING. As you have said, my lord, he is
chief heir next my grace,

And, if I die tomorrow, next he shall
succeed my place.

AMBIDEXTER. And, if it please your grace,
O king, I heard him say,

For your death unto the God day and
night he did pray;

He would live so virtuously and get him
such a praise

That Fame by trump his due deserts in
honor should upraise;

He said your grace deservéd had the
cursing of all men, 680

That ye should never after him get any
praise again.

KING. Did he speak thus of my grace in
such despiteful wise?

Or else dost thou presume to fill my
princely ears with lies?

LORD. I cannot think it in my heart that
he would report so.

KING. How sayst thou? Speak the truth:
was it so or no?

AMBIDEXTER. I think so, if it please your
grace, but I cannot tell.

KING. Thou play'st with both hands, now
I perceive well!

But, for to put all doubts aside and to
make him leese his hope,

He shall die by dint of sword or else by
choking rope.

Shall he succeed when I am gone, to have
more praise than I? 690

Were he father, as brother mine, I swear
that he shall die!

To palace mine I will therefore, his death
for to pursue.

Exit [King with the Lord].

AMBIDEXTER. Are ye gone? Straightway
I will follow you.—

[*To the audience.*] How like ye now, my
masters? Doth not this gear cotton? [1]

The proverb old is verified: "Soon ripe,
and soon rotten!"

He will not be quiet till his brother be
killed;

His delight is wholly to have his blood
spilled.

Marry, sir, I told him a notable lie!

If it were to do again, I durst [not] do it, I!

[1] Affair succeed.

Marry, when I had done, to it I durst
not stand; 700

Thereby ye may perceive I use to play
with each hand.

But how now, cousin Cutpurse, with
whom play you?

Take heed, for his hand is groping even
now!

Cousin, take heed, if you do secretly
grope;

If ye be taken, cousin, ye must look
through a rope. *Exit.*

Enter Lord Smirdis alone.

[SMIRDIS.] I am wandering alone, here and
there to walk;

The court is so unquiet, in it I take
no joy.

Solitary to myself now I may talk.

If I could rule, I wist what to say.

Enter Cruelty and Murder with bloody hands.

CRUELTY. My coequal partner, Murder,
come away; 710

From me long thou mayst not stay.

MURDER. Yes, from thee I may stay, but
not thou from me;

Therefore I have a prerogative above
thee.

CRUELTY. But in this case we must together abide.

Come, come! Lord Smirdis I have spied.

Lay hands on him with all festination, [2]

That on him we may work our indignation! [*They seize him.*]

SMIRDIS. How now, my friends? What
have you to do with me?

MURDER. King Cambises hath sent us
unto thee,

Commanding us straightly, without
mercy or favor, 720

Upon thee to bestow our behavior,

With cruelty to murder you and make
you away.

SMIRDIS. Yet pardon me, I heartily you
pray!

Consider, the king is a tyrant tyran-
nious,

And all his doings be damnable and pernicious.

Favor me therefore; I did him never
offend.

[2] Speed.

CRUELTY. No favor at all! Your life is at an end!
Even now I strike, his body to wound. *Strike him in divers places.*[1]
Behold, now his blood springs out on the ground!
A little bladder of vinegar pricked.[2]
MURDER. Now he is dead, let us present him to the king. 730
CRUELTY. Lay to your hand, away him to bring. *Exeunt.*

Enter Ambidexter.

AMBIDEXTER. O the passion of God, yonder is a heavy court!
Some weeps, some wails—and some make great sport.
Lord Smirdis by Cruelty and Murder is slain;
But Jesus! for want of him how some do complain!
If I should have had a thousand pound I could not forbear weeping.
Now Jesus have his blessed soul in keeping!
Ah, good lord, to think on him, how it doth me grieve!
I cannot forbear weeping, ye may me believe. *Weep.*
O my heart, how my pulses do beat! 740
With sorrowful lamentations I am in such a heat!
Ah, my heart, how for him it doth sorrow!
Nay, I have done, in faith, now. And God give ye good morrow!
Ha, ha! Weep? Nay, laugh, with both hands to play!
The king through his cruelty hath made him away;
But hath not he wrought a most wicked deed,
Because king after him he should not proceed,
His own natural brother, and having no more,
To procure his death by violence sore?
In spite, because his brother should never be king, 750
His heart, being wicked, consented to this thing.

Now he hath no more brothers nor kin-red[3] alive.
If the king use this gear still, he cannot long thrive.

Enter Hob and Lob.

HOB. God's hat, neighbor, come away! It's time to market to go!
LOB. God's vast,[4] neighbor, zay ye zo?
The clock hath stricken vive, ich[5] think, by Lakin![6]
Bum vay,[7] vrom sleep cham not very well waken!
But, neighbor Hob, neighbor Hob, what have ye to zell?
HOB. Bum troth, neighbor Lob, to you I chill tell:
Chave two goslings and a chine of pork— 760
There is no vatter between this and York.
Chave a pot of strawberries and a calve's head;
A zennight zince, tomorrow, it hath been dead.
LOB. Chave a score of eggs and of butter a pound:
Yesterday a nest of goodly young rabbits I vound;
Chave vorty things mo, of more and of less—
My brain is not very good them to express.
But, God's hat, neighbor, wot'st[8] what?
HOB. No, not well, neighbor; what's that?
LOB. Bum vay, neighbor, master king is a zhrode[9] lad! 770
Zo God help me, and halidom,[10] I think the vool be mad!
Zome zay he deal cruelly: his brother he did kill,
And also a goodly young lad's heart-blood he did spill.
HOB. Vorbod of God,[11] neighbor! Has he played zuch a voolish deed?
AMBIDEXTER. Goodman Hob and Goodman Lob, God be your speed!
As you two towards market do walk,

---

[1] In the original this stage direction is printed in the margin at line 723.
[2] In the original this stage direction is printed in the margin at line 727.
[3] Kindred.
[4] Fast. In the following rustic dialect, initial *z = s* and initial *v = f*.
[5] I. See *Roister Doister*, I, iii, 100, n.
[6] Ladykin; *i.e.*, the Virgin.
[7] By my faith.   [8] Knowest.   [9] Shrewd.
[10] By my holiness.   [11] God forbid!

Of the king's cruelty I did hear you talk.
I insure you he is a king most vile and
  pernicious;
His doings and life are odious and vicious.
Lob. It were a good deed zomebody would
  break his head.   780
Hob. Bum vay, neighbor Lob, I chuld he
  were dead!
Ambidexter. So would I, Lob and Hob,
  with all my heart!—
  [*To audience.*] Now with both hands will
  you see me play my part.—
Ah, ye whoreson [1] traitorly knaves,
Hob and Lob, out upon you, slaves!
Lob. And thou call'st me knave, thou art
  another!
My name is Lob, and Hob my next
  neighbor.
Ambidexter. Hob and Lob! Ah, ye coun-
  try patches, [2]
Ah, ye fools, ye have made wrong
  matches!
Ye have spoken treason against the
  king's grace!   790
For it I will accuse ye before his face;
Then for the same ye shall be martyred.
At the least ye shall be hanged, drawn,
  and quartered!
Hob. O gentleman, ye shall have two
  pear-pies, and tell not of me!
Lob. By God, a vat goose chill give thee.
I think no hurt, by my vather's soul I
  zwear!
Hob. Chave lived well all my lifetime, my
  neighbors among,
And now chould be loath to come to zuch
  wrong—
To be hanged and quartered, the grief
  would be great!
Lob. A foul evil on thee, Hob! Who bid
  thee on it treat?   800
Vor it was thou that first did him
  name.
Hob. Thou liest like a varlet and thou
  zayst the zame!
It was zuch a foolish Lob as thou.
Lob. Speak many words, and, by Cod's
  nails I vow,
Upon thy pate my staff I will lay!
Ambidexter. [*Aside.*] By the Mass, I will
  cause them to make a fray.—
Yea, Lob, thou sayst true: all came
  through him.

Lob. Bum vay, thou hod,[3] a little would
  make me ye trim!
Give thee a zwap on thy nose till thy
  heart ache!
Hob. If thou darest, do it! Else, man,
  cry "creak!" [4]   810
I trust, before thou hurt me,
With my staff chili make a Lob of
  thee!
*Here let them fight with their staves, not come
  near another by three or four yards; the
  Vice set them on as hard as he can; one
  of their wives come out, and all-to* [5] *beat
  the Vice; he run away.*

*Enter Marian-May-Be-Good, Hob's Wife,
  running in with a broom, and part them.*

Marian. O the body of me! Husband
  Hob, what mean ye to fight?
For the passion of God, no more blows
  smite!
Neighbors and friends so long, and now
  to fall out?
What! in your age to seem so stout?
If I had not parted ye, one had killed
  another.
Lob. I had not cared, I swear by God's
  Mother!
Marian. Shake hands again at the re-
  quest of me;
As ye have been friends, so friends still
  be.   820
Hob. Bum troth, cham content and zayst
  word, neighbor Lob.
Lob. I am content; agreed, neighbor
  Hob!
*Shake hands and laugh heartily one at
                              another.*
Marian. So, get you to market; no longer
  stay.
And with yonder knave let me make a
  fray.
Hob. Content, wife Marian; chill do as
  thou dost say.
But buss me, ich pray thee, at going
  away!   *Exeunt Hob, Lob.*
Marian. Thou whoreson knave and prick-
  eared boy, why didst thou let them
  fight?
If one had killed another here, couldst
  thou their deaths requite?

[3] Hob(?).   [4] *I.e.*, confess yourself beaten
[5] Thoroughly.

---

[1] Rascally.   [2] Clowns, bumpkins.

It bears a sign by this thy deed a cow-
ardly knave thou art,
Else wouldst thou draw that weapon
thine, like a man,[1] them to part. 830
AMBIDEXTER. What,   Marian-May-Be-
Good, are you come prattling?
Ye may hap get a box on the ear with
your talking!
If they had killed one another, I had not
cared a pease.
*Here let her swinge him in her broom; she
gets him down, and he her down; thus
one on the top of another make pastime.*
MARIAN. Ah, villain, myself on thee I
must ease!
Give me a box on the ear? That will I try.
Who shall be master, thou shalt see by-
and-by!
AMBIDEXTER. O, no more, no more, I be-
seech you heartily!
Even now I yield, and give you the
mast'ry.
                Run his way out while she is down.
MARIAN. Ah, thou knave! dost thou throw
me down and run thy [2] way?
If he were here again, O, how I would
him pay!   840
I will after him, and, if I can him meet,
With these my nails his face I will greet.
                                    [*Exit.*]

*Enter Venus leading out her son Cupid,
blind. He must have a bow and two
shafts, one headed with gold and th'
other with lead.*

VENUS. Come forth, my son. Unto my
words attentive ears resign;
What I pretend,[3] see you frequent, to
force this game of mine.
The king a kinswoman hath, adorned
with beauty store; [4]
And I wish that Diana's gifts they twain
shall keep no more,
But use my silver sugared game their
joys for to augment.
When I do speak, to wound his heart,
Cupid my son, consent,
And shoot at him the shaft of love that
bears the head of gold,
To wound his heart in lover's wise, his
grief for to unfold.   850

Though kin she be unto his grace, that
nature me expel,
Against the course thereof he may in my
game please me well.
Wherefore, my son, do not forget; forthwith pursue the deed!
CUPID. Mother, I mean for to obey as
you have whole decreed;
But you must tell me, mother dear,
when I shall arrow draw,
Else your request to be attained will not
be worth a straw;
I am blind and cannot see, but still do
shoot by guess.
The poets well, in places, store [5] of my
might do express.
VENUS. Cupid my son, when time shall
serve that thou shalt do this deed,
Then warning I to thee will give; but see
thou shoot with speed.   860

Enter a Lord, a Lady, and a Waiting-maid.

[FIRST] LORD. Lady dear, to king akin,
forthwith let us proceed
To trace abroad the beauty fields, as erst
we had decreed.
The blowing buds whose savory scents
our sense will much delight,
The sweet smell of musk white-rose to
please the appetite,
The chirping birds whose pleasant tunes
therein shall here record
That our great joy we shall it find in
field to walk abroad,
On lute and cittern there to play a heavenly harmony;
Our ears shall hear, heart to content, our
sports to beautify.
LADY. Unto your words, most comely lord,
myself submit do I;
To trace with you in field so green I mean
not to deny.   870
                Here trace up and down, playing.
MAID. And I, your waiting-maid, at hand
with diligence will be,
For to fulfill with heart and hand, when
you shall command me.

Enter King, Lord, and Knight.

KING. Come on, my lord and knight,
abroad; our mirth let us employ.
Since he is dead, this heart of mine in
corpse I feel it joy.

---

[1] Suggested by Manly. Original reads *knave*.
[2] Emended by Manly; original has *the*.
[3] Intend.   [4] Store of beauty.
[5] Greatness, abundance.

Should brother mine have reignéd king
when I had yielded breath?
A thousand brothers I rather had to put
them all to death.
But, O behold, where I do see a lord and
lady fair!
For beauty she most worthy is to sit in
prince's chair.
VENUS. Shoot forth, my son! Now is
the time that thou must wound his
heart.
CUPID. Content you, mother; I will do
my part.   880
Shoot there, and go out Venus and Cupid.
KING. Of truth, my lord, in eye of mine
all ladies she doth excel.
Can none report what dame she is, and to
my grace it tell?
LORD. Redoubted prince, pleaseth your
grace, to you she is akin,
Cousin-german, nigh of birth, by mother's side come in.
KNIGHT. And that her waiting-maiden is,
attending her upon.
He is a lord of prince's court, and will be
there anon.
They sport themselves in pleasant field,
to former uséd use.
KING. My lord and knight, of truth I
speak. My heart it cannot choose
But with my lady I must speak and so
express my mind.—
My lord and ladies, walking there, if you
will favor find,   890
Present yourselves unto my grace, and
by my side come stand.
FIRST LORD. We will fulfill, most mighty
king, as your grace doth command.
KING. Lady dear, intelligence my grace
hath got of late,
You issued out of mother's stock and kin
unto my state.
According to rule of birth you are cousin-
german mine;
Yet do I wish that farther off this kinred
I could find;
For Cupid he, that eyeless boy, my heart
hath so enflamed
With beauty, you me to content the like
cannot be named;
For, since I entered in this place and on
you fixed mine eyes,
Most burning fits about my heart in
ample wise did rise.   900

The heat of them such force doth yield,
my corpse they scorch, alas!
And burns the same with wasting heat,
as Titan doth the grass.
And, sith this heat is kindled so and
fresh in heart of me,
There is no way but of the same the
quencher you must be.
My meaning is that beauty yours my
heart with love doth wound;
To give me love mind [1] to content, my
heart hath you out found;
And you are she must be my wife, else
shall I end my days.
Consent to this, and be my queen, to
wear the crown with praise!
LADY. If it please your grace, O mighty
king, you shall not this request.
It is a thing that nature's course doth
utterly detest,   910
And high it would the God displease; of
all, that is the worst.
To grant your grace to marry so, it is
not I that durst.
Yet humble thanks I render now unto
you, mighty king,
That you vouchsafe to great estate so
gladly would me bring.
Were it not it were offense, I would it
not deny,
But such great honor to achieve my
heart I would apply.
Therefore, O king, with humble heart in
this I pardon crave;
My answer is: in this request your mind
ye may not have.
KING. May I not? Nay, then, I will, by
all the gods I vow!
And I will marry thee as wife. This is
mine answer now!   920
Who dare say nay what I pretend, who
dare the same withstand,
Shall lose his head, and have report as
traitor through my land.
There is no nay. I will you have, and
you my queen shall be!
LADY. Then, mighty king, I crave your
grace to hear the words of me:
Your counsel take of lordings' wit; the
laws aright peruse;
If I with safe may grant this deed, I will
it not refuse.

[1] Desire.

KING. No, no! What I have said to you,
  I mean to have it so.
For counsel theirs I mean not, I, in this
  respect to go;
But to my palace let us go, the marriage
  to prepare;
For, to avoid [1] my will in this, I can it
  not forbear.   930
LADY. O God, forgive me, if I do amiss!
  The king by compulsion enforceth me
  this.
MAID. Unto the gods for your estate I
  will not cease to pray,
That you may be a happy queen, and see
  most joyful day.
KING. Come on, my lords; with gladsome
  hearts let us rejoice with glee!
Your music show to joy this deed at the
  request of me!
BOTH. For to obey your grace's words our
  honors do agree.   *Exeunt.*

Enter Ambidexter.

AMBIDEXTER. O the passion of me! Marry,
  as ye say, yonder is a royal court!
There is triumphing and sport upon
  sport,
Such loyal lords, with such lordly exercise,   940
Frequenting such pastime as they can
  devise,
Running at tilt, jousting, with running
  at the ring,
Masking and mumming, with each kind
  of thing,
Such dancing, such singing, with musical
  harmony!
Believe me, I was loath to absent their
  company.
But will you believe? Jesu, what haste
  they made till they were married!
Not for a million of pounds one day
  longer they would have tar[ri]ed!
O, there was a banquet royal and super-
  excellent!
Thousands and thousands at that banquet was spent.
I muse of nothing but how they can be
  married so soon.   950
I care not if I be married before tomorrow at noon,
If marriage be a thing that so may be
  had.

[1] Make void, give up.

[*To a girl in the audience.*] How say you,
  maid? To marry me will ye be glad?
Out of doubt, I believe it is some excellent
  treasure;
Else to the same belongs abundant pleas-
  ure.
Yet with mine ears I have heard some
  say,
"That ever I was married, now cursèd
  be the day!"
Those be they [that] [2] with curst [3] wives
  be matched.
That husband for hawk's meat [4] of [5]
  them is up-snatched.
Head broke with a bedstaff, face all-to
  bescratched—   960
"Knave!" "Slave!" and "Villain!"—a
  coiled coat [6] now and then.
When the wife hath given it, she will say,
  "Alas, good man!"
Such were better unmarried, my masters,
  I trow,
Than all their life after be matched with
  a shrow.[7]

Enter Preparation.

[PREPARATION.] With speed I am sent all
  things to prepare,
My message to do as the king did de-
  clare.
His grace doth mean a banquet to
  make,
Meaning in this place repast for to take.
Well, the cloth shall be laid, and all
  things in readiness,
To court to return when done is my
  business.   970
AMBIDEXTER. A proper man and also fit
For the king's estate to prepare a ban-
  quet!
PREPARATION. What, Ambidexter? Thou
  art not unknown!
A mischief on all good faces, so that I
  curse not mine own!
Now, in the knave's name, shake hands
  with me.
AMBIDEXTER. Well said, goodman pouch-
  mouth; your reverence I see.
I will teach ye, if your manners no better
  be.

[2] Supplied from first edn.
[3] Shrewish.
[4] Something seized greedily.
[5] By.
[6] A beating.
[7] Shrew.

Ah, ye slave, the king doth me a gentleman allow;
Therefore I look that to me ye should
bow.   *Fight.*
PREPARATION. Good Master Ambidexter,
pardon my behavior;   980
For this your deeds you are a knave, for
your labor!
AMBIDEXTER. Why, ye stale counterly [1]
villain, nothing but "knave"? *Fight.*
PREPARATION. I am sorry your mastership
offended I have;
Shake hands, that between us agreement
may be.
I was overshot with myself, I do see.
Let me have your help this furniture to
provide.
The king from this place will not long
abide.   *Set the fruit on the board.*
AMBIDEXTER. Content; it is the thing that
I would wish.
I myself will go fetch one dish.
*Let the Vice fetch a dish of nuts, and let them
fall in the bringing of them in.*
PREPARATION. Cleanly, Master Ambidex-
ter, for fair on the ground they lie. 990
AMBIDEXTER. I will have them up again
by-and-by.
PREPARATION. To see all in readiness I
will put you in trust;
There is no nay, to the court needs I
must.   *Exit Preparation.*
AMBIDEXTER. Have ye no doubt but all
shall be well.—
Marry, sir, as you say, this gear doth
excel!
All things is in a readiness, when they
come hither,
The king's grace and the queen both togither.—
[*To the audience.*] I beseech ye, my masters, tell me, is it not best
That I be so bold as to bid a guest?
He is as honest a man as ever spurred
cow—   1000
My cousin Cutpurse, I mean; I beseech
ye, judge you.
Believe me, cousin, if to be the king's
guest ye could be taken,
I trust that offer will never be for-
saken.
But, cousin, because to that office ye are
not like to come,

[1] Fit for the Counter, a prison.

Frequent your exercises—a horn [2] on
your thumb,
A quick eye, a sharp knife, at hand a
receiver.[3]
But then take heed, cousin, ye be a
cleanly conveyor.
Content yourself, cousin; for this banquet
you are unfit,
When such as I at the same am unworthy
to sit.

Enter King, Queen, and his Train.

KING. My queen and lords, to take re-
past, let us attempt the same.   1010
Here is the place; delay no time, but to
our purpose frame.
QUEEN. With willing hearts your whole
behest we mind for to obey.
ALL. And we, the rest of prince's train, will
do as you do say.   *Sit at the banquet.*
KING. Methink mine ears doth wish the
sound of music's harmony;
Here, for to play before my grace, in place
I would them spy.   *Play at the banquet.*
AMBIDEXTER. They be at hand, sir, with
stick and fiddle;
They can play a new dance, called " Hey-
diddle-diddle."
KING. My queen, perpend. What I pro-
nounce, I will not violate,
But one thing which my heart makes
glad I mind to explicate.
You know in court uptrainéd is a lion
very young;   1020
Of one litter two whelps [4] beside, as yet
not very strong.
I did request one whelp to see and this
young lion fight;
But lion did the whelp convince by
strength of force and might.
His brother whelp, perceiving that the
lion was too good,
And he by force was like to see the other
whelp his [5] blood,
With force to lion he did run, his brother
for to help.
A wonder great it was to see that friendship in a whelp!
So then the whelps between them both
the lion did convince.

[2] A thimble of horn, worn by cutpurses.
[3] A confederate to whom stolen goods were
handed.   [4] Dogs, in this case.
[5] *Whelp his* is an old form of the possessive.

Which thing to see before mine eyes did
glad the heart of prince.
At this tale told, let the Queen weep.
QUEEN. These words to hear makes stilling
tears issue from crystal eyes. 1030
KING. What dost thou mean, my spouse,
to weep for loss of any prize? [1]
QUEEN. No, no, O king, but, as you see,
friendship in brother's whelp;
When one was like to have repulse, the
other yielded help.
And was this favor showed in dogs, to
shame of royal king?
Alack, I wish these ears of mine had not
once heard this thing!
Even so should you, O mighty king, to
brother been a stay,
And not, without offense to you, in such
wise him to slay.
In all assays it was your part his cause
to have defended,
And whosoever had him misused to have
them reprehended.
But faithful love was more in dog than it
was in your grace. 1040
KING. O cursed caitiff, vicious and vile,
I hate thee in this place!
This banquet is at an end; take all these
things away.
Before my face thou shalt repent the
words that thou dost say.
O wretch most vile, didst thou the cause
of brother mine so tender
The loss of him should grieve thy heart,
he being none offender?
It did me good his death to have—so will
it to have thine!
What friendship he had at my hands, the
same even thou shalt find.
I give consent, and make a vow, that
thou shalt die the death!
By Cruel's sword and Murder fell even
thou shalt lose thy breath.
Ambidexter, see with speed to Cruelty
ye go; 1050
Cause him hither to approach, Murder
with him also.
AMBIDEXTER. I ready am for to fulfill if
that it be your grace's will.
KING. Then naught oblite [2] my message
given; absent thyself away.
AMBIDEXTER. Then in this place I will no
longer stay.—

[Aside to the Queen.] If that I durst, I
would mourn your case;
But, alas! I dare not, for fear of his
grace. *Exit Ambidex[ter].*
KING. Thou cursed Jill! [3] by all the gods I
take an oath and swear
That flesh of thine these hands of mine
in pieces small could tear!
But thou shalt die by dent [4] of sword;
there is no friend ne fee
Shall find remorse at prince's hand to
save the life of thee! 1060
QUEEN. O mighty king and husband mine,
vouchsafe to hear me speak,
And license give to spouse of thine her
patient mind to break.
For tender love unto your grace my
words I did so frame;
For pure love doth heart of king me vio-
late and blame.
And to your grace is this offense that I
should purchase death?
Then cursed time that I was queen to
shorten this my breath!
Your grace doth know by marriage true
I am your wife and spouse,
And one to save another's health at
troth-plight made our vows.
Therefore, O king, let loving queen at
thy hand find remorse;
Let pity be a mean to quench that cruel
raging force, 1070
And pardon, plight [5] from prince's mouth,
yield grace unto your queen,
That amity with faithful zeal may ever
be us between.
KING. Ah, caitiff vile! to pity thee my
heart it is not bent;
Ne yet to pardon your offense it is not
mine intent.
FIRST LORD. Our mighty prince, with
humble suit of your grace this I crave,
That this request it may take place, your
favor for to have.
Let mercy yet abundantly the life of
queen preserve,
Sith she in most obedient wise your
grace's will doth serve.
As yet your grace but while with her hath
had cohabitation,
And sure this is no desert why to yield
her indignation. [6] 1080

[1] Contest.   [2] Forget.
[3] Wench.   [5] Plighted, pledged.
[4] Dint.   [6] Indignity.

Therefore, O king, her life prolong, to joy
   her days in bliss!

SECOND LORD. Your grace shall win immortal fame in granting unto this.

She is a queen whose goodly hue excels
   the royal rose,

For beauty bright Dame Nature she a
   large gift did dispose.

For comeliness who may compare? Of
   all she bears the bell.[1]

This should give cause to move your
   grace to love her very well.

Her silver breast in those your arms to
   sing the songs of love—

Fine qualities most excellent to be in her
   you prove;

A precious pearl of price to prince, a
   jewel passing all!

Therefore, O king, to beg remorse on both
   my knees I fall;   1090

To grant her grace to have her life, with
   heart I do desire.

KING. You villains twain, with raging
   force ye set my heart on fire!

If I consent that she shall die, how dare
   ye crave her life?

You two to ask this at my hand doth
   much enlarge my strife.

Were it not for shame, you two should
   die, that for her life do sue.

But favor mine from you is gone, my
   lords, I tell you true.

I sent for Cruelty of late; if he would
   come away,

I would commit her to his hands his
   cruel part to play.

Even now I see where he doth come; it
   doth my heart delight.

Enter Cruelty and Murder.

CRUELTY. Come, Murder, come; let us go
   forth with might;   1100

Once again the king's commandment we
   must fulfill.

MURDER. I am contented[2] to do it with a
   good will.

KING. Murder and Cruelty, for both of
   you I sent,

With all festination your offices to frequent.

Lay hold on the queen; take her to your
   power,

And make her away within this hour!

Spare for no fear; I do you full permit.
So I from this place do mean for to flit.

BOTH. With courageous hearts, O king, we
   will obey.

KING. Then come, my lords, let us depart
   away.   1110

BOTH THE LORDS. With heavy hearts we
   will do all your grace doth say.

             Exeunt King and Lord[s].

CRUELTY. Come, lady and queen, now are
   you in our handling;

In faith, with you we will use no dandling.

MURDER. With all expedition I, Murder,
   will take place;

Though thou be a queen, ye be under my
   grace.

QUEEN. With patience I will you both
   obey.[3]

CRUELTY. No more words, but go with us
   away!

QUEEN. Yet before I die, some psalm to
   God let me sing.

BOTH. We be content to permit you that
   thing.

QUEEN. Farewell, you ladies of the court,
   with all your masking hue!   1120

I do forsake these broidered guards, and
   all the fashions new,

The court and all the courtly train,
   wherein I had delight;

I banished am from happy sport, and all
   by spiteful spite;

Yet with a joyful heart to God a psalm
   I mean to sing,

Forgiving all [men][4] and the king of
   each kind of thing. *Sing,[5] and exeunt.*

Enter Ambidexter weeping.

AMBIDEXTER. Ah, ah, ah, ah! I cannot
   choose but weep for the queen!

Nothing but mourning now at the court
   there is seen.

O, O, my heart, my heart! O, my bum
   will break!

Very grief so torments me that scarce I
   can speak.

Who could but weep for the loss of such
   a lady?   1130

That cannot I do, I swear by mine honesty.

But, Lord! so the ladies mourn, crying
   "Alack!"

---

[1] Wins the prize.   [2] Original reads *contended.*
[3] Original interchanges *obey* and *away* of next
line.   [4] Supplied by Manly.   [5] The song is lost.

Nothing is worn now but only black.
I believe all [the] [1] cloth in Watling
  Street to make gowns would not serve.
If I make a lie, the devil let ye sterve! [2]
All ladies mourn, both young and old;
There is not one that weareth a point's
  worth of gold.
There is a sort for fear for the king do
  pray
That would have him dead, by the Mass,
  I dare say. [3]
What a king was he that hath used such
  tyranny!   1140
He was akin to Bishop Bonner, [4] I think
  verily!
For both their delights was to shed blood,
But never intended to do any good.
Cambises put a judge to death—that was
  a good deed;
But to kill the young child was worse to
  proceed;
To murder his brother, and then his own
  wife—
So help me God and halidom, it is pity
  of his life!
Hear ye? I will lay twenty thousand
  pound
That the king himself doth die by some
  wound;
He hath shed so much blood that his will
  be shed.   1150
If it come to pass, in faith, then he is
  sped.

Enter the King, without a goun, a sword
  thrust up into his side, bleeding.

KING. Out, alas! What shall I do? My
  life is finished!
Wounded I am by sudden chance; my
  blood is minishéd.
Gog's heart, what means might I make
  my life to preserve?
Is there naught to be my help, nor is
  there naught to serve?
Out upon the court and lords that there
  remain!
To help my grief in this my case will
  none of them take pain?

[1] Supplied by Hazlitt.   [2] Die.
[3] *I.e.*, there is a group who pray for the king
out of fear, but wish him dead.
[4] Bishop of London, who was hated because
of his persecution of the Protestants.

Who but I, in such a wise, his death's
  wound could have got?
As I on horseback up did leap, my sword
  from scabbard shot,
And ran me thus into the side, as you
  right well may see.   1160
A marvel's chance unfortunate, that in
  this wise should be!
I feel myself a-dying now; of life bereft
  am I;
And Death hath caught me with his
  dart; for want of blood I spy. [5]
Thus, gasping, here on ground I lie; for
  nothing I do care.
A just reward for my misdeeds my death
  doth plain declare.
            Here let him quake and stir.
AMBIDEXTER. How now, noble king? Pluck
  up your heart!
What, will you die, and from us depart?
Speak to me and ye be alive!
He cannot speak. But behold, how with
  Death he doth strive.   [*King dies.*]
Alas, good king! Alas, he is gone! 1170
The devil take me if for him I make any
  moan.
I did prognosticate of his end, by the
  Mass!
Like as I did say, so is it come to pass.
I will be gone. If I should be found here,
That I should kill him it would appear.
For fear with his death they do me
  charge,
Farewell, my masters, I will go take
  barge.
I mean to be packing; now is the tide;
Farewell, my masters, I will no longer
  abide!   *Exit Ambidexter.*

Enter three Lords.

FIRST LORD. Behold, my lord, it is even
  so as he to us did tell.   1180
His grace is dead, upon the ground, by
  dint of sword most fell.
SECOND LORD. As he in saddle would have
  leaped, his sword from sheath did go,
Goring him up into the side. His life was
  ended so.
THIRD LORD. His blood so fast did issue
  out that naught could him prolong;
Yet, before he yielded up the ghost, his
  heart was very strong.

[5] Spyre, 'spire, expire(?).

FIRST LORD. A just reward for his misdeeds the God above hath wrought,
For certainly the life he led was to be
counted naught.
SECOND LORD. Yet a princely burial he
shall have, according to his estate;
And more of him here at this time we
have not to dilate.
THIRD LORD. My lords, let us take him
up and carry him away.   1190
BOTH. Content we are with one accord to
do as you do say.   *Exeunt all.*

EPILOGUE

Right gentle audience, here have you pe-
rused
The tragical history of this wicked king.
According to our duty, we have not refused,
But to our best intent expressed every-
thing.
We trust none is offended for this our
doing.
Our author craves likewise, if he have
squared [1] amiss,
By gentle admonition to know where
the fault is.
His good will shall not be neglected to
amend the same.

Shaped, built.

Praying all to bear, therefore, with this
simple deed
Until the time serve a better he may
frame;   10
Thus yielding you thanks, to end we
decreed
That you so gently have suffered us to
proceed,
In such patient wise as to hear and see,
We can but thank ye therefor; we can do
no more, we!

As duty binds us, for our noble queen let
us pray,
And for her honorable council, the truth
that they may use,
To practice justice and defend her grace
each day;
To maintain God's word they may not
refuse,
To correct all those that would her grace
and grace's laws abuse;
Beseeching God over us she may reign
long,   20
To be guided by truth and defended from
wrong.

AMEN, QUOD [2] THOMAS PRESTON.

[2] Quoth, said.

THOMAS NORTON AND THOMAS SACKVILLE

The Tragedy of Gorboduc is historically significant as the first regular English tragedy and the first English play to be written almost entirely in blank verse. Acted by the law students of the Inner Temple during their Christmas festival in 1561/2 and again before Queen Elizabeth at Whitehall Palace, January 18, 1561/2, it was surreptitiously printed by William Griffith in 1565, but an authorized edition was issued by John Day in 1570. In 1590 Edward Allde published a reprint of the edition of 1565. The title page of the 1565 edition informs us that three acts were written by Thomas Norton and the last two by Thomas Sackville. Howard Baker in his *Induction to Tragedy* (Baton Rouge, 1939) has concluded, however, after studying the somewhat divergent political philosophies of the two authors, that the first scene was probably Sackville's and the last Norton's, with the rest of the play done as the title page stated. Sara R. Watson, in *"Gorboduc* and the Theory of Tyrannicide" (*MLR*, 1939), reached a similar conclusion independently. The probable bibliographical history of the text was studied by I. B. Cauthen in *"Gorboduc, Ferrex, and Porrex:* The First Two Quartos," in *Essays on Shakespeare and the Elizabethan Drama in Honor of Hardin Craig* (Columbia, Missouri, 1962).

Thomas Norton was born in London in 1532, was admitted to the Inner Temple in 1555, became a successful lawyer, and served as a member of Parliament for Gatton, Berwick, and London at various times from 1558 to 1580. He married a daughter of the great Archbishop Thomas Cranmer. In 1570 he was made an M. A. by Cambridge University, which was probably the scene of his undergraduate training. In the next year he was appointed Remembrancer of the City of London. He was an active anti-Roman Catholic in Parliament, went to Rome in 1579 to collect information against the Catholics, and two years later was appointed official censor of Catholic citizens. For his examinations and tortures of Catholics he acquired the nickname "Rackmaster-General" and was committed to the Tower of London for a short time in 1584 on a charge of treason because of his rabid Puritan attacks on the episcopacy. Much of his time, however, was devoted to literature. He wrote Latin and English poetry, including versions of twenty-eight psalms printed in the Psalter of Sternhold and Hopkins. He produced a number of controversial pamphlets against the Roman Catholics and a political tract on a Roman Catholic rebellion under Elizabeth which, because of the theme of *Gorboduc*, has some special interest. He also translated a number of works, including Calvin's *Institutes of the Christian Religion*. But his Puritan fanaticism eventually led him, in his later years, to open hostility toward the stage. He died in 1584.

Thomas Sackville was born at Buckhurst, Surrey, about 1530. He was the son of Sir Richard Sackville, a first cousin to Anne Boleyn, mother of Queen Elizabeth. He became a barrister at the Inner Temple, and received his M.A. from Cambridge in 1571. In 1563 he had contributed to *The Mirror for Magistrates* his well-known "Induction" and "The Complaint of Henry, Duke of Buckingham," which gave promise of a brilliant literary future. But he soon forsook literature for a political career. In 1558, 1559, and 1563 he was an M.P. for Westmoreland, East Grimstead, and Aylesbury. Then, after an extensive tour of Europe, where he suffered an unpleasant but brief imprisonment for his rashly expressed Protestant opinions, he was called home by his father's death and became heir to a vast estate. Almost immediately he was knighted and simultaneously created Baron Buckhurst. Queen Elizabeth's favor advanced him rapidly on a career of public service. He took part in various diplomatic missions at home and abroad, especially in France and the Netherlands; in 1591 he was elected Chancellor of Oxford University; and in 1599 took Lord Burghley's place as Lord High Treasurer. His rival for the Chancellorship, and one of his chief political opponents, had been the dashing young Earl of Essex, one of Elizabeth's later favorites, and in 1601, as Lord High Steward, he perhaps derived some satisfaction from pronouncing the sentence of execution on the younger man for treason. This event may well have aroused echoes in his memory of the days when he had helped to write *Gorboduc*, with its warning against civil war. Under James I he became a member of the Privy Council in 1603 and was also made Lord High Treasurer for life. In 1604 he was created Earl of Dorset. Still politically active, he died suddenly at the Council table at Whitehall in 1608.

Although *Gorboduc* must indubitably be classified as a tragedy, it has equal claims to being regarded as a history or chronicle play, and is discussed at some length as such by Ribner in his *The English History Play in the Age of Shakespeare*. Ribner concludes that the highest form of the historical play, illustrated by *Gorboduc*, emerged from the medieval morality. Although Bishop John Bale's *King John* was the first real English history play following this tradition, *Gorboduc* was completely free from pure morality abstractions in its characters.

The primary, if not the only, source for the story of *Gorboduc* as used by the collaborators was Geoffrey of Monmouth's famous *Historia Regum Britanniae*, or *History of the Kings of Britain*, completed about 1148 and of course available in sixteenth century editions. In 1910 H. A. Watt (*BUW*) had suggested that the probable source of the play was a 1559 edition of Richard Grafton's *Chronicle* of England; but in 1957 R. A. Peters pointed out ("*Gorboduc* and Grafton's *Chronicle*," *NQ*) that no such edition of Grafton is known, and that the only chronicle that could have been used was one of the twin editions of John Hardynge's *Chronicle* of 1543/44. Moreover, the story of Gorboduc in these editions is told in the first part of the chronicle, the verse portion by Hardynge, and not in Grafton's prose continuation. In any case it is apparent that the playwrights, like the chroniclers, accepted the apocryphal story as authentic history. The play is replete with allusions to the Trojan War and its religious mythology is consistently classical, not Christian. Some of the names, however, have morality overtones, since "Eubulus" means "good counsellor," and "Philander" "the friend of man." "Dordon," however, seems to have no such abstract significance, nor do "Arostus," "Hermon," and "Tyndar," the evil counsellors against whom the good counsellors are balanced. Ribner suggests that the evil counsellors would be easily recognized by an Elizabethan audience as descendants of the old Vice, and that the destruction of each of the protagonists, through accepting the wrong advice, is also typical of the moralities. Other names seem to be of ancient British origin. Ribner also believes that Sackville was probably responsible for the choice of the subject matter of the play because of his well-known historical interests, shown in his collecting material for *The Mirror for Magistrates*.

The arguments among critics and scholars as to the extent of the influence of Seneca upon *Gorboduc* have been long and often rather violent, from Sir Philip Sidney's compliment, "climbing to the heighth of Seneca his style," onward. The modern debate has ranged from the pioneer studies of H. Schmidt in 1887 and J. W. Cunliffe in 1893 and 1912 (who perhaps overestimated its importance) to those of Howard Baker (*Induction to Tragedy*, Louisiana State University Press, 1940) and Peter Ure ("Some Differences between Senecan and Elizabethan Tragedy," *DUJ*, 1948), who are inclined to minimize its influence and stress native medieval influences instead. More moderate points of view have been expressed by F. L. Lucas in *Seneca and Elizabethan Tragedy* (Cambridge, 1922); Marvin T. Herrick in "The Senecan Influence in *Gorboduc*" (*Studies in Speech and Drama in Honor of Alexander M. Drummond*, Ithaca, 1944);

W. A. Armstrong in *The Influence of Seneca and Machiavelli on the Elizabethan Tyrant* (1948); Henry W. Wells in "Senecan Influence on Elizabethan Tragedy" (*SAB*, 1944); and Paul Becquet in "L'influence de Sénèque sur *Gorboduc*" in *Études Anglaises* for 1961.

Certain aspects of *Gorboduc* are clearly Senecan.   In form the Senecan influence imposed a sense of structure which was previously absent.   The division into five acts, each of which is divided into two balanced scenes and ends with a classical chorus which sums up the action and draws a moral from it, derives from the Senecan drama. In style the presence of Seneca is also felt in the generally formal and rhetorical quality, the long didactic and sententious speeches with their balanced and periodic structure, the stichomythic dialogue, the use of a Nuntius (or messenger) to announce events of consequence and often of violence and sensational horror rather than to show them on stage, and the emphasis on revenge as a tragic motif.   On the other hand, there is less emphasis on the Stoic attitude toward life and suffering than in many later plays.   And the dumb show which opens each act and presents in pantomime the symbolical import of the coming action is not Senecan.   These dumb shows have generally been traced back to the *intermedii*, or allegorical representations between the acts, of Italian tragedy; but another theory traces them to the pageantry of the medieval miracle play and similar spectacles, as does Dieter Mehl in *The Elizabethan Dumb Show* (London, 1965), following the theories of George R. Kernodle (*From Art to Theater*, University of Chicago Press, 1947).   In 1935 B. R. Pearson also surveyed the whole subject of "The Dumb-Show in Elizabethan Drama" (*RES*), beginning with *Gorboduc*.   In the play's departure from the three dramatic unities of time, place, and action, it also fails to follow the rigid Senecan model.   The fifth act especially, in its apparent violation of even the basic unity of action, seems to be a notable departure from the classical principle.   Willard Farnham, however, in *The Medieval Heritage of Elizabethan Tragedy*, has suggested that perhaps the authors regarded the whole British kingdom as being a sort of tragic protagonist rather than any of the individual characters.

The tragic theory of Norton and Sackville seems to come close to that of the Aristotelian tragic flaw, since Gorboduc and his sons bring on their own destruction by errors of judgment and ambition.   As Farnham points out, the catastrophes of the leading characters differ from the endings of most medieval morality plays, in which the hero realized his mistakes before it was too late, repented, and, after a period of penance, was restored to happiness and salvation.   The theory differed even more from that of the medieval Wheel of Fortune and the "*De Casibus*" stories, according to which great men fell from their places not so much from some weakness or error in themselves as from the arbitary operation of a capricious and malicious fate.   (See S. F. Johnson, "The Tragic Hero in Early Elizabethan Drama," *Studies in English Renaissance Drama, in Honor of Karl J. Holzknecht*, New York University Press, 1959.)   At the end of Gorboduc, however, as Ribner reminds us, there is an affirmation of faith in God's ultimate goodness and divine plan for the universe, if only man will take heed of His warnings.

A warning constitutes the basic purpose of *Gorboduc:* a veiled but clear caution to Queen Elizabeth of the dangers of civil war in its most terrible aspects if she dies without a definite provision for succession to the throne.   Past history is used for secular purposes: to advocate to the ruler the value of listening to advisers and of following Parliamentary principles.   Just a year before the performance of the play, the House of Commons had presented to Elizabeth a petition to limit the succession in such a way; in fact, Baker has suggested the possibility that the Calvinist Norton was himself the author of the petition, and has assigned the more monarchical and Italianate parts of the play to the more traveled young courtier, Sackville.   S. A. Small, in "The Political Import of the Norton Half of *Gorbobuc*" (*PMLA*, 1931), has argued that Norton in the first part of the play took the Puritan and Huguenot position and drove home the lesson that rulers should obey the good advice of statesmen in matters affecting the welfare of the realm, and thus prepared the way for Sackville to ask for the limitation of the succession in the last act. Sara Watson has further suggested that Norton was following the doctrine enunciated by the Puritan Christopher Goodman in *How Superior Powers Ought to Be Obeyed* (1558), to the effect that even kings need not be obeyed and in fact may be forcibly removed from office if they do not follow God's will in seeking the welfare of the people. Gertrude C. Reese, in "The Question of the Succession in Elizabethan Drama" (*UTSE*, 1942), has concluded that *Gorboduc* upholds the sanctity of an established succession confirmed by Parliament against any "pretended right," and has speculated that the playwrights were supporting the claim of the Protestant Lady Katherine Grey of the Suffolk line, named to succeed Elizabeth in the contested will of Henry VIII.

Although in their adoption of blank verse as their prosodic medium the dramatists made a revolutionary advance, Baker has called attention to the fact that a few months earlier Norton had rendered into blank verse two passages from Virgil quoted by Calvin in his *Institutes*. Baker has also maintained that the form did not come from an imitation of unrhymed classical meters, but had its roots in medieval poetry. Moody E. Prior, in *The Language of Tragedy*, has made the most thorough examination of the play from the prosodic, rhetorical, and poetic point of view, and has pointed out that earlier uses of blank verse, beginning with Surrey's original experiment in his translation of the *Aeneid*, all apparently had the epic in mind—an air which clung to English dramatic blank verse for some time. Thomas Newton in his collection of previous translations of Seneca in *Seneca His Ten Tragedies* in 1581 still regarded "fourteeners" "as the proper English equivalent for the Latin tragic style," and blank verse did not become really established for some years. Though the verse of Norton and Sackville may seem stiff today, it is "the deliberate formality of pattern which is the principal adornment of the language." Prior offers examples of the use of repetition, alliteration, rhetorical schemes, "sentences," and so on, and ends by calling attention to the almost complete and surprising absence of metaphor. R. Y. Turner, in "Pathos and the *Gorboduc* Tradition" (*HLQ*, 1962), has also discussed various rhetorical devices in Elizabethan drama beginning with *Gorboduc*, especially the lament. Somehow critics seem generally to have overlooked the peculiar use of irregularly placed rhymes in the opening speeches of the play, and of various rhymed stanza forms in the choruses. These more lyrical effects are supported by the introduction of the music of various instruments into the dumb shows (violins followed by cornets, flutes, hautboys, and finally drums and flutes together). The music was usually consistent with the atmosphere of the coming action, but J. H. Summerwell has questioned the appropriateness of violins in the opening dumb show ("Violence and/or Violins," *NQ*, 1957). Inasmuch as this dumb show introduces the first "wild men" to the English theater proper, although the type had appeared before in sword dances and mummings (Robert H. Goldsmith, "The Wild Man on the English Stage," *MLR*, 1958), Summerwell may be right in expecting wilder music than violins would seem to provide in this show. (F. W. Sternfeld, in *Music in Shakespearean Tragedy*, London, 1963, has surveyed the use of both instrumental and vocal music from *Gorboduc* to Shakespeare.)

This text of the play is based on the second edition, 1570, as reprinted by J. W. Cunliffe in his *Early Classical Tragedies* (Oxford, 1912).

THE TRAGEDY OF [GORBODUC;
OR OF][1] FERREX AND PORREX[2]

BY

THOMAS NORTON AND THOMAS SACKVILLE

THE P[RINTER] TO THE READER

Where this tragedy was for furniture of part of the grand Christmas in the Inner Temple first written about nine years ago by the Right Honorable Thomas, now Lord Buckhurst, and by T. Norton, and after showed before her majesty, and never intended by the authors thereof to be published; yet one W. G., getting a copy thereof at some young man's hand that lacked a little money and much discretion, in [10 the last great plague, an[no] 1565, about five years past, while the said lord was out of England, and T. Norton far out of London, and neither of them both made privy, put it forth exceedingly corrupted—even as if by means of a broker, for hire, he should have enticed into his house a fair maid and done her villainy, and after all-to[3] bescratched her face, torn her apparel, bewrayed and disfigured her, and then [20 thrust her out of doors dishonested. In such plight, after long wandering, she came at length home to the sight of her friends, who scant knew her but by a few tokens and marks remaining. They—the authors, I mean—though they were very much displeased that she so ran abroad without leave, whereby she caught her shame, as many wantons do, yet seeing the case, as it is, remediless, have for common hon- [30 esty and shamefastness new appareled, trimmed, and attired her in such form as she was before. In which better form since she hath come to me, I have harbored her for her friends' sake and her own; and I do not doubt her parents, the authors, will not now be discontent that she go abroad among you, good readers, so it be in honest company. For she is by my encouragement and others' somewhat less ashamed of [40 the dishonesty done to her, because it was by fraud and force. If she be welcome among you, and gently entertained, in favor of the house from whence she is descended and of her own nature courteously disposed to offend no man, her friends will thank you for it. If not, but that she shall be still reproached with her former mishap, or quarreled at by envious persons, she, poor gentlewoman, will surely play [50 Lucrece's part, and of herself die for shame; and I shall wish that she had tarried still at home with me, where she was welcome, for she did never put me to more charge but this one poor black gown lined with white that I have now given her to go abroad among you withal.

THE ARGUMENT OF THE TRAGEDY [4]

Gorboduc, King of Britain, divided his realm in his lifetime to his sons, Ferrex and Porrex. The sons fell to dissension. The younger killed the elder. The mother, that more dearly loved the elder, for revenge killed the younger. The people, moved with the cruelty of the fact,[5] rose

Same Was Showed on Stage before the Queen's Majesty, about Nine Years Past, viz., the xviii Day of January, 1561. By the Gentlemen of the Inner Temple. Seen and Allowed, etc."

[1] Added by Adams. The title of the 1565 edn. runs: "The Tragedy of Gorboduc, Whereof Three Acts Were Written by Thomas Norton, and the Two Last by Thomas Sackville."

[2] The title continues: "Set Forth without Addition or Alteration but Altogether As the

[3] Thoroughly.

[4] In the original this argument, or synopsis of plot, is printed on the back of the title-page.

[5] Deed.

in rebellion and slew both father and mother. The nobility assembled and most terribly destroyed the rebels. And [10 afterwards, for want of issue of the prince, whereby the succession of the crown became uncertain, they fell to civil war, in which both they and many of their issues were slain, and the land for a long time almost desolate and miserably wasted.

THE NAMES OF THE SPEAKERS

GORBODUC, *King of Great Britain.*
VIDENA, *queen and wife to King Gorboduc.*
FERREX, *elder son to King Gorboduc.*
PORREX, *younger son to King Gorboduc.*
CLOTYN, *Duke of Cornwall.*
FERGUS, *Duke of Albany.*
MANDUD, *Duke of Logris.*
GWENARD, *Duke of Cumberland.*
EUBULUS, *secretary to the king.*
AROSTUS, *a counselor to the king.*
DORDAN, *a counselor assigned by the king to his eldest son, Ferrex.*

PHILANDER, *a counselor assigned by the king to his youngest son, Porrex. Both being of the old king's counsel before.*
HERMON, *a parasite remaining with Ferrex.*
TYNDAR, *a parasite remaining with Porrex.*
NUNTIUS, *a messenger of the elder brother's death.*
NUNTIUS, *a messenger of Duke Fergus' rising in arms.*
MARCELLA, *a lady of the queen's privy-chamber.*
CHORUS, *four ancient and sage men of Britain.*

[SCENE: *Britain.*

TIME: *Legendary.*]

THE ORDER OF THE DUMB SHOW BEFORE THE FIRST ACT, AND THE SIGNIFICATION THEREOF

First, the music of violins began to play, during which came in upon the stage six wild men, clothed in leaves. Of whom the first bare in his neck a fagot of small sticks, which they all, both severally and together, assayed with all their strength to break; but it could not be broken by them. At the length one of them pulled out one of the sticks and brake it, and the rest, plucking out all the other sticks one after another, did easily break them, the same being severed which, being conjoined, they had before attempted in vain. After they had this done, they departed the stage, and the music ceased. Hereby was signified that a state knit in unity doth continue strong against all force, but, being divided, is easily destroyed; as befell upon Duke Gorboduc dividing his land to his two sons, which he before held in monarchy, and upon the dissension of the brethren, to whom it was divided.

ACTUS PRIMUS. SCENA PRIMA.

[*A room in Gorboduc's palace.*]

Viden[a], Ferrex.

VID. The silent night, that brings the quiet pause
From painful travails of the weary day,
Prolongs my careful[1] thoughts, and makes me blame
The slow Aurore, that so for love or shame
Doth long delay to show her blushing face;
And now the day renews my griefful plaint.

FER. My gracious lady and my mother dear,
Pardon my grief for your so grievéd mind
To ask what cause tormenteth so your heart.

VID. So great a wrong and so unjust despite,　　10
Without all cause against all course of kind![2]

[1] Full of care.
[2] Nature.

FER. Such causeless wrong and so unjust despite
May have redress or, at the least, revenge.
VID. Neither, my son; such is the froward will,
The person such, such my mishap and thine.
FER. Mine know I none, but grief for your distress.
VID. Yes, mine for thine, my son.   A father? No.
In kind a father, not in kindliness.
FER. My father? Why, I know nothing at all
Wherein I have misdone unto his grace.   20
VID. Therefore, the more unkind to thee and me.
For, knowing well, my son, the tender love
That I have ever borne and bear to thee,
He, grieved thereat, is not content alone
To spoil thee of my sight, my chiefest joy;
But thee, of thy birthright and heritage,
Causeless, unkindly, and in wrongful wise,
Against all law and right, he will bereave:
Half of his kingdom he will give away.
FER. To whom?
VID.   Even to Porrex, his younger son;   30
Whose growing pride I do so sore suspect
That, being raised to equal rule with thee,
Methinks I see his envious heart to swell,
Filled with disdain and with ambitious hope.
The end the gods do know, whose altars I
Full oft have made in vain of cattle slain
To send the sacred smoke to heaven's throne,
For thee, my son, if things do so succeed,
As now my jealous mind misdeemeth sore.
FER. Madam, leave care and careful plaint for me.   40
Just hath my father been to every wight;
His first unjustice he will not extend
To me, I trust, that give no cause thereof;
My brother's pride shall hurt himself, not me.
VID. So grant the gods! But yet thy father so

Hath firmly fixed his unmoved mind
That plaints and prayers can no whit avail;
For those have I assayed, but even this day
He will endeavor to procure assent
Of all his council to his fond devise.[1]   50
FER. Their ancestors from race to race[2] have borne
True faith to my forefathers and their seed;
I trust they eke will bear the like to me.
VID. There resteth all. But if they fail thereof,
And if the end bring forth an ill success,
On them and theirs the mischief shall befall,
And so I pray the gods requite it them;
And so they will, for so is wont to be.
When lords and trusted rulers under kings,
To please the present fancy of the prince,   60
With wrong transpose the course of governance,
Murders, mischief, or civil sword at length,
Or mutual treason, or a just revenge,
When right succeeding line returns again,
By Jove's just judgment and deserved wrath,
Brings them to cruel and reproachful death,
And roots their names and kindreds from the earth.
FER. Mother, content you, you shall see the end.
VID. The end? Thy end, I fear! Jove end me first!   [Exeunt.]

ACTUS PRIMUS. SCENA SECUNDA.

[The council chamber in Gorboduc's palace.]

Gorboduc, Arostus, Philander, Eubulus.

GORB. My lords, whose grave advice and faithful aid
Have long upheld my honor and my realm,
And brought me to this age from tender years,
Guiding so great estate with great renowm,

1 Foolish design.
2 From generation to generation.

Now more importeth me [1] than erst [2] to use
Your faith and wisdom, whereby yet I reign;
That, when by death my life and rule shall cease,
The kingdom yet may with unbroken course
Have certain prince, by whose undoubted right
Your wealth and peace may stand in quiet stay;   10
And eke that they whom nature hath prepared
In time to take my place in princely seat,
While in their father's time their pliant youth
Yields to the frame of skillful governance,
May so be taught and trained in noble arts
As what their fathers, which have reigned before,
Have with great fame derived down to them,
With honor they may leave unto their seed;
And not be thought, for their unworthy life,
And for their lawless swerving out of kind,   20
Worthy to lose what law and kind them gave;
But that they may preserve the common peace,
The cause that first began and still maintains
The lineal course of kings' inheritance,
For me, for mine, for you, and for the state
Whereof both I and you have charge and care.
Thus do I mean to use your wonted faith
To me and mine and to your native land.
My lords, be plain without all wry [3] respect
Or poisonous craft to speak in pleasing wise,   30
Lest, as the blame of ill-succeeding things
Shall light on you, so light the harms also.

Aros. Your good acceptance so, most noble king,
Of such our faithfulness as heretofore
We have employed in duties to your grace
And to this realm, whose worthy head you are,
Well proves that neither you mistrust at all,
Nor we shall need in boasting wise to show
Our truth to you, nor yet our wakeful care
For you, for yours, and for our native land.   40
Wherefore, O king—I speak as one for all,
Sith [4] all as one do bear you egal [5] faith—
Doubt not to use our counsels and our aids,
Whose honors, goods, and lives are whole avowed
To serve, to aid, and to defend your grace.
Gorb. My lords, I thank you all? This is the case:
Ye know, the gods, who have the sovereign care
For kings, for kingdoms, and for commonweals,
Gave me two sons in my more lusty age,
Who now in my decaying years are grown   50
Well towards riper state of mind and strength
To take in hand some greater princely charge.
As yet they live and spend [their] [6] hopeful days
With me and with their mother here in court.
Their age now asketh other place and trade,
And mine also doth ask another change—
Theirs to more travail, mine to greater ease.
When fatal death shall end my mortal life,
My purpose is to leave unto them twain
The realm divided into two sundry parts: 60
The one, Ferrex, mine elder son, shall have;

[1] It is more important for me.
[2] Formerly.   [3] Twisted, dissembled.

[4] Since.   [5] Equal.   [6] From 1565 edn.

The other shall the younger, Porrex, rule.
That both my purpose may more firmly
    stand,
And eke that they may better rule their
    charge,
I mean forthwith to place them in the
    same,
That in my life they may both learn to
    rule,
And I may joy to see their ruling well.
This is, in sum, what I would have ye
    weigh:
First, whether ye allow my whole devise,
And think it good for me, for them, for
    you,   70
And for our country, mother of us all;
And if ye like it and allow it well,
Then for their guiding and their gov-
    ernance
Show forth such means of circumstance
As ye think meet to be both known and
    kept.
Lo, this is all. Now tell me your advice.
Aros. And this is much, and asketh great
    advice.
But for my part, my sovereign lord and
    king,
This do I think: your majesty doth know
How under you, in justice and in
    peace,   80
Great wealth and honor long we have
    enjoyed,
So as we cannot seem with greedy minds
To wish for change of prince or gov-
    ernance;
But, if we like your purpose and devise,
Our liking must be deeméd to proceed
Of rightful reason and of heedful care,
Not for ourselves, but for the common
    state,
Sith our own state doth need no better
    change.
I think in all as erst your grace hath
    said.
First, when you shall unload your aged
    mind   90
Of heavy care and troubles manifold,
And lay the same upon my lords, your
    sons,
Whose growing years may bear the bur-
    den long—
And long I pray the gods to grant it
    so!—
And in your life, while you shall so behold

Their rule, their virtues, and their noble
    deeds,
Such as their kind behighteth [1] to us all,
Great be the profits that shall grow
    thereof.
Your age in quiet shall the longer last;
Your lasting age shall be their longer
    stay;   100
For cares of kings that rule as you have
    ruled,
For public wealth and not for private joy,
Do waste man's life and hasten crooked
    age,
With furrowed face and with enfeebled
    limbs,
To draw on creeping death a swifter pace.
They two, yet young, shall bear the
    parted reign
With greater ease than one, now old,
    alone
Can wield the whole, for whom much
    harder is
With lessened strength the double weight
    to bear.
Your eye, your counsel, and the grave
    regard   110
Of father, yea, of such a father's name,
Now at beginning of their sundered reign,
When is the hazard of their whole success,
Shall bridle so their force of youthful
    heats
And so restrain the rage of insolence,
Which most assails the young and noble
    minds,
And so shall guide and train in tempered
    stay
Their yet green bending wits with rev-
    erend awe,
As—now inured with virtues at the
    first—
Custom, O king, shall bring delightful-
    ness.   120
By use of virtue, vice shall grow in hate.
But, if you so dispose it that the day
Which ends your life shall first begin
    their reign,
Great is the peril what will be the end,
When such beginning of such liberties,
Void of such stays as in your life do lie,
Shall leave them free to randon [2] of their
    will,
An open prey to traitorous flattery,
The greatest pestilence of noble youth;

[1] Promises.   [2] Random. rove.

Which peril shall be past if, in your
    life,   130
Their tempered youth with aged father's
    awe
Be brought in ure [1] of skillful stayédness;
And, in your life, their lives disposéd so
Shall length your noble life in joyfulness.
Thus think I that your grace hath wisely
    thought,
And that your tender care of common
    weal [2]
Hath bred this thought, so to divide
    your land,
And plant your sons to bear the present
    rule,
While you yet live to see their ruling well,
That you may longer live by joy
    therein.   140
What furder [3] means behooveful are and
    meet,
At greater leisure may your grace devise,
When all have said, and when we be
    agreed
If this be best, to part the realm in twain,
And place your sons in present govern-
    ment;
Whereof, as I have plainly said my mind,
So would I hear the rest of all my lords.
PHIL. In part I think as hath been said
    before;
In part, again, my mind is otherwise.
As for dividing of this realm in twain, 150
And lotting out the same in egal parts
To either of my lords, your grace's sons,
That think I best for this your realm's
    behoof,
For profit and advancement of your sons,
And for your comfort and your honor eke.
But so to place them while your life do
    last,
To yield to them your royal governance,
To be above them only in the name
Of father, not in kingly state also,
I think not good for you, for them, nor
    us.   160
This kingdom, since the bloody civil field
Where Morgan slain did yield his con-
    quered part
Unto his cousin's sword in Camberland,
Containeth all that whilom [4] did suffice
Three noble sons of your forefather
    Brute;

So your two sons it may suffice also.
The mo [5] the stronger, if they gree [6] in
    one.
The smaller compass that the realm doth
    hold,
The easier is the sway thereof to weld,[7]
The nearer justice to the wrongéd
    poor,   170
The smaller charge, and yet enough for
    one.
And when the region is divided so
That brethren be the lords of either part,
Such strength doth nature knit between
    them both,
In sundry bodies by conjoinéd love,
That, not as two, but one of doubled
    force,
Each is to other as a sure defense;
The nobleness and glory of the one
Doth sharp the courage of the other's
    mind,
With virtuous envy to contend for
    praise.   180
And such an egalness hath nature made
Between the brethren of one father's
    seed
As an unkindly wrong it seems to be
To throw the brother subject under feet
Of him whose peer he is by course of
    kind;
And nature, that did make this egalness,
Oft so repineth at so great a wrong
That oft she raiseth up a grudging grief
In younger brethren at the elder's state,
Whereby both towns and kingdoms have
    been razed,   190
And famous stocks of royal blood de-
    stroyed.
The brother, that should be the brother's
    aid,
And have a wakeful care for his defense,
Gapes for his death, and blames the
    lingering years
That draw not forth his end with faster
    course;
And, oft impatient of so long delays,
With hateful slaughter he prevents [8] the
    fates,
And heaps a just reward for brother's
    blood,
With endless vengeance, on his stock for
    aye.

[1] Use, practice.   [3] Further.   [5] More.   [7] Wield, govern.
[2] Welfare.   [4] Formerly.   [6] Agree.   [8] Anticipates.

Such mischiefs here are wisely met
　　withal,　　　　　　　　　　　　200
If egal state may nourish egal love,
Where none hath cause to grudge at
　　other's good.
But now the head to stoop beneath them
　　both,
Ne [1] kind, ne reason, ne good order bears.
And oft it hath been seen, where nature's
　　course
Hath been perverted in disordered wise,
When fathers cease to know that they
　　should rule,
The children cease to know they should
　　obey;
And often over-kindly tenderness
Is mother of unkindly stubbornness. 210
I speak not this in envy or reproach,
As if I grudged the glory of your sons,
Whose honor I beseech the gods increase;
Nor yet as if I thought there did remain
So filthy cankers in their noble breasts,
Whom I esteem—which is their greatest
　　praise—
Undoubted children of so good a king.
Only I mean to show by certain rules,
Which kind hath graft within the mind
　　of man,
That nature hath her order and her
　　course,　　　　　　　　　　　　220
Which, being broken, doth corrupt the
　　state
Of minds and things, even in the best of
　　all.
My lords, your sons, may learn to rule
　　of you;
Your own example in your noble court
Is fittest guider of their youthful years.
If you desire to see some present joy
By sight of their well ruling in your life,
See them obey—so shall you see them
　　rule.
Whoso obeyeth not with humbleness
Will rule with outrage and with inso-
　　lence.　　　　　　　　　　　　230
Long may they rule, I do beseech the
　　gods,
But long may they learn, ere they begin
　　to rule.
If kind and fates would suffer,[2] I would
　　wish
Them aged princes and immortal kings.
Wherefore, most noble king, I well assent

Between your sons that you divide your
　　realm,
And, as in kind, so match them in degree.
But, while the gods prolong your royal
　　life,
Prolong your reign; for thereto [3] live you
　　here,
And therefore have the gods so long
　　forborne　　　　　　　　　　　240
To join you to themselves, that still you
　　might
Be prince and father of our commonweal.
They, when they see your children ripe
　　to rule,
Will make them room, and will remove
　　you hence,
That yours, in right ensuing of your life,
May rightly honor your immortal name.
EUB. Your wonted true regard of faithful
　　hearts
Makes me, O king, the bolder to presume
To speak what I conceive within my
　　breast,
Although the same do not agree at all 250
With that which other here my lords
　　have said,
Nor which yourself have seeméd best to
　　like.
Pardon I crave, and that my words be
　　deemed
To flow from hearty zeal unto your grace,
And to the safety of your commonweal.
To part your realm unto my lords, your
　　sons,
I think not good for you, ne yet for them,
But worst of all for this our native land.
Within one land one single rule is best:
Divided reigns do make divided
　　hearts,　　　　　　　　　　　260
But peace preserves the country and the
　　prince.
Such is in man the greedy mind to reign,
So great is his desire to climb aloft,
In worldly stage the stateliest parts to
　　bear,
That faith and justice and all kindly love
Do yield unto desire of sovereignty,
Where egal state doth raise an egal hope
To win the thing that either would attain.
Your grace rememb'reth how in passéd
　　years
The mighty Brute, first prince of all this
　　land.　　　　　　　　　　　　270

[1] Not, nor.　　　　　　　　[2] Allow.

[3] For this purpose.

Possessed the same and ruled it well in
  one;
He, thinking that the compass did suf-
  fice
For his three sons three kingdoms eke to
  make,
Cut it in three, as you would now in
  twain.
But how much British blood hath since
  been spilt
To join again the sundered unity,
What princes slain before their timely
  hour,
What waste of towns and people in the
  land,
What treasons heaped on murders and
  on spoils—
Whose just revenge even yet is scarcely
  ceased—   280
Ruthful remembrance is yet raw in mind.
The gods forbid the like to chance again!
And you, O king, give not the cause
  thereof.
My Lord Ferrex, your elder son, per-
  haps—
Whom kind and custom gives a rightful
  hope
To be your heir and to succeed your
  reign—
Shall think that he doth suffer greater
  wrong
Than he perchance will bear, if power
  serve.
Porrex, the younger, so upraised in state,
Perhaps in courage will be raised also. 290
If flattery then, which fails not to assail
The tender minds of yet unskillful youth,
In one shall kindle and increase disdain,
And envy in the other's heart inflame,
This fire shall waste their love, their lives,
  their land,
And ruthful ruin shall destroy them both.
I wish not this, O king, so to befall,
But fear the thing that I do most abhor.
Give no beginning to so dreadful end;
Keep them in order and obedience,   300
And let them both, by now obeying you,
Learn such behavior as beseems their
  state—
The elder, mildness in his governance;
The younger, a yielding contentedness.
And keep them near unto your presence
  still,
That they, restrainéd by the awe of you,

May live in compass of well tempered
  stay,
And pass the perils of their youthful
  years.
Your aged life draws on to feebler time,
Wherein you shall less able be to bear
The travails that in youth you have sus-
  tained,   311
Both in your person's and your realm's
  defense.
If planting now your sons in furder parts,
You send them furder from your present
  reach,
Less shall you know how they them-
  selves demean;
Traitorous corrupters of their pliant
  youth
Shall have unspied a much more free
  access;
And, if ambition and inflamed disdain
Shall arm the one, the other, or them
  both,
To civil war or to usurping pride,   320
Late shall you rue that you ne recked [1]
  before.
Good is, I grant, of all to hope the best,
But not to live still [2] dreadless of the
  worst.
So trust the one that the other be fore-
  seen.
Arm not unskillfulness with princely
  power,
But you that long have wisely ruled the
  reins
Of royalty within your noble realm,
So hold them, while the gods for our
  avails [3]
Shall stretch the thread of your pro-
  longéd days.
Too soon he clamb [4] into the flaming
  car,   330
Whose want of skill did set the earth on
  fire.
Time and example of your noble grace
Shall teach your sons both to obey and
  rule.
When time hath taught them, time shall
  make them place,
The place that now is full; and so I pray
Long it remain to comfort of us all.
GORB. I take your faithful hearts in thank-
  ful part.

[1] Did not heed.   [3] Profit.
[2] Always.   [4] Climbed.

But, sith I see no cause to draw my mind
To fear the nature of my loving sons,
Or to misdeem that envy or disdain   340
Can there work hate where nature plant-
   eth love,
In one self purpose do I still abide.
My love extendeth egally to both;
My land sufficeth for them both also.
Humber shall part the marches [1] of their
   realms:
The southern part the elder shall possess;
The northern shall Porrex, the younger,
   rule.
In quiet I will pass mine aged days,
Free from the travail and the painful
   cares   349
That hasten age upon the worthiest kings.
But, lest the fraud, that ye do seem to
   fear,
Of flattering tongues, corrupt their tender
   youth,
And writhe them to the ways of youthful
   lust,
To climbing pride, or to revenging hate,
Or to neglecting of their careful charge
Lewdly to live in wanton recklessness,
Or to oppressing of the rightful cause,
Or not to wreak the wrongs done to the
   poor,
To tread down truth, or favor false
   deceit,
I mean to join to either of my sons   360
Some one of those whose long approved
   faith
And wisdom tried may well assure my
   heart
That mining fraud shall find no way to
   creep
Into their fencéd ears with grave advice.
This is the end; and so I pray you all
To bear my sons the love and loyalty
That I have found within your faithful
   breasts.
AROS. You nor your sons, our sovereign
   lord, shall want
Our faith and service while our lives do
   last.   [*Exeunt.*]

CHORUS

When settled stay doth hold the royal
   throne   370
   In steadfast place, by known and
   doubtless [2] right,

And chiefly when descent on one alone
   Makes single and unparted reign to
   light,
Each change of course unjoints the whole
   estate,
And yields it thrall to ruin by debate.[3]

The strength that, knit by fast accord in
   one,
   Against all foreign power of mighty
   foes,
Could of itself defend itself alone,
   Disjoinéd once, the former force doth
   lose.
The sticks, that sundered brake so soon
   in twain,   380
In fagot bound attempted were in vain.

Oft tender mind that leads the partial eye
   Of erring parents in their children's
   love,
Destroys the wrongly loved child
   thereby.
   This doth the proud son of Apollo
   prove,
Who, rashly set in chariot of his sire,
Inflamed the parchéd earth with heav-
   en's fire.

And this great king, that doth divide
   his land
   And change the course of his descend-
   ing crown,
And yields the reign into his children's
   hand,   390
   From blissful state of joy and great
   renown,
A mirror shall become to princes all,
To learn to shun the cause of such a fall.[4]

THE ORDER AND SIGNIFICATION OF THE DUMB SHOW BEFORE THE SECOND ACT

*First, the music of cornets began to play,
   during which came in upon the stage a
   king accompanied with a number of his
   nobility and gentlemen. And, after he
   had placed himself in a chair of estate
   prepared for him, there came and kneeled
   before him a grave and aged gentleman,
   and offered up a cup unto him of wine
   in a glass, which the king refused. After*

[1] Borders.   [2] Undoubted.

[3] Strife.
[4] None of the choruses are divided into stanzas
in the original.

*him comes a brave and lusty young gentle-
man, and presents the king with a cup
of gold filled with poison, which the king
accepted, and, drinking the same, immediately fell down dead upon the stage,
and so was carried thence away by his
lords and gentlemen, and then the music
ceased. Hereby was signified that, as
glass by nature holdeth no poison, but is
clear and may easily be seen through ne
boweth* [1] by any art, so a faithful counselor holdeth no treason, but is plain and
open, ne yieldeth to any undiscreet affection, but giveth wholesome counsel, which
the ill-advised prince refuseth. The delightful gold filled with poison betokeneth
flattery, which under fair seeming of
pleasant words beareth deadly poison,
which destroyeth* [2] the prince that receiveth it. As befell in the two brethren,
Ferrex and Porrex, who, refusing the
wholesome advice of grave counselors,
credited these young parasites and
brought to themselves death and destruction thereby.*

ACTUS SECUNDUS. SCENA PRIMA.

[*The court of Ferrex.*]

Ferrex, Hermon, Dordan.

FER. I marvel much what reason led the
    king,
My father, thus, without all my desert,
To reave me [3] half the kingdom, which
    by course
Of law and nature should remain to me.
HER. If you with stubborn and untaméd
    pride
Had stood against him in rebelling wise,
Or if with grudging mind you had envied
So slow a sliding of his aged years,
Or sought before your time to haste the
    course
Of fatal death upon his royal head, 10
Or stained your stock with murder of
    your kin,
Some face of reason might perhaps have
    seemed
To yield some likely cause to spoil ye
    thus.

[1] Bendeth.
[2] From 1565 edn. Original reads *destroyed*.
[3] Bereave me of, rob me of.

FER. The wreakful [4] gods pour on my
    cursed head
Eternal plagues and never-dying woes,
The hellish prince adjudge my damned
    ghost
To Tantale's thirst, or proud Ixion's
    wheel,
Or cruel gripe [5] to gnaw my growing
    heart,
To during [6] torments and unquenchéd
    flames,
If ever I conceived so foul a thought, 20
To wish his end of life or yet of reign.
DOR. Ne yet your father, O most noble
    prince,
Did ever think so foul a thing of you;
For he, with more than father's tender
    love,
While yet the fates do lend him life to
    rule—
Who long might live to see your ruling
    well—
To you, my lord, and to his other son,
Lo, he resigns his realm and royalty;
Which never would so wise a prince have
    done
If he had once misdeemed that in your
    heart 30
There ever lodgéd so unkind a thought.
But tender love, my lord, and settled
    trust
Of your good nature and your noble mind
Made him to place you thus in royal
    throne,
And now to give you half his realm to
    guide;
Yea, and that half which, in abounding
    store
Of things that serve to make a wealthy
    realm,
In stately cities, and in fruitful soil,
In temperate breathing of the milder
    heaven,
In things of needful use, which friendly
    sea 40
Transports by traffic from the foreign
    parts,
In flowing wealth, in honor, and in force,
Doth pass the double value of the part
That Porrex hath allotted to his reign.
Such is your case, such is your father's
    love.

[4] Vengeful.   [5] Griffin.   [6] Enduring.

FER. Ah! love, my friends? Love wrongs not whom he loves!

DOR. Ne yet he wrongeth you that giveth you
So large a reign ere that the course of time
Bring you to kingdom by descended right,
Which time perhaps might end your time before.   50

FER. Is this no wrong, say you, to reave from me
My native right of half so great a realm,
And thus to match his younger son with me
In egal power and in as great degree?
Yea, and what son? The son whose swelling pride
Would never yield one point of reverence,
When I, the elder and apparent heir,
Stood in the likelihood to possess the whole;
Yea, and that son which from his childish age
Envieth mine honor and doth hate my life.   60
What will he now do, when his pride, his rage,
The mindful malice of his grudging heart
Is armed with force, with wealth, and kingly state?

HER. Was this not wrong—yea, ill-advised wrong—
To give so mad a man so sharp a sword,
To so great peril of so great mishap,
Wide open thus to set so large a way?

DOR. Alas, my lord, what griefful thing is this,
That of your brother you can think so ill?
I never saw him utter likely sign   70
Whereby a man might see or once misdeem
Such hate of you ne such unyielding pride.
Ill is their counsel, shameful be their end,
That raising such mistrustful fear in you,
Sowing the seed of such unkindly hate,
Travail by treason to destroy you both.
Wise is your brother and of noble hope,
Worthy to wield a large and mighty realm.
So much a stronger friend have you thereby,
Whose strength is your strength if you gree in one.   80

HER. If nature and the gods had pinched so
Their flowing bounty and their noble gifts
Of princely qualities, from you, my lord,
And poured them all at once in wasteful wise
Upon your father's younger son alone,
Perhaps there be [1] that in your prejudice [2]
Would say that birth should yield to worthiness.
But sith in each good gift and princely art
Ye are his match, and, in the chief of all,
In mildness and in sober governance   90
Ye far surmount; and sith there is in you
Sufficing skill and hopeful towardness
To weld the whole and match your elder's praise,
I see no cause why ye should lose the half.
Ne would I wish you yield to such a loss,
Lest your mild sufferance of so great a wrong
Be deemed cowardish and simple dread,
Which shall give courage to the fiery head
Of your young brother to invade the whole.
While yet therefore sticks in the people's mind   100
The loathed wrong of your disheritance;
And ere your brother have, by settled power,
By guileful cloak of an alluring show,
Got him some force and favor in the realm;
And, while the noble queen, your mother, lives,
To work and practice all for your avail,
Attempt redress by arms, and wreak yourself
Upon his life that gaineth by your loss,
Who now to shame of you and grief of us
In your own kingdom triumphs over you.   110
Show now your courage meet for kingly state,
That they which have avowed to spend their goods,
Their lands, their lives and honors in your cause,

[1] Supply *those*.   [2] To your damage.

May be the bolder to maintain your part,
When they do see that coward fear in you
Shall not betray ne fail their faithful
  hearts.
If once the death of Porrex end the strife,
And pay the price of his usurped reign,
Your mother shall persuade [1] the angry
  king.
The lords, your friends, eke shall appease
  his rage;   120
For they be wise, and well they can
  foresee
That ere long time your aged father's
  death
Will bring a time when you shall well
  requite
Their friendly favor or their hateful spite,
Yea, or their slackness to advance your
  cause.
" Wise men do not so hang on passing
  state
Of present princes, chiefly in their age,
But they will further cast their reaching
  eye,
To view and weigh the times and reigns
  to come." [2]
Ne is it likely, though the king be
  wroth,   130
That he yet will or that the realm will
  bear
Extreme revenge upon his only son;
Or, if he would, what one is he that dare
Be minister to such an enterprise?
And here you be now placéd in your
  own,
Amid your friends, your vassals, and your
  strength.
We shall defend and keep your person
  safe,
Till either counsel turn his tender mind,
Or age or sorrow end his weary days.
But, if the fear of gods and secret
  grudge   140
Of nature's law, repining at the fact,
Withhold your courage from so great
  attempt,
Know ye that lust of kingdoms hath no
  law.
The gods do bear and well allow in kings
The thinges [3] they abhor in rascal routs. [4]

[1] Win over.
[2] Quotation marks were commonly used to
call attention to sententious sayings.
[3] Dissyllabic.   [4] The rabble.

"When kings on slender quarrels run to
  wars,
And then in cruel and unkindly wise
Command thefts, rapes, murders of in-
  nocents,
The spoil of towns, ruins of mighty
  realms,
Think you such princes do suppose them-
  selves   150
Subject to laws of kind and fear of gods?"
Murders and violent thefts in private
  men
Are heinous crimes and full of foul re-
  proach,
Yet none offense, but decked with glo-
  rious name
Of noble conquests in the hands of kings.
But, if you like not yet so hot devise,
Ne list to take such vantage of the time,
But, though with peril of your own estate,
You will not be the first that shall invade,
Assemble yet your force for your de-
  fense,   160
And for your safety stand upon your
  guard.
DOR. O heaven! was there ever heard or
  known
So wicked counsel to a noble prince?
Let me, my lord, disclose unto your
  grace
This heinous tale, what mischief it con-
  tains:
Your father's death, your brother's, and
  your own—
Your present murder and eternal shame.
Hear me, O king, and suffer not to sink
So high a treason in your princely breast.
FER. The mighty gods forbid that ever I
Should once conceive such mischief in
  my heart.   171
Although my brother hath bereft my
  realm,
And bear perhaps to me an hateful mind,
Shall I revenge it with his death there-
  fore?
Or shall I so destroy my father's life
That gave me life? The gods forbid, I
  say.
Cease you to speak so any more to me;
Ne you, my friend, with answer once
  repeat
So foul a tale. In silence let it die.
What lord or subject shall have hope at
  all   180

That under me they safely shall enjoy
Their goods, their honors, lands, and
    liberties,
With whom neither one only brother
    dear
Ne father dearer could enjoy their lives?
But, sith I fear my younger brother's
    rage,
And sith perhaps some other man may
    give
Some like advice, to move his grudging
    head
At mine estate—which counsel may per-
    chance
Take greater force with him than this
    with me—
I will in secret so prepare myself   190
As, if his malice or his lust to reign
Break forth in arms or sudden violence,
I may withstand his rage and keep mine
    own.   [*Exeunt Ferrex and Hermon.*]
DOR. I fear the fatal time now draweth on
When civil hate shall end the noble line
Of famous Brute and of his royal seed.
Great Jove, defend [1] the mischiefs now
    at hand!
O, that the secretary's wise advice
Had erst been heard when he besought
    the king
Not to divide his land, nor send his
    sons   200
To further parts from presence of his
    court,
Ne yet to yield to them his governance!
Lo, such are they now in the royal throne
As was rash Phaëton in Phœbus' car;
Ne then the fiery steeds did draw the
    flame
With wilder randon [2] through the kindled
    skies
Than traitorous counsel now will whirl
    about
The youthful heads of these unskillful
    kings.
But I hereof their father will inform;
The reverence of him perhaps shall
    stay   210
The growing mischiefs while they yet are
    green.
If this help not, then woe unto them-
    selves,
The prince, the people, the divided land!
    [*Exit.*]

[1] Prevent.   [2] Impetuosity.

ACTUS SECUNDUS. SCENA SECUNDA.

[*The court of Porrex.*]

Porrex, Tyndar, Philander.

POR. And is it thus? And doth he so
    prepare
Against his brother as his mortal foe?
And now while yet his aged father lives?
Neither regards he him, nor fears he me?
War would he have? And he shall have
    it so!
TYN. I saw, myself, the great preparéd
    store
Of horse, of armor, and of weapons there;
Ne bring I to my lord reported tales
Without the ground of seen and searchéd
    truth.
Lo, secret quarrels run about his court 10
To bring the name of you, my lord, in
    hate.
Each man, almost, can now debate the
    cause,
And ask a reason of so great a wrong—
Why he, so noble and so wise a prince,
Is, as unworthy, reft his heritage,
And why the king, misled by crafty
    means,
Divided thus his land from course of
    right.
The wiser sort hold down their griefful
    heads;
Each man withdraws from talk and
    company
Of those that have been known to favor
    you.   20
To hide the mischief of their meaning
    there,
Rumors are spread of your preparing
    here.
The rascal numbers of unskillful sort
Are filled with monstrous tales of you
    and yours.
In secret I was counseled by my friends
To haste me thence, and brought you,
    as you know,
Letters from those that both can truly
    tell
And would not write unless they knew it
    well.
PHIL. My lord, yet ere you move unkindly
    war,
Send to your brother to demand the
    cause.   30

Perhaps some traitorous tales have filled
  his ears
With false reports against your noble
  grace;
Which, once disclosed, shall end the
  growing strife
That else, not stayed with wise foresight
  in time,
Shall hazard both your kingdoms and
  your lives.
Send to your father eke; he shall appease
Your kindled minds and rid you of this
  fear.
POR. Rid me of fear? 1 fear him not at all;
Ne will to him ne to my father send.
If danger were for one to tarry there,   40
Think ye it safety to return again?
In mischiefs such as Ferrex now intends,
The wonted courteous laws to messengers
Are not observed, which in just war they
  use.
Shall I so hazard any one of mine?
Shall I betray my trusty friends to him,
That have disclosed his treason unto me?
Let him entreat that fears; I fear him nct.
Or shall I to the king, my father, send?
Yea, and send now, while such a mother
  lives,   50
That loves my brother and that hateth
  me?
Shall I give leisure, by my fond ¹ delays,
To Ferrex to oppress me all unware?
I will not; but I will invade his realm
And seek the traitor prince within his
  court.
Mischief for mischief is a due reward.
His wretched head shall pay the worthy
  price
Of this his treason and his hate to me.
Shall I abide, and treat, and send, and
  pray,
And hold my yelden ² throat to traitor's
  knife,   60
While I, with valiant mind and conquer-
  ing force,
Might rid myself of foes and win a realm?
Yet rather, when I have the wretch's
  head,
Then to the king, my father, will I send.
The bootless case may yet appease his
  wrath;
If not, I will defend me as I may.
          [Exeunt Porrex and Tyndar.]

¹ Foolish.   ² Yielded, submissive.

PHIL. Lo, here the end of these two youth-
  ful kings,
The father's death, the ruin of their
  realms!
"O most unhappy state of counselors,
That light on so unhappy lords and times
That neither can their good advice be
  heard,   71
Yet must they bear the blames of ill
  success."
But I will to the king, their father, haste,
Ere this mischief come to the likely end;
That, if the mindful wrath of wreakful
  gods—
Since mighty Ilion's fall not yet appeased
With these poor remnants of the Trojan
  name—
Have not determined by unmovéd fate
Out of this realm to raze the British line,
By good advice, by awe of father's name,
By force of wiser lords, this kindled
  hate   81
May yet be quenched ere it consume us
  all.   [Exit.]

CHORUS
When youth, not bridled with a guiding
    stay,
  Is left to randon of their own delight,
And welds whole realms by force of
    sovereign sway,
  Great is the danger of unmastered
    might,
Lest skilless rage throw down, with
    headlong fall,
  Their lands, their states, their lives,
    themselves and all.

When growing pride doth fill the swelling
    breast,
  And greedy lust ³ doth raise the climb-
    ing mind,   90
O, hardly may the peril be repressed.
  Ne fear of angry gods, ne lawes' ⁴ kind,
Ne country's care can firéd hearts re-
    strain,
When force hath arméd envy and disdain.

When kings of foresight ⁵ will neglect the
    rede ⁶
  Of best advice, and yield to pleasing
    tales

³ Desire.   ⁵ Of set purpose.
⁴ Dissyllabic.   ⁶ Counsel.

That do their fancies' noisome humor
    feed,
Ne reason nor regard of right avails.
Succeeding heaps of plagues shall teach,
    too late,   99
To learn the mischiefs of misguided state.

Foul fall the traitor false that under-
    mines
    The love of brethren to destroy them
        both.
Woe to the prince that pliant ear inclines
    And yields his mind to poisonous tale
        that floweth
From flattering mouth!   And woe to
    wretched land
That wastes itself with civil sword in
    hand!

Lo, thus it is, poison in gold to take,
And wholesome drink in homely cup
    forsake.

The Order and Signification of the
    Dumb Show before the Third Act

First, the music of flutes began to play, dur-
*   ing which came in upon the stage a*
*   company of mourners, all clad in black,*
*   betokening death and sorrow to ensue*
*   upon the ill-advised misgovernment and*
*   dissension of brethren, as befell upon the*
*   murder of Ferrex by his younger brother.*
*   After the mourners had passed thrice*
*   about the stage, they departed, and then*
*   the music ceased.*

Actus Tertius. Scena Prima.

[*The court of Gorboduc.*]

Gorboduc, Eubulus, Arostus, Philander,
*   Nuntius.*[1]

Gorb. O cruel fates, O mindful wrath of
    gods,
    Whose vengeance neither Simois' stained
        streams
    Flowing with blood of Trojan princes
        slain,
    Nor Phrygian fields made rank with
        corpses dead
    Of Asian kings and lords, can yet ap-
        pease;
    Ne slaughter of unhappy Priam's race,
    Nor Ilion's fall, made level with the soil,

[1] Last two enter later.

Can yet suffice; but still continued rage
Pursues our lives, and from the farthest
    seas
Doth chase the issues of destroyed
    Troy.   10
"O, no man happy till his end be seen."
If any flowing wealth and seeming joy
In present years might make a happy
    wight,
Happy was Hecuba, the woefullest wretch
That ever lived to make a mirror of;
And happy Priam, with his noble sons;
And happy I, till now, alas, I see
And feel my most unhappy wretched-
    ness.
Behold, my lords, read ye this letter
    here.
Lo, it contains the ruin of our realm, 20
If timely speed provide not hasty help.
Yet, O ye gods, if ever woeful king
Might move ye, kings of kings, wreak it
    on me
And on my sons, not on this guiltless
    realm!
Send down your wasting flames from
    wrathful skies,
To reave me and my sons the hateful
    breath.
Read, read, my lords; this is the matter
    why
I called ye now to have your good advice.

The letter from Dordan, the counselor of the
*   elder prince.*

Eubulus readeth the letter.

"My sovereign lord, what I am loath to
    write,
But loathest am to see, that I am
    forced   30
By letters now to make you understand.
My Lord Ferrex, your eldest son, misled
By traitorous fraud of young untempered
    wits,
Assembleth force against your younger
    son,
Ne can my counsel yet withdraw the heat
And furious pangs of his inflaméd head.
Disdain, saith he, of his disheritance
Arms him to wreak the great pretended
    wrong
With civil sword upon his brother's life.
If present help do not restrain this
    rage,   40

This flame will waste your sons, your
    land, and you.
Your majesty's faithful and most humble
    subject,

                   DORDAN."
AROS. O king, appease your grief and stay
    your plaint;
    Great is the matter, and a woeful case,
    But timely knowledge may bring timely
        help.
    Send for them both unto your presence
        here.
    The reverence of your honor, age, and
        state,
    Your grave advice, the awe of father's
        name,
    Shall quickly knit again this broken
        peace.
    And, if in either of my lords, your sons, 50
    Be such untaméd and unyielding pride
    As will not bend unto your noble hests; [1]
    If Ferrex, the elder son, can bear no peer,
    Or Porrex, not content, aspires to more
    Than you him gave above his native
        right,
    Join with the juster side; so shall you
        force
    Them to agree, and hold the land in
        stay.
EUB. What meaneth this?   Lo, yonder
    comes in haste
    Philander from my lord, your younger
    son.

           [*Enter Philander.*]

GORB. The gods send joyful news!
PHIL.   The mighty Jove   60
    Preserve your majesty, O noble king.
GORB. Philander, welcome! But how doth
    my son?
PHIL. Your son, sir, lives, and healthy I
    him left.
    But yet, O king, the want of lustful
        health
    Could not be half so griefful to your
        grace
    As these most wretched tidings that I
        bring.
GORB. O heavens, yet more? Not end of
    woes to me?
PHIL. Tyndar, O king, came lately from
    the court

[1] Behests, commands.

Of Ferrex to my lord, your younger son,
And made report of great preparéd
    store   70
For war, and saith that it is wholly meant
Against Porrex, for high disdain that he
Lives now a king, and egal in degree
With him that claimeth to succeed the
    whole,
As by due title of descending right.
Porrex is now so set on flaming fire,
Partly with kindled rage of cruel wrath,
Partly with hope to gain a realm thereby,
That he in haste prepareth to invade 79
His brother's land, and with unkindly war
Threatens the murder of your elder son;
Ne could I him persuade that first he
    should
Send to his brother to demand the cause,
Nor yet to you to stay this hateful strife.
Wherefore, sith there no more I can be
    heard,
I come myself now to inform your grace,
And to beseech you, as you love the life
And safety of your children and your
    realm,
Now to employ your wisdom and your
    force
To stay this mischief ere it be too late. 90
GORB. Are they in arms?   Would he not
    send to me?
Is this the honor of a father's name?
In vain we travail to assuage their minds,
As if their hearts, whom neither brother's
    love,
Nor father's awe, nor kingdom's cares
    can move,
Our counsels could withdraw from raging
    heat.
Jove slay them both, and end the curséd
    line.
For, though perhaps fear of such mighty
    force
As I, my lords, joined with your noble
    aids,
May yet raise, shall repress their present
    heat,   100
The secret grudge and malice will remain;
The fire, not quenched, but kept in close
    restraint,
Fed still within, breaks forth with double
    flame.
Their death and mine must pease [2] the
    angry gods.

[2] Appease.

PHIL. Yield not, O king, so much to weak
  despair;
  Your sons yet live, and long, I trust,
  they shall.
If fates had taken you from earthly life
Before beginning of this civil strife,
Perhaps your sons in their unmastered
  youth,
Loose from regard of any living wight, 110
Would run on headlong, with unbridled
  race,
To their own death and ruin of this
  realm.
But, sith the gods, that have the care for
  kings,
Of things and times dispose the order so
That in your life this kindled flame
  breaks forth,
While yet your life, your wisdom, and
  your power
May stay the growing mischief, and
  repress
The fiery blaze of their enkindled heat,
It seems—and so ye ought to deem
  thereof—
That loving Jove hath tempered so the
  time   120
Of this debate to happen in your days,
That you yet living may the same ap-
  pease,
And add it to the glory of your latter
  age,
And they your sons may learn to live in
  peace.
Beware, O king, the greatest harm of all,
Lest by your wailful plaints your has-
  tened death
Yield larger room unto their growing
  rage.
Preserve your life, the only hope of stay.
And, if your highness herein list to use
Wisdom or force, counsel or knightly
  aid,   130
Lo, we, our persons, powers, and lives
  are yours.
Use us till death, O king; we are your
  own.
EUB. Lo, here the peril that was erst fore-
  seen,
  When you, O king, did first divide your
  land,
  And yield your present reign unto your
  sons.
But now, O noble prince, now is no time

To wail and plain,[1] and waste your woeful
  life;
Now is the time for present good advice.
Sorrow doth dark the judgment of the
  wit.
"The heart unbroken and the courage
  free   140
From feeble faintness of bootless despair
Doth either rise to safety or renowm
By noble valure [2] of unvanquished mind,
Or yet doth perish in more happy sort."
Your grace may send to either of your
  sons
Some one both wise and noble personage,
Which with good counsel and with
  weighty name
Of father shall present before their eyes
Your hest, your life, your safety, and
  their own,
The present mischief of their deadly
  strife.   150
And, in the while, assemble you the force
Which your commandment and the
  speedy haste
Of all my lords here present can prepare.
The terror of your mighty power shall
  stay
The rage of both, or yet of one at least.

[Enter Nuntius.]

NUN. O king, the greatest grief that ever
  prince did hear,
That ever woeful messenger did tell,
That ever wretched land hath seen be-
  fore,
I bring to you: Porrex, your younger son,
With sudden force invaded hath the
  land   160
That you to Ferrex did allot to rule,
And with his own most bloody hand he
  hath
His brother slain, and doth possess his
  realm.
GORB. O heavens, send down the flames of
  your revenge!
  Destroy, I say, with flash of wreakful
  fire
  The traitor son, and then the wretched
  sire!
  But let us go, that yet perhaps I may
  Die with revenge and pease the hateful
  gods.   *[Exeunt.]*

[1] Complain.   [2] Valor, worth.

CHORUS

The lust of kingdom knows no sacred
    faith,
    No rule of reason, no regard of
        right,   170
No kindly love, no fear of heaven's
    wrath,
    But, with contempt of gods and man's
        despite,
Through bloody slaughter doth prepare
    the ways
To fatal scepter and accursed reign.
The son so loathes the father's lingering
    days,
    Ne dreads his hand in brother's blood
        to stain.
O wretched prince, ne dost thou yet
    record
    The yet fresh murthers done within
        the land
Of thy forefathers, when the cruel sword
Bereft Morgan his life with cousin's
    hand?   180
Thus fatal plagues pursue the guilty race
    Whose murderous hand, imbrued with
        guiltless blood,
Asks vengeance still before the heaven's
    face,
    With endless mischiefs on the cursèd
        brood.
The wicked child thus brings to woeful
    sire
    The mournful plaints to waste his very
        life.
Thus do the cruel flames of civil fire
    Destroy the parted reign with hateful
        strife;
And hence doth spring the well from
    which doth flow
The dead black streams of mourning,
    plaints, and woe.   190

THE ORDER AND SIGNIFICATION OF THE
    DUMB SHOW BFFORE THE FOURTH
    ACT

First, the music of hautboys began to play,
    during which there came forth from un-
    der the stage, as though out of hell,
    three Furies, Alecto, Megæra, and Tisi-
    phone, clad in black garments sprinkled
    with blood and flames, their bodies girt
    with snakes, their heads spread with
    serpents instead of hair, the one bear-

ing in her hand a snake, the other a
    whip, and the third a burning firebrand,
    each driving before them a king and a
    queen, which, moved by Furies, unnat-
    urally had slain their own children. The
    names of the kings and queens were
    these: Tantalus, Medea, Athamas, Ino,
    Cambises, Althea. After that the Furies
    and these had passed about the stage
    thrice, they departed, and then the music
    ceased. Hereby was signified the un-
    natural murders to follow; that is to
    say, Porrex slain by his own mother,
    and of King Gorboduc and Queen
    Viden[a], killed by their own subjects.

ACTUS QUARTUS. SCENA PRIMA.

[A room in Gorboduc's palace.]

Viden[a] sola.

VID. Why should I live, and linger forth my
    time
In longer life to double my distress?
O me, most woeful wight, whom no mishap
Long ere this day could have bereavéd
    hence!
Mought [1] not these hands, by fortune or by
    fate,
Have pierced this breast, and life with iron
    reft?
Or in this palace here, where I so long
Have spent my days, could not that happy
    hour
Once, once have happed, in which these
    hugy frames
With death by fall might have oppressèd
    me?   10
Or should not this most hard and cruel soil,
So oft where I have pressed my wretched
    steps,
Sometime had ruth of mine accursèd life
To rend in twain, [and] [2] swallow me
    therein?
So had my bones possessèd now in peace
Their happy grave within the closèd
    ground,
And greedy worms had gnawn this pinéd
    heart
Without my feeling pain; so should not now
This living breast remain the ruthful tomb
Wherein my heart, yelden to death, is
    gravéd; [3]   20

[1] Might.
[2] Supplied from 1565 edn.   [3] Buried.

Nor dreary thoughts, with pangs of pining grief,
My doleful mind had not afflicted thus.
O my beloved son! O my sweet child!
My dear Ferrex, my joy, my life's delight!
Is my beloved son, is my sweet child,
My dear Ferrex, my joy, my life's delight,
Murdered with cruel death?   O hateful wretch!
O heinous traitor both to heaven and earth!
Thou, Porrex, thou this damnéd deed hast wrought;
Thou, Porrex, thou shalt dearly by [1] the same.   30
Traitor to kin and kind, to sire and me,
To thine own flesh, and traitor to thyself!
The gods on thee in hell shall wreak their wrath,
And here in earth this hand shall take revenge
On thee, Porrex, thou false and caitiff wight.
If after blood so eager were thy thirst,
And murderous mind had so possessed thee,
If such hard heart of rock and stony flint
Lived in thy breast that nothing else could like [2]
Thy cruel tyrant's thought but death and blood,   40
Wild savage beasts, mought not their slaughter serve
To feed thy greedy will, and in the midst
Of their entrails to stain thy deadly hands
With blood deserved, and drink thereof thy fill?
Or if naught else but death and blood of man
Mought please thy lust, could none in Britain land—
Whose heart betorn out of his panting breast
With thine own hand, or work what death thou wouldest—
Suffice to make a sacrifice to pease
That deadly mind and murderous thought in thee,   50
But he who in the selfsame womb was wrapped,
Where thou in dismal hour receivedst life?
Or if needs, needs thy hand must slaughter make,
Moughtest thou not have reached a mortal wound,

[1] Aby; pay the penalty for.   [2] Please.

And with thy sword have pierced this cursed womb
That the accursed Porrex brought to light,
And given me a just reward therefor?
So Ferrex yet sweet life mought have enjoyed
And to his aged father comfort brought,
With some young son in whom they both might live.   60
But whereunto waste I this ruthful speech,
To thee that hast thy brother's blood thus shed?
Shall I still think that from this womb thou sprung,
That I thee bare, or take thee for my son?
No, traitor, no; I thee refuse for mine.
Murderer, I thee renounce; thou art not mine.
Never, O wretch, this womb conceived thee,
Nor never bode [3] I painful throes for thee.
Changeling to me thou art, and not my child,   69
Nor to no wight that spark of pity knew.
Ruthless, unkind, monster of nature's work,
Thou never sucked the milk of woman's breast,
But from thy birth the cruel tiger's teats
Have nursed thee; nor yet of flesh and blood
Formed is thy heart, but of hard iron wrought;
And wild and desert woods bred thee to life.
But canst thou hope to scape my just revenge,
Or that these hands will not be wroke [4] on thee?
Dost thou not know that Ferrex' mother lives,
That loved him more dearly than herself?   80
And doth she live, and is not venged on thee?   [Exit.]

ACTUS QUARTUS.   SCENA SECUNDA.

[The court of Gorboduc.]

Gorboduc, Arostus, Eubulus, Porrex, Marcella. [5]

GORB.   We marvel much whereto this ling'ring stay
   Falls out so long.   Porrex unto our court,
   By order of our letters, is returned,

[3] Suffered.   [5] Wreaked, avenged.
[4] Last three enter later.

And Eubulus received from us behest,[1]
At his arrival here, to give him charge
Before our presence straight to make re-
pair;
And yet we have no word whereof he
stays.

AROS. Lo, where he comes, and Eubulus
with him.

[*Enter Eubulus and Porrex.*]

EUB. According to your highness' hest to
me,
Here have I Porrex brought, even in such
sort   10
As from his wearied horse he did alight,
For that your grace did will such haste
therein.

GORB. We like and praise this speedy will
in you
To work the thing that to your charge
we gave.
Porrex, if we so far should swerve from
kind,
And from those bounds which law of
nature sets,
As thou hast done by vile and wretched
deed,
In cruel murder of thy brother's life,
Our present hand could stay no longer
time,
But straight should bathe this blade in
blood of thee   20
As just revenge of thy detested crime.
No, we should not offend the law of
kind,
If now this sword of ours did slay thee
here;
For thou hast murdered him whose
heinous death
Even nature's force doth move us to re-
venge
By blood again; and justice forceth us
To measure death for death, thy due
desert.
Yet sithens [2] thou art our child, and sith
as yet
In this hard case what word thou canst
allege
For thy defense by us hath not been
heard,   30
We are content to stay our will for that

Which justice bids us presently to work,
And give thee leave to use thy speech at
full,
If aught thou have to lay for thine excuse.

POR. Neither, O king, I can or will deny
But that this hand from Ferrex life hath
reft—
Which fact how much my doleful heart
doth wail,
O, would it mought as full appear to
sight
As inward grief doth pour it forth to me!
So yet perhaps, if ever ruthful heart,   40
Melting in tears within a manly breast,
Through deep repentance of his bloody
fact,
If ever grief, if ever woeful man
Might move regret with sorrow of his
fault,
I think the torment of my mournful case,
Known to your grace, as I do feel the
same,
Would force even Wrath herself to pity
me.
But as the water, troubled with the mud,
Shows not the face which else the eye
should see,
Even so your ireful mind with stirréd
thought   50
Cannot so perfectly discern my cause.
But this unhap, amongst so many heaps,[3]
I must content me with, most wretched
man,
That to myself I must reserve my woe
In pining thoughts of mine accurséd fact,
Since I may not show here my smallest
grief,
Such as it is, and as my breast endures,
Which I esteem the greatest misery
Of all mishaps that fortune now can send.
Not that I rest in hope with plaint and
tears   60
To purchase life; for to the gods I clepe [4]
For true record of this my faithful
speech:
Never this heart shall have the thought-
ful dread
To die the death that by your grace's
doom,
By just desert, shall be pronounced to me;
Nor never shall this tongue once spend
the speech

---

[1] Suggested by Thorndike; all preceding edns.
have *by hest*.
[2] Since (probably pronounced as one syllable).

[3] Among so many heaps (of unhaps). *Cf.* V,
ii, 109.
[4] Call.

Pardon to crave, or seek by suit to live.
I mean not this as though I were not
   touched
With care of dreadful death, or that I
   held
Life in contempt, but that I know the
   mind   70
Stoops to no dread, although the flesh be
   frail.
And for my guilt, I yield the same so
   great
As in myself I find a fear to sue
For grant of life.
GORB.   In vain, O wretch,
   thou showest
A woeful heart! Ferrex now lies in grave,
Slain by thy hand.
POR.   Yet this, O father,
   hear,
And then I end. Your majesty well
   knows
That when my brother Ferrex and my-
   self
By your own hest were joined in gov-
   ernance
Of this your grace's realm of Britain
   land,   80
I never sought nor travailed for the same;
Nor by myself nor by no friend I
   wrought,
But from your highness' will alone it
   sprung,
Of your most gracious goodness bent to
   me.
But how my brother's heart even then
   repined
With swollen disdain against mine egal
   rule,
Seeing that realm which by descent
   should grow
Wholly to him allotted half to me!
Even in your highness' court he now re-
   mains,
And with my brother then in nearest
   place,   90
Who can record what proof thereof was
   showed,
And how my brother's envious heart ap-
   peared.
Yet I that judgéd it my part to seek
His favor and good will, and loath to
   make
Your highness know the thing which
   should have brought

Grief to your grace and your offense to
   him,
Hoping my earnest suit should soon have
   won
A loving heart within a brother's breast,
Wrought in that sort that for a pledge
   of love
And faithful heart he gave to me his
   hand.   100
This made me think that he had ban-
   ished quite
All rancor from his thought, and bare to
   me
Such hearty love as I did owe to him.
But, after once we left your grace's court,
And from your highness' presence lived
   apart,
This egal rule still, still did grudge him so
That now those envious sparks, which
   erst lay raked
In living cinders of dissembling breast,
Kindled so far within his heart disdain
That longer could he not refrain from
   proof   110
Of secret practice to deprive me life
By poison's force, and had bereft me so,
If mine own servant, hired to this fact
And moved by truth with hate to work
   the same,
In time had not bewrayed [1] it unto me.
When thus I saw the knot of love unknit,
All honest league and faithful promise
   broke,
The law of kind and truth thus rent in
   twain,
His heart on mischief set, and in his
   breast
Black treason hid, then, then did I de-
   spair   120
That ever time could win him friend to
   me;
Then saw I how he smiled with slaying
   knife
Wrapped under cloak; then saw I deep
   deceit
Lurk in his face and death prepared for
   me.
Even nature moved me then to hold my
   life
More dear to me than his, and bade this
   hand—
Since by his life my death must needs
   ensue

[1] Betrayed, divulged.

And by his death my life to be pre-
served—
To shed his blood and seek my safety so.
And wisdom willéd me without pro-
tract [1]   130
In speedy wise to put the same in ure.
Thus have I told the cause that movéd
me
To work my brother's death; and so I
yield
My life, my death, to judgment of your
grace.

GORB. O cruel wight, should any cause
prevail
To make thee stain thy hands with
brother's blood?
But what of thee we will resolve to do
Shall yet remain unknown. Thou in the
mean
Shalt from our royal presence banished be,
Until our princely pleasure furder shall
To thee be showed. Depart therefore
our sight,   141
Accurséd child! [*Exit Porrex.*] What
cruel destiny,
What froward fate hath sorted us this
chance,
That, even in those where we should
comfort find,
Where our delight now in our aged days
S[h]ould rest and be, even there our only
grief
And deepest sorrows to abridge our life,
Most pining cares, and deadly thoughts
do grow?

AROS. Your grace should now, in these
grave years of yours,
Have found ere this the price of mortal
joys: 150
How short they be, how fading here in
earth,
How full of change, how brittle our es-
tate,
Of nothing sure, save only of the death
To whom both man and all the world
doth owe
Their end at last. Neither should na-
ture's power
In other sort against your heart prevail
Than as the naked hand whose stroke
assays
The armed breast where force doth light
in vain.

[1] Delay.

GORB. Many can yield right sage and
grave advice
Of patient sprite[2] to others wrapped in
woe,   160
And can in speech both rule and conquer
kind,
Who, if by proof they might feel nature's
force,
Would show themselves men as they are
indeed,
Which now will needs be gods. But what
doth mean
The sorry cheer of her that here doth
come?

[*Enter Marcella.*]

MAR. O, where is ruth,[3] or where is pity
now?
Whither is gentle heart and mercy fled?
Are they exiled out of our stony breasts,
Never to make return? Is all the world
Drownéd in blood, and sunk in cru-
elty?   170
If not in women mercy may be found,
If not, alas, within the mother's breast,
To her own child, to her own flesh and
blood,
If ruth be banished thence, if pity there
May have no place, if there no gentle
heart
Do live and dwell, where should we seek
it then?

GORB. Madam, alas, what means your
woeful tale?

MAR. O silly[4] woman I, why to this hour
Have kind and fortune thus deferred my
breath,
That I should live to see this doleful
day?   180
Will ever wight believe that such hard
heart
Could rest within the cruel mother's
breast,
With her own hand to slay her only son?
But out, alas! these eyes beheld the
same—
They saw the dreary sight, and are be-
come
Most ruthful records of the bloody fact.
Porrex, alas, is by his mother slain,
And with her hand—a woeful thing to
tell—

[2] Spirit.   [3] Compassion.   [4] Helpless.

While slumb'ring on his careful bed he
rests,
His heart stabbed in with knife, is reft of
life.   190
GORB. O Eubulus, O, draw this sword of
ours,
And pierce this heart with speed! O
hateful light,
O loathsome life, O sweet and welcome
death!
Dear Eubulus, work this, we thee be-
seech!
EUB. Patient [1] your grace; perhaps he liv-
eth yet,
With wound received, but not of certain
death.
GORB. O, let us then repair unto the place,
And see if Porrex live or thus be slain.
          [Exeunt Gorboduc and Eubulus.]
MAR. Alas, he liveth not! It is too true
That, with these eyes, of him a peerless
prince,   200
Son to a king, and in the flower of youth,
Even with a twink a senseless stock I
saw.[2]
AROS. O damned deed!
MAR.   But hear his ruth-
ful end:
The noble prince, pierced with the sud-
den wound,
Out of his wretched slumber hastely
start,[3]
Whose strength now failing, straight he
overthrew,[4]
When in the fall his eyes, even new
unclosed,
Beheld the queen, and cried to her for
help.
We then, alas, the ladies which that time
Did there attend, seeing that heinous
deed,   210
And hearing him oft call the wretched
name
Of mother, and to cry to her for aid
Whose direful hand gave him the mortal
wound,
Pitying, alas—for nought else could we
do—
His ruthful end, ran to the woeful bed,

Despoiled straight his breast, and, all we
might,
Wiped in vain with napkins next at hand
The sudden streams of blood that flushéd
fast
Out of the gaping wound. O, what a look,
O, what a ruthful, steadfast eye me-
thought   220
He fixed upon my face, which to my
death
Will never part fro [5] me, when with a
braid [6]
A deep-fet [7] sigh he gave, and there-
withal,
Clasping his hands, to heaven he cast his
sight;
And straight—pale death pressing within
his face—
The flying ghost his mortal corpse for-
sook.
AROS. Never did age bring forth so vile a
fact.
MAR. O hard and cruel hap, that thus as-
signed
Unto so worthy a wight so wretched end;
But most hard cruel heart, that could
consent   230
To lend the hateful destinies that hand
By which, alas, so heinous crime was
wrought!
O queen of adamant! O marble breast!
If not the favor of his comely face,
If not his princely cheer and countenance,
His valiant active arms, his manly breast,
If not his fair and seemly personage,
His noble limbs in such proportion cast
As would have rapt a silly woman's
thought—
If this mought not have moved thy
bloody heart   240
And that most cruel hand the wretched
weapon
Even to let fall, and kissed him in the
face,
With tears for ruth to reave such one by
death,
Should nature yet consent to slay her
son?
O mother, thou to murder thus thy child!
Even Jove with justice must with light-
ning flames
From heaven send down some strange
revenge on thee.

---

[1] Used as a reflexive verb.
[2] An awkward passage. The sense seems to be:
"It is too true that with these eyes even in an
instant I saw a senseless corpse made of him," etc.
[3] Hastily started.   [4] Fell over.
[5] From.   [6] A start.   [7] Deep-fetched.

Ah, noble prince, how oft have I beheld
Thee mounted on thy fierce and tram-
  pling steed,
Shining in armor bright before the
  tilt,   250
And with thy mistress' sleeve tied on
  thy helm,
And charge thy staff [1]—to please thy
  lady's eye—
That bowed the headpiece of thy friendly
  foe;
How oft in arms on horse to bend the
  mace,
How oft in arms on foot to break the
  sword,
Which never now these eyes may see
  again!
AROS. Madam, alas, in vain these plaints
  are shed;
Rather with me depart, and help to
  swage [2]
The thoughtful griefs that in the aged
  king
Must needs by nature grow by death of
  this   260
His only son, whom he did hold so
  dear.
MAR. What wight is that which saw that
  I did see,
And could refrain to wail with plaint
  and tears?
Not I, alas! That heart is not in me.—
But let us go, for I am grieved anew
To call to mind the wretched father's
  woe.   [*Exeunt.*]

CHORUS

When greedy lust in royal seat to reign
  Hath reft all care of gods and eke of
  men,
And cruel heart, wrath, treason, and
  disdain,
  Within ambitious breast are lodgéd,
  then   270
Behold how mischief wide herself displays,
And with the brother's hand the brother
  slays.

When blood thus shed doth stain the
  heaven's face,
  Crying to Jove for vengeance of the
  deed,

[1] Level thy lance.   [2] Assuage.

The mighty god even moveth from his
  place
  With wrath to wreak. Then sends he
  forth with speed
The dreadful Furies, daughters of the
  night,
  With serpents girt, carrying the whip
  of ire,
With hair of stinging snakes, and shining
  bright
  With flames and blood, and with a
  brand of fire.   280
These, for revenge of wretched murder
  done,
Do make the mother kill her only son.

Blood asketh blood, and death must
  death requite;
  Jove, by his just and everlasting doom,
Justly hath ever so requited it.
  The times before record, and times to
  come
Shall find it true, and so doth present
  proof
Present before our eyes for our behoof.

O happy wight that suffers not the snare
  Of murderous mind to tangle him in
  blood;   290
And happy he that can in time beware
  By other's harms and turn it to his
  good.
But woe to him that, fearing not to
  offend,
Doth serve his lust and will not see the
  end.

THE ORDER AND SIGNIFICATION OF THE DUMB SHOW BEFORE THE FIFTH ACT

*First, the drums and flutes began to sound,
  during which there came forth upon the
  stage a company of harquebusiers and
  of armed men, all in order of battle.
  These, after their pieces discharged, and
  that the armed men had three times
  marched about the stage, departed, and
  then the drums and flutes did cease.
  Hereby was signified tumults, rebellions,
  arms, and civil wars to follow, as fell
  in the realm of Great Britain, which,
  by the space of fifty years and more,
  continued in civil war between the nobility after the death of King Gorboduc*

and of his issues, for want of certain
limitation in succession of the crown,
till the time of Dunwallo Molmutius,
who reduced the land to monarchy.

ACTUS QUINTUS. SCENA PRIMA.

[*The court of Gorboduc.*]

Clotyn, Mandud, Gwenard, Fergus, Eubulus.

CLOT. Did ever age bring forth such ty-
    rants' hearts?
The brother hath bereft the brother's life;
The mother, she hath dyed her cruel
    hands
In blood of her own son; and now at last
The people, lo, forgetting truth and love,
Contemning quite both law and loyal
    heart,
Even they have slain their sovereign lord
    and queen.
MAND. Shall this their traitorous crime
    unpunished rest?
Even yet they cease not, carried on with
    rage,
In their rebellious routs, to threaten
    still   10
A new bloodshed unto the prince's kin,
To slay them all, and to uproot the race
Both of the king and queen; so are they
    moved
With Porrex' death, wherein they falsely
    charge
The guiltless king without desert at all,
And traitorously have murdered him
    therefor,
And eke the queen.
GWEN.   Shall subjects dare
    with force
To work revenge upon their prince's fact?
Admit the worst that may—as sure in
    this
The deed was foul, the queen to slay
    her son—   20
Shall yet the subject seek to take the
    sword,
Arise against his lord, and slay his king?
O wretched state where those rebellious
    hearts
Are not rent out even from their living
    breasts,
And with the body thrown unto the
    fowls,
As carrion food, for terror of the rest!

FERG. There can no punishment be
    thought too great
For this so grievous crime. Let speed
    therefore
Be used therein, for it behooveth so.
EUB. Ye all, my lords, I see, consent in
    one,   30
And I as one consent with ye in all.
I hold it more than need, with sharpest
    law
To punish this tumultuous bloody rage.
For nothing more may shake the com-
    mon state
Than sufferance of uproars without re-
    dress,
Whereby how some kingdoms of mighty
    power,
After great conquests made, and flour-
    ishing
In fame and wealth, have been to ruin
    brought.
I pray to Jove that we may rather wail
Such hap in them than witness in our-
    selves.   40
Eke fully with the duke my mind agrees,
Though kings forget to govern as they
    ought,
Yet subjects must obey as they are
    bound.
But now, my lords, before ye farder
    wade,[1]
Or spend your speech, what sharp re-
    venge shall fall
By justice' plague on these rebellious
    wights,
Methinks ye rather should first search
    the way
By which in time the rage of this uproar
Mought be repressed, and these great
    tumults ceased.
Even yet the life of Britain land doth
    hang   50
In traitors' balance of unegal weight.
Think not, my lords, the death of Gor-
    boduc
Nor yet Videna's blood will cease their
    rage.
Even our own lives, our wives, and chil-
    dren dear,
Our country, dearest of all, in danger
    stands,
Now to be spoiled, now, now made des-
    olate,
[1] Proceed.

And by ourselves a conquest to ensue.
For, give once sway unto the people's lusts
To rush forth on, and stay them not in time,
And, as the stream that rolleth down the hill,   60
So will they headlong run with raging thoughts
From blood to blood, from mischief unto mo,
To ruin of the realm, themselves, and all—
So giddy are the common people's minds,
So glad of change, more wavering than the sea.
Ye see, my lords, what strength these rebels have,
What hugy number is assembled still;
For, though the traitorous fact for which they rose
Be wrought and done, yet lodge they still in field;
So that, how far their furies yet will stretch,   70
Great cause we have to dread. That we may seek
By present battle to repress their power,
Speed must we use to levy force therefor;
For either they forthwith will mischief work,
Or their rebellious roars forthwith will cease.
These violent things may have no lasting long.
Let us, therefore, use this for present help:
Persuade by gentle speech, and offer grace
With gift of pardon, save unto the chief,
And that upon condition that forthwith   80
They yield the captains of their enterprise,
To bear such guerdon of their traitorous fact
As may be both due vengeance to themselves
And wholesome terror to posterity.
This shall, I think, scatter the greatest part,
That now are holden, with desire of home,

Wearied in field with cold of winter's nights,
And some, no doubt, stricken with dread of law.
When this is once proclaimed, it shall make
The captains to mistrust the multitude,   90
Whose safety bids them to betray their heads;
And so much more, because the rascal routs
In things of great and perilous attempts
Are never trusty to the noble race.
And, while we treat and stand on terms of grace,
We shall both stay their fury's rage the while,
And eke gain time, whose only help sufficeth
Withouten war to vanquish rebels' power.
In the meanwhile, make you in readiness
Such band of horsemen as ye may prepare.   100
Horsemen, you know, are not the commons' strength,
But are the force and store of noblemen,
Whereby the unchosen and unarmèd sort
Of skilless rebels, whom none other power
But number makes to be of dreadful force,
With sudden brunt may quickly be oppressed.
And, if this gentle mean of proffered grace
With stubborn hearts cannot so far avail
As to assuage their desperate courages,
Then do I wish such slaughter to be made   110
As present age and eke posterity
May be adrad [1] with horror of revenge
That justly then shall on these rebels fall.
This is, my lords, the sum of mine advice.
CLOT. Neither this case admits debate at large,
And, though it did, this speech that hath been said
Hath well abridged the tale I would have told.
Fully with Eubulus do I consent
In all that he hath said; and, if the same

---

[1] Adread, afraid.

To you, my lords, may seem for best
advice,   120
I wish that it should straight be put in
ure.
MAND. My lords, then let us presently [1]
depart,
And follow this that liketh us so well.
[*Exeunt Clotyn, Mandud, Gwenard, and
Eubulus.*]
FERG. If ever time to gain a kingdom here
Were offered man, now it is offered me.
The realm is reft both of their king and
queen;
The offspring of the prince is slain and
dead;
No issue now remains, the heir unknown;
The people are in arms and mutinies;
The nobles they are busied how to
cease   130
These great rebellious tumults and up-
roars;
And Britain land, now desert, left alone,
Amid these broils uncertain where to
rest,
Offers herself unto that noble heart
That will or dare pursue to bear her
crown.
Shall I, that am the Duke of Albany,
Descended from that line of noble blood
Which hath so long flourished in worthy
fame
Of valiant hearts, such as in noble breasts
Of right should rest above the baser
sort,   140
Refuse to venture life to win a crown?
Whom shall I find enemies that will
withstand
My fact herein, if I attempt by arms
To seek the same now in these times of
broil?
These dukes' [2] power can hardly well
appease
The people that already are in arms.
But, if perhaps my force be once in
field,
Is not my strength in power above the
best
Of all these lords now left in Britain land?
And though they should match me with
power of men,   150
Yet doubtful is the chance of battles
joined.
If victors of the field we may depart,

Ours is the scepter then of Great Britain;
If slain amid the plain this body lie,
Mine enemies yet shall not deny me
this,
But that I died giving the noble charge
To hazard life for conquest of a crown.
Forthwith, therefore, will I in post de-
part
To Albany, and raise in armor there
All power I can; and here my secret
friends   160
By secret practice shall solicit still
To seek to win to me the people's hearts.
[*Exit.*]

ACTUS QUINTUS. SCENA SECUNDA.

[*The same.*]

*Eubulus, Clotyn, Mandud, Gwenard, Arostus,
Nuntius.* [3]

EUB. O Jove, how are these people's hearts
abused!
What blind fury thus headlong carries
them,
That, though so many books, so many
rolls
Of ancient time, record what grievous
plagues
Light on these rebels aye, [4] and though so
oft
Their ears have heard their aged fathers
tell
What just reward these traitors still re-
ceive,
Yea, though themselves have seen deep
death and blood,
By strangling cord and slaughter of the
sword,
To such assigned, yet can they not beware,   10
Yet cannot stay their lewd rebellious
hands,
But suffering, lo, foul treason to distain [5]
Their wretched minds, forget their loyal
heart,
Reject all truth, and rise against their
prince?
A ruthful case, that those whom duty's
bond,
Whom grafted law, by nature, truth, and
faith,
Bound to preserve their country and
their king,

---

[1] At once.   [2] Dissyllabic.

[3] The last five enter later.   [4] Forever.   [5] Stain.

Born to defend their commonwealth and
  prince,
Even they should give consent thus to
  subvert
Thee, Britain land, and from thy womb
  should spring,   20
O native soil, those that will needs de-
  stroy
And ruin thee and eke themselves in fine.[1]
For lo, when once the dukes had offered
  grace
Of pardon sweet, the multitude misled
By traitorous fraud of their ungracious
  heads,
One sort that saw the dangerous success
Of stubborn standing in rebellious war,
And knew the difference of prince's power
From headless number of tumultuous
  routs,
Whom common country's care and pri-
  vate fear   30
Taught to repent the error of their rage,
Laid hands upon the captains of their
  band,
And brought them bound unto the
  mighty dukes.
And other sort, not trusting yet so well
The truth of pardon, or mistrusting more
Their own offense than that they could
  conceive
Such hope of pardon for so foul misdeed,
Or for that they their captains could not
  yield,
Who, fearing to be yielded, fled before,
Stale[2] home by silence of the secret
  night.   40
The third unhappy and enragéd sort
Of desperate hearts who, stained in
  princes' blood,
From traitorous furor could not be with-
  drawn
By love, by law, by grace, ne yet by fear,
By proffered life, ne yet by threatened
  death,
With minds hopeless of life, dreadless of
  death,
Careless of country, and aweless of God,
Stood bent to fight, as Furies did them
  move
With violent death to close their traitor-
  ous life.
These all by power of horsemen were op-
  pressed,   50

And with revenging sword slain in the
  field,
Or with the strangling cord hanged on
  the trees,
Where yet their carrion carcasses do
  preach
The fruits that rebels reap of their uproars,
And of the murder of their sacred prince.
But lo, where do approach the noble
  dukes
By whom these tumults have been thus
  appeased.

[*Enter Clotyn, Mandud, Gwenard, and
  Arostus.*]

CLOT. I think the world will now at length
  beware
And fear to put on arms against their
  prince.
MAND. If not, those traitorous hearts that
  dare rebel,   60
Let them behold the wide and hugy fields
With blood and bodies spread of rebels
  slain,
The lofty trees clothed with the corpses
  dead,
That, strangled with the cord, do hang
  thereon.
AROS. A just reward, such as all times
  before
Have ever lotted[3] to those wretched folks.
GWEN. But what means he that cometh
  here so fast?

[*Enter Nuntius.*]

NUN. My lords, as duty and my troth doth
  move,
And of my country work a care in me,
That, if the spending of my breath
  availed   70
To do the service that my heart desires,
I would not shun to embrace a present
  death,
So have I now, in that wherein I thought
My travail mought perform some good
  effect,
Ventered[4] my life to bring these tidings
  here.
Fergus, the mighty Duke of Albany,
Is now in arms and lodgeth in the field
With twenty thousand men; hither he
  bends

---

[1] Finally.   [2] Stole

Allotted.   [4] Ventured.

His speedy march, and minds to invade
the crown.
Daily he gathereth strength, and spreads
abroad　　　　　　　　　　　　　80
That to this realm no certain heir re-
mains,
That Britain land is left without a guide,
That he the scepter seeks for nothing
else
But to preserve the people and the land,
Which now remain as ship without a
stern.
Lo, this is that which I have here to say.
CLOT. Is this his faith? And shall he falsely
thus
Abuse the vantage of unhappy times?
O wretched land, if his outrageous pride,
His cruel and untempered willfulness, 90
His deep dissembling shows of false pre-
tense,
Should once attain the crown of Britain
land!
Let us, my lords, with timely force resist
The new attempt of this our common
foe,
As we would quench the flames of com-
mon fire.
MAND. Though we remain without a cer-
tain prince
To weld the realm or guide the wand'ring
rule,
Yet now the common mother of us all,
Our native land, our country, that con-
tains
Our wives, children, kindred, ourselves,
and all　　　　　　　　　　　　100
That ever is or may be dear to man,
Cries unto us to help ourselves and her.
Let us advance our powers to repress
This growing foe of all our liberties.
GWEN. Yea, let us so, my lords, with hasty
speed.
And ye, O gods, send us the welcome
death
To shed our blood in field, and leave us
not
In loathsome life to linger out our days,
To see the hugy heaps of these unhaps
That now roll down upon the wretched
land,　　　　　　　　　　　　110
Where empty place of princely govern-
ance,
No certain stay now left of doubtless
heir,

Thus leaves [1] this guideless realm an open
prey
To endless storms and waste of civil war.
AROS. That ye, my lords, do so agree in
one,
To save your country from the violent
reign
And wrongfully usurpéd tyranny
Of him that threatens conquest of you all,
To save your realm, and in this realm
yourselves,
From foreign thraldom of so proud a
prince,　　　　　　　　　　　　120
Much do I praise; and I beseech the gods
With happy honor to requite it you.
But, O my lords, sith now the heaven's
wrath
Hath reft this land the issue of their
prince;
Sith of the body of our late sovereign
lord
Remains no mo since the young kings
be slain,
And of the title of descended crown
Uncertainly the divers minds do think
Even of the learned sort, and more un-
certainly
Will partial fancy and affection deem, 130
But most uncertainly will climbing pride
And hope of reign withdraw to sundry
parts
The doubtful right and hopeful lust to
reign;
When once this noble service is achieved
For Britain land, the mother of ye all;
When once ye have with armed force
repressed
The proud attempts of this Albanian
prince
That threatens thraldom to your native
land;
When ye shall vanquishers return from
field
And find the princely state an open
prey　　　　　　　　　　　　140
To greedy lust and to usurping power,
Then, then, my lords, if ever kindly care
Of ancient honor of your ancestors,
Of present wealth and noblesse of your
stocks,
Yea, of the lives and safety yet to come
Of your dear wives, your children, and
yourselves,

[1] Original reads *leave.*

Might move your noble hearts with
   gentle ruth,
Then, then, have pity on the torn estate;
Then help to salve the well-near hopeless
   sore;
Which ye shall do if ye yourselves with-
   hold   150
The slaying knife from your own mother's
   throat.
Her shall you save, and you, and yours
   in her,
If ye shall all with one assent forbear
Once to lay hand or take unto yourselves
The crown, by color of pretended right,
Or by what other means soever it be,
Till first by common counsel of you all
In parliament the regal diadem
Be set in certain place of governance—
In which your parliament, and in your
   choice,   160
Prefer the right, my lords, without re-
   spect
Of strength or friends or whatsoever
   cause
That may set forward any other's part.
For right will last, and wrong cannot en-
   dure.
Right mean I his or hers upon whose
   name
The people rest by mean of native line,
Or by the virtue of some former law,
Already made their title to advance.
Such one, my lords, let be your chosen
   king,
Such one so born within your native
   land,   170
Such one prefer, and in no wise admit
The heavy yoke of foreign governance;
Let foreign titles yield to public wealth.
And with that heart wherewith ye now
   prepare
Thus to withstand the proud invading
   foe,
With that same heart, my lords, keep out
   also
Unnatural thralldom of stranger's reign;
Ne suffer you, against the rules of kind,
Your mother land to serve a foreign
   prince.
Eub. Lo, here the end of Brutus' royal
   line,   180
And lo, the entry to the woeful wreck
And utter ruin of this noble realm!
The royal king and eke his sons are slain;

No ruler rests within the regal seat;
The heir to whom the scepter longs [1] un-
   known,
That [2] to each force of foreign princes'
   power,
Whom vantage of our wretched state may
   move
By sudden arms to gain so rich a realm,
And to the proud and greedy mind at
   home,
Whom blinded lust to reign leads to as-
   pire,   190
Lo, Britain realm is left an open prey,
A present spoil by conquest to ensue.
Who seeth not now how many rising
   minds
Do feed their thoughts with hope to
   reach a realm?
And who will not by force attempt to
   win
So great a gain, that hope persuades to
   have?
A simple color [3] shall for title serve.
Who wins the royal crown will want no
   right,
Nor such as shall display by long descent
A lineal race to prove him lawful
   king.   200
In the meanwhile these civil arms shall
   rage,
And thus a thousand mischiefs shall un-
   fold,
And far and near spread [4] thee, O Britain
   land.
All right and law shall cease, and he that
   had
Nothing today, tomorrow shall enjoy
Great heaps of gold, and he that flowed
   in wealth,
Lo, he shall be bereft of life and all;
And happiest he that then possesseth
   least.
The wives shall suffer rape; the maids
   deflowered
And children fatherless shall weep and
   wail;   210
With fire and sword thy native folk shall
   perish;
One kinsman shall bereave another's life;
The father shall unwitting slay the son;
The son shall slay the sire and know it
   not;

[1] Belongs.   [3] Pretense.
[2] So that.   [4] Spread over.

Women and maids the cruel soldier's
  sword
Shall pierce to death; and silly children,
  lo,
That playing [1] in the streets and fields
  are found,
By violent hands shall close their latter
  day.
Whom shall the fierce and bloody soldier
Reserve to life? Whom shall he spare
  from death?   220
Even thou, O wretched mother, half
  alive,
Thou shalt behold thy dear and only child
Slain with the sword while he yet sucks
  thy breast.
Lo, guiltless blood shall thus each where
  be shed.
Thus shall the wasted soil yield forth no
  fruit,
But dearth and famine shall possess the
  land.
The towns shall be consumed and burnt
  with fire,
The peopled cities shall wax desolate;
And thou, O Britain, whilom in renowm,
Whilom in wealth and fame, shalt thus
  be torn,   230
Dismembered thus, and thus be rent in
  twain,
Thus wasted and defaced, spoiled and
  destroyed.
These be the fruits your civil wars will
  bring.
Hereto it comes when kings will not
  consent
To grave advice, but follow willful will.
This is the end when in fond princes'
  hearts
Flattery prevails and sage rede hath no
  place.
These are the plagues when murder is the
  mean
To make new heirs unto the royal crown.
Thus wreak the gods when that the
  mother's wrath   240
Naught but the blood of her own child
  may swage.
These mischiefs spring when rebels will
  arise
To work revenge and judge their prince's
  fact.

[1] From 1565 edn. Original reads *play*.

This, this ensues, when noble men do fail
In loyal truth, and subjects will be kings.
And this doth grow, when lo, unto the
  prince
Whom death or sudden hap of life be-
  reaves,
No certain heir remains—such certain
  heir,
As not all-only [2] is the rightful heir,
But to the realm is so made known to be,
And troth thereby vested in subjects'
  hearts   251
To owe faith there where right is known
  to rest.
Alas, in parliament what hope can be,
When is of parliament no hope at all,
Which, though it be assembled by consent,
Yet is not likely with consent to end?
While each one for himself, or for his
  friend,
Against his foe shall travail what he may,
While now the state, left open to the man
That shall with greatest force invade the
  same,   260
Shall fill ambitious minds with gaping
  hope,
When will they once with yielding hearts
  agree?
Or in the while, how shall the realm be
  used?
No, no; then parliament should have
  been holden,
And certain heirs appointed to the crown,
To stay the title of established right,
And in the people plant obedience,
While yet the prince did live whose name
  and power
By lawful summons and authority   269
Might make a parliament to be of force,
And might have set the state in quiet stay.
But now, O happy man whom speedy
  death
Deprives of life, ne is enforced to see
These hugy mischiefs and these miseries,
These civil wars, these murders, and
  these wrongs
Of justice! Yet must God in fine restore
This noble crown unto the lawful heir:
For right will always live, and rise at
  length,
But wrong can never take deep root to
  last.   [*Exeunt.*]

[2] Alonely, solely.

THE END OF THE TRAGEDY OF KING GORBODUC.

GEORGE GASCOIGNE

George Gascoigne, the author of the first extant English play to be written completely in prose, even though it was actually a translation from the Italian, became an author only after he had failed at several other pursuits, had squandered his estate, and was ready to settle down and live a reformed life. In his ability, versatility, and volatility he was representative of one type of Renaissance man whose active and restless life of the body did not preclude an active and restless life of the mind.

C. T. Prouty, whose *George Gascoigne, Elizabethan Courtier, Soldier, and Poet* (Columbia University Press, 1942) has brought together, extended, and surpassed the results of the biographical researches of other students (J. W. Cunliffe, R. W. Chambers, C. H. Herford, B. M. Ward, R. P. Cawley, Genevieve Ambrose, Florence E. Teager, John C. Hankins, Genevieve A. Oldfield, and Fitzgerald Flournoy, for example), remarks at the outset of his book than often the work of "little men" helps us to a better understanding of the work of greater men to come. Such is the case of Gascoigne in relation to later and greater Elizabethan writers like Lyly, Marlowe, Shakespeare, Greene, and Nashe.

George Gascoigne came from a flourishing and prosperous Bedfordshire family, originally from Yorkshire. His grandfather, Sir William Gascoigne, had been comptroller of the household of the powerful Cardinal Thomas Wolsey and, after Wolsey's fall, steward to John Neville, Lord Latimer. Earlier he had twice been sheriff in Bedfordshire. Sir William's son, Sir John, had made a good marriage; had sat in Parliament for Bedford in 1542, 1553, and 1557; and had served as justice of the peace. His first child, George, was probably born about 1539, according to Prouty's calculations. The boy apparently inherited much of the temperaments of both his father and his mother. His father was property-conscious, stubborn, irascible, aggressive, and addicted to physical quarrels and women (in his will he left a good annuity to one of his female servants). His mother was also of a quick-tempered and litigious nature, and excluded neither her sister nor her sons from her legal disputes. With such a heritage, it is not strange that the boy proved unsettled, unpredictable, and imprudent. The family was also Roman Catholic in the midst of Protestants, though the son eventually rebelled against his religion as well as against his parents.

From some of George's many later autobiographical poems, it appears that he had some of his early schooling in Westmoreland and that he went on to Cambridge University—probably Trinity College, since he wrote in high terms of his educational debt to Stephen Nevynson, who was a Fellow and a tutor there from 1547 to 1561. Prouty speculates that Gascoigne was at Cambridge—although not necessarily in the University—between 1547 and 1555, and suggests that his name does not appear in any of the surviving records because he was the son of a mere knight, and therefore a commoner. In 1555 Gascoigne entered Gray's Inn, but if at the outset he ever had any serious interest in the law as a profession it soon disappeared. While at Gray's, however, he was Burgess from his Bedford borough in Queen Mary's last Parliament, and attended Queen Elizabeth's coronation as deputy for his father.

This experience in London made the young man determine to try his luck at the court itself, where for a time he lived a gay life and dissipated his income so thoroughly that he had to borrow from his father to pay his debts. He shuttled between London and the family's estates at Willington, Cardington, and Walthamstow, where he tried rather unsuccessfully to learn something about farm management. He even dropped in at Gray's Inn again in 1564 or 1565 to resume his study of the law, but he did not persist. As a result of one of many lawsuits, this time with the Earl of Bedford, he actually found himself for a time lodged in Bedford jail. It was during this period that he wrote his two major dramatic works, *Jocasta* and *Supposes*.

In 1561, while still trying to be a courtier, he contracted a trouble-filled marriage to Elizabeth Bretton, widow of William Bretton and mother of Nicholas Bretton, who was to become a well-known minor poet. Elizabeth was also, presumably, the recent wife of Edward Boyes. At least Boyes thought she was his wife (but for unknown reasons she did not) when she decided to marry Gascoigne. One night in 1562 the two husbands and their retainers fought "a great fray in Redcross Street," and the case, involving Bretton's property and his children, dragged on through the courts for many years, though a court decree allowed Elizabeth to validate her marriage to Gascoigne. Gascoigne's behavior in his efforts to keep Bretton's property for himself and his wife and away from Boyes and Bretton's children seems to have been rather shady.

When Sir John Gascoigne died in April 1568, the terms of his deathbed will led many people (including George Whetstone, the poet-dramatist, author of the tragicomedy *Promos and Cassandra*, and the composer of "Remembrance," a pithy biographical epitaph of his friend Gascoigne) to conclude that the father had disinherited his son. Prouty dissents, however, pointing out that although Sir John censured his son severely, this censure seems to have been for his conduct in financial affairs and not for his morals. All of the many lawsuits that Gascoigne was entangled in were decided against him until in 1571 his name drops from the court records.

Clearly it was time for the young man to try some new and more rewarding career. This opportunity came through the rebellion of the Dutch against their Spanish oppressors in 1572. Gascoigne became a member of the first band of English volunteers, unofficially sanctioned by the Queen, and saw action in several badly planned and poorly managed engagements. On his empty-handed return to England, he apparently decided that his pen could be more useful than the plough, the sword, the lawyer's wig, or the courtier's dress. He had been writing verses in private, which had been well received in court and legal circles, where he had friends, and therefore decided to publish his poems and try to obtain a wealthy and influential patron such as Lord Grey of Wilton or Anthony Browne, Viscount Montague. But even while the book was going through the press, he found himself enmeshed in new troubles, which were summed up in an anonymous letter sent to the Privy Council, ostensibly to prevent him from taking his recently won seat in Parliament as Burgess from Midhurst. The main charges against him were: (1) the debts owed by him to "a greate nomber of personnes"; (2) "he is a defamed person and noted as well for Manslaughter as for other greate crymes" (probably a reference to some otherwise unnoted duel); (3) "he is a common Rymer and a deviser of slaunderous Pasquelles againste divers personnes of greate callinge"; and (4) "he is a notorious Ruffianne and especiallie noted to be both a spie, an Atheist and godlesse personne." Even though his book, *A Hundreth Sundry Flowers*, was almost off the press, March 1573 was obviously a wise time for Gascoigne to take off for the Dutch war again. But he was no luckier than before. His ship was wrecked in landing at Brill. Although he may have participated in the attempts to relieve Harlem and Middleburgh, and is called "captain" in the letters and notes of Barnaby Rich, he quarreled with his commander, Colonel Thomas Morgan, and joined the forces of Prince William of Orange at Delft. But he and his men had a very unpleasant time there, and so he was put in charge of a hoy, or small coating vessel, and was probably in the fleet that harassed the Spanish coming from Antwerp. Here he was more successful, and received a special gift of three hundred guilders from the Prince in addition to his pay. Nevertheless, he soon became implicated in some suspicious maneuvers involving the relief of Leyden, was captured by the Spanish, and, after being held prisoner with some other captains for four months, was sent back to England. He returned to find that his book was out, that it had aroused violent objections in some quarters, and that his enemies, whoever they were (probably his creditors and the "divines" of the church party), were still hounding him.

All these adventures and misadventures were enough to make a man now well into his thirties stop and think, and George Gascoigne became, as Prouty heads his chapter, "The Repentant Sinner." In the attempt to mollify his attackers, Gascoigne brought out an expurgated, rearranged, and enlarged edition of his book, entitled *The Posies*, and provided it with prefatory verses and letters confessing his disillusionment with a world in which it is every man for himself, acknowledging his errors, and announcing his intention to lead a new life. Prouty is willing to accept his reform as sincere and quotes from Willard Farnham's chapter, "Gothic Espousal and Contempt of the World," in *The Medieval Heritage of Elizabethan Tragedy*, in support of his opinion. However this may be, George Gascoigne spent the last part of his short life as a literary man, writing pious and moralistic works like his refurbished *The Complaint of Phylomene* (1576), a translation of Pope Innocent III's *De Contemptu Mundi*, which was Part I of a long tract entitled *The Drum of Doomsday* and was dedicated to his old enemy the Earl of Bedford. Another of his moralistic treatises had the appealing title of *A Delicate Diet, for Dainty-Mouthed Drunkards* (1576). In the same year he dedicated *The Steel Glass*, another moralistic poem, to Lord Grey of Wilton. This was the first original nondramatic poem in blank verse in English.

In the previous year (1575) he had published *The Glass of Government*, the only English specimen of the Dutch prodigal son play. He had probably observed this type of play while in the Netherlands and it may well have attracted him because of his own recent experiences as a wayward young man. Shortly afterward he had a part in Elizabeth's favorite, the Earl of Leicester's magnificent entertainment for the Queen at Kenilworth during her famous "progress" about her adulating kingdom. He apparently did the major share of the writing of *The Princely Pleasures at the Court at Kenilworth*, which, although such spectacles had already been given at court in London, is the first complete surviving example of any Elizabethan masque or revel. Unfortunately the weather did not permit the actual performance of his own particular masque about Diana's nymph Zabeta (a compliment to the Virgin Queen Elizabeth), but on the third day he had an opportunity to appear before the Queen as Sylvanus, a "Savage man," or "wild man" (already seen in *Gorboduc*), and to declaim several lines of submission to her on his knees. A little later he strengthened his position as she set out for a hunt; in the character of Sylvanus he ran by the side of her horse reciting his speech, which was graciously received. When the Queen later moved on to Woodstock, Gascoigne composed "The Tale of Hermetes the Hermit," and on New Year's Day presented her with an elaborate manuscript of it in English, Latin, Italian, and French, which he himself had illustrated with emblems. In its preface he repeated his confession of past misdeeds and asked for understanding and forgiveness. As a result, in the late summer of 1576 the government sent him back to the Low Countries to report on the state of affairs there. He was in time to witness the sack of Antwerp by discontented Spanish mutineers and wrote a vivid description of it in his pamphlet, *The Spoil of Antwerp*. But he did not live long to enjoy the fruits of his new life. He had been in bad health for some time, and died at Stamford on October 7, 1577, either at the Bretton manor of Burghe or at the home of his friend and fellow-poet, George Whetstone. In his "Remembrance" poem, Whetstone drew an affecting picture of the deathbed scene and Gascoigne's farewell speech to his wife and son William.

Gascoigne's two most important contributions to the English drama were *Jocasta* and *Supposes*, both of them acted at Gray's Inn sometime during the year 1566. Yet it must be repeated that neither was an original work, since both were translations from Gascoigne's favorite language, Italian. The success of *Gorboduc* at the Inner Temple and at Whitehall the year before had perhaps stimulated Gascoigne and his friend and collaborator, Francis Kinwelmarsh, to a friendly rivalry in composing an English version of the story of Jocasta. They did not, however, actually go back to Euripides's *Phoenissae*, as the title page implied, but rather, as J. P. Mahaffy in his study of *Euripides* in 1874 first recognized, used the 1549 version by Lodovico Dolce in his *Giocasta*. Nevertheless, as Prouty maintains, we must not discount the fact that "*Jocasta* remains, even though twice removed, the first hint of Greek tragedy in the English tongue," or that "the translators differed from their confreres at the Inns of Court and preferred Greek to Roman tragedy." The young student-lawyers were probably attracted to *Giocasta* because of its reflection of the ideas and style of Seneca, who was close to Euripides in many ways. But the translation by Gascoigne and Kinwelmarsh was not slavish, and their alterations and additions in style, realistic detail, and structure for greater dramatic effectiveness give the play some claim to originality. It was the second play in English to use blank verse.

Gascoigne alone was responsible for translating—almost adapting—*Supposes* from the Italian of the "divine Ariosto," who had written his *I Suppositi* in prose in 1509 and then, about twenty years later, turned it into verse. In making use of the best features of both versions and adding some of his own in his prose redaction, Gascoigne showed both a skilful dramatic sense and a strong interest in English style. Ariosto himself, of course, had been much influenced by the *Captivi* of Plautus and the *Eunuchus* of Terence, with some contributions from other Roman comedies. He had also brought together the almost stock elements of the young master's exchange of roles with his servant, his entering in disguise the house of his sweetheart, the false substitute for the real father, the discovery of a long lost son identified by a mole on his shoulder, the parasite, and the rich old wooer who developed into the stock character called the pantaloon in Italian comedy. E. K. Chambers in *The Elizabethan Stage* and Lily B. Campbell in *Scenes and Machines on the English Stage during the Renaissance* (Columbia University Press, 1923) have discussed the probable staging of the play in a private theater.

All in all, Gascoigne was never really a professional man of letters, at least not to the extent of depending for his income on the sale of his writings. His status as an aristocrat would have made such a direct commercialization of his art impossible. But the indirect approach, through patronage and offices, was what he was aiming at when he died while still under forty. The motto that he placed on some of his title pages was "*Tam Marti Quam Mercurio;*" that is, "As Much for Mars as for Mercury." His claim of an equal devotion to arms and wit perhaps sums up his own desire for fame as well as anything can, though perhaps his best claim for recognition and remembrance lies in Shakespeare's probable use of the basic plot in *Supposes* for the underplot of Bianca and Lucentio in *The Taming of the Shrew*.

Supposes was first printed about 1572–73. An improved edition was included in *The Posies* in 1575, a miscellany of different types of work, at least in the main Gascoigne's. A reprint of the text of 1575 by R. W. Bond in his *Early Plays from the Italian* (Oxford, 1911) is the basis of the present text, though J. W. Cunliffe's edition of the play in his *Works of Gascoigne* (Cambridge University Press, 1907–10) has been used for comparison.

SUPPOSES[1]

BY

GEORGE GASCOIGNE

THE NAMES OF THE ACTORS

BALIA, *the nurse.*
POLYNESTA, *the young woman.*
CLEANDER, *the doctor,[2] suitor to Polynesta.*
PASIPHILO, *the parasite.*
CARION, *the doctor's man.*
DULIPPO, *feigned servant, and lover of Polynesta.*
EROSTRATO, *feigned master, and suitor to Polynesta.*
DALIO and CRAPINO } *servants to feigned Erostrato.*

SIENESE, *a gentleman stranger.*
PAQUETTO and PETRUCHIO } *his servants.*
DAMON, *father to Polynesta.*
NEVOLA and TWO OTHER HIS SERVANTS.
PSITERIA, *an old hag in his house.*
PHILOGANO, *a Sicilian gentleman, father to Erostrato.*
LITIO, *his servant.*
FERRARESE, *an innkeeper of Ferrara.*

The comedy presented as it were in Ferrara.

[TIME: *About 1500.*]

THE PROLOGUE OR ARGUMENT

I suppose you are assembled here supposing to reap the fruit of my travails;[3] and, to be plain, I mean presently to present you with a comedy called *Supposes,*[4] the very name whereof may peradventure drive into every of your heads a sundry suppose, to suppose the meaning of our Supposes. Some, percase,[5] will suppose we mean to occupy your ears with sophistical handling of subtile suppositions; some other will [10 suppose we go about to decipher unto you some quaint conceits,[6] which hitherto have been only supposed, as it were, in shadows;[7] and some I see smiling as though they supposed we would trouble you with the vain suppose of some wanton suppose.[8] But, understand, this our Suppose is nothing else but a mistaking or imagination of one thing for another. For you shall see the master supposed for the servant, the [20 servant for the master; the freeman for a slave, and the bondslave for a freeman; the stranger for a well-known friend, and the familiar for a stranger. But what? I suppose that even already you suppose me very fond[9] that have so simply disclosed unto you the subtilties of these our Supposes; where otherwise, indeed, I suppose you should have heard almost the last of our Supposes before you could [30 have supposed any of them aright. Let this then suffice.

ACTUS I. SCENA i.[10]

Balia, the nurse, [followed by] Polynesta, the young woman.

[BAL.] Here is nobody. Come forth, Polynesta. Let us look about, to be sure lest any man hear our talk; for I think within the house the tables, the planks,

---

[1] The original title continues: "A Comedy Written in the Italian Tongue by Ariosto, Englished by George Gascoigne, of Gray's Inn, Esquire, and There Presented. 1566."
[2] Of law.   [3] Labors.
[4] Ariosto's title, *I Suppositi,* carried the meaning of "substitutions" rather than of "suppositions."
[5] Perchance.
[6] Ingeniously elaborated conceptions.
[7] Pictures.   [8] "Prostitute" (Adams).
[9] Foolish.
[10] The whole action, which occupies only a few hours, takes place in a street between the houses of Damon and Erostrato.

the beds, the portals,[1] yea, and the cupboards themselves have ears.

POLY. You might as well have said the windows and the doors. Do you not see how they hearken?

BAL. Well, you jest fair; but I would [10 advise you take heed! I have bidden you a thousand times beware. You will be spied one day talking with Dulippo.

POLY. And why should I not talk with Dulippo as well as with any other, I pray you?

BAL. I have given you a wherefore for this why many times. But go to! Follow your own advice till you overwhelm us all with sudden mishap. 20

POLY. A great mishap, I promise you! Marry, God's blessing on their heart that set such a brooch on my cap.[2]

BAL. Well, look well about you! A man would think it were enough for you secretly to rejoice that by my help you have passed so many pleasant nights together. And yet, by my troth, I do it more than half against my will, for I would rather you had settled your fancy in [30 some noble family. Yea, and it is no small grief unto me that, rejecting the suits of so many nobles and gentlemen, you have chosen for your darling a poor servant of your father's, by whom shame and infamy is the best dower you can look for to attain.

POLY. And, I pray you, whom may I thank but gentle nurse, that continually praising him, what for his personage,[3] [40 his courtesy, and, above all, the extreme passions [4] of his mind—in fine, you would never cease till I accepted him, delighted in him, and at length desired him with no less affection than he erst [5] desired me.

BAL. I cannot deny but at the beginning I did recommend him unto you (as, indeed, I may say that for myself I have a pitiful heart), seeing the depth of his unbridled affection, and that continually [50 he never ceased to fill mine ears with lamentable complaints.

POLY. Nay, rather that he filled your purse with bribes and rewards, nurse!

BAL. Well, you may judge of nurse as you list.[6] Indeed, I have thought it always a deed of charity to help the miserable young men whose tender youth consumeth with the furious flames of love. But, be you sure, if I had thought you [60 would have passed to the terms you now stand in, pity nor pension,[7] penny nor paternoster,[8] should ever have made nurse once to open her mouth in the cause.

POLY. No? Of honesty, I pray you, who first brought him into my chamber, who first taught him the way to my bed but you? Fie, nurse, fie! Never speak of it for shame! You will make me tell a wise tale anon.[9] 70

BAL. And have I these thanks for my good will? Why then, I see well I shall be counted the cause of all mishap.

POLY. Nay, rather the author of my good hap, gentle nurse. For I would thou knewest I love not Dulippo, nor any of so mean estate, but have bestowed my love more worthily than thou deemest. But I will say no more at this time. 79

BAL. Then I am glad you have changed your mind yet.

POLY. Nay, I neither have changed nor will change it.

BAL. Then I understand you not. How said you?

POLY. Marry, I say that I love not Dulippo, nor any such as he; and yet I neither have changed nor will change my mind.

BAL. I cannot tell. You love to lie [90 with Dulippo very well. This gear [10] is Greek to me. Either it hangs not well together or I am very dull of understanding. Speak plain, I pray you.

POLY. I can speak no plainer; I have sworn to the contrary.

BAL. How! Make you so dainty [11] to tell it nurse, lest she should reveal it? You have trusted me as far as may be (I may show to you) in things that touch your [100 honor if they were known, and make you strange to tell me this? I am sure it is but a trifle in comparison of those things whereof heretofore you have made me privy.

POLY. Well, it is of greater importance

[1] Passages.
[2] I.e., "put such a feather in my cap."
[3] Bodily form.
[4] Heroic sentiments.   [5] First.

[6] Please.   [7] Payment.   [8] Prayer.   [9] Soon.
[10] Affair.   [11] Are you so squeamish?

than you think, nurse; yet would I tell it you—under condition and promise that you shall not tell it again, nor give any sign or token to be suspected that you know it. [110

BAL. I promise you, of my honesty. Say on.

POLY. Well, hear you me then. This young man whom you have always taken for Dulippo is a noble-born Sicilian, his right name Erostrato, son to Philogano, one of the worthiest men in that country.

BAL. How, Erostrato? Is it not our neighbor, which ——

POLY. Hold thy talking, nurse, and [120 hearken to me that I may explain the whole case unto thee. The man whom to this day you have supposed to be Dulippo is, as I say, Erostrato, a gentleman that came from Sicilia to study in this city; *The first suppose and ground of all the supposes.* and even at his first arrival met me in the street, fell enamored of me, and of such vehement force were the passions he suffered that immediately he cast aside [130 both long gown and books, and determined on me only to apply his study. And to the end he might the more commodiously both see me and talk with me, he exchanged both name, habit, clothes, and credit with his servant Dulippo, whom only he brought with him out of Sicilia. And so, with the turning of a hand, of Erostrato, a gentleman, he became Dulippo, a serving-man, and soon after [140 sought service of my father and obtained it.

BAL. Are you sure of this?

POLY. Yea, out of doubt. On the other side, Dulippo took upon him the name of Erostrato, his master, the habit, the credit, books, and all things needful to a student, and in short space profited very much, and is now esteemed as you see.

BAL. Are there no other Sicilians here nor none that pass this way, which [150 may discover them?

POLY. Very few that pass this way, and few or none that tarry here any time.

BAL. This hath been a strange adventure! But, I pray you, how hang these things together—that the student, whom you say to be the servant and not the master, is become an earnest suitor to you and requireth you of your father in marriage? 160

POLY. That is a policy devised between them to put Doctor Dotipole [1] out of conceit [2]—the old dotard!—he that so instantly doth lie upon [3] my father for me. But look where he comes—as God help me, it is he. Out upon him! What a lusky yonker [4] is this! Yet I had rather be a nun a thousand times than be cumbered with such a coistrel. [5] 169

BAL. Daughter, you have reason. But let us go in before he come any nearer.

Polynesta goeth in, and Balia stayeth a little while after, speaking a word or two to the doctor, and then departeth.

SCENA ii.

Cleander, doctor; Pasiphilo, parasite; Balia, nurse.

[CLE.] Were these dames [6] here, or did mine eyes dazzle?

PASI. Nay, sir, here were Polynesta and her nurse.

CLE. Was my Polynesta here? Alas, I knew her not!

BAL. [*Aside.*] He must have better eyesight that should marry your Polynesta—or else he may chance to oversee the best point in his tables [7] sometimes. [*Exit.*] 10

PASI. Sir, it is no marvel; the air is very misty today. I myself knew her better by her apparel than by her face.

CLE. In good faith, and I thank God, I have mine eyesight good and perfit [8]— little worse than when I was but twenty years old.

PASI. How can it be otherwise? You are but young.

CLE. I am fifty years old. 20

PASI. [*Aside.*] He tells [9] ten less than he is.

CLE. What sayst thou of ten less?

PASI. I say I would have thought you ten less; you look like one of six-and-thirty, or seven-and-thirty at the most.

CLE. I am no less than I tell.

PASI. You are like enough to live fifty more Show me your hand.

[1] A common name for a blockhead.
[2] *I.e.*, humble his pride.
[3] So insistently urges. [4] Lazy youngster.
[5] Rascal. [6] Great ladies.
[7] "*I.e.*, be made a cuckold; metaphor from backgammon" (Bond).
[8] Perfect. [9] Counts.

CLE. Why, is Pasiphilo a chiro- [30 mancer? [1]

PASI. What is not Pasiphilo? I pray you, show me it a little.

CLE. Here it is.

PASI. O, how straight and infract [2] is this line of life! You will live to the years of Melchisedec.

CLE. Thou wouldest say Methusalem.

PASI. Why, is it not all one?

CLE. I perceive you are no very [40 good Bibler, Pasiphilo.

PASI. Yes, sir, an excellent good bibbler,[3] specially in a bottle. O, what a mount of Venus here is! But this light serveth not very well. I will behold it another day, when the air is clearer, and tell you somewhat, peradventure, to your contentation.[4]

CLE. You shall do me great pleasure. But tell me, I pray thee, Pasiphilo, [50 whom dost thou think Polynesta liketh better, Erostrato or me?

PASI. Why, you, out of doubt! She is a gentlewoman of a noble mind, and maketh greater accompt of the reputation she shall have in marrying your worship, than that poor scholar, whose birth and parentage God knoweth, and very few else.

CLE. Yet he taketh it upon him bravely [5] in this country. 60

PASI. Yea, where no man knoweth the contrary. But let him brave it, boast his birth, and do what he can, the virtue and knowledge that is within this body of yours is worth more than all the country he came from.

CLE. It becometh not a man to praise himself; but indeed I may say, and say truly, that my knowledge hath stood me in better stead at a pinch than could all [70 the goods in the world. I came out of Otranto when the Turks won it, and first I came to Padua, after [6] hither, where, by reading,[7] counseling, and pleading, within twenty years I have gathered and gained as good as ten thousand ducats.

PASI. Yea, marry, this is the right knowledge! Philosophy, Poetry, Logic, and all the rest are but pickling [8] sciences in comparison to this. 80

CLE. But pickling indeed; whereof we have a verse:

The trade of law doth fill the boist'rous bags; [9]
They swim in silk, when others roist [10] in rags.

PASI. O excellent verse! Who made it? Virgil?

CLE. Virgil? Tush, it is written in one of our glosses.[11]

PASI. Sure, whosoever wrote it, the moral is excellent, and worthy to be [90 written in letters of gold. But to the purpose! I think you shall never recover the wealth that you lost at Otranto.

CLE. I think I have doubled it, or rather made it four times as much. *Another sup-* But, indeed, I lost mine only *pose.* son there, a child of five years old.

PASI. O great pity!

CLE. Yea, I had rather have lost all the goods in the world. 100

PASI. Alas! alas! by God! And grafts of such a stock are very gayson [12] in these days.

CLE. I know not whether he were slain, or the Turks took him and kept him as a bondslave.

PASI. Alas, I could weep for compassion! But there is no remedy but patience. You shall get many by this young damsel, with the grace of God. 110

CLE. Yea, if I get her.

PASI. Get her? Why doubt you of that?

CLE. Why? Her father holds me off with delays, so that I must needs doubt.

PASI. Content yourself, sir. He is a wise man and desirous to place his daughter well. He will not be too rash in his determination; he will think well of the matter. And let him think, for the longer he thinketh, the more good of you shall he [120 think. Whose wealth, whose virtue, whose skill, or whose estimation can he compare to yours in this city?

CLE. And hast thou not told him that I would make his daughter a dower of two thousand ducats?

PASI. Why, even now. I came but from thence since.[13]

---

[1] Palmist.
[2] Unbroken.
[3] Tippler.
[4] Satisfaction.
[5] Lives showily.
[6] Afterward.
[7] Lecturing.
[8] Trifling.
[9] Large pouches to hold the back hair of the wigs worn by judges.
[10] Bluster.
[11] Commentaries on the law.
[12] Geason, rare.
[13] Straightway.

CLE. What said he?

PASI. Nothing but that Erostrato [130 had proffered the like.

CLE. Erostrato? How can he make any dower, and his father yet alive?

PASI. Think you I did not tell him so? Yes, I warrant you, I forgot nothing that may furder [1] your cause. And doubt you not, Erostrato shall never have her—unless it be in a dream.

CLE. Well, gentle Pasiphilo, go thy ways and tell Damon I require nothing but [140 his daughter; I will none of his goods; I shall enrich her of mine own; and, if this dower of two thousand ducats seem not sufficient, I will make it five hundreth more, yea, a thousand, or whatsoever he will demand, rather than fail. Go to, Pasiphilo! Show thyself friendly in working this feat for me; spare for no cost. Since I have gone thus far, I will be loath to be outbidden. Go! 150

PASI. Where shall I come to you again?

CLE. At my house.

PASI. When?

CLE. When thou wilt.

PASI. Shall I come at dinner time?

CLE. I would bid thee to dinner, but it is a saint's even, which I have ever fasted.

PASI. [Aside.] Fast till thou famish!

CLE. Hark!

PASI. [Aside.] He speaketh of a dead [160 man's fast.[2]

CLE. Thou hearest me not.

PASI. [Aside.] Nor thou understandest me not.

CLE. I dare say thou art angry I bid thee not to dinner, but come if thou wilt; thou shalt take such as thou findest.

PASI. What! think you I know not where to dine?

CLE. Yes, Pasiphilo, thou art not to [170 seek.[3]

PASI. No, be you sure; there are enow will pray me.

CLE. That I know well enough, Pasiphilo. But thou canst not be better welcome in any place than to me. I will tarry for thee.

PASI. Well, since you will needs, I will come.

CLE. Despatch then, and bring no [180 news but good.

PASI. [Aside.] Better than my reward, by the Rood!

Cleander exit; Pasiphilo restat.[4]

SCENA iii.

Pasiphilo, Dulippo.[5]

[PASI.] O miserable, covetous wretch! He findeth an excuse by St. Nicholas' fast, because [6] I should not dine with him— as though I should dine at his own dish! He maketh goodly feasts, I promise you! It is no wonder though he think me bound unto him for my fare; for, over and besides that his provision is as scant as may be, yet there is great difference between his diet and mine. I never so much as [10 sip of the wine that he tasteth; I feed at the board's end with brown bread. Marry, I reach always to his own dish, for there are no more but that only on the table. Yet he thinks that for one such dinner I am bound to do him all the service that I can, and thinks me sufficiently rewarded for all my travail with one such festival promotion! And yet, peradventure, some men think I have great gains under him, [20 but I may say, and swear, that this dozen year I have not gained so much in value as the points at my hose,[7] which are but three, with codpiece-point and all. He thinks that I may feed upon his favor and fair words, but, if I could not otherwise provide for one, Pasiphilo were in a wise case.[8] Pasiphilo hath mo [9] pastures to pass in than one, I warrant you! I am of household with this scholar Eros- [30 trato, his rival, as well as with Domine [10] Cleander—now with the one, and then with the other, according as I see their caters [11] provide good cheer at the market—and I find the means so to handle the matter that I am welcome to both. If the one see me talk with the other, I make him believe it is to hearken news in the furtherance of his cause, and thus I become a broker on both sides. Well, [40 let them both apply the matter as well as

[1] Further.
[2] *I.e.*, one which, like Cleander's own, is never broken. [3] Not deficient in that respect.
[4] Remains.
[5] Enters later.
[6] By cause; why.
[7] Laces on my breeches.
[8] In a bad way.
[9] More.
[10] Master.
[11] Caterers.

they can, for indeed I will travail for none of them both, yet will I seem to work wonders on each hand. But is not this one of Damon's servants that cometh forth? It is. Of him I shall understand where his master is. Whither goeth this joyly [1] gallant?

[Enter Dulippo from Damon's house.]

DUL. I come to seek somebody that may accompany my master at dinner. [50 He is alone and would fain have good company.

PASI. Seek no further. You could never have found one better than me.

DUL. I have no commission to bring so many.

PASI. How,[2] many? I will come alone.

DUL. How canst thou come alone that hast continually a legion of ravening wolves within thee? 60

PASI. Thou dost, as servants commonly do, hate all that love to visit their masters.

DUL. And why?

PASI. Because they have too many teeth, as you think.

DUL. Nay, because they have too many tongues.

PASI. Tongues? I pray you, what did my tongue ever hurt you?

DUL. I speak but merrily with you, [70 Pasiphilo. Go in; my master is ready to dine.

PASI. What, dineth he so early?

DUL. He that riseth early, dineth early.

PASI. I would I were his man. Master Doctor never dineth till noon, and how delicately then, God knoweth! I will be bold to go in, for I count myself bidden.

DUL. You were best so.

Pasiphilo intrat; [3] *Dul[ippo] restat.*

Hard hap had I when I first be- [80 gan this unfortunate enterprise! For I supposed the readiest medicine to my miserable affects [4] had been to change name, clothes, and credit with my servant, and to place myself in Damon's service; thinking that, as shivering cold by glowing fire, thirst by drink, hunger by pleasant repasts, and a thousand such like

passions find remedy by their contraries, so my restless desire might have found [90 quiet by continual contemplation. But, alas, I find that only love is unsatiable, for, as the fly playeth with the flame till at last she is cause of her own decay, so the lover that thinketh with kissing and coll- ing [5] to content his unbridled appetite, is commonly seen the only cause of his own consumption. Two years are now past since, under the color [6] of Damon's service, I have been a sworn servant to Cupid [100 —of whom I have received as much favor and grace as ever man found in his service. I have free liberty at all times to behold my desired, to talk with her, to embrace her, yea, be it spoken in secret, to lie with her. I reap the fruits of my desire; yet, as my joys abound, even so my pains in- crease. I fare like the covetous man that, having all the world at will, is never yet content. The more I have, the more I [110 desire. Alas! what wretched estate have I brought myself unto, if in the end of all my far fetches [7] she be given by her father to this old doting doctor, this buzzard, this bribing villain, that by so many means seeketh to obtain her at her father's hands! I know she loveth me best of all others. But what may that prevail when perforce she shall be constrained to marry another? Alas! the pleasant taste of my sugared [120 joys doth yet remain so perfect in my remembrance that the least sop of sorrow seemeth more sour than gall in my mouth. If I had never known delight, with better contentation might I have passed these dreadful dolors. And if this old *mump- simus* [8]—whom the pox consume!—should win her, then may I say, "Farewell the pleasant talk, the kind embracings, yea, farewell the sight of my Polynesta!" [130 For he, like a jealous wretch, will pen her up, that I think the birds of the air shall not win the sight of her. I hoped to have cast a block in his way by the means that my servant, who is supposed to be Eros- trato and with my habit and credit is well esteemed, should proffer himself a suitor—at the least to countervail the doctor's proffers. But my master, knowing the wealth of the one and doubting the [140

---

[1] Elegant, well-dressed.
[2] In what way?
[3] Goes in.
[4] Feelings.
[5] "Necking," embracing.
[6] Pretense.
[7] Clever plots.
[8] Obstinate dolt.

state [1] of the other, is determined to be fed no longer with fair words, but to accept the doctor, whom he right well knoweth, for his son-in-law. Well, my servant promised me yesterday to devise yet again some new conspiracy to drive Master Doctor out of conceit, and to lay a snare that the fox himself might be caught in! What it is, I know not, nor I saw him not since he went about it. I will go see if he be [150 within, that at least if he help me not, he may yet prolong my life for this once. But here cometh his lackey. Ho, Jackpack, where is Erostrato?

Here must Crapine be coming in with a basket and a stick in his hand.

Scena iv.

Crapino, the lackey; Dulippo.

[Cra.] Erostrato? Marry, he is in his skin!

Dul. Ah, whoreson [2] boy! I say, how shall I find Erostrato?

Cra. Find [3] him? How mean you—by the week or by the year?

Dul. You crackhalter! [4] If I catch you by the ears, I shall make you answer me directly.

Cra. Indeed?   10

Dul. Tarry me a little.

Cra. In faith, sir, I have no leisure.

Dul. Shall we try who can run fastest?

Cra. Your legs be longer than mine; you should have given me the advantage.

Dul. Go to! Tell me where is Erostrato?

Cra. I left him in the street, where he gave me this casket—this basket, I would have said—and bade me bear it to [20 Dalio, and return to him at the duke's palace.

Dul. If thou see him, tell him I must needs speak with him immediately; or abide awhile! I will go seek him myself rather than be suspected by going to his house.

Crapino departeth, and Dulippo also; after, Dulippo cometh in again seeking Erostrato.

Finis Actus i.

[1] Estate.
[2] Rascally.
[3] Punning on *find*, to board, support.
[4] Gallows bird.

Actus II. Scena i.

Dulippo, Erostrato. [5]

[Dul.] I think if I had as many eyes as Argus I could not have sought a man more narrowly in every street and every by-lane. There are not many gentlemen, scholars, nor merchants in the city of Ferrara but I have met with them, except him. Peradventure he is come home another way. But look where he cometh at the last!

[Enter Erostrato.]

Ero. In good time have I spied my good master!   10

Dul. For the love of God, call me "Dulippo," not "master." Maintain the credit that thou hast hitherto kept, and let me alone.

Ero. Yet, sir, let me sometimes do my duty unto you, especially where nobody heareth.

Dul. Yea, but so long the parrot useth to cry "knap" [6] in sport that at the last she calleth her master "knave" in [20 earnest; so long you will use to call me "master," that at the last we shall be heard. What news?

Ero. Good!

Dul. Indeed?

Ero. Yea, excellent. We have as good as won the wager.

Dul. O, how happy were I if this were true!

Ero. Hear you me. Yesternight in [30 the evening I walked out and found Pasiphilo, and with small entreating I had him home to supper; where, by such means as I used, he became my great friend, and told me the whole order of our adversary's determination, yea, and what Damon doth intend to do also; and hath promised me that from time to time, what he can espy he will bring me word of it.

Dul. I cannot tell whether you [40 know him or no. He is not to trust unto— a very flattering and a lying knave.

Ero. I know him very well; he cannot deceive me. And this that he hath told me I know must needs be true.

Dul. And what was it in effect?

Ero. That Damon had purposed to give

[5] Enters later.   [6] Knave, rascal.

his daughter in marriage to this *Another sup-*
doctor upon the dower that he *pose.*
hath proffered. 50

DUL. Are these your good news, your
excellent news?

ERO. Stay awhile; you will understand
me before you hear me.

DUL. Well, say on.

ERO. I answered to that, I was ready to
make her the like dower.

DUL. Well said.

ERO. Abide; you hear not the worst yet.

DUL. O God, is there any worse [60
behind?

ERO. Worse? Why, what assurance could
you suppose that I might make without
some special consent from Philogano, my
father?

DUL. Nay, you can tell; you are better
scholar than I.

ERO. Indeed, you have lost your time,
for the books that you toss [1] nowadays
treat of small science! 70

DUL. Leave thy jesting and proceed.

ERO. I said, further, that I received
letters lately from my father, whereby I
understood that he would be here very
shortly to perform all that I had proffered.
Therefore I required him to request Damon
on my behalf that he would stay his promise to the doctor for a fortnight or more.

DUL. This is somewhat yet, for by this
means I shall be sure to linger and live [80
in hope one fortnight longer. But, at the
fortnight's end when Philogano cometh not,
how shall I then do? Yea, and though he
came, how may I any way hope of his consent, when he shall see that to follow this
amorous enterprise I have set aside all
study, all remembrance of my duty, and
all dread of shame? Alas, alas, I may go
hang myself!

ERO. Comfort yourself, man, and [90
trust in me. There is a salve for every sore,
and doubt you not, to this mischief we
shall find a remedy.

DUL. O, friend, revive me, that hitherto,
since I first attempted this matter, have
been continually dying.

ERO. Well, hearken awhile then. This
morning I took my horse and rode into the
fields to solace myself; and, as I passed the
ford beyond St. Anthony's Gate, I met [100

[1] Turn the leaves of.

at the foot of the hill a gentleman riding
with two or three men; and, as methought
by his habit and his looks, he should be
none of the wisest. He saluted me, and I
him. I asked him from whence he came,
and whither he would. He answered that
he had come from Venice, then from Padua,
now was going to Ferrara, and so to his
country, which is Siena. As soon as I
knew him to be a Sienese, suddenly [110
lifting up mine eyes, as it were with an admiration,[2] I said unto him, "Are you a
Sienese, and come to Ferrara?" "Why
not?" said he. Quoth I, half and more
with a trembling voice, "Know you the
danger that should ensue if you be known
in Ferrara to be a Sienese?" He, more than
half amazed, desired me earnestly to tell
him what I meant.

DUL. I understand not whereto this [120
tendeth.

ERO. I believe you. But hearken to me.

DUL. Go to, then.

ERO. I answered him in this sort: "Gentleman, because I have heretofore found
very courteous entertainment in your
country, being a student there, I accompt
myself, as it were, bound to a Sienese, and
therefore if I knew of any mishap towards
any of that country, God forbid but I [130
should disclose it. And I marvel that you
knew not of the injury that your countrymen offered this other day to the ambassadors of County [3] Hercules."

DUL. What tales he telleth me! What
appertain these to me?

ERO. If you will hearken awhile, you
shall find them no tales, but that they appertain to you more than you think for.

DUL. Forth. 140

ERO. I told him further, these ambassadors of County Hercules had divers
mules, wagons, and charettes,[4] laden with
divers costly jewels, gorgeous furniture, and
other things, which they carried as presents,
passing that way, to the King of Naples;
the which were not only stayed in Siene
by the officers whom you call customers,[5]
but searched, ransacked, tossed, and
turned, and in the end exacted for trib- [150
ute, as if they had been the goods of a
mean merchant.

[2] Wondering look.   [4] Carts.
[3] Count.   [5] Customs officers.

DUL. Whither the devil will he? Is it possible that this gear appertain anything to my cause? I find neither head nor foot in it.

ERO. O, how impatient you are! I pray you, stay awhile.

DUL. Go to yet awhile, then.

ERO. I proceeded that upon these [160 causes the duke sent his chancellor to declare the case unto the senate there, of whom he had the most uncourteous answer that ever was heard; whereupon he was so enraged with all of that country that for revenge he had sworn to spoil as many of them as ever should come to Ferrara, and to send them home in their doublet and their hose.

DUL. And, I pray thee, how could- [170 est thou upon the sudden devise or imagine such a lie, and to what purpose?

ERO. You shall hear by-and-by [1] a thing as fit for our purpose as any could have happened.

DUL. I would fain hear you conclude.

ERO. You would fain leap over the stile before you come at the hedge. I would you had heard me, and seen the gestures that I enforced to make him believe this! [180

DUL. I believe you, for I know you can counterfeit well.

ERO. Further, I said, the duke had charged, upon great penalties, that the inn-holders and victualers should bring word daily of as many Sieneses as came to their houses. The gentleman, being, as I guessed at the first, a man of small *sapientia*,[2] when he heard these news, would have turned his horse another way.   190

DUL. By likelihood he was not very wise when he would believe that of his country which, if it had been true, every man must needs have known it.

ERO. Why not, when he had not been in his country for a month past, and I told him this had happened within these seven days?

DUL. Belike [3] he was of small experience.

ERO. I think, of as little as may be. [200 But best of all for our purpose, and good adventure it was, that I met with such an one. Now hearken, I pray you.

DUL. Make an end, I pray thee.

ERO. He, as I say, when he heard these

words, would have turned the bridle; and I, feigning a countenance as though I were somewhat pensive and careful for him, paused awhile, and after, with a great sigh, said to him: "Gentleman, for the cour- [210 tesy that, as I said, I have found in your country, and because your affair shall be the better despatched, I will find the means to lodge you in my house, and you shall say to every man that you are a Sicilian of Cathanea, your name Philogano, father to me—that am indeed of that country and city—called here Erostrato. And I, to pleasure you, will during your abode here do you reverence as you were my [220 father."

DUL. Out upon me! What a gross-headed fool am I! Now I perceive whereto this tale tendeth.

ERO. Well, and how like you of it?

DUL. Indifferently.[4] But one thing I doubt.

ERO. What is that?

DUL. Marry, that when he hath been here two or three days, he shall hear of [230 every man that there is no such thing between the duke and the town of Siene.

ERO. As for that, let me alone. I do entertain and will entertain him so well that within these two or three days I will disclose unto him all the whole matter, and doubt not but to bring him in for performance of as much as I have promised to Damon. For what hurt can it be to him, when he shall bind [5] a strange name and [240 not his own?

DUL. What! Think you he will be entreated to stand bound for a dower of two thousand ducats by the year?

ERO. Yea, why not, if it were ten thousand, as long as he is not indeed the man that is bound?

DUL. Well, if it be so, what shall we be the nearer to our purpose?

ERO. Why, when we have done as [250 much as we can, how can we do any more?

DUL. And where have you left him?

ERO. At the inn, because of his horses. He and his men shall lie in my house.

DUL. Why brought you him not with you?

ERO. I thought better to use your advice first.

_____
[1] Immediately.   [2] Wisdom.   [3] Perhaps.

[4] Moderately well.   [5] Assume.

DUL. Well. go take him home. Make him all the cheer you can; spare for no [260 cost. I will allow it.

ERO. Content. Look where he cometh.

DUL. Is this he? Go meet him. By my troth, he looks even like a good soul! He that fisheth for him might be sure to catch a cod's head![1] I will rest here awhile to decipher him.

Erostrato espieth the Sienese and goeth towards him; Dulippo standeth aside.

SCENA ii.

The Sienese; Paquetto and Petruchio, his servants; Erostrato.

[SIEN.] He that traveleth in this world passeth by many perils.

PAQ. You say true, sir. If the boat had been a little more laden *Another sup-* this morning at the ferry, we *pose.*
had been all drowned, for I think there are none of us that could have swum.

SIEN. I speak not of that.

PAQ. O, you mean the foul way that we had since we came from this Padua. I [10 promise you, I was afraid twice or thrice that your mule would have lien [2] fast in the mire.

SIEN. Jesu, what a blockhead thou art! I speak of the peril we are in presently since we came into this city.

PAQ. A great peril, I promise you, that we were no sooner arrived but you found a friend that brought you from the inn and lodged you in his own house!   20

SIEN. Yea, marry, God reward the gentle young man that we met, for else we had been in a wise case by this time. But have done with these tales. *A doltish* And take you heed, and you *suppose.*
also, sirrah, take heed that none of you say we be Sieneses; and remember that you call me Philogano of Cathanea.

PAQ. Sure, I shall never remember these outlandish words! I could well re- [30 member Haccanea.[3]

SIEN. I say, "Cathanea," and not "Haccanea," with a vengeance!

PAQ. Let another name it, then, when need is, for I shall never remember it.

SIEN. Then hold thy peace, and take heed thou name not Siene.

PAQ. How say you if I feign myself dumb, as I did once in the house of Crisobolus?   40

SIEN. Do as thou thinkest best. [*Erostrato advances.*] But look where cometh the gentleman whom we are so much bound unto.

ERO. Welcome, my dear father Philogano.

SIEN. Gramercy, my good son Erostrato.

ERO. That is well said. Be mindful of your tongue, for these Ferrareses be [50 as crafty as the devil of hell.

SIEN. No, no; be you sure we will do as you have bidden us!

ERO. For, if you should name Siene, they would spoil you immediately, and turn you out of the town with more shame than I would should befall you for a thousand crowns.

SIEN. I warrant you, I was giving them warning as I came to you; and I doubt [60 not but they will take good heed.

ERO. Yea, and trust not the servants of my household too far, for they are Ferrareses all, and never knew my father, nor came never in Sicilia.—This is my house. Will it please you to go in? I will follow.

They go in. Dulippo tarrieth, and espieth the Doctor coming in with his Man.

SCENA iii.

Dulippo alone.

[DUL.] This gear hath had no evil beginning. If it continue so and fall to happy end! But is not this the silly doctor with the side [4] bonnet—the doting fool that dare presume to become a suitor to such a peerless paragon? O, how covetousness doth blind the common sort of men! Damon, more desirous of the dower than mindful of his gentle and gallant daughter, hath determined to make him his [10 son-in-law, who for his age may be his father-in-law, and hath greater respect to the abundance of goods than to his own natural child. He beareth well in mind to fill his own purse, but he little rememb'reth

---

[1] Fool.   [2] Lain.

[3] "Possibly a pun on *hackney* . . . a prostitute" (Adams).

[4] Large.

that his daughter's purse shall be continually empty—unless Master Doctor fill it with double duck eggs.[1] Alas, I jest, and have no joy! I will stand here aside and laugh a little at this lobcock.[2] 20
Dulippo espieth the Doctor and his Man coming.

SCENA iv.

Carion, the Doctor's Man; Cleander; Dulippo [, who stands aside].

[CAR.] Master, what the devil mean you to go seek guests at this time of the day? The mayor's officers have dined ere this time, which are alway the last in the market.

CLE. I come to seek Pasiphilo, to the end he may dine with me.

CAR. As though six mouths, and the cat for the seventh, be not sufficient to eat an harlotry shotterell,[3] a penny-[10 worth of cheese, and half a score spurlings![4] This is all the dainties you have dressed for you and your family.

CLE. Ah, greedy gut, art thou afeard thou shalt want?

CAR. I am afeard indeed! It is not the first time I have found it so.

DUL. [*Aside.*] Shall I make some sport with this gallant? What shall I say to him? 20

CLE. Thou art afeard, belike, that he will eat thee and the rest.

CAR. Nay, rather that he will eat your mule, both hair and hide.

CLE. Hair and hide? And why not flesh and all?

CAR. Because she hath none! If she had any flesh, I think you had eaten her yourself by this time.

CLE. She may thank you, then, for [30 your good attendance.

CAR. Nay, she may thank you for your small allowance.

DUL. [*Aside.*] In faith, now, let me alone.

CLE. Hold thy peace, drunken knave, and espy me Pasiphilo.

DUL. [*Aside.*] Since I can do no better,

I will set such a stance [5] between him and Pasiphilo that all this town shall not [40 make them friends.

CAR. Could you not have sent to seek him, but you must come yourself? Surely you come for some other purpose, for, if you would have had Pasiphilo to dinner, I warrant you he would have tarried here an hour since.[6]

CLE. Hold thy peace! Here is one of Damon's servants. Of him I *Another sup-* shall understand where he is. *pose.*
Good fellow, art not thou one of Damon's servants? 52

DUL. Yes, sir, at your knamandement.[7]

CLE. Gramercy. Tell me, then, hath Pasiphilo been there this day or no?

DUL. Yes, sir, and I think he be there still. Ah, ah, ah!

CLE. What [8] laughest thou?

DUL. At a thing that every man may not laugh at. 60

CLE. What?

DUL. Talk that Pasiphilo had with my master this day.

CLE. What talk, I pray thee?

DUL. I may not tell it.

CLE. Doth it concern me?

DUL. Nay, I will say nothing.

CLE. Tell me.

DUL. I can say no more.

CLE. I would but know if it concern [70 me. I pray thee tell me.

DUL. I would tell you if I were sure you would not tell it again.

CLE. Believe me, I will keep it close. Carion, give us leave a little; go aside.
[*Carion stands aside.*]

DUL. If my master should know that it came by me, I were better die a thousand deaths.

CLE. He shall never know it. Say on.

DUL. Yea, but what assurance shall [80 I have?

CLE. I lay thee my faith and honesty in pawn.

DUL. A pretty pawn! The fulkers [9] will not lend you a farthing on it.

CLE. Yea, but amongst honest men it is more worth than gold.

1 "Pun on 'duckets,' and also with a further and coarse meaning" (Adams).
   2 Lubber.   4 Sparlings, smelts.
   3 Scurvy pike.

5 Distance, disagreement.
6 He would have been waiting here an hour ago.
7 Commandment. So all early edns.
8 Why.   9 Pawnbrokers.

Dul. Yea, marry, sir, but where be they? But will you needs have me tell it unto you? 90

Cle. Yea, I pray thee, if it anything appertain to me.

Dul. Yes, it is of you. And I would gladly tell it you, because I would not have such a man of worship so scorned by a villain ribald.[1]

Cle. I pray thee tell me then.

Dul. I will tell you, so that you will swear never to tell it to Pasiphilo, to my master, nor to any other body. 100

Car. [Aside.] Surely it is some toy[2] devised to get some money of him.

Cle. I think I have a book here.

Car. [Aside.] If he knew him as well as I, he would never go about it, for he may as soon get one of his teeth from his jaws with a pair of pinchers as a penny out of his purse with such a conceit.

Cle. Here is a letter will serve the turn. I swear to thee by the contents hereof [110 never to disclose it to any man.

Dul. I will tell you. I am sorry to see how Pasiphilo doth abuse you, persuading you that always he laboreth for you, where, indeed, he lieth on my master continually, as it were with tooth and nail, for a stranger, a scholar, born in Sicilia. They call him Roscus, or Arsekiss—he hath a mad name; I can never hit upon it.

Cle. And thou reckonest it as madly. Is it not Erostrato? 121

Dul. That same. I should never have remembered it. And the villain[3] speaketh all the evil of you that can be devised.

Cle. To whom?

Dul. To my master; yea, and to Polynesta herself sometimes.

Cle. Is it possible? Ah, slave! And what saith he?

Dul. More evil than I can imagine: [130 that you are the miserablest and most niggardly man that ever was.

Cle. Sayeth Pasiphilo so by me?

Dul. And that as often as he cometh to your house he is like to die for hunger, you fare so well.

Cle. That the devil take him else!

Dul. And that you are the testiest man,

and most divers[4] to please, in the whole world, so that he cannot please you un- [140 less he should even kill himself with continual pain.

Cle. O devilish tongue!

Dul. Furthermore, that you cough continually and spit, so that a dog cannot abide it.

Cle. I never spit nor cough more than thus—vho, vho; and that but since I caught this murre.[5] But who is free from it?

Dul. You say true, sir. Yet further, [150 he saith your armholes stink, your feet worse than they, and your breath worst of all.

Cle. If I quite[6] him not for this gear!

Dul. And that you are bursten in the cods.[7]

Cle. O villain! He lieth! And if I were not in the street thou shouldest see them.

Dul. And he saith that you desire [160 this young gentlewoman as much for other men's pleasure as for your own.

Cle. What meaneth he by that?

Dul. Peradventure that by her beauty you would entice many young men to your house.

Cle. Young men? To what purpose?

Dul. Nay, guess you that.

Cle. Is it possible that Pasiphilo speaketh thus of me? 170

Dul. Yea, and much more.

Cle. And doth Damon believe him?

Dul. Yea, more than you would think; in such sort that long ere this he would have given you a flat repulse, but Pasiphilo entreated him to continue you a suitor for his advantage.

Cle. How for his advantage?

Dul. Marry, that during your suit he might still have some reward for his [180 great pains.

Cle. He shall have a rope, and yet that is more than he deserveth. I had thought to have given him these hose when I had worn them a little nearer, but he shall have a &c.[8]

Dul. In good faith, sir, they were but lost on him. Will you anything else with me, sir?

---

[1] Lewd scoundrel. [2] Trick.
[3] So other edns. than original, which has villainy.

[4] Diverse, perverse, difficult.
[5] Catarrh. [7] Scrotum.
[6] Requite. [8] To be filled out by the actor.

CLE. Nay, I have heard too much [190 of [1] thee already.

DUL. Then I will take my leave of you.

CLE. Farewell! But tell me, may I not know thy name?

DUL. Sir, they call me Foul-fall-you.

CLE. An ill-favored name, by my troth! Art thou this countryman? [2]

DUL. No, sir, I was born by a castle men call Scab-catch-you. Fare you well, sir!   [*Exit.*] 200

CLE. Farewell! O God, how have I been abused! What a spokesman! What a messenger had I provided!

CAR. Why, sir, will you tarry for Pasiphilo till we die for hunger?

CLE. Trouble me not. That the devil take you both!

CAR. [*Aside.*] These news, whatsoever they be, like him not.

CLE. Art thou so hungry yet? I pray [210 to God thou be never satisfied!

CAR. By the Mass, no more I shall, as long as I am your servant.

CLE. Go, with mischance!

CAR. Yea, and a mischief to you and to all such covetous wretches!   [*Exeunt.*]

FINIS ACTUS II.

ACTUS III. SCENA i.

Dalio, the cook; Crapine, the lackey; Erostrato; Dulippo.[3]

[DAL.] By that time we come to the house I trust that of these twenty eggs in the basket we shall find but very few whole. But it is a folly to talk to him. What the devil! Wilt thou never lay that stick out of thy hand? He fighteth with the dogs, beateth the bears; at everything in the street he findeth occasion to tarry. If he spy a slipstring [4] by the way—such another as himself, a page, a lackey, or a [10 dwarf—the devil of hell cannot hold him in chains but he will be doing with him. I cannot go two steps but I must look back for my yonker. Go to, haltersick! [5] If you break one egg, I may chance break &c.

CRA. What will you break? Your nose in mine, &c.?

DAL. Ah, beast!

CRA. If I be a beast, yet I am no horned [6] beast.   20

DAL. Is it even so? Is the wind in that door? If I were unloaden, I would tell you whether I be a horned beast or no.

CRA. You are alway laden either with wine or with ale.

DAL. Ah, spiteful boy! Shall I suffer him?   [*Strikes him.*]

CRA. Ah, cowardly beast, darest thou strike and say never a word?

DAL. Well, my master shall know of [30 this gear. Either he shall redress it or he shall lose one of us.

CRA. Tell him the worst thou canst by me.

Erostra[to] et Du[lippo] ex improviso.[7]

ERO. What noise, what a rule [8] is this?

CRA. Marry, sir, he striketh me because I tell him of his swearing.

DAL. The villain lieth deadly! He reviles me because I bid him make haste.

ERO. Holla! no more of this. Dalio, [40 do you make in a readiness those pigeons, stock doves, and also the breast of veal; and let your vessel be as clear as glass against I return, that I may tell you which I will have roasted and which boiled. [*Exit Dalio.*] Crapine, lay down that basket and follow me. O, that I could tell where to find Pasiphilo!—But look where he cometh that can tell me of him.

Dulippo is espied by Erostrato.

DUL. What have you done with [50 Philogano, your father?

ERO. I have left him within. I would fain speak with Pasiphilo. Can you tell me where he is?

DUL. He dined this day with my master, but whither he went from thence I know not. What would you with him?

ERO. I would have him go tell Damon that Philogano, my father, is come, and ready to make assurance of as much as [60 he will require. Now shall I teach Master Doctor a school point. He travaileth to none other end but to catch *cornua*,[9] and he shall have them, for, as old as he is, and

---

[1] From.   [2] A man of this country.

[3] Last two enter later.

[4] Eluder of the gallows.

[5] Haltersack, gallows bird.

[6] Alluding to the horns of a cuckold.

[7] Enter unexpectedly. (But Erostrato does not notice Dulippo immediately.)   [9] Horns; also cuckoldry.

[8] Conduct, unruliness.

as many subtilties as he hath learned in the law, he cannot go beyond me one ace.

DUL. O dear friend, go thy ways, seek Pasiphilo, find him out, and conclude somewhat to our contentation.

ERO. But where shall I find him?   70

DUL. At the feasts, if there be any, or else in the market with the poulters or the fishmongers.

ERO. What should he do with them?

DUL. Marry, he watcheth whose caters buy the best meat. If any buy a fat capon, a good breast of veal, fresh salmon, or any such good dish, he followeth to the house, and either with some news or some stale jest, he will be sure to make himself [80 a guest.

ERO. In faith, and I will seek there for him.

DUL. Then must you needs find him, and, when you have done, I will make you laugh.

ERO. Whereat?

DUL. At certain sport I made today with Master Doctor.

ERO. And why not now?

DUL. No, it asketh further leisure. [90 I pray thee despatch and find out Pasiphilo, that honest man.

Dulippo tarrieth.   Erostrato goeth out [with Crapine].

SCENA ii.

Dulippo alone.

[DUL.] This amorous cause that hangeth in controversy between Domine Doctor and me may be compared to them that play at primero:[1] of whom someone, peradventure, shall leese[2] a great sum of money before he win one stake, and at last, half in anger, shall set up his rest, win it, and after that another, another, and another, till at last he draw the most part of the money to his heap, the other by [10 little and little still diminishing his rest, till at last he be come as near the brink as erst the other was; yet again, peradventure, fortune smiling on him, he shall, as it were by piecemeal, pull out the guts of his fellow's bags, and bring him barer than he himself was tofore;[3] and so in play continue still, fortune favoring now this way, now that way, till at last the one of them

is left with as many crosses[4] as God [20 hath brethren.[5]   O, how often have I thought myself sure of the upper hand herein!—but I triumphed before the victory.   And then how oft again have I thought the field lost!   Thus have I been tossed, now over, now under, even as fortune list to whirl the wheel, neither sure to win nor certain to lose the wager. And this practice that now my servant hath devised, although hitherto it hath not [30 succeeded amiss, yet can I not count myself assured of it; for I fear still that one mischance or other will come and turn it topsy-turvy.   But look where my master cometh.

Damon, coming in, espieth Dulippo and calleth him.

SCENA iii.

Damon, Dulippo, Nevola, and two mo Servants.[6]

[DAM.] Dulippo!

DUL. Here, sir.

DAM. Go in and bid Nevola and his fellows come hither, that I may tell them what they shall go about. And go you into my study; there upon the shelf you shall find a roll of writings which John of the Dean[7] made to my father when he sold him the Grange farm, endorsed with both their names. Bring it hither to me.   10

DUL. It shall be done, sir.   [*Exit.*]

DAM. Go. I will prepare other manner of writings for you than you are aware of. O fools, that trust any man but themselves nowadays! O spiteful fortune! Thou dost me wrong, I think, that from the depth of hell-pit thou hast sent me this servant to be the subversion of me and all mine!— Come hither, sirs, and hear what I shall say unto you. (*The Servants come in.*) [20 Go into my study, where you shall find Dulippo. Step to him all at once, take him, and, with a cord that I have laid on the table for the nonce, bind him hand and foot, carry him into the dungeon under the stairs, make fast the door, and bring me the key—it hangeth by upon a pin on the wall. Despatch, and do this gear as privily as

---

[1] Game of cards.   [2] Lose.   [3] Before.

[4] Coins.   [6] Last three enter later.
[5] *I.e.*, none at all.   [7] Valley.

you can. And thou, Nevola, come hither
to me again with speed.　　　　　　30

NEV. Well, I shall. [*Exit with Servants.*]

DAM. Alas, how shall I be revenged of
this extreme despite? If I punish my servant according to his devilish deserts, I
shall heap further cares upon mine own
head. For to such detestable offenses no
punishment can seem sufficient but only
death, and in such cases it is not lawful for
a man to be his own carver. The laws are
ordained, and officers appointed to min- [40
ister justice for the redress of wrongs; and,
if to the potestates [1] I complain me, I shall
publish mine own reproach to the world.
Yea, what should it prevail [2] me to use all
the punishments that can be devised? The
thing, once done, cannot be undone. My
daughter is deflowered, and I utterly dishonested.[3] How can I then wipe that blot
off my brow? And on whom shall I seek
revenge? Alas, alas, I myself have been [50
the cause of all these cares, and have deserved to bear the punishment of all these
mishaps! Alas, I should not have committed my dearest darling in custody to so
careless a creature as this old nurse; for we
see by common proof that these old women
be either peevish [4] or pitiful, either easily
inclined to evil or quickly corrupted with
bribes and rewards. O wife, my good wife,
that now liest cold in the grave, now [60
may I well bewail the want of thee, and,
mourning, now may I bemoan that I miss
thee! If thou hadst lived, such was thy
government of the least things that thou
wouldest prudently have provided for the
preservation of this pearl. A costly jewel
may I well accompt her, that hath been
my chief comfort in youth, and is now become the corrosive of mine age! O Polynesta, full evil hast thou requited the [70
clemency of thy careful father! And yet
to excuse thee guiltless before God and to
condemn thee guilty before the world, I
can count none other but my wretched
self the caitiff [5] and causer of all my cares.
For of all the duties that are requisite in
human life, only obedience is by the parents to be required of the child, where, on
the other side, the parents are bound, first
to beget them, then to bring them forth, [80

after to nourish them, to preserve them
from bodily perils in the cradle, from danger
of soul by godly education, to match them
in consort [6] inclined to virtue, to banish
them all idle and wanton company, to
allow them sufficient for their sustentation,
to cut off excess (the open gate of sin),
seldom or never to smile on them unless it
be to their encouragement in virtue, and
finally to provide them marriages in [90
time convenient, lest, neglected of us, they
learn to set either too much or too little
by themselves. Five years are past since
I might have married her, when by continual excuses I have prolonged it to my
own perdition. Alas, I should have considered she is a collop [7] of my own flesh.
What should I think to make her a princess? Alas, alas, a poor kingdom have
I now caught to endow her with! It is [100
too true that of all sorrows this is the head
source and chief fountain of all furies: the
goods of the world are incertain, the gains
[little] [8] to be rejoiced at, and the loss not
greatly to be lamented; only the children,
cast away, cutteth the parents' throat with
the knife of inward care, which knife will
kill me surely—I make none other accompt.

Damon's Servants come to him again.

SCENA iv.

Nevola, Damon, Pasiphilo.[9]

[NEV.] Sir, we have done as you bade us,
and here is the key.

DAM. Well, go then, Nevola, and seek
Master Casteling, the jailor; he dwelleth by
St. Antony's Gate. Desire him to lend
me a pair of the fetters he useth for his
prisoners; and come again quickly.

NEV. Well, sir.

DAM. Hear you. If he ask what I
would do with them, say you cannot [10
tell. And tell neither him nor any other
what is become of Dulippo.

Damon goeth out.

[NEV.] I warrant you, sir.—Fie upon the
devil! It is a thing almost unpossible
for a man nowadays to handle money but
the metal will stick on his *Another sup-*
fingers. I marveled alway at *pose.*
this fellow of mine, Dulippo, that of the

---

[1] Chief magistrates.　　　　[2] Avail.
[3] Dishonored.　[4] Silly, weak.　[5] Captive.

[6] Companionship.　　[8] Suggested by Bond.
[7] Slice, chip.　　[9] Enters later.

wages he received he could maintain himself so bravely appareled, but now [20 I perceive the cause. He had the disbursing and receipt of all my master's affairs, the keys of the graner;[1] Dulippo here, Dulippo there; [in] favor with my master, in favor with his daughter—what would you more? He was *magister facto-tum*.[2] He was as fine as the crusado,[3] and we silly wretches as coarse as canvas. Well, behold what it is come to in the end! He had been better to have done less. 30

Pasi[philo] subito et improviso venit.[4]

PASI. Thou sayst true, Nevola! He hath done too much, indeed.

NEV. From whence comest thou, in the devil's name?

PASI. Out of the same house thou camest from, but not out of the same door.

NEV. We had thought thou hadst been gone long since.

PASI. When I arose from the table, I felt a rumbling in my belly, which [40 made me run to the stable, and there I fell on sleep[5] upon the straw and have lien there ever since. And thou—whither goest thou?

NEV. My master hath sent me on an errand in great haste.

PASI. Whither, I pray thee?

NEV. Nay, I may not tell. Farewell.
[*Exit.*]

PASI. As though I need any further instructions! O God, what news I heard [50 even now, as I lay in the stable! O good Erostrato, and poor Cleander, that have so earnestly stroven for this *Another sup-* damsel! Happy is he that can *pose.* get her, I promise you! He shall be sure of mo than one at a clap that catcheth her—either Adam or Eve within her belly. O God, how men may be deceived in a woman! Who would have believed the contrary but that she had [60 been a virgin? Ask the neighbors, and you shall hear very good report of her. Mark her behaviors, and you would have judged her very maidenly—seldom seen abroad but in place of prayer and there very devout, and no gazer at outward sights, no

blazer of her beauty above in the windows, no stale[6] at the door for the bypassers. You would have thought her a holy young woman. But much good do it Domine [70 Doctor! He shall be sure to lack no CORN[7] in a dear year, whatsoever he have with her else. I beshrew me if I let[8] the marriage any way. But is not this the old scabbed quean[9] that I heard disclosing all this gear to her master as I stood in the stable ere now? It is she. Whither goeth, Psiteria?

Pasiphilo espieth Psiteria coming.

SCENA V.

Psiteria, Pasiphilo.

[PSIT.] To a gossip[10] of mine hereby.

PASI. What, to tattle of the goodly stir that thou kept'st concerning Polynesta?

PSIT. No, no. But how knew you of that gear?

PASI. You told me.

PSIT. I? When did I tell you?

PASI. Even now when you told it to Damon. I both saw you and heard you, though you saw not me. A good part, [10 I promise you, to accuse the poor wench, kill the old man with care, over and besides the danger you have brought Dulippo and the nurse unto, and many mo! Fie! fie!

PSIT. Indeed, I was to blame, but not so much as you think.

PASI. And how not so much? Did I not hear you tell?

PSIT. Yes, but I will tell you how it [20 came to pass. I have known for a great while that this Dulippo and Polynesta have lien together, and all by the means of the nurse; yet I held my peace and never told it. Now this other day the nurse fell on scolding with me, and twice or thrice called me "drunken old whore" and such names that it was too bad; and I called her "bawd" and told her that I knew well enough how often she had brought [30 Dulippo to Polynesta's bed. Yet all this while I thought not that anybody had heard me; but it befell clean contrary, for my master was on the other side of

---

[1] Granary.   [2] Master Do-all.   [3] A coin.
[4] Pasiphilo enters suddenly and unexpectedly.
[5] Asleep.

[6] Decoy.
[7] Pun on the Latin word for *horn*.
[8] Hinder.   [9] Vile slut.   [10] Crony.

the wall and heard all our talk, whereupon he sent for me and forced me to confess all that you heard.

PASI. And why wouldest thou tell him? I would not for &c.

PSIT. Well, if I had thought my [40 master would have taken it so, he should rather have killed me.

PASI. Why, how could he take it?

PSIT. Alas, it pitieth me to see the poor young woman, how she weeps, wails, and tears her hair, not esteeming her own life half so dear as she doth poor Dulippo's; and her father, he weeps on the other side, that it would pierce an heart of stone with pity. But I must be gone.　　50

PASI. Go! That the gunpowder consume thee, old trot![1]　　[Exeunt.]

FINIS ACTUS III.

ACTUS IV. SCENA i.

Erostrato, feigned [,accompanied by Crapine].

[ERO.] What shall I do? Alas! what remedy shall I find for my rueful estate? What escape or what excuse may I now devise to shift over[2] our subtile supposes? For, though to this day I have usurped the name of my master, and that without check or control of any man, now shall I be openly deciphered, and that in the sight of every man. Now shall it openly be known whether I be Erostrato the [10 gentleman, or Dulippo the servant. We have hitherto played our parts in abusing[3] others, but now cometh the man that will not be abused—the right Philogano, the right father of the right Erostrato. Going to seek Pasiphilo and hearing that he was at the water gate, behold I espied my fellow Litio, and by-and-by my old master Philogano setting forth his first step on land. I to fuge,[4] and away [20 hither as fast as I could to bring word to the right Erostrato of his right father Philogano, that to so sudden a mishap some subtile shift might be upon the sudden devised. But what can be imagined to serve the turn, although we had months' respite to beat our brains about it, since we are commonly known—at the least supposed—in this town, he for Dulippo,

a slave and servant to Damon, and I [30 for Erostrato, a gentleman and a student? But behold, run, Crapine, to yonder old woman before she get within the doors, and desire her to call out Dulippo. But hear you—if she ask who would speak with him, say thyself and none other.

Erostrato espieth Psiteria coming, and sendeth his Lackey to her.

SCENA ii.

Crapine, Psiteria, Erostrato, feigned.

[CRA.] Honest woman! you gossip! thou rotten whore! Hearest thou not, old witch?

PSIT. A rope stretch your young bones! Either you must live to be as old as I or be hanged while you are young.

CRA. I pray thee, look if Dulippo be within.

PSIT. Yes, that he is, I warrant him!

CRA. Desire him, then, to come hither and speak a word with me. He shall [10 not tarry.

PSIT. Content yourself; he is otherwise occupied.

CRA. Yet tell him so, gentle girl.

PSIT. I tell you, he is busy.

CRA. Why, is it such a matter to tell him so, thou crooked crone?

PSIT. A rope stretch you, marry!

CRA. A pox eat you, marry!

PSIT. Thou wilt be hanged, I war- [20 rant thee, if thou live to it.

CRA. And thou wilt be burnt, I warrant thee, if the canker consume thee not.

PSIT. If I come near you, hempstring,[5] I will teach you to sing sol fa![6]

CRA. Come on! and if I get a stone I will scare crows with you.

PSIT. Go, with a mischief! I think thou be some devil that would tempt me. [Exit.]

ERO. Crapine! Hear you? Come [30 away. Let her go, with a vengeance! Why come you not? Alas, look where my master Philogano cometh! What shall I do? Where shall I hide me? He shall not see me in these clothes, nor before I have spoken with the right Erostrato.

Erostrato espieth Philogano coming and
runneth about to hide him

_____

[1] Hag.　[2] Conceal.　[3] Deceiving.　[4] Flight.

[5] Gallows bird.　　　[6] I.e., scream.

Scena iii.

Philogano; Ferrarese, the innkeeper; Litio, a servant.

[Phi.] Honest man, it is even so. Be you sure there is no love to be compared like the love of the parents towards their children. It is not long since I thought that a very weighty matter should not have made me come out of Sicilia; and yet now I have taken this tedious toil and travail upon me, only to see my son and to have him home with me.

Fer. By my faith, sir, it hath been a [10 great travail indeed, and too much for one of your age.

Phi. Yea, be you sure. I came in company with certain gentlemen of my country, who had affairs to despatch as far as to Ancona, from thence by water to Ravenna, and from Ravenna hither, continually against the tide.

Fer. Yea, and I think that you had but homely lodging by the way. 20

Phi. The worst that ever man had. But that was nothing to the stir that the searchers [1] kept with me when I came aboard the ship. Jesus, how often they untrussed my male [2] and ransacked a little capcase [3] that I had, tossed and turned all that was within it, searched my bosom, yea, my breeches, that I assure you I thought they would have flayed me to search between the fell [4] and the flesh [30 for fardings.[5]

Fer. Sure, I have heard no less, and that the merchants bob [6] them sometimes; but they play the knaves still.

Phi. Yea, be you well assured; such an office is the inheritance of a knave, and an honest man will not meddle with it.

Fer. Well, this passage shall seem pleasant unto you when you shall find your child in health and well. But, I pray you, [40 sir, why did you not rather send for him into Sicilia than to come yourself, specially since you had none other business? Peradventure you had rather endanger yourself by this noisome [7] journey than hazard to draw him from his study.

Phi. Nay, that was not the matter, for I had rather have him give over his study altogether and come home.

Fer. Why, if you minded not to [50 make him learned, to what end did you send him hither at the first?

Phi. I will tell you. When he was at home, he did as most young men do—he played many mad pranks and did many things that liked me not very well; and I, thinking that by that time he had seen the world he would learn to know himself better, exhorted him to study and put in his election what place he would go to. [60 At the last he came hither, and I think he was scarce here so soon as I felt the want of him, in such sort as from that day to this I have passed few nights without tears. I have written to him very often that he should come home, but continually he refused, still beseeching me to continue his study, wherein he doubted not, as he said, but to profit greatly.

Fer. Indeed, he is very much com- [70 mended of all men, and specially of the best reputed students.

Phi. I am glad he hath not lost his time, but I care not greatly for so much knowledge. I would not be without the sight of him again so long for all the learning in the world. I am old now, and, if God should call me in his absence, I promise you I think it would drive me into desperation. 80

Fer. It is commendable in a man to love his children, but to be so tender over them is more womanlike.

Phi. Well, I confess it is my fault. And yet I will tell you another cause of my coming hither, more weighty than this. Divers of my country have been here since he came hither, by whom I have sent unto him, and some of them have been thrice, some four or five times at his house, [90 and yet could never speak with him. I fear he applies his study so that he will not leese the minute of an hour from his book. What, alas, he might yet talk with his countrymen for a while! He is a young man, tenderly brought up, and, if he fare thus continually night and day at his book, it may be enough to drive him into a frenzy.

Fer. Indeed, enough were as good [100

---

[1] Customs officers.
[2] Opened my trunk.
[3] Bag.
[4] Skin.
[5] Farthings, *i.e.*, taxable goods.
[6] Deceive, cheat.
[7] Annoying.

as a feast. Lo you, sir, here is your son Erostrato's house. I will knock.

PHI. Yea, I pray you knock.

[Knocks on the door.]

FER. They hear not.

PHI. Knock again.

FER. I think they be on sleep.

LIT. If this gate were your grandfather's soul, you could not knock more softly. Let me come! [Knocks violently.] Ho, ho! Is there anybody within?　110

Dalio cometh to the window, and there maketh them answer.

SCENA iv.

Dalio, the cook; Ferrarese, the innholder; Philogano; Litio, his man.

[DAL.] What devil of hell is there? I think he will break the gates in pieces!

LIT. Marry, sir, we had thought you had been on sleep within, and therefore we thought best to wake you. What doth Erostrato?

DAL. He is not within.

PHI. Open the door, good fellow, I pray thee.

DAL. If you think to lodge here, [10 you are deceived, I tell you; for here are guests enow already.

PHI. A good fellow, and much for thy master['s] honesty, by our Lady! And what guests, I pray thee?

DAL. Here is Philogano, my *Another sup-*master's father, lately come *pose.* out of Sicilia.

PHI. Thou speakest truer than thou art aware of. He will be, by that time thou [20 hast opened the door. Open, I pray thee heartily.

DAL. It is a small matter for me to open the door, but here is no lodging for you. I tell you plain, the house is full.

PHI. Of whom?

DAL. I told you. Here is Philogano, my master's father, come from Cathanea.

PHI. And when came he?

DAL. He came three hours since, or [30 more. He alighted at the Angel and left his horses there. Afterward my master brought him hither.

PHI. Good fellow, I think thou hast good sport to mock me.

DAL. Nay, I think you have good sport

to make me tarry here, as though I have nothing else to do. I am matched with an unruly mate in the kitchen. I will go look to him another while.　40

PHI. I think he be drunken.

FER. Sure he seems so. See you not how red he is about the gills?

PHI. Abide, fellow. What Philogano is it whom thou talkest of?

DAL. An honest gentleman, father to Erostrato, my master.

PHI. And where is he?

DAL. Here within.

PHI. May we see him?　50

DAL. I think you may if you be not blind.

PHI. Go to! Go tell him here is one would speak with him.

DAL. Marry, that I will willingly do.

Dalio draweth his head in at the window.[1]

PHI. I cannot tell what I should say to this gear. Litio, what thinkest thou of it?

LIT. I cannot tell you what I should say, sir. The world is large and long; there [59 may be mo Philoganos and mo *Another sup-*Erostratos than one, yea, and *pose.* mo Ferraras, mo Sicilias, and mo Cathaneas. Peradventure this is not that Ferrara which you sent your son unto.

PHI. Peradventure thou art a fool, and he was another that answered us even now.—But be you sure, honest man, that you mistake not the house?

FER. Nay, then God help! Think you I know not Erostrato's house? Yes, and [70 himself also. I saw him here no longer since than yesterday. But here comes one that will tell us tidings of him. I like his countenance better than the other's that answered at the window erewhile.

The Sienese cometh out.

SCENA v.

Sienese, Philogano, [Ferrarese, Litio,] Dalio.

[SIEN.] Would you speak with me, sir?

PHI. Yea, sir; I would fain know whence you are.

SIEN. Sir, I am a Sicilian, at your commandment.

PHI. What part of Sicilia?

SIEN. Of Cathanea.

[1] This direction appears at the end of the scene in all early edns.

Phi. What shall I call your name?

Sien. My name is Philogano.

Phi. What trade do you occupy? 10

Sien. Merchandise.

Phi. What merchandise brought you hither?

Sien. None. I came only to see a son that I have here whom I saw not these two years.

Phi. What call they your son?

Sien. Erostrato.

Phi. Is Erostrato your son?

Sien. Yea, verily.

Phi. And are you Philogano? 20

Sien. The same.

Phi. And a merchant of Cathanea?

Sien. What need I tell you so often? I will not tell you a lie.

Phi. Yes, you have told me a false lie, and thou art a villain, and no better!

Sien. Sir, you offer me great wrong with these injurious words.

Phi. Nay, I will do more than I have yet proffered to do, for I will prove thee a [30 liar and a knave to take upon thee that thou art not.

Sien. Sir, I am Philogano of Cathanea, out of all doubt. If I were not, *A stout sup-* I would be loath to tell you so. *pose.*

Phi. O, see the boldness of this brute beast! What a brazen face he setteth on it!

Sien. Well, you may believe me if you list. What wonder you?

Phi. I wonder at thy impudency; for [40 thou, nor nature that framed thee, can ever counterfeit thee to be me, ribald villain and lying wretch that thou art!

Dal. Shall I suffer a knave to abuse my master's father thus? [*Draws A pleasant his sword.*] Hence, villain! *suppose.* Hence, or I will sheathe this good faw-chion [1] in your paunch! If my master Erostrato find you prating here on this fashion to his father, I would not be in [50 your coat for mo cony skins [2] than I gat these twelve months. Come you in again, sir, and let this cur bark here till he burst!

Dalio pulleth the Sienese in at the doors.

Scena vi.

Philogano, Litio, Ferrarese.

[Phi.] Litio, how likest thou this gear?

Lit. Sir, I like it as evil as may be. But have you not often heard tell of the false-

[1] Falchion. [2] Rabbit skins.

hood of Ferrara? And now may you see, it falleth out accordingly.

Fer. Friend, you do not well to slander the city. These men are no Ferrareses, you may know by their tongue.

Lit. Well, there is never a barrel better herring between you both.[3] But indeed [10 your officers are most to blame, that suffer such faults to escape unpunished.

Fer. What know the officers of this? Think you they know of every fault?

Lit. Nay, I think they will know as little as may be, specially when they have no gains by it. But they ought to have their ears as open to hear of such offenses as the inn gates be to receive guests.

Phi. Hold thy peace, fool! 20

Lit. By the Mass, I am afeard that we shall be proved fools, both two.

Phi. Well, what shall we do?

Lit. I would think best we should go seek Erostrato himself.

Fer. I will wait upon you willingly, and, either at the schools or at the convocations, we shall find him.

Phi. By our Lady, I am weary. I will run no longer about to seek him. I am [30 sure hither he will come at the last.

Lit. Sure, my mind gives *A true sup-* me that we shall find a new *pose.* Erostrato ere it be long.

Fer. Look where he is! Whither runs he? Stay you awhile; I will go tell him that you are here. Erostrato! Erostrato! ho, Erostrato! I would speak with you! *Erostrato is espied upon the stage running about.*

Scena vii.

Feigned Erostrato, Ferrarese, Philogano, Litio, Dalio.

[Ero. (*Aside.*)] Now can I hide me no longer. Alas! what shall I do? I will set a good face on, to bear out the matter.

Fer. O Erostrato, Philogano, your father, is come out of Sicilia.

Ero. Tell me that I know not. I have been with him, and seen him already.

Fer. Is it possible? And it seemeth by him that you know not of his coming.

[3] Proverb meaning, "There is no difference between you two."

Ero. Why, have you spoken with [10 him? When saw you him, I pray you?

Fer. Look you where he stands. Why go you not to him? Look you, Philogano; behold your dear son Erostrato.

Phi. Erostrato? This is not Erostrato. This seemeth rather to be Dulippo—and it is Dulippo indeed.

Lit. Why, doubt you of that?

Ero. What saith this honest man?

Phi. Marry, sir, indeed you are so [20 honorably clad it is no marvel if you look big.

Ero. To whom speaketh he?

Phi. What! God help! Do you not know me?

Ero. As far as I remember, sir, I never saw you before.

Phi. Hark, Litio, here is good gear! This honest man will not know me!

Ero. Gentleman, you take your [30 marks amiss.

Lit. Did I not tell you of the *A shameless* falsehood of Ferrara, master? *suppose.* Dulippo hath learned to play the knave indifferently well since he came hither.

Phi. Peace, I say.

Ero. Friend, my name is not Dulippo. Ask you thoroughout this town of great and small; they know me. Ask this honest man that is with you, if you will not [40 believe me.

Fer. Indeed, I never knew him otherwise called than Erostrato; and so they call him, as many as know him.

Lit. Master, now you may see the falsehood of these fellows. This *A needless* honest man, your host, is of *suppose.* counsel with him, and would face us down that it is Erostrato. Beware of these mates! [1] 50

Fer. Friend, thou doest me wrong to suspect me, for sure I never heard him otherwise called than Erostrato.

Ero. What name could you hear me called by but by my right name? But I am wise enough to stand prating here with this old man! I think he be mad.

[*Enter Dalio and other Servants, armed.*]

Phi. Ah, runagate! Ah, villain traitor! Dost thou use thy master thus?. What hast thou done with my son, villain? [60

[1] Fellows

Dal. Doth this dog bark here still? And will you suffer him, master, thus to revile you?

Ero. Come in, come in. What wilt thou do with this pestil? [2]

Dal. I will rap the old cackabed [3] on the costard. [4]

Ero. Away with it! And you, sirrah, lay down these stones! Come in at door, every one of you. Bear with him, for [70 his age. I pass not of [5] his evil words.

Erostrato taketh all his Servants in at the
doors.

Scena viii.

Philogano, Ferrarese, Litio.

[Phi.] Alas, who shall relieve my miserable estate? To whom shall I complain, since he whom I brought up of a child, yea, and cherished him as if he had been mine own, doth now utterly deny to know me? And you, whom I took for an honest man and he that should have brought me to the sight of my son, are compact [6] with this false wretch, and would face me down that he is Erostrato. Alas, you might have [10 some compassion of mine age, *Another sup-* to the misery I am now in, and *pose.* that I am a stranger desolate of all comfort in this country; or, at the least, you should have feared the vengeance of God, the supreme judge, which knoweth the secrets of all hearts, in bearing this false witness with him whom heaven and earth do know to be Dulippo and not Erostrato.

Lit. If there be many such witnesses [20 in this country, men may go about to prove what they will in controversies here.

Fer. Well, sir, you may judge of me as it pleaseth you; and how the matter cometh to pass I know not, but, truly, ever since he came first hither I have known him by the name of Erostrato, the son of Philogano, a Cathanese. Now, whether he be so indeed or whether he be Dulippo, as you allege, let that be proved by them that knew [30 him before he came hither. But I protest before God that which I have said is neither a matter compact with him nor any

[2] Pestle, pig's leg.
[3] Vulgar term of abuse.
[4] Apple, head.
[5] Care not for.
[6] In conspiracy.

other, but even as I have heard him called and reputed of all men.

PHI. Out and alas! He whom I sent hither with my son to be his servant and to give attendance on him, hath either cut his throat or by some evil means made [39 him away, and hath not only *A shrewd sup-* taken his garments, his books, *pose.* his money, and that which he brought out of Sicilia with him, but usurpeth his name also, and turneth to his own commodity the bills of exchange that I have always allowed for my son's expenses. O miserable Philogano, O unhappy old man! O eternal God, is there no judge, no officer, no higher powers whom I may complain unto for redress of these wrongs? 50

FER. Yes, sir, we have potestates, we have judges, and, above all, we have a most just prince. Doubt you not but you shall have justice, if your cause be just.

PHI. Bring me then to the judges, to the potestates, or to whom you think best; for I will disclose a pack of the greatest knavery, a fardel [1] of the foulest falsehood, that ever was heard of!

LIT. Sir, he that will go to the law [60 must be sure of four things: first, a right and a just cause; then, a righteous advocate to plead; next, favor *coram judice;* [2] and, above all, a good purse to procure it.

FER. I have not heard that the law hath any respect to favor; what you mean by it I cannot tell.

PHI. Have you no regard to his words; he is but a fool.

FER. I pray you, sir, let him tell me [70 what is favor.

LIT. Favor call I to have a friend near about the judge, who may so solicit thy cause as, if it be right, speedy sentence may ensue without any delays; if it be not good, then to prolong it, till at the last thine adversary, being weary, shall be glad to compound with thee.

FER. Of thus much (although I never heard thus much in this country before) [80 doubt you not, Philogano: I will bring you to an advocate that shall speed you accordingly.

PHI. Then shall I give myself, as it were, a prey to the lawyers, whose insatiable jaws I am not able to feed, although I had

here all the goods and lands which I possess in mine own country—much less, being a stranger in this misery. I know their cautels [3] of old. At the first time I come [90 they will so extol my cause as though it were already won; but within a sevennight or ten days, if I do not continually feed them, as the crow doth her brats, twenty times in an hour, they will begin to wax cold and to find cavils in my cause, saying that at the first I did not well instruct them; till, at the last, they will not only draw the stuffing out of my purse but the marrow out of my bones. 100

FER. Yea, sir; but this man that I tell you of is half a saint.

LIT. And the other half a devil, I hold [4] a penny!

PHI. Well said, Litio. Indeed, I have but small confidence in their smooth looks.

FER. Well, sir, I think this whom I mean is no such manner of man. But if he were, there is such hatred and evil- *Another sup-* will between him and this *pose.* gentleman (whether he be Erostrato or [111 Dulippo, whatsoever he be) that I warrant you he will do whatsoever he can do for you, were it but to spite him.

PHI. Why, what hatred is betwixt them?

FER. They are both in love and suitors to one gentlewoman, the daughter of a wealthy man in this city.

PHI. Why, is the villain become of such estimation that he dare presume to be [120 a suitor to any gentlewoman of a good family?

FER. Yea, sir, out of all doubt.

PHI. How call you his adversary?

FER. Cleander, one of the excellentest doctors in our city.

PHI. For God's love, let us go to him!

FER. Go we then. [*Exeunt.*]

FINIS ACTUS IV.

ACTUS V. SCENA i.

Feigned Erostrato.

[ERO.] What a mishap was this, that before I could meet with Erostrato I have light even full in the lap of Philogano, where I was constrained to deny my name, to deny my master, and to feign that I knew him not, to contend with him, and to

---

[1] Bundle.   [2] Before the judge.   [3] Artifices.   [4] Wager.

revile him in such sort that, hap what hap can, I can never hap well in favor with him again! Therefore, if I could come to speak with the right Erostrato, I will renounce [10 unto him both habit and credit, and away as fast as I can trudge into some strange country where I may never see Philogano again—alas, he that of a little child hath brought me up unto this day and nourished me as if I had been his own, and, indeed, to confess the *Another sup-* truth, I have no father to *pose.*
trust unto but him. But look where Pasiphilo cometh, the fittest man in the world [20 to go on my message to Erostrato.

Erostrato espieth Pasiphilo coming towards him.

Scena ii.

Pasiphilo, Erostrato.

[Pasi.] Two good news have I heard today already: one, that Erostrato prepared a great feast this night; the other, that he seeketh for me. And I, to ease him of his travail, lest he should run up and down seeking me, and because no man loveth better than I to have an errand where good cheer is, come in posthaste even home to his own house. And look where he is.

Ero. Pasiphilo, thou must do one [10 thing for me, if thou love me.

Pasi. If I love you not, who loves you? Command me.

Ero. Go then a little there, to Damon's house; ask for Dulippo, and tell him—

Pasi. Wot [1] you what? I cannot speak with him. He is in prison.

Ero. In prison! How cometh that to pass? Where is he in prison?

Pasi. In a vile dungeon, there, within [20 his master's house.

Ero. Canst thou tell wherefore?

Pasi. Be you content to know he is in prison. I have told you too much.

Ero. If ever you will do anything for me, tell me.

Pasi. I pray you, desire me not. What were you the better if you knew?

Ero. More than thou thinkest, Pasiphilo, by God.　　　　　　30

Pasi. Well, and yet it stands me upon,[2] more than you think, to keep it secret.

[1] Know.　　　[2] It is incumbent upon me.

Ero. Why, Pasiphilo, is this the trust I have had in you? Are these the fair promises you have a[l]ways made me?

Pasi. By the Mass, I would I had fasted this night with Master Doctor rather than have come hither.

Ero. Well, Pasiphilo, either tell me, or, at few words, never think to be welcome [40 to this house from henceforth.

Pasi. Nay, yet I had rather leese all the gentlemen in this town. But, if I tell you anything that displease you, blame nobody but yourself now.

Ero. There is nothing can grieve me more than Dulippo's mishap—no, not mine own; and therefore I am sure thou canst tell me no worse tidings.

Pasi. Well, since you would needs [50 have it, I will tell you. He *Another* was taken abed with your *plain and* beloved Polynesta. *homely sup-*
Ero. Alas, and doth Damon *pose.*
know it?

Pasi. An old trot in the house disclosed it to him; whereupon he took both Dulippo and the nurse, which hath been the broker of all this bargain, and clapped them both in a cage—where, I think, they shall [60 have sour [3] sops to [4] their sweetmeats.

Ero. Pasiphilo, go thy ways into the kitchen; command the cook to boil and roast what liketh thee best. I make thee supervisor of this supper.

Pasi. By the Mass, if you should have studied this sevennight you could not have appointed me an office to please me better! You shall see what dishes I will devise.

Pasiphilo goeth in; Erostrato tarrieth.

Scena iii.

Feigned Erostrato alone.

[Ero.] I was glad to rid him out of the way, lest he should see me burst out of these swelling tears, which hitherto with great pain I have prisoned in my breast, and lest he should hear the echo of my doubled sighs, which bounce from the bottom of my heavy heart. O cursèd I! O cruel fortune, that so many dispersed griefs as were sufficient to subvert a legion of lovers hast suddenly assem- [10

[3] From 1573 edn. Original has *sorowe.*
[4] In addition to.

bled within my careful carcass to fret this fearful heart in sunder with desperation! Thou that hast kept my master all his youth within the realm of Sicilia, reserving the wind and waves in a temperate calm— as it were at his command—now to convey his aged limbs hither, neither sooner nor later, but even in the worst time that may be! If, at any time before, thou haddest conducted him, this enterprise [20 had been cut off without care in the beginning; and, if never so little longer thou hadst lingered [1] his journey, this happy day might then have fully finished our drifts [2] and devises. But, alas, thou hast brought him even in the very worst time, to plunge us all in the pit of perdition! Neither art thou content to entangle me alone in thy ruinous ropes, but thou must also catch the right Erostrato in thy [30 crooked claws, to reward us both with open shame and rebuke. Two years hast thou kept secret our subtile supposes, even this day to decipher them with a sorrowful success. What shall I do? Alas, what shift shall I make? It is too late now to imagine any further deceit, for every minute seemeth an hour till I find some succor for the miserable captive Erostrato. Well, since there is no other remedy, I [40 will go to my master Philogano, and to him will I tell the whole truth of the matter, that at the least he may provide in time before his son feel the smart of some sharp revenge and punishment. This is the best, and thus will I do. Yet I know that for mine own part I shall do bitter penance for my faults forepassed! But such is the good will and duty that I bear to Erostrato as even with the loss [50 of my life I must not stick to adventure anything which may turn to his commodity. But what shall I do? Shall I go seek my master about the town, or shall I tarry his return hither? If I meet him in the streets, he will cry out upon me, neither will he hearken to anything that I shall say till he have gathered all the people wondering about me as it were at an owl. Therefore I were better to abide here. And yet, [60 if he tarry long, I will go seek him rather than prolong the time to Erostrato's peril.

Pasiphilo returneth to Erostrato.

[1] Delayed.　　　　　　　　　　[2] Plots.

SCENA iv.

Pasiphilo, feigned Erostrato.

[PASI. (*To Dalio within.*)] Yea, dress them, but lay them not to the fire till they will be ready to sit down.—This gear goeth in order, but if I had not gone in, there had fallen a foul fault.

ERO. And what fault, I pray thee?

PASI. Marry, Dalio would have laid the shoulder of mutton and the capon both to the fire at once, like a fool! He did not consider that the one would have more [10 roasting than the other.

ERO. Alas, I would this were the greatest fault.

PASI. Why? And either the one should have been burned before the other had been roasted, or else he must have drawn them off the spit, and they would have been served to the board either cold or raw.

ERO. Thou hast reason, Pasiphilo.

PASI. Now, sir, if it please you, I will [20 go into the town and buy oranges, olives, and caphers; [3] for without such sauce the supper were more than half lost.

ERO. There are [4] within already, doubt you not; there shall lack nothing that is necessary.　　　　　　　*Erostrato exit.*

PASI. Since I told him these news of Dulippo, he is clean beside himself. He hath so many hammers in his head that his brains are ready to burst. And let them [30 break. So I may sup with him tonight, what care I? But is not this *A knavish Dominus noster Cleandrus* [5] that *suppose.* cometh before? Well said. By my truth, we will teach Master Doctor to wear a cornered cap [6] of a new fashion. By God, Polynesta shall be his! He shall have her, out of doubt; for I have told Erostrato such news of her that he will none of her.

Cleander and Philogano come in, talking of the matter in controversy.

SCENA v.

Cleander, Philogano, Litio, Pasiphilo.

[CLE.] Yea, but how will ye prove that he is not Erostrato, having such presumptions to the contrary? Or how shall it be thought that you are Philogano, when another taketh upon him this same name,

[3] Capers.　　　　　　　　[5] Our master, Cleander.
[4] Supply *some.*　　　　　　[6] Horns of the cuckold.

and for proof bringeth him for a witness which hath been ever reputed here for Erostrato?

PHI. I will tell you, sir. Let me be kept here fast in prison, and at my [10 charges let there be some man sent into Sicilia that may bring hither with him two or three of the honestest men in Cathanea, and by them let it be proved if I or this other be Philogano, and whether he be Erostrato or Dulippo my servant; and, if you find me contrary,[1] let me suffer death for it.

PASI. I will go salute Master Doctor.

CLE. It will ask great labor and great [20 expenses to prove it this way, but it is the best remedy that I can see.

PASI. God save you, sir!

CLE. And reward you as you have deserved.

PASI. Then shall he give me your favor continually.

CLE. He shall give you a halter, knave and villain that thou art!

PASI. I know I am a knave, but no [30 villain. I am your servant.

CLE. I neither take thee for my servant nor for my friend.

PASI. Why, wherein have I offended you, sir?

CLE. Hence to the gallows, knave!

PASI. What! Soft and fair, sir, I pray you. "*I præ, sequar;*"[2] you are mine elder.

CLE. I will be even with you, be you sure, honest man.　　　　　　　　40

PASI. Why, sir? I never offended you.

CLE. Well, I will teach you. Out of my sight, knave!

PASI. What! I am no dog, I would you wist.[3]

CLE. Pratest thou yet, villain? I will make thee—

PASI. What will you make me? I see well the more a man doth suffer you, the worse you are.　　　　　　　　50

CLE. Ah, villain, if it were not for this gentleman, I would tell you what I—

PASI. Villain? Nay, I am as honest a man as you.

CLE. Thou liest in thy throat, knave!

PHI. O, sir, stay your wisdom.

PASI. What! Will you fight? Marry, come on!

CLE. Well, knave, I will meet with you another time. Go your way.　　　　60

PASI. Even when you list, sir, I will be your man.

CLE. And if I be not even with thee, call me cut![4]

PASI. Nay, by the Mass, all is one. I care not, for I have nothing. If I had either lands or goods, peradventure you would pull me into the law.　　　[*Exit.*]

PHI. Sir, I perceive your patience is moved.　　　　　　　　70

CLE. This villain! But let him go. I will see him punished as he hath deserved. Now to the matter. How said you?

PHI. This fellow hath disquieted you, sir. Peradventure you would *Lawyers* be loath to be troubled any *are never* further.　　　　　　　*weary to get*

CLE. Not a whit. Say on, *money.* and let him go—with a vengeance!

PHI. I say, let them send at my [80 charge to Cathanea.

CLE. Yea, I remember that well, and it is the surest way as this case requireth. But tell me, how is he your servant, and how come you by him? Inform me fully in the matter.

PHI. I will tell you, sir. When the Turks won Otranto—

CLE. O, you put me in remembrance of my mishaps!　　　　　　90

PHI. How, sir?

CLE. For I was driven among the rest out of the town (it is my native country), and there I lost more than ever I shall recover again while I live.

PHI. Alas, a pitiful case, by St. Anne!

CLE. Well, proceed.

PHI. At that time, as I said, there were certain of our country that scoured those coasts upon the seas with a good bark, [100 well appointed for the purpose, and had espial of a Turkey vessel that came laden from thence with great abundance of riches.

CLE. And peradventure most *A gentle* of mine.　　　　　　　*suppose.*

PHI. So they boarded them, and in the end overcame them, and brought the goods to Palermo, from whence they came; and amongst other things that they had was this villain, my servant, a [110 boy at that time, I think not past five years old.

CLE. Alas, I lost one of that same age there!

PHI. And I, being there, and liking the child's favor well, proffered them four and twenty ducats for him, and had him.

CLE. What! was the child a Turk? Or had the Turks brought him from Otranto?

PHI. They said he was a child of [120 Otranto. But what is that to the matter? Once four and twenty ducats he cost me—that I wot well.

CLE. Alas, I speak it not for that, sir. I would it were he whom I mean.

PHI. Why, whom mean you, sir?

LIT. Beware, sir; be not too *A crafty* lavish!   *suppose.*

CLE. Was his name Dulippo then or had he not another name?   130

LIT. Beware what you say, sir!

PHI. What the devil hast thou to do!—Dulippo? No, sir, his name was Carino.

LIT. Yea, well said! Tell all, and more too; do!

CLE. O Lord, if it be as I think, how happy were I! And why did you change his name then?

PHI. We called him Dulippo because when he cried, as children do some- [140 times, he would always cry on that name, Dulippo.

CLE. Well, then I see well it is my own only child, whom I lost when I lost my country! He was named Carino after his grandfather; and this Dulippo, whom he always remembered in his lamenting, was his foster-father that nourished him and brought him up.

LIT. Sir, have I not told you enough [150 of the falsehood of Ferrara? This gentleman will not only pick your purse, but beguile you of your servant also, and make you believe he is his son.

CLE. Well, good fellow, I have not used to lie.

LIT. Sir, no; but everything hath a beginning.

CLE. Fie! Philogano, have you not the least suspect [1] that may be of me.   160

LIT. No, marry; but it were good he had the most suspect that may be.

[1] Suspicion.

CLE. Well, hold thou thy peace a little, good fellow. I pray you tell me, Philogano, had the child any remembrance of his father's name, his mother's name, or the name of his family?

PHI. He did remember them, and could name his mother also, but sure I have forgotten the name.   170

LIT. I remember it well enough!

PHI. Tell it then.

LIT. Nay, that I will not, marry! You have told him too much already.

PHI. Tell it, I say, if thou can.

LIT. Can? Yes, by the Mass, I can well enough! But I will have my tongue pulled out rather than tell it unless he tell it first. Do you not perceive, sir, what he goeth about?   180

CLE. Well, I will tell you then. My name you know already; my wife, his mother's, name was Sophronia; the house that I came of they call Spiagia.

LIT. I never heard him speak of Spiagia, but indeed I have heard him say his mother's name was Sophronia. But what of that? A great matter, I promise you! It is like enough that you two have compact together to deceive my master. [190

CLE. What needeth me more evident tokens? This is my son out of doubt, whom I lost eighteen years since, and a thousand thousand times have I lamented for him. He should have also a mold [2] on his left shoulder.

LIT. He hath a mold there indeed, and an hole in another place, too—I would your nose were in it!

CLE. Fair words, fellow Litio! O, [200 I pray you, let us go talk with him! O fortune, how much am I bound to thee if I find my son!

PHI. Yea, how little am I beholden to fortune, that know not where my son is become; and you, whom I chose to be mine advocate, will now, by the means of this Dulippo, become mine adversary!

CLE. Sir, let us first go find mine, [209 and, I warrant you, yours will *A right sup-* be found also ere it be long. *pose.*

PHI. God grant! Go we then.

CLE. Since the door is open, I will never knock nor call, but we will be bold to go in.

[2] Mole.

LIT. [*To Philogano.*] Sir, take you heed lest he lead you to some mischief.

PHI. Alas, Litio, if my son be lost, what care I what become of me?

LIT. Well, I have told you my mind, sir. Do you as you please.   221

Exeunt. Damon and Psiteria come in.

SCENA vi.

Damon, Psiteria.

[DAM.] Come hither, you old callet,[1] you tattling huswife! That the devil cut out your tongue! Tell me, how could Pasiphilo know of this gear but by you?

PSIT. Sir, he never knew it of me; he was the first that told me of it.

DAM. Thou liest, old drab! But I would advise you tell me the truth, or I will make those old bones rattle in your skin.

PSIT. Sir, if you find me contrary, [10 kill me.

DAM. Why, where should he talk with thee?

PSIT. He talked with me of it here in the street.

DAM. What did you here?

PSIT. I was going to the weaver's for a web of cloth you have there.

DAM. And what cause could Pasiphilo have to talk of it, unless thou began the [20 matter first?

PSIT. Nay, he began with me, sir, reviling me because I had told you of it. I asked him how he knew of it, and he said he was in the stable when you examined me erewhile.

DAM. Alas, alas, what shall I do then? In at doors, old whore! I will pluck that tongue of thine out by the roots one day. [*Exit Psiteria.*] Alas, it grieveth me [30 more that Pasiphilo knoweth it than all the rest. He that will have a thing kept secret, let him tell it to Pasiphilo! The people shall know it, and as many as have ears, and no mo. By this time he hath told it in a hundreth places! Cleander was the first, Erostrato the second; and so from one to another throughout the city. Alas, what dower, what marriage shall I now prepare for my daughter? O poor [40 dolorous Damon, more miserable than misery itself! Would God it were true

[1] Whore.

that Polynesta told me ere-while—that he who hath deflowered her is of no servile estate, as hitherto he hath been *The first suppose brought to conclusion.* supposed in my service, but that he is a gentleman, born of a good parentage in Sicilia. Alas, small riches should content me if he be but of an honest family! But [50 I fear that he hath devised these toys to allure my daughter's love. Well, I will go examine her again. My mind giveth me that I shall perceive by her tale whether it be true or not. But is not this Pasiphilo that cometh out of my neighbor's house? What the devil aileth him to leap and laugh so like a fool in the highway?

Pasiphilo cometh out of the house laughing.

SCENA vii.

Pasiphilo,[2] Damon.

[PASI. (*To himself.*)] O God, that I might find Damon at home!

DAM. What the devil would he with me?

PASI. [*To himself.*] That I may be the first that shall bring him these news!

DAM. What will he tell me, in the name of God?

PASI. [*To himself.*] O Lord, how happy am I!—Look where he is.

DAM. What news, Pasiphilo, that [10 thou art so merry?

PASI. Sir, I am merry to make you glad. I bring you joyful news!

DAM. And that I have need of, Pasiphilo.

PASI. I know, sir, that you are a sorrowful man for this mishap that hath chanced in your house. Peradventure you thought I had not known of it. But let it pass! Pluck up your sprites,[3] and rejoice! For [20 he that hath done you this injury is so well born and hath so rich parents that you may be glad to make him your son-in-law.

DAM. How knowest thou?

PASI. His father, Philogano, one of the worthiest men in all Cathanea, is now come to the city, and is here in your neighbor's house.

DAM. What, in Erostrato's house?

PASI. Nay, in Dulippo's house. For [30 where you have always supposed this gentleman to be Erostrato, it is not so; but

[2] Original prints *Philogano.*   [3] Spirits.

your servant, whom you have imprisoned, hitherto supposed to be Dulippo, he is indeed Erostrato, and that other is Dulippo. And thus they have always, even since their first arrival in this city, exchanged names, to the end that Erostrato, the master, under the name of Dulippo, a servant, might be entertained in your house [40 and so win the love of your daughter.

DAM. Well, then I perceive it is even as Polynesta told me.

PASI. Why, did she tell you so?

DAM. Yea, but I thought it but a tale.

PASI. Well, it is a true tale. And here they will be with you by-and-by—both Philogano, this worthy man, and Master Doctor Cleander.

DAM. Cleander? What to do?   50

PASI. Cleander? Why thereby lies another tale—the most fortunate adventure that ever you heard! Wot you what? This other Dulippo, whom all this while we supposed to be Erostrato, is found to be the son of Cleander, whom he lost at the loss of Otranto, and was after sold in Sicilia to this Philogano. The strangest case that ever you heard! A man might make a comedy of it. They will come even [60 straight and tell you the whole circumstance of it themselves.

DAM. Nay, I will first go hear the story of this Dulippo, be it Dulippo or Erostrato, that I have here within, before I speak with Philogano.

PASI. So shall you do well, sir. I will go tell them that they may stay awhile.— But look where they come.

Damon goeth in; Sienese, Cleander, and Philogano come upon the stage.

SCENA viii.

Sienese, Cleander, [Carino,] [1] Philogano.

[SIEN.] Sir, you shall not need to excuse the matter any further. Since I have received no greater injury than by words, let them pass like wind. I take them well in worth and am rather well pleased than offended. For it shall both be a good warning to me another time how to trust every man at the first sight, yea, and I shall have good game hereafter to tell this pleasant story another day in mine own country. [10

---

[1] *I.e.*, the real Dulippo.

CLE. Gentleman, you have reason; and be you sure that as many as hear it will take great pleasure in it. And you, Philogano, may think that God in heaven above hath ordained your coming hither at this present to the end I might recover my lost son, whom by no other means I could ever have found out.

PHI. Surely, sir, I think no less; for I think that not so much as a leaf falleth [20 from the tree without the ordinance of God. But let us go seek Damon, for methinketh every day a year, every hour a day, and every minute too much, till I see my Erostrato.

CLE. I cannot blame you. Go we then. Carino, take you that gentleman home in the meantime. The fewer the better to be present at such affairs.

Pasiphilo stayeth their going in.

SCENA ix.

Pasiphilo,[2] Cleander.

[PASI.] Master Doctor, will you not show me this favor, to tell me the cause of your displeasure?

CLE. Gentle Pasiphilo, I must needs confess I have done thee wrong, and that I believed tales of thee, which indeed I find now contrary.

PASI. I am glad, then, that it proceeded rather of ignorance than of malice.

CLE. Yea, believe me, Pasiphilo.   10

PASI. O, sir, but yet you should not have given me such foul words.

CLE. Well, content thyself, Pasiphilo. I am thy friend, as I have always been; for proof whereof, come sup with me tonight, and from day to day this sevennight be thou my guest. But behold, here cometh Damon out of his house.

Here they come all together.

SCENA x.

Cleander, Philogano, Damon, Erostrato, Pasiphilo, Polynesta; Nevola and other Servants.[3]

[CLE. (*To Damon.*)] We are come unto you, sir, to turn your sorrow into joy and gladness—the sorrow, we mean, that of force you have sustained since this mishap

---

[2] Original has *Philogano*.   [3] Enter later.

of late fallen in your house. But be you of good comfort, sir, and assure yourself that this young man, which youthfully and not maliciously hath committed this amorous offense, is very well able, with consent of this worthy man, his father, to make [10 you sufficient amends, being born in Cathanea of Sicilia, of a noble house, no way inferior unto you, and of wealth, by the report of such as know it, far exceeding that of yours.

PHI. And I here, in proper person, do present unto you, sir, not only my assured friendship and brotherhood, but do earnestly desire you to accept my poor child, though unworthy, as your son-in-law. [20 And for recompense of the injury he hath done you, I proffer my whole lands in dower to your daughter; yea, and more would, if more I might.

CLE. And I, sir, who have hitherto so earnestly desired your daughter in marriage, do now willingly yield up and quit claim to this young man, who, both for his years and for the love he beareth her, is most meetest to be her husband. For [30 where I was desirous of a wife by whom I might have issue, to leave that little which God hath sent me, now have I little need, that, thanks be to God, have found my dearly beloved son, whom I lost of a child at the siege of Otranto.

DAM. Worthy gentleman, your friendship, your alliance, and the nobility of your birth are such as I have much more cause to desire them of you than you to re- [40 quest of me that which is already granted. Therefore I gladly and willingly receive the same, and think myself most happy now

of all my life past that I have gotten so toward [1] a son-in-law to myself and so worthy a father-in-law to my daughter. Yea, and much the greater is my contentation since this worthy gentleman, Master Cleander, doth hold himself satisfied. And now, behold your son! 50

ERO. O father!

PASI. Behold the natural love of the child to the father. For inward joy he cannot pronounce one word; instead whereof he sendeth sobs and tears to tell the effect of his inward intention.[2] But why do you abide here abroad? Will it please you to go into the house, sir?

DAM. Pasiphilo hath said well. Will it please you to go in, sir? 60

[Enter Nevola with fetters.]

NEV. Here I have brought you, sir, both fetters and bolts.

DAM. Away with them, now!

Nev. Yea, but what shall I do with them?

DAM. Marry, I will tell thee, Nevola. To make a right end of our supposes, lay one of those bolts in the fire, and make thee a suppository as long as mine arm— God save the sample!—[*Turns to the audience.*] Nobles and gentlemen, if you [71 suppose that our Supposes have given you sufficient cause of delight, show some token whereby we may suppose you are content.

Et plauserunt.[3]

[1] Promising.
[2] From 1573 edn. Original reads *invention*.
[3] And they applauded.

FINIS.

JOHN LYLY

As in the case of many other important Elizabethan dramatists, John Lyly was almost forgotten from the middle of the seventeenth century to the latter part of the nineteenth. But from that time on his rehabilitation was so complete that when R. W. Bond produced his monumental three-volume edition of *The Complete Works of John Lyly* in 1902 he was unable to restrain his enthusiasm. In his opening biographical essay he extolled Lyly for his leadership in diverse fields: as almost the first Englishman with an acute sense of prose form and certainly the first to make his countrymen feel that the writing of prose was an art; as the first real English novelist; as the first "regular" English dramatist, "the true inventor and introducer of dramatic style, conduct, and dialogue," and "the first to produce any body of important plays," "the herald of an epoch, the master of the king" (that is, of Shakespeare, who owed so much to Lyly); as "the first to establish prose in comedy" (in original comedy, not translation); as "the first to write plays both cleanly and coherent, bright and smooth; the first to present to us on the stage woman in all her charm and wit, grace and laughter; the first to utilize and insist on love-making as the grand perennial source of interest in fiction and drama alike; the first founder, finally, of that 'college of witcrackers' who have lightened for Englishmen the weight and seriousness of life. . . ." John Dover Wilson in his *John Lyly* (Cambridge University Press, 1905) and A. G. Feuillerat in his similarly titled book (Cambridge University Press, 1910) went almost as far as Bond; and Felix E. Schelling in his great pioneer two-volume history of *Elizabethan Drama* (Boston, 1908) called him the "first professional dramatist" to depend primarily on his pen to earn a living, as well as "the first conscious and constructive artist in the list of English playwrights."

The reader today, then, might well expect that such an original and talented author would have been not only recognized but highly rewarded by his contemporaries. Lyly was recognized, but was not as highly rewarded as he thought he deserved.

As implied in the college matriculation records, John Lyly was born between October 9, 1553, and October 8, 1554. He was probably born at Canterbury and was the son of George Lyly, a prebendary of the cathedral, who was himself the son of William Lyly (or Lilly), a famous master of St. Paul's Grammar School, London, and author of the chief Latin grammar of the period. It is no wonder, then, that John Lyly's writings revealed such a strong classical and educational background. The boy entered Magdalen College, Oxford, in 1569, and took his B.A. in 1573, following it with his M.A. in 1575. As was often the case at the time, Cambridge University also incorporated him an M.A. in 1579, though it is not clear whether he actually studied for the degree. His college career was not completely smooth, studious, and uneventful, however, since soon after his entrance he seems to have been "rusticated," or suspended, for a time. Nevertheless, he retained sufficient boldness, if not effrontery, to petition unsuccessfully his influential patron, Lord Burghley, to request the Queen to procure him a Fellowship at Magdalen over the heads of the college authorities.

The year before Cambridge granted him his M.A. (and perhaps this was the reason why it did so), Lyly published his famous *Euphues: The Anatomy of Wit*, a work intended to set a new pattern for English prose. On a thin thread of fiction he wove into the book miscellaneous dissertations on all kinds of subjects, such as education and contemporary manners. The book created such a furor that in 1580 Lyly wrote a sequel, *Euphues and His England*. The literary style of these works, which contributed the word *euphuism* to the English language, was imitated in romantic novels by others for many years. Although the euphuistic elements in Lyly's own writing decreased as he grew older (see C. G. Child, *Lyly and Euphuism*, Leipzig, 1894), a good specimen of it can be found in Endymion's long speech in the first scene of Lyly's play *Endymion*.

After Cambridge Lyly went to London to carve a career for himself. He became secretary to Burghley's son-in-law, Edward de Vere, the Earl of Oxford, who perhaps influenced him to try his hand at writing plays, since he had a troupe of boy actors and ambitions as a playwright himself. Lyly's dramatic work was part of his disappointing effort to advance his fortunes at court, especially in connection with the office of the Revels, but it was also designed for the professional theater. The records of the activities and interrelations of the boy companies by whom his plays were acted are complicated and often obscure. (See Harold N. Hillebrand, *The Child Actors: A Chapter in Elizabethan Stage History*, *UIS*, 1926.) *Campaspe* and *Sappho and Phao* were printed in 1584 as having been acted early in the year at court by the Children of the Chapel and the Boys of St. Paul's Choir, but official payment for the two performances was made to Oxford's "Servants" under Lyly. Possibly the boy company under Oxford's patronage was combined with the other two companies in this year to perform court plays written by Lyly and Oxford. According to the prologues, however, Lyly's two plays were also publicly acted at the "private" theater of Blackfriars, where the Children of the Chapel had given periodic performances for profit since 1576. Apparently Lyly and Oxford acquired an interest in this playhouse just as it was closed by a suit in 1584. Later Lyly wrote plays for Paul's Boys, as the title pages show, clearly for both court and public performances, until the public acting of the boys came to an end by law in 1591. These plays, with the dates of publication (though some were written earlier), were *Endymion* (1591), *Galathea* (1592), *Midas* (1592), *Mother Bombie* (1594), his only realistic play of contemporary life, and *Love's Metamorphosis* (1601). *The Woman in the Moon* (1597) has no indication of the company and may have been the result of some other connection.

In addition to his theatrical activities, Lyly was Esquire of the Body to Elizabeth in 1588. He became engaged in the Martin Marprelate controversy between the Puritans and the Anglican bishops. He wrote at least one pamphlet on the bishops' side, *Pap with a Hatchet* (1589), and probably some plays, now lost. He sat in Parliament, without distinction, four times between 1589 and 1601. While still quite young he had been encouraged by the Queen, as he put it, to "ayme all my courses att the Revells, I dare not saye with a promise, butt a hopefull item of the reversion." This office of Master of the Revels he never attained, although, as Schelling says, "none could have been more fit for the Mastership." He may, however, have held the post of Vice-Master of the Children of St. Paul's; at least the pedantic scholar, Gabriel Harvey, wrote sarcastically, "He hath not played the Vice-master of Poules, and the Foolemaster of the Theater for naughtes." Bernard M. Wagner (*TLS*, September 28, 1933) showed through the records of St. Martin's, Ludgate, that Lyly was living in that parish close to the St. Paul's choir school between 1587 and 1592, and that four of his children were baptized there; later he moved to Maxborough, where two more children were baptized. All these family burdens were too much for his purse. Warren B. Austin in "John Lyly and Queen Elizabeth" (*NQ*, 1939) printed a letter from Toby Matthew, Bishop of Durham, to Sir Julius Caesar, one of the Masters of Bequests, dated February 9, 1604/5, in which Matthew reminded the other of the many unredeemed promises made to Lyly by the Queen. Now that a new ruler was on the throne the bishop begged Caesar to plead Lyly's cause with James, "the rather in regard of his yeres fast growing on and his insupportable charge of many children, all unbestowed, besides the debt wherein he standeth." Perhaps Bond's conjecture that Lyly received a grant of Crown land in 1605 can be strengthened by the conjecture that James responded to this petition. But in any case Lyly never received the final recognition that he craved and deserved. He died thwarted, impoverished, and in obscure circumstances in 1606.

It is in keeping with his effort to please the court and the public that Lyly's dramatic work marks the first stage in the development toward the Elizabethan popular drama of superb literary quality which was to follow. In the words of Bond, Lyly struck a "balance between classic precedent and romantic freedom." Titles of lost plays suggest that court taste had turned from the stricter classicism of academic circles to romance, sometimes disguised by the use of classical story. Lyly used as a basis for most of his plots love stories drawn from ancient history or mythology, most often from Ovid, adding at times pastoral or sylvan settings, and always reflecting the ideals of courtly circles. Indirect effects of classical influence, possibly in part derived from Italian sources, are seen in both structure and style of the plays. There are good motivation of action, variety and skilful complication of incidents, and suspense, especially in the love story. G. Wilson Knight, in "Lyly" (*RES*, 1939), has discussed Lyly's use of love as the "whole theme" of his plays, and has emphasized his use of central dominating figures and central symbols, "both throwing forward to Shakespeare." Bernard F. Huppé, in "Allegory of Love in Lyly's Court Comedies" (*ELH*, 1946), has found the basis of Lyly's conception of love in the pronouncement of Euphues that "true and virtuous love is to be grounded upon time, reason, favor, and virtue," and has shown how the moral and the amoral, chastity and passion, are constantly at strife in the plays— chastity of course being fortified by the example of the Virgin Queen. Alice Willcox, in "Medical References in the Dramas of John Lyly" (*Annals of Medical History*, 1938), has glanced at the matter from another angle. She has shown that, although Lyly's use of medical terms and his treatment of the humors were extensive, his viewpoint was generally conventional, except that in *Endymion* (I, iii, and II, ii) he was ahead of his time in casting doubt on the theory that the liver is the seat of love.

A simplified form of the famous euphuistic prose style, with new elements of wit and the conceit appropriate to brisk dialogue, combined with a frequently poetic language, makes Lyly's dramatic prose significant for the future of Elizabethan drama. In his pages, with their quotations from the classics and their parody of the forms and devices of logic, Lyly developed roles appropriate to his actors as school boys, and the amount of singing in the plays gives scope for them as choir boys. M. R. Best, however, in "A Note on the Songs in Lyly's Plays" (*NQ*, 1965), has drawn attention to certain songs which critics have suggested as somehow related to the songs published by Blount in his *Six Court Comedies* of Lyly in 1632, has summarized the evidence about the songs and their probable writers, and has used this evidence as support for G. K. Hunter's theory (*John Lyly: The Humanist as Courtier*, London, 1962) that Blount obtained the songs from the music library of St. Paul's choir and that they were not all by Lyly himself.

In *Endymion* the main incidents of the long sleep and the kiss of Cynthia, drawn from Ovid's *Ars Amatoria* and Lucian's *True History*, furnished a basis for Lyly's best blend of classic story, love intrigue, courtly and sylvan setting, satire and wit. A long tradition of freely interpreting classical myth as shadowing historical events or embodying allegory was responsible for popularizing myths in the Renaissance. They were used in poetry generally, but perhaps chiefly in pageants and plays, to present—for either flattery or satire—contemporary events or figures. The names of most of the characters in *Endymion* reveal not only the playwright's background in classical literature and languages but also the liberties he took with them. In the Greek myth of Endymion it was Selene, the moon, who fell in love with the handsome son of Zeus and the nymph Calyce and cast him into a perpetual sleep so that she could come down at her own desire and kiss him without his knowledge. The original Semele was another of the sweethearts of Zeus, but was consumed by lightning when he granted her request to appear to her as the god of thunder as he did to Hera. But Semele was later translated from the underworld to Olympus. Eumenides also underwent a considerable transformation, since the name was actually the propitiatory Greek term for the Erinyes, or Furies. Since the word literally means "the kindly ones," Lyly has adapted it to stand for friendship. Cynthia (also known as Selene and Artemis) was, of course, the Greek moon-goddess, the symbol of virginity, whereas Tellus was the Italian deity of Earth and the goddess of marriage and fertility. Pythagoras underwent no change, but remained the Greek philosopher and mathematician who also had some magical powers. Dares appeared in the *Iliad* as a priest of Hephaestus. Dipsas was the name of a Greek serpent whose bite was supposed to produce intense thirst. Bagoa was perhaps derived from Bagoas, a eunuch and poisoner in ancient Persia. Sir Thopas (or topaz) was a knight—"the flower of royal chivalry," as Chaucer described him in his own story in *The Canterbury Tales*. (Daniel C. Boughner, in "The Background of Lyly's Sir Thopas," *PMLA*, 1939, found in this minor character a combination of elements from the *miles gloriosus* of Latin comedy, from the *capitano millantatore* and the *pedante* of the Italian stage, and from contemporary English life.) Lyly lifted other names for his hybrid cast almost bodily from ordinary Greek and Latin words: Geron is Greek for "an old man," and Gyptes obviously means simply "the Egyptian"; and the names of the remaining three women come straight from the Latin—Floscula "a little flower," Scintilla "a spark," and Favilla "an ember." In fact, Lyly himself directed attention to the meanings of the last two names when these maids first appear in II, ii.

Many attempts have been made to unravel the apparent allegory of the play. Certainly Lyly availed himself fully of the fashion of flattering Elizabeth as Cynthia and possibly also commented indirectly on events in the court. In 1843 Halpin argued that Endymion's story represented the Earl of Leicester's love for Elizabeth and his relations to others at court. Feuillerat and Bond speculated that the play was concerned with the complications involving Elizabeth with her cousin and prisoner, Mary Queen of Scots, and with Mary's son, James VI of Scotland, in his ambition to become Elizabeth's successor. Percy W. Long (*MP*, 1911), however, cast serious doubts on Feuillerat's interpretation, and E. K. Chambers supported him. The most ingenious and historically well-informed of all these interpretations is that of Josephine W. Bennett, who suggested in "Oxford and *Endymion*" (*PMLA*, 1942) that, although of course Cynthia stood for Elizabeth, Endymion represented the Earl of Oxford, Lyly's patron, Tellus was Anne Vavasour, and Corsites Sir Henry Lee. Mrs. Bennett tried to show the parallels in the situation in which the Earl was accused in 1581 by Anne, one of the Queen's gentlewomen, of being the father of a son she had borne. F. S. Boas (*YWES*, 1942) pointed out, however, that this event had taken place so many years earlier that it would no longer have been topical, and that Oxford's boy players had no part in presenting the play, since it was acted by the Children of Paul's. Long, in fact, argued that the allegory is primarily one of Platonic love, in which Endymion passes from love of Tellus (Earth), or earthly beauty, to adoration of Cynthia as a symbol of heavenly beauty; and Huppé went so far as to dismiss all historical interpretations of the allegorical aspects of all Lyly's plays.

Endymion, probably composed some time between 1585 and 1568, was entered on the Stationers' Register on October 4, 1591, and was published anonymously later that year. The play was printed as Lyly's by Blount in *Six Court Comedies* of 1632, and the style leaves no doubt as to Lyly's authorship. The text of the present edition is based on Bond's reprint of the quarto of 1591 in his *Complete Works* of Lyly.

ENDYMION, THE MAN IN THE MOON[1]

[BY

JOHN LYLY

DRAMATIS PERSONÆ

ENDYMION, *in love with Cynthia.*
EUMENIDES, *his friend, in love with Semele.*
CORSITES, *a captain, in love with Tellus.*
PANELION ⎱ *lords of Cynthia's court.*
ZONTES ⎰
PYTHAGORAS, *a philosopher.*
GYPTES, *an Egyptian soothsayer.*
GERON, *an old man, husband to Dipsas.*
SIR TOPHAS, *a braggart.*
DARES, *page to Endymion.*
SAMIAS, *page to Eumenides.*
EPITON, *page to Sir Tophas.*

MASTER CONSTABLE.
FIRST *and* SECOND WATCHMAN.

CYNTHIA, *the queen.*
TELLUS, *her rival, in love with Endymion.*
FLOSCULA, *her friend.*
SEMELE, *a lady at the court.*
SCINTILLA ⎱ *maids at the court.*
FAVILLA ⎰
DIPSAS, *an old enchantress.*
BAGOA, *her servant.*
FAIRIES.
THREE LADIES *and an* OLD MAN *in the dumb show.*

SCENE: *Cynthia's realm.*

TIME: *Mythical.*]

THE PROLOGUE

MOST high and happy princess, we must tell you a tale of the Man in the Moon, which, if it seem ridiculous for the method, or superfluous for the matter, or for the means incredible, for three faults we can make but one excuse: it is a tale of the Man in the Moon.

It was forbidden in old time to dispute of Chimera because it was a fiction. We hope in our times none will apply [10 pastimes,[2] because they are fancies; for there liveth none under the sun that knows what to make of the Man in the Moon. We present neither comedy, nor tragedy, nor story, nor anything but that whosoever heareth may say this: "Why, here is a tale of the Man in the Moon."

ACTUS PRIMUS. SCENA PRIMA.

[A grove near the cell of Endymion.]

Endymion, Eumenides.

END. I find, Eumenides, in all things both variety to content and satiety to glut, saving only in my affections, which are so staid, and withal so stately that I can neither satisfy my heart with love, nor mine eyes with wonder. My thoughts, Eumenides, are stitched to the stars, which, being as high as I can see, thou mayst imagine how much higher they are than I can reach. 10

EUM. If you be enamored of anything above the moon, your thoughts are ridiculous, for that [3] things immortal are not subject to affections; if allured or enchanted with these transitory things under the moon, you show yourself senseless to attribute such lofty titles to such low [4] trifles.

END. My love is placed neither under the moon nor above.

EUM. I hope you be not sotted[1] [20 upon the Man in the Moon.

END. No; but settled either to die or possess the moon herself.

EUM. Is Endymion mad, or do I mistake? Do you love the moon, Endymion?

END. Eumenides, the moon.

EUM. There was never any so peevish[2] to imagine the moon either capable of affection or shape of a mistress; for as impossible it is to make love fit to her hu- [30 mor, which no man knoweth, as a coat to her form, which continueth not in one bigness whilst she is measuring. Cease off, Endymion, to feed so much upon fancies. That melancholy blood must be purged which draweth you to a dotage no less miserable than monstrous.

END. My thoughts have no veins, and yet, unless they be let blood, I shall perish.   40

EUM. But they have vanities, which being reformed, you may be restored.

END. O fair Cynthia, why do others term thee unconstant whom I have ever found unmovable? Injurious time, corrupt manners, unkind men, who, finding a constancy not to be matched in my sweet mistress, have christened her with the name of wavering, waxing, and waning! Is she inconstant that keepeth a settled [50 course, which, since her first creation, altereth not one minute in her moving? There is nothing thought more admirable or commendable in the sea than the ebbing and flowing; and shall the moon, from whom the sea taketh this virtue, be accounted fickle for increasing and decreasing? Flowers in their buds are nothing worth till they be blown, nor blossoms accounted[3] till they be ripe fruit; [60 and shall we then say they be changeable for that they grow from seeds to leaves, from leaves to buds, from buds to their perfection? Then why be not twigs that become trees, children that become men, and mornings that grow to evenings, termed wavering, for that they continue not at one stay?[4] Ay, but Cynthia, being in her fulness, decayeth, as not delighting

in her greatest beauty, or withering [70 when she should be most honored. When malice cannot object anything, folly will, making that a vice which is the greatest virtue. What thing (my mistress excepted) being in the pride of her beauty and latter minute of her age, that waxeth young again? Tell me, Eumenides, what is he that, having a mistress of ripe years and infinite virtues, great honors, and unspeakable beauty, but would wish that [80 she might grow tender again, getting youth by years, and never-decaying beauty by time; whose fair face neither the summer's blaze can scorch, nor winter's blast chap, nor the numbering of years breed altering of colors? Such is my sweet Cynthia, whom time cannot touch because she is divine, nor will offend because she is delicate. O Cynthia, if thou shouldest always continue at thy fulness, both gods and [90 men would conspire to ravish thee. But thou, to abate the pride of our affections, dost detract from thy perfections, thinking it sufficient if once in a month we enjoy a glimpse of thy majesty; and then, to increase our griefs, thou dost decrease thy gleams, coming out of thy royal robes, wherewith thou dazzlest our eyes, down into thy swathe clouts,[5] beguiling our eyes. And then—   100

EUM. Stay there, Endymion. Thou that committest idolatry wilt straight blaspheme if thou be suffered. Sleep would do thee more good than speech. The moon heareth thee not or, if she do, regardeth thee not.

END. Vain Eumenides, whose thoughts never grow higher than the crown of thy head! Why troublest thou me, having neither head to conceive the cause of [110 my love or a heart to receive the impressions? Follow thou thine own fortunes, which creep on the earth, and suffer me to fly to mine, whose fall, though it be desperate, yet shall it come by daring. Farewell!
                                   [*Exit.*]

EUM. Without doubt Endymion is bewitched; otherwise in a man of such rare virtues there could not harbor a mind of such extreme madness. I will follow him, lest in this fancy of the moon he de- [120 prive himself of the sight of the sun. *Exit.*

[1] Besotted, infatuated.   [3] Computed.
[2] Silly.   [4] State.
                              [5] Swaddling clothes.

SCENA SECUNDA.

[*The gardens of Cynthia's palace.*]

Tellus, Floscula.

TELLUS. Treacherous and most perjured Endymion, is Cynthia the sweetness
of thy life and the bitterness of my death?
What revenge may be devised so full of
shame as my thoughts are replenished
with malice? Tell me, Floscula, if false-
ness in love can possibly be punished with
extremity of hate. As long as sword, fire,
or poison may be hired, no traitor to my
love shall live unrevenged. Were thy [10
oaths without number, thy kisses without
measure, thy sighs without end, forged to
deceive a poor credulous virgin, whose
simplicity had been worth thy favor and
better fortune? If the gods sit unequal[1]
beholders of injuries, or laughers at lovers' deceits, then let mischief be as well
forgiven in women as perjury winked at
in men.

FLOSC. Madam, if you would com- [20
pare the state of Cynthia with your own,
and the height of Endymion his [2] thoughts
with the meanness of your fortune, you
would rather yield than contend, being
between you and her no comparison; and
rather wonder than rage at the greatness
of his mind, being affected with a thing
more than mortal.

TELLUS. No comparison, Floscula? And
why so? Is not my beauty divine, [30
whose body is decked with fair flowers, and
whose veins are vines, yielding sweet liquor to
the dullest spirits; whose ears are corn,
to bring strength; and whose hairs are
grass, to bring abundance? Doth not
frankincense and myrrh breathe out of
my nostrils, and all the sacrifice of the
gods breed in my bowels? Infinite are my
creatures, without which neither thou nor
Endymion nor any could love or live.　　40

FLOSC. But know you not, fair lady,
that Cynthia governeth all things? Your
grapes would be but dry husks, your corn
but chaff, and all your virtues vain, were
it not Cynthia that preserveth the one in
the bud and nourisheth the other in the
blade, and by her influence both comforteth all things, and by her authority com-

mandeth all creatures. Suffer, then, Endymion to follow his affections, though to [50
obtain her be impossible, and let him
flatter himself in his own imaginations,
because they are immortal.

TELLUS. Loath I am, Endymion, thou
shouldest die, because I love thee well;
and that thou shouldest live, it grieveth
me, because thou lovest Cynthia too well.
In these extremities what shall I do?
Floscula, no more words; I am resolved.
He shall neither live nor die!　　　　　60

FLOSC. A strange practice,[3] if it be
possible.

TELLUS. Yes, I will entangle him in
such a sweet net that he shall neither find
the means to come out, nor desire it. All
allurements of pleasure will I cast before
his eyes, insomuch that he shall slake
that love which he now voweth to Cynthia, and burn in mine, of which he seemeth careless. In this languishing, be- [70
tween my amorous devices and his own
loose desires, there shall such dissolute
thoughts take root in his head and over
his heart grow so thick a skin that neither
hope of preferment nor fear of punishment nor counsel of the wisest nor company of the worthiest shall alter his humor
nor make him once to think of his honor.

FLOSC. A revenge incredible, and, if it
may be, unnatural.　　　　　　　　80

TELLUS. He shall know the malice of
a woman to have neither mean nor end;
and of a woman deluded in love to have
neither rule nor reason. I can do it; I
must; I will! All his virtues will I shadow
with vices. His person—ah, sweet person!—
shall he deck with such rich robes as he
shall forget it is his own person; his sharp
wit—ah, wit too sharp that hath cut off all
my joys!—shall he use in flattering of [90
my face and devising sonnets in my favor.
The prime of his youth and pride of his
time shall be spent in melancholy passions,
careless behavior, untamed thoughts, and
unbridled affections.

FLOSC. When this is done, what then?
Shall it continue till his death, or shall he
dote forever in this delight?

TELLUS. Ah, Floscula, thou rendest
my heart in sunder in putting me in [100
remembrance of the end.

---

[1] Prejudiced.　　　　[2] *I.e.*, Endymion's.　　　　[3] Stratagem.

FLOSC. Why, if this be not the end, all the rest is to no end.

TELLUS. Yet suffer me to imitate Juno, who would turn Jupiter's lovers to beasts on the earth, though she knew afterwards they should be stars in heaven.

FLOSC. Affection that is bred by enchantment is like a flower that is wrought in silk— in color and form most like, but [110 nothing at all in substance or savor.

TELLUS. It shall suffice me, if the world talk, that I am favored of Endymion.

FLOSC. Well, use your own will; but you shall find that love gotten with witchcraft is as unpleasant as fish taken with medicines [1] unwholesome.

TELLUS. Floscula, they that be so poor that they have neither net nor hook will rather poison dough than pine with [120 hunger; and she that is so oppressed with love that she is neither able with beauty nor wit to obtain her friend, will rather use unlawful means than try untolerable pains. I will do it.   *Exit.*

FLOSC. Then about it! Poor Endymion, what traps are laid for thee because thou honorest one that all the world wond'reth at! And what plots are cast to make thee unfortunate that studiest of all men [130 to be the faithfulest!   *Exit.*

SCENA TERTIA.

[*The same.*]

Dares, Samias, Sir Tophas, Epiton.[2]

DAR. Now our masters are in love up to the ears, what have we to do but to be in knavery up to the crowns?

SAM. O, that we had Sir Tophas, that brave squire, in the midst of our mirth—*et ecce autem,*[3] "Will you see the devil?"—

Enter Sir Tophas [and Epiton].

TOP. Epi!

EPI. Here, sir!

TOP. I brook not this idle humor of [10 love; it tickleth not my liver, from whence the lovemongers in former ages seemed to infer they should proceed.

EPI. Love, sir, may lie in your lungs— and I think it doth, and that is the cause you blow and are so pursy.

TOP. Tush, boy, I think it but some device of the poet to get money.

EPI. A poet? What's that?

TOP. Dost thou not know what a [20 poet is?

EPI. No.

TOP. Why, fool, a poet is as much as one should say—a poet.—But soft, yonder be two wrens; shall I shoot at them?

EPI. They are two lads!

TOP. Larks or wrens, I will kill them.

EPI. Larks! Are you blind? They are two little boys.

TOP. Birds or boys, they are both [30 but a pittance for my breakfast; therefore have at them, for their brains must as it were embroider my bolts.[4]

SAM. Stay your courage, valiant knight, for your widsom is so weary that it stayeth itself.

DAR. Why, Sir Tophas, have you forgotten your old friends?

TOP. Friends? *Nego argumentum.*[5]

SAM. And why not friends?   40

TOP. Because *amicitia* (as in old annuals[6] we find) is *inter pares.*[7] Now, my pretty companions, you shall see how unequal you be to me. But I will not cut you quite off—you shall be my half-friends for reaching to my middle; so far as from the ground to the waist I will be your friend.

DAR. Learnedly! But what shall become of the rest of your body, from the waist to the crown?   50

TOP. My children, *quod supra vos, nihil ad vos.*[8] You must think the rest immortal, because you cannot reach it.

EPI. Nay, I tell ye my master is more than a man.

DAR. And thou less than a mouse.

TOP. But what be you two?

SAM. I am Samias, page to Eumenides.[9]

DAR. And I Dares, page to Endymion.

TOP. Of what occupation are your [60 masters?

---

[1] Caught with poisoned bait (here, dough balls).
[2] Last two enter later.
[3] And behold indeed!

[4] Flat-headed arrows.
[5] I deny the proof.
[6] Annals (?).
[7] Friendship is among equals.
[8] What is above you is nothing to you.
[9] Bond correctly transposes the names of the masters, in this and the following line.

DAR. Occupation, you clown! Why, they are honorable, and warriors.

TOP. Then are they my prentices.

DAR. Thine? And why so?

TOP. I was the first that ever devised war, and therefore by Mars himself given me for my arms a whole armory; and thus I go, as you see, clothed with artillery. It is not silks—milksops!—nor [70 tissues, nor the fine wool of Seres,[1] but iron, steel, swords, flame, shot, terror, clamor, blood, and ruin, that rocks asleep my thoughts, which never had any other cradle but cruelty. Let me see, do you not bleed?

DAR. Why so?

TOP. Commonly my words wound.

SAM. What then do your blows?

TOP. Not only wound,[2] but also con- [80 found.

SAM. How dar'st thou come so near thy master, Epi? Sir Tophas, spare us!

TOP. You shall live: you, Samias, because you are little; you, Dares, because you are no bigger; and both of you, because you are but two, for commonly I kill by the dozen, and have for every particular adversary a peculiar weapon.

SAM. May we know the use, for our [90 better skill in war?

TOP. You shall. Here is a burbolt [3] for the ugly beast the blackbird.

DAR. A cruel sight!

TOP. Here is the musket for the untamed or, as the vulgar sort term it, the wild mallard.

SAM. O desperate attempt!

EPI. Nay, my master will match them.

DAR. Ay, if he catch them. 100

TOP. Here is a spear and shield, and both necessary, the one to conquer, the other to subdue or overcome the terrible trout, which, although he be under the water, yet tying a string to the top of my spear and an engine of iron to the end of my line, I overthrow him, and then herein I put him.

SAM. O wonderful war!—[Aside.] Dares, didst thou ever hear such a dolt? 110

DAR. [Aside.] All the better; we shall have good sport hereafter, if we can get leisure.

SAM. [Aside.] Leisure! I will rather lose my master's service than his company! Look how he struts!—But what is this? Call you it your sword?

TOP. No, it is my scimitar, which I, by construction often studying to be compendious, call my smiter. 120

DAR. What, are you also learned, sir?

TOP. Learned? I am all Mars and Ars.[4]

SAM. Nay, you are all mass and ass.

TOP. Mock you me? You shall both suffer, yet with such weapons as you shall make choice of the weapon wherewith you shall perish. Am I all a mass or lump? Is there no proportion in me? Am I all ass? Is there no wit in me? Epi, prepare them to the slaughter. 130

SAM. I pray, sir, hear us speak! We call you mass, which your learning doth well understand is all man, for *mas, maris* is a man. Then *as*, as you know, is a weight, and we for your virtues account you a weight.

TOP. The Latin hath saved your lives, the which a world of silver could not have ransomed. I understand you, and pardon you. 140

DAR. Well, Sir Tophas, we bid you farewell, and at our next meeting we will be ready to do you service.

TOP. Samias, I thank you; Dares, I thank you; but especially I thank you both.

SAM. [Aside.] Wisely! Come, next time we'll have some pretty gentlewomen with us to walk, for without doubt with them he will be very dainty. 150

DAR. Come, let us see what our masters do; it is high time.

Exeunt [Samias and Dares].

TOP. Now will I march into the field, where, if I cannot encounter with my foul enemies, I will withdraw myself to the river, and there fortify for fish, for there resteth no minute free from fight.

Exit [Sir Tophas with Epiton].

SCENA QUARTA.

[Another part of the same.]

Tellus, Floscula, Dipsas.

TELLUS. Behold, Floscula, we have met with the woman by chance that we

---

[1] Chinese silk. Original reads *Ceres;* changed by Bond.　[2] Early edns. read *confound.*　[3] Birdbolt.

[4] War and art.

sought for by travel.[1]   I will break my
mind to her without ceremony or circumstance, lest we lose that time in advice
that should be spent in execution.

FLOSC. Use your discretion; I will in
this case neither give counsel nor consent,
for there cannot be a thing more monstrous
than to force affection by sorcery, [10
neither do I imagine anything more impossible.

TELLUS. Tush, Floscula, in obtaining
of love, what impossibilities will I not try?
And for the winning of Endymion, what
impieties will I not practice?—Dipsas,
whom as many honor for age as wonder
at for cunning, listen in few words to my
tale, and answer in one word to the purpose,
for that neither my burning desire [20
can afford long speech, nor the short time
I have to stay many delays. Is it possible
by herbs, stones, spells, incantation, enchantment, exorcisms, fire, metals, planets,
or any practice, to plant affection where
it is not, and to supplant it where it is?

DIPSAS. Fair lady, you may imagine
that these hoary hairs are not void of
experience, nor the great name that goeth
of my cunning to be without cause. I [30
can darken the sun by my skill and remove the moon out of her course; I can
restore youth to the aged and make hills
without bottoms; there is nothing that I
cannot do but that only which you would
have me do; and therein I differ from the
gods, that I am not able to rule hearts,
for, were it in my power to place affection
by appointment, I would make such evil
appetites, such inordinate lusts, such [40
cursed desires, as all the world should be
filled both with superstitious heats and extreme love.

TELLUS. Unhappy Tellus, whose desires are so desperate that they are neither
to be conceived of any creature, nor to be
cured by any art!

DIPSAS. This I can: breed slackness
in love, though never root it out. What is
he whom you love, and what she that [50
he honoreth?

TELLUS. Endymion, sweet Endymion,
is he that hath my heart; and Cynthia,
too-too fair Cynthia, the miracle of nature, of time, of fortune, is the lady that

[1] Travail (?), labor.

he delights in, and dotes on every day,
and dies for ten thousand times a day.

DIPSAS. Would you have his love either
by absence or sickness aslaked?[2] Would
you that Cynthia should mistrust him, [60
or be jealous of him without color?[3]

TELLUS. It is the only thing I crave
that, seeing my love to Endymion, unspotted, cannot be accepted, his truth to
Cynthia, though it be unspeakable, may
be suspected.

DIPSAS. I will undertake it, and over
take[4] him, that all his love shall be doubted
of, and therefore become desperate. But
this will wear out with time, that [70
treadeth all things down but truth.

TELLUS. Let us go.

DIPSAS. I follow.   *Exeunt.*

ACTUS SECUNDUS. SCENA PRIMA

[*A grove near the cell of Endymion.*]

Endymion, Tellus.[5]

END. O fair Cynthia! O unfortunate
Endymion! Why was not thy birth as
high as thy thoughts, or her beauty less
than heavenly; or why are not thine honors
as rare as her beauty, or thy fortunes as
great as thy deserts? Sweet Cynthia, how
wouldst thou be pleased, how possessed?
Will labors, patient of all extremities, obtain thy love? There is no mountain so
steep that I will not climb, no monster [10
so cruel that I will not tame, no action
so desperate that I will not attempt.
Desirest thou the passions of love, the
sad and melancholy moods of perplexed
minds, the not-to-be-expressed torments
of racked thoughts? Behold my sad tears,
my deep sighs, my hollow eyes, my broken
sleeps, my heavy countenance! Wouldst
thou have me vowed only to thy beauty
and consume every minute of time in [20
thy service? Remember my solitary life
almost these seven years. Whom have I
entertained but mine own thoughts and
thy virtues? What company have I used
but contemplation? Whom have I wondered at but thee? Nay, whom have I
not contemned for thee? Have I not crept
to those on whom I might have trodden,

[2] Slaked, abated.   [4] Overcome.
[3] Reason, excuse.   [5] Enters later.

only because thou didst shine upon them? Have not injuries been sweet to me if [30 thou vouchsafest I should bear them? Have I not spent my golden years in hopes, waxing old with wishing, yet wishing nothing but thy love? With Tellus, fair Tellus, have I dissembled, using her but as a cloak for mine affections, that others, seeing my mangled and disordered mind, might think it were for one that loveth me, not for Cynthia, whose perfection alloweth no companion nor comparison. [40 In the midst of these distempered thoughts of mine thou art not only jealous of my truth, but careless, suspicious, and secure,[1] which strange humor maketh my mind as desperate as thy conceits [2] are doubtful. I am none of those wolves that bark most when thou shinest brightest, but that fish (thy fish, Cynthia, in the flood Araris)[3] which at thy waxing is as white as the driven snow, and at thy [50 waning as black as deepest darkness. I am that Endymion, sweet Cynthia, that have carried my thoughts in equal balance with my actions, being always as free from imagining ill as enterprising; that Endymion whose eyes never esteemed anything fair but thy face, whose tongue termed nothing rare but thy virtues, and whose heart imagined nothing miraculous but thy government; yea, that Endymion, [60 who, divorcing himself from the amiableness of all ladies, the bravery [4] of all courts, the company of all men, hath chosen in a solitary cell to live, only by feeding on thy favor, accounting in the world—but thyself—nothing excellent, nothing immortal. Thus mayst thou see every vein, sinew, muscle, and artery of my love, in which there is no flattery, nor deceit, error, nor art. But soft, here cometh Tellus. [70 I must turn my other face to her, like Janus, lest she be as suspicious as Juno.

Enter Tellus [,Floscula, and Dipsas].

TELLUS. Yonder I espy Endymion. I will seem to suspect nothing, but soothe him, that, seeing I cannot obtain the depth of his love, I may learn the height of his

---

[1] Overconfident.　　[2] Fancies, imaginings, ideas.
[3] Emended by Baker. Original reads *Aranis*. A characteristic Lylian use of Pliny's unnatural *Natural Philosophy*.　　　　　[4] Splendor.

dissembling. Floscula and Dipsas, withdraw yourselves out of our sight, yet be within the hearing of our saluting.—　79
　　　　[Exeunt Floscula and Dipsas.]
How now, Endymion, always solitary? No company but your own thoughts, no friend but melancholy fancies?

END. You know, fair Tellus, that the sweet remembrance of your love is the only companion of my life, and thy presence, my paradise, so that I am not alone when nobody is with me, and in heaven itself when thou art with me.

TELLUS. Then you love me, Endymion?

END. Or else I live not, Tellus.　90

TELLUS. Is it not possible for you, Endymion, to dissemble?

END. Not, Tellus, unless I could make me a woman.

TELLUS. Why, is dissembling joined to their sex inseparable, as heat to fire, heaviness to earth, moisture to water, thinness to air?

END. No, but found in their sex as common as spots upon doves, moles [100 upon faces, caterpillars upon sweet apples, cobwebs upon fair windows.

TELLUS. Do they all dissemble?

END. All but one.

TELLUS. Who is that?

END. I dare not tell; for, if I should say you, then would you imagine my flattery to be extreme; if another, then would you think my love to be but indifferent.　110

TELLUS. You will be sure I shall take no vantage of your words. But, in sooth, Endymion, without more ceremonies, is it not Cynthia?

END. You know, Tellus, that of the gods we are forbidden to dispute, because their deities come not within the compass of our reasons; and of Cynthia we are allowed not to talk but to wonder, because her virtues are not within the reach [120 of our capacities.

TELLUS. Why, she is but a woman.

END. No more was Venus.

TELLUS. She is but a virgin.

END. No more was Vesta.

TELLUS. She shall have an end.

END. So shall the world.

TELLUS. Is not her beauty subject to time?

END. No more than time is to [130 standing still.

TELLUS. Wilt thou make her immortal?

END. No, but incomparable.

TELLUS. Take heed, Endymion, lest like the wrastler in Olympia, that, striving to lift an impossible weight, catched an incurable strain, thou, by fixing thy thoughts above thy reach, fall into a disease without all recure.[1] But I see thou art now in love with Cynthia. 140

END. No, Tellus; thou knowest that the stately cedar, whose top reacheth unto the clouds, never boweth his head to the shrubs that grow in the valley; nor ivy, that climbeth up by the elm, can ever get hold of the beams of the sun. Cynthia I honor in all humility, whom none ought or dare adventure to love, whose affections are immortal, and virtues infinite. Suffer me, therefore, to gaze on the moon, [150 at whom, were it not for thyself, I would die with wondering.   *Exeunt.*

SCENA SECUNDA.

[*The gardens of Cynthia's palace.*]

Dares, Samias, Scintilla, Favilla.

DAR. Come, Samias, diddest thou ever hear such a sighing, the one for Cynthia, the other for Semele, and both for moonshine in the water?

SAM. Let them sigh, and let us sing. How say you, gentlewomen, are not our masters too far in love?

SCINT. Their tongues, happily,[2] are dipped to the root in amorous words and sweet discourses, but I think their [10 hearts are scarce tipped on the side with constant desires.

DAR. How say you, Favilla, is not love a lurcher,[3] that taketh men's stomachs away that they cannot eat, their spleen that they cannot laugh, their hearts that they cannot fight, their eyes that they cannot sleep, and leaveth nothing but livers to make nothing but lovers?

FAVIL. Away, peevish boy! A rod [20 were better under thy girdle than love in thy mouth. It will be a forward cock that croweth in the shell.

DAR. Alas, good old gentlewoman, how it becometh you to be grave!

SCINT. Favilla, though she be but a spark,[4] yet is she fire.

FAVIL. And you, Scintilla, be not much more than a spark, though you would be esteemed a flame. 30

SAM. [*Aside to Dares.*] It were good sport to see the fight between two sparks.

DAR. [*Aside to Samias.*] Let them to it, and we will warm us by their words.

SCINT. You are not angry, Favilla?

FAVIL. That is, Scintilla, as you list to take it.

SAM. That, that!

SCINT. This it is to be matched with girls who, coming but yesterday from [40 making of babies,[5] would before tomorrow be accounted matrons.

FAVIL. I cry your matronship mercy. Because your pantables[6] be higher with cork, therefore your feet must needs be higher in the insteps. You will be mine elder because you stand upon a stool and I on the floor.

SAM. Good, good!

DAR. [*To Samias.*] Let them alone, [50 and see with what countenance they will become friends.

SCINT. Nay, you think to be the wiser, because you mean to have the last word.

SAM. [*To Dares.*] Step between them lest they scratch.—In faith, gentlewomen, seeing we came out to be merry, let not your jarring mar our jests; be friends. How say you?

SCINT. I am not angry, but it spited [60 me to see how short she was.

FAVIL. I meant nothing till she would needs cross me.

DAR. Then, so let it rest.

SCINT. I am agreed.

FAVIL. And I. [*Weeping.*] Yet I never took anything so unkindly in my life.

SCINT. [*Weeping.*] 'Tis I have the cause, that never offered the occasion.

DAR. Excellent, and right like a [70 woman!

SAM. A strange sight to see water come out of fire!

---

[1] Recovery.
[2] Haply, perhaps.
[3] Lurker, thief.
[4] Punning on *spark*, a person of gay disposition.
[5] Doils.
[6] Pantofles, slippers.

DAR. It is their property to carry in their eyes fire and water, tears and torches, and in their mouths honey and gall.

SCINT. You will be a good one if you live. But what is yonder formal fellow?

Enter Sir Tophas [, followed by Epiton].

DAR. Sir Tophas, Sir Tophas, of whom we told you. If you be good wenches, [80 make as though you love him, and wonder at him.

FAVIL. We will do our parts.

DAR. But first let us stand aside, and let him use his garb,[1] for all consisteth in his gracing.[2]   [*The four retire.*]

TOP. Epi!

EPI. At hand, sir.

TOP. How likest thou this martial life, where nothing but blood besprinkleth [90 our bosoms? Let me see, be our enemies[3] fat?

EPI. Passing fat; and I would not change this life to be a lord; and yourself passeth all comparison, for other captains kill and beat, and there is nothing you kill but you also eat.

TOP. I will draw out their guts out of their bellies, and tear the flesh with my teeth, so mortal is my hate, and so [100 eager my unstaunched stomach.

EPI. [*Aside.*] My master thinks himself the valiantest man in the world if he kill a wren; so warlike a thing he accompteth to take away life, though it be from a lark.

TOP. Epi, I find my thoughts to swell and my spirit to take wings, insomuch that I cannot continue within the compass of so slender combats.   110

FAVIL.   This passeth!
SCINT. } [*Aside.*] Why, is he not mad?
SAM.   No, but a little vainglorious.

TOP. Epi!

EPI. Sir?

TOP. I will encounter that black and cruel enemy that beareth rough and untewed[4] locks upon his body, whose sire throweth down the strongest walls, [120

whose legs are as many as both ours, on whose head are placed most horrible horns by nature as a defense from all harms.

EPI. What mean you, master, to be so desperate?

TOP. Honor inciteth me, and very hunger compelleth me.

EPI. What is that monster?

TOP. The monster *Ovis*. I have said; let thy wits work.   130

EPI. I cannot imagine it. Yet let me see: a black enemy with rough locks— it may be a sheep, and *Ovis* is a sheep; his sire so strong—a ram is a sheep's sire, that being also an engine of war; horns he hath, and four legs—so hath a sheep. Without doubt, this monster is a black sheep. Is it not a sheep that you mean?

TOP. Thou hast hit it. That monster will I kill and sup with.   140

SAM. [*Aside.*] Come, let us take him off.—[*Samias, Dares, Favilla, and Scintilla advance.*] Sir Tophas, all hail!

TOP. Welcome, children. I seldom cast mine eyes so low as to the crowns of your heads, and therefore pardon me that I spake not all this while.

DAR. No harm done. Here be fair ladies come to wonder at your person, your valor, your wit, the report where- [150 of hath made them careless of their own honors, to glut their eyes and hearts upon yours.

TOP. Report cannot but injure me, for that, not knowing fully what I am, I fear she hath been a niggard in her praises.

SCINT. No, gentle knight, Report hath been prodigal; for she hath left you no equal, nor herself credit, so much hath she told—yet no more than we now see. [160

DAR. [*Aside.*] A good wench!

FAVIL. If there remain as much pity toward women as there is in you courage against your enemies, then shall we be happy, who, hearing of your person, came to see it, and, seeing it, are now in love with it.

TOP. Love me, ladies? I easily believe it, but my tough heart receiveth no impression with sweet words. Mars may [170 pierce it; Venus shall not paint on it.

FAVIL. A cruel saying.

SAM. [*Aside.*] There's a girl!

---

[1] Show his demeanor.
[2] All depends on honoring him.
[3] *I.e.*, the fish Epiton carries.
[4] Uncombed.

DAR. Will you cast these ladies away, and all for a little love? Do but speak kindly!

TOP. There cometh no soft syllable within my lips; custom hath made my words bloody and my heart barbarous. That pelting [1] word love, how wat'rish [180 it is in my mouth; it carrieth no sound. Hate, horror, death are speeches that nourish my spirits. I like honey, but I care not for the bees; I delight in music, but I love not to play on the bagpipes; I can vouchsafe to hear the voice of women, but to touch their bodies, I disdain it as a thing childish and fit for such men as can digest nothing but milk.

SCINT. A hard heart! Shall we die [190 for your love and find no remedy?

TOP. I have already taken a surfeit.

EPI. Good master, pity them.

TOP. Pity them, Epi? No, I do not think that this breast shall be pestered with such a foolish passion.—What is that the gentlewoman carrieth in [2] a chain?

EPI. Why, it is a squirrel.

TOP. A squirrel? O gods, what things are made for money! 200

DAR. [Aside.] Is not this gentleman overwise?

FAVIL. [Aside.] I could stay all day with him, if I feared not to be shent.[3]

SCINT. [Aside.] Is it not possible to meet again?

DAR. [Aside.] Yes, at any time.

FAVIL. [Aside.] Then let us hasten home. 209

SCINT. Sir Tophas, the god of war deal better with you than you do with the god of love.

FAVIL. Our love we may dissemble—digest [4] we cannot; but I doubt not but time will hamper you and help us.

TOP. I defy time, who hath no interest in my heart. Come, Epi, let me to the battle with that hideous beast. Love is pap, and hath no relish in my taste because it is not terrible.— 220

DAR. Indeed, a black sheep is a perilous beast. But let us in till another time.

FAVIL. I shall long for that time.

Exeunt.

[1] Paltry, contemptible.
[2] On.
[3] Scolded.   [4] Digest, stomach, put up with.

[*A grove near the cell of Endymion.*]

Endymion, Dipsas, Bagoa.[5]

END. No rest, Endymion? Still uncertain how to settle thy steps by day or thy thoughts by night? Thy truth is measured by thy fortune, and thou art judged unfaithful because thou art unhappy. I will see if I can beguile myself with sleep, and, if no slumber will take hold in my eyes, yet will I embrace the golden thoughts in my head, and wish to melt by musing; that, as ebony, which no fire [10 can scorch, is yet consumed with sweet savors, so my heart, which cannot be bent by the hardness of fortune, may be bruised by amorous desires. On yonder bank never grew anything but lunary,[6] and hereafter I will never have any bed but that bank. O Endymion, Tellus was fair, but what availeth beauty without wisdom? Nay, Endymion, she was wise, but what availeth wisdom without honor? She [20 was honorable, Endymion; belie her not. Ay, but how obscure is honor without fortune! Was she not fortunate whom so many followed? Yes, yes, but base is fortune without majesty. Thy majesty, Cynthia, all the world knoweth and wondereth at, but not one in the world that can imitate it or comprehend it. No more. Endymion! Sleep or die! Nay, die, for to sleep, it is impossible.—And yet I [30 know not how it cometh to pass, I feel such a heaviness both in mine eyes and heart that I am suddenly benumbed, yea, in every joint. It may be weariness, for when did I rest? It may be deep melancholy, for when did I not sigh? Cynthia! Ay, so—I say, Cynthia! *He falls asleep.*

[*Enter Dipsas and Bagoa.*]

DIPSAS. Little dost thou know, Endymion, when thou shalt wake, for, hadst thou placed thy heart as low in love as [40 thy head lieth now in sleep, thou mightest have commanded Tellus, whom now, instead of a mistress, thou shalt find a tomb. These eyes must I seal up by art, not nature, which are to be opened neither by art nor nature. Thou that lay'st down with

[5] Last two enter later.   [6] Moonwort.

golden locks shalt not awake until they be turned to silver hairs; and that chin on which scarcely appeareth soft down shall be filled with bristles as hard as [50 broom. Thou shalt sleep out thy youth and flowering time, and become dry hay before thou knewest thyself green grass; and ready by age to step into the grave when thou wakest, that was youthful in the court when thou laid'st thee down to sleep. The malice of Tellus hath brought this to pass, which, if she could not have entreated of me by fair means, she would have commanded by menacing, for [60 from her gather we all our simples to maintain our sorceries.—Fan with this hemlock over his face, and sing the enchantment for sleep, whilst I go in and finish those ceremonies that are required in our art. Take heed ye touch not his face, for the fan is so seasoned that whoso it toucheth with a leaf shall presently die, and over whom the wind of it breatheth, he shall sleep forever.   *Exit.* [70

BAGOA. Let me alone; I will be careful. What hap hadst thou, Endymion, to come under the hands of Dipsas! O fair Endymion, how it grieveth me that that fair face must be turned to a withered skin and taste the pains of death before it feel the reward of love! I fear Tellus will repent that which the heavens themselves seemed to rue. But I hear Dipsas coming! I dare not repine, lest she make me [80 pine, and rock me into such a deep sleep that I shall not awake to my marriage.

Enter Dipsas.

DIPSAS. How now, have you finished?
BAGOA. Yea.
DIPSAS. Well then, let us in. And see that you do not so much as whisper that I did this, for, if you do, I will turn thy hairs to adders and all thy teeth in thy head to tongues. Come away, come away!   *Exeunt.* [90

A DUMB SHOW[1]

Music sounds. Three Ladies enter: one with a knife and a looking-glass, who, by

[1] This scene, representing the dream of Endymion, first appeared in Blount's edition of 1632. *Cf.* Endymion's account of the incident, V, i, 109 ff.

the procurement [2] of one of the other two, offers to stab Endymion as he sleeps; but the third wrings her hands, lamenteth, offering still to prevent it, but dares not.

At last, the first Lady, looking in the glass, casts down the knife.   *Exeunt.*

Enters an Ancient Man with books with three leaves; offers the same twice. Endymion refuseth. He rendeth two, and offers the third, where he stands awhile; and then Endymion offers to take it.

       Exit [the Old Man].

ACTUS TERTIUS. SCENA PRIMA.
[*The gardens of Cynthia's palace.*]

Cynthia, Three Lords [*Eumenides, Zontes, and Panelion*], *Tellus* [*,Semele, Corsites*].

CYNTH. Is the report true that Endymion is stricken into such a dead sleep that nothing can either wake him or move him?

EUM. Too true, madam, and as much to be pitied as wondered at.

TELLUS. As good sleep and do no harm as wake and do no good.

CYNTH. What maketh you, Tellus, to be so short? The time was, Endymion [10 only was.

EUM. It is an old saying, madam, that a waking dog doth afar off bark at a sleeping lion.

SEM. It were good, Eumenides, that you took a nap with your friend, for your speech beginneth to be heavy.

EUM. Contrary to your nature, Semele, which hath been always accounted light.

CYNTH. What, have we here before [20 my face these unseemly and malapert overthwarts![3] I will tame your tongues and your thoughts, and make your speeches answerable to your duties, and your conceits fit for my dignity, else will I banish you both my person and the world.

EUM. Pardon I humbly ask; but such is my unspotted faith to Endymion that whatsoever seemeth a needle to prick his finger is a dagger to wound my heart. [30

CYNTH. If you be so dear to him, how happeneth it you neither go to see him, nor search for remedy for him?

[2] Instigation, urging.
[3] Impertinent wranglings.

EUM. I have seen him to my grief, and sought recure with despair, for that I cannot imagine who should restore him that is the wonder to all men. Your highness, on whose hands the compass of the earth is at command, though not in possession, may show yourself both worthy [40 your sex, your nature, and your favor, if you redeem that honorable Endymion, whose ripe years foretell rare virtues, and whose unmellowed conceits promise ripe counsel.

CYNTH. I have had trial of Endymion, and conceive greater assurance of his age than I could hope of his youth.

TELLUS. But timely,[1] madam, crooks that tree that will be a cammock,[2] and [50 young it pricks that will be a thorn; and therefore he that began without care to settle his life, it is a sign without amendment he will end it.

CYNTH. Presumptuous girl, I will make thy tongue an example of unrecoverable displeasure. Corsites, carry her to the castle in the desert, there to remain and weave.   59

CORS. Shall she work stories or poetries?

CYNTH. It skilleth[3] not which. Go to! In both, for she shall find examples infinite in either what punishment long tongues have. Eumenides, if either the soothsayers in Egypt, or the enchanters in Thessaly, or the philosophers in Greece, or all the sages of the world can find remedy, I will procure it. Therefore, despatch with all speed: you, Eumenides, into [70 Thessaly; you, Zontes, into Greece, because you are acquainted in Athens; you, Panelion, to Egypt; saying that Cynthia sendeth, and, if you will, commandeth.

EUM. On bowed knee I give thanks, and with wings on my legs I fly for remedy.

ZON. We are ready at your highness' command, and hope to return to your full content.

CYNTH. It shall never be said that [80 Cynthia, whose mercy and goodness filleth the heavens with joys and the world with marvels, will suffer either Endymion or any to perish, if he may be protected.

[1] Early.
[2] Tree artificially bent.
[3] Matters.

EUM. Your majesty's words have been always deeds, and your deeds virtues.

Exeunt.

SCENA SECUNDA.

[Before the castle of Corsites in a desert.]

Corsites, Tellus.

CORS. Here is the castle, fair Tellus, in which you must weave, till either time end your days, or Cynthia her displeasure. I am sorry so fair a face should be subject to so hard a fortune, and that the flower of beauty, which is honored in courts, should here wither in prison.

TELLUS. Corsites, Cynthia may restrain the liberty of my body; of my thoughts she cannot, and therefore do I [10 esteem myself most free, though I am in greatest bondage.

CORS. Can you then feed on fancy, and subdue the malice of envy by the sweetness of imagination?

TELLUS. Corsites, there is no sweeter music to the miserable than despair; and therefore the more bitterness I feel, the more sweetness I find; for so vain were liberty, and so unwelcome the following [20 of higher fortune, that I choose rather to pine in this castle than to be a prince in any other court.

CORS. A humor contrary to your years and nothing agreeable to your sex—the one commonly allured with delights, the other always with sovereignty.

TELLUS. I marvel, Corsites, that you, being a captain, who should sound nothing but terror and suck nothing but blood, [30 can find in your heart to talk such smooth words, for that it agreeth not with your calling to use words so soft as that of love.

CORS. Lady, it were unfit of wars to discourse with women, into whose minds nothing can sink but smoothness; besides, you must not think that soldiers be so rough-hewn, or of such knotty mettle, that beauty cannot allure, and you, [40 being beyond perfection, enchant.

TELLUS. Good Corsites, talk not of love, but let me to my labor. The little beauty I have shall be bestowed on my loom, which I now mean to make my lover.

Cors. Let us in, and what favor Corsites can show, Tellus shall command.

Tellus. The only favor I desire is now and then to walk.　　　　　*Exeunt.*

Scena Tertia.

[*The gardens of Cynthia's palace.*]

Sir Tophas and Epi[ton].

Top. Epi!

Epi. Here, sir.

Top. Unrig me. Heigh-ho!

Epi. What's that?

Top. An interjection, whereof some are of mourning: as *eho, vah.*[1]

Epi. I understand you not.

Top. Thou seest me.

Epi. Ay.

Top. Thou hear'st me.　　　　　10

Epi. Ay.

Top. Thou feelest me.

Epi. Ay.

Top. And not understand'st me?

Epi. No.

Top. Then am I but three-quarters of a noun substantive. But alas, Epi, to tell thee the troth, I am a noun adjective.

Epi. Why?

Top. Because I cannot stand with- [20 out another.

Epi. Who is that?

Top. Dipsas.

Epi. Are you in love?

Top. No; but love hath, as it were, milked my thoughts and drained from my heart the very substance of my accustomed courage. It worketh in my head like new wine, so as I must hoop my sconce with iron, lest my head break, and so I be- [30 wray[2] my brains. But, I pray thee, first discover me in all parts, that I may be like a lover, and then will I sigh and die. Take my gun and give me a gown: "*Cedant arma togæ.*"[3]

Epi. Here.

Top. Take my sword and shield and give me beard-brush and scissors: "*Bella gerant alii; tu, Pari, semper ama.*"[4]

Epi. Will you be trimmed, sir?　　40

Top. Not yet; for I feel a contention within me whether I shall frame the bodkin beard or the bush.[5] But take my pike and give me pen: "*Dicere quæ puduit, scribere jussit amor.*"[6]

Epi. I will furnish you, sir.

Top. Now, for my bow and bolts give me ink and paper, for my smiter a penknife; for

Scalpellum, calami, atramentum, charta, libelli,　　　　　50
Sint semper studiis arma parata meis.[7]

Epi. Sir, will you give over wars and play with that bable[8] called love?

Top. Give over wars? No, Epi, "*Militat omnis amans, et habet sua castra Cupido.*"[9]

Epi. Love hath made you very eloquent, but your face is nothing fair.

Top. "*Non formosus erat, sed erat facundus Ulysses.*"[10]

Epi. Nay, I must seek a new master [60 if you can speak nothing but verses.

Top. "*Quicquid conabar dicere, versus erat.*"[11] Epi, I feel all *Ovid de Arte Amandi* lie as heavy at my heart as a load of logs. O, what a fine, thin hair hath Dipsas! What a pretty, low forehead! What a tall and stately nose! What little, hollow eyes! What great and goodly lips! How harmless she is, being toothless! Her fingers fat and short, adorned with long nails [70 like a bitter![12] In how sweet a proportion

---

[1] The discussion of grammatical terms in this and the following lines is modeled upon passages in William Lilly's famous Latin grammar.

[2] Uncover.

[3] From Cicero, *De officiis*, i, 22, 76: "Let arms give place to the toga."

[4] Combination of verses from Ovid, *Heroides*, xiii, 84; xvii, 254: "Let others wage wars; thou, O Paris, must always love."

[5] Shape the beard like a dagger or leave it untrimmed.

[6] Ovid, *Heroides*, iv, 10: "Those things which one has hesitated to say, Love has bidden to write."

[7] Lines apparently invented by Lyly: A penknife, quills, ink, paper, booklets—let these weapons [*i.e.*, implements] be always in readiness for my studies.

[8] Bauble.

[9] Ovid, *Amores*, i, 9, 1: "Every lover goes to war, and Cupid holds his camp."

[10] Ovid, *Ars amatoria*, ii, 123: "Ulysses was not handsome, but he was eloquent."

[11] Ovid, *Tristia*, iv, 10, 26: "Whatever I was trying to express was poetry."

[12] Bittern.

her cheeks hang down to her breasts like dugs and her paps to her waist like bags! What a low stature she is, and yet what a great foot she carrieth! How thrifty must she be in whom there is no waist! How virtuous is she like to be over whom no man can be jealous!

EPI. Stay, master, you forget yourself.

TOP. O Epi, even as a dish melteth [80 by the fire, so doth my wit increase by love.

EPI. Pithily, and to the purpose! But what, begin you to nod?

TOP. Good Epi, let me take a nap; for, as some man may better steal a horse than another look over the hedge, so divers shall be sleepy when they would fainest take rest. *He sleeps.* [89

EPI. Who ever saw such a woodcock![1] Love Dipsas! Without doubt all the world will now account him valiant, that ventureth on her whom none durst undertake. But here cometh two wags.

Enter Dares and Samias.

SAM. Thy master hath slept his share.

DAR. I think he doth it because he would not pay me my board wages.

SAM. It is a thing most strange, and I think mine will never return, so that we must both seek new masters, for we [100 shall never live by our manners.

EPI. If you want masters, join with me and serve Sir Tophas, who must needs keep more men because he is toward marriage.

SAM. What, Epi, where's thy master?

EPI. Yonder, sleeping in love.

DAR. Is it possible?

EPI. He hath taken his thoughts a hole lower, and saith, seeing it is the fashion of the world, he will vail [2] bonnet to beauty.

SAM. How is he attired? 111

EPI. Lovely.

DAR. Whom loveth this amorous knight?

EPI. Dipsas.

SAM. That ugly creature? Why, she is a fool, a scold, fat, without fashion, and quite without favor.

EPI. Tush, you be simple; my master hath a good marriage.

DAR. Good? As how? 120

EPI. Why, in marrying Dipsas he shall have every day twelve dishes of meat to his dinner, though there be none but Dipsas with him: four of flesh, four of fish, four of fruit.

SAM. As how, Epi?

EPI. For flesh these: woodcock, goose, bitter, and rail.

DAR. Indeed, he shall not miss if Dipsas be there. 130

EPI. For fish these: crab, carp, lump, and pouting.

SAM. Excellent, for of my word she is both crabbish, lumpish, and carping.

EPI. For fruit these: fretters,[3] medlars, hartichokes,[4] and lady-longings. Thus you see he shall fare like a king, though he be but a beggar.

DAR. Well, Epi, dine thou with him, for I had rather fast than see her face. [140 But, see, thy ma[ster] is asleep; let us have a song to wake this amorous knight.

EPI. Agreed.

SAM. Content.

THE FIRST SONG [5]

EPI. Here snores Tophas,
That amorous ass,
Who loves Dipsas,
With face so sweet,
Nose and chin meet.

ALL THREE. { At sight of her each Fury
skips 150
And flings into her lap
their whips.

DAR. Holla, holla in his ear.

SAM. The witch, sure, thrust her fingers there.

EPI. Cramp him, or wring the fool by th' nose;

DAR. Or clap some burning flax to his toes.

SAM. What music's best to wake him?

EPI. Baw-wow, let bandogs shake him!

DAR. Let adders hiss in 's ear!

SAM. Else earwigs wriggle there!

EPI. No, let him batten! When his tongue 160
Once goes, a cat is not worse strung.

ALL THREE. { But if he ope nor mouth
nor eyes,
He may in time sleep himself wise.

[3] An unidentified fruit. [4] Artichokes.
[5] All the songs in the play appeared first in Blount's edn.

[1] Fool. [2] Doff.

Top. [*Waking.*] Sleep is a binding of the senses, love a loosing.

Epi. [*Aside.*] Let us hear him awhile.

Top. There appeared in my sleep a goodly owl, who, sitting upon my shoulder, cried, "Twit, twit," and before mine eyes presented herself the express image of [170 Dipsas. I marveled what the owl said, till at the last I perceived "Twit, twit"— "To it, to it," only by contraction—admonished by this vision to make account of my sweet Venus.

Sam. Sir Tophas, you have overslept yourself.

Top. No, youth, I have but slept over my love.   179

Dar. Love? Why, it is impossible that into so noble and unconquered a courage love should creep, having first a head as hard to pierce as steel, then to pass to a heart armed with a shirt of mail.

Epi. Ay, but my master yawning one day in the sun, Love crept into his mouth before he could close it, and there kept such a tumbling in his body that he was glad to untruss the points [1] of his heart and entertain Love as a stranger.   190

Top. If there remain any pity in you, plead for me to Dipsas.

Dar. Plead? Nay, we will press her to it.—[*Aside to Samias.*] Let us go with him to Dipsas, and there shall we have good sport.—But, Sir Tophas, when shall we go? For I find my tongue voluble, and my heart venturous, and all myself like myself.   199

Sam. [*Aside to Dares.*] Come, Dares, let us not lose him till we find our masters, for, as long as he liveth, we shall lack neither mirth nor meat.

Epi. We will travice.[2] Will you go, sir?

Top. "*I præ; sequar.*"[3]   *Exeunt.*

Scena Quarta.

[*Near a fountain in the desert.*]

Eumenides, Geron.

Eum. Father, your sad music, being tuned on the same key that my hard fortune is, hath so melted my mind that I

[1] Untie the laces.   [2] Traverse, proceed.
[3] Terence, *Andria*, I, i, 144: "Go ahead; I'll follow."

wish to hang at your mouth's end till my life end.

Ger. These tunes, gentleman, have I been accustomed with these fifty winters, having no other house to shroud myself but the broad heavens. And so familiar with me hath use made misery that I [10 esteem sorrow my chiefest solace, and welcomest is that guest to me that can rehearse the saddest tale or the bloodiest tragedy.

Eum. A strange humor. Might I inquire the cause?

Ger. You must pardon me if I deny to tell it, for, knowing that the revealing of griefs is, as it were, a renewing of sorrow, I have vowed therefore to conceal them, [20 that I might not only feel the depth of everlasting discontentment, but despair of remedy. But whence are you? What fortune hath thrust you to this distress?

Eum. I am going to Thessaly, to seek remedy for Endymion, my dearest friend, who hath been cast into a dead sleep almost these twenty years, waxing old and ready for the grave, being almost but newly come forth of the cradle.   30

Ger. You need not for recure travel far, for whoso can clearly see the bottom of this fountain shall have remedy for anything.

Eum. That, methinketh, is unpossible. Why, what virtue can there be in water?

Ger. Yes, whosoever can shed the tears of a faithful lover shall obtain anything he would. Read these words engraven about the brim.   40

Eum. Have you known this by experience, or is it placed here of purpose to delude men?

Ger. I only would have experience of it, and then should there be an end of my misery; and then would I tell the strangest discourse that ever yet was heard.

Eum. Ah, Eumenides!

Ger. What lack you, gentleman? Are you not well?   50

Eum. Yes, father, but a qualm that often cometh over my heart doth now take hold of me. But did never any lovers come hither?

Ger. Lusters, but not lovers; for often have I seen them weep, but never could I hear they saw the bottom.

Eum. Came there women also?

Ger. Some.

Eum. What did they see?   60

Ger. They all wept, that the fountain overflowed with tears, but so thick became the water with their tears that I could scarce discern the brim, much less behold the bottom.

Eum. Be faithful lovers so scant?

Ger. It seemeth so, for yet heard I never of any.

Eum. Ah, Eumenides, how art thou perplexed! Call to mind the beauty of [70 thy sweet mistress and the depth of thy never-dying affections. How oft hast thou honored her, not only without spot, but suspicion of falsehood! And how hardly hath she rewarded thee without cause or color of despite.[1] How secret hast thou been these seven years, that hast not, nor once darest not, to name her, for [2] discontenting her. How faithful, that hast offered to die for her, to please her! Un- [80 happy Eumenides!

Ger. Why, gentleman, did you once love?

Eum. Once? Ay, father, and ever shall.

Ger. Was she unkind and you faithful?

Eum. She of all women the most froward, and I of all creatures the most fond.

Ger. You doted then, not loved, for affection is grounded on virtue, and virtue is never peevish; or on beauty, and [90 beauty loveth to be praised.

Eum. Ay, but, if all virtuous ladies should yield to all that be loving, or all amiable gentlewomen entertain all that be amorous, their virtues would be accounted vices, and their beauties deformities; for that love can be but between two, and that not proceeding of [3] him that is most faithful but most fortunate.

Ger. I would you were so faithful [100 that your tears might make you fortunate.

Eum. Yea, father, if that my tears clear not this fountain, then may you swear it is but a mere mockery.

Ger. So saith every one yet that wept.

Eum. Ah, I faint, I die! Ah, sweet Semele, let me alone, and dissolve,[4] by weeping, into water.

[Gazes into the fountain.]

Ger. This affection [5] seemeth strange. If he see nothing, without doubt this [110 dissembling passeth,[6] for nothing shall draw me from the belief.

Eum. Father, I plainly see the bottom, and there in white marble engraven these words: *Ask one for all, and but one thing at all.*

Ger. O fortunate Eumenides (for so have I heard thee call thyself), let me see.— I cannot discern any such thing. I think thou dreamest.   120

Eum. Ah, father, thou art not a faithful lover, and therefore canst not behold it.

Ger. Then ask, that I may be satisfied by the event, and thyself blessed.

Eum. Ask? So I will. And what shall I do but ask, and whom should I ask but Semele, the possessing of whose person is a pleasure that cannot come within the compass of comparison; whose golden locks seem most curious [7] when they seem [130 most careless; whose sweet looks seem most alluring when they are most chaste; and whose words the more virtuous they are, the more amorous they be accounted? I pray thee, Fortune, when I shall first meet with fair Semele, dash my delight with some light disgrace, lest, embracing sweetness beyond measure, I take a surfeit without recure. Let her practice her accustomed coyness that I may diet myself upon [140 my desires; otherwise the fulness of my joys will diminish the sweetness, and I shall perish by them before I possess them.

Why do I trifle the time in words? The least minute being spent in the getting of Semele is more worth than the whole world; therefore let me ask. What now, Eumenides! Whither art thou drawn? Hast thou forgotten both friendship and duty, care of Endymion, and the com- [150 mandment of Cynthia? Shall he die in a leaden sleep because thou sleepest in a golden dream? Ay, let him sleep ever, so I slumber but one minute with Semele. Love knoweth neither friendship nor kindred.

Shall I not hazard the loss of a friend for the obtaining of her for whom I would often lose myself? Fond [8] Eumenides, shall the enticing beauty of a most disdainful lady be of more force than the [160

---

[1] With no occasion or reason for ill will.

[2] For fear of.   [3] Caused by.   [4] Let me dissolve.

[5] Passion.   [7] Artfully arranged.

[6] This hypocrisy is excessive.   [8] Foolish

rare fidelity of a tried friend? The love of men to women is a thing common and of course; the friendship of man to man infinite and immortal.—Tush! Semele doth possess my love.—Ay, but Endymion hath deserved it. I will help Endymion. I found Endymion unspotted in his truth.—Ay, but I shall find Semele constant in her love. I will have Semele.—What shall I do? Father, thy gray hairs are ambas- [170 sadors of experience. Which shall I ask?

GER. Eumenides, release Endymion, for all things, friendship excepted, are subject to fortune. Love is but an eyeworm, which only tickleth the head with hopes and wishes; friendship the image of eternity, in which there is nothing movable, nothing mischievous. As much difference as there is between beauty and virtue, bodies and shadows, colors and life, so great [180 odds is there between love and friendship.

Love is a chameleon, which draweth nothing into the mouth but air, and nourisheth nothing in the body but lungs. Believe me, Eumenides, desire dies in the same moment that beauty sickens, and beauty fadeth in the same instant that it flourisheth. When adversities flow, then love ebbs; but friendship standeth stiffly in storms. Time draweth wrinkles in [190 a fair face, but addeth fresh colors to a fast friend, which neither heat, nor cold, nor misery, nor place, nor destiny can alter or diminish. O friendship, of all things the most rare, and therefore most rare because most excellent, whose comforts in misery is always sweet, and whose counsels in prosperity are ever fortunate! Vain love, that, only coming near to friendship in name, would seem to be the [200 same or better in nature!

EUM. Father, I allow your reasons, and will therefore conquer mine own. Virtue shall subdue affections, wisdom lust, friendship beauty. Mistresses are in every place, and as common as hares in Athos, bees in Hybla, fowls in the air; but friends to be found are like the phœnix in Arabia, but one; or the philadelphi [1] in Arays, never above two. I will have Endymion. [210 Sacred fountain, in whose bowels are hidden divine secrets, I have increased your waters with the tears of unspotted thoughts,

[1] Shrubs on which the flowers grow in pairs.

and therefore let me receive the reward you promise. Endymion, the truest friend to me, and faithfulest lover to Cynthia, is in such a dead sleep that nothing can wake or move him.

GER. Dost thou see anything?

EUM. I see in the same pillar these [220 words: *When she whose figure of all is the perfectest, and never to be measured—always one, yet never the same—still inconstant, yet never wavering—shall come and kiss Endymion in his sleep, he shall then rise; else never.* This is strange.

GER. What see you else?

EUM. There cometh over mine eyes either a dark mist, or upon the fountain a deep thickness, for I can perceive [230 nothing. But how am I deluded, or what difficult—nay, impossible—thing is this?

GER. Methinketh it easy.

EUM. Good father, and how?

GER. Is not a circle of all figures the perfectest?

EUM. Yes.

GER. And is not Cynthia of all circles the most absolute?

EUM. Yes.   240

GER. Is it not impossible to measure her, who still worketh by her influence, never standing at one stay?

EUM. Yes.

GER. Is she not always Cynthia, yet seldom in the same bigness; always wavering in her waxing or waning, that our bodies might the better be governed, our seasons the dailier give their increase; yet never to be removed from her course, [250 as long as the heavens continue theirs?

EUM. Yes.

GER. Then who can it be but Cynthia, whose virtues, being all divine, must needs bring things to pass that be miraculous? Go, humble thyself to Cynthia; tell her the success, of which myself shall be a witness. And this assure thyself, that she that sent to find means for his safety will now work her cunning.   260

EUM. How fortunate am I, if Cynthia be she that may do it!

GER. How fond art thou, if thou do not believe it!

EUM. I will hasten thither that I may entreat on my knees for succor, and embrace in mine arms my friend.

GER. I will go with thee, for unto Cynthia must I discover all my sorrows, who also must work in me a contentment.

EUM. May I now know the cause? [271

GER. That shall be as we walk, and I doubt not but the strangeness of my tale will take away the tediousness of our journey.

EUM. Let us go.

GER. I follow.   *Exeunt.*

ACTUS QUARTUS. SCENA PRIMA.

[*Before the castle of Corsites in a desert.*]

Tellus; Corsites.[1]

TELLUS. I marvel Corsites giveth me so much liberty—all the world knowing his charge[2] to be so high and his nature to be most strange—who hath so ill entreated ladies of great honor that he hath not suffered them to look out of windows, much less to walk abroad. It may be he is in love with me, for (Endymion, hardhearted Endymion, excepted) what is he that is not enamored of my beauty? [10 But what respectest thou the love of all the world? Endymion hates thee. Alas, poor Endymion, my malice hath exceeded my love, and thy faith to Cynthia quenched my affections. Quenched, Tellus? Nay, kindled them afresh; insomuch that I find scorching flames for dead embers, and cruel encounters of war in my thoughts instead of sweet parleys. Ah, that I might once again see Endymion! Accursed [20 girl, what hope hast thou to see Endymion, on whose head already are grown gray hairs, and whose life must yield to nature before Cynthia end her displeasure? Wicked Dipsas and most devilish Tellus, the one for cunning too exquisite, the other for hate too intolerable! Thou wast commanded to weave the stories and poetries wherein were showed both examples and punishments of tattling tongues, and [30 thou hast only embroidered[3] the sweet face of Endymion, devices of love, melancholy imaginations, and what not, out of thy work, that thou shouldst study to pick out of thy mind. But here cometh Corsites. I must seem yielding and stout;

full of mildness, yet tempered with a majesty, for, if I be too flexible, I shall give him more hope than I mean; if too froward, enjoy less liberty than I would. [40 Love him I cannot, and therefore will practice that which is most contrary[4] to our sex, to dissemble.

Enter Corsites.

COR. Fair Tellus, I perceive you rise with the lark, and to yourself sing with the nightingale.

TELLUS. My lord, I have no playfellow but fancy. Being barred of all company, I must question with myself, and make my thoughts my friends.   50

COR. I would you would account my thoughts also your friends, for they be such as are only busied in wondering at your beauty and wisdom; and some such as have esteemed your fortune too hard; and divers of that kind that offer to set you free, if you will set them free.

TELLUS. There are no colors so contrary as white and black, nor elements so disagreeing as fire and water, nor [60 anything so opposite as men's thoughts and their words.

COR. He that gave Cassandra the gift of prophesying, with the curse that, spake she never so true, she should never be believed, hath I think poisoned the fortune of men, that, uttering the extremities of their inward passions, are always suspected of outward perjuries.

TELLUS. Well, Corsites, I will flatter [70 myself and believe you. What would you do to enjoy my love?

COR. Set all the ladies of the castle free, and make you the pleasure of my life. More I cannot do; less I will not.

TELLUS. These be great words, and fit your calling, for captains must promise things impossible. But will you do one thing for all?

COR. Anything, sweet Tellus, that [80 am ready for all.

TELLUS. You know that on the lunary bank sleepeth Endymion.

COR. I know it.

TELLUS. If you will remove him from that place by force, and convey him into

---

[1] Enters later.

[2] Military position.   [3] Embroidered.

[4] Bond suggests *customary.*

some obscure cave by policy, I give you here the faith of an unspotted virgin that you only shall possess me as a lover, and in spite of malice have me for a wife.　　90

COR. Remove him, Tellus? Yes, Tellus, he shall be removed, and that so soon as [1] thou shalt as much commend my diligence as my force. I go.

TELLUS. Stay, will yourself attempt it?

COR. Ay, Tellus; as I would have none partaker of my sweet love, so shall none be partners of my labors. But I pray thee go at your best leisure, for Cynthia begin- neth to rise, and, if she discover our [100 love, we both perish, for nothing pleaseth her but the fairness of virginity. All things must be not only without lust but without suspicion of lightness.

TELLUS. I will depart, and go you to Endymion.

COR. I fly, Tellus, being of all men the most fortunate.　　　　　　　　*Exit.*

TELLUS. Simple Corsites, I have set thee about a task, being but a man, [110 that the gods themselves cannot perform, for little dost thou know how heavy his head lies, how hard his fortune. But such shifts must women have to deceive men, and, under color of things easy, entreat that which is impossible; otherwise we should be cumbered with importunities, oaths, sighs, letters, and all implements of love, which to one resolved to the contrary are most loathsome. I will in, and laugh [120 with the other ladies at Corsites' sweating.
　　　　　　　　　　　　　　　Exit.

SCENA SECUNDA.

[*The gardens of Cynthia's palace.*]

Samias and Dares; Epiton. [2]

SAM. Will thy master never awake?

DAR. No; I think he sleeps for a wager. But how shall we spend the time? Sir Tophas is so far in love that he pineth in his bed and cometh not abroad.

SAM. But here cometh Epi in a pelting chafe. [3]

[*Enter Epiton.*]

EPI. A pox of all false proverbs, and were a proverb a page, I would have him by the ears!　　　　　　　　　　　10

SAM. Why art thou angry?

EPI. Why? You know it is said, "The tide tarrieth no man."

SAM. True.

EPI. A monstrous lie; for I was tied two hours, and tarried for one to unloose me.

DAR. Alas, poor Epi!

EPI. Poor? No, no, you base, con- ceited slaves, I am a most complete [20 gentleman, although I be in disgrace with Sir Tophas.

DAR. Art thou out with him?

EPI. Ay, because I cannot get him a lodging with Endymion. He would fain take a nap for forty or fifty years.

DAR. A short sleep, considering our long life.

SAM. Is he still in love?

EPI. In love? Why, he doth noth- [30 ing but make sonnets!

SAM. Canst thou remember any one of his poems?

EPI. Ay, this is one:

The beggar Love, that knows not where
　　to lodge,
　　At last within my heart, when I slept,
　　　　　　　　　　　　　He crept.

I waked, and so my fancies began to
　　fodge. [4]

SAM. That's a very long verse.

EPI. Why, the other was short. The [40 first is called from the thumb to the little finger; the second from the little finger to the elbow; and some he hath made to reach to the crown of his head, and down again to the sole of his foot. It is set to the tune of the Black Saunce; [5] *ratio est,* [6] because Dipsas is a black saint.

DAR. Very wisely. But pray thee, Epi, how art thou complete, and, being from thy master, what occupation wilt thou [50 take?

EPI. Know, [7] my hearts, I am an ab- solute *microcosmus,* a petty world of my- self: my library is my head, for I have no other books but my brains; my wardrope [8] on my back, for I have no more apparel

---

[1] That.　　　[2] Enters later.　　　[3] Petty rage.

[4] Move.
[5] The Black Sanctus was a hymn to Saint Satan in ridicule of the monks.
[6] The reason is.
[7] Emended by Baker. Early edns. read *No.*
[8] Wardrobe.

than is on my body; my armory at my fingers' ends, for I use no other artillery than my nails; my treasure in my purse. "*Sic omnia mea mecum porto.*" [1]   60

DAR. Good!

EPI. Now, sirs, my palace is paved with grass and tiled with stars, for "*Cælo tegitur qui non habet urnam*" [2]—"he that hath no house must lie in the yard."

SAM. A brave resolution! But how wilt thou spend thy time?

EPI. Not in any melancholy sort; for mine exercise I will walk horses.

DAR. Too bad!   70

EPI. Why, is it not said, "It is good walking when one hath his horse in his hand"?

SAM. Worse and worse! But how wilt thou live?

EPI. By angling. O, 'tis a stately occupation to stand four hours in a cold morning, and to have his nose bitten with frost before his bait be mumbled with a fish.

DAR. A rare attempt! But wilt thou [80 never travel?

EPI. Yes, in a western barge,[3] when, with a good wind and lusty pugs,[4] one may go ten miles in two days.

SAM. Thou art excellent at thy choice. But what pastime wilt thou use? None?

EPI. Yes, the quickest of all.

SAM. What, dice?

EPI. No, when I am in haste, one-and-twenty games at chess, to pass a few [90 minutes.

DAR. A life for a little lord, and full of quickness.[5]

EPI. Tush, let me alone! But I must needs see if I can find where Endymion lieth, and then go to a certain fountain hard by, where they say faithful lovers shall have all things they will ask. If I can find out any of these, *Ego et magister meus erimus in tuto*—I and my master [100 shall be friends. He is resolved to weep some three or four pailfuls to avoid [6] the rheum of love that wambleth [7] in his stomach.

[1] Quoted by Cicero in *Paradoxa Stoicorum*, i, 1: "Thus all my possessions I carry with me."
[2] Lucan, vii, 819.
[3] *I.e.*, on the Thames.
[4] Bargemen.
[5] Liveliness.
[6] Empty.   [7] Rumbles.

Enter the Watch.

SAM. Shall we never see thy master, Dares?

DAR. Yes; let us go now, for tomorrow Cynthia will be there.

EPI. I will go with you. But how shall we see for the watch?   110

SAM. Tush, let me alone! I'll begin to them. Masters, God speed you.

1 WATCH. Sir boy, we are all sped already.

EPI. [*Aside.*] So methinks, for they smell all of drink, like a beggar's beard.

DAR. But I pray, sirs, may we see Endymion?

2 WATCH. No, we are commanded in Cynthia's name that no man shall see [120 him.

SAM. No man? Why, we are but boys.

1 WATCH. Mass, neighbors, he says true, for, if I swear I will never drink my liquor by the quart, and yet call for two pints, I think with a safe conscience I may carouse both.

DAR. Pithily, and to the purpose!

2 WATCH. Tush, tush, neighbors, take me with you.[8]   130

SAM. [*Aside.*] This will grow hot.

DAR. [*Aside.*] Let them alone.

2 WATCH. If I say to my wife, "Wife, I will have no raisins in my pudding," she puts in currants. Small raisins are raisins, and boys are men; even as my wife should have put no raisins in my pudding, so shall there no boys see Endymion.

DAR. Learnedly!

EPI. Let Master Constable speak; [140 I think he is the wisest among you.

MA. CONST. You know, neighbors, 'tis an old said [9] saw, "Children and fools speak true."

ALL *say:* True.

MA. CONST. Well, there you see the men be the fools, because it is provided from the children.

DAR. Good!

MA. CONST. Then say I, neighbors, [150 that children must not see Endymion, because children and fools speak true.

EPI. O wicked application!

SAM. Scurvily brought about!

[8] Let me understand you.
[9] Sad, serious.

1 WATCH. Nay, he says true, and therefore till Cynthia have been here, he shall
not be uncovered. Therefore, away!

DAR. [*Aside to Samias and Epiton.*] A
watch, quoth you! A man may watch
seven years for a wise word, and yet [160
go without it. Their wits are all as rusty as
their bills.[1] But come on, Ma[ster] Const[able], shall we have a song before we go?

MA. CONST. With all my heart.

THE SECOND SONG

WATCH. Stand! Who goes there?
We charge you, appear
Fore our constable here,
In the name of the Man in the Moon.
To us billmen relate
Why you stagger so late, 170
And how you come drunk so soon.
   PAGES. What are ye, scabs?[2]
   WATCH. The watch;
This the constable.
   PAGES. A patch![3]
   MA. CONST. Knock 'em down unless
     they all stand!
If any run away,
'Tis the old watchman's play,
To reach him a bill of his hand.
   PAGES. O gentlemen, hold;
Your gowns freeze with cold, 179
And your rotten teeth dance in your head.
   EPI. Wine nothing shall cost ye;
   SAM. Nor huge fires to roast ye;
   DAR. Then soberly let us be led.
   MA. CONST. Come, my brown bills, we'll
     roar,[4]
Bounce loud at tavern door,
   OMNES. And i' th' morning steal all to
     bed!
                    Exeunt.

SCENA TERTIA.

[*A grove near Endymion's cell.*]

Corsites solus. [*Endymion sleeps on the bank
in the grove.*]

CORS. I am come in sight of the lunary
bank. Without doubt Tellus doteth upon
me, and cunningly, that I might not perceive her love, she hath set me to a task
that is done before it is begun. Endymion,
you must change your pillow, and if you
be not weary of sleep, I will carry you

[1] Halberds.
[2] Rascals, sheriff's officers.
[3] Fool. [4] Revel.

where at ease you shall sleep your fill. It
were good that without more ceremonies
I took him, lest, being espied, I be en- [10
trapped, and so incur the displeasure of
Cynthia, who commonly setteth watch
that Endymion have no wrong. (*He lifts.*)
What now, is your mastership so heavy,
or are you nailed to the ground? Not stir
one whit? Then use all thy force, though
he feel it and wake. What, stone-still?
Turned, I think, to earth with lying so
long on the earth. Didst not thou, Corsites,
before Cynthia, pull up a tree that [20
forty years was fastened with roots and
wreathed in knots to the ground? Didst
not thou with main force pull open the
iron gates which no ram or engine could
move? Have my weak thoughts made
brawn-fallen my strong arms? Or is it the
nature of love or the quintessence of the
mind to breed numbness or litherness,[5] or
I know not what languishing in my joints
and sinews, being but the base strings [30
of my body? Or doth the remembrance of
Tellus so refine my spirits into a matter
so subtle and divine that the other fleshy
parts cannot work whilst they muse?
Rest thyself, rest thyself; nay, rent[6] thyself in pieces, Corsites, and strive, in spite
of love, fortune, and nature, to lift up this
dulled body, heavier than dead and more
senseless than death.

Enter Fairies.

But what are these so fair fiends that [40
cause my hairs to stand upright and spirits to fall down? Hags—out, alas, nymphs,
I crave pardon! Ay me, out! What do I
hear?

*The Fairies dance and with a song pinch
him, and he falleth asleep. They kiss
Endymion and depart.*

THE THIRD SONG BY FAIRIES

OMNES. Pinch him, pinch him, black and
   blue,
Saucy mortals must not view
What the Queen of Stars is doing,
Nor pry into our fairy wooing.
   1 FAIRY. Pinch him blue,
   2 FAIRY. And pinch him black; 50
   3 FAIRY. Let him not lack

[5] Flaccidity, sloth. [6] Rend, tear.

Sharp nails to pinch him blue and red,
Till sleep has rocked his addle head.
  4 FAIRY. For the trespass he hath done,
Spots o'er all his flesh shall run.
Kiss Endymion, kiss his eyes,
Then to our midnight hay-de-guise.[1]

Exeunt.

Cynthia, Floscula, Semele, Panelion, Zontes,
Pythagoras, Gyptes.

CYNTH. You see, Pythagoras, what ridiculous opinions you hold, and I doubt
not but you are now of another mind.   60
  PYTHAG. Madam, I plainly perceive
that the perfection of your brightness hath
pierced through the thickness that covered
my mind; insomuch that I am no less glad
to be reformed than ashamed to remember
my grossness.
  GYPTES. They are thrice fortunate that
live in your palace where truth is not in
colors but life, virtues not in imagination but execution.   70
  CYNTH. I have always studied to have
rather living virtues than painted gods,
the body of truth than the tomb. But let
us walk to Endymion; it may be it lieth
in your arts to deliver him. As for Eumenides, I fear he is dead.
  PYTHAG. I have alleged all the natural
reasons I can for such a long sleep.
  GYPTES. I can do nothing till I see him.
  CYNTH. Come, Floscula; I am sure   [80
you are glad that you shall behold Endymion.
  FLOSC. I were blessed, if I might have
him recovered.
  CYNTH. Are you in love with his person?
  FLOSC. No, but with his virtue.
  CYNTH. What say you, Semele?
  SEM. Madam, I dare say nothing for
fear I offend.
  CYNTH. Belike you cannot speak   [90
except you be spiteful; but as good be silent
as saucy. Panelion, what punishment were
fit for Semele, in whose speech and thoughts
is only contempt and sourness?
  PANEL. I love not, madam, to give any
judgment; yet, sith [2] your highness commandeth, I think to commit her tongue
close prisoner to her mouth.
  CYNTH. Agreed. Semele, if thou speak
this twelvemonth, thou shalt forfeit   [100

thy tongue.—Behold Endymion! Alas,
poor gentleman, hast thou spent thy youth
in sleep, that once vowed all to my service? Hollow eyes, gray hairs, wrinkled
cheeks, and decayed limbs! Is it destiny
or deceit that hath brought this to pass?
If the first, who could prevent thy wretched
stars? If the latter, I would I might know
thy cruel enemy. I favored thee, Endymion, for thy honor, thy virtues, thy af-   [110
fections. But [3] to bring thy thoughts within
the compass of thy fortunes, I have seemed
strange, that I might have thee stayed; [4]
and now are thy days ended before my
favor begin! But whom have we here?
Is it not Corsites?
  ZON. It is, but more like a leopard than
a man.
  CYNTH. Awake him.   [*Zontes wakens*
Corsites.] How now, Corsites, what   [120
make [5] you here? How came you deformed?
Look on thy hands, and then thou seest
the picture of thy face.
  CORS. Miserable wretch, and accursed!
How am I deluded! Madam, I ask pardon
for my offense, and you see my fortune
deserveth pity.
  CYNTH. Speak on; thy offense cannot
deserve greater punishment. But see thou
rehearse the truth, else shalt thou not   [130
find me as thou wishest me.
  CORS. Madam, as it is no offense to be
in love, being a man mortal, so I hope can
it be no shame to tell with whom, my
lady being heavenly. Your majesty committed to my charge fair Tellus, whose
beauty in the same moment took my
heart captive that I undertook to carry
her body prisoner. Since that time have
I found such combats in my thoughts   [140
between love and duty, reverence and
affection, that I could neither endure the
conflict nor hope for the conquest.
  CYNTH. In love? A thing far unfitting
the name of a captain, and, as I thought,
the tough and unsmoothed nature of Corsites. But forth!
  CORS. Feeling this continual war, I
thought rather by parley to yield than by
certain danger to perish. I unfolded   [150
to Tellus the depth of my affections, and
framed my tongue to utter a sweet tale of
love, that was wont to sound nothing but

---

[1] Rustic dance.   [2] Since.   [3] Only.   [4] Checked (*i.e.*, in his ambitions).   [5] Do.

threats of war. She, too fair to be true and too false for one so fair, after a nice [1] denial, practiced a notable deceit, commanding me to remove Endymion from this cabin,[2] and carry him to some dark cave; which I, seeking to accomplish, found impossible, and so by fairies or fiends [160 have been thus handled.

CYNTH. How say you, my lords, is not Tellus always practicing of some deceits? In sooth, Corsites, thy face is now too foul for a lover, and thine heart too fond for a soldier. You may see when warriors become wantons how their manners alter with their faces. Is it not a shame, Corsites, that, having lived so long in Mars his camp, thou shouldest now be rocked [170 in Venus' cradle? Dost thou wear Cupid's quiver at thy girdle and make lances of looks? Well, Corsites, rouse thyself and be as thou hast been; and let Tellus, who is made all of love, melt herself in her own looseness.

CORS. Madam, I doubt not but to recover my former state, for Tellus' beauty never wrought such love in my mind as now her deceit hath despite; and yet to be [180 revenged of a woman were a thing than love itself more womanish.

GYPTES. These spots, gentleman, are to be worn out, if you rub them over with this lunary, so that in place where you received this main,[3] you shall find a medicine.

CORS. I thank you for that. The gods bless[4] me from love and these pretty ladies that haunt this green.   190

FLOSC. Corsites, I would Tellus saw your amiable face.

ZON. How spitefully Semele laugheth, that dare not speak!

CYNTH. Could you not stir Endymion with that doubled strength of yours?

CORS. Not so much as his finger with all my force.

CYNTH. Pythagoras and Gyptes, what think you of Endymion? What rea- [200 son is to be given, what remedy?

PYTHAG. Madam, it is impossible to yield reason for things that happen not in compass of nature. It is most certain that some strange enchantment hath bound all his senses.

CYNTH. What say you, Gyptes?

GYPTES. With Pythagoras, that it is enchantment, and that so strange that no art can undo it (for that heaviness [210 argueth a malice unremovable in the enchantress) and that no power can end it, till she die that did it, or the heavens show some means more than miraculous.

FLOSC. O Endymion, could spite itself devise a mischief so monstrous as to make thee dead with life, and living being altogether dead? Where others number their years, their hours, their minutes, and step to age by stairs, thou only hast [220 thy years and times in a cluster, being old before thou remem'rest thou wast young.

CYNTH. No more, Floscula; pity doth him no good. I would anything else might, and I vow by the unspotted honor of a lady he should not miss it. But is this all, Gyptes, that is to be done?

GYPTES. All as yet. It may be that either the enchantress shall die or else be discovered. If either happen, I will [230 then practice the utmost of my art. In the mean season, about this grove would I have a watch, and the first living thing that toucheth Endymion to be taken.

CYNTH. Corsites, what say you? Will you undertake this?

CORS. Good madam, pardon me! I was overtaken[5] too late. I should rather break into the middest of a main battle than again fall into the hands of those [240 fair babies.[6]

CYNTH. Well, I will provide others. Pythagoras and Gyptes, you shall yet remain in my court, till I hear what may be done in this matter.

PYTHAG. We attend.

CYNTH. Let us go in.   *Exeunt.*

ACTUS QUINTUS. SCENA PRIMA.

[*The same.*]

Samias, Dares.

SAM. Eumenides hath told such strange tales as I may well wonder at them, but never believe them.

---

[1] Overscrupulous, fastidious.
[2] Shelter (represented by the overhanging inner stage?).   [3] Maim.   [4] Protect.
[5] Overpowered.   [6] *I.e.*, the fairies.

DAR. The other old man, what a sad speech used he, that caused us almost all to weep. Cynthia is so desirous to know the experiment of her own virtue,[1] and so willing to ease Endymion's hard fortune, that she no sooner heard the discourse but she made herself in a readiness to [10 try the event.

SAM. We will also see the event. But whist, here cometh Cynthia with all her train! Let us sneak in amongst them.

Enter Cynthia, Floscula, Semele, [Eumenides,] Panelion, etc.

CYNTH. Eumenides, it cannot sink into my head that I should be signified by that sacred fountain, for many things are there in the world to which those words may be applied.

EUM. Good madam, vouchsafe but [20 to try; else shall I think myself most unhappy that I asked not my sweet mistress.

CYNTH. Will you not yet tell me her name?

EUM. Pardon me, good madam, for if Endymion awake, he shall; myself have sworn never to reveal it.

CYNTH. Well, let us to Endymion. I will not be so stately, good Endymion, not to stoop to do thee good; and, if thy [30 liberty consist in a kiss from me, thou shalt have it. And, although my mouth hath been heretofore as untouched as my thoughts, yet now to recover thy life, though to restore thy youth it be impossible, I will do that to Endymion which yet never mortal man could boast of heretofore, nor shall ever hope for hereafter. *She kisseth him.*

EUM. Madam, he beginneth to stir!

CYNTH. Soft, Eumenides; stand still! [40

EUM. Ah, I see his eyes almost open!

CYNTH. I command thee once again, stir not! I will stand behind him.

PANEL. What do I see? Endymion almost awake?

EUM. Endymion! Endymion! Art thou deaf or dumb, or hath this long sleep taken away thy memory? Ah, my sweet Endymion, seest thou not Eumenides, thy faithful friend, thy faithful Eumenides, who [50 for thy safety hath been careless of his own content? Speak, Endymion! Endymion! Endymion!

END. Endymion? I call to mind such a name.

EUM. Hast thou forgotten thyself, Endymion? Then do I not marvel thou rememb'rest not thy friend. I tell thee thou art Endymion, and I Eumenides. Behold also Cynthia, by whose favor thou art [60 awaked, and by whose virtue thou shalt continue thy natural course.

CYNTH. Endymion, speak, sweet Endymion! Knowest thou not Cynthia?

END. O heavens, whom do I behold? Fair Cynthia, divine Cynthia?

CYNTH. I am Cynthia, and thou Endymion.   68

END. "Endymion"! What do I hear? What! a gray beard, hollow eyes, withered body, decayed limbs—and all in one night?

EUM. One night! Thou hast here slept forty years—by what enchantress as yet it is not known—and behold, the twig to which thou laid'st thy head is now become a tree. Callest thou not Eumenides to remembrance?

END. Thy name I do remember by the sound, but thy favor[2] I do not yet call to mind; only divine Cynthia, to whom [80 time, fortune, destiny, and death are subject, I see and remember, and in all humility I regard and reverence.

CYNTH. You have good cause to remember Eumenides, who hath for thy safety forsaken his own solace.

END. Am I that Endymion who was wont in court to lead my life, and in jousts, tourneys, and arms, to exercise my youth? Am I that Endymion?   90

EUM. Thou art that Endymion, and I Eumenides. Wilt thou not yet call me to remembrance?

END. Ah, sweet Eumenides, I now perceive thou art he, and that myself have the name of Endymion; but that this should be my body I doubt, for how could my curled locks be turned to gray hairs and my strong body to a dying weakness, having waxed old, and not knowing it? [100

CYNTH. Well, Endymion, arise. [*Endymion attempts to rise, but sinks back.*] A while sit down, for that thy limbs are stiff and not able to stay thee, and tell what hast thou seen in thy sleep all this while, what dreams, visions, thoughts, and for-

---

[1] Make trial of her power.

[2] Appearance, face.

tunes; for it is impossible but in so long time thou shouldest see things strange.

END. Fair Cynthia, I will rehearse what I have seen, humbly desiring that, [110 when I exceed in length, you give me warning, that I may end; for to utter all I have to speak would be troublesome, although happily the strangeness may somewhat abate the tediousness.

CYNTH. Well, Endymion, begin.

END. Methought I saw a lady passing fair, but very mischievous, who in the one hand carried a knife with which she offered to cut my throat, and in the other a [120 looking-glass, wherein seeing how ill anger became ladies, she refrained from intended violence. She was accompanied with other damsels, one of which, with a stern countenance, and as it were with a settled malice engraven in her eyes, provoked her to execute mischief; another, with visage sad, and constant only in sorrow, with her arms crossed and watery eyes, seemed to lament my fortune, but durst not offer to pre- [130 vent the force. I started in my sleep, feeling my very veins to swell and my sinews to stretch with fear, and such a cold sweat bedewed all my body that death itself could not be so terrible as the vision.

CYNTH. A strange sight! Gyptes, at our better leisure, shall expound it.

END. After long debating with herself, mercy overcame anger, and there appeared in her heavenly face such a divine maj- [140 esty mingled with a sweet mildness that I was ravished with the sight above measure, and wished that I might have enjoyed the sight without end. And so she departed with the other ladies, of which the one retained still an unmovable cruelty, the other a constant pity.

CYNTH. Poor Endymion, how wast thou affrighted! What else?   149

END. After her, immediately appeared an aged man with a beard as white as snow, carrying in his hand a book with three leaves, and speaking, as I remember, these words: "Endymion, receive this book with three leaves, in which are contained counsels, policies, and pictures," and with that he offered me the book, which I rejected; wherewith, moved with a disdainful pity, he rent the first leaf in a thousand shivers. The second time he [160

offered it, which I refused also; at which, bending his brows, and pitching his eyes fast to the ground, as though they were fixed to the earth and not again to be removed, then suddenly casting them up to the heavens, he tore in a rage the second leaf, and offered the book only with one leaf. I know not whether fear to offend or desire to know some strange thing moved me. I took the book, and so the old [170 man vanished.

CYNTH. What diddest thou imagine was in the last leaf?

END. There—ay, portrayed to life— with a cold quaking in every joint, I beheld many wolves barking at thee, Cynthia, who, having ground their teeth to bite, did with striving bleed themselves to death. There might I see Ingratitude with an hundred eyes gazing for benefits, [180 and with a thousand teeth gnawing on the bowels wherein she was bred. Treachery stood all clothed in white, with a smiling countenance, but both her hands bathed in blood. Envy with a pale and meager face (whose body was so lean that one might tell [1] all her bones, and whose garment was so tottered [2] that it was easy to number every thread) stood shooting at stars, whose darts fell down again on [190 her own face. There might I behold drones, or beetles—I know not how to term them— creeping under the wings of a princely eagle, who, being carried into her nest, sought there to suck that vein that would have killed the eagle. I mused that things so base should attempt a fact [3] so barbarous, or durst imagine a thing so bloody. And many other things, madam, the repetition whereof may at your better [200 leisure seem more pleasing, for bees surfeit sometimes with honey, and the gods are glutted with harmony, and your highness may be dulled with delight.

CYNTH. I am content to be dieted; therefore, let us in. Eumenides, see that Endymion be well tended, lest, either eating immoderately or sleeping again too long, he fall into a deadly surfeit or into his former sleep.   210

See this also be proclaimed: that whosoever will discover this practice shall

---

[1] Count.
[2] Tattered.
[3] Deed, act.

have of Cynthia infinite thanks and no small rewards.

Exit [with all but Floscula, Eumenides, Semele, and Endymion].

FLOSC. Ah, Endymion, none so joyful as Floscula of thy restoring.

EUM. Yes, Floscula, let Eumenides be somewhat gladder, and do not that wrong to the settled friendship of a man as to compare it with the light affection [220 of a woman. Ah, my dear friend Endymion, suffer me to die with gazing at thee!

END. Eumenides, thy friendship is immortal and not to be conceived; and thy good will, Floscula, better than I have deserved. But let us all wait on Cynthia. I marvel Semele speaketh not a word.

EUM. Because if she do, she loseth her tongue!

END. But how prospereth your love?

EUM. I never yet spake word since [231 your sleep.

END. I doubt not but your affection is old and your appetite cold.

EUM. No, Endymion, thine hath made it stronger, and now are my sparks grown to flames and my fancies almost to frenzies. But let us follow, and within we will debate all this matter at large.   *Exeunt.*

SCENA SECUNDA.

[*The gardens of Cynthia's palace.*]

Sir Tophas, Epiton.

TOP. Epi, Love hath justled my liberty from the wall, and taken the upper hand of my reason.

EPI. Let me then trip up the heels of your affection and thrust your good will into the gutter.

TOP. No, Epi, Love is a lord of misrule and keepeth Christmas in my corpse.[1]

EPI. No doubt there is good cheer. What dishes of delight doth his lord- [10 ship feast you withal?

TOP. First, with a great platter of plum porridge of pleasure, wherein is stewed the mutton of mistrust.

EPI. Excellent love lap.[2]

TOP. Then cometh a pie of patience, a hen of honey, a goose of gall, a capon of care, and many other viands, some sweet

and some sour, which proveth love to be, as it was said of in old years, *dulce* [20 *venenum.*[3]

EPI. A brave banquet!

TOP. But, Epi, I pray thee feel on my chin; something pricketh me. What dost thou feel or see?

EPI. There are three or four little hairs.

TOP. I pray thee call it my beard. How shall I be troubled when this young spring [4] shall grow to a great wood!

EPI. O, sir, your chin is but a quiller[5] [30 yet; you will be most majestical when it is full-fledge. But I marvel that you love Dipsas, that old crone.

TOP. "*Agnosco veteris vestigia flammæ*"[6]—"I love the smoke of an old fire."

EPI. Why, she is so cold that no fire can thaw her thoughts.

TOP. It is an old goose, Epi, that will eat no oats; old kine will kick, old rats gnaw cheese, and old sacks will have [40 much patching. I prefer an old cony before a rabbit-sucker,[7] and an ancient hen before a young chicken-peeper.

EPI. [*Aside.*] *Argumentum ab antiquitate;*[8] my master loveth antique work.

TOP. Give me a pippin that is withered like an old wife!

EPI. Good, sir.

TOP. Then—*a contrario sequitur argumentum*[9]—give me a wife that looks [50 like an old pippin.

EPI. [*Aside.*] Nothing hath made my master a fool but flat scholarship.

TOP. Knowest thou not that old wine is best?

EPI. Yes.

TOP. And thou knowest that like will be like?

EPI. Ay.

TOP. And thou knowest that Venus [60 loved the best wine?

EPI. So.

TOP. Then I conclude that Venus was an old woman in an old cup of wine, for "*Est Venus in vinis, ignis in igne fuit.*"[10]

---

[1] Body.   [2] Love broth.

[3] Sweet poison.   [5] An unfledged bird.
[4] Sprout.   [6] Virgil, *Æneid*, iv, 23.
[7] An old rabbit before a sucking one.
[8] Argument from antiquity.
[9] From the contrary follows the proof.
[10] Adapted from Ovid, *Ars amat.*, i, 244, meaning, "Love is in wines as surely as fire is [lit., *was*] in fire."

EPI. "*O lepidum caput*,"[1] O madcap master! You were worthy to win Dipsas, were she as old again, for in your love you have worn the nap of your wit quite off and made it threadbare. But soft, who [70 comes here?

[*Enter Samias and Dares.*]

TOP. My solicitors.

SAM. All hail, Sir Tophas. How feel you yourself?

TOP. Stately in every joint, which the common people term stiffness. Doth Dipsas stoop? Will she yield? Will she bend?

DAR. O, sir, as much as you would wish, for her chin almost toucheth her knees.   80

EPI. Master, she is bent, I warrant you.

TOP. What conditions doth she ask?

SAM. She hath vowed she will never love any that hath not a tooth in his head less than she.

TOP. How many hath she?

DAR. One.

EPI. That goeth hard, master, for then you must have none.   90

TOP. A small request, and agreeable to the gravity of her years. What should a wise man do with his mouth full of bones like a charnel[2]-house? The turtle[3] true hath ne'er a tooth.

SAM. [*Aside to Epiton.*] Thy master is in a notable vein, that will lose his teeth to be like a turtle.

EPI. [*Aside to Samias.*] Let him lose his tongue, too; I care not!   100

DAR. Nay, you must also have no nails, for she long since hath cast hers.

TOP. That I yield to. What a quiet life shall Dipsas and I lead when we can neither bite nor scratch! You may see, youths, how age provides for peace.

SAM. [*Aside to Epiton.*] How shall we do to make him leave his love, for we never spake to her?

DAR. [*Aside to Samias.*] Let me [110 alone.—[*To Sir Tophas.*] She is a notable witch, and hath turned her maid Bagoa to an aspen tree, for bewraying her secrets.

TOP. I honor her for her cunning, for now when I am weary of walking on two legs, what a pleasure may she do me to turn me to some goodly ass, and help me to four.

DAR. Nay, then I must tell you the troth: her husband, Geron, is come [120 home, who this fifty years hath had her to wife.

TOP. What do I hear? Hath she an husband? Go to the sexton and tell him Desire is dead, and will him to dig his grave. O heavens, an husband! What death is agreeable to my fortune?

SAM. Be not desperate, and we will help you to find a young lady.

TOP. I love no grissels;[4] they are [130 so brittle they will crack like glass, or so dainty that if they be touched they are straight of the fashion of wax. "*Animus majoribus instat*" [5]—"I desire old matrons." What a sight would it be to embrace one whose hair were as orient as the pearl, whose teeth shall be so pure a watchet[6] that they shall stain the truest turkis,[7] whose nose shall throw more beams from it than the fiery carbuncle, whose eyes [140 shall be environed about with redness exceeding the deepest coral, and whose lips might compare with silver for the paleness! Such a one if you can help me to, I will by piecemeal curtal[8] my affections towards Dipsas, and walk my swelling thoughts till they be cold.

EPI. Wisely provided! How say you, my friends, will you angle for my master's cause?   150

SAM. Most willingly.

DAR. If we speed him not shortly, I will burn my cap. We will serve him of the spades, and dig an old wife out of the grave that shall be answerable to his gravity.

TOP. Youths, adieu. He that bringeth me first news, shall possess mine inheritance.

[*Exit.*]

DAR. What, is thy master landed?

EPI. Know you not that my master [160 is *liber tenens?*

SAM. What's that?

---

[1] Terence, *Adelphi*, v, ix, 9: "O fine head!"
[2] Original reads *channel*.
[3] Turtledove.

[4] Griseldas, young girls.
[5] Ovid, *Ars Amat.*, ii, 535.
[6] Pale blue.

[7] Turquoise.
[8] Curtail.

EPI. A freeholder. But I will after him.

SAM. And we to hear what news of Endymion for the conclusion.   *Exeunt.*

SCENA TERTIA.

[*The same.*]

Panelion, Zontes.

PANEL. Who would have thought that Tellus, being so fair by nature, so honorable by birth, so wise by education, would have entered into a mischief to the gods so odious, to men so detestable, and to her friend so malicious!

ZON. If Bagoa had not bewrayed it, how then should it have come to light? But we see that gold and fair words are of force to corrupt the strongest men, and [10 therefore able to work silly women like wax.

PANEL. I marvel what Cynthia will determine in this cause.

ZON. I fear, as in all causes: hear of it in justice, and then judge of it in mercy; for how can it be that she that is unwilling to punish her deadliest foes with disgrace will revenge injuries of her train with death?   20

PANEL. That old witch, Dipsas, in a rage, having understood her practice to be discovered, turned poor Bagoa to an aspen tree. But let us make haste and bring Tellus before Cynthia, for she was coming out after us.

ZON. Let us go.   *Exeunt.*

Cynthia, Semele, Floscula, Dipsas, Endymion, Eumenides [,*Geron, Pythagoras, Gyptes, Sir Tophas*].

CYNTH. Dipsas, thy years are not so many as thy vices, yet more in number than commonly nature doth afford or [30 justice should permit. Hast thou almost these fifty years practiced that detested wickedness of witchcraft? Wast thou so simple as for to know the nature of simples of all creatures to be most sinful?

Thou hast threatened to turn my course awry and alter by thy damnable art the government that I now possess by the eternal gods; but know thou, Dipsas, and let all the enchanters know, that Cyn- [40 thia, being placed for light on earth, is also

protected by the powers of heaven. Breathe out thou mayst words; gather thou mayst herbs; find out thou mayst stones agreeable to thine art; yet of no force to appall my heart, in which courage is so rooted, and constant persuasion of the mercy of the gods so grounded, that all thy witchcraft I esteem as weak as the world doth thy case wretched.   50

This noble gentleman, Geron, once thy husband but now thy mortal hate, didst thou procure to live in a desert, almost desperate; Endymion, the flower of my court and the hope of succeeding time, hast thou bewitched by art, before thou wouldest suffer him to flourish by nature.

DIPSAS. Madam, things past may be repented, not recalled. There is nothing so wicked that I have not done, nor [60 anything so wished for as death; yet among all the things that I committed, there is nothing so much tormenteth my rented and ransacked thoughts as that in the prime of my husband's youth I divorced him by my devilish art; for which if to die might be amends, I would not live till tomorrow; if to live and still be more miserable would better content him, I would wish of all creatures to be oldest and [70 ugliest.

GER. Dipsas, thou hast made this difference between me and Endymion, that being both young, thou hast caused me to wake in melancholy, losing the joys of my youth, and him to sleep, not rememb'ring youth.

CYNTH. Stay, here cometh Tellus; we shall now know all.

[*Enter Panelion and Zontes, with Corsites and Tellus.*]

CORS. I would to Cynthia thou [80 couldest make as good an excuse in truth as to me thou hast done by wit.

TELLUS. Truth shall be mine answer, and therefore I will not study for an excuse.

CYNTH. Is it possible, Tellus, that so few years should harbor so many mischiefs? Thy swelling pride have I borne, because it is a thing that beauty maketh blameless, which the more it exceedeth fairness in measure, the more it stretch- [90 eth itself in disdain. Thy devices against Corsites I smile at, for that wits, the

sharper they are, the shrewder [1] they are;
but this unacquainted [2] and most unnatural practice with a vile enchantress
against so noble a gentleman as Endymion
I abhor as a thing most malicious, and will
revenge as a deed most monstrous.

And as for you, Dipsas, I will send you
into the desert amongst wild beasts, [100
and try whether you can cast lions, tigers,
boars, and bears into as dead a sleep as
you did Endymion, or turn them to trees,
as you have done Bagoa. But tell me,
Tellus, what was the cause of this cruel
part, far unfitting thy sex, in which nothing should be but simpleness, and much
disagreeing from thy face, in which nothing seemed to be but softness?

TELLUS. Divine Cynthia, by whom [110
I receive my life and am content to end
it, I can neither excuse my fault without
lying, nor confess it without shame; yet
were it possible that in so heavenly
thoughts as yours there could fall such
earthly motions as mine, I would then
hope, if not to be pardoned without extreme punishment, yet to be heard without great marvel.

CYNTH. Say on, Tellus; I cannot [120
imagine anything that can color such a
cruelty.

TELLUS. Endymion, that Endymion,
in the prime of his youth, so ravished my
heart with love that to obtain my desires
I could not find means, nor to recite them,
reason.

What was she that favored not Endymion, being young, wise, honorable, and virtuous? Besides, what metal was she [130
made of (be she mortal) that is not affected
with the spice, nay, infected with the
poison of that not-to-be-expressed, yet
always-to-be-felt love, which breaketh the
brains and never bruiseth the brow, consumeth the heart and never toucheth the
skin, and maketh a deep scar to be seen
before any wound at all be felt? My heart,
too tender to withstand such a divine
fury, yielded to love. Madam, I, [140
not without blushing, confess [I] yielded
to love.

CYNTH. A strange effect of love, to
work such an extreme hate. How say you,
Endymion? All this was for love?

[1] More mischievous.　　　　[2] Unheard of.

END. I say, madam, then the gods
send me a woman's hate.

CYNTH. That were as bad, for then by
contrary you should never sleep. But on,
Tellus; let us hear the end.　　　　150

TELLUS. Feeling a continual burning
in all my bowels, and a bursting almost
in every vein, I could not smother the inward fire, but it must needs be perceived
by the outward smoke; and, by the flying
abroad of divers sparks, divers judged of
my scalding flames. Endymion, as full of
art as wit, marking mine eyes (in which
he might see almost his own), my sighs
(by which he might ever hear his [160
name sounded), aimed at my heart, in
which he was assured his person was im-
printed, and by questions wrung out that
which was ready to burst out. When he saw
the depth of my affections, he sware that
mine in respect of his were as fumes to
Ætna, valleys to Alps, ants to eagles, and
nothing could be compared to my beauty
but his love and eternity. Thus drawing
a smooth shoe upon a crooked foot, [170
he made me believe that (which all of
our sex willingly acknowledge) I was beautiful, and to wonder (which indeed is a
thing miraculous) that any of his sex should
be faithful.

CYNTH. Endymion, how will you clear
yourself?

END. Madam, by mine own accuser.

CYNTH. Well, Tellus, proceed; but [179
briefly, lest, taking delight in uttering thy
love, thou offend us with the length
of it.

TELLUS. I will, madam, quickly make
an end of my love and my tale. Finding
continual increase of my tormenting
thoughts, and that the enjoying of my
love made deeper wounds than the entering into it, I could find no means to ease
my grief but to follow Endymion, and
continually to have him in the ob- [190
ject of mine eyes who had me slave and
subject to his love.

But in the moment that I feared his falsehood and fried myself most in mine affections, I found—ah, grief, even then I
lost myself!—I found him in most melancholy and desperate terms, cursing his
stars, his state, the earth, the heavens,
the world, and all for the love of—

CYNTH. Of whom? Tellus, speak [200 boldly.

TELLUS. Madam, I dare not utter, for fear to offend.

CYNTH. Speak, I say; who dare take offense, if thou be commanded by Cynthia?

TELLUS. For the love of Cynthia.

CYNTH. For my love, Tellus? That were strange. Endymion, is it true?

END. In all things, madam, Tellus doth not speak false.   210

CYNTH. What will this breed to in the end? Well, Endymion, we shall hear all.

TELLUS. I, seeing my hopes turned to mishaps, and a settled dissembling towards me, and an unmovable desire to Cynthia, forgetting both myself and my sex, fell into this unnatural hate; for, knowing your virtues, Cynthia, to be immortal, I could not have an imagination to withdraw him; [1] and, finding mine [220 own affections unquenchable, I could not carry the mind that any else should possess what I had pursued. For, though in majesty, beauty, virtue, and dignity I always humbled and yielded myself to Cynthia, yet in affections I esteemed myself equal with the goddesses; and all other creatures, according to their states, with myself; for stars to their bigness have their lights, and the sun hath no more; [230 and little pitchers, when they can hold no more, are as full as great vessels that run over. Thus, madam, in all truth have I uttered the unhappiness of my love and the cause of my hate, yielding wholly to that divine judgment which never erred for want of wisdom or envied for too much partiality.

CYNTH. How say you, my lords, to this matter? But what say you, En- [240 dymion? Hath Tellus told troth?

END. Madam, in all things but in that she said I loved her and swore to honor her.

CYNTH. Was there such a time whenas for my love thou didst vow thyself to death, and in respect of it loathed thy life? Speak, Endymion; I will not revenge it with hate.

END. The time was, madam, and is, and ever shall be, that I honored [250 your highness above all the world, but to stretch it so far as to call it love I never

[1] Hope to draw him away.

durst. There hath none pleased mine eye but Cynthia, none delighted mine ears but Cynthia, none possessed my heart but Cynthia. I have forsaken all other fortunes to follow Cynthia, and here I stand ready to die, if it please Cynthia. Such a difference hath the gods set between our states that all must be duty, [260 loyalty, and reverence; nothing (without it vouchsafe your highness) be termed love. My unspotted thoughts, my languishing body, my discontented life, let them obtain by princely favor that which to challenge they must not presume, only wishing of impossibilities; with imagination of which I will spend my spirits, and to myself, that no creature may hear, softly call it love; and, if any urge to utter what I [270 whisper, then will I name it honor. From this sweet contemplation if I be not driven. I shall live of all men the most content, taking more pleasure in mine aged thoughts than ever I did in my youthful actions.

CYNTH. Endymion, this honorable respect of thine shall be christened love in thee, and my reward for it, favor. Persevere, Endymion, in loving me, and I account more strength in a true heart [280 than in a walled city. I have labored to win all, and study to keep such as I have won; but those that neither my favor can move to continue constant, nor my offered benefits get to be faithful, the gods shall either reduce to truth, or revenge their treacheries with justice. Endymion, continue as thou hast begun, and thou shalt find that Cynthia shineth not on thee in vain. [Endymion regains his youth.] [290

END. Your highness hath blessed me, and your words have again restored my youth; methinks I feel my joints strong and these moldy hairs to molt, and all by your virtue, Cynthia, into whose hands the balance that weigheth time and fortune are committed.

CYNTH. What, young again! Then it is pity to punish Tellus.

TELLUS. Ah, Endymion, now I [300 know thee and ask pardon of thee; suffer me still to wish thee well.

END. Tellus, Cynthia must command what she will.

FLOSC. Endymion, I rejoice to see thee in thy former estate.

END. Good Floscula, to thee also am I in my former affections.

EUM. Endymion, the comfort of my life, how am I ravished with a joy match- [310 less, saving only the enjoying of my mistress!

CYNTH. Endymion, you must now tell who Eumenides shrineth for his saint.

END. Semele, madam.

CYNTH. Semele, Eumenides? Is it Semele, the very wasp of all women, whose tongue stingeth as much as an adder's tooth?

EUM. It is Semele, Cynthia, the [320 possessing of whose love must only prolong my life.

CYNTH. Nay, sith Endymion is restored, we will have all parties pleased. Semele, are you content after so long trial of his faith, such rare secrecy, such unspotted love, to take Eumenides? Why speak you not? Not a word?

END. Silence, madam, consents; that is most true.   330

CYNTH. It is true, Endymion. Eumenides, take Semele; take her, I say.

EUM. Humble thanks, madam; now only do I begin to live.

SEM. A hard choice, madam, either to be married if I say nothing, or to lose my tongue if I speak a word. Yet do I rather choose to have my tongue cut out than my heart distempered—I will not have him.

CYNTH. Speaks the parrot? She [340 shall nod hereafter with signs. Cut off her tongue, nay, her head, that, having a servant of honorable birth, honest manners, and true love, will not be persuaded!

SEM. He is no faithful lover, madam, for then would he have asked his mistress.

GER. Had he not been faithful, he had never seen into the fountain, and so lost his friend and mistress.

EUM. Thine own thoughts, sweet [350 Semele, witness against thy words, for what hast thou found in my life but love? And as yet what have I found in my love but bitterness? Madam, pardon Semele, and let my tongue ransom hers.

CYNTH. Thy tongue, Eumenides? What, shouldst thou live wanting a tongue to blaze the beauty of Semele? Well, Semele, I will not command love, for it cannot be enforced; let me entreat it.   360

SEM. I am content your highness shall command, for now only do I think Eumenides faithful, that is willing to lose his tongue for my sake; yet loath, because it should do me better service. Madam, I accept of Eumenides.

CYNTH. I thank you, Semele.

EUM. Ah, happy Eumenides, that hast a friend so faithful and a mistress so fair! With what sudden mischief will the [370 gods daunt this excess of joy? Sweet Semele, I live or die as thou wilt.

CYNTH. What shall become of Tellus? Tellus, you know Endymion is vowed to a service from which death cannot remove him. Corsites casteth still a lovely [1] look towards you. How say you, will you have your Corsites, and so receive pardon for all that is past?

TELLUS. Madam, most willingly.   380

CYNTH. But I cannot tell whether Corsites be agreed.

CORS. Ay, madam, more happy to enjoy Tellus than the monarchy of the world.

EUM. Why, she caused you to be pinched with fairies!

CORS. Ay, but her fairness hath pinched my heart more deeply.

CYNTH. Well, enjoy thy love.   But what have you wrought in the castle, [390 Tellus?

TELLUS. Only the picture of Endymion.

CYNTH. Then so much of Endymion as his picture cometh to, possess and play withal.

CORS. Ah, my sweet Tellus, my love shall be as thy beauty is, matchless.

CYNTH. Now it resteth, Dipsas, that if thou wilt forswear that vile art of enchanting, Geron hath promised again to re- [400 ceive thee; otherwise, if thou be wedded to that wickedness, I must and will see it punished to the uttermost.

DIPSAS. Madam, I renounce both substance and shadow of that most horrible and hateful trade, vowing to the gods continual penance, and to your highness obedience.

CYNTH. How say you, Geron?   Will you admit her to your wife?   410

GER. Ay, with more joy than I did the first day, for nothing could happen to make me happy but only her forsaking

[1] Loving.

that lewd [1] and detestable course. Dipsas, I embrace thee.

DIPSAS. And I thee, Geron, to whom I will hereafter recite the cause of these my first follies.

CYNTH. Well, Endymion, nothing resteth now but that we depart. Thou hast my favor; Tellus her friend; Eumenides [421 in paradise with his Semele; Geron contented with Dipsas.

TOP. Nay, soft; I cannot handsomely go to bed without Bagoa.

CYNTH. Well, Sir Tophas, it may be there are more virtues in me than myself knoweth of, for Endymion I awaked, and at my words he waxed young. I will try whether I can turn this tree again to [430 thy true love.

TOP. Turn her to a true love or false, so she be a wench I care not.

CYNTH. Bagoa, Cynthia putteth an end to thy hard fortunes; for, being turned to a tree for revealing a truth, I will recover thee again, if in my power be the effect of truth. [Bagoa recovers human shape.]

TOP. Bagoa, a bots [2] upon thee!

CYNTH. Come, my lords, let us in. [440 You, Gyptes and Pythagoras, if you can content yourselves in our court, to fall from vain follies of philosophers to such virtues as are here practiced, you shall be entertained according to your deserts, for Cynthia is no stepmother to strangers.

[1] Base. [2] Worms.

PYTHAG. I had rather in Cynthia's court spend ten years than in Greece one hour.

GYPTES. And I choose rather to [450 live by the sight of Cynthia than by the possessing of all Egypt.

CYNTH. Then follow.

EUM. We all attend. *Exeunt.*

FINIS.

THE EPILOGUE

A MAN walking abroad, the Wind and Sun strove for sovereignty, the one with his blast, the other with his beams. The Wind blew hard; the man wrapped his garment about him harder. It blustered more strongly; he then girt it fast to him. "I cannot prevail," said the Wind. The Sun, casting her crystal beams, began to warm the man; he unloosed his gown. Yet it shined brighter; he then put it [10 off. "I yield," said the Wind, "for, if thou continue shining, he will also put off his coat."

Dread sovereign, the malicious that seek to overthrow us with threats do but stiffen our thoughts and make them sturdier in storms; but, if your highness vouchsafe with your favorable beams to glance upon us, we shall not only stoop, but with all humility lay both our hands and [20 hearts at your majesty's feet.

GEORGE PEELE

George Peele was one of a loosely organized group of Elizabethan writers, including John Lyly, Robert Greene, Thomas Nashe, and Thomas Lodge, who in modern times have been dubbed the "University Wits." This title is used to distinguish them from the many other university-trained authors, sometimes even churchmen, whose appeal was either to more popular and simple-minded audiences or to their more serious and sober-minded countrymen. The appeal of these Wits was chiefly to the taste for the sophisticated, the fantastic, the imaginative, and the romantic. David H. Horne, in his biographical and critical study of Peele in *The Life and Minor Works of George Peele* (New Haven, 1952), stated: "The purpose of the present study is not to whitewash Peele but, if the facts warrant it, to neutralize the scarlet and blue of his reputation and perhaps to eliminate a bit of the Greene. The time has come to cease regarding the University Wits as universal rakes."

Bernard M. Wagner (in a letter to the *TLS*, September 28, 1933) fixed, approximately, the birth-date of Peele by announcing the discovery of the boy's baptism entry in the register of the Church of St. James, Garlickhithe, London, on July 27, 1556. Two years later the family moved to the parish of St. Olave, Jewry, and then in 1562 the old Grey Friars monastery in Newgate, which had recently been converted into a philanthropic and municipally supported asylum for orphans and "decayed old people," and given the new (later to be famous) name, Christ's Hospital. James Peele, the boy's father, had been appointed its chief administrative officer, or clerk (perhaps because he was both an accountant and a teacher), and he remained in this position until 1582. In addition to being the author of the earliest surviving textbook on double-entry bookkeeping, James Peele, an energetic and versatile man in spite of continuing pecuniary difficulties, apparently also rather fancied himself as a literary man. He wrote his second book on accounting and arithmetic in dramatic dialogue form, interspersed with verses, and also worked on several city and mayoral pageants. This interest may well have rubbed off on his son. George's mother, Anne, died in 1579, and her husband quickly married again. Horne concludes that George Peele's family connections could not have helped him much either in the City or in court, since his whole background was that of the middle-class London tradesman, and that his early education in the hospital (though it consisted chiefly of Greek, Latin, Hebrew, religion, and some rhetoric) brought him mostly into contact with the lower classes—an environment which he apparently was only too glad to escape as soon as possible.

At any rate, at the end of March 1571, a few days after the Governors had given him a special grant of more books by Erasmus, Tully (Cicero), Terence, Horace, and Ovid, he and a fellow-student left on horseback for Broadgates Hall (now Pembroke College), Oxford. Later he transferred to Christ Church College. Here he probably lived a pretty austere life, even though his father may have gone into debt to keep him in school. Nothing is known about his ability as a student, except that he was admitted to the B.A. on June 12, 1577; "determined" (underwent the normal series of disputations to determine a new Bachelor's fitness) in Lent of the next year; and finally, having completed his studies in moral and natural philosophy in a year less than the normal time, received his M.A. in 1579. Horne concludes that, although the university community had recently undergone a "laxity in moral and mental tone," there is nothing to show that Peele was especially affected by it or that he led the life of a playboy there.

It was at Christ Church, which was a well-known place for the writing and producing of plays, mostly in Latin, that the boy first discovered an interest in the theater. And it was apparently at this time that Peele made a translation of one of the *Iphigenia* plays by Euripides, which may have been presented in the Great Hall of the college. However this may be, it was to this translation that we owe the first important personal picture of the young man. William Gager, perhaps the best known author of Latin plays at Oxford at this time, was so impressed by his friend Peele's work that he wrote two Latin eulogies to him. In these he confessed that he was amazed at Peele's "serious remarks mixed with clever jests," and ended the first poem by begging him "to go on binding the ancient poets to you. If you can gratify the ancients, you'll easily gratify the moderns." Both of these things Peele did his best to accomplish. In his second poem, Gager included a vignette of his friend, describing him as "strangely short of leg, dark of complexion, and red-haired." Some years later one of *The Merry Conceited Jests of George Peele* implied that he also wore a beard and had a high-pitched voice like a woman's. Plainly, young Peele was not physically prepossessing, and had to depend for appeal on his personality and his quill.

Between attaining his B.A. and his M.A., Peele became involved in certain events which some early biographers, like A. H. Bullen, made use of to attribute to him the character of a fast-living, dissipated, undependable young man. There is a mysterious entry in the Court Book of Christ's Hospital in 1579 stating that James Peele had promised to "discharge" from his house his son George "and all other his household wch haue bene chargable to him." Horne, however, disputes the possible scandalous implications of this entry, and maintains that the occasion may have been perfectly innocent. Sometime between March and October of 1580, after Peele had returned to Oxford, he married sixteen-year-old Ann Cooke, the only child of a merchant of St. Aldgate's parish near the college. For the next four years he and his child-wife were embroiled in a series of lawsuits in the Chancellor's Court at Oxford to settle the estate of his father-in-law, who had died just before Peele's marriage. The situation entailed frequent traveling between London and Oxford, where he and his family lived at the college. Horne speculates that during this time Peele may have been associated with some college office, such as that of Censor, which would have involved the supervising of plays, and that he may have been working on some of his early surviving poems, such as *The Tale of Troy*, which perhaps helped to prepare him later for his first play, *The Arraignment of Paris*.

In 1581 he left Oxford to take up permanent residence in London, first near the Inns of Court in Holborn just outside the City wall. Nevertheless, he returned to Oxford intermittently for various reasons, the most interesting of which was that in May 1583 he became one of the directors of the entertainments given at Oxford in honor of Albertus Alasco, Count Palatine of Seradia, Poland. While his friend Gager did the writing, Peele helped to supervise the erection of the stage, the scenery, the costuming, the fireworks, and so on. This experience was soon to stand him in good stead as a professional playwright for the public theaters—a decision which he apparently made in the late 1580s, about which time his wife may have died. He would then have been living on the Bankside and may have married a second time, since Dowling ("A Few Points concerning Peele" [*NQ*, 1933]) discovered an entry in the register of St. Olave, Southwark, of the marriage in 1591 of a George Peele to one Mary Yates, or Gates. If this George Peele was the dramatist, his ill luck with the law followed him. His new wife was the widow of a soldier who had sued the government for back pay for service in the Netherlands, and some dubious dealings seem to have gone on, although with little tangible result.

Although he probably decided to become a playwright in the late 1580s, the question of just how busy Peele was as a man of the public theater—where his plays were performed by companies connected with the Lord High Admiral, the Queen, and Philip Henslowe—has kept scholars busy. Some have even speculated that he became an

actor, but Horne discounts this theory on the assumption that no writer of the "scholarly set" would have so lowered himself—and Peele was soon to be signing himself
"Gentleman" as well as "Master of Arts in Oxenford" on some of his title pages. The
number of extant plays provably from his pen is only five; but, as Horne remarks,
"Indeed, if we believe all the literary historians who have published 'discoveries' concerning Peele, he wrote most of the anonymous plays of the period and had a hand in
some of Shakespeare's." Horne would agree with Arthur M. Sampley, who in two
articles rejected Peele's hand in such plays. In "Verbal Tests for Peele's Plays" (*SP*,
1933) Sampley collected and evaluated 133 words and phrases which had been offered
by J. M. Robertson and H. Dugdale Sykes as evidence of Peele's contribution to *Titus
Andronicus, Alphonsus, Emperor of Germany, The Troublesome Reign of King John*, and
King Leir, and found practically all of them in identical, or almost identical, form in
older dramatists. Sampley later verified his conclusions by examining some of these
and other conjectural plays in "Plot Structure in Peele's Plays as a Test of Authorship"
(*PMLA*, 1936), and decided that most of the anonymous plays were too well constructed
to have been written by Peele. Other scholars have dealt with the possible authorship
of these doubtful plays, especially *Alphonsus*, and all their discussions throw considerable light on the widespread practice of collaboration in the Elizabethan theater.

The canon of Peele's indubitable plays as accepted by Horne is as follows: *The
Arraignment of Paris* (written between 1581 and 1584, printed 1584); *The Battle of
Alcazar* (written 1588–89, printed 1594); *The Love of King David and Fair Bethsabe*
(written between 1592 and 1594, printed 1599); *The Famous Chronicle of King Edward
the First* (written about 1593, printed 1593); and *The Old Wives' Tale* (written about
1593–94, printed 1595). Two lost plays are also generally admitted to the canon: *The
Hunting of Cupid* (written between 1581 and 1585, printed 1591) and *The Turkish
Mahomet and Hiren the Fair Greek* (written before 1594). Dowling, in "The Date and
Order of Peele's Plays" (*NQ*, 1933), and Thorleif Larsen, in "A Bibliography of the
Writings of George Peele" (*MP*, 1934), have made contributions to the same subject.
The very titles of these plays suggest the variety of Peele's interests, since they include
the classical pastoral, the melodrama, the romantic tragedy, the history play, and the
folk play. During the period of his dramatic writing, he also continued to write poetry
with some profusion, largely of the occasional type involving well-known people and
events.

On January 17, 1596, Peele sent his young daughter on a mission to the Lord High
Treasurer, Lord Burghley. She carried with her the manuscript of his youthful poem,
The Tale of Troy, as a sort of intercessional offering and introduction to a begging letter,
in which her father pleaded for help, since "long sickness had enfeebled him." Apparently the letter failed to untie any purse strings. Perhaps, even if it had, help would
have come too late since, on November 9, 1596, an entry in the register of St. James's,
Clerkenwell, recorded the death of "George Peele, householder"—presumably the poet-
dramatist. The "long sickness" referred to in his letter was probably the same as
Francis Meres alluded to facetiously in his *Palladis Tamia, Wit's Treasury*, a pithy
review of English authors from Chaucer to the present. Meres ended his account of
Peele with the sharp epitaph: "As Anacreon the poet died by the pot: so George Peele
by the pox." This bald charge that syphilis was the cause of Peele's death, taken
together with the posthumously published *The Merry Conceited Jests of George Peele*
(1607) and references and admonitions in Robert Greene's *Groatsworth of Wit Bought
with a Million of Repentance* (1592), was largely responsible for the bad reputation Peele
had among scholars and critics until Horne undertook his campaign of rehabilitation.

Some of Tucker Brooke's epithets can be taken as representative of the rest—from
Alexander Dyce, George Saintsbury, and A. H. Bullen to F. E. Schelling and Mark
Eccles. To Brooke, Peele was "a bad man and a surpassing poet," an "unredeemed
scapegrace," a "product of London streets and gutters," "always on the edge of beggary
and never far from the prospect of jail." Horne, however, by comparing the *Jests* with

other jest books of the period, has concluded that most of the frequently scurrilous anecdotes associated with Peele were either traditional or generic, although a few of the stories contain bits of authentic biographical information that might lend credibility to the rest. The collector or editor clearly did not have a high opinion of Peele's character, since the playwright was, like so many of his contemporaries, a well-known patron of taverns, a boon companion, an improvident accumulator of debts, and a neglecter of his wife and family. But although the collector's picture was derogatory it was not defamatory, and it scarcely justified the smudged reputation given Peele after his death.

THE ARRAIGNMENT OF PARIS

The Arraignment of Paris, the earliest pastoral play to survive (though the Revels accounts record titles of lost plays which would seem to have been of this nature), was given before Elizabeth by the Children of the Chapel between 1581/2 and 1583/4. It was published anonymously in 1584, apparently without entry on the Stationers' Register. Its authorship is established through Nashe's allusion to it in his *Menaphon* and by the attribution to Peele of two of its songs in the anthology, *England's Parnassus*. No specific source is known, but the general idea of showing what might have happened between the times when Ate dropped the golden apple among the three jealous goddesses and when the Trojan War actually began may have come to Peele while writing his *Tale of Troy*. Since he was living among law students at the time, the idea of a trial would be natural to him. In "The Background of Peele's *The Arraignment of Paris*" (*NQ*, 1956) Inga-Stina Ekeblad shows "how very common the judgement theme was, not only in literature and pageantry in general, but precisely in its special application to Elizabeth," and calls attention also to the judgment scene in Book X of *The Golden Ass* of Apuleius as a possible source. Paulilli's *Il Giuditio di Paride* not only had a parallel title but also may have suggested some conventional devices. The names of the four shepherds may well have come from Edmund Spenser's recently published *The Shepherd's Calendar* (1579).

Peele's play marked his only association with the child actors and with the Revels. The play has originality in its situation, although its construction is disjointed and the subplot involving Thestylis, Colin, and the other shepherds is dropped without showing any reason why it was ever introduced. The play is also notable for its masque-like stage effects and for its versification. Although some of its lines and rhymes hobble a bit, there is great variety of poetic form in that different metrical forms are assigned to different characters. Peele also introduced lyrical songs for the choir boys, including one of the echo songs so much in vogue at the time. But his road to fame did not lie through the court drama, in spite of his outrageous flattery of the Queen in the last scene. Nor did it come from the Lord Mayor's pageants, with which he maintained a long connection (as his father had done), although only two of his productions (in 1585 and 1591) survive.

The present text of *The Arraignment* is based on the Malone Society reprint, prepared by H. H. Child.

THE ARRAIGNMENT OF PARIS[1]

[BY
GEORGE PEELE

DRAMATIS PERSONÆ

SATURN	JUNO
JUPITER	PALLAS
NEPTUNE	VENUS
PLUTO	DIANA
APOLLO	POMONA
MARS	FLORA
BACCHUS	RHANIS
MERCURY	ATE
VULCAN	CLOTHO
PAN	LACHESIS
FAUNUS	ATROPOS
SILVANUS	THE MUSES
PARIS	A NYMPH OF DIANA
COLIN	ŒNONE
HOBBINOL	HELEN
DIGGON	THESTYLIS
THENOT	

CUPIDS, CYCLOPS, SHEPHERDS, KNIGHTS, A
CHURL, *etc.*

SCENE: *A vale in Ida.*

TIME: *Mythical.*]

Ate, Prologus.[2]

Condemnéd soul, Ate, from lowest hell
And deadly rivers of the infernal Jove,
Where bloodless ghosts in pains of endless
    date
Fill ruthless ears with never-ceasing cries,
Behold, I come in place, and bring beside
The bane of Troy! Behold, the fatal fruit,
Raught[3] from the golden tree of Proser-
    pine!
Proud Troy must fall, so bid the gods
    above,
And stately Ilium's lofty towers be razed
By conquering hands of the victorious
    foe;   10
King Priam's palace waste with flaming fire,
Whose thick and foggy smoke, piercing
    the sky,
Must serve for messenger of sacrifice,
T' appease the anger of the angry heav-
    ens;
And Priam's younger son, the shepherd
    swain,
Paris, th' unhappy organ[4] of the Greeks.
So loath and weary of her heavy load,
The Earth complains unto the hellish
    prince,
Surcharged with the burden that she
    nill[5] sustain.
Th' unpartial daughters of Necessity   20
Bin aides[6] in her suit; and so the twine
That holds old Priam's house, the thread
    of Troy,
Dame Atropos with knife in sunder cuts.
Done be the pleasure of the powers above,

---

[1] The original title continues: "A Pastoral.
Presented before the Queen's Majesty by the
Children of Her Chapel."
[2] *I.e.*, speaking as Prologue.
[3] Reached, taken.

[4] Provocation (?).
[5] Will not.
[6] Are aids. Such archaisms as these plurals
(with the final *-es* here pronounced as a syllable)
are fairly common throughout the play to represent shepherds' speech.

Whose hests [1] men must obey; and I my part
Perform in Ida vales. Lordings, adieu;
Imposing silence for your task, I end,
Till just assembly of the goddesses
Make me begin the tragedy of Troy.
                    Exit Ate cum aureo pomo. [2]

Act[us] I. Scena i.

[A vale in Ida.] [3]

Pan, Faunus, and Silvanus, with their Attendants, enter to give welcome to the Goddesses. Pan's Shepherd hath a lamb, Faunus' Hunter hath a fawn, Silvanus' Woodman with an oaken bough laden with acorns.

Pan incipit. [4]

PAN. Silvanus, either Flora doth us wrong
    Or Faunus made us tarry all too long,
    For by this morning mirth it should appear
    The Muses or the goddesses be near.
FAUN. My fawn was nimble, Pan, and whipped apace—
    'Twas happy that we caught him up at last—
    The fattest, fairest fawn in all the chase;
    I wonder how the knave could skip so fast.
PAN. And I have brought a twagger for the nonce, [5]
    A bunting [6] lamb; nay, pray, you feel no bones.   10
    Believe me now, my cunning much I miss
    If ever Pan felt fatter lamb than this.
SIL. Sirs, you may boast your flocks and herds that bin both fresh and fair,
    Yet hath Silvanus walks, [7] iwis, [8] that stand in wholesome air;
    And, lo, the honor of the woods, the gallant oaken bough,
    Do I bestow, laden with acorns and with mast enow! [9]

PAN. Peace, man, for shame! Shalt have both lambs and dams and flocks and herds and all,
    And all my pipes to make the[e] glee; we meet not now to brawl.
FAUN. There's no such matter, Pan! We are all friends assembled hether, [10]
    To bid Queen Juno and her feres [11] most humbly welcome hether.   20
    Diana, mistress of our woods, her presence will not want; [12]
    Her courtesy to all her friends, we wot, [13] is nothing scant.

Act[us] I. Scena ii.

Pomona entereth with her fruit. Manentibus Pan cum reliquis. [14]

POM. Yea, Pan, no farther yet, and had the start of me?
    Why, then, Pomona with her fruit comes time enough, I see.
    Come on awhile; with country store, like friends, we venter [15] forth.
    Thinkest, Faunus, that these goddesses will take our gifts in worth? [16]
FAUN. Yea, doubtless, for shall tell thee, dame, 'twere better give a thing,
    A sign of love, unto a mighty person or a king,
    Than to a rude and barbarous swain, but bad and basely born;
    For gently takes the gentleman that [17] oft the clown will scorn.
PAN. Say'st truly, Faunus. I myself have given good tidy [18] lambs
    To Mercury—may say to thee—to Phœbus, and to Jove,   10
    When to a country mops, [19] forsooth, chave [20] offered all their dams,
    And piped and prayed for little worth. and ranged about the grove.
POM. God Pan, that makes your flock so thin, and makes you look so lean,
    To kiss in corners.

---

[1] Behests, commands.
[2] Ate goes out with the golden apple.
[3] The setting is the same throughout the play
[4] Pan begins.
[5] A male lamb for the occasion.
[6] With budding horns.   [8] Certainly.
[7] Tracts of forest.   [9] Nuts enough.

[10] Hither.   [12] Be lacking.
[11] Companions.   [13] Know.
[14] Pan with the others remaining.
[15] Venture.
[16] "In good part" (Bullen).
[17] That which.
[18] Plump; fit for sacrifice.
[19] Wench, from Mopsa, a common name for a shepherdess or a rustic girl.
[20] Dialect for *ich have*, I have.

PAN.   Well said, wench! Some other thing you mean.

POM. Yea, jest it out till it go alone; but marvel where we miss

Fair Flora all this merry morn.

FAUN.   Some news; see where she is.

ACT[US] I. SCENA iii.

Flora entereth to the country gods.

PAN. Flora, well met, and for thy taken pain,

Poor country gods, thy debtors we remain.

FLO. Believe me, Pan, not all thy lambs and yoes,[1]

Nor, Faunus, all thy lusty bucks and does

(But that I am instructed well to know

What service to the hills and dales I owe)

Could have enforced me to so strange a toil,

Thus to enrich this gaudy, gallant [2] soil.

FAUN. But tell me, wench, hast done't so trick [3] indeed

That heaven itself may wonder at the deed?   10

FLO. Not Iris, in her pride and bravery,[4]

Adorns her arch [5] with such variety,

Nor doth the milk-white way in frosty night

Appear so fair and beautiful in sight

As done [6] these fields and groves and sweetest bowers,

Bestrewed and decked with parti-colored flowers.

Along the bubbling brooks and silver glide [7]

That at the bottom doth in silence slide,

The watery flowers and lilies on the banks,

Like blazing comets, burgeon all in ranks;   20

Under the hawthorn and the poplar tree,

Where sacred Phœbe may delight to be,

The primrose and the purple hyacinth,

The dainty violet and the wholesome minth,[8]

The double daisy and the cowslip, queen

Of summer flowers, do overpeer the green;

And round about the valley as ye pass,

Ye may ne [9] see for peeping flowers the grass—

That [10] well the mighty Juno and the rest   29

May boldly think to be a welcome guest

On Ida hills, when to approve the thing

The Queen of Flowers prepares a second spring.

SIL. Thou gentle nymph, what thanks shall we repay

To thee that makest our fields and woods so gay?

FLO. Silvanus, when it is thy hap to see,

My workmanship in portraying all the three—

First stately Juno with her port and grace,

Her robes, her lawns, her crownet,[11] and her mace—

Would make thee muse [12] this picture to behold

Of yellow oxlips bright as burnished gold.   40

POM. A rare device; and Flora well, perdy,[13]

Did paint her yellow for her jealousy.

FLO. Pallas in flowers of hue and colors red,

Her plumes, her helm, her lance, her Gorgon's head,

Her trailing tresses that hang flaring round,

Of July flowers so graffèd [14] in the ground

That, trust me, sirs, who did the cunning see,

Would at a blush [15] suppose it to be she.

PAN. Good Flora, by my flock, 'twere very good

To dight [16] her all in red resembling blood.   50

FLO. Fair Venus of sweet violets in blue,

With other flowers infixed for change of hue;

Her plumes, her pendants, bracelets, and her rings,

Her dainty fan, and twenty other things,

---

[1] Ewes.   [3] Neatly.
[2] Excellent.   [4] Finery.
[5] Rainbow, personified in Iris.
[6] Do, an archaic plural.   [7] Current.   [8] Mint.

[9] Not.   [13] *Par Dieu.*
[10] So that.   [14] Grafted.
[11] Coronet.   [15] Glance.
[12] Marvel.   [16] Dress.

Her lusty mantle waving in the wind,
And every part in color and in kind;[1]
And for her wreath of roses, she nill dare
With Flora's cunning counterfeit compare;
So that what living wight shall chance to see
These goddesses, each placed in her degree, 60
Portrayed by Flora's workmanship alone,
Must say that art and nature met in one.

SIL. A dainty draught[2] to lay her down in blue,
The color commonly betokening "true."

FLO. This piece of work, compact with many a flower,
And well laid in at entrance of the bower,
Where Phœbe means to make this meeting royal,
Have I prepared to welcome them withal.

POM. And are they yet dismounted, Flora, say,
That we may wend to meet them on the way? 70

FLO. That shall not need. They are at hand by this,
And the conductor of the train hight[3] Rhanis.
Juno hath left her chariot long ago,
And hath returned her peacocks by her rainbow,
And bravely, as becomes the wife of Jove,
Doth honor by her presence to our grove.
Fair Venus she hath let her sparrows fly,
To tend on her and make her melody;
Her turtles[4] and her swans unyokéd be,
And flicker near her side for company. 80
Pallas hath set her tigers loose to feed,
Commanding them to wait when she hath need.
And hitherward with proud and stately pace,
To do us honor in the sylvan chase,

They march, like to the pomp of heaven above,
Juno, the wife and sister of King Jove,
The warlike Pallas, and the Queen of Love.

PAN. Pipe, Pan, for joy, and let thy shepherds sing;
Shall never age forget this memorable thing.

FLO. Clio, the sagest of the Sisters Nine, 90
To do observance to this dame divine,
Lady of learning and of chivalry,
Is here arrived in fair assembly;[5]
And, wand'ring up and down th' unbeaten ways,
Ring through the wood sweet songs of Pallas' praise.

POM. Hark, Flora, Faunus! Here is melody,
A charm[6] of birds, and more than ordinary.

An artificial charm of birds being heard within, Pan speaks.

PAN. The silly[7] birds make mirth; then should we do them wrong,
Pomona, if we nill bestow an echo to their song.   *An echo to their song.*

THE SONG

(A choir within and without.)

GODS. O Ida, O Ida, O Ida, happy hill! 100
This honor done to Ida, may it continue still!

MUSES. [*Within.*] Ye country gods that in this Ida wone,[8]
Bring down your gifts of welcome,
For honor done to Ida.

GODS. Behold, in sign of joy we sing,
And signs of joyful welcome bring,
For honor done to Ida.

MUSES. [*Within.*] The Muses give you melody to gratulate this chance,[9]
And Phœbe, chief of sylvan chase, commands you all to dance.

GODS. (*Dance.*) Then[10] round in a circle our sportance must be; 110
Hold hands in a hornpipe, all gallant in glee.

MUSES. [*Within.*] Reverence, reverence, most humble reverence!

GODS. Most humble reverence!

---

[1] *I.e.*, suitable and natural.
[2] Rare device in painting.
[3] Is called.
[4] Turtledoves.
[5] Last syllable pronounced as two.
[6] Chorus.
[7] Simple.
[8] Dwell.
[9] To greet this occasion.
[10] Original reads *the*.

ACT[US] I. SCENA iv.

Pallas, Juno, and Venus enter, Rhanis lead-
ing the way.　Pan alone sings.

THE SONG

The god of shepherds and his mates
With country cheer salutes your states,
Fair, wise, and worthy as you be,
And thank the gracious ladies three
　　For honor done to Ida. *The birds sing.*

The song being done, Juno speaks.

JUNO. Venus, what shall I say?　For,
　　though I be a dame divine,
This welcome and this melody exceeds
　　these wits of mine.
VEN. Believe me, Juno, as I hight the
　　Sovereign of Love,
These rare delights in pleasures pass the
　　banquets of King Jove.
PAL. Then, Venus, I conclude, it easily
　　may be seen　　　　　　　　　　10
That in her chaste and pleasant walks
　　fair Phœbe is a queen.
RHA. Divine Pallas, and you sacred
　　dames,
Juno and Venus, honored by your
　　names,
Juno, the wife and sister of King Jove,
Fair Venus, lady-president of love,
If any entertainment in this place
That can afford but homely, rude, and
　　base,
It please your godheads to accept in
　　gree,[1]
That gracious thought our happiness
　　shall be.
My mistress Dian, this right well I
　　know,　　　　　　　　　　　　20
For love that to this presence she doth
　　owe,
Accounts more honor done to her this
　　day
Than ever whilom[2] in these woods of
　　Ida.
And for our country gods, I dare be
　　bold,
They make such cheer, your presence
　　to behold,
Such jouissance,[3] such mirth, and merri-
　　ment,

As nothing else their mind might more
　　content.
And that you do believe it to be so,
Fair goddesses, your lovely looks do
　　show.
It rests in fine, for to confirm my talk,　30
Ye deign to pass along to Dian's walk,
Where she among her troop of maids
　　attends
The fair arrival of her welcome friends.
FLO. And we will wait with all observ-
　　ance due,
And do just honor to this heavenly crew.
PAN. The god of shepherds, Juno, ere thou
　　go,
Intends a lamb on thee for to bestow.
FAUN. Faunus, high ranger in Diana's
　　chase,
Presents a fawn to Lady Venus' grace.
SIL. Silvanus gives to Pallas' deity　　40
This gallant bough raught from the
　　oaken tree.
POM. To them that doth this honor to
　　our fields
Her mellow apples poor Pomona yields.
JUNO. And, gentle gods, these signs of
　　your good will
We take in worth, and shall accept them
　　still.
VEN. And, Flora, this to thee among the
　　rest:
Thy workmanship comparing with the
　　best,
Let it suffice thy cunning to have [pow-
　　er][4]
To call King Jove from forth his heavenly
　　bower.
Hadst thou a lover, Flora, credit me,　50
I think thou wouldst bedeck him gal-
　　lantly.
But wend we on; and, Rhanis, lead the
　　way,
That kens the painted paths of pleasant
　　Ida.　　　　　　　　　　*Exeunt omnes.*

ACT[US] I. SCENA V ET ULTIMA.[5]

Paris and Œnone.

PAR. Œnone, while[6] we bin disposed to
　　walk,
Tell me what shall be subject of our
　　talk.

---

[1] With good will.　　[2] Formerly.　　[3] Jollity.

[4] Suggested by Dyce.　　[5] And last.　　[6] Until.

Thou hast a sort [1] of pretty tales in store;
Dare say no nymph in Ida woods hath more.
Again, beside thy sweet alluring face,
In telling them thou hast a special grace.
Then, prithee, sweet, afford some pretty thing,
Some toy that from thy pleasant wit doth spring.

Œn. Paris, my heart's contentment and my choice,
Use thou thy pipe, and I will use my voice;   10
So shall thy just request not be denied,
And time well spent, and both be satisfied.

Par. Well, gentle nymph, although thou do me wrong,
That can ne tune my pipe unto a song,
Me list [2] this once, Œnone, for thy sake,
This idle task on me to undertake.

They sit under a tree together.

Œn. And whereon, then, shall be my roundelay?
For thou hast heard my store long since, dare say: [3]
How Saturn did divide his kingdom tho [4]
To Jove, to Neptune, and to Dis below;   20
How mighty men made foul successless war
Against the gods and state of Jupiter;
How Phorcys' imp, that was so trick and fair,
That tangled Neptune in her golden hair,
Became a Gorgon for her lewd misdeed—
A pretty fable, Paris, for to read,
A piece of cunning, trust me, for the nonce,
That wealth and beauty alter men to stones;
How Salmacis, resembling idleness,
Turns men to women all through wantonness;   30
How Pluto raught Queen Ceres' daughter thence

And what did follow of that love-offense;
Of Daphne turned into the laurel tree,
That shows a mirror of virginity;
Now fair Narcissus, tooting on his shade, [5]
Reproves disdain, and tells how form doth vade; [6]
How cunning Philomela's needle tells
What force in love, what wit in sorrow dwells;
What pains unhappy souls abide in hell,
They say, because on earth they lived not well—   40
Ixion's wheel, proud Tantal's pining woe,
Prometheus' torment, and a many mo; [7]
How Danaus' daughters ply their endless task;
What toil the toil of Sisyphus doth ask.
All these are old and known, I know; yet if thou wilt have any,
Choose some of these, for, trust me, else Œnone hath not many.

Par. Nay, what thou wilt; but, sith [8] my cunning not compares with thine,
Begin some toy [9] that I can play upon this pipe of mine.

Œn. There is a pretty sonnet, [10] then— we call it "Cupid's Curse:"   49
"They that do change old love for new, pray gods they change for worse!"
The note is fine and quick withal; the ditty will agree,
Paris, with that same vow of thine upon our poplar tree.

Par. No better thing; begin it then. Œnone, thou shalt see
Our music figure of [11] the love that grows twixt thee and me.

They sing, and, while Œnone singeth, he pipeth. Incipit Œnone.

Œn. Fair and fair, and twice so fair,
    As fair as any may be,
The fairest shepherd on our green,
    A love for any lady.
Par. Fair and fair, and twice so far,
    As fair as any may be,   60
Thy love is fair for thee alone,
    And for no other lady.

---

[1] Collection.   [2] It pleases me.
[3] Original has *Fabula* in margin here, and the following thirteen stories are numbered.
[4] Then.

[5] Gazing on his reflection.   [7] More.
[6] Fade, vanish.   [8] Since.
[9] Trifle, here a light musical air.
[10] Song.   [11] Portray.

Œn. My love is fair, my love is gay,
　　As fresh as bin the flowers in May,
　　And of my love my roundelay,
　　My merry, merry, merry roundelay,
　　　Concludes with Cupid's curse:
　　They that do change old love for new,
　　Pray gods they change for worse!
Ambo simul.[1] They that do change, etc.　70
Œn. Fair and fair, etc.
Par. Fair and fair, etc.　Thy love is fair,
　　etc.

Œn. My love can pipe, my love can sing,
　　My love can many a pretty thing,
　　And of his lovely praises ring
　　My merry, merry roundelays;
　　　Amen to Cupid's curse:
　　They that do change, etc.
Par. They that do change, etc.
Ambo. Fair and fair, etc.　Finis camenæ.[2]

*The song being ended, they rise, and Œnone
speaks.*

Œn. Sweet shepherd, for Œnone's sake
　　be cunning[3] in this song,　　　81
And keep thy love, and love thy choice,
　　or else thou dost her wrong.
Par. My vow is made and witnessèd;
　　the poplar will not start,[4]
Nor shall the nymph Œnone's love from
　　forth my breathing heart.
I will go bring thee on thy way, my
　　flock are here behind,
And I will have a lover's fee; they say,
　　"Unkissed, unkind."　　*Exeunt ambo.*

Act[us] II. Scena i.

Venus, Juno, Pallas.

Ven. (*Ex abrupto.*[5]) But pray you, tell
　　me, Juno, was it so,
As Pallas told me here the tale of Echo?
Jun. She was a nymph indeed, as Pallas
　　tells,
A walker,[6] such as in these thickets
　　dwells;
And as she told what subtle, juggling
　　pranks
She played with Juno, so she told her
　　thanks:[7]

[1] Both together.
[2] The end of the song.
[3] Skillful, expert.
[4] *I.e.*, tremble in token of a false vow.
[5] Abruptly.
[6] Forest-dweller.
[7] An ironical phrase for *dismissed her.*

A tattling trull to come at every call,
And now, forsooth, nor tongue nor life
　　at all.
And, though perhaps she was a help to
　　Jove,
And held me chat[8] while he might court
　　his love,　　　　　　　　　10
Believe me, dames, I am of this opinion,
He took but little pleasure in the minion;
And whatsoe'er his scapes[9] have been
　　beside,
Dare say for him, a[10] never strayed so
　　wide.
A lovely nut-brown lass or lusty trull
Have power perhaps to make a god a
　　bull.
Ven. Gramercy, gentle Juno, for that
　　jest;
I'faith, that item was worth all the rest.
Pal. No matter, Venus, howsoe'er you
　　scorn,
My father Jove at that time ware the
　　horn.[11]　　　　　　　　20
Jun. Had every wanton god above, Venus,
　　not better luck,
Then heaven would be a pleasant park,
　　and Mars a lusty buck.
Ven. Tut, Mars hath horns to butt withal,
　　although no bull a shows.
A never needs to mask in nets; a fears
　　no jealous froes.[12]
Jun. Forsooth the better is his turn, for,
　　if a speak too loud,
Must find some shift to shadow him, a
　　net or else a cloud.
Pal. No more of this, fair goddesses; un-
　　rip not so your shames,
To stand all naked to the world, that
　　been such heavenly dames.
Jun. Nay, Pallas, that's a common trick
　　with Venus, well we know;
And all the gods in heaven have seen her
　　naked long ago.　　　　　30
Ven. And then she was so fair and bright,
　　and lovely and so trim,
As Mars is but for Venus' tooth,[13] and
　　she will sport with him.
And, but me list not here to make com-
　　parison with Jove,
Mars is no ranger, Juno, he, in every
　　open grove.

[8] In conversation.　[9] Escapades.　[10] He.
[11] Wore the horn—the proverbial sign of the
cuckold.　[12] Women.　[13] Taste, pleasure.

PAL. Too much of this! We wander far;
    the skies begin to scowl.
  Retire we to Diana's bower; the weather
    will be foul.

The storm being past of thunder and light-
ning, and Ate having trundled the ball
into place, crying, "Fatum Trojæ," [1]
Juno taketh the ball up and speaketh.

JUN. Pallas, the storm is past and gone,
    and Phœbus clears the skies,
  And, lo, behold a ball of gold, a fair and
    worthy prize!
VEN. [*Reading.*] This posy [2] wills the ap-
    ple to the fairest given be;
  Then is it mine, for Venus hight the
    fairest of the three.   40
PAL. The fairest here, as fair is meant,
    am I; ye do me wrong;
  And, if the fairest have it must, to me it
    doth belong.
JUN. Then Juno may it not enjoy, so
    everyone says no;
  But I will prove myself the fairest, ere
    I lose it so.   *They read the posy.*
  The brief [3] is this, *Detur pulcherrimæ*—
  Let this unto the fairest given be,
  The fairest of the three—and I am she.
PAL. (*Reads.*) *Detur pulcherrimæ*—
  Let this unto the fairest given be,
  The fairest of the three—and I am she. 50
VEN. (*Reads.*) *Detur pulcherrimæ*—
  Let this unto the fairest given be,
  The fairest of the three—and I am
    she.
JUN. My face is fair; but yet the majesty
  That all the gods in heaven have seen
    in me
  Have made them choose me of the
    planets seven
  To be the wife of Jove and Queen of
    Heaven;
  If then this prize be but bequeathed to
    beauty,
  The only she that wins this prize am I.
VEN. That Venus is the fairest, this doth
    prove: 60
  That Venus is the lovely Queen of Love.
  The name of Venus is indeed but beauty,
  And men me fairest call per excellency; [4]
  If then this prize be but bequeathed to
    beauty,
  The only she that wins this prize am I.

PAL. To stand on terms of beauty as you
    take it,
  Believe me, ladies, is but to mistake it.
  The beauty that this subtle prize must
    win,
  No outward beauty hight, but dwells
    within;
  And sift it as you please, and you shall
    find   70
  This beauty is the beauty of the mind.
  This fairness, Virtue hight in general,
  That many branches hath in special;
  This beauty Wisdom hight, whereof am I
  By heaven appointed goddess worthily.
  And look, how much the mind, the bet-
    ter part,
  Doth overpass the body in desert, [5]
  So much the mistress of those gifts di-
    vine
  Excels thy beauty, and that state of
    thine.
  Then, if this prize be thus bequeathed
    to beauty,   80
  The only she that wins this prize am I.
VEN. Nay, Pallas, by your leave you
    wander clean.
  We must not conster [6] hereof as you
    mean,
  But take the sense as it is plainly meant;
  And let the fairest ha't, I am content.
PAL. Our reasons will be infinite, I trow,
  Unless unto some other point we grow.
  But first here's none, methinks, dis-
    posed to yield,
  And none but will with words maintain
    the field.
JUN. Then, if you will, to avoid a tedious
    grudge,   90
  Refer it to the sentence of a judge;
  Whoe'er he be that cometh next in place,
  Let him bestow the ball and end the
    case.
VEN. So can it not go wrong with me at
    all. [7]
PAL. I am agreed, however it befall.
  And yet by common doom, [8] so may it
    be,
  I may be said the fairest of the three.
JUN. Then yonder, lo, that shepherd swain
    is he,
  That must be umpire in this controversy!

[1] The fate of Troy.
[2] Inscription.
[3] Writing.
[4] Above all.
[5] Pronounced *desart.*
[6] Construe.
[7] Emended by Dyce. Original reads *not at all.*
[8] Judgment.

ACT[US] II. SCENA ii.

Paris alone. Manentibus Pal[lade], Junone,
Venere.

VEN. Juno, in happy time, I do accept
   the man;
   It seemeth by his looks some skill of
   love he can.[1]
PAR. [*Aside.*] The nymph is gone, and I,
   all solitary,
   Must wend to tend my charge, oppressed
   with melancholy.
   This day (or else me fails my shepherd's
   skill)
   Will tide [2] me passing good or passing ill.
JUN. Shepherd, abash not, though at sud-
   den thus
   Thou be arrived by ignorance among us,
   Not earthly but divine, and goddesses
   all three;
   Juno, Pallas, Venus, these our titles be. 10
   Nor fear to speak for reverence of the
   place,
   Chosen to end a hard and doubtful case.
   This apple, lo (nor ask thou whence it
   came),
   Is to be given unto the fairest dame.
   And fairest is, nor she, nor she, but she
   Whom, shepherd, thou shalt fairest name
   to be.
   This is thy charge; fulfill without of-
   fense,
   And she that wins shall give thee recom-
   pense.
PAL. Dread not to speak, for we have
   chosen thee,
   Sith in this case we can no judges be.   20
VEN. And, shepherd, say that I the fair-
   est am,
   And thou shalt win good guerdon for
   the same.
JUN. Nay, shepherd, look upon my stately
   grace,
   Because the pomp that longs [3] to Juno's
   mace
   Thou mayst not see; and think Queen
   Juno's name,
   To whom old shepherds title works of
   fame,[4]
   Is mighty, and may easily suffice,
   At Phœbus' hand, to gain a golden prize.

---

[1] Knows.   [2] Betide, befall.   [3] Belongs.
[4] *I.e.*, to whom old poets address famous
works.

And for thy meed, sith I am queen of
   riches,
Shepherd, I will reward thee with great
   monarchies,   30
Empires, and kingdoms, heaps of massy
   gold,
Scepters and diadems curious to behold,
Rich robes, of sumptuous workman-
   ship and cost,
And thousand things whereof I make
   no boast.
The mold whereon thou treadest shall
   be of Tagus' sands,
And Xanthus shall run liquid gold for
   thee to wash thy hands;
And, if thou like to tend thy flock, and
   not from them to fly,
Their fleeces shall be curléd gold to
   please their master's eye.
And last, to set thy heart on fire, give
   this one fruit to me,
And, shepherd, lo, this tree of gold will
   I bestow on thee!   40

JUNO'S SHOW

Hereupon did rise a tree of gold, laden
with diadems and crowns of gold.

The ground whereon it grows, the grass,
   the root of gold,
The body and the bark of gold, all
   glist'ring to behold,
The leaves of burnished gold, the fruits
   that thereon grow
Are diadems set with pearl in gold, in
   gorgeous glist'ring show;
And, if this tree of gold in lieu may not
   suffice,
Require a grove of golden trees, so Juno
   bear the prize.   *The tree sinketh.*
PAL. Me list not tempt thee with decaying
   wealth,
   Which is embased by want of lusty
   health;
   But, if thou have a mind to fly above,
   Ycrowned [5] with fame, near to the seat
   of Jove,   50
   If thou aspire to wisdom's worthiness,
   Whereof thou mayst not see the bright-
   ness,
   If thou desire honor of chivalry,
   To be renowned for happy victory,
   To fight it out, and in the champaign [6]
   field

---

[5] Old form of the past participle.   [6] Open.

To shroud thee under Pallas' warlike
shield,
To prance on barbéd steeds—this honor,
lo,
Myself for guerdon shall on thee bestow!
And for encouragement, that thou mayst
see
What famous knights Dame Pallas'
warriors be,   60
Behold in Pallas' honor here they come,
Marching along with sound of thund'-
ring drum.

PALLAS' SHOW

Hereupon did enter nine Knights in armor,
treading a warlike almain,[1] *by drum and*
fife, and then having marched forth again,
Venus speaketh.

VEN. Come, shepherd, come, sweet shep-
herd, look on me;
These been too hot alarums,[2] these, for
thee.
But, if thou wilt give me the golden
ball,
Cupid my boy shall ha't to play withal,
That, whensoe'er this apple he shall see,
The God of Love himself shall think
on thee,
And bid thee look and choose, and he
will wound
Whereso thy fancy's[3] object shall be
found;   70
And lightly when he shoots he doth
not miss.
And I will give thee many a lovely kiss,
And come and play with thee on Ida
here;
And, if thou wilt a face that hath no peer,
A gallant girl, a lusty minion trull,
That can give sport to thee thy belly-
ful,
To ravish all thy beating veins with
joy,
Here is a lass of Venus' court, my boy,

Helen ent'reth with four Cupids.

Here, gentle shepherd, here's for thee
a piece,
The fairest face, the flower of gallant
Greece.   80

[1] Dance.   [2] Calls to arms.   [3] Love's.

VENUS' SHOW

Here Helen ent'reth in her bravery, with four
Cupids attending on her, each having his
fan in his hand to fan fresh air in her
face. She singeth as followeth:

Se Diana nel cielo è una stella,
Chiara e lucente, piena di splendore,
Che porge luc' all' affanato cuore;

Se Diana nel ferno è una dea,
Che da conforto all' anime dannate
Che per amor son morte desperate;

Se Diana, ch' in terra è delle ninfe
Reina imperativa di dolci fiori,
Tra bosch' e selve da morte a pastori;

Io son un Diana dolce e rara,   90
Che con li guardi io posso far guerra
A Dian' in fern', in cielo, e in terra.[4]   *Exit.*

The song being ended, Helen departeth, and
Paris speaketh.

PAR. Most heavenly dames, was never
man as I,
Poor shepherd swain, so happy and un-
happy;
The least of these delights that you de-
vise,
Able to rap[5] and dazzle human eyes.
But, since my silence may not pardoned
be,
And I appoint which is the fairest she,
Pardon, most sacred dames, sith one,
not all,
By Paris' doom must have this golden
ball.   100
Thy beauty, stately Juno, dame divine,
That like to Phœbus' golden beams doth
shine,

[4] If Diana is a star in heaven,
bright and shining, full of splendor,
giving light to the grieving heart;

If Diana is a goddess in hell,
who gives comfort to the tormented souls
who on account of love have died in despair;

If Diana, who on earth is of the nymphs
the reigning queen of sweet flowers,
amid woods and groves gives death to shepherds;

I am a Diana gentle and rare,
for with my glances I can make war
upon Diana in hell, in heaven, and on earth.

[5] Affect with rapture.

Approves itself to be most excellent;
But that fair face that doth me most
    content,
Sith fair, fair dames, is neither she nor she,
But she whom I shall fairest deem to be,
That face is hers that hight the Queen
    of Love,
Whose sweetness doth both gods and
    creatures move.
      He giveth the golden ball to Venus.
And, if the fairest face deserve the ball,
Fair Venus, ladies, bears it from ye all.
VEN. And in this ball doth Venus more
    delight   111
Than in her lovely boy fair Cupid's
    sight.
Come, shepherd, come; sweet Venus is
    thy friend,
No matter how thou other gods offend.
Venus taketh Paris with her. Exeunt [ambo].
JUN. But he shall rue and ban the dis-
    mal day
Wherein his Venus bare the ball away;
And heaven and earth just witnesses
    shall be
I will revenge it on his progeny.
PAL. Well, Juno, whether we be lief [1] or
    loath,   119
Venus hath got the apple from us both.
                 Exeunt ambo.

ACT[US] III. SCENA i.

*Colin, th' enamored shepherd, singeth his
                passion of love.*

THE SONG

O gentle Love, ungentle for thy deed,
    Thou makest my heart
    A bloody mark
With piercing shot to bleed!
Shoot soft, sweet Love, for fear thou shoot
    amiss,
    For fear too keen
    Thy arrows been,
And hit the heart where my beloved is.
Too fair that fortune were, nor never I
    Shall be so blessed,   10
    Among the rest,
That Love shall seize on her by sympathy.
Then since with Love my prayers bear no
    boot,[2]
    This doth remain
    To cease my pain,
I take the wound, and die at Venus' foot.
              Exit Colin.

[1] Willing.   [2] Profit.

ACT[US] III. SCENA ii.

Hobbinol, Diggon, Thenot.

HOB. Poor Colin, woeful man, thy life
    forespoke [3] by love,
What uncouth [4] fit, what malady, is
    this that thou dost prove? [5]
DIG. Or [6] Love is void of physic clean,
    or Love's our common wrack,
That gives us bane [7] to bring us low,
    and let[s] us medicine lack.
HOB. That ever Love had reverence
    'mong silly shepherd swains!
Belike [8] that humor hurts them most
    that most might be their pains.
THE. Hobbin, it is some other god that
    cherisheth their [9] sheep,
For sure this Love doth nothing else
    but make our herdmen weep.
DIG. And what a hap is this, I pray, when
    all our woods rejoice,
For Colin thus to be denied his young
    and lovely choice!   10
THE. She hight indeed so fresh and fair
    that well it is for thee,
Colin—and kind [10] hath been thy friend—
    that Cupid could not see.
HOB. And whither wends yon thriveless [11]
    swain? Like to the stricken deer,
Seeks he dictamum [12] for his wound with-
    in our forest here?
DIG. He wends to greet the Queen of Love,
    that in these woods doth wone,
With mirthless lays to make complaint
    to Venus of her son.
THE. Ah, Colin, thou art all deceived!
    She dallies with the boy,
And winks at all his wanton pranks,
    and thinks thy love a toy.
HOB. Then leave him to his luckless love;
    let him abide his fate.
The sore is rankled all too far; our com-
    fort comes too late.   20
DIG. Though Thestylis the scorpion be
    that breaks his sweet assault,
Yet will Rhamnusia [13] vengeance take
    on her disdainful fault.

[3] Predetermined.   [6] Either.
[4] Strange.   [7] Poison.
[5] Experience.   [8] Perhaps.
[9] Emended by Dyce. Original reads *her*.
[10] Nature.   [11] Unfortunate.
[12] Dictamnum, a healing herb.
[13] Nemesis.

THE. Lo, yonder comes the lovely nymph,
that in these Ida vales
  Plays with Amyntas' lusty boy and
  coys [1] him in the dales!
HOB. Thenot, methinks her cheer is
changed; her mirthful looks are laid;
  She frolics not. Pray God the lad have
  not beguiled the maid!

ACT[US] III. SCENA iii.

*Œnone ent'reth with a wreath of poplar on
her head. Manent Pastores.* [2]

ŒN. Beguiled, disdained, and out of love!
Live long, thou poplar tree,
  And let thy letters grow in length, to
  witness this with me.
Ah, Venus, but for reverence unto thy
sacred name,
  To steal a silly maiden's love, I might
  account it blame!
And, if the tales be true I hear, and
blush for to recite,
  Thou dost me wrong to leave the plains
  and dally out of sight.
False Paris, this was not thy vow, when
thou and I were one,
  To range and change old love for new;
  but now those days be gone.
But I will find the goddess out, that she
thy vow may read,
  And fill these woods with my laments
  for thy unhappy deed.   10
HOB. So fair a face, so foul a thought to
harbor in his breast!
  Thy hope consumed, poor nymph, thy
  hap is worse than all the rest.
ŒN. Ah, shepherds, you bin full of wiles,
and whet your wits on books,
  And rap poor maids with pipes and
  songs, and sweet alluring looks!
DIG. Misspeak [3] not all for his amiss; [4]
there bin that keepen [5] flocks,
  That never chose but once, nor yet
  beguiléd love with mocks.
ŒN. False Paris, he is none of those;
his trothless double deed
  Will hurt a many shepherds else that
  might go nigh to speed. [6]

[1] Caresses.
[2] The shepherds remain.
[3] Reproach.
[4] Fault.
[5] Those who keep.
[6] Prosper (in love).

THE. Poor Colin, that is ill for thee, that
art as true in trust
  To thy sweet smart as to his nymph
  Paris hath been unjust.   20
ŒN. Ah, well is she hath Colin won, that
nill no other love!
  And woe is me. My luck is loss, my
  pains no pity move.
HOB. Farewell, fair nymph, sith he must
heal alone that gave the wound;
  There grows no herb of such effect upon
  Dame Nature's ground.

Exeunt Pastores.

[ACTUS III. SCENA iv.]

*Manet Œnone.   Mercu[ry] ent'r[eth] with
Vulcan's Cyclops.* [7]

MER. Here is a nymph that sadly sits,
and she belike
  Can tell some news, Pyracmon, of the
  jolly swain we seek.
Dare wage my wings, the lass doth love,
she looks so bleak and thin;
  And 'tis for anger or for grief—but I
  will talk begin.
ŒN. [*Aside.*] Break out, poor heart, and
make complaint, the mountain flocks
to move,
  What proud repulse and thankless scorn
  thou hast received of love.
MER. She singeth; sirs, be hushed awhile.

Œnone singeth as she sits.

ŒNONE'S COMPLAINT

Melpomene, the Muse of tragic songs,
With mournful tunes, in stole of dismal hue,
Assist a silly nymph to wail her woe,   10
And leave thy lusty company behind.
Thou luckless wreath! Becomes not me to
  wear
The poplar tree for triumph of my love.
Then, as my joy, my pride of love, is left,
Be thou unclothéd of thy lovely green;
And in thy leaves my fortune written be,
And them some gentle wind let blow
  abroad,
That all the world may see how false of love
False Paris hath to his Œnone been.

*The song ended, Œnone sitting still, Mercury
speaketh.*

MER. Good day, fair maid; weary belike
with following of your game,   20
  I wish thee cunning at thy will, to spare
  or strike the same.

[7] Used in this play for both singular and plural.

ŒN. I thank you, sir; my game is quick,[1] and rids [2] a length of ground,
And yet I am deceived, or else a had a deadly wound.
MER. Your hand perhaps did swarve [3] awry.
ŒN. Or else it was my heart.
MER. Then sure a plied his footmanship.
ŒN. A played a ranging part.
MER. You should have given a deeper wound.
ŒN. I could not that for pity.
MER. You should have eyed him better, then.
ŒN. Blind Love was not so witty.
MER. Why, tell me, sweet, are you in love?
ŒN. O,[4] would I were not so!
MER. Ye mean because a does ye wrong?
ŒN. Perdy, the more my woe.
MER. Why, mean ye Love, or him ye loved?
ŒN. Well may I mean them both. 30
MER. Is Love to blame?
ŒN. The Queen of Love hath made him false his troth.[5]
MER. Mean ye, indeed, the Queen of Love?
ŒN. Even wanton Cupid's dame.
MER. Why, was thy love so lovely then?
ŒN. His beauty hight [6] his shame—
The fairest shepherd on our green.
MER. Is he a shepherd, than?[7]
ŒN. And sometime kept a bleating flock.
MER. Enough, this is the man.
Where wones he, then?
ŒN. About these woods, far from the poplar tree.
MER. What poplar mean ye?
ŒN. Witness of the vows betwixt him and me.
And come and wend a little way, and you shall see his skill.
MER. Sirs, tarry you.
ŒN. Nay, let them go.
MER. Nay, not unless you will.
Stay, nymph, and hark what I say of him thou blamest so, 40
And, credit me, I have a sad discourse to tell thee ere I go.

Know then, my pretty mops, that I hight Mercury,
The messenger of heaven, and hether fly,
To seize upon the man whom thou dost love,
To summon him before my father Jove,
To answer matter of great consequence;
And Jove himself will not be long from hence.
ŒN. Sweet Mercury, and have poor Œnon's cries
For Paris' fault ypierced th' unpartial skies?
MER. The same is he, that jolly shepherd's swain. 50
ŒN. His flock do graze upon Aurora's plain;
The color of his coat is lusty green;
That would these eyes of mine had never seen
His ticing[8] curléd hair, his front[9] of ivory,
Then had not I, poor I, bin unhappy.
MER. No marvel, wench, although we cannot find him,
When all-too late[10] the Queen of Heaven doth mind him.
But, if thou wilt have physic for thy sore,
Mind him who list, remember thou him no more;
And find some other game, and get thee gone; 60
For here will lusty suitors come anon,
Too hot and lusty for thy dying vein,
Such as ne'er wont[11] to make their suits in vain.
  Exit Mer[cury] cum Cyclop[e].
ŒN. I will go sit and pine under the poplar tree,
And write my answer to his vow, that every eye may see. *Exit.*

ACT[US] III. SCENA v.

Venus, Paris, and a company of Shepherds.

VEN. Shepherds, I am content, for this sweet shepherd's sake,
A strange revenge upon the maid and her disdain to take.

---

[1] Alive. [2] Traverses. [3] Swerve.
[4] Suggested by Child. Original reads *or.*
[5] Break his promise. [6] Promised, assured.
[7] Then, a common Elizabethan spelling here retained for the rime.
[8] Enticing. [9] Forehead.
[10] Very lately.
[11] Suggested by Dyce; original reads *were monte.*

Let Colin's corpse be brought in place,
and buried [1] in the plain,
And let this be the verse, "The love
whom Thestylis hath slain."
And, trust me, I will chide my son for
partiality,
That gave the swain so deep a wound,
and let her scape him by.

Pasto[r]. Alas, that ever Love was blind,
to shoot so far amiss!

Ven. Cupid, my son, was more to blame;
the fault not mine, but his.

*Pastores exeunt. Manet Ven[us] cum Pa-
r[ide].*

Par. O madam, if yourself would deign
the handling of the bow,
Albeit it be a task, yourself more skill,
more justice know.   10

Ven. Sweet shepherd, didst thou ever
love?

Par.   Lady, a little once.

Ven. And art thou changed?

Par.   Fair Queen of Love,
I loved not all attonce.[2]

Ven. Well, wanton, wert thou wounded
so deep as some have been,
It were a cunning cure to heal, and rueful to be seen.

Par. But tell me, gracious goddess, for
a start [3] and false offense
Hath Venus or her son the power at
pleasure to dispense? [4]

Ven. My boy, I will instruct thee in a
piece of poetry
That haply erst [5] thou hast not heard:
in hell there is a tree
Where once a day do sleep the souls of
false forsworen lovers,
With open hearts; and thereabout in
swarms the number hovers   20
Of poor forsaken ghosts, whose wings
from off this tree do beat
Round drops of fiery Phlegiton to scorch
false hearts with heat.
This pain did Venus and her son en-
treat the Prince of Hell
T' impose to such as faithless were to
such as loved them well.
And therefore this, my lovely boy, fair
Venus doth advise thee:

Be true and steadfast in thy love; beware thou do disguise [6] thee,
For he that makes but love a jest, when
pleaseth him to start,
Shall feel those fiery water drops consume his faithless heart.

Par. Is Venus and her son so full of
justice and severity?

Ven. Pity it were that love should not
be linkéd with indifferency.   30
However lovers can exclaim for hard
success in love,
Trust me, some more than common
cause that painful hap doth move;
And Cupid's bow is not alone his triumph, but his rod.
Nor is he only but a boy—he hight a
mighty god;
And they that do him reverence have
reason for the same;
His shafts keep heaven and earth in
awe, and shape rewards for shame.

Par. And hath he reason to maintain why
Colin died for love?

Ven. Yea, reason good, I warrant thee;
in right it might behove.[7]

Par. Then be the name of Love adored;
his bow is full of might,
His wounds are all but for desert, his
laws are all but right.   40

[Ven.] Well, for this once me list [8] apply
my speeches to thy sense,[9]
And Thestylis shall feel the pain for
Love's supposed offense.

*The Shepherds bring in Colin's hearse, sing-
ing:*

Welladay, welladay, poor Colin, thou art
going to the ground,
The love whom Thestylis hath slain—
Hard heart, fair face, fraught with dis-
dain,
Disdain in love a deadly wound.
Wound her, sweet Love, so deep again,
That she may feel the dying pain
Of this unhappy shepherd's swain,   49
And die for love as Colin died, as Colin died.

Finis camenæ.

Ven. Shepherds, abide; let Colin's corpse
be witness of the pain
That Thestylis endures in love, a plague
for her disdain.

---

[1] Emended by Dyce. Original reads *burned.*
[2] At once.
[3] Deviation (from right).
[4] Give dispensation.   [5] Before.

[6] Alter.   [7] It was needful.   [8] It pleases me.
[9] *I.e.,* adapt my commands to thy judgment.

Behold the organ of our wrath, this
rusty churl is he;
She dotes on his ill-favored face, so
much accursed is she.
*She singeth an old song called "The Wooing
of Colman."*

*A foul, crooked Churl enters, and Thestylis,
a fair lass, wooeth him. He crabbedly
refuseth her, and goeth out of place. She
tarrieth behind.*

PAR. Ah, poor unhappy Thestylis, un-
pitied is thy pain!
VEN. Her fortune not unlike to hers [1]
whom cruel thou hast slain.
Thestylis singeth, and the Shepherds reply.

THE SONG

[THEST.] The strange affects [2] of my tor-
mented heart,
Whom cruel love hath woeful prisoner
caught,
Whom cruel hate hath into bondage
brought,
Whom wit no way of safe escape hath
taught,   60
Enforce me say, in witness of my smart,
There is no pain to [3] foul disdain in
hardy suits of love.
SHEP. There is no pain, etc.
THEST. Cruel, farewell.
SHEP. Cruel, farewell.
THEST. Most cruel thou, of all that nature
framed.
SHEP. Most cruel, etc.
THEST. To kill thy love with thy disdain.
SHEP. To kill thy love with thy disdain.
THEST. Cruel Disdain, so live thou named.
SHEP. Cruel Disdain, etc.   71
THEST. And let me die of Iphis' pain.
SHEP. A life too good for thy disdain.
THEST. Sith this my stars to me allot,
And thou thy love hast all forgot.
                              Exit Thest[ylis].
SHEP. And thou, etc.

*The grace of this song is in the Shepherds'
echo to her verse.*
VEN. Now, shepherds, bury Colin's
corpse, perfume his hearse with flowers,
And write what justice Venus did amid
these woods of yours.
                The Shepherds carry out Colin. [4]

[1] Emended by Dyce. Original reads *his*.
[2] Feelings; original has *effects*.
[3] Comparable to.
[4] In the original this direction appears immediately after the song.

How now, how cheers my lovely boy
after this dump [5] of love?
PAR. Such dumps, sweet lady, as bin
these are deadly dumps to prove.   80
VEN. Cease, shepherd; there [6] are other
news after this melancholy.
My mind presumes some tempest toward [7] upon the speech of Mercury.

ACT[US] III. SCENA vi.

*Mercury with Vulcan's Cyclops enter. Ma-
nentibus Ven[ere] cum Par[ide].*

MER. Fair Lady Venus, let me pardoned
be,
That have of long been well-beloved of
thee,
If, as my office bids, myself first brings
To my sweet madam these unwelcome
tidings.
VEN. What news, what tidings, gentle
Mercury,
In middest of my delights to trouble
me?
MER. At Juno's suit, Pallas assisting her,
Sith both did join in suit to Jupiter,
Action is entered in the court of heaven;
And me, the swiftest of the planets
seven,   10
With warrant they have thence des-
patched away
To apprehend and find the man, they
say,
That gave from them that selfsame ball
of gold,
Which, I presume, I do in place behold;
Which man, unless my marks be taken
wide, [8]
Is he that sits so near thy gracious side.
This being so, it rests he go from hence,
Before the gods to answer his offense.
VEN. What tale is this? Doth Juno and
her mate
Pursue this shepherd with such deadly
hate,   20
As what was then our general agree-
ment
To stand unto, they nill be now content?
Let Juno jet, [9] and Pallas play her part;
What here I have, I won it by desert;

[5] Mournful song.
[6] Original reads *these*.
[7] Near at hand.
[8] Unless I am wide of the mark.
[9] Strut.

And heaven and earth shall both con-
　founded be,
Ere wrong in this be done to him or me.
Mer. This little fruit, if Mercury can
　spell,[1]
Will send, I fear, a world of souls to
　hell.
Ven. What mean these Cyclops, Mercury?
　Is Vulcan waxed so fine,
To send his chimney-sweepers forth to
　fetter any friend of mine?—　　30
Abash not, shepherd, at the thing; my-
　self thy bail will be.—
He shall be present at the court of
　Jove, I warrant thee.
Mer. Venus, give me your pledge.
Ven.　　My ceston,[2] or my fan, or both?
Mer. (*Taketh her fan.*) Nay, this shall
　serve, your word to me as sure as is
　your oath,
At Diana's bower! And, lady, if my wit
　or policy
May profit him, for Venus' sake let him
　make bold with Mercury.
　　　　Exit [with the Cyclops].
Ven. Sweet Paris, whereon dost thou
　muse?
Par. The angry heavens, for this fatal jar,
Name me the instrument of dire and
　deadly war.
*Explicit Actus Tertius.　Exeunt Venus et
　　　　　　　　　　　　Paris.*

Act[us] IV.　Scena i.

Vulcan, following one of Diana's Nymphs.

Vul. Why, nymph, what need ye run so
　fast? What though but black I be?
I have more pretty knacks to please
　than every eye doth see;
And though I go not so upright, and
　though I am a smith,
To make me gracious you may have
　some other thing therewith.

Act[us] IV.　Scena ii.

Bacchus, Vulcan, Nymph.

Bac. Yea, Vulcan, will ye so indeed?—
　Nay, turn and tell him, trull,
He hath a mistress of his own to take
　his bellyful.

Vul. Why, sir, if Phœbe's dainty nymph
　please lusty Vulcan's tooth,
Why may not Vulcan tread awry as well
　as Venus doth?
Nym. Ye shall not taint your troth for
　me. You wot it very well,
All that be Dian's maids are vowed to
　halter apes[3] in hell.[4]
Bac. I' faith, i' faith, my gentle mops, but
　I do know a cast[5]—
Lead apes who list—that we would help
　t'unhalter them as fast.
Nym. Fie, fie, your skill is wondrous great!
　Had thought the God of Wine
Had tended but his tubs and grapes,
　and not been half so fine.　　10
Vul. Gramercy for that quirk, my girl.
Bac.　　That's one of dainty's frumps.[6]
Nym. I pray, sir, take't with all amiss;
　our cunning comes by lumps.
Vul. Sh'ath capped his answer in the Q.[7]
Nym.　　How says a, has she so?
As well as she that capped your head
　to keep you warm below.
Vul. Yea, then you will be curst,[8] I see.
Bac.　　Best let her even alone.
Nym. Yea, gentle gods, and find some
　other string to harp upon.
Bac. Some other string! Agreed, i'faith,
　some other pretty thing;
'Twere shame fair maids should idle
　be. How say you, will ye sing?
Nym. Some rounds or merry roundelays;
　we sing no other songs.
Your melancholic notes not to our
　country mirth belongs.　　20
Vul. Here comes a crew will help us
　trim.[9]

Actus IV.　Scena iii.

Mercury with the Cyclops.

Mer. Yea, now our task is done.
Bac. Then, merry Mercury, more than
　time this round were well begun.
They sing "Hey down, down, down," etc.

*The song done, she windeth a horn in Vul-
　can's ear, and runneth out.　Manent
　Vulc[an], Bac[chus], Mer[cury], Cyclops.*

[3] Emended by Dyce. Original reads *apples.*
[4] Proverbial reward of spinsterhood.
[5] Trick.　　　　　　　　　　[7] Question.
[6] Mocks, sneers.　　　　　　[8] Shrewish.
[9] Balance the parts (of the song).

[1] Foretell.　　　　　　　　[2] Cestus, girdle.

VUL. A harlotry,[1] I warrant her!

BAC. 　　　　A peevish, elvish shroe![2]

MER. Have seen as far to come as near,
　for all her ranging so.
　But, Bacchus, time well-spent; I wot
　our sacred father Jove
　With Phœbus and the God of War are
　met in Dian's grove.

VUL. Then we are here before them yet;
　but stay—the earth doth swell!
　God Neptune, too (this hap is good),
　doth meet the Prince of Hell.

*Pluto ascendeth from below in his chair;
　　Neptune ent'reth at another way.*

PLU. What jars are these that call the
　gods of heaven and hell below?

NEP. It is a work of wit and toil to rule
　a lusty shroe.　　　　　　　　　10

ACT[US] IV.　SCENA iv.

*Enter Jupiter, Saturn, Apollo, Mars, Pluto,
　Neptune, Bacchus, Vulcan, Mer[cury],
　Juno, Pallas, Diana, Cyclops.　Jupiter
　speaketh.*

JUP. Bring forth the man of Troy, that
　he may hear
　Whereof he is to be arraignéd here.

NEP. Lo, where a comes, prepared to plead
　his case,
　Under conduct of lovely Venus' grace!

[Enter Venus with Paris.]

MER. I have not seen a more alluring boy.

APOL. So beauty hight the wrack of
　Priam's Troy.

*The Gods being set in Diana's bower, Juno,
　Pallas, Diana, Venus, and Paris stand
　　　　　　on sides before them.*

VEN. Lo, sacred Jove, at Juno's proud
　complaint,
　As erst I gave my pledge to Mercury,
　I bring the man whom he did late at-
　taint,[3]
　To answer his indictment orderly;　　10
　And crave this grace of this immortal
　senate,
　That ye allow the man his advocate.

PAL. That may not be; the laws of heaven
　deny
　A man to plead or answer by attorney.

VEN. Pallas, thy doom is all too peremptory.

APOL. Venus, that favor is denied him
　flatly:
　He is a man, and therefore by our laws,
　Himself, without his aid, must plead
　his cause.

VEN. Then bash not,[4] shepherd, in so
　good a case;
　And friends thou hast, as well as foes,
　in place.　　　　　　　　　　20

JUN. Why, Mercury, why do ye not in-
　dict him?

VEN. Soft, gentle Juno, I pray you, do
　not bite him.

JUN. Nay, gods, I trow you are like to
　have great silence
　Unless this parrot be commanded hence.

JUP.[5] Venus, forbear, be still.—Speak,
　Mercury.

VEN. If Juno jangle, Venus will reply.

MER. Paris, King Priam's son, thou art
　arraigned of partiality,
　Of sentence partial and unjust, for that
　without indifferency,[6]
　Beyond desert or merit fair, as thine
　accusers say,
　From them to Lady Venus here thou
　gavest the prize away.　　　　30
　What is thine answer?

PARIS' ORATION TO THE COUNCIL OF THE GODS

[PAR.] Sacred and just, thou great and
　dreadful Jove,
　And you thrice-reverend powers, whom
　love nor hate
　May wrest awry, if this to me, a man,
　This fortune fatal[7] be, that I must plead
　For safe excusal of my guiltless thought,
　The honor more makes my mishap the less
　That I, a man, must plead before the
　gods—
　Gracious forbearers[8] of the world's
　amiss—
　For her, whose beauty how it hath en-
　ticed,　　　　　　　　　　　40
　This heavenly senate may with me aver.
　But sith nor that nor this may do me boot,
　And for myself myself must speaker be,
　A mortal man amidst this heavenly
　presence,

---

[1] "Baggage."　[2] Shrew.　[3] Accuse, arrest.

[4] Be not abashed.　　　　[7] Decreed.
[5] Original reads *Jov.*　　[8] Tolerators.
[6] Impartiality.

Let me not shape a long defense to them
That been beholders of my guiltless
thoughts.
Then for the deed that I may not deny,
Wherein consists the full of mine of-
fense,
I did upon command; if then I erred,
I did no more than to a man belonged. 50
And if, in verdit [1] of their forms divine,
My dazzled eye did swarve or surfeit
more
On Venus' face than any face of theirs,
It was no partial fault, but fault of his,
Belike, whose eyesight not so perfect
was
As might discern the brightness of the
rest.
And, if it were permitted unto men,
Ye gods, to parley with your secret
thoughts,
There been that sit upon that sacred
seat
That would with Paris err in Venus'
praise.   60
But let me cease to speak of error here,
Sith what my hand, the organ of my
heart,
Did give with good agreement of mine
eye,
My tongue is void with process to main-
tain. [2]
PLU. A jolly shepherd, wise and eloquent!
PAR. First, then, arraigned of partiality,
Paris replies, "Unguilty of the fact;" [3]
His reason is, because he knew no more
Fair Venus' ceston than Dame Juno's
mace,
Nor never saw wise Pallas' crystal
shield.   70
Then, as I looked, I loved and liked
attonce,
And, as it was referred from them to
me,
To give the prize to her whose beauty
best
My fancy did commend, so did I praise
And judge as might my dazzled eye
discern.
NEP. A piece of art, that cunningly,
perdy,
Refers the blame to weakness of his eye.

PAR. Now—for I must add reason for
my deed—
Why Venus rather pleased me of the
three: 79
First, in the entrails [4] of my mortal ears,
The question standing upon beauty's
blaze, [5]
The name of her that hight the Queen
of Love,
Methought [6] in beauty should not be
excelled.
Had it been destinéd to majesty—
Yet will I not rob Venus of her grace—
Then stately Juno might have borne
the ball.
Had it to wisdom been intituléd,
My human wit had given it Pallas then.
But, sith unto the fairest of the three
That power that threw it for my far-
ther ill   90
Did dedicate this ball, and safest durst
My shepherd's skill adventure, as I
thought,
To judge of form and beauty rather
than
Of Juno's state or Pallas' worthiness,
That learned to ken the fairest of the
flock,
And praiséd beauty but by nature's
aim,
Behold, to Venus Paris gave this fruit,
A daysman [7] chosen there by full consent;
And heavenly powers should not repent
their deeds.
Where it is said beyond desert of hers 100
I honored Venus with this golden prize,
Ye gods, alas, what can a mortal man
Discern betwixt the sacred gifts of
heaven?
Or, if I may with reverence reason thus,
Suppose I gave—and judged corruptly
then,
For hope of that that best did please
my thought—
This apple, not for beauty's praise alone,
I might offend, sith I was pardonéd, [8]
And tempted more than ever creature
was
With wealth, with beauty, and with
chivalry,   110

---

[1] Verdict.
[2] Unable to explain in a detailed story.
[3] Deed.
[4] Turnings.   [5] Blazon, proclamation.
[6] Emended by Dyce.   Original reads *my*·
thought.   [7] Judge.
[8] Released from liability to punishment.

And so preferred beauty before them all,
The thing that hath enchanted heaven
　itself.
And for the one, contentment is my
　wealth;
A shell of salt will serve a shepherd swain,
A slender banquet in a homely scrip,[1]
And water running from the silver
　spring.
For arms, they dread no foes that sit so
　low;
A thorn[2] can keep the wind from off
　my back;
A sheepcote thatched, a shepherd's
　palace hight.
Of tragic muses shepherds con[3] no
　skill;　　　　　　　　　　　　　120
Enough is them, if Cupid been dis-
　pleased,
To sing his praise on slender oaten pipe.
And thus, thrice-reverend, have I told
　my tale,
And crave the torment of my guiltless
　soul
To be measured by my faultless thought.
If warlike Pallas or the Queen of Heaven
Sue to reverse my sentence by appeal,
Be it as please your majesties divine;
The wrong, the hurt, not mine, if any
　be,
But hers whose beauty claimed the prize
　of me.　　　　　　　　　　　130
　　Paris having ended, Jupiter speaketh.
JUP. Venus, withdraw your shepherd for
　a space,
Till he again be called for into place.
　　　　　　　Exeunt Venus et Paris.
Juno, what will ye after this reply,
But doom with sentence of indifferency?
And, if you will but justice in the cause,
The man must quited[4] be by heaven's
　laws.
JUN. Yea, gentle Jove, when Juno's suits
　are moved,
Then heaven may see how well she is
　beloved!
APOL. But, madam, fits it majesty divine
In any sort from justice to decline?　　140
PAL. Whether the man be guilty, yea or
　no,
That doth not hinder our appeal, I
　trow.

JUN. Phœbus, I wot, amid this heavenly
　crew,
There be that have to say as well as you.
APOL. And, Juno, I with them, and they
　with me,
In law and right must needfully agree.
PAL. I grant ye may agree, but be content
To doubt upon regard of[5] your agree-
　ment.
PLU. And, if ye marked, the man in his
　defense
Said thereof as a might with rever-
　ence.　　　　　　　　　　　150
VUL. And did ye very well, I promise ye.
JUN. No doubt, sir, you could note it
　cunningly.
SAT. Well, Juno, if ye will appeal, ye may;
But first despatch the shepherd hence
　away.
MARS. Then Vulcan's dame is like to have
　the wrong.
JUN. And that in passion[6] doth to Mars
　belong!
JUP. Call Venus and the shepherd in
　again.　　　　　　*[Exit Mercury.]*
BAC. And rid[7] the man that he may
　know his pain.[8]
APOL. His pain, his pain, his never-dying
　pain,　　　　　　　　　　　159
A cause to make a many mo complain.

Mercury bringeth in Venus and Paris.

JUP. Shepherd, thou hast been heard with
　equity and law,
And, for[9] thy stars do thee to other call-
　ing draw,
We here dismiss thee hence, by order
　of our senate;
Go take thy way to Troy, and there
　abide thy fate.
VEN. Sweet shepherd, with such luck in
　love, while thou dost live,
As may the Queen of Love to any lover
　give!
PAR. My luck is loss, howe'er my love do
　speed.
I fear me Paris shall but rue his deed.
　　　　　　　　　　Paris exit.
APOL. From Ida woods now wends the
　shepherd's boy,
That in his bosom carries fire to Troy. 170

---

[1] Wallet.　　　　　　　[3] Know, have.
[2] Thorn tree.　　　　　[4] Freed.
[5] Hesitate in respect to.　[8] Sentence, fate.
[6] Sorrow.　　　　　　[9] Because.
[7] Free.

JUP. Venus, these ladies do appeal, you
  see,
  And that they may appeal the gods
    agree.
  It resteth, then, that you be well content
  To stand in this unto our final judg-
    ment;
  And, if King Priam's son did well in
    this,
  The law of heaven will not lead amiss.
VEN. But, sacred Jupiter, might thy
  daughter choose,
  She might with reason this appeal re-
    fuse;
  Yet, if they be unmovéd in their shames,
  Be it a stain and blemish to their
    names, 180
  A deed too far unworthy of the place,
  Unworthy Pallas' lance or Juno's mace;
  And, if to beauty it bequeathéd be,
  I doubt not but it will return to me.
              She layeth down the ball.
PAL. Venus, there is no more ado than
  so;
  It resteth where the gods do it bestow.
NEP. But, ladies—under favor of your
  rage—
  Howe'er it be, you play upon the van-
    tage.[1]
JUP. Then, dames, that we more freely
  may debate,
  And hear th' indifferent sentence of
    this senate, 190
  Withdraw you from this presence for
    a space,
  Till we have throughly questioned of
    the case.
  Dian shall be your guide; nor shall you
    need
  Yourselves t' inquire how things do
    here succeed;
  We will, as we resolve, give you to know,
  By general doom how everything doth go.
DIAN. Thy will, my wish.—Fair ladies,
  will ye wend?
JUN. Beshrew her whom this sentence
  doth offend.
VEN. Now, Jove, be just; and, gods, you
  that be Venus' friends,
  If you have ever done her wrong, then
    may you make amends. 200
Manent dii.[2] *Exeunt Diana, Pallas, Juno,*
                  Venus.

[1] Have the advantage.   [2] The gods remain.

JUP. Venus is fair; Pallas and Juno too.
VUL. But tell me now, without some
  more ado,
  Who is the fairest she, and do not
    flatter.
PLU. Vulcan, upon comparison hangs all
  the matter;
  That done, the quarrel and the strife
    were ended.
MARS. Because 'tis known the quarrel
  is pretended.
VUL. Mars, you have reason for your
  speech, perdy;
  My dame, I trow, is fairest in your
    eye.
MARS. Or, Vulcan, I should do her double
  wrong.
SAT. About a toy we tarry here so long. 210
  Give it by voices; voices give the
    odds;
  A trifle so to trouble all the gods!
NEP. Believe me, Saturn, be it so for me.
BAC. For me.
PLU.   For me.
MARS.   For me, if Jove agree.
MER. And, gentle gods, I am indifferent;
  But then I know who's likely to be
    shent.[3]
APOL. Thrice-reverend gods, and thou,
  immortal Jove,
  If Phœbus may, as him doth much be-
    hove,
  Be licenséd, according to our laws,
  To speak uprightly in this doubted [4]
    cause 220
  (Sith women's wits work men's unceas-
    ing woes)
  To make them friends, that now bin
    friendless foes,
  And peace to keep with them, with us,
    and all,
  That make their title to this golden
    ball—
  Nor think, ye gods, my speech doth de-
    rogate
  From sacred power of this immortal
    senate—
  Refer this sentence where it doth be-
    long.
  In this, say I, fair Phœbe hath the
    wrong;
  Not that I mean her beauty bears the
    prize, 229

[3] Reproved.   [4] Dreaded.

But that the holy law of heaven denies
One god to meddle in another's power;
And this befell so near Diana's bower
As, for th' appeasing this unpleasant grudge,
In my conceit [1] she hight the fittest judge.
If Jove comptrol [2] not Pluto's hell with charms,
If Mars have sovereign power to manage arms,
If Bacchus bear no rule in Neptune['s] sea,
Nor Vulcan's fire doth Saturn's scythe obey,
Suppress not then, gainst law and equity,
Diana's power in her own territory,　240
Whose regiment, [3] amid her sacred bowers,
As proper hight as any rule of yours.
Well may we so wipe all the speech away
That Pallas, Juno, Venus hath to say,
And answer that, by justice of our laws,
We were not suffered to conclude the cause.
And this to me most egal [4] doom appears—
A woman to be judge among her feres.
MER. Apollo hath found out the only mean
To rid the blame from us and trouble clean.　250
VUL. We are beholding [5] to his sacred wit.
JUP. I can commend and well allow of it;
And so derive [6] the matter from us all,
That Dian have the giving of the ball.
VUL. So Jove may clearly excuse him in the case,
Where Juno else would chide and brawl apace.　*All they rise to [7] go forth.*
MER. And now it were some cunning to divine
To whom Diana will this prize resign.
VUL. Sufficeth me, it shall be none of mine!
BAC. Vulcan, though thou be black, th'art nothing fine.　260
VUL. Go bathe thee, Bacchus, in a tub of wine;
The ball's as likely to be mine as thine!
Exeunt omnes. Explicit Act[us] Quartus.

[1] Opinion.　　[3] Rule.　　[5] Beholden, indebted.
[2] Control.　　[4] Equal.　　[6] Divert
[7] Emended by Bullen. Original reads *and.*

ACT[US] V ET ULTIMI SCENA i.[8]

Diana, Pallas, Juno, Venus.

DIAN. Lo, ladies, far beyond my hope and will, you see,
This thankless office is imposed to me;
Wherein, if you will rest as well content
As Dian will be judge indifferent,
My egal doom shall none of you offend,
And of this quarrel make a final end.
And therefore, whether you be lief or loath,
Confirm your promise with some sacred oath.
PAL. Phœbe, chief mistress of this sylvan chase,
Whom gods have chosen to conclude the case　10
That yet in balance undecided lies,
Touching bestowing of this golden prize,
I give my promise and mine oath withal,
By Styx, by heaven's power imperial,
By all that 'longs to Pallas' deity,
Her shield, her lance, ensigns of chivalry,
Her sacred wreath of olive and of bay,
Her crested helm, and else what Pallas may,
That wheresoe'er this ball of purest gold,
That chaste Diana here in hand doth hold,　20
Unpartially her wisdom shall bestow,
Without mislike or quarrel any mo
Pallas shall rest content and satisfied,
And say the best desert doth there abide.
JUN. And here I promise and protest withal,
By Styx, by heaven's power imperial,
By all that longs to Juno's deity,
Her crown, her mace, ensigns of majesty,
Her spotless marriage rites, her league divine,
And by that holy name of Proserpine,　30
That wheresoe'er this ball of purest gold,
That chaste Diana here in hand doth hold,
Unpartially her wisdom shall bestow,
Without mislike or quarrel any mo
Juno shall rest content and satisfied,
And say the best desert doth there abide.
VEN. And, lovely Phœbe, for I know thy doom

[8] The first scene of the fifth and last act.

Will be no other than shall thee become,
Behold, I take thy dainty hand to kiss,
And with my solemn oath confirm my
    promise,   40
By Styx, by Jove's immortal empery,
By Cupid's bow, by Venus' myrtle tree,
By Vulcan's gift, my ceston and my
    fan,
By this red rose, whose color first began
When erst my wanton boy (the more
    his blame)
Did draw his bow awry and hurt his
    dame,
By all the honor and the sacrifice
That from Cithæron and from Paphos
    rise,

The con- ⎫ That wheresoe'er, ⎫
clusion   ⎬   etc.   ⎬ *ut supra.*[1]
above   ⎭ Venus shall rest,   ⎭
               etc.

Diana, having taken their oaths, speaketh.
Diana describeth the nymph Eliza, a
*   figure of the queen.*[2]
DIAN. It is enough, and, goddesses, at-
    tend: 51
    There wones within these pleasant
        shady woods,
    Where neither storm nor sun's dis-
        temperature
    Have power to hurt by cruel heat or
        cold,
    Under the climate of the milder heaven,
    Where seldom lights Jove's angry thun-
        derbolt,
    For favor of that sovereign earthly
        peer,
    Where whistling winds make music
        'mong the trees,
    Far from disturbance of our country
        gods,
    Amids the cypress-springs, a gracious
        nymph,   60
    That honor[s] Dian for her chastity,
    And likes the labors well of Phœbe's
        groves.
    The place Elysium hight, and of the
        place
    Her name that governs there Eliza is—
    A kingdom that may well compare with
        mine,
    An ancient seat of kings, a second Troy,

Ycompassed round with a commodious
    sea;
Her people are yclepéd [3] *Angeli,*
Or, if I miss, a letter is the most.   69
She giveth laws of justice and of peace;
And on her head, as fits her fortune best,
She wears a wreath of laurel, gold, and
    palm;
Her robes of purple and of scarlet dye;
Her veil of white, as best befits a maid.
Her ancestors live in the House of Fame.
She giveth arms of happy victory,
And flowers to deck her lions crowned
    with gold.
This peerless nymph, whom heaven and
    earth beloves,
This paragon, this only, this is she,   79
In whom do meet so many gifts in one,
On whom our country gods so often
    gaze,
In honor of whose name the Muses
    sing—
In state Queen Juno's peer, for power
    in arms
And virtues of the mind Minerva's mate,
As fair and lovely as the Queen of Love,
As chaste as Dian in her chaste desires.
The same is she, if Phœbe do no wrong,
To whom this ball in merit doth belong.
PAL. If this be she whom some Zabeta
    call,
    To whom thy wisdom well bequeaths
        the ball,   90
    I can remember, at her day of birth,
    How Flora with her flowers strewed the
        earth,
    How every power with heavenly maj-
        esty
    In person honored that solemnity.
JUN. The lovely Graces were not far
    away;
    They threw their balm for triumph [4]
        of the day.
VEN. The Fates, against their kind, be-
    gan a cheerful song,
    And vowed her life with favor to prolong.
    Then first gan [5] Cupid's eyesight wexen [6]
        dim;
    Belike Eliza's beauty blinded him.   100
    To this fair nymph, not earthly, but
        divine,
    Contents it me my honor to resign.

PAL. To this fair queen, so beautiful and
    wise,
  Pallas bequeaths her title in the prize.
JUN. To her whom Juno's looks so well
    become,
  The Queen of Heaven yields at Phœbe's [1]
    doom;
  And glad I am Diana found the art,
  Without offense so well to please desert.
DIAN. Then mark my tale: the usual
    time is nigh,
  When wont [2] the dames of life and des-
    tiny,   110
  In robes of cheerful colors, to repair
  To this renownéd queen so wise and
    fair,
  With pleasant songs this peerless nymph
    to greet.
  Clotho lays down her distaff at her
    feet;
  And Lachesis doth pull the thread at
    length;
  The third with favor gives it stuff and
    strength,
  And, for [3] contrary kind, affords her
    leave,
  As her best likes, her web of life to
    weave.
  This time we will attend, and in the
    mean while
  With some sweet song the tediousness
    beguile.   120
*The music sound, and the Nymphs within
sing or solfa with voices and instruments
awhile. Then enter Clotho, Lachesis,
and Atropos, singing as follows, the
state [4] being in place:*

THE SONG

CLOTH. *Humanæ vitæ filum sic volvere
  Parcæ.*
LACH. *Humanæ vitæ filum sic tendere
  Parcæ.*
ATRO. *Humanæ vitæ filum sic scindere
  Parcæ.*
CLOTH. *Clotho colum bajulat.*
LACH.   *Lachesis trahit.*
ATRO.   *Atropos occat.*

[1] Emended by Dyce. Original reads *Phœbus.*
[2] Are wont, accustomed.
[3] Probably a misprint for *far. Cf.* l. 152 for
the phrase *far indeed contrary kind (i.e.,* nature)
and also l. 144 for the Latin equivalent.
[4] Chair of state.

TRES SIMUL. *Vive diu, felix votis homi-
  numque deumque,
  Corpore, mente, libro, doctissima, candida,
  casta.* [5]
*They lay down their properties at the Queen's
                     feet.*
CLOTH. *Clotho colum pedibus,*
LACH. *Lachesis tibi pendula fila,*
ATRO. *Et fatale tuis manibus ferrum Atro-
  pos offert.*
[TRES SIMUL.] *Vive diu, felix, etc.* [6]   130
*The song being ended, Clotho speaks to the
                    Queen.*
CLOTH. Gracious and wise, fair queen of
    rare renown,
  Whom heaven and earth beloves, amid
    thy train—
  Noble and lovely peers—to honor thee
  And do thee favor more than may belong
  By nature's law to any earthly wight,[7]
  Behold continuance of our yearly due.
  Th' unpartial dames of destiny, we meet,
  As have the gods and we agreed in one,
  In reverence of Eliza's noble name;
  And humbly, lo, her distaff Clotho
    yields!   140
LACH. Her spindle Lachesis, and her fa-
    tal reel,
  Lays down in reverence at Eliza's feet.
  *Te tamen in terris unam tria numina
    Divam
  Invita statuunt naturæ lege sorores,
  Et tibi, non aliis, didicerunt parcere
    Parcæ.* [8]

[5] CLOTH. Thus the Fates spin the thread of
  human life.
LACH. Thus the Fates measure the thread of
  human life.
ATRO. Thus the Fates cut the thread of human life.
CLOTH. Clotho bears the distaff.
LACH.   Lachesis measures.
ATRO.   Atropos cuts.
THE THREE TOGETHER. Live long, happy in
  the prayers of men and gods,
  Chaste in body, pure in mind, most skilled in
  learning.
[6] CLOTH. Clotho [places] the distaff at thy
  feet,
LACH. Lachesis [gives] thee the pendent threads,
ATRO. And Atropos puts into your hands the
  fateful shears.
[THE THREE TOGETHER.] Live long, happy, etc.
[7] Person.
[8] The three divine sisters, despite the law of
nature, appoint thee a goddess unique, though on
earth; and thee and no others have the Fates
learned to spare.

ATRO. Dame Atropos, according as her feres,
To thee, fair queen, resigns her fatal knife.
Live long the noble phœnix of our age,
Our fair Eliza, our Zabeta fair! 149
DIAN. And lo, beside this rare solemnity
And sacrifice these dames are wont to do,
A favor, far indeed contrary kind,
Bequeathéd is unto thy worthiness—
She delivereth the ball of gold to the Queen's own hands.
This prize from heaven and heavenly goddesses!
Accept it, then, thy due by Dian's doom,
Praise of the wisdom, beauty, and the state,

That best becomes thy peerless excellency.
VEN. So, fair Eliza, Venus doth resign
The honor of this honor to be thine.
JUN. So is the Queen of Heaven content likewise 160
To yield to thee her title in the prize.
PAL. So Pallas yields the praise hereof to thee,
For wisdom, princely state, and peerless beauty.

EPILOGUS

OMNES SIMUL. *Vive diu felix, votis hominumque deumque,*
Corpore, mente, libro, doctissima, candida, casta. *Exeunt omnes.*
FINIS.

GEORGE PEELE

THE OLD WIVES' TALE

The Old Wives' Tale, entered on the Stationers' Register in 1595 and printed in the same year as being by "G.P." (identified by William Herbert in his revision of Joseph Ames's *Typographical Antiquities* in 1785–90), has occasioned scholarly students considerable perplexity on several scores. For one thing, since it is considerably shorter than most Elizabethan plays, there has been speculation that the present text represents an abbreviated and mutilated version of the original play, perhaps cut down by the Queen's Men for one of their provincial tours. (See Harold Jenkins, *MLN*, 1939, and Horne.) There has also been much critical disagreement as to Peele's intentions in writing the play: Is it to be regarded as a fantastic and romantic comedy or as a satire or even a burlesque of this genre? A considerable part of the controversy has centered on the identification of the blustering, pedantic braggart, Huanebango, whose name has been taken by some as a parody of the name of the great romantic hero of the medieval French *chanson de geste*, Huon of Bordeaux. Philip Henslowe's diary of his theatrical transactions records the performance of a play entitled *Hewen of Burdoche* on December 28, 1593. In "The Date of Peele's *The Old Wives' Tale*" (*MP*, 1932), Larsen developed the previous theory that Huanebango was intended as a caricature of Spenser's friend, the learned and quarrelsome classical scholar Gabriel Harvey. Harvey had quarreled with Lyly in 1589 and with Nashe and Greene in 1592/3, and had been mocked as "Gabriel Huffe-Snuffe" by Nashe. The fact that Harvey had violently advocated the use of the hexameter and of Latin quantity verse as the standard English meter (a form adopted by Richard Stanyhurst in his translation of the first four books of the *Aeneid* in 1583) and that Peele put tags from Stanyhurst into the mouth of Huanebango lends some validity to this claim.

But even though Huanebango is recognized as a topical satirical portrait, this identification alone is not sufficient to turn the whole play into simply a burlesque of romantic comedy and make it the first English literary satire of the drama, as Schelling, G. P. Baker, Tucker Brooke, and P. H. Cheffaud (in his *George Peele*, Paris, 1913) have regarded it. More recent critics, like Gwenan Jones ("The Intention of Peele's *Old Wives' Tale*, *AS*, 1925), Larsen ("*The Old Wives' Tale* by George Peele," *TRSC*, 1935), and Robert L. Blair (*An Edition of George Peele's "Old Wives' Tale*," a University of Illinois Ph.D. dissertation, 1956), have preferred to regard it as essentially a romantic fantasy with satirical overtones. A. K. McIlwraith in his comments on the play in *Five Elizabethan Comedies* (Oxford University Press, 1934) suggested that the most appreciative point of view from which to read it would be to look at it as a sort of dream fairy-tale, as implied by Old Madge and her listeners in the induction and the conclusion. Thus, even in the play's present form, its superficial weaknesses in plot, coherence, motivation, and characterization would turn into virtues, and be supported by the lyric element of the songs, the homely humor of the rural characters, and, especially, the use of both English and classical folklore.

Peele's obviously thorough steeping in folklore has long been recognized. The play is essentially a medley of motives and incidents drawn from folk tales. Thus the main incident—the pursuit of Delia and her rescue from the conjuror—gives the earliest extant version of a tale found also in a section of Christopher Middleton's *Chinon of England* (1597) and in Milton's *Comus*. All three are modified forms of the folk tale

243

Childe Rowland, in which the youngest of three brothers rescues his sister from the elf king after the other two have failed. In the play the successful brother is replaced by a suitor and his helper, who come from a tale of "The Lady and the Monster" type. Peele probably followed some form of it closely, for the main incidents and most of the details of the Eumenides plot appear in one version or another of a modern folk tale which is best known as one of the components of *Jack the Giant Killer*. A stock motive in a tale of this type is that of "The Grateful Dead," which Peele used in its most conventional form—the ghostly helper exacting a promise of half the hero's gains and as a test of loyalty demanding that the rescued lady be cut in two. In this form the motive is found, much earlier than in the play, *Oliver of Castile*, translated from the French and printed in England in 1518. Still another folk tale introduced into the play is *The Three Heads of the Well*, with its contrasted sisters, which is linked to the main thread by the marriage of the sisters to two who have failed in the quest for Delia. While Peele possibly found many of these various incidents already combined in some folk tale which he followed, evidently he made modifications in details. For instance, the contrast between the husbands of the two sisters in *The Three Heads of the Well* has been subordinated in the play to the treatment of them as stock comic figures, one a clown and the other a braggart. Although the induction, as in *The Taming of the Shrew* and *The Knight of the Burning Pestle*, satirizes the taste of the audience, its primary purpose here is to indicate the source of the material in folk tale. The name Sacrapant and some of the lines in the play came from Greene's *Orlando Furioso*, derived from Ariosto. Blair has also suggested that Peele, perhaps from his boyhood, may have been familiar with the Irish tales of "Beauty and the World" and "The King of Ireland's Son"—a possibility of some interest in view of what Horne calls Peele's "hibernian physical characteristics" and the belief of S. E. Winbolt (modern historian and Senior Classical Master of Christ's Hospital, in *George Peele*, London, n.d.) that the full name of George Peele's father may have been James Riley Peele. John Crow, in "Folklore in Elizabethan Drama" (*F*, 1947), has concentrated attention on *The Old Wives' Tale* and has brought many of these elements together, adding such other possible sources as "The White Bear of England's Wood."

The present text is based on W. W. Greg's reprint for the Malone Society (1907), compared with A. H. Bullen's edition of Peele's *Works* in 1888.

THE OLD WIVES' TALE[1]

BY

GEORGE PEELE

[DRAMATIS PERSONÆ

SACRAPANT, *the conjurer.*
FIRST BROTHER, *named* CALYPHA.
SECOND BROTHER, *named* THELEA.
EUMENIDES, *the Wandering Knight.*
OLD MAN, *named* ERESTUS.
LAMPRISCUS.
HUANEBANGO.
COREBUS, *or* BOOBY, *the clown.*
WIGGEN.
CHURCHWARDEN, *named* STEVEN LOACH.
SEXTON.
GHOST OF JACK.
FRIAR, HARVESTMEN, *and* HARVESTWOMEN,
   TWO FURIES, *and* FIDDLERS.

DELIA, *sister to Calypha and Thelea.*
VENELIA, *betrothed to Erestus.*
ZANTIPPA, *the Curst*[2] *Daughter of Lampriscus.*
CELANTA, *the Foul Wench, another daughter.*
HOSTESS.
ANTIC
FROLIC
FANTASTIC
A SMITH, *named*   *Characters of induction*
  CLUNCH   *and interscenes.*
OLD WOMAN, *his*
  wife, named
  MADGE

SCENE: *England and a part of Greece, near Thessaly.*

TIME: *Mythical.*]

Enter Antic, Frolic, and Fantastic.[3]

ANT. How now, fellow Frolic![4] What, all amort?[5] Doth this sadness become thy madness? What though we have lost our way in the woods, yet never hang the head as though thou hadst no hope to live till tomorrow; for Fantastic and I will warrant thy life tonight for twenty in the hundred.

FROL. Antic and Fantastic, as I am frolic franion,[6] never in all my life was I so dead slain. What, to lose our way in [10 the wood, without either fire or candle, so uncomfortable! *O cælum! O terra!*[7] *O Maria! O Neptune!*

FANT. Why makes thou it so strange, seeing Cupid hath led our young master to the fair lady, and she is the only saint that he hath sworn to serve?

FROL. What resteth[8] then but we commit him to his wench, and each of us take his stand up in a tree, and sing out our [20 ill fortune to the tune of "O man in desperation"?

ANT. Desperately spoken, fellow Frolic, in the dark; but, seeing it falls out thus, let us rehearse the old proverb:

"Three merry men, and three merry men,
  And three merry men be we;
I in the wood, and thou on the ground,
  And Jack sleeps in the tree."

FANT. Hush! A dog in the wood, or [30 a wooden[9] dog! O comfortable hearing! I had even as lief the chamberlain of the White Horse had called me up to bed.

---

[1] The traditional title of the play is retained, although *wives* was a common possessive singular, and although the original entry in the Stationers' Register for April 16, 1595, reads: "A booke or interlude, intituled a pleasant Conceipte called the owlde wifes tale." The title continues: "A Pleasant Conceited Comedy, Played by the Queen's Majesty's Players. Written by G. P."
[2] Peevish.
[3] In the original there is no scene division or indication of setting. The action represents what Madge and her group visualize.
[4] Original has *Franticke.*
[5] Dejected.   [6] An idle, carefree fellow.
[7] O heaven! O earth!
[8] Remaineth.   [9] Punning on *wood*, mad.

245

FROL. Either hath this trotting cur gone out of his circuit, or else are we near some

Enter a Smith, with a lantern and candle.

village, which should not be far off, for I perceive the glimmering of a glowworm, a candle, or a cat's eye, my life for a half-penny! In the name of my own father, be thou ox or ass that appearest, tell us [40 what thou art.

SMITH. What am I? Why, I am Clunch the smith. What are you? What make [1] you in my territories at this time of the night?

ANT. What do we make, dost thou ask? Why, we make faces for fear, such as, if thy mortal eyes could behold, would make thee water the long seams of thy side slops,[2] smith.   50

FROL. And, in faith, sir, unless your hospitality do relieve us, we are like to wander, with a sorrowful heigh-ho, among the owlets and hobgoblins of the forest. Good Vulcan, for Cupid's sake that hath cozened us all, befriend us as thou mayst; and command us howsoever, wheresoever, whensoever, in whatsoever, for ever and ever.

SMITH. Well, masters, it seems to [60 me you have lost your way in the wood; in consideration whereof, if you will go with Clunch to his cottage, you shall have house-room and a good fire to sit by, although we have no bedding to put you in.

ALL. O blessed smith, O bountiful Clunch!

SMITH. For your further entertainment, it shall be as it may be, so and so.
                                Hear a dog bark.
Hark![3] This is Ball, my dog, that [70 bids you all welcome in his own language. Come, take heed for stumbling on the threshold.—Open door, Madge; take in guests.

Enter Old Woman.

OLD WOM. Welcome, Clunch, and good fellows all, that come with my goodman. For my goodman's sake, come on, sit down. Here is a piece of cheese and a pudding of my own making.

---

[1] Do.   [2] Loose breeches.
[3] The scene is now at the cottage.

ANT. Thanks, gammer; a good ex- [80 ample for the wives of our town.

FROL. Gammer, thou and thy goodman sit lovingly together. We come to chat, and not to eat.

SMITH. Well, masters, if you will eat nothing, take away. Come, what do we to pass away the time? Lay a crab in the fire to roast for lamb's wool.[4] What, shall we have a game at trump or ruff [5] to drive away the time? How say you?   90

FANT. This smith leads a life as merry as a king with Madge his wife. Sirrah Frolic, I am sure thou art not without some round [6] or other; no doubt but Clunch can bear his part.

FROL. Else think you me ill brought up; so set to it when you will.   *They sing.*

SONG

Whenas the rye reach to the chin,
And chopcherry, chopcherry ripe [7] within,
Strawberries swimming in the cream, 100
And schoolboys playing in the stream;
Then O, then O, then O, my true love said,
Till that time come again,
She could not live a maid.

ANT. This sport does well, but methinks, gammer, a merry winter's tale would drive away the time trimly. Come, I am sure you are not without a score.

FANT. I' faith, gammer, a tale of an hour long were as good as an hour's sleep.   110

FROL. Look you, gammer, of the giant and the king's daughter, and I know not what. I have seen the day, when I was a little one, you might have drawn me a mile after you with such a discourse.

OLD WOM. Well, since you be so importunate, my goodman shall fill the pot and get him to bed. They that ply their work must keep good hours. One of you go lie with him; he is a clean-skinned [120 man, I tell you, without either spavin or windgall. So I am content to drive away the time with an old wives' winter's tale.

FANT. No better hay in Devonshire. O' my word, gammer, I'll be one of your audience.

---

[4] Ale mixed with the pulp of roasted crab-apples.
[5] Card games.   [6] Song.
[7] A game of catching a suspended cherry with the teeth.

FROL. And I another, that's flat.

ANT. Then must I to bed with the good-man.—*Bona nox*,[1] gammer. Good night, Frolic. 130

SMITH. Come on, my lad, thou shalt take thy unnatural rest with me.

Exeunt Antic and the Smith.

FROL. Yet this vantage shall we have of them in the morning, to be ready at the sight thereof extempore.

OLD WOM. Now this bargain, my masters, must I make with you, that you will say hum and ha to my tale. So shall I know you are awake.

BOTH. Content, gammer; that will [140 we do.

OLD WOM. Once upon a time, there was a king, or a lord, or a duke, that had a fair daughter, the fairest that ever was, as white as snow and as red as blood; and once upon a time his daughter was stolen away, and he sent all his men to seek out his daughter, and he sent so long that he sent all his men out of his land.

FROL. Who dressed his dinner, then? [150

OLD WOM. Nay, either hear my tale, or kiss my tail.

FANT. Well said! On with your tale, gammer.

OLD WOM. O Lord, I quite forgot! There was a conjurer, and this conjurer could do anything, and he turned himself into a great dragon, and carried the king's daughter away in his mouth to a castle that he made of stone, and there he [160 kept her I know not how long, till at last all the king's men went out so long that her two brothers went to seek her. O, I forget! She—he, I would say—turned a proper young man to a bear in the night, and a man in the day, and keeps [2] by a cross that parts three several ways, and he made his lady run mad.—God's me bones, who comes here?

Enter the Two Brothers.

FROL. Soft, gammer, here some [170 come to tell your tale for you.

FANT. Let them alone; let us hear what they will say.

1 BRO. Upon these chalky cliffs of Albion We are arrived now with tedious toil,

[1] Good night.
[2] Dwells (referring to the young man).

And compassing the wide world round about,
To seek our sister, to seek fair Delia forth,
Yet cannot we so much as hear of her.

2 BRO. O fortune cruel, cruel and unkind!
Unkind in that we cannot find our sister, 180
Our sister, hapless in her cruel chance!
Soft! Who have we here?

Enter Senex [Old Man] at the Cross, stooping to gather.

1 BRO. Now, father, God be your speed! What do you gather there?

OLD MAN. Hips and haws, and sticks and straws, and things that I gather on the ground, my son.

1 BRO. Hips and haws, and sticks and straws! Why, is that all your food, father?

OLD MAN. Yea, son. 190

2 BRO. Father, here is an alms penny for me; and, if I speed in that I go for, I will give thee as good a gown of gray as ever thou diddest wear.

1 BRO. And, father, here is another alms penny for me; and, if I speed in my journey, I will give thee a palmer's staff of ivory and a scallop shell of beaten gold.

OLD MAN. Was she fair?

2 BRO. Ay, the fairest for white, [200 and the purest for red, as the blood of the deer or the driven snow.

OLD MAN. Then hark well, and mark well, my old spell:
Be not afraid of every stranger;
Start not aside at every danger;
Things that seem are not the same;
Blow a blast at every flame;
For, when one flame of fire goes out,
Then comes your wishes well about.
If any ask who told you this good, 210
Say the white bear of England's wood.

1 BRO. Brother, heard you not what the old man said?
"Be not afraid of every stranger;
Start not aside for every danger;
Things that seem are not the same;
Blow a blast at every flame;
[For, when one flame of fire goes out,
Then comes your wishes well about.]
If any ask who told you this good,
Say the white bear of England's wood." 220

2 BRO. Well, if this do us any good,

Well fare the white bear of England's
wood! 　　　*Ex[eunt the Two Brothers]*.
OLD MAN. Now sit thee here, and tell a
heavy tale.

Sad in thy mood, and sober in thy cheer,
Here sit thee now, and to thyself relate
The hard mishap of thy most wretched
state.
In Thessaly I lived in sweet content,
Until that fortune wrought my over-
throw;
For there I wedded was unto a dame
That lived in honor, virtue, love, and
fame. 　　　　　　　　　　230
But Sacrapant, that cursed sorcerer,
Being besotted with my beauteous love,
My dearest love, my true betrothed wife,
Did seek the means to rid me of my life.
But, worse than this, he with his chant-
ing spells
Did turn me straight unto an ugly bear;
And, when the sun doth settle in the west,
Then I begin to don my ugly hide.
And all the day I sit, as now you see,
And speak in riddles, all inspired with
rage, 　　　　　　　　　　240
Seeming an old and miserable man;
And yet I am in April of my age.

*Enter Venelia his lady, mad, and goes in
again.*

See where Venelia, my betrothed love,
Runs madding, all enraged, about the
woods,
All by his cursed and enchanting spells.—

Enter Lampriscus with a pot of honey.

But here comes Lampriscus, my discontented neighbor. How now, neighbor! You
look toward the ground as well as I; you
muse on something.

LAMP. Neighbor, on nothing but on [250
the matter I so often moved to you. If you
do anything for charity, help me; if for
neighborhood or brotherhood, help me.
Never was one so cumbered as is poor
Lampriscus. And, to begin, I pray receive
this pot of honey to mend your fare.

OLD MAN. Thanks, neighbor, set it
down. Honey is always welcome to the
bear. And now, neighbor, let me hear the
cause of your coming. 　　　　　260

LAMP. I am, as you know, neighbor, a

man unmarried, and lived so unquietly
with my two wives that I keep every year
holy the day wherein I buried them both.
The first was on Saint Andrew's day,[1] the
other on Saint Luke's.[2]

OLD MAN. And now, neighbor, you of
this country say your custom is out. But
on with your tale, neighbor.

LAMP. By my first wife, whose [270
tongue wearied me alive, and sounded in
my ears like the clapper of a great bell,
whose talk was a continual torment to all
that dwelt by her or lived nigh her, you
have heard me say I had a handsome
daughter.

OLD MAN. True, neighbor.

LAMP. She it is that afflicts me with her
continual clamors, and hangs on me like a
bur. Poor she is, and proud she is; as [280
poor as a sheep new-shorn, and as proud
of her hopes as a peacock of her tail well
grown.

OLD MAN. Well said, Lampriscus! You
speak it like an Englishman.

LAMP. As curst as a wasp and as froward as a child new-taken from the
mother's teat; she is to my age as smoke
to the eyes or as vinegar to the teeth.

OLD MAN. Holily praised, neighbor. [290
As much for the next.

LAMP. By my other wife I had a daughter so hard-favored, so foul and ill-faced,
that I think a grove full of golden trees,
and the leaves of rubies and diamonds,
would not be a dowry answerable to her
deformity.

OLD MAN. Well, neighbor, now you
have spoke, hear me speak. Send them to
the well for the water of life; there shall [300
they find their fortunes unlooked for.
Neighbor, farewell. 　　　　　*Exit.*

LAMP. Farewell, and a thousand! And
now goeth poor Lampriscus to put in execution this excellent counsel. 　　*Exit.*[3]

FROL. Why, this goes round without a
fiddling stick. But, do you hear, gammer,
was this the man that was a bear in the
night and a man in the day?

OLD WOM. Ay, this is he; and this [310

---

[1] Lovers' lucky day.
[2] "St. Luke was jocularly regarded as the
patron saint of cuckolds" (Bullen).
[3] Original reads *Exeunt*.

man that came to him was a beggar, and dwelt upon a green. But soft! Who comes here? O, these are the harvestmen. Ten to one they sing a song of mowing.

Enter the Harvestmen a-singing, with this song double repeated.

All ye that lovely lovers be,
Pray you for me.
Lo, here we come a-sowing, a-sowing,
And sow sweet fruits of love;
In your sweet hearts well may it prove!
Exeunt.

Enter Huanebango with his two-hand sword, and Booby, the clown.

FANT. Gammer, what is he?   320
OLD WOM. O, this is one that is going to the conjurer. Let him alone; hear what he says.

HUAN. Now, by Mars and Mercury, Jupiter and Janus, Sol and Saturnus, Venus and Vesta, Pallas and Proserpina, and by the honor of my house, Polimacker-oeplacidus, it is a wonder to see what this love will make silly fellows adventure, even in the wane of their wits and infancy of [330 their discretion. Alas, my friend, what fortune calls thee forth to seek thy fortune among brazen gates, enchanted towers, fire and brimstone, thunder and lightning? Beauty, I tell thee, is peerless, and she precious whom thou affectest. Do off these desires, good countryman; good friend, run away from thyself; and, so soon as thou canst, forget her, whom none must inherit but he that can monsters tame, labors [340 achieve, riddles absolve, loose enchantments, murther magic, and kill conjuring— and that is the great and mighty Huanebango.

BOOBY. Hark you, sir, hark you. First know I have here the flirting [1] feather, and have given the parish the start for the long stock.[2] Now, sir, if it be no more but running through a little lightning and thunder, and "riddle me, riddle me what's this?" [350 I'll have the wench from the conjurer, if he were ten conjurers.

[1] Swaying.
[2] Either *startled the parish with my long stockings* or *started the style for long stockings in the parish.*

HUAN. I have abandoned the court and honorable company, to do my devoir against this sore sorcerer and mighty magician. If this lady be so fair as she is said to be, she is mine, she is mine; *meus, mea, meum, in contemptum omnium grammaticorum.*[3]

BOOBY. *O falsum Latinum!* The fair [360 maid is *minum, cum apurtinantibus gibletes* [4] and all.

HUAN. If she be mine, as I assure myself the heavens will do somewhat to reward my worthiness, she shall be allied to none of the meanest gods, but be invested in the most famous stock of Huanebango—Polimackeroeplacidus, my grandfather; my father, Pergopolineo; my mother, Dionora de Sardinia, famously descended.   370

BOOBY. Do you hear, sir? Had not you a cousin that was called Gusteceridis?

HUAN. Indeed, I had a cousin that sometime followed the court infortunately, and his name Bustegusteceridis.

BOOBY. O Lord, I know him well! He is the knight of the neat's feet.

HUAN. O, he loved no capon better! He hath oftentimes deceived his boy of his dinner. That was his fault, good Buste- [380 gusteceridis.

BOOBY. Come, shall we go along?

[Enter Old Man.]

Soft! Here is an old man at the cross; let us ask him the way thither.—Ho, you gaffer![5] I pray you tell where the wise man, the conjurer, dwells.

HUAN. Where that earthly goddess keepeth her abode, the commander of my thoughts and fair mistress of my heart.

OLD MAN. Fair enough, and far [390 enough from thy fingering, son.

HUAN. I will follow my fortune after mine own fancy, and do according to mine own discretion.

OLD MAN. Yet give something to an old man before you go.

HUAN. Father, methinks a piece of this cake might serve your turn.

OLD MAN. Yea, son.

HUAN. Huanebango giveth no [400 cakes for alms; ask of them that give gifts

[3] Mine, mine, mine, in contempt of all grammarians. [4] Mine, with her appurtenant parts.
[5] Grandfather, old man.

for poor beggars.—Fair lady, if thou wert once shrined in this bosom, I would buckler[1] thee haratantara. *Exit.*

BOOBY. Father, do you see this man? You little think he'll run a mile or two for such a cake, or pass[2] for a pudding. I tell you, father, he has kept such a begging of me for a piece of this cake! Whoo! He comes upon me with "a superfantial [410 substance, and the foison[3] of the earth," that I know not what he means. If he came to me thus, and said, "My friend Booby," or so, why, I could spare him a piece with all my heart; but, when he tells me how God hath enriched me above other fellows with a cake, why, he makes me blind and deaf at once. Yet, father, here is a piece of cake for you, as hard as the world goes.[4] 420

OLD MAN. Thanks, son, but list to me:
He shall be deaf when thou shalt not see.
Farewell, my son. Things may so hit,
Thou mayst have wealth to mend thy wit.

BOOBY. Farewell, father, farewell; for I must make haste after my two-hand sword that is gone before. *Exeunt omnes.*

Enter Sacrapant in his study.

SACR. The day is clear, the welkin bright
and gray,
The lark is merry and records her notes;
Each thing rejoiceth underneath the
sky 430
But only I, whom heaven hath in hate,
Wretched and miserable Sacrapant.
In Thessaly was I born and brought up;
My mother Meroe hight,[5] a famous
witch,
And by her cunning I of her did learn
To change and alter shapes of mortal men.
There did I turn myself into a dragon,
And stole away the daughter to the king,
Fair Delia, the mistress of my heart,
And brought her hither to revive the
man 440
That seemeth young and pleasant to
behold,
And yet is aged, crooked, weak, and
numb.
Thus by enchanting spells I do deceive

Those that behold and look upon my
face;
But well may I bid youthful years adieu.

Enter Delia with a pot in her hand.

See where she comes from whence my
sorrows grow!
How now, fair Delia, where have you
been?

DEL. At the foot of the rock for running water, and gathering roots for your dinner, sir. 450

SACR. Ah, Delia, fairer art thou than the running water, yet harder far than steel or adamant!

DEL. Will it please you to sit down, sir?

SACR. Ay, Delia, sit and ask me what thou wilt,
Thou shalt have it brought into thy lap.

DEL. Then, I pray you, sir, let me have the best meat from the King of England's table, and the best wine in all France, brought in by the veriest knave in all [460 Spain.

SACR. Delia, I am glad to see you so pleasant. Well, sit thee down.—
Spread, table, spread
Meat, drink, and bread!
Ever may I have
What I ever crave,
When I am spread,
For meat for my black cock,
And meat for my red. 470

Enter a Friar with a chine of beef and a pot of wine.

Here, Delia, will ye fall to?

DEL. Is this the best meat in England?

SACR. Yea.

DEL. What is it?

SACR. A chine of English beef, meat for a king and a king's followers.

DEL. Is this the best wine in France?

SACR. Yea.

DEL. What wine is it?

SACR. A cup of neat wine of Or- [480 leans, that never came near the brewers in England.

DEL. Is this the veriest knave in all Spain?

SACR. Yea.

DEL. What is he, a friar?

SACR. Yea, a friar indefinite, and a knave infinite.

[1] Protect.   [2] Care.
[3] Plentiful harvest. Booby imitates the stilted language of Huanebango.
[4] Though times are hard.   [5] Was called.

DEL. Then, I pray ye, Sir Friar, tell me before you go which is the most greed- [490 iest Englishman?

FRIAR. The miserable and most covetous usurer.

SACR. Hold thee there, friar. *Exit Friar.*
But soft! Who have we here? Delia, away, be gone!

Enter the Two Brothers.

Delia, away, for beset are we!—
But heaven [n]or hell shall rescue her for [1] me.
[*Exeunt Delia and Sacrapant.*]

1 BRO. Brother, was not that Delia did appear?
Or was it but her shadow that was here?

2 BRO. Sister, where art thou? Delia, come again! 500
He calls, that of thy absence doth complain.—
Call out, Calypha, that she may hear,
And cry aloud, for Delia is near.

ECHO. Near.

1 BRO. Near! O, where? Hast thou any tidings?

ECHO. Tidings.

2 BRO. Which way is Delia, then—or that, or this?

ECHO. This.

1 BRO. And may we safely come where Delia is?

ECHO. Yes. 510

2 BRO. Brother, remember you the white bear of England's wood?
"Start not aside for every danger;
Be not afeard of every stranger;
Things that seem are not the same."

1 BRO. Brother, why do we not then courageously enter?

2 BRO. Then, brother, draw thy sword and follow me.

Enter the Conjurer; it lightens and thunders; the 2 Brother falls down.

1 BRO. What, brother, dost thou fall?

SACR. Ay, and thou too, Calypha. 520

Fall 1 Brother. Enter two Furies.

Adeste, dæmones! [2] Away with them!
Go carry them straight to Sacrapanto's cell,
There in despair and torture for to dwell.

[1] Because of.　　　　[2] Come, spirits!

These are Thenores' sons of Thessaly,
That come to seek Delia, their sister, forth;
But, with a potion I to her have given,
My arts hath made her to forget herself.
He removes a turf and shows a light in a glass. [3]
See here the thing which doth prolong my life.
With this enchantment I do anything;
And, till this fade, my skill shall still endure, 530
And never none shall break this little glass,
But she that's neither wife, widow, nor maid.
Then cheer thyself; this is thy destiny,
Never to die but by a dead man's hand.
Exeunt.

Enter Eumenides, the Wandering Knight, and the Old Man at the Cross.

EUM. Tell me, Time, tell me, just Time,
When shall I Delia see?
When shall I see the lodestar of my life?
When shall my wand'ring course end with her sight,
Or I but view my hope, my heart's delight?—
Father, God speed! If you tell fortunes, [540
I pray, good father, tell me mine.

OLD MAN. Son, I do see in thy face
Thy blessed fortune work apace.
I do perceive that thou hast wit;
Beg of thy fate to govern it,
For wisdom governed by advice
Makes many fortunate and wise.
Bestow thy alms, give more than all,
Till dead men's bones come at thy call.
Farewell, my son! Dream of no rest [550
Till thou repent that [4] thou didst best.
Exit Old M[an].

EUM. This man hath left me in a labyrinth:
He biddeth me give more than all,
"Till dead men's bones come at thy call;"
He biddeth me dream of no rest,
Till I repent that I do best.
[*He lies down and sleeps.*]

[3] "The 'Life-Index,' so called, of popular tales, connected with the equally popular *motif* of the 'Thankful Dead'" (Gummere).
[4] Of that which.

Enter Wiggen, Corebus,[1] Churchwarden, and Sexton.

WIG. You may be ashamed, you whoreson [2] scald [3] sexton and churchwarden, if you had any shame in those shameless faces of yours, to let a poor man lie so [560 long above ground unburied. A rot on you all, that have no more compassion of a good fellow when he is gone!

CHURCH.[4] What, would you have us to bury him, and to answer it ourselves to the parish?

SEX. Parish me no parishes! Pay me my fees, and let the rest run on in the quarter's accounts, and put it down for one of your good deeds, o' God's name, for I [570 am not one that curiously [5] stands upon merits.

COR. You whoreson, sodden-headed sheep's-face, shall a good fellow do less service and more honesty to the parish, and will you not, when he is dead, let him have Christmas [6] burial?

WIG. Peace, Corebus! As sure as Jack was Jack, the frolic'st franion amongst you, and I, Wiggen, his sweet sworn [580 brother, Jack shall have his funerals, or some of them shall lie on God's dear earth for it, that's once.[7]

CHURCH. Wiggen, I hope thou wilt do no more than thou dar'st answer.

WIG. Sir, sir, dare or dare not, more or less, answer or not answer, do this, or have this.

Wiggen sets upon the parish [8] with a pikestaff.

SEX. Help, help, help!

Eumenides awakes and comes to them.

EUM. Hold thy hands, good fellow. [590

COR. Can you blame him, sir, if he take Jack's part against this shake-rotten parish that will not bury Jack?

EUM. Why, what was that Jack?

COR. Who, Jack, sir? Who, our Jack, sir? As good a fellow as ever trod upon neat's-leather.

WIG. Look you, sir, he gave fourscore and nineteen mourning gowns to the parish

when he died, and, because he would [600 not make them up a full hundred, they would not bury him. Was not this good dealing?

CHURCH. O Lord, sir, how he lies! He was not worth a halfpenny, and drunk out every penny; and now his fellows, his drunken companions, would have us to bury him at the charge of the parish. And [9] we make many such matches, we may pull down the steeple, sell the bells, and [610 thatch the chancel. He shall lie above ground till he dance a galliard about the churchyard, for Steven Loach.

WIG. *Sic argumentaris, Domine* Loach:[10] "and we make many such matches, we may pull down the steeple, sell the bells, and thatch the chancel!"—In good time, sir, and hang yourselves in the bell ropes when you have done. *Domine, opponens præpono tibi hanc quæstionem,*[11] whether [620 will you have the ground broken or your pates broken first? For one of them shall be done presently, and, to begin mine, I'll seal it upon your coxcomb.

EUM. Hold thy hands, I pray thee, good fellow; be not too hasty.

COR. You capon's face, we shall have you turned out of the parish one of these days, with never a tatter to your arse. Then you are in worse taking than [630 Jack.

EUM. Faith, and he is bad enough. This fellow does but the part of a friend, to seek to bury his friend. How much will bury him?

WIG. Faith, about some fifteen or sixteen shillings will bestow him honestly.

SEX. Ay, even thereabouts, sir.

EUM. Here, hold it then. [*Starts to give money; then speaks to himself.*] And [640 I have left me but one poor three halfpence. Now do I remember the words the old man spake at the cross, "Bestow all thou hast," and this is all, "till dead men's bones come at thy call."—Here, hold it. [*Gives money.*] And so farewell.

WIG. God and all good be with you, sir! Nay, you cormorants, I'll bestow one peal of [12] Jack at mine own proper costs and charges.   650

---

[1] Previously, Booby, the clown.
[2] Rascally.   [4] Original has *Simon.*
[3] Scabby.   [5] Carefully.
[6] Corebus' blunder for *Christian.*
[7] "That's settled once for all" (Bullen).
[8] Sexton.

[9] If.   [10] Thus you argue, Master Loach.
[11] Master, responding, I put before you this question.   [12] Peal of bells on.

COR. You may thank God the long staff and the bilbo-blade crossed not your coxcomb. Well, we'll to the church-stile [1] and have a pot, and so trill-lill.

BOTH [CHURCHWARDEN AND SEXTON]. Come, let's go. *Exeunt.*

FANT. But, hark you, gammer, methinks this Jack bore a great sway in the parish. 658

OLD WOM. O, this Jack was a marvelous fellow! He was but a poor man, but very well beloved. You shall see anon what this Jack will come to.

Enter the Harvestmen singing, with Women in their hands.

FROL. Soft! Who have we here? Our amorous harvesters.[2]

FANT. Ay, ay, let us sit still, and let them alone.

Here they begin to sing, the song doubled.

Lo, here we come a-reaping, a-reaping,
To reap our harvest fruit,
And thus we pass the year so long,
And never be we mute. 670
Exit the Harvestmen.

Enter Huanebango and Corebus, the clown.

FROL. Soft! Who have we here?

OLD WOM. O, this is a choleric gentleman! All you that love your lives, keep out of the smell of his two-hand sword. Now goes he to the conjurer.

FANT. Methinks the conjurer should put the fool into a juggling-box.

HUAN. Fee, fa, fum, here is the Englishman—
Conquer him that can—
Came for his lady bright, 680
To prove himself a knight,
And win her love in fight.

COR. Who-haw, Master Bango, are you here? Hear you, you had best sit down here and beg an alms with me.

HUAN. Hence, base cullion![3] Here is he that commandeth ingress and egress with

his weapon, and will enter at his voluntary, whosoever saith no.

A voice and flame of fire; Huanebango falleth down.

VOICE. No! 690

OLD WOM. So with that they kissed, and spoiled the edge of as good a two-hand sword as ever God put life in. Now goes Corebus in, spite of the conjurer.

Enter the Conjurer [with two Furies] and strike Corebus blind.

SACR. Away with him into the open fields,
To be a ravening prey to crows and kites.
[*The Furies carry Huanebango out.*]
And, for this villain, let him wander up and down
In naught but darkness and eternal night.

COR. Here hast thou slain Huan, a slashing knight,
And robbéd poor Corebus of his sight.
Exit.

SACR. Hence, villain, hence!— 701
Now I have unto Delia given a potion of forgetfulness,
That, when she comes, she shall not know her brothers.
Lo, where they labor, like to country slaves
With spade and mattock on this enchanted ground!
Now will I call her by another name;
For never shall she know herself again,
Until that Sacrapant hath breathed his last.
See where she comes.

Enter Delia.

Come hither, Delia, take this goad. 710
Here hard at hand two slaves do work and dig for gold;
Gore them with this, and thou shalt have enough. *He gives her a goad.*

DEL. Good sir, I know not what you mean.

SACR. [*Aside.*] She hath forgotten to be Delia,
But not forgot the same she should forget;
But I will change her name.—
Fair Berecynthia, so this country calls you,
Go ply these strangers, wench; they dig for gold. *Exit Sacrapant.*

DEL. O heavens, how am I beholding[4] to this fair young man!

---

[1] Gummere quotes Overbury's *Characters:* "For at every church stile commonly ther's an ale-house."

[2] Original has *harvest starres.*   [3] Fellow.

[4] Beholden, indebted.

But I must ply these strangers to their
work.   720
See where they come.

*Enter the Two Brothers in their shirts, with
spades, digging.*

1 Bro. O brother, see where Delia is!
2 Bro. O Delia, happy are we to see thee
here!
Del. What tell you me of Delia, prating
swains?
I know no Delia, nor know I what you
mean.
Ply you your work, or else you're like to
smart.
1 Bro. Why, Delia, know'st thou not thy
brothers here?
We come from Thessaly to seek thee
forth;
And thou deceivest thyself, for thou art
Delia.   729
Del. Yet more of Delia? Then take this,
and smart. [*Pricks them with the goad.*]
What, feign you shifts for to defer your
labor?
Work, villains, work; it is for gold you dig.
2 Bro. Peace, brother, peace! This vild [1]
enchanter
Hath ravished Delia of her senses clean,
And she forgets that she is Delia.
1 Bro. Leave, cruel thou, to hurt the
miserable.—
Dig, brother, dig, for she is hard as steel.
*Here they dig, and descry the light under a
little hill.*
2 Bro. Stay, brother; what hast thou
descried?
Del. Away, and touch it not; it is something that my lord hath hidden there.
                        She covers it again.

Enter Sacrapant.

Sacr. Well said!   Thou plyest these
pioners [2] well.—Go, get you in, you
laboring slaves.—   740
Come, Berecynthia, let us in likewise,
And hear the nightingale record her
notes.   *Exeunt omnes.*

*Enter Zantippa, the Curst Daughter, to the
well, with a pot in her hand.* [3]

Zant. Now for a husband, house, and
home. God send a good one or none, I pray

God! My father hath sent me to the well
for the water of life, and tells me, if I give
fair words, I shall have a husband.

*Enter [Celanta,] the Foul Wench, to the well
for water with a pot in her hand.*

But here comes Celanta, my sweet sister.
I'll stand by and hear what she says. [749
Cel. My father hath sent me to the
well for water, and he tells me, if I speak
fair, I shall have a husband and none of the
worst. Well, though I am black,[4] I am sure
all the world will not forsake me; and, as
the old proverb is, though I am black, I am
not the devil.
Zant. Marry-gup with a murrain,[5] I
know wherefore thou speakest that. But
go thy ways home as wise as thou [759
cam'st, or I'll set thee home with a wanion.[6]
*Here she strikes her pitcher against her sis-
ter's, and breaks them both, and goes
her way.*
Cel. I think this be the curstest quean
in the world. You see what she is, a little
fair but as proud as the devil, and the
veriest vixen that lives upon God's earth.
Well, I'll let her alone, and go home and
get another pitcher, and for all this get me
to the well for water.   *Exit*

*Enter two Furies out of the Conjurer's cell
and lays Huanebango by the Well of
Life [and then exeunt]. Enter Zantippa
with a pitcher to the well.*

Zant. Once again for a husband; and
in faith, Celanta, I have got the start [769
of you. Belike husbands grow by the well-
side. Now my father says I must rule my
tongue. Why, alas, what am I then? A
woman without a tongue is as a soldier without his weapon. But I'll have my water
and be gone.
*Here she offers to dip her pitcher in, and a
Head speaks in the well.*
Head. Gently dip, but not too deep;
For fear you make the golden beard [7] to
weep,
Fair maiden, white and red,
Stroke me smooth, and comb my head;
And thou shalt have some cockle-bread.[8]

[4] Ugly.
[5] Plague take you!   [6] Vengeance.
[7] Original has *birde*, but see l. 959.
[8] Bread kneaded in a peculiar fashion and used
as a love charm.

[1] Vile.   [2] Diggers.
[3] This scene is a reworking of *The Three Heads
of the Well.*

ZANT. What is this: "Fair maiden, white and red, 781
Comb me smooth, and stroke my head,
And thou shalt have some cockle-bread"?
"Cockle," callest thou it, boy? Faith,
I'll give you cockle-bread!

She breaks her pitcher upon his head; then it thunders and lightens, and Huanebango rises up. Huanebango is deaf and cannot hear.

HUAN. Philida phileridos, Pamphilida florida flortos,
Dub dub-a-dub, bounce, quoth the guns, with a sulphurous huff-snuff; [1]
Waked with a wench, pretty peat, [2] pretty love, and my sweet pretty pigsnie, [3]
Just by thy side shall sit surnamed great Huanebango;
Safe in my arms will I keep thee, threat Mars or thunder Olympus. 790

ZANT. [*Aside.*] Foh, what greasy groom have we here? He looks as though he crept out of the backside of the well, and speaks like a drum perished at the west end. [4]

HUAN. O, that I might—but I may not, woe to my destiny therefore! [5]—
Kiss that I clasp, but I cannot. Tell me, my destiny, wherefore?

ZANT. [*Aside.*] Whoop! Now I have my dream. Did you never hear so great a wonder as this? Three blue beans in a blue bladder—rattle, bladder, rattle. 800

HUAN. [*Aside.*] I'll now set my countenance, and to her in prose. It may be this rim-ram-ruff [6] is too rude an encounter.—Let me, fair lady, if you be at leisure, revel with your sweetness, and rail upon that cowardly conjurer that hath cast me, or congealed me rather, into an unkind sleep, and polluted my carcass.

ZANT. [*Aside.*] Laugh, laugh, Zantippa; thou hast thy fortune, a fool and a hus- [810 band under one.

HUAN. Truly, sweetheart, as I seem, about some twenty years, the very April of mine age.

ZANT. [*Aside.*] Why, what a prating ass is this!

HUAN. Her coral lips, her crimson chin, Her silver teeth so white within,

Her golden locks, her rolling eye,
Her pretty parts, let them go by, 820
Heigh-ho, hath wounded me,
That I must die this day to see!

ZANT. By Gog's [7] bones, thou art a flouting knave. "Her coral lips, her crimson chin"! ka, wilshaw! [8]

HUAN. True, my own, and my own because mine, and mine because mine, ha, ha! Above a thousand pounds in possibility, and things fitting thy desire in possession. 830

ZANT. [*Aside.*] The sot thinks I ask of his lands. Lob be your comfort, [9] and cuckold be your destiny!—Hear you, sir; and, if you will have us, you had best say so betime.

HUAN. True, sweetheart, and will royalize thy progeny with my pedigree.

Exeunt omnes.

Enter Eumenides, the Wandering Knight.

EUM. Wretched Eumenides, still unfortunate,
Envied by fortune and forlorn by fate, 839
Here pine and die, wretched Eumenides!
Die in the spring, the April of my age?
Here sit thee down, repent what thou hast done.
I would to God that it were ne'er begun.

Enter [the Ghost of] Jack.

JACK. You are well overtaken, sir.
EUM. Who's that?
JACK. You are heartily well met, sir.
EUM. Forbear, I say. Who is that which pincheth me?
JACK. Trusting in God, good Master Eumenides, that you are in so good [850 health as all your friends were at the making hereof, God give you good morrow, sir! Lack you not a neat, handsome, and cleanly young lad, about the age of fifteen or sixteen years, that can run by your horse, and, for a need, make your mastership's shoes as black as ink? How say you, sir?
EUM. Alas, pretty lad, I know not how to keep myself, and much less a serv-

[1] Apparently a parody of Stanyhurst's hexameters.
[2] Pet.
[3] Pig's eye, darling.
[4] *I.e.*, brokenly.
[5] A quotation from Harvey's *Encomium Lauri.*
[6] Chaucer's phrase for alliteration.
[7] God's.
[8] Quotha wilta-shalta, *i.e.*, quoth he willy-nilly.
[9] "May you be brought into 'Lob's pound,' the thralldom of the hen-pecked married man" (Bullen).

ant, my pretty boy, my state is so [860 bad.

JACK. Content yourself, you shall not be so ill a master but I'll be as bad a servant. Tut, sir, I know you, though you know not me. Are not you the man, sir, deny it if you can, sir, that came from a strange place in the land of Catita, where Jackanapes flies with his tail in his mouth, to seek out a lady as white as snow and as red as blood? Ha, ha! Have I [870 touched you now?

EUM. [Aside.] I think this boy be a spirit.—How know'st thou all this?

JACK. Tut, are not you the man, sir, deny it if you can, sir, that gave all the money you had to the burying of a poor man, and but one three halfpence left in your purse? Content you, sir, I'll serve you, that is flat.   879

EUM. Well, my lad, since thou art so impor[tu]nate, I am content to entertain thee, not as a servant, but a copartner in my journey. But whither shall we go, for I have not any money more than one bare three halfpence?

JACK. Well, master, content yourself, for, if my divination be not out, that shall be spent at the next inn or alehouse we come to, for, master, I know you are passing hungry; therefore I'll go before and [890 provide dinner until that you come. No doubt but you'll come fair and softly after.

EUM. Ay, go before; I'll follow thee.

JACK. But do you hear, master? Do you know my name?

EUM. No, I promise thee, not yet.

JACK. Why, I am Jack.   *Exit*[1] *Jack.*

EUM. Jack! Why, be it so then.

Enter the Hostess and Jack, setting meat on the table; and Fiddlers come[2] *to play. Eumenides walketh up and down, and will eat no meat.*

HOST. How say you, sir? Do you please to sit down?   900

EUM. Hostess, I thank you, I have no great stomach.

HOST. Pray, sir, what is the reason your master is so strange? Doth not this meat please him?

JACK. Yes, hostess, but it is my mas-

[1] Original reads *Exeunt.*
[2] Original reads *came.*

ter's fashion to pay before he eats; therefore, a reckoning, good hostess.

HOST. Marry, shall you, sir, presently.
                                                         Exit.

EUM. Why, Jack, what dost thou [910 mean? Thou knowest I have not any money; therefore, sweet Jack, tell me, what shall I do?

JACK. Well, master, look in your purse.

EUM. Why, faith, it is a folly, for I have no money.

JACK. Why, look you, master; do so much for me.

EUM. [*Looking into his purse.*]   Alas, Jack, my purse is full of money!   920

JACK. "Alas," master! Does that word belong to this accident? Why, methinks I should have seen you cast away your cloak, and in a bravado danced a galliard round about the chamber. Why, master, your man can teach you more wit than this.

[Enter Hostess.]

Come, hostess, cheer up my master.

HOST. You are heartily welcome; and, if it please you to eat of a fat capon, a fairer bird, a finer bird, a sweeter bird, [930 a crisper bird, a neater bird, your worship never eat of.

EUM. Thanks, my fine, eloquent hostess.

JACK. But hear you, master, one word by the way. Are you content I shall be halves in all you get in your journey?

EUM. I am, Jack; here is my hand.

JACK. Enough, master, I ask no more.

EUM. Come, hostess, receive your [939 money; and I thank you for my good entertainment.   [*Gives money.*]

HOST. You are heartily welcome, sir.

EUM. Come, Jack, whither go we now?

JACK. Marry, master, to the conjurer's presently.[3]

EUM. Content, Jack.—Hostess, farewell.   *Exe[unt] om[nes].*

Enter Corebus and Celanta, the Foul Wench, to the well for water.

COR. Come, my duck, come. I have now got a wife. Thou art fair, art thou not?   950

CEL. My Corebus, the fairest alive; make no doubt of that.

COR. Come, wench, are we almost at the well?   [3] At once.

CEL. Ay, Corebus, we are almost at the well now. I'll go fetch some water. Sit down while I dip my pitcher in.

VOICE. Gently dip, but not too deep,
For fear you make the golden beard to weep.

A Head comes up with ears of corn, and she combs them in her lap.

Fair maiden, white and red,   960
Comb me smooth, and stroke my head,
And thou shalt have some cockle-bread.

A Head comes up full of gold; she combs it into her lap.[1]

Gently dip, but not too deep,
For fear thou make the golden beard to weep.
Fair maid, white and red,
Comb me smooth, and stroke my head,
And every hair a sheaf shall be,
And every sheaf a golden tree.

CEL. O, see, Corebus, I have combed a great deal of gold into my lap, [970 and a great deal of corn!

COR. Well said, wench! Now we shall have just enough. God send us coiners to coin our gold. But, come, shall we go home, sweetheart?

CEL. Nay, come, Corebus, I will lead you.

COR. So, Corebus, things have well hit;
Thou hast gotten wealth to mend thy wit.
Exit [Corebus with Celanta].

Enter Jack and the Wandering Knight.

JACK. Come away, master, come. [980

EUM. Go along, Jack; I'll follow thee. Jack, they say it is good to go cross-legged, and say his prayers backward. How sayest thou?

JACK. Tut, never fear, master; let me alone. Here sit you still; speak not a word. And, because[2] you shall not be enticed with his enchanting speeches, with this same wool I'll stop your ears. And so, master, sit still, for I must to the conjurer. [990
Exit Jack.

Enter the Conjurer to the Wandering Knight.

SACR. How now! What man art thou that sits so sad?
Why dost thou gaze upon these stately trees

Without the leave and will of Sacrapant?
What, not a word but mum?
Then, Sacrapant, thou art betrayed.

Enter Jack, invisible, and taketh off Sacrapant's wreath from his head and his sword out of his hand.

What hand invades the head of Sacrapant?
What hateful Fury doth envy my happy state?
Then, Sacrapant, these are thy latest days.
Alas, my veins are numbed, my sinews shrink,
My blood is pierced, my breath fleeting away,   1000
And now my timeless date is come to end!
He in whose life his actions hath been so foul,
Now in his death to hell descends his soul.   *He dieth.*

JACK. O, sir, are you gone? Now I hope we shall have some other coil.[3]—Now, master, how like you this? The conjurer he is dead, and vows never to trouble us more. Now get you to your fair lady, and see what you can do with her.—Alas, he heareth me not all this while; but [1010 I will help that.
He pulls the wool out of his ears.

EUM. How now, Jack! What news?

JACK. Here, master, take this sword, and dig with it at the foot of this hill.
He digs and spies a light.

EUM. How now, Jack! What is this?

JACK. Master, without this the conjurer could do nothing; and so long as this light lasts, so long doth his art endure, and, this being out, then doth his art decay.   1020

EUM. Why, then, Jack, I will soon put out this light.

JACK. Ay, master, how?

EUM. Why, with a stone I'll break the glass, and then blow it out.

JACK. No, master, you may as soon break the smith's anvil as this little vial; nor the biggest blast that ever Boreas blew cannot blow out this little light but she that is neither maid, wife, nor widow. [1030 Master, wind this horn, and see what will happen.

---

[1] This stage direction occurs in original after l. 968.   [2] So that.

[3] Trouble.

*He winds the horn.   Here enters Venelia,
and breaks the glass, and blows out the
light, and goeth in again.*

So, master, how like you this? This is she
that ran madding in the woods, his betrothed love that keeps the cross. And
now, this light being out, all are restored to
their former liberty. And now, master, to
the lady that you have so long looked for.
*He draweth a curtain, and there Delia sitteth
asleep.*

EUM. God speed, fair maid, sitting alone—
    there is once;   1039
    God speed, fair maid—there is twice;
    God speed, fair maid—that is thrice.
DEL. Not so, good sir, for you are by.
JACK. Enough, master, she hath spoke;
now I will leave her with you.   [*Exit.*]
EUM. Thou fairest flower of these western
    parts,
    Whose beauty so reflecteth in my sight
    As doth a crystal mirror in the sun,
    For thy sweet sake I have crossed the
        frozen Rhine; [1]
    Leaving fair Po, I sailed up Danuby
    As far as Saba, whose enhancing streams
    Cuts twixt the Tartars and the Rus-
        sians;   1051
    These have I crossed for thee, fair Delia.
    Then grant me that which I have sued
        for long.
DEL. Thou gentle knight, whose fortune
    is so good
    To find me out and set my brothers free,
    My faith, my heart, my hand I give to
        thee.
EUM. Thanks, gentle madam.   But here
comes Jack.   Thank him, for he is the best
friend that we have.   1059

Enter Jack, with a head in his hand.

How now, Jack!   What hast thou there?
JACK. Marry, master, the head of the
conjurer.
EUM. Why, Jack, that is impossible; he
was a young man.
JACK. Ah, master, so he deceived them
that beheld him!   But he was a miserable,
old, and crooked man, though to each
man's eye h[e see]med young and fresh;
for, master, this conjurer took the shape

[1] "This and the next three lines are found,
with slight variations, in Greene's *Orlando
Furioso*" (Dyce)

of the old man that kept the cross,   [1070
and that old man was in the likeness of the
conjurer.   But now, master, wind your horn.

*He winds his horn.   Enter Venelia, the Two
Brothers, and [Erestus,] he that was at
the cross.*

EUM. Welcome, Erestus!   Welcome, fair
    Venelia!
    Welcome, Thelea and Calypha both!
    Now have I her that I so long have
        sought;
    So saith fair Delia, if we have your con-
        sent.
1 BRO. Valiant Eumenides, thou well de-
        servest
    To have our favors; so let us rejoice
    That by thy means we are at liberty.
    Here may we joy each in other's sight,
    And this fair lady have her Wand'ring
        Knight.   1081
JACK. So, master, now ye think you
have done, but I must have a saying to
you.   You know you and I were partners,
I to have half in all you got.
EUM. Why, so thou shalt, Jack.
JACK. Why, then, master, draw your
sword, part your lady, let me have half
of her presently.
EUM. Why, I hope, Jack, thou dost   [1090
but jest.   I promised thee half I got, but
not half my lady.
JACK. But what else, master?   Have you
not gotten her?   Therefore divide her
straight, for I will have half; there is no
remedy.
EUM. Well, ere I will falsify my word
unto my friend, take her all.   Here, Jack,
I'll give her thee.
JACK. Nay, neither more nor less,   [1100
master, but even just half.
EUM. Before I will falsify my faith unto
my friend, I will divide her.   Jack, thou
shalt have half.
1 BRO. Be not so cruel unto our sister,
gentle knight.
2 BRO. O, spare fair Delia!   She deserves
no death.
EUM. Content yourselves; my word is
passed to him.—Therefore prepare   [1110
thyself, Delia, for thou must die.
DEL. Then farewell, world!   Adieu, Eu
    menides!

He offers to strike, and Jack stays him.

JACK. Stay, master; it is sufficient I have tried your constancy. Do you now remember since you paid for the burying of a poor fellow?

EUM. Ay, very well, Jack.

JACK. Then, master, thank that good deed for this good turn; and so God be with you all!   *Jack leaps down in the ground.*

EUM. Jack, what, art thou gone? Then farewell, Jack!—   1121
Come, brothers, and my beauteous Delia,
Erestus, and thy dear Venelia,
We will to Thessaly with joyful hearts.

ALL. Agreed! We follow thee and Delia.
                                        Exeunt omnes.

FANT. What, gammer, asleep?

OLD WOM. By the Mass, son, 'tis almost day, and my windows shuts at the cock's crow.   1129

FROL. Do you hear, gammer, methinks this Jack bore a great sway amongst them.

OLD WOM. O, man, this was the ghost of the poor man that they kept such a coil to bury; and that makes him to help the Wand'ring Knight so much. But come, let us in; we will have a cup of ale and a toast this morning, and so depart.[1]

FANT. Then you have made an end of your tale, gammer?   [1140

OLD WOM. Yes, faith. When this was done, I took a piece of bread and cheese, and came my way; and so shall you have, too, before you go, to your breakfast.
                                        [Exeunt.]

[1] Separate.

ROBERT GREENE

Although it was a somewhat unsuitable epithet for him, Robert Greene, like his friend George Peele, was labeled a "University Wit." Greene loved to describe himself as "Academiae Utriusque Magister in Artibus" ("Master of Arts of Both Universities"), but he lived a life which was as far from that of the academic ivory tower as it is possible to get. He was born into a lower-middle-class family in Norwich, and was baptized there on July 11, 1558. He apparently attended the Norwich Free Grammar School since, as Kenneth Mildenberger, correcting previous archivists, has pointed out in "Robert Green at Cambridge" (*MLN*, 1951), this school had "exhibitions," or scholarships, at Corpus Christi College, and in the central university register there is an entry of the matriculation of Robert Greene, sizar, there in the Easter term of 1573. Since there is a similar entry of his matriculation at St. John's College on November 26, 1575, he apparently transferred there after establishing himself in the university at C.C.C., and received his B.A. in 1579–80. But by 1583 he was at Clare Hall, where he got his first M.A. Five years later Oxford conferred the same degree on him.

Greene had no reticence about himself or anything else and was an autobiographical writer of the first water. Even though he was prone to embellish facts to make a better story, there is no better way of introducing him than to let him speak for himself, as he did in a series of confessional pamphlets and prodigal son stories at the end of his very short career. (Like George Gascoigne, he underwent a sudden conversion and repentance at the end of his life.) These works by Greene include his *Mourning Garment* (1590), *Never Too Late* (1590), *Farewell to Folly* (1591), *Groatsworth of Wit, Bought with a Million of Repentance* (1592), and *Repentance* (1592). Of these the most personally revealing is probably his *Repentance*, written on his deathbed. Here he disclosed that he was born in Norwich, of parents known for their "grauitie and honest life," to whose "wholesome aduertisements" he turned a deaf ear. Nevertheless he went up to Cambridge where, as he put it:

I light amongst wags as lewd as my selfe, with whome I consumed the flower of my youth, who drew mee to travell into Italy, and Spaine, in which places I sawe and practizde such villainie as is abhominable to declare. Thus by their counsaile I sought to furnish myselfe with coine, which I procured by cunning sleights from my Father and my friends, and my Mother pampered mee so long, and secretly helped me to the oyle of Angels, that I grew hereby prone to all mischiefe: so that, beeing then conuersant with notable Braggarts, boon companions, and ordinary spend-thrifts, that practized sundry superficiall studies, I became as a Sien grafted into the same stocke, whereby I did absolutely participate of their nature and qualities. At my return into England, I ruffeled out in my silks, in the habit of *Malcontent*, and seemed so discontent, that no place would please me to abide in, nor no vocation cause mee to stay my selfe in: but after I had by degrees proceeded Maister of Arts, I left the Vniversitie and away to London, where (after I had continued some short time, and driuen my self out of credit with sundry of my friends) I became an Author of Playes, and a penner of Loue Pamphlets, so that I soone grew famous in that qualitie, that who for that trade growne so ordinary about London as *Robin Greene*.

He soon married "a Gentlemans daughter of good account, with whom I liued for a while: but for as much as she would perswade me from my wilful wickednes, after I had a child by her, I cast her off, hauing spent vp the marriage money which I obtained

261

by her. Then I left her at six or seuen, who went into Lincolneshire, and I to London."
This son, ironically named Fortunatus, lived only two years. Actually Greene had left
his wife to take up with the sister of a notorious London gang leader named Ball, from
whom he learned a great deal more about the underworld.

The "Love Pamphlets," as their author called them, consisted of a series of prose
romances beginning in 1580–83 with the two parts of *Mamillia, A Mirror or Looking
Glass for the Ladies of England*, written in the currently popular euphuistic style, and
ending with the much more attractive *Pandosto* (1588) and *Menaphon* (1589). Since
these were written largely under the influence of the Italian *novella* and the pastoral
and Greek romance, they revealed nothing of the seamy and bohemian side of London
life which he was learning to know so well. Late in 1591 and early in 1592 Greene exploited this more realistic aspect of life in a hastily published series of pamphlets on the
London underworld: *A Notable Discovery of Cozenage, The Second Part of Cony-Catching,
a Third and Last Part, A Disputation between a He and a She Cony-Catcher, The Black
Book's Messenger*, and probably the ironical *A Defense of Cony-Catching*. A cony was
a rabbit—by transfer any gullible victim of a trickster or cheater. Greene, knowing all
the snares and devices and being essentially a journalist, was well able to appeal to the
already well-established popular taste for such sensational "rogue literature."

In 1592, when he was only thirty-four, he went to what his friend Tom Nashe immortally described as "that fatal banquet of Rhenish wine and pickled herring." The
"surfeit," as the sarcastic Gabriel Harvey called it, was apparently too much for his
already weakened constitution. Although at first he feared no permanent ill effects,
the illness dragged on for over a month. The printer of the *Repentance*, as well as Nashe
and Harvey, whose enmity he had incurred through his participation in the Marprelate
controversy, wrote their generally agreeing accounts of his death. He had lost most of
his friends and would have died in the streets if a shoemaker named Isam and his wife,
assisted by the mother of Greene's illegitimate son, had not taken him into their house
in Dowgate. At the end Greene wanted to pray, but he heard a voice crying "Robin
Greene, thou art damned," much as he had in a religious experience earlier when he
listened to a sermon of a minister in St. Andrew's Church, Norwich. On the night of
September 2, 1592, a friend brought him news from his wife, who sent him commendations and reported that she was in good health. Greene's conscience so troubled him
that he immediately sent a faltering note back to her through Isam, beginning, "Sweet
Wife, as ever there was any good will or friendship between thee and me see this bearer
(my Host) satisfied of his debt. I owe him tenne pound, and but for him I had perished
in the streetes. Forget and forgive my wronges done unto thee, and Almighty God have
mercie on my soule. . . ." He died the next day in the presence of the Isams. Mistress Isam emotionally crowned him with a symbolic garland of bay leaves, and he was
buried in the New Churchyard near Bedlam the following day.

Greene left varying opinions and epitaphs behind him. Nashe, in *Four Letters
Confuted*, his reply to Harvey's *Four Letters, and Certain Sonnets: Especially Touching
Robert Greene, and Other Parties, by Him Abused*, described his friend as having "A jolly
long red peake [i.e., beard], like a spire of a steeple," which "hee cherisht continually
without cutting, whereat a man might hang a Jewel, it was so sharp and pendant."
Nashe added that Greene had left a "very faire Cloake, with sleeves of. . . greene,"
and "a greasy pair of silk stockings." He also called him a "good fellowe," though a
considerable drinker, a man who cared more about having enough in his purse for a
"good cuppe of wine" than he did for "winning credite by his workes," but still a man
of "more vertues than vices." Greene's fellow-playwright, Henry Chettle, in his
Kind-Heart's Dream, told how he had recopied the *Groatsworth* so that the printer could
read it, and described the dead man as "a man of indifferent years, of face amible, of
body well proportioned, his attire after the habite of a scholler-like gentleman, onely his
hair somewhat long, . . . of singular pleasaunce, the verye supporter, and. . . the
only comedian, of a vulgar writer, in this country." On the opposite page of the ledger,

Harvey wrote immediately after Greene's death: "Loe a wilde head, ful of mad brain and a thousand crotchets: A scholler, a Discourser, a Courtier, a ruffian, a Gamester, a Lover. . . ." In this churlish opinion Harvey was supported by his friend Christopher Bird. While Greene was dying, Bird called him, in "A Due Commendation of the Quipping Autor": "A rakehell: A makeshift: a scribbling foole:/A famous boyard [i.e., a blindly reckless fellow], in Citty, and Schoole." Since Greene had a sharp tongue as well as a fluent pen, he was the kind of man who makes strong friends and violent enemies. Even William Shakespeare was the victim of one of his famous barbs; at least, the following passage in the *Groatsworth* is almost universally interpreted as being aimed at the newcomer in the English theater: ". . . there is an upstart crow, beautified with our feathers, that with his *Tygers heart wrapt in a Players hide*, supposes he is as well able to bumbast out a blanke verse as the best of you: and being an absolute *Johannes Factotum*, is in his owne conceit the only Shake-scene in a countrie." Perhaps the barb was made in envy because, as Greene admitted in the preface to *Perimedes the Blacksmith* (1588), he had been derided for not being able to make his own verses "jet upon the stage in tragicall buskins."

John Clarke Jordan, in *Robert Greene* (Columbia University Press, 1915), the most complete study of Greene so far, follows Greene's own suggestion by dividing his literary career into three parts. These parts were indicated by certain Latin mottoes selected by Greene for use on his title pages: Horace's "Omne Tulit Punctum Qui Miscuit Utile Dulci" ("He Has Everyone's Applause Who Mingles the Useful with the Sweet"); "Sero sed Serio" ("Late, but in Earnest"); and "Nascimur pro Patria" ("We Are Born for [the Good of] Our Country"). In exemplifying these mottoes in print, Greene wrote so prolifically over a period of less than ten years that when Alexander Grosart decided to collect *The Complete Works of Robert Greene* in 1881–83, he found that they filled fifteen volumes. J. Churton Collins, however, found that he could contain *The Plays and Poems of Robert Greene* in two volumes (Oxford, 1905), a fact which perhaps indicates that the writing of plays was only a minor aspect of the literary output of this extraordinary Elizabethan.

The plays that can safely be assigned to Greene, although their chronology is not certain, are *The Comical History of Alphonsus, King of Arragon*, an extravagant imitation, almost a parody, of Marlowe's *Tamburlaine*, as played by Lord Strange's Men about 1588 (published in 1599); *A Looking Glass for London and England*, in which Greene and his collaborator, Thomas Lodge, presented a warning and moral lesson to England under the guise of retelling the story of Nineveh, its king, Rasni, and the prophet Hosea (written about 1588; printed in 1594); *The History of Orlando Furioso, One of the Twelve Peers of France*, based in part on Ariosto's romantic epic, played first by the Queen's Men before the Queen about 1588–89, then resold to the Admiral's Men in a piece of sharp practice while the other company went on tour, and published in 1594; *The Honorable History of Friar Bacon and Friar Bungay*, to be discussed below; and *The Scottish History of James the Fourth*, purportedly a true chronicle, but actually a rather charming fiction based on a story in Cinthio's *Hecatomithi* (probably written about 1590–91, entered on the Stationers' Register in 1594, but not clearly published till 1598). Among the other plays which have been attributed to Greene by various scholars on rather uncertain evidence are *George a Greene*, *The Tragical Reign of Selimus, A Knack To Know a Knave*, and the First and Second Parts of *Henry VI*.

The first record of *Friar Bacon*, the play on which Greene's reputation as a playwright now chiefly depends, is Henslowe's note of a performance of it as an old play in 1592, given by Lord Strange's Men at the Rose Theater. Much scholarly discussion of Greene's plays in general has focused on the relationships between them and Marlowe's. (See Una Ellis-Fermor in "Marlowe and Greene: A Note on Their Relations as Dramatic Artists," *Studies in Honor of T. W. Baldwin*, University of Illinois Press, 1958; and Irving Ribner, in "Greene's Attack on Marlowe: Some Light on *Alphonsus* and *Selimus*," *SP*, 1955.) The view until rather recently has been that

Marlowe's *Doctor Faustus* preceded Greene's *Friar Bacon*, which was hurriedly written to take advantage of the popularity of Marlowe's play and of stories about magicians in general. Since many scholars, such as W. W. Greg, have been inclined to date *Doctor Faustus* as late as 1592, this theory would require a considerable cramping of time to fit the events. Daniel Seltzer, in his important critical edition of *Friar Bacon* (Regents Renaissance Drama series, University of Nebraska Press, 1963), has summed up the arguments on both sides, and come to the conclusion that the positions of the two plays should be reversed. He even suggests that perhaps, since Greene received his second M.A. degree from Oxford in 1588, he may then "have decided to write a play about his new alma mater's great natural philosopher," Roger Bacon. If so, however, it must be admitted that Greene's picture of the pedantry and vanity in universities was not all flattery, as seen in the allusion of Miles, Bacon's clumsy student, to Alexander Barclay's social satire, *The Ship of Fools*, which he says he will conjure from Oxford, "With colleges and schools, well-loaden with fools" (vii, 100–1). Seltzer's argument is too complicated to go into here, but it is based partially on the suggestion of W. W. Greg, in his edition of *Henslowe's Diary* (London, 1904), that when Prince Edward says to the Earl of Lincoln, "Lacy, thou know'st next Friday is S. James' " (i, 156), he is only telling the truth if the play was first performed in 1589. The generally highly patriotic tone of the play might also help to place it shortly after the defeat of the Spanish Armada, even if there is no direct reference to this event. At any rate, a date of 1589 would give Greene priority in dramatizing such material and make him a much more original writer than he was regarded before, even though the play was not printed (probably from an acting copy) until 1594.

As has been realized for a long time, Greene's major printed source for his play was an anonymous prose romance entitled *The Famous History of Friar Bacon, Containing the Wonderful Things That He Did in His Life: Also the Manner of His Death; with the Lives and Deaths of the Two Conjurors Bungye and Vandermast, Very Pleasant and Delightful To Be Read.* At least this is the title of the earliest extant edition, a chapbook of 1627, although it is supposed to have been published originally in the middle of the sixteenth century. (See Waldo F. McNeir, "Traditional Elements in the Character of Greene's Friar Bungay," *SP*, 1948.) Greene may also have drawn minor details from Holinshed, Bale, Foxe, Bruno, among others, as well as from medieval stories about magicians and wizards like Merlin, Oberon, and Virgil. (See McNeir; also P. Z. Round, "Greene's Materials for *Friar Bacon and Friar Bungay*," *MLR*, 1926, and J. D. McCallum, "Greene's *Friar Bacon and Friar Bungay*, *MLN*, 1920.) But, as Seltzer observed, in transforming the material in the chapbook for dramatic use, Greene made several interesting and effective changes. Except for the title "Friar" he removed all references to Bacon as a churchman, as well as Bacon's insistence that his powers were based on science and not on magic, where Greene places them. Moreover, Greene also puts less stress on Bacon's patriotic intentions until the end of the play, where he also introduces a strongly religious element through Bacon's repentance. Similarly, he shifts the emphasis on the roles of some of the leading characters, such as the two friars, and Lacy and Edward.

Until recently it has also been the custom to say that in *Doctor Faustus* Marlowe illustrated the power and effects of the practice of black magic, and in *Friar Bacon* Greene portrayed the power and effects of white magic. But in 1952 Frank Town dissented in an article entitled " 'White Magic' in *Friar Bacon* and *Doctor Faustus*" (*MLN*), citing Bale's *Illustrium Maioris Britanniae Scriptorum Summarium*, which describes Bacon as a prestidigitator and necromantic magician, who worked marvels not through the power of God but by the operation of evil spirits. In Greene's play, Friar Bacon admits that he actually summons evil spirits from the depths to do his bidding before he finally repents his wrongdoing and abandons his practice. So Towne would seem to be right in concluding that "to make him out a 'harmless' white magician surely does violence to the rationale of the play." Seltzer follows up this idea in some detail, pointing out that in the opening scenes of the play Bacon is even willing to use his sorcerer's powers to help the amorous and unscrupulous Prince Edward in his plan to "enjoy" Margaret without marrying her—although Edward ultimately reforms when he meets a more suitable mate in Elinor. As Seltzer says, "Even though the seriousness of Bacon's art is eventually lightened through the comic decorum of the play, it is important to remember its basically dangerous significance," since occultism—nearly universally believed in during the Renaissance—was almost unanimously regarded as unchristian and diabolical. It was, in Seltzer's words, "an easy step from [people's] yearning to understand things past ordinary perception—the goal, for example, of the Friar Bacon in the anonymous play, *John of Bordeaux* (very likely by Greene)—to the inordinate desire for knowledge which causes Faustus. . . to call upon the powers of hell." (See McNeir, *PMLA*, 1949, on the authorship of *John of Bordeaux*.) Adolphus Ward has also studied the origins of Bacon's necromantic formulae in his one-volume edition of *Doctor Faustus and Friar Bacon*.

It has also been customary to speak of Margaret as the first good example of a well-developed, realistic, and appealing heroine in the English drama. Kenneth Muir, however, in "Robert Greene as Dramatist," in *Essays on Shakespeare and Elizabethan Drama*, has dissented by insisting that she is not really a three-dimensional person and that her character has been sacrificed to situation. He also believes that the play's plot construction hardly justifies Nashe's praise of Greene as a master of plot. Seltzer, however, disagrees on both counts, and shows how Greene has skilfully brought all the characters in both plots "under the wholesome influence" of Margaret, just as, "at one juncture or another, they come in contact with Bungay." To Seltzer, Margaret is a combination of two types of medieval and Renaissance heroine—the lady of true nobility living in lowly surroundings and the Patient Griselda, who was found in folklore long before Boccaccio, Petrarch, and Chaucer gave their versions of the tale. However, Margaret's humbleness and constancy to her love, in spite of Lacy's cruel testing, are so exaggerated, as is her courtly language, that at times they become amusing rather than affecting. This exaggeration may be accounted for by the fact that the whole spirit and atmosphere of the play were utterly alien to the sordidness of the real life Greene had been living. In spite of weaknesses, however, Greene, like Lyly and Peele, was another Elizabethan who helped show the way to Shakespeare.

The Malone Society reprint of the 1594 quarto, prepared by W. W. Greg, is the basis of the present text.

THE HONORABLE HISTORY OF FRIAR BACON AND FRIAR BUNGAY[1]

BY

ROBERT GREENE

[*DRAMATIS PERSONÆ*

KING HENRY THE THIRD.
EDWARD, *Prince of Wales, his son.*
EMPEROR OF GERMANY.
KING OF CASTILE.
LACY, *Earl of Lincoln* ⎫
WARREN, *Earl of Sussex* ⎬ *Edward's friends.*
ERMSBY, *a gentleman* ⎭
RALPH SIMNELL, *the king's fool.*
FRIAR ROGER BACON.
MILES, *his poor scholar.*
FRIAR BUNGAY.
JAQUES VANDERMAST, *a German magician.*
BURDEN ⎫
MASON ⎬ *doctors of Oxford.*
CLEMENT ⎭
LAMBERT ⎫
SERLSBY ⎬ *gentlemen.*

TWO SCHOLARS, *their sons.*
THE KEEPER OF FRESSINGFIELD.
HIS FRIEND.
THOMAS ⎫
RICHARD ⎬ *rustics.*
CONSTABLE.
A POST BOY.
LORDS, COUNTRY CLOWNS, *etc.*

ELINOR, *daughter to the King of Castile*
MARGARET,[2] *the keeper's daughter.*
JOAN, *a country wench.*
HOSTESS OF THE BELL AT HENLEY.

A DEVIL.
A SPEAKER FOR THE BRAZEN HEAD.
A SPIRIT IN THE SHAPE OF HERCULES.

SCENE: *England.*

TIME: *Thirteenth Century.*]

[SCENE i.

Framlingham.]

*Enter Edward the First,[3] malcontented, with
Lacy, Earl of Lincoln, John Warren,
Earl of Sussex, and Ermsby, gentle-
man; Rafe[4] Simnell, the king's fool.*

LACY. Why looks my lord like to a troubled sky
When heaven's bright shine is shadowed
with a fog?
Alate[5] we ran the deer, and through
the lawns[6]

Stripped[7] with our nags the lofty frolic
bucks
That scudded fore the teasers[8] like the
wind.
Ne'er was the deer of merry Fressing-
field
So lustily pulled down by jolly mates,
Nor shared the farmers such fat venison,
So frankly dealt,[9] this hundred years
before;
Nor have I seen my lord more frolic in
the chase,   10
And now—changed to a melancholy
dump.[10]
WARREN. After the prince got to the
keeper's lodge,

---

[1] The original title continues: "As It Was
Played by Her Majesty's Servants."
[2] In the original usually spelled *Margret*.
[3] Should be Prince Edward, since Henry III is
still king at the end of the play.
[4] Variant of *Ralph*. [5] Of late, lately. [6] Glades.

[7] Outstripped.   [9] Generously divided.
[8] Hunting dogs.   [10] Fit of abstraction.

267

And had been jocund in the house awhile,
Tossing off ale and milk in country cans,
Whether it was the country's sweet content,
Or else the bonny damsel filled us drink,
That seemed so stately in her stammel [1] red,
Or that a qualm did cross his stomach then,
But straight he fell into his passions.

ERMSBY. Sirrah Rafe, what say you to your master? 20
Shall he thus all amort [2] live malcontent?

RAFE. Hearest thou, Ned?—Nay, look if he will speak to me!

EDWARD. What say'st thou to me, fool?

RAFE. I prithee, tell me, Ned, art thou in love with the keeper's daughter?

EDWARD. How if I be, what then?

RAFE. Why, then, sirrah, I'll teach thee how to deceive Love.

EDWARD. How, Rafe? 30

RAFE. Marry, sirrah Ned, thou shalt put on my cap and my coat and my dagger, and I will put on thy clothes and thy sword; and so thou shalt be my fool.

EDWARD. And what of this?

RAFE. Why, so thou shalt beguile Love, for Love is such a proud scab [3] that he will never meddle with fools nor children. Is not Rafe's counsel good, Ned?

EDWARD. Tell me, Ned Lacy, didst thou mark the maid, 40
How lively in her country weeds she looked?
A bonnier wench all Suffolk cannot yield.
All Suffolk! Nay, all England holds none such!

RAFE. Sirrah Will Ermsby, Ned is deceived.

ERMSBY. Why, Rafe?

RAFE. He says all England hath no such, and I say, and I'll stand to it, there is one better in Warwickshire.

WARREN. How provest thou that, Rafe?

RAFE. Why, is not the abbot a [51 learned man, and hath read many books, and thinkest thou he hath not more learning than thou to choose a bonny wench?

Yes, I warrant thee, by his whole grammar. [4]

ERMSBY. A good reason, Rafe.

EDWARD. I tell thee, Lacy, that her sparkling eyes
Do lighten forth sweet love's alluring fire;
And in her tresses she doth fold the looks
Of such as gaze upon her golden hair; 61
Her bashful white, mixed with the morning's red,
Luna doth boast upon her lovely cheeks;
Her front is Beauty's table, [5] where she paints
The glories of her gorgeous excellence;
Her teeth are shelves of precious margarites, [6]
Richly enclosed with ruddy coral cleeves. [7]
Tush, Lacy, she is Beauty's overmatch,
If thou survey'st her curious imagery. [8]

LACY. I grant, my lord, the damsel is as fair 70
As simple Suffolk's homely towns can yield;
But in the court be quainter [9] dames than she,
Whose faces are enriched with honor's taint, [10]
Whose beauties stand upon the stage of fame,
And vaunt their trophies in the courts of love.

EDWARD. Ah, Ned, but hadst thou watched her as myself,
And seen the secret beauties of the maid,
Their courtly coyness were but foolery.

ERMSBY. Why, how watched you her, my lord?

EDWARD. Whenas she swept like Venus through the house, 80
And in her shape fast folded up my thoughts,
Into the milk house went I with the maid,
And there amongst the cream bowls she did shine
As Pallas 'mongst her princely huswifery. [11]

[1] Woolen cloth.
[2] À la mort, spiritless.
[3] Merry wag.
[4] Learning.
[5] Tablet.
[6] Pearls.
[7] Cliffs.
[8] Rare appearance.
[9] Daintier, more fastidious.
[10] Tint.
[11] Housekeeping.

She turned her smock over her lily arms,
And dived them into milk to run her
    cheese;
But, whiter than the milk, her crystal
    skin,
Checked with lines of azure, made her [1]
    blush
That art or nature durst bring for com-
    pare.
Ermsby, if thou hadst seen, as I did
    note it well,   90
How Beauty played the huswife, how
    this girl,
Like Lucrece, laid her fingers to the work,
Thou wouldest with Tarquin hazard
    Rome and all
To win the lovely maid of Fressingfield.

RAFE. Sirrah Ned, wouldst fain have
her?

EDWARD. Ay, Rafe.

RAFE. Why, Ned, I have laid the plot
in my head; thou shalt have her already.

EDWARD. I'll give thee a new coat, and
learn me that.[2]   101

RAFE. Why, sirrah Ned, we'll ride to
Oxford to Friar Bacon. O, he is a brave
scholar, sirrah; they say he is a brave
nigromancer,[3] that he can make women of
devils, and he can juggle cats into coster-
mongers.

EDWARD. And how then, Rafe?

RAFE. Marry, sirrah, thou shalt go to
him, and because [4] thy father Harry [110
shall not miss thee, he shall turn me into
thee; and I'll to the court, and I'll prince it
out; and he shall make thee either a silken
purse full of gold or else a fine-wrought
smock.

EDWARD. But how shall I have the
maid?

RAFE. Marry, sirrah, if thou be'st a
silken purse full of gold, then on Sundays
she'll hang thee by her side, and you [120
must not say a word. Now, sir, when
she comes into a great press of people, for
fear of the cutpurse, on a sudden she'll
swap thee into her plackerd;[5] then, sirrah,
being there, you may plead for yourself.

ERMSBY. Excellent policy!

EDWARD. But how if I be a wrought
smock?

RAFE. Then she'll put thee into her
chest and lay thee into lavender, and [130
upon some good day she'll put thee on;
and at night when you go to bed, then being
turned from a smock to a man, you may
make up the match.

LACY. Wonderfully wisely counseled,
Rafe.

EDWARD. Rafe shall have a new coat.

RAFE. God thank you—when I have
it on my back, Ned.

EDWARD. Lacy, the fool hath laid a per-
fect plot,   140
Forwhy [6] our country Margaret is so
    coy
And stands so much upon her honest
    points[7]
That marriage or no market with the
    maid
Ermsby, it must be nigroma[n]tic spells
And charms of art[8] that must enchain
    her love,
Or else shall Edward never win the girl.
Therefore, my wags, we'll horse us in
    the morn,
And post to Oxford to this jolly friar.
Bacon shall by his magic do this deed.

WARREN. Content, my lord; and that's
    a speedy way   150
To wean these headstrong puppies from
    the teat.

EDWARD. I am unknown, not taken for
    the prince;
They only deem us frolic courtiers,
That revel thus among our liege's game;
Therefore I have devised a policy.
Lacy, thou know'st next Friday is
    S[aint] James',[9]
And then the country flocks to Harles-
    ton Fair;
Then will the keeper's daughter frolic
    there,
And overshine the troop of all the maids
That come to see and to be seen that
    day.   160
Haunt thee disguised among the coun-
    try swains;
Feign th'art a farmer's son, not far
    from thence;
Espy her loves, and who she liketh best;
Cote[10] him, and court her, to control
    the clown;[11]

---

[1] *I.e.*, any other woman.
[2] If you teach me that.
[3] Necromancer.
[4] In order that.
[5] Thrust thee into her skirt pocket.
[6] Because.   [8] Magic.   [9] July 25.   [10] Outstrip.
[7] Chaste principles.   [11] Overmaster the rustic.

Say that the courtier tired [1] all in green,
That helped her handsomely to run her
　　cheese,
And filled her father's lodge with venison,
Commends him, and sends fairings, [2]
　　to herself.
Buy something worthy of her parentage,
Not worth her beauty, for, Lacy, then
　　the fair　　　　　　　　　　　　170
Affords no jewel fitting for the maid.
And, when thou talkest of me, note if
　　she blush.
O, then she loves! But, if her cheeks
　　wax pale,
Disdain it is. Lacy, send [3] how she fares,
And spare no time nor cost to win her loves.
LACY. I will, my lord, so execute this charge
As if that Lacy were in love with her.
EDWARD. Send letters speedily to Ox-
　　ford of the news.
RAFE. And, sirrah Lacy, buy me a
thousand thousand million of fine bells.
LACY. What wilt thou do with them,
Rafe?　　　　　　　　　　　　　182
RAFE. Marry, every time that Ned sighs
for the keeper's daughter, I'll tie a bell
about him; and so within three or four
days I will send word to his father Harry
that his son and my master Ned is be-
come Love's morris dance.
EDWARD. Well, Lacy, look with care unto
　　thy charge,　　　　　　　　　189
And I will haste to Oxford to the friar,
That he by art and thou by secret gifts
Mayst make me lord of merry Fressing-
　　field.
LACY. God send your honor your heart's
　　desire.　　　　　　　　　*Exeunt.*

[SCENE ii.

Friar Bacon's study at Brasenose College,
Oxford.]

Enter Friar Bacon, with Miles, his poor
　　scholar, with books under his arm; with
　　them Burden, Mason, Clement, three
　　　　　　　　　　　　doctors.

BACON. Miles, where are you?
MILES. *Hic sum, dostissime et reveren-*
dissime doctor. [4]

BACON. *Attulisti nos libros meos de*
necromantia? [5]
MILES. *Ecce quam bonum et quam*
jocundum, habitares libros in unum! [6]
BACON. Now, masters of our academic
　　state,
That rule in Oxford, viceroys in your
　　place,
Whose heads contain maps of the liberal
　　arts,　　　　　　　　　　　　10
Spending your time in depth of learned
　　skill,
Why flock you thus to Bacon's secret
　　cell,
A friar newly stalled [7] in Brazen-nose?
Say what's your mind, that I may make
　　reply.
BURDEN. Bacon, we hear that long we
　　have suspect,
That thou art read in magic's mystery—
In pyromancy, to divine by flames;
To tell, by hydroma[n]tic, ebbs and tides;
By aeromancy to discover doubts,
To plain out [8] questions, as Apollo did. 20
BACON. Well, Master Burden, what of
all this?
MILES. Marry, sir, he doth but fulfill,
by rehearsing of these names, the fable of
the Fox and the Grapes; that which is
above us pertains nothing to us.
BURDEN. I tell thee, Bacon, Oxford makes
　　report—
Nay, England and the court of Henry
　　says—
Th'art making of a brazen head by art,
Which shall unfold strange doubts and
　　aphorisms, [9]　　　　　　　　30
And read a lecture in philosophy;
And, by the help of devils and ghastly
　　fiends,
Thou mean'st, ere many years or days
　　be past,
To compass England with a wall of
　　brass.
BACON. And what of this?
MILES. What of this, master? Why,
he doth speak mystically, for he knows,
if your skill fail to make a brazen head, yet
Mother Waters' strong ale will fit his turn
to make him have a copper nose.　　40

---

[1] Attired.　　　　[2] Gifts bought at the fair.
[3] Send news of.
[4] Here I am, most learned and venerable doctor. (The Latin throughout the play is corrupt.
Translations are approximate.)

[5] Have you brought us my books on magic?
[6] How good and how pleasant it is to live
together among books!　　[7] Installed.　　[8] Explain.
[9] Statement of scientific principles.

CLEMENT. Bacon, we come not grieving
at thy skill,
But joying that our academy yields
A man supposed the wonder of the
world;
For, if thy cunning work these miracles,
England and Europe shall admire[1] thy
fame,
And Oxford shall in characters of brass
And statues such as were built up in
Rome
Eternize Friar Bacon for his art.
MASON. Then, gentle friar, tell us thy
intent.
BACON. Seeing you come as friends unto
the friar,   50
Resolve you,[2] doctors, Bacon can by
books
Make storming Boreas thunder from
his cave,
And dim fair Luna to a dark eclipse.
The great archruler, potentate of hell,
Trembles when Bacon bids him or his
fiends
Bow to the force of his pentagoron.[3]
What art can work, the frolic friar
knows;
And therefore will I turn my magic
books,
And strain out nigromancy to the deep.[4]
I have contrived and framed a head of
brass   60
(I made Belcephon hammer out the
stuff),
And that by art shall read philosophy.
And I will strengthen England by my
skill,
That, if ten Cæsars lived and reigned
in Rome,
With all the legions Europe doth con-
tain,
They should not touch a grass of English
ground.
The work that Ninus reared at Babylon,
The brazen walls framed by Semiramis,
Carved out like to the portal of the sun,
Shall not be such as rings the English
strand   70
From Dover to the market place of Rye.
BURDEN. Is this possible?

MILES. I'll bring ye two or three wit-
nesses.
BURDEN. What be those?
MILES. Marry, sir, three or four as
honest devils and good companions as
any be in hell.
MASON. No doubt but magic may do
much in this;   79
For he that reads but mathematic rules
Shall find conclusions that avail to
work
Wonders that pass the common sense
of men.
BURDEN. But Bacon roves a blow beyond
his reach,[5]
And tells of more than magic can per-
form,
Thinking to get a fame by fooleries.
Have I not passed as far in state of
schools,
And read of many secrets?   Yet to
think
That heads of brass can utter any voice,
Or more, to tell of deep philosophy—
This is a fable Æsop had forgot.   90
BACON. Burden, thou wrong'st me in
detracting thus;
Bacon loves not to stuff himself with
lies.
But tell me fore these doctors, if thou
dare,
Of certain questions I shall move to
thee.
BURDEN. I will; ask what thou can.
MILES. Marry, sir, he'll straight be
on your pickpack,[6] to know whether the
feminine or the masculine gender be most
worthy.[7]   99
BACON. Were you not yesterday, Mas-
ter Burden, at Henley upon the Thames?
BURDEN. I was. What then?
BACON. What book studied you thereon
all night?
BURDEN. I?   None at all; I read not
there a line.
BACON. Then, doctors, Friar Bacon's art
knows naught.
CLEMENT. What say you to this, Master
Burden? Doth he not touch you?
BURDEN. I pass not of[8] his frivolous
speeches.   111

---

[1] Wonder at.   [2] Understand.
[3] Pentagonon, a five-pointed emblem with
magical powers.
[4] Exert my magic to the utmost.

[5] Shoots at a target beyond his range.
[6] Pickaback.   [8] Care not for.
[7] As in William Lilly's Latin grammar.

MILES. Nay, Master Burden, my master, ere he hath done with you, will turn you from a doctor to a dunce, and shake you so small that he will leave no more learning in you than is in Balaam's ass.

BACON. Masters, for that learned Burden's skill is deep,

And sore he doubts of Bacon's cabalism,

I'll show you why he haunts to Henley oft:

Not, doctors, for to taste the fragrant air,   120

But there to spend the night in alchemy,

To multiply with secret spells of art.

Thus private steals he learning from us all.

To prove my sayings true, I'll show you straight

The book he keeps at Henley for himself.

MILES. Nay, now my master goes to

MILES. Nay, now my master goes to conjuration, take heed!

BACON. Masters, stand still; fear not, I'll show you but his book. (*Here he conjures.*)

Per omnes deos infernales, Belcephon! [1]   130

Enter a Woman with a shoulder of mutton on a spit, and a Devil.

MILES. O master, cease your conjuration, or you spoil all, for here's a she-devil come with a shoulder of mutton on a spit. You have marred the devil's supper; but no doubt he thinks our college fare is slender, and so hath sent you his cook with a shoulder of mutton, to make it exceed.[2]

HOSTESS. O, where am I, or what's become of me?

BACON. What art thou?   140

HOSTESS. Hostess at Henley, mistress of the Bell.

BACON. How camest thou here?

HOSTESS. As I was in the kitchen 'mongst the maids,

Spitting the meat against supper for my guess,[3]

A motion [4] moved me to look forth of door.

No sooner had I pried[5] into the yard,

But straight a whirlwind hoisted me from thence,

And mounted me aloft unto the clouds.

As in a trance, I thought nor feared naught,

Nor know I where or whither I was ta'en,   150

Nor where I am nor what these persons be.

BACON. No?   Know you not Master Burden?

HOSTESS. O, yes, good sir, he is my daily guest.—

What, Master Burden, 't was but yesternight

That you and I at Henley played at cards.

BURDEN. I know not what we did!— A pox of all conjuring friars!

CLEMENT. Now, jolly friar, tell us, is this the book

That Burden is so careful to look on?

BACON. It is.—But, Burden, tell me now,

Thinkest thou that Bacon's nigromantic skill   161

Cannot perform his head and wall of brass,

When he can fetch thine hostess in such post?

MILES. I'll warrant you, master, if Master Burden could conjure as well as you, he would have his book every night from Henley to study on at Oxford.

MASON. Burden, what, are you mated[6] by this frolic friar?—

Look how he droops; his guilty conscience

Drives him to bash,[7] and makes his hostess blush.   170

BACON. Well, mistress, for I will not have you missed,

You shall to Henley to cheer up your guests

Fore supper gin.[8]—Burden, bid her adieu;

Say farewell to your hostess fore she goes.—

Sirrah, away, and set her safe at home.

HOSTESS. Master Burden, when shall we see you at Henley?

Exeunt Hostess and the Devil.

BURDEN. The devil take thee and Henley too!   179

MILES. Master, shall I make a good motion?

---

[1] By all the infernal gods, Belcephon!
[2] Become better.   [3] Guests.   [4] Impulse.
[5] Peered.

[6] Confounded.   [7] Be abashed.   [8] Begin.

BACON. What's that?

MILES. Marry, sir, now that my hostess is gone to provide supper, conjure up another spirit, and send Doctor Burden flying after.

BACON. Thus, rulers of our academic state,
You have seen the friar frame his art by proof;
And as the college calléd Brazen-nose
Is under him, and he the master there,
So surely shall this head of brass be framed,   191
And yield forth strange and uncouth [1] aphorisms,
And hell and Hecate shall fail the friar,
But I will circle England round with brass.

MILES. So be it *et nunc et semper*,[2] amen.   *Exeunt omnes.*

[SCENE iii.

Harleston Fair.]

Enter Margaret, the Fair Maid of Fressingfield, with Thomas, [Richard,] and Joan, and other clowns; Lacy disguised in country apparel.

THOMAS. By my troth, Margaret, here's a weather is able to make a man call his father whoreson. If this weather hold, we shall have hay good cheap,[3] and butter and cheese at Harleston will bear no price.

MARGARET. Thomas, maids, when they come to see the fair,
Count not to make a cope [4] for dearth of hay.
When we have turned our butter to the salt,
And set our cheese safely upon the racks,
Then let our fathers price it as they please.   10
We country sluts of merry Fressingfield
Come to buy needless naughts to make us fine,
And look that young men should be frank this day,
And court us with such fairings as they can.
Phœbus is blithe, and frolic looks from heaven,

As when he courted lovely Semele,
Swearing the peddlers shall have empty packs,
If that fair weather may make chapmen buy.

LACY. But, lovely Peggy, Semele is dead,
And therefore Phœbus from his palace pries,   20
And, seeing such a sweet and seemly saint,
Shows all his glories for to court yourself.

MARGARET. This is a fairing, gentle sir, indeed,
To soothe me up with such smooth flattery;
But, learn of me, your scoff's too broad before.[5]—
Well, Joan, our beauties must abide their jests;
We serve the turn in jolly Fressingfield.

JOAN. Margaret, a farmer's daughter for a farmer's son!
I warrant you, the meanest of us both
Shall have a mate to lead us from the church.   30
But, Thomas, what's the news? What, in a dump?
Give me your hand; we are near a peddler's shop.
Out with your purse; we must have fairings now.

THOMAS. Faith, Joan, and shall. I'll bestow a fairing on you, and then we will to the tavern, and snap off a pint of wine or two.

All this while Lacy whispers Margaret in the ear.

MARGARET. Whence are you, sir? Of Suffolk? For your terms
Are finer than the common sort of men.

LACY. Faith, lovely girl, I am of Beccles by,[6]   40
Your neighbor, not above six miles from hence,
A farmer's son, that never was so quaint[7]
But that he could do courtesy to such dames.
But trust me, Margaret, I am sent in charge
From him that reveled in your father's house,

---

[1] Unusual.
[2] Now and forever.
[3] At a good price.
[4] Bargain.
[5] *I.e.*, obvious.
[6] From near Beccles.
[7] Odd, boorish.

And filled his lodge with cheer and
venison,
Tired in green. He sent you this rich
purse;
His token that he helped you run your
cheese,
And in the milk house chatted with
yourself.

MARGARET. To me?   You forget your-
self.[1]   50

LACY. Women are often weak in memory.

MARGARET. O, pardon, sir, I call to mind
the man.
'Twere little manners to refuse his gift,
And yet I hope he sends it not for love;
For we have little leisure to debate of
that.

JOAN. What, Margaret, blush not; maids
must have their loves!

THOMAS. Nay, by the Mass, she looks
pale as if she were angry.

RICHARD. Sirrah, are you of Beccles?
I pray, how doth Goodman Cob? My [60
father bought a horse of him.—I'll tell
you, Margaret, a [2] were good to be a
gentleman's jade, for of all things the
foul hilding [3] could not abide a dung cart.

MARGARET. [Aside.] How different is this
farmer from the rest
That erst as yet [4] have pleased my
wand'ring sight!
His words are witty, quickened with
a smile,
His courtesy gentle, smelling of the
court;
Facile and debonair in all his deeds,
Proportioned as was Paris, when, in
gray,[5]   70
He courted Œnon in the vale by Troy.
Great lords have come and pleaded for
my love—
Who but the keeper's lass of Fressing-
field?
And yet methinks this farmer's jolly[6]
son
Passeth[7] the proudest that hath pleased
mine eye.
But, Peg, disclose not that thou art in
love,
And show as yet no sign of love to him,

Although thou well wouldst wish him
for thy love.
Keep that to thee till time doth serve
thy turn,
To show the grief wherein thy heart
doth burn.—   80
Come, Joan and Thomas, shall we to
the fair?
You, Beccles man, will not forsake us
now?

LACY. Not whilst I may have such quaint
girls as you.

MARGARET. Well, if you chance to come
by Fressingfield,
Make but a step into the keeper's lodge,
And such poor fare as woodmen can
afford,
Butter and cheese, cream and fat venison,
You shall have store, and welcome
therewithal.

LACY. Gramercies, Peggy; look for me
ere long.   *Exeunt omnes.*

[SCENE iv.

Hampton Court.]

*Enter Henry the Third, the Emperor, the
King of Castile, Elinor, his daughter,
Jaques Vandermast, a German.*

HENRY. Great men of Europe. monarchs
of the West,
Ringed with the walls of old Oceanus,
Whose lofty surge is[8] like the battle-
ments
That compassed high-built Babel in
with towers,
Welcome, my lords, welcome, brave
western kings,
To England's shore, whose promontory
cleeves
Shows Albion is another little world.
Welcome says English Henry to you
all;
Chiefly unto the lovely Elinor,
Who dared for Edward's sake cut
through the seas,   10
And venture as Agenor's damsel[9] through
the deep,
To get the love of Henry's wanton son.

CASTILE. England's rich monarch, brave
Plantagenet,

---

[1] Surely you mistake.   [3] Good-for-nothing.
[2] He.   [4] Until now.
[5] Traditional garb of shepherds.
[6] *Jolie*, handsome, gay.   [7] Surpasseth.
[8] Original has *surges*.
[9] Europa, carried off by Zeus.

The Pyren Mounts swelling above the
    clouds
That ward the wealthy Castile in with
    walls
Could not detain the beauteous Elinor;
But, hearing of the fame of Edward's
    youth,
She dared to brook Neptunus' haughty
    pride,
And bide the brunt of froward Æolus.
Then may fair England welcome her
    the more.   20
ELINOR. After that English Henry by
    his lords
Had sent Prince Edward's lovely coun-
    terfeit,[1]
A present to the Castile Elinor,
The comely portrait of so brave a man,
The virtuous fame discoursèd of his
    deeds,
Edward's courageous resolution,
Done at the Holy Land fore Damas'[2]
    walls,
Led both mine eye and thoughts in
    equal links
To like so of the English monarch's son
That I attempted perils for his sake.   30
EMPEROR. Where is the prince, my lord?
HENRY. He posted down, not long since,
    from the court
To Suffolk side, to merry Framlingham,
To sport himself amongst my fallow
    deer;
From thence, by packets sent to Hamp-
    ton House,
We hear the prince is ridden with his
    lords
To Oxford, in the academy there
To hear dispute amongst the learned
    men.
But we will send forth letters for my son,
To will him come from Oxford to the
    court.   40
EMPEROR. Nay, rather, Henry, let us,
    as we be,
Ride for to visit Oxford with our train.
Fain would I see your universities,
And what learned men your academy
    yields.
From Hapsburg have I brought a
    learned clerk
To hold dispute with English orators.

This doctor, surnamed Jaques Vander-
    mast,
A German born, passed into Padua,
To Florence and to fair Bolonia,
To Paris, Rheims, and stately Orleans, 50
And, talking there with men of art,
    put down
The chiefest of them all in aphorisms,
In magic, and the mathematic rules.
Now let us, Henry, try him in your
    schools.
HENRY. He shall, my lord; this motion
    likes me well
We'll progress[3] straight to Oxford with
    our trains,
And see what men our academy brings.—
And, wonder Vandermast, welcome to
    me.
In Oxford shalt thou find a jolly friar
Called Friar Bacon, England's only
    flower.   60
Set him but nonplus in his magic spells,
And make him yield in mathematic
    rules,
And for thy glory I will bind thy brows,
Not with a poet's garland made of bays,
But with a coronet of choicest gold.
Whilst then[4] we f[l]it to Oxford with
    our troops,
Let's in and banquet in our English
    court.   *Exit [with his Train].*

[SCENE V.

An Oxford street.]

*Enter Rafe Simnell in Edward's apparel;
Edward, Warren, Ermsby, disguised.*

RAFE. Where be these vagabond knaves,
that they attend no better on their master?

EDWARD. If it please your honor, we
are all ready at an inch.[5]

RAFE. Sirrah Ned, I'll have no more
post horse to ride on. I'll have another
fetch.[6]

ERMSBY. I pray you, how is that, my
lord?   10

RAFE. Marry, sir, I'll send to the Isle
of Ely for four or five dozen of geese, and
I'll have them tied six and six together
with whipcord. Now upon their backs
will I have a fair field bed[7] with a canopy;

[1] Picture.   [2] Damascus'.
[3] Journey in state.

[4] Until the time that. [5] At any instant. [6] Trick.
[7] Portable bed used in campaigns.

and so, when it is my pleasure, I'll flee into what place I please. This will be easy.

WARREN. Your honor hath said well.
But shall we to Brazen-nose College before we pull off our boots?   20

ERMSBY. Warren, well motioned; we will
    to the friar
Before we revel it within the town.—
Rafe, see you keep your countenance
    like a prince.

RAFE. Wherefore have I such a company of cutting [1] knaves to wait upon me,
but to keep and defend my countenance
against all mine enemies? Have you not
good swords and bucklers?

Enter Bacon and Miles.

ERMSBY. Stay, who comes here?

WARREN. Some scholar; and we'll   [30
ask him where Friar Bacon is.

BACON. Why, thou arrant dunce, shall
I never make thee good scholar? Doth
not all the town cry out and say, "Friar
Bacon's subsizar[2] is the greatest blockhead in all Oxford"? Why, thou canst not
speak one word of true Latin.

MILES. No, sir? Yes, what is this else?
Ego sum tuus homo—"I am your man."
I warrant you, sir, as good Tully's   [40
phrase as any is in Oxford.

BACON. Come on, sirrah! What part
of speech is *Ego?*

MILES. *Ego*, that is "I"; marry, *nomen
substantivo.*

BACON. How prove you that?

MILES. Why, sir, let him prove himself, and a will; "I" can be heard, felt,
and understood.   49

BACON. O gross dunce!   *Here beat him.*

EDWARD. Come, let us break off this
dispute between these two.—Sirrah, where
is Brazen-nose College?

MILES. Not far from Coppersmiths'
Hall.

EDWARD. What, dost thou mock me?

MILES. Not I, sir. But what would
you at Brazen-nose?

ERMSBY. Marry, we would speak with
Friar Bacon.   60

MILES. Whose men be you?

ERMSBY. Marry, scholar, here's our
master.

RAFE. Sirrah, I am the master of these
good fellows. Mayst thou not know me to
be a lord by my reparel?

MILES. Then here's good game for the
hawk; for here's the master fool and a
covey of coxcombs. One wise man, I
think, would spring [3] you all.   70

EDWARD. Gog's [4] wounds! Warren,
kill him!

WARREN. Why, Ned, I think the
devil be in my sheath; I cannot get out
my dagger.

ERMSBY. Nor I mine. 'Swones,[5] Ned,
I think I am bewitched.

MILES. A company of scabs! The
proudest of you all draw your weapon, if he
can.—[*Aside.*] See how boldly I speak, [80
now my master is by.

EDWARD. I strive in vain; but, if my sword
    be shut
And conjured fast by magic in my sheath,
Villain, here is my fist!
        Strike him a box on the ear.

MILES. O, I beseech you, conjure his
hands too, that he may not lift his arms
to his head, for he is light-fingered!

RAFE. Ned, strike him; I'll warrant [6]
thee, by mine honor.

BACON. What means the English prince
    to wrong my man?   90

EDWARD. To whom speakest thou?

BACON. To thee.

EDWARD. Who art thou?

BACON. Could you not judge when all
    your swords grew fast
That Friar Bacon was not far from
    hence?
Edward, King Henry's son and Prince
    of Wales,
Thy fool disguised cannot conceal thy-
    self.
I know both Ermsby and the Sussex
    earl,
Else Friar Bacon had but little skill.
Thou comest in post from merry Fres-
    singfield,   100
Fast-fancied [7] to the keeper's bonny
    lass,
To crave some succor of the jolly friar;

---

[1] Swaggering.
[2] Student who worked for his board and tui-
tion.

[3] Springe, ensnare.   [6] Back, support.
[4] God's.   [7] Bound by love.
[5] Swounds, God's wounds.

And Lacy, Earl of Lincoln, hast thou left
To treat [1] fair Margaret to allow thy
    loves.
But friends are men, and love can baffle
    lords;
The earl both woos and courts her for
    himself.
WARREN. Ned, this is strange; the friar
    knoweth all.
ERMSBY. Apollo could not utter more than
    this.
EDWARD. I stand amazed to hear this
    jolly friar
Tell even the very secrets of my
    thoughts.—   110
But, learned Bacon, since thou knowest
    the cause
Why I did post so fast from Fressing-
    field,
Help, friar, at a pinch, that I may have
The love of lovely Margaret to myself,
And, as I am true Prince of Wales, I'll give
Living and lands to strength thy col-
    lege state.
WARREN. Good friar, help the prince in
    this.
RAFE. Why, servant Ned, will not the
friar do it? Were not my sword glued to
my scabbard by conjuration, I would [120
cut off his head, and make him do it by
force.
MILES. In faith, my lord, your man-
hood and your sword is all alike; they are
so fast conjured that we shall never see
them.
ERMSBY. What, doctor, in a dump?
    Tush, help the prince,
And thou shalt see how liberal he will
    prove.
BACON. Crave not such actions greater
    dumps than these?
I will, my lord, strain out my magic
    spells;   130
For this day comes the earl to Fressing-
    field,
And fore that night shuts in the day
    with dark,
They'll be betrothéd each to other fast.
But come with me; we'll to my study
    straight,
And in a glass prospective [2] I will show
What's done this day in merry Fres-
    singfield.

[1] Entreat.   [2] Magic mirror.

EDWARD. Gramercies, Bacon; I will
    quite [3] thy pain.
BACON. But send your train, my lord,
    into the town.
My scholar shall go bring them to their
    inn.
Meanwhile we'll see the knavery of
    the earl.   140
EDWARD. Warren, leave me, and, Erms-
    by, take the fool;
Let him be master, and go revel it
Till I and Friar Bacon talk awhile.
WARREN. We will, my lord.
RAFE. Faith, Ned, and I'll lord it out
till thou comest. I'll be Prince of Wales
over all the blackpots [4] in Oxford.   *Exeunt.*

[SCENE vi.

Bacon's study.]

Bacon and Edward goes into the study.

BACON. Now, frolic Edward, welcome
    to my cell.
Here tempers Friar Bacon many toys, [5]
And holds this place his consistory
    court,
Wherein the devils plead homage to
    his words.
Within this glass prospective thou shalt
    see
This day what's done in merry Fres-
    singfield
Twixt lovely Peggy and the Lincoln
    earl.
EDWARD. Friar, thou glad'st me. Now
    shall Edward try
How Lacy meaneth to his sovereign
    lord.
BACON. Stand there and look directly
    in the glass.   10

Enter Margaret and Friar Bungay. [6]

What sees my lord?
EDWARD. I see the keeper's lovely lass
    appear,
As bright-sun [7] as the paramour of
    Mars,
Only attended by a jolly friar.

[3] Requite, reward.   [4] Leather wine jugs.
[5] Perfects many trifles.
[6] The persons in the magic glass are seen but
not heard by Edward.
[7] Brightsome (?).

BACON. Sit still, and keep the crystal in your eye.

MARGARET. But tell me, Friar Bungay, is it true
That this fair courteous country swain,
Who says his father is a farmer nigh,
Can be Lord Lacy, Earl of Lincolnshire?
BUNGAY. Peggy, 'tis true; 'tis Lacy for my life,   20
Or else mine art and cunning both doth fail,
Left by Prince Edward to procure his loves;
For he in green, that holp you run your cheese,
Is son to Henry, and the Prince of Wales.
MARGARET. Be what he will, his lure is but for lust.
But did Lord Lacy like poor Margaret,
Or would he deign to wed a country lass,
Friar, I would his humble handmaid be,
And for great wealth quite him with courtesy.
BUNGAY. Why, Margaret, dost thou love him?   30
MARGARET. His personage, like the pride of vaunting Troy,
Might well avouch to shadow[1] Helen's 'scape.[2]
His wit is quick and ready in conceit,
As Greece afforded in her chiefest prime,
Courteous, ah, friar, full of pleasing smiles!
Trust me, I love too much to tell thee more;
Suffice, to me he's England's paramour.[3]
BUNGAY. Hath not each eye that viewed thy pleasing face
Surnaméd thee the Fair Maid of Fressingfield?
MARGARET. Yes, Bungay; and would God the lovely earl   40
Had that in esse[4] that so many sought.
BUNGAY. Fear not, the friar will not be behind
To show his cunning to entangle love.

EDWARD. I think the friar courts the bonny wench;
Bacon, methinks he is a lusty churl.
BACON. Now look, my lord.

Enter Lacy [disguised as before].

EDWARD. Gog's wounds, Bacon, here comes Lacy!
BACON. Sit still, my lord, and mark the comedy.

BUNGAY. Here's Lacy; Margaret, step aside awhile.   [*They withdraw.*]
LACY. Daphne, the damsel that caught Phœbus fast,   50
And locked him in the brightness of her looks,
Was not so beauteous in Apollo's eyes
As is fair Margaret to the Lincoln earl.
Recant thee, Lacy. Thou art put in trust.
Edward, thy sovereign's son, hath chosen thee,
A secret[5] friend, to court her for himself,
And darest thou wrong thy prince with treachery?
Lacy, love makes no exception of a friend,
Nor deems it of a prince but as a man.
Honor bids thee control him in his lust.
His wooing is not for to wed the girl,   61
But to entrap her and beguile the lass.
Lacy, thou lovest; then brook not such abuse,
But wed her, and abide thy prince's frown,
For better die than see her live disgraced.
MARGARET. Come, friar, I will shake him from his dumps.—   [*Comes forward.*]
How cheer you, sir? A penny for your thought!
You're early up, pray God it be the near.[6]
What, come from Beccles in a morn so soon?
LACY. Thus watchful[7] are such men as live in love,   70
Whose eyes brook broken slumbers for their sleep.
I tell thee, Peggy, since last Harleston fair
My mind hath felt a heap of passions.
MARGARET. A trusty man, that court it for your friend!
Woo you still for the courtier all in green?
I marvel that he sues not for himself.

---

[1] Excuse.   [3] Darling.
[2] Original reads *cape*.   [4] In actuality.
[5] Close.   [7] Sleepless.
[6] A common expression meaning *the nearer to your purpose.*

LACY. Peggy, I pleaded first to get your grace for him;

But, when mine eyes surveyed your beauteous looks,

Love, like a wag,[1] straight dived into my heart,

And there did shrine the idea[2] of yourself. 80

Pity me, though I be a farmer's son;

And measure not my riches, but my love.

MARGARET. You are very hasty; for to garden well,

Seeds must have time to sprout before they spring.

Love ought to creep as doth the dial's shade,

For timely[3] ripe is rotten too-too soon.

BUNGAY. [Coming forward.]   Deus hic.[4]

Room for a merry friar!

What, youth of Beccles, with the keeper's lass?

'Tis well. But, tell me, hear you any news?

MARGARET. No, friar. What news?   90

BUNGAY. Hear you not how the pursuivants do post

With proclamations through each country town?

LACY. For what, gentle friar?   Tell the news.

BUNGAY. Dwell'st thou in Beccles, and hear'st not of these news?

Lacy, the Earl of Lincoln, is late fled

From Windsor court, disguiséd like a swain,

And lurks about the country here unknown.

Henry suspects him of some treachery,

And therefore doth proclaim in every way

That who can take the Lincoln earl shall have, 100

Paid in the Exchequer, twenty thousand crowns.

LACY. The Earl of Lincoln! Friar, thou art mad!

It was some other; thou mistakest the man.

The Earl of Lincoln! Why, it cannot be!

MARGARET. Yes, very well, my lord, for you are he.

The keeper's daughter took you prisoner.

Lord Lacy, yield; I'll be your jailer once.

EDWARD. How familiar they be, Bacon!

BACON. Sit still, and mark the sequel of their loves.

LACY. Then am I double prisoner to thyself. 110

Peggy, I yield! But are these news in jest?

MARGARET. In jest with you, but earnest unto me,

Forwhy these wrongs do wring me at the heart.

Ah, how these earls and noble men of birth

Flatter and feign, to forge poor women's ill!

LACY. Believe me, lass, I am the Lincoln earl;

I not deny but, tired thus in rags,

I lived disguised to win fair Peggy's love.

MARGARET. What love is there where wedding ends not love?

LACY. I meant, fair girl, to make thee Lacy's wife. 120

MARGARET. I little think that earls will stoop so low.

LACY. Say, shall I make thee countess ere I sleep?

MARGARET. Handmaid unto the earl, so please himself;

A wife in name, but servant in obedience.

LACY. The Lincoln countess, for it shall be so!

I'll plight the bands,[5] and seal it with a kiss.

EDWARD. Gog's wounds, Bacon, they kiss! I'll stab them!

BACON. O, hold your hands, my lord! It is the glass!

EDWARD. Choler to see the traitors gree[6] so well 129

Made me think the shadows substances.

BACON. 'Twere a long poinard,[7] my lord, to reach between

Oxford and Fressingfield.   But sit still and see more.

---

[1] Mischievous boy.   [3] Prematurely.
[2] Image.   [4] God here.
[5] Pledge the bans.   [6] Agree.   [7] Poniard.

BUNGAY. Well, Lord of Lincoln, if your
loves be knit,
And that your tongues and thoughts do
both agree,
To avoid ensuing jars, I'll hamper up [1]
the match.
I'll take my portace [2] forth and wed you
here;
Then go to bed and seal up your desires.
LACY. Friar, content.—Peggy, how like
you this?
MARGARET. What likes my lord is pleasing unto me.
BUNGAY. Then handfast [3] hand, and I
will to my book.   140

BACON. What sees my lord now?
EDWARD. Bacon, I see the lovers hand
in hand,
The friar ready with his portace there
To wed them both. Then am I quite
undone!
Bacon, help now, if e'er thy magic served;
Help, Bacon! Stop the marriage now,
If devils or nigromancy may suffice,
And I will give thee forty thousand
crowns.
BACON. Fear not, my lord, I'll stop the
jolly friar   149
For [4] mumbling up his orisons this day.

LACY. Why speak'st not, Bungay? Friar,
to thy book!
  Bungay is mute, crying, "Hud, hud."
MARGARET. How lookest thou, friar, as
a man distraught!
Reft of thy senses. Bungay? Show by
signs,
If thou be dumb, what passions holdeth
thee.
LACY. He's dumb indeed. Bacon hath
with his devils
Enchanted him, or else some strange
disease
Or apoplexy hath possessed his lungs.
But, Peggy, what he cannot with his
book,
We'll twixt us both unite it up in heart.
MARGARET. Else let me die, my lord, a
miscreant.   160

EDWARD. Why stands Friar Bungay [5] so
amazed? [6]
BACON. I have struck him dumb, my
lord; and, if your honor please,
I'll fetch this Bungay straightway from
Fressingfield
And he shall dine with us in Oxford here.
EDWARD. Bacon, do that, and thou con-
tentest me.

LACY. Of courtesy, Margaret, let us lead
the friar
Unto thy father's lodge, to comfort him
With broths, to bring him from this
hapless trance.
MARGARET. Or else, my lord, we were
passing unkind   169
To leave the friar so in his distress.

*Enter a Devil, and carry Bungay on his
back.*

O, help, my lord! A devil, a devil, my
lord!
Look how he carries Bungay on his back!
Let's hence, for Bacon's spirits be
abroad.
              Exeunt [Margaret and Lacy].

EDWARD. Bacon, I laugh to see the jolly
friar
Mounted upon the devil, and how the
earl
Flees with his bonny lass for fear.
As soon as Bungay is at Brazen-nose,
And I have chatted with the merry
friar,
I will in post hie me to Fressingfield,
And quite these wrongs on Lacy ere it
be long.   180
BACON. So be it, my lord. But let us to
our dinner,
For, ere we have taken our repast awhile,
We shall have Bungay brought to
Brazen-nose.   *Exeunt.*

[SCENE vii.
The Regent House at Oxford.]

*Enter   three   doctors,   Burden,   Mason,
Clement.*

MASON. Now that we are gathered in
the Regent House,
It fits us talk about the king's repair,

---

[1] Make fast.   [2] Breviary for outdoor use.
[3] Join; used of marriage contracts.   [4] From.
[5] Original reads *Bacon.*
[6] Bewildered.   [7] Visit.

For he, troopéd with [1] all the western
 kings
That lie alongst the Danzig seas by
 east,
North by the clime of frosty Germany,
The Almain [2] monarch, and the Saxon
 duke, [3]
Castile and lovely Elinor with him,
Have in their jests resolved for Oxford
 town.
BURDEN. We must lay plots of stately
 tragedies,
Strange comic shows such as proud
 Roscius   10
Vaunted before the Roman emperors—
CLEMENT. To welcome all the western
 potentates.
But more: the king by letters hath fore-
 told
That Frederick, the Almain emperor,
Hath brought with him a German of
 esteem,
Whose surname is Don Jaques Vander-
 mast,
Skillful in magic and those secret arts.
MASON. Then must we all make suit
 unto the friar,
To Friar Bacon, that he vouch [4] this
 task,
And undertake to countervail in skill   20
The German; else there's none in Ox-
 ford can
Match and dispute with learned Vander-
 mast.
BURDEN. Bacon, if he will hold the Ger-
 man play,
We'll teach him what an English friar
 can do.
The devil, I think, dare not dispute
 with him.
CLEMENT. Indeed, Mas' Doctor, he pleas-
 uréd you,
In that he brought your hostess with
 her spit
From Henley, posting unto Brazen-nose!
BURDEN. A vengeance on the friar for his
 pains!
But, leaving that, let's hie to Bacon
 straight,   30
To see if he will take this task in hand.

CLEMENT. Stay, what rumor is this?
The town is up in a mutiny. What hurly-
burly is this?

Enter a Constable, with Rafe, Warren,
Ermsby, and Miles.

CONSTABLE. Nay, masters, if you were
ne'er so good, you shall before the doctors
to answer your misdemeanor.
BURDEN. What's the matter, fellow?
CONSTABLE. Marry, sir, here's a company of rufflers, that, drinking in   [40
the tavern, have made a great brawl,
and almost killed the vintner.
MILES. *Salve,* [5] Doctor Burden!   This
 lubberly lurden, [6]
Ill-shaped and ill-faced, disdained and
 disgraced,
What he tells unto *vobis mentitur de*
 nobis. [7]
BURDEN. Who is the master and chief
of this crew?
MILES. *Ecce asinum mundi fugura ro-*
 tundi, [8]
Neat, sheat, [9] and fine, as brisk as a cup
 of wine.
BURDEN. What are you?   50
RAFE. I am, father doctor, as a man
would say, the bellwether of this company; these are my lords, and I the Prince
of Wales.
CLEMENT. Are you Edward, the king's
son?
RAFE. Sirrah Miles, bring hither the
tapster that drew the wine, and, I warrant, when they see how soundly I have
broke his head, they'll say 'twas done   [60
by no less man than a prince.
MASON. I cannot believe that this is
the Prince of Wales.
WARREN. And why so, sir?
MASON. For they say the prince is a
brave and a wise gentleman.
WARREN. Why, and thinkest thou, doctor, that he is not so?
Dar'st thou detract and derogate from
 him,
Being so lovely and so brave a youth?
ERMSBY. Whose face, shining with many
 a sugared smile,   70

[1] Accompanied by.   [2] German.
[3] Original reads *Scocon duke.* This character
does not actually appear, although again referred
to.   [4] Avouch, make good.

[5] Save you!   [6] Blockhead.
[7] Whatever he tells you, he is lying about us.
[8] Behold the jackass of the round-shaped world.
[9] Trim (?); lively (?).

Bewrays [1] that he is bred of princely race.

MILES. And yet, Master Doctor, to speak like a proctor,
And tell unto you what is veriment [2] and true;
To cease of this quarrel, look but on his apparel;
Then mark but my talis, he is great Prince of Walis,
The chief of our *gregis*, and *filius regis* [3];
Then ware what is done, for he is Henry's white [4] son.

RAFE. Doctors, whose doting nightcaps are not capable of my ingenious dignity, know that I am Edward Plantage- [80 net, whom if you displease will make a ship that shall hold all your colleges, and so carry away the Niniversity with a fair wind to the Bankside in Southwark. —How say'st thou, Ned Warren? Shall I not do it?

WARREN. Yes, my good lord; and, if it please your lordship, I will gather up all your old pantofles, [5] and with the cork make you a pinnace of five hundred [90 ton, that shall serve the turn marvelous well, my lord.

ERMSBY. And I, my lord, will have pioners [6] to undermine the town, that the very gardens and orchards be carried away for your summer walks.

MILES. And I, with *scientia* and great *diligentia*,
Will conjure and charm, to keep you from harm;
That, *utrum horum mavis*, [7] your very great *navis*, [8]
Like Bartlet's [9] ship, from Oxford do skip   100
With colleges and schools, full-loaden with fools.
Quid dices ad hoc, [10] worshipful *Domine Dawcock*? [11]

CLEMENT. Why, hare-brained courtiers, are you drunk or mad,
To taunt us up with such scurrility?

Deem you us men of base and light esteem,
To bring us such a fop for Henry's son?—
Call out the beadles and convey them hence
Straight to Bocardo; [12] let the roisters lie
Close clapped in bolts, until their wits be tame.

ERMSBY. Why, shall we to prison, [110 my lord?

RAFE. What sayst, Miles, shall I honor the prison with my presence?

MILES. No, no! Out with your blades, and hamper these jades;
Have a flirt [13] and a crash, now play revel-dash, [14]
And teach these *sacerdos* [15] that the Bocardos,
Like peasants and elves, are meet for themselves.

MASON. To the prison with them, constable!

WARREN. Well, doctors, seeing I have sported me
With laughing at these mad and merry wags,   120
Know that Prince Edward is at Brazennose,
And this, attiréd like the Prince of Wales,
Is Rafe, King Henry's only lovéd fool,
I, Earl of Sussex, [16] and this Ermsby,
One of the privy chamber to the king,
Who, while the prince with Friar Bacon stays,
Have reveled it in Oxford as you see.

MASON. My lord, pardon us, we knew not what you were.
But courtiers may make greater scapes [17] than these.
Will 't please your honor dine with me today?   130

WARREN. I will, Master Doctor, and satisfy the vintner for his hurt; only I must desire you to imagine him all this forenoon the Prince of Wales.

MASON. I will, sir.

RAFE. And upon that I will lead the way; only I will have Miles go before me,

---

[1] Betrays.   [2] Truth.
[3] The chief of our company and son of the king.   [4] Dear.   [5] Slippers.   [6] Diggers.
[7] Whichever of these you prefer.   [8] Ship.
[9] Miles's mistake for Barclay, the translator of Brandt's *Ship of Fools*.
[10] What do you say to this?
[11] Jackdaw, dolt.

[12] A prison at Oxford.   [15] Priests.
[13] Quick blow.   [16] Original reads *Essex*.
[14] Rowdy game.   [17] Escapades.

because I have heard Henry say that wisdom must go before majesty.

Exeunt omnes.

[SCENE viii.

Fressingfield.]

Enter Prince Edward with his poinard in his hand, Lacy, and Margaret.

EDWARD. Lacy, thou canst not shroud thy trait'rous thoughts,
Nor cover, as did Cassius, all his wiles;
For Edward hath an eye that looks as far
As Lynceus from the shores of Grecia.
Did not I sit in Oxford by the friar,
And see thee court the maid of Fressingfield,
Sealing thy flattering fancies with a kiss?
Did not proud Bungay draw his portace forth,
And, joining hand in hand, had married you,
If Friar Bacon had not stroke [1] him dumb,   10
And mounted him upon a spirit's back,
That we might chat at Oxford with the friar?
Traitor, what answer'st?   Is not all this true?

LACY. Truth all, my lord; and thus I make reply:
At Harleston Fair, there courting for your grace,
Whenas mine eye surveyed her curious shape,
And drew the beauteous glory of her looks
To dive into the center of my heart,
Love taught me that your honor did but jest,   19
That princes were in fancy [2] but as men;
How that the lovely maid of Fressingfield
Was fitter to be Lacy's wedded wife
Than concubine unto the Prince of Wales.

EDWARD. Injurious Lacy, did I love thee more
Than Alexander his Hephestion?
Did I unfold the passion[s] of my love,
And lock them in the closet of thy thoughts?
Wert thou to Edward second to himself,
Sole friend, and partner of his secret loves?
And could a glance of fading beauty break   30
The enchainéd fetters of such private friends?
Base coward, false, and too effeminate
To be corrival [3] with a prince in thoughts!
From Oxford have I posted since I dined,
To quite a traitor fore that Edward sleep.

MARGARET. 'Twas I, my lord, not Lacy stepped awry;
For oft he sued and courted for yourself,
And still wooed for the courtier all in green.   38
But I, whom fancy made but overfond,
Pleaded myself with looks as if I loved;
I fed mine eye with gazing on his face,
And still bewitched loved Lacy with my looks.
My heart with sighs, mine eyes pleaded with tears,
My face held pity and content at once,
And more I could not cipher out [4] by signs
But that I loved Lord Lacy with my heart.
Then, worthy Edward, measure with thy mind
If women's favors will not force men fall,
If beauty and if darts of piercing love
Are not of force to bury thoughts of friends.   50

EDWARD. I tell thee, Peggy, I will have thy loves;
Edward or none shall conquer Margaret.
In frigates bottomed with rich Sethin [5] planks,
Topped with the lofty firs of Lebanon,
Stemmed and incased with burnished ivory,
And overlaid with plates of Persian wealth,
Like Thetis shalt thou wanton on the waves,
And draw the dolphins to thy lovely eyes,

[1] Struck.   [2] Love.   [3] Partner.   [4] Express.   [5] Shittim.

To dance lavoltas [1] in the purple streams.
Sirens, with harps and silver psalteries, 60
Shall wait with music at thy frigate's
    stem,
And entertain fair Margaret with their [2]
    lays.
England and England's wealth shall
    wait on thee;
Britain shall bend unto her prince's
    love,
And do due homage to thine excellence,
If thou wilt be but Edward's Margaret.
MARGARET. Pardon, my lord; if Jove's
    great royalty
Sent me such presents as to Danaë,
If Phœbus, tired [3] in Latona's webs,
Come courting from the beauty of his
    lodge, 70
The dulcet tunes of frolic Mercury
Nor [4] all the wealth heaven's treasury
    affords
Should make me leave Lord Lacy or
    his love.
EDWARD. I have learned at Oxford, then,
    this point of schools: [5]
Ablata causa, tollitur effectus.[6]
Lacy, the cause that Margaret cannot
    love
Nor fix her liking on the English prince,
Take him away, and then the effects
    will fail.
Villain, prepare thyself; for I will bathe
My poinard in the bosom of an earl. 80
LACY. Rather than live, and miss fair
    Margaret's love,
Prince Edward, stop not at the fatal
    doom,
But stab it home. End both my loves
    and life.
MARGARET. Brave Prince of Wales, hon-
    ored for royal deeds,
'Twere sin to stain fair Venus' courts
    with blood;
Love's conquests ends, my lord, in
    courtesy.
Spare Lacy, gentle Edward; let me die,
For so both you and he do cease your
    loves.

EDWARD. Lacy shall die as traitor to his
    lord.
LACY. I have deserved it, Edward; act
    it well. 90
MARGARET. What hopes the prince to
    gain by Lacy's death?
EDWARD. To end the loves twixt him
    and Margaret.
MARGARET. Why, thinks King Henry's
    son that Margaret's love
Hangs in the uncertain balance of
    proud time?
That death shall make a discord of our
    thoughts?
No, stab the earl, and, fore the morn-
    ing sun
Shall vaunt him thrice over the lofty
    east,
Margaret will meet her Lacy in the
    heavens.
LACY. If aught betides to lovely Margaret
That wrongs or wrings her honor from
    content, 100
Europe's rich wealth nor England's
    monarchy
Should not allure Lacy to overlive.[7]
Then, Edward, short my life, and end
    her loves.
MARGARET. Rid [8] me, and keep a friend
    worth many loves.
LACY. Nay, Edward, keep a love worth
    many friends.
MARGARET. And, if thy mind be such as
    fame hath blazed,
Then, princely Edward, let us both
    abide[9]
The fatal resolution of thy rage.
Banish thou fancy and embrace re-
    venge,
And in one tomb knit both our car-
    casses, 110
Whose hearts were linkéd in one perfect
    love.
EDWARD. [*Aside*.] Edward, art thou
    that famous Prince of Wales
Who at Damasco beat the Saracens,
And brought'st home triumph on thy
    lance's point,
And shall thy plumes be pulled by Venus
    down?
Is it princely to dissever lovers' leagues,
To part such friends as glory in their
    loves?

[1] Lively dances.
[2] Original reads *her*.
[3] Attired. Original has *tied*.
[4] Emended by Dyce. Original reads *not*.
[5] Principle of scholastic argument.
[6] The cause being removed, the effect is taken away.
[7] Outlive, survive.   [8] Get rid of.   [9] Suffer.

Leave, Ned, and make a virtue of this fault,
And further Peg and Lacy in their loves.
So in subduing fancy's passion,   120
Conquering thyself, thou gett'st the richest spoil.—
Lacy, rise up! Fair Peggy, here's my hand!
The Prince of Wales hath conquered all his thoughts,
And all his loves he yields unto the earl.
Lacy, enjoy the maid of Fressingfield;
Make her thy Lincoln countess at the church,
And Ned, as he is true Plantagenet,
Will give her to thee frankly for thy wife.

LACY. Humbly I take her of my sovereign,
As if that Edward gave me England's right,   130
And riched me with the Albion diadem.

MARGARET. And doth the English prince mean true?
Will he vouchsafe to cease his former loves,
And yield the title of a country maid
Unto Lord Lacy?

EDWARD. I will, fair Peggy, as I am true lord.

MARGARET. Then, lordly sir, whose conquest is as great
In conquering love as Cæsar's victories,
Margaret, as mild and humble in her thoughts
As was Aspasia unto Cyrus' self,   140
Yields thanks, and, next Lord Lacy, doth enshrine
Edward the second secret in her heart.[1]

EDWARD. Gramercy, Peggy. Now that vows are passed,
And that your loves are not [to] be revolt,[2]
Once, Lacy, friends again, come, we will post
To Oxford; for this day the king is there,
And brings for Edward Castile Elinor.
Peggy, I must go see and view my wife;
I pray God I like her as I loved thee.
Beside, Lord Lincoln, we shall hear dispute   150

Twixt Friar Bacon and learned Vandermast.
Peggy, we'll leave you for a week or two.

MARGARET. As it please Lord Lacy; but love's foolish looks
Think footsteps miles and minutes to be hours.

LACY. I'll hasten, Peggy, to make short return.—
But, please your honor, go unto the lodge.
We shall have butter, cheese, and venison;
And yesterday I brought for Margaret
A lusty bottle of neat claret wine.
Thus can we feast and entertain your grace.   160

EDWARD. 'Tis cheer, Lord Lacy, for an emperor,
If he respect the person and the place.
Come, let us in; for I will all this night
Ride post until I come to Bacon's cell.
                                    Exeunt.

[SCENE ix.

Oxford.]

Enter Henry, Emperor, Castile, Elinor, Vandermast, Bungay.

EMPEROR. Trust me, Plantagenet, these Oxford schools
Are richly seated near the riverside,
The mountains full of fat and fallow deer,
The battling [3] pastures lade [4] with kine and flocks,
The town gorgeous with high-built colleges,
And scholars seemly in their grave attire,
Learned in searching principles of art.—
What is thy judgment, Jaques Vandermast?

VANDER. That lordly are the buildings of the town,
Spacious the rooms, and full of pleasant walks;   10
But for the doctors, how that they be learned,
It may be meanly, for aught I can hear.

BUNGAY. I tell thee, German, Hapsburg holds none such,
None read so deep as Oxenford contains.

[1] *I.e.,* the second (next to Lacy) in her affection.   [2] Withdrawn, overturned.   [3] Nourishing.   [4] Laden.

There are within our academic state
Men that may lecture it in Germany
To all the doctors of your Belgic schools.
HENRY. Stand to him, Bungay; charm
  this Vandermast,
And I will use thee as a royal king.
VANDER. Wherein darest thou dispute with
  me? 20
BUNGAY. In what a doctor and a friar can.
VANDER. Before rich Europe's worthies
  put thou forth
  The doubtful question unto Vander-
  mast.
BUNGAY. Let it be this: Whether the
spirits of pyromancy or geomancy be most
predominant in magic?
VANDER. I say, of pyromancy.
BUNGAY. And I, of geomancy.
VANDER. The cabalists that write of
  magic spells,
As Hermes, Melchie, and Pythagoras, 30
Affirm that, 'mongst the quadruplicity
Of elemental essence,[1] terra is but thought
To be a *punctum* squaréd to[2] the rest;
And that the compass of ascending
  elements
Exceed in bigness as they do in height;
Judging the concave circle of the sun
To hold the rest in his circumference.
If, then, as Hermes says, the fire be
  great'st,
Purest, and only giveth shapes to
  spirits,
Then must these *dæmones*[3] that haunt
  that place 40
Be every way superior to the rest.
BUNGAY. I reason not of elemental shapes,
Nor tell I of the concave latitudes,
Noting their essence nor their quality,
But of the spirits that pyromancy calls,
And of the vigor of the geomantic
  fiends.
I tell thee, German, magic haunts the
  grounds,
And those strange necromantic spells,
That work such shows and wondering
  in the world,
Are acted by those geomantic spirits 50
That Hermes called *terræ filii*.[4]
The fiery spirits are but transparent
  shades,

That lightly pass as heralds to bear
  news;
But earthly fiends, closed in the lowest
  deep,
Dissever mountains, if they be but
  charged,
Being more gross and massy in their
  power.
VANDER. Rather these earthly geomantic
  spirits
Are dull and like the place where they
  remain;
For, when proud Lucifer fell from the
  heavens,
The spirits and angels that did sin with
  him 60
Retained their local essence as their
  faults,
All subject under Luna's continent.
They which offended less hang in the
  fire,
And second faults did rest within the
  air;
But Lucifer and his proud-hearted
  fiends
Were thrown into the center of the
  earth,
Having less understanding than the
  rest,
As having greater sin and lesser grace.
Therefore such gross and earthly spirits
  do serve
For jugglers, witches, and vild[5] sor-
  cerers; 70
Whereas the pyromantic genii
Are mighty, swift, and of far-reaching
  power.
But, grant that geomancy hath most
  force,
Bungay, to please these mighty poten-
  tates,
Prove by some instance what thy art
  can do.
BUNGAY. I will.
EMPEROR. Now, English Harry, here be-
  gins the game;
We shall see sport between these learned
  men.
VANDER. What wilt thou do?
BUNGAY. Show thee the tree, leaved with
  refinéd gold, 80
Whereon the fearful **dragon** held his
  seat,

---

[1] The four elements of fire, air, earth, and
water.   [2] An atom compared with.
[3] Spirits.   [4] Sons of the earth.
[5] Vile, low in rank.

That watched the garden called Hesperides,
Subdued and won by conquering Her·
cules.
VANDER. Well done!

*Here Bungay conjures, and the tree appears
with the Dragon shooting fire.*

HENRY. What say you, royal lordings,
to my friar?
Hath he not done a point of cunning
skill?
VANDER. Each scholar in the nigromantic
spells
Can do as much as Bungay hath performed.
But as Alcmena's bastard razed this
tree,
So will I raise him up as when he lived, 90
And cause him pull the dragon from
his seat,
And tear the branches piecemeal from
the root.—
Hercules! *Prodi, prodi,*[1] Hercules!

Hercules appears in his lion's skin.

HERCULES. *Quis me vult?* [2]
VANDER. Jove's bastard son, thou Libyan Hercules,
Pull off the sprigs from off the Hesperian tree,
As once thou didst to win the golden
fruit.
HERCULES. *Fiat.*[3]
     Here he begins to break the branches.
VANDER. Now, Bungay, if thou canst
by magic charm 99
The fiend appearing like great Hercules
From pulling down the branches of the
tree,
Then art thou worthy to be counted
learned.
BUNGAY. I cannot.
VANDER. Cease, Hercules, until I give
thee charge.—
Mighty commander of this English isle,
Henry, come from the stout Plantagenets,
Bungay is learned enough to be a friar;
But, to compare with Jaques Vandermast,

Oxford and Cambridge must go seek
their cells
To find a man to match him in his art. 110
I have given nonplus to the Paduans,
To them of Sien, Florence, and Bologna,
Rheims, Louvain, and fair Rotherdam,
Frankfort, Lutrech,[4] and Orleans.
And now must Henry, if he do me right,
Crown me with laurel, as they all have
done.

Enter Bacon.

BACON. All hail to this royal company,
That sit to hear and see this strange
dispute!—
Bungay, how stand'st thou as a man
amazed!
What, hath the German acted more
than thou? 120
VANDER. What art thou that questions
thus?
BACON. Men call me Bacon.
VANDER. Lordly thou look'st, as if that
thou wert learned;
Thy countenance as if science held her
seat
Between the circled arches of thy brows.
HENRY. Now, monarchs, hath the German
found his match.
EMPEROR. Bestir thee, Jaques; take not
now the foil,[5]
Lest thou dost lose what foretime thou
didst gain.
VANDER. Bacon, wilt thou dispute?
BACON. No, unless he were more learned
than Vandermast; 130
For yet, tell me, what hast thou done?
VANDER. Raised Hercules to ruinate that
tree
That Bungay mounted by his magic
spells.
BACON. Set Hercules to work.
VANDER. Now, Hercules, I charge thee
to thy task;
Pull off the golden branches from the
root.
HERCULES. I dare not. Seest thou not
great Bacon here,
Whose frown doth act more than thy
magic can?
VANDER. By all the thrones and dominations, 139

[1] Come forth.   [2] Who wishes me?
[3] Let it be done.

[4] Utrecht, or Lutetia (Paris) (?).
[5] Fall, a wrestling term.

Virtues, powers, and mighty hierarchies,
I charge thee to obey to Vandermast.
HERCULES. Bacon, that bridles head-
strong Belcephon,
And rules Asmenoth, guider of the north,
Binds me from yielding unto Vander-
mast.
HENRY. How now, Vandermast! Have
you met with your match?
VANDER. Never before was't known to
Vandermast
That men held devils in such obedient
awe.
Bacon doth more than art, or else I
fail.
EMPEROR. Why, Vandermast, art thou
overcome?—
Bacon, dispute with him, and try his
skill.   150
BACON. I come not, monarchs, for to
hold dispute
With such a novice as is Vandermast;
I come to have your royalties to dine
With Friar Bacon here in Brazen-nose.
And, for this German troubles but the
place,
And holds this audience with a long
suspense,
I'll send him to his academy hence.—
Thou Hercules, whom Vandermast did
raise,
Transport the German unto Hapsburg
straight,
That he may learn by travail, gainst[1]
the spring,[2]   160
More secret dooms and aphorisms of art.
Vanish the tree, and thou away with
him!
Exit the Spirit with Vandermast and the tree.
EMPEROR. Why, Bacon, whither dost
thou send him?
BACON. To Hapsburg; there your high-
ness at return
Shall find the German in his study safe.
HENRY. Bacon, thou hast honored Eng-
land with thy skill,
And made fair Oxford famous by thine
art;
I will be English Henry to thyself.
But tell me, shall we dine with thee
today?
BACON. With me, my lord. And, while I
fit my cheer,   170

See where Prince Edward comes to welcome you,
Gracious as the morning star of heaven.
                                Exit.

Enter Edward, Lacy, Warren, Ermsby.
EMPEROR. Is this Prince Edward, Henry's
royal son?
How martial is the figure of his face,
Yet lovely and beset with amorets![3]
HENRY. Ned, where hast thou been?
EDWARD. At Framlingham, my lord, to
try your bucks
If they could scape the teasers or the
toil.
But, hearing of these lordly potentates
Landed and progressed up to Oxford
town,   180
I posted to give entertain[4] to them—
Chief, to the Almain monarch; next to
him,
And joint with him, Castile and Saxony
Are welcome as they may be to the
English court.
Thus for the men. But see, Venus ap-
pears,
Or one that overmatcheth Venus in
her shape!—
Sweet Elinor, beauty's high-swelling
pride,
Rich nature's glory and her wealth at
once,
Fair of all fairs, welcome to Albion;
Welcome to me, and welcome to thine
own,   190
If that thou deign'st the welcome from
myself.
ELINOR. Martial Plantagenet, Henry's
high-minded son,
The mark that Elinor did count her aim,
I liked thee fore I saw thee. Now I
love,
And so as in so short a time I may;
Yet so as time shall never break that
so,
And therefore so accept of Elinor.
CASTILE. Fear not, my lord, this couple
will agree,
If love may creep into their wanton
eyes.
And therefore, Edward, I accept thee
here,   200
Without suspense, as my adopted son.

---

[1] In preparation for.   [2] Original reads *springs*.   [3] Loving looks.   [4] Reception.

HENRY. Let me, that joy in these consort-
　　ing greets
And glory in these honors done to Ned,
Yield thanks for all these favors to my
　　son,
And rest a true Plantagenet to all.

Enter Miles with a cloth and trenchers and
　　　　　　　　　　　　　　　　　salt.

MILES.[1] *Salvete, omnes reges,*[2] that govern
　　your *greges* [3]
In Saxony and Spain, in England and
　　in Almain!
For all this frolic rable [4] must I cover
　　thee, table,[5]
With trenchers, salt, and cloth; and
　　then look for your broth.　　　209
EMPEROR. What pleasant fellow is this?
HENRY. 'Tis, my lord, Doctor Bacon's
poor scholar.
MILES. [*Aside.*] My master hath made
me sewer [6] of these great lords; and, God
knows, I am as serviceable at a table as
a sow is under an apple tree. 'Tis no matter; their cheer shall not be great, and
therefore what skills [7] where the salt stand,[8]
before or behind?　　　　　　[*Exit.*]
CASTILE. These scholars knows more skill
　　in axioms,　　　　　　　　220
How to use quips and sleights of soph-
　　istry,
Than for to cover [9] courtly for a king.

Enter Miles with a mess of pottage and
　　　broth; and, after him, Bacon.

MILES. [10] Spill, sir? Why, do you think
I never carried twopenny chop [11] before
in my life?—
By your leave, *nobile decus,*[12] for here
　　comes Doctor Bacon's *pecus,*[13]
Being in his full age, to carry a mess of
　　pottage.

---

[1] The following speech appears as prose in the
original.
[2] Hail, all you kings.　　[5] The table (?).
[3] Peoples.　　　　　　　[6] Butler.
[4] Rabble.　　　　　　　[7] What does it matter?
[8] A large saltcellar usually marked the dividing line between superior and inferior guests.
[9] Set a table.
[10] All of the following speech is printed as prose
in the original.
[11] Chopped meat in broth (?).
[12] Your worshipful honor.
[13] Beast of burden.

BACON. Lordings, admire [14] not if your
　　cheer be this,
For we must keep our academic fare;
No riot where philosophy doth reign.
And therefore, Henry, place these po-
　　tentates,　　　　　　　　231
And bid them fall unto their frugal
　　cates.[15]
EMPEROR. Presumptuous friar! What,
　　scoff'st thou at a king?
What, dost thou taunt us with thy
　　peasants' fare,
And give us cates fit for country
　　swains?—
Henry, proceeds this jest of thy consent,
To twit us with such a pittance of such
　　price?
Tell me, and Frederick will not grieve
　　thee long.
HENRY. By Henry's honor, and the royal
　　faith
The English monarch beareth to his
　　friend,　　　　　　　　　240
I knew not of the friar's feeble fare,
Nor am I pleased he entertains you
　　thus.
BACON. Content thee, Frederick, for I
　　showed the cates
To let thee see how scholars use to feed,
How little meat refines our English
　　wits.—
Miles, take away, and let it be thy dinner.
MILES. Marry, sir, I will. This day shall
　　be a festival day with me,
For I shall exceed in the highest degree.
　　　　　　　　　　　　　　Exit Miles.
BACON. I tell thee, monarch, all the Ger-
　　man peers
Could not afford thy entertainment
　　such,　　　　　　　　　250
So royal and so full of majesty,
As Bacon will present to Frederick.
The basest waiter that attends thy cups
Shall be in honors greater than thyself;
And for thy cates, rich Alexandria
　　drugs,[16]
Fetched by carvels from Egypt's rich-
　　est straits,
Found in the wealthy strond of Africa,
Shall royalize the table of my king.
Wines richer than the 'Gyptian courte-
　　san

---

[14] Wonder.　　　　　　　　[16] Spices.
[15] Delicacies, morsels.

Quaffed to Augustus' kingly counter-
   match,[1]   260
Shall be caroused in English Henry's
   feast;
Kandy shall yield the richest of her
   canes;
Persia, down her Volga by canoes,
Send down the secrets of her spicery;
The Afric dates, mirabiles [2] of Spain,
Conserves and suckets [3] from Tiberias,
Cates from Judea, choicer than the
   lamp [4]
That fired Rome with sparks of glut-
   tony,
Shall beautify the board for Frederick.
And therefore grudge not at a friar's
   feast.   *[Exeunt.]*

[SCENE x.

Fressingfield.]

Enter two gentlemen, Lambert and Serlsby,
               with the Keeper.

LAMBERT. Come, frolic keeper of our
   liege's game,
Whose table spread hath ever venison
And jacks [5] of wine to welcome passen-
   gers,
Know I am in love with jolly Margaret,
That overshines our damsels as the moon
Dark'neth the brightest sparkles of
   the night.
In Laxfield here my land and living
   lies.
I'll make thy daughter jointer [6] of it
   all,
So thou consent to give her to [7] my wife;
And I can spend five hundreth marks
   a year.   10
SERLSBY. I am the lands-lord, keeper, of
   thy holds;
By copy [8] all thy living lies in me;
Laxfield did never see me raise my due.
I will enfeoff fair Margaret in all
So she will take her to a lusty squire.
KEEPER. Now, courteous gentles, if the
   keeper's girl
Hath pleased the liking fancy of you
   both,

And with her beauty hath subdued your
   thoughts,
'Tis doubtful to decide the question.
It joys me that such men of great esteem
Should lay their liking on this base
   estate,   21
And that her state should grow so for-
   tunate
To be a wife to meaner men than you.
But sith [9] such squires will stoop to
   keeper's fee,
I will, to avoid displeasure of you both,
Call Margaret forth, and she shall make
   her choice.   *Exit.*
LAMBERT. Content, keeper; send her un-
   to us.
Why, Serlsby, is thy wife so lately dead,
Are all thy loves so lightly passéd over,
As thou canst wed before the year be
   out?   30
SERLSBY. I live not, Lambert, to content
   the dead,
Nor was I wedded but for life to her.
The grave [10] ends and begins a married
   state.

Enter Margaret.

LAMBERT. Peggy, the lovely flower of
   all towns,
Suffolk's fair Helen, and rich England's
   star,
Whose beauty, tempered with her hus-
   wifery,
Makes England talk of merry Fressing-
   field!
SERLSBY. I cannot trick it up with poesies,
Nor paint my passions with compari-
   sons,   39
Nor tell a tale of Phœbus and his loves;
But this believe me: Laxfield here is
   mine,
Of ancient rent seven hundred pounds
   a year,
And, if thou canst but love a country
   squire,
I will enfeoff thee, Margaret, in all.
I cannot flatter; try me, if thou please.
MARGARET. Brave neighboring squires,
   the stay of Suffolk's clime,
A keeper's daughter is too base in gree [11]
To match with men accompted [12] of
   such worth.

[1] Rival.   [5] Pitchers.
[2] Myrobalans, dried plums.   [6] Joint-possessor.
[3] Sweetmeats.   [7] For.
[4] Ward suggests *lamprey.*   [8] Copyhold.

[9] Since.   [11] Degree.
[10] Original reads *graves.*   [12] Accounted.

But might I not displease, I would reply.

LAMBERT. Say, Peggy; naught shall make us discontent. 50

MARGARET. Then, gentles, note that love hath little stay,
Nor can the flames that Venus sets on fire
Be kindled but by fancy's motion.
Then pardon, gentles, if a maid's reply
Be doubtful, while [1] I have debated with myself,
Who, or of whom, love shall constrain me like.

SERLSBY. Let it be me; and trust me, Margaret,
The meads environed with the silver streams,
Whose battling pastures fatt'neth all my flocks,
Yielding forth fleeces stapled [2] with such wool 60
As Leominster [3] cannot yield more finer stuff,
And forty kine with fair and burnished heads,
With strouting [4] dugs that paggle [5] to the ground,
Shall serve thy dairy, if thou wed with me.

LAMBERT. Let pass the country wealth, as flocks and kine,
And lands that wave with Ceres' golden sheaves,
Filling my barns with plenty of the fields.
But, Peggy, if thou wed thyself to me,
Thou shalt have garments of embroidered [6] silk,
Lawns, and rich networks for thy head-attire. 70
Costly shall be thy fair abiliments,[7]
If thou wilt be but Lambert's loving wife.

MARGARET. Content you, gentles; you have proffered fair,
And more than fits a country maid's degree;
But give me leave to counsel me a time,
For fancy blooms not at the first assault.

Give me but ten days' respite, and I will reply,
Which or to whom myself affectionates.

SERLSBY. Lambert, I tell thee, thou art importunate; 79
Such beauty fits not such a base esquire.
It is for Serlsby to have Margaret.

LAMBERT. Think'st thou with wealth to overreach me?
Serlsby, I scorn to brook thy country braves.[8]
I dare thee, coward, to maintain this wrong,
At dint of rapier, single in the field.

SERLSBY. I'll answer, Lambert, what I have avouched!—
Margaret, farewell; another time shall serve. *Exit Serlsby.*

LAMBERT. I'll follow!—Peggy, farewell to thyself;
Listen how well I'll answer for thy love.
Exit Lambert.

MARGARET. How Fortune tempers lucky haps with frowns, 90
And wrongs me with the sweets of my delight!
Love is my bliss, and love is now my bale.
Shall I be Helen in my forward [9] fates,
As I am Helen in my matchless hue,
And set rich Suffolk with my face afire?
If lovely Lacy were but with his Peggy,
The cloudy darkness of his bitter frown
Would check the pride of these aspiring squires.
Before the term of ten days be expired,
Whenas they look for answer of their loves, 100
My lord will come to merry Fressingfield,
And end their fancies and their follies both.
Till when, Peggy, be blithe and of good cheer.

Enter a Post with a letter and a bag of gold.

POST. Fair lovely damsel, which way leads this path?
How might I post me unto Fressingfield?
Which footpath leadeth to the keeper's lodge?

MARGARET. Your way is ready, and this path is right.

---

[1] Until.
[2] Fibered.
[3] The original spelling, *Lempster*, indicates the pronunciation.
[4] Swelling.
[5] Hang loosely down.
[6] Embroidered.
[7] Habiliments.
[8] Boasts, insults.
[9] Froward.

Myself do dwell hereby in Fressingfield,
And, if the keeper be the man you seek,
I am his daughter. May I know the
  cause? 110
POST. Lovely, and once beloved of my
  lord—
No marvel if his eye was lodged so
  low,
When brighter beauty is not in the
  heavens—
The Lincoln earl hath sent you letters
  here,
And, with them, just an hundred pounds
  in gold.
Sweet, bonny wench, read them and
  make reply.
MARGARET. The scrolls that Jove sent
  Danaë,
Wrapped in rich closures [1] of fine bur-
  nished gold,
Were not more welcome than these
  lines to me.
Tell me, whilst that I do unrip the
  seals, 120
Lives Lacy well? How fares my lovely
  lord?
POST. Well, if that wealth may make men
  to live well.

The letter, and Margaret reads it.

"The blooms of the almond tree grow in
a night, and vanish in a morn; the flies
hœmeræ,[2] fair Peggy, take life with the
sun, and die with the dew; fancy, that
slippeth in with a gaze, goeth out with
a wink; and too timely loves have ever
the shortest length. I write this as thy
grief, and my folly, who at Fressing- [130
field loved that which time hath taught
me to be but mean dainties. Eyes are
dissemblers, and fancy is but queasy.
Therefore know, Margaret, I have chosen
a Spanish lady to be my wife, chief waiting-
woman to the Princess Elinor—a lady
fair, and no less fair than thyself, honorable and wealthy. In that I forsake thee,
I leave thee to thine own liking; and for
thy dowry I have sent thee an hundred [140
pounds, and ever assure thee of my favor,
which shall avail thee and thine much.
  Farewell. Not thine, nor his own,
        EDWARD LACY."

[1] Coverings.
[2] Ephemeræ.

Fond [3] Ate, doomer of bad-boding fates,
That wraps proud Fortune in thy snaky
  locks,
Didst thou enchant my birthday with
  such stars
As lightened mischief from their in-
  fancy?
If heavens had vowed, if stars had made
  decree, 149
To show on me their froward influ-
  ence,
If Lacy had but loved, heavens, hell,
  and all
Could not have wronged the patience
  of my mind.
POST. It grieves me, damsel; but the earl
  is forced
To love the lady by the king's command.
MARGARET. The wealth combined within
  the English shelves,[4]
Europe's commander, nor the English
  king
Should not have moved the love of
  Peggy from her lord.
POST. What answer shall I return to
  my lord?
MARGARET. First, for thou cam'st from
  Lacy whom I loved—
Ah, give me leave to sigh at every
  thought!— 160
Take thou, my friend, the hundred
  pound he sent,
For Margaret's resolution craves no
  dower.
The world shall be to her as vanity;
Wealth, trash; love, hate; pleasure,
  despair.
For I will straight to stately Framling-
  ham,
And in the abbey there be shorn a nun,
And yield my loves and liberty to God.
Fellow, I give thee this, not for the
  news,
For those be hateful unto Margaret,
But for th'art Lacy's man, once Mar-
  garet's love. 170
POST. What I have heard, what passions
  I have seen,
I'll make report of them unto the earl.
            Exit Post.
MARGARET. Say that she joys his fancies
  be at rest,
And prays that his misfortune may be
  hers. *Exit.*

[3] Foolish, capricious.
[4] Sandbanks, beaches.

[SCENE xi.

Bacon's study.]

Enter Friar Bacon, drawing the curtains with a white stick, a book in his hand, and a lamp lighted by him; and the Brazen Head, and Miles with weapons by him.

BACON. Miles, where are you?

MILES. Here, sir.

BACON. How chance you tarry so long?

MILES. Think you that the watching of the Brazen Head craves no furniture? I warrant you, sir, I have so armed myself that, if all your devils come, I will not fear them an inch.

BACON. Miles, thou knowest that I have dived into hell,

And sought the darkest palaces of fiends;   10

That with my magic spells great Belcephon

Hath left his lodge and kneeléd at my cell;

The rafters of the earth rent from the poles,

And three-formed Luna hid her silver looks,

Trembling upon her concave continent,

When Bacon read upon his magic book.

With seven years' tossing nigromantic charms,

Poring upon dark Hecat's principles,

I have framed out a monstrous head of brass,

That, by the enchanting forces of the devil,   20

Shall tell out strange and uncouth aphorisms,

And girt fair England with a wall of brass.

Bungay and I have watched these threescore days,

And now our vital spirits crave some rest.

If Argus lived, and had his hundred eyes,

They could not overwatch Phobetor's[1] night.

Now, Miles, in thee rests Friar Bacon's weal;

The honor and renown of all his life

Hangs in the watching of this Brazen Head.

Therefore I charge thee by the immortal God,   30

That holds the souls of men within his fist,

This night thou watch, for, ere the morning star

Sends out his glorious glister on the north,

The head will speak.   Then, Miles, upon thy life,

Wake me; for then by magic art I'll work

To end my seven years' task with excellence.

If that a wink but shut thy watchful eye,

Then farewell Bacon's glory and his fame!

Draw close the curtains, Miles.   Now, for thy life,

Be watchful, and—   40

Here he falleth asleep.

MILES. So! I thought you would talk yourself asleep anon; and 'tis no marvel, for Bungay on the days, and he on the nights, have watched just these ten-and-fifty days.   Now this is the night, and 'tis my task, and no more.   Now, Jesus bless me, what a goodly head it is! And a nose!   You talk of *nos autem glorificare,*[2] but here's a nose that I warrant may be called *nos autem popelare* for the people [50 of the parish.   Well, I am furnished with weapons.   Now, sir, I will set me down by a post, and make it as good as a watchman to wake me if I chance to slumber.   I thought, Goodman Head, I would call you out of your *memento.*

Sit down and knock your head.

Passion o' God, I have almost broke my pate!   Up, Miles, to your task; take your brown bill[3] in your hand.   Here's some of your master's hobgoblins abroad.   60

With this a great noise.   The Head speaks.

HEAD. Time is!

MILES. Time is!   Why, Master Brazen Head, have you such a capital nose, and answer you with syllables, "Time is"? Is this all my master's cunning, to spend seven years' study about "Time is"? Well, sir, it may be we shall have some better orations of it anon.   Well, I'll watch

[1] Morpheus's.   [2] Miles's impossible Latin pun on a liturgical phrase.   [3] Halbert.

you as narrowly as ever you were watched,
and I'll play with you as the nightingale [70
with the slowworm:[1] I'll set a prick
against my breast. [*Places the halbert against
his breast.*] Now rest there, Miles. [*He
falls over.*] Lord, have mercy upon me!
I have almost killed myself! [*A great
noise.*] Up, Miles; list how they rumble.

HEAD. Time was!

MILES. Well, Friar Bacon, you spent
your seven years' study well, that can
make your head speak but two words [80
at once. "Time was"! Yea, marry, time was
when my master was a wise man, but
that was before he began to make the
Brazen Head. You shall lie while your
arse ache, and your head speak no better.
Well, I will watch, and walk up and down,
and be a peripatetian and a philosopher
of Aristotle's stamp. [*A great noise.*]
What, a fresh noise? Take thy pistols in
hand, Miles!   90

*Here the Head speaks, and a lightning
flasheth forth, and a hand appears that
breaketh down the Head with a hammer.*

HEAD. Time is past!

MILES. Master, master, up! Hell's
broken loose! Your head speaks; and
there's such a thunder and lightning that
I warrant all Oxford is up in arms. Out
of your bed, and take a brown bill in
your hand. The latter day is come!

BACON. Miles, I come. O, passing warily
watched!

Bacon will make thee next himself in
love.

When spake the head?   100

MILES. When spake the head! Did not
you say that he should tell strange principles of philosophy? Why, sir, it speaks
but two words at a time.

BACON. Why, villain, hath it spoken
oft?

MILES. Oft! Ay, marry, hath it, thrice;
but in all those three times it hath uttered
but seven words.

BACON. As how?   110

MILES. Marry, sir, the first time he
said, "Time is," as if Fabius Cumenta-
tor[2] should have pronounced a sentence;
he said, "Time was;" and the third time,

with thunder and lightning, as in great
choler, he said, "Time is past."

BACON. 'Tis past indeed!   A villain!
Time is past!

My life, my fame, my glory, all are
past.—

Bacon, the turrets of thy hope are ruined
down;   119

Thy seven years' study lieth in the dust!

Thy Brazen Head lies broken through
a slave

That watched, and would not when the
head did will.—

What said the head first?

MILES. Even, sir, "Time is."

BACON. Villain, if thou hadst called to
Bacon then,

If thou hadst watched, and waked the
sleepy friar,

The Brazen Head had uttered aphorisms,

And England had been circled round
with brass.

But proud Astmeroth,[3] ruler of the
North,   129

And Demogorgon, master of the fates,

Grudge that a mortal man should work
so much.

Hell trembled at my deep, commanding
spells;

Fiends frowned to see a man their overmatch;

Bacon might boast more than a man
might boast.

But now the braves of Bacon hath an
end;

Europe's conceit[4] of Bacon hath an end;

His seven years' practice sorteth[5] to
ill end;

And, villain, sith my glory hath an end,

I will appoint thee fatal to some end.[6]

Villain, avoid! Get thee from Bacon's
sight!   140

Vagrant, go roam and range about the
world,

And perish as a vagabond on earth!

MILES. Why, then, sir, you forbid me
your service?

BACON. My service, villain, with a fatal
curse

That direful plagues and mischief fall
on thee!

---

[1] Small snake.

[2] Miles's distortion of *Cunctator*, i.e., the
Roman general nicknamed "the delayer."

[3] Same as *Asmenoth*.

[4] Conception, opinion.

[5] Comes.   [6] To some fatal end (?).

MILES. 'Tis no matter; I am against[1] you with the old proverb, "The more the fox is cursed, the better he fares."[2] God be with you, sir. I'll take but a book in my hand, a wide-sleeved gown on my [150 back, and a crowned cap on my head, and see if I can want promotion. [*Exit.*]

BACON. Some fiend or ghost haunt on thy weary steps
Until they do transport thee quick to hell;
For Bacon shall have never merry day,
To lose the fame and honor of his Head.
Exit.

[SCENE xii.

At court.]

*Enter Emperor, Castile, Henry, Elinor,
Edward, Lacy, Rafe.*

EMPEROR. Now, lovely prince, the prince of Albion's wealth,
How fares the Lady Elinor and you?
What, have you courted and found Castile fit
To answer England in equivalence?
Will 't be a match twixt bonny Nel and thee?

EDWARD. Should Paris enter in the courts of Greece,
And not lie fettered in fair Helen's looks,
Or Phœbus scape those piercing amorets
That Daphne glancéd at his deity?
Can Edward then sit by a flame and freeze,   10
Whose heat puts Helen and fair Daphne down?
Now, monarchs, ask the lady if we gree.

HENRY. What, madam, hath my son found grace or no?

ELINOR. Seeing, my lord, his lovely counterfeit,
And hearing how his mind and shape agreed,
I come not, trooped with all this warlike train,
Doubting of love, but so affectionate
As[3] Edward hath in England what he won in Spain.

[1] Before.
[2] With puns on *coursed* (*pursued*) and *fares* (*goes*).   [3] That.

CASTILE. A match, my lord; these wantons needs must love.
Men must have wives, and women will be wed.   20
Let's haste the day to honor up the rites.

RAFE. Sirrah Harry, shall Ned marry Nell?

HENRY. Ay, Rafe; how then?

RAFE. Marry, Harry, follow my counsel: send for Friar Bacon to marry them, for he'll so conjure him and her with his nigromancy that they shall love together like pig and lamb whilst they live.

CASTILE. But hear'st thou, Rafe? [30 Art thou content to have Elinor to thy lady?

RAFE. Ay, so she will promise me two things.

CASTILE. What's that, Rafe?

RAFE. That she will never scold with Ned, nor fight with me.—Sirrah Harry, I have put her down with a thing unpossible.

HENRY. What's that, Rafe?   40

RAFE. Why, Harry, didst thou ever see that a woman could both hold her tongue and her hands? No! But when egg pies grows on apple trees, then will thy gray mare prove a bagpiper.

EMPEROR. What says the Lord of Castile and the Earl of Lincoln, that they are in such earnest and secret talk?

CASTILE. I stand, my lord, amazéd at his talk,
How he discourseth of the constancy
Of one surnamed, for beauty's excellence,   51
The Fair Maid of merry Fressingfield.

HENRY. 'Tis true, my lord, 'tis wondrous for to hear;
Her beauty passing Mars's paramour,
Her virgin's right as rich as Vesta's was.
Lacy and Ned hath told me miracles.

CASTILE. What says Lord Lacy? Shall she be his wife?

LACY. Or else Lord Lacy is unfit to live.—
May it please your highness give me leave to post
To Fressingfield, I'll fetch the bonny girl,   60

And prove, in true appearance at the court,
What I have vouchéd often with my tongue.
HENRY. Lacy, go to the querry [1] of my stable,
And take such coursers as shall fit thy turn.
Hie thee to Fressingfield, and bring home the lass;
And, for her fame flies through the English coast,
If it may please the Lady Elinor,
One day shall match your excellence and her.
ELINOR. We Castile ladies are not very coy. [2]
Your highness may command a greater boon; 70
And glad were I to grace the Lincoln earl
With being partner of his marriage day.
EDWARD. Gramercy, Nell, for I do love the lord,
As he that's second to myself in love.
RAFE. You love her?—Madam Nell, never believe him you, though he swears he loves you.
ELINOR. Why, Rafe?
RAFE. Why, his love is like unto a tapster's glass that is broken with every [80 touch; for he loved the Fair Maid of Fressingfield once out of all ho. [3]— Nay, Ned, never wink upon me; I care not, I.
HENRY. Rafe tells all; you shall have a good secretary of him.—
But, Lacy, haste thee post to Fressingfield;
For, ere thou hast fitted all things for her state,
The solemn marriage day will be at hand.
LACY. I go, my lord. *Exit Lacy.*
EMPEROR. How shall we pass this day, my lord? 90
HENRY. To horse, my lord. The day is passing fair;
We'll fly the partridge or go rouse the deer.
Follow, my lords; you shall not want for sport. *Exeunt.*

[SCENE xiii.

Bacon's study.]

Enter Friar Bacon with Friar Bungay to his cell.

BUNGAY. What means the friar that frolicked it of late,
To sit as melancholy in his cell
As if he had neither lost nor won today?
BACON. Ah, Bungay, my Brazen Head is spoiled,
My glory gone, my seven years' study lost!
The fame of Bacon, bruited through the world,
Shall end and perish with this deep disgrace.
BUNGAY. Bacon hath built foundation of [4] his fame
So surely on the wings of true report,
With acting strange and uncouth miracles, 10
As this cannot infringe what he deserves.
BACON. Bungay, sit down, for by prospective skill
I find this day shall fall out ominous:
Some deadly act shall tide [5] me ere I sleep;
But what and wherein little can I guess.
BUNGAY. My mind is heavy, whatsoe'er shall hap.

Enter two Scholars, sons to Lambert and Serlsby. Knock.

BACON. Who's that knocks?
BUNGAY. Two scholars that desires to speak with you.
BACON. Bid them come in.— 19
Now, my youths, what would you have?
1 SCHOLAR. Sir, we are Suffolk men and neighboring friends;
Our fathers in their countries lusty squires;
Their lands adjoin. In Crackfield [6] mine doth dwell,
And his in Laxfield. We are college mates,
Sworn brothers, as our fathers lives as friends.

[1] Equerry.
[2] Distant. disdainful.
[3] Out of all bounds.
[4] Original reads *on.*
[5] Betide.
[6] Now Cratfield.

BACON. To what end is all this?

2 SCHOLAR. Hearing your worship kept
within your cell
A glass prospective, wherein men might
see
Whatso their thoughts or hearts' desire could wish,
We come to know how that our fathers
fare.   30

BACON. My glass is free for every honest
man.
Sit down, and you shall see ere long
how
Or in what state your friendly father
lives.
Meanwhile, tell me your names.

1 SCHOLAR.[1] Mine Lambert.

2 SCHOLAR. And mine Serlsby.

BACON. Bungay, I smell there will be a
tragedy.

*Enter [in the glass] Lambert and Serlsby
with rapiers and daggers.*

LAMBERT. Serlsby, thou hast kept thine
hour like a man.
Th'art worthy of the title of a squire,
That durst, for proof of thy affection   40
And for thy mistress' favor, prize[2]
thy blood.
Thou know'st what words did pass at
Fressingfield,
Such shameless braves as manhood can-
not brook.
Ay, for I scorn to bear such piercing
taunts,
Prepare thee, Serlsby; one of us will die.

SERLSBY. Thou see'st I single [meet] thee
[in] the field,[3]
And what I spake, I'll maintain with
my sword.
Stand on thy guard; I cannot scold it
out.
And, if thou kill me, think I have a son
That lives in Oxford in the Broadgates
Hall,   50
Who will revenge his father's blood with
blood.

LAMBERT. And, Serlsby, I have there a
lusty boy
That dares at weapon buckle with thy
son,

And lives in Broadgates too, as well as
thine.
But draw thy rapier, for we'll have a
bout.

BACON. Now, lusty younkers, look within
the glass,
And tell me if you can discern your
sires.

1 SCHOLAR. Serlsby, 'tis hard; thy father
offers wrong,
To combat with my father in the field.

2 SCHOLAR. Lambert, thou liest; my fa-
ther's is the abuse,[4]   60
And thou shalt find it, if my father
harm.[5]

BUNGAY. How goes it, sirs?

1 SCHOLAR. Our fathers are in combat,
hard by Fressingfield.

BACON. Sit still, my friends, and see the
event.

LAMBERT. Why stand'st thou, Serlsby?
Doubt'st thou of thy life?
A veney,[6] man! Fair Margaret craves
so much.

SERLSBY. Then this for her!

1 SCHOLAR. Ah, well thrust!

2 SCHOLAR. But mark the ward.[7]

They fight and kill each other.

LAMBERT. O, I am slain!   70

SERLSBY. And I.—Lord, have mercy on
me!

1 SCHOLAR. My father slain!—Serlsby,
ward that!

2 SCHOLAR. And so is mine!—Lambert,
I'll quite thee well.
The two Scholars stab one another.[8]

BUNGAY. O, strange stratagem![9]

BACON. See, friar, where the fathers[10] both
lie dead!—
Bacon, thy magic doth effect this massacre.
This glass prospective worketh many
woes;

---

[4] *I.e.*, my father is the offended one.   [6] Bout.
[5] Come to harm.   [7] Guard.
[8] Stage direction appears before the 2 Scholar's speech in original.
[9] Violent deed.   [10] Scholars (?).

---

[1] Original reads *Lambert.*
[2] Risk.   [3] Insertions by Dyce.

And therefore, seeing these brave lusty
  Brutes,[1]
These friendly youths, did perish by
  thine art,
End all thy magic and thine art at
  once.   80
The poniard that did end the fatal [2]
  lives
Shall break the cause efficiat of [3] their
  woes.
So fade the glass, and end with it the
  shows
That nigromancy did infuse the crystal
  with.   *He breaks the glass.*
BUNGAY. What means learned Bacon
  thus to break his glass?
BACON. I tell thee, Bungay, it repents
  me sore
That ever Bacon meddled in this art.
The hours I have spent in pyromantic
  spells,
The fearful tossing in the latest night
Of papers full of nigromantic charms,   90
Conjuring and adjuring devils and
  fiends,
With stole and alb and strange pentag-
  onon;
The wresting [4] of the holy name of God,
As Sother, Eloim, and Adonai,
Alpha, Manoth, and Tetragrammaton,
With praying to the fivefold powers
  of heaven,
Are instances that Bacon must be
  damned
For using devils to countervail his God.—
Yet, Bacon, cheer thee; drown not in
  despair.
Sins have their salves; repentance can
  do much.   100
Think Mercy sits where Justice holds
  her seat,
And from those wounds those bloody
  Jews did pierce,
Which by thy magic oft did bleed afresh,
From thence for thee the dew of mercy
  drops
To wash the wrath of high Jehovah's
  ire,
And make thee as a new-born babe from
  sin.—
Bungay, I'll spend the remnant of my
  life

In pure devotion, praying to my God
That he would save what Bacon vainly
  lost.   *Exit [with Bungay].*

[SCENE xiv.

Fressingfield.]

*Enter Margaret in nun's apparel; Keeper,
       her father; and their Friend.*

KEEPER. Margaret, be not so headstrong
  in these vows!
O, bury not such beauty in a cell,
That England hath held famous for
  the hue!
Thy father's hair, like to the silver
  blooms
That beautify the shrubs of Africa,
Shall fall before the dated time of death,
Thus to forgo his lovely Margaret.
MARGARET. Ah, father, when the harmony
  of heaven
Soundeth the measures of a lively faith,
The vain illusions of this flattering
  world   10
Seems odious to the thoughts of Mar-
  garet.
I lovéd once—Lord Lacy was my love;
And now I hate myself for that I loved,
And doted more on him than on my God.
For this I scourge myself with sharp
  repents.
But now the touch of such aspiring sins
Tells me all love is lust but love of
  heavens;
That beauty used for love is vanity.
The world contains naught but alluring
  baits,   19
Pride, flattery, and inconstant thoughts.
To shun the pricks of death, I leave the
  world,
And vow to meditate on heavenly bliss,
To live in Framlingham a holy nun,
Holy and pure in conscience and in
  deed;
And for to wish all maids to learn of me
To seek heaven's joy before earth's
  vanity.
FRIEND. And will you then, Margaret,
be shorn a nun, and so leave us all?
MARGARET. Now farewell, world, the
  engine of all woe!
Farewell to friends and father! Wel-
  come, Christ!   30

[1] Britons (or heroes?).   [3] Effecting.
[2] Fated.   [4] Misusing.

Adieu to dainty robes! This base attire
Better befits an humble mind to God
Than all the show of rich abiliments.
Love, O love, and, with fond love, fare-
well,
Sweet Lacy, whom I lovéd once so dear.
Ever be well, but never in my thoughts,
Lest I offend to think on Lacy's love.
But even to that, as to the rest, farewell!

*Enter Lacy, Warren, Ermsby, booted and
spurred.*

LACY. Come on, my wags, we're near
the keeper's lodge.
Here have I oft walked in the wat'ry
meads,   40
And chatted with my lovely Margaret.
WARREN. Sirrah Ned, is not this the
keeper?
LACY. 'Tis the same.
ERMSBY. The old lecher hath gotten holy
mutton [1] to him—a nun, my lord!
LACY. Keeper, how farest thou? Holla,
man, what cheer?
How doth Peggy, thy daughter and my
love?
KEEPER. Ah, good my lord! O, woe is me
for Peg!
See where she stands clad in her nun's
attire,
Ready for to be shorn in Framling-
ham.   50
She leaves the world because she left
your love.
O, good my lord, persuade her if you
can!
LACY. Why, how now, Margaret! What,
a malcontent?
A nun? What holy father taught you
this,
To task yourself to such a tedious life
As die a maid? 'Twere injury to me
To smother up such beauty in a cell.
MARGARET. Lord Lacy, thinking of thy
former miss,[2]
How fond [3] the prime of wanton years
were spent
In love—O, fie upon that fond con-
ceit,   60
Whose hap and essence hangeth in the
eye!—

[1] Loose woman.   [2] Error.   [3] Foolishly.

I leave both love and love's content
at once,
Betaking me to Him that is true love,
And leaving all the world for love of
Him.
LACY. Whence, Peggy, comes this meta-
morphosis?
What, shorn a nun, and I have from the
court
Posted with coursers to convey thee
hence
To Windsor, where our marriage shall
be kept?
Thy wedding robes are in the tailor's
hands.
Come, Peggy, leave these peremptory
vows.   70
MARGARET. Did not my lord resign his
interest,
And make divorce twixt Margaret and
him?
LACY. 'Twas but to try sweet Peggy's
constancy.
But will fair Margaret leave her love and
lord?
MARGARET. Is not heaven's joy before
earth's fading bliss,
And life above sweeter than life in love?
LACY. Why, then, Margaret will be shorn
a nun?
MARGARET. Margaret hath made a vow
which may not be revoked.
WARREN. We cannot stay, my lord; and,
if she be so strict,   79
Our leisure grants us not to woo afresh.
ERMSBY. Choose you, fair damsel; yet
the choice is yours,
Either a solemn nunnery or the court,
God or Lord Lacy. Which contents you
best,
To be a nun or else Lord Lacy's wife?
LACY. A good motion.—Peggy, your an-
swer must be short.
MARGARET. The flesh is frail. My lord
doth know it well,
That when he comes with his enchanting
face,
Whatsoe'er betide, I cannot say him
nay.
Off goes the habit of a maiden's heart,
And, seeing fortune will, fair Framling-
ham,   90
And all the show of holy nuns, farewell!
Lacy for me, if he will be my lord.

LACY. Peggy, thy lord, thy love, thy
 husband!
 Trust me, by truth of knighthood, that
 the king
 Stays for to marry matchless Elinor,
 Until I bring thee richly to the court,
 That one day may both marry her and
 thee.—
 How sayst thou, keeper? Art thou glad
 of this?
KEEPER. As if the English king had given
 The park and deer of Fressingfield to
 me.   100
ERMSBY. I pray thee, my Lord of Sus-
 sex, why art thou in a brown study?
WARREN. To see the nature of women—
 that be they never so near God, yet they
 love to die in a man's arms.
LACY. What have you fit for breakfast?
 We have hied
 And posted all this night to Fressingfield.
MARGARET. Butter and cheese, and um-
 bles [1] of a deer,
 Such as poor keepers have within their
 lodge.
LACY. And not a bottle of wine?   110
MARGARET. We'll find one for my lord.
LACY. Come, Sussex, let's in; we shall
 have more,
 For she speaks least, to hold her promise
 sure.   *Exeunt.*

[SCENE xv.

Bacon's study.]

Enter a Devil to seek Miles.

DEVIL. How restless are the ghosts of
 hellish spirits,
 When every charmer with his magic
 spells
 Calls us from ninefold-trenchéd Phleg-
 eton,[2]
 To scud and overscour the earth in post
 Upon the speedy wings of swiftest winds!
 Now Bacon hath raised me from the
 darkest deep,
 To search about the world for Miles
 his man,
 For Miles, and to torment his lazy bones
 For careless watching of his Brazen
 Head.
 See where he comes. O, he is mine!   10

[1] Numbles; heart, liver, etc.
[2] Emended by Dyce. Original reads *Blegiton.*

Enter Miles with a gown and a cornercap.

MILES. A scholar, quoth you! Marry,
 sir, I would I had been made a bottle
 maker when I was made a scholar; for I
 can get neither to be a deacon, reader, nor
 schoolmaster, no, not the clerk of a parish.
 Some call me dunce; another saith my head
 is as full of Latin as an egg's full of oatmeal. Thus I am tormented, that the
 devil and Friar Bacon haunts me.—
 Good Lord, here's one of my master's [20
 devils! I'll go speak to him.—What,
 Master Plutus, how cheer you?
DEVIL. Dost thou know me?
MILES. Know you, sir! Why, are not
 you one of my master's devils that were
 wont to come to my master, Doctor Bacon,
 at Brazen-nose?
DEVIL. Yes, marry, am I.
MILES. Good Lord, M[aster] Plutus,
 I have seen you a thousand times at my [30
 master's, and yet I had never the manners
 to make you drink. But, sir, I am glad
 to see how conformable you are to the
 statute.—[*To audience.*] I warrant you,
 he's as yeomanly a man as you shall see.
 Mark you, masters, here's a plain, honest
 man, without welt or guard.[3]—But I pray
 you, sir, do you come lately from hell?
DEVIL. Ay, marry; how then?
MILES. Faith, 'tis a place I have de- [40
 sired long to see. Have you not good tip-
 pling houses there? May not a man have
 a lusty fire there, a pot of good ale, a pair [4]
 of cards, a swingeing [5] piece of chalk,[6]
 and a brown toast that will clap a white
 waistcoat [7] on a cup of good drink?
DEVIL. All this you may have there.
MILES. You are for me, friend, and I
 am for you. But I pray you, may I not
 have an office there?   50
DEVIL. Yes, a thousand! What wouldst
 thou be?
MILES. By my troth, sir, in a place
 where I may profit myself. I know hell
 is a hot place, and men are marvelous dry,
 and much drink is spent there. I would be
 a tapster.
DEVIL. Thou shalt.
MILES. There's nothing lets [8] me from

[3] Facing or trimming.   [4] Pack.
[5] Striking, huge.
[6] Used in marking up alehouse accounts.
[7] *I.e.,* foam.   [8] Hinders.

going with you, but that 'tis a long [60
journey, and I have never a horse.

DEVIL. Thou shalt ride on my back.

MILES. Now surely here's a courteous
devil, that, for to pleasure his friend, will
not stick to make a jade of himself.—
But I pray you, goodman friend, let me
move a question to you.

DEVIL. What's that?

MILES. I pray you, whether is your pace
a trot or an amble?   70

DEVIL. An amble.

MILES. 'Tis well; but take heed it be
not a trot. But 'tis no matter, I'll prevent
it.   [*Puts on spurs.*]

DEVIL. What dost?

MILES. Marry, friend, I put on my
spurs; for, if I find your pace either a trot
or else uneasy, I'll put you to a false gallop;
I'll make you feel the benefit of my
spurs.   80

DEVIL. Get up upon my back.

MILES. O Lord, here's even a goodly
marvel, when a man rides to hell on the
devil's back!   *Exeunt, roaring.*

[SCENE xvi.

At court.]

*Enter the Emperor with a pointless sword;
next, the King of Castile, carrying a
sword with a point; Lacy, carrying the
globe; Ed[ward]; Warr[en], carrying a rod
of gold with a dove on it; Ermsby with
a crown and scepter; the Queen [i.e.,
Princess Elinor] with the Fair Maid of
Fressingfield on her left hand; Henry;
Bacon; with other Lords attending.*

EDWARD. Great potentates, earth's miracles for state,
Think that Prince Edward humbles at
your feet,
And, for these favors, on his martial
sword
He vows perpetual homage to yourselves,
Yielding these honors unto Elinor.

HENRY. Gramercies, lordings. Old Plan-
tagenet,
That rules and sways the Albion diadem,
With tears discovers these conceivéd
joys,
And vows requital, if his men-at-arms,

The wealth of England, or due honor,
done   10
To Elinor, may quite his favorites.
But all this while what say you to the
dames
That shine like to the crystal lamps of
heaven?

EMPEROR. If but a third were added to
these two,
They did surpass those gorgeous images
That gloried Ida with rich beauty's
wealth.[1]

MARGARET. 'Tis I, my lords who humbly
on my knee
Must yield her orisons to mighty Jove
For lifting up his handmaid to this state,
Brought from her homely cottage to
the court,   20
And graced with kings, princes, and
emperors;
To whom (next to the noble Lincoln
earl)
I vow obedience, and such humble love
As may a handmaid to such mighty
men.

ELINOR. Thou martial man that wears
the Almain crown,
And you the western potentates of
might,
The Albion princess, English Edward's
wife,
Proud that the lovely star of Fressingfield,
Fair Margaret, countess to the Lincoln earl,
Attends on Elinor—gramercies, lord,
for her—   30
'Tis I give thanks for Margaret to you
all,
And rest,[2] for her, due bounden to yourselves.

HENRY. Seeing the marriage is solemnizéd,
Let's march in triumph to the royal
feast.—
But why stands Friar Bacon here so
mute?

BACON. Repentant for the follies of my
youth,
That magic's secret mysteries misled,
And joyful that this royal marriage
Portends such bliss unto this matchless
realm.

[1] *I.e.,* Juno, Pallas, and Venus.   [2] Remain.

HENRY. Why, Bacon, what strange event
    shall happen to this land?   40
  Or what shall grow from Edward and
    his queen?
BACON. I find by deep prescience of mine
    art,
  Which once I tempered in my secret cell,
  That here where Brute did build his
    Troynovant,[1]
  From forth the royal garden of a king
  Shall flourish out so rich and fair a bud [2]
  Whose brightness shall deface proud
    Phœbus' flower,
  And overshadow Albion with her leaves.
  Till then Mars shall be master of the
    field,
  But then the stormy threats of wars
    shall cease.   50
  The horse shall stamp as careless of the
    pike;
  Drums shall be turned to timbrels of
    delight;
  With wealthy favors plenty shall enrich
  The strond that gladded wand'ring
    Brute to see,
  And peace from heaven shall harbor in
    these leaves
  That gorgeous beautifies this matchless
    flower.
  Apollo's hellitropian [3] then shall stoop,
  And Venus' hyacinth shall vail [4] her top;

Juno shall shut her gilliflowers up,
  And Pallas' bay shall 'bash her bright-
    est green;   60
  Ceres' carnation, in consort with those,
  Shall stoop and wonder at Diana's rose.
HENRY. This prophecy is mystical.—
  But, glorious commanders of Europa's
    love,
  That makes fair England like that
    wealthy isle
  Circled with Gihon and swift [5] Euphrates,
  In royalizing Henry's Albion
  With presence of your princely mighti-
    ness,
  Let's march. The tables all are spread,
  And viands such as England's wealth
    affords   70
  Are ready set to furnish out the boards.
  You shall have welcome, mighty po-
    tentates.
  It rests to furnish up this royal feast.
  Only your hearts be frolic, for the time
  Craves that we taste of naught but
    jouissance.[6]
  Thus glories England over all the West.
                Exeunt omnes.

FINIS FRIAR BACON, MADE BY ROBERT
    GREENE, MASTER OF ARTS.

"Omne tulit punctum qui miscuit utile dulci."[7]

---

[1] London, which according to legend was
founded by Brutus, descendant of Æneas.
[2] Referring to Queen Elizabeth.
[3] Heliotrope.   [4] Lower.

[5] Dyce's emendation. Original reads *first.*
[6] Pleasure.
[7] "He has everybody's approval who mingles
the useful with the agreeable" (Horace).

GEORGE A GREENE

The first cause of the attribution of the anonymous *George a Greene* to Robert Greene came from the discovery of two notes in different seventeenth century hands on the title page of a copy of the 1599 edition formerly in the Chatsworth Collection. These notes read: "Writen by . . . a minister, who ac[ted] the piners pt in it himselfe. Teste W. Shakespea[re];" and "Ed. Juby saith that the play was made by Ro. Gree[ne]." These notes are suspect, and it has been suggested by Samuel A. Tannenbaum that they may have been forged by a former owner of the book, or even by John Payne Collier himself, who first announced the discovery and whose forgeries in other cases have been detected. Greg, on the other hand, has maintained that they are in the hand of Sir George Buc, Master of the Revels from 1608 to 1622. If they are Buc's, the second note, perhaps correcting the first or perhaps adding to it, furnishes contemporary evidence, since Juby, an actor prominent from 1594 to 1618, would have known playhouse traditions. Examining all aspects of the problem impartially, Charles A. Pennel, in "The Authenticity of the *George a Greene* Title-Page Inscriptions" (*JEGP*, 1965), has pointed out that Collier did not use the inscriptions to prove the authorship of the play, that he miscopied them, and that he misdated Juby's connection with the Admiral's Men. The chief modern scholar of standing who has come out dogmatically for Greene's authorship is H. Dugdale Sykes, in "Robert Greene and *George a Greene, the Pinner of Wakefield*" (*RES*, 1931), and in a letter to J. LeGay Brereton (*ibid.*, 1933). Sykes based his case on a comparison of vocabulary and parallel passages in this play and in *Friar Bacon, Alphonsus*, and *James IV*, and concluded that these put Greene's authorship "beyond a doubt." F. S. Boas (*YWES*, 1931) ended his note on the first article by saying: "Sykes has certainly strengthened the case for Greene's authorship." Few others, except Churton Collins, have been willing to go this far, although Dyce, Grosart, and Dickinson, along with Collins, have printed it among his presumed works. Oscar Mertins in his Breslau dissertation, *Robert Greene und The Play of George-a-Greene* (1885), rejected it; C. N. Gayley in his *Representative English Comedies* (New York, 1903) was noncommittal; and Jordan was dubious, as was Muir.

Clarence L. Wentworth, in "A Probable Source for *George a Greene*" (*TLS*, July 4, 1936), brought out parallels between the story of the Earl of Kendal in the play and the career of the Scotch Earl of Atholl, who conspired against James I of Scotland; but Irving Ribner in *The English Historical Play* maintained that "the king is no more specifically referred to than as King Edward, the nobles are entirely fictitious, and all are involved in an entirely unhistorical plot."

The superiority of the stalwart hero of some trade to the unprincipled nobleman or even to the old woodland outlaw and folk hero, Robin Hood, was a fairly frequent theme of ballad and tale, and *George a Greene* has many suggestions of the style and conventions of the popular ballad. Even though George beats all the belligerent shoemakers single-handedly, their recognition as members of the "gentle craft" by the King himself is evidence of the independence of the new Elizabethan democracy.

It is perhaps for this very reason that the play is interesting today, in spite of its crudities of versification and the spasmodic nature of its plot development, which are probably accounted for by its having been cut and corrupted by some traveling company.

The present text is based on the Malone Society reprint of the edition of 1599, prepared by F. W. Clarke.

GEORGE A[1] GREENE, THE PINNER OF WAKEFIELD[2]

[*DRAMATIS PERSONÆ*

EDWARD, *King of England.*[3]
EARL OF WARWICK.
JAMES, *King of Scotland.*[3]
LORD HUMES.
EARL OF KENDAL ⎫
LORD BONFIELD ⎪
SIR NICHOLAS MANNERING ⎬ *rebels.*
SIR GILBERT ARMSTRONG ⎭
MUSGROVE, *keeper of Sandown Castle.*
CUDDY, *his son.*
GEORGE A GREENE, *the pinner*[4] *of Wake-field.*
JENKIN, *a clown* ⎫ *servants to*
WILY, *a boy* ⎬ *George a Greene.*

GRIME.
WOODROFFE, *the justice of Wakefield.*
ROBIN HOOD.
SCARLET ⎫ *Robin Hood's men.*
MUCH ⎬
JOHN TAYLOR, *post of King James.*
NED A BARLEY, *a small boy.*
A SHOEMAKER.

JANE A BARLEY, *mother of Ned.*
BETTRIS, *daughter to Grime.*
MAID MARIAN.
TOWNSMEN, SHOEMAKERS, SOLDIERS, MESSENGER, *etc.*

SCENE: *England.*

TIME: *Indefinite.*]

[SCENE i.

Near Bradford.]

Enter the Earl of Kendal; with him the Lord Bonfield, Sir Gilbert Armstrong, [Sir Nicholas Mannering,] and John [Taylor].

KEND. Welcome to Bradford, martial gentlemen,
L[ord] Bonfield and Sir Gilbert Armstrong both;
And all my troops, even to my basest groom,
Courage and welcome, for the day is ours!
Our cause is good—it is for the land's avail.
Then let us fight and die for England's good!
OMNES. We will, my lord!

KEND. As I am Henry Momford, Kendal's earl,
You honor me with this assent of yours;
And here upon my sword I make protest
For to relieve the poor or die myself. 11
And know, my lords, that James, the King of Scots,
Wars hard upon the borders of this land.—
Here is his post.—Say, John Taylor,
What news with King James?
JOHN. War, my lord! Tall[5] and good news, I trow;[6]
For King Jamie vows to meet you the twenty-sixth of this month,
God willing; marry, doth he, sir.
KEND. My friends, you see what we have to win.—
Well, John, commend me to King James 20
And tell him I will meet him the twenty-sixth of this month
And all the rest; and so, farewell.
Exit John.

Bonfield, why stand'st thou as a man in dumps?

Courage! For, if I win, I'll make thee duke.

I, Henry Momford, will be king myself;

And I will make thee Duke of Lancaster,

And Gilbert Armstrong Lord of Doncaster.

BON. Nothing, my lord, makes me amazed [1] at all

But that our soldiers finds our victuals scant.

We must make havoc of those country swains; 30

For so will the rest tremble and be afraid,

And humbly send provision to your camp.

GILB. My Lord Bonfield gives good advice.

They make a scorn,[2] and stand upon [3] the king;

So what is brought is sent from them perforce.

Ask Mannering else.

KEND. What sayest thou, Mannering?

MAN. Whenas [4] I showed your high commission,

They made this answer,

Only to send provision for your horses. 40

KEND. Well, hie thee to Wakefield, bid the town

To send me all provision that I want,

Lest I, like martial Tamburlaine, lay waste

Their bordering countries,

And leaving none alive that contradicts my commission.

MAN. Let me alone, my lord; I'll make them

Vail [5] their plumes; for whatsoe'er he be,

The proudest knight, justice, or other, that gainsayeth

Your word, I'll clap him fast,[6] to make the rest to fear.

KEND. Do so, Nick. Hie thee thither presently,[7] 50

And let us hear of thee again tomorrow.

MAN. Will you not remove, my lord?

KEND. No, I will lie at Bradford all this night

And all the next.—Come, Bonfield, let us go,

And listen out [8] some bonny lasses here.

Exeunt omnes.

[SCENE ii.

Wakefield.]

Enter the Justice, a Townsman, George a Greene, and Sir Nicholas Mannering with his commission.

JUST. M[aster] Mannering, stand aside, whilst we confer

What is best to do.—

Townsmen of Wakefield, the Earl of Kendal

Here hath sent for victuals;

And in aiding him we show ourselves

No less than traitors to the king;

Therefore let me hear, townsmen,

What is your consents.[9]

TOWNS. Even as you please, we are all content.

JUST. Then, M[aster] Mannering, we are resolved. 10

MAN. As how?

JUST. Marry, sir, thus.

We will send the Earl of Kendal no victuals,

Because he is a traitor to the king,

And in aiding him we show ourselves no less.

MAN. Why, men of Wakefield, are you waxen mad,

That present danger cannot whet your wits

Wisely to make provision of yourselves?

The earl is thirty thousand men strong in power,

And what town soever him resist, 20

He lays it flat and level with the ground.

Ye silly men, you seek your own decay;

Therefore send my lord such provision as he wants,

So he will spare your town, and come no nearer

Wakefield than he is.

JUST. Master Mannering, you have your answer;

You may be gone.

MAN. Well, Woodroffe, for so I guess is thy name,

---

[1] Perplexed.
[2] *I.e.*, they scorn us.
[3] With.
[4] When.
[5] Lower.
[6] Imprison.
[7] At once.
[8] Get news of.
[9] Opinion.

I'll make thee curse thy overthwart [1]
denial;
And all that sit upon the bench this day
Shall rue the hour they have withstood
my lord's   31
Commission.
JUST. Do thy worst; we fear thee not.
MAN. See you these seals? Before you
pass the town,
I will have all things my lord doth want,
In spite of you.
GEORGE. Proud dapper Jack,[2] vail bonnet
to
The bench
That represents the person of the king,
Or, sirrah, I'll lay thy head before thy
feet!   40
MAN. Why, who art thou?
GEORGE. Why, I am George a Greene,
True liegeman to my king,
Who scorns that men of such esteem as
these
Should brook the braves [3] of any traitor-
ous squire.
You of the bench, and you, my fellow-
friends,
Neighbors, we subjects all unto the
king,
We are English born, and therefore Ed-
ward's friends,
Vowed unto him even in our mothers'
womb,
Our minds to God, our hearts unto our
king.   50
Our wealth, our homage, and our car-
casses
Be all King Edward's. Then, sirrah,
we have
Nothing left for traitors but our swords,
Whetted to bathe them in your bloods,
And die against you, before we send you
any victuals.
JUST. Well spoken, George a Greene!
TOWNS. Pray let George a Greene speak
for us.
GEORGE. Sirrah, you get no victuals here,
Not if a hoof of beef would save your
lives.
MAN. Fellow, I stand amazed at thy pre-
sumption.   60
Why, what art thou that darest gainsay
my lord,

Knowing his mighty puissance and his
stroke?
Why, my friend, I come not barely of
myself,
For, see, I have a large commission.
GEORGE. Let me see it, sirrah.
             [*Takes the commission.*]
Whose seals be these?
MAN. This is the Earl of Kendal's seal-
at-arms,
This Lord Charnel Bonfield's,
And this Sir Gilbert Armstrong's.
GEORGE. I tell thee, sirrah, did good King
Edward's son   70
Seal a commission against the king his
father,
Thus would I tear it in despite of him,
             He tears the commission.
Being traitor to my sovereign.
MAN. What, hast thou torn my lord's
commission?
Thou shalt rue it, and so shall all Wake-
field.
GEORGE. What, are you in choler? I will
give you pills
To cool your stomach.[4]
Seest thou these seals?
Now, by my father's soul, which was a
yeoman
When he was alive, eat them,   80
Or eat my dagger's point, proud squire.
MAN. But thou dost but jest, I hope.
GEORGE. Sure, that shall you see before
we two part.
MAN. Well, and [5] there be no remedy, so,
George—
             [*Swallows one of the seals.*]
One is gone; I pray thee, no more now.
GEORGE. O, sir, if one be good, the others
cannot hurt!
         [*Mannering swallows the other seals.*]
So, sir; now you may go tell the Earl of
Kendal,
Although I have rent his large com-
mission,
Yet of courtesy I have sent all his seals
Back again by you.   90
MAN. Well, sir, I will do your arrant.[6]
                 Exit.
GEORGE. Now let him tell his lord that he
hath
Spoke with George a Greene,
Right [7] pinner of merry Wakefield town,

[1] Perverse.   [3] Endure the threats.
[2] Knave.
[4] Angry temper.   [5] If.   [6] Errand.   [7] True.

That hath physic for a fool,

Pills for a traitor that doth wrong his
sovereign.

Are you content with this that I have
done?

JUST. Aye, content, George;

For highly hast thou honored Wakefield
town　　　　　　　　　　　　　　　　99

In cutting of proud Mannering so short.

Come, thou shalt be my welcome guest
today,

For well thou hast deserved reward and
.favor.　　　　　　　　　*Exeunt omnes.*

[SCENE iii.

Before Musgrove's castle.]

*Enter Old Musgrove and Young Cuddy, his
son.*

CUDDY. Now, gentle father, list unto thy
son,

And for my mother's love,

That erst [1] was blithe and bonny in
thine eye,

Grant one petition that I shall demand.

MUS. What is that, my Cuddy?

CUDDY. Father, you know the ancient enmity of late

Between the Musgroves and the wily
Scots,

Whereof they have oath

Not to leave one alive that strides a
lance. [2]

O father, you are old and, waning, age
unto the grave.　　　　　　　　　10

Old William Musgrove, which whilom [3]
was thought

The bravest horseman in all Westmoreland,

Is weak, and forced to stay his arm upon
a staff,

That erst could wield a lance.

Then, gentle father, resign the hold [4]
to me;

Give arms to youth, and honor unto age.

MUS. Avaunt, false-hearted boy!　My
joints do quake

Even with anguish of thy very words.

Hath William Musgrove seen an hundred
years,

Have I been feared and dreaded of the
Scots,　　　　　　　　　　　　　　20

[1] Formerly.
[2] *I.e.,* even the children.

That, when they heard my name in any
road, [5]

They fled away, and posted thence
amain, [6]

And shall I die with shame now in mine
age?

No, Cuddy, no.　Thus resolve I:

Here have I lived, and here will Musgrove die.　　　　　　　*Exeunt omnes.*

[SCENE iv.

Before Grime's house at Bradford.]

*Enter Lord Bonfield, Sir Gilbert Armstrong,
M[aster] Grime, and Bettris, his daughter.*

BON. Now, gentle Grime, God-a-mercy [7]
for our good cheer;

Our fare was royal, and our welcome
great;

And, sith [8] so kindly thou hast entertained us,

If we return with happy victory,

We will deal as friendly with thee in
recompense.

GRIME. Your welcome was but duty,
gentle lord;

For wherefore have we given us our
wealth

But to make our betters welcome when
they come?

[*Aside.*] O, this goes hard when traitors
must be flattered!

But life is sweet, and I cannot withstand it.　　　　　　　　　　　10

God, I hope, will revenge the quarrel
of my king.—

GILB. What said you, Grime?

GRIME. I say, Sir Gilbert, looking on my
daughter,

I curse the hour that e'er I got [9] the girl;

For, sir, she may have many wealthy
suitors,

And yet she disdains them all to have

Poor George a Greene unto her husband.

BON. On that, good Grime, I am talking
with thy

Daughter;

But she, in quirks and quiddities of
love,　　　　　　　　　　　　　20

Sets me to school, she is so overwise.—

[5] Raid.
[6] At full speed.
[7] God reward you; thank you.
[8] Since.
[9] Begot.

But, gentle girl, if thou wilt forsake
The pinner and be my love, I will ad-
vance thee high.
To dignify those hairs of amber hue,
I'll grace them with a chaplet made of
pearl,
Set with choice rubies, sparks,[1] and dia-
monds,
Planted upon a velvet hood, to hide
that head
Wherein two sapphires burn like spar-
kling fire.
This will I do, fair Bettris, and far more,
If thou wilt love the Lord of Doncaster.
BETTRIS. Heigh-ho! My heart is in a
higher place,   31
Perhaps on the earl, if that be he.
See where he comes, or [2] angry or in
love,
Forwhy [3] his color [4] looketh discontent.
KEND. [_Entering._] Come, Nick, follow me.

Enter the Earl of Kendal and Nicholas
Mannering.

BON. How now, my lord? What news?
KEND. Such news, Bonfield, as will make
thee laugh,
And fret thy fill, to hear how Nick was
used.
Why, the justices stand on their terms.
Nick, as you know, is haughty in his
words;   40
He laid the law unto the justices
With threat'ning braves, that one looked
on another,
Ready to stoop; but that a churl came
in,
One George a Greene, the pinner of the
town,
And with his dagger drawn laid hands
on Nick,
And by no beggars [5] swore that we were
traitors,
Rent our commission, and upon a brave
Made Nick to eat the seals or brook the
stab.
Poor Mannering, afraid, came posting
hither straight.
BETTRIS. O lovely George, fortune be
still [6] thy friend!   50

And as thy thoughts be high, so be thy
mind
In all accords, even to thy heart's de-
sire!
BON. What says fair Bettris?
GRIME. My lord, she is praying for George
a Greene.
He is the man, and she will none but him.
BON. But him? Why, look on me, my
girl!
Thou knowest that yesternight I courted
thee,
And swore at my return to wed with
thee.
Then tell me, love, shall I have all thy
fair? [7]
BETTRIS. I care not for earl, nor yet for
knight,   60
Nor baron that is so bold;
For George a Greene, the merry pinner,
He hath my heart in hold.
BON. Bootless, my lord, are many vain
replies.
Let us hie us to Wakefield, and send her
the pinner's head.
KEND. It shall be so.—Grime, gramercy.
Shut up thy daughter; bridle her af-
fects.[8]
Let me not miss her when I make return;
Therefore look to her, as to thy life, good
Grime.
GRIME. I warrant you, my lord.   70
        Ex[eunt] Grime and Bettris.
KEND. And, Bettris, leave a base pinner
for to love an earl.
Fain would I see this pinner, George a
Greene.
It shall be thus:
Nick Mannering shall lead on the battle,[9]
And we three will go to Wakefield in
some disguise.
But howsoever, I'll have his head today.
        Ex[eunt] omnes.

[SCENE V.

Before Sir John a Barley's castle.]

Enter the King of Scots, Lord Humes, with
Soldiers, and Johnny [Taylor].

JAMES.[10] Why, Johnny, then the Earl of
Kendal is blithe,

---

[1] Precious stones.
[2] Either.
[3] Because.
[4] Appearance.
[5] By no small oath.
[6] Always.
[7] Beauty.   [8] Affections.   [9] Army.
[10] In the original _King_ is used here and at line
6 to designate the speaker.

And hath brave men that troop along
with him?

JOHNNY. Ay, marry, my liege, and hath
good men
That come along with him,
And vows to meet you at Scrasblesea,
God willing.

JAMES. If good S[aint] Andrew lend King
Jamie leave,
I will be with him at the pointed [1] day.
But, soft!—Whose pretty boy art thou?

Enter Jane a Barley's Son.

NED. Sir, I am son unto Sir John a Barley,
Eldest, and all that e'er my mother
had;   10
Edward my name.

JAMES. And whither art thou going,
pretty Ned?

NED. To seek some birds, and kill them,
if I can.
And now my schoolmaster is also gone,
So have I liberty to ply my bow;
For, when he comes, I stir not from my
book.

JAMES. Lord Humes, but mark the visage
of this child.
By him I guess the beauty of his mother;
None but Leda could breed Helena.
Tell me, Ned, who is within with thy
mother?   20

NED. Not [2] but herself and household
servants, sir.
If you would speak with her, knock at
this gate.

JAMES. Johnny, knock at that gate.
                   [*John knocks.*]

Enter Jane a Barley upon the walls.

JANE. O, I am betrayed! What multitudes
be these?

JAMES. Fear not, fair Jane, for all these
men are mine,
And all thy friends, if thou be friend to
me.
I am thy lover, James the King of Scots,
That oft have sued and wooed with
many letters,
Painting my outward passions with my
pen,
Whenas my inward soul did bleed for
woe.   30

[1]Appointed.   [2] Naught (?).

Little regard was given to my suit,
But haply thy husband's presence
wrought it.
Therefore, sweet Jane, I fitted me to
time,
And, hearing that thy husband was from
home,
Am come to crave what long I have desired.

NED. Nay, soft you,[3] sir! You get no en-
trance here,
That seek to wrong Sir John a Barley so,
And offer such dishonor to my mother.

JAMES. Why, what dishonor, Ned?

NED. Though young, yet often have I
heard   40
My father say
No greater wrong than to be made
cuckold.
Were I of age, or were my body strong,
Where he ten kings, I would shoot him
to the heart
That should attempt to give Sir John
the horn.[4]
Mother, let him not come in.
I will go lie at Jockie Miller's house.

JAMES. Stay him!

JANE. Ay, well said; Ned, thou hast given
the king
His answer,   50
For, were the ghost of Cæsar on the
earth,
Wrapped in the wonted glory of his
honor,
He should not make me wrong my hus-
band so.
But good King James is pleasant,[5] as I
guess,
And means to try what humor I am in;
Else would he never have brought an
host of men
To have them witness of his Scottish lust.

JAMES. Jane, in faith, Jane!

JANE. Never reply, for I protest by the
highest
Holy God,   60
That doometh just revenge for things
amiss,
King James, of all men, shall not have
my love.

JAMES. Then list to me: Saint Andrew
be my boot,[6]

[3] Stop.   [4] Proverbial sign of the cuckold.
[5] Jocular.   [6] Aid.

But I'll raze thy castle to the very ground
Unless thou open the gate, and let me in.
JANE. I fear thee not, King Jamie; do thy
    worst.
This castle is too strong for thee to scale;
Besides, tomorrow will Sir John come
    home.
JAMES. Well, Jane, since thou disdain'st
    King James' love,
I'll draw thee on with sharp and deep
    extremes;   70
For, by my father's soul, this brat of
    thine
Shall perish here before thine eyes,
Unless thou open the gate, and let me in.
JANE. O deep extremes! My heart begins
    to break!
My little Ned looks pale for fear!
Cheer thee, my boy; I will do much for
    thee.
NED. But not so much as to dishonor me.
JANE. And if thou diest, I cannot live,
    sweet Ned.
NED. Then die with honor, mother, dy-
    ing chaste.
JANE. I am armed: 80
My husband's love, his honor, and his
    fame
Joins [1] victory by virtue.
Now, King James, if mother's tears can-
    not allay thine ire,
Then butcher him, for I will never yield.
The son shall die before I wrong the
    father.
JAMES. Why, then, he dies.

Alarum within. Enter a Messenger.

MESSENGER. My lord, Musgrove is at
    hand.
JAMES. Who, Musgrove?   The devil he
    is! Come,
My horse!   *Exeunt omnes.*

[SCENE vi.

The same.]

*Enter Old Musgrove with King James
                  prisoner.*

MUS. Now, King James, thou art my
    prisoner.
JAMES. Not thine, but fortune's prisoner!

[1] Enjoins.

Enter Cuddy.

CUDDY. Father, the field is ours.   Their
    colors we
Have seized,
And Humes is slain—I slew him hand
    to hand.
MUS. God and Saint George!
CUDDY. O father, I am sore athirst!
JANE. Come in, young Cuddy, come and
    drink thy fill.
Bring in King Jamie with you as a guest;
For all this broil was cause [2] he could
    not enter.   10
                  Exeunt omnes.

[SCENE vii.

Wakefield.]

Enter George a Greene alone.

GEORGE. The sweet content of men that
    live in love
Breeds fretting humors in a restless mind;
And fancy,[3] being checked by fortune's
    spite,
Grows too impatient in her sweet de-
    sires—
Sweet to those men whom love leads on
    to bliss,
But sour to me whose hap is still amiss.

Enter [Jenkin,] the clown.

JEN. Marry, amen, sir.
GEORGE. Sir, what do you cry "amen" at?
JEN. Why, did not you talk of love?
GEORGE. How do you know that?   10
JEN. Well, though I say it that should not
    say it,
There are few fellows in our parish
So nettled with love as I have been of
    late.
GEORGE. Sirrah, I thought no less when
    the other morning
You rose so early to go to your wenches.
Sir, I had thought you had gone about
    my honest business.
JEN. Trow, you have hit it; for, master,
    be it known
To you,
There is some good will betwixt Madge
    the sousewife[4]

[2] Because, so that.
[3] Love.   [4] Seller of souse, or pickled pork.

And I;   20
Marry, she hath another lover.
GEORGE. Canst thou brook any rivals
    in thy love?
JEN. A rider? No, he is a sow-gelder and
    goes afoot.
But Madge pointed to meet me in your
    wheat close.[1]
GEORGE. Well, did she meet you there?
JEN. Never make question of that.
And first I saluted her with a green
    gown,[2]
And after fell as hard a-wooing
As if the priest had been at our backs
    to have married us.
GEORGE. What, did she grant?   30
JEN. Did she grant? Never make question
    of that.
And she gave me a shirt collar
Wrought over with no counterfeit stuff.
GEORGE. What, was it gold?
JEN. Nay, 'twas better than gold.
GEORGE. What was it?
JEN. Right Coventry blue.[3]
We[4] had no sooner come there but wot[5]
    you who came by?
GEORGE. No, who?
JEN. Clim, the sow-gelder.   40
GEORGE. Came he by?
JEN. He spied Madge and I sit together.
He leapt from his horse, laid his hand
    on his dagger, and
Began to swear.
Now I seeing he had a dagger,
And I nothing but this twig in my
    hand,
I gave him fair words and said nothing.
He comes to me, and takes me by the
    bosom.
"You whoreson[6] slave," said he, "hold
    my horse.
And look he take no cold in his feet." 50
"No, marry, shall he, sir," quoth I;
"I'll lay my cloak underneath him."
I took my cloak, spread it all along,
And his horse on the midst of it.
GEORGE. Thou clown, didst thou set his
    horse upon
Thy cloak?
JEN. Ay, but mark how I served him:

Madge and he was no sooner gone down
    into the ditch
But I plucked out my knife,
Cut four holes in my cloak, and made
    his horse stand   60
On the bare ground.
GEORGE. 'Twas well done. Now, sir, go
    and survey my fields.
If you find any cattle in the corn, to
    pound[7] with them!
JEN. And, if I find any in the pound,
I shall turn them out.

                          Exit Jenkin.

Enter the Earl of Kendal, Lord Bonfield,
    Sir Gilbert, all disguised, with a Train
                          of Men.

KEND. Now we have put the horses in
    the corn,
Let us stand in some corner for to hear
What braving terms the pinner will
    breathe
When he spies our horses in the corn.
                [*They conceal themselves.*]

Enter Jenkin[8] blowing of his horn.

JEN. O master, where are you? We have
a prize.   71
GEORGE. A prize! What is it?
JEN. Three goodly horses in our wheat
close.
GEORGE. Three horses in our wheat
close? Whose be they?
JEN. Marry, that's a riddle to me, but
they are there, velvet horses, and I never
saw such horses before. As my duty was,
I put off my cap, and said as followeth: [80
"My masters, what do you make[9] in
our close?" One of them, hearing me ask
what he made there, held up his head and
neighed, and after his manner laughed as
heartily as if a mare had been tied to his
girdle. "My masters," said I, "it is no
laughing matter; for, if my master take you
here, you go as round as a top to the
pound." Another untoward jade, hearing
me threaten him to the pound and to [90
tell you of them, cast up both his heels, and
let such a monstrous great fart that was
as much as in his language to say, " A fart

---

[1] Field.   [2] Tumbled her in the grass.
[3] Superior blue embroidery thread made at
Coventry, with a pun on *black and blue*.
[4] Original reads *who*.   [5] Know.   [6] Rascally.

[7] Public enclosure for stray cattle.
[8] Original reads *Jack*, possibly the name of the
actor of the part.   [9] Do.

for the pound, and a fart for George a
Greene!" Now I, hearing this, put on my
cap, blew my horn, called them all jades,
and came to tell you.

GEORGE. Now, sir, go and drive me those
three horses
To the pound.

JEN. Do you hear? I were best take a
constable　　　　　　　　　　　　　100
With me.

GEORGE. Why so?

[JEN.] Why, they, being gentlemen's
horses, may stand on their
Reputation, and will not obey me.

GEORGE. Go, do as I bid you, sir.

JEN. Well, I may go.

The Earl of Kendal, the Lord Bonfield, and
*　　　Sir Gilbert Armstrong meet them.*

KEND. Whither away, sir?

JEN. Whither away? I am going to put
the horses
In the pound.

KEND. Sirrah, those three horses belong
to us, and we put　　　　　　　110
Them in, and they must tarry there and
eat their fill.

JEN. Stay, I will go tell my master.—
Hear you, master? We have another
prize:
Those three horses be in your wheat close
still,
And here be three geldings more.

GEORGE. What be these?

JEN. These are the masters of the horses.

GEORGE. Now, gentlemen—I know not
your degrees,
But more you cannot be, unless you be
kings—
Why wrong you us of Wakefield with
your horses?　　　　　　　　120
I am the pinner, and, before you pass,
You shall make good the trespass they
have done.

KEND. Peace, saucy mate, prate not to us!
I tell thee, pinner, we are gentlemen.

GEORGE. Why, sir, so may I, sir, although
I give no arms.[1]

KEND. Thou? How art thou a gentleman?

JEN. And such is my master, and he may
give as good

[1] Bear no coat of arms.

Arms as ever your great-grandfather
could give.

KEND. Pray thee, let me hear how.

JEN. Marry, my master may give for his
arms　　　　　　　　　　　　　130
The picture of April in a green jerkin,
With a rook on one fist and an horn on
the other;
But my master gives his arms the wrong
way,
For he gives the horn on his fist,
And your grandfather, because he would
not lose his
Arms,
Wears the horn on his own head.

KEND. Well, pinner, sith our horses be in,
In spite of thee they now shall feed their
fill,
And eat until our leisures serve to go.　140

GEORGE. Now, by my father's soul,
Were good King Edward's horses in the
corn,
They shall amend the scath[2] or kiss[3] the
pound;
Much more yours, sir, whatsoe'er you be.

KEND. Why, man, thou knowest not us.
We do belong to Henry Momford, Earl of
Kendal,
Men that, before a month be full expired,
Will be King Edward's betters in the
land.

GEORGE. King Edward's better! Rebel,
thou liest!　　　　　*George strikes him.*

BON. Villain, what has thou done? Thou
hast stroke[4]　　　　　　　　150
An earl.

GEORGE. Why, what care I? A poor man
that is true
Is better than an earl, if he be false.
Traitors reap no better favors at my
hands.

KEND. Ay, so methinks; but thou shalt
dear aby[5] this blow.—
Now or never lay hold on the pinner!

Enter all the Ambush.

GEORGE. Stay, my lords, let us parley on
these broils.—
[*Aside.*] Not Hercules against two, the
proverb is,
Nor I against so great a multitude.

[2] Harm.　　　　　[3] Be imprisoned in (slang).
[4] Struck.　　　　　　[5] Dearly pay for.

Had not your troops come marching as
　they did, 160
I would have stopped your passage unto
　London.
But now I'll fly to secret policy.
KEND. What dost thou murmur, George?
GEORGE. Marry, this, my lord; I muse,[1]
If thou be Henry Momford, Kendal's
　earl,
That thou wilt do poor G[eorge] a Greene
　this wrong,
Ever to match me with a troop of men.
KEND. Why dost thou strike me then?
GEORGE. Why, my lord, measure me but
　by yourself:
Had you a man had served you long,
And heard your foe misuse you behind
　your back, 171
And would not draw his sword in your
　defense,
You would cashier him.
Much more, King Edward is my king;
And before I'll hear him so wronged,
I'll die within this place,
And maintain good whatsoever I have
　said.
And, if I speak not reason in this case,
What I have said I'll maintain in this
　place.
BON. A pardon, my lord, for this pinner,
For, trust me, he speaketh like a man of
　worth. 181
KEND. Well, George, wilt thou leave
　Wakefield and
Wend with me,
I'll freely put up all and pardon thee.
GEORGE. Ay, my lord, considering [2] me one
　thing:
You will leave these arms, and follow
　your good king.
KEND. Why, George, I rise not against
　King Edward,
But for the poor that is oppressed by
　wrong;
And, if King Edward will redress the
　same,
I will not offer him disparagement, 190
But otherwise; and so let this suffice.
Thou hear'st the reason why I rise in
　arms.
Now, wilt thou leave Wakefield and
　wend with me,
I'll make thee captain of a hardy band,

[1] Marvel.　　　　　　　[2] Granting, noting.

And, when I have my will, dub thee a
　knight.
GEORGE. Why, my lord, have you any
　hope to win?
KEND. Why, there is a prophecy doth say
That King James and I shall meet at
　London,
And make the king vail[3] bonnet to us both.
GEORGE. If this were true, my lord, this
　were a mighty reason. 200
KEND. Why, it is a miraculous prophecy,
　and cannot fail.
GEORGE. Well, my lord, you have almost
　turned me.—
Jenkin, come hither.
JEN. Sir?
GEORGE. Go your ways home, sir,
And drive me those three horses home
　unto my house,
And pour them down a bushel of good
　oats.
JEN. Well, I will.—[Aside]. Must I give
　these scurvy horses
Oats? Exit Jenkin.
GEORGE. Will it please you to command
　your train aside? 210
KEND. Stand aside. Exit the Train.
GEORGE. Now list to me:
Here in a wood not far from hence,
There dwells an old man in a cave alone,
That can foretell what fortunes shall
　befall you,
For he is greatly skillful in magic art.
Go you three to him early in the morning,
And question him. If he says good,
Why, then, my lord, I am the foremost
　man!
We will march up with your camp to
　London. 220
KEND. George, thou honorest me in this.
But where shall we find him out?
GEORGE. My man shall conduct you to the
　place.
But, good my lords, tell me true what the
　wise man saith.
KEND. That will I, as I am Earl of Kendal.
GEORGE. Why, then, to honor G[eorge] a
　Greene the more,
Vouchsafe a piece of beef at my poor
　house.
You shall have wafer cakes your fill,
A piece of beef hung up since Martle-
　mas.[4]

[3] Remove.　　　[4] Martinmas, November 11.

If that like you not, take what you bring,
  for me! [1]   230
KEND. Gramercies, George.
                       Exeunt omnes.

[SCENE viii.

Before Grime's house at Bradford.]

*Enter George a Greene's boy, Wily, disguised
    like a woman, to M[aster] Grime's.*

WILY. O, what is love? It is some mighty
  power,
  Else could it never conquer G[eorge] a
    Greene.
  Here dwells a churl that keeps away his
    love.
  I know the worst, and, if I be espied,
  'Tis but a beating; and, if I by this
    means
  Can get fair Bettris forth her father's
    door,
  It is enough. Venus for me, and all gods
    above [2]
  Be aiding to my wily enterprise!
              He knocks at the door.

Enter Grime.

GRIME. How now! Who knocks there?
  What would you have?
  From whence came you? Where do you
    dwell?   10
WILY. I am, forsooth, a sempster's [3] maid
  hard by,
  That hath brought work home to your
    daughter.
GRIME. Nay, are you not some crafty
  quean[4]
  That comes from George a Greene, that
    rascal,
  With some letters to my daughter?
  I will have you searched.
WILY. Alas, sir, it is Hebrew unto me
  To tell me of George a Greene or any
    other!
  Search me, good sir,
  And, if you find a letter about me,   20
  Let me have the punishment that is
    due.
GRIME. Why are you muffled? I like you
  the worse
  For that.

WILY. I am not, sir, ashamed to show my
  face;
  Yet loath I am my cheeks should take the
    air—
  Not that I am chary of my beauty's
    hue,
  But that I am troubled with the tooth-
    ache sore.   *[Uncovers his face.]*
GRIME. *[Aside.]* A pretty wench, of smil-
  ing countenance!
  Old men can like, although they cannot
    love;
  Ay, and love, though not so brief[5] as
    young men can.—   30
  Well, go in, my wench, and speak with
    my daughter.   *Exit [Wily].*
  I wonder much at the Earl of Kendal,
  Being a mighty man, as still he is;
  Yet for to be a traitor to his king
  Is more than God or man will well
    allow.
  But what a fool am I to talk of him!
  My mind is more here of the pretty
    lass.
  Had she brought some forty pounds to
    town,
  I could be content to make her my
    wife.
  Yet I have heard it in a proverb said,   40
  He that is old and marries with a lass,
  Lies but at home, and proves himself an
    ass.

Enter Bettris in Wily's apparel, to Grime.

  How now, my wench! How is't? What,
    not a word?
  Alas, poor soul, the toothache plagues
    her sore!
  Well, my wench, here is an angel[6] for to
    buy thee pins,
  And I pray thee use mine house,
  The oft'ner, the more welcome. Farewell.
                       Exit.
BETTRIS. O blesséd love, and blesséd for-
  tune both!
  But, Bettris, stand not here to talk of
    love,
  But hie thee straight unto thy George a
    Greene.   50
  Never went roebuck swifter on the downs
  Than I will trip it till I see my George.
                       Exit.

---

[1] For all I care.   [3] Seamstress'.
[2] Original reads *all goes alone.* [4] Hussy.
[5] Readily.   [6] Gold coin.

[SCENE ix.

Before a cave near Wakefield.]

*Enter the Earl of Kendal, L[ord] Bonfield,
Sir Gilbert, and Jenkin, the clown.*

KEND. Come away, Jenkin.

JEN. Come, here is his house.—Where be
you, ho?

GEORGE. [*Within.*] Who knocks there?

KEND. Here are two or three poor men,
father,
   Would speak with you.

GEORGE. [*Within.*] Pray, give your man
leave to lead me forth.

KEND. Go, Jenkin, fetch him forth.

JEN. Come, old man.

Enter George a Greene, disguised.

KEND. Father, here is three poor men come
to question
   Thee a word in secret that concerns their
   lives.   10

GEORGE. Say on, my sons.

KEND. Father, I am sure you hear the
news,
   How that the Earl of Kendal wars
   against the king.
   Now, father, we three are gentlemen by
   birth,
   But younger brethren that want reven-
   ues,
   And for the hope we have to be preferred,
   If that we knew that we shall win,
   We will march with him;
   If not, we will not march a foot to
   London more.
   Therefore, good father, tell us what shall
   happen,   20
   Whether the king or the Earl of Kendal
   shall win.

GEORGE. The king, my son.

KEND. Art thou sure of that?

GEORGE. Ay, as sure as thou art Henry
Momford,
   The one L[ord] Bonfield, the other Sir
   Gilbert.

KEND. Why, this is wondrous, being blind
of sight,
   His deep perseverance [1] should be such to
   know us.

GILB. Magic is mighty and foretelleth
great matters.

Indeed, father, here is the earl come to
see thee,
   And therefore, good father, fable not
   with him.   30

GEORGE. Welcome is the earl to my poor
cell,
   And so are you, my lords; but let me
   counsel you
   To leave these wars against your king,
   And live in quiet.

KEND. Father, we come not for advice in
war,
   But to know whether we shall win or
   leese. [2]

GEORGE. Lose, gentle lords, but not by
good King Edward;
   A baser man shall give you all the foil. [3]

KEND. Ay, marry, father, what man is
that?

GEORGE. Poor George a Greene, the pinner.   40

KEND. What shall he?

GEORGE. Pull all your plumes, and sore
dishonor you.

KEND. He! As how?

GEORGE. Nay, the end tries all; but so
it will fall out.

KEND. But so it shall not, by my honor!
Christ!
   I'll raise my camp, and fire Wakefield
   town,
   And take that servile pinner, George a
   Greene,
   And butcher him before King Edward's
   face.

GEORGE. Good my lord, be not offended,
   For I speak no more than art reveals
   to me.   50
   And for greater proof
   Give your man leave to fetch me my staff.

KEND. Jenkin, fetch him his walking staff.

JEN. Here is your walking staff.

GEORGE. I'll prove it good upon your
carcasses;
   A wiser wizard never met you yet,
   Nor one that better could foredoom
   your fall.
   Now I have singled you here alone, [4]
   I care not, though you be three to one.
                  [*Throws off his disguise.*]

KEND. Villain, hast thou betrayed us?   60

----

[1] Perceiverance, perception.

[2] Lose.   [3] Defeat.

[4] *I.e.*, as an animal is selected from a herd for
hunting.

GEORGE. Momford, thou liest! Never was I traitor yet;

Only devised this guile to draw you on For to be combatants.

Now conquer me, and then march on to London!

But shall go hard but I will hold you task.[1]

GILB. Come, my lord, cheerly; I'll kill him hand to hand.

KEND. A thousand pound to him that strikes that stroke!

GEORGE. Then give it me, for I will have the first.

Here they fight; George kills Sir Gilbert and takes the other two prisoners.

BON. Stay, George; we do appeal.

GEORGE. To whom?   70

BON. Why, to the king!

For rather had we bide what he appoints, Than here be murthered by a servile groom.

KEND. What wilt thou do with us?

GEORGE. Even as Lord Bonfield wished,[2] You shall unto the king;

And, for that purpose, see where the justice is placed.

Enter Justice.

JUST. Now, my Lord of Kendal, where be all your threats?

Even as the cause, so is the combat fallen;

Else one could never have conquered three.   80

KEND. I pray thee, Woodroffe, do not twit me;

If I have faulted, I must make amends.

GEORGE. Master Woodroffe, here is not a place for many

Words;

I beseech ye, sir, discharge all his soldiers,

That every man may go home unto his own house.

JUST. It shall be so. What wilt thou do, George?

GEORGE. Master Woodroffe, look to your charge;

Leave me to myself.

JUST. Come, my lords.   ˙90

Exit all but George.

[1] If I do not keep you busy.

[2] Original reads *wist*.

GEORGE. Here sit thou, George, wearing a willow wreath,

As one despairing of thy beauteous love.

Fie, George, no more!

Pine not away for that which cannot be.

I cannot joy in any earthly bliss

So long as I do want my Bettris.

Enter Jenkin.

JEN. Who see a master of mine?

GEORGE. How now, sirrah! Whither away?

JEN. Whither away? Why, who do you take me to be?

GEORGE. Why, Jenkin, my man.   100

JEN. I was so once indeed, but now the case is altered.

GEORGE. I pray thee, as how?

JEN. Were not you a fortune teller today?

GEORGE. Well, what of that?

JEN. So sure am I become a juggler.

What will you say if I juggle your sweetheart?

GEORGE. Peace, prating losel![3] Her jealous father

Doth wait over her with such suspicious eyes

That, if a man but dally by her feet,

He thinks it straight a witch[4] to charm his daughter.   110

JEN. Well, what will you give me if I bring her hither?

GEORGE. A suit of green and twenty crowns besides.

JEN. Well, by your leave, give me room.

You must give me something that you have lately worn.

GEORGE. Here is a gown. Will that serve you?   [*Gives his gown.*]

JEN. Ay, this will serve me. Keep out of my circle,

Lest you be torn in pieces with shedevils.—

Mistress Bettris—once, twice, thrice!

He throws the gown [5] in, and she comes out.

O, is this no cunning?

GEORGE. Is this my love, or is it but her shadow?   120

JEN. Ay, this is the shadow, but here is the substance.

[3] Worthless fellow.

[4] Spell.

[5] Original reads *ground*.

GEORGE. Tell me, sweet love, what good fortune
Brought thee hither?
For one it was that favored George a Greene.
BETTRIS. Both love and fortune brought me to my George,
In whose sweet sight is all my heart's content.
GEORGE. Tell me, sweet love, how cam'st thou from thy
Father's?
BETTRIS. A willing mind hath many slips in love.   129
It was not I, but Wily, thy sweet boy.
GEORGE. And where is Wily now?
BETTRIS. In my apparel, in my chamber still.
GEORGE. Jenkin, come hither.   Go to Bradford,
And listen out your fellow Wily.—
Come, Bettris, let us in,
And in my cottage we will sit and talk.
Exeunt omnes.

[SCENE x.

Edward's court at London.]

Enter King Edward, the King of Scots, Lord Warwick, Young Cuddy, and their Train.

EDWARD. Brother of Scotland, I do hold it hard,
Seeing a league of truce was late confirmed
Twixt you and me, without displeasure offered
You should make such invasion in my land.
The vows of kings should be as oracles,
Not blemished with the stain of any breach,
Chiefly [1] where fealty and homage willeth it.
JAMES. Brother of England, rub not the sore afresh;
My conscience grieves me for my deep misdeed.
I have the worst; of thirty thousand men,   10
There scaped not full five thousand from the field.

[1] Especially.

EDWARD. [*To Cuddy.*] Gramercy, Musgrove, else it had gone hard.
Cuddy, I'll quite [2] thee well ere we two part.
JAMES. But had not his old father, William Musgrove,
Played twice the man, I had not now been here.
A stronger man I seldom felt before;
But one of more resolute valiance
Treads not, I think, upon the English ground.
EDWARD. I wot well. Musgrove shall not lose his hire.
CUDDY. And it please your grace, my father was   20
Fivescore and three at midsummer last past;
Yet had King Jamie been as good as George a Greene,
Yet Billy Musgrove would have fought with him.
EDWARD. As George a Greene? I pray thee, Cuddy,
Let me question thee.
Much have I heard, since I came to my crown;
Many in manner of a proverb say,
"Were he as good as G[eorge] a Greene, I would strike him sure."
I pray thee, tell me, Cuddy, canst thou inform me,
What is that George a Greene?   30
CUDDY. Know, my lord, I never saw the man,
But mickle [3] talk is of him in the country.
They say he is the pinner of Wakefield town,
But for his other qualities, I let alone.
WAR. May it please your grace, I know the man too well.
EDWARD. Too well? Why so, Warwick?
WAR. For once he swinged me till my bones did ache.
EDWARD. Why, dares he strike an earl?
WAR. An earl, my lord? Nay, he will strike a king,
Be it not King Edward.   40
For stature he is framed
Like to the picture of stout Hercules,
And for his carriage passeth Robin Hood.

[2] Requite, reward.   [3] Much.

The boldest earl or baron of your land
That offereth scath unto the town of
  Wakefield,
George will arrest his pledge unto the
  pound;[1]
And whoso resisteth bears away the
  blows,
For he himself is good enough for three.
EDWARD. Why, this is wondrous, my
  L[ord] of Warwick!
Sore do I long to see this George a
  Greene.   50
But leaving him, what shall we do, my
  lord,
For to subdue the rebels in the north?
They are now marching up to Don-
  caster.—

Enter one with the Earl of Kendal prisoner.

Soft! Who have we there?
CUDDY. Here is a traitor, the Earl of
  Kendal.
EDWARD. Aspiring traitor, how dar'st
  thou once
Cast thine eyes upon thy sovereign
That honored thee with kindness and
  with favor?
But I will make thee bye[2] this treason
  dear.
KEND. Good my lord—   60
EDWARD. Reply not, traitor![3]—
Tell me, Cuddy, whose deed of honor
Won the victory against this rebel?
CUDDY. George a Greene, the pinner of
  Wakefield.
EDWARD. George a Greene! Now shall I
  hear news
Certain, what this pinner is.
Discourse it briefly, Cuddy, how it be-
  fell.
CUDDY. Kendal and Bonfield, with Sir
  Gilbert Armstrong,
Came to Wakefield town disguised,
And there spoke ill of your grace;   70
Which George but hearing, felled them
  at his feet,
And, had not rescue come into the place,
George had slain them[4] in his close of
  wheat.

[1] *I.e.*, keep him in the pound as a hostage.
[2] Aby, pay for.
[3] In the original this line and the preceding are
printed on one line.
[4] Original reads *him.*

EDWARD. But, Cuddy, canst thou not
  tell
Where I might give and grant some-
  thing
That might please and highly gratify
  the pinner's thoughts?
CUDDY. This at their parting George did
  say to me:[5]
"If the king vouchsafe of this my serv-
  ice,
Then, gentle Cuddy, kneel upon thy
  knee,
And humbly crave a boon of him for
  me."   80
EDWARD. Cuddy, what is it?
CUDDY. It is his will your grace would
  pardon them,
And let them live, although they have
  offended.
EDWARD. I think the man striveth to be
  glorious.[6]
Well, George hath craved it, and it shall
  be granted,
Which none but he in England should
  have gotten.—
Live, Kendal, but as prisoner;
So shalt thou end thy days within the
  Tower.
KEND. Gracious is Edward to offending
  subjects.
JAMES. My Lord of Kend[al], you are
  welcome to the court.   90
EDWARD. Nay, but "ill-come" as it falls
  out now;
Ay, "ill-come" indeed, were it not for
  George a Greene.
But, "gentle king," for so you would
  aver,
And, "Edward's betters," I salute you
  both,
[*He mockingly vails bonnet to them.*[7]]
And here I vow by good Saint George,
You will gain but little when your sums
  are counted!
I sore do long to see this George a
  Greene.
And, for because I never saw the north,
I will forthwith go see it;
And, for that to none I will be known, 100

[5] The contradiction between this statement
and l. 31 may be due to the careless rewriting
of the play for use by a touring company.
[6] Vainglorious.
[7] Suggested by Adams as a fulfillment of the
prophecy in sc. vii, ll. 197–99.

We will disguise ourselves and steal down
　secretly,
Thou and I, King James, Cuddy, and
　two or three,
And make a merry journey for a
　month.—
Away, then, conduct him to the Tower —
Come on, King James, my heart must
　needs be merry,
If fortune makes such havoc of our foes.
　　　　　　　　　　Ex[eunt] omnes.

[SCENE xi.

Sherwood Forest.]

*Enter Robin Hood, Maid Marian, Scarlet,
　and Much, the miller's son.*

ROBIN. Why is not lovely Marian blithe
　of cheer?
What ails my leman,[1] that she gins[2]
　to lour?
Say, good Marian, why art thou so sad?
MARIAN. Nothing, my Robin, grieves me
　to the heart
But, whensoever I do walk abroad,
I hear no songs but all of George a
　Greene;
Bettris, his fair leman, passeth me,
And this, my Robin, galls my very soul.
ROBIN. Content [thee].[3]　What wreaks[4]
　it us though George a
Greene be stout,　　　　　　　　　　10
So long as he does proffer us no scath?
Envy doth seldom hurt but to itself;
And therefore, Marian, smile upon thy
　Robin.
MARIAN. Never will Marian smile upon
　her Robin,
Nor lie with him under the greenwood
　shade,
Till that thou go to Wakefield on a green,
And beat the pinner for the love of me.
ROBIN. Content thee, Marian; I will ease
　thy grief.
My merry men and I will thither stray;
And here I vow that, for the love of thee,
I will beat George a Greene, or he shall
　beat me.　　　　　　　　　　　　21
SCARLET. As I am Scarlet, next to Little
　John,
One of the boldest yeomen of the crew,

So will I wend with Robin all along,
And try this pinner what he dares do.
MUCH. As I am Much, the miller's son,
That left my mill to go with thee
(And nill[5] repent that I have done;
This pleasant life contenteth me),
In aught I may, to do thee good,　　30
I'll live and die with Robin Hood.
MARIAN. And, Robin, Marian she will go
　with thee
To see fair Bettris how bright she is of
　blee.[6]
ROBIN. Marian, thou shalt go with thy
　Robin.—
Bend up your bows, and see your strings
　be tight,
The arrows keen, and everything be ready,
And each of you a good bat[7] on his neck,
Able to lay a good man on the ground.
SCARLET. I will have Friar Tuck's.
MUCH. I will have Little John's.　　40
ROBIN. I will have one made of an ashen
　plank,[8]
Able to bear a bout or two.—
Then come on, Marian, let us go,
For, before the sun doth show the morn-
　ing day,
I will be at Wakefield to see this pinner,
　George a Greene.　　*Exeunt omnes.*

[SCENE xii.

Bradford.]

*Enter a Shoemaker sitting upon the stage at
　work; Jenkin to him [,carrying a staff].*

JEN. My masters, he that hath neither
　meat nor money,
And hath lost his credit with the ale-wife,
For anything I know, may go supper-
　less to bed.—
But soft! Who is here? Here is a shoe-
　maker;
He knows where is the best ale.
Shoemaker, I pray thee tell me,
Where is the best ale in the town?
SHOE. Afore, afore, follow thy nose!
At the sign of the Eggshell.
JEN. Come, shoemaker, if thou wilt,　10
And take thy part of a pot.
SHOE. [*Rising.*]　Sirrah, down with your
　staff!
Down with your staff!

---

[1] Sweetheart.　　　　[3] Supplied by Dyce.
[2] Begins.　　　　　　[4] Recks, matters.
[5] Will not.　　[6] Complexion.　　[7] Staff.
[8] Emended by Mitford. Original reads *plunk.*

JEN. Why, how now! Is the fellow mad?
  I pray thee tell me, why should I hold
    down my staff?
SHOE. You will down with him, will you
    not, sir?
JEN. Why, tell me wherefore?
SHOE. My friend, this is the town of
    merry Bradford,[1]
  And here is a custom held
  That none shall pass with his staff on
    his shoulders   20
  But he must have a bout with me;
  And so shall you, sir.
JEN. And so will not I, sir!
SHOE. That will I try. Barking dogs bite
    not the sorest.
JEN. [Aside.] I would to God I were once
    well rid of him.
SHOE. Now, what, will you down with
    your staff?
JEN. Why, you are not in earnest, are
    you?
SHOE. If I am not, take that!
                                [Strikes him.]
JEN. You whoreson, cowardly scab,
  It is but the part of a clapperdudgeon [2]
  To strike a man in the street.   31
  But darest thou walk to the town's
    end with me?
SHOE. Ay, that I dare do; but stay till I
    lay in my
  Tools, and I will go with thee to the
    town's end
  Presently.[3]
JEN. [Aside.] I would I knew how to be
    rid of this fellow.
SHOE. Come, sir, will you go to the
    town's end now, sir?
JEN. Ay, sir, come.—
                         [They cross the stage.]
  Now we are at the town's end. What
    say you now?
SHOE. Marry, come, let us even have a
    bout.   40
JEN. Ha, stay a little; hold thy hands,
    I pray thee!
SHOE. Why, what's the matter?
JEN. Faith, I am underpinner of a town,
  And there is an order, which if I do not
    keep,
  I shall be turned out of mine office.
SHOE. What is that, sir?

JEN. Whensoever I go fight with any-
    body,
  I use to flourish my staff thrice about
    my head
  Before I strike, and then show no
    favor.
SHOE. Well, sir, and till then I will not
    strike thee.   50
JEN. Well, sir, here is once, twice—
  Here is my hand; I will never do it the
    third time.
SHOE. Why, then, I see we shall not fight.
JEN. Faith, no! Come, I will give thee
    two pots
  Of the best ale, and be friends.
SHOE. [Aside.] Faith, I see it is as hard
    to get water out of a flint
  As to get him to have a bout with me;
  Therefore I will enter into him for some
    good cheer.—
  My friend, I see thou art a faint-hearted
    fellow;
  Thou hast no stomach [4] to fight;   60
  Therefore let us go to the alehouse and
    drink.
JEN. Well, content! Go thy ways, and
    say thy prayers;
  Thou scap'st my hands today.
                              Exeunt omnes.

[SCENE xiii.

Wakefield.]

Enter George a Greene and Bettris.

GEORGE. Tell me, sweet love, how is thy
    mind content?
  What, canst thou brook to live with
    George a Greene?
BETTRIS. O, George, how little pleasing
    are these words!
  Came I from Bradford for the love of
    thee,
  And left my father for so sweet a friend!
  Here will I live until my life do end.

Enter Robin Hood, and Marian, and his
                                      Train.

GEORGE. Happy am I to have so sweet
    a love.—
  But what are these come tracing [5] here
    along?

_____

[1] Original reads *Wakefield.*
[2] Beggar.   [3] Immediately   [4] Courage.   [5] Walking.

BETTRIS. Three men come striking through the corn,
My love.   10

GEORGE. Back again, you foolish travelers,
For you are wrong, and may not wend this way.

ROBIN. That were great shame.
Now, by my soul, proud sir,
We be three tall yeomen, and thou art but one.—
Come, we will forward in despite of him.

GEORGE. Leap the ditch, or I will make you skip.
What, cannot the highway serve your turn,
But you must make a path over the corn?

ROBIN. Why, art thou mad? Dar'st thou encounter three?   20
We are no babes, man; look upon our limbs.

GEORGE. Sirrah, the biggest limbs have not the stoutest hearts.
Were ye as good as Robin Hood and his three merry men,
I'll drive you back the same way that ye came.
Be ye men, ye scorn to encounter me all at once;
But be ye cowards, set upon me all three,
And try the pinner what he dares perform.

SCARLET. Were thou as high in deeds
As thou art haughty in words,
Thou well mightest be a champion for a king.   30
But empty vessels have the loudest sounds,
And cowards prattle more than men of worth.

GEORGE. Sirrah, darest thou try me?

SCARLET. Ay, sirrah, that I dare.
They fight, and George a Grèene beats him.

MUCH. How now! What, art thou down?—
Come, sir, I am next.
They fight, and George a Greene beats him.

ROBIN. Come, sirrah, now to me! Spare me not,
For I'll not spare thee.

GEORGE. Make no doubt I will be as liberal to thee.
                    They fight. Robin Hood stays.[1]

[1] Desists, rests.

ROBIN. Stay, George, for here I do protest   40
Thou art the stoutest champion that ever I laid
Hands upon.

GEORGE. Soft you, sir! By your leave, you lie;
You never yet laid hands on me.

ROBIN. George, wilt thou forsake Wakefield,
And go with me?
Two liveries will I give thee every year,
And forty crowns shall be thy fee.

GEORGE. Why, who art thou?

ROBIN. Why, Robin Hood!   50
I am come hither with my Marian
And these my yeomen for to visit thee.

GEORGE. Robin Hood! Next to King Edward
Art thou lief [2] to me.
Welcome, sweet Robin; welcome, Maid Marian;
And welcome, you, my friends.
Will you to my poor house?
You shall have wafer cakes your fill,
A piece of beef hung up since Martlemas,
Mutton and veal. If this like you not,   60
Take that you find, or that you bring, for me.

ROBIN. God-a-mercies, good George,
I'll be thy guest today.

GEORGE. Robin, therein thou honorest me.
I'll lead the way.   *Exeunt omnes.*

[SCENE xiv.

Bradford.]

Enter King Edward and King James disguised, with two staves.

EDWARD. Come on, King James; now we are
Thus disguised,
There is none, I know, will take us to be kings.
I think we are now in Bradford,
Where all the merry shoemakers dwell.

Enter a Shoemaker [with his Comrades].

SHOE. Down with your staves, my friends,
Down with them!

EDWARD. Down with our staves? I pray thee, why so?

[2] Dear.

Shoe. My friend, I see thou art a stranger here,
Else wouldest thou not have questioned
  of the thing.   10
This is the town of merry Bradford,
And here hath been a custom kept of
  old,
That none may bear his staff upon his
  neck,
But trail it all along throughout the
  town,
Unless they mean to have a bout with
  me.
Edward. But hear you, sir, hath the king
Granted you this custom?
Shoe. King or kaiser, none shall pass
  this way,
Except King Edward;
No, not the stoutest groom that haunts
  his court.   20
Therefore down with your staves!
Edward. [Aside.] What were we best to
  do?
James. [Aside.] Faith, my lord, they are
  stout fellows;
And, because we will see some sport,
We will trail our staves.
Edward. Hear'st thou, my friend?
Because we are men of peace and travel-
  ers,
We are content to trail our staves.
Shoe. The way lies before you; go along.

Enter Robin Hood and George a Greene,
                    disguised.

Robin. See, George, two men are passing
Through the town,   31
Two lusty men, and yet they trail their
  staves.
George. Robin, they are some peasants
Tricked in yeoman's weeds.—Hollo,
  you two travelers!
Edward. Call you us, sir?
George. Ay, you. Are ye not big enough
  to bear
Your bats upon your necks,
But you must trail them along the
  streets?
Edward. Yes, sir, we are big enough;
  but here is a custom
Kept, that none may pass, his staff
  upon his neck,   40
Unless he trail it at the weapon's point.

Sir, we are men of peace, and love to
  sleep
In our whole skins, and therefore quiet-
  ness is best.
George. Base-minded peasants, worth-
  less to be men!
What, have you bones and limbs to
  strike a blow,
And be your hearts so faint you cannot
  fight?
Were't not for shame, I would shrub [1]
  your shoulders well,
And teach you manhood against [2] an-
  other time.
Shoe. Well preached, Sir Jack! Down
  with your staff!
Edward. Do you hear, my friends? And
  you be wise,   50
Keep down your staves,
For all the town will rise upon you.
George. Thou speakest like an honest,
  quiet fellow.
But hear you me. In spite of all the
  swains
Of Bradford town, bear me your staves
  upon your necks,
Or, to begin withal, I'll baste you both
  so well,
You were never better basted in your
  lives.
Edward. We will hold up our staves.
George a Greene fights with the Shoemakers,
          and beats them all down.
George. What, have you any more?
Call all your town forth, cut and long-
  tail. [3]   60
  The Shoemakers spy [4] *George a Greene.*
Shoe. What, George a Greene, is it you?
A plague found [5] you!
I think you longed to swinge me well.
Come, George, we will crush [6] a pot
  before we part.
George. A pot, you slave! We will have
  an hundred.—
Here, Will Perkins, take my purse;
Fetch me a stand [7] of ale, and set in the
  market place,
That all may drink that are athirst this
  day;

[1] Scrub, beat.   [2] In preparation for.
[3] Docked and undocked (said of dogs and horses); hence, all classes of people.
[4] Recognize.   [6] Drink.
[5] Confound.   [7] Cask.

For this is for a fee to welcome Robin
Hood
To Bradford town.   70
*They bring out the stand of ale and fall
a-drinking.*
Here, Robin, sit thou here; for thou art
the best man
At the board this day.
You that are strangers, place yourselves
where you will.
Robin, here's a carouse to good King
Edward's self;
And they that love him not, I would
we had
The basting of them a little.

*Enter the Earl of Warwick with other Noble-
men, bringing out the King's garments;
then George a Greene and the rest kneel
down to the King.*

EDWARD. Come, masters, all fellows!—
Nay, Robin, you are the best man at
the board today.—
Rise up, George.
GEORGE. Nay, good my liege, ill-nurtured
we were, then.   80
Though we Yorkshire men be blunt of
speech,
And little skilled in court or such quaint
fashions,
Yet nature teacheth us duty to our king;
Therefore I humbly beseech you pardon
George a Greene.
ROBIN. And, good my lord, a pardon for
poor Robin;
And for us all a pardon, good King Ed-
ward.
SHOE. I pray you, a pardon for the shoe-
makers.
EDWARD. I frankly grant a pardon to you
all.   [*They rise.*]
And, George a Greene, give me thy hand;
There's none in England that shall do
thee wrong.   90
Even from my court I came to see thy-
self;
And now I see that fame speaks naught
but truth.
GEORGE. I humbly thank your royal
majesty.
That which I did against the Earl of
Kendal,
It was but a subject's duty to his sov-
ereign,

And therefore little merit such good
words.
EDWARD. But, ere I go, I'll grace thee with
good deeds.
Say what King Edward may perform,
And thou shalt have it, being in Eng-
land's bounds.
GEORGE. I have a lovely leman,   100
As bright of blee as is the silver moon,
And old Grime her father will not let
her match
With me, because I am a pinner,
Although I love her, and she me, dearly.
EDWARD. Where is she?
GEORGE. At home at my poor house,
And vows never to marry unless her
father
Give consent; which is my great grief,
my lord.
EDWARD. If this be all, I will despatch it
straight;
I'll send for Grime and force him give
his grant;   110
He will not deny King Edward such a
suit.

Enter Jenkin and speaks.

[JEN.] Ho, who saw a master of mine?
O, he is gotten into company, and a body
should rake
Hell for company!
GEORGE. Peace, ye slave!   See where
King Edward is.
EDWARD. George, what is he?
GEORGE. I beseech your grace pardon
him; he is my man.
SHOE. Sirrah, the king hath been drink-
ing with us,
And did pledge us too.
JEN. Hath he so?   Kneel!   I dub you
"gentlemen."   120
SHOE. Beg it of the king, Jenkin.
JEN. I will.—I beseech your worship grant
me one thing.
EDWARD. What is that?
JEN. Hark in your ear.
He whispers the King in the ear.
EDWARD. Go your ways, and do it.
JEN. Come, down on your knees; I have
got it.
SHOE. Let us hear what it is first.
JEN. Marry, because you have drunk
with the king,

And the king hath so graciously pledged
  you,
You shall be no more called shoe-
  makers,   130
But you and yours, to the world's end,
Shall be called "the trade of the gentle [1]
  craft."
SHOE. I beseech your majesty reform
  this
Which he hath spoken.
JEN. I beseech your worship consume
  this
Which he hath spoken.
EDWARD. Confirm it, you would say.—
  Well, he hath done it for you; it is suf-
  ficient.
Come, George, we will go to Grime,
And have thy love.   140
JEN. I am sure your worship will
  abide;
For yonder is coming old Musgrove
And mad Cuddy, his son.—
Master, my fellow Wily comes dressed
  like a woman,
And Master Grime will marry Wily.
Here they come.

*Enter Musgrove and Cuddy; and Master
Grime, Wily, Maid Marian, and Bettris.*

EDWARD. Which is thy old father, Cuddy?
CUDDY. This, if it please your majesty.
                        [*Musgrove kneels.*]
EDWARD. Ah, old Musgrove, stand[2] up;
  It fits not such gray hairs to kneel.
MUS. [*Rising.*] Long live my sovereign!
  Long and happy be his days!   151
Vouchsafe, my gracious lord, a simple
  gift
At Billy Musgrove's hand.
King James at Middleham [3] Castle
  gave me this;
This won the honor, and this give I
  thee.   [*Gives sword to Edward.*]
EDWARD. God-a-mercy, Musgrove, for
  this friendly gift;
And, for thou felledst a king with this
  same weapon,
This blade shall here dub valiant Mus-
  grove knight.

[1] Genteel, elegant.
[2] Original reads *kneel.*
[3] The original form *Meddellom* shows the pronunciation.

MUS. Alas, what hath your highness
  done? I am poor.
EDWARD. To mend thy living take thou
  Middleham Castle,   160
The hold of both. And if thou want
  living, complain;
Thou shalt have more to maintain thy
  estate.—
George, which is thy love?
GEORGE. This, if please your majesty.
EDWARD. Art thou her aged father?
GRIME. I am, and it like your majesty.
EDWARD. And wilt not give thy daughter
  unto George?
GRIME. Yes, my lord, if he will let me
  marry
With this lovely lass.
EDWARD. What sayst thou, George?   170
GEORGE. With all my heart, my lord, I
  give consent.
GRIME. Then do I give my daughter unto
  George.
WILY. Then shall the marriage soon be
  at an end.
Witness, my lord, if that I be a woman;
                    [*Throws off his disguise.*]
For I am Wily, boy to George a Greene,
Who for my master wrought this subtle
  shift.
EDWARD. What, is it a boy?—What sayst
  thou to this, Grime?
GRIME. Marry, my lord, I think this boy
  hath
More knavery than all the world be-
  sides.
Yet am I content that George shall
  both have   180
My daughter and my lands.
EDWARD. Now, George, it rests I gratify
  thy worth;
And therefore here I do bequeath to
  thee,
In full possession, half that Kendal
  hath;
And whatas [4] Bradford holds of me in
  chief,
I give it frankly unto thee forever.
Kneel down, George.
GEORGE. What will your majesty do?
EDWARD. Dub thee a knight, George.
GEORGE. I beseech your grace, grant me
  one thing.   190
EDWARD. What is that?
    [4] Whatsoever.

GEORGE. Then let me live and die a yeoman still.

So was my father, so must live his son.
For 'tis more credit to men of base degree
To do great deeds than men of dignity.

EDWARD. Well, be it so, George.

JAMES. I beseech your grace, despatch with me,
And set down my ransom.

EDWARD. George a Greene, set down the King of Scots
His ransom.   200

GEORGE. I beseech your grace, pardon me;
It passeth my skill.

EDWARD. Do it; the honor's thine.

GEORGE. Then let King James make good
Those towns which he hath burnt upon the borders;
Give a small pension to the fatherless,
Whose fathers he caused murthered in those wars;

Put in pledge for these things to your grace,
And so return.

[EDWARD.] King James, are you content? [1]

JAMES. I am content, and like [2] your majesty,   211
And will leave good castles in security.

EDWARD. I crave no more.—Now, George a Greene,
I'll to thy house; and when I have supped, I'll go to ask
And see if Jane a Barley be so fair
As good King James reports her for to be.
And for the ancient custom of *Vail staff*, keep it still;
Claim privilege from me.
If any ask a reason why or how,
Say English Edward vailed his staff to you.

[1] In the original this sentence is given to George a Greene, completing the last line of his speech.   [2] If it please.

FINIS.

THOMAS KYD

The three most frequently mentioned plays in the Elizabethan age were *Tamburlaine*, *Hamlet*, and *The Spanish Tragedy*. Of these three only William Shakespeare claimed authorship on his title page, and the names of Marlowe and Kyd must be reached chiefly by indirection. During Kyd's lifetime Robert Greene had alluded slightingly to him in his *Groatsworth of Wit* in 1592, and Thomas Nashe had dropped a tantalizing clue to his authorship in his "Epistle" preceding his friend Greene's *Menaphon* in 1589. This was addressed "To the Gentlemen Students of Both Universities," and in it Nashe revealed the contemptuous envy he and his fellow university graduates had for the group of more popular authors who had never gone to college. Wrote Nashe:

I'le. . . talke a little in friendship with a few of our triviall translators. It is a common practise now a daies amongst a sort of shifting companions, that runne through every arte and thrive by none, to leave the trade of *Noverint* whereto they were borne, and busie themselves with the indevors of Art, that could scarcelie latinize their necke-verse if they should have neede; yet English *Seneca* read by candle light yeeldes manie good sentences, as *Bloud is a begger*, and so foorth: and if you intreate him faire in a frostie morning, hee will affoord you whole *Hamlets*, I should say handfulls of tragicall speaches. But O griefe, *tempus edax rerum*, what's that will last alwaies? The sea exhaled by droppes will in continuance be drie, and *Seneca* let bloud line by line and page by page, at length must needes die to our stage; which makes his famisht followers to imitate the Kidde in *Aesop*, who enamored with the Foxes newfangles, forsooke all hopes of life to leape into a new occupation; and these men renowncing all possibilities of credit or estimation, to intermeddle with Italian translations: wherein how poorelie they have plodded, (as those that are neither provenzall men, nor are able to distinguish Articles) let all indifferent Gentlemen that have travailed in that tongue, discerne by their twopenie pamphlets. . . .

Several highly reputable scholars, like R. B. McKerrow, W. W. Greg, E. K. Chambers, Philip Edwards, and G. I. Duthie, have refused to admit the clear applicability of this passage to Kyd, maintaining that it is a description of a group or a type rather than an individual. But other scholars of equal standing, like F. G. Fleay, F. S. Boas, and Alfred Harbage, have found the parallels between the veiled allusions and puns and the known facts of Kyd's life and background very clear—so clear that they have been willing to accept the applications of Nashe's other remarks to otherwise unknown aspects of Kyd's life and writings as almost equally inescapable. Arthur Freeman, the author of the latest and most thorough study of Kyd (*Thomas Kyd/Facts and Problems*, Oxford, 1967), examined the arguments on both sides, and especially Nashe's phrase, "the Kidde in *Aesop*" (even though this fable is not in Aesop but in Spenser), and came to this conclusion: "But if the specific jeers which precede and follow the citation can be linked with any certainty to Kyd, the strength of the association increases to the point of plausibility, and even probability." Felix Carrère has also discussed the question in his *Le Théâtre de Thomas Kyd: Contribution à l'Étude du Drame Elizabethain* (Toulouse, 1951).

Freeman has pieced together these rather meager known facts about Kyd's life: He was baptized in the Church of St. Mary Woolnoth, London, on November 6, 1558. The register describes him as the "son of Francis Kidd, *Citizen and Writer of the Courte Letter of London*." Writers of the "Court Letter" were scriveners or notaries who had their own guild, which maintained high and proud standards of literacy. At the time of Thomas's birth, his father had been a freeman of the Company of Scriveners for about a year, and by 1580 had risen to be its warden, with several apprentices in his shop. He was also churchwarden at St. Mary's in 1575–76. Although in 1571 he and three other Londoners were involved in a Chancery suit for fraud concerning the possession of a tavern or inn in Cornhill, the suit was apparently settled out of court to the satisfaction of all. Francis Kyd's wife was named Anna (or Anne, or Agnes). Besides Thomas there were two other children, a boy and a girl. The family was, with little doubt, respectable and fairly well to do. They lived in a prosperous section of town, and one of their neighbors and friends was Francis Coldocke, a prominent bookseller and publisher. Thomas Hacket, the bookseller who later published one of Kyd's translations, was another Lombard Street neighbor.

Thomas was apparently expected to follow his father's profession, as suggested by Nashe in his slurring reference to those "shifting companions . . . who leave the trade of *Noverint*, whereto they were borne"—"*Noverint*" being the first word in the phrase with which legal writs and documents began: "*Noverint universi per praesentes;*" that is, "Know all men by these presents." On October 26, 1565, at the age of seven, he was enrolled in the nearby, well-known, and remarkable Merchant Taylors' School, of which the humanist Richard Mulcaster was the famous and learned headmaster and which Edmund Spenser was still attending as a "poor scholar." Here Kyd seems to have made good use of his educational opportunities; in addition to Latin, which all students were expected to learn, he also learned French and Italian sufficiently well to publish somewhat inaccurate translations which Nashe pretended to regard as "triviall." Kyd may also have learned enough Greek to have penned some lost speeches in it for *The Spanish Tragedy*, but although he introduced one common Spanish phrase into the same play, he apparently did not learn that language. (See Boas, *The Works of Thomas Kyd*, Oxford, 1955.) Most of the characters in *The Spanish Tragedy* actually have Italian names.

How long the boy stayed at the Merchant Taylors' School is unknown, although he probably left school about 1583, and it seems clear that he never attended a university. Nor is there any sound evidence that he ever traveled abroad, since his references to Continental geography are somewhat shaky. Perhaps he returned for a time to his father's shop as apprentice. At any rate, in the early 1580s he seems to have associated himself with the theater, especially with the Queen's Players. Thomas Dekker's pamphlet, *A Knight's Conjuring* (1607), after describing Spenser and his spiritual father Chaucer in conversation in the Elysian Fields, continues: "In another companie sat Learned Watson, industrious Kyd, ingenious Atchlow, and (tho hee had beene a player, molded out of their pennes) yet because he had been their louer, and a register to the Muses, inimitable Bentley. . . ." Still a third group consisted of Marlowe, Greene, and Peele, joined later by Nashe and Chettle. Thomas Watson and Thomas Achelly (the name is spelled in a dozen different ways) were poets and, it seems, playwrights, though little known ones. "Inimitable Bentley," however, was John Bentley, one of the best actors before Edward Alleyn and Richard Burbage. Bentley died in 1585, at the age of thirty-two, and if he had been "molded" out of the pens of Watson, Kyd, and Achelly (that is, he acted in plays by them), Kyd must have been writing well before that date. (See T. W. Baldwin, "Thomas Kyd's Early Company Connections," *PQ*, 1927). Freeman points out that Dekker's grouping not only seems to place Kyd and his friends in an older class than the other but also in a more sober one, since Dekker pictures it as gathered about "the holy well, some of them singing Paeans to Apollo, som of them hymnes to the rest of the goddes . . . ," whereas the other group was standing laughing "vnder the shades of a large vyne." What plays Kyd could have written for the Queen's Men before 1585 is problematical, but Freeman lists titles of lost plays which he may have had a hand in.

Although Kyd was described by Dekker as the "industrious Kyd," the fruits of his industry have not been easy to identify. In addition to *The Spanish Tragedy*, it is generally believed, as Nashe implies in his "whole *Hamlets*, I should say handfulls of tragicall speaches," that Kyd anticipated Shakespeare in using François de Belleforest's version of the story of Hamlet in his *Histoires Tragiques* (1570) for an early, now lost, play on Hamlet (called *Ur-Hamlet* by the Germans). Probably inspired by the Countess of Pembroke's translation of *Marc Antoine* (1592) by Robert Garnier, called the "French Seneca," Kyd translated the same author's *Cornelie* as *Pompey the Great, His Fair Cornelia's Tragedy*. This was printed in 1593 and is the only extant play to bear his name. (For a broader discussion of this general subject, see Matthew P. McDiarmid's "The Influence of Robert Garnier on Some Elizabethan Tragedies," *EA*, 1958. Fredson T. Bowers discusses the evidence for Kyd's *Ur-Hamlet* in *The Elizabethan Revenge Tragedy*, Princeton, 1940.) Kyd is also believed by some to be the author of *The Rare Triumphs of Love and Fortune* (1589), *Arden of Feversham* (1592), and *The Tragedy of Soliman and Perseda* (1592), a condensed version of which becomes the climactic play within a play at the end of *The Spanish Tragedy*. The first dated book ascribed to Kyd on the basis of his signed initials is *The Householder's Philosophy* (1588), based on a story by Tasso and published by his old neighbor Thomas Hacket. He is also credited with having written several prose pamphlets, some of which are signed or initialed.

During the period of these writings, the events of Kyd's nonliterary life, so far as they are known, became focused on the year 1593. In this year there was not only a heavy outbreak of the plague, which closed the London playhouses, but also an outburst of hatred against the foreigners who had been flooding the country. One way in which this xenophobia expressed itself was through the writing of ballads and the affixing of printed posters and written libels on the walls of buildings, even of churchyards. For some unknown reason Kyd was one of the first suspects, and in May he was arrested and thrown into prison. When his rooms were searched, the officers discovered among his papers a manuscript of what they described as "vile hereticall Conceiptes denyinge the deity of Jhesus Christe our Savior." Not until 1923 did anyone show that these fragments were actually copied from an early sixteenth century Unitarian treatise reprinted in John Proctor's *The Fall of the Late Arrian*, 1549. (See W. D. Briggs, "On a Document concerning Christopher Marlowe," *SP*, 1923, and G. T. Buckley, "Who Was the Late Arrian?," *MLN*, 1934.) When these papers were discovered by the officers, they magnified Kyd's guilt. In spite of his terrified insistence that he knew nothing about them and his explanation that they must be Christopher Marlowe's and must have become "shufled with some of myne (vnknown to me) by some occasion of o[u]r wrytinge in one chamber twoe yeares synce" (when Marlowe was employed by Kyd's own patron for the writing of plays), the Privy Council was apparently not convinced. Nor did his horrified repudiation of the idea that either he or his patron could approve of the character or the religious opinions of Marlowe, who was also "intemp[er]ate & of a cruel hart," make any impression.

Although the handwriting of the manuscript is unidentifiable, Marlowe was also brought under investigation; but, probably because of his connection with the English intelligence service, he was released after interrogation. Kyd, however, was kept prisoner and perhaps even put on the rack; shortly after Marlowe's murder he wrote to Sir John Puckering, Keeper of the Great Seal and *de facto* head of the Privy Council, and spoke humbly of his "paines and vndeserved tortures," which would have "ingendred more impatience" in other people than it did in him. Apparently this letter and another which he wrote to Puckering primarily to "intreate some speaches from yo[u] in my favor to my Lorde" (that is, his patron) had no appreciable effect. The "Lorde" or patron preferred by Freeman to other candidates (such as Charles Howard, Lord Admiral, and Henry Herbert, Earl of Pembroke) is Henry, fourth Earl of Sussex and father of Robert Radcliffe, Lord Fitzwalters, the young husband of the young Countess of Sussex, to whom Kyd dedicated his *Cornelia*. The character of the Earl, as well as his patronage of a minor company of players, seems to fit what Kyd says in his letter about his six years of service to him and his family position as a secretary or tutor. But in spite of the pathetic picture Kyd drew in his dedication to the young Countess concerning his "afflictions of minde," his "misery," and "the bitter times and privie broken passions" from which he was suffering, the Radcliffe family apparently decided to have nothing more to do with him, and he died not long afterward, a broken and ruined man. He was buried in the churchyard of St. Mary Colchurch on August 15, 1594. Freeman believes that the document which Josef Schick discovered in 1899 showing that in December 1594 Kyd's parents renounced administration of their son's estate does not necessarily prove that they repudiated him; it may merely have been their way of escaping payment of his debts.

As usual, there are bibliographical and textural problems connected with *The Spanish Tragedy*. It was not until 1773 that Thomas Hawkins, in *The Origin of the English Drama* (Oxford, 1773), called attention to an incidental remark by Thomas Heywood in his *Apology for Actors* (1612) that named Kyd openly as the author of the play. The date assigned to its composition has varied from 1582 to 1590, but few now would place it before 1586 or 1587. Thomas W. Ross, in his old-spelling edition of the play for The Fountainwell Drama Texts (Berkeley and Edinburgh, 1968), suggests "sometime in the late 1580s." Alfred Harbage prefers the 1587 date because of the lack of even a remote or obscure reference of the Spanish Armada in a play which is set in Spain and contains a notable passage on past English victories over the Spanish ("Intrigue in Elizabethan Tragedy," *Essays on Shakespeare and Elizabethan Drama*, University of Missouri Press, 1962). S. F. Johnson agreed with Philip Edwards in his Revels edition of the play (London, 1959) that Josef Schick's attempts in his Temple Classics edition (London, 1898) to find direct allusions to current Spanish-Portuguese relations were "ludicrous," although the anti-Spanish bias of the whole play is evident (*"The Spanish Tragedy;* or Babylon Revisited," *ibid.*). But Freeman disagrees. Harbage also discounts McKerrow's questioning of the identification of Kyd in Nashe's "Epistle," finds Edwards's date of about 1590 dubious, and is not convinced by Baldwin's argument "for a date at the beginning of the decade" (*On the Literary Genetics of Shakespeare's Plays*, University of Illinois Press, 1959). 1586–87, Harbage says, is, "coincidentally, . . . about the midpoint of the 'five and twenty or thirty' years ago given by Ben Jonson in his induction to *Bartholomew Fair* (1614) as the era of *Titus Andronicus* and 'Jeronimo.' "

The known history of *The Spanish Tragedy* opens with Henslowe's record of frequent performances in 1592. License to print was granted in October of that year. What is apparently the earliest extant edition is undated, and exists in a unique copy in the British Museum; but Thomas W. Ross, in attempting to account for some of the typographical peculiarities in the setting up of the text, suggests "ca. 1592" ("Kyd's *The Spanish Tragedy:* A Bibliographical Hypothesis," *BRMMLA*, 1968). The earliest dated printing is 1594. Both editions, however, refer to a "first impression," now lost. In 1597 Henslowe recorded a number of performances of the play as new, perhaps on account of revision. In September 1601 and June 1602 he paid Jonson for additions to *Jeronimo*, possibly in competition with the closely related *Hamlet*, which Shakespeare was reviving for the Lord Chamberlain's players at the same time, and with several new revenge plays of other companies modeled on these two. In 1602 another edition appeared with "new additions," which develop certain impassioned parts, and which have been assigned to Jonson on the basis of Henslowe's payments. The amounts paid, however, would suggest a more thorough revision, and the style of the additions is regarded as against Jonson's authorship. H. W. Crundell and H. G. Howarth have tried to make out a case for Thomas Dekker ("The 1602 Additions to *The Spanish Tragedy*," *NQ*, 1933 and 1934, and *TLS*, February 13, 1937). The question has also arisen as to whether these additions were intended to replace or enlarge certain passages in the original (Levin L. Schücking, "*The Spanish Tragedy* Additions," *TLS*, June 12, 1937, and *Die Zusatze zur "Spanish Tragedy*," Leipzig, 1938). Boas (*TLS*, June 26, 1937) agreed with Schücking's replacement theory except for the scene where Hieronimo finds his son's dead body and the scene of the Painter. Freeman very simply explains these inconsistencies by assuming that they are due to a careless and hurried transcript of passages from an acting text or prompt book.

The play had an extraordinary popularity. It ran into many editions (at least one of them pirated), was freely imitated, was the subject of numerous allusions (especially by way of stage satire and parody), and finally made its way to Germany. It has been supposed that Kyd himself attempted to capitalize on the popularity of his play by writing what might be called a first part, although the extant *First Part of Jeronimo*, a comedy, is certainly by another hand.

The romantic plot, for which no source has been traced, is strongly colored by the influence of Senecan tragedy, although Freeman (in spite of Nashe's "English *Seneca* read by candle light") finds no proof that Kyd was familiar with the Jasper Heywood edition of *Seneca* in 1581. This Senecan influence (whether directly by the Latin or at second hand through the English) appears in the use of a chorus and a ghost (although they do not really operate in the Senecan fashion), in the sententious and balanced speeches illustrating all the accepted rhetorical devices, in the declamation, and in the melodramatic treatment of character. In fact, this classical influence extends so far that the whole religious background is reminiscent of ancient mythology in spite of the obvious fact that Spain was not only a Christian country but a strongly Roman Catholic one. Howard Baker, however, has maintained that the Ghost of Andrea and the personification of Revenge are not so much classical figures as adaptations of stock characters from medieval metrical tragedies and moralities ("Ghosts and Guides," *MP*, 1935).

Freeman states that Kyd has composed his plot not so much in the Spanish genre as in the Italian, which was well-known in England through the collections of such tales by Pettie, Painter, Wotton, and others. He admits, however, that no specific sources are known, and concludes that "we must credit him with powers of invention unparalleled among the dramatists of his time." Nevertheless, he proceeds to examine several possible minor contributions and aids to Kyd's inventiveness. He mentions, for instance, Kyd's use of one of the stories in Henry Wotton's translation of Jacques Yver's *A Courtly Controversy of Cupid's Cautels*, published in 1578 by Kyd's old neighbor Coldocke, as the basis for Hieronimo's play within a play. He also discovers, in another story in the same book, "an almost perfect analogue of the relationship of Horatio, Bel-imperia, Lorenzo, and the captive prince Balthazar." He accepts and expands Schick's earlier investigations into recent Portuguese-Spanish history by referring both to modern histories of Spain and to contemporary sixteenth century accounts of land and naval battles, as well as to popular English accounts of English heroes of the past. As for the character of Lorenzo, Freeman agrees with previous commentators that he embodies the characteristics of one type of Machiavellian villain, but suggests that, in addition, "Kyd may have had recourse to contemporary examples of practicing politicians." He also quotes Bowers and Baldwin on the similarity between Lorenzo's method of disposing of Pedringano and a slanderous pamphlet on the way the Earl of Leicester had got rid of one Gates, a thief employed by him for disreputable businesses.

The Spanish Tragedy has been regarded for ages as the real instigator and prototype of the tragedy of blood and revenge, a subject discussed at length by Bowers. Most recent discussion, however, has focused on the Elizabethan concepts of the ethics, duties, and morality of revenge. Essentially, the conflict has centered on whether revenge is primarily a public or a private concern—whether the state, supported by the teachings of the church, should be the sole instrument for the apprehension and punishment of the criminal, or revenger, or whether the individual wronged had the primary function of accomplishing vengeance, especially if murder was involved. The latter was the primitive and still popular tradition (especially, the Elizabethans believed, in Italy and France) though lip service was generally paid to the former. From the latter point of view, too, the question naturally arose as to whether the revenger was really a criminal. Here, obviously, the role of the father, Hieronimo, is immediately concerned, and many have agreed with Bowers that, beginning in Act III, he is turned from a justified hero into an Italianate villain. Harbage, feeling that the intrigue action of the play, with its mixture of tragedy and comedy, furnished the main appeal to the Elizabethan audience, concluded that today we can no longer approve of Hieronimo's conduct, and therefore cannot accept Kyd's play as true tragedy. Most of the recent critics, however, have disagreed and have attempted to show why Hieronimo was forced against his will into the course of private vengeance. J. D. Ratliff, in "Hieronimo Explains Himself" (*SP*, 1957), used the Marshal's soliloquy in III, xii, to show why he abandoned the Christian attitude toward revenge. His status as Marshal of Spain and as a judge, the secrecy of the murder of his son, and his rebuff by Lorenzo and the King when he sought justice forced him to take matters into his own hands. Moreover, the way in which the Ghost in the epilogue consigns all of Hieronimo's victims to the most horrible of torments in terms of the classical Hades, whereas he calls Hieronimo "good," Isabella and Bel-imperia "fair," and Horatio his "friend," show that at least Kyd himself regarded the Marshal as a justified and honorable revenger. S. F. Johnson, too, felt that Bowers had not sufficiently recognized Kyd's "brilliant invention" of Hieronimo's tragic dilemma as the officially appointed minister of justice forced by circumstances to take justice into his own hands, or his actual following of the Mosaic code of "an eye for an eye," which Protestants like Calvin and others believed to be as much the word of God as anything else in the two Testaments. Ernest de Chickera reexamined the problem of "Divine Justice and Private Revenge" (*MLR*, 1962) and decided that if certain of the major scenes and speeches were analyzed more closely we would see "divine vengeance or justice operating purposefully, thus fulfilling God's pledge to revenge or punish," and that Hieronimo was forced eventually into private revenge only because the King, God's proper instrument, was too weak to act as he should. In 1965 David Laird made a further examination of Hieronimo's ideas on revenge ("Hieronimo's Dilemma," *SP*, 1965); and in the same year Einar J. Jensen, somewhat annoyed by the whole controversy, entitled an article in *JEGP* "Kyd's *Spanish Tragedy:* The Play Explains Itself," and insisted that Hieronimo "must himself resort to policy and intrigue in order to gain the revenge which is his legitimate due." Whatever the villain-hero judgment on Hieronimo, there is almost unanimous agreement with Tucker Brooke (*Introduction to Tudor Drama*, Oxford, 1933) that in Lorenzo Kyd had created "the first of a line of Machiavellian villains," echoes of whom reappeared in Marlowe's Barabas, the "Jew of Malta," and Young Mortimer in *Edward II;* in Shakespeare's *Titus Andronicus, Richard II*, and *King Lear;* in Chettle's *Tragedy of Hoffman;* and in the plays of Webster and Tourneur.

The chief remaining crux of the tragedy concerns the play within a play, one of several ideas which Shakespeare borrowed from Kyd's *The Spanish Tragedy* or his *Ur-Hamlet*. In "The Play within a Play: An Elizabethan Dramatic Device" (*E & S*, 1960), Arthur Brown reviewed the recurrence of this contrivance from Kyd's introduction of it through its adoption by many of the most important dramatists of the time. Freeman also discussed its evolution from the prologues in Greek tragedy through the Italian *intermedii* and English dumb shows. The main question concerned not only Hieronimo's insistence that each of the characters in the inner play speak in a different language, but also Kyd's note in the printed text to his "Gentlemen" readers that he thought it "good" that here his "sundry languages . . . be set down in English, more largely, for the easier understanding to every public reader." Critics have wondered why this concession was more desirable for public readers than for public audiences, many members of which were probably less highly educated than the play's readers. Both readers and audiences, moreover, should have been thoroughly prepared for a polyglot piece by the way in which Kyd had already shown off his linguistic ability and education through the many Latin quotations, interspersed with some Italian and Spanish phrases, with which he had embellished his dialogue. Schücking had gone so far as to suggest that the whole thing was little more than an advertizement of the 1592 edition of *Soliman and Perseda*, but Boas had combatted this suggestion and maintained that the words referred only to the ensuing playlet (*TLS*, June 19–July 17, 1937). Muriel C. Bradbrook speculated that the inner play might actually have been acted in foreign tongues because Elizabethan groundlings delighted in hearing "the sound of a strange language," but then discounted her own suggestion (*Themes and Conventions of Elizabethan Tragedy*, Cambridge University Press, 1935). Philip Edwards was even more dubious, believing that the playlet was performed in English, or even pantomimed, since the printed text told the story "more largely." P. W. Biesterfeldt, in his monograph *Die Dramatische Technik von Thomas Kyds* (Halle, 1936), compromised and held that the characters did speak in "sundry languages," but that they supplemented the dialogue with broad pantomime, as in a dumb show. S. F. Johnson, however, made the most provocative suggestion of all in calling attention to the way in which Kyd prepared his audience by having Hieronimo tell how, when young in Toledo, he had written a tragedy to be acted by "gentlemen and scholars too," but would considerately provide the King with a book containing the "argument" of the play, even though it was now, as Balthazar pointed out, to be acted "by princes and courtiers,/Such as can tell how to speak." Nevertheless Hieronimo, in his brief soliloquy after instructing his cast, prophesies that he will now see the fall of Babylon, "Wrought by the heavens in this confusion." From this reference to the fate of Babylon, Johnson worked out an intricate but closely reasoned analogy, "both with the confusion of tongues wrought by the Lord at Babel (*Genesis*, 11) and with the horrible destruction of both the historical and symbolic Babylons as prophesied in *Isaiah*, 13, *Jeremiah*, 51, and *Revelation*, 18. To Protestant interpreters, the symbolic Babylon was of course Rome, the whore of Babylon being equated with the Antichrist, in turn equated with the Pope, one of whose agents in Kyd's day was the King of Spain. . . ." After a further development of the Babel-Babylon theme, Johnson suggested that the gruesome act of Hieronimo in biting out his tongue (accomplished perhaps, as Charles Prouty suggested in his edition of the play for the Crofts Classics in 1951, by substituting for it a slice of raw liver) could be seen as a "symbolic refusal to participate in the confusion of the world after Babel," as well as to "identify Hieronimo as admirably Stoic, for he is imitating the legendary action of Zeno of Elea, the traditional founder of the Stoic School." Freeman, however, has pointed out similar episodes in Greek, Latin, and English works. He also is puzzled to find a reason for Hieronimo's silence, since there is no longer anything to conceal.

These aspects of *The Spanish Tragedy* considered together have split critics into two groups. Moody E. Prior, in *The Language of Tragedy*, remarked: "That Hieronimo is not one of the great dramatic figures is chiefly due to the technical immaturity of Kyd," in spite of the "remarkable originality of so much of the play," including the colloquial flexibility of much of his blank verse along with his retention of so many of the old rhetorical patterns. B. L. Joseph, in his edition of the play for the New Mermaids series in 1964, went much further and criticized Kyd for his failure to use his virtuosity of language to "communicate a full imagining of character in action in the respective situations." To him there is "too much contrivance and too little organic growth" in the shaping of the plot. He concludes: "Fundamentally, its failure as a work of the imagination derives from its postulated theme."

On the other hand, William H. Wiatt has defended even the Alexandro-Villuppo scenes as necessary to make the audience better understand the powerful reasons for Hieronimo's delaying revenge until he is sure of the trustworthiness of his evidence ("The Dramatic Function of the Alexandro-Villuppo Episode in *The Spanish Tragedy*," *NQ*, 1958). Biesterfeldt had meticulously analyzed the play as the outstanding example of the combination of features from the Senecan drama and the popular stage, and defended its structure by maintaining that it was the printer who was responsible for dividing it into four acts instead of the conventional five. And G. Gregory Smith had praised Kyd as "the first English dramatist who writes dramatically" and who "was well served by his realism" as well as by his "human" and "probable" dialogue (*Cambridge History of English Literature*, Cambridge University Press, 1910). Finally, Freeman has taken the judicious position that "In general, among critics of the drama of the Elizabethan period, Kyd has been treated as a literary figure of considerable historical importance, and almost negligible poetical worth—a traditional view which may easily result in a corresponding overestimation of Kyd's aesthetic and poetic capabilities now and in the immediate future, if only to redress a bad balance."

The present text is based on the recension of the undated quarto in the British Museum (printed by Allde for White) made by Schick in his variorum edition of the play (Berlin, 1901), except that the additions have been taken from the Malone Society reprint of the edition of 1602 prepared by Greg. Boas's standard edition of *The Works of Thomas Kyd* (Oxford, 1901) has also been consulted.

THE SPANISH TRAGEDY[1]

[BY

THOMAS KYD

DRAMATIS PERSONÆ

GHOST OF ANDREA, *a Spanish courtier* } *induction and chorus.*
REVENGE

KING OF SPAIN.
DON CYPRIAN, *Duke of Castile, his brother.*
LORENZO, *Don Cyprian's son.*
PAGE OF LORENZO.
HIERONIMO, *Marshal of Spain.*
HORATIO, *his son.*
SPANISH GENERAL.
DEPUTY.
VICEROY OF PORTUGAL.
BALTHAZAR, *his son.*
SERBERINE, *Balthazar's servant.*
DON PEDRO, *the viceroy's brother.*
ALEXANDRO } *Portuguese noblemen.*
VILLUPPO
PORTUGUESE AMBASSADOR.
TWO PORTUGUESE.
DON BAZULTO, *an old man.*

PEDRINGANO, *Bel-imperia's servant.*
CHRISTOPHIL, *Bel-imperia's custodian.*
THREE CITIZENS.
MESSENGER.
HANGMAN.
ARMY, ROYAL SUITES, NOBLEMEN, OFFICERS, HALBERDIERS, SERVANTS, THREE WATCHMEN, ETC.

BEL-IMPERIA, *Don Cyprian's daughter.*
ISABELLA, *Hieronimo's wife.*
MAID OF ISABELLA.

Three KINGS *and three* KNIGHTS, *in the first dumb show;* HYMEN *and two* TORCHBEARERS *in the second.*

BAZARDO, *a painter* } *in the additions to the play.*
PEDRO *and* JAQUES,
Hieronimo's servants

SCENE: *Spain and Portugal.*

TIME: *Contemporary.*]

ACTUS PRIMUS.

[INDUCTION, *or* CHORUS]

*Enter the Ghost of Andrea, and with him
Revenge.*

GHOST. When this eternal substance of my
    soul
Did live imprisoned in my wanton flesh,
Each in their function serving other's
    need,
I was a courtier in the Spanish court.
My name was Don Andrea, my descent,
Though not ignoble, yet inferior far
To gracious fortunes of my tender youth.

For there in prime and pride of all my
    years,
By duteous service and deserving love,
In secret I possessed a worthy dame, 10
Which hight [2] sweet Bel-imperia by
    name.
But in the harvest of my summer joys
Death's winter nipped the blossoms of
    my bliss,
Forcing divorce betwixt my love and me.
For in the late conflict with Portingale
My valor drew me into danger's mouth
Till life to death made passage through
    my wounds.
When I was slain, my soul descended
    straight
To pass the flowing stream of Acheron;

[1] The title continues: "Containing the Lamentable End of Don Horatio and Bel-imperia, with the Pitiful Death of Old Hieronimo." In the 1615 edn. a sub-title is substituted: "Or Hieronimo Is Mad Again."

[2] Who was called.

335

But churlish Charon, only boatman
 there, 20
Said that, my rites of burial not per-
 formed,
I might not sit amongst his passengers.
Ere Sol had slept three nights in Thetis'
 lap,
And slaked his smoking chariot in her
 flood,
By Don Horatio, our knight marshal's
 son,
My funerals and obsequies were done.
Then was the ferryman of hell content
To pass me over to the slimy strand
That leads to fell Avernus' ugly waves.
There, pleasing Cerberus with honeyed
 speech, 30
I passed the perils of the foremost porch.
Not far from hence, amidst ten thousand
 souls,
Sat Minos, Æacus, and Rhadamanth,
To whom no sooner gan [1] I make ap-
 proach
To crave a passport for my wand'ring
 ghost,
But Minos, in graven leaves of lottery,
Drew forth the manner of my life and
 death.
"This knight," quoth he, "both lived
 and died in love,
And for his love tried fortune of the wars,
And by war's fortune lost both love and
 life." 40
"Why then," said Æacus, "convey him
 hence,
To walk with lovers in our fields of love,
And spend the course of everlasting time
Under green myrtle trees and cypress
 shades."
"No, no," said Rhadamanth, "it were
 not well
With loving souls to place a martialist.
He died in war, and must to martial
 fields,
Where wounded Hector lives in lasting
 pain,
And Achilles' Myrmidons do scour the
 plain." 49
Then Minos, mildest censor [2] of the three,
Made this device to end the difference:
"Send him," quoth he, "to our infernal
 king,
To doom him as best seems his majesty."

To this effect my passport straight was
 drawn.
In keeping on my way to Pluto's court,
Through dreadful shades of ever-
 glooming night,
I saw more sights than thousand tongues
 can tell,
Or pens can write, or mortal hearts can
 think.
Three ways there were.   That on the
 right-hand side 59
Was ready way unto the foresaid fields,
Where lovers live and bloody martialists,
But either sort contained within his
 bounds.
The left-hand path, declining fearfully,
Was ready downfall to the deepest hell,
Where bloody Furies shakes their whips
 of steel,
And poor Ixion turns an endless wheel;
Where usurers are choked with melting
 gold,
And wantons are embraced with ugly
 snakes,
And murderers groan with never-killing
 wounds,
And perjured wights scalded in boiling
 lead, 70
And all foul sins with torments over-
 whelmed.
Twixt these two ways I trod the middle
 path,
Which brought me to the fair Elysian
 green,
In midst whereof there stands a stately
 tower,
The walls of brass, the gates of adamant.
Here finding Pluto with his Proserpine,
I showed my passport, humbled on my
 knee,
Whereat fair Proserpine began to smile,
And begged that only she might give
 my doom.
Pluto was pleased, and sealed it with a
 kiss. 80
Forthwith, Revenge, she rounded [3] thee
 in th' ear,
And bade thee lead me through the gates
 of horn,
Where dreams have passage in the silent
 night.
No sooner had she spoke, but we were
 here—

[1] Did.   [2] Judge.   [3] Whispered.

I wot [1] not how—in twinkling of an eye.

REVENGE. Then know, Andrea, that thou
 art arrived
 Where thou shalt see the author of thy
  death,
 Don Balthazar, the prince of Portingale,
 Deprived of life by Bel-imperia.
 Here sit we down to see the mystery,[2] 90
 And serve for Chorus in this tragedy.

[SCENA PRIMA.

The Spanish court.]

*Enter Spanish King, General, Castile, and
       Hieronimo.*

KING. Now say, l[ord] general, how fares
 our camp?

GEN. All well, my sovereign liege, except
 some few
 That are deceased by fortune of the war.

KING. But what portends thy cheerful
 countenance,
 And posting to our presence thus in
  haste?
 Speak, man, hath fortune given us victory?

GEN. Victory, my liege, and that with little
 loss.

KING. Our Portingales will pay us tribute
 then?

GEN. Tribute and wonted homage therewithal.

KING. Then blessed be heaven and guider
 of the heavens,   10
 From whose fair influence such justice
  flows.

CAS. "*O multum dilecte Deo, tibi militat
 æther,*
*Et conjuratæ curvato poplite gentes
Succumbunt: recti soror est victoria
 juris.*" [3]

KING. Thanks to my loving brother of
 Castile.—
 But, general, unfold in brief discourse
 Your form of battle and your war's suc-
  cess,
 That, adding all the pleasure of thy news
 Unto the height of former happiness,

[1] Know.   [2] Play.
[3] "O thou much loved of God, for thee heaven
wars, and the peoples of earth, united, submit on bended knee. The triumph of justice
is the sister of righteousness" (adapted from
Claudian's *De Tertio Consulatu Honorii*, ll. 96–
98).

 With deeper wage and greater dignity 20
 We may reward thy blissful chivalry.

GEN. Where Spain and Portingale do
 jointly knit
 Their frontiers, leaning on each other's
  bound,
 There met our armies in their proud
  array,
 Both furnished well, both full of hope
  and fear,
 Both menacing alike with daring shows,
 Both vaunting sundry colors of device,
 Both cheerly sounding trumpets, drums,
  and fifes,
 Both raising dreadful clamors to the sky
 That valleys, hills, and rivers made re-
  bound,   30
 And heaven itself was frighted with the
  sound.
 Our battles both were pitched in squad-
  ron form,
 Each corner strongly fenced with wings
  of shot,
 But, ere we joined and came to push of
  pike,
 I brought a squadron of our readiest shot
 From out our rearward [4] to begin the
  fight;
 They brought another wing t' encounter
  us.
 Meanwhile, our ordinance[5] played on
  either side,
 And captains strove to have their valors
  tried.
 Don Pedro, their chief horsemen's colo-
  nel,   40
 Did with his cornet[6] bravely make at-
  tempt
 To break the order of our battle ranks;
 But Don Rogero, worthy man of war,
 Marched forth against him with our
  musketeers,
 And stopped the malice of his fell ap-
  proach.
 While they maintain hot skirmish to and
  fro,
 Both battles join, and fall to handy-
  blows,[7]
 Their violent shot resembling th' ocean's
  rage,
 When, roaring loud and with a swelling
  tide,

[4] Rear division.   [6] Troop of horse.
[5] Ordnance.   [7] Hand-to-hand fighting.

It beats upon the rampiers [1] of huge
rocks,   50
And gapes to swallow neighbor-bounding
lands.
Now, while Bellona rageth here and
there,
Thick storms of bullets ran like winter's
hail,
And shivered lances dark the troubled
air.
          Pede pes et cuspide cuspis;
Arma sonant armis, vir petiturque viro. [2]
On every side drop captains to the
ground,
And soldiers, some ill maimed, some slain
outright.
Here falls a body sindered [3] from his
head;
There legs and arms lie bleeding on the
grass,   60
Mingled with weapons and unboweled
steeds,
That scattering overspread the purple
plain.
In all this turmoil, three long hours and
more,
The victory to neither part inclined,
Till Don Andrea, with his brave lan-
ciers,
In their main battle made so great a
breach
That, half dismayed, the multitude re-
tired.
But Balthazar, the Portingales' young
prince,
Brought rescue, and encouraged them
to stay.
Herehence [4] the fight was eagerly re-
newed,   70
And in that conflict was Andrea slain—
Brave man at arms, but weak to [5] Baltha-
zar.
Yet while the prince, insulting [6] over
him,
Breathed out proud vaunts, sounding to
our reproach,
Friendship and hardy valor joined in one
Pricked forth Horatio, our knight mar-
shal's son,

To challenge forth that prince in single
fight.
Not long between these twain the fight
endured,
But straight the prince was beaten from
his horse,
And forced to yield him prisoner to his
foe.   80
When he was taken, all the rest they fled,
And our carbines pursued them to the
death,
Till, Phœbus waving [7] to the western
deep,
Our trumpeters were charged to sound
retreat.
KING. Thanks, good l[ord] general, for
these good news;
And, for some argument of more to come,
Take this and wear it for thy sovereign's
sake.   *Give him his chain.*
But tell me now, hast thou confirmed a
peace?
GEN. No peace, my liege, but peace con-
ditional,
That, if with homage tribute be well
paid,   90
The fury of your forces will be stayed;
And to this peace their viceroy hath
subscribed,   *Give the K[ing] a paper.*
And made a solemn vow that, during
life,
His tribute shall be truly paid to Spain.
KING. These words, these deeds, become
thy person well.
But now, knight marshal, frolic with
thy king,
For 'tis thy son that wins this battle's
prize.
HIER. Long may he live to serve my sov-
ereign liege,
And soon decay, unless he serve my
liege.
KING. Nor thou nor he shall die without
reward.   *A tucket* [8] *afar off.* 100
What means this warning of this trump-
et's sound?
GEN. This tells me that your grace's men
of war,
Such as war's fortune hath reserved
from death,
Come marching on towards your royal
seat,
To show themselves before your majesty,

---

[1] Rampires, ramparts, embankments.
[2] Foot against foot and spear against spear,
arms clash on arms, hero is assailed by hero
(a combination of phrases from Statius, Virgil,
and Curtius).   [3] Sundered.   [4] From this point.
[5] Compared to.   [6] Triumphing scornfully.
[7] Waning, sinking.   [8] Flourish of trumpets.

For so I gave in charge at my depart,
Whereby by demonstration shall appear
That all, except three hundred or few
  more,
Are safe returned, and by their foes en-
  riched.

The Army enters, Balthazar, between Lorenzo
                          and Horatio, captive.

KING. A gladsome sight! I long to see
  them here. *They enter and pass by.* 110
Was that the warlike prince of Portingale
That by our nephew was in triumph
  led?
GEN. It was, my liege, the prince of Portin-
  gale.
KING. But what was he that on the other
  side
Held him by th' arm as partner of the
  prize?
HIER. That was my son, my gracious sov-
  ereign,
Of whom though from his tender infancy
My loving thoughts did never hope but
  well,
He never pleased his father's eyes till
  now,
Nor filled my heart with overcloying
  joys.   120
KING. Go, let them march once more about
  these walls,
That, staying them, we may confer and
  talk
With our brave prisoner and his double
  guard.   [*Exit a Messenger.*]
Hieronimo, it greatly pleaseth us
That in our victory thou have a share,
By virtue of thy worthy son's exploit.

                Enter again.

Bring hither the young prince of Portin-
  gale.
The rest march on; but, ere they be dis-
  missed,
We will bestow on every soldier
Two ducats and on every leader ten, 130
That they may know our largess wel-
  comes them.
Exeunt all but [*the King,*] *Bal*[*thazar,*]
            Lor[*enzo*], *Hor*[*atio*].
Welcome, Don Balthazar! Welcome,
  nephew!

And thou, Horatio, thou art welcome
  too.
Young prince, although thy father's hard
  misdeeds,
In keeping back the tribute that he owes,
Deserve but evil measure at our hands,
Yet shalt thou know that Spain is hon-
  orable.
BAL. The trespass that my father made in
  peace
Is now controlled [1] by fortune of the
  wars,
And, cards once dealt, it boots not ask
  why so.   140
His men are slain—a weakening to his
  realm;
His colors seized—a blot unto his name;
His son distressed—a corsive [2] to his
  heart.
These punishments may clear his late
  offense.
KING. Ay, Balthazar, if he observe this
  truce,
Our peace will grow the stronger for
  these wars.
Meanwhile live thou, though not in lib-
  erty,
Yet free from bearing any servile yoke,
For in our hearing thy deserts were great,
And in our sight thyself art gracious. 150
BAL. And I shall study to deserve this
  grace.
KING. But tell me—for their holding
  makes me doubt—
To which of these twain art thou pris-
  oner?
LOR. To me, my liege.
HOR.   To me, my sovereign.
LOR. This hand first took his courser by
  the reins.
HOR. But first my lance did put him from
  his horse.
LOR. I seized his weapon, and enjoyed it
  first.
HOR. But first I forced him lay his weap-
  ons down.
KING. Let go his arm, upon our privilege.
                          Let him go.
Say, worthy prince, to whether [3] didst
  thou yield?   160
BAL. To him in courtesy; to this perforce.
He spake me fair; this other gave me
  strokes.

---

[1] Checked.   [2] Corrosive.   [3] Which one.

He promised life; this other threatened
    death.
He won my love; this other conquered
    me—
And, truth to say, I yield myself to both.
HIER. But that I know your grace for
    just and wise,
And might seem partial in this difference,
Enforced by nature and by law of arms,
My tongue should plead for young
    Horatio's right.   169
He hunted well that was a lion's death,
Not he that in a garment wore his skin;
So hares may pull dead lions by the
    beard.
KING. Content thee, marshal, thou shalt
    have no wrong;
And, for thy sake, thy son shall want no
    right.
Will both abide the censure [1] of my
    doom?
LOR. I crave no better than your grace
    awards.
HOR. Nor I, although I sit beside my
    right.
KING. Then by my judgment thus your
    strife shall end:
You both deserve, and both shall have
    reward.
Nephew, thou took'st his weapon and
    his horse;   180
His weapons and his horse are thy re-
    ward.
Horatio, thou didst force him first to
    yield;
His ransom therefore is thy valor's fee.
Appoint the sum, as you shall both agree.
But, nephew, thou shalt have the prince
    in guard,
For thine estate best fitteth such a guest.
Horatio's house were small for all his
    train.
Yet, in regard thy substance passeth his,
And that just guerdon may befall desert,
To him we yield the armor of the
    prince.   190
How likes Don Balthazar of this device?
BAL. Right well, my liege, if this proviso
    were
That Don Horatio bear us company,
Whom I admire and love for chivalry.
KING. Horatio, leave him not that loves
    thee so.—

[1] Judgment.

Now let us hence to see our soldiers paid,
And feast our prisoner as our friendly
    guest.   *Exeunt.*

[SCENA SECUNDA.
The Portuguese court.]

Enter Viceroy, Alexandro, Villuppo.

VIC. Is our ambassador despatched for
    Spain?
ALEX. Two days, my liege, are past since
    his depart.
VIC. And tribute payment gone along with
    him?
ALEX. Ay, my good lord.
VIC. Then rest we here awhile in our un-
    rest,
And feed our sorrows with some inward
    sighs,
For deepest cares break never into tears.
But wherefore sit I in a regal throne?
This better fits a wretch's endless moan.
                  Falls to the ground.
Yet this is higher than my fortunes
    reach,   10
And therefore better than my state de-
    serves.
Ay, ay, this earth, image of melancholy,
Seeks him whom fates adjudge to misery.
Here let me lie; now am I at the lowest.
Qui jacet in terra, non habet unde cadat.
In me consumpsit vires Fortuna nocendo;
Nil superest ut jam possit obesse magis. [2]
Yes, Fortune may bereave me of my
    crown—
Here, take it now. Let Fortune do her
    worst,
She will not rob me of this sable weed. 20
O, no, she envies none but pleasant
    things.
Such is the folly of despiteful chance!
Fortune is blind, and sees not my deserts;
So is she deaf, and hears not my laments;
And could she hear, yet is she willful-mad,
And therefore will not pity my distress.
Suppose that she could pity me, what
    then?
What help can be expected at her hands
Whose foot [is] [3] standing on a rolling
    stone,

[2] He who lies upon the ground hath not
whence he may fall. On me hath Fortune exhausted her powers of injury. There remains
no further damage that she can inflict (source
unknown).   [3] Added by Dodsley.

And mind more mutable than fickle
winds?   30
Why wail I, then, where's hope of no
redress?
O, yes, complaining makes my grief seem
less.
My late ambition hath distained [1] my
faith;
My breach of faith occasioned bloody
wars;
Those bloody wars have spent my treas-
ure;
And with my treasure my people's blood;
And with their blood, my joy and best
beloved,
My best beloved, my sweet and only son.
O, wherefore went I not to war myself?
The cause was mine; I might have died
for both.   40
My years were mellow; his but young
and green.
My death were natural, but his was
forced.
ALEX. No doubt, my liege, but still the
prince survives.
VIC. Survives! Ay, where?
ALEX. In Spain, a prisoner by mischance
of war.
VIC. Then they have slain him for his
father's fault.
ALEX. That were a breach to common
law of arms.
VIC. They reck no laws that meditate re-
venge.
ALEX. His ransom's worth will stay from
foul revenge.
VIC. No; if he lived, the news would soon
be here.   50
ALEX. Nay, evil news fly faster still than
good.
VIC. Tell me no more of news, for he is
dead.
VIL. My sovereign, pardon the author of
ill news,
And I'll bewray [2] the fortune of thy son.
VIC. Speak on, I'll guerdon thee, whate'er
it be.
Mine ear is ready to receive ill news,
My heart grown hard gainst mischief's
battery.
Stand up, I say, and tell thy tale at large.
VIL. Then hear that truth which these
mine eyes have seen.

When both the armies were in battle
joined,   60
Don Balthazar, amidst the thickest
troops,
To win renown did wondrous feats of
arms.
Amongst the rest, I saw him, hand to
hand,
In single fight with their lord general,
Till Alexandro, that here counterfeits
Under the color of a duteous friend,
Discharged his pistol at the prince's back
As though he would have slain their
general—
But therewithal Don Balthazar fell down,
And, when he fell, then we began to
fly;   70
But, had he lived, the day had sure been
ours.
ALEX. O wicked forgery! O traitorous mis-
creant!
VIC. Hold thou thy peace! But now, Vil-
luppo, say,
Where then became [3] the carcass of my
son?
VIL. I saw them drag it to the Spanish
tents.
VIC. Ay, ay, my nightly dreams have told
me this.—
Thou false, unkind, unthankful, traitor-
ous beast,
Wherein had Balthazar offended thee
That thou shouldst thus betray him to
our foes?
Was't Spanish gold that bleared so
thine eyes   80
That thou couldst see no part of our
deserts?
Perchance, because thou art Terceira's
lord,
Thou hadst some hope to wear this
diadem,
If first my son and then myself were
slain.
But thy ambitious thought shall break
thy neck.
Ay, this was it that made thee spill his
blood,
   Take the crown and put it on again.
But I'll now wear it till thy blood be
spilt.
ALEX. Vouchsafe, dread sovereign, to hear
me speak.

[1] Stained, defiled.   [2] Disclose.   [3] What became of.

Vic. Away with him! His sight is second hell.

Keep him till we determine of his death.   [*They take him out.*] 90

If Balthazar be dead, he shall not live.

Villuppo, follow us for thy reward.
                                        Exit Vice[roy].

Vil. Thus have I with an envious, forgéd tale

Deceived the king, betrayed mine enemy,

And hope for guerdon of my villainy.
                                        Exit.

[Scena Tertia.

Hieronimo's garden.[1]]

Enter Horatio and Bel-imperia.

Bel. Signior Horatio, this is the place and hour,

Wherein I must entreat thee to relate

The circumstance of Don Andrea's death,

Who, living, was my garland's sweetest flower,

And in his death hath buried my delights.

Hor. For love of him and service to yourself,

I nill[2] refuse this heavy, doleful charge;

Yet tears and sighs, I fear, will hinder me.

When both our armies were enjoined in fight,

Your worthy chevalier amidst the thick'st,   10

For glorious cause still aiming at the fairest,

Was at the last by young Don Balthazar

Encountered hand to hand. Their fight was long,

Their hearts were great, their clamors menacing,

Their strength alike, their strokes both dangerous.

But wrathful Nemesis, that wicked power,

Envying at Andrea's praise and worth,

Cut short his life to end his praise and worth.

She, she herself, disguised in armor's mask—

As Pallas was before proud Pergamus—   20

Brought in a fresh supply of halberdiers,

Which paunched[3] his horse, and dinged[4] him to the ground.

Then young Don Balthazar with ruthless rage,

Taking advantage of his foe's distress,

Did finish what his halberdiers begun,

And left not till Andrea's life was done.

Then, though too late, incensed with just remorse,[5]

I with my band set forth against the prince

And brought him prisoner from his halberdiers.

Bel. Would thou hadst slain him that so slew my love!   30

But then was Don Andrea's carcass lost?

Hor. No, that was it for which I chiefly strove,

Nor stepped I back till I recovered him.

I took him up, and wound him in mine arms;

And, welding[6] him unto my private tent,

There laid him down, and dewed him with my tears,

And sighed and sorrowed as became a friend.

But neither friendly sorrow, sighs, nor tears

Could win pale Death from his usurpéd right.

Yet this I did, and less I could not do: 40

I saw him honored with due funeral.

This scarf I plucked from off his lifeless arm,

And wear it in remembrance of my friend.

Bel. I know the scarf. Would he had kept it still!

For, had he lived, he would have kept it still,

And worn it for his Bel-imperia's sake,

For 'twas my favor at his last depart.

But now wear thou it both for him and me,

For after him thou hast deserved it best.

---

[1] If II, ii, 42–43, refers to I, iii, 48–54, the scene here is Hieronimo's garden, and, according to ll. 110–15, close to the place of the banquet in I, iv. Possibly, however, I, iii and iv, are to be regarded as one scene, beginning in some indefinite locality and shifting to a banqueting hall.

[2] Ne will; will not.

[3] Stabbed in the belly.   [5] Sorrow.
[4] Knocked down.   [6] Wielding, carrying.

But, for thy kindness in his life and
  death,							50
Be sure, while Bel-imperia's life endures,
She will be Don Horatio's thankful
  friend.
Hor. And, madam, Don Horatio will not
  slack
Humbly to serve fair Bel-imperia.
But now, if your good liking stand
  thereto,
I'll crave your pardon to go seek the
  prince,
For so the duke, your father, gave me
  charge.					*Exit.*
Bel. Ay, go, Horatio, leave me here
  alone,
For solitude best fits my cheerless mood.
Yet what avails to wail Andrea's
  death,							60
From whence Horatio proves my second
  love?
Had he not loved Andrea as he did,
He could not sit in Bel-imperia's
  thoughts.
But how can love find harbor in my
  breast
Till I revenge the death of my beloved?
Yes, second love shall further my re-
  venge!
I'll love Horatio, my Andrea's friend,
The more to spite the prince that
  wrought his end;
And, where Don Balthazar, that slew
  my love,
Himself now pleads for favor at my
  hands,							70
He shall, in rigor of my just disdain,
Reap long repentance for his murderous
  deed.
For what was't else but murderous
  cowardice,
So many to oppress one valiant knight,
Without respect of honor in the fight?
And here he comes that murdered my
  delight.

Enter Lorenzo and Balthazar.

Lor. Sister, what means this melancholy
  walk?
Bel. That for a while I wish no company.
Lor. But here the prince is come to visit
  you.
Bel. That argues that he lives in lib-
  erty.							80

Bal. No, madam, but in pleasing servi-
  tude.
Bel. Your prison then, belike, is your
  conceit.[1]
Bal. Ay, by conceit my freedom is en-
  thralled.
Bel. Then with conceit enlarge [2] yourself
  again.
Bal. What if conceit have laid my heart
  to gage? [3]
Bel. Pay that you borrowed, and recover
  it.
Bal. I die, if it return from whence it lies.
Bel. A heartless man, and live? A mir-
  acle!
Bal. Ay, lady, love can work such mir-
  acles.
Lor. Tush, tush, my lord! Let go these
  ambages,[4]						90
And in plain terms acquaint her with
  your love.
Bel. What boots complaint, when there's
  no remedy?
Bal. Yes, to your gracious self must I com-
  plain,
In whose fair answer lies my remedy;
On whose perfection all my thoughts
  attend;
On whose aspect mine eyes find beauty's
  bower;
In whose translucent breast my heart is
  lodged.
Bel. Alas, my lord, these are but words of
  course,[5]
And but devise[d] to drive me from this
  place.
She in going in lets fall her glove, which
  		Horatio, coming out, takes up.
Hor. Madam, your glove.				100
Bel. Thanks, good Horatio; take it for thy
  pains.
Bal. Signior Horatio stooped in happy
  time!
Hor. I reaped more grace than I deserved
  or hoped.
Lor. My lord, be not dismayed for what
  is past;
You know that women oft are humorous.[6]
These clouds will overblow with little
  wind;

[1] Thought, imagination.	[4] Roundabout phrases.
[2] Free.			[5] Formal phrases.
[3] As security.			[6] Variable, capricious.

Let me alone, I'll scatter them myself.
Meanwhile, let us devise to spend the
time
In some delightful sports and reveling.
Hor. The king, my lords, is coming hither
straight   110
To feast the Portingale ambassador;
Things were in readiness before I came.
Bal. Then here it fits us to attend the king,
To welcome hither our ambassador,
And learn my father and my country's
health.

[Scena Quarta.

The banqueting hall in the Spanish court.]

*Enter the banquet, Trumpets, the King, and
Ambassador.*

King. See, lord ambassador, how Spain
entreats [1]
Their prisoner Balthazar, thy viceroy's
son.
We pleasure more in kindness than in
wars.
Amb. Sad is our king, and Portingale la-
ments,
Supposing that Don Balthazar is slain.
Bal. So am I—slain by beauty's tyranny!
You see, my lord, how Balthazar is slain:
I frolic with the Duke of Castile's son,
Wrapped every hour in pleasures of the
court,
And graced with favors of his majesty. [10
King. Put off your greetings till our feast
be done;
Now come and sit with us, and taste our
cheer.   *Sit to the banquet.*
Sit down, young prince; you are our
second guest.
Brother, sit down; and, nephew, take
your place.
Signior Horatio, wait thou upon our cup,
For well thou has deserved to be hon-
ored.
Now, lordings, fall to. Spain is Portugal,
And Portugal is Spain; we both are
friends;
Tribute is paid, and we enjoy our right.
But where is old Hieronimo, our mar-
shal?   20
He promised us, in honor of our guest,
To grace our banquet with some pom-
pous jest.[2]

[1] Treats.   [2] Stately entertainment.

*Enter Hieronimo, with a drum, three
Knights, each [with] his scutcheon; then
he fetches three Kings; they take their
crowns and them captive.*

Hieronimo, this masque contents mine
eye,
Although I sound not well the mystery.
Hier. The first armed knight that hung
his scutcheon up
*He takes the scutcheon and gives it to the
King.*
Was English Robert, Earl of Gloucester,
Who, when King Stephen bore sway in
Albion,
Arrived with five-and-twenty thousand
men
In Portingale, and by success of war.
Enforced the king, then but a Saracen, 30
To bear the yoke of the English mon-
archy.
King. My lord of Portingale, by this you
see
That which may comfort both your king
and you,
And make your late discomfort seem the
less.
But say, Hieronimo, what was the next?
Hier. The second knight that hung his
scutcheon up   *He doth as he did before.*
Was Edmund, Earl of Kent in Albion,
When English Richard wore the diadem.
He came likewise, and razéd Lisbon
walls,
And took the King of Portingale in
fight,   40
For which and other suchlike service
done
He after was created Duke of York.
King. This is another special argument
That Portingale may deign to bear our
yoke,
When it by little England hath been
yoked.
But now, Hieronimo, what were the last?
Hier. The third and last, not least, in our
account,   *Doing as before.*
Was, as the rest, a valiant Englishman,
Brave John of Gaunt, the Duke of Lan-
caster,
As by his scutcheon plainly may ap-
pear.   50
He with a puissant army came to Spain
And took our King of Castile prisoner.

AMB. This is an argument for our viceroy
  That Spain may not insult for her suc-
    cess,
  Since English warriors likewise conquered
    Spain,
  And made them bow their knees to
    Albion.
KING. Hieronimo, I drink to thee for this
    device,
  Which hath pleased both the ambassador
    and me.
  Pledge me, Hieronimo, if thou love the
    king.   *Takes the cup of Horatio.*
  My lord, I fear we sit but overlong,   60
  Unless our dainties were more delicate,
  But welcome are you to the best we have.
  Now let us in, that you may be des-
    patched.
  I think our council is already set.
                    Exeunt omnes.

[CHORUS]

ANDREA. Come we for this from depth of
    underground,
  To see him feast that gave me my
    death's wound?
  These pleasant sights are sorrow to my
    soul—
  Nothing but league,[1] and love, and ban-
    queting!
REVENGE. Be still, Andrea; ere we go from
    hence,
  I'll turn their friendship into fell de-
    spite,   70
  Their love to mortal hate, their day to
    night,
  Their hope into despair, their peace to
    war,
  Their joys to pain, their bliss to misery.

ACTUS SECUNDUS. [SCENA PRIMA.

A room in Don Cyprian's palace.]

Enter Lorenzo and Balthazar.

LOR. My lord, though Bel-imperia seem
    thus coy,
  Let reason hold you in your wonted joy.
  In time the savage bull sustains the
    yoke,[2]

[1] Friendship.
[2] Lines 3–6, 9–10, are modeled on Sonnet 47
of Watson's *Hecatompathia.*

In time all haggard [3] hawks will stoop to
    lure,
In time small wedges cleave the hardest
    oak,
In time the flint is pierced with softest
    shower,
And she in time will fall from her dis-
    dain,
And rue the sufferance of your friendly
    pain.
BAL. No, she is wilder and more hard
    withal
  Than beast or bird or tree or stony
    wall.   10
  But wherefore blot I Bel-imperia's name?
  It is my fault, not she, that merits blame.
  My feature is not to content her sight,
  My words are rude and work her no
    delight.
  The lines I send her are but harsh and ill,
  Such as do drop from Pan and Marsyas'
    quill.
  My presents are not of sufficient cost,
  And, being worthless, all my labor's lost.
  Yet might she love me for my valiancy—
  Ay, but that's slandered by captivity.   20
  Yet might she love me to content her
    sire—
  Ay, but her reason masters his desire.
  Yet might she love me as her brother's
    friend—
  Ay, but her hopes aim at some other end.
  Yet might she love me to uprear her
    state—
  Ay, but perhaps she hopes some nobler
    mate.
  Yet might she love me as her beauty's
    thrall—
  Ay, but I fear she cannot love at all.
LOR. My lord, for my sake leave this
    ecstasy,[4]
  And doubt not but we'll find some
    remedy.   30
  Some cause there is that lets you not be
    loved;
  First that must needs be known, and
    then removed.
  What if my sister love some other knight?
BAL. My summer's day will turn to win-
    ter's night.
LOR. I have already found a stratagem
  To sound the bottom of this doubtful
    theme.
[3] Wild.   [4] Frenzy.

My lord, for once you shall be ruled by
  me;
Hinder me not, whate'er you hear or see.
By force or fair means will I cast about
To find the truth of all this question
  out. 40
Ho, Pedringano!
PED.   Signior!
LOR.   *Vien qui presto.*[1]

Enter Pedringano.

PED. Hath your lordship any service to
  command me?
LOR. Ay, Pedringano, service of import,
  And—not to spend the time in trifling
  words—
  Thus stands the case: it is not long, thou
  know'st,
  Since I did shield thee from my father's
  wrath,
  For thy conveyance[2] in Andrea's love,
  For which thou wert adjudged to punish-
  ment.
  I stood betwixt thee and thy punishment,
  And, since, thou knowest how I have
  favored thee. 50
  Now to these favors will I add reward,
  Not with fair words, but store of golden
  coin,
  And lands and living joined with dig-
  nities,
  If thou but satisfy my just demand.
  Tell truth, and have me for thy lasting
  friend.
PED. Whate'er it be your lordship shall de-
  mand,
  My bounden duty bids me tell the truth,
  If case[3] it lie in me to tell the truth.
LOR. Then, Pedringano, this is my de-
  mand:
  Whom loves my sister Bel-imperia? 60
  For she reposeth all her trust in thee.
  Speak, man, and gain both friendship and
  reward.
  I mean, whom loves she in Andrea's
  place?
PED. Alas, my lord, since Don Andrea's
  death
  I have no credit with her as before,
  And therefore know not if she love or no.
LOR. Nay, if thou dally, then I am thy foe,
                  [*Draw his sword.*][4]

And fear shall force what friendship
  cannot win.
Thy death shall bury what thy life con-
  ceals;
Thou diest for more esteeming her than
  me. 70
PED. O, stay, my lord!
LOR. Yet speak the truth, and I will
  guerdon thee,
  And shield thee from whatever can
  ensue,
  And will conceal whate'er proceeds from
  thee.
  But, if thou dally once again, thou diest.
PED. If Madam Bel-imperia be in love—
LOR. What, villain! If's and and's?
                  [*Offer to kill him.*][4]
PED. O, stay, my lord! She loves Horatio.
                  Balthazar starts back.
LOR. What, Don Horatio, our knight
  marshal's son?
PED. Even him, my lord. 80
LOR. Now say but how know'st thou he
  is her love,
  And thou shalt find me kind and lib-
  eral.
  Stand up, I say, and fearless tell the
  truth.
PED. She sent him letters, which myself
  perused,
  Full fraught with lines and arguments of
  love,
  Preferring him before Prince Balthazar.
LOR. Swear on this cross[5] that what thou
  sayst is true,
  And that thou wilt conceal what thou
  hast told.
PED. I swear to both, by Him that made
  us all.
LOR. In hope thine oath is true, here's thy
  reward; 90
  But, if I prove thee perjured and unjust,
  This very sword whereon thou took'st
  thine oath
  Shall be the worker of thy tragedy.
PED. What I have said is true, and shall—
  for me—
  Be still concealed from Bel-imperia.
  Besides, your honor's liberality
  Deserves my duteous service, even till
  death.
LOR. Let this be all that thou shalt do for
  me:

1 Come here quickly.
2 Trickery.
3 In case.
4 From 1602 edn.
5 *I.e.*, sword hilt.

Be watchful when and where these lovers
meet,

And give me notice in some secret
sort.　　　　　　　　　　　　　100

PED. I will, my lord.

LOR. Then shalt thou find that I am
liberal.

Thou know'st that I can more advance
thy state

Than she. Be therefore wise, and fail me
not.

Go and attend her, as thy custom is,

Lest absence make her think thou dost
amiss.　　　　　　*Exit Pedringano.*

Why, so: *tam armis quam ingenio.*[1]

Where words prevail not, violence prevails;

But gold doth more than either of them
both.

How likes Prince Balthazar this stratagem?　　　　　　　　　　　110

BAL. Both well and ill. It makes me glad
and sad:

Glad that I know the hinderer of my
love—

Sad that I fear she hates me whom I
love;

Glad that I know on whom to be revenged—

Sad that she'll fly me if I take revenge.

Yet must I take revenge or die myself,

For love resisted grows impatient.

I think Horatio be my destined plague.

First, in his hand he brandishéd a sword,

And with that sword he fiercely wagéd
war,　　　　　　　　　　　120

And in that war he gave me dangerous
wounds,

And by those wounds he forcéd me to
yield,

And by my yielding I became his slave.

Now in his mouth he carries pleasing
words,

Which pleasing words do harbor sweet
conceits,

Which sweet conceits are limed with sly
deceits,

Which sly deceits smooth Bel-imperia's
ears,

And through her ears dive down into her
heart,

And in her heart set him where I should
stand.

[1] As much by force as by wisdom.

Thus hath he ta'en my body by his
force,　　　　　　　　　　　130

And now by sleight would captivate my
soul.

But in his fall I'll tempt the destinies,

And either lose my life or win my love.

LOR. Let's go, my lord; your staying stays
revenge.

Do you but follow me, and gain your love.

Her favor must be won by his remove.
　　　　　　　　　　　　Exeunt.

[SCENA SECUNDA.

The same.]

Enter Horatio and Bel-imperia.

HOR. Now, madam, since by favor of your
love

Our hidden smoke is turned to open flame,

And that with looks and words we feed
our thought

(Two chief contents, where more cannot
be had),

Thus, in the midst of love's fair blandish-
ments,

Why show you sign of inward languish-
ments?

*Pedringano showeth all to the Prince and
Lorenzo, placing them in secret.*

BEL. My heart, sweet friend, is like a ship
at sea.

She wisheth port, where, riding all at ease,

She may repair what stormy times have
worn,

And, leaning on the shore, may sing with
joy　　　　　　　　　　　　10

That pleasure follows pain, and bliss
annoy.

Possession of thy love is th' only port

Wherein my heart, with fears and hopes
long tossed,

Each hour doth wish and long to make
resort,

There to repair the joys that it hath lost,

And, sitting safe, to sing in Cupid's choir

That sweetest bliss is crown of love's
desire.

Balthazar [and Lorenzo] above.

BAL. O, sleep, mine eyes; see not my love
profaned.

Be deaf, my ears; hear not my discontent.

Die, heart; another joys what thou deservest.　　　　　　　　　　20

Lor. Watch still, mine eyes, to see this love disjoined;
Hear still, mine ears, to hear them both lament;
Live, heart, to joy at fond Horatio's fall.

Bel. Why stands Horatio speechless all this while?
Hor. The less I speak, the more I meditate.
Bel. But whereon dost thou chiefly meditate?
Hor. On dangers past, and pleasures to ensue.

Bal. On pleasures past, and dangers to ensue.

Bel. What dangers and what pleasures dost thou mean?
Hor. Dangers of war, and pleasures of our love.   30

Lor. Dangers of death, but pleasures none at all.

Bel. Let dangers go; thy war shall be with me,
But such a war as breaks no bond of peace.
Speak thou fair words, I'll cross them with fair words;
Send thou sweet looks, I'll meet them with sweet looks;
Write loving lines, I'll answer loving lines;
Give me a kiss, I'll countercheck thy kiss.
Be this our warring peace, or peaceful war.
Hor. But, gracious madam, then appoint the field,
Where trial of this war shall first be made.   40

Bal. Ambitious villain, how his boldness grows!

Bel. Then be thy father's pleasant bower the field,
Where first we vowed a mutual amity.
The court were dangerous; that place is safe.
Our hour shall be when Vesper gins to rise,
That summons home distressful travelers.[1]

[1] The meaning *travailers, workers*, is also possible.

There none shall hear us but the harmless birds;
Happily [2] the gentle nightingale
Shall carol us asleep, ere we be ware,
And, singing with the prickle at her breast,   50
Tell our delight and mirthful dalliance.
Till then each hour will seem a year and more.
Hor. But, honeysweet and honorable love,
Return we now into your father's sight;
Dangerous suspicion waits on our delight.

Lor. Ay, danger mixed with jealous despite
Shall send thy soul into eternal night.
                   Exeunt.

[Scena Tertia.

The Spanish court.]

Enter King of Spain, Portingale Ambassador, Don Cyprian, etc.

King. Brother of Castile, to the prince's love
What says your daughter Bel-imperia?
Cyp. Although she coy it,[3] as becomes her kind,
And yet dissemble that she loves the prince,
I doubt not, I, but she will stoop in time.
And, were she froward, which she will not be,
Yet herein shall she follow my advice,
Which is to love him, or forgo my love.
King. Then, lord ambassador of Portingale,
Advise thy king to make this marriage up   10
For strengthening of our late-confirméd league.
I know no better means to make us friends.
Her dowry shall be large and liberal.
Besides that she is daughter and half-heir
Unto our brother here, Don Cyprian,
And shall enjoy the moiety of his land,
I'll grace her marriage with an uncle's gift,
And this it is: in case the match go forward,

[2] Haply, perhaps.   [3] Pretend to be shy.

The tribute which you pay shall be re-
leased;
And, if by Balthazar she have a son,　20
He shall enjoy the kingdom after us.
AMB. I'll make the motion to my sovereign
liege,
And work it, if my counsel may prevail.
KING. Do so, my lord, and, if he give
consent,
I hope his presence here will honor us
In celebration of the nuptial day;
And let himself determine of the time.
AMB. Will 't please your grace command
me aught beside?
KING. Commend me to the king, and so
farewell.
But where's Prince Balthazar to take his
leave?　　　　　　　　　　　　　30
AMB. That is performed already, my good
lord.
KING. Amongst the rest of what you have
in charge,
The prince's ransom must not be forgot.
That's none of mine, but his that took
him prisoner,
And well his forwardness deserves re-
ward.
It was Horatio, our knight marshal's son.
AMB. Between us there's a price already
pitched,
And shall be sent with all convenient
speed.
KING. Then once again farewell, my lord.
AMB. Farewell, my Lord of Castile, and the
rest.　　　　　　　　　　　　*Exit.*　40
KING. Now, brother, you must take some
little pains
To win fair Bel-imperia from her will.
Young virgins must be ruled by their
friends.
The prince is amiable and loves her well.
If she neglect him and forgo his love,
She both will wrong her own estate and
ours.
Therefore, whiles I do entertain the
prince
With greatest pleasure that our court
affords,
Endeavor you to win your daughter's
thought.
If she give back,[1] all this will come to
naught.　　　　　　　　　　　　50
　　　　　　　　　　　　　　　Exeunt.

[1] Decline.

Enter Horatio, Bel-imperia, and Pedringano.

HOR. Now that the night begins with
sable wings
To overcloud the brightness of the sun,
And that in darkness pleasures may be
done,
Come, Bel-imperia, let us to the bower,
And there in safety pass a pleasant hour.
BEL. I follow thee, my love, and will not
back,
Although my fainting heart controls my
soul.
HOR. Why, make you doubt of Pedrin-
gano's faith?
BEL. No, he is as trusty as my second
self.—
Go, Pedringano, watch without the
gate,　　　　　　　　　　　　10
And let us know if any make approach.
PED. [*Aside.*] Instead of watching, I'll de-
serve more gold
By fetching Don Lorenzo to this match.
　　　　　　　　　　Exit Ped[ringano].
HOR. What means my love?
BEL. 　　　　　　　I know not what myself,
And yet my heart foretells me some mis-
chance.
HOR. Sweet, say not so; fair fortune is our
friend,
And heavens have shut up day to pleas-
ure us.
The stars, thou seest, hold back their
twinkling shine,
And Luna hides herself to pleasure us.
BEL. Thou hast prevailed; I'll conquer my
misdoubt,　　　　　　　　　　20
And in thy love and counsel drown my
fear.
I fear no more; love now is all my
thoughts.
Why sit we not, for pleasure asketh ease?
HOR. The more thou sitt'st within these
leafy bowers,
The more will Flora deck it with her
flowers.
BEL. Ay, but, if Flora spy Horatio here,
Her jealous eye will think I sit too near.
HOR. Hark, madam, how the birds record
by night,
For joy that Bel-imperia sits in sight.
[2] Sing.

BEL. No, Cupid counterfeits the nightingale, 30
To frame sweet music to Horatio's tale.

HOR. If Cupid sing, then Venus is not far.
Ay, thou art Venus, or some fairer star.

BEL. If I be Venus, thou must needs be
Mars;
And, where Mars reigneth, there must
needs be wars.

HOR. Then thus begin our wars. Put forth
thy hand,
That it may combat with my ruder hand.

BEL. Set forth thy foot to try the push of
mine.

HOR. But first my looks shall combat
against thine.

BEL. Then ward thyself: I dart this kiss
at thee. 40

HOR. Thus I retort the dart thou threw'st
at me.

BEL. Nay, then, to gain the glory of the
field
My twining arms shall yoke and make
thee yield.

HOR. Nay, then, my arms are large and
strong withal.
Thus elms by vines are compassed, till
they fall.

BEL. O, let me go, for in my troubled eyes
Now mayst thou read that life in passion
dies.

HOR. O, stay awhile, and I will die with
thee;
So shalt thou yield, and yet have conquered me.

BEL. Who's there? Pedringano?—We are
betrayed! 50

Enter Lorenzo, Balthazar, Serberine, Pedrin-
gano, disguised.

LOR. My lord, away with her; take her
aside.—
O, sir, forbear! Your valor is already
tried.—
Quickly despatch, my masters.
They hang him in the arbor.

HOR. What, will you murder me?

LOR. Ay, thus, and thus! These are the
fruits of love. *They stab him.*

BEL. O, save his life, and let me die for
him!
O, save him, brother! Save him, Balthazar!
I loved Horatio, but he loved not me.

BAL. But Balthazar loves Bel-imperia.

LOR. Although his life were still ambitious,
proud,
Yet is he at the highest now he is dead. 60

BEL. Murder! Murder! Help, Hieronimo,
help!

LOR. Come, stop her mouth; away with
her. *Exeunt.*

Enter Hieronimo in his shirt, etc.

HIER. What outcries pluck me from my
naked bed,
And chill my throbbing heart with
trembling fear,
Which never danger yet could daunt
before?
Who calls Hieronimo? Speak, here I am.
I did not slumber; therefore 'twas no
dream.
No, no, it was some woman cried for help,
And here within this garden did she cry,
And in this garden must I rescue her.— 70
But stay, what murd'rous spectacle is
this?
A man hanged up and all the murderers
gone!
And in my bower, to lay the guilt on me!
This place was made for pleasure, not
for death. *He cuts him down.*
Those garments that he wears I oft have
seen—
Alas, it is Horatio, my sweet son!
O, no, but he that whilom [1] was my son!
O, was it thou that calledst me from my
bed?
O, speak, if any spark of life remain.
I am thy father. Who hath slain my
son? 80
What savage monster, not of human
kind,
Hath here been glutted with thy harm-
less blood,
And left thy bloody corpse dishonored
here,
For me, amidst these dark and deathful
shades,
To drown thee with an ocean of my tears?
O heavens, why made you night to cover
sin?
By day this deed of darkness had not
been.
O earth, why didst thou not in time
devour

[1] Formerly.

The vild [1] profaner of this sacred bower?
O poor Horatio, what hadst thou mis-
done,   9C
To leese [2] thy life ere life was new begun?
O wicked butcher, whatsoe'er thou wert,
How could thou strangle virtue and
desert?
Ay me most wretched, that have lost my
joy,
In leesing my Horatio, my sweet boy!

Enter Isabel[la].

ISAB. My husband's absence makes my
heart to throb.—
Hieronimo!
HIER. Here, Isabella, help me to lament,
For sighs are stopped, and all my tears
are spent.
ISAB. What world of grief! My son
Horatio!   100
O, where's the author of this endless
woe?
HIER. To know the author were some ease
of grief,
For in revenge my heart would find relief.
ISAB. Then is he gone? And is my son gone
too?
O, gush out, tears, fountains and floods
of tears;
Blow, sighs, and raise an everlasting
storm,
For outrage fits our curséd wretchedness! [3]
Ay me, Hieronimo, sweet husband, speak!
HIER. He supped with us tonight, frolic
and merry,
And said he would go visit Balthazar 110
At the duke's palace—there the prince
doth lodge.
He had no custom to stay out so late;
He may be in his chamber. Some go see.
Roderigo, ho!

Enter Pedro and Jaques.

ISAB. Ay me, he raves!—Sweet Hier-
onimo!
HIER. True, all Spain takes note of it.
Besides, he is so generally beloved;
His majesty the other day did grace him

[1] Vile.   [2] Lose.
[3] The first of the additions begins here and
extends through l. 160. Some modern editors
have attempted without success to improve the
form of the verse in these additions by changing
the division of lines. Here the line division of
the original has been kept in all the additions.

With waiting on his cup. These be favors
Which do assure me [he] [4] cannot be
short-lived.
ISAB. Sweet Hieronimo!   120
HIER. I wonder how this fellow got his
clothes!—
Sirrah, sirrah, I'll know the truth of all.
Jaques, run to the Duke of Castile's
presently,
And bid my son Horatio to come home.
I and his mother have had strange
dreams tonight.
Do ye hear me, sir?
JAQUES. Ay, sir.
HIER. Well, sir, be gone. Pedro, come
hither. Know'st thou who this is?
PED. Too well, sir.
HIER. Too well! Who, who is it? Peace,
Isabella! Nay, blush not, man.   130
PED. It is my lord Horatio.
HIER. Ha, ha! St. James, but this doth
make me laugh,
That there are more deluded than my-
self.
PED. Deluded?
HIER. Ay, I would have sworn myself,
within this hour,
That this had been my son Horatio,
His garments are so like. Ha! Are they
not great persuasions?
ISAB. O, would to God it were not so!
HIER. Were not, Isabella? Dost thou
dream it is?   139
Can thy soft bosom entertain a thought
That such a black deed of mischief should
be done
On one so pure and spotless as our son?
Away, I am ashamed.
ISAB. Dear Hieronimo, cast a more serious
eye upon thy grief;
Weak apprehension gives but weak
belief.
HIER. It was a man, sure, that was hanged
up here;
A youth, as I remember. I cut him down.
If it should prove my son now after all—
Say you? Say you?—Light! Lend me
a taper;
Let me look again.—   150
O God! Confusion, mischief, torment,
death, and hell,
Drop all your stings at once in my cold
bosom,

[4] From 1603 edn.

That now is stiff with horror. Kill me
　quickly!
Be gracious to me, thou infective [1] night,
And drop this deed of murder down on
　me.
Gird in my waste of grief with thy large
　darkness,
And let me not survive to see the light
May put me in the mind I had a son.

Isab. O sweet Horatio! O my dearest
　son!

Hier. How strangely had I lost my way
　to grief!　　　　　　　　　　　160
　Sweet, lovely rose, ill-plucked before thy
　　time,
　Fair, worthy son, not conquered, but
　　betrayed,
　I'll kiss thee now, for words with tears
　　are stayed.

Isab. And I'll close up the glasses of his
　sight,
　For once these eyes were only my de-
　　light.

Hier. Seest thou this handkercher be-
　smeared with blood?
　It shall not from me, till I take revenge.
　Seest thou those wounds that yet are
　　bleeding fresh?
　I'll not entomb them, till I have revenged.
　Then will I joy amidst my discontent; 170
　Till then my sorrow never shall be spent.

Isab. The heavens are just; murder can-
　not be hid.
　Time is the author both of truth and
　　right,
　And time will bring this treachery to
　　light.

Hier. Meanwhile, good Isabella, cease thy
　plaints,
　Or, at the least, dissemble them awhile.
　So shall we sooner find the practice [2] out,
　And learn by whom all this was brought
　　about.
　Come, Isabel, now let us take him up,
　　　　　　　　　　They take him up.
　And bear him in from out this cursèd
　　place.　　　　　　　　　　180
　I'll say his dirge; singing fits not this case.

O aliquis mihi quas pulchrum ver educat
　　herbas,　　　　　　Hiero[nimo] sets his
　　　　　　　　　　　　breast unto his sword.
Misceat, et nostro detur medicina dolori;

[1] Infectious.　　　　　　　　[2] Plot.

Aut, si qui faciunt annorum oblivia,
　　succos
Præbeat; ipse metam magnum quæcunque
　　per orbem
Gramina Sol pulchras effert in luminis oras;
Ipse bibam quicquid meditatur saga veneni,
Quicquid et herbarum vi cæca nenia nectit:
Omnia perpetiar, lethum quoque, dum
　　semel omnis
Noster in extincto moriatur pectore sen-
　　sus.　　　　　　　　　　190
Ergo tuos oculos nunquam, mea vita,
　　videbo?
Et tua perpetuus sepelivit lumina somnus?
Emoriar tecum: sic, sic, juvat ire sub
　　umbras.
At tamen absistam properato cedere letho,
Ne mortem vindicta tuam tam nulla
　　sequatur. [3]

　　　Here he throws it from him
　　　and bears the body away.

[Chorus]

Andrea. Brought'st thou me hither to in-
　crease my pain?
　I looked that Balthazar should have
　　been slain,
　But 'tis my friend Horatio that is slain,
　And they abuse fair Bel-imperia,
　On whom I doted more than all the
　　world,　　　　　　　　　　200
　Because she loved me more than all the
　　world.

Revenge. Thou talk'st of harvest when
　the corn is green.
　The end is crown of every work well
　　done;

[3] O, let some one mingle for me herbs which
beautiful spring brings forth, and let a medicine
be given for my pain. Or let one furnish whatever juices provide forgetfulness of the years.
Myself shall reap whatever grasses throughout
the great world the sun brings forth to the fair
shores of light. Myself shall drink whatever
poison a witch devises and whatever of herbs
the incantation weaves by secret power. All
things shall I suffer patiently, even death, provided once for all all feeling die in my extin-
guished breast. And so shall I never see your
eyes, my life? And hath perpetual sleep buried
your orbs? I shall die with you: so, so it pleases
me to go down to the shades. But yet I shall
abstain from going in hastened death [i.e., by
suicide], lest by so doing no vengeance should
follow your death (a patchwork of verses from
Virgil, Lucretius, Horace, Tibullus, Catullus,
etc.).

The sickle comes not till the corn be ripe.
Be still, and, ere I lead thee from this place,
I'll show thee Balthazar in heavy case.

ACTUS TERTIUS. [SCENA PRIMA.

The Portuguese court.]

*Enter Viceroy of Portingale, Nobles, Alex-
andro, Villuppo.*

VIC. Infortunate condition of kings,
Seated amidst so many helpless doubts!
First we are placed upon extremest height,
And oft supplanted with exceeding hate,
But ever subject to the wheel of chance.
And at our highest never joy we so
As we both doubt and dread our over-
throw.
So striveth not the waves with sundry winds
As Fortune toileth in the affairs of kings,
That would be feared, yet fear to be beloved, 10
Sith ¹ fear or love to kings is flattery.²
For instance, lordings, look upon your king,
By hate deprivéd of his dearest son,
The only hope of our successive line.
[1] NOB. I had not thought that Alex-
andro's heart
Had been envenomed with such extreme hate;
But now I see that words have several works,
And there's no credit in the countenance.
VIL. No; for, my lord, had you beheld the train ³
That feignéd love had colored in his looks, 20
When he in camp consorted ⁴ Balthazar,
Far more inconstant had you thought the sun,
That hourly coasts ⁵ the center of the earth,
Than Alexandro's purpose to the prince.
VIC. No more, Villuppo, thou hast said enough,
And with thy words thou slayest our wounded thoughts.

Nor shall I longer dally with the world,
Procrastinating Alexandro's death.
Go, some of you, and fetch the traitor forth
That, as he is condemnéd, he may die. 30

*Enter Alexandro with a Nobleman and
Halberts.*

NOB. In such extremes will naught but patience serve.
ALEX. But in extremes what patience shall I use?
Nor discontents it me to leave the world,
With whom there nothing can prevail but wrong.
NOB. Yet hope the best.
ALEX.   'Tis heaven is my hope.
As for the earth, it is too much infect
To yield me hope of any of her mold.
VIC. Why linger ye? Bring forth that daring fiend,
And let him die for his accurséd deed.
ALEX. Not that I fear the extremity of death 40
(For nobles cannot stoop to servile fear)
Do I, O king, thus discontented live.
But this, O, this, torments my laboring soul,
That thus I die suspected of a sin
Whereof, as heavens have known my secret thoughts,
So am I free from this suggestion.
VIC. No more, I say! To the tortures! When? ⁶
Bind him, and burn his body in those flames, *They bind him to the stake.*
That shall prefigure those unquenchéd fires
Of Phlegeton, preparéd for his soul. 50
ALEX. My guiltless death will be avenged on thee,
On thee, Villuppo, that hath maliced ⁷ thus,
Or for thy meed hast falsely me accused.
VIL. Nay, Alexandro, if thou menace me,
I'll lend a hand to send thee to the lake ⁸
Where those thy words shall perish with thy works,
Injurious traitor! Monstrous homicide!

¹ Since.
² The preceding passage is based on Seneca's
gamemnon, ll. 57–73.   ⁴ Accompanied.
³ Deception.   ⁵ Moves round.

⁶ An expression of impatience.
⁷ Entertained malice.
⁸ *I.e.,* Avernus.

Enter Ambassador.

[AMB.] Stay, hold awhile;
And here—with pardon of his majesty—
Lay hands upon Villuppo.

VIC.   Ambassador, 60
What news hath urged this sudden entrance?

AMB. Know, sovereign l[ord], that Balthazar doth live.

VIC. What sayest thou? Liveth Balthazar our son?

AMB. Your highness' son, L[ord] Balthazar, doth live,
And, well entreated in the court of Spain,
Humbly commends him to your majesty.
These eyes beheld, and these my followers';
With these, the letters of the king's commends[1]   *Gives him letters.*
Are happy witnesses of his highness' health.

The King looks on the letters, and proceeds.

VIC. "Thy son doth live; your tribute is received.   70
Thy peace is made, and we are satisfied.
The rest resolve upon as things proposed
For both our honors and thy benefit."

AMB. These are his highness' farther articles.   *He gives him more letters.*

VIC. Accursèd wretch, to intimate these ills
Against the life and reputation
Of noble Alexandro! Come, my lord, unbind him.—
Let him unbind thee, that is bound to death,
To make a quital[2] for thy discontent.
                    They unbind him.

ALEX. Dread lord, in kindness[3] you could do no less   80
Upon report of such a damnèd fact.[4]
But thus we see our innocence hath saved
The hopeless life which thou, Villuppo, sought
By thy suggestions to have massacred.

VIC. Say, false Villuppo, wherefore didst thou thus
Falsely betray Lord Alexandro's life—
Him whom thou knowest that no unkindness else

But even the slaughter of our dearest son
Could once have moved us to have misconceived?

ALEX. Say, treacherous Villuppo, tell the king: 90
Wherein[5] hath Alexandro used thee ill?

VIL. Rent with remembrance of so foul a deed,
My guilty soul submits me to thy doom;
For not for Alexandro's injuries,
But for reward and hope to be preferred,
Thus have I shamelessly hazarded his life.

VIC. Which, villain, shall be ransomed with thy death,
And not so mean[6] a torment as we here
Devised for him who, thou said'st, slew our son,
But with the bitterest torments and extremes   100
That may be yet invented for thine end.
                    Alex[andro] seems to entreat.
Entreat me not.—Go, take the traitor hence.—   *Exit Vil[luppo].*
And, Alexandro, let us honor thee
With public notice of thy loyalty.—
To end those things articulated here
By our great lord, the mighty King of Spain,
We with our council will deliberate.
Come, Alexandro, keep us company.
                    Exeunt.

[SCENA SECUNDA.

Near the place of Bel-imperia's confinement.]

Enter Hieronimo.

HIER. O eyes! No eyes, but fountains fraught with tears!
O life! No life, but lively form of death!
O world! No world, but mass of public wrongs,
Confused and filled with murder and misdeeds!
O sacred heavens, if this unhallowed deed,
If this inhuman and barbarous attempt,
If this incomparable murder thus
Of mine, but now no more my son,
Shall unrevealed and unrevengèd pass,

[1] Commendations.   [2] Requital.   [3] Nature.
[4] Deed.   [5] Emended by Hazlitt. Early edns. read *or wherein.*   [6] Moderate.

How should we term your dealings to be
  just,   10
If you unjustly deal with those that in
  your justice trust?
The night, sad secretary[1] to my moans,
With direful visions wake my vexéd soul,
And with the wounds of my distressful
  son
Solicit me for notice of his death.
The ugly fiends do sally forth of hell,
And frame my steps to unfrequented
  paths,
And fear my heart with fierce inflaméd
  thoughts.
The cloudy day my discontents records,
Early begins to register my dreams,   20
And drive me forth to seek the murderer.
Eyes, life, world, heavens, hell, night,
  and day,
See, search, show, send some man, some
  mean, that may—   *A letter falleth.*
What's here? A letter? Tush! It is not
  so!—
A letter written to Hieronimo! *Red ink.*
"For want of ink, receive this bloody
  writ.
Me hath my hapless brother hid from
  thee.
Revenge thyself on Balthazar and him,
For these were they that murderéd thy
  son.
Hieronimo, revenge Horatio's death,   30
And better fare than Bel-imperia doth."
What means this unexpected miracle?
My son slain by Lorenzo and the prince!
What cause had they Horatio to malign?
Or what might move thee, Bel-imperia,
To accuse thy brother, had he been the
  mean?
Hieronimo, beware!   Thou art be-
  trayed,
And to entrap thy life this train is laid.
Advise thee therefore; be not credulous.
This is deviséd to endanger thee,   40
That thou, by this, Lorenzo shouldst
  accuse;
And he, for thy dishonor done, should
  draw
Thy life in question and thy name in
  hate.
Dear was the life of my beloved son,
And of his death behoves me be revenged;
Then hazard not thine own, Hieronimo,
But live t' effect thy resolution.

I therefore will by circumstances[2] try
What I can gather to confirm this writ;
And, hearkening near the Duke of Cas-
  tile's house,   50
Close, if I can, with Bel-imperia,
To listen more, but nothing to bewray.

Enter Pedringano.

Now, Pedringano!
PED.   Now, Hieronimo!
HIER. Where's thy lady?
PED.   I know not. Here's my lord.

Enter Lorenzo.

LOR. How now, who's this? Hieronimo?
HIER.   My lord!
PED. He asketh for my lady Bel-imperia.
LOR. What to do, Hieronimo? The duke,
  my father, hath
  Upon some disgrace awhile removed her
    hence;
  But, if it be aught I may inform her of,
  Tell me, Hieronimo, and I'll let her know
    it.   60
HIER. Nay, nay, my lord, I thank you; it
  shall not need.
  I had a suit unto her, but too late,
  And her disgrace makes me unfortunate.
LOR. Why so, Hieronimo? Use me.[3]
HIER. Who? You, my lord?
  I reserve your favor for a greater honor;
  This is a very toy,[4] my lord, a toy.
LOR. All's one, Hieronimo; acquaint me
  with it.
HIER. I' faith, my lord, 'tis an idle thing,
  I must confess;
  I ha' been too slack, too tardy, too re-
    miss unto your honor.   70
LOR. How now, Hieronimo?
HIER. In troth, my lord, it is a thing of
  nothing,
  The murder of a son, or so—
  A thing of nothing, my lord!
LOR.   Why then, farewell.
HIER. My grief no heart, my thoughts no
  tongue can tell.   *Exit.*

---

[1] Confidant.   [2] Roundabout methods.
[3] The passage from this point through "nothing, my lord!" in l.74 is substituted in the
1602 edn. for the following speech of Hieronimo
in the original:
  O, no, my lord, I dare not; it must not be.
  I humbly thank your lordship.
[4] Trifle.

LOR. Come hither, Pedringano, seest thou this?

PED. My lord, I see it, and suspect it too.

LOR. This is that damnéd villain Serberine
That hath, I fear, revealed Horatio's death.

PED. My lord, he could not, 'twas so lately done;   80
And, since, he hath not left my company.

LOR. Admit he have not, his condition's such
  As fear or flattering words may make him false.
  I know his humor,[1] and therewith repent
  That e'er I used him in this enterprise.
  But, Pedringano, to prevent the worst,
  And 'cause I know thee secret as my soul,
  Here, for thy further satisfaction, take thou this,   *Gives him more gold.*
  And hearken to me. Thus it is devised:
  This night thou must (and, prithee, so resolve)   90
  Meet Serberine at S[aint] Luigi's Park—
  Thou know'st 'tis here hard by behind the house.
  There take thy stand, and see thou strike him sure,
  For die he must, if we do mean to live.

PED. But how shall Serberine be there, my lord?

LOR. Let me alone; I'll send to him to meet
  The prince and me, where thou must do this deed.

PED. It shall be done, my l[ord], it shall be done;
  And I'll go arm myself to meet him there.

LOR. When things shall alter, as I hope they will,   100
  Then shalt thou mount for this; thou knowest my mind.
                            Exit Ped[ringano].
  Che le Ieron![2]

Enter Page.

PAGE.   My lord?

LOR.   Go, sirrah,
  To Serberine, and bid him forthwith meet

---

[1] Disposition, character.
[2] Unintelligible. Probably a call to the page.

The prince and me at S[aint] Luigi's Park,
Behind the house, this evening, boy.

PAGE.   I go, my lord.

LOR. But, sirrah, let the hour be eight a-clock.
Bid him not fail.

PAGE.   I fly, my lord. *Exit.*

LOR. Now to confirm the complot thou hast cast
Of all these practices, I'll spread the watch,
Upon precise commandment from the king,   110
Strongly to guard the place where Pedringano
This night shall murder hapless Serberine.
Thus must we work that will avoid distrust;
Thus must we practice to prevent mishap;
And thus one ill another must expulse.
This sly inquiry of Hieronimo
For Bel-imperia breeds suspicion,
And this suspicion bodes a further ill.
As for myself, I know my secret fault,
And so do they. But I have dealt for them.   120
They that for coin their souls endangeréd,
To save my life, for coin shall venture theirs;
And better it's that base companions die
Than by their life to hazard our good haps.
Nor shall they live, for me to fear their faith.
I'll trust myself, myself shall be my friend;
For die they shall; slaves are ordainéd
to no other end.   *Exit.*

[SCENA TERTIA.

Saint Luigi's Park.]

Enter Pedringano, with a pistol.

[PED.] Now, Pedringano, bid thy pistol hold;
And hold on, Fortune; once more favor me.
Give but success to mine attempting spirit,
And let me shift for taking of mine aim.

Here is the gold. This is the gold pro-
posed.
It is no dream that I adventure for,
But Pedringano is possessed thereof.
And he that would not strain his con-
science
For him that thus his liberal purse hath
stretched,
Unworthy such a favor, may he fail,   10
And, wishing, want when such as I pre-
vail.
As for the fear of apprehension,
I know, if need should be, my noble
lord
Will stand between me and ensuing
harms.
Besides, this place is free from all sus-
pect.
Here therefore will I stay and take my
stand.

Enter the Watch.

1 [WATCH.] I wonder much to what intent it is
That we are thus expressly charged to
watch.
2 [WATCH.] 'Tis by commandment in the
king's own name.
3 [WATCH.] But we were never wont to
watch and ward   20
So near the duke his brother's house
before.
2 [WATCH.] Content yourself. Stand close;
there's somewhat in 't.

Enter Serberine.

SER. Here, Serberine, attend and stay
thy pace,
For here did Don Lorenzo's page appoint
That thou by his command shouldst
meet with him.
How fit a place—if one were so disposed—
Methinks this corner is, to close¹ with
one.
PED. Here comes the bird that I must
seize upon.
Now, Pedringano, or never, play the
man!
SER. I wonder that his lordship stays
so long,   30
Or wherefore should he send for me so
late?

PED. For this, Serberine!—and thou shalt
ha't.   *Shoots the dag.*²
So, there he lies; my promise is performed.

The Watch.

1 [WATCH.] Hark, gentlemen, this is a
pistol shot.
2 [WATCH.] And here's one slain! Stay
the murderer.
PED. Now by the sorrows of the souls in
hell,   *He strives with the Watch.*
Who first lays hand on me, I'll be his
priest.
3 [WATCH.] Sirrah, confess, and therein
play the priest.
Why hast thou thus unkindly³ killed
the man?
PED. Why? Because he walked abroad
so late.   40
3 [WATCH.] Come, sir, you had been better kept your bed
Than have committed this misdeed so
late.
2 [WATCH.] Come, to the marshal's with
the murderer!
1 [WATCH.] On to Hieronimo's! Help me
here
To bring the murdered body with us
too.
PED. Hieronimo? Carry me before whom
you will.
Whate'er he be, I'll answer him and
you;
And do your worst, for I defy you all.
     Exeunt.

[SCENA QUARTA.

A room in Don Cyprian's palace.]

Enter Lorenzo and Balthazar.

BAL. How now, my lord, what makes
you rise so soon?
LOR. Fear of preventing our mishaps too
late.
BAL. What mischief is it that we not mistrust?⁴
LOR. Our greatest ills we least mistrust,
my lord,
And inexpected harms do hurt us
most.

¹ Grapple.   ³ Unnaturally.
² Pistol.   ⁴ Suspect.

BAL. Why, tell me, Don Lorenzo, tell me, man,

If aught concerns our honor and your own.

LOR. Nor you, nor me, my lord, but both in one;

For I suspect—and the presumption's great—

That by those base confederates in our fault   10

Touching the death of Don Horatio,

We are betrayed to old Hieronimo.

BAL. Betrayed, Lorenzo? Tush! It cannot be.

LOR. A guilty conscience, urgéd with the thought

Of former evils, easily cannot err.

I am persuaded—and dissuade me not—

That all's revealéd to Hieronimo.

And therefore know that I have cast it thus—

[Enter Page.] [1]

But here's the page. How now? What news with thee?

PAGE. My lord, Serberine is slain.

BAL.   Who? Serberine, my man?   20

PAGE. Your highness' man, my lord.

LOR.   Speak, page, who murdered him?

PAGE. He that is apprehended for the fact.

LOR. Who?

PAGE. Pedringano.

BAL. Is Serberine slain, that loved his lord so well?

Injurious villain, murderer of his friend!

LOR. Hath Pedringano murdered Serberine?

My lord, let me entreat you to take the pains

To exasperate and hasten his revenge[2]

With your complaints unto my l[ord] the king.   30

This their dissension breeds a greater doubt.

BAL. Assure thee, Don Lorenzo, he shall die,

Or else his highness hardly shall deny.[3]

Meanwhile I'll haste the marshal-sessions,

For die he shall for this his damnéd deed.

          Exit Balt[hazar].

---

[1] From 1615 edn.   [2] Revenge on him.
[3] *I.e.*, shall with difficulty deny my demand.

LOR. Why so, this fits our former policy,

And thus experience bids the wise to deal.

I lay the plot; he prosecutes the point.

I set the trap; he breaks the worthless twigs,

And sees not that wherewith the bird was limed.   40

Thus hopeful men, that mean to hold their own,

Must look like fowlers to their dearest friends.

He runs to kill whom I have holp [4] to catch,

And no man knows it was my reaching fatch.[5]

'Tis hard to trust unto a multitude,

Or anyone, in mine opinion,

When men themselves their secrets will reveal.

Enter a Messenger with a letter.

Boy!

PAGE. My lord.

LOR. What's he?

MES.   I have a letter to your lordship.

LOR. From whence?

MES.   From Pedringano that's imprisoned.   51

LOR. So he is in prison then?

MES.   Ay, my good lord.

LOR. What would he with us?—He writes us here

To stand good lord, and help him in distress.—

Tell him I have his letters, know his mind,

And what we may, let him assure him of.

Fellow, begone; my boy shall follow thee.   *Exit Mes[senger].*

This works like wax; yet once more try thy wits.

Boy, go, convey this purse to Pedringano.

Thou know'st the prison. Closely [6] give it him,   60

And be advised that none be there about.

Bid him be merry still, but secret;

And, though the marshal-sessions be today,

---

[4] Helped.   [5] Deep-reaching trick.   [6] Secretly.

Bid him not doubt of his delivery.
Tell him his pardon is already signed,
And thereon bid him boldly be re-
solved;
For, were he ready to be turnéd off[1]—
As 'tis my will the uttermost be tried—
Thou with his pardon shalt attend him
still.
Show him this box; tell him his pardon's
in't;　　　　　　　　　　　　　　　70
But open't not, an if [2] thou lov'st thy
life,
But let him wisely keep his hopes un-
known.
He shall not want while Don Lorenzo
lives.
Away!
PAGE. I go, my lord, I run.
LOR. But, sirrah, see that this be cleanly [3]
done.　　　　　　　　　　*Exit Page.*
Now stands our fortune on a tickle
point,
And now or never ends Lorenzo's doubts.
One only thing is uneffected yet,
And that's to see the executioner.　　80
But to what end? I list not trust the
air
With utterance of our pretense [4] therein,
For fear the privy whisp'ring of the
wind
Convey our words amongst unfriendly
ears,
That lie too open to advantages.[5]
E quel che voglio io, nessun lo sa;
Intendo io; quel mi basterà.[6]　　　*Exit.*

[SCENA QUINTA.

A street.]

Enter Boy with the box.

[BOY.] My master hath forbidden me to
look in this box, and, by my troth, 'tis
likely, if he had not warned me, I should
not have had so much idle time; for we
men's-kind in our minority are like women
in their uncertainty—that they are most
forbidden, they will soonest attempt. So
I now.—By my bare honesty, here's noth-

---

[1] Hanged.
[2] An emphatic form of *if*.
[3] Adroitly.
[4] Intention.
[5] Opportunities.
[6] And what I wish, that no one knows. I
intend it; that will be enough for me (source
unknown).

ing but the bare empty box! Were it not
sin against secrecy, I would say it [10
were a piece of gentlemanlike knavery.
I must go to Pedringano, and tell him his
pardon is in this box; nay, I would have
sworn it, had I not seen the contrary. I
cannot choose but smile to think how the
villain will flout the gallows, scorn the
audience, and descant on the hangman,
and all presuming of his pardon from
hence. Will 't not be an odd jest for me
to stand and grace every jest he makes, [20
pointing my finger at this box, as who
would say, "Mock on, here's thy warrant"? Is 't not a scurvy jest that a man
should jest himself to death? Alas, poor
Pedringano, I am in a sort sorry for thee;
but, if I should be hanged with thee, I
cannot weep.　　　　　　　　　*Exit.*

[SCENA SEXTA.

The Court of Justice.]

Enter Hieronimo and the Deputy.

HIER. Thus must we toil in other men's
extremes,
That know not how to remedy our
own,
And do them justice, when unjustly
we,
For all our wrongs, can compass no
redress.
But shall I never live to see the day
That I may come, by justice of the
heavens,
To know the cause that may my cares
allay?
This toils [7] my body, this consumeth
age,
That only I to all men just must be,
And neither gods nor men be just to
me.　　　　　　　　　　　　　　10
DEP. Worthy Hieronimo, your office asks
A care to punish such as do transgress.
HIER. So is 't my duty to regard his death
Who, when he lived, deserved my
dearest blood.
But come, for that we came for! Let's
begin,
For here lies that which bids me to be
gone.

---

[7] Taxes.

Enter Officers, [Hangman,] Boy, and Ped-
ringano, with a letter in his hand, bound.

DEP. Bring forth the prisoner, for the
    court is set.
PED. Gramercy, boy, but it was time to
    come,
For I had written to my lord anew
A nearer matter that concerneth him,   20
For fear his lordship had forgotten me.
But sith he hath remembered me so
    well—
Come, come, come on, when shall we
    to this gear? ¹
HIER. Stand forth, thou monster, mur-
    derer of men,
And here, for satisfaction of the world,
Confess thy folly, and repent thy fault;
For there's thy place of execution.
PED. This is short work. Well, to your
    marshalship
First I confess—nor fear I death there-
    for—
I am the man; 'twas I slew Serberine.   30
But, sir, then you think this shall be
    the place
Where we shall satisfy you for this gear?
DEP. Ay, Pedringano.
PED.   Now I think not so.
HIER. Peace, impudent, for thou shalt
    find it so;
For blood with blood shall, while I sit
    as judge,
Be satisfiéd, and the law discharged.
And, though myself cannot receive the
    like,
Yet will I see that others have their
    right.
Despatch! The fault's approvéd ² and
    confessed,
And by our law he is condemned to die. 40
HANG. Come on, sir, are you ready?
PED. To do what, my fine, officious
    knave?
HANG. To go to this gear.
PED. O, sir, you are too forward. Thou
wouldst fain furnish me with a halter, to
disfurnish me of my habit.³ So I should
go out of this gear, my raiment, into that
gear, the rope. But, hangman, now I spy
your knavery, I'll not change without
boot;⁴ that's flat.   50

HANG. Come, sir.
PED. So, then, I must up?
HANG. No remedy.
PED. Yes, but there shall be for my
coming down.
HANG. Indeed, here's a remedy for that.
PED. How? Be turned off?
HANG. Ay, truly. Come, are you ready?
I pray, sir, despatch; the day goes away.
PED. What, do you hang by the hour?
If you do, I may chance to break your
old custom.   62
HANG. Faith, you have reason, for I
am like to break your young neck.
PED. Dost thou mock me, hangman?
Pray God, I be not preserved to break
your knave's pate for this.
HANG. Alas, sir, you are a foot too low
to reach it, and I hope you will never
grow so high while I am in the office.   70
PED. Sirrah, dost see yonder boy with
the box in his hand?
HANG. What, he that points to it with
his finger?
PED. Ay, that companion.
HANG. I know him not. But what of
him?
PED. Dost thou think to live till his
old doublet will make thee a new truss?⁵
HANG. Ay, and many a fair year after, [80
to truss up many an honester man than
either thou or he.
PED. What hath he in his box, as thou
think'st?
HANG. Faith, I cannot tell, nor I care
not greatly. Methinks you should rather
hearken to your soul's health.
PED. Why, sirrah hangman, I take it
that that is good for the body is likewise
good for the soul; and, it may be, in [90
that box is balm for both.
HANG. Well, thou art even the merriest piece of man's flesh that e'er groaned
at my office door!
PED. Is your roguery become an office
with a knave's name?
HANG. Ay, and that shall all they witness that see you seal it with a thief's
name.
PED. I prithee, request this good [100
company to pray with me.

---

¹ Business.   ² Proved.
³ The hangman received the criminal's garments.   ⁴ Profit, with a pun.

⁵ The term was used both for a close-fitting
body garment and for tight, short breeches or
drawers.

HANG. Ay, marry, sir, this is a good
motion.—My masters, you see here's a
good fellow.

PED. Nay, nay, now I remember me,
let them alone till some other time, for
now I have no great need.

HIER. I have not seen a wretch so impudent.

O monstrous times, where murder's
set so light,

And where the soul, that should be
shrined in heaven,　　　　　110

Solely delights in interdicted things,

Still wand'ring in the thorny passages,

That intercepts itself of [1] happiness.

Murder! O bloody monster! God forbid

A fault so foul should scape unpunishéd.

Despatch, and see this execution done!—

This makes me to remember thee, my
son.　　　　　*Exit Hiero[nimo].*

PED. Nay, soft, no haste.

DEP. Why, wherefore stay you?　Have
you hope of life?

PED. Why, ay!　　　　　120

HANG. As how?

PED. Why, rascal, by my pardon from
the king.

HANG. Stand you on that?　Then you
shall off with this.　*He turns him off.*

DEP. So, executioner!—Convey him hence,

But let his body be unburied.

Let not the earth be chokéd or infect

With that which heaven contemns, and
men neglect.　　　　　*Exeunt.*

[SCENA SEPTIMA.

A room in Hieronimo's house.]

Enter Hieronimo.

[HIER.] Where shall I run to breathe
abroad my woes,

My woes, whose weight hath weariéd
the earth,

Or mine exclaims,[2] that have surcharged
the air

With ceaseless plaints for my deceaséd
son?

The blust'ring winds, conspiring with my
words,

At my lament have moved the leafless
trees,

Disrobed the meadows of their flowered
green,

[1] Bars itself from.　　　　[2] Exclamations.

Made mountains marsh with spring tides
of my tears,

And broken through the brazen gates of
hell.

Yet still tormented is my tortured soul 10

With broken sighs and restless passions,

That, wingéd, mount, and hovering in
the air,

Beat at the windows of the brightest
heavens,

Soliciting for justice and revenge.

But they are placed in those imperial[3]
heights,

Where, countermured[4] with walls of diamond,

I find the place impregnable; and they

Resist my woes, and give my words no
way.

Enter Hangman with a letter.

HANG. O Lord, sir! God bless you, sir!
The man, sir, Petergade, sir, he that 　[20
was so full of merry conceits—

HIER. Well, what of him?

HANG. O Lord, sir, he went the wrong
way; the fellow had a fair commission to
the contrary.　Sir, here is his passport.　I
pray you, sir, we have done him wrong.

HIER. I warrant thee; give it me.

HANG. You will stand between the
gallows and me?

HIER. Ay, ay.　　　　　30

HANG. I thank your l[ord] worship.
　　　　　Exit Hangman.

HIER. And yet, though somewhat nearer
me concerns,

I will, to ease the grief that I sustain,

Take truce with sorrow while I read on
this.

"My lord, I write, as mine extremes
required,

That you would labor my delivery.

If you neglect, my life is desperate,

And in my death I shall reveal the troth.

You know, my lord, I slew him for your
sake,

And was confederate with the prince and
you;　　　　　40

Won by rewards and hopeful promises,

I holp to murder Don Horatio too."—

Holp he to murder mine Horatio?

And actors in th' accurséd tragedy

Wast thou, Lorenzo, Balthazar and thou,

[3] Empyreal(?).　　　　[4] Doubly walled.

Of whom my son, my son, deserved so
 well?
What have I heard? What have mine
 eyes beheld?
O sacred heavens, may it come to pass
That such a monstrous and detested
 deed,
So closely smothered, and so long con-
 cealed,   50
Shall thus by this be vengéd or revealed?
Now see I what I durst not then sus-
 pect,
That Bel-imperia's letter was not feigned.
Nor feignéd she, though falsely they have
 wronged
Both her, myself, Horatio, and them-
 selves.
Now may I make compare twixt hers
 and this,
Of every accident I ne'er could find
Till now, and now I feelingly perceive
They did what heaven unpunished would
 not leave.
O false Lorenzo! Are these thy flattering
 looks?   60
Is this the honor that thou didst my
 son?
And Balthazar—bane to thy soul and
 me!—
Was this the ransom he reserved thee
 for?
Woe to the cause of these constrainéd
 wars!
Woe to thy baseness and captivity!
Woe to thy birth, thy body, and thy
 soul,
Thy curséd father, and thy conquered
 self!
And banned with bitter execrations be
The day and place where he did pity
 thee!
But wherefore waste I mine unfruitful
 words,   70
When naught but blood will satisfy my
 woes?
I will go plain me [1] to my lord the king,
And cry aloud for justice through the
 court,
Wearing the flints with these my with-
 ered feet;
And either purchase justice by entreats,
Or tire them all with my revenging
 threats.   *Exit.*

[1] Complain.

[SCENA OCTAVA.

The same.]

Enter Isabell[a] and her Maid.

ISAB. So that you say this herb will purge
 the eye,
And this, the head?
Ah, but none of them will purge the
 heart!
No, there's no medicine left for my dis-
 ease,
Nor any physic to recure the dead.
       She runs lunatic.
Horatio! O, where's Horatio?
MAID. Good madam, affright not thus
 yourself
With outrage [2] for your son Horatio.
He sleeps in quiet in the Elysian fields.
ISAB. Why, did I not give you gowns and
 goodly things,   10
Bought you a whistle and a whipstalk [3]
 too,
To be revengéd on their villainies?
MAID. Madam, these humors do torment
 my soul.
ISAB. My soul—poor soul, thou talks of
 things
Thou know'st not what—my soul hath
 silver wings,
That mounts me up unto the highest
 heavens.·
To heaven? Ay, there sits my Horatio,
Backed with a troop of fiery cherubins,
Dancing about his newly healéd wounds,
Singing sweet hymns and chanting heav-
 enly notes,   20
Rare harmony to greet his innocence,
That died, ay, died, a mirror in our days.
But say, where shall I find the men, the
 murderers,
That slew Horatio? Whither shall I run
To find them out that murderéd my son?
         Exeunt.

[SCENA NONA.

*Outside the place of Bel-imperia's con-
finement.*]

Bel-imperia at a window.

BEL. What means this outrage that is offered me?
Why am I thus sequestered from the
 court?

[2] Outcry.   [3] Whipstock.

No notice! Shall I not know the cause
Of these my secret and suspicious ills?
Accurséd brother, unkind murderer,
Why bends thou thus thy mind to martyr
me?
Hieronimo, why writ I of thy wrongs,
Or why art thou so slack in thy revenge?
Andrea, O Andrea! That thou saw'st
Me for thy friend Horatio handled thus,
And him for me thus causeless mur-
deréd!—   11
Well, force perforce, I must constrain
myself
To patience, and apply me [1] to the time,
Till heaven, as I have hoped, shall set
me free.

Enter Christophil.

CHRIS. Come, Madam Bel-imperia, this
may not be.   *Exeunt.*

Enter Lorenzo, Balthazar, and the Page.[2]

LOR. Boy, talk no further. Thus far things
go well.
Thou art assuréd that thou sawest him
dead?
PAGE. Or else, my lord, I live not.
LOR.   That's enough.
As for his resolution in his end,
Leave that to him with whom he so-
journs now.   20
Here, take my ring and give it Christo-
phil,
And bid him let my sister be enlarged,
And bring her hither straight.—
                              Exit Page.
This that I did was for a policy,
To smooth and keep the murder secret,
Which, as a nine-days' wonder, being
o'erblown,
My gentle sister will I now enlarge.
BAL. And time, Lorenzo, for my lord the
duke,
You heard, inquired for her yesternight.
LOR. Why, and, my lord, I hope you heard
me say   30
Sufficient reason why she kept away.
But that's all one. My lord, you love her?
BAL.   Ay.

LOR. Then in your love beware. Deal
cunningly;
Salve all suspicions; only soothe me up,[3]
And, if she hap to stand on terms [4] with
us—
As for her sweetheart and concealment
so—
Jest with her gently. Under feignéd jest
Are things concealed that else would
breed unrest.
But here she comes.

Enter Bel-imperia.

                              Now, sister—
BEL.   Sister? No!
Thou art no brother, but an enemy;   40
Else wouldst thou not have used thy
sister so:
First, to affright me with thy weapons
drawn,
And with extremes abuse my company; [5]
And then to hurry me, like whirlwind's
rage,
Amidst a crew of thy confederates,
And clap me up where none might come
at me,
Nor I at any to reveal my wrongs.
What madding [6] fury did possess thy
wits?
Or wherein is 't that I offended thee?
LOR. Advise you better, Bel-imperia,   50
For I have done you no disparagement—
Unless, by more discretion than deserved,
I sought to save your honor and mine own.
BEL. Mine honor? Why, Lorenzo, wherein
is 't
That I neglect my reputation so
As you, or any, need to rescue it?
LOR. His highness and my father were
resolved
To come confer with old Hieronimo
Concerning certain matters of estate
That by the viceroy was determinéd. 60
BEL. And wherein was mine honor touched
in that?
BAL. Have patience, Bel-imperia; hear the
rest.
LOR. Me, next in sight, as messenger they
sent
To give him notice that they were so
nigh.

---

[1] Conform myself.
[2] It is conventional to make a new scene here.
Lorenzo and Balthazar probably enter on the
lower stage, however, as Bel-imperia leaves the
upper.

[3] Support me.   [6] Raving.
[4] Insist on her rights.
[5] Do violence to my companion.

Now when I came, consorted with the
prince,
And unexpected in an arbor there
Found Bel-imperia with Horatio—
BEL.   How then?
LOR. Why then, remembering that old dis-
grace,
Which you for Don Andrea had en-
dured,
And now were likely longer to sustain 70
By being found so meanly accompanied,
Thought rather—for I knew no readier
mean—
To thrust Horatio forth my father's way.
BAL. And carry you obscurely somewhere
else,
Lest that his highness should have found
you there.
BEL. Even so, my lord?   And you are
witness
That this is true which he entreateth of?
You, gentle brother, forged this for my
sake,
And you, my lord, were made his instru-
ment?
A work of worth, worthy the noting
too!   80
But what's the cause that you concealed
me since?
LOR. Your melancholy, sister, since the
news
Of your first favorite Don Andrea's
death
My father's old wrath hath exasperate.
BAL. And better was 't for you, being in
disgrace,
To absent yourself, and give his fury
place.
BEL. But why had I no notice of his ire?
LOR. That were to add more fuel to your
fire,
Who burnt like Ætna for Andrea's loss.
BEL. Hath not my father then inquired
for me?   90
LOR. Sister, he hath, and thus excused I
thee.   *He whispereth in her ear.*
But, Bel-imperia, see the gentle prince;
Look on thy love, behold young Baltha-
zar,
Whose passions by thy presence are
increased,
And in whose melancholy thou mayst see
Thy hate, his love; thy flight, his follow-
ing thee.

BEL. Brother, you are become an orator—
I know not, I, by what experience—
Too politic for me, past all compare,
Since last I saw you. But content your-
self;   100
The prince is meditating higher things.
BAL. 'Tis of thy beauty, then, that con-
quers kings;
Of those thy tresses, Ariadne's twines,
Wherewith my liberty thou hast sur-
prised;
Of that thine ivory front,[1] my sorrow's
map,
Wherein I see no haven to rest my hope.
BEL. To love and fear, and both at once,
my lord,
In my conceit, are things of more im-
port
Than women's wits are to be busied
with.
BAL. 'Tis I that love.
BEL.   Whom?
BAL.   Bel-imperia. 110
BEL. But I that fear.
BAL.   Whom?
BEL.   Bel-imperia.
LOR. Fear yourself?
BEL.   Ay, brother.
LOR.   How?
BEL.   As those
That what they love are loath and fear
to lose.
BAL. Then, fair, let Balthazar your keeper
be.
BEL. No, Balthazar doth fear as well as
we:
Et[2] *tremulo metui pavidum junxere timo-
rem*—
Et vanum stolidæ proditionis opus.[3] *Exit.*
LOR. Nay, and you argue things so cun-
ningly,
We'll go continue this discourse at
court.
BAL. Led by the lodestar of her heavenly
looks,   120
Wends poor oppressèd Balthazar,
As o'er the mountains walks the wan-
derer,
Incertain to effect his pilgrimage.
                              Exeunt.

[1] Brow.
[2] Emended by Hazlitt. Early edns. read *Est.*
[3] And to quivering fear they added trembling
terror—and the vain task of stupid betrayal
(source unknown).

[SCENA DECIMA.

A street.]

Enter two Portingales, and Hieronimo
meets them.

1 [PORT.] By your leave, sir.

HIER.[1] 'Tis neither as you think, nor as
you think,
Nor as you think. You're wide all.
These slippers are not mine; they were
my son Horatio's.
My son? And what's a son?
A thing begot within a pair of minutes—
thereabout;
A lump bred up in darkness, and doth
serve
To ballace [2] these light creatures we call
women;
And, at nine months' end, creeps forth
to light.
What is there yet in a son   10
To make a father dote, rave, or run mad?
Being born, it pouts, cries, and breeds
teeth.
What is there yet in a son? He must be
fed,
Be taught to go, and speak. Ay, or yet
Why might not a man love a calf as well,
Or melt in passion o'er a frisking kid,
As for a son? Methinks a young bacon
Or a fine little smooth horse colt
Should move a man as much as doth a
son,
For one of these, in very little time,   20
Will grow to some good use, whereas a
son,
The more he grows in stature and in
years,
The more unsquared, unbeveled,[3] he
appears,
Reckons his parents among the rank of
fools,
Strikes care upon their heads with his
mad riots,
Makes them look old before they meet
with age.
This is a son! And what a loss were this,
considered truly?—
O, but my Horatio grew out of reach of
these
Insatiate humors. He loved his loving
parents;

He was my comfort and his mother's
joy,   30
The very arm that did hold up our house;
Our hopes were storéd up in him.
None but a damnéd murderer could hate
him.
He had not seen the back of nineteen
year,
When his strong arm unhorsed the proud
Prince Balthazar,
And his great mind, too full of honor,
Took him unto [4] mercy, that valiant but
ignoble Portingale!
Well, heaven is heaven still,
And there is Nemesis, and Furies,
And things called whips,   40
And they sometimes do meet with mur-
derers.
They do not always scape, that is some
comfort.
Ay, ay, ay; and then time steals on, and
steals, and steals,
Till violence leaps forth like thunder
Wrapped in a ball of fire,
And so doth bring confusion to them all.—
Good leave have you; nay, I pray you go,
For I'll leave you, if you can leave me so.

2 [PORT.] Pray you, which is the next[5] way
to my lord the duke's?

HIER. The next way from me.

1 [PORT.]   To his house, we mean. 50

HIER. O, hard by; 'tis yon house that you
see.

2 [PORT.] You could not tell us if his son
were there?

HIER. Who, my Lord Lorenzo?

1 [PORT.]   Ay, sir.

He [Hieronimo] goeth in at one door and
comes out at another.

HIER.   O, forbear!
For other talk for us far fitter were.
But, if you be importunate to know
The way to him, and where to find him
out,
Then list to me, and I'll resolve your
doubt.
There is a path upon your left-hand side
That leadeth from a guilty conscience
Unto a forest of distrust and fear,   60
A darksome place, and dangerous to pass.
There shall you meet with melancholy
thoughts,
Whose baleful humors if you but uphold,

---

[1] The following speech except the last two
lines is an addition.   [2] Ballast.   [3] Unpolished.
[4] Early edns. read *us to*.   [5] Nearest.

It will conduct you to despair and
death—
Whose rocky cliffs when you have once
beheld,
Within a hugy dale of lasting night,
That, kindled with the world's iniquities,
Doth cast up filthy and detested fumes—
Not far from thence, where murderers
have built
A habitation for their curséd souls, 70
There, in a brazen caldron, fixed by Jove
In his fell wrath, upon a sulphur flame,
Yourselves shall find Lorenzo bathing
him
In boiling lead and blood of innocents.
1 [PORT.] Ha, ha, ha!
HIER. Ha, ha, ha! Why, ha, ha, ha! Fare-
well, good ha, ha, ha!   *Exit.*
2 [PORT.] Doubtless this man is passing lu-
natic,
Or imperfection of his age doth make him
dote.
Come, let's away to seek my lord the
duke.   [*Exeunt.*] [1]

[SCENA UNDECIMA.

The Spanish court.]

*Enter Hieronimo, with a poniard in one
hand and a rope in the other.*

HIER. Now, sir, perhaps I come and see the
king;
The king sees me, and fain would hear
my suit.
Why, is not this a strange and seld-seen [2]
thing,
That standers-by with toys should
strike me mute?
Go to, I see their shifts, and say no more.
Hieronimo, 'tis time for thee to trudge.
Down by the dale that flows with purple
gore
Standeth a fiery tower. There sits a judge
Upon a seat of steel and molten brass,
And twixt his teeth he holds a fire-
brand,   10
That leads unto the lake where hell doth
stand.
Away, Hieronimo! To him be gone;
He'll do thee justice for Horatio's death.
Turn down this path, [3] thou shalt be with
him straight;

[1] From 1602 edn.   [3] *I.e.,* the poniard.
[2] Seldom seen.

Or this [4] and then thou need'st not take
thy breath.
This way, or that way?—Soft and fair!
Not so!
For, if I hang or kill myself, let's know
Who will revenge Horatio's murder then?
No, no! Fie, no! Pardon me, I'll none
of that.
      He flings away the dagger and halter.
This way I'll take; and this way comes
the king,   *He takes them up again.* 20
And here I'll have a fling at him, that's
flat;
And, Balthazar, I'll be with thee to
bring, [5]
And thee, Lorenzo! Here's the king—
nay, stay;
And here, ay, here—there goes the hare
away.

*Enter   King,   Ambassador,   Castile,   and
Lorenzo.*

KING. Now show, ambassador, what our
viceroy saith.
    Hath he received the articles we sent?
HIER. Justice, O, justice to Hieronimo!
LOR. Back! Seest thou not the king is
busy?
HIER.   O, is he so?
KING. Who is he that interrupts our
business?
HIER. Not I. [*Aside.*] Hieronimo, beware!
Go by, go by! [6]   30
AMB. Renowméd king, he hath received
and read
Thy kingly proffers and thy promised
league;
And, as a man extremely overjoyed
To hear his son so princely entertained,
Whose death he had so solemnly be-
wailed,
This for thy further satisfaction
And kingly love he kindly lets thee
know.
First, for the marriage of his princely son
With Bel-imperia, thy beloved niece,
The news are more delightful to his
soul   40
Than myrrh or incense to the offended
heavens.

[4] *I.e.,* the rope.   [5] Get the upper hand of thee.
[6] A phrase which was widely quoted in Elizabethan literature; probably used to denote impatience.

In person, therefore, will he come himself,
To see the marriage rites solemnizéd,
And, in the presence of the court of Spain.
To knit a sure inextricable ¹ band
Of kingly love and everlasting league
Betwixt the crowns of Spain and Portin-
  gale.
There will he give his crown to Balthazar,
And make a queen of Bel-imperia.
KING. Brother, how like you this our vice-
  roy's love?   50
CAS. No doubt, my lord, it is an argu-
  ment
Of honorable care to keep his friend,
And wondrous zeal to Balthazar his son;
Nor am I least indebted to his grace
That bends his liking to my daughter
  thus.
AMB. Now last, dread lord, here hath his
  highness sent
(Although he send not that his son re-
  turn)
His ransom due to Don Horatio.
HIER. Horatio! Who calls Horatio?
KING. And well remembered, thank his
  majesty!   60
Here, see it given to Horatio.
HIER. Justice, O, justice, justice, gentle
  king!
KING. Who is that? Hieronimo?
HIER. Justice, O, justice! O my son, my
  son!
My son, whom naught can ransom or
  redeem!
LOR. Hieronimo, you are not well-advised.
HIER. Away, Lorenzo, hinder me no more,
For thou hast made me bankrupt of my
  bliss.
Give me my son! You shall not ransom
  him!
Away! I'll rip the bowels of the earth, 70
                  He diggeth with his dagger.
And ferry over to th' Elysian plains,
And bring my son to show his deadly
  wounds.
Stand from about me!
I'll make a pickax of my poniard,
And here surrender up my marshalship,
For I'll go marshal up the fiends in hell
To be avengéd on you all for this.
KING. What means this outrage?
Will none of you restrain his fury?

¹ Emended by Hawkins. Original reads *in-
execrable.*

HIER. Nay, soft and fair! You shall not
  need to strive.   80
Needs must he go that the devils drive.
                                          Exit.
KING. What accident hath happed Hier-
  onimo?
I have not seen him to demean him so.
LOR. My gracious lord, he is with extreme
  pride,
Conceived of young Horatio his son,
And covetous of having to himself
The ransom of the young prince Balthazar,
Distract, and in a manner lunatic.
KING. Believe me, nephew, we are sorry
  for 't.
This is the love that fathers bear their
  sons.   90
But, gentle brother, go give to him this
  gold,
The prince's ransom; let him have his due.
For what he hath, Horatio shall not want.
Happily Hieronimo hath need thereof.
LOR. But, if he be thus helplessly distract,
'Tis requisite his office be resigned,
And given to one of more discretion.
KING. We shall increase his melancholy so.
'Tis best that we see further in it first,
Till when, ourself will exempt [him] ² the
  place.   100
And, brother, now bring in the ambassa-
  dor,
That he may be a witness of the match
Twixt Balthazar and Bel-imperia,
And that we may prefix a certain time
Wherein the marriage shall be solemnized,
That we may have thy lord, the viceroy,
  here.
AMB. Therein your highness highly shall
  content
His majesty, that longs to hear from
  hence.
KING. On, then, and hear you, lord am-
  bassador—   *Exeunt.*

[SCENA DUODECIMA.
Hieronimo's garden.]

³*Enter Jaques and Pedro.*

JAQ. I wonder, Pedro, why our master thus
At midnight sends us with our torches
  light,

² Added by Boas; meaning to excuse him from
his duties.
³ The following scene through l.156 is an
addition. The line division is often confused.

When man and bird and beast are all at
  rest,
Save those that watch for rape and
  bloody murder.
PED. O Jaques, know thou that our mas-
  ter's mind
Is much distraught since his Horatio died,
And—now his aged years should sleep in
  rest,
His heart in quiet—like a desperate man,
Grows lunatic and childish for his son.
Sometimes, as he doth at his table sit, 10
He speaks as if Horatio stood by him;
Then starting in a rage, falls on the
  earth,
Cries out, "Horatio, where is my Hora-
  tio?"
So that with extreme grief and cutting
  sorrow
There is not left in him one inch of
  man.—
See, where he comes.

Enter Hieronimo.

HIER. I pry through every crevice of each
  wall,
Look on each tree, and search through
  every brake,
Beat at the bushes, stamp our grandam
  earth,
Dive in the water, and stare up to
  heaven,   20
Yet cannot I behold my son Horatio.—
How now, who's there? Sprites, sprites?—
PED. We are your servants that attend
  you, sir.
HIER. What make you with your torches
  in the dark?
PED. You bid us light them, and attend
  you here.
HIER. No, no, you are deceived! Not I;
  you are deceived!
Was I so mad to bid you light your
  torches now?
Light me your torches at the mid of noon,
Whenas the sun-god rides in all his glory;
Light me your torches then.
PED.   Then we burn daylight. 30
HIER. Let it be burnt! Night is a murder-
  ous slut,
That would not have her treasons to be
  seen;
And yonder pale-faced Hecate there, the
  moon,

Doth give consent to that is done in
  darkness;
And all those stars that gaze upon her
  face
Are aglots [1] on her sleeve, pins on her
  train;
And those that should be powerful and
  divine
Do sleep in darkness when they most
  should shine.
PED. Provoke them not, fair sir, with
  tempting words.
The heavens are gracious, and your mis-
  eries and sorrow   40
Makes you speak you know not what.
HIER. Villain, thou liest! And thou doest
  naught
But tell me I am mad. Thou liest! I am
  not mad!
I know thee to be Pedro, and he Jaques.
I'll prove it to thee; and, were I mad, how
  could I?
Where was she that same night when my
  Hor[atio] was murdered?
She should have shone—search thou the
  book.
Had the moon shone, in my boy's face
  there was a kind of grace,
That I know—nay, I do know—had the
  murderer seen him,
His weapon would have fall'n and cut
  the earth,   50
Had he been framed of naught but blood
  and death.
Alack, when mischief doth it knows not
  what,
What shall we say to mischief?

Enter Isabella.

ISAB. Dear Hieronimo, come in a-doors;
O, seek not means so to increase thy
  sorrow.
HIER. Indeed, Isabella, we do nothing here.
I do not cry—ask Pedro, and ask Jaques.
Not I indeed; we are very merry, very
  merry.
ISAB. How?   Be merry here, be merry
  here?
Is not this the place, and this the very
  tree,   60
Where my Horatio died, where he was
  murdered?

[1] Metal ornaments. From 1610 edn. Original
reads *aggots.*

HIER. Was—do not say what. Let her
  weep it out.
This was the tree. I set it of a kernel;
And, when our hot Spain could not let
  it grow,
But that the infant and the human sap
Began to wither, duly twice a morning
Would I be sprinkling it with fountain
  water.
At last it grew and grew, and bore and
  bore,
Till at the length it grew a gallows, and
  did bear our son.
It bore thy fruit and mine—O wicked,
  wicked plant!   70
      One knocks within at the door.
See who knocks there.
PED.   It is a painter, sir.
HIER. Bid him come in, and paint some
  comfort,
For surely there's none lives but painted
  comfort.
Let him come in!—One knows not what
  may chance.
God's will that I should set this tree!
But even so, masters ungrateful servants
  rear from naught,
And then they hate them that did bring
  them up.

          Enter the Painter.

PAIN. God bless you, sir.
HIER. Wherefore? Why, thou scornful
  villain?
  How, where, or by what means should I
  be blessed?   80
ISAB. What wouldst thou have, good fel-
  low?
PAIN.   Justice, madam.
HIER. O ambitious beggar! Wouldst thou
  have that
  That lives not in the world?
Why, all the undelved mines cannot buy
An ounce of justice, 'tis a jewel so in-
  estimable.
I tell thee, God hath engrossed all jus-
  tice in his hands,
And there is none but what comes from
  him.
PAIN. O, then I see that God must right
  me for my murdered son.
HIER. How, was thy son murdered?
PAIN. Ay, sir. No man did hold a son so
  dear.   90

HIER. What, not as thine? That's a lie
  As massy as the earth. I had a son
  Whose least unvalued hair did weigh
  A thousand of thy sons; and he was
  murdered.
PAIN. Alas, sir, I had no more but he.
HIER. Nor I, nor I! But this same one of
  mine
  Was worth a legion. But all is one.
Pedro, Jaques, go in a-doors; Isabella, go!
And this good fellow here and I
Will range this hideous orchard up and
  down   100
Like to two lions reavéd of their young.
Go in a-doors, I say.
      Exeunt. The Painter and he sits down.
                Come, let's talk wisely now.
  Was thy son murdered?
PAIN.   Ay, sir.
HIER.   So was mine.
  How dost take it? Art thou not some-
  times mad?
  Is there no tricks [1] that comes before
  thine eyes?
PAIN. O Lord, yes, sir. [2]
HIER. Art a painter? Canst paint me a
  tear, or a wound,
  A groan, or a sigh? Canst paint me such
  a tree as this?
PAIN. Sir, I am sure you have heard of
  my painting; my name's Bazardo.
HIER. Bazardo! Afore God, an excellent
  fellow. Look you, sir,   110
Do you see, I'd have you paint me [for]
  my gallery
In your oil colors matted, [3] and draw me
  five
Years younger than I am—do ye see, sir,
  let five
Years go; let them go—like the marshal
  of Spain,
My wife Isabella standing by me,
With a speaking look to my son Horatio,
Which should intend to this or some
  suchlike purpose:
"God bless thee, my sweet son;" and
  my hand leaning upon his head, thus,
  sir, do you see? May it be done?

[1] Illusions.
[2] The remainder of the added passage is so
chaotic in form that it has been printed as
prose by some editors.
[3] Meaning doubtful; probably either *set in a
mat* or *a mount*, or *lacking in luster*.

Pain. Very well, sir.

Hier. Nay, I pray mark me, sir. Then,
sir, would I have you paint me this
tree, this very tree.　　　120
Canst paint a doleful cry?

Pain. Seemingly, sir.

Hier. Nay, it should cry; but all is one.
Well, sir, paint me a youth, run thorough and thorough with villains'
swords, hanging upon this tree.
Canst draw a murderer?

Pain. I'll warrant you, sir;
I have the pattern of the most noto-
rious villains that ever lived in all
Spain.

Hier. O, let them be worse, worse. Stretch
thine art,
And let their beards be of Judas his own
color,[1]
And let their eyebrows jutty over—in
any case observe that.　　　130
Then, sir, after some violent noise,
Bring me forth in my shirt, and my gown
under mine arm, with my torch in my
hand, and my sword reared up thus,
and with these words:
"What noise is this? Who calls Hieronimo?"
May it be done?

Pain. Yea, sir.

[Hier.] Well, sir, then bring me forth,
bring me thorough alley and alley,
still with a distracted countenance going along, and let my hair heave up
my nightcap.
Let the clouds scowl, make the moon
dark, the stars extinct, the winds blowing, the bells tolling, the owl shrieking,
the toads croaking, the minutes jer-
ring,[2] and the clock striking twelve.
And then at last, sir, starting, behold a
man hanging, and tottering, and tottering as you know the wind will weave
a man, and I, with a trice[3] to cut
him down,
And, looking upon him by the advantage
of my torch, find it to be my son
Horatio.
There you may [show][4] a passion, there
you may show a passion!　　　140
Draw me like old Priam of Troy,

Crying, "The house is afire! The house
is afire!"
As the torch over my head. Make me
curse,
Make me rave, make me cry, make me
mad,
Make me well again, make me curse hell,
Invocate heaven, and, in the end, leave me
In a trance, and so forth.

Pain. And is this the end?

Hier. O no, there is no end! The end is
death and madness,
As I am never better than when I am
mad.　　　150
Then methinks I am a brave fellow;
Then I do wonders. But reason abuseth
me,
And there's the torment, there's the hell.
At the last, sir, bring me to one of the
murderers.
Were he as strong as Hector, thus would I
Tear and drag him up and down.

He beats the Painter in, then comes out again
with a book in his hand.[5]

"*Vindicta mihi!*"[6]
Ay, heaven will be revenged of every ill,
Nor will they suffer murder unrepaid.
Then stay, Hieronimo; attend their
will,　　　160
For mortal men may not appoint their
time!—
"*Per scelus semper tutum est sceleribus*
iter."[7]
Strike, and strike home, where wrong is
offered thee,
For evils unto ills conductors be,
And death's the worst of resolution.
For he that thinks with patience to con-
tend
To quiet life, his life shall easily end.—
"*Fata si miseros juvant, habes salutem;*
Fata si vitam negant, habes sepulchrum:"[8]
If destiny thy miseries do ease,　　　170
Then hast thou health, and happy shalt
thou be;

---

[1] *I.e.*, red, according to medieval tradition.
[2] Jarring, ticking.
[3] Moment.　　　[4] Added by Dodsley.

[5] This stage direction is a substitute for
"Enter Hieronimo, with a book in his hand" in
the earlier editions.
[6] "Vengeance is mine" (*Romans*, xii.19).
[7] "The path to crimes is always made safe by
crime" (from Seneca's *Agamemnon*, l. 115).
[8] "If the Fates aid the unfortunate, you have
safety; if the Fates deny you life, you have a
tomb" (from Seneca's *Troades*, ll. 511–512).
Paraphrased in the following four lines.

If destiny deny thee life, Hieronimo,
Yet shalt thou be assuréd of a tomb;
If neither, yet let this thy comfort be:
Heaven covereth him that hath no burial.
And, to conclude, I will revenge his death!
But how? Not, as the vulgar wits of men,
With open, but inevitable ills,[1]
As by a secret, yet a certain mean,
Which under kindship[2] will be cloakéd
   best.   180
Wise men will take their opportunity,
Closely and safely fitting things to time.
But in extremes advantage hath no time,
And therefore all times fit not for revenge.
Thus therefore will I rest me in unrest,
Dissembling quiet in unquietness,
Not seeming that I know their villainies,
That my simplicity may make them
   think
That ignorantly I will let all slip,
For ignorance, I wot, and well they
   know,   190
"*Remedium malorum iners est.*"[3]
Nor aught avails it me to menace them
Who, as a wintry storm upon a plain,
Will bear me down with their nobility.
No, no, Hieronimo, thou must enjoin
Thine eyes to observation, and thy
   tongue
To milder speeches than thy spirit
   affords,
Thy heart to patience, and thy hands to
   rest,
Thy cap to courtesy, and thy knee to
   bow,
Till to revenge thou know when, where,
   and how.   *A noise within.*   200
How now, what noise? What coil[4] is that
   you keep?

Enter a Servant.

SER. Here are a sort[5] of poor petitioners
   That are importunate, and[6] it shall
   please you, sir,
   That you should plead their cases to the
   king.
HIER. That I should plead their several
   actions?
   Why, let them enter, and let me see
   them.

---

[1] Injuries, attacks.   [2] Kindness.
[3] "Ignorance is a cowardly remedy for misfortunes" (from Seneca's *Œdipus*, l. 515).
[4] Disturbance.   [5] Company.   [6] If.

Enter three Citizens and an Old Man.

1 [CIT.] So, I tell you this: for learning and
   for law
   There is not any advocate in Spain
   That can prevail, or will take half the
   pain
   That he will, in pursuit of equity.   210
HIER. Come near, you men, that thus
   importune me.—
[*Aside.*] Now must I bear a face of gravity;
   For thus I used, before my marshalship,
   To plead in causes as corregidor.[7]—
   Come on, sirs, what's the matter?
2 [CIT.]   Sir, an action.
HIER. Of battery?
1 [CIT.]   Mine of debt.
HIER.   Give place.
2 [CIT.] No, sir, mine is an action of the
   case.[8]
3 [CIT.] Mine an *ejectione firmæ*[9] by a
   lease.
HIER. Content you, sirs. Are you
   determinéd   219
   That I should plead your several actions?
1 [CIT.] Ay, sir, and here's my declaration.
2 [CIT.] And here's my band.[10]
3 [CIT.]   And here's my lease.
   They give him papers.
HIER. But wherefore stands yon silly man
   so mute,
   With mournful eyes and hands to heaven
   upreared?
   Come hither, father, let me know thy
   cause.
SENEX.[11] O worthy sir, my cause, but
   slightly known,
   May move the hearts of warlike Myrmi-
   dons,
   And melt the Corsic rocks with ruthful
   tears.
HIER. Say, father, tell me what's thy suit.
SENEX. No, sir, could my woes   230
   Give way unto my most distressful words,
   Then should I not in paper, as you see,
   With ink bewray what blood began in me.
HIER. What's here? "The humble sup-
   plication
   Of Don Bazulto for his murdered son."

---

[7] Advocate; properly, magistrate.
[8] "A universal remedy given for all personal
wrongs . . . so called because the plaintiff's
whole case . . . is set forth at length in the
original writ" (Blackstone).
[9] A writ to eject a tenant.   [10] Bond.
[11] *I.e.*, Old Man; also *Baz.* in speech heads.

SENEX. Ay, sir.

HIER.   No, sir, it was my murdered
     son.

O, my son, my son; O, my son Horatio!

But mine, or thine, Bazulto, be content.

Here, take my handkercher and wipe
     thine eyes,

Whiles wretched I in thy mishaps may
     see   240

The lively portrait of my dying self.

          He draweth out a bloody napkin.

O, no, not this! Horatio, this was thine,

And, when I dyed it in thy dearest blood,

This was a token twixt thy soul and me

That of thy death revengéd I should be.

But here, take this, and this—what,
     my purse?—

Ay, this, and that, and all of them are
     thine,

For all as one are our extremities.

1 [CIT.] O, see the kindness of Hieronimo!

2 [CIT.] This gentleness shows him a gen-
     tleman.   250

HIER. See, see, O, see thy shame,
     Hieronimo!

See here a loving father to his son!

Behold the sorrows and the sad laments

That he delivereth for his son's decease!

If love's effects so strives in lesser things,

If love enforce such moods in meaner
     wits,

If love express such power in poor estates,

Hieronimo, whenas a raging sea,

Tossed with the wind and tide, o'er-
     turnest then

The upper billows, course of waves to
     keep,   260

Whilst lesser waters labor in the deep,

Then shamest thou not, Hieronimo, to
     neglect

The sweet revenge of thy Horatio?

Though on this earth justice will not be
     found,

I'll down to hell, and in this passion

Knock at the dismal gates of Pluto's
     court,

Getting by force, as once Alcides did,

A troop of furies and tormenting hags

To torture Don Lorenzo and the rest.

Yet lest the triple-headed porter should

Deny my passage to the slimy strand, 271

The Thracian poet thou shalt counter-
     feit.

Come on, old father, be my Orpheus,

And, if thou canst [1] no notes upon the
     harp,

Then sound the burden [2] of thy sore
     heart's grief,

Till we do gain that Proserpine may
     grant

Revenge on them that murderéd my son.

Then will I rent and tear them, thus and
     thus,

Shivering their limbs in pieces with my
     teeth.   *Tear the papers.*

1 [CIT.] O sir, my declaration!

          Exit Hieronimo, and they after.

2 [CIT.]   Save my bond! 280

          Enter Hieronimo.

2 [CIT.] Save my bond!

3 [CIT.] Alas, my lease! It cost me ten
     pound,

And you, my lord, have torn the same.

HIER. That cannot be; I gave it never a
     wound.

Show me one drop of blood fall from the
     same!

How is it possible I should slay it then?

Tush, no; run after, catch me if you can.

*Exeunt all but the Old Man. Bazulto re-
     mains till Hieronimo enters again, who,
          staring him in the face, speaks.*

HIER. And art thou come, Horatio, from
     the depth,

To ask for justice in this upper earth,

To tell thy father thou art unrevenged,

To wring more tears from Isabella's
     eyes,   291

Whose lights are dimmed with overlong
     laments?

Go back, my son; complain to Æacus,

For here's no justice. Gentle boy, begone,

For justice is exiléd from the earth.

Hieronimo will bear thee company.

Thy mother cries on righteous Rhada-
     manth

For just revenge against the murderers.

SENEX. Alas, my lord, whence springs this
     troubled speech?

HIER. But let me look on my Horatio. 300

Sweet boy, how art thou changed in
     death's black shade!

Had Proserpine no pity on thy youth,

But suffered thy fair crimson-colored
     spring

With withered winter to be blasted thus?

[1] Knowest.   [2] Bass accompaniment.

Horatio, thou art older than thy father.
Ah, ruthless fate,[1] that favor[2] thus
   transforms!

BAZ. Ah, my good lord, I am not your
   young son.

HIER. What, not my son? Thou then a
   Fury art,
Sent from the empty kingdom of black
   night
To summon me to make appearance 310
Before grim Minos and just Rhada-
   manth,
To plague Hieronimo that is remiss,
And seeks not vengeance for Horatio's
   death.

BAZ. I am a grievéd man, and not a ghost,
   That came for justice for my murdered
   son.

HIER. Ay, now I know thee, now thou
   namest my son.
Thou art the lively image of my grief;
Within thy face my sorrows I may see.
Thy eyes are gummed with tears, thy
   cheeks are wan,
Thy forehead troubled, and thy mut-
   t'ring lips   320
Murmur sad words abruptly broken off
By force of windy sighs thy spirit
   breathes.
And all this sorrow riseth for thy son,
And selfsame sorrow feel I for my son.
Come in, old man, thou shalt to Isabel.
Lean on my arm; I thee, thou me, shalt
   stay,
And thou, and I, and she will sing a song,
Three parts in one, but all of discords
   framed.—
Talk not of chords, but let us now be
   gone,
For with a cord Horatio was slain. 330
                        Exeunt.

[SCENA TERTIA DECIMA.

The Spanish court.]

Enter King of Spain, the Duke, Viceroy, and
Lorenzo, Balthazar, Don Pedro, and
                        Bel-imperia.

KING. Go, brother, it is the Duke of
   Castile's cause;
Salute the viceroy in our name.

CAS.   I go.

[1] Emended by Dodsley. Original reads *Father*.
[2] Appearance.

VIC. Go forth, Don Pedro, for thy
   nephew's sake,
And greet the Duke of Castile.

PED.   It shall be so.

KING. And now to meet these Portuguese,
For as we now are, so sometimes were
   these,
Kings and commanders of the western
   Indies.—
Welcome, brave viceroy, to the court of
   Spain,
And welcome all his honorable train!
'Tis not unknown to us for why you
   come,   10
Or have so kingly crossed the seas.
Sufficeth it, in this we note the troth
And more than common love you lend
   to us.
So is it that mine honorable niece
(For it beseems us now that it be known)
Already is betrothed to Balthazar;
And by appointment and our condescent[3]
Tomorrow are they to be marriéd.
To this intent we entertain thyself,
Thy followers, their pleasure, and our
   peace.   20
Speak, men of Portingale, shall it be so?
If ay, say so; if not, say flatly no.

VIC. Renowméd king, I come not, as thou
   think'st,
With doubtful followers, unresolvéd men,
But such as have upon thine articles
Confirmed thy motion, and contented me.
Know, sovereign, I come to solemnize
The marriage of thy belovéd niece,
Fair Bel-imperia, with my Balthazar—
With thee, my son, whom sith I live to
   see,   30
Here take my crown, I give it her and
   thee,
And let me live a solitary life,
In ceaseless prayers,
To think how strangely heaven hath thee
   preserved.

KING. See, brother, see, how nature strives
   in him!
Come, worthy viceroy, and accompany
Thy friend with thine extremities.[4]
A place more private fits this princely
   mood.

VIC. Or here, or where your highness
   thinks it good.
    Exeunt all but Cas[tile] and Lor[enzo].

[3] Consent.   [4] Unrestrained expression of feelings.

CAS. Nay, stay, Lorenzo, let me talk with you. 40
Seest thou this entertainment of these kings?
LOR. I do, my lord, and joy to see the same.
CAS. And knowest thou why this meeting is?
LOR. For her, my lord, whom Balthazar doth love,
And to confirm their promised marriage.
CAS. She is thy sister?
LOR. Who, Bel-imperia? Ay,
My gracious lord, and this is the day
That I have longed so happily to see.
CAS. Thou wouldst be loath that any fault of thine 49
Should intercept her in her happiness?
LOR. Heavens will not let Lorenzo err so much.
CAS. Why then, Lorenzo, listen to my words.
It is suspected, and reported too,
That thou, Lorenzo, wrong'st Hieronimo,
And in his suits towards his majesty
Still keep'st him back, and seeks to cross his suit.
LOR. That I, my lord—?
CAS. I tell thee, son, myself have heard it said,
When, to my sorrow, I have been ashamed
To answer for thee, though thou art my son. 60
Lorenzo, knowest thou not the common love
And kindness that Hieronimo hath won
By his deserts within the court of Spain?
Or seest thou not the k[ing] my brother's care
In his behalf, and to procure his health?
Lorenzo, shouldst thou thwart his passions,
And he exclaim against thee to the king,
What honor were 't in this assembly,
Or what a scandal were't among the kings
To hear Hieronimo exclaim on thee! 70
Tell me—and look thou tell me truly too—
Whence grows the ground of this report in court?
LOR. My l[ord], it lies not in Lorenzo's power

To stop the vulgar,[1] liberal of their tongues.
A small advantage makes a water-breach,
And no man lives that long contenteth all.
CAS. Myself have seen thee busy to keep back
Him and his supplications from the king.
LOR. Yourself, my l[ord], hath seen his passions 79
That ill beseemed the presence of a king;
And, for I pitied him in his distress,
I held him thence with kind and courteous words
As free from malice to Hieronimo
As to my soul, my lord.
CAS. Hieronimo, my son, mistakes thee then.
LOR. My gracious father, believe me, so he doth.
But what's a silly man, distract in mind,
To think upon the murder of his son?
Alas, how easy is it for him to err! 89
But for his satisfaction and the world's,
'Twere good, my l[ord], that Hieronimo and I
Were reconciled, if he misconster[2] me.
CAS. Lorenzo, thou hast said; it shall be so.
Go one of you, and call Hieronimo.

Enter Balthazar and Bel-imperia.

BAL. Come, Bel-imperia, Balthazar's content,
My sorrow's ease and sovereign of my bliss,
Sith heaven hath ordained thee to be mine,
Disperse those clouds and melancholy looks,
And clear them up with those thy sun-bright eyes,
Wherein my hope and heaven's fair beauty lies. 100
BEL. My looks, my lord, are fitting for my love,
Which, new-begun, can show [no][3] brighter yet.
BAL. New-kindled flames should burn as morning sun.
BEL. But not too fast, lest heat and all be done.
I see my lord my father.

¹ Common people. ³ From 1602 edn.
² Misconstrue.

BAL.   Truce, my love;
I will go salute him.
CAS.   Welcome, Balthazar.
Welcome, brave prince, the pledge of
Castile's peace!
And welcome, Bel-imperia!—How now,
girl?
Why comest thou sadly to salute us thus?
Content thyself, for I am satisfied.   110
It is not now as when Andrea lived;
We have forgotten and forgiven that,
And thou art gracéd with a happier
love.—
But, Balthazar, here comes Hieronimo;
I'll have a word with him.

Enter Hieronimo and a Servant.

HIER. And where's the duke?
SER.   Yonder.
HIER.   Even so.—
[*Aside.*] What new device have they
devoised, trow? [1]
Pocas palabras! [2] Mild as the lamb!
Is 't I will be revenged? No, I am not
the man.—
CAS. Welcome, Hieronimo.   120
LOR. Welcome, Hieronimo.
BAL. Welcome, Hieronimo.
HIER. My lords, I thank you for Horatio.
CAS. Hieronimo, the reason that I sent
To speak with you, is this—
HIER.   What, so short?
Then I'll be gone; I thank you for 't.
CAS. Nay, stay, Hieronimo!—Go call him,
son.
[LOR.] Hieronimo, my father craves a word
with you.
HIER. With me, sir? Why, my l[ord], I
thought you had done.   129
LOR. [*Aside.*] No. Would he had!
CAS.   Hieronimo, I hear
You find yourself aggrievéd at my son,
Because you have not access unto the
king,
And say 'tis he that intercepts your suits.
HIER. Why, is not this a miserable thing,
my lord?
CAS. Hieronimo, I hope you have no cause,
And would be loath that one of your
deserts
Should once have reason to suspect my
son,
Considering how I think of you myself.

1 Think you?   2 Few words.

HIER. Your son Lorenzo? Whom, my
noble lord?
The hope of Spain, mine honorable
friend?   140
Grant me the combat of them, if they
dare.   *Draws out his sword.*
I'll meet him face to face, to tell me so!
These be the scandalous reports of such
As love not me, and hate my lord too
much.
Should I suspect Lorenzo would prevent
Or cross my suit, that loved my son so
well?
My lord, I am ashamed it should be
said.
LOR. Hieronimo, I never gave you cause.
HIER. My good lord, I know you did
not.
CAS.   There then pause;
And for the satisfaction of the world, 150
Hieronimo, frequent my homely house,
The Duke of Castile, Cyprian's ancient
seat,
And, when thou wilt, use me, my son,
and it.
But here, before Prince Balthazar and
me,
Embrace each other, and be perfect
friends.
HIER. Ay, marry, my lord, and shall.
Friends, quoth he? See, I'll be friends
with you all—
Specially with you, my lovely lord;
For divers causes it is fit for us
That we be friends. The world's sus-
picious,   160
And men may think what we imagine
not.
BAL. Why, this is friendly done, Hiero-
nimo.
LOR. And that I hope. Old grudges are
forgot?
HIER. What else? It were a shame it
should not be so.
CAS. Come on, Hieronimo, at my re-
quest;
Let us entreat your company today.
                              Exeunt.
HIER. Your lordship's to command.—Pha[
keep your way.
*Mi. Chi mi fa? Piu Correzza Che no sule
Tradito viha otrade vule.* [3]   *Exit.* 169

3 He who caresses me more than is his custom
has betrayed me or hopes to betray me.

[CHORUS]

Enter Ghost and Revenge.

GHOST. Awake, Erichtho! Cerberus, awake!
Solicit Pluto, gentle Proserpine!
To combat, Acheron and Erebus!
For ne'er, by Styx and Phlegeton in hell,
O'er-ferried Charon to the fiery lakes
Such fearful sights as poor Andrea sees.[1]
Revenge, awake!
REVENGE.   Awake? For why?
GHOST. Awake, Revenge, for thou art ill-
advised
To sleep away what thou art warned to
watch!
REVENGE. Content thyself, and do not
trouble me.
GHOST. Awake, Revenge, if love—as love
hath had—   180
Have yet the power or prevalence in hell!
Hieronimo with Lorenzo is joined in
league,
And intercepts our passage to revenge.
Awake, Revenge, or we are woebegone!
REVENGE. Thus worldlings ground[2] what
they have dreamed upon.
Content thyself, Andrea.   Though I
sleep,
Yet is my mood soliciting their souls.
Sufficeth thee that poor Hieronimo
Cannot forget his son Horatio.
Nor dies Revenge, although he sleep
awhile;   190
For, in unquiet, quietness is feigned,
And slumb'ring is a common worldly
wile.
Behold, Andrea, for an instance, how
Revenge hath slept, and then imagine
thou
What 'tis to be subject to destiny.

Enter a Dumb Show.

GHOST. Awake, Revenge; reveal this mys-
tery.
REVENGE. The two first the nuptial
torches bore
As brightly burning as the midday's sun;
But after them doth Hymen hie as fast,
Clothéd in sable and a saffron robe,   200
And blows them out, and quencheth
them with blood,
As discontent that things continue so.

_____
[1] Lines 171–74, corrupt in the original, have
been emended by Schick.   [2] Rely on.

GHOST. Sufficeth me; thy meaning's under-
stood,
And thanks to thee and those infernal
powers
That will not tolerate a lover's woe.
Rest thee, for I will sit to see the rest.
REVENGE. Then argue not, for thou hast
thy request.   *Exeunt.*

ACTUS QUARTUS. [SCENA PRIMA.

A room in Don Cyprian's palace.]

Enter Bel-imperia and Hieronimo.

BEL. Is this the love thou bear'st Horatio?
Is this the kindness that thou counter-
feits?
Are these the fruits of thine incessant
tears?
Hieronimo, are these thy passions,
Thy protestations and thy deep laments,
That thou wert wont to weary men
withal?
O unkind father! O deceitful world!
With what excuses canst thou show thy-
self—
With what dishonor and the hate of
men—
From this dishonor and the hate of
men,   10
Thus to neglect the loss and life of him
Whom both my letters and thine own
belief
Assures thee to be causeless slaughteréd?
Hieronimo, for shame, Hieronimo,
Be not a history to aftertimes
Of such ingratitude unto thy son.
Unhappy mothers of such children then!
But monstrous fathers to forget so soon
The death of those whom they with care
and cost
Have tendered so, thus careless should
be lost.   20
Myself, a stranger in respect of thee,
So loved his life as still I wish their
deaths.
Nor shall his death be unrevenged by
me,
Although I bear it out for fashion's sake,
For here I swear, in sight of heaven and
earth,
Shouldst thou neglect the love thou
shouldst retain,
And give it over and devise no more,

Myself should send their hateful souls
to hell
That wrought his downfall with extrem-
est death.
HIER. But may it be that Bel-imperia 30
Vows such revenge as she hath deigned
to say?
Why, then I see that heaven applies our
drift,[1]
And all the saints do sit soliciting
For vengeance on those curséd murder-
ers.
Madam, 'tis true, and now I find it so,
I found a letter, written in your name,
And, in that letter, how Horatio died.
Pardon, O, pardon, Bel-imperia,
My fear and care in not believing it;
Nor think I thoughtless think upon a
mean 40
To let his death be unrevenged at full.
And here I vow—so you but give consent,
And will conceal my resolution—
I will ere long determine of their deaths
That causeless thus have murder[é]d my
son.
BEL. Hieronimo, I will consent, conceal,
And aught that may effect for thine
avail,
Join with thee to revenge Horatio's
death.
HIER. On, then; [and] whatsoever I devise,
Let me entreat you, grace my practices,
Forwhy [2] the plot's already in mine
head. 51
Here they are.

Enter Balthazar and Lorenzo.

BAL.   How now, Hieronimo?
What, courting Bel-imperia?
HIER.   Ay, my lord;
Such courting as, I promise you,
She hath my heart, but you, my lord,
have hers.
LOR. But now, Hieronimo, or never,
We are to entreat your help.
HIER.   My help?
Why, my good lords, assure yourselves
of me,
For you have given me cause—ay, by
my faith, have you!
BAL. It pleased you, at the entertainment
of the ambassador, 60

To grace the king so much as with a
show.
Now, were your study so well furnishéd,
As, for the passing of the first night's
sport,
To entertain my father with the like,
Or any suchlike pleasing motion,[3]
Assure yourself, it would content them
well.
HIER. Is this all?
BAL.   Ay, this is all.
HIER. Why then, I'll fit you; say no more.
When I was young, I gave my mind
And plied myself to fruitless poetry, 70
Which, though it profit the professor
naught,
Yet is it passing pleasing to the world.
LOR. And how for that?
HIER.   Marry, my good lord, thus
(And yet methinks, you are too quick
with us):
When in Toledo there I studiéd,
It was my chance to write a tragedy—
See here, my lords—
               He shows them a book.
Which, long forgot, I found this other day.
Now would your lordships favor me so
much
As but to grace me with your acting
it—   80
I mean each one of you to play a part—
Assure you it will prove most passing
strange,
And wondrous plausible[4] to that as-
sembly.
BAL. What, would you have us play a
tragedy?
HIER. Why, Nero thought it no dispar-
agement,
And kings and emperors have ta'en de-
light
To make experience of their wits in
plays.[5]
LOR. Nay, be not angry, good Hieronimo;
The prince but asked a question.
BAL. In faith, Hieronimo, an you be in
earnest,   90
I'll make one.
LOR.   And I another.
HIER. Now, my good lord, could you en-
treat

---

[1] Approves our plan.   [2] Because.
[3] Puppet show.   [4] Applaudable.
[5] These lines, which are quoted by Heywood,
give the clue to Kyd's authorship.

Your sister Bel-imperia to make one?
For what's a play without a woman in it?
BEL. Little entreaty shall serve me, Hiero-
nimo,
For I must needs be employed in your
play.
HIER. Why, this is well. I tell you, lord-
ings,
It was determinéd to have been acted
By gentlemen and scholars too,
Such as could tell what to speak.
BAL.   And now 100
It shall be played by princes and court-
iers,
Such as can tell how to speak,
If, as it is our country manner,
You will but let us know the argument.
HIER. That shall I roundly. The chron-
icles of Spain
Record this written of a knight of
Rhodes:
He was betrothed, and wedded at the
length,
To one Perseda, an Italian dame,
Whose beauty ravished all that her be-
held,
Especially the soul of Soliman,   110
Who at the marriage was the chiefest
guest.[1]
By sundry means sought Soliman to
win
Perseda's love, and could not gain the
same.
Then gan he break his passions to a
friend,
One of his bashaws, whom he held full
dear.
Her had this bashaw long solicited,
And saw she was not otherwise to be
won
But by her husband's death, this knight
of Rhodes,
Whom presently by treachery he slew.
She, stirred with an exceeding hate
therefor,   120
As cause of this, slew Soliman
And, to escape the bashaw's tyranny,
Did stab herself. And this the tragedy.
LOR. O excellent!
BEL.   But say, Hieronimo,
What then became of him that was the
bashaw?

<hr>

[1] Cf. the play *Soliman and Perseda*, attributed
to Kyd.

HIER. Marry, thus: moved with remorse
of his misdeeds,
Ran to a mountain top, and hung him-
self.
BAL. But which of us is to perform that
part?
HIER. O, that will I, my lords; make no
doubt of it.
I'll play the murderer, I warrant you, 130
For I already have conceited that.
BAL. And what shall I?
HIER. Great Soliman, the Turkish em-
peror.
LOR. And I?
HIER.   Erastus, the knight of Rhodes.
BEL. And I?
HIER.   Perseda, chaste and resolute.
And here, my lords, are several abstracts
drawn,
For each of you to note your parts,
And act it, as occasion's offered you.
You must provide a Turkish cap,
A black mustachio and a falchion;   140
        Gives a paper to Bal[thazar].
You with a cross, like to a knight of
Rhodes;
        Gives another to Lor[enzo].
And, madam, you must attire yourself
    He giveth Bel[-imperia] another.
Like Phœbe, Flora, or the huntress,[2]
Which to your discretion shall seem
best.
And, as for me, my lords, I'll look to
one,
And, with the ransom that the viceroy
sent,
So furnish and perform this tragedy
As all the world shall say Hieronimo
Was liberal in gracing of it so.
BAL. Hieronimo, methinks a comedy were
better.   150
HIER. A comedy?
Fie! Comedies are fit for common wits;
But to present a kingly troop withal,
Give me a stately-written tragedy,
Tragedia cothurnata,[3] fitting kings,
Containing matter, and not common
things.
My lords, all this must be performed,
As fitting for the first night's reveling.
The Italian tragedians were so sharp
of wit

<hr>

[2] *I.e.*, Diana.
[3] Wearing the buskin of the tragic actor.

That in one hour's meditation   160
They would perform anything in action.

Lor. And well it may, for I have seen
the like
In Paris 'mongst the French tragedians.

Hier. In Paris? Mass! And well remem-
beréd!
There's one thing more that rests for us
to do.

Bal. What's that, Hieronimo? Forget
not anything.

Hier. Each one of us
Must act his part in unknown lan-
guages,
That it may breed the more variety:
As you, my lord, in Latin, I in Greek,   170
You in Italian; and, for because I know
That Bel-imperia hath practicéd the
French,
In courtly French shall all her phrases
be.

Bel. You mean to try my cunning then,
Hieronimo?

Bal. But this will be a mere confusion
And hardly shall we all be understood.

Hier. It must be so, for the conclusion
Shall prove the invention and all was
good.
And I myself in an oration,
And with a strange and wondrous show
besides,   180
That I will have there behind a cur-
tain,
Assure yourself, shall make the matter
known.
And all shall be concluded in one scene,
For there's no pleasure ta'en in tedious-
ness.

Bal. [Aside.] How like you this?

Lor. [Aside.]   Why, thus, my lord:
We must resolve to soothe his humors
up.

Bal. On then, Hieronimo. Farewell till
soon.

Hier. You'll ply this gear?

Lor.   I warrant you.
          Exeunt all but Hiero[nimo].

Hier.   Why, so!
Now shall I see the fall of Babylon,
Wrought by the heavens in this con-
fusion.   190
And, if the world like not this tragedy,
Hard is the hap of old Hieronimo. *Exit.*

Hieronimo's garden.]

Enter Isabella with a weapon.

[Isab.] Tell me no more!—O monstrous
homicides!
Since neither piety or pity moves
The king to justice or compassion,
I will revenge myself upon this place,
Where thus they murdered my belovéd
son.   *She cuts down the arbor.*
Down with these branches and these
loathsome boughs
Of this unfortunate and fatal pine!
Down with them, Isabella; rent them
up,
And burn the roots from whence the
rest is sprung!
I will not leave a root, a stalk, a tree,   10
A bough, a branch, a blossom, nor a
leaf,
No, not an herb within this garden
plot—
Accurséd complot of my misery!
Fruitless forever may this garden be,
Barren the earth, and blissless whosoever
Imagines not to keep it unmanured![1]
An eastern wind, commixed with noi-
some airs,
Shall blast the plants and the young
saplings;
The earth with serpents shall be pesteréd,
And passengers, for fear to be infect,   20
Shall stand aloof, and, looking at it,
tell,
"There, murdered, died the son of Isa-
bel."
Ay, here he died, and here I him em-
brace.
See, where his ghost solicits with his
wounds
Revenge on her that should revenge his
death.
Hieronimo, make haste to see thy son,
For sorrow and despair hath cited me
To hear Horatio plead with Rhada-
manth.
Make haste, Hieronimo, to hold ex-
cused[2]
Thy negligence in pursuit of their
deaths   30
Whose hateful wrath bereaved him of
his breath.

[1] Uncultivated.   [2] Make excuses for.

Ah, nay, thou dost delay their deaths,
Forgives the murderers of thy noble
   son,
And none but I bestir me—to no end!
And, as I curse this tree from further
   fruit,
So shall my womb be cursèd for his
   sake,
And with this weapon will I wound the
   breast,
The hapless breast, that gave Horatio
   suck.   *She stabs herself.*

[SCENA TERTIA.

A room in Don Cyprian's palace.]

Enter Hieronimo; he knocks up[1] the curtain.
        Enter the Duke of Castile.

CAS. How now, Hieronimo, where's your
   fellows,
  That you take all this pain?
HIER. O, sir, it is for the author's credit
  To look that all things may go well.
  But, good my lord, let me entreat your
   grace
  To give the king the copy of the play.
  This is the argument of what we show.
CAS. I will, Hieronimo.
HIER. One thing more, my good lord.
CAS. What's that?
HIER.   Let me entreat your grace   10
  That, when the train are passed into the
   gallery,
  You would vouchsafe to throw me down
   the key.
CAS. I will, Hieronimo.   *Exit Cas[tile].*
HIER. What, are you ready, Balthazar?
  Bring a chair and a cushion for the king.

    Enter Balthazar, with a chair.

Well done, Balthazar! Hang up the title:
"Our scene is Rhodes." What, is your
   beard on?
BAL. Half on; the other is in my hand.
HIER. Despatch, for shame. Are you so
   long?   *Exit Balthazar.*
Bethink thyself, Hieronimo,   20
Recall thy wits, recount thy former
   wrongs
Thou hast received by murder of thy
   son,
And lastly, not least, how Isabel,
Once his mother and thy dearest wife,
All woebegone for him, hath slain herself.

Behoves thee then, Hieronimo, to be
   revenged!
The plot is laid of dire revenge.
On then, Hieronimo, pursue revenge,
For nothing wants but acting of revenge!
             Exit Hieronimo.

*Enter Spanish King, Viceroy, the Duke of
   Castile, and their Train [to the gallery].*[2]

KING. Now, viceroy, shall we see the
   tragedy   30
  Of Soliman, the Turkish emperor,
  Performed of pleasure by your son the
   prince,
  My nephew Don Lorenzo, and my niece.
VIC. Who? Bel-imperia?
KING. Ay, and Hieronimo, our marshal,
  At whose request they deign to do't
   themselves.
  These be our pastimes in the court of
   Spain.
  Here, brother, you shall be the book-
   keeper.
  This is the argument of that they show.
            He giveth him a book.
(*Gentlemen, this play of Hieronimo, in* [40
*sundry languages, was thought good to be set
down in English, more largely, for the easier
understanding to every public reader.*)

*Enter Balthazar, Bel-imperia, and Hiero-
                nimo.*

BAL. Bashaw, that Rhodes is ours, yield
   heavens the honor,
  And holy Mahomet, our sacred prophet!
  And be thou graced with every excellence
  That Soliman can give, or thou desire.
  But thy desert in conquering Rhodes is
   less
  Than in reserving this fair Christian
   nymph,
  Perseda, blissful lamp of excellence,   50
  Whose eyes compel, like powerful ada-
   mant,
  The warlike heart of Soliman to wait.

KING. See, viceroy, that is Balthazar, your
   son,
  That represents the emperor Soliman.
  How well he acts his amorous passion!
VIC. Ay, Bel-imperia hath taught him
   that.
[1] Hammers together.   [2] Added by Manly.

CAS. That's because his mind runs all on
　Bel-imperia.

HIER. Whatever joy earth yields, betide
　your majesty.
BAL. Earth yields no joy without Perseda's
　love.
HIER. Let then Perseda on your grace
　attend.　　　　　　　　　　　　　60
BAL. She shall not wait on me, but I on
　her.
　Drawn by the influence of her lights, I
　yield.
　But let my friend, the Rhodian knight,
　come forth,
　Erasto, dearer than my life to me,
　That he may see Perseda, my beloved.

Enter Erasto.

KING. Here comes Lorenzo. Look upon
　the plot
　And tell me, brother, what part plays he?

BEL. Ah, my Erasto, welcome to Perseda.
LOR. Thrice happy is Erasto that thou
　livest;
　Rhodes' loss is nothing to Erasto's joy. 70
　Sith his Perseda lives, his life survives.
BAL. Ah, bashaw, here is love between
　Erasto
　And fair Perseda, sovereign of my soul.
HIER. Remove Erasto, mighty Soliman,
　And then Perseda will be quickly won.
BAL. Erasto is my friend, and, while he
　lives,
　Perseda never will remove her love.
HIER. Let not Erasto live to grieve great
　Soliman.
BAL. Dear is Erasto in our princely eye.
HIER. But, if he be your rival, let him
　die.　　　　　　　　　　　　　80
BAL. Why, let him die!—So love com-
　mandeth me;
　Yet grieve I that Erasto should so die.
HIER. Erasto, Soliman saluteth thee,
　And lets thee wit by me his highness' will,
　Which is, thou shouldst be thus em-
　ployed.　　　　　　　　　*Stab him.*
BEL.　　　　　Ay me!
　Erasto! See, Soliman, Erasto's slain!
BAL. Yet liveth Soliman to comfort thee.
　Fair queen of beauty, let not favor die,
　But with a gracious eye behold his
　grief　　　　　　　　　　　　89

That with Perseda's beauty is increased,
If by Perseda [hi]s grief be not released.
BEL. Tyrant, desist soliciting vain suits.
　Relentless are mine ears to thy laments
　As thy butcher is pitiless and base,
　Which seized on my Erasto, harmless
　knight.
　Yet by thy power thou thinkest to
　command,
　And to thy power Perseda doth obey;
　But, were she able, thus she would
　revenge
　Thy treacheries on thee, ignoble prince;
　　　　　　　　　　　　Stab him.
　And on herself she would be thus re-
　venged.　　　　　　　　*Stab herself.*

KING. Well said!—Old marshal, this was
　bravely done!　　　　　　　　101
HIER. But Bel-imperia plays Perseda
　well!
VIC. Were this in earnest, Bel-imperia,
　You would be better to my son than so.
KING. But now what follows for Hiero-
　nimo?
HIER. Marry, this follows for Hieronimo.
　Here break we off our sundry languages,
　And thus conclude I in our vulgar tongue.
　Happily you think—but bootless are
　your thoughts—
　That this is fabulously counterfeit, 110
　And that we do as all tragedians do—
　To die today (for fashioning our scene,
　The death of Ajax or some Roman peer),
　And, in a minute starting up again,
　Revive to please tomorrow's audience.
　No, princes; know I am Hieronimo,
　The hopeless father of a hapless son,
　Whose tongue is tuned to tell his latest
　tale,
　Not to excuse gross errors in the play.
　I see, your looks urge instance of these
　words;　　　　　　　　　　120
　Behold the reason urging me to this!
　　　Shows [the painting of?] his dead son.
　See here my show; look on this spectacle!
　Here lay my hope, and here my hope
　hath end;
　Here lay my heart, and here my heart
　was slain;
　Here lay my treasure, here my treasure
　lost;
　Here lay my bliss, and here my bliss
　bereft.

But hope, heart, treasure, joy, and bliss,
All fled, failed, died, yea, all decayed
  with this.
From forth these wounds came breath
  that gave me life;
They murdered me that made these fatal
  marks.   130
The cause was love, whence grew this
  mortal hate;
The hate—Lorenzo and young Baltha-
  zar;
The love—my son to Bel-imperia.
But night, the coverer of accursed
  crimes,
With pitchy silence hushed these trai-
  tors' harms,
And lent them leave, for they had sorted [1]
  leisure
To take advantage in my garden plot
Upon my son, my dear Horatio.
There merciless they butchered up my
  boy,
In black, dark night, to pale, dim, cruel
  death.   140
He shrieks. I heard—and yet, methinks,
  I hear—
His dismal outcry echo in the air.
With soonest speed I hasted to the noise,
Where hanging on a tree I found my son,
Through-girt [2] with wounds, and slaugh-
  tered as you see.
And grieved I, think you, at this spec-
  tacle?
Speak, Portuguese, whose loss resembles
  mine.
If thou canst weep upon thy Balthazar,
'Tis like I wailed for my Horatio.   149
And you, my l[ord], whose reconciled son
Marched in a net, and thought himself
  unseen,
And rated me for brainsick lunacy,
With "God amend that mad Hiero-
  nimo!"—
How can you brook our play's catastro-
  phe?
And here behold this bloody handker-
  cher,
Which at Horatio's death I weeping
  dipped
Within the river of his bleeding wounds.
It as propitious, see, I have reserved,
And never hath it left my bloody
  heart,

Soliciting remembrance of my vow   160
With these, O, these accursed murderers,
Which now performed, my heart is
  satisfied.
And to this end the bashaw I became
That might revenge me on Lorenzo's life,
Who therefore was appointed to the part,
And was to represent the knight of
  Rhodes
That I might kill him more conveniently.
So, viceroy, was this Balthazar, thy son,
That Soliman which Bel-imperia,
In person of Perseda, murdered,   170
So[le]ly appointed to that tragic part
That she might slay him that offended
  her.
Poor Bel-imperia missed her part in this:
For, though the story saith she should
  have died,
Yet I of kindness, and of care to her,
Did otherwise determine of her end;
But love of him whom they did hate too
  much
Did urge her resolution to be such.
And, princes, now behold Hieronimo,
Author and actor in this tragedy,   180
Bearing his latest fortune in his fist,
And will as resolute conclude his part
As any of the actors gone before.
And, gentles, thus I end my play.
Urge no more words; I have no more to
  say.   *He runs to hang himself.*
KING. O, hearken, viceroy! Hold, Hiero-
  nimo!
Brother, my nephew and thy son are
  slain!
VIC. We are betrayed; my Balthazar is
  slain!
Break ope the doors; run, save Hiero-
  nimo.
              [*They break in and hold Hieronimo.*][3]
Hieronimo, do but inform the king of
  these events;   190
Upon mine honor, thou shalt have no
  harm.
HIER. Viceroy, I will not trust thee with
  my life,
Which I this day have offered to my son.
Accursed wretch!
Why stay'st thou him that was resolved
  to die?
KING. Speak, traitor! Damned, bloody
  murderer, speak!

[1] Selected.   [2] Pierced.   [3] From 1602 edn.

For now 1 have thee, I will make thee
speak.
Why has thou done this undeserving[1]
deed?

VIC. Why hast thou murderéd my Balthazar?

CAS. Why hast thou butchered both my
children thus?[2]   200

HIER. But are you sure they are dead?

CAS.   Ay, slave, too sure.

HIER. What, and yours too?

VIC. Ay, all are dead; not one of them
survive.

HIER. Nay, then I care not. Come, and we
shall be friends.
Let us lay our heads together;
See, here's a goodly noose will hold them
all.

VIC. O damnéd devil, how secure[3] he is!

HIER. Secure? Why, dost thou wonder
at it?
I tell thee, viceroy, this day I have seen
revenged,
And in that sight am grown a prouder
monarch   210
Than ever sat under the crown of Spain.
Had I as many lives as there be stars,
As many heavens to go to as those lives,

[1] Undeserved.
[2] Lines 201–249 are substituted in the 1602
HIER. O, good words!
As dear to me was my Horatio
As yours, or yours, or yours, my l[ord], to you.
My guiltless son was by Lorenzo slain,
And by Lorenzo and that Balthazar
Am I at last revengéd thoroughly,
Upon whose souls may heavens be yet avenged
With greater far than these afflictions.
CAS. But who were thy confederates in this?
VIC. That was thy daughter Bel-imperia,
For by her hand my Balthazar was slain.
I saw her stab him.
KING.   Why speakest thou not?
HIER. What lesser liberty can kings afford
Than harmless silence? Then afford it me.
Sufficeth, I may not, nor I will not tell thee.
KING. Fetch forth the tortures. Traitor as
thou art,
I'll make thee tell.
HIER. Indeed? Thou mayest torment me as
his wretched son
Hath done in murd'ring my Horatio,
But never shalt thou force me to reveal
The thing which I have vowed inviolate.
And therefore, in despite of all thy threats,
Pleased with their deaths, and eased with their
revenge,
First take my tongue, and afterwards my
heart.   [3] Assured.   [4] Familiar.

I'd give them all, ay, and my soul to boot,
But I would see thee ride in this red pool.

CAS. Speak, who were thy confederates in
this?

VIC. That was thy daughter Bel-imperia,
For by her hand my Balthazar was
slain.
I saw her stab him.

HIER. O, good words! As dear to me was
my Horatio,   220
As yours, or yours, or yours, my lord, to
you.
My guiltless son was by Lorenzo slain,
And by Lorenzo and that Balthazar
Am I at last revengéd thoroughly,
Upon whose souls may heavens be yet
revenged
With greater far than these afflictions.
Methinks, since I grew inward[4] with
revenge,
I cannot look with scorn enough on
death.

KING. What, dost thou mock us, slave?—
Bring tortures forth.

HIER. Do, do, do; and meantime I'll tor-
ture you.   230
You had a son, as I take it, and your son
Should ha' been married to your
daughter. Ha, was't not so?—
You had a son too; he was my liege's
nephew.
He was proud and politic. Had he lived,
He might ha' come to wear the crown of
Spain.
I think 'twas so; 'twas I that killed him.
Look you, this same hand, 'twas it that
stabbed
His heart—do you see, this hand?—
For one Horatio, if you ever knew him, a
youth,
One that they hanged up in his father's
garden;   240
One that did force your valiant son to
yield,
While your more valiant son did take him
prisoner.

VIC. Be deaf, my senses; I can hear no
more.

KING. Fall, heaven, and cover us with thy
sad ruins.

CAS. Roll all the world within thy pitchy
cloud.

HIER. Now do I applaud what I have
acted.

Nunc mers cadæ manus. [1]

Now to express the rupture of my
　　part—

First take my tongue, and afterward my
　　heart.　　*He bites out his tongue.*　249

KING. O, monstrous resolution of a wretch!

See, viceroy, he hath bitten forth his
　　tongue

Rather than to reveal what we required.

CAS. Yet can he write.

KING. And, if in this he satisfy us not,

We will devise th' extremest kind of
　　death

That ever was invented for a wretch.

*Then he makes signs for a knife to mend
　　　　　　　　　　　　　　his pen.*

CAS. O, he would have a knife to mend his
　　pen.

VIC. Here, and advise thee that thou write
　　the troth.—

Look to my brother! Save Hieronimo!

He with a knife stabs the Duke and himself.

KING. What age hath ever heard such
　　monstrous deeds?　　　　　　　260

My brother, and the whole succeeding
　　hope

That Spain expected after my decease!

Go, bear his body hence, that we may
　　mourn

The loss of our beloved brother's death,

That he may be entombed whate'er be-
　　fall.

I am the next, the nearest, last of all.

VIC. And thou, Don Pedro, do the like for
　　us.

Take up our hapless son, untimely
　　slain;

Set me with him, and he with woeful
　　me,　　　　　　　　　　　　　　269

Upon the mainmast of a ship unmanned,

And let the wind and tide haul me
　　along

To Scylla's barking and untaméd gulf,

Or to the loathsome pool of Acheron,

To weep my want for my sweet Baltha-
　　zar.

Spain hath no refuge for a Portingale.

*The trumpets sound a dead march, the King
　　of Spain mourning after his brother's
　　body, and the King of Portingale bearing
　　　　　　　　　　　the body of his son.*

[1] Reading *iners cadat* for *mers cadæ*, the meaning seems to be, "Now let my hand fall lifeless"
(source unknown).

[CHORUS]

Enter Ghost and Revenge.

GHOST. Ay, now my hopes have end in
　　their effects,

When blood and sorrow finish my desires:

Horatio murdered in his father's bower;

Vild Serberine by Pedringano slain;

False Pedringano hanged by quaint de-
　　vice;

Fair Isabella by herself misdone;

Prince Balthazar by Bel-imperia stabbed;

The Duke of Castile and his wicked son

Both done to death by old Hieronimo;

My Bel-imperia fall'n as Dido fell;　　10

And good Hieronimo slain by himself.

Ay, these were spectacles to please my
　　soul!

Now will I beg at lovely Proserpine

That, by the virtue of her princely doom,[2]

I may consort my friends in pleasing sort,

And on my foes work just and sharp re-
　　venge.

I'll lead my friend Horatio through those
　　fields

Where never-dying wars are still inured;[3]

I'll lead fair Isabella to that train [4]　19

Where pity weeps, but never feeleth pain;

I'll lead my Bel-imperia to those joys

That vestal virgins and fair queens pos-
　　sess;

I'll lead Hieronimo where Orpheus plays,

Adding sweet pleasure to eternal days.

But say, Revenge (for thou must help,
　　or none),

Against the rest how shall my hate be
　　shown?

REVENGE. This hand shall hale them down
　　to deepest hell,

Where none but furies, bugs,[5] and tor-
　　tures dwell.

GHOST. Then, sweet Revenge, do this at
　　my request:

Let me be judge, and doom them to un-
　　rest.　　　　　　　　　　　　　30

Let loose poor Tityus from the vulture's
　　gripe,

And let Don Cyprian supply his room;

Place Don Lorenzo on Ixion's wheel,

And let the lover's endless pains surcease

(Juno forgets old wrath, and grants
　　him ease);

[2] Decree.　　　　　　[4] Company.
[3] Carried on.　　　　　[5] Bugbears, terrors.

Hang Balthazar about Chimera's neck,
And let him there bewail his bloody love,
Repining at our joys that are above;
Let Serberine go roll the fatal stone,
And take from Sisyphus his endless
   moan;   40
False Pedringano, for his treachery,
Let him be dragged through boiling
   Acheron,
And there live, dying still in endless
   flames,

Blaspheming gods and all their holy
   names.
REVENGE. Then haste we down to meet
   thy friends and foes,
To place thy friends in ease, the rest in
   woes,
For here, though death hath [1] end their
   misery,
I'll there begin their endless tragedy.
Exeunt.

[1] 1623 edn. has *doth.*

ARDEN OF FEVERSHAM

The authorship of *Arden of Feversham* has been a source of much conjecture. In 1770 Edward Jacob reprinted the play with a brief preface in which, without advancing any evidence of value, he attributed it to Shakespeare. In spite of much able criticism written in support of Shakespearean authorship in the nineteenth century, this view is now discredited. In his edition of Kyd's works, Boas held, as Fleay had argued many years earlier, that the author was an imitator of Kyd rather than Kyd himself. But later, in reviewing A. K. McIlwraith's *Five Elizabethan Tragedies* (Oxford, 1938), which decided that the attribution to Kyd was possible, Boas announced that he thought Marlowe "more probable" (*YWES*, 1938). Tucker Brooke, however, in *The Tudor Drama* (Boston, 1911), had called it the finest of Kyd's plays. And Kyd's claim has also been supported by Charles Crawford ("The Authorship of *Arden of Feversham*," *SJ*, 1903, and *Collectanea*, Stratford-on-Avon, 1906) and by H. Dugdale Sykes in *Sidelights on Shakespeare* (Stratford-on-Avon, 1919). Sykes gives the following recapitulation of his evidence:

The play echoes the phrasing not only of Kyd's earlier dramas, but of his later work as well. It uses his vocabulary and exhibits the characteristic features of his diction even to the least conspicuous of his mannerisms. It was written by a dramatist who, like Kyd, had a technical knowledge of legal documents and legal procedure. It deals with just such a crime as he had chosen for the subject of a prose tract [*The Murder of John Brewen*]. Like *Soliman and Perseda* it borrows from Marlowe's *Edward II*. Like *The Spanish Tragedy* and *Soliman and Perseda* it shows the influence of Seneca and of Garnier. Like them it was published anonymously by Edward White. It is with some confidence that I submit that there is here conclusive proof that it is Kyd's play.

Although able scholars have accepted this argument, the case for Kyd is very doubtful. Sykes's impressionistic method of determining authorship has been shown to be fallacious in similar cases. Here the argument from diction is especially questionable: first, because he does not confine himself to Kyd's one authentic original play, *The Spanish Tragedy*, for comparison, but speaks of *Arden of Feversham* as echoing Kyd's "earlier dramas" and "later work"; and, second, because there was extensive borrowing of effective phrases and devices in plays around 1590.

Other candidates for at least a hand in the play have included Anthony Munday (H. W. Crundell, "*Arden of Feversham*," *NQ*, 1934) and an otherwise totally unknown person named Cloy. The latter suggestion came from W. J. Lawrence, who found an item in the sales catalogue of the library of Dr. John Monro in April 1792 listing "Cloy's *Tragedy of Arden of Feversham*, 1633" (*TLS*, June 28, 1934). Lawrence admitted, however, that the name "Cloy" as a surname is otherwise unknown, but pointed out that on August 27, 1623, Sir Henry Herbert, Master of the Revels, granted a license to Bartholomew Cloys and his three assistants to create and perform various puppet shows. E. H. C. Oliphant, who had previously held out for a joint authorship of Kyd and Marlowe, found this lead worth following up (*TLS*, June 18, 1936), although Charles L. Stainer had suggested that "Cloy" might have been a misprint for "Clay," and recalled that Jonson in *A Tale of a Tub* (1633) had ridiculed a "John Clay." V. Scholderer made the sensible suggestion that the name read as "Cloy" for listing in the catalogue might well have referred to the former owner of the copy, and that perhaps

"Cloy's" was simply a misreading of "Oldys," that is, William Oldys, the well-known eighteenth century scholar and bibliographer. The obvious solution to this whole muddle is simply to regard *Arden of Feversham* as the work of *auctor ignotus*.

The play is founded on an actual murder committed in 1551, a murder so notorious that Holinshed almost a generation later gave a lengthy account of it in his *Chronicles*. Glenn H. Blayney found an almost simultaneously printed reference to the murder in the *Breviat Chronicle* in 1551 or 1552 ("*Arden of Feversham*—An Early Reference," *NQ*, 1955). The dramatist apparently used the Holinshed chronicle, but he may have been acquainted with other accounts or even with local legends. Significant variations from Holinshed are the addition of the confidant Franklin, the omission of Arden's winking at his wife's infidelity, and the use of a fog to frustrate the plans of Shakebag and Will. The free use of chronicle material around 1592, especially for tragedy, may have influenced the selection of this story for dramatization. The author handles it realistically, almost journalistically, presenting, as he claims in the epilogue, "a naked tragedy" without embellishments of style. Perhaps the fact that the story deals with characters of the middle and lower classes rather than with kings and nobles common in tragedy drawn from romance and history led the author to avoid the pomp and rhetoric prevailing in the tragedy of the period. The success of the play, with its dramatic force and its vivid impressions of moods and places, probably had much to do with the vogue of the type.

Henry H. Adams, in his *English Domestic or Homiletic Tragedy, 1575 to 1642* (Columbia University Press, 1943), calls *Arden* the "most famous of all Elizabethan domestic tragedies, and unquestionably the best." It is also the first important representative to survive. As Adams sees the genre, Elizabethan domestic tragedy always had a didactic objective, and the only constant attributes of all such plays were the choice of a hero, the moralizing, and the religious teaching. Moreover, typical domestic tragedy always followed a general pattern found in *Arden* ("the sequence being sin, discovery, repentance, punishment, and expectation of divine mercy"). Whenever the playwright varied from his source, he rearranged his events "to stress the ethical implications of the story. The entire construction of the play is that of a moral demonstration, and at every stage of the action the hand of Providence can be discerned." Adams feels that the treatment of the character of Arden from the dramatic point of view is understandable only when sixteenth-century religious conceptions are applied to the play. "Throughout the action, the fortunes of Arden correspond to his state of grace." The author therefore focuses on Arden's legalized land stealing and his treatment of the former occupants of the land as the cause of his death. Although Adams describes him as "not an attractive figure at any time," Arden is really a more complex—even contradictory—character than this statement implies and scarcely seems to deserve the gory death he finally receives. The murderers, however, have earned their mass punishment; and Black Will and Shakebag, the conscienceless villains who escape, come to a bad end. Even an innocent man, the goldsmith Bradshaw, goes down in the general holocaust. Clark is the only one whose end remains unknown. *Arden of Feversham* is a suspenseful pursuit play which maintains interest in spite of its simplicity and frequent crudeness.

The play was entered on the Stationers' Register on April 3, 1592, and was printed anonymously for Edward White in the same year. There had been a quarrel between White and another publisher, Abel Jeffes, over the rights to publish *Arden* and *The Spanish Tragedy*. The register recorded the entry of *Arden* by White on April 9, 1592. On December 18 a court decree decided that since White had printed *The Spanish Tragedy*, belonging to Jeffes, and Jeffes had printed *Arden*, belonging to White, both impressions should be confiscated and the profits devoted "to the use of the poore of the company." Although this order called for confiscation, not destruction, no copy of Jeffes's edition of *Arden* has survived (Hugh Macdonald and D. Nichol Smith, Malone Society edition of the 1592 quarto of *Arden*, 1947). Greg attempted to unravel this confusion by suggesting that probably in the spring of 1592 Jeffes got hold of a somewhat corrupt manuscript of *The Spanish Tragedy* and printed it toward the end of July without registering it. In the meantime, Greg speculates, White had obtained an excellent version (perhaps through the actors themselves) and immediately printed it. Then Jeffes, to protect what he regarded as his rights, entered the play on the Stationers' Register on October 8. White then accused Jeffes of infringing his rights in *Arden*, whereupon the court stepped in. It was the White editions, with comparatively good texts, which survived. (See Greg, Malone Society edition of *The Spanish Tragedy*, 1948.) Other editions appeared in 1599 and 1633.

The present text is based on John S. Farmer's reproduction of the quarto of 1592 in the Tudor Facsimile Texts and on Tucker Brooke's reprint in *The Shakespeare Apocrypha* (Oxford, 1918).

THE LAMENTABLE AND TRUE TRAG= EDY OF M[ASTER] ARDEN OF FEVERSHAM IN KENT[1]

[*DRAMATIS PERSONÆ*

LORD CHEINY.
THOMAS ARDEN, *a gentleman of Feversham.*
FRANKLIN, *his friend.*
MICHAEL, *Arden's servant.*
MOSBIE, *lover of Arden's wife.*
MAYOR OF FEVERSHAM.
ADAM FOWLE, *landlord of the Flower-de-Luce.*
CLARKE, *a painter.*
GREENE, *a tenant.*

BRADSHAW, *a goldsmith.*
DICK REEDE, *a sailor.*
BLACK WILL ⎱ *murderers.*
SHAKEBAG ⎰

ALICE, *Arden's wife.*
SUSAN, *Mosbie's sister.*

ATTENDANTS OF LORD CHEINY, THE WATCH,
A SAILOR, A PRENTICE, A FERRYMAN.

SCENE: *Feversham, London, and the surrounding country.*

TIME: *1551.*]

[SCENE i.

Before and in Arden's house.]

Enter Arden and Franklin.

FRANK. Arden, cheer up thy spirits, and
    droop no more!
My gracious lord, the Duke of Somerset,
Hath freely given to thee and to thy
    heirs,
By letters patents from his majesty,
All the lands of the Abbey of Feversham.
Here are the deeds, sealed and subscribed
    with his name and the king's.
               [*Gives the papers.*]
Read them, and leave this melancholy
    mood.
ARD. Franklin, thy love prolongs my
    weary life;

And but for thee how odious were this
    life,
That shows me nothing, but torments
    my soul,   10
And those foul objects that offend mine
    eyes,
Which makes me wish that for this veil
    of heaven
The earth hung over my head and cov-
    ered me!
Love letters passed twixt Mosbie and my
    wife,
And they have privy meetings in the
    town.
Nay, on his finger did I spy the ring
Which at our marriage day the priest put
    on.
Can any grief be half so great as this?
FRANK. Comfort thyself, sweet friend. It
    is not strange   19
That women will be false and wavering.
ARD. Ay, but to dote on such a one as he
Is monstrous, Franklin, and intolerable.
FRANK. Why, what is he?
ARD. A botcher,[2] and no better at the first,

[1] The title continues: "Who Was Most Wick-edly Murdered by the Means of His Disloyal and Wanton Wife, Who for the Love She Bare to One Mosbie Hired Two Desperate Ruffians, Black Will and Shakebag, to Kill Him. Wherein Is Showed the Great Malice and Dissimulation of a Wicked Woman, the Unsatiable Desire of Filthy Lust, and the Shameful End of All Murderers."

[2] A patcher of old clothes, a tailor.

391

Who, by base brokage getting some small
  stock,
Crept into service of a nobleman,
And by his servile flattery and fawning
Is now become the steward of his house,
And bravely jets it [1] in his silken gown.
FRANK. No nobleman will count'nance
  such a peasant.   30
ARD. Yes, the Lord Clifford, he that loves
  not me.
But through his favor let him not grow
  proud;
For, were he by the lord protector
  backed,
He should not make me to be pointed at.
I am by birth a gentleman of blood,
And that injurious ribald that attempts
To violate my dear wife's chastity
(For dear I hold her love, as dear as
  heaven)
Shall on the bed which he thinks to defile
See his dissevered joints and sinews torn,
Whilst on the planchers [2] pants his weary
  body,   41
Smeared in the channels of his lustful
  blood.
FRANK. Be patient, gentle friend, and
  learn of me
To ease thy grief and save her chastity.
Entreat her fair; sweet words are fittest
  engines
To race [3] the flint walls of a woman's
  breast.
In any case be not too jealous, [4]
Nor make no question of her love to thee;
But, as securely, [5] presently [6] take horse,
And lie with me at London all this term;
For women, when they may, will not,   51
But, being kept back, straight grow out-
  rageous.
ARD. Though this abhors from [7] reason, yet
  I'll try it,
And call her forth and presently take
  leave.—How! Alice!

Here enters Alice.

ALICE. Husband, what mean you to get
  up so early?
Summer nights are short, and yet you
  rise ere day.

[1] Struts.   [5] As if unsuspicious.
[2] Planks, wooden floor.   [6] Immediately.
[3] Raze.   [7] Is at variance with.
[4] Common form for *jealous*

Had I been wake, you had not rise [8] so
  soon.
ARD. Sweet love, thou know'st that we
  two, Ovid-like,
Have often chid the morning when it gan
  to peep,
And often wished that dark Night's pur-
  blind steeds   60
Would pull her by the purple mantle
  back,
And cast her in the ocean to her love.
But this night, sweet Alice, thou hast
  killed my heart:
I heard thee call on Mosbie in thy sleep.
ALICE. 'Tis like I was asleep when I named
  him,
For, being awake, he comes not in my
  thoughts.
ARD. Ay, but you started up and suddenly,
Instead of him, caught me about the
  neck.
ALICE. Instead of him? Why, who was
  there but you?   69
And where but one is, how can I mistake?
FRANK. Arden, leave [9] to urge her overfar.
ARD. Nay, love, there is no credit in a
  dream;
Let it suffice I know thou lovest me well.
ALICE. Now I remember whereupon it
  came:
Had we no talk of Mosbie yesternight?
FRANK. Mistress Alice, I heard you name
  him once or twice.
ALICE. And thereof came it, and therefore
  blame not me.
ARD. I know it did, and therefore let it
  pass.
I must to London, sweet Alice, presently.
ALICE. But, tell me, do you mean to stay
  there long?   80
ARD. No longer there till my affairs be
  done.
FRANK. He will not stay above a month at
  most.
ALICE. A month? Ay me! Sweet Arden,
  come again
Within a day or two, or else I die.
ARD. I cannot long be from thee, gentle
  Alice.
Whilst Michael fetch our horses from the
  field,
Franklin and I will down unto the quay,

[8] An old form of the past participle.
[9] Cease.

For I have certain goods there to unload.
Meanwhile prepare our breakfast, gentle
Alice,
For yet ere noon we'll take horse and
away.   90
                Exeunt Arden and Franklin.
ALICE. Ere noon he means to take horse
and away!
Sweet news is this. O, that some airy
spirit
Would in the shape and likeness of a
horse
Gallop with Arden cross the ocean,
And throw him from his back into the
waves!
Sweet Mosbie is the man that hath my
heart,
And he usurps it, having naught but this,
That I am tied to him by marriage.
Love is a god, and marriage is but words;
And therefore Mosbie's title is the best.
Tush! whether it be or no, he shall be
mine,   101
In spite of him, of Hymen, and of rites.

Here enters Adam of the Flower-de-Luce.

And here comes Adam of the Flower-de-
Luce.
I hope he brings me tidings of my love.—
How now, Adam, what is the news with
you?
Be not afraid; my husband is now from
home.
ADAM. He whom you wot [1] of, Mosbie,
Mistress Alice,
Is come to town, and sends you word by
me
In any case you may not visit him.
ALICE. Not visit him?   110
ADAM. No, nor take no knowledge of his
being here.
ALICE. But, tell me, is he angry or dis-
pleased?
ADAM. Should seem so, for he is wondrous
sad.
ALICE. Were he as mad as raving Hercules,
I'll see him, I; and, were thy house of
force,[2]
These hands of mine should race it to
the ground,
Unless that thou wouldst bring me to
my love.

[1] Know.   [2] Fortified.

ADAM. Nay, and [3] you be so impatient, I'll
be gone.
ALICE. Stay, Adam, stay; thou wert wont
to be my friend.
Ask Mosbie how I have incurred his
wrath;   120
Bear him from me these pair of silver
dice,
With which we played for kisses many a
time,
And, when I lost, I won, and so did he
(Such winning and such losing Jove send
me!);
And bid him, if his love do not decline,
[To] [4] come this morning but along my
door,
And as a stranger but salute me there.
This may he do without suspect [5] or fear.
ADAM. I'll tell him what you say, and so
farewell.   *Exit Adam.*
ALICE. Do, and one day I'll make amends
for all.—   130
I know he loves me well, but dares not
come,
Because my husband is so jealous,
And these my marrow [6]-prying neigh-
bors' blab
Hinder our meetings, when we would
confer.
But, if I live, that block shall be removed,
And, Mosbie, thou that comes to me by
stealth
Shalt neither fear the biting speech of
men
Nor Arden's looks. As surely shall he die
As I abhor him and love only thee.

Here enters Michael.

How now, Michael, whither are you go-
ing?   140
MICH. To fetch my master's nag.
I hope you'll think on me.
ALICE. Ay; but, Michael, see you keep
your oath,
And be as secret as you are resolute.
MICH. I'll see he shall not live above a
week.
ALICE. On that condition, Michael, here is
my hand;
None shall have Mosbie's sister but thy-
self.

[3] If.   [4] Added in 1633 edn.
[5] Suspicion.   [6] Later quartos have *narrow.*

MICH. I understand the painter here hard by
  Hath made report that he and Sue is sure.[1]
ALICE. There's no such matter, Michael; believe it not.   150
MICH. But he hath sent a dagger sticking in a heart,
  With a verse or two stolen from a painted cloth,[2]
  The which I hear the wench keeps in her chest.
  Well, let her keep it! I shall find a fellow
  That can both write and read and make rime too.
  And if I do—well, I say no more.
  I'll send from London such a taunting letter
  As[3] [she][4] shall eat the heart he sent with salt
  And fling the dagger at the painter's head.
ALICE. What needs all this? I say that Susan's thine.   160
MICH. Why, then I say that I will kill my master,
  Or anything that you will have me do.
ALICE. But, Michael, see you do it cunningly.
MICH. Why, say I should be took, I'll ne'er confess
  That you know anything; and Susan, being a maid,
  May beg me from the gallows of the shrieve.[5]
ALICE. Trust not to that, Michael.
MICH. You cannot tell me; I have seen it, I.
  But, mistress, tell her, whether I live or die,
  I'll make her more worth than twenty painters can,   170
  For I will rid mine elder brother away,
  And then the farm of Bolton is mine own.
  Who would not venture upon house and land,
  When he may have it for a right-down[6] blow?

[1] Betrothed.   [3] That.
[2] Hangings for a room.   [4] Supplied by Delius.
[5] Sheriff. "It was a popular belief that an offer of marriage from a virgin might save a criminal from the gallows" (Oliphant).
[6] Downright.

Here enters Mosbie.

ALICE. Yonder comes Mosbie! Michael, get thee gone,
  And let not him nor any know thy drifts.[7]
                                    Exit Michael.
  Mosbie, my love!
MOS. Away, I say, and talk not to me now!
ALICE. A word or two, sweetheart, and then I will.
  'Tis yet but early days;[8] thou needest not fear.   180
MOS. Where is your husband?
ALICE. 'Tis now high water, and he is at the quay.
MOS. There let him be; henceforward know me not.
ALICE. Is this the end of all thy solemn oaths?
  Is this the fruit thy reconcilement buds?
  Have I for this given thee so many favors,
  Incurred my husband's hate, and, out alas,
  Made shipwreck of mine honor for thy sake?
  And dost thou say, "Henceforward know me not"?
  Remember, when I locked thee in my closet,[9]   190
  What were thy words and mine. Did we not both
  Decree to murder Arden in the night?
  The heavens can witness, and the world can tell,
  Before I saw that falsehood look of thine,
  Fore I was tangled with thy ticing[10] speech,.
  Arden to me was dearer than my soul—
  And shall be still. Base peasant, get thee gone,
  And boast not of thy conquest over me,
  Gotten by witchcraft and mere[11] sorcery!
  For what hast thou to countenance[12] my love,   200
  Being descended of a noble house,
  And matched already with a gentleman
  Whose servant thou mayst be? And so farewell.
MOS. Ungentle and unkind Alice, now I see
  That which I ever feared, and find too true:

[7] Plots.   [10] Enticing.
[8] Early in the day.   [11] Absolute.
[9] Private chamber.   [12] Be in keeping with.

A woman's love is as the lightning-
flame,
Which even in bursting forth consumes
itself.
To try thy constancy have I been
strange.
Would I had never tried, but lived in
hope!

ALICE. What needs thou try me whom
thou never found false?   210

MOS. Yet pardon me, for love is jealous.

ALICE. So list [1] the sailor to the mermaid's
song;
So looks the traveler to the basilisk.
I am content for to be reconciled,
And that, I know, will be mine over-
throw.

MOS. Thine overthrow? First let the world
dissolve.

ALICE. Nay, Mosbie, let me still enjoy
thy love,
And, happen what will, I am resolute.
My saving husband hoards up bags of
gold   219
To make our children rich, and now is he
Gone to unload the goods that shall be
thine,
And he and Franklin will to London
straight.

MOS. To London, Alice? If thou'lt be
ruled by me,
We'll make him sure enough for coming
there.

ALICE. Ah, would we could!

MOS. I happened on a painter yesternight,
The only cunning man of Christendom,
For he can temper poison with his oil,
That whoso looks upon the work he
draws
Shall, with the beams that issue from
his [2] sight,   230
Suck venom to his breast and slay him-
self.
Sweet Alice, he shall draw thy counter-
feit,
That Arden may, by gazing on it, perish.

ALICE. Ay, but, Mosbie, that is dangerous,
For thou, or I, or any other else,
Coming into the chamber where it hangs,
may die.

MOS. Ay, but we'll have it covered with a
cloth
And hung up in the study for himself.

ALICE. It may not be, for, when the picture's drawn,   239
Arden, I know, will come and show it me.

MOS. Fear not; we'll have that shall serve
the turn.   [*They cross the stage.*]
This is the painter's house; I'll call him
forth.

ALICE. But, Mosbie, I'll have no such picture, I.

MOS. I pray thee leave it to my discretion.
How, Clarke!

Here enters Clarke.

O, you are an honest man of your word;
you served me well.

CLARKE. Why, sir, I'll do it for you at
any time,
Provided, as you have given your word,
I may have Susan Mosbie to my wife.
For, as sharp-witted poets, whose sweet
verse
Make heavenly gods break off their nec-
tar draughts   250
And lay their ears down to the lowly
earth,
Use humble promise to their sacred muse,
So we that are the poets' favorites
Must have a love. Ay, Love is the
painter's muse,
That makes him frame a speaking coun-
tenance,
A weeping eye that witnesses heart's
grief.
Then tell me, Master Mosbie, shall I
have her?

ALICE. 'Tis pity but he should; he'll use
her well.

MOS. Clarke, here's my hand; my sister
shall be thine.

CLARKE. Then, brother, to requite this
courtesy,   260
You shall command my life, my skill,
and all.

ALICE. Ah, that thou couldst be secret!

MOS. Fear him not. Leave; I have talked
sufficient.

CLARKE. You know not me that ask such
questions.
Let it suffice I know you love him well,
And fain would have your husband made
away;
Wherein, trust me, you show a noble
mind.

[1] Listens.   [2] Its.

That rather than you'll live with him
you hate,
You'll venture life, and die with him
you love.
The like will I do for my Susan's sake. 270
ALICE. Yet nothing could enforce me to
the deed
But Mosbie's love.   Might I without
control
Enjoy thee still, then Arden should not
die;
But, seeing I cannot, therefore let him
die.
MOS. Enough, sweet Alice; thy kind words
makes me melt.
Your trick of poisoned pictures we dis-
like;
Some other poison would do better far.
ALICE. Ay, such as might be put into his
broth,
And yet in taste not to be found at all.
CLARKE. I know your mind, and here I
have it for you.   280
Put but a dram of this into his drink,
Or any kind of broth that he shall eat,
And he shall die within an hour after.
ALICE. As I am a gentlewoman, Clarke,
next day
Thou and Susan shall be married.
MOS. And I'll make her dowry more than
I'll talk of, Clarke.
CLARKE. Yonder's your husband. Mosbie,
I'll be gone.

Here enters Arden and Franklin.

ALICE. In good time [1] see where my hus-
band comes.
Master Mosbie, ask him the question
yourself.   *Exit Clarke.*
MOS. Master Arden, being at London yes-
ternight,   290
The Abbey lands, whereof you are now
possessed,
Were offered me on some occasion
By Greene, one of Sir Antony Ager's men.
I pray you, sir, tell me, are not the lands
yours?
Hath any other interest herein?
ARD. Mosbie, that question we'll decide
anon.
Alice, make ready my breakfast; I must
hence.   *Exit Alice.*

[1] At the right moment.

As for the lands, Mosbie, they are mine
By letters patents from his majesty. 299
But I must have a mandate for my wife;
They say you seek to rob me of her love.
Villain, what makes thou in her com-
pany?
She's no companion for so base a groom.
MOS. Arden, I thought not on her; I came
to thee;
But rather than I pocket up this wrong—
FRANK. [*Interposing.*] What will you do,
sir?
MOS. Revenge it on the proudest of you
both.
Then Arden draws forth Mosbie's sword.
ARD. So, sirrah.   You may not wear a
sword—
The statute makes against artificers. [2]
I warrand that I do. [3] Now use your bod-
kin,   310
Your Spanish needle, and your pressing
iron,
For this shall go with me. And mark my
words—
You goodman botcher, 'tis to you I
speak—
The next time that I take thee near my
house,
Instead of legs I'll make thee crawl on
stumps.
MOS. Ah, Master Arden, you have injured
me;
I do appeal to God and to the world.
FRANK. Why, canst thou deny thou wert
a botcher once?
MOS. Measure me what I am, not what I
was.
ARD. Why, what art thou now but a velvet
drudge,   320
A cheating steward, and base-minded
peasant?
MOS. Arden, now thou hast belched and
vomited
The rancorous venom of thy misswoln
heart,
Hear me but speak. As I intend to live
With God and his elected saints in
heaven,
I never meant more to solicit her;
And that she knows, and all the world
shall see.

[2] Provides against the wearing of swords by
handicraftsmen.
[3] I have warrant for what I do.

I loved her once—sweet Arden, pardon
   me.
I could not choose; her beauty fired my
   heart!
But time hath quenched these over-
   raging coals;   330
And, Arden, though I now frequent thy
   house,
'Tis for my sister's sake, her waiting-
   maid,
And not for hers. Mayest thou enjoy
   her long!
Hell-fire and wrathful vengeance light
   on me,
If I dishonor her or injure thee.
ARD. Mosbie, with these thy protestations
   The deadly hatred of my heart is ap-
   peased,
And thou and I'll be friends, if this prove
   true.
As for the base terms I gave thee late,
Forget them, Mosbie; I had cause to
   speak,   340
When all the knights and gentlemen of
   Kent
Make common table talk of her and thee.
MOS. Who lives that is not touched with
   slanderous tongues?
FRANK. Then, Mosbie, to eschew the
   speech of men,
Upon whose general bruit [1] all honor
   hangs,
Forbear his house.
ARD. Forbear it! Nay, rather frequent it
   more.
The world shall see that I distrust her
   not.
To warn him on the sudden from my
   house
Were to confirm the rumor that is
   grown.   350
MOS. By my faith, sir, [2] you say true,
And therefore will I sojourn here awhile,
Until our enemies have talked their fill;
And then, I hope, they'll cease, and at
   last confess
How causeless they have injured her and
   me.
   [*They pass to a room on the inner stage.*]
ARD. And I will lie at London all this term
To let them see how light I weigh their
   words.

[1] Report.
[2] All early edns. read *By faith, my sir.*

Here enters Alice.

ALICE. Husband, sit down; your breakfast
   will be cold.
ARD. Come, M[aster] Mosbie, will you sit
   with us?
MOS. I cannot eat, but I'll sit for com-
   pany.   360
ARD. Sirrah Michael, see our horse be
   ready.
ALICE. Husband, why pause ye? Why eat
   you not?
ARD. I am not well. There's something
   in this broth
That is not wholesome. Didst thou make
   it, Alice?
ALICE. I did, and that's the cause it likes
   not you.
Then she throws down the broth on the ground.
   There's nothing that I do can please your
   taste.
You were best to say I would have poi-
   soned you.
I cannot speak or cast aside my eye,
But he imagines I have stepped awry.
Here's he that you cast in my teeth so
   oft;   370
Now will I be convinced or purge myself.
I charge thee speak to this mistrustful
   man,
Thou that wouldst see me hang, thou,
   Mosbie, thou.
What favor hast thou had more than a
   kiss
At coming or departing from the town?
MOS. You wrong yourself and me to cast
   these doubts;
Your loving husband is not jealous.
ARD. Why, gentle Mistress Alice, cannot
   I be ill
But you'll accuse yourself?—
Franklin, thou hast a box of mithri-
   date;   380
I'll take a little to prevent the worst.
FRANK. Do so, and let us presently take
   horse;
My life for yours, ye shall do well enough.
ALICE. Give me a spoon; I'll eat of it my-
   self.
Would it were full of poison to the brim,
Then should my cares and troubles have
   an end!
Was ever silly [3] woman so tormented?

[3] Simple.

ARD. Be patient, sweet love; I mistrust
    not thee.
ALICE. God will revenge it, Arden, if thou
    dost;
    For never woman loved her husband
    better than I do thee.   390
ARD. I know it, sweet Alice. Cease to
    complain,
    Lest that in tears I answer thee again.
FRANK. Come, leave this dallying, and let
    us away.
ALICE. Forbear to wound me with that
    bitter word;
    Arden shall go to London in my arms.
ARD. Loath am I to depart, yet I must go.
ALICE. Wilt thou to London, then, and
    leave me here?
    Ah, if thou love me, gentle Arden, stay.
    Yet, if thy business be of great im-
    port,   399
    Go, if thou wilt; I'll bear it as I may.
    But write from London to me every week,
    Nay, every day, and stay no longer there
    Than thou must needs, lest that I die for
    sorrow.
ARD. I'll write unto thee every other tide.
    And so farewell, sweet Alice, till we meet
    next.
ALICE. Farewell, husband, seeing you'll
    have it so;
    And, M[aster] Franklin, seeing you take
    him hence,
    In hope you'll hasten him home, I'll give
    you this.   *And then she kisseth him.*
FRANK. And if he stay, the fault shall not
    be mine.
    Mosbie, farewell, and see you keep your
    oath.   410
MOS. I hope he is not jealous of me now.
ARD. No, Mosbie, no; hereafter think of
    me
    As of your dearest friend, and so farewell.
    Exeunt Arden, Franklin, and Michael.
ALICE. I am glad he is gone; he was about
    to stay,
    But did you mark me then how I brake
    off?
MOS. Ay, Alice, and it was cunningly per-
    formed.
    But what a villain is that painter Clarke!
ALICE. Was it not a goodly poison that he
    gave?
    Why, he's as well now as he was be-
    fore.   419

It should have been some fine confection
That might have given the broth some
    dainty taste.
This powder was too gross and populous.[1]
MOS. But, had he eaten but three spoon-
    fuls more,
Then had he died and our love continued.
ALICE. Why, so it shall, Mosbie, albeit he
    live.
MOS. It is unpossible, for I have sworn
Never hereafter to solicit thee,
Or, whilst he lives, once more importune
    thee.
ALICE. Thou shalt not need; I will impor-
    tune thee.
What? Shall an oath make thee forsake
    my love?   430
As if I have not sworn as much myself
And given my hand unto him in the
    church!
Tush, Mosbie; oaths are words, and
    words is wind,
And wind is mutable. Then, I conclude,
'Tis childishness to stand upon an oath.
MOS. Well proved, Mistress Alice; yet by
    your leave
I'll keep mine unbroken whilst he lives.
ALICE. Ay, do, and spare not; his time is
    but short;
For, if thou beest as resolute as I,
We'll have him murdered as he walks the
    streets.   440
In London, many alehouse ruffians keep,[2]
Which, as I hear, will murther men for
    gold.
They shall be soundly feed to pay him
    home.

Here enters Greene.

MOS. Alice, what's he that comes yonder?
    Knowest thou him?
ALICE. Mosbie, begone! I hope 'tis one
    that comes
To put in practice our intended drifts.
                                Exit Mosbie.
GREENE. Mistress Arden, you are well
    met.
I am sorry that your husband is from
    home,
Whenas[3] my purposed journey was to
    him;   449
Yet all my labor is not spent in vain,

[1] Thick.   [2] Lodge.   [3] Since.

For I suppose that you can full discourse
And flat resolve [1] me of the thing I seek.

ALICE. What is it, Master Greene? If that I may
Or can with safety, I will answer you.

GREENE. I heard your husband had the grant of late,
Confirmed by letters patents from the king,
Of all the lands of the Abbey of Feversham,
Generally intitled,[2] so that all former grants
Are cut off, whereof I myself had one;
But now my interest by that is void.   460
This is all, Mistress Arden. Is it true or no? [3]

ALICE. True, Master Greene; the lands are his in state,[4]
And whatsoever leases were before
Are void for term of Master Arden's life.
He hath the grant under the chancery seal.

GREENE. Pardon me, Mistress Arden, I must speak,
For I am touched. Your husband doth me wrong
To wring me from the little land I have.
My living is my life; only that
Resteth remainder of my portion.   470
Desire of wealth is endless in his mind,
And he is greedy-gaping still [5] for gain;
Nor cares he though young gentlemen do beg,
So he may scrape and hoard up in his pouch.
But, seeing he hath taken my lands, I'll value life
As careless as he is careful for to get;
And tell him this from me, I'll be revenged,
And so as he shall wish the Abbey lands
Had rested still within their former state.   479

ALICE. Alas, poor gentleman, I pity you,
And woe is me that any man should want!
God knows 'tis not my fault. But wonder not

Though he be hard to others, when to me—
Ah, Master Greene, God knows how I am used!

GREENE. Why, Mistress Arden, can the crabbéd churl
Use you unkindly? Respects he not your birth,
Your honorable friends, nor what you brought?
Why, all Kent knows your parentage and what you are.

ALICE. Ah, M[aster] Greene, be it spoken in secret here,   489
I never live good day with him alone.
When he is at home, then have I froward looks,
Hard words, and blows to mend the match withal;
And, though I might content as good a man,
Yet doth he keep in every corner trulls;
And, weary with his trugs [6] at home,
Then rides he straight to London; there, forsooth,
He revels it among such filthy ones
As counsels him to make away his wife.
Thus live I daily in continual fear,
In sorrow, so despairing of redress   500
As every day I wish with hearty prayer
That he or I were taken forth the world.

GREENE. Now trust me, Mistress Alice, it grieveth me
So fair a creature should be so abused.
Why, who would have thought the civil sir so sullen?
He looks so smoothly. Now, fie upon him, churl!
And, if he live a day, he lives too long.
But frolic, woman! I shall be the man
Shall set you free from all this discontent;
And, if the churl deny my interest   510
And will not yield my lease into my hand,
I'll pay him home, whatever hap to me.

ALICE. But speak you as you think?

GREENE. Ay, God's my witness, I mean plain dealing,
For I had rather die than lose my land.

ALICE. Then, Master Greene, be counseléd by me.
Endanger not yourself for such a churl,

---

[1] Completely satisfy.   [2] Deeded.
[3] From 1599 edn. Original has *nor*.
[4] By law.   [5] Always.   [6] Wenches.

But hire some cutter [1] for to cut him
short,

And here's ten pound to wager them
withal.

When he is dead, you shall have twenty
more,   520

And the lands whereof my husband is
possessed

Shall be intitled as they were before.

GREENE. Will you keep promise with me?

ALICE. Or count me false and perjured
whilst I live.

GREENE. Then here's my hand; I'll have
him so despatched.

I'll up to London straight; I'll thither
post,

And never rest till I have compassed it.
Till then farewell.

ALICE. Good fortune follow all your for-
ward thoughts,   529

Exit Greene.

And whosoever doth attempt the deed,

A happy hand I wish, and so farewell.—

All this goes well. Mosbie, I long for
thee

To let thee know all that I have contrived.

Here enters Mosbie and Clarke.

MOS. How now, Alice, what's the news?

ALICE. Such as will content thee well,
sweetheart.

MOS. Well, let them pass awhile, and tell
me, Alice,

How have you dealt and tempered with [2]
my sister?

What, will she have my neighbor, Clarke,
or no?

ALICE. What, M[aster] Mosbie! Let him
woo himself!

Think you that maids look not for fair
words?   540

Go to her, Clarke; she's all alone within.

Michael, my man, is clean out of her
books.

CLARKE. I thank you, Mistress Arden. I
will in;

And, if fair Susan and I can make a
gree,[3]

You shall command me to the uttermost,

As far as either goods or life may stretch.

Exit Clarke.

MOS. Now, Alice, let's hear thy news.

ALICE. They be so good that I must laugh
for joy

Before I can begin to tell my tale.

MOS. Let's hear them, that I may laugh
for company.   550

ALICE. This morning, M[aster] Greene—
Dick Greene, I mean,

From whom my husband had the Abbey
land—

Came hither, railing, for to know the
truth

Whether my husband had the lands by
grant.

I told him all, whereat he stormed amain

And swore he would cry quittance with [4]
the churl,

And, if he did deny his interest,

Stab him, whatsoever did befall himself.

Whenas [5] I saw his choler thus to rise,

I whetted on the gentleman with words;

And, to conclude, Mosbie, at last we
grew   561

To composition [6] for my husband's death.

I gave him ten pound to hire knaves,

By some device to make away the churl;

When he is dead, he should have twenty
more

And repossess his former lands again.

On this we greed, and he is ridden
straight

To London to bring his death about.

MOS. But call you this good news?

ALICE. Ay, sweetheart, be they not?   570

MOS. 'Twere cheerful news to hear the
churl were dead;

But trust me, Alice, I take it passing ill

You would be so forgetful of our state

To make recount of it to every groom.

What! to acquaint each stranger with our
drifts,

Chiefly in case of murther, why, 'tis the
way

To make it open unto Arden's self

And bring thyself and me to ruin both.

Forewarned, forearmed; who threats his
enemy,

Lends him a sword to guard himself
withal.   580

ALICE. I did it for the best.

MOS. Well, seeing 'tis done, cheerly [7] let
it pass.

---

[1] Cutthroat.   [2] Reach an agreement.
[2] Worked upon.

[4] Be even with.   [5] When.
[6] Agreement.   [7] Cheerfully.

You know this Greene; is he not religious? [1]
A man, I guess, of great devotion?

ALICE. He is.

MOS. Then, sweet Alice, let it pass; I
have a drift
Will quiet all, whatever is amiss.

Here enters Clarke and Susan.

ALICE. How now, Clarke?   Have you
found me false?
Did I not plead the matter hard for you?

CLARKE. You did.   590

MOS. And what? Wilt be a match?

CLARKE. A match, i' faith, sir; ay, the
day is mine.
The painter lays his colors to the life;
His pencil draws no shadows in his love.
Susan is mine.

ALICE. You make her blush.

MOS. What, sister, is it Clarke must be
the man?

SUS. It resteth in your grant. Some words
are passed,
And happily [2] we be grown unto a match,
If you be willing that it shall be so. 600

MOS. Ah, Master Clarke, it resteth at my
grant;
You see my sister's yet at my dispose.
But, so you'll grant me one thing I shall
ask,
I am content my sister shall be yours.

CLARKE. What is it, M[aster] Mosbie?

MOS. I do remember once in secret talk
You told me how you could compound
by art
A crucifix impoisoned,
That whoso look upon it should wax
blind
And with the scent be stifled, that ere
long   610
He should die poisoned that did view it
well.
I would have you make me such a
crucifix,
And then I'll grant my sister shall be
yours.

CLARKE. Though I am loath, because it
toucheth life,
Yet, rather or I'll leave sweet Susan's
love,
I'll do it, and with all the haste I may.
But for whom is it?

[1] Conscientious.   [2] Haply, perchance.

ALICE. Leave that to us. Why, Clarke, is
it possible
That you should paint and draw it out
yourself,   619
The colors being baleful and impoisoned,
And no ways prejudice [3] yourself withal?

MOS. Well questioned,   Alice.—Clarke,
how answer you that? [4]

CLARKE. Very easily: I'll tell you straight
How I do work of these impoisoned drugs.
I fasten on my spectacles so close
As nothing can any way offend my sight;
Then, as I put a leaf within my nose,
So put I rhubarb to avoid the smell,
And softly as another work I paint.

MOS. 'Tis very well. But against when
shall I have it?   630

CLARKE. Within this ten days.

MOS.   'Twill serve the turn.
Now, Alice, let's in and see what cheer
you keep.
I hope, now M[aster] Arden is from home,
You'll give me leave to play your hus-
band's part.

ALICE. Mosbie, you know, who's master
of my heart,
He well may be the master of the house.
                                E[x]eunt.

[SCENE ii.

The road between Feversham and London.]

Here enters Greene and Bradshaw.

BRAD. See you them that comes yonder,
M[aster] Greene?

GREENE. Ay, very well.   Do you know
them?

Here enters Black Will and Shakebag.

BRAD. The one I know not, but he seems a
knave,
Chiefly for bearing the other company;
For such a slave, so vile a rogue as he,
Lives not again upon the earth.
Black Will is his name.   I tell you,
M[aster] Greene,
At Boulogne he and I were fellow soldiers,
Where he played such pranks
As all the camp feared him for his
villainy.   10
I warrant you he bears so bad a mind
That for a crown he'll murther any man.

[3] Endanger.
[4] Here and in a few later passages the line
divisions have been regularized.

GREENE. The fitter is he for my purpose, marry!

WILL. How now, fellow Bradshaw? Whither away so early?

BRAD. O Will, times are changed. No fellows now,
Though we were once together in the field;
Yet thy friend to do thee any good I can.

WILL.[1] Why, Bradshaw, was not thou and I fellow soldiers at Boulogne, [20 where I was a corporal, and thou but a base mercenary groom? No fellows now, because you are a goldsmith and have a little plate in your shop! You were glad to call me "fellow Will," and with a cursy[2] to the earth, "One snatch, good corporal," when I stole the half ox from John the victualer, and domineered[3] with it amongst good fellows in one night.   29

BRAD. Ay, Will, those days are past with me.

WILL. Ay, but they be not past with me, for I keep that same honorable mind still. Good neighbor Bradshaw, you are too proud to be my fellow, but, were it not that I see more company coming down the hill, I would be fellows with you once more, and share crowns with you too. But let that pass, and tell me whither you go.   40

BRAD. To London, Will, about a piece of service
Wherein happily thou mayst pleasure me.

WILL. What is it?

BRAD. Of late Lord Cheiny lost some plate,
Which one did bring and sold it at my shop,
Saying he served Sir Antony Cooke.
A search was made, the plate was found with me,
And I am bound to answer at the size.[4]
Now, Lord Cheiny solemnly vows,
If law will serve him, he'll hang me for his plate.   50
Now I am going to London upon hope
To find the fellow. Now, Will, I know
Thou art acquainted with such companions.

WILL. What manner of man was he?

BRAD. A lean-faced, writhen[5] knave,
Hawk-nosed and very hollow-eyed,
With mighty furrows in his stormy brows;
Long hair down his shoulders curled;
His chin was bare, but on his upper lip
A mutchado,[6] which he wound about his ear.   60

WILL. What apparel had he?

BRAD. A watchet[7] satin doublet all-to[8] torn
(The inner side did bear the greater show),
A pair of threadbare velvet hose, seam-rent,
A worsted stocking rent above the shoe,
A livery cloak, but all the lace was off;
'Twas bad, but yet it served to hide the plate.

WILL. Sirrah Shakebag, canst thou remember since we trolled the bowl[9] at Sittingburgh, where I broke the tap- [70 ster's head of the Lion with a cudgel-stick?

SHAKE. Ay, very well, Will.

WILL. Why, it was with the money that the plate was sold for. Sirrah Bradshaw, what wilt thou give him that can tell thee who sold thy plate?

BRAD. Who, I pray thee, good Will?

WILL. Why, 'twas one Jack Fitten. He's now in Newgate for stealing a horse, and shall be arraigned the next size.   80

BRAD. Why, then let Lord Cheiny seek Jack Fitten forth,
For I'll back and tell him who robbed him of his plate.
This cheers my heart. M[aster] Greene, I'll leave you,
For I must to the Isle of Sheppy with speed.

GREENE. Before you go, let me entreat you
To carry this letter to Mistress Arden of Feversham
And humbly recommend me to herself.

BRAD. That will I, M[aster] Greene, and so farewell.—
Here, Will, there's a crown for thy good news.   *Exit Bradshaw.*

WILL. Farewell, Bradshaw; I'll [90

---

[1] The passages printed as prose throughout the play are printed as rough verse in the original (with the exception of the letters).
[2] Curtsey.   [4] Assizes.
[3] Lived like a lord, feasted.

[5] Twisted.   [7] Pale blue.
[6] Mustache.   [8] Completely.
[9] Passed the drinking cup.

drink no water for thy sake whilst this lasts.
—Now, gentleman, shall we have your company to London?

GREENE. Nay, stay, sirs.
A little more I needs must use your help,
And in a matter of great consequence,
Wherein if you'll be secret and profound,
I'll give you twenty angels for your pains.

WILL. How? Twenty angels? Give my fellow George Shakebag and me twenty [100 angels, and, if thou'lt have thy own father slain, that thou mayst inherit his land, we'll kill him.

SHAKE. Ay, thy mother, thy sister, thy brother, or all thy kin.

GREENE. We'l, this it is: Arden of Feversham
Hath highly wronged me about the Abbey land,
That no revenge but death will serve the turn.
Will you two kill him? Here's the angels down,
And I will lay the platform [1] of his death.   110

WILL. Plat me no platforms. Give me the money, and I'll stab him as he stands pissing against a wall, but I'll kill him.

SHAKE. Where is he?

GREENE. He is now at London, in Aldersgate Street.

SHAKE. He's dead as if he had been condemned by an act of parliament, if once Black Will and I swear his death.

GREENE. Here is ten pound, and, [120 when he is dead, ye shall have twenty more.

WILL. My fingers itches to be at the peasant. Ah, that I might be set awork thus through the year, and that murther would grow to an occupation, that a man might, without danger of law—Zounds, I warrant I should be warden of the company! Come, let us be going, and we'll bait [2] at Rochester, where I'll give thee a gallon of sack to hansel [3] the match withal.   *Exeunt.*   131

[SCENE iii.

A street near St. Paul's, London.]

Here enters Michael.

MICH. I have gotten such a letter as will touch the painter; and thus it is:

[1] Plan.   [2] Stop to feed.   [3] Confirm.

Here enters Arden and Franklin and hears Michael read this letter.

"My duty remembered, Mistress Susan, hoping in God you be in good health, as I Michael was at the making hereof. This is to certify you that as the turtle [4] true, when she hath lost her mate, sitteth alone, so I, mourning for your absence, do walk up and down Paul's till one day I fell asleep and lost my master's pantofles. [5] [10 Ah, Mistress Susan, abolish that paltry painter, cut him off by the shins with a frowning look of your crabbed countenance, and think upon Michael, who, drunk with the dregs of your favor, will cleave as fast to your love as a plaster of pitch to a galled horseback. Thus hoping you will let my passions penetrate, or rather impetrate [6] mercy of your meek hands, I end.   20
        Yours,
            MICHAEL, or else not MICHAEL."

ARD. Why, you paltry knave,
Stand you here loitering, knowing my affairs,
What haste my business craves to send to Kent?

FRANK. Faith, friend Michael, this is very ill,
Knowing your master hath no more but you,
And do ye slack his business for your own?

ARD. Where is the letter, sirrah? Let me see it.   *Then he gives him the letter.*
See, Master Franklin, here's proper stuff: 30
Susan my maid, the painter, and my man,
A crew of harlots, [7] all in love, forsooth.
Sirrah, let me hear no more of this.
Now for thy life once write to her a word!

Here enters Greene, Will, and Shakebag.

Wilt thou be married to so base a trull?
'Tis Mosbie's sister. Come I once at home,
I'll rouse her from remaining in my house.

[4] Turtledove.   [6] Obtain by entreaty.
[5] Slippers.   [7] Worthless persons of either sex.

Now, M[aster] Franklin, let us go walk
in Paul's;
Come but a turn or two, and then away.
Exeunt [Arden, Franklin, and Michael].
GREENE. The first is Arden, and that's his
man;   40
The other is Franklin, Arden's dearest
friend.
WILL. Zounds, I'll kill them all three.
GREENE. Nay, sirs, touch not his man in
any case;
But stand close, and take you fittest
standing,
And, at his coming forth, speed [1] him.
To the Nag's Head; there is this coward's
haunt.
But now I'll leave you till the deed be
done.   *Exit Greene.*
SHAKE. If he be not paid his own, ne'er
trust Shakebag.
WILL. Sirrah Shakebag, at his coming
forth
I'll run him through, and then to the
Blackfriars,   50
And there take water and away.
SHAKE. Why, that's the best; but see
thou miss him not.
WILL. How can I miss him, when I
think on the forty angels I must have
more?

Here enters a Prentice.

PREN. [*Aside.*] 'Tis very late; I were best
shut up my stall,
For here will be old filching,[2] when the
press
Comes forth of Paul's.
*Then lets he down his window, and it breaks
Black Will's head.*
WILL. Zounds, draw, Shakebag, draw!
I am almost killed.   60
PREN. We'll tame you, I warrant.
WILL. Zounds, I am tame enough al-
ready.

Here enters Arden, Fran[klin], and Michael.

ARD. What troublesome fray or mutiny
is this?
FRANK. 'Tis nothing but some brabbling
paltry fray,
Devised to pick men's pockets in the
throng.

[1] Despatch.   [2] Abundant stealing.

ARD. Is't nothing else? Come, Franklin,
let us away.   *Exeunt.*
WILL. What mends [3] shall I have for my
broken head?
PREN. Marry, this mends: that, if you
get you not away all the sooner, you [70
shall be well beaten and sent to the
Counter.[4]   *Exit Prentice.*
WILL. Well, I'll be gone, but look to
your signs, for I'll pull them down all.
Shakebag, my broken head grieves me
not so much as by this means Arden hath
escaped.

Here enters Greene.

I had a glimpse of him and his compan-
ion.   79
GREENE. Why, sirs, Arden's as well
as I. I met him and Franklin going merrily
to the ordinary.[5] What, dare you not do
it?
WILL. Yes, sir, we dare do it; but,
were my consent to give again, we would
not do it under ten pound more. I value
every drop of my blood at a French crown.
I have had ten pound to steal a dog, and
we have no more here to kill a man. But [89
that a bargain is a bargain, and so forth,
you should do it yourself.
GREENE. I pray thee, how came thy
head broke?
WILL. Why, thou seest it is broke, dost
thou not?
SHAKE. Standing against a stall, watching Arden's coming, a boy let down his
shop window and broke his head, whereupon arose a brawl, and in the tumult
Arden escaped us and passed by un- [100
thought on. But forbearance is no acquittance; another time we'll do it, I warrant
thee.
GREENE. I pray thee, Will, make clean
thy bloody brow,
And let us bethink us on some other
place
Where Arden may be met with handsomely.
Remember how devoutly thou hast
sworn
To kill the villain; think upon thine oath.
WILL. Tush, I have broken five hundred
oaths!

[3] Amends.   [4] A London prison.   [5] Tavern.

But wouldst thou charm me to effect
　this deed,　　　　　　　　　　110
Tell me of gold, my resolution's fee;
Say thou seest Mosbie kneeling at my
　knees,
Off'ring me service for my high attempt,
And sweet Alice Arden, with a lap of
　crowns,
Comes with a lowly cursy to the earth,
Saying, "Take this but for thy quarter-
　age;[1]
Such yearly tribute will I answer [2] thee."
Why, this would steel soft-mettled cow-
　ardice,
With which Black Will was never tainted
　with.
I tell thee, Greene, the forlorn trav-
　eler　　　　　　　　　　　　　120
Whose lips are glued with summer's
　parching heat
Ne'er longed so much to see a running
　brook
As I to finish Arden's tragedy.
Seest thou this gore that cleaveth to
　my face?
From hence ne'er will I wash this bloody
　stain,
Till Arden's heart be panting in my hand.
GREENE. Why, that's well said; but what
　saith Shakebag?
SHAKE. I cannot paint my valor out with
　words;
　But, give me place and opportunity,
Such mercy as the starven lioness,　130
When she is dry-sucked of her eager
　young,
Shows to the prey that next encounters
　her,
On Arden so much pity would I take.
GREENE. So should it fare with men of
　firm resolve.
And now, sirs, seeing this accident
Of meeting him in Paul's hath no suc-
　cess,
Let us bethink us on some other place
Whose earth may swallow up this Ar-
　den's blood.

Here enters Michael.

See, yonder comes his man.　And wot
　you what?
The foolish knave is in love with Mos-
　bie's sister,　　　　　　　　　140

And for her sake, whose love he cannot
　get
Unless Mosbie solicit his suit,
The villain hath sworn the slaughter
　of his master.
We'll question him, for he may stead [3]
　us much.—
How now, Michael, whither are you
　going?
MICH. My master hath new supped,
　And I am going to prepare his chamber.
GREENE. Where supped M[aster] Arden?
　MICH. At the Nag's Head, at the
eighteenpence ordinary.[4]　How now,　[150
M[aster] Shakebag?　What, Black Will!
God's dear Lady, how chance your face is
so bloody?
　WILL. Go to, sirrah, there is a chance
in it; this sauciness in you will make you
be knocked.
MICH. Nay, and you be offended, I'll be
　gone.
GREENE. Stay, Michael; you may not
　scape us so.
　Michael, I know you love your m[aster]
　well.
MICH. Why, so I do; but wherefore urge
　you that?　　　　　　　　　160
GREENE. Because I think you love your
　mistress better.
[MICH.] So think not I; but say, i' faith,
　what if I should?
SHAKE. Come to the purpose, Michael;
　we hear
You have a pretty love in Feversham.
MICH. Why, have I two or three, what's
　that to thee?
WILL. You deal too mildly with the
　peasant.　Thus it is:
'Tis known to us you love Mosbie's
　sister;
We know besides that you have ta'en
　your oath
To further Mosbie to your mistress'
　bed,
And kill your m[aster] for his sister's
　sake.　　　　　　　　　170
Now, sir, a poorer coward than yourself
Was never fostered in the coast of Kent.
How comes it then that such a knave as
　you
Dare swear a matter of such conse-
　quence?

---

[1] Quarterly payment.　　　[2] Render.

[3] Help.　　　　[4] Here, a dining room.

GREENE. Ah, Will—

WILL. Tush, give me leave; there's no
more but this:

Sith [1] thou hast sworn, we dare discover
all;

And, hadst thou or shouldst thou utter
it,

We have devised a complat [2] under
hand,

Whatever shall betide to any of us, 180

To send thee roundly to the devil of
hell.

And therefore thus: I am the very man,

Marked in my birth hour by the destinies,

To give an end to Arden's life on earth;

Thou but a member [3] but to whet the
knife

Whose edge must search the closet of his
breast.

Thy office is but to appoint the place,

And train thy m[aster] to his tragedy;

Mine to perform it when occasion
serves. 189

Then be not nice,[4] but here devise with us

How and what way we may conclude
his death.

SHAKE. So shalt thou purchase Mosbie
for thy friend,

And by his friendship gain his sister's
love.

GREENE. So shall thy mistress be thy
favorer,

And thou disburdened of the oath thou
made.

MICH. Well, gentlemen, I cannot but confess,

Sith you have urged me so apparently,

That I have vowed my M[aster] Arden's
death;

And he whose kindly love and liberal
hand

Doth challenge naught but good deserts
of me, 200

I will deliver over to your hands.

This night come to his house at Aldersgate;

The doors I'll leave unlocked against [5]
you come.

No sooner shall ye enter through the
latch,

Over the threshold to the inner court,

But on your left hand shall you see the
stairs

That leads directly to my m[aster's]
chamber.

There take him and dispose him as ye
please.

Now it were good we parted company. 209

What I have promiséd, I will perform.

WILL. Should you deceive us, 'twould
go wrong with you.

MICH. I will accomplish all I have revealed.

WILL. Come, let's go drink; choler makes
me as dry as a dog.

*Exeunt Will, Gre[ene], and Shak[ebag].
Manet [6] Michael.*

MICH. Thus feeds the lamb securely on
the down,

Whilst through the thicket of an arbor
brake

The hunger-bitten wolf o'erpries [7] his
haunt

And takes advantage to eat him up.

Ah, harmless Arden, how, how hast
thou misdone,

That thus thy gentle life is leveled at?

The many good turns that thou hast
done to me, 220

Now must I quittance [8] with betraying
thee.

I, that should take the weapon in my
hand

And buckler thee from ill-intending foes,

Do lead thee with a wicked, fraudful
smile,

As unsuspected, to the slaughterhouse.

So have I sworn to Mosbie and my mistress;

So have I promised to the slaughter-
men;

And, should I not deal currently [9] with
them,

Their lawless rage would take revenge
on me.

Tush, I will spurn at mercy for this
once. 230

Let pity lodge where feeble women
lie;

I am resolved, and Arden needs must
die. *Exit Michael.*

[1] Since.
[2] Complot, plan.
In expectation of the time when.
[3] Helper.
[4] Squeamish.
[6] Remains.
[7] Looks over.
[8] Requite.
[9] Genuinely, honestly.

[SCENE iv.

A room in Franklin's house at Aldersgate.]
Here enters Arden and Fran[klin].

ARD. No, Franklin, no. If fear or stormy threats,
If love of me or care of womanhood,
If fear of God or common speech of men,
Who mangle credit with their wounding words,
And couch dishonor as dishonor buds,
Might join repentance in her wanton thoughts,
No question then but she would turn the leaf
And sorrow for her dissolution.[1]
But she is rooted in her wickedness,
Perverse and stubborn, not to be reclaimed;   10
Good counsel is to her as rain to weeds,
And reprehension makes her vice to grow
As Hydra's head that flourished[2] by decay.
Her faults, methink, are painted in my face,
For every searching eye to overread;
And Mosbie's name, a scandal unto mine,
Is deeply trenchéd in my blushing brow.
Ah, Franklin, Franklin, when I think on this,
My heart's grief rends my other powers
Worse than the conflict at the hour of death.   20
FRANK. Gentle Arden, leave this sad lament.
She will amend, and so your griefs will cease;
Or else she'll die, and so your sorrows end.
If neither of these two do happily fall,
Yet let your comfort be that others bear
Your woes, twice doubled all, with patience.
ARD. My house is irksome; there I cannot rest.
FRANK. Then stay with me in London; go not home.
ARD. Then that base Mosbie doth usurp my room
And makes his triumph of my being thence.   30

At home or not at home, where'er I be,
Here, here it lies [*Points to his heart.*], ah, Franklin, here it lies
That will not out till wretched Arden dies.

Here enters Michael.

FRANK. Forget your griefs awhile. Here comes your man.
ARD. What a-clock is 't, sirrah?
MICH. Almost ten.
ARD. See, see, how runs away the weary time!
Come, M[aster] Franklin, shall we go to bed?
Exeunt Arden and Michael. Manet Franklin.
FRANK. I pray you, go before; I'll follow you.—
Ah, what a hell is fretful jealousy!   40
What pity-moaning[3] words, what deep-fetched sighs,
What grievous groans and overlading woes
Accompanies this gentle gentleman!
Now will he shake his care-oppresséd head,
Then fix his sad eyes on the sullen earth,
Ashamed to gaze upon the open world.
Now will he cast his eyes up towards the heavens,
Looking that ways for redress of wrong;
Sometimes he seeketh to beguile his grief
And tells a story with his careful[4] tongue;   50
Then comes his wife's dishonor in his thoughts
And in the middle cutteth off his tale,
Pouring fresh sorrow on his weary limbs.
So woebegone, so inly charged with woe,
Was never any lived and bare it so.

Here enters Michael.

MICH. My m[aster] would desire you come to bed.
FRANK. Is he himself already in his bed?
Exit Fran[klin]. Manet Mic[hael].
MICH. He is, and fain would have the light away.—
Conflicting thoughts, encampéd in my breast,

[1] Degeneration.
[2] Suggested by Delius; early edns. read *perished.*
[3] In the original *moning,* possibly a misprint for *mouing* (*i.e., moving*).   [4] Full of care.

Awake me with the echo of their
  strokes,   60
And I, a judge to censure either side,
Can give to neither wishéd victory.
My master's kindness pleads to me for life
With just demand, and I must grant it
  him;
My mistress she hath forced me with an
  oath,
For Susan's sake, the which I may not
  break,
For that is nearer than a master's love.
That grim-faced fellow, pitiless Black
  Will,
And Shakebag, stern in bloody strata-
  gem—
Two rougher ruffians never lived in
  Kent—   70
Have sworn my death, if I infringe my
  vow,
A dreadful thing to be considered of.
Methinks I see them with their bol-
  stered [1] hair,
Staring and grinning in thy gentle face,
And in their ruthless hands their daggers
  drawn,
Insulting o'er thee [2] with a peck of oaths,
Whilst thou, submissive, pleading for
  relief,
Art mangled by their ireful instruments.
Methinks I hear them ask where Michael
  is,
And pitiless Black Will cries, "Stab the
  slave!   80
The peasant will detect[3] the tragedy!"
The wrinkles in his foul death-threat'ning
  face
Gapes open wide, like graves to swallow
  men.
My death to him is but a merriment,
And he will murther me to make him
  sport.
He comes, he comes!   Ah, M[aster]
  Franklin, help!
Call up the neighbors, or we are but dead!

Here enters Fran[klin] and Arden.

FRANK. What dismal outcry calls me from
  my rest?
ARD. What hath occasioned such a fearful
  cry?   89
Speak, Michael! Hath any injured thee?

¹ Disheveled.   ³ Reveal.
² From 1633 edn. Original reads *there*.

MICH. Nothing, sir; but, as I fell asleep,
  Upon the threshold leaning to the stairs,
  I had a fearful dream that troubled me,
  And in my slumber thought I was beset
  With murtherer thieves that came to
    rifle me.
  My trembling joints witness my inward
    fear.
  I crave your pardons for disturbing you.
ARD. So great a cry for nothing I ne'er
  heard.
  What? Are the doors fast locked and all
    things safe?
MICH. I cannot tell; I think I locked the
  doors.   100
ARD. I like not this, but I'll go see my-
  self.—   [*He tries the doors.*]
  Ne'er trust me but the doors were all un-
    locked.
  This negligence not half contenteth me.
  Get you to bed, and, if you love my favor,
  Let me have no more such pranks as
    these.
  Come, M[aster] Franklin, let us go to bed.
FRANK. Ay, by my faith; the air is very
  cold.—
  Michael, farewell; I pray thee dream no
    more.   *Exeunt.*

[SCENE V.

Before Franklin's house.]

Here enters Will, Gre[ene], and Shak[ebag]. [4]

SHAKE. Black night hath hid the pleasures
  of the day,
  And sheeting darkness overhangs the
    earth,
  And with the black fold of her cloudy
    robe
  Obscures[5] us from the eyesight of the
    world,
  In which sweet silence such as we tri-
    umph.
  The lazy minutes linger on their time,
  Loath to give due audit to the hour,
  Till in the watch[6] our purpose be com-
    plete
  And Arden sent to everlasting night.
  Greene, get you gone, and linger here
    about,   10

⁴ The stage direction follows 1.1 in the
  original.
⁵ From 1633 edn. Earlier edns. read *obscure*.
⁶ Time division of the night.

And at some hour hence come to us again,
Where we will give you instance [1] of his death.

GREENE. Speed to my wish, whose will so-e'er says no; [2]
And so I'll leave you for an hour or two.
Exit Gre[ene].

WILL. I tell thee, Shakebag, would this thing were done.
I am so heavy that I can scarce go;
This drowsiness in me bodes little good.

SHAKE. How now, Will? Become a Precisian? [3]
Nay, then let's go sleep, when bugs [4] and fears
Shall kill our courages with their fancy's work.   20

WILL. Why, Shakebag, thou mistakes me much,
And wrongs me too in telling me of fear.
Were 't not a serious thing we go about,
It should be slipped [5] till I had fought with thee,
To let thee know I am no coward, I.
I tell thee, Shakebag, thou abusest me.

SHAKE. Why, thy speech bewrayed an inly kind of fear,
And savored of a weak, relenting spirit.
Go forward now in that we have begun,
And afterwards attempt [6] me when thou darest.   30

WILL. And, if I do not, heaven cut me off!
But let that pass, and show me to this house,
Where thou shalt see I'll do as much as Shakebag.

SHAKE. This is the door; but, soft, methinks 'tis shut.
The villain Michael hath deceivéd us.

WILL. Soft, let me see, Shakebag; 'tis shut indeed.
Knock with thy sword; perhaps the slave will hear.

SHAKE. It will not be. The white-livered peasant is gone to bed,
And laughs us both to scorn.

WILL. And he shall buy his merriment as dear   40

As ever coistrel [7] bought so little sport.
Ne'er let this sword assist me when I need,
But rust and canker after I have sworn,
If I, the next time that I meet the hind,
Lop not away his leg, his arm, or both.

SHAKE. And let me never draw a sword again,
Nor prosper in the twilight, cockshut light, [8]
When I would fleece the wealthy passenger, [9]
But lie and languish in a loathsome den,
Hated and spit at by the goers-by,   50
And in that death may die unpitiéd,
If I, the next time that I meet the slave,
Cut not the nose from off the coward's face
And trample on it for this villainy.

WILL. Come, let's go seek out Greene. I know he'll swear.

SHAKE. He were a villain, and [10] he would not swear.
'Twould make a peasant swear amongst his boys,
That ne'er durst say before but "yea" and "no,"
To be thus flouted of a coisterel.

WILL. Shakebag, let's seek out Greene, and in the morning   60
At the alehouse butting [11] Arden's house
Watch the outcoming of that prick-eared cur,
And then let me alone to handle him.
Exeunt.

[SCENE vi.

A room in Franklin's house.]

Here enters Ard[en], Fra[nklin], and Michael.

ARD. Sirrah, get you back to Billensgate [12]
And learn what time the tide will serve our turn;
Come to us in Paul's. First go make the bed,
And afterwards go hearken for the flood. [13]
Exit Michael.

Come, M[aster] Franklin, you shall go with me.

---

[1] Evidence.
[2] *I.e.*, no matter who wills the contrary.
[3] Puritan.   [5] Let go, put aside.
[4] Bugaboos.   [6] Make trial of, attack.
[7] Varlet.
[8] Time when woodcocks (*i.e.*, gulls) are caught.
[9] Passer-by.   [11] Abutting on.   [12] Billingsgate.
[10] If.   [13] Flood tide.

This night I dreamed that, being in a park,
A toil [1] was pitched to overthrow the deer,
And I upon a little rising hill
Stood whistly [2] watching for the herd's approach.
Even there, methoughts, a gentle slumber took me,   10
And summoned all my parts to sweet repose;
But in the pleasure of this golden rest
An ill-thewed foster [3] had removed the toil
And rounded me with that beguiling home [4]
Which late, methought, was pitched to cast [5] the deer.
With that he blew an evil-sounding horn,
And at the noise another herdman came,
With fauchon [6] drawn, and bent it at my breast,
Crying aloud, "Thou art the game we seek!"
With this I waked and trembled every joint,   20
Like one obscuréd in a little bush,
That sees a lion foraging about,
And, when the dreadful forest-king is gone
He pries about with timorous suspect
Throughout the thorny casements of the brake,
And will not think his person dangerless,
But quakes and shewers, [7] though the cause be gone.
So, trust me, Franklin, when I did awake,
I stood in doubt whether I waked or no—
Such great impression took [8] this fond [9] surprise.   30
God grant this vision bedeem [10] me any good.

FRANK. This fantasy doth rise from Michael's fear,
Who being awakéd with the noise he made,
His troubled senses yet could take no rest;
And this, I warrant you, procured your dream.

ARD. It may be so; God frame it to the best.
But oftentimes my dreams presage too true.

FRANK. To such as note their nightly fantasies,
Some one in twenty may incur belief.
But use it not: [11] 'tis but a mockery.   40

ARD. Come, M[aster] Franklin, we'll now walk in Paul's
And dine together at the ordinary,
And by my man's direction draw to the quay,
And with the tide go down to Feversham.
Say, M[aster] Franklin, shall it not be so?

FRANK. At your good pleasure, sir;
I'll bear you company.   *Exeunt.*

[SCENE vii.

A street in Aldersgate.]

Here enters Michael at one door. Here enters Greene, Will, and Shakebag at another door.

WILL. Draw, Shakebag, for here's that villain Michael.

GREENE. First, Will, let's hear what he can say.

WILL. Speak, milksop slave, and never after speak!

MICH. For God's sake, sirs, let me excuse myself!
For here I swear, by heaven and earth and all,
I did perform the outmost [12] of my task,
And left the doors unbolted and unlocked.
But see the chance: Franklin and my master
Were very late conferring in the porch,
And Franklin left his napkin [13] where he sat   10
With certain gold knit in it, as he said.
Being in bed, he did bethink himself,
And coming down he found the doors unshut.
He locked the gates, and brought away the keys,
For which offense my master rated me.
But now I am going to see what flood it is,

For with the tide my m[aster] will away,
Where you may front [1] him well on
  Rainham Down,
A place well fitting such a stratagem.
WILL. Your excuse hath somewhat molli-
  fied my choler.   20
  Why now, Greene, 'tis better now nor [2]
  e'er it was.
GREENE. But, Michael, is this true?
MICH. As true as I report it to be true.
SHAKE. Then, Michael, this shall be your
  penance:
  To feast us all at the Salutation,
  Where we will plat [3] our purpose
  throughly.
GREENE. And, Michael, you shall bear no
  news of this tide,
  Because [4] they two may be in Rainham
  Down
  Before your m[aster].
MICH. Why, I'll agree to anything you'll
  have me,   30
  So you will except of my company.[5]
                                    Exeunt.

[SCENE viii.

A room in Arden's house at Feversham.]

Here enters Mosbie.

MOS. Disturbéd thoughts drives me from
  company
  And dries my marrow with their watch-
  fulness;
  Continual trouble of my moody brain
  Feebles my body by excess of drink,
  And nips me as the bitter northeast
  wind
  Doth check the tender blossoms in the
  spring.
  Well fares the man, howe'er his cates [6] do
  taste,
  That tables not with foul suspicion;
  And he but pines amongst his delicates,
  Whose troubled mind is stuffed with dis-
  content.   10
  My golden time was when I had no
  gold.
  Though [7] then I wanted, yet I slept
  secure;
  My daily toil begat me night's repose,

My night's repose made daylight fresh
  to me.
But, since I climbed the top bough of the
  tree
And sought to build my nest among the
  clouds,
Each gentle, stary [8] gale doth shake my
  bed,
And makes me dread my downfall to the
  earth.
But whither doth contemplation carry
  me?
The way I seek to find, where pleasure
  dwells,   20
Is hedged behind me that I cannot
  back,
But needs must on, although to danger's
  gate.
Then, Arden, perish thou by that decree;
For Greene doth ear [9] the land and weed
  thee up
To make my harvest nothing but pure
  corn.
And for his pains I'll heave him up
  awhile,
And after smother him to have his
  wax—
Such bees as Greene must never live to
  sting.
Then is there Michael and the painter
  too,
Chief actors to Arden's overthrow,   30
Who, when they shall see me sit in
  Arden's seat,
They will insult upon me for my meed,[10]
Or fright me by detecting [11] of his end.
I'll none of that, for I can cast a bone
To make these curs pluck out each
  other's throat,
And then am I sole ruler of mine own.
Yet Mistress Arden lives; but she's my-
  self,
And holy church rites makes us two but
  one.
But what for that? I may not trust you,
  Alice.
You have supplanted Arden for my
  sake,   40
And will extirpen [12] me to plant another.
'Tis fearful sleeping in a serpent's bed,
And I will cleanly rid my hands of her.

[1] From 1633 edn.; original reads *frons.*
[2] Than.   [3] Plot.   [4] In order that.
[5] Excuse me from accompanying you.
[6] Dainties.   [7] Original reads *thought.*
[8] Stirry (?); stirring (?).   [11] Betraying.
[9] Plow.   [12] Extirpate.
[10] Assail me for my bribe (?).

Here enters Alice.

But here she comes, and I must flatter her.—

How now, Alice? What, sad and passionate? [1]

Make me partaker of thy pensiveness;
Fire divided burns with lesser force.

ALICE. But I will dam that fire in my breast
 Till by the force thereof my part consume. Ah, Mosbie!

Mos. Such deep pathaires,[2] like to a cannon's burst   50
 Discharged against a ruinated wall,
 Breaks my relenting heart in thousand pieces.
 Ungentle Alice, thy sorrow is my sore;
 Thou know'st it well, and 'tis thy policy
 To forge distressful looks to wound a breast
 Where lies a heart that dies where thou art sad.
 It is not love that loves to anger love.

ALICE. It is not love that loves to murther love.

Mos. How mean you that?

ALICE. Thou knowest how dearly Arden lovéd me.   60

Mos. And then?

ALICE. And then—conceal the rest, for 'tis too bad,
 Lest that my words be carried with the wind,
 And published in the world to both our shames.
 I pray thee, Mosbie, let our springtime wither;
 Our harvest else will yield but loathsome weeds.
 Forget, I pray thee, what hath passed betwix us,
 For now I blush and tremble at the thoughts!

Mos. What, are you changed?

ALICE. Ay, to my former happy life again,   70
 From title of an odious strumpet's name
 To honest Arden's wife, not Arden's honest [3] wife.
 Ha, Mosbie, 'tis thou hast rifled me of that
 And made me sland[e]rous to all my kin;

[1] Full of emotion. [2] Sighs (?). [3] Chaste.

Even in my forehead is thy name engraven,
A mean artificer, that low-born name.
I was bewitched; woe worth the hapless hour
And all the causes that enchanted me!

Mos. Nay, if thou ban,[4] let me breathe curses forth,
 And, if you stand so nicely[5] at your fame,[6]   80
 Let me repent the credit I have lost.
 I have neglected matters of import
 That would have stated[7] me above thy state,
 Forslowed[8] advantages, and spurned at time;
 Ay, Fortune's right hand Mosbie hath forsook
 To take a wanton giglot[9] by the left.
 I left the marriage of an honest maid,
 Whose dowry would have weighed down all thy wealth,
 Whose beauty and demeanor far exceeded thee—
 This certain good I lost for changing bad,   90
 And wrapped my credit in thy company.
 I was bewitched—that is no theme of thine!—
 And thou unhallowed hast enchanted me.
 But I will break thy spells and exorcisms,
 And put another sight upon these eyes
 That showed my heart a raven for a dow.[10]
 Thou art not fair—I viewed thee not till now;
 Thou art not kind—till now I knew thee not.
 And now the rain hath beaten off thy gilt,
 Thy worthless copper shows thee counterfeit.   100
 It grieves me not to see how foul thou art,
 But mads me that ever I thought thee fair.
 Go, get thee gone, a copesmate[11] for thy hinds;
 I am too good to be thy favorite.

ALICE. Ay, now I see, and too soon find it true,

[4] Curse. [7] Placed. [10] Dove.
[5] Fastidiously. [8] Delayed. [11] Companion.
[6] Reputation. [9] Wench.

Which often hath been told me by my
friends,
That Mosbie loves me not but for my
wealth,
Which, too incredulous, I ne'er believed.
Nay, hear me speak, Mosbie, a word or
two; 109
I'll bite my tongue if it speak bitterly.
Look on me, Mosbie, or I'll kill myself;
Nothing shall hide me from thy stormy
look.
If thou cry war, there is no peace for me.
I will do penance for offending thee,
And burn this prayer book, where I here
use
The holy word that had converted me.
See, Mosbie, I will tear away the leaves,
And all the leaves, and in this golden
cover
Shall thy sweet phrases and thy letters
dwell;
And thereon will I chiefly meditate, 120
And hold no other sect but such devotion.
Wilt thou not look? Is all thy love over-
whelmed?
Wilt thou not hear? What malice stops
thine ears?
Why speaks thou not? What silence ties
thy tongue?
Thou hast been sighted [1] as the eagle is,
And heard [2] as quickly as the fearful hare,
And spoke [3] as smoothly as an orator,
When I have bid thee hear or see or
speak,
And art thou sensible in none of these?
Weigh all thy good turns with this little
fault, 130
And I deserve not Mosbie's muddy looks.
A fence[4] of trouble is not thickened still.[5]
Be clear again; I'll ne'er more trouble
thee.
Mos. O, no, I am a base artificer;
My wings are feathered for a lowly flight.
Mosbie? Fie! No, not for a thousand
pound.
Make love to you? Why, 'tis unpardon-
able;
We beggars must not breathe where
gentles[6] are.

[1] Endowed with sight.   [6] Gentlefolk.
[2] Endowed with hearing.
[3] Endowed with speech.
[4] Read *fount*?   [5] The sense seems to be: "A troubled pool is not always turbid."

Alice. Sweet Mosbie is as gentle as a king,
And I too blind to judge him otherwise.
Flowers do sometimes spring in fallow
lands, 141
Weeds in gardens, roses grow on thorns;
So, whatsoe'er my Mosbie's father was,
Himself [is][7] valued gentle by his worth.
Mos. Ah, how you women can insinuate,
And clear a trespass with your sweet-set
tongue!
I will forget this quarrel, gentle Alice,
Provided I'll be tempted so no more.

Here enters Bradshaw.

Alice. Then with thy lips seal up this
new-made match. 149
Mos. Soft, Alice, for here comes somebody.
Alice. How now, Bradshaw, what's the
news with you?
Brad. I have little news, but here's a letter
That M[aster] Greene importuned me to
give you.
Alice. Go in, Bradshaw; call for a cup of
beer. *Exit [Bradshaw].*
'Tis almost supper time; thou shalt stay
with us.
Then she reads the letter.
"We have missed of our purpose at Lon-
don, but shall perform it by the way. We
thank our neighbor Bradshaw.
Yours,
Richard Greene." 160
How likes my love the tenor of this letter?
Mos. Well, were his date complete and
expired!
Alice. Ah, would it were! Then comes
my happy hour;
Till then my bliss is mixed with bitter
gall.
Come, let us in to shun suspicion.
Mos.[8] Ay, to the gates of death to follow
thee. *Exeunt.*

[Scene ix.

Near Rainham Down, Rochester.]

Here enters Greene, Will, and Shakebag.

Shake. Come, Will, see thy tools be in a
readiness!
Is not thy powder dank, or will thy flint
strike fire?

[7] Supplied by Jacob.
[8] From 1633 edn. Original has *Alice.*

WILL. Then ask me if my nose be on my face,
Or whether my tongue be frozen in my mouth.
Zounds, here's a coil! [1]
You were best swear me on the intergatories [2]
How many pistols I have took in hand,
Or whether I love the smell of gunpowder,
Or dare abide the noise the dag [3] will make,
Or will not wink at flashing of the fire. 10
I pray thee, Shakebag, let this answer thee,
That I have took more purses in this down
Than e'er thou handledst pistols in thy life.
SHAKE. Ay, happily thou hast picked more in a throng;
But, should I brag what booties I have took,
I think the overplus that's more than thine
Would mount to a greater sum of money
Than either thou or all thy kin are worth.
Zounds, I hate them (as I hate a toad)
That carry a muscado [4] in their tongue,
And scarce a hurting weapon in their hand. 21
WILL. O Greene, intolerable!
It is not for mine honor to bear this.
Why, Shakebag, I did serve the king at Boulogne,
And thou canst brag of nothing that thou hast done.
SHAKE. Why, so can Jack of Feversham,
That sounded [5] for a fillip on the nose,
When he that gave it him holloed in his ear,
And he supposed a cannon-bullet hit him.
Then they fight.
GREENE. I pray you, sirs, list to Æsop's talk: 30
Whilst two stout dogs were striving for a bone,
There comes a cur and stole it from them both;
So, while you stand striving on these terms of manhood,
Arden escapes us, and deceive[s] us all.

SHAKE. Why, he begun.
WILL.   And thou shalt find I'll end;
I do but slip it until better time.
But, if I do forget—
Then he kneels down and holds up his hands to heaven.
GREENE. Well, take your fittest standings, and once more
Lime your twigs to catch this weary [6] bird. 39
I'll leave you, and at your dags' discharge
Make towards, like the longing water dog
That coucheth till the fowling piece be off,
Then seizeth on the prey with eager mood.
Ah, might I see him stretching forth his limbs,
As I have seen them beat their wings ere now!
SHAKE. Why, that thou shalt see, if he come this way.
GREENE. Yes, that he doth, Shakebag, I'll warrant thee.
But brawl not when I am gone in any case.
But, sirs, be sure to speed him when he comes,
And in that hope I'll leave you for an hour. *Exit Gre[ene].* 50

Here enters Arden, Fran[klin], and Mic[hael].

MICH. 'Twere best that I went back to Rochester.
The horse halts downright; it were not good
He traveled in such pain to Feversham.
Removing of a shoe may happily help it.
ARD. Well, get you back to Rochester; but, sirrah, see
Ye overtake us ere we come to Rainham Down,
For it will be very late ere we get home.
MICH. [*Aside.*] Ay, God he knows, and so doth Will and Shakebag,
That thou shalt never go further than that down;
And therefore have I pricked the horse on purpose, 60
Because I would not view the massacre.
Exit Michael.

---

[1] Bother.   [3] Pistol.   [5] Swooned.
[2] Interrogatories.   [4] Musket.

[5] Troublesome, vexatious.   Jacob suggests *wary.*

ARD. Come, M[aster] Franklin, onwards
with your tale.

FRANK. I assure you, sir, you task me
much.

A heavy blood is gathered at my heart,
And on the sudden is my wind so short
As hindereth the passage of my speech;
So fierce a qualm yet ne'er assailéd me.

ARD. Come, M[aster] Franklin, let us go
on softly.

The annoyance of the dust or else some
meat

You eat [1] at dinner cannot brook [2] [with] [3]
you.　　　　　　　　　　　　　70

I have been often so, and soon amended.

FRANK. Do you remember where my tale
did leave?

ARD. Ay, where the gentleman did check [4]
his wife.

FRANK. She being reprehended for the
fact, [5]

Witness produced that took her with the
deed,

Her glove brought in which there she left
behind,

And many other assured arguments,

Her husband asked her whether it were
not so.

ARD. Her answer then? I wonder how she
looked,

Having forsworn it with such vehement
oaths,　　　　　　　　　　　80

And at the instant so approved [6] upon her.

FRANK. First did she cast her eyes down
to the earth,

Watching the drops that fell amain from
thence;

Then softly draws she forth her handkercher,

And modestly she wipes her tear-stained
face;

Then hemmed she out, to clear her voice
should seem,

And with a majesty addressed herself
To encounter all their accusations.—

Pardon me, M[aster] Arden, I can no
more;

This fighting at my heart makes short
my wind.　　　　　　　　　　90

ARD. Come, we are almost now at Rainham Down.

Your pretty tale beguiles the weary way;
I would you were in state to tell it out.

SHAKE. [Aside.] Stand close, Will; I hear
them coming.

Here enters Lord Cheiny with his Men.

WILL. [Aside.] Stand to it, Shakebag, and
be resolute.

LORD C. Is it so near night as it seems,
Or will this black-faced evening have a
shower?—

What, M[aster] Arden? You are well
met;

I have longed this fortnight's day to
speak with you.

You are a stranger, man, in the Isle of
Sheppy.　　　　　　　　　　　100

ARD. Your honor's always! Bound to do
you service!

LORD C. Come you from London, and
ne'er a man with you?

ARD. My man's coming after, but here's
My honest friend that came along with
me.

LORD C. My lord protector's man I take
you to be.

FRANK. Ay, my good lord, and highly
bound to you.

LORD C. You and your friend come home
and sup with me.

ARD. I beseech your honor, pardon me;
I have made a promise to a gentleman,
My honest friend, to meet him at my
house.　　　　　　　　　　　110

The occasion is great, or else would I
wait on you.

LORD C. Will you come tomorrow and dine
with me,

And bring your honest friend along with
you?

I have divers matters to talk with you
about.

ARD. Tomorrow we'll wait upon your
honor.

LORD C. One of you stay my horse at the
top of the hill.—

What! Black Will? For whose purse
wait you?

Thou wilt be hanged in Kent, when all
is done.

WILL. Not hanged, God save your honor;
I am your bedesman, [7] bound to pray for
you.　　　　　　　　　　　120

---

[1] Preterit.
[2] Agree.
[3] Added in 1633 edn.
[4] Reprove.
[5] Deed.
[6] Proved.
[7] One who says prayers for charity received.

LORD C. I think thou ne'er saidest prayer
in all thy life.—

One of you give him a crown.—

And, sirrah, leave this kind of life;

If thou beest tainted [1] for a penny matter,

And come in question, surely thou wilt
truss.[2]—

Come, M[aster] Arden, let us be going;

Your way and mine lies four mile together.

Exeunt. Manet Black Will and Shakebag.

WILL. The devil break all your necks at
four miles' end!

Zounds, I could kill myself for very
anger!

His lordship chops me in,[3]   130

Even when my dag was leveled at his
heart.

I would his crown were molten down his
throat.

SHAKE. Arden, thou hast wondrous holy
luck.

Did ever man escape as thou hast done?

Well, I'll discharge my pistol at the
sky,

For by this bullet Arden might not die.

Here enters Greene.

GREENE. What, is he down? Is he despatched?

SHAKE. Ay, in health towards Feversham,
to shame us all.

GREENE. The devil he is! Why, sirs, how
escaped he?

SHAKE. When we were ready to shoot, 140
Comes my Lord Cheiny to prevent his
death.

GREENE. The Lord of Heaven hath preserved him.

WILL. Preserved a fig! The L[ord] Cheiny
hath preserved him,

And bids him to a feast to his house at
Shorlow.

But by the way once more I'll meet with
him,

And, if all the Cheinies in the world say
no,

I'll have a bullet in his breast tomorrow.

Therefore come, Greene, and let us to
Feversham.

GREENE. Ay, and excuse ourselves to Mistress Arden.

O, how she'll chafe when she hears of
this!   150

SHAKE. Why, I'll warrant you she'll think
we dare not do it.

WILL. Why, then let us go, and tell her
all the matter,

And plat the news [4] to cut him off tomorrow.   *Exeunt.*

[SCENE X.

Arden's house at Feversham.]

*Here enters Arden and his Wife, Franklin,
and Michael.*

ARD. See how the hours, the guardant [5]
of heaven's gate,

Have by their toil removed the darksome
clouds,

That Sol may well discern the trampled
pace [6]

Wherein he wont to guide his golden car.

The season fits; come, Franklin, let's
away.

ALICE. I thought you did pretend some
special hunt

That made you thus cut short the time
of rest.

ARD. It was no chase that made me rise
so early,

But, as I told thee yesternight, to go

To the Isle of Sheppy,   10

There to dine with my Lord Cheiny;

For so his honor late commanded me.

ALICE. Ay, such kind husbands seldom
want excuses;

Home is a wild cat to a wandering wit.

The time hath been—would God it were
not past!—

That honor's title nor a lord's command

Could once have drawn you from these
arms of mine.

But my deserts or your desires [7] decay,

Or both; yet if true love may seem desert,

I merit still to have thy company.   20

FRANK. Why, I pray you, sir, let her go
along with us.

I am sure his honor will welcome her

And us the more for bringing her along.

---

[1] Accused.   [3] Thrusts in, interrupts.
[2] Hang.

[4] Plot a new means.   [6] Course, path.
[5] Guardian.
[7] Suggested by Warnke. Original reads *deserves.*

ARD. Content; sirrah, saddle your mistress' nag.

ALICE. No, begged favor merits little
thanks.

If I should go, our house would run away,
Or else be stolen; therefore I'll stay behind.

ARD. Nay, see how mistaking you are!
I pray thee, go.

ALICE. No, no, not now.

ARD. Then let me leave thee satisfied in
this,   30
That time nor place nor persons alter
me,
But that I hold thee dearer than my life.

ALICE. That will be seen by your quick
return.

ARD. And that shall be ere night, and if
I live.
Farewell, sweet Alice; we mind to sup
with thee.   *Exit Al[ice].*

FRANK. Come, Michael, are our horses
ready?

MICH. Ay, your horse are ready, but I
am not ready, for I have lost my purse, with
six-and-thirty shillings in it, with taking up
of [1] my m[aster's] nag.   40

FRANK. Why, I pray you, let us go before,
Whilst he stays behind to seek his purse.

ARD. Go to, sirrah; see you follow us to
the Isle of Sheppy
To my Lord Cheiny's, where we mean to
dine.

Exeunt Arden and Franklin. Manet Michael.

MICH. So, fair weather after you, for before you lies Black Will and Shakebag in
the broom close,[2] too close for you. They'll
be your ferrymen to long home.[3]

Here enters the Painter.

But who is this? The painter, my corrival, that would needs win M[istress]   [50
Susan.

CLARKE. How now, Michael? How doth
my mistress and all at home?

MICH. Who? Susan Mosbie? She is your
mistress too?

CLARKE. Ay, how doth she and all the
rest?

MICH. All's well but Susan; she is sick.

CLARKE. Sick? Of what disease?

MICH. Of a great fear.   6(

CLARKE. A fear of what?

MICH. A great fever.

CLARKE. A fever? God forbid!

MICH. Yes, faith, and of a lordaine,[4] too,
as big as yourself.

CLARKE. O, Michael, the spleen prickles
you. Go to; you carry an eye over Mistress Susan.

MICH. Ay, faith, to keep her from the
painter.   70

CLARKE. Why more from a painter than
from a serving creature like yourself?

MICH. Because you painters make but a
painting-table of a pretty wench, and spoil
her beauty with blotting.

CLARKE. What mean you by that?

MICH. Why, that you painters paint
lambs in the lining of wenches' petticoats,
and we serving-men put horns to them
to make them become sheep.   80

CLARKE. Such another word will cost
you a cuff or a knock.

MICH. What, with a dagger made of a
pencil? Faith, 'tis too weak, and therefore
thou too weak to win Susan.

CLARKE. Would Susan's love lay upon
this stroke! *Then he breaks Michael's head.*

Here enters Mosbie, Greene, and Alice.

ALICE. I'll lay my life, this is for Susan's
love.
Stayed you behind your m[aster] to this
end?   89
Have you no other time to brabble in
But now when serious matters are in
hand?—
Say, Clarke, hast thou done the thing
thou promised?

CLARKE. Ay, here it is. The very touch is
death!

ALICE. Then this, I hope, if all the rest do
fail,
Will catch M[aster] Arden,
And make him wise in death that lived a
fool.
Why should he thrust his sickle in our
corn,
Or what hath he to do with thee, my love,
Or govern me that am to rule my-
self?

---

[1] Making gambol.   [3] *I.e.*, the grave.
[2] Field.

[4] Clown, with a play on *lurdan*, meaning "fever
of idleness."

Forsooth, for credit sake, I must leave
thee!   100
Nay, he must leave to live that we may
love,
May live, may love; for what is life but
love?
And love shall last as long as life remains,
And life shall end before my love depart.
Mos. Why, what's love without true
constancy?
Like to a pillar built of many stones,
Yet neither with good mortar well com-
pact
Nor cement [1] to fasten it in the joints,
But that it shakes with every blast of
wind,
And, being touched, straight falls unto
the earth,   110
And buries all his [2] haughty pride in dust.
No, let our love be rocks of adamant,
Which time nor place nor tempest can
asunder. [3]
Greene. Mosbie, leave protestations now,
And let us bethink us what we have to do.
Black Will and Shakebag I have placed
In the broom close, watching Arden's
coming.
Let's to them and see what they have
done.   *Exeunt.*

[Scene xi.

*The Kentish coast opposite the Isle of
Sheppy.*]

Here enters Ard[en] and Fra[nklin].

Ard. O ferryman, where art thou?

Here enters the Ferryman.

Fer. Here, here! Go before to the boat,
and I will follow you.
Arden. We have great haste; I pray
thee, come away.
Fer. Fie, what a mist is here!
Ard. This mist, my friend, is mystical,
Like to a good companion's smoky brain
That was half drowned with new ale
overnight.
Fer. 'Twere pity but his skull were [10
opened to make more chimney room.
Frank. Friend, what's thy opinion of
this mist?
Fer. I think 'tis like to a curst [4] wife in a

[1] From 1633 edn. Original reads *semell.*
[2] Its.   [3] Part.   [4] Cross, shrewish.

little house, that never leaves her husband
till she have driven him out at doors with
a wet pair of eyes. Then looks he as if his
house were afire, or some of his friends
dead.
Ard. Speaks thou this of thine own [20
experience?
Fer. Perhaps, ay; perhaps, no; for my
wife is as other women are, that is to say,
governed by the moon.
Frank. By the moon? How, I pray
thee?
Fer. Nay, thereby lies a bargain, and
you shall not have it fresh and fasting. [5]
Ard. Yes, I pray thee, good ferryman.
Fer. Then for this once. Let it be [30
midsummer moon, but yet my wife has
another moon.
Frank. Another moon?
Fer. Ay, and it hath influences and
eclipses.
Ard. Why, then, by this reckoning you
sometimes play the man in the moon?
Fer. Ay, but you had not best to meddle with that moon, lest I scratch you by
the face with my bramble bush.   40
Ard. I am almost stifled with this fog.
Come, let's away.
Frank. And, sirrah, as we go, let us have
some more of your bold yeomandry. [6]
Fer. Nay, by my troth, sir, but flat
knavery.   *Exeunt.*

[Scene xii.

Another part of the coast.]

*Here enters Will at one door, and Shakebag
at another.*

Shake. O, Will, where art thou?
Will. Here, Shakebag, almost in hell's
mouth, where I cannot see my way for
smoke.
Shake. I pray thee, speak still that we
may meet by the sound, for I shall fall
into some ditch or other, unless my feet
see better than my eyes.
Will. Didst thou ever see better
weather to run away with another man's [10
wife, or play with a wench at potfinger? [7]
Shake. No; this were a fine world for
chandlers if this weather would last, for

[5] Before eating; in your eagerness; for nothing (?).   [7] Game otherwise unknown.
[6] Yeoman's talk.

then a man should never dine nor sup without candlelight. But, sirrah Will, what horses are those that passed?

WILL. Why, didst thou hear any?

SHAKE. Ay, that I did.

WILL. My life for thine, 'twas Arden and his companion, and then all our [20 labor's lost.

SHAKE. Nay, say not so, for, if it be they, they may happily lose their way as we have done, and then we may chance meet with them.

WILL. Come, let us go on like a couple of blind pilgrims.

Then Shakebag falls into a ditch.

SHAKE. Help, Will, help! I am almost drowned!

Here enters the Ferryman.

FER. Who's that that calls for help? 30

WILL. 'Twas none here; 'twas thou thyself.

FER. I came to help him that called for help. Why, how now? Who is this that's in the ditch? You are well enough served to go without a guide such weather as this.

WILL. Sirrah, what companies hath passed your ferry this morning?

FER. None but a couple of gentle- [40 men, that went to dine at my Lord Cheiny's.

WILL. Shakebag, did not I tell thee as much?

FER. Why, sir, will you have any letters carried to them?

WILL. No, sir; get you gone.

FER. Did you ever see such a mist as this?

WILL. No, nor such a fool as will [50 rather be hought [1] than get his way.

FER. Why, sir, this is no Hough-Monday; [2] you are deceived.—What's his name, I pray you, sir?

SHAKE. His name is Black Will.

FER. I hope to see him one day hanged upon a hill.   *Exit Ferryman.*

SHAKE. See how the sun hath cleared the foggy mist,

Now we have missed the mark of our intent.

[1] Hamstrung.
[2] Hock Monday, a festival shortly after Easter.

Here enters Greene, Mosbie, and Alice.

MOS. Black Will and Shakebag, what make [3] you here? 60

What, is the deed done? Is Arden dead?

WILL. What could a blinded man perform in arms?

Saw you not how till now the sky was dark,

That neither horse nor man could be discerned?

Yet did we hear their horses as they passed.

GREENE. Have they escaped you, then, and passed the ferry?

SHAKE. Ay, for a while; but here we two will stay,

And at their coming back meet with them once more.

Zounds, I was ne'er so toiled [4] in all my life

In following so slight a task as this. 70

MOS. How cam'st thou so berayed? [5]

WILL. With making false footing in the dark.

He needs would follow them without a guide.

ALICE. Here's to pay for a fire and good cheer.

Get you to Feversham to the Flower-de-Luce,

And rest yourselves until some other time.

GREENE. Let me alone; it most concerns my state.

WILL. Ay, Mistress Arden, this will serve the turn,

In case we fall into a second fog.

Exeunt Greene, Will, and Shake[bag].

MOS. These knaves will never do it; let us give it over. 80

ALICE. First tell me how you like my new device:

Soon, when my husband is returning back,

You and I both marching arm in arm,

Like loving friends, we'll meet him on the way,

And boldly beard and brave him to his teeth.

When words grow hot and blows begin to rise,

[3] Do.   [4] Entangled or fatigued.
[5] Befouled with mud.

I'll call those cutters forth your tenement,
Who, in a manner to take up the fray,
Shall wound my husband Hornsby [1] to
   the death.
Mos. Ah, fine device! Why, this deserves
   a kiss.   *Exeunt.* 90

[Scene xiii.

Near the Flower-de-Luce in Feversham.]

Here enters Dick Reede and a Sailor.

Sail. Faith, Dick Reede, it is to little end.
   His conscience is too liberal, and he too
      niggardly
   To part from anything may do thee good.
Reede. He is coming from Shorlow, as I
      understand.
   Here I'll intercept him, for at his house
   He never will vouchsafe to speak with
      me.
   If prayers and fair entreaties will not
      serve,
   Or make no batt'ry in his flinty breast,

Here enters Fra[nklin], Ard[en], and Michael.

   I'll curse the carl, and see what that will
      do.
   See where he comes to further my in-
      tent!—   10
M[aster] Arden, I am now bound to the
   sea.
My coming to you was about the plat of
   ground
Which wrongfully you detain from me.
Although the rent of it be very small,
Yet will it help my wife and children,
Which here I leave in Feversham, God
   knows,
Needy and bare. For Christ's sake, let
   them have it!
Ard. Franklin, hearest thou this fellow
      speak?
   That which he craves I dearly bought of
      him,
   Although the rent of it was ever
      mine.—   20
   Sirrah, you that ask these questions,
   If with thy clamorous impeaching [2]
      tongue
   Thou rail on me, as I have heard thou
      dost,

I'll lay thee up so close a twelvemonth's
   day,
As thou shalt neither see the sun nor
   moon.
Look to it, for, as surely as I live,
I'll banish pity if thou use me thus.
Reede. What, wilt thou do me wrong and
      threat me too?
   Nay, then, I'll tempt thee, Arden; do thy
      worst.
   God, I beseech thee, show some mir-
      acle   30
   On thee or thine, in plaguing thee for this.
   That plot of ground which thou detains
      from me—
   I speak it in an agony of spirit—
   Be ruinous and fatal unto thee!
   Either there be butchered by thy dearest
      friends,
   Or else be brought for men to wonder at,
   Or thou or thine miscarry in that place,
   Or there run mad and end thy cursèd
      days!
Frank. Fie, bitter knave, bridle thine
      envious [3] tongue;
   For curses are like arrows shot up-
      right,   40
   Which, falling down, light on the shoot-
      er's [4] head.
Reede. Light where they will! Were I
      upon the sea,
   As oft I have in many a bitter storm,
   And saw a dreadful southern flaw at
      hand,
   The pilot quaking at the doubtful [5]
      storm,
   And all the sailors praying on their knees,
   Even in that fearful time would I fall
      down,
   And ask of God, whate'er betide of me,
   Vengeance on Arden or some misevent [6]
   To show the world what wrong the carl
      hath done.   50
   This charge I'll leave with my distressful
      wife;
   My children shall be taught such prayers
      as these;
   And thus I go, but leave my curse with
      thee.   *Exeunt Reede and Sailor.*
Ard. It is the railingest knave in Chris-
      tendom,

[1] Cuckold.   [2] Accusing.
[3] Spiteful.
[4] From 1633 edn. Original reads *sutors.*
[5] Fearful.   [6] Mischance.

And oftentimes the villain will be mad.
It greatly matters not what he says,
But I assure you I ne'er did him
  wrong.
FRANK. I think so, M[aster] Arden.
ARD. Now that our horses are gone home
  before,
My wife may happily meet me on the
  way.   60
For God knows she is grown passing kind
  of late,
And greatly changéd from the old humor
Of her wonted frowardness,
And seeks by fair means to redeem old
  faults.
FRANK. Happy the change that alters for
  the best!
But see in any case you make no speech
Of the cheer we had at my Lord
  Cheiny's,
Although most bounteous and liberal,
For that will make her think herself more
  wronged,
In that we did not carry her along;   70
For sure she grieved that she was left
  behind.
ARD. Come, Franklin, let us strain to
  mend our pace,
And take her unawares playing the cook;

Here enters Alice and Mosbie.

For I believe she'll strive to mend our
  cheer.
FRANK. Why, there's no better creatures
  in the world
Than women are when they are in good
  humors.
ARD. Who is that? Mosbie? What, so
  familiar?
Injurious strumpet, and thou ribald
  knave,
Untwine those arms.
ALICE. Ay, with a sugared kiss let them
  untwine.   80
ARD. Ah, Mosbie, perjured beast! Bear
  this and all!
Mos. And yet no hornéd beast; the horns
  are thine.
FRANK. O monstrous! Nay, then 'tis time
  to draw.
      [*Arden, Franklin, and Mosbie draw.*]
ALICE. Help, help! They murther my husband.

Here enters Will and Shak[ebag].

SHAKE. Zounds, who injures M[aster]
  Mosbie?   [*He and Mosbie are wounded.*]
—Help, Will! I am hurt.
Mos. I may thank you, Mistress Arden,
  for this wound.
     Exeunt Mosbie, Will, and Shakebag.
ALICE. Ah, Arden, what folly blinded
  thee?
Ah, jealous harebrain man, what hast
  thou done!   90
When we, to welcome thee,[1] intended
  sport,
Came lovingly to meet thee on thy way,
Thou drew'st thy sword, enraged with
  jealousy,
And hurt thy friend whose thoughts were
  free from harm—
All for a worthless kiss and joining arms,
Both done but merrily to try thy pa-
  tience.
And me unhappy that devised the jest,
Which, though begun in sport, yet ends
  in blood!
FRANK. Marry, God defend me from such
  a jest!
ALICE. Couldst thou not see us friendly
  smile on thee,   100
When we joined arms and when I kissed
  his cheek?
Hast thou not lately found me overkind?
Didst thou not hear me cry, they murther
  thee?
Called I not help to set my husband free?
No, ears and all were witched. Ah, me ac-
  cursed,
To link in liking with a frantic man!
Henceforth I'll be thy slave, no more thy
  wife,
For with that name I never shall content
  thee.
If I be merry, thou straightways thinks
  me light;
If sad, thou sayest the sullens [2] trouble
  me;   110
If well attired, thou thinks I will be gad-
  ding;
If homely, I seem sluttish in thine eye.
Thus am I still, and shall be while [3] I die.
Poor wench, abused by thy misgovern-
  ment!

[1] Original reads *thy.*   [3] Until.
[2] Dumps.

ARD. But is it for truth that neither thou nor he
Intendedst malice in your misdemeanor?
ALICE. The heavens can witness of our harmless thoughts.
ARD. Then pardon me, sweet Alice,
And forgive this fault!   119
Forget but this and never see the like.
Impose me penance, and I will perform it,
For in thy discontent I find a death,
A death tormenting more than death itself.
ALICE. Nay, hadst thou loved me as thou dost pretend,
Thou wouldst have marked the speeches of thy friend,
Who going wounded from the place, he said
His skin was pierced only through my device.
And, if sad sorrow taint thee for this fault,
Thou wouldst have followed him, and seen him dressed,
And cried him mercy whom thou hast misdone.   130
Ne'er shall my heart be eased till this be done.
ARD. Content thee, sweet Alice, thou shalt have thy will,
Whate'er it be. For that I injured thee
And wronged my friend, shame scourgeth my offense.
Come thou thyself, and go along with me,
And be a mediator twixt us two.
FRANK. Why, M[aster] Arden, know you what you do?
Will you follow him that hath dishonored you?
ALICE. Why, canst thou prove I have been disloyal?
FRANK. Why, Mosbie taunts your [1] husband with the horn.   140
ALICE. Ay, after he had reviled him
By the injurious name of perjured beast!
He knew no wrong could spite a jealous man
More than the hateful naming of the horn.
FRANK. Suppose 'tis true; yet is it dangerous
To follow him whom he hath lately hurt.
ALICE. A fault confessed is more than half amends;

But men of such ill spirit as yourself
Work crosses and debates twixt man and wife.
ARD. I pray thee, gentle Franklin, hold thy peace.   150
I know my wife counsels me for the best.
I'll seek out Mosbie where his wound is dressed,
And salve his hapless quarrel if I may.
                          Exeunt Arden and Alice.
FRANK. He whom the devil drives must go perforce.
Poor gentleman, how soon he is bewitched!
And yet, because his wife is the instrument,
His friends must not be lavish in their speech.   *Exit Fran[klin].*

[SCENE xiv.

A room in Arden's house.]

Here enters Will, Shakebag, and Greene.

WILL. Sirrah Greene, when was I so long in killing a man?
GREENE. I think we shall never do it. Let us give it over.
SHAKE. Nay, zounds! We'll kill him, though we be hanged at his door for our labor.
WILL. Thou knowest, Greene, that I have lived in London this twelve years, where I have made some go upon wooden [10 legs for taking the wall on me;[2] divers with silver noses for saying, "There goes Black Will!" I have cracked as many blades as thou hast done nuts.
GREENE. O monstrous lie!
WILL: Faith, in a manner I have. The bawdyhouses have paid me tribute; there durst not a whore set up unless she have agreed with me first for opening her shop windows. For a cross word of a tapster [20 I have pierced one barrel after another with my dagger, and held him be [3] the ears till all his beer hath run out. In Thames Street a brewer's cart was like to have run over me. I made no more ado, but went to the clerk and cut all the natches off his tails [4] and beat them about his head. I and my company have taken the constable from his watch, and carried him

---

[1] From 1633 edn. Original reads *traunt you.*
[2] For pushing me into the street.   [3] By.
[4] Notches off his tallies (sticks on which his accounts were kept).

about the fields on a coltstaff.[1] I have   [30
broken a sergeant's head with his own
mace, and bailed whom I list with my
sword and buckler. All the tenpenny
alehouses would stand every morning with
a quart pot in his hand, saying, "Will it
please your worship drink?" He that had
not done so, had been sure to have had his
sign pulled down and his lattice borne away
the next night. To conclude, what have I
not done? Yet cannot do this. Doubt-   [40
less he is preserved by miracle.

Here enters Alice and Michael.

GREENE. Hence, Will!   Here comes
M[istress] Arden.
ALICE. Ah, gentle Michael, art thou sure
    they're friends?
MICH. Why, I saw them when they both
    shook hands.
When Mosbie bled, he even wept for
    sorrow,
And railed on Franklin that was cause
    of all.
No sooner came the surgeon in at doors,
But my m[aster] took to his purse and
    gave him money,
And, to conclude, sent me to bring you
    word   50
That Mosbie, Franklin, Bradshaw, Adam
    Fowle,
With divers of his neighbors and his
    friends,
Will come and sup with you at our house
    this night.
ALICE. Ah, gentle Michael, run thou
    back again,
And, when my husband walks into the
    fair,
Bid Mosbie steal from him and come
    to me;
And this night shall thou and Susan be
    made sure.
MICH. I'll go tell him.
ALICE. And, as thou goest, tell John cook
    of our guests,
And bid him lay it on—spare for no
    cost.   *Exit Michael.*   60
WILL. Nay, and there be such cheer, we
    will bid ourselves.—
Mistress Arden, Dick Greene and I do
    mean to sup with you.

[1] Staff used for carrying tubs.

ALICE. And welcome shall you be.   Ah,
    gentlemen,
How missed you of your purpose yester-
    night?
GREENE. 'Twas long of [2] Shakebag, that
    unlucky villain.
SHAKE. Thou dost me wrong; I did as
    much as any.
WILL. Nay then, M[istress] Alice, I'll
    tell you how it was.
When he should have locked with both
    his hilts,[3]
He in a bravery [4] flourished over his head;
With that comes Franklin at him lust-
    ily,   70
And hurts the slave; with that he slinks
    away.
Now his way had been to have come
hand and feet, one and two round, at his
costard; [5] he like a fool bears his sword-
point half a yard out of danger. I lie here
for my life. [*Takes a position of defense.*]
If the devil come, and he have no more
strength than fence,[6] he shall never beat
me from this ward.[7]
I'll stand to it, a buckler in a skillful
    hand   80
Is as good as a castle; nay,
'Tis better than a sconce,[8] for I have
    tried it.
Mosbie, perceiving this, began to faint.
With that comes Arden with his arm-
    ing sword,[9]
And thrust him through the shoulder in
    a trice.
ALICE. Ay, but I wonder why you both
    stood still.
WILL. Faith, I was so amazed, I could
    not strike.
ALICE. Ah, sirs, had he yesternight been
    slain,
For every drop of his detested blood
I would have crammed [10] in angels [11] in
    thy fist,   90
And kissed thee, too, and hugged thee
    in my arms.
WILL. Patient yourself; we cannot help
    it now.

[2] Because of.
[3] Sword. *Hilts* was often used for singular.
[4] Bravado.   [7] Guard.
[5] Apple, head.   [8] Fort.
[6] Fencing skill.   [9] A two-handed sword.
[10] From 1633 edn.; original reads *would
cramme.*   [11] Coins.

Greene and we two will dog him through the fair,
And stab him in the crowd, and steal away.

Here enters Mosbie.

ALICE. It is unpossible; but here comes he
That will, I hope, invent some surer means.
Sweet Mosbie, hide thy arm; it kills my heart.
MOS. Ay, Mistress Arden, this is your favor.
ALICE. Ah, say not so, for, when I saw thee hurt,
I could have took the weapon thou lett'st fall,   100
And run at Arden, for I have sworn
That these mine eyes, offended with his sight,
Shall never close till Arden's be shut up.
This night I rose and walked about the chamber,
And twice or thrice I thought to have murthered him.
MOS. What, in the night? Then had we been undone.
ALICE. Why, how long shall he live?
MOS. Faith, Alice, no longer than this night.—
Black Will and Shakebag, will you two
Perform the complot that I have laid? 110
WILL. Ay, or else think me as a villain.
GREENE. And rather than you shall want,[1] I'll help, myself.
MOS. You, M[aster] Greene, shall single Franklin forth,
And hold him with a long tale of strange news,
That he may not come home till supper time.
I'll fetch M[aster] Arden home, and we, like friends,
Will play a game or two at tables [2] here.
ALICE. But what of all this? How shall he be slain?
MOS. Why, Black Will and Shakebag, locked within the countinghouse,
Shall, at a certain watchword given, rush forth.   120
WILL. What shall the watchword be?

MOS. "Now I take you"—that shall be the word.
But come not forth before in any case.
WILL. I warrant you. But who shall lock me in?
ALICE. That will I do; thou'st keep the key thyself.
MOS. Come, M[aster] Greene; go you along with me.
See all things ready, Alice, against we come.
ALICE. Take no care for that; send you him home,
                    Exeunt Mosbie and Greene.
And, if he e'er go forth again, blame me.
Come, Black Will, that in mine eyes art fair;   130
Next unto Mosbie do I honor thee.
Instead of fair words and large promises
My hands shall play you golden harmony.[3]
How like you this? Say, will you do it, sirs?
WILL. Ay, and that bravely, too. Mark my device:
Place Mosbie, being a stranger, in a chair,
And let your husband sit upon a stool,
That I may come behind him cunningly,   138
And with a towel pull him to the ground,
Then stab him till his flesh be as a sine;[4]
That done, bear him behind the Abbey,
That those that find him murthered may suppose
Some slave or other killed him for his gold.
ALICE. A fine device! You shall have twenty pound,
And, when he is dead, you shall have forty more,
And, lest you might be suspected staying here,
Michael shall saddle you two lusty geldings;
Ride whither you will, to Scotland, or to Wales,
I'll see you shall not lack, where'er you be.
WILL. Such words would make one kill a thousand [5] men!   150
Give me the key! Which is the countinghouse?

---

[1] Fail.   [2] Backgammon.
[3] *I.e.*, give you money.   [4] Seine, sieve.
[5] Original reads *1000* without the article.

ALICE. Here would I stay and still en-
courage you,
But that I know how resolute you are.
SHAKE. Tush, you are too faint-hearted;
we must do it.
ALICE. But Mosbie will be there, whose
very looks
Will add unwonted courage to my
thought,
And make me the first that shall adven-
ture on him.
WILL. Tush, get you gone; 'tis we must
do the deed.
When this door opens next, look for
his death.
                [*Exeunt Will and Shakebag.*]
ALICE. Ah, would he now were here that
it might open!   160
I shall no more be closed in Arden's
arms,
That like the snakes of black Tisiphone
Sting me with their embracings. Mos-
bie's arms
Shall compass me, and, were I made a
star,
I would have none other spheres but
those.
There is no nectar but in Mosbie's lips!
Had chaste Diana kissed him, she like
me
Would grow lovesick, and from her
wat'ry bower
Fling down Endymion and snath [1] him
up.
Then blame not me that slay a silly
man   170
Not half so lovely as Endymion.

Here enters Michael.

MICH. Mistress, my master is coming
hard by.
ALICE. Who comes with him?
MICH. Nobody but Mosbie.
ALICE. That's well, Michael. Fetch in
the tables, and, when thou hast done,
stand before the countinghouse door.
MICH. Why so?   179
ALICE. Black Will is locked within to
do the deed.
MICH. What? Shall he die tonight?
ALICE. Ay, Michael.
MICH. But shall not Susan know it?

ALICE. Yes, for she'll be as secret as
ourselves.
MICH. That's brave.[2] I'll go fetch the
tables.
ALICE. But, Michael, hark to me a word
or two.
When my husband is come in, lock the
street door;   190
He shall be murthered or [3] the guests
come in.   *Exit Mic[hael].*

Here enters Arden and Mosbie.

Husband, what mean you to bring
Mosbie home?
Although I wished you to be reconciled,
'Twas more for fear of you than love of
him.
Black Will and Greene are his compan-
ions,
And they are cutters, and may cut you
short;
Therefore I thought it good to make you
friends.
But wherefore do you bring him hither
now?
You have given me my supper with his
sight.[4]
MOS. M[aster] Arden, methinks your
wife would have me gone.   200
ARD. No, good M[aster] Mosbie; women
will be prating.
Alice, bid him welcome; he and I are
friends.
ALICE. You may enforce me to it if you
will;
But I had rather die than bid him welcome.
His company hath purchased me ill
friends,
And therefore will I ne'er frequent it
more.
MOS. [*Aside.*] O, how cunningly she can
dissemble!
ARD. Now he is here, you will not serve
me so.
ALICE. I pray you be not angry or displeased;
I'll bid him welcome, seeing you'll have
it so.   210
You are welcome, M[aster] Mosbie; will
you sit down?

[2] Splendid.   [4] *I.e.*, taken my appetite away.
[3] Before.

[1] Snatch.

Mos. I know I am welcome to your loving husband;
But for yourself you speak not from your heart.
Alice. And, if I do not, sir, think I have cause.
Mos. Pardon me, M[aster] Arden; I'll away.
Ard. No, good M[aster] Mosbie.
Alice. We shall have guests enough, though you go hence.
Mos. I pray you, M[aster] Arden, let me go.
Ard. I pray thee, Mosbie, let her prate her fill.
Alice. The doors are open, sir; you may be gone.   220
Mich. [Aside.] Nay, that's a lie, for I have locked the doors.
Ard. Sirrah, fetch me a cup of wine; I'll make them friends.
And, gentle M[istress] Alice, seeing you are so stout,[1]
You shall begin. Frown not; I'll have it so.
Alice. I pray you meddle with that you have to do.
Ard. Why, Alice, how can I do too much for him
Whose life I have endangered without cause?
Alice. 'Tis true; and, seeing 'twas partly through my means,
I am content to drink to him for this once.
Here, M[aster] Mosbie—and, I pray you, henceforth   230
Be you as strange to me as I to you.
Your company hath purchased me ill friends,
And I for you, God knows, have undeserved
Been ill spoken of in every place;
Therefore henceforth frequent my house no more.
Mos. I'll see your husband in despite of you.
Yet, Arden, I protest to thee by heaven,
Thou ne'er shalt see me more after this night.
I'll go to Rome rather than be forsworn.
Ard. Tush, I'll have no such vows made in my house.   240

Alice. Yes, I pray you, husband, let him swear;
And, on that condition, Mosbie, pledge me here.
Mos. Ay, as willingly as I mean to live.
Ard. Come, Alice, is our supper ready yet?
Alice. It will by then you have played a game at tables.
Ard. Come, M[aster] Mosbie, what shall we play for?
Mos. Three games for a French crown, sir, and [2] please you.
Ard. Content.
                    Then they play at the tables.

[Enter Will and Shakebag.]

Will. [Aside.] Can he not take him yet? What a spite is that!
Alice. [Aside.] Not yet, Will. Take heed he see thee not.   250
Will. [Aside.] I fear he will spy me as I am coming.
Mich. [Aside.] To prevent that, creep betwixt my legs.
Mos. One ace, or else I lose the game.
Ard. Marry, sir, there's two for failing.[3]
Mos. Ah, M[aster] Arden, "now I can take you."
                    Then Will pulls him down with a towel.
Ard. Mosbie! Michael! Alice! What will you do?
Will. Nothing but take you up, sir, nothing else.
Mos. There's for the pressing iron you told me of.   [Stabs him.]
Shake. And there's for the ten pound in my sleeve.   [Stabs him.]
Alice. What! Groans thou? Nay, then give me the weapon!   260
Take this for hind'ring Mosbie's love and mine!   [She stabs him.]
Mich. O, mistress!
Will. Ah, that villain will betray us all.
Mos. Tush, fear him not; he will be secret.
Mich. Why, dost thou think I will betray myself?
Shake. In Southwark dwells a bonny northern lass,
The widow Chambley; I'll to her house now,

---

[1] Stubborn, proud.   [2] An't, if it.   [3] If one is not sufficient.

And, if she will not give me harborough,[1]
I'll make booty of the quean[2] even to her
   smock.

WILL. Shift for yourselves; we two will
   leave you now.   270

ALICE. First lay the body in the countinghouse.

Then they lay the body in the countinghouse.

WILL. We have our gold; Mistress Alice,
   adieu;
   Mosbie, farewell, and, Michael, farewell
   too.   *Exeunt.*

Enter Susan.

SUS. Mistress, the guests are at the doors.
   Hearken, they knock. What, shall I let
   them in?

ALICE. Mosbie, go thou, and bear them
   company.   *Exit M[osbie].*
   And, Susan, fetch water and wash away
   this blood.

SUS. The blood cleaveth to the ground
   and will not out.

ALICE. But with my nails I'll scrape away
   the blood.—
   The more I strive, the more the blood
   appears!   280

SUS. What's the reason, m[istress], can you
   tell?

ALICE. Because I blush not at my husband's death.

Here enters Mosbie.

MOS. How now? What's the matter? Is
   all well?

ALICE. Ay, well, if Arden were alive again.
   In vain we strive, for here his blood remains.

MOS. Why, strew rushes on it, can you
   not?
   This wench doth nothing. Fall unto the
   work.

ALICE. 'Twas thou that made me murther
   him.

MOS.   What of that?

ALICE. Nay, nothing, Mosbie, so it be not
   known.

MOS. Keep thou it close, and 'tis unpossible.   290

ALICE. Ah, but I cannot! Was he not slain
   by me?
   My husband's death torments me at the
   heart.

MOS. It shall not long torment thee, gentle
   Alice.
   I am thy husband; think no more of him.

Here enters Adam Fowle and Brad[shaw].

BRAD. How now, M[istress] Arden? What
   ail you weep?[3]

MOS. Because her husband is abroad so
   late.
   A couple of ruffians threatened him yesternight,
   And she, poor soul, is afraid he should be
   hurt.

ADAM. Is 't nothing else? Tush, he'll be
   here anon.

Here enters Greene.

GREENE. Now, M[istress] Arden, lack you
   any guests?   300

ALICE. Ah, M[aster] Greene, did you see
   my husband lately?

GREENE. I saw him walking behind the
   Abbey even now.

Here enters Franklin.

ALICE. I do not like this being out so
   late.—
   M[aster] Franklin, where did you leave
   my husband?

FRANK. Believe me, I saw him not since
   morning.
   Fear you not; he'll come anon. Meantime
   You may do well to bid his guests sit
   down.

ALICE. Ay, so they shall. M[aster] Bradshaw, sit you there;
   I pray you, be content; I'll have my will.
   M[aster] Mosbie, sit you in my husband's
   seat.   310

MICH. [*Aside.*] Susan, shall thou and I
   wait on them?
   Or, and thou sayst the word, let us sit
   down too.

SUS. [*Aside.*] Peace, we have other matters now in hand.
   I fear me, Michael, all will be bewrayed.

MICH. [*Aside.*] Tush, so it be known
   that I shall marry thee in the morning,
   I care not though I be hanged ere night.
   But to prevent the worst I'll buy some
   ratsbane.   319

---

[1] Harbor.   [2] Hussy.   [3] *I.e.,* what ails you that you weep?

Sus. [*Aside.*] Why, Michael, wilt thou poison thyself?

Mich. [*Aside.*] No, but my mistress, for I fear she'll tell.

Sus. [*Aside.*] Tush, Michael, fear not her; she's wise enough.

Mos. Sirrah Michael, give's a cup of beer.—

M[istress] Arden, here's to your husband.

Alice.   My husband!

Frank. What ails you, woman, to cry so suddenly?

Alice. Ah, neighbors, a sudden qualm came over my heart;

My husband's being forth torments my mind.   330

I know something's amiss; he is not well

Or else I should have heard of him ere now.

Mos. [*Aside.*] She will undo us through her foolishness.

Greene. Fear not, M[istress] Arden; he's well enough.

Alice. Tell not me; I know he is not well.

He was not wont for to stay thus late.

Good M[aster] Franklin, go and seek him forth,

And, if you find him, send him home to me,

And tell him what a fear he hath put me in.

Frank. [*Aside.*] I like not this; I pray God all be well.—   340

Exeunt Fra[nklin], Mos[bie], and Gre[ene].

I'll seek him out, and find him if I can.

Alice. [*Aside.*] Michael, how shall I do to rid the rest away?

Mich. [*Aside.*] Leave that to my charge; let me alone.—

'Tis very late, M[aster] Bradshaw,

And there are many false knaves abroad,

And you have many narrow lanes to pass.

Brad. Faith, friend Michael, and thou sayest true.

Therefore I pray thee light's forth and lend's a link.[1]

Exeunt Brad[shaw], Adam, and Michael.

Alice. Michael, bring them to the doors, but do not stay;   349

You know I do not love to be alone.—

Go, Susan, and bid thy brother come.

But wherefore should he come? Here is naught but fear;

Stay, Susan, stay, and help to counsel me.

[1] Torch.

Sus. Alas, I counsel! Fear frights away my wits.

Then they open the countinghouse door, and look upon Arden.

Alice. See, Susan, where thy quondam master lies,

Sweet Arden, smeared in blood and filthy gore.

Sus. My brother, you, and I shall rue this deed.

Alice. Come, Susan, help to lift his body forth,

And let our salt tears be his obsequies.

Here enters Mosbie and Greene.

Mos. How now, Alice, whither will you bear him?   360

Alice. Sweet Mosbie, art thou come? Then weep that will;

I have my wish in that I joy thy sight.

Greene. Well, it hoves[2] us to be circumspect.

Mos. Ay, for Franklin thinks that we have murthered him.

Alice. Ay, but he cannot prove it for his life.

We'll spend this night in dalliance and in sport.

Here enters Michael.

Mich. O mistress, the mayor and all the watch

Are coming towards our house with glaives and bills![3]

Alice. Make the door fast; let them not come in.

Mos. Tell me, sweet Alice, how shall I escape?   370

Alice. Out at the back door, over the pile of wood,

And for one night lie at the Flower-de-Luce.

Mos. That is the next way to betray myself.

Greene. Alas, M[istress] Arden, the watch will take me here,

And cause suspicion where else would be none.

Alice. Why, take that way that M[aster] Mosbie doth;

But first convey the body to the fields.

Then they bear the body into the fields.

[2] Behooves.   [3] Swords and halberts.

Mos. Until tomorrow, sweet Alice, now
    farewell.
And see you confess nothing in any case.
GREENE. Be resolute, M[istress] Alice; be-
    tray us not,   380
But cleave to us as we will stick to you.
           Exeunt Mosbie and Greene.
ALICE. Now, let the judge and juries do
    their worst.
My house is clear, and now I fear them
    not.
SUS. As we went, it snowéd all the way,
    Which makes me fear our footsteps will
    be spied.
ALICE. Peace, fool, the snow will cover
    them again.
SUS. But it had done before we came back
    again.
ALICE. Hark, hark, they knock!   Go,
    Michael, let them in.

Here enters the Mayor and the Watch.

How now, M[aster] Mayor, have you
    brought my husband home?
MAYOR. I saw him come into your house
    an hour ago.   390
ALICE. You are deceived; it was a Lon-
    doner.
MAYOR. Mistress Arden, know you not
    one that is called Black Will?
ALICE. I know none such.   What mean
    these questions?
MAYOR. I have the council's warrand to
    apprehend him.
ALICE. [*Aside.*] I am glad it is no worse. —
Why, M[aster] Mayor, think you I har-
    bor any such?
MAYOR. We are informed that here he is;
And therefore pardon us, for we must
    search.
ALICE. Ay, search, and spare you not,
    through every room.
Were my husband at home, you would
    not offer this.   400

Here enters Franklin.

M[aster] Franklin, what mean you come
    so sad?
FRANK. Arden, thy husband and my
    friend, is slain!
ALICE. Ah, by whom? M[aster] Franklin,
    can you tell?

FRANK. I know not; but behind the Ab-
    bey
There he lies murthered in most piteous
    case.
MAYOR. But, M[aster] Franklin, are you
    sure 'tis he?
FRANK. I am too sure; would God I were
    deceived.
ALICE. Find out the murtherers; let them
    be known.
FRANK. Ay, so they shall. Come you along
    with us.
ALICE. Wherefore?
FRANK.   Know you this hand towel
    and this knife?   410
SUS. [*Aside.*] Ah, Michael, through this
    thy negligence
Thou hast betrayéd and undone us all.
MICH. [*Aside.*] I was so afraid I knew-not
    what I did;
I thought I had thrown them both into
    the well.
ALICE. It is the pig's blood we had to
    supper.
But wherefore stay you? Find out the
    murtherers.
MAYOR. I fear me you'll prove one of
    them yourself.
ALICE. I one of them? What mean such
    questions?
FRANK. I fear me he was murthered in
    this house
And carried to the fields, for from that
    place   420
Backwards and forwards may you see
The print of many feet within the
    snow.
And look about this chamber where we
    are,
And you shall find part of his guiltless
    blood,
For in his slipshoe [1] did I find some
    rushes,
Which argueth he was murthered in this
    room.
MAYOR. Look in the place where he was
    wont to sit.
See, see! His blood! It is too manifest.
ALICE. It is a cup of wine that Michael
    shed.
MICH. Ay, truly.   430
FRANK. It is his blood, which, strumpet,
    thou hast shed!
[1] Slipper.

But, if I live, thou and thy complices
Which have conspired and wrought his
  death shall rue it.
ALICE. Ah, M[aster] Franklin, God and
  heaven can tell
I loved him more than all the world be-
  side.
  But bring me to him; let me see his body.
FRANK. Bring that villain and Mosbie's
  sister too;
And one of you go to the Flower-de-Luce,
And seek for Mosbie, and apprehend him
  too.   *Exeunt.*

[SCENE XV.

An obscure street in Southwark.]

Here enters Shakebag solus.

SHAKE. The widow Chambley in her hus-
  band's days I kept;
And, now he's dead, she is grown so stout
She will not know her old companions.
I came thither, thinking to have had
Harbor as I was wont,
And she was ready to thrust me out at
  doors.
But, whether she would or no, I got me up,
And, as she followed me, I spurned her
  down the stairs,
And broke her neck, and cut her tapster's
  throat,
And now I am going to fling them in the
  Thames.   10
I have the gold; what care I though it be
  known!
I'll cross the water and take sanctuary.
                         Exit Shakebag.

[SCENE XVI.

A room in Arden's house.]

*Here enters the Mayor, Mosbie, Alice, Frank-
lin, Michael, and Susan.*

MAYOR. See, M[istress] Arden, where your
  husband lies.
Confess this foul fault and be penitent.
ALICE. Arden, sweet husband, what shall
  I say?
The more I sound his name, the more he
  bleeds;
This blood condemns me, and in gushing
  forth
Speaks as it falls, and asks me why I did it.

Forgive me, Arden; I repent me now,
And, would my death save thine, thou
  shouldst not die.
Rise up, sweet Arden, and enjoy thy love,
And frown not on me when we meet in
  heaven;   10
In heaven I love thee, though on earth
  I did not.
MAYOR. Say, Mosbie, what made thee
  murther him?
FRANK. Study not for an answer; look not
  down.
His purse and girdle found at thy bed's
  head
Witness sufficiently thou didst the deed.
It bootless is to swear thou didst it not.
MOS. I hired Black Will and Shakebag,
  ruffians both,
And they and I have done this mur-
  therous deed.
But wherefore stay we? Come and bear
  me hence.
FRANK. Those ruffians shall not escape; I
  will up to London,   20
And get the council's warrand to appre-
  hend them.   *Exeunt.*

[SCENE XVII.

The Kentish coast.]

Here enters Will.

WILL. Shakebag, I hear, hath taken sanc-
  tuary,
But I am so pursued with hues and cries
For petty robberies that I have done
That I can come unto no sanctuary.
Therefore must I in some oyster boat
At last be fain to go aboard some hoy,[1]
And so to Flushing. There is no staying
  here.
At Sittinburgh the watch was like to take
  me,
And, had not I with my buckler covered
  my head,
And run full blank at all adventures,[2] 10
I am sure I had ne'er gone further than
  that place,
For the constable had twenty warrands
  to apprehend me;
Besides that, I robbed him and his man
  once at Gadshill.
Farewell, England; I'll to Flushing now.
                         Exit Will.

[1] Small boat.   [2] *I.e.*, taken all risks.

[SCENE xviii.

A courtroom at Feversham.]

Here enters the Mayor, Mosbie, Alice, Michael, Susan, and Bradshaw.

MAYOR. Come, make haste and bring away the prisoners.

BRAD. M[istress] Arden, you are now going to God,
And I am by the law condemned to die
About a letter I brought from M[aster] Greene.
I pray you, M[istress] Arden, speak the truth.
Was I ever privy to your intent or no?

ALICE. What should I say? You brought me such a letter,
But I dare swear thou knewest not the contents.
Leave now to trouble me with worldly things,
And let me meditate upon my Savior Christ,   10
Whose blood must save me for the blood I shed.

MOS. How long shall I live in this hell of grief?
Convey me from the presence of that strumpet.

ALICE. Ah, but for thee I had never been strumpet.
What cannot oaths and protestations do,
When men have opportunity to woo?
I was too young to sound thy villainies,
But now I find it and repent too late.

SUS. Ah, gentle brother, wherefore should I die?   19
I knew not of it till the deed was done.

MOS. For thee I mourn more than for myself;
But let it suffice, I cannot save thee now.

MICH. And, if your brother and my mistress
Had not promised me you in marriage,
I had ne'er given consent to this foul deed.

MAYOR. Leave to accuse each other now,
And listen to the sentence I shall give.
Bear Mosbie and his sister to London straight,
Where they in Smithfield must be executed;   29
Bear M[istress] Arden unto Canterbury,
Where her sentence is she must be burnt,
Michael and Bradshaw in Feversham must suffer death.

ALICE. Let my death make amends for all my sins.

MOS. Fie upon women!—this shall be my song.
But bear me hence, for I have lived too long.

SUS. Seeing no hope on earth, in heaven is my hope.

MICH. Faith, I care not, seeing I die with Susan.

BRAD. My blood be on his head that gave the sentence.

MAYOR. To speedy execution with them all!   *Exeunt.*

[EPILOGUE]

Here enters Franklin.

FRANK. Thus have you seen the truth of Arden's death.
As for the ruffians, Shakebag and Black Will,
The one took sanctuary, and, being sent for out,
Was murthered in Southwark as he passed
To Greenwich, where the lord protector lay.
Black Will was burnt in Flushing on a stage;
Greene was hangéd at Osbridge in Kent;
The painter fled and how he died we know not.
But this above the rest is to be noted:
Arden lay murthered in that plot of ground   10
Which he by force and violence held from Reede,
And in the grass his body's print was seen
Two years and more after the deed was done.
Gentlemen, we hope you'll pardon this naked tragedy,
Wherein no filéd [1] points are foisted in
To make it gracious to the ear or eye;
For simple truth is gracious enough,
And needs no other points of glozing stuff.   *[Exit.]*

FINIS.

[1] Polished.

CHRISTOPHER MARLOWE

Christopher Marlowe's reputation, even more than John Lyly's, has undergone remarkable transformations. He was the subject of wild rumors and exaggerated critical denunciation, as well as praise, during his short life, but he became almost forgotten in the later seventeenth and eighteenth centuries. His name does not appear in the indexes to Allardyce Nicoll's three-volume history of the English drama from the Restoration to 1800. But in Nicoll's four-volume series on the more romantic nineteenth-century drama Marlowe's name begins to reappear, and the literary scholars also started to rediscover him. Editions of his collected works were issued by G. Robinson, A. Dyce, F. Cunningham, H. Breyman and A. Wagner, A. H. Bullen and Havelock Ellis.

In the twentieth century English and American scholars have caused such a flood of articles, biographies, and editions of both individual and collected works that even the most indefatigable student feels submerged. The most important of these complete editions are those by C. F. Tucker Brooke (Oxford, 1910) and R. H. Case *et al.* in six volumes (London, 1931–3, 1961). Charles Crawford has published a seven-volume *Marlow Concordance* through Henry de Vocht's *Materials for the Study of the Old English Drama* (Louvain, 1911–32); and Samuel A. Tannenbaum has edited *Christopher Marlowe: A Concise Bibliography* (Scholars' Facsimile Reprints, 1937), later superseded by that of John Bakeless in *The Tragicall History of Christopher Marlowe* (Harvard, 1942). Of the spate of full-length biographical studies the most important are as follows: Una M. Ellis-Fermor, *Christopher Marlowe* (London, 1927); F. S. Boas, *Marlowe and His Circle* (Oxford, 1929, 1931) and *Christopher Marlowe: A Biographical and Critical Study* (Oxford, 1940); Mark W. Eccles, *Christopher Marlowe in London* (Harvard University Press, 1934); Philip Henderson, *And Morning in His Eyes* (London, 1937); John Bakeless, *Christopher Marlowe: The Man in His Time* (New York, 1937) and *The Tragicall History of Christopher Marlowe* (Harvard University Press, 1942); Paul H. Kocher, *Christopher Marlowe: A Study of His Thought, Learning, and Character* (University of North Carolina, 1946); Michel Poirier, *Christopher Marlowe* (London, 1951); and Harry Levin's largely critical *The Overreacher: A Study of Christopher Marlowe* (Harvard, 1952).

Twentieth-century biographical and critical articles are almost too numerous to count, though mention must certainly be made of *Marlowe: A Collection of Critical Essays*, consisting of fourteen articles by Marlowe authorities, edited by Clifford Leech (London and New York, 1964). There must have been something in the character, life, and writings of Christopher Marlowe which makes a special appeal to our age. As a typical Renaissance man, he lived life fully and dangerously for a brief twenty-nine years, and his age, like our own, was one of world turbulence and discovery, of a roving, questioning spirit, and of a stormy conflict between skepticism and conventional beliefs.

In the sixteenth century there were so many variant spellings and pronunciations of the name which finally became established as Marlowe that researchers have often had difficulty in discriminating among their owners. The name appears on various records not only as Marlowe, but also as Marlow, Marloe, Marley, Marly, Marlye, Morley, Marlin, Marlen, and M'lyn. But there is little doubt that the man whom we know as Christopher Marlowe was born into the family of a respectable burgess in the parish of St. George the Martyr in the cathedral town of Canterbury, Kent, on February 6,

1564. He was the second child and first son of John Marlowe, a member of the shoe-makers' and tanners' guild, and of Catherine Arthur, probably the daughter of Christo-pher Arthur, rector of St. Peter's church there, after whom the boy was presumably named.

In January 1579, Christopher "Marley" was awarded a scholarship for boys between nine and fifteen at the ancient King's School, and his name appears in some of the treasurer's accounts. Since he was almost fifteen when he was given the award, he apparently stayed only about two years. But since *The History of the King's School, Canterbury*, by C. E. Woodruff and H. J. Cape (London, 1908), showed that the Dean and Chapter of the school encouraged the production of tragedies, comedies, and interludes by "the schoolmaster and scholars," it is likely that the boy's interest in the theater was aroused at this time. When Matthew Parker, Archbishop of Canterbury, died in 1575, his will provided for the establishment of three scholarships for King's School boys from Canterbury at Corpus Christi College, Cambridge, and Marlowe (known first as Marlin or Marlen, but later as Marley) received one of these, although he was matriculated in March 1581 only as a pensioner (G. C. Moore-Smith, *MLR*, 1909). He had actually come into residence, however, in the second term. Bakeless, in his *Christopher Marlowe*, tells of going through the Corpus Christi and university libraries and noting the books there which may have been read by Marlowe as sources for some of his later plays. And Ethel Seaton, in "Marlowe's Light Reading" (*Elizabethan and Jacobean Studies Presented to Frank Percy Wilson*, Oxford, 1959), has found evidence in the plays them-selves of three mainsprings of Marlowe's reading in medieval literature, though not all necessarily while he was still in college: general reminiscences of the romances, espe-cially the popular or English ones, and of the Alexander saga; the Troy legend; and more historical material, such as *Godfrey of Boulogne*.

Even in his college days, Marlowe reacted violently against the religious and con-ventional family atmosphere in which he had been reared. At first his record of pay-ments and fees showed him to be quite regular in residence, as might have been expected from a young man who, according to the implication of Parker's will, was expected to take ministerial orders. But during part of 1582 his attendance became spotty, and during the academic year 1584–85 he was absent more than half the time. Neverthe-less, he proceeded B.A. in 1584, and M.A. in 1587, although irregularities shown in certain of the university records indicate that he was in trouble with the college author-ities in the interim. In fact, various rumors about his activities seem to have been floating about the Cambridge campus, a partial answer to which was provided by J. Leslie Hotson in his trail-blazing *The Death of Christopher Marlowe* (London and Har-vard, 1925). Hotson discovered an entry in the register of the Privy Council for June 29, 1587, as follows:

Whereas it was reported that Christopher Morley was determined to haue gone beyond the seas to Reames and there to remaine Their L[ordship]s thought good to certifie that he had no such intent, but that in all his acc[i]ons he had behaued him selfe orderlie and dis-creetelie wherebie he had done her Ma[jes]tie good service, and deserued to be rewarded for his faithfull dealinge: Their L[ordship]s request was that the rumor thereof should be allaied by all possible meanes, and that he should be furthered in the degree he was to take this next Commencem[en]t: Because it was not her Ma[jes]t[ie]s pleasure that anie one emploied as he had been in matters touching the benefitt of his Countrie should be defamed by those that are ignorant in th'affaires he went about.

This certification of good conduct not only cleared Marlowe of the charge that he had intended to go over to the Roman Catholic church (Rheims was one of the major head-quarters of English Roman Catholics on the Continent), but reinstated him in the good graces of the college authorities and also implied that he might have been engaged in some sort of secret-service mission (Boas, *Marlowe and His Circle*). Ironically, the only known specimen of Marlowe's handwriting is the witnessing of a will of a Canterbury woman, which explained another absence from Cambridge (Bakeless, *Tragicall History*).

When Marlowe left Cambridge to take up permanent residence in London, he soon began to get himself talked about as a hot-tempered young ruffler who was not to be trifled with in either physical or intellectual conflict. In October 1589 he found it necessary to get two friends, Richard Kitchen and Humphrey Rowland (both of whom had bad records), to become sureties, under heavy financial penalties, that "Christopher Marley, gentleman," would "personally appear at the next Sessions of Newgate to answer everything that may be alleged against him on the part of the Queen, and shall not depart without the permission of the Court" (Hotson, "Marlowe among the Churchwardens," *Atlantic Monthly*, July 1926). Similarly, Mark Eccles (*Christopher Marlowe in London, HSE*, 1934) discovered several records in the Public Record Office which revealed that in September of the same year Marlowe was seriously involved in a quarrel between his friend the poet Thomas Watson and William Bradley, the son of the landlord of the Bishop Inn. Bradley, who had already demanded "sureties of the peace" against Watson and two of his other friends and who knew Marlowe to be close to them all, attacked Marlowe (apparently without overt provocation) when he happened to meet him in Hog Lane in the parish of St. Giles without Cripplegate. Watson, who was near by, saw the fight, rushed to his friend's help, and in the scuffle killed Bradley. Both Watson and Marlowe were arrested "on suspicion of murder" and committed to Newgate. Both pleaded self-defense and were eventually released (although Watson had to be pardoned by the Queen); and Marlowe returned to his rooms in Norton Folgate. While in prison he met some interesting prisoners, notably one John Poole, a coiner or counterfeiter, who gave him some ideas about coining English and French money (Eccles, "Marlowe in Newgate," *TLS*, Sept 6, 1934). Nevertheless, in spite of these not too creditable episodes, Marlowe apparently retained sufficient government confidence for him to be continued in its employment.

Marlowe's eventual behind-the-scenes employer was probably Sir Francis Walsingham, Secretary of State and the organizer of the English intelligence service. But soon after his arrival in London Marlowe had gained as a literary patron Sir Thomas Walsingham, son of a cousin of Sir Francis. Sir Thomas, also patron of Thomas Watson and George Chapman, was likewise involved in the spy network. Marlowe also somehow found his way into a small circle of freethinkers and free talkers centering around Sir Walter Raleigh and his friend and dependent, the mathematician and astronomer Thomas Harriot. The group also included Walter Warner, a mathematical friend of Harriot; Matthew Royden, a minor poet; and perhaps others of less importance. In a not altogether sound study, "Raleigh and Marlowe: A Study in Elizabethan Fustian" (Fordham University Press, 1941), Eleanor G. Clark attempted to show the influence of Raleigh's thought and career on Marlowe's plays. Marlowe for a time also formed a close association with Thomas Kyd, the author of *The Spanish Tragedy;* in fact, as Kyd stated, they had been "wrytinge in one chamber two yeares synce," that is, in the early summer of 1591. All these relationships and events were to come together in the series of catastrophic coincidences which led to Marlowe's death on May 30, 1593. This fascinating mystery story is too complicated to be more than briefly summarized here.

At one of the meetings of Raleigh and his group, Marlowe—according to the testimony of an informer, Richard Chomley—read what Chomley called "the Atheist lecture"—not an unexpected subject in view of the reputation Marlowe already had among the pious as a scoffer and blasphemer. In fact, he was referred to as "that Atheist Tamburlaine" by Robert Greene in 1588. Actually he was not an atheist in the proper sense; his writings clearly show that he believed in a God. But he did indulge in a searching and irreverent criticism of both the Old and the New Testaments, pointing out in jesting fashion some of their irrational inconsistencies, impossibilities, and absurdities—calling Moses, for instance, nothing but a "juggler" in performing his miracles. It was basically the institutions and beliefs of contemporary orthodox religion that he rejected. But when Thomas Kyd's room was raided, one of the heretical documents found there was part of an Arian or Socinian treatise of half a century past (see W. Dinsmore Briggs, *SP*, 1923), which Kyd fearfully explained was really the property of Marlowe and had become accidentally mixed up with his own papers. Another informer, Richard Baines, also testified to Marlowe's "atheistic" utterances and his "horrible blasphemes;" but Paul H. Kocher, in "Marlowe's Atheist Lecture" (*JEGP*, 1940), has surmised that if a few minor transpositions are made in the order of Marlowe's statements as summarized by Baines, it would appear that the informer was merely reporting the Raleigh lecture, which had become widely circulated. Kocher later amplified this theme in "Backgrounds for Marlowe's Atheist Lecture" (*Renaissance Studies in Honor of Hardin Craig*, Stanford University Press, 1941), in which he placed the so-called "lecture" in a setting of extracts from contemporary religious and irreligious treatises. The Misses Lynette and Eveline Feasy have also discussed "The Validity of the Baines Document" (*NQ*, 1949); they agreed with Kocher's general conclusions, but have added other possible sources of their own. F. S. Boas, following up a suggestion in an article by L. Antheunis in a Flemish periodical, has attempted an identification of Baines with an Englishman who studied for the Roman Catholic priesthood at Rheims in 1581. While there, Boas says, Baines conceived the idea of getting a reward from Elizabeth for revealing Roman Catholic plots against her and even of poisoning the members of the seminary. His plot was betrayed by a confederate and he was jailed for ten months, but after signing a full confession in 1583 he disappeared. Boas thinks that if such a man got back to England he would have been the kind to inform against Marlowe ("Informer against Marlowe," *TLS*, Sept. 16, 1949).

At any rate, on May 18, 1593, the Privy Council sent a messenger to Sir Thomas Walsingham's estate at Scadbury to seek out Marlowe for arrest and interrogation—probably because Kyd, who had been taken into custody a few days earlier, had accused Marlowe of being the owner of the "Arian treatise." Nevertheless, during all this time Marlowe seems to have remained in government service, whether or not the messenger succeeded in bringing him before the Privy Council.

The next we hear of him is that on May 30 he was invited to meet with three men at the tavern of a widow, Eleanor Bull, at Deptford, just outside London. The three men, all of bad reputation but all associated in one way or another with Thomas Walsingham, were Robert Poley, Ingram Frezer or Frizer, and Nicholas Skeres. Poley, a rather decayed gentleman, had a long record as both spy and counterspy, had spent time in prison, and had played a minor role in Anthony Babington's abortive plot to murder Elizabeth and enthrone Mary Queen of Scots. Frizer, now in Thomas Walsingham's service, had been involved—so far as the records are concerned—only in some shady financial dealings. Skeres, distinctly below the others in social caste but a hanger-on of Frizer, had been mentioned in a letter to Burghley among other "maisterles men & cut-purses," and was a minor London thief and shoplifter. What brought this choice assortment of suspicious characters together in Mistress Bull's house has never been clear. One Elizabethan commentator suggested a "banquet," another a session at "tables" (backgammon), and others a conference on some forthcoming plan or plot. Since the meeting lasted quietly from ten in the morning until after supper before its disastrous denouement, perhaps all three took place. At any rate, the gathering was abruptly brought to an end when Marlowe was stabbed to death by Frizer. Conflicting rumors about Marlowe's death soon began to float about London. Gabriel Harvey was clearly off the mark in his epilogue to "A New Letter of Notable Contents" (1593) when he implied that Marlowe died of the plague, which was rampant that year. Frances Meres was a little closer to the truth when he wrote in his usual allusive style in *Palladis Tamia* (1598) that "As the poet *Lycophron* was shot to death by a certain riual of his: so *Christopher Marlowe* was stabd to death by a bawdy seruing man, a riuall of his in his lewde loue." Other writers, many of them moralists, had their own explanations and drew their own lessons as to God's vengeance on a blasphemer.

Over three centuries had passed, however, before Leslie Hotson opened up a new and more solid approach to the mystery. In 1925 Hotson announced his discovery of the documents in the coroner's inquest—which had taken place two days after Marlowe's death before William Danby, coroner of the Queen's household, and sixteen citizens drawn from various districts of London. After supper, according to this official account, a dispute had arisen between Frizer and Christopher "Morley" about "le recknynge." While Frizer was lying on a bed, with Poley and Skeres sitting closely on each side of him, Marlowe had suddenly and maliciously drawn Frizer's own dagger, which was at his back, and given him two long but superficial wounds on the head. In his struggle to regain his own weapon, Frizer inflicted a wound above his assailant's right eye which penetrated two inches into the brain. Marlowe died instantly. On June 28, Frizer received a pardon for the murder on grounds of self-defense.

This evidence might have settled the matter, but instead it precipitated a controversy which still boils. Eugenie de Kalb started it all with a letter on "The Death of Marlowe" to the *Times Literary Supplement* (May 21, 1925), questioning the physical possibility of such a struggle in view of the given positions of all four men. In another article on "Robert Poley's Movements as a Messenger of the Court, 1588 to 1601" (*RES*, 1933) she examined thirty-six extracts from official documents concerning Poley, and concluded: That "his presence at that scene in Deptford Strand was most irregular, is subtly conveyed by his masters, who forestall inquiry with the statement, occurring nowhere else among the entries of payments to the messengers, of his 'being in her majesties service all the aforesaid time.' " Miss de Kalb not only speculated about the possible political implications of the meeting, but even suggested that Frizer and the others were actually employed by Lady Walsingham to murder Marlowe because he possessed information dangerous to her. In this speculation Miss de Kalb has been supported by Bakeless; but Boas, in his note on Bakeless's biography (*YWES*, 1942), has found her theory untenable. At any rate, Christopher Marlowe lived—and died— a fascinating enigma.

To most Elizabethan theater-goers the play was much more important than its author. And most playwrights seem to have agreed with them, since the desire to achieve literary fame through placing their names on title pages seems to have been relatively inconsequential. Nor was there any certainty concerning the relationship between the date of composition or production and the date of publication. This situation was so patent in the case of Marlowe that, in spite of the efforts of some modern scholars to establish a canon and a chronology for his plays, others have lost patience with the whole endeavor. In 1938 F. S. Boas, in commenting on Kocher's attempt to set up a time order for the years which elapsed between the first draft of *Dido, Queen of Carthage*, and the composition of the unfinished poem, *Hero and Leander*, wrote: "In these words there is the tacit assumption, which is highly questionable, that Marlowe's writings can be arranged in their chronological order" ("The Development of Marlowe's Character," *PQ*, 1938). In 1964 Bernard Harris (Boas's successor as the drama editor of *The Year's Work in English Studies*), in reviewing J. B. Steane's attempt to establish a complete canon in his *Marlowe: A Critical Study* (Cambridge University Press), grumbled that "in the present state of Marlowe criticism this is scarcely to be expected, if it is ever, indeed, to be desired." Earlier, Rupert Taylor had offered "A Tentative Chronology of Marlowe and Some Other Elizabethan Plays" (*PMLA*, 1936), which Boas discredited because it brought Marlowe's dramatic activities to an end three years before his death; and in 1940 Boas praised Marion Bodwell Smith's *Marlowe's Imagery and the Marlowe Canon* (University of Pennsylvania Press) for "her painstaking methods and her lucid scheme of classification," but concluded that her results were disputable. Perhaps Kenneth Muir's conclusions in "The Chronology of Marlowe's Plays" (*Proceedings of the Leeds Philosophical Society* for 1943) are as useful as any. Muir arranges the plays in the following sequence: *Dido* (1586–87; revised, 1591–92); *Tamburlaine* (1587; printed, 1590); *The Jew of Malta* (1589); *Doctor Faustus* (1590); *Edward II* (1591); and *The Massacre at Paris* (1592). Anonymous plays that have also been ascribed to Marlowe on various conjectural grounds are *Arden of Feversham*, different parts of *Henry VI*, *A Larum for London*, *The True Tragedy of Richard III*, and some others.

TAMBURLAINE, PART I

Just as more critical and scholarly attention has been devoted in the twentieth century to Marlowe than to any other Elizabethan dramatist except Shakespeare, so more has been written about *Tamburlaine* (a two-part play, only the first of which is reprinted here) than about any of Marlowe's other plays, including *Doctor Faustus*. The reason probably is that *Tamburlaine* reflects more aspects of Renaissance political thought and attitudes. In addition to discussions of it by editors of his complete works or plays and by full-scale biographers, there have been dozens of articles on all phases of its thinking and style, besides several independent editions of the play itself. The most useful and thorough of these independent editions are those of Una Ellis-Fermor (London, 1930; revised, 1951) and of John D. Jump (University of Nebraska Press, 1967). Yet the only contemporary evidence of Marlowe's authorship is either indirect—in the form of veiled allusions—or internal—in its ideas, its poetic language, and its reflection of a personality. No writers assign it specifically to Marlowe until the end of the next century. The last clear record of its performance before the twentieth century is in Henslowe's diary in 1595, though allusions in the early seventeenth century indicate that it was probably still alive on the stage and certainly alive in playbook form. But in spite of its nineteenth-century rebirth in the library, apparently its first revival on stage did not occur until 1919, when a cut version was given at Yale. This production led to similar revivals and readings in the nonprofessional theater.

In his dramatization of the headlong career of the Mongolian (or Scythian, or Tartar— the terms are used more or less interchangeably) conqueror, Tamburlaine, the playwright had several sources to draw on. The name of this supermanly hero was Timur the Lame, so called for the lameness he apparently acquired while he was still a young marauder, if not a bandit. Marlowe carefully repressed this infirmity so as not to detract from his protagonist's greatness and perfection. (For a comparison of Marlowe's character with his historical original, see Leslie Spence in "Tamburlaine and Marlowe," *PMLA*, 1927.) These available sources, however, were not always the more reliable ones of the early Byzantine historians or of certain Italian, Spanish, and German travelers, but were rather recensions, elaborations, and embellishments of these accounts by the Spaniard, Pedro Mexia (1543) (as translated into Italian, French, and English) or by the Italian, Pietro Perondino [writing in Latin as Petrus Perondinus (1553)], supplemented perhaps by the story of the travels of an Armenian named Haytoun (translated into French in 1501). But it is probable that Marlowe worked directly from such English sources as a chapter in Thomas Fortescue's *The Forest* (1574), a translation of Mexia, and George Whetstone's *The English Mirror* (1586), a translation of Perondinus. It is also possible that Marlowe knew Jean Bodin's account of Tamburlaine in *Six Livres de la Republique* (1576) and that he had seen Richard Knolles's as yet unpublished *A General History of the Turks*, since manuscripts were frequently circulated in literary circles. (See Thomas C. Izard, "The Principal Source for Marlowe's *Tamburlaine*," *MLN*, 1943; Ethel Seaton, "Fresh Sources for Marlowe," *RES*, 1929; Hugh G. Dick, "*Tamburlaine* Sources Once More," *SP*, 1949.) For Part II Marlowe supplemented his reading by drawing on a history of Hungary, an episode in Ariosto's *Orlando Furioso*, and an English work on fortification (also in manuscript). For geography throughout the play he relied on the world atlas by Abraham Ortelius.

Theatrum Orbis Terrarum, published in Antwerp in 1570. But Marlowe allowed himself many liberties in the use, rejection, or modification of episodes or details; in his treatment of the geography of Asia, eastern Europe, and Asia Minor (which he often speaks of as Africa) when dealing with battles recorded in history; and in his choice of characters' proper names (except the unfortunate Bajazeth), which he drew from various sources and historical periods, or even invented (including Zenocrate, since only one early record mentions that Tamburlaine had a wife). (M. M. Wehling, in "Marlowe's Mnemonic Nominalogy, with Especial Reference to *Tamburlaine*," *MLN*, 1958, has tried to show how the characteristics of many of these persons are brought out by examining the derivations of their names, particularly from the Greek.) In his frequent references to "bullets" Marlowe does not seem to realize that gunpowder in the modern sense was unknown to the Tartars, who depended primarily on bows and swords, though they were apparently familiar with siege engines and some sort of explosives. This cavalier treatment of historical fact in the interest of the creation of higher human truths receives the approval of Wilbur Sanders in *The Dramatist and the Received Idea: Studies in the Plays of Marlowe and Shakespeare* (Cambridge University Press, 1968), in which the author attacks what he calls the triviality of much source-and-influence study.

Nevertheless, Tucker Brooke has described *Tamburlaine* as "the source and original of the English history play" and "the classic instance of chivalrous romance turned drama" (*The Tudor Drama*, Boston, 1911); and Irving Ribner has called it the "first clear treatment of an actual historical figure within the form of the heroic play." Ribner, in *The English History Play* and "Marlowe's 'Tragicke Glasse'" in *Essays on Shakespeare and Elizabethan Drama*, has dealt with the play as the work of a man "with a mature philosophy of history," using it to present important political doctrines, quite unlike those in *Gorboduc* or *Cambises*. Like Poggio Bracciolini and his followers, Marlowe has placed this play in the humanist tradition of "the new Renaissance prince who, by his own ability and without regard for any supernatural power, could conquer the world and revitalize empires." In other words, Marlowe discarded the old idea of history as being guided by God or Providence, and preached that it is governed by the two forces of human will and fortune. He did not use fortune in the medieval Christian manner as the instrument of God's guidance of human affairs, but in the classical conception of a lawless element in the universe which can, for a time at least, be controlled by human wisdom and power. Marlowe's hero, therefore, is like the heroes of Polybius, Francesco Guicciardini, and Niccolo Machiavelli (though Kocher in his study of Marlowe's thought has rather discounted the extent of Machiavelli's influence). With such a philosophy of the extreme self-expression of the individual, it is perfectly natural and proper that a lowly Scythian shepherd should have an ambition to rule the whole world—and almost succeed in his ruthless intentions. These intentions become justified because of the more perfect government he sets up in the conquered lands, even though it is an absolutist government quite in accord with Tudor standards. Tamburlaine is stopped in his often-bloody career only by his death, which ends Part II.

Roy W. Battenhouse, in his article, "Tamburlaine, the 'Scourge of God'" (*PMLA*, 1941), attempted to use this death, which occurs shortly after Tamburlaine has defied the gods, Mahomet, and the Koran, as part of his argument that Marlowe, the quondam theology student, was really writing a moral and Christian play as a counterblast to "the libels of Kyd and Baines." Actually Marlowe himself establishes no clear connection between Tamburlaine's death and his "atheistic" defiance. Somewhat similarly, Helen L. Gardner ("The Second Part of *Tamburlaine the Great*," *MLR*, 1942) has argued that Marlowe's intentions in Part II differ so much from those of Part I that Part II is not simply a continuation, designed to capitalize on the first part's popularity, but that it presents a force that in the end destroys the hero, a force which "can be called Necessity or God, according to one's interpretation of Marlowe's religious thought." The Misses Feasy also (in a series of articles in *NQ* for 1950 and 1951) have discovered echoes in *Tamburlaine* of passages in various homilies, church services, and Biblical wisdom and prophetic books (especially *Isaiah* and *Revelation*) and have suggested that while at Cambridge Marlowe, as a prospective clergyman, could have come under the influence of certain liberal anti-Calvinistic theologians such as Peter Baro and William Harsnett. John P. Cutts, in "The Ultimate Source of Tamburlaine's White, Red, Black, and Death?" (*NQ*, 1958), has also speculated on the influence of *Revelation* on Marlowe.

Johnstone Parr has approached the subject of Tamburlaine's death from two still different angles—astrology and Renaissance medical theories—and comes to the conclusion that "the catastrophe of Tamburlaine is not at all out of joint with his character; for his peculiar distemper has been occasioned by his innate passions, and in the light of sixteenth century psycho-physiology it was perfectly obvious to an intelligent Elizabethan that the wrathful Scythian should have been despatched in such a manner." (See Parr's *Tamburlaine's Malady and Other Essays on Astrology in Elizabethan Drama*, University of Alabama Press, 1953; also Francis R. Johnson's article on Marlowe's Ptolemaic cosmology in "Marlowe's Astronomy and Skepticism," *ELH*, 1946.)   Don Cameron Allen, in "Renaissance Remedies for Fortune: Marlowe and the *Fortunati*" (*SP*, 1941), had earlier come to a somewhat similar conclusion and explained Tamburlaine's complex character by connecting him with the doctrine of the *fortunati*, as expressed by the Italian Giovanni Pontano in 1518-19.   According to this doctrine, certain men are born fortunate and are inevitably successful.   In reply to Egidio da Viterbo's objection that this theory left no place for Providence, Pontano answered that fortune is governed by the stars.   Allen used this concept to explain what he regarded as the structural defect of the play—its apparent absence of climaxes—and said that the lives of the *fortunati* in comparison with those of ordinary men are all climaxes.   From still a different angle, T. M. Pearce, in "Marlowe and Castiglione" (*MLQ*, 1951), has seen Tamburlaine conforming in most of his characteristics to the description of the ideal courtier in *Il Cortegiano*.   Pearce (in another article in *MLQ* for 1954) has also followed up the theme of educational training and discipline by analyzing Tamburlaine's rigorous treatment of his three sons in Part II according to the theories of Roger Ascham, Sir Thomas Elyot, Sir Humphrey Gilbert, and others. Since Marlowe had translated the first book of Lucan's *Pharsalia* (probably while still under the classical influence of college, just as he had perhaps sketched the first draft of *Tamburlaine* while there), William Blissett, in "Lucan's Caesar and the Elizabethan Villain" (*SP*, 1956), has seen strong traces of this "villain-hero" in Tamburlaine.   R. T. Tailor, in "Maximinus and Tamburlaine" (*NQ*, 1957), has pointed to a "curious parallel" between the attributes and careers of Tamburlaine and the Roman emperor, as presented by Machiavelli in *The Prince*.   Though Ribner, in "Marlowe's 'Tragicke Glasse'," has hesitated to find a "genuinely tragic conflict" in *Tamburlaine*, Douglas Cole, in *Suffering and Evil in the Plays of Christopher Marlowe* (Princeton, 1962), concluded that Marlowe's treatment of the subject "contains at its core a trenchantly ironic view of man's aspirations and the hell of suffering that they are able to produce even on earth."   In ultimate reaction against theories which read an openly didactic intention into *Tamburlaine*, Robert Kimbrough, in "*I Tamburlaine*: A Speaking Picture in a Tragic Glass" (*Renaissance Drama*, Northwestern University Press, 1960), concluded that Marlowe had written a carefully constructed play, combining pageantry, blank verse, and ethical study, in a way to please playgoers, and had done so in such a way that, unlike plays in the morality tradition, it eschewed open preachment of its moral, even in its ending, and thus started a new trend in playwriting. It is remarkable, too, as Philip Henderson has noted, that even though Marlowe had translated Ovid's *Amores* (probably in college), his plays were singularly lacking in any prurient emphasis on sex, in spite of the robust frankness of the Elizabethan age in general toward the subject.   However, one need not go as far as he and Muriel Bradbrook (*The School of*

Night, Cambridge University Press, 1936) do in identifying Tamburlaine with the active principle in life and Zenocrate with the contemplative imagination.

In *Tamburlaine* Marlowe effected the greatest achievement so far in the style of English poetic drama, even if one believes that Thomas Kyd preceded him in his use of dramatic blank verse. *Tamburlaine* was principally responsible for Ben Jonson's invention of the phrase, Marlowe's "mighty line," which has resounded down the ages (see especially Bakeless's chapter on the subject). This achievement went far beyond previous uses of the blank verse line in its greater flexibility and impact. Although Marlowe's lines generally follow a regular metrical pattern in their use of the caesura and the end-stop, they also frequently introduce an Alexandrine, a truncated line, or a run-on line. It is his poetic style in a larger sense, however, that distinguishes his writing from that of his predecessors and most of his contemporaries. It not only makes successful use of alliteration and assonance, but the language is highly metaphorical as well as rhetorical—though it sometimes descends to youthful rant and bombast. (Marlowe's peculiar use of hyperbole gave rise to Levin's title, *The Overreacher*.) The effectiveness of Marlowe's dramatic verse is also largely due to the richness of his diction and the resonances of his skilful manipulations of the exotic and polysyllabic names of places and people, with appropriate descriptive epithets. (For valuable general discussions of Marlowe's poetic style, see Brooke, "Marlowe's Versification and Style," *SP*, 1922; Prior, *The Language of Tragedy;* and Donald Peet, "The Rhetoric of *Tamburlaine*," *ELH*, 1959.)

Several prose passages in the midst of the verse perhaps also make for variety and contrast, although they do not always seem to be used for consistent reasons. Perhaps some of them may have something to do with the prefatory apology of Marlowe's printer, which explains his removal of some "fond and frivolous gestures" from the printed text. These probably consisted of comical, even farcical, passages inserted by Marlowe or someone else for the delectation of the groundlings. This raises the question as to whether Marlowe possessed a sense of humor. Clifford Leech in "Marlowe's Humor," in *Essays on Shakespeare and Elizabethan Drama*, adopts on the whole T. S. Eliot's assertion that Marlowe's "most powerful and mature tone" was that of a "savage comic humour," and remarks that "Ultimately there will come, perhaps, a recognition of the important part played by savage humor in *Tamburlaine* and in *Doctor Faustus*," even though they are tragic plays.

William Archer, iconoclastic as always where the English drama before his own period is concerned, explained his reason for not including Marlowe in his discussion of "The Elizabethan Legend" (*The Old Drama and the New*, London, 1922): "I shall entirely pass over those whom we may call the primitives—Marlowe, Kyd, Greene, Peele and Lodge—and take notice only of writers who came to the front after the purely tentative period was past, and the formula of the age had fairly established itself. In doing so I intend no disrespect to that master of the 'mighty line,' Christopher Marlowe. He was a great poet, and might, had he lived, have grown into a great dramatist. But it is evident that in his work the differentiation between epic and drama is as yet imperfectly accomplished."

The basis of the present text is the 1590 edition, as presented in C. F. Tucker Brooke's variorum edition of *The Works of Christopher Marlowe* (Oxford, 1910).

TAMBURLAINE THE GREAT

[BY

CHRISTOPHER MARLOWE

THE FIRST PART

DRAMATIS PERSONÆ

MYCETES, *King of Persia.*
COSROE, *his brother.*
ORTYGIUS ⎫
CENEUS ⎪
MEANDER ⎬ *Persian lords and leaders.*
MENAPHON ⎪
THERIDAMAS ⎭
TAMBURLAINE, *a Scythian shepherd.*
TECHELLES ⎫ *his followers.*
USUMCASANE ⎭
BAJAZETH, *Emperor of the Turks.*
KING OF ARABIA.
KING OF FEZ.
KING OF MOROCCO.
KING of ARGIER.[2]

SOLDAN of EGYPT.
GOVERNOR of DAMASCUS.
AGYDAS ⎫ *Median lords.*
MAGNETES ⎭
CAPOLIN, *an Egyptian captain.*
PHILEMUS, *a messenger.*
BASSOES,[3] LORDS, CITIZENS, MOORS,
    SOLDIERS, *and* ATTENDANTS.

ZENOCRATE, *daughter of the Soldan of
    Egypt.*
ANIPPE, *her maid.*
ZABINA, *wife of Bajazeth.*
EBEA, *her maid.*
VIRGINS OF DAMASCUS.

SCENE: *Western Asia.*

TIME: *Fourteenth Century.*]

TO THE GENTLEMEN READERS, AND OTHERS THAT TAKE PLEASURE IN READING HISTORIES.

Gentlemen, and courteous readers whosoever: I have here published in print for your sakes the two tragical discourses of the Scythian shepherd, Tamburlaine, that became so great a conqueror and so mighty a monarch. My hope is that they will be now no less acceptable unto you to read after your serious affairs and studies than they have been, lately, delightful for many of you to see, when the same were [10] showed in London upon stages. I have, purposely, omitted and left out some fond[4] and frivolous gestures, digressing and, in my poor opinion, far unmeet for the matter, which I thought might seem more tedious unto the wise than any way else to be regarded, though haply they have been of some vain, conceited fondlings[5] greatly gaped at, what times they were showed upon the stage in their graced deformities; [20] nevertheless, now, to be mixtured in print with such matter of worth, it would prove a great disgrace to so honorable and stately a history. Great folly were it in me to commend unto your wisdoms either the eloquence of the author that writ them, or the worthiness of the matter itself; I therefore leave unto your learned censures[6] both the one and the other, and myself, the poor

[1] The title continues: "Who, from a Scythian Shepherd, by His Rare and Wonderful Conquests Became a Most Puissant and Mighty Monarch, and (for His Tyranny and Terror in War) Was Termed the Scourge of God. Divided into Two Tragical Discourses, as They Were Sundry Times Showed upon Stages in the City of London, by the Right Honorable the Lord Admiral His Servants. Now First and Newly Published."
[2] Algiers.   [3] Bashaws.
[4] Foolish.   [5] Fools.   [6] Judgments.

443

printer of them, unto your most cour- [30
teous and favorable protection, which if you
vouchsafe to accept, you shall evermore
bind me to employ what travail and service
I can to the advancing and pleasuring of
your excellent degree.

Yours, most humble at commandment,
R[ichard] J[ones], Printer.

THE PROLOGUE

FROM jigging veins of riming mother wits
And such conceits as clownage keeps in pay,
We'll lead you to the stately tent of war,
Where you shall hear the Scythian Tam-
  burlaine
Threat'ning the world with high astound-
  ing terms,
And scourging kingdoms with his conquer-
  ing sword.
View but his picture in this tragic glass,
And then applaud his fortunes as you
  please.

ACTUS I. SCENA i.

[The Persian court.]

*Mycetes, Cosroe, Meander, Theridamas,
Ortygius, Ceneus, [Menaphon,] with
Others.*

MYC. Brother Cosroe, I find myself ag-
  grieved,
Yet insufficient to express the same,
For it requires a great and thund'ring
  speech.
Good brother, tell the cause unto my
  lords;
I know you have a better wit than I.
Cos. Unhappy Persia, that in former age
Hast been the seat of mighty conquerors
That, in their prowess and their policies,
Have triumphed over Afric and the
  bounds
Of Europe, where the sun dares scarce
  appear   10
For freezing meteors and congealéd cold,
Now to be ruled and governed by a man
At whose birthday Cynthia with Saturn
  joined,
And Jove, the Sun, and Mercury denied
To shed their [1] influence in his fickle
  brain!

[1] Suggested by Dyce. Original has *his.*

Now Turks and Tartars shake their
  swords at thee,
Meaning to mangle all thy provinces.
MYC. Brother, I see your meaning well
  enough,
And thorough [2] your planets I perceive
  you think
I am not wise enough to be a king;   20
But I refer me to my noblemen
That know my wit, and can be witnesses.
I might command you to be slain for this.
Meander, might I not?
MEAN. Not for so small a fault, my sov-
  ereign lord.
MYC. I mean it not, but yet I know I
  might.
Yet live; yea, live. Mycetes wills it so.
Meander, thou, my faithful counselor,
Declare the cause of my conceivéd grief,
Which is, God knows, about that Tam-
  burlaine,   30
That, like a fox in midst of harvest
  time,
Doth prey upon my flocks of passengers, [3]
And, as I hear, doth mean to pull my
  plumes;
Therefore 'tis good and meet for to be
  wise.
MEAN. Oft have I heard your majesty
  complain
Of Tamburlaine, that sturdy Scythian
  thief,
That robs your merchants of Persepolis,
Treading by land unto the Western Isles,
And in your confines with his lawless
  train
Daily commits incivil [4] outrages,   40
Hoping (misled by dreaming prophecies)
To reign in Asia, and with barbarous
  arms
To make himself the monarch of the
  East.
But, ere he march in Asia, or display
His vagrant ensign in the Persian fields,
Your grace hath taken order by Theri-
  damas,
Charged with a thousand horse, to appre-
  hend
And bring him captive to your highness'
  throne.
MYC. Full true thou speak'st, and like
  thyself, my lord,

[2] Through.   [4] Barbarous.
[3] Travelers, traders.

Whom I may term a Damon for thy
   love.   50
Therefore 'tis best, if so it like you all,
To send my thousand horse incontinent [1]
To apprehend that paltry Scythian.
How like you this, my honorable lords?
Is it not a kingly resolution?
Cos. It cannot choose, because it comes
   from you.
Myc. Then hear thy charge, valiant Theri-
   damas,
The chiefest captain of Mycetes' host,
The hope of Persia, and the very legs
Whereon our state doth lean, as on a
   staff   60
That holds us up, and foils our neighbor
   foes.
Thou shalt be leader of this thousand
   horse,
Whose foaming gall with rage and high
   disdain
Have sworn the death of wicked Tam-
   burlaine.
Go frowning forth; but come thou smiling
   home,
As did Sir Paris with the Grecian dame.
Return with speed—time passeth swift
   away;
Our life is frail, and we may die today.
Ther. Before the moon renew her bor-
   rowed light,
Doubt not, my lord and gracious sov-
   ereign,   70
But Tamburlaine and that Tartarian
   rout
Shall either perish by our warlike hands
Or plead for mercy at your highness'
   feet.
Myc. Go, stout Theridamas; thy words
   are swords,
And with thy looks thou conquerest all
   thy foes.
I long to see thee back return from
   thence,
That I may view these milk-white steeds
   of mine,
All loaden with the heads of killéd men,
And from their knees even to their hoofs
   below,
Besmeared with blood that makes a
   dainty [2] show.   80
Ther. Then now, my lord, I humbly take
   my leave.

Myc. Therid[amas], farewell ten thousand
   times!   *Exit* [*Theridamas*]
Ah, Menaphon, why stayest thou thus
   behind,
When other men press forward for re-
   nown?
Go, Menaphon, go into Scythia,
And foot by foot follow Theridamas.
Cos. Nay, pray you let him stay; a greater
   [task] [3]
Fits Menaphon than warring with a
   thief.
Create him prorex [4] of [all] [5] Africa,
That he may win the Babylonians'
   hearts,   90
Which will revolt from Persian govern-
   ment,
Unless they have a wiser king than you.
Myc. "Unless they have a wiser king than
   you"!
These are his words. Meander, set them
   down.
Cos. And add this to them—that all
   Asia
Lament to see the folly of their king.
Myc. Well, here I swear by this my royal
   seat—
Cos. You may do well to kiss it then!
Myc. Embossed with silk as best beseems
   my state,
To be revenged for these contemptuous
   words.   100
O, where is duty and allegiance now?
Fled to the Caspian or the Ocean main?
What, shall I call thee brother? No, a foe.
Monster of nature, shame unto thy
   stock,
That dar'st presume thy sovereign for to
   mock!
Meander, come! I am abused, Meander.
Exit [*with his Train*]. *Manent* [6] *Cosroe
   et Menaphon.*
Mena. How now, my lord? What, mated [7]
   and amazed
To hear the king thus threaten like him-
   self?
Cos. Ah, Menaphon, I pass [8] not for his
   threats.
The plot is laid by Persian noblemen 110
And captains of the Median garrisons
To crown me Emperor of Asia.

---

[1] Immediately.   [2] Fine, rare.

[3] Added by Robinson.   [5] From 1605 edn.
[4] Viceroy.   [6] Remain.
[7] Checkmated, confounded.   [8] Care.

But this it is that doth excruciate
The very substance of my vexéd soul—
To see our neighbors, that were wont to
quake
And tremble at the Persian monarch's
name,
Now sits and laughs our regiment [1] to
scorn;
And, that which might resolve [2] me into
tears,
Men from the farthest equinoctial line
Have swarmed in troops into the Eastern
India,   120
Lading their ships with gold and precious
stones,
And made their spoils from all our prov-
inces.
MENA. This should entreat your highness
to rejoice,
Since fortune gives you opportunity
To gain the title of a conqueror
By curing of this maiméd empery.
Afric and Europe bordering on your land,
And continent [3] to your dominions,
How easily may you, with a mighty host,
Pass into Grecia, as did Cyrus once,   130
And cause them to withdraw their forces
home,
Lest you subdue the pride of Christen-
dom!   [Trumpet within.]
Cos. But, Menaph[on], what means this
trumpet's sound?
MENA. Behold, my lord, Ortygius and the
rest
Bringing the crown to make you em-
peror!

Enter Ortygius and Ceneus [4] bearing a
crown, with Others.

ORTY. Magnificent and mighty Prince Cos-
roe,
We, in the name of other Persian states [5]
And commons of this mighty monarchy,
Present thee with th' imperial diadem.
CEN. The warlike soldiers and the gentle-
men,   140
That heretofore have filled Persepolis
With Afric captains taken in the field,
Whose ransom made them march in coats
of gold,

With costly jewels hanging at their ears,
And shining stones upon their lofty
crests,
Now living idle in the walléd towns,
Wanting both pay and martial discipline,
Begin in troops to threaten civil war,
And openly exclaim against the king.
Therefore, to stay all sudden muti-
nies,   150
We will invest your highness emperor,
Whereat the soldiers will conceive more
joy
Than did the Macedonians at the spoil
Of great Darius and his wealthy host.
Cos. Well, since I see the state of Persia
droop
And languish in my brother's govern-
ment,
I willingly receive th' imperial crown,
And vow to wear it for my country's
good,
In spite of them [6] shall malice [7] my es-
tate.
ORTY. And, in assurance of desired suc-
cess,   160
We here do crown thee Monarch of the
East,
Emperor of Asia and of Persia,
Great Lord of Media and Armenia,
Duke of Africa and Albania,
Mesopotamia and of Parthia,
East India and the late-discovered isles,
Chief Lord of all the wide, vast Euxine
sea,
And of the ever-raging Caspian lake!
Long live Cosroe, mighty emperor!
Cos. And Jove may [8] never let me longer
live   170
Than I may seek to gratify your love,
And cause the soldiers that thus honor
me
To triumph over many provinces!
By whose desires of discipline in arms
I doubt not shortly but to reign sole
king,
And with the army of Theridamas,
Whither we presently will fly, my lords,
To rest secure against my brother's force.
ORTY. We knew, my lord, before we
brought the crown,
Intending your investion [9] so near   180

[1] Rule, government.
[2] Dissolve.
[3] Contiguous.
[4] Emended by Dyce. Original reads *Cornerus*.
[5] Persons of state.
[6] Them who.
[7] Bear malice to, seek to injure.
[8] May Jove.
[9] Investiture.

The residence of your despiséd brother,
The lord[s] would not be too exasperate [1]
To injure or suppress your worthy title;
Or, if they would, there are in readiness
Ten thousand horse to carry you from hence,
In spite of all suspected enemies.

Cos. I know it well, my lord, and thank you all.

Orty. Sound up the trumpets then. God save the king!   *Exeunt.*

Actus I. Scena ii.

[Tamburlaine's camp in Scythia.]

Tamburlaine leading Zenocrate; Techelles, Usumcasane, [Agydas, Magnetes;] other Lords and Soldiers loaden with treasure.

Tam. Come, lady, let not this appall your thoughts.
The jewels and the treasure we have ta'en
Shall be reserved, and you in better state
Than if you were arrived in Syria,
Even in the circle of your father's arms,
The mighty Soldan of Egyptia.

Zen. Ah, shepherd, pity my distresséd plight
(If, as thou seemst, thou art so mean a man)
And seek not to enrich thy followers
By lawless rapine from a silly [2] maid   10
Who, traveling with these Median lords
To Memphis, from my uncle's country of Media,
Where all my youth I have been governéd,
Have passed the army of the mighty Turk,
Bearing his privy signet and his hand
To safe conduct us thorough Africa.

Mag. And, since we have arrived in Scythia,
Besides rich presents from the puissant Cham,
We have his highness' letters to command
Aid and assistance, if we stand in need.   20

Tam. But now you see these letters and commands
Are countermanded by a greater man;

And through my provinces you must expect
Letters of conduct from my mightiness,
If you intend to keep your treasure safe.
But, since I love to live at liberty,
As easily may you get the soldan's crown
As any prizes out of my precinct,
For they are friends that help to wean my state
Till men and kingdoms help to strengthen it,   30
And must maintain my life exempt from servitude.—
But, tell me, madam, is your grace betrothed?

Zen. I am, my lord—for so you do import. [3]

Tam. I am a lord, for so my deeds shall prove,
And yet a shepherd by my parentage.
But, lady, this fair face and heavenly hue
Must grace his bed that conquers Asia,
And means to be a terror to the world,
Measuring the limits of his empery
By east and west, as Phœbus doth his course.   40
Lie here, ye weeds that I disdain to wear!
This complete armor and this curtle-ax [4]
Are adjuncts more beseeming Tamburlaine.
And, madam, whatsoever you esteem
Of this success [5] and loss unvaluéd, [6]
Both may invest you Empress of the East;
And these that seem but silly country swains
May have the leading of so great an host
As with their weight shall make the mountains quake,
Even as when windy exhalations,   50
Fighting for passage, tilt within the earth.

Tech. As princely lions, when they rouse themselves,
Stretching their paws, and threat'ning herds of beasts,
So in his armor looketh Tamburlaine.
Methinks I see kings kneeling at his feet,
And he, with frowning brows and fiery looks,
Spurning their crowns from off their captive heads.

---

[1] Old form of past participle.
[2] Simple, innocent.
[3] Bear yourself.
[4] Cutlass.
[5] Event.
[6] Invaluable.

USUM. And making thee and me, Techelles, kings,
That even to death will follow Tamburlaine.
TAM. Nobly resolved, sweet friends and followers! 60
These lords, perhaps, do scorn our estimates,
And think we prattle with distempered spirits;
But, since they measure our deserts so mean,
That in conceit [1] bear empires on our spears,
Affecting thoughts coequal with the clouds,
They shall be kept our forcéd followers,
Till with their eyes they view us emperors.
ZEN. The gods, defenders of the innocent,
Will never prosper your intended drifts, [2]
That thus oppress poor friendless passengers. 70
Therefore at least admit us liberty,
Even as thou hop'st to be eternizéd [3]
By living Asia's mighty emperor.
AGYD. I hope our lady's treasure and our own
May serve for ransom to our liberties.
Return our mules and empty camels back,
That we may travel into Syria,
Where her betrothéd lord, Alcidamus,
Expects th' arrival of her highness' person.
MAG. And, wheresoever we repose ourselves, 80
We will report but well of Tamburlaine.
TAM. Disdains Zenocrate [4] to live with me?
Or you, my lords, to be my followers?
Think you I weigh this treasure more than you?
Not all the gold in India's wealthy arms
Shall buy the meanest soldier in my train.
Zenocrate, lovelier than the love of Jove,
Brighter than is the silver Rhodope, [5]
Fairer than whitest snow on Scythian hills,
Thy person is more worth to Tamburlaine 90

[1] Idea, fancy, imagination. [3] Made immortal.
[2] Plans, schemes.
[4] Final *e* usually pronounced.
[5] Suggested by Dyce; original has *Rhodolfe*.

Than the possession of the Persian crown,
Which gracious stars have promised at my birth.
A hundreth Tartars shall attend on thee,
Mounted on steeds swifter than Pegasus.
Thy garments shall be made of Median silk,
Enchased with precious jewels of mine own,
More rich and valurous [6] than Zenocrate's.
With milk-white harts upon an ivory sled
Thou shalt be drawn amidst the frozen pools,
And scale the icy mountains' lofty tops, 100
Which with thy beauty will be soon resolved.
My martial prizes with five hundred men,
Won on the fifty-headed Volga's waves,
Shall all we offer to Zenocrate—
And then myself to fair Zenocrate.
TECH. What now!—In love?
TAM. Techelles, women must be flatteréd,
But this is she with whom I am in love.

Enter a Soldier.

SOLD. News! News!
TAM. How now, what's the matter? 110
SOLD. A thousand Persian horsemen are at hand,
Sent from the king to overcome us all.
TAM. How now, my lords of Egypt, and Zenocrate!
Now must your jewels be restored again,
And I that triumphed so be overcome?
How say you, lordings? Is not this your hope?
AGYD. We hope yourself will willingly restore them.
TAM. Such hope, such fortune, have the thousand horse.
Soft ye, [7] my lords and sweet Zenocrate!
You must be forcéd from me ere you go. 120
A thousand horsemen? We five hundred foot?
An odds too great for us to stand against!
But are they rich? And is their armor good?

[6] Valuable.
[7] Wait, stop.

SOLD. Their pluméd helms are wrought
with beaten gold,
Their swords enameled, and about their
necks
Hangs massy chains of gold down to the
waist,
In every part exceeding brave [1] and rich.
TAM. Then shall we fight courageously
with them,
Or look [2] you I should play the orator?
TECH. No; cowards and faint-hearted run-
aways　　　130
Look for orations when the foe is near.
Our swords shall play the orators for us.
USUM. Come! Let us meet them at the
mountain foot,
And with a sudden and an hot alarum
Drive all their horses headlong down the
hill.
TECH. Come, let us march!
TAM. Stay, Techelles! Ask a parley first.

The Soldiers enter.

Open the mails,[3] yet guard the treasure
sure;
Lay out our golden wedges to the
view
That their reflections may amaze the
Persians;　　　140
And look we friendly on them when they
come.
But, if they offer word or violence,
We'll fight five hundred men-at-arms to
one
Before we part with our possession.
And gainst the general we will lift our
swords,
And either lanch [4] his greedy, thirsting
throat,
Or take him prisoner, and his chain shall
serve
For manacles till he be ransomed home.
TECH. I hear them come. Shall we en-
counter them?
TAM. Keep all your standings and not stir
a foot;　　　150
Myself will bide the danger of the brunt.

Enter Theridamas with Others.

THER. Where is this Scythian Tambur-
laine?
TAM. Whom seek'st thou, Persian?—I am
Tamburlaine.

THER. Tamburlaine?—
[*Aside.*] A Scythian shepherd so em-
bellishéd
With nature's pride and richest furni-
ture!
His looks do menace heaven and dare the
gods;
His fiery eyes are fixed upon the earth,
As if he now devised some stratagem,
Or meant to pierce Avernus' darksome
vaults　　　160
To pull the triple-headed dog from hell.
TAM. [*Aside.*] Noble and mild this Persian
seems to be,
If outward habit judge [5] the inward man.
TECH. [*Aside.*] His deep affections [6] make
him passionate.
TAM. [*Aside.*] With what a majesty he
rears his looks!—
In thee, thou valiant man of Persia,
I see the folly of thy emperor.
Art thou but captain of a thousand horse,
That, by characters graven in thy brows
And by thy martial face and stout as-
pect,　　　170
Deserv'st to have the leading of an host?
Forsake thy king, and do but join with
me,
And we will triumph over all the world.
I hold the Fates bound fast in iron chains,
And with my hand turn Fortune's
wheel about;
And sooner shall the sun fall from his
sphere
Than Tamburlaine be slain or overcome.
Draw forth thy sword, thou mighty
man-at-arms,
Intending but to race [7] my charméd skin,
And Jove himself will stretch his hand
from heaven　　　180
To ward the blow and shield me safe
from harm.
See how he rains down heaps of gold in
showers,
As if he meant to give my soldiers pay!
And, as a sure and grounded argument
That I shall be the monarch of the East,
He sends this soldan's daughter, rich
and brave,
To be my queen and portly [8] emperess.
If thou wilt stay with me, renowméd
man,

[5] Indicate.　　　[7] Rase, scratch.
[6] Feelings.　　　[8] Stately.

[1] Fine.　[2] Expect, wish.　[3] Baggage.　[4] Lance, cut.

And lead thy thousand horse with my
conduct,
Besides thy share of this Egyptian
prize, 190
Those thousand horse shall sweat with
martial spoil
Of conquered kingdoms and of cities
sacked.
Both we will walk upon the lofty clifts; [1]
And Christian merchants [2] that with
Russian stems
Plow up huge furrows in the Caspian sea
Shall vail [3] to us as·lords of all the lake.
Both we will reign as consuls of the earth,
And mighty kings shall be our senators.
Jove sometime maskéd in a shepherd's
weed;
And by those steps that he hath scaled
the heavens 200
May we become immortal like the gods!
Join with me now in this my mean
estate
(I call it mean because, being yet ob-
scure,
The nations far removed admire [4] me
not),
And, when my name and honor shall be
spread
As far as Boreas claps his brazen wings,
Or fair Boötes sends his cheerful light,
Then shalt thou be competitor [5] with
me,
And sit with Tamburlaine in all his maj-
esty.
THER. Not Hermes, prolocutor to the
gods, 210
Could use persuasions more pathetical.[6]
TAM. Nor are Apollo's oracles more true
Than thou shalt find my vaunts sub-
stantial.
TECH. We are his friends, and, if the Per-
sian king
Should offer present dukedoms to our
state,
We think it loss to make exchange for
that
We are assured of by our friend's suc-
cess.
USUM. And kingdoms at the least we all
expect,
Besides the honor in assured conquests,

Where kings shall crouch unto our con-
quering swords, 220
And hosts of soldiers stand amazed at
us,
When with their fearful tongues they
shall confess
These are the men that all the world
admires.
THER. What strong enchantments tice [7]
my yielding soul!
Are these resolvéd noble Scythians?
But shall I prove a traitor to my king?
TAM. No, but the trusty friend of Tam-
burlaine.
THER. Won with thy words, and con-
quered with thy looks,
I yield myself, my men, and horse to
thee,
To be partaker of thy good or ill 230
As long as life maintains Theridamas.
TAM. Theridamas, my friend, take here
my hand,
Which is as much as if I swore by heaven
And called the gods to witness of my
vow!
Thus shall my heart be still combined
with thine
Until our bodies turn to elements,
And both our souls aspire [8] celestial
thrones.
Techelles and Casane, welcome him!
TECH. Welcome, renowméd Persian, to us
all!
USUM. Long may Theridamas remain
with us! 240
TAM. These are my friends, in whom I
more rejoice
Than doth the King of Persia in his
crown,
And by the love of Pylades and Orestes,
Whose statues [9] we adore in Scythia,
Thyself and them shall never part from
me
Before I crown you kings in Asia.
Make much of them, gentle Theridamas,
And they will never leave thee till the
death.
THER. Nor thee nor them, thrice noble
Tamburlaine,
Shall want my heart to be with glad-
ness pierced 250
To do you honor and security.

[1] Cliffs.
[2] Merchantmen.
[3] Lower their topsails in salute.
[4] Wonder at.
[5] Partner.
[6] Moving.
[7] Entice.
[8] Aspire to.
[9] Probably *statues*

TAM. A thousand thanks, worthy Theridamas.—

And now, fair madam and my noble
lords,

If you will willingly remain with me,

You shall have honors as your merits
be;

Or else you shall be forced with slavery.

AGYD. We yield unto thee, happy Tamburlaine.

TAM. For you then, madam, I am out
of doubt.

ZEN. I must be pleased perforce. Wretched
Zenocrate!   *Exeunt.*

ACTUS II. SCENA i.

[*Cosroe's camp.*]

*Cosroe, Menaphon, Ortygius, Ceneus, with
other Soldiers.*

COS. Thus far are we towards Theridamas

And valiant Tamburlaine, the man of
fame,

The man that in the forehead of his
fortune

Bears figures of renown and miracle.

But tell me, that hast seen him, Menaphon,

What stature wields [1] he, and what
personage?

MENA. Of stature tall, and straightly fash-
ionéd,

Like his desire, lift [2] upwards and divine;

So large of limbs, his joints so strongly
knit,

Such breadth of shoulders as might
mainly bear   10

Old Atlas' burthen. Twixt his manly
pitch, [3]

A pearl [4] more worth than all the world
is placed,

Wherein by curious sovereignty of art

Are fixed his piercing instruments of
sight,

Whose fiery circles bear encompasséd

A heaven of heavenly bodies in their
spheres,

That guides his steps and actions to
the throne,

Where honor sits invested royally.

Pale of complexion, wrought in him with
passion,

Thirsting with sovereignty, with love of
arms,   20

His lofty brows, in folds, do figure [5]
death

And, in their smoothness, amity and
life.

About them hangs a knot of amber hair,

Wrappéd in curls, as fierce Achilles' was,

On which the breath of heaven delights
to play,

Making it dance with wanton majesty.

His arms and fingers, long and sinewy, [6]

Betokening valor and excess of strength—

In every part proportioned like the
man—

Should make the world subdued to Tamburlaine.   30

COS. Well hast thou portrayed in thy
terms of life [7]

The face and personage of a wondrous
man.

Nature doth strive with fortune and
his stars

To make him famous in accomplished
worth;

And well his merits show him to be
made

His fortune's master and the king of
men,

That could persuade at such a sudden
pinch,

With reasons of his valor and his life,

A thousand sworn and overmatching
foes.

Then, when our powers in points of
swords are joined   40

And closed in compass of the killing
bullet,

Though strait the passage and the port [8]
be made

That leads to palace of my brother's life,

Proud is his fortune if we pierce it not.

And, when the princely Persian diadem

Shall overweigh his weary, witless head,

And fall like mellowed fruit with shakes
of death,

In fair Persia, noble Tamburlaine

Shall be my regent and remain as king.

---

[1] Possesses.   [2] Lifted.

[3] Height (falconry); here, shoulders.

[4] *I.e.*, the head.

[5] Foreshadow.

[6] Suggested by Dyce; original has *snowy*.

[7] Lively terms.   [8] Portal, gate.

ORTY. In happy hour we have set the crown   50
Upon your kingly head, that seeks our honor
In joining with the man ordained by heaven
To further every action to the best.
CEN. He that with shepherds and a little spoil
Durst, in disdain of wrong and tyranny,
Defend his freedom gainst a monarchy,
What will he do supported by a king,
Leading a troop of gentlemen and lords,
And stuffed with treasure for his highest thoughts!
COS. And such shall wait on worthy Tamburlaine.   60
Our army will be forty thousand strong,
When Tamburlaine and brave Theridamas
Have met us by the river Araris,
And all conjoined to meet the witless king
That now is marching near to Parthia.
And with unwilling soldiers faintly armed,
To seek revenge on me and Tamburlaine—
To whom, sweet Menaphon, direct me straight.
MEN. I will, my lord.   *Exeunt.*

ACTUS II. SCENA ii.

[*Mycetes' camp in the Caucasus.*]

Mycetes, Meander, with other Lords and Soldiers.

MYC. Come, my Meander, let us to this gear.[1]
I tell you true, my heart is swoln with wrath
On this same thievish villain, Tamburlaine,
And of [2] that false Cosroe, my traitorous brother.
Would it not grieve a king to be so abused
And have a thousand horsemen ta'en away,

And, which is worst, to have his diadem
Sought for by such scald [3] knaves as love him not?
I think it would. Well then, by heavens I swear,
Aurora shall not peep out of her doors, 10
But I will have Cosroe by the head,
And kill proud Tamburlaine with point of sword.
Tell you the rest, Meander; I have said.
MEAN. Then having passed Armenian deserts now,
And pitched [4] our tents under the Georgian hills,
Whose tops are covered with Tartarian thieves,
That lie in ambush, waiting for a prey,
What should we do but bid them battle straight,
And rid the world of those detested troops,
Lest, if we let them linger here awhile, 20
They gather strength by power of fresh supplies?
This country swarms with vile, outrageous men
That live by rapine and by lawless spoil,
Fit soldiers for the wicked Tamburlaine;
And he that could with gifts and promises
Inveigle him that led a thousand horse,
And make him false [5] his faith unto his king,
Will quickly win such as are like himself.
Therefore cheer up your minds; prepare to fight.
He that can take or slaughter Tamburlaine   30
Shall rule the province of Albania.
Who brings that traitor's head, Theridamas',
Shall have a government in Media,
Beside the spoil of him and all his train.
But, if Cosroe—as our spials [6] say,
And as we know—remains with Tamburlaine,
His highness' pleasure is that he should live,
And be reclaimed with princely lenity.

---

[1] Business.   [2] On.
[3] Scabby, base.   [5] Betray.
[4] Original has *pitch.*   [6] Spies.

[Enter a Spy.]

A Spy. An hundred horsemen of my company,
 Scouting abroad upon these champion [1]
 plains,   40
 Have viewed the army of the Scythians,
 Which make reports it far exceeds the
 king's.
Mean. Suppose they be in number infinite,
 Yet, being void of martial discipline,
 All running headlong after greedy spoils,
 And more regarding gain than victory,
 Like to the cruel brothers of the earth,
 Sprung of the teeth of dragons venomous,
 Their careless swords shall lanch their
 fellows' throats,
 And make us triumph in their overthrow.   50
Myc. Was there such brethren, sweet
 Meander, say,
 That sprung of teeth of dragons venomous?
Mean. So poets say, my lord.
Myc. And 'tis a pretty toy to be a poet.
 Well, well, Meander, thou art deeply
 read,
 And, having thee, I have a jewel sure.
 Go on, my lord, and give your charge,
 I say;
 Thy wit will make us conquerors today.
Mean. Then, noble soldiers, to entrap
 these thieves,
 That live confounded in disordered
 troops,   60
 If wealth or riches may prevail with
 them,
 We have our camels laden all with gold,
 Which you that be but common soldiers
 Shall fling in every corner of the field;
 And, while the baseborn Tartars take
 it up,
 You, fighting more for honor than for
 gold,
 Shall massacre those greedy-minded
 slaves,
 And, when their scattered army is subdued,
 And you march on their slaughtered
 carcasses,
 Share equally the gold that bought their
 lives,   70

[1] Champaign, level.

And live like gentlemen in Persia.
 Strike up the drum and march courageously!
 Fortune herself doth sit upon our crests.
Myc. He tells you true, my masters; so
 he does.
 Drums, why sound ye not, when Meand[er] speaks?   *Exeunt.*

Actus II. Scena iii.

[Tamburlaine's camp.]

Cosroe, Tamburlaine, Theridamas, Techelles,
 Usumcasane, Ortygius, with Others.

Cos. Now, worthy Tamburlaine, have I
 reposed
 In thy approvéd fortunes all my hope.
 What think'st thou, man, shall come of
 our attempts?
 For, even as from assuréd oracle,
 I take thy doom [2] for satisfaction.
Tam. And so mistake you not a whit, my
 lord;
 For fates and oracles [of] heaven have
 sworn
 To royalize the deeds of Tamburlaine,
 And make them blessed that share in
 his attempts.
 And doubt you not but, if you favor
 me,   10
 And let my fortunes and my valor sway
 To some direction in your martial deeds,
 The world will strive with hosts of men-at-arms,
 To swarm unto the ensign I support.
 The host of Xerxes, which by fame is
 said
 To drink the mighty Parthian Araris,
 Was but a handful to that we will have.
 Our quivering lances, shaking in the
 air,
 And bullets, like Jove's dreadful thunderbolts,
 Enrolled in flames and fiery smoldering
 mists,   20
 Shall threat the gods more than Cyclopian wars;
 And, with our sun-bright armor as we
 march,
 We'll chase the stars from heaven and
 dim their eyes
 That stand and muse at our admiréd
 arms.

[2] Opinion.

THER. You see, my lord, what working
   words he hath;
   But, when you see his actions stop his
      speech,
   Your speech will stay [1] or so extol his
      worth
   As I shall be commended and excused
   For turning my poor charge to his di-
      rection.
   And these his two renowméd friends,
      my lord,   30
   Would make one thrust and strive to be
      retained
   In such a great degree of amity.
TECH. With duty and with amity we
      yield
   Our utmost service to the fair Cosroe.
COS. Which I esteem as portion of my
      crown.
   Usumcasane and Techelles both,
   When she [2] that rules in Rhamnis'
      golden gates,
   And makes a passage for all prosperous
      arms,
   Shall make me solely Emperor of Asia,
   Then shall your meeds and valors be
      advanced   40
   To rooms of honor and nobility.
TAM. Then haste, Cosroe, to be king
      alone,
   That I with these, my friends, and all
      my men
   May triumph in our long-expected
      fate.
   The king, your brother, is now hard
      at hand;
   Meet with the fool, and rid your royal
      shoulders
   Of such a burthen as outweighs the
      sands
   And all the craggy rocks of Caspia.

[Enter a Messenger.]

MESS. My lord, we have discovered the
      enemy
   Ready to charge you with a mighty
      army.   50
COS. Come, Tamburlaine! Now whet thy
      wingéd sword,
   And lift thy lofty arm into the clouds

That it may reach the King of Persia's
      crown,
   And set it safe on my victorious head.
TAM. See where it is, the keenest cuttle-
      ax [3]
   That e'er made passage thorough Per-
      sian arms.
   These are the wings shall make it fly
      as swift
   As doth the lightning or the breath of
      heaven,
   And kill as sure as it swiftly flies.   59
COS. Thy words assure me of kind success.
   Go, valiant soldier, go before and charge
   The fainting army of that foolish king.
TAM. Usumcasane and Techelles, come!
   We are enough to scare the enemy,
   And more than needs to make an em-
      peror.   [Exeunt.]

[ACTUS II. SCENA iv.

Part of the battlefield.]

*To the battle, and Mycetes comes out alone
   with his crown in his hand, offering
                              to hide it.*

MYC. Accursed be he that first invented
      war.
   They knew not, ah, they knew not,
      simple men,
   How those [4] were hit by pelting cannon
      shot
   Stand staggering like a quivering aspen
      leaf
   Fearing the force of Boreas' boist'rous
      blasts.
   In what a lamentable case were I
   If nature had not given me wisdom's
      lore!
   For kings are clouts [5] that every man
      shoots at,
   Our crown the pin [6] that thousands seek
      to cleave.
   Therefore in policy I think it good   10
   To hide it close—a goodly stratagem,
   And far from any man that is a fool.
   So shall I not be known; or, if I be,
   They cannot take away my crown from
      me.
   Here will I hide it in this simple hole.

---

[1] *I.e.*, you will be speechless.
[2] "Nemesis, who had a temple at Rhamnus"
(Bullen).
[3] Curtle-ax, cutlass.
[4] Those who.
[5] Center of an archer's target.
[6] Peg fastening the clout.

Enter Tamburlaine.

TAM. What, fearful coward, straggling
from the camp
  When kings themselves are present in
the field?

MYC. Thou liest!

TAM.   Base villain, dar'st thou
give the lie?

MYC. Away; I am the king! Go; touch me
not!
  Thou break'st the law of arms, unless
thou kneel   20
  And cry me, "Mercy, noble king!"

TAM. Are you the witty King of Persia?

MYC. Ay, marry am I. Have you any
suit to me?

TAM. I would entreat you to speak but
three wise words.

MYC. So I can when I see my time.

TAM. Is this your crown?

MYC. Ay, didst thou ever see a fairer?

TAM. You will not sell it, will ye?   30

MYC. Such another word and I will
have thee executed. Come, give it me!

TAM. No; I took it prisoner.

MYC. You lie; I gave it you.

TAM. Then 'tis mine.

MYC. No; I mean I let you keep it.

TAM. Well, I mean you shall have it again.
  Here, take it for awhile. I lend it thee
  Till I may see thee hemmed with arméd
men.
  Then shalt thou see me pull it from thy
head.   40
  Thou art no match for mighty Tambur-
laine.   [*Exit.*]

MYC. O gods! Is this Tamburlaine the
thief?
  I marvel much he stole it not away.

Sound trumpets to the battle, and he runs in.

[ACTUS II. SCENA v.

Tamburlaine's camp.]

*Cosroe, Tamburlaine, Theridamas, Mena-
phon, Meander, Ortygius, Techelles,
Usumcasane, with Others.*

TAM. Hold thee, Cosroe! Wear two imperial crowns!
  Think thee invested now as royally,
  Even by the mighty hand of Tamburlaine,

As if as many kings as could encompass
thee
  With greatest pomp had crowned thee
emperor.

COS. So do I, thrice renowméd man-at-
arms,
  And none shall keep the crown but Tam-
burlaine.
  Thee do I make my regent of Persia,
  And general lieftenant [1] of my armies.
  Meander, you that were our brother's
guide   10
  And chiefest counselor in all his acts,
  Since he is yielded to the stroke of war,
  On your submission we with thanks
excuse,
  And give you equal place in our affairs.

MEAN. Most happy emperor, in humblest
terms
  I vow my service to your majesty,
  With utmost virtue of my faith and duty

COS. Thanks, good Meander. Then, Cos-
roe, reign
  And govern Persia in her former pomp!
  Now send ambassage to thy neighbor
kings,   20
  And let them know the Persian king is
changed
  From one that knew not what a king
should do,
  To one that can command what longs [2]
thereto.
  And now we will to fair Persepolis,
  With twenty thousand expert soldiers.
  The lords and captains of my brother's
camp
  With little slaughter take Meander's
course,
  And gladly yield them to my gracious
rule.
  Ortygius and Menaphon, my trusty
friends,
  Now will I gratify your former good,   30
  And grace your calling with a greater
sway.

ORTY. And, as we ever aimed [3] at your
behoof, [4]
  And sought your state all honor it de-
served,
  So will we with our powers and our lives
  Endeavor to preserve and prosper it.

---

[1] Lieutenant.   [2] Belongs.
[3] From 1605 edn. Original reads *and.*
[4] Advantage.

Cos. I will not thank thee, sweet Ortygius;
Better replies shall prove my purposes.
And now, Lord Tamburlaine, my broth-
er's camp
I leave to thee and to Theridamas,
To follow me to fair Persepolis.   40
Then will we march to all those Indian
mines
My witless brother to the Christians lost,
And ransom [1] them with fame and
usury. [2]
And, till thou overtake me, Tamburlaine,
Staying to order all the scattered troops,
Farewell, lord regent and his happy
friends!
I long to sit upon my brother's throne.
MENA. Your majesty shall shortly have
your wish,
And ride in triumph through Persepolis.
Exeunt. Manent Tamb[urlaine], Tech[elles],
Ther[idamas], Usum[casane].
TAM. "And ride in triumph through Per-
sepolis"!   50
Is it not brave to be a king, Techelles?
Usumcasane and Theridamas,
Is it not passing brave to be a king,
"And ride in triumph through Persep-
olis"?
TECH. O, my lord, 'tis sweet and full of
pomp.
USUM. To be a king is half to be a god.
THER. A god is not so glorious as a king.
I think the pleasure they enjoy in heaven
Cannot compare with kingly joys in
earth.
To wear a crown enchased with pearl and
gold,   60
Whose virtues carry with it life and
death;
To ask and have, command and be
obeyed;
When looks breed love, with looks to gain
the prize—
Such power attractive shines in princes'
eyes!
TAM. Why, say, Theridamas, wilt thou be
a king?
THER. Nay, though I praise it, I can live
without it.
TAM. What says my other friends? Will
you be kings?
TECH. Ay, if I could, with all my heart,
my lord.

TAM. Why, that's well said, Techelles.
So would I,
And so would you, my masters, would
you not?   70
USUM. What then, my lord?
TAM. Why then, Casane, shall we wish for
aught
The world affords in greatest novelty,
And rest attemptless, faint, and desti-
tute?
Methinks we should not. I am strongly
moved
That, if I should desire the Persian
crown,
I could attain it with a wondrous ease.
And would not all our soldiers soon con-
sent,
If we should aim at such a dignity?
THER. I know they would with our per-
suasions.   80
TAM. Why then, Theridamas, I'll first
assay
To get the Persian kingdom to myself;
Then thou for Parthia; they for Scythia
and Media;
And, if I prosper, all shall be as sure
As if the Turk, the pope, Afric, and
Greece,
Came creeping to us with their crowns
apace.
TECH. Then shall we send to this triumph-
ing king,
And bid him battle for his novel crown?
USUM. Nay, quickly then, before his room
be hot.
TAM. 'Twill prove a pretty jest, in faith,
my friends.   90
THER. A jest to charge on twenty thou-
sand men?
I judge the purchase [3] more important
far.
TAM. Judge by thyself, Theridamas, not
me,
For presently Techelles here shall haste
To bid him battle ere he pass too far,
And lose more labor than the gain will
quite. [4]
Then shalt thou see the Scythian Tam-
burlaine
Make but a jest to win the Persian
crown.
Techelles, take a thousand horse with
thee,

[1] Deliver.   [2] Profit.

[3] Undertaking.   [4] Requite.

And bid him turn him[1] back to war with
us,   100
That only made him king to make us
    sport.
We will not steal upon him cowardly,
But give him warning and more warriors.
Haste thee, Techelles; we will follow
    thee.—
What saith Theridamas?
THER.   Go on for me.   *Exeunt.*

ACTUS II. SCENA vi.

[*Cosroe's camp.*]

*Cosroe, Meander, Ortygius, Menaphon, with
                        other Soldiers.*

COS. What means this devilish shepherd to
    aspire
With such a giantly presumption
To cast up hills against the face of
    heaven,
And dare the force of angry Jupiter?
But, as he thrust them underneath the
    hills,
And pressed out fire from their burning
    jaws,
So will I send this monstrous slave to hell,
Where flames shall ever feed upon his
    soul.
MEAN. Some powers divine, or else in-
    fernal, mixed
Their angry seeds at his conception,   10
For he was never sprung of human race,
Since with the spirit of his fearful pride
He dare so doubtlessly[2] resolve of[3] rule,
And by profession[4] be ambitious.
ORTY. What god, or fiend, or spirit of the
    earth,
Or monster turnéd to a manly shape,
Or of what mold or mettle he be made,
What star or state soever govern him,
Let us put on our meet, encount'ring[5]
    minds
And, in detesting such a devilish thief,   20
In love of honor and defense of right,
Be armed against the hate of such a foe,
Whether from earth, or hell, or heaven he
    grow.
COS. Nobly resolved, my good Ortygius!
And, since we all have sucked one whole-
    some air,

And with the same proportion of ele-
    ments
Resolve, I hope we are resembled,[6]
Vowing our loves to equal death and life.
Let's cheer our soldiers to encounter him,
That grievous image of ingratitude,   30
That fiery thirster after sovereignty,
And burn him in the fury of that flame
That none can quench[7] but blood and
    empery.
Resolve, my lords and loving soldiers,
    now
To save your king and country from
    decay.
Then strike up, drum; and all the stars
    that make
The loathsome circle of my dated life,
Direct my weapon to his barbarous heart,
That thus opposeth him against the gods,
And scorns the powers that govern
    Persia!   [*Exeunt.*]   40

[ACTUS II. SCENA vii.

A plain.]

*Enter to the battle, and after the battle enter
    Cosroe, wounded, Theridamas, Tam-
    burlaine, Techelles, Usumcasane, with
                                    Others.*

COS. Barbarous and bloody Tamburlaine,
Thus to deprive me of my crown and life!
Treacherous and false Theridamas,
Even at the morning of my happy state,
Scarce being seated in my royal throne,
To work my downfall and untimely end!
An uncouth[8] pain torments my grievéd
    soul,
And death arrests the organ of my voice,
Who, ent'ring at the breach thy sword
    hath made,
Sacks every vein and artier[9] of my
    heart.   10
Bloody and insatiate Tamburlaine!
TAM. The thirst of reign and sweetness of a
    crown
That caused the eldest son of heavenly
    Ops
To thrust his doting father from his
    chair,
And place himself in the emperial[10]
    heaven,

---

[1] Original reads *his.*   [4] Open avowal.
[2] Fearlessly.   [5] Warlike.
[3] Upon.

[6] Alike.   [8] Strange.
[7] Quench.   [9] Artery.
[10] Imperial or empyreal?

Moved me to manage arms against thy
state.
What better president [1] than mighty
Jove?
Nature, that framed us of four elements,
Warring within our breasts for regiment,
Doth teach us all to have aspiring
minds. 20
Our souls, whose faculties can compre-
hend
The wondrous architecture of the world,
And measure every wand'ring planet's
course,
Still climbing after knowledge infinite,
And always moving as the restless
spheres,
Wills us to wear ourselves and never rest
Until we reach the ripest fruit of all,
That perfect bliss and sole felicity,
The sweet fruition of an earthly crown.
THER. And that made me to join with
Tamburlaine, 30
For he is gross and like the massy earth,
That moves not upwards, nor by princely
deeds
Doth mean to soar above the highest sort.
TECH. And that made us the friends of
Tamburlaine,
To lift our swords against the Persian
king.
USUM. For, as when Jove did thrust old
Saturn down,
Neptune and Dis gained each of them a
crown,
So do we hope to reign in Asia,
If Tamburlaine be placed in Persia.
COS. The strangest men that ever nature
made! 40
I know not how to take their tyrannies.
My bloodless body waxeth chill and cold,
And with my blood my life slides through
my wound.
My soul begins to take her flight to hell,
And summons all my senses to depart.
The heat and moisture, which did feed
each other,
For want of nourishment to feed them
both,
Is dry and cold; and now doth ghastly
Death,
With greedy talents [2] gripe my bleeding
heart,
And like a harpy tires [3] on my life. 50

[1] Precedent. [2] Talons. [3] Preys.

Theridamas and Tamburlaine, I die!
And fearful vengeance light upon you
both!
[Dies.] He [4] takes the crown and puts it on.
TAM. Not all the curses which the Furies
breathe
Shall make me leave so rich a prize as
this.
Theridamas, Techelles, and the rest,
Who think you now is King of Persia?
ALL. Tamburlaine! Tamburlaine
TAM. Though Mars himself, the angry god
of arms,
And all the earthly potentates conspire
To dispossess me of this diadem, 60
Yet will I wear it in despite of them,
As great commander of this eastern
world,
If you but say that Tamburlaine shall
reign.
ALL. Long live Tamburlaine and reign in
Asia!
TAM. So now it is more surer on my head
Than if the gods had held a parliament,
And all pronounced me King of Persia.
[Exeunt.]

FINIS ACTUS SECUNDI.

ACTUS III. SCENA i.

[Before Constantinople.]

Bajazeth, the Kings of Fez, Morocco, and
Argier, with Others, in great pomp.

BAJ. Great kings of Barbary and my
portly bassoes,
We hear the Tartars and the eastern
thieves,
Under the conduct of one Tamburlaine,
Presume a bickering [5] with your emperor,
And thinks to rouse us from our dreadful
siege
Of the famous Grecian Constantinople.
You know our army is invincible;
As many circumciséd Turks we have,
And warlike bands of Christians renied, [6]
As hath the ocean or the Terrene sea [7] [10
Small drops of water when the moon be-
gins
To join in one her semicircled horns.
Yet would we not be braved with foreign
power,

[4] I.e., Tamburlaine. [6] Apostates.
[5] Battle. [7] The Mediterranean.

Nor raise our siege before the Grecians
  yield,
Or breathless lie before the city walls.
Fez. Renowméd emperor and mighty
  general,
What if you sent the bassoes of your
  guard
To charge him to remain in Asia,
Or else to threaten death and deadly arms
As from the mouth of mighty Baja-
  zeth?   20
Baj. Hie thee, my basso, fast to Persia.
Tell him thy lord, the Turkish emperor,
Dread lord of Afric, Europe, and Asia,
Great king and conqueror of Grecia,
The ocean, Terrene, and the coal-black
  sea,[1]
The high and highest monarch of the
  world,
Wills and commands—for say not I
  entreat—
Not once to set his foot in Africa,
Or spread his colors in Grecia,
Lest he incur the fury of my wrath.   30
Tell him I am content to take a truce,
Because I hear he bears a valiant mind.
But if, presuming on his silly power,
He be so mad to manage arms with me,
Then stay thou with him. Say I bid thee
  so.
And if, before the sun have measured
  heaven
With triple circuit, thou regreet us not,
We mean to take his morning's next arise
For messenger he will not be reclaimed,
And mean to fetch thee in despite of
  him.   40
Basso. Most great and puissant monarch
  of the earth,
Your basso will accomplish your behest,
And show your pleasure to the Persian,
As fits the legate of the stately Turk.
                          Exit Bass[o].
Arg. They say he is the King of Persia;
But, if he dare attempt to stir your siege,
'Twere requisite he should be ten times
  more,
For all flesh quakes at your magnificence.
Baj. True, Argier, and tremble at my
  looks.
Mor. The spring is hindered by your
  smothering host,   50
For neither rain can fall upon the earth,

Nor sun reflex[2] his virtuous beams
  thereon,
The ground is mantled with such multi-
  tudes.
Baj. All this is true as holy Mahomet;
And all the trees are blasted with our
  breaths.
Fez. What thinks your greatness best to
  be achieved
In pursuit of the city's overthrow?
Baj. I will the captive pioners[3] of Argier
Cut off the water that by leaden pipes
Runs to the city from the mountain
  Carnon.   60
Two thousand horse shall forage up and
  down,
That no relief or succor come by land;
And all the sea my galleys countermand.[4]
Then shall our footmen lie within the
  trench,
And with their cannons, mouthed like
  Orcus' gulf,
Batter the walls, and we will enter in.
And thus the Grecians shall be con-
  queréd.   *Exeunt.*

Actus III. Scena ii.

[*Tamburlaine's camp.*]

Agydas, Zenocrate, Anippe, with Others.

[Agyd.] Madam Zenocrate, may I presume
  To know the cause of these unquiet fits,
  That work such trouble to your wonted
    rest?
  'Tis more than pity such a heavenly face
  Should by heart's sorrow wax so wan and
    pale,
  When your offensive rape[5] by Tambur-
    laine—
  Which of your whole displeasures should
    be most—
  Hath seemed to be digested long ago.
Zen. Although it be digested long ago,
  As his exceeding favors have deserved, 10
  And might content the Queen of Heaven,
    as well
  As it hath changed my first conceived
    disdain,
  Yet, since, a farther passion feeds my
    thoughts
  With ceaseless and disconsolate conceits,

[1] The Black Sea.
[2] Throw.
[3] Miners.
[4] Control.
[5] Capture.

Which dyes my looks so lifeless as they
   are,
And might, if my extremes had full
   events,[1]
Make me the ghastly counterfeit of
   death.
AGYD. Eternal heaven sooner be dissolved,
And all that pierceth Phœbe's silver eye,
Before such hap fall to Zenocrate!   20
ZEN. Ah, life and soul, still hover in his
   breast
And leave my body senseless as the earth,
Or else unite you to his life and soul,
That I may live and die with Tambur-
   laine!

*Enter [, unseen,] Tamburlaine with Techelles
   and Others.*
AGYD. With Tamburlaine? Ah, fair Zeno-
   crate,
Let not a man so vile and barbarous,
That holds you from your father in
   despite,
And keeps you from the honors of a
   queen,
Being supposed his worthless concubine,
Be honored with your love but for neces-
   sity.   30
So, now [2] the mighty soldan hears of you,
Your highness needs not doubt but in
   short time
He will with Tamburlaine's destruction
Redeem you from this deadly servitude.
ZEN. Leave to wound me with these words,
And speak of Tamburlaine as he deserves.
The entertainment we have had of him
Is far from villainy [3] or servitude,
And might in noble minds be counted
   princely.
AGYD. How can you fancy one that looks
   so fierce,   40
Only disposed to martial stratagems,
Who, when he shall embrace you in his
   arms,
Will tell how many thousand men he
   slew,
And, when you look for amorous dis-
   course,
Will rattle forth his facts [4] of war and
   blood,
Too harsh a subject for your dainty
   ears?

ZEN. As looks the Sun through Nilus' flow-
   ing stream,
Or when the Morning holds him in her
   arms,
So looks my lordly love, fair Tambur-
   laine;
His talk much sweeter than the Muses'
   song   50
They sung for honor gainst Pierides,
Or when Minerva did with Neptune
   strive,
And higher would I rear my estimate
Than Juno, sister to the highest god,
If I were matched with mighty Tambur-
   laine.
AGYD. Yet be not so inconstant in your
   love,
But let the young Arabian live in hope
After your rescue to enjoy his choice.
You see, though first the King of Persia,
Being a shepherd, seemed to love you
   much,   60
Now in his majesty he leaves those
   looks,
Those words of favor, and those com-
   fortings,
And gives no more than common cour-
   tesies.
ZEN. Thence rise the tears that so distain [5]
   my cheeks,
Fearing[6] his love through my unworthi-
   ness.—
*Tamburlaine goes to her and takes her away
   lovingly by the hand, looking wrathfully
   on Agydas, and says nothing. [Exeunt
   all but Agydas.]*
AGYD. Betrayed by fortune and suspicious
   love,
Threatened with frowning wrath and
   jealousy,
Surprised with fear of hideous revenge,
I stand aghast; but most astoniéd[7]   69
To see his choler shut in secret thoughts,
And wrapped in silence of his angry soul,
Upon his brows was portrayed ugly
   death,
And in his eyes the fury of his heart,
That shine as comets, menacing revenge,
And casts a pale complexion on his
   cheeks.
As, when the seaman sees the Hyades
Gather an army of Cimmerian clouds
(Auster and Aquilon with wingéd steeds,

---

[1] If my extremities were carried to their out-
come.   [2] Now that.   [3] Serfdom.   [4] Deeds.
   [5] Stain.   [6] Fearing to lose.   [7] Astonished.

All sweating, tilt about the watery heav-
ens,
With shivering spears enforcing thunder-
claps,   80
And from their shields strike flames of
lightening),
All fearful folds his sails and sounds the
main,[1]
Lifting his prayers to the heavens for aid
Against the terror of the winds and
waves,
So fares Agydas for the late-felt frowns
That sent a tempest to my daunted
thoughts,
And makes my soul divine her over-
throw.

*Enter [Usumcasane and] Techelles with a
naked dagger.*

TECH. See you, Agydas, how the king
salutes you.
He bids you prophesy what it imports.
                                   Exit.[2]
AGYD. I prophesied before, and now I
prove   90
The killing frowns of jealousy and love.
He needed not with words confirm my
fear,
For words are vain where working tools
present
The naked action of my threatened end.
It says, Agydas, thou shalt surely die,
And of extremities elect the least;
More honor and less pain it may procure
To die by this resolvéd hand of thine
Than stay the torments he and heaven
have sworn.
Then haste, Agydas, and prevent the
plagues   100
Which thy prolongéd fates may draw
on thee.
Go, wander free from fear of tyrant's
rage,
Removéd from the torments and the hell
Wherewith he may excruciate thy soul;
And let Agydas by Agydas die,
And with this stab slumber eternally.
                          [Stabs himself.][3]
TECH. Usumcasane, see how right the man
Hath hit the meaning of my lord the
king.

[1] Takes sea soundings.
[2] He and Usumcasane stand aside.
[3] Supplied from 1605 edn.

USUM. Faith, and, Techelles, it was manly
done.
And, since he was so wise and honor-
able,   110
Let us afford him now the bearing
hence,
And crave his triple-worthy burial.
TECH. Agreed, Casane; we will honor him.
            [Exeunt, bearing out the body.]

ACTUS III. SCENA iii.

[The same.]

*Tamburlaine, Techelles, Usumcasane, Theri-
damas, Basso, Zenocrate, [Anippe,] with
Others.*

TAM. Basso, by this thy lord and master
knows
I mean to meet him in Bithynia.
See how he comes! Tush, Turks are full
of brags,
And menace more than they can well
perform.
He meet me in the field, and fetch thee
hence?
Alas, poor Turk! His fortune is too weak
T' encounter with the strength of Tam-
burlaine.
View well my camp, and speak indiffer-
ently.[4]
Do not my captains and my soldiers
look
As if they meant to conquer Africa?[5]   10
BASSO. Your men are valiant, but their
number few,
And cannot terrify his mighty host.
My lord, the great commander of the
world,
Besides fifteen contributory kings,
Hath now in arms ten thousand Janis-
saries,
Mounted on lusty Mauritanian steeds,
Brought to the war by men of Tripoli;
Two hundred thousand footmen that
have served
In two set battles fought in Grecia;
And for the expedition of this war,   20
If he think good, can from his garri-
sons
Withdraw as many more to follow him.
TECH. The more he brings, the greater is
the spoil.

[4] Impartially.
[5] Bithynia was actually in Asia Minor.

For, when they perish by our warlike
hands,
We mean to seat our footmen on their
steeds,
And rifle all those stately Janisars.

TAM. But will those kings accompany
your lord?

BASSO. Such as his highness please; but
some must stay
To rule the provinces he late subdued.

TAM. [To his Captains.] Then fight courageously; their crowns are yours!   30
This hand shall set them on your conquering heads,
That made me Emperor of Asia.

USUM. Let him bring millions infinite
of men,
Unpeopling Western Africa and Greece,
Yet we assure us of the victory.

THER. Even he that in a trice vanquished
two kings
More mighty than the Turkish emperor,
Shall rouse him out of Europe and pur-
sue
His scattered army till they yield or die.

TAM. Well said, Theridamas.   Speak in
that mood;   40
For will and shall best fitteth Tambur-
laine,
Whose smiling stars gives him assuréd
hope
Of martial triumph ere he meet his foes.
I that am termed the scourge and wrath
of God,
The only fear and terror of the world,
Will first subdue the Turk, and then
enlarge
Those Christian captives, which you
keep as slaves,
Burdening their bodies with your heavy
chains,
And feeding them with thin and slender
fare,
That naked row about the Terrene sea, 50
And, when they chance to breathe and
rest a space,
Are punished with bastones [1] so griev-
ously
That they lie panting on the galley's
side,
And strive for life at every stroke they
give.
These are the cruel pirates of Argier,

[1] Cudgels.   [2] Runaways, apostates.

That damnéd train, the scum of Africa,
Inhabited with straggling runagates, [2]
That make quick havoc of the Christian
blood.
But, as I live, that town shall curse the
time
That Tamburlaine set foot in Africa.   60

*Enter Bajazeth with his Bassoes and con-
tributory Kings [; Zabina and Ebea].*

BAJ. Bassoes and Janissaries of my guard,
Attend upon the person of your lord,
The greatest potentate of Africa.

TAM. Techelles and the rest, prepare your
swords;
I mean t' encounter with that Bajazeth.

BAJ. Kings of Fez, Moroccus, and Argier,
He calls me Bajazeth, whom you call
lord!
Note the presumption of this Scythian
slave!
I tell thee, villain, those that lead my
horse
Have to their names titles of dignity,   70
And dar'st thou bluntly call me Baja-
zeth?

TAM. And know thou, Turk, that those
which lead my horse
Shall lead thee captive thorough Africa.
And dar'st thou bluntly call me Tamburlaine?

BAJ. By Mahomet my kinsman's sep-
ulcher
And by the holy Alcoran, [3] I swear
He shall be made a chaste and lustless
eunuch,
And in my sarell [4] tend my concubines;
And all his captains that thus stoutly
stand
Shall draw the chariot of my emperess, 80
Whom I have brought to see their over-
throw.

TAM. By this my sword that conquered
Persia,
Thy fall shall make me famous through
the world.
I will not tell thee how I'll handle thee,
But every common soldier of my camp
Shall smile to see thy miserable state.

FEZ. What means the mighty Turkish
emperor,
To talk with one so base as Tamburlaine?

[3] The Koran.   [4] Seraglio.

Mor. Ye Moors and valiant men of Bar-
bary,
How can ye suffer these indignities?   90
Arg. Leave words, and let them feel your
lances' points
Which glided through the bowels of
the Greeks.
Baj. Well said, my stout contributory
kings!
Your threefold army and my hugy host
Shall swallow up these baseborn Persians.
Tech. Puissant, renowmed, and mighty
Tamburlaine,
Why stay we thus prolonging all their
lives?
Ther. I long to see those crowns won by
our swords,
That we may reign as kings of Africa.
Usum. What coward would not fight for
such a prize?   100
Tam. Fight all courageously, and be you
kings;
I speak it, and my words are oracles.
Baj. Zabina, mother of three braver boys
Than Hercules, that in his infancy
Did pash [1] the jaws of serpents ven-
omous;
Whose hands are made to gripe a war-
like lance,
Their shoulders broad for complete
armor fit,
Their limbs more large and of a bigger
size
Than all the brats ysprung [2] from Ty-
phon's loins;
Who, when they come unto their fa-
ther's age,   110
Will batter turrets with their manly
fists—
Sit here upon this royal chair of state,
And on thy head wear my imperial
crown
Until I bring this sturdy Tamburlaine
And all his captains bound in captive
chains.
Zab. Such good success happen to Ba-
jazeth!
Tam. Zenocrate, the loveliest maid alive,
Fairer than rocks of pearl and precious
stone,
The only paragon [3] of Tamburlaine,
Whose eyes are brighter than the lamps
of heaven   120

[1] Dash to pieces.   [2] Old past participle.   [3] Mate.

And speech more pleasant than sweet
harmony;
That with thy looks canst clear the
darkened sky,
And calm the rage of thund'ring Jupi-
ter,
Sit down by her, adornéd with my
crown,
As if thou wert the empress of the world.
Stir not, Zenocrate, until thou see
Me march victoriously with all my men,
Triumphing over him and these his
kings,
Which I will bring as vassals to thy feet;
Till then take thou my crown, vaunt
of my worth,   130
And manage words with her, as we will
arms.
Zen. And may my love, the King of
Persia,
Return with victory and free from
wound!
Baj. Now shalt thou feel the force of
Turkish arms,
Which lately made all Europe quake
for fear.
I have of Turks, Arabians, Moors, and
Jews
Enough to cover all Bithynia.
Let thousands die; their slaughtered
carcasses
Shall serve for walls and bulwarks to
the rest;
And, as the heads of Hydra, so my
power,   140
Subdued, shall stand as mighty as be-
fore.
If they should yield their necks unto
the sword,
Thy soldiers' arms could not endure to
strike
So many blows as I have heads for
thee.
Thou knowest not, foolish-hardy Tam-
burlaine,
What 'tis to meet me in the open field,
That leave no ground for thee to march
upon.
Tam. Our conquering swords shall mar-
shal us the way
We used to march upon the slaughtered
foe,
Trampling their bowels with our horses'
hoofs—   156

Brave horses bred on the white Tartarian hills.
My camp is like to Julius Cæsar's host,
That never fought but had the victory;
Nor in Pharsalia was there such hot war
As these my followers willingly would have.
Legions of spirits fleeting [1] in the air
Direct our bullets and our weapons' points,
And make our strokes to wound the senseless lure, [2]
And, when she sees our bloody colors spread,   159
Then Victory begins to take her flight,
Resting herself upon my milk-white tent.—
But come, my lords, to weapons let us fall;
The field is ours, the Turk, his wife, and all.   *Exit with his Followers.*
BAJ. Come, kings and bassoes, let us glut our swords,
That thirst to drink the feeble Persians' blood.   *Exit with his Followers.*
ZAB. Base concubine, must thou be placed by me,
That am the empress of the mighty Turk?
ZEN. Disdainful Turkess and unreverend boss, [3]
Call'st thou me concubine, that am betrothed
Unto the great and mighty Tamburlaine?   170
ZAB. To Tamburlaine, the great Tartarian thief!
ZEN. Thou wilt repent these lavish words of thine,
When thy great basso-master and thyself
Must plead for mercy at his kingly feet,
And sue to me to be your advocates. [4]
ZAB. And sue to thee? I tell thee, shameless girl,
Thou shalt be laundress to my waiting maid!—
How lik'st thou her, Ebea? Will she serve?

EBEA. Madam, she thinks perhaps she is too fine,
But I shall turn her into other weeds,   180
And make her dainty fingers fall to work.
ZEN. Hear'st thou, Anippe, how thy drudge doth talk?
And how my slave, her mistress, menaceth?
Both for their sauciness shall be employed
To dress the common soldiers' meat and drink,
For we will scorn they should come near ourselves.
ANIP. Yet sometimes let your highness send for them
To do the work my chambermaid disdains.
          They sound the battle within and stay. [5]
ZEN. Ye gods and powers that govern Persia,
And made my lordly love her worthy king,   190
Now strengthen him against the Turkish Bajazeth,
And let his foes, like flocks of fearful roes
Pursued by hunters, fly his angry looks,
That I may see him issue conqueror!
ZAB. Now, Mahomet, solicit God himself,
And make him rain down murthering shot from heaven
To dash the Scythians' brains, and strike them dead,
That dare to manage arms with him
That offered jewels to thy sacred shrine,
When first he warred against the Christians!   200
          To the battle again.
ZEN. By this the Turks lie welt'ring in their blood,
And Tamburlaine is Lord of Africa.
ZAB. Thou art deceived. I heard the trumpets sound
As when my emperor overthrew the Greeks,
And led them captive into Africa.
Straight will I use thee as thy pride deserves.
Prepare thyself to live and die my slave!
ZEN. If Mahomet should come from heaven and swear

---

[1] Floating.
[2] Dyce suggests: "And make *your* strokes to wound the senseless *air*."
[3] Fat woman.
[4] Wagner suggests *advocatess*.
[5] Cease, pause. This battle actually took place in 1402 at Angora (Ankara).

My royal lord is slain or conqueréd,
Yet should he not persuade me other-
   wise   210
But that he lives and will be conqueror.
Bajazeth flies and he [1] *pursues him. The*
   battle short, and they enter. Bajazeth is
                          overcome.
TAM. Now, king of bassoes, who is con-
   queror?
BAJ. Thou, by the fortune of this damnéd
   soil.
TAM. Where are your stout contributory
   kings?

Enter Techelles, Theridamas, Usumcasane.

TECH. We have their crowns; their bodies
   strow the field.
TAM. Each man a crown? Why, kingly
   fought, i' faith!
Deliver them into my treasury.
ZEN. Now let me offer to my gracious
   lord
His royal crown again, so highly won.
TAM. Nay, take the Turkish crown from
   her, Zenocrate,   220
And crown me Emperor of Africa.
ZAB. No, Tamburlaine; though now thou
   gat the best,
Thou shalt not yet be lord of Africa.
THER. Give her the crown, Turkess; you
   were best.
He takes it from her and gives it Zenocrate.
ZAB. Injurious villains, thieves, runa-
   gates,
How dare you thus abuse my majesty?
THER. Here, madam, you are empress;
   she is none.
TAM. Not now, Theridamas; her time is
   past.
The pillars that have bolstered up those
   terms [2]
Are fallen in clusters at my conquering
   feet.   230
ZAB. Though he be prisoner, he may be
   ransomed.
TAM. Not all the world shall ransom Ba-
   jazeth.
BAJ. Ah, fair Zabina, we have lost the
   field!
And never had the Turkish emperor
So great a foil by any foreign foe.
Now will the Christian miscreants be glad,

Ringing with joy their superstitious
   bells,
And making bonfires for my overthrow.
But, ere I die, those foul idolaters
Shall make me bonfires with their
   filthy bones,   240
For, though the glory of this day be
   lost,
Afric and Greece have garrisons enough
To make me sovereign of the earth
   again.
TAM. Those walléd garrisons will I sub-
   due,
And write myself great Lord of Africa.
So from the East unto the furthest
   West
Shall Tamburlaine extend his puissant
   arm.
The galleys and those pilling [3] brigan-
   dines
That yearly sail to the Venetian gulf
And hover in the Straits for Christians'
   wrack   250
Shall lie at anchor in the isle Asant,
Until the Persian fleet and men of war,
Sailing along the oriental sea,
Have fetched [4] about the Indian conti-
   nent,
Even from Persepolis to Mexico,
And thence unto the straits of Jubal-
   ter, [5]
Where they shall meet and join their
   force in one,
Keeping in awe the Bay of Portingale, [6]
And all the ocean by the British shore;
And by this means I'll win the world
   at last.   260
BAJ. Yet set a ransom on me, Tambur-
   laine.
TAM. What, think'st thou Tamburlaine
   esteems thy gold?
I'll make the kings of India, ere I die,
Offer their mines to sue for peace to me,
And dig for treasure to appease my
   wrath.
Come, bind them both, and one lead
   in the Turk;
The Turkess let my love's maid lead
   away.   *They bind them.*
BAJ. Ah, villains, dare ye touch my sacred
   arms?
O Mahomet!—O sleepy Mahomet!

[1] *I.e.*, Tamburlaine.   [2] Bases of statues.

[3] Pillaging.   [4] Sailed.   [5] Gibraltar.
[6] Bay of Portugal, *i.e.*, Bay of Biscay.

ZAB. O curséd Mahomet, that makest us
thus　　　　　　　　　　　　　　　270
　The slaves to Scythians rude and bar-
　　barous!
TAM. Come, bring them in, and for this
happy conquest
　Triumph and solemnize a martial feast.
　　　　　　　　　　　　　　Exeunt.

FINIS ACTUS TERTII.

ACTUS IV. SCENA i.

[*The Egyptian court.*]

Soldan of Egypt, with three or four Lords,
　　Capolin [*,and a Messenger*].

SOLD. Awake, ye men of Memphis! Hear
the clang
　Of Scythian trumpets! Hear the basi-
　　lisks [1]
　That, roaring, shake Damascus' turrets
　　down!
　The rogue of Volga holds Zenocrate,
　The soldan's daughter, for his concubine,
　And with a troop of thieves and vaga-
　　bonds
　Hath spread his colors to our high dis-
　　grace,
　While you, faint-hearted, base Egyp-
　　tians,
　Lie slumbering on the flowery banks of
　　Nile,
　As crocodiles that unaffrighted rest,　10
　While thund'ring cannons rattle on their
　　skins.
MESS. Nay, mighty soldan, did your great-
ness see
　The frowning looks of fiery Tamburlaine,
　That with his terror and imperious eyes
　Commands the hearts of his associates,
　It might amaze your royal majesty.
SOLD. Villain, I tell thee, were that Tam-
burlaine
　As monstrous as Gorgon,[2] prince of hell,
　The soldan would not start a foot from
　　him.
　But speak, what power hath he?
MESS.　　　　　　　Mighty lord,　20
　Three hundred thousand men in armor
　　clad,
　Upon their prancing steeds disdainfully
　With wanton paces trampling on the
　　ground;

[1] Cannon.　　　　　　　[2] Demogorgon.

Five hundred thousand footmen threat'-
ning shot,
　Shaking their swords, their spears, and
　　iron bills,
　Environing their standard round, that
　　stood
　As bristle-pointed as a thorny wood.
　Their warlike engines and munition
　Exceed the forces of their martial men.
SOLD. Nay, could their numbers counter-
vail[3] the stars,　　　　　　30
　Or ever-drizzling drops of April showers,
　Or withered leaves that autumn shaketh
　　down,
　Yet would the soldan by his conquering
　　power
　So scatter and consume them in his rage
　That not a man should live to rue their
　　fall.
CAP. So might your highness had you
time to sort[4]
　Your fighting men and raise your royal
　　host;
　But Tamburlaine, by expedition,
　Advantage takes of your unreadiness.
SOLD. Let him take all th' advantages he
can.　　　　　　　　　　　40
　Were all the world conspired to fight for
　　him,
　Nay, were he devil, as he is no man,
　Yet in revenge of fair Zenocrate,
　Whom he detaineth in despite of us,
　This arm should send him down to Ere-
　　bus
　To shroud his shame in darkness of the
　　night.
MESS. Pleaseth your mightiness to under-
stand,
　His resolution far exceedeth all.
　The first day when he pitcheth down his
　　tents,
　White is their hue, and on his silver
　　crest　　　　　　　　　　50
　A snowy feather spangled white he
　　bears,
　To signify the mildness of his mind,
　That, satiate with spoil, refuseth blood.
　But, when Aurora mounts the second
　　time,
　As red as scarlet is his furniture.
　Then must his kindled wrath be
　　quenched with blood,
　Not sparing any that can manage arms

[3] Equal.　　　　　　　[4] Select.

But, if these threats move not submission,
Black are his colors, black pavilion;
His spear, his shield, his horse, his
armor, plumes,   60
And jetty feathers menace death and
hell.
Without respect of sex, degree, or age,
He razeth all his foes with fire and sword.
$OLD. Merciless villain, peasant, ignorant
Of lawful arms or martial discipline!
Pillage and murder are his usual trades;
The slave usurps the glorious name of
war.
See, Capolin, the fair Arabian king,
That hath been disappointed by this
slave
Of my fair daughter and his princely
love,   70
May have fresh warning to go war with
us,
And be revenged for her disparagement.
                                      [*Exeunt.*]

Actus IV. Scena ii.

[*Tamburlaine's camp outside Damascus.*]

Tamburlaine, Techelles, Theridamas, Usum-
casane, Zenocrate, Anippe, two Moors
drawing Bajazeth in his cage, and his
Wife following him.

TAM. Bring out my footstool!
                They take him out of the cage.
BAJ. Ye holy priests of heavenly Ma-
homet,
That, sacrificing, slice and cut your flesh,
Staining his altars with your purple
blood,
Make heaven to frown and every fixéd
star
To suck up poison from the moorish fens,
And pour it in this glorious [1] tyrant's
throat!
TAM. The chiefest God, first mover of that
sphere
Enchased[2] with thousands ever-shining
lamps,
Will sooner burn the glorious frame of
heaven   10
Than it should so conspire my over-
throw.
But, villain, thou that wishest this to me,

Fall prostrate on the low disdainful
earth,
And be the footstool of great Tambur-
laine,
That I may rise into my royal throne.
BAJ. First shalt thou rip my bowels with
thy sword,
And sacrifice my heart to death and hell,
Before I yield to such a slavery.
TAM. Base villain, vassal, slave to Tam-
burlaine,
Unworthy to embrace or touch the
ground   20
That bears the honor of my royal
weight,
Stoop, villain, stoop! Stoop! For so he
bids
That may command thee piecemeal to be
torn,
Or scattered like the lofty cedar trees
Struck with the voice of thund'ring
Jupiter.
BAJ. Then, as I look down to the damnéd
fiends,
Fiends, look on me! And thou, dread
god of hell,
With ebon scepter strike this hateful
earth,
And make it swallow both of us at once!
                He gets up upon him to his chair.
TAM. Now clear the triple region of the
air,   30
And let the majesty of heaven behold
Their scourge and terror tread on em-
perors.
Smile, stars, that reigned at my nativity,
And dim the brightness of their neighbor
lamps!
Disdain to borrow light of Cynthia!
For I, the chiefest lamp of all the earth,
First rising in the east with mild aspect,
But fixéd now in the meridian line,
Will send up fire to your turning spheres,
And cause the sun to borrow light of
you.   40
My sword stroke[3] fire from his coat of
steel,
Even in Bithynia, when I took this Turk,
As when a fiery exhalation,
Wrapped in the bowels of a freezing
cloud,
Fighting for passage, make[s] the welkin
crack,

---

[1] Vainglorious.   [2] Set.   [3] Struck.

And casts a flash of lightning to the earth.
But, ere I march to wealthy Persia,
Or leave Damascus and th' Egyptian fields,
As was the fame of Clymene's brainsick son,[1]
That almost brent [2] the axletree of heaven, 50
So shall our swords, our lances, and our shot
Fill all the air with fiery meteors.
Then, when the sky shall wax as red as blood,
It shall be said I made it red myself,
To make me think of naught but blood and war.

ZAB. Unworthy king, that by thy cruelty
Unlawfully usurpest the Persian seat,
Dar'st thou, that never saw an emperor
Before thou met my husband in the field,
Being thy captive, thus abuse his state, 60
Keeping his kingly body in a cage,
That roofs of gold and sun-bright palaces
Should have prepared to entertain his grace,
And treading him beneath thy loathsome feet,
Whose feet the kings of Africa have kissed?

TECH. You must devise some torment worse, my lord,
To make these captives rein their lavish tongues.

TAM. Zenocrate, look better to your slave!

ZEN. She is my handmaid's slave, and she shall look
That these abuses flow not from her tongue. 70
Chide her, Anippe!

ANIP. Let these be warnings for you then, my slave,
How you abuse the person of the king;
Or else I swear to have you whipped, stark-naked.

BAJ. Great Tamburlaine, great in my overthrow,
Ambitious pride shall make thee fall as low
For treading on the back of Bajazeth,

[1] *I.e.*, Phaëton. Original reads *Clymeus*.
[2] Burnt.

That should be horséd on four mighty kings.

TAM. Thy names and titles and thy dignities
Are fled from Bajazeth and remain with me, 80
That will maintain it against a world of kings.
Put him in again!
[*They put him back into the cage.*]

BAJ. Is this a place for mighty Bajazeth?
Confusion light on him that helps thee thus!

TAM. There, whiles he lives, shall Bajazeth be kept,
And, where I go, be thus in triumph drawn;
And thou, his wife, shalt feed him with the scraps
My servitures [3] shall bring thee from my board,
For he that gives him other food than this
Shall sit by him and starve to death himself. 90
This is my mind and I will have it so.
Not all the kings and emperors of the earth,
If they would lay their crowns before my feet,
Shall ransom him or take him from his cage.
The ages that shall talk of Tamburlaine,
Even from this day to Plato's wondrous year,
Shall talk how I have handled Bajazeth.
These Moors, that drew him from Bithynia
To fair Damascus, where we now remain,
Shall lead him with us wheresoe'er we go. 100
Techelles and my loving followers,
Now may we see Damascus' lofty towers,
Like to the shadows of pyramides,[4]
That with their beauties graced the Memphian fields.
The golden stature [5] of their feathered bird
That spreads her wings upon the city walls
Shall not defend it from our battering shot.
The townsmen mask in silk and cloth of gold,

[3] Servitors. [4] Quadrisyllabic. [5] Statue.

And every house is as a treasury.
The men, the treasure, and the town is
    ours. 110
THER. Your tents of white now pitched
    before the gates,
And gentle flags of amity displayed,
I doubt not but the governor will yield,
Offering Damascus to your majesty.
TAM. So shall he have his life, and all the
    rest.
But, if he stay until the bloody flag
Be once advanced on my vermilion tent,
He dies, and those that kept us out so
    long.
And, when they see me march in black
    array,
With mournful streamers hanging down
    their heads, 120
Were in that city all the world contained,
Not one should scape, but perish by our
    swords.
ZEN. Yet would you have some pity for
    my sake,
Because it is my country's, and my
    father's!
TAM. Not for the world, Zenocrate, if I
    have sworn.
Come; bring in the Turk!   *Exeunt.*

ACTUS IV. SCENA iii.

[*The Egyptian court.*]

Soldan, Arabia, Capolin, with steeming [1]
colors and Soldiers.

SOLD. Methinks we march as Meleager did,
Environéd with brave Argolian knights,
To chase the savage Cal[y]donian boar,
Or Cephalus with lusty Theban youths
Against the wolf that angry Themis sent
To waste and spoil the sweet Aonian
    fields,
A monster of five hundred thousand
    heads,
Compact of rapine, piracy, and spoil.
The scum of men, the hate and scourge of
    God,
Raves in Egyptia and annoyeth us. 10
My lord, it is the bloody Tamburlaine,
A sturdy felon and a base-bred thief,
By murder raiséd to the Persian crown,
That dares control us in our territories.
To tame the pride of this presumptuous
    beast,

[1] Bright, gleaming.

Join your Arabians with the soldan's
    power;
Let us unite our royal bands in one,
And hasten to remove Damascus' siege.
It is a blemish to the majesty
And high estate of mighty emperors 20
That such a base, usurping vagabond
Should brave a king, or wear a princely
    crown.
ARAB. Renowméd soldan, have ye lately
    heard
The overthrow of mighty Bajazeth
About the confines of Bithynia,
The slavery wherewith he persecutes
The noble Turk and his great emperess?
SOLD. I have, and sorrow for his bad
    success.
But, noble lord of great Arabia,
Be so persuaded that the soldan is 30
No more dismayed with tidings of his fall
Than in the haven when the pilot stands
And views a stranger's ship rent in the
    winds,
And shiveréd against a craggy rock.
Yet, in compassion of his wretched state,
A sacred vow to heaven and him I make,
Confirming it with Ibis' holy name,
That Tamburlaine shall rue the day, the
    hour,
Wherein he wrought such ignominious
    wrong
Unto the hallowed person of a prince, 40
Or kept the fair Zenocrate so long
As concubine, I fear, to feed his lust.
ARAB. Let grief and fury hasten on re-
    venge;
Let Tamburlaine for his offenses feel
Such plagues as heaven and we can pour
    on him.
I long to break my spear upon his crest,
And prove the weight of his victorious
    arm,
For fame, I fear, hath been too prodigal
In sounding through the world his partial
    praise.
SOLD. Capolin, hast thou surveyed our
    powers? 50
CAP. Great Emperors of Egypt and
    Arabia,
The number of your hosts united is
A hundred and fifty thousand horse,
Two hundred thousand foot, brave men-
    at-arms,
Courageous, and full of hardiness,

As frolic as the hunters in the chase
Of savage beasts amid the desert woods.
ARAB. My mind presageth fortunate suc-
    cess;
    And, Tamburlaine, my spirit doth fore-
    see
    The utter ruin of thy men and thee.   60
SOLD. Then rear your standards; let your
    sounding drums
    Direct our soldiers to Damascus' walls.
    Now, Tamburlaine, the mighty soldan
    comes,
    And leads with him the great Arabian
    king
    To dim thy baseness and obscurity,
    Famous for nothing but for theft and
    spoil;
    To raze and scatter thy inglorious crew
    Of Scythians and slavish Persians.
                                    Exeunt.

ACTUS IV. SCENA iv.[1]

[*Tamburlaine's camp outside Damascus.*]

*The banquet; and to it cometh Tamburlaine,
    all in scarlet, [Zenocrate,] Theridamas,
    Techelles, Usumcasane, the Turk [Ba-
    jazeth in his cage, Zabina], with Others.*

TAM. Now hang our bloody colors by Da-
    mascus,
    Reflexing hues of blood upon their heads,
    While they walk quivering on their city
    walls,
    Half dead for fear before they feel my
    wrath;
    Then let us freely banquet and carouse [2]
    Full bowls of wine unto the God of War,
    That means to fill your helmets full of
    gold,
    And make Damascus' spoils as rich to
    you
    As was to Jason Colchos' golden fleece.—
    And now, Bajazeth, hast thou any
    stomach?   10
BAJ. Ay, such a stomach, cruel Tambur-
    laine, as I could willingly feed upon thy
    blood-raw heart.
TAM. Nay, thine own is easier to come
    by; pluck out that, and 'twill serve thee
    and thy wife. Well, Zenocrate, Techelles,
    and the rest, fall to your victuals.
BAJ. Fall to, and never may your meat
    digest!

Ye Furies, that can mask invisible,
Dive to the bottom of Avernus' pool,   20
And in your hands bring hellish poison
    up
And squeeze it in the cup of Tambur-
    laine!
Or, wingéd snakes of Lerna, cast your
    stings,
And leave your venoms in this tyrant's
    dish!
ZAB. And may this banquet prove as
    ominous
    As Progne's to th' adulterous Thracian
    king,
    That fed upon the substance of his child!
ZEN. My lord, how can you suffer these
    Outrageous curses by these slaves of
    yours?
TAM. To let them see, divine Zenocrate,   30
    I glory in the curses of my foes,
    Having the power from the emperial
    heaven
    To turn them all upon their proper heads.
TECH. I pray you give them leave,
    madam; this speech is a goodly refreshing
    to them.
THER. But, if his highness would let
    them be fed, it would do them more good.
TAM. Sirrah, why fall you not to? Are
    you so daintily brought up you cannot   [40
    eat your own flesh?
BAJ. First, legions of devils shall tear
    thee in pieces!
USUM. Villain, knowest thou to whom
    thou speakest?
TAM. O, let him alone. Here, eat, sir.
    Take it from my sword's point, or I'll thrust
    it to thy heart.
                He [3] *takes it and stamps upon it.*
THER. He stamps it under his feet, my
    lord.   50
TAM. Take it up, villain, and eat it, or I
    will make thee slice the brawns of thy arms
    into carbonadoes [4] and eat them.
USUM. Nay, 'twere better he killed his
    wife, and then she shall be sure not to be
    starved, and he be provided for a month's
    victual beforehand.
TAM. Here is my dagger. Despatch her
    while she is fat, for, if she live but awhile
    longer, she will fall into a consumption   [60
    with fretting, and then she will not be
    worth the eating.

---

[1] Original has 5.   [2] Drink.   [3] *I.e.*, Bajazeth.   [4] Steaks.

THER. Dost thou think that Mahomet will suffer this?

TECH. 'Tis like he will, when he cannot let [1] it.

TAM. Go to; fall to your meat!—What, not a bit? Belike he hath not been watered today; give him some drink.

They give him water to drink, and he flings it on the ground.

Fast, and welcome, sir, while [2] hunger [70] make you eat. How now, Zenocrate, doth not the Turk and his wife make a goodly show at a banquet?

ZEN. Yes, my lord.

THER. Methinks 'tis a great deal better than a consort [3] of music.

TAM. Yet music would do well to cheer up Zenocrate. Pray thee, tell why art thou so sad? If thou wilt have a song, the Turk shall strain his voice. But why is it?   80

ZEN. My lord, to see my father's town besieged,

The country wasted where myself was born,

How can it but afflict my very soul?

If any love remain in you, my lord,

Or if my love unto your majesty

May merit favor at your highness' hands,

Then raise your siege from fair Damascus' walls,

And with my father take a friendly truce.

TAM. Zenocrate, were Egypt Jove's own land,

Yet would I with my sword make Jove to stoop.   90

I will confute those blind geographers

That make a triple region in the world,

Excluding regions which I mean to trace, [4]

And with this pen [5] reduce them to a map,

Calling the provinces, cities, and towns,

After my name and thine, Zenocrate.

Here at Damascus will I make the point

That shall begin the perpendicular;

And wouldst thou have me buy thy father's love

With such a loss? Tell me, Zenocrate. 100

ZEN. Honor still wait on happy Tamburlaine!

Yet give me leave to plead for him, my lord.

TAM. Content thyself. His person shall be safe

And all the friends of fair Zenocrate,

If with their lives they will be pleased to yield

Or may be forced to make me emperor;

For Egypt and Arabia must be mine.—

Feed, you slave! Thou mayst think thyself happy to be fed from my trencher.

BAJ. My empty stomach, full of idle heat,   110

Draws bloody humors from my feeble parts,

Preserving life by hasting cruel death.

My veins are pale, my sinews hard and dry,

My joints benumbed; unless I eat, I die.

ZAB. Eat, Bajazeth. Let us live in spite of them, looking [6] some happy power will pity and enlarge [7] us.

TAM. Here, Turk, wilt thou have a clean trencher?

BAJ. Ay, tyrant, and more meat.   120

TAM. Soft, sir; you must be dieted; too much eating will make you surfeit.

THER. So it would, my lord, specially having so small a walk and so little exercise.

Enter a second course of crowns.

TAM. Theridamas, Techelles, and Casane, here are the cates [8] you desire to finger, are they not?

THER. Ay, my lord, but none save kings must feed with these.

TECH. 'Tis enough for us to see [130] them, and for Tamburlaine only to enjoy them.

TAM. Well, here is now to the Soldan of Egypt, the King of Arabia, and the Governor of Damascus. Now take these three crowns, and pledge me, my contributory kings. I crown you here, Theridamas, King of Argier; Techelles, King of Fez; and Usumcasane, King of Moroccus. How say you to this, Turk? These are not your [140] contributory kings.

BAJ. Nor shall they long be thine, I warrant them.

TAM. Kings of Argier, Moroccus, and of Fez,

[1] Prevent.   [4] Travel over.
[2] Until.   [5] *I.e.*, sword.
[3] Company of musicians.

[6] Expecting.   [7] Free.   [8] Delicacies

You that have marched with happy Tam-
burlaine
As far as from the frozen place of heaven
Unto the wat'ry morning's ruddy hour,[1]
And thence by land unto the torrid zone,
Deserve these titles I endow you with
By value [2] and by magnanimity.[3]
Your births shall be no blemish to your
fame,   150
For virtue is the fount whence honor
springs,
And they are worthy she investeth kings.
THER. And, since your highness hath so
well vouchsafed,
If we deserve them not with higher
meeds [4]
Than erst our states and actions have
retained,
Take them away again and make us
slaves.
TAM. Well said, Theridamas; when holy
fates
Shall stablish me in strong Egyptia,
We mean to travel to th' antartic [5] pole,
Conquering the people underneath our
feet,   160
And be renowmed as never emperors
were.
Zenocrate, I will not crown thee yet,
Until with greater honors I be graced.
                     [*Exeunt.*]

FINIS ACTUS QUARTI.

ACTUS V. SCENA i.

[*Outside the walls of Damascus.*]

*The Governor of Damasco, with three or four
Citizens, and four Virgins with branches
of laurel in their hands.*

GOV. Still doth this man, or rather god, of
war,
Batter our walls and beat our turrets
down,
And to resist with longer stubbornness
Or hope of rescue from the soldan's
power
Were but to bring our willful overthrow,
And make us desperate of our threatened
lives.
We see his tents have now been alteréd

[1] *I.e..* dawn, the east.
[2] Worth, goodness.
[3] Courage.
[4] Merits.
[5] Antarctic. From 1592 edn. Original reads
intatique.

With terrors to the last and cruelest
hue.
His coal-black colors everywhere ad-
vanced
Threaten our city with a general spoil. 10
And, if we should with common rites of
arms
Offer our safeties to his clemency,
I fear the custom, proper to his sword,
Which he observes as parcel[6] of his fame,
Intending so to terrify the world,
By any innovation or remorse
Will never be dispensed with till our
deaths.
Therefore, for these our harmless vir-
gins' sakes,
Whose honors and whose lives rely on
him,
Let us have hope that their unspotted
prayers,   20
Their blubbered cheeks, and hearty,
humble moans,
Will melt his fury into some remorse,[7]
And use us like a loving conqueror.
[1] VIRG. If humble suits or imprecations,[8]
Uttered with tears of wretchedness and
blood
Shed from the heads and hearts of all
our sex
(Some made you wives, and some your
children),
Might have entreated your obdurate
breasts
To entertain some care of our securities
Whiles[9] only danger beat upon our
walls,   30
These more than dangerous warrants
of our death
Had never been erected as they be,
Nor you depend on such weak helps as
we.
GOV. Well, lovely virgins, think our
country's care,
Our love of honor, loath to be enthralled
To foreign powers and rough imperious
yokes,
Would not with too much cowardice
or fear,
Before all hope of rescue were denied,
Submit yourselves and us to servitude.
Therefore, in that your safeties and our
own,   40

[6] An essential part.
[7] Pity.
[8] Prayers.
[9] During the time that.

Your honors, liberties, and lives were
    weighed
In equal care and balance with our own,
Endure as we the malice of our stars,
The wrath of Tamburlaine, and power
    of wars;
Or be the means the overweighing [1]
    heavens
Have kept to qualify [2] these hot ex-
    tremes,
And bring us pardon in your cheerful
    looks.
2 VIRG. Then here before the majesty of
    heaven
And holy patrons of Egyptia,
With knees and hearts submissive we
    entreat   50
Grace to our words and pity to our looks
That this device may prove propitious,
And through the eyes and ears of Tam-
    burlaine
Convey events [3] of mercy to his heart.
Grant that these signs of victory we
    yield
May bind the temples of his conquering
    head,
To hide the folded furrows of his brows,
And shadow his displeaséd countenance
With happy looks of ruth and lenity.
Leave us, my lord and loving country-
    men;   60
What simple virgins may persuade, we
    will.
GOV. Farewell, sweet virgins, on whose
    safe return
Depends our city, liberty, and lives.
         Exeunt [all but the Virgins].

ACTUS V. SCENA ii.

[*The same.*]

[*The Virgins are approached by*] *Tambur-
    laine, Techelles, Theridamas, Usumca-
    san[e], with Others; Tamburlaine all in
    black and very melancholy.*

TAM. What, are the turtles [4] frayed [5] out
    of their nests?
    Alas, poor fools! Must you be first
    shall feel
The sworn destruction of Damascus?

They know my custom. Could they
    not as well
Have sent ye out when first my milk-
    white flags,
Through which sweet Mercy threw her
    gentle beams,
Reflexing them on your disdainful eyes,
As now, when fury and incenséd hate
Flings slaughtering terror from my coal-
    black tents,
And tells for truth submissions comes
    too late?   10
1 VIRG. Most happy king and emperor
    of the earth,
Image of honor and nobility,
For whom the powers divine have made
    the world,
And on whose throne the holy Graces
    sit,
In whose sweet person is comprised the
    sum
Of nature's skill and heavenly majesty,
Pity our plights! O, pity poor Damascus!
Pity old age, within whose silver hairs
Honor and reverence evermore have
    reigned!
Pity the marriage bed, where many a
    lord,   20
In prime and glory of his loving joy,
Embraceth now with tears of ruth and
    blood
The jealous [6] body of his fearful wife,
Whose cheeks and hearts, so punished
    with conceit
To think thy puissant, never-stayéd
    arm
Will part their bodies, and prevent their
    souls
From heavens of comfort yet their age
    might bear,
Now wax all pale and withered to the
    death,
As well for grief our ruthless governor
Hath thus refused the mercy of thy
    hand   30
(Whose scepter angels kiss and furies
    dread)
As for their liberties, their loves, or
    lives!
O, then for these, and such as we our-
    selves,
For us, for infants, and for all our bloods,
That never nourished thought against
    thy rule,

[1] Overruling.
[2] Mollify.
[3] Effects.
[4] Turtledoves.
[5] Frightened.
[6] Apprehensive.

Pity, O, pity, sacred emperor,
The prostrate service of this wretched
　town,
And take in sign thereof this gilded
　wreath,
Whereto each man of rule hath given
　his hand,
And wished, as worthy subjects, happy
　means　　　　　　　　　　　　　40
To be investers of thy royal brows
Even with the true Egyptian diadem!
TAM. Virgins, in vain ye labor to pre-
　vent
That which mine honor swears shall
　be performed.
Behold my sword! What see you at
　the point?
[1] VIRG. Nothing but fear and fatal
　steel, my lord.
TAM. Your fearful minds are thick and
　misty then;
For there sits Death, there sits impe-
　rious Death,
Keeping his circuit [1] by the slicing
　edge.
But I am pleased you shall not see him
　there;　　　　　　　　　　　　50
He now is seated on my horsemen's
　spears,
And on their points his fleshless body
　feeds.
Techelles, straight go charge a few of
　them
To charge these dames, and show my
　servant, Death,
Sitting in scarlet on their arméd spears.
OMNES. O, pity us!
TAM. Away with them, I say, and show
　them Death!　　*They take them away.*
I will not spare these proud Egyp-
　tians,
Nor change my martial observations[2]
For all the wealth of Gihon's golden
　waves,　　　　　　　　　　　　60
Or for the love of Venus, would she
　leave
The angry god of arms and lie with
　me.
They have refused the offer of their
　lives,
And know my customs are as peremp-
　tory
As wrathful planets, death, or destiny.

[1] Law court.　　　[2] Observances, customs.

Enter Techelles.

What, have your horsemen shown the
　virgins Death?
TECH. They have, my lord, and on Da-
　mascus' walls
Have hoisted up their slaughtered car-
　casses.
TAM. A sight as baneful to their souls,
　I think,
As are Thessalian drugs or mithri-
　date[3]—　　　　　　　　　　　70
But go, my lords, put the rest to the
　sword.
　　　　　Exeunt [all except Tamburlaine].
Ah, fair Zenocrate, divine Zenocrate,
Fair is too foul an epithet for thee,
That in thy passion[4] for thy country's
　love,
And fear to see thy kingly father's harm,
With hair disheveled wip'st thy watery
　cheeks,
And, like to Flora in her morning's
　pride,
Shaking her silver treshes[5] in the air
Rain'st on the earth resolvéd pearl in
　showers,
And sprinklest sapphires on thy shin-
　ing face,　　　　　　　　　　　80
Where Beauty, mother to the Muses,
　sits
And comments[6] volumes with her ivory
　pen,
Taking instructions from thy flowing
　eyes,
Eyes, when that Ebena steps to heaven,
In silence of thy solemn evening's walk,
Making the mantle of the richest night,
The moon, the planets, and the meteors,
　light!
There angels in their crystal armors
　fight
A doubtful battle with my tempted
　thoughts
For Egypt's freedom, and the soldan's
　life—　　　　　　　　　　　　90
His life that so consumes Zenocrate,
Whose sorrows lay more siege unto my
　soul
Than all my army to Damascus' walls;
And neither Persians' sovereign nor
　the Turk

[3] Usually an antidote against poison; here, a
poison.
[4] Suffering.　　　　　[5] Tresses.
　　　　　　　　　　　　[6] Writes.

Troubled my senses with conceit of foil [1]
So much by much as doth Zenocrate.
What is beauty, saith my sufferings, then?
If all the pens that ever poets held
Had fed the feeling of their masters' thoughts,
And every sweetness that inspired their hearts,　　　　100
Their minds, and muses on admired themes;
If all the heavenly quintessence they still [2]
From their immortal flowers of poesy,
Wherein, as in a mirror, we perceive
The highest reaches of a human wit;
If these had made one poem's period, [3]
And all combined in beauty's worthiness,
Yet should there hover in their restless heads
One thought, one grace, one wonder, at the least,　　　　109
Which into words no virtue can digest.
But how unseemly is it for my sex,
My discipline of arms and chivalry,
My nature, and the terror of my name,
To harbor thoughts effeminate and faint!
Save only that in beauty's just applause,
With whose instinct the soul of man is touched
(And every warrior that is rapt with love
Of fame, of valor, and of victory
Must needs have beauty beat on his conceits),
I, thus conceiving and subduing both　120
That which hath stopped the tempest of the gods,
Even from the fiery-spangled veil of heaven,
To feel the lovely warmth of shepherds' flames,
And march [4] in cottages of strowéd weeds,
Shall give the world to note, for all my birth,
That virtue [5] solely is the sum of glory,
And fashions men with true nobility.—
Who's within there?

[1] Thought of defeat.　　[2] Distill.　　[3] Climax.
[4] Move about.　　[5] Strength, manly qualities.

Enter two or three [Attendants].

Hath Bajazeth been fed today?
A[TTE]N. Ay, my lord.　　　　130
TAM. Bring him forth; and let us know the town be ransacked.
　　　　　　　　　　[Exeunt Attendants.]

Enter Techelles, Theridamas, Usumcasan[e], and Others.

TECH. The town is ours, my lord, and fresh supply
Of conquest and of spoil is offered us.
TAM. That's well, Techelles. What's the news?
TECH. The soldan and the Arabian king together
March on us with such eager violence
As if there were no way but one with us.
TAM. No more there is not, I warrant thee, Techelles.
　　　　They bring in the Turk [and Zabina].
THER. We know the victory is ours, my lord;　　　　140
But let us save the reverend soldan's life
For fair Zenocrate, that so laments his state.
TAM. That will we chiefly see unto, Theridamas,
For sweet Zenocrate, whose worthiness
Deserves a conquest over every heart.—
And now, my footstool, if I lose the field,
You hope of liberty and restitution.
Here let him stay, my masters, from the tents,
Till we have made us ready for the field.
Pray for us, Bajazeth; we are going.　　150
Exeunt [all except Bajazeth and Zabina].
BAJ. Go, never to return with victory!
Millions of men encompass thee about,
And gore thy body with as many wounds!
Sharp, forkéd arrows light upon thy horse!
Furies from the black Cocytus lake
Break up the earth, and with their fire-brands
Enforce thee run upon the baneful pikes!
Volleys of shot pierce through thy charméd skin,

And every bullet dipped in poisoned
  drugs,   159
Or roaring cannons sever all thy joints,
Making thee mount as high as eagles
  soar!
ZAB. Let all the swords and lances in the
  field
Stick in his breast as in their proper
  rooms!
At every pore let blood come dropping
  forth,
That ling'ring pains may massacre his
  heart,
And madness send his damnéd soul to
  hell!
BAJ. Ah, fair Zabina, we may curse his
  power,
The heavens may frown, the earth for
  anger quake,
But such a star hath influence in his
  sword
As rules the skies and countermands
  the gods   170
More than Cimmerian Styx or destiny;
And then shall we in this detested
  guise,
With shame, with hunger, and with
  horror lie,[1]
Griping our bowels with retorquéd[2]
  thoughts,
And have no hope to end our ecstasies.[3]
ZAB. Then is there left no Mahomet, no
  God,
No fiend, no fortune, nor no hope of
  end
To our infamous, monstrous slaveries?
Gape, earth, and let the fiends infernal
  view
A hell as hopeless and as full of fear   180
As are the blasted banks of Erebus,
Where shaking ghosts with ever-howling
  groans
Hover about the ugly ferryman,
To get a passage to Elysian!
Why should we live? O, wretches, beg-
  gars, slaves!
Why live we, Bajazeth, and build up
  nests
So high within the region of the air
By living long in this oppression
That all the world will see and laugh to
  scorn

The former triumphs of our mighti-
  ness   190
In this obscure, infernal servitude?
BAJ. O life, more loathsome to my vexéd
  thoughts
Than noisome parbreak[4] of the Stygian
  snakes,
Which fills the nooks of hell with stand-
  ing air,
Infecting all the ghosts with cureless
  griefs!
O dreary engines[5] of my loathéd sight,
That sees my crown, my honor, and my
  name
Thrust under yoke and thralldom of a
  thief,
Why feed ye still on day's accurséd beams
And sink not quite into my tortured
  soul?   200
You see my wife, my queen and em-
  peress,
Brought up and proppéd by the hand of
  Fame,
Queen of fifteen contributory queens,
Now thrown to rooms[6] of black abjec-
  tion,
Smeared with blots of basest drudgery,
And villainess[7] to shame, disdain, and
  misery.
Accurséd Bajazeth, whose words of
  ruth,
That would with pity cheer Zabina's
  heart,
And make our souls resolve in ceaseless
  tears,
Sharp hunger bites upon, and gripes
  the root   210
From whence the issues of my thoughts
  do break!
O poor Zabina, O my queen, my queen,
Fetch me some water for my burning
  breast,
To cool and comfort me with longer date
That in the shortened sequel of my life
I may pour forth my soul into thine arms
With words of love, whose moaning
  intercourse
Hath hitherto been stayed with wrath
  and hate
Of our expressless,[8] banned[9] inflic-
  tions.

---

[1] Original has *aie*.   [3] Frenzies.
[2] Twisted inward.

[4] Vomit.   [7] Slave.
[5] Instruments, *i.e.*, eyes.   [8] Inexpressible.
[6] Positions.   [9] Cursed.

ZAB. Sweet Bajazeth, I will prolong thy
  life   220
As long as any blood or spark of breath
Can quench or cool the torments of
  my grief.   *She goes out.*
BAJ. Now, Bajazeth, abridge thy bane-
  ful days,
And beat thy brains out of thy conquered
  head,
Since other means are all forbidden me
That may be ministers of my decay.
O highest lamp of ever-living Jove,
Accursèd day, infected with my griefs,
Hide now thy stainèd face in endless
  night,
And shut the windows of the lightsome
  heavens!   230
Let ugly Darkness with her rusty coach,
Engirt with tempests, wrapped in pitchy
  clouds,
Smother the earth with never-fading
  mists,
And let her horses from their nostrils
  breathe
Rebellious winds and dreadful thunder-
  claps,
That in this terror Tamburlaine may
  live,
And my pined[1] soul, resolved in liquid
  air,
May still excruciate his tormented
  thoughts!
Then let the stony dart of senseless
  cold
Pierce through the center of my withered
  heart,   240
And make a passage for my loathèd
  life!
  He brains himself against the cage.

  Enter Zabina.

ZAB. What do mine eyes behold? My
  husband dead!
His skull all riven in twain! His brains
  dashed out,
The brains of Bajazeth, my lord and
  sovereign!
O Bajazeth, my husband and my lord!
O Bajazeth, O Turk, O emperor!
Give him his liquor? Not I. Bring milk
and fire, and my blood I bring him again!—
Tear me in pieces! Give me the sword

with a ball of wildfire upon it!—Down   [250
with him, down with him!—Go to my child!
Away, away, away! Ah, save that infant,
save him, save him!—I, even I, speak to
her.—The sun was down; streamers white,
red, black, here, here, here!—Fling the
meat in his face!—Tamburlaine, Tamburlaine!—Let the soldiers be buried.—Hell!
Death! Tamburlaine! Hell!—Make ready
my coach, my chair, my jewels. I come,
I come, I come!   260
She runs against the cage and brains herself.

  [Enter] Zenocrate with Anippe.

[ZEN.] Wretched Zenocrate, that livest
  to see
Damascus' walls dyed with Egyptian
  blood,
Thy father's subjects and thy country-
  men;
Thy streets strowed with dissevered
  joints of men
And wounded bodies gasping yet for
  life!
But most accursed, to see the sun-bright
  troop
Of heavenly virgins and unspotted
  maids,
Whose looks might make the angry god
  of arms
To break his sword and mildly treat
  of love,   269
On horsemen's lances to be hoisted up
And guiltlessly endure a cruel death!
For every fell and stout[2] Tartarian steed,
That stamped on others with their thun-
  d'ring hoofs,
When all their riders charged their
  quivering spears,
Began to check[3] the ground and rein
  themselves,
Gazing upon the beauty of their looks.
Ah, Tamburlaine, wert thou the cause
  of this
That term'st Zenocrate thy dearest
  love,
Whose lives were dearer to Zenocrate
Than her own life, or aught save thine
  own love?—   280
But see another bloody spectacle!
Ah, wretched eyes, the enemies of my
  heart,

---

[1] Tormented.   [2] Fierce and proud.   [3] Push against.

How are ye glutted with these grievous
  objects,
And tell my soul more tales of bleeding
  ruth!
See, see, Anippe, if they breathe or no.
ANIP. No breath, nor sense, nor motion
  in them both.
Ah, madam, this their slavery hath en-
  forced,
And ruthless cruelty of Tamburlaine.
ZEN. Earth, cast up fountains from thy
  entrails,
And wet thy cheeks for their untimely
  deaths!   290
Shake with their weight in sign of fear
  and grief!
Blush, Heaven, that gave them honor
  at their birth
And let them die a death so barbarous!
Those that are proud of fickle empery
And place their chiefest good in earthly
  pomp,
Behold the Turk and his great emperess!
Ah, Tamburlaine, my love, sweet Tam-
  burlaine,
That fights for scepters and for slippery
  crowns,
Behold the Turk and his great emper-
  ess!
Thou, that in conduct of thy happy
  stars   300
Sleep'st every night with conquests on
  thy brows,
And yet wouldst shun the wavering
  turns of war,
In fear and feeling of the like distress
Behold the Turk and his great emperess!
Ah, mighty Jove and holy Mahomet,
Pardon my love!—O, pardon his con-
  tempt
Of earthly fortune and respect of pity,
And let not conquest, ruthlessly pur-
  sued,
Be equally against his life incensed   309
In this great Turk and hapless emper-
  ess!
And pardon me that was not moved
  with ruth
To see them live so long in misery!
Ah, what may chance to thee, Zenocrate?
ANIP. Madam, content yourself, and be
  resolved;
Your love hath Fortune so at his com-
  mand

That she shall stay and turn her wheel
  no more,
As long as life maintains his mighty
  arm
That fights for honor to adorn your
  head.

Enter [Philemus,] a Messenger.

ZEN. What other heavy news now brings
  Philemus?
PHIL. Madam, your father, and the Ara-
  bian king,   320
The first affecter [1] of your excellence,
Comes now, as Turnus gainst Æneas
  did,
Arméd with lance into the Egyptian
  fields,
Ready for battle gainst my lord, the king
ZEN. Now shame and duty, love and fear
  presents
A thousand sorrows to my martyred soul.
Whom should I wish the fatal victory
When my poor pleasures are divided
  thus
And racked by duty from my curséd
  heart?   329
My father and my first-betrothéd love
Must fight against my life and present
  love,
Wherein the change I use condemns my
  faith,
And makes my deeds infamous through
  the world.
But as the gods, to end the Troyans'
  toil,
Prevented [2] Turnus of Lavinia
And fatally enriched Æneas' love,
So, for a final issue to my griefs,
To pacify my country and my love
Must Tamburlaine by their resistless
  powers
With virtue of a gentle victory   340
Conclude a league of honor to my hope;
Then, as the powers divine have pre-
  ordained,
With happy safety of my father's life
Send like defense of fair Arabia.

*They sound to the battle [within], and Tam-
  burlaine enjoys the victory. After,
                      Arabia enters wounded.*

ARAB. What curséd power guides the
  murthering hands

[1] Lover.   [2] Deprived.

Of this infamous tyrant's soldiers
That no escape may save their enemies,
Nor fortune keep themselves from vic-
   tory?
Lie down, Arabia, wounded to the death,
And let Zenocrate's fair eyes behold
That, as for her thou bear'st these
   wretched arms,   351
Even so for her thou diest in these arms,
Leaving thy blood for witness of thy
   love.
ZEN. Too dear a witness for such love, my
   lord!
Behold Zenocrate, the cursèd object,
Whose fortunes never masterèd her
   griefs;
Behold her wounded, in conceit, for
   thee,
As much as thy fair body is for me,
ARAB. Then shall I die with full, con-
   tented heart,
Having beheld divine Zenocrate,   360
Whose sight with joy would take away
   my life
As now it bringeth sweetness to my
   wound,
If I had not been wounded as I am.
Ah, that the deadly pangs I suffer now
Would lend an hour's license to my
   tongue,
To make discourse of some sweet acci-
   dents
Have chanced [1] thy merits in this worth-
   less [2] bondage,
And that I might be privy to the state
Of thy deserved contentment, and thy
   love.   369
But, making now a virtue of thy sight
To drive all sorrow from my fainting
   soul,
Since death denies me further cause of
   joy,
Deprived of care, my heart with com-
   fort dies,
Since thy desirèd hand shall close mine
   eyes.   [Dies.]

Enter Tamburlaine, leading the Soldan,
   Techelles, Theridamas, Usumcasane,
                            with Others.

TAM. Come, happy father of Zenocrate,
A title higher than thy soldan's name.

[1] Befallen.   [2] Unworthy.

Though my right hand have thus en-
   thrallèd thee,
Thy princely daughter here shall set
   thee free,
She that hath calmed the fury of my
   sword,
Which had ere this been bathed in
   streams of blood   380
As vast and deep as Euphrates or Nile.
ZEN. O sight thrice welcome to my joy-
   ful soul,
To see the king, my father, issue safe
From dangerous battle of my conquer-
   ing love!
SOLD. Well met, my only dear Zenocrate,
Though with the loss of Egypt and my
   crown.
TAM. 'Twas I, my lord, that gat the vic-
   tory,
And therefore grieve not at your over-
   throw,
Since I shall render all into your hands,
And add more strength to your domin-
   ions   390
Than ever yet confirmed th' Egyptian
   crown.
The God of War resigns his room to me,
Meaning to make me general of the
   world.
Jove, viewing me in arms, looks pale
   and wan,
Fearing my power should pull him from
   his throne.
Where'er I come, the Fatal Sisters
   sweat
And grisly Death, by running to and
   fro,
To do their ceaseless homage to my
   sword.
And here in Afric, where it seldom
   rains,
Since I arrived with my triumphant
   host,   400
Have swelling clouds, drawn from wide-
   gasping wounds,
Been oft resolved in bloody, purple
   showers,
A meteor that might terrify the earth,
And make it quake at every drop it
   drinks.
Millions of souls sit on the banks of
   Styx,
Waiting the back return of Charon's
   boat;

Hell and Elysian swarm with ghosts of men
That I have sent from sundry foughten fields,
To spread my fame through hell and up to heaven.
And see, my lord, a sight of strange import: 410
Emperors and kings lie breathless at my feet.
The Turk and his great empress, as it seems,
Left to themselves while we were at the fight,
Have desperately despatched their slavish lives;
With them Arabia, too, hath left his life—
All sights of power to grace my victory.
And such are objects fit for Tamburlaine,
Wherein, as in a mirror, may be seen
His honor, that consists in shedding blood,
When men presume to manage arms with him. 420
SOLD. Mighty hath God and Mahomet made thy hand,
Renowmèd Tamburlaine, to whom all kings
Of force [1] must yield their crowns and emperies;
And I am pleased with this my overthrow,
If, as beseems a person of thy state,
Thou hast with honor used Zenocrate.
TAM. Her state and person wants no pomp, you see;
And for all blot of foul inchastity
I record [2] heaven her heavenly self is clear.
Then let me find no further time to grace 430
Her princely temples with the Persian crown,
But here these kings that on my fortunes wait,
And have been crowned for provèd worthiness,
Even by this hand that shall establish them,
Shall now, adjoining all their hands with mine,

[1] Of necessity.   [2] Take to witness.

Invest her here my Queen of Persia.
What saith the noble soldan and Zenocrate?
SOLD. I yield with thanks and protestations
Of endless honor to thee for her love.
TAM. Then doubt I not but fair Zenocrate 440
Will soon consent to satisfy us both.
ZEN. Else should I much forget myself, my lord.
THER. Then let us set the crown upon her head,
That long hath lingered for so high a seat.
TECH. My hand is ready to perform the deed,
For now her marriage time shall work us rest.
USUM. And here's the crown, my lord, help set it on.
TAM. Then sit thou down, divine Zenocrate;
And here we crown thee Queen of Persia 449
And all the kingdoms and dominions
That late the power of Tamburlaine subdued.
As Juno, when the giants were suppressed,
That darted mountains at her brother Jove,
So looks my love, shadowing in her brows
Triumphs and trophies for my victories;
Or as Latona's daughter, bent to arms,
Adding more courage to my conquering mind.
To gratify the sweet Zenocrate,
Egyptians, Moors, and men of Asia,
From Barbary unto the western Indie,
Shall pay a yearly tribute to thy sire; 461
And from the bounds of Afric to the banks
Of Ganges shall his mighty arm extend.
And now, my lords and loving followers
That purchased kingdoms by your martial deeds,
Cast off your armor, put on scarlet robes,
Mount up your royal places of estate,
Environèd with troops of noblemen,
And there make laws to rule your provinces.

Hang up your weapons on Alcides'
  post,[1]   470
For Tamburlaine takes truce with all
  the world.
Thy first-betrothéd love, Arabia,
Shall we with honor, as beseems, entomb
With this great Turk and his fair em-
  peress.

[1] Doorpost of the temple.

Then, after all these solemn exequies,
We will our celebrated rites of marriage solemnize.   [*Exeunt.*]

Finis Actus Quinti et Ultimi Hujus
      Primæ Partis.[2]

[2] The end of the fifth and last act of this first
part.

CHRISTOPHER MARLOWE

DOCTOR FAUSTUS

Like so many Elizabethan plays, *The Tragical History of the Life and Death of Doctor Faustus* presents many editorial and bibliographical puzzles. The first extant record of a performance is in 1594, the year after Marlowe's death, when Edward Alleyn and the Lord Admiral's Men were having a great success with it at the Rose on the Bankside. Although it was not a new play then, no one knows for certain just how old it was. The old and long-persistent theory was that it was one of the first plays from Marlowe's pen (perhaps 1588 or 1589); but recent scholarly opinion has tended toward later and later dates, anywhere between 1590 and 1592, and well after Greene's *Friar Bacon*. Now two dominant schools of thought exist—one basically subjective and psychologically oriented and the other objective and source-oriented. The subjectivists split among themselves and argue in different directions. As John D. Jump puts it in his 1962 edition of the play, one group of subjectivists maintains that "Marlowe's plays, taken in the order 1 and 2 *Tamburlaine, Doctor Faustus, The Jew of Malta,* and *Edward II,* illustrate a progressive decline of humanist faith." But another group believes that "If the plays are taken in the order 1 and 2 *Tamburlaine, The Jew of Malta, Edward II,* and *Doctor Faustus,* they can be seen to illustrate an increasingly defiant assertion of individualism, followed by the eventual recognition of its necessary limitations." The objective approach can be used to support either order, but is probably stronger for a late date for *Faustus.* It depends for evidence entirely on Marlowe's relationship to his main source, the first full-length presentation of the story of Faustus for sixteenth-century readers.

There seems to be no doubt that there had actually been a George or John Faustus active in the early sixteenth century, but the first accounts of him were relatively brief and contradictory, presenting him in various lights, from a mere wandering scholar and fortune-teller of questionable morality to a magician whose pact with the devil led to his dreadful death. In 1587, however, a lengthy and circumstantial story with a title beginning *Historia von D. Iohañ Faustus* . . . (now known as the "German Faust-buch") was published at Frankfurt-am-Main by an anonymous German Protestant. Five years later an Englishman, signing himself only "P. F." but calling himself a gentleman, produced his translation of the German, with many additions of his own. These additions make it certain that Marlowe used the English version rather than the German, since many passages in his play are based on episodes and phraseology absent from the original German. The title of the earliest extant edition of P. F.'s account began: *The History of the Damnable Life and Deserved Death of Doctor John Faustus* . . . . It is possible that Marlowe could have seen this book in manuscript before its publication, or that there had been an earlier published edition (as argued by Paul H. Kocher in "The Early Date for Marlowe's *Faustus,*" *MLN,* 1943), in which case he could have written his play before 1592; if he did not see it, then 1592 sets a limiting date. Kocher, in "The Witchcraft Basis in Marlowe's *Faustus*" (*MP,* 1938), showed that Marlowe supplemented this source material with his own knowledge of Renaissance, medieval, and classical ideas about witchcraft. And Beatrice Dawe Browne contended that Marlowe was also influenced by the legends about the first century Samaritan Gnostic, Simon Magus the magician ("Marlowe, Faustus, and Simon Magus," *PMLA,* 1937).

(For a detailed discussion of all these matters, see the introduction to W. W. Greg's parallel-text edition of *Marlowe's Doctor Faustus/1604–1616*, Oxford, 1950.)

The situation is further complicated by two facts: that no printed version of Marlowe's play is extant before 1604, though it had been entered on the Stationers' Register early in 1601, and that the 1604 version is a third shorter than the next extant edition of 1616. Until very recently it was the almost universal opinion that the short version, in spite of a text manifestly corrupt in many passages, gave the closest possible approach to Marlowe's original, and that the 1616 version had simply expanded the earlier one by adding new episodes and comic passages to appeal more fully to Jacobean tastes. This explanation was supported by the fact that already, in November 1602, Henslowe had paid £4 to William Birde and Samuel Rowley, hack writers, "for ther adicyones in doctor fostes." In 1950, however, W. W. Greg published his four hundred page parallel-text edition of the play, in which he proved to the satisfaction of most scholars that in reality the longer version, though also corrupt in some places, represented Marlowe's original play, and that the earlier and shorter version was actually a sort of pirated text which had been put together, perhaps for touring purposes, by actors or reporters relying on their memories. Apparently, in setting up the 1616 version, the printer made some use of the earlier text, and Boas based his choice of the 1616 text for his 1932 edition on the speculation that two different Marlovian manuscripts were extant, each leading to a different playbook. About the same time, Leo Kirschbaum had independently reached similar conclusions ("The Good and Bad Quartos of *Doctor Faustus*," *The Library*, 1946). Nevertheless, as late as 1964, Warren D. Smith defended the 1604 text because he felt it showed more clearly the "vast discrepancy between the actuality of the experience of the hero . . . and his anticipation as he signs the fatal document" ("The Nature of Evil in *Doctor Faustus*," *MLR*, 1964). For the benefit of those readers who also prefer a better balance between the comical and the serious scenes, or who might wish to compare the two versions, it may be said that the longer version derives chiefly from the following scenes, which either do not appear at all in the 1604 text or are expansions of it: II, iii; III, i-ii; IV, i-vii; V, i-ii. Minor differences in dialogue or in phraseology also occur in other scenes.

Another of the play's problems which have bothered ordinary readers as well as scholars is the seemingly incongruous mixture of farce and even horseplay with the serious intellectual theorizing and ultimate agonizing tragedy of Faustus. The most frequent and obvious explanation is that these passages could not have been by Marlowe (who was supposed to have no sense of humor), and that they were foisted on the play by one or more collaborators, not necessarily selected or approved by him. Greg was inclined to accept the comic scenes in the papal and imperial courts as having been written by Rowley, with the collaboration of Marlowe, but thought that those commissioned by Henslowe to Rowley and Birde were presumably lost. Assuming that Rowley was the author of the 1616 text's episode concerning "Saxon Bruno" as the Emperor's candidate for the papacy, Leslie M. Oliver suggested that the source of this comic and satirical scene was John Foxe's *Acts and Monuments* . . . , popularly known as "Foxe's Book of Martyrs" ("Rowley, Foxe, and the *Faustus* Additions," *MLN*, 1945). Kocher, by assembling a large number of parallel passages in the 1604 prose scenes of the play and in Nashe's prose works, speculated on "Nashe's Authorship of the Prose Scenes in *Faustus*" (*HLQ*, 1942). As time has passed, however, more and more critics have been defending these farcical scenes as necessary to the total design of the play, instead of apologizing for them as excrescences and concessions to the groundlings. Greg took this position in "The Damnation of Faustus" (*MLN*, 1946), and insisted that, whoever wrote them, they must have been part of Marlowe's original intention and under his control. F. P. Wilson, in *Marlowe and the Early Shakespeare* (Oxford, 1952), took the same position, and so did Robert Ornstein in "The Comic Synthesis in *Doctor Faustus*" (*ELH*, 1955), asserting that the intention of the comedy in the play is both didactic and comic and clarifies our perception of the moral values involved. The measure of Faustus's tragic fall is the increasing discrepancy between his aspirations and his achievements, and the tragic and the comic approach each other until "the difference between hero and clown is one of degree, not kind." Ribner, in "Marlowe's 'Tragicke Glasse,' " and John H. Crabtree, Jr., in "The Comedy in Marlowe's *Doctor Faustus*" (*Furman University Studies*, 1961), reached these same conclusions. Muriel C. Bradbrook, however, offered the most provocative comment in her article on "Marlowe's *Doctor Faustus* and the Eldritch Tradition" (*Essays on Shakespeare and Elizabethan Drama*). While admitting that "much of the conjuring which fills the middle of the play may now seem irrelevant and tasteless," she suggested tying the comic and tragic scenes together according to the principles of "the eldritch tradition" (a Scotch term for the weird and the uncanny).

> Eldritch diabolism, while both comic and terrific, is amoral . . . . The cackle of ghoulish laughter is essential to winter's tales of sprites and goblins, phantoms and illusions . . . . Faustus's own tricks vary from those of the common conjurer to those of the eldritch 'shape-changer'; his transformations, though devoid of the moral significance which burns in the scenes of choice, combine the comic and the horrific, being designed to raise at once a shudder and a guffaw.

Adding that in Marlowe's day this kind of mirth was often combined "with anti-papal stories, with scurrilities and fabliaux in the popular jestbooks of the common press," she concluded that the "savage comic humor" which T. S. Eliot had discerned in Marlowe was in the eldritch tradition, and displayed itself most clearly in *Doctor Faustus* and parts of *The Jew of Malta*.

The remaining major problem propounded by the play and, ideologically, the most important of all, concerns Marlowe's own attitude toward Faustus and the attitude he wished his audience to take toward him. Should Faustus be regarded as a "hero" or simply a "protagonist"—even, at times, an "antagonist"? Is this a Christian or an anti-Christian play? Was the author still the "atheist" many continued to call him after his death, or was he a repentant sinner, pleading for understanding and mercy? Is the surface "moral" the true moral? Again there are two schools of thought on the matter.

From the Christian point of view, Leo Kirschbaum, for example, in "Marlowe's *Faustus: A Reconsideration*" (*RES*, 1943), insisted that "there is no more obvious Christian doctrine in all Elizabethan literature than *Doctor Faustus*;" and Ribner, in "Marlowe's 'Tragicke Glasse', " went almost as far: "If he had lived longer, perhaps Marlowe might have written a play of true Christian affirmation, but he did not do so in *Doctor Faustus*, . . . though in *Doctor Faustus* he seemed to be moving closer than ever to traditional Christianity." Kocher put it in a slightly different way in his book on Marlowe: "However desperate his desire to be free, he was bound to Christianity by the surest of chains—hatred mingled with reluctant longing, and fascination much akin to fear." Hardly any critic would dissent from the view that one of the main themes of the play is the conflict between salvation and damnation of Faustus's soul, and Leonard H. Frey has called attention to the focusing of this theme in his "Antithetical Balance in the Opening and Close of *Doctor Faustus*" (*MLQ*, 1963). Another way of looking at the same situation is to focus on Faustus's conscience, as Lily B. Campbell has done in "*Doctor Faustus*: A Case of Conscience" (*PMLA*, 1952). She noted that the play's ending in the sin of despair was similar to the celebrated and much-publicized contemporary case of the Italian lawyer, Francis Spira. Miss Campbell also called attention to the influence of the morality play as shown in the presence of the Good and Evil Angels, the Seven Deadly Sins, and the Old Man. Arieh Sachs similarly argued that the "spiritual crime of Faustus is a religious despair of salvation, seen as springing from the primordial guilt of Pride, but sufficiently recurrent in the play to justify our regarding it as Faustus's main transgression" ("The Religious Despair of Doctor Faustus," *JEGP*, 1964).

Before either of these articles appeared, John C. McCloskey had written on "The Theme of Despair in Marlowe's *Faustus*" (*CE*, 1942). Joseph T. McCullen found the main root of this despair in Faustus's limited and defective knowledge, due chiefly to the sin of Sloth ("*Doctor Faustus* and Renaissance Learning," *MLR*, 1955). In concluding that "it is as reasonable to consider *Doctor Faustus* a moral play as to conclude that it is largely a drama of Revolt," McCullen introduced the second attitude toward Faustus—that is, as the Renaissance scholar and rebel. Nan C. Carpenter found this theme of "lust for learning" focused in the debate between Faustus and the Knight in the Emperor's court (" 'Miles' vs. 'Clericus' in Marlowe's *Faustus*," *NQ*, 1952). Boas emphasized the same aspect of Renaissance learning and expressed the most widely accepted interpretation of Marlowe's own attitude toward his "hero" when he wrote: "The fascination of the play lies in the fact that while Marlowe shows that Faustus cannot escape the terrible penalty of his pact with the devil, he represents him not as 'a wretched creature,' but as the embodiment of the 'soaring Renaissance aspiration to exploit newly-revealed sources of beauty, knowledge, and power' " (review of Kirschbaum's article, *YWES*, 1943). Clifford Davidson found a special significance in the fact that Marlowe had located his setting in Wittenberg, in "the intellectual milieu of the Wittenberg Reformers, the focus of whose religious views centered upon man's salvation" ("Doctor Faustus of Wittenberg," *SP*, 1962). Many critics, such as Roma Gill in her edition of the play for the New Mermaids series in 1965, have pointed to the inadequacy of Faustus's goals and achievements when measured against his aspirations as another aspect of his tragedy. The only episode in which Faustus comes close to consummating his ambitions is in his lyrical vision of Helen of Troy—and even here, some critics, like Ribner, raise the question of whether the figure Mephostophilis summons for him is the real Helen or only a succuba. (A valuable discussion of the play, its background, ideas, and problems, is in the monograph by J. P. Brockbank: *Marlowe: Dr. Faustus*, London, 1962.)

The present text follows, in general, that of 1616 as established by John D. Jump in his edition of the play for the Revels series in 1962; but some use has also been made of Greg and of Roma Gill's edition in the New Mermaids series (1965).

THE TRAGICAL HISTORY OF THE LIFE AND DEATH OF DOCTOR FAUSTUS[1]

BY

CHRISTOPHER MARLOWE

[DRAMATIS PERSONÆ

CHORUS.
DR. JOHN FAUSTUS.
WAGNER, *his servant, a student.*
VALDES } *his friends, magicians.*
CORNELIUS
THREE SCHOLARS, *students under* Faustus.
AN OLD MAN.
POPE ADRIAN.
RAYMOND, *King of Hungary.*
BRUNO, *the rival pope.*
CARDINALS OF FRANCE *and* PADUA.
THE ARCHBISHOP OF RHEIMS.
CHARLES V, *Emperor of Germany.*
MARTINO
FREDERICK } *knights at the Emperor's court.*
BENVOLIO
DUKE OF SAXONY.
DUKE OF VANHOLT.
DUCHESS OF VANHOLT.

ROBIN, *also called the* CLOWN.
DICK.
A VINTNER.
A HORSE-COURSER.[2]
A CARTER.
THE HOSTESS *at an inn.*
THE GOOD ANGEL.
THE BAD ANGEL.
MEPHOSTOPHILIS.
LUCIFER.
BELZEBUB.
SPIRITS *presenting*
  THE SEVEN DEADLY SINS,
  ALEXANDER THE GREAT,
  ALEXANDER'S PARAMOUR,
  DARIUS, *King of Persia,*
  HELEN OF TROY.
Devils, Bishops, Monks, Soldiers, *and*
  Attendants.

PLACE: *Germany.*

TIME: *Early sixteenth century.*]

PROLOGUE

Enter Chorus.

CHORUS. Not marching in the fields of
  Thrasimene,

Where Mars did mate[3] the warlike
  Carthagens,
Nor sporting in the dalliance of love
In courts of kings, where state is over-
  turned,
Nor in the pomp of proud audacious
  deeds,
Intends our Muse to vaunt his heavenly
  verse:

---

[1] The title of the 1604 edition reads: "The Tragical History of Dr. Faustus. As It Hath Been Acted by the Right Honorable The Earl of Nottingham His Servants. Written by Ch. Marl."

[2] Dealer in horses.   [3] Join.

487

Only this, Gentles—we must now perform
The form[1] of Faustus' fortunes, good or bad.
And now to patient judgments we appeal,
And speak for Faustus in his infancy. [10
Now is he born, of parents base of stock,
In Germany, within a town called Rhode;[2]
At riper years to Wittenberg he went,
Whereas[3] his kinsmen chiefly brought him up;
So much he profits in divinity,
The fruitful plot of scholarism graced,
That shortly he was graced with doctor's name,[4]
Excelling all, whose sweet delight disputes
In th' heavenly matters of theology,
Till, swollen with cunning,[5] of a self-conceit,   20
His waxen wings did mount above his reach,
And, melting, heavens conspired his overthrow:
For, falling to a devilish exercise,
And glutted now with learning's golden gifts,
He surfeits upon curséd necromancy.
Nothing so sweet as magic is to him,
Which he prefers before his chiefest bliss.[6]
And this the man that in his study sits!

Exit.

ACT I. SCENE i.

Faustus in his study [reading].

FAUST. Settle thy studies, Faustus, and begin
To sound the depth of that thou wilt profess;[7]
Having commenced,[8] be a divine in show,[9]
Yet level at the end of every art,
And live and die in Aristotle's works.

Sweet *Analytics,* 'tis thou hast ravished me.
"Bene disserere est finis logices:"
Is to dispute well logic's chiefest end?
Affords this art no greater miracle?
Then read no more, thou hast attained that end;   10
A greater subject fitteth Faustus' wit.
Bid *on kai me on*[10] farewell. Galen, come:
Seeing, *"ubi desinit philosophus, ibi incipit medicus."*[11]
Be a physician, Faustus, heap up gold,
And be eternized[12] for some wondrous cure.
"Summum bonum medicinæ sanitas:"
The end of physic is our body's health.
Why, Faustus, hast thou not attained that end?
Is not thy common talk sound aphorisms?[13]
Are not thy bills[14] hung up as monuments,   20
Whereby whole cities have escaped the plague,
And thousand desperate maladies been cured?
Yet art thou still but Faustus, and a man.
Couldst thou make men to live eternally,
Or, being dead, raise them to life again,
Then this profession were to be esteemed.
Physic, farewell! Where is Justinian?
*"Si una eademque res legatur duobus,
Alter rem, alter valorem rei,"*[15] etc.
A petty case of paltry legacies!   30
"Exhereditare filium non potest pater nisi—"[16]
Such is the subject of the Institute
And universal body of the law.
This study fits a mercenary drudge,
Who aims at nothing but external trash,
Too servile and illiberal for me.
When all is done, divinity is best:
Jerome's Bible,[17] Faustus, view it well:
"Stipendium peccati mors est." Ha!
"Stipendium," etc.

---

[1] Course.
[2] Now Stadtroda, in central Germany.
[3] Where.
[4] At Cambridge a new Doctor of Divinity was enrolled in the Book of Grace.
[5] Learning.
[6] *I.e.,* hope of salvation.
[7] Study and teach.
[8] Graduated.
[9] Appearance.

[10] Being and not being.
[11] Where the philosopher stops, there the doctor begins.
[12] Immortalized.
[13] Medical maxims.   [14] Prescriptions.
[15] If one and the same thing is bequeathed to two persons, one gets the thing, the other the value of the thing.
[16] A father cannot disinherit his son unless—
[17] The Vulgate.

The reward of sin is death? That's
hard.   40
*"Si peccasse negamus, fallimur, et nulla
est in nobis veritas:"*
If we say that we have no sin, we deceive
ourselves, and there is no truth in us.
Why then, belike, we must sin, and so
consequently die.
Ay, we must die an everlasting death.
What doctrine call you this? *"Che
sarà, sarà:"*
What will be, shall be.   Divinity,
adieu!—
These metaphysics of magicians   50
And necromantic books are heavenly:
Lines, circles, signs, letters, and char-
acters!
Ay, these are those that Faustus most
desires.
O, what a world of profit and delight,
Of power, of honor, of omnipotence,
Is promised to the studious artisan![1]
All things that move between the quiet
poles
Shall be at my command: emperors and
kings
Are but obeyed in their several provinces,
Nor can they raise the wind, or rend the
clouds;   60
But his dominion that exceeds[2] in this
Stretcheth as far as doth the mind of
man:
A sound magician is a mighty god.
Here, Faustus, try thy brains to gain a
deity.—

Enter Wagner.

Wagner! Commend me to my dearest
friends,
The German Valdes and Cornelius;
Request them earnestly to visit me.
WAG. I will, sir.   *Exit.*
FAUST. Their conference will be a greater
help to me
Than all my labors, plod I ne'er so
fast.   70

Enter the Angel and Spirit.

GOOD A. O Faustus, lay that damnéd book
aside,
And gaze not on it lest it tempt thy
soul,

---

[1] Student of a liberal art.
[2] Excels.

And heap God's heavy wrath upon thy
head!
Read, read the Scriptures; that is
blasphemy.
BAD A. Go forward, Faustus, in that
famous art
Wherein all nature's treasury[3] is con-
tained:
Be thou on earth as Jove is in the sky,
Lord and commander of these elements.
                          Exeunt [Angels].
FAUST. How am I glutted with conceit[4] of
this!
Shall I make spirits fetch me what I
please?   80
Resolve me of all ambiguities?[5]
Perform what desperate enterprise I
will?
I'll have them fly to India[6] for gold;
Ransack the ocean for orient pearl,
And search all corners of the new-found
world
For pleasant fruits and princely deli-
cates.[7]
I'll have them read me strange phi-
losophy,
And tell the secrets of all foreign kings;
I'll have them wall all Germany with
brass,
And make swift Rhine circle fair Witten-
berg;   90
I'll have them fill the public schools[8] with
silk,[9]
Wherewith the students shall be bravely[10]
clad.
I'll levy soldiers with the coin they bring,
And chase the Prince of Parma from our
land,
And reign sole king of all our provinces.
Yea, stranger engines[11] for the brunt of
war
Than was the fiery keel at Antwerp's
bridge,
I'll make my servile spirits to invent.
Come, German Valdes and Cornelius,
And make me blessed with your sage
conference.   100

---

[3] Treasure.
[4] Saturated with the thought.
[5] Free me from all uncertainties.
[6] Perhaps the American Indies.
[7] Delicacies.
[8] University lecture rooms.
[9] Emended by Dyce. Quartos read *skill*.
[10] Timely.   [11] Machines.

Enter Valdes and Cornelius.

Valdes, sweet Valdes, and Cornelius,
Know that your words have won me at
    the last
To practise magic and concealéd arts;
Yet not your words only, but mine own
    fantasy,
That will receive no object for my head
But[1] ruminates on necromantic skill.
Philosophy is odious and obscure;
Both law and physic are for petty wits;
Divinity is basest of the three,
Unpleasant, harsh, contemptible, and
    vile.   110
'Tis magic, magic that hath ravished me.
Then, gentle friends, aid me in this
    attempt,
And I, that have with concise syllogisms
Gravelled the pastors of the German
    church
And made the flowering pride of Witten-
    berg
Swarm to my problems,[2] as th'infernal
    spirits
On sweet Musæus when he came to hell,
Will be as cunning as Agrippa was,
Whose shadows[3] made all Europe honor
    him.
VALD. Faustus, these books, thy wit, and
    our experience   120
Shall make all nations to canonise us.
As Indian Moors[4] obey their Spanish
    lords,
So shall the spirits of every element
Be always serviceable to us three;
Like lions shall they guard us when we
    please,
Like Almaine rutters[5] with their horse-
    men's staves,
Or Lapland giants trotting by our sides;
Sometimes like women or unwedded
    maids,
Shadowing more beauty in their airy
    brows
Than have the white breasts of the Queen
    of Love.   130
From Venice shall they drag huge
    argosies
And from America the golden fleece

That yearly stuffs old Philip's treasury,
If learnéd Faustus will be resolute.
FAUST. Valdes, as resolute am I in this,
As thou to live; therefore object it not.
CORN. The miracles that magic will per-
    form
Will make thee vow to study nothing
    else.
He that is grounded in astrology,
Enriched with tongues,[6] well seen[7] in
    minerals,   140
Hath all the principles magic doth
    require.
Then doubt not, Faustus, but to be
    renowned,
And more frequented[8] for this mystery
Than heretofore the Delphian oracle.
The spirits tell me they can dry the sea,
And fetch the treasure of all foreign
    wrecks;
Yea, all the wealth that our forefathers
    hid
Within the massy[9] entrails of the earth.
Then tell me, Faustus, what shall we
    three want?
FAUST. Nothing, Cornelius! O, this cheers
    my soul!   150
Come, show me some demonstrations
    magical,
That I may conjure in some lusty[10]
    grove,
And have these joys in full possession.
VALD. Then haste thee to some solitary
    grove,
And bear wise Bacon's and Abanus'
    works,
The Hebrew Psalter, and New Testa-
    ment;
And whatsoever else is requisite,
We will inform thee ere our conference
    cease.
CORN. Valdes, first let him know the words
    of art,
And then, all other ceremonies learned,
                                            160
Faustus may try his cunning by himself.
VALD. First I'll instruct him in the rudi-
    ments,
And then wilt thou be perfecter than I.
FAUST. The come and dine with me, and
    after meat

[1] Supply *that which*.
[2] Disputations.
[3] Spirits.
[4] American Indians.
[5] German cavalry.

[6] Languages.   [9] Solid.
[7] Informed.   [10] Pleasant.
[8] Sought after.

We'll canvass every quiddity[1] thereof:
For ere I sleep, I'll try what I can do.
This night I'll conjure though I die
therefore.

Exeunt omnes.

ACT I. SCENE ii.

[*Before Faustus' house.*]

Enter two Scholars.

1 SCH. I wonder what's become of
Faustus, that was wont to make our schools
ring with *sic probo.*[2]

2 SCH. That shall we presently[3] know;
here comes his boy.

Enter Wagner.

1 SCH. How now, sirrah! Where's thy
master?

WAG. God in heaven knows.

2 SCH. Why, dost not thou know then?

WAG. Yes, I know, but that follows   [10
not.

1 SCH. Go to, sirrah! Leave your jesting,
and tell us where he is.

WAG. That follows not by force of argument, which you, being licentiates,[4] should
stand upon; therefore, acknowledge your
error and be attentive.

2 SCH. Then you will not tell us?

WAG. You are deceived, for I will tell
you; yet if you were not dunces, you   [20
would never ask me such a question. For
is he not *corpus naturale*?[5] And is not that
mobile?[5] Then wherefore should you ask
me such a question? But that I am by
nature phlegmatic, slow to wrath, and
prone to lechery—to love, I would say—
it were not for you to come within forty
foot of the place of execution,[6] although I
do not doubt but to see you both hanged
the next sessions. Thus having tri-   [30
umphed over you, I will set my countenance like a precisian,[7] and begin to speak
thus: "Truly, my dear brethren, my master
is within at dinner, with Valdes and Cornelius, as this wine, if it could speak,
would inform your worships; and so the
Lord bless you, preserve you, and keep you,
my dear brethren."   *Exit.*

1 SCH. Nay, then, I fear he is fallen into
that damned art for which they two   [40
are infamous through the world.

2 SCH. Were he a stranger, and not
allied to me, yet should I grieve for him.
But come, let us go and inform the Rector,
and see if he by his grave counsel can
reclaim him.

1 SCH. I fear me, nothing will reclaim
him now.

2 SCH. Yet let us see what we can do.
Exeunt.

ACT I. SCENE iii.

[*A grove.*]

*Thunder. Enter Lucifer and four Devils
above. Faustus to them, with this speech.*

FAUST. Now that the gloomy shadow of
the earth,
Longing to view Orion's drizzling look,
Leaps from th'antarctic world unto the
sky,
And dims the welkin with her pitchy
breath,
Faustus, begin thine incantations,
And try if devils will obey thy hest,[8]
Seeing thou hast prayed and sacrificed to
them.
Within this circle is Jehovah's name,
Forward and backward anagrammatized,
Th'abbreviated names of holy saints,   [10
Figures of every adjunct[9] to the heavens,
And characters of signs and erring stars,[10]
By which the spirits are enforced to rise.
Then fear not, Faustus, but be resolute
And try the uttermost magic can
perform.

(*Thunder.*)

*Sint mihi dei Acherontis propitii, valeat
numen triplex Jehovæ; ignei, aerii,
aquatici, terreni spiritus salvete! Orientis
princeps, Belzebub inferni ardentis mon-
archa, et Demogorgon, propitiamus vos,   [20
ut appareat, et surgat Mephostophilis.*

(*Dragon*)[11]

---

[1] Detail, essence.   [2] Thus I prove it.   [3] At once.
[4] Graduates, licensed to study for higher
degrees.
[5] A natural body; a movable body. Terms
used in the physics of the day.
[6] The room within, where Faustus is dining.
[7] Puritan.

[8] Behest, command.   [9] Star.
[10] Signs of the Zodiac and planets.
[11] Leo Kirshbaum, "Mephostophilis and the
Lost Dragon," *RES* for 1942, suggests that this
may be a warning to the property man to prepare the dragon, in the form of which the Devil,
Mephostophilis, is to enter.

Quid tu moraris?   Per Jehovam, Gehen-
nam, et consecratam aquam, quam nunc [20
spargo; signumque crucis quod nunc facio;
et per vota nostra, ipse nunc surgat nobis
dicatus Mephostophilis.[1]

Enter a Devil.

I charge thee to return and change thy
    shape;
Thou art too ugly to attend on me.
Go and return an old Franciscan friar;
That holy shape becomes a devil best.
                    Exit Devil.   [30
I see there's virtue in my heavenly words!
Who would not be proficient in this art?
How pliant is this Mephostophilis,
Full of obedience and humility!
Such is the force of magic and my spells.
Now, Faustus, thou art conjuror lau-
    reate,
That canst command great Mephos-
    tophilis.
Quin   redis,   Mephostophilis,   fratris
imagine?[2]

Enter Mephostophilis [as a Franciscan friar].

MEPH. Now, Faustus, what wouldst thou
    have me do?
FAUST. I charge thee wait upon me whilst
    I live   40
To do whatever Faustus shall command.
Be it to make the moon drop from her
    sphere,
Or the ocean to overwhelm the world.
MEPH. I am a servant to great Lucifer,
And may not follow thee without his
    leave;
No more than he commands, must we
    perform.
FAUST. Did not he charge thee to appear
    to me?
MEPH. No, I came now hither of mine own
    accord.

[1] May the gods of Acheron be propitious to
me. Away with the three-fold godhead of
Jehovah. Welcome, spirts of fire, air, water, and
earth. We ask your favor, O prince of the East,
Belzebub, monarch of burning hell, and Demogorgon, that Mephostophilis may appear and
rise.   Why dost thou delay?   By Jehovah,
Gehenna, and the holy water which I now
sprinkle, and the sign of the cross which I now
make, and by our vows, may Mephostophilis
himself now rise, commanded by us.
[2] Why dost thou not return, Mephostophilis,
in the likeness of a friar?

FAUST. Did not my conjuring speeches
    raise thee? Speak!
MEPH. That was the cause, but yet *per*
    accidens:[3]   50
For when we hear one rack the name of
    God,
Abjure the Scriptures, and his savior
    Christ,
We fly in hope to get his glorious soul;
Nor will we come unless he use such
    means
Whereby he is in danger to be damned.
Therefore the shortest cut for conjuring
Is stoutly to abjure the Trinity
And pray devoutly to the prince of hell.
FAUST. So Faustus hath
Already done, and holds this princi-
    ple: 60
There is no chief but only Belzebub,
To whom Faustus doth dedicate himself.
This word "damnation" terrifies not him,
For he confounds hell in Elysium.[4]
His ghost be with the old philosophers.[5]
But, leaving these vain trifles of men's
    souls,
Tell me, what is that Lucifer, thy lord?
MEPH. Arch-regent and commander of all
    spirits.
FAUST. Was not that Lucifer an angel
    once?
MEPH. Yes, Faustus, and most dearly
    loved of God.   70
FAUST. How comes it then that he is prince
    of devils?
MEPH. O, by aspiring pride and insolence,
For which God threw him from the face
    of heaven.
FAUST. And what are you that live with
    Lucifer?
MEPH. Unhappy spirits that fell with
    Lucifer,
Conspired against our God with Lucifer,
And are for ever damned with Lucifer.
FAUST. Where are you damned?
MEPH.   In hell.
FAUST. How comes it then that thou art
    out of hell?   80

[3] By chance.
[4] *I.e.*, he makes no distinction between the
Christian and the pagan concepts of the afterlife.
[5] *I.e.*, those who, like him, disbelieved in an
eternity of punishment. The line seems to come
from a saying of Averroes, '*Sit anima mea cum*
philosophis' (*cf.* J. C. Maxwell, NQ, 1949; J. M.
Steadman, NQ, 1962).

MEPH. Why, this is hell, nor am I out of it.
  Think'st thou that I, who saw the face
    of God,
  And tasted the eternal joys of heaven,
  Am not tormented with ten thousand
    hells,
  In being deprived of everlasting
    bliss?
  O Faustus, leave these frivolous de-
    mands,
  Which strike a terror to my fainting soul.
FAUST. What, is great Mephostophilis so
    passionate¹
  For being deprivéd of the joys of heaven?
  Learn thou of Faustus manly forti-
    tude,   90
  And scorn those joys thou never shalt
    possess.
  Go bear these tidings to great Lucifer:
  Seeing Faustus hath incurred eternal
    death,
  By desperate thoughts against Jove's
    deity,
  Say he surrenders up to him his soul,
  So he will spare him four and twenty
    years,
  Letting him live in all voluptuousness,
  Having thee ever to attend on me,
  To give me whatsoever I shall ask;
  To tell me whatsoever I demand;   100
  To slay mine enemies, and aid my friends,
  And always be obedient to my will.
  Go, and return to mighty Lucifer,
  And meet me in my study, at midnight,
  And then resolve me of thy master's
    mind.
MEPH. I will, Faustus.   Exit.
FAUST. Had I as many souls as there be
    stars,
  I'd give them all for Mephostophilis.
  By him, I'll be great conqueror of the
    world,
  And make a bridge th[o]rough the mov-
    ing air   110
  To pass the ocean with a band of men;
  I'll join the hills that bind the Afric
    shore,
  And make that country continent to
    Spain,
  And both contributory to my crown.
  The emperor shall not live but by my
    leave,
  Nor any potentate of Germany.
  ¹ Moved.

Now that I have obtained what I desired
I'll live in speculation of this art
Till Mephostophilis return again.   Exit.

ACT I. SCENE iv.

[A street.]

Enter Wagner and the Clown.

WAG. Come hither, sirrah boy.
CLO. Boy? O disgrace to my person!
Zounds,² boy in your face! You have seen
many boys with such pickadevants,³ I am
sure.
WAG. Sirrah, hast thou no comings in?
CLO. Yes, and goings out too, you may
see, sir. [Points to his clothes.]
WAG. Alas, poor slave, see how poverty
jests in his nakedness. The villain is [10
bare and out of service, and so hungry that
I know he would give his soul to the devil
for a shoulder of mutton, though it were
blood-raw.
CLO. Not so neither! I had need to have
it well roasted, and good sauce to it, if I
pay so dear, I can tell you.
WAG. Sirrah, wilt thou be my man and
wait on me? And I will make thee go, like
Qui mihi discipulus.⁴   20
CLO. What, in verse?
WAG. No slave, in beaten⁵ silk, and
stavesacre.⁶
CLO. Stavesacre? That's good to kill
vermin; then, belike, if I serve you, I shall
be lousy.
WAG. Why, so thou shalt be, whether
thou dost it or no, for, sirrah, if thou dost
not presently bind thyself to me for seven
years, I'll turn all the lice about thee [30
into familiars,⁷ and make them tear thee
in pieces.
CLO. Nay, sir, you may save yourself a
labor, for they are as familiar with me, as
if they paid for their meat and drink, I can
tell you.
WAG. Well, sirrah, leave your jesting, and
take these guilders.   [Gives money.]

² God's wounds.
³ French pic à devant; pointed beards.
⁴ "You who are my pupil"; the opening words
of a Latin poem by the schoolmaster and gram-
marian William Lilly.
⁵ Stamped with metal and embroidered.
⁶ Powdered larkspur seeds, used as a lice-killer.
⁷ Familiar spirits.

Clo. Gridirons, what be they?

Wag. Why, French crowns. 40

Clo. Mass, but for the name of French crowns a man were as good have as many English counters.[1]

Wag. So, now thou art to be at an hour's warning, whensoever and wheresoever the devil shall fetch thee.

Clo. Here, take your guilders again. I'll none of 'em.

Wag. Not I, thou art pressed.[2] Prepare thyself, for I will presently raise up [50 two devils to carry thee away: Baliol and Belcher!

Clo. Let your Balio and your Belcher come here, and I'll knock them, they were never so knocked since they were devils. Say I should kill one of them, what would folks say? "Do ye see yonder tall[3] fellow in the round slop,[4] he has killed the devil!" So I should be called Kill-devil all the parish over. 60

Enter two Devils, and the Clown runs up and down crying.

Wag. How now, sir, will you serve me now?

Clo. Ay, good Wagner, take the devils away then.

Wag. Spirits away!

Exeunt [Devils].

Now, sirrah, follow me.

Clo. I will, sir; but hark you, master, will you teach me this conjuring occupation?

Wag. Ay, sirrah, I'll teach thee to [70 turn thyself to a dog, or a cat, or a mouse, or a rat, or anything.

Clo. A dog, or a cat, or a mouse, or a rat? O brave, Wagner.

Wag. Villain, call me Master Wagner, and see that you walk attentively, and let your right eye be always diametrally[5] fixed upon my left heel, that thou may'st *quasi vestigias nostras insistere.*[6]

Clo. Well, sir, I warrant you. [80

Exeunt.

[1] Worthless tokens; French crowns were easily counterfeited.
[2] Enlisted.
[3] Brave.
[4] Wide breeches.
[5] Diametrically.
[6] As if to walk in our footsteps.

Act II. Scene i.

Enter Faustus in his study.

Faust. Now, Faustus, must thou needs be damned
And canst thou not be saved.
What boots it then to think on God or heaven?
Away with such vain fancies and despair.
Despair in God, and trust in Belzebub.
Now go not backward; no, Faustus, be resolute.
Why waverest thou? O, something soundeth in mine ears:
"Abjure this magic; turn to God again."
Ay, and Faustus will turn to God again.
To God? He loves thee not. 10
The God thou servest is thine own appetite
Wherein is fixed the love of Belzebub;
To him, I'll build an altar and a church,
And offer lukewarm blood of newborn babes.

Enter the two Angels.

Good A. Sweet Faustus leave that execrable art.
Faust. Contrition, prayer, repentance—what of these?
Good A. O, they are means to bring thee unto heaven.
Bad A. Rather illusions, fruits of lunacy,
That make men foolish that do trust them most.
Good A. Sweet Faustus, think of heaven, and heavenly things. 20
Bad A. No, Faustus, think of honor and of wealth. *Exeunt Angels.*
Faust. Wealth!
Why, the signory of Emden shall be mine.
When Mephostophilis shall stand by me,
What god can hurt me? Faustus, thou art safe.
Cast no more doubts; Mephostophilis, come
And bring glad tidings from great Lucifer.
Is't not midnight? Come, Mephostophilis;
Veni,[7] *veni, Mephostophilis.*

[7] Come.

Enter Mephostophilis.

Now tell me what saith Lucifer, thy   [30
    lord?

MEPH. That I shall wait on Faustus whilst
    he lives,

So he will buy my service with his soul.

FAUST. Already Faustus hath hazarded
    that for thee.

MEPH. But now thou must bequeath it
    solemnly,

And write a deed of gift with thine own
    blood,

For that security craves Lucifer.

If thou deny it, I must back to hell.

FAUST. Stay, Mephostophilis, and tell me,
    What good will my soul do thy lord?

MEPH. Enlarge his kingdom.   40

FAUST. Is that the reason why he tempts
    us thus?

MEPH. *Solamen miseris, socios habuisse
    doloris.*[1]

FAUST. Have you any pain that torture
    others?

MEPH. As great as have the human souls
    of men.

But tell me, Faustus, shall I have thy soul?

And I will be thy slave and wait on thee,

And give thee more than thou hast wit
    to ask.

FAUST. Ay, Mephostophilis, I'll give it him.

MEPH. Then, Faustus, stab thine arm
    courageously,

And bind thy soul, that at some certain
    day   50

Great Lucifer may claim it as his own,

And then be thou as great as Lucifer.

FAUST. Lo, Mephostophilis, for love of thee
    [*Stabs his arm.*]

Faustus hath cut his arm, and with his
    proper[2] blood

Assures his soul to be great Lucifer's,

Chief lord and regent of perpetual night.

View here this blood that trickles from
    mine arm,

And let it be propitious for my wish.

MEPH. But, Faustus,

Write it in manner of a deed of gift.   [60

FAUST. Ay, so I will.   [*Writes.*]
    But, Mephostophilis,

My blood congeals, and I can write no
    more.

MEPH. I'll fetch thee fire to dissolve it
    straight.   *Exit.*

FAUST. What might the staying of my
    blood portend?

Is it unwilling I should write this bill?

Why streams it not, that I may write
    afresh?

"Faustus gives to thee his soul." Ah,
    there it stayed!

Why should'st thou not? Is not thy
    soul thine own?

Then write again: "Faustus gives to thee
    his soul."

*Enter Mephostophilis with the
    Chafer[3] of Fire.*

MEPH. See, Faustus, here is fire. Set it
    on.   70

FAUST. So, now the blood begins to clear
    again.   [*Writes again.*]

Now will I make an end immediately.

MEPH. [*Aside.*] What will not I do to
    obtain his soul!

FAUST. *Consummatum est:*[4] this bill is
    ended,

And Faustus hath bequeathed his soul to
    Lucifer.

But what is this inscription on mine arm?

Homo, fuge![5] Whither should I fly?

If unto God, he'll throw me down to hell.

My senses are deceived; here's nothing
    writ.

O yes, I see it plain, even here is
    writ,   80

Homo, fuge! Yet shall not Faustus fly.

MEPH. I'll fetch him somewhat to delight
    his mind.
    Exit.

*Enter Devils, giving crowns and rich apparel
to Faustus. They dance, and then depart.
    Enter Mephostophilis.*

FAUST. What means this show? Speak,
    Mephostophilis.

MEPH. Nothing, Faustus, but to delight
    thy mind,

And let thee see what magic can perform.

FAUST. But may I raise such spirits when
    I please?

[1] It is a solace to the wretched to have had
companions in sorrow.
[2] Own.

[3] Portable grate.
[4] It is finished; the last words of Christ on the
cross.
[5] Fly, O man.

Meph. Ay, Faustus, and do greater things than these.

Faust. Then, Mephostophilis, receive this scroll,
A deed of gift, of body and of soul—
But yet conditionally, that thou perform 90
All covenants and articles between us both.

Meph. Faustus, I swear by hell and Lucifer
To effect all promises between us made.

Faust. Then hear me read it, Mephostophilis.
"On the conditions following:— First, that Faustus may be a spirit in form and substance. Secondly, that Mephostophilis shall be his servant, and at his command. Thirdly, that Mephostophilis shall do for him, and bring him what- [100 soever. Fourthly, that he shall be in his chamber or house invisible. Lastly, that he shall appear to the said John Faustus, at all times, in what form or shape soever he please.—I, John Faustus of Wittenberg, doctor, by these presents, do give both body and soul to Lucifer, Prince of the East, and his minister, Mephostophilis, and furthermore grant unto them that, four and twenty years being expired, the [110 articles above written inviolate, full power to fetch or carry the said John Faustus, body and soul, flesh, blood, or goods, into their habitation wheresoever.
By me, John Faustus."

Meph. Speak, Faustus, do you deliver this as your deed?

Faust. Ay, take it, and the devil give thee good on't.

Meph. Now, Faustus, ask what thou wilt.

Faust. First will I question with thee about hell:
Tell me, where is the place that men call hell? 120

Meph. Under the heavens.

Faust. Ay, so are all things else; but whereabouts?

Meph. Within the bowels of these elements,
Where we are tortured, and remain for ever.
Hell hath no limits, nor is circumscribed
In one self place;[1] but where we are is hell,
And where hell is, there must we ever be.

[1] One particular place.

And, to be short, when all the world dissolves,
And every creature shall be purified,
All places shall be hell that is not heaven. 130

Faust. I think hell's a fable.

Meph. Ay, think so still, till experience change thy mind.

Faust. Why, dost thou think that Faustus shall be damned?

Meph. Ay, of necessity, for here's the scroll
In which thou hast given thy soul to Lucifer.

Faust. Ay, and body too, but what of that?
Think'st thou that Faustus is so fond[2] to imagine
That after this life there is any pain?
No, these are trifles, and mere old wives' tales.

Meph. But I am an instance to prove the contrary, 140
For I tell thee I am damned, and now in hell.

Faust. Nay, and[3] this be hell, I'll willingly be damned.
What, sleeping, eating, walking, and disputing?
But leaving this, let me have a wife, the fairest maid in Germany, for I am wanton and lascivious, and cannot live without a wife.

Meph. How, a wife? I prithee, Faustus, talk not of a wife.

Faust. Nay, sweet Mephostophilis, fetch me one, for I will have one.

Meph. Well, thou wilt have one. Sit there till I come. 150
I'll fetch thee a wife in the devil's name.
[Exit.]

Enter with a Devil dressed like a woman, with fireworks.

Meph. Tell me, Faustus, how dost thou like thy wife?

Faust. A plague on her for a hot whore!
No, I'll no wife.

Meph. Marriage is but a ceremonial toy,
And if thou lovest me think no more of it.
I'll cull thee out the fairest courtesans
And bring them every morning to thy bed.

[2] Foolish.　　　　[3] If.

She whom thine eye shall like, thy heart
  shall have,
Were she as chaste as was Penelope,
As wise as Saba,[1] or as beautiful   [160
As was bright Lucifer before his fall.
Hold, take this book, peruse it thor-
  oughly.
The iterating of these lines brings gold;
The framing of this circle on the ground
Brings thunder, whirlwinds, storm, and
  lightning;
Pronounce this thrice devoutly to thyself,
And men in harness[2] shall appear to thee,
Ready to execute what thou command'st.
FAUST. Thanks, Mephostophilis; yet fain
would I have a book wherein I might   [170
behold all spells and incantations, that I
might raise up spirits when I please.
MEPH. Here they are in this book.
                    There turn to them.
FAUST. Now would I have a book where
I might see all characters and planets of
the heavens, that I might know their
motions and dispositions.[3]
MEPH. Here they are too.
                    Turn to them.
FAUST. Nay, let me have one book more,
and then I have done, wherein I   [180
might see all plants, herbs, and trees that
grow upon the earth.
MEPH. Here they be.
FAUST. O, thou art deceived.
MEPH. Tut, I warrant thee.
                    Turn to them.
                    Exeunt.

ACT II. SCENE ii.

*Enter Faustus in his study
and Mephostophilis.*

FAUST. When I behold the heavens, then
  I repent
And curse thee, wicked Mephostophilis,
Because thou hast deprived me of those
  joys.
MEPH. 'Twas thine own seeking, Faustus.
  Thank thyself.
But think'st thou heaven is such a
  glorious thing?
I tell thee, Faustus, it is not half so fair

[1] The Queen of Sheba.
[2] Armor.
[3] Situations in relation to their influence on
men.

As thou, or any man that breathes on
  earth.
FAUST. How prov'st thou that?
MEPH. 'Twas made for man; then he's
  more excellent.
FAUST. If heaven was made for man, 'twas
  made for me.   10
I will renounce this magic and repent.

Enter the two Angels.

GOOD A. Faustus, repent; yet God will
  pity thee.
BAD A. Thou art a spirit; God cannot pity
  thee.
FAUST. Who buzzeth in mine ears I am a
  spirit?
Be I a devil, yet God may pity me,
Yea, God will pity me if I repent.
EVIL A. Ay, but Faustus never shall
  repent.   *Exeunt Angels.*
FAUST. My heart's so hardened I cannot
  repent!
Scarce can I name salvation, faith, or
  heaven,
But fearful echoes thunders in mine
  ears,   20
"Faustus, thou art damned." Then
  swords and knives,
Poison, guns, halters, and envenomed
  steel
Are laid before me to dispatch myself.
And long ere this, I should have done the
  deed,
Had not sweet pleasure conquered deep
  despair.
Have not I made blind Homer sing to me
Of Alexander's love, and Œnon's death?
And hath not he that built the walls of
  Thebes
With ravishing sound of his melodious
  harp
Made music with my Mephostophilis? [30
Why should I die then, or basely despair?
I am resolved! Faustus shall not repent.
Come, Mephostophilis, let us dispute
  again,
And reason of divine astrology.
Speak, are there many spheres above the
  moon?
Are all celestial bodies but one globe,
As is the substance of this centric earth?
MEPH. As are the elements, such are the
  heavens,

Even from the moon unto the empyreal
   orb,
Mutually folded in each other's
   spheres,   40
And jointly move upon one axletree,
Whose termine[1] is termed the world's
   wide pole.
Nor are the names of Saturn, Mars, or
   Jupiter,
Feigned, but are erring stars.

FAUST. But have they all one motion,
both *situ et tempore?*[2]

MEPH. All move from east to west in
four and twenty hours, upon the poles of
the world, but differ in their motions upon
the poles of the zodiac.   50

FAUST. These slender questions Wagner
   can decide!
Hath   Mephostophilis   no   greater
   skill?
Who knows not the double motion of the
   planets?
That the first is finished in a natural day,
   the second thus:
Saturn in thirty years; Jupiter in twelve;
Mars in four; the Sun, Venus, and Mercury in a year; the Moon in twenty-
   eight days. These are freshmen's suppositions. But tell me, hath every sphere
   a dominion or *intelligentia?*[3]   60

MEPH. Ay.

FAUST. How many heavens, or spheres,
are there?

MEPH. Nine: the seven planets, the
firmament, and the empyreal heaven.

FAUST. But is there not *cælum igneum?
et cristallinum?*[4]

MEPH. No, Faustus, they be but fables.

FAUST. Resolve me then in this one
question: why are not conjunctions, [70
oppositions, aspects, eclipses, all at one
time, but in some years we have more, in
some less?

MEPH. *Per inæqualem motum, respectu
totius.*[5]

FAUST. Well, I am answered. Now tell
me who made the world?

MEPH. I will not.

FAUST. Sweet Mephostophilis, tell me.

MEPH. Move[6] me not, Faustus.   80

FAUST. Villain, have not I bound thee
to tell me anything?

MEPH. Ay, that is not against our kingdom. This is. Thou art damned; think
thou on hell.

FAUST. Think, Faustus, upon God, that
   made the world.

MEPH. Remember this!   *Exit.*

FAUST. Ay, go, accursèd spirit, to ugly hell.
'Tis thou hast damned distressèd Faus-
   tus' soul.   90
Is't not too late?

Enter the two Angels.

BAD A. Too late.

GOOD A. Never too late, if Faustus will
   repent.

BAD A. If thou repent, devils will tear
thee in pieces.

GOOD A. Repent, and they shall never
raze[7] thy skin.   *Exeunt Angels.*

FAUST. O Christ, my savior, my savior,
   Help to save distressèd Faustus' soul!

Enter Lucifer, Belzebub, and Mephostophilis.

LUC. Christ cannot save thy soul, for he is
   just;
There's none but I have interest in the
   same.   100

FAUST. O, what art thou that look'st so
   terribly?

LUC. I am Lucifer, and this is my companion prince in hell.

FAUST. O Faustus, they are come to fetch
   thy soul!

BELZ. We are come to tell thee thou dost
injure us.

LUC. Thou call'st on Christ contrary to thy
promise.

BELZ. Thou should'st not think on God.

LUC.   Think on the devil.

BELZ. And his dam too.

FAUST. Nor will I henceforth. Pardon me
   for this,
And Faustus vows never to look to
   heaven,   110
Never to name God, or to pray to him,
To burn his scriptures, slay his ministers,
And make my spirits pull his churches
   down.

[1] Limit (astronomical).
[2] In space and in time.
[3] Intelligence, spirit.
[4] The sphere of fire? And of crystal?
[5] Because of their uneven motion in regard
to the whole.

[6] Vex.   [7] Scratch.

Luc. So shalt thou show thyself, an obedient servant,

And we will highly gratify[1] thee for it.

Belz. Faustus, we are come from hell in person to show thee some pastime. Sit down and thou shalt behold the Seven Deadly Sins appear to thee in their proper shapes and likenesses. 120

Faust. That sight will be as pleasing unto me as Paradise was to Adam the first day of his creation.

Luc. Talk not of Paradise or creation, but mark the show. Go, Mephostophilis, fetch them in.

Enter the Seven Deadly Sins.

Belz. Now, Faustus, examine them of their several names and dispositions.

Faust. That shall I soon. What art thou, the first? 130

Pride. I am Pride. I disdain to have any parents. I am like to Ovid's flea, I can creep into every corner of a wench. Sometimes, like a periwig, I sit upon her brow; next, like a necklace, I hang about her neck; then, like a fan of feathers, I kiss her lips; and then, turning myself to a wrought[2] smock, do what I list. But fie, what a smell is here! I'll not speak another word unless the ground be perfumed, [140 and covered with cloth of arras.[3]

Faust. Thou art a proud knave indeed. What art thou, the second?

Covet. I am Covetousness, begotten of an old churl in a leather bag; and might I now obtain my wish, this house, you, and all should turn to gold, that I might lock you safe into my chest. O my sweet gold!

Faust. And what art thou, the third?

Envy. I am Envy, begotten of a [150 chimney sweeper and an oyster wife. I cannot read, and therefore wish all books burnt. I am lean with seeing others eat. O, that there would come a famine over all the world, that all might die, and I live alone, then thou shouldst see how fat I'd be. But must thou sit, and I stand? Come down, with a vengeance!

Faust. Out, envious wretch! But what art thou, the fourth? 160

Wrath. I am Wrath. I had neither father nor mother; I leapt out of a lion's

mouth when I was scarce an hour old, and ever since have run up and down the world with these case[4] of rapiers, wounding myself when I could get none to fight withal. I was born in hell, and look to it, for some of you shall be my father.

Faust. And what art thou, the fifth?

Glut. I am Gluttony. My parents [170 are all dead, and the devil a penny they have left me but a small pension, and that buys me thirty meals a day, and ten bevers[5]—a small trifle to suffice nature. I come of a royal pedigree: my father was a gammon of bacon, and my mother was a hogshead of claret wine. My godfathers were these: Peter Pickled-Herring and Martin Martlemass-Beef. O, but my god-mother, she was a jolly gentlewoman, [180 and well loved in every good town and city; her name was Mistress Margery March-Beer. Now,[6] Faustus, thou hast heard all my progeny,[7] wilt thou bid me to supper?

Faust. No, I'll see thee hanged; thou wilt eat up all my victuals.

Glut. Then the devil choke thee.

Faust. Choke thyself, Glutton. What art thou, the sixth? 190

Sloth. Hey ho! I am Sloth. I was be-gotten on a sunny bank, where I have lain ever since, and you have done me great injury to bring me from thence; let me be carried thither again by Gluttony and Lechery. Hey ho, I'll not speak a word more for a king's ransom.

Faust. And what are you, Mistress Minx, the seventh and last?

Lech. Who, I? I, sir? I am one [200 that loves an inch of raw mutton[8] better than an ell of fried stockfish,[9] and the first letter of my name begins with Lechery.

Luc. Away to hell, away! On, piper!

Exeunt the Seven Sins.

Faust. O, how this sight doth delight my soul.

Luc. But, Faustus, in hell is all manner of delight.

Faust. O, might I see hell, and return again safe, how happy were I then. 210

Luc. Faustus, thou shalt; at midnight I will send for thee.

---

[1] Reward.　　[2] Embroidered.　　[3] Tapestry.

[4] A pair.
[5] Snacks.
[6] Now that.
[7] Lineage.
[8] *I.e.*, virility.
[9] *I.e.*, impotence.

Meanwhile peruse this book, and view
   it throughly,
And thou shalt turn thyself into what
   shape thou wilt.
FAUST. Thanks, mighty Lucifer.
This will I keep as chary[1] as my life.
LUC. Now, Faustus, farewell.
FAUST. Farewell, great Lucifer! Come,
Mephostophilis.

Exeunt omnes, several ways.

ACT II. SCENE iii.

[*An innyard.*]

Enter the Clown [Robin].

CLO. What, Dick, look to the horses
there till I come again. I have gotten one
of Doctor Faustus' conjuring books, and
now we'll have such knavery, as't passes.[2]

Enter Dick.

DICK. What, Robin, you must come
away and walk the horses.
ROBIN. I walk the horses! I scorn't,
'faith, I have other matters in hand. Let
the horses walk themselves and they will.
[*Reads.*] "A *per se* a; t. h. e. the; o *per*   [10
se o; deny orgon, gorgon," Keep further
from me, O thou illiterate and unlearned
ostler.
DICK. 'Snails, what hast thou got there?
A book? Why, thou canst not tell ne'er a
word on't.
ROBIN. That thou shalt see presently.
Keep out of the circle, I say, lest I send
you into the hostry[3] with a vengeance.
DICK. That's like, 'faith. You had   [20
best leave your foolery, for an my master
come, he'll conjure you, 'faith.
ROBIN. My master conjure me? I'll
tell thee what, an my master come here,
I'll clap as fair a pair of horns on's head
as e'er thou sawest in thy life.
DICK. Thou needest not do that, for my
mistress hath done it.
ROBIN. Ay, there be of us here, that
have waded as deep into matters as   30
other men, if they were disposed to talk.
DICK. A plague take you, I thought you
did not sneak up and down after her for
nothing. But I prithee tell me, in good
sadness,[4] Robin, is that a conjuring book?

ROBIN. Do but speak what thou'lt have
me to do, and I'll do't. If thou'lt dance
naked, put off thy clothes, and I'll conjure
thee about presently; or if thou'lt go but
to the tavern with me, I'll give thee   [40
white wine, red wine, claret wine, sack,
muscadine, malmsey, and whippincrust.[5]
Hold, belly, hold, and we'll not pay one
penny for it.
DICK. O brave! Prithee, let's to it
presently, for I am as dry as a dog.
ROBIN. Come then, let's away. *Exeunt.*

CHORUS I.

Enter the Chorus.

CHORUS. Learned Faustus,
   To find the secrets of astronomy,
   Graven in the book of Jove's high
      firmament,
   Did mount him up to scale Olympus'
      top;
   Where sitting in a chariot burning
      bright,
   Drawn by the strength of yokéd dragons'
      necks,
   He views the clouds, the planets, and the
      stars,
   The tropics, zones, and quarters of the
      sky,
   From the bright circle of the hornéd
      moon,
   Even to the height of Primum
      Mobile.[6]   10
   And whirling round with this circum-
      ference,
   Within the concave compass of the pole,
   From east to west his dragons swiftly
      glide,
   And in eight days did bring him home
      again.
Not long he stayed within his quiet house
To rest his bones after his weary toil,
But new exploits do hale him out again.
And mounted then upon a dragon's back,
That with his wings did part the subtle
   air,
He now is gone to prove cosmo-
   graphy,   20
That measures coasts and kingdoms of
   the earth,

---

[1] Carefully.   [3] Hostelry, inn.
[2] As beats everything.   [4] Seriously.
[5] Corruption of *hippocras;* a spiced wine.
[6] The outermost sphere, which was supposed
to give motion to all the others.

And as I guess will first arrive at Rome
To see the Pope and manner of his court,
And take some part of holy Peter's feast,
The which this day is highly solemnized.

Exit.

ACT III. SCENE i.

[*The Pope's Privy Chamber.*]

Enter Faustus and Mephostophilis.

FAUST. Having now, my good Mephos-
tophilis,
Passed with delight the stately town of
Trier,
Environed round with airy mountain
tops,
With walls of flint, and deep entrenchéd
lakes,
Not to be won by any conquering prince,
From Paris next, coasting the realm of
France,
We saw the river Main fall into Rhine,
Whose banks are set with groves of
fruitful vines.
Then up to Naples, rich Campania,
With buildings fair, and gorgeous to the
eye,   10
Whose streets straight forth,[1] and paved
with finest brick,
Quarter the town in four equivalents.
There saw we learnéd Maro's[2] golden
tomb,
The way he cut an English mile in length
Thorough a rock of stone in one night's
space.
From thence to Venice, Padua, and the
rest,
In midst of which a sumptúous temple
stands,
That threats the stars with her aspiring
top,
Whose frame is paved with sundry
colored stones,
And roofed aloft with curious work in
gold.   20
Thus hitherto hath Faustus spent his
time.
But tell me now, what resting place is
this?
Hast thou, as erst[3] I did command,
Conducted me within the walls of Rome?

MEPH. I have, my Faustus, and for proof
thereof,
This is the goodly palace of the Pope;
And 'cause we are no common guests,
I choose his privy chamber for our use.

FAUST. I hope his holiness will bid us
welcome.

MEPH. All's one, for we'll be bold with his
venison.   30
But now, my Faustus, that thou may'st
perceive
What Rome contains for to delight thine
eyes,
Know that this city stands upon seven
hills,
That underprop the groundwork of the
same.
Just through the midst runs flowing
Tiber's stream,
With winding banks that cut it in two
parts,
Over the which four stately bridges lean,
That make safe passage to each part of
Rome.
Upon the bridge called Ponte Angelo
Erected is a castle passing strong,   40
Where thou shalt see such store of
ordinance[4]
As that the double cannons forged of
brass
Do match the number of the days con-
tained
Within the compass of one complete
year,
Besides the gates and high pyramidës
That Julius Cæsar brought from Africa.

FAUST. Now by the kingdoms of infernal
rule,
Of Styx, of Acheron, and the fiery lake
Of ever-burning Phlegethon, I swear
That I do long to see the monuments   [50
And situation of bright-splendent Rome.
Come, therefore; let's away.

MEPH. Nay, stay, my Faustus. I know
you'd see the Pope
And take some part of holy Peter's feast,
The which in state and high solemnity
This day is held through Rome and Italy
In honor of the Pope's triumphant
victory.

FAUST. Sweet Mephostophilis, thou pleasest me.
Whilst I am here on earth, let me be
cloyed

---

[1] In straight lines.
[2] Virgil was regarded as a
magician in the Middle Ages.
[3] Earlier.
[4] Ordnance.

With all things that delight the heart of
   man.   60
My four and twenty years of liberty
I'll spend in pleasure and in dalliance,
That Faustus' name, whilst this bright
   frame doth stand,
May be admired[1] through the furthest
   land.
MEPH. 'Tis well said, Faustus. Come
   then. Stand by me
And thou shalt see them come immedi-
   ately.
FAUST. Nay, stay, my gentle Mephos-
   tophilis,
And grant me my request, and then I
   go.
Thou knowest within the compass of
   eight days,
We viewed the face of heaven, of earth
   and hell.   70
So high our dragons soared into the
   air
That, looking down, the earth appeared
   to me
No bigger than my hand in quantity.
There did we view the kingdoms of the
   world,
And what might please mine eye, I there
   beheld.
Then in this show let me an actor
   be,
That this proud Pope may Faustus'
   cunning see.
MEPH. Let it be so, my Faustus, but first
   stay
And view their triumphs[2] as they pass
   this way;
And then devise what best contents thy
   mind,   80
By cunning in thine art to cross the Pope
Or dash the pride of this solemnity;
To make his monks and abbots stand like
   apes
And point like antics[3] at his triple crown;
To beat the beads about the friars' pates,
Or clap huge horns upon the cardinals'
   heads;
Or any villainy thou canst devise,
And I'll perform it, Faustus. Hark, they
   come.
This day shall make thee be admired in
   Rome.

[1] Wondered at.
[2] Ceremonies.   [3] Buffoons.

Enter the Cardinals and Bishops, some bear-
ing crosiers, some the pillars;[4] Monks and
Friars singing their procession.[5] Then the
Pope and Raymond, King of Hungary, with
Bruno led in chains.

POPE. Cast down our footstool.
RAY.   Saxon Bruno, stoop,   90
   Whilst on thy back his holiness ascends
Saint Peter's chair and state pontifical.
BRUNO. Proud Lucifer, that state belongs
   to me;
But thus I fall to Peter, not to thee.
POPE. To me and Peter shalt thou grovel-
   ling lie,
And crouch before the papal dignity.
Sound trumpets, then, for thus Saint
   Peter's heir
From Bruno's back ascends Saint Peter's
   chair.   *A flourish while he ascends.*
Thus, as the gods creep on with feet of
   wool,
Long ere with iron hands they punish
   men,   100
So shall our sleeping vengeance now arise
And smite with death thy hated enter-
   prise.
Lord Cardinals of France and Padua,
Go forthwith to our holy consistory
And read amongst the statutes decretal
What by the holy council held at Trent
The sacred synod hath decreed for him
That doth assume the papal government,
Without election and a true consent.
Away, and bring us word with
   speed.   110
1 CARD. We go, my Lord.
                        Exeunt Cardinals.
POPE. Lord Raymond!

[The Pope and Raymond converse.]

FAUST. Go, haste thee, gentle Mephos-
   tophilis.
Follow the cardinals to the consistory,
And, as they turn their superstitious
   books,
Strike them with sloth and drowsy
   idleness,
And make them sleep so sound that in
   their shapes
Thyself and I may parley with this Pope,

[4] Ornamental columns, symbolizing the support of the church.
[5] Religious office.

This proud confronter of the Emperor,
And in despite of all his holiness   120
Restore this Bruno to his liberty
And bear him to the states of Germany.

MEPH. Faustus, I go.

FAUST.   Dispatch it soon.
The Pope shall curse that Faustus came
to Rome.

        Exeunt Faustus and Mephostophilis.

BRUNO. Pope Adrian, let me have some
right of law.
I was elected by the Emperor.

POPE. We will depose the Emperor for
that deed
And curse the people that submit to him.
Both he and thou shalt' stand excom-
municate
And interdict from Church's privi-
lege   130
And all society of holy men.
He grows too proud in his authority,
Lifting his lofty head above the clouds,
And like a steeple overpeers the Church.
But we'll pull down his haughty inso-
lence;
And as Pope Alexander, our progenitor,[1]
Trod on the neck of German Frederick,
Adding this golden sentence to our praise,
That Peter's heirs should tread on
emperors
And walk upon the dreadful adder's
back,   140
Treading the lion and the dragon down,
And fearless spurn the killing basilisk,
So will we quell that haughty schismatic
And by authority apostolical
Depose him from his regal government.

BRUNO. Pope Julius swore to princely
Sigismund,
For him and the succeeding popes of
Rome,
To hold the emperors their lawful lords.

POPE. Pope Julius did abuse the Church's
rites,
And therefore none of his decrees can
stand.   150
Is not all power on earth bestowed on us?
And therefore though we would we can-
not err.
Behold this silver belt, whereto is fixed
Seven golden keys fast sealed with seven
seals,

In token of our seven-fold power from
heaven,
To bind or loose, lock fast, condemn, or
judge,
Resign,[2] or seal, or whatso pleaseth us.
Then he, and thou, and all the world
shall stoop
Or be assuréd of our dreadful curse,
To light as heavy as the pains of
hell.   160

        *Enter Faustus and Mephostophilis
        like the cardinals.*

MEPH. [*Aside.*] Now tell me, Faustus, are
we not fitted well?

FAUST. [*Aside.*] Yes, Mephostophilis, and
two such cardinals
Ne'er served a holy pope as we shall do.
But whilst they sleep within the con-
sistory,
Let us salute his reverend Fatherhood.

RAY. Behold, my Lord, the cardinals are
returned.

POPE. Welcome, grave fathers. Answer
presently.
What have our holy council there decreed
Concerning Bruno and the Emperor,
In quittance of their late conspiracy   [170
Against our state and papal dignity?

FAUST. Most sacred patron of the Church
of Rome,
By full consent of all the synod
Of priests and prelates, it is thus decreed:
That Bruno and the German Emperor
Be held as lollards[3] and bold schismatics
And proud disturbers of the Church's
peace.
And if that Bruno by his own assent,
Without enforcement of[4] the German
peers,
Did seek to wear the triple diadem   [180
And by your death to climb Saint Peter's
chair,
The statutes decretal have thus decreed
He shall be straight condemned of heresy
And on a pile of faggots burnt to death.

POPE. It is enough. Here, take him to
your charge
And bear him straight to Ponte Angelo
And in the strongest tower enclose him
fast.

[2] Annul.
[3] Heretics.
[4] Compulsion from.

[1] Predecessor.

Tomorrow, sitting in our consistory,
With all our college of grave cardinals,
We will determine of his life or
  death. 190
Here, take his triple crown along with
  you
And leave it in the Church's treasury.
Make haste again, my good lord
  cardinals,
And take our blessing apostolical.
MEPH. [*Aside.*] So, so, was never devil
  thus blessed before!
FAUST. [*Aside.*] Away, sweet Mephos-
  tophilis, be gone.
The cardinals will be plagued for this
  anon.
  Exeunt Faustus and Mephostophilis
  [with Bruno].
POPE. Go presently, and bring a banquet
  forth,
That we may solemnize Saint Peter's
  feast,
And with Lord Raymond, King of
  Hungary, 200
Drink to our late and happy victory.
  Exeunt.

ACT III. SCENE ii.

A sennet[1] while the banquet is brought in;
and then enter Faustus and Mephostophilis
in their own shapes.

MEPH. Now, Faustus, come. Prepare thy-
  self for mirth.
The sleepy cardinals are hard at hand
To censure Bruno, that is posted hence,
And on a proud-paced steed, as swift as
  thought,
Flies o'er the Alps to fruitful Germany,
There to salute the woeful Emperor.
FAUST. The Pope will curse them for their
  sloth today,
That slept both Bruno and his crown
  away.
But now, that Faustus may delight his
  mind,
And by their folly make some merri-
  ment, 10
Sweet Mephostophilis, so charm me here,
That I may walk invisible to all,
And do whate'er I please, unseen of any.
MEPH. Faustus, thou shalt. Then kneel
  down presently.

[1] A flourish on the trumpets.

Whilst on thy head I lay my hand
And charm thee with this magic wand,
First wear this girdle, then appear
Invisible to all are here.
The planets seven, the gloomy air,
Hell, and the Furies' forkéd hair, 20
Pluto's blue fire, and Hecat's tree,
With magic spells so compass thee
That no eye may thy body see.
So, Faustus, now for[2] all their holiness,
Do what thou wilt; thou shalt not be
  discerned.
FAUST. Thanks, Mephostophilis. Now,
  friars, take heed
Lest Faustus make your shaven crowns
  to bleed.
MEPH. Faustus, no more. See where the
  cardinals come.

Sound a sennet.
Enter Pope and all the Lords.
Enter the Cardinals with a book.

POPE. Welcome, Lord Cardinals. Come,
  sit down.
Lord Raymond, take your seat. Friars,
  attend 30
And see that all things be in readiness
As best beseems this solemn festival.
1 CARD. First, may it please your sacred
  Holiness,
To view the sentence of the reverend
  synod
Concerning Bruno and the Emperor?
POPE. What needs this question? Did I
  not tell you
Tomorrow we would sit i'th'consistory
And there determine of his punishment?
You brought us word even now, it was
  decreed
That Bruno and the curséd Emperor [40
Were by the holy council both con-
  demned
For loathéd lollards and base schismatics.
Then wherefore would you have me view
  that book?
1 CARD. Your Grace mistakes; you gave
  us no such charge.
POPE. Deny it not. We all are witnesses
That Bruno here was late delivered you,
With his rich triple crown to be reserved
And put into the Church's treasury.
AMBO[3] CARDS. By holy Paul, we saw them
  not.

[2] In spite of.   [3] Both.

POPE. By Peter, you shall die   50
  Unless you bring them forth immedi-
    ately.
  Hale them to prison, lade[1] their limbs
    with gyves.[2]
  False prelates, for this hateful treachery
  Cursed be your souls to hellish misery.
    [*Exeunt Cardinals with some Friars.*]
FAUST. [*Aside.*] So, they are safe. Now,
  Faustus, to the feast.
  The Pope had never such a frolic guest.
POPE. Lord Archbishop of Rheims, sit
  down with us.
ARCH. I thank your Holiness.
FAUST. Fall to! The devil choke you an
  you spare.
POPE. Who's that spoke? Friars, look
  about!   60
  Lord Raymond, pray fall to; I am
    beholding[3]
  To the Bishop of Milan for this so rare
    a present.
FAUST. I thank you, sir.   *Snatch it.*
POPE. How now? Who snatched the
  meat from me?
  Villains, why speak you not?
  My good Lord Archbishop, here's a most
    dainty dish,
  Was sent me from a cardinal in France.
FAUST. I'll have that too.   [*Snatch it.*]
POPE. What lollards do attend our Holiness
  That we receive such great indig-
    nity?   70
  Fetch me some wine.
FAUST. Ay, pray do, for Faustus is a-dry.
POPE. Lord Raymond, I drink unto your
  grace.
FAUST. I pledge your grace.   [*Snatch cup.*]
POPE. My wine gone too! Ye lubbers,
  look about
  And find the man that doth this villainy,
  Or by our sanctitude you all shall die.
  I pray, my lords, have patience at this
    troublesome banquet.
ARCH. Please it your Holiness, I think
  it be some ghost crept out of purgatory,
  and now is come unto your Holiness for
  his pardon.   80
POPE. It may be so.
  Go then, command our priests to sing a
    dirge

  To lay the fury of this same troublesome
    ghost.
  Once again, my lord, fall to.
          The Pope crosseth himself.
FAUST. How now? Must every bit be
  spiced with a cross?
  Nay then, take that.
          Faustus hits him a box of the ear.
POPE. O, I am slain! Help me, my lords!
  O, come and help to bear my body hence.
  Damned be this soul forever for this
    deed.   90
          Exeunt the Pope and his train.
MEPH. Now, Faustus, what will you do
now? For I can tell you you'll be cursed
with bell, book, and candle.
FAUST. Bell, book, and candle; candle,
  book, and bell;
  Forward and backward, to curse Faustus
  to hell.

Enter the Friars with bell, book, and candle
for the dirge.

1 FRIAR. Come, brethren, let's about our
  business with good devotion.
          Sing this:
  Cursed be he that stole his Holiness'
    meat from the table.
    Maledicat Dominus.[4]
  Cursed be he that struck his Holiness a
    blow on the face.
    Maledicat Dominus.
  Cursed be he that took Friar Sandelo a
    blow on the pate.   100
    Maledicat Dominus.
  Cursed be he that disturbeth our holy
    dirge.
    Maledicat Dominus.
  Cursed be he that took away his Holi-
    ness' wine.
    Maledicat Dominus.
[*Faustus and Mephostophilis*] *beat the*
  Friars, fling fireworks among them,
    and exeunt.

ACT III. SCENE iii.

Enter Clown [*Robin*] *and Dick, with a cup.*

DICK. Sirrah Robin, we were best look
that your devil can answer the stealing of
this same cup, for the vintner's boy follows
us at the hard heels.[5]

---

[1] Load.
[2] Chains.
[3] Beholden, indebted.

[4] May the Lord curse him.
[5] Close on our heels.

ROBIN. 'Tis no matter, let him come; an he follow us, I'll so conjure him, as he was never conjured in his life, I warrant him. Let me see the cup.

Enter Vintner.

DICK. Here 'tis—yonder he comes! Now, Robin, now or never show thy [10 cunning.

VINT. O, are you here? I am glad I have found you. You are a couple of fine companions![1] Pray, where's the cup you stole from the tavern?

ROBIN. How, how? We steal a cup! Take heed what you say; we look not like cup-stealers, I can tell you.

VINT. Never deny't, for I know you have it, and I'll search you.   20

ROBIN. Search me? Ay, and spare not— hold the cup, Dick—come, come, search me, search me.   [*Vintner searches Robin.*]

VINT. Come on, sirrah, let me search you now.   [*They pass the cup back and forth.*]

DICK. Ay, ay, do, do—hold the cup, Robin—I fear not your searching; we scorn to steal your cups, I can tell you.

[*Vintner searches Dick.*]

VINT. Never outface me for the matter, for sure the cup is between you two.   30

ROBIN. Nay, there you lie, 'tis beyond us both.

VINT. A plague take you! I thought 'twas your knavery to take it away. Come, give it me again.

ROBIN. Ay much! When, can you tell? Dick, make me a circle, and stand close at my back, and stir not for thy life. Vintner, you shall have your cup anon—say nothing, Dick! *O per se, O; Demogorgon,* [40 *Belcher, and Mephostophilis!*

Enter Mephostophilis.

MEPH. You princely legions of infernal rule,
How am I vexéd by these villains' charms!
From Constantinople have they brought me now,
Only for pleasure of these damnéd slaves.
[*Exit Vintner.*]

ROBIN. By lady, sir, you have had a shrewd[2] journey of it. Will it please you

to take a shoulder of mutton to supper, and a tester[3] in your purse, and go back again?

DICK. Ay, I pray you heartily, sir,   [50 for we called you but in jest, I promise you.

MEPH. To purge the rashness of this curséd deed,
First, be thou turnéd to this ugly shape,
For apish deeds transforméd to an ape.

ROBIN. O brave, an ape! I pray, sir, let me have the carrying of him about to show some tricks.

MEPH. And so thou shalt. Be thou transforméd to a dog and carry him upon thy back. Away, be gone!   60

ROBIN. A dog? That's excellent! Let the maids look well to their porridge-pots, for I'll into the kitchen presently. Come, Dick, come.
Exeunt the two Clowns.

MEPH. Now with the flames of ever-burning fire,
I'll wing myself, and forthwith fly amain[4]
Unto my Faustus, to the great Turk's court.   *Exit.*

CHORUS 2.

Enter Chorus.

CHORUS. When Faustus had with pleasure ta'en the view
Of rarest things and royal courts of kings,
He stayed his course, and so returnéd home,
Where such as bare his absence but with grief—
I mean his friends and near'st companions—
Did gratulate his safety with kind words;
And in their conference of what befell,
Touching his journey through the world and air,
They put forth questions of astrology,
Which Faustus answered with such learnéd skill   10
As they admired and wondered at his wit.
Now is his fame spread forth in every land.
Amongst the rest, the Emperor is one,
Carolus the Fifth, at whose palace now
Faustus is feasted 'mongst his noblemen.
What there he did in trial of his art,
I leave untold. Your eyes shall see performed.

[1] Rascals.   [2] Hard.   [3] Sixpence.   [4] With full speed.

Act IV. Scene i.

[The courtyard of the Emperor's palace.]

Enter Martino and Frederick at several doors.

MART. What ho, officers, gentlemen,
  Hie to the presence[1] to attend the
    Emperor!
  Good Frederick, see the rooms be voided
    straight;
  His Majesty is coming to the hall.
  Go back, and see the state[2] in readiness.
FRED. But where is Bruno, our elected
    Pope,
  That on a fury's back came post from
    Rome?
  Will not his Grace consort[3] the Emperor?
MART. O yes, and with him comes the
    German conjuror,
  The learnéd Faustus, fame of Witten-
    berg,   10
  The wonder of the world for magic art;
  And he intends to show great Carolus
  The race of all his stout progenitors,
  And bring in presence of his Majesty
  The royal shapes and warlike semblances
  Of Alexander and his beauteous par-
    amour.
FRED. Where is Benvolio?
MART. Fast asleep, I warrant you.
  He took his rouse[4] with stoups[5] of
    Rhenish wine
  So kindly yesternight to Bruno's
    health   20
  That all this day the sluggard keeps his
    bed.
FRED. See, see, his window's ope; we'll call
  to him.
MART. What ho, Benvolio!

*Enter Benvolio above at a window, in his
nightcap; buttoning.*

BEN. What a devil ail you two?
MART. Speak softly, sir, lest the devil hear
  you,
  For Faustus at the court is late arrived
  And at his heels a thousand furies wait,
  To accomplish whatsoever the doctor
    please.
BEN. What of this?

[1] Audience chamber.
[2] Throne.
[3] Accompany.
[4] Caroused.
[5] Flagons.

MART. Come, leave thy chamber first,
  and thou shalt see   30
  This conjuror perform such rare exploits
  Before the Pope and royal Emperor
  As never yet was seen in Germany.
BEN. Has not the Pope enough of con-
    juring yet?
  He was upon the devil's back late enough;
  And if he be so far in love with him
  I would he would post with him to Rome
    again.
FRED. Speak, wilt thou come and see this
  sport?
BEN. Not I.
MART. Wilt thou stand in thy window and
  see it then?   40
BEN. Ay, and I fall not asleep i'th'mean-
  time.
MART. The Emperor is at hand, who comes
  to see
  What wonders by black spells may com-
    passed be.
BEN. Well, go you attend the Emperor;
I am content for this once to thrust my
head out at a window. For they say, if a
man be drunk overnight, the devil cannot
hurt him in the morning. If that be true,
I have a charm in my head, shall control
him as well as the conjuror, I warrant you.
    [Exeunt Frederick and Martino.]

Act IV. Scene ii.

[The same.]

*A sennet. Charles the German Emperor,
Bruno [, Duke of] Saxony, Faustus,
Mephostophilis, Frederick, Martino,
and Attendants.*

[Benvolio remains in the window.]

EMP. Wonder of men, renowned magician,
  Thrice-learnéd Faustus, welcome to our
    court.
  This deed of thine, in setting Bruno free
  From his and our professéd enemy,
  Shall add more excellence unto thine art
  Than if by powerful necromantic spells
  Thou could'st command the world's
    obedience.
  Forever be beloved of Carolus.
  And if this Bruno thou hast late re-
    deemed,
  In peace possess the triple diadem   10
  And sit in Peter's chair, despite of chance,

Thou shalt be famous through all Italy
And honored of the German Emperor.
FAUST. These gracious words, most royal
　　Carolus,
Shall make poor Faustus to his utmost
　　power
Both love and serve the German
　　Emperor
And lay his life at holy Bruno's feet.
For proof whereof, if so your grace be
　　pleased,
The doctor stands prepared, by power of
　　art,
To cast his magic charms that shall pierce
　　through   20
The ebon gates of ever-burning hell
And hale the stubborn furies from their
　　caves
To compass whatsoe'er your grace
　　commands.
BEN. 'Blood, he speaks terribly; but for
all that, I do not greatly believe him. He
looks as like a conjuror as the Pope to a
costermonger.
EMP. Then, Faustus, as thou late didst
　　promise us,
We would behold that famous conqueror,
Great Alexander, and his paramour,[1] [30
In their true shapes and state ma-
　　jestical,
That we may wonder at their excellence.
FAUST. Your Majesty shall see them
　　presently.
Mephostophilis, away!
And with a solemn noise of trumpets'
　　sound
Present before this royal Emperor
Great Alexander and his beauteous
　　paramour.
MEPH. Faustus, I will.
　　　　　　　　　　　　　　　　　Exit.
BEN. Well, master doctor, an your devils
come not away quickly, you shall have　[40
me asleep presently. Zounds, I could eat
myself for anger, to think I have been such
an ass all this while, to stand gaping
after the devil's governor and can see
nothing.
FAUST. I'll make you feel something anon,
　　if my art fail me not.
My lord, I must forewarn your Majesty
That, when my spirits present the royal
　　shapes

[1] Wife; i.e., Roxana.

Of Alexander and his paramour,
Your grace demand no questions of the
　　king,   50
But in dumb silence let them come and go.
EMP. Be it as Faustus please, we are
content.
BEN. Ay, ay, and I am content too.
And thou bring Alexander and his par-
amour before the Emperor, I'll be Actæon
and turn myself to a stag.
FAUST. And I'll play Diana, and send
you the horns presently.

*Sennet. Enter at one door the Emperor
Alexander, at the other Darius. They meet,
Darius is thrown down, Alexander kills
him, takes off his crown, and offering to
go out, his Paramour meets him, he embraceth
her, and sets Darius' crown upon her
head, and coming back, both salute the
Emperor, who, leaving his state, offers to
embrace them, which Faustus seeing, suddenly stays him.*
Then trumpets cease and music sounds.

My gracious lord, you do forget yourself.
These are but shadows, not substan-
　　tial.   60
EMP. O, pardon me! My thoughts are so
　　ravished
With sight of this renownéd emperor
That in mine arms I would have com-
　　passed him.
But, Faustus, since I may not speak to
　　them,
To satisfy my longing thoughts at full,
Let me this tell thee: I have heard it said
That this fair lady, whilst she lived on
　　earth,
Had on her neck a little wart or mole.
How may I prove that saying to be true?
FAUST. Your Majesty may boldly go and
　　see.   70
EMP. Faustus, I see it plain.
And in this sight thou better pleasest me
Than if I gained another monarchy.
FAUST. Away, be gone!　　　*Exit Show.*
See, see, my gracious lord, what strange
beast is yon, that thrusts his head out at
window?
EMP. O wondrous sight! See, Duke of
　　Saxony,
Two spreading horns most strangely
　　fastenéd
Upon the head of young Benvolio.　　80

Sax. What, is he asleep, or dead?

Faust. He sleeps, my lord, but dreams not of his horns.

Emp. This sport is excellent. We'll call and wake him.

What ho, Benvolio!

Ben. A plague upon you, let me sleep awhile.

Emp. I blame thee not to sleep much, having such a head of thine own.

Sax. Look up, Benvolio, 'tis the Emperor calls.

Ben. The Emperor? Where? O zounds, my head!

Emp. Nay, and thy horns hold, 'tis [90 no matter for thy head, for that's armed sufficiently.

Faust. Why, how now, sir knight? What, hanged by the horns? This is most horrible! Fie, fie, pull in your head for shame, let not all the world wonder at you.

Ben. Zounds, doctor, is this your villainy?

Faust. O, say not so, sir. The doctor has no skill,

No art, no cunning, to present these lords,

Or bring before this royal Emperor [100 The mighty monarch, warlike Alexander? If Faustus do it, you are straight resolved

In bold Actæon's shape to turn a stag. And therefore, my lord, so please your Majesty,

I'll raise a kennel of hounds shall hunt him so

As all his footmanship[1] shall scarce prevail

To keep his carcase from their bloody fangs.

Ho, Belimote, Argiron, Asterote!

Ben. Hold, hold! Zounds, he'll raise up a kennel of devils, I think, anon. [110 Good my lord, entreat for me. 'Sblood, I am never able to endure these torments.

Emp. Then, good master doctor,

Let me entreat you to remove his horns; He has done penance now sufficiently.

Faust. My gracious lord, not so much for injury done to me, as to delight your Majesty with some mirth, hath Faustus justly requited this injurious knight; which being all I desire, I am content [120

[1] Skill in running.

to remove his horns. Mephostophilis, transform him—and hereafter, sir, look you speak well of scholars.

Ben. Speak well of ye! 'Sblood, and scholars be such cuckold-makers to clap horns of honest men's heads o' this order, I'll ne'er trust smooth faces and small ruffs[2] more. But an I be not revenged for this, would I might be turned to a gaping oyster, and drink nothing but salt water.   130

Emp. Come, Faustus, while the Emperor lives,

In recompense of this thy high desert, Thou shalt command the state of Germany

And live beloved of mighty Carolus.

Exeunt omnes.

Act IV. Scene iii.

[Near a grove.]

Enter Benvolio, Martino, Frederick, and Soldiers.

Mart. Nay, sweet Benvolio, let us sway thy thoughts

From this attempt against the conjuror.

Ben. Away, you love me not, to urge me thus.

Shall I let slip so great an injury,

When every servile groom jests at my wrongs,

And in their rustic gambols proudly[3] say, "Benvolio's head was graced with horns today"?

O, may these eyelids never close again, Till with my sword I have that conjuror slain.

If you will aid me in this enterprise, [10 Then draw your weapons, and be resolute:

If not, depart. Here will Benvolio die, But[4] Faustus' death shall quit[5] my infamy.

Fred. Nay, we will stay with thee, betide what may,

And kill that doctor if he come this way.

Ben. Then, gentle Frederick, hie thee to the grove,

And place our servants and our followers Close in an ambush there behind the trees.

[2] Beardless scholars in academic robes.
[3] Insolently.   [4] Unless.   [5] Requite.

By this[1] (I know) the conjuror is near.
I saw him kneel and kiss the Emperor's
    hand,   20
And take his leave, laden with rich
    rewards.
Then, soldiers, boldly fight. If Faustus
    die,
Take you the wealth; leave us the
    victory.
FRED. Come, soldiers, follow me unto the
    grove;
Who kills him shall have gold and end-
    less love.
            Exit Frederick with the Soldiers.
BEN. My head is lighter than it was by
    th'horns,
But yet my heart's more ponderous than
    my head,
And pants until I see that conjuror dead.
MART. Where shall we place ourselves,
    Benvolio?
BEN. Here will we stay to bide the first
    assault.   30
O, were that damnéd hell-hound but in
    place,[2]
Thou soon should'st see me quit my foul
    disgrace.

            Enter Frederick.

FRED. Close, close, the conjuror is at hand,
And all alone, comes walking in his gown.
Be ready then, and strike the peasant
    down.
BEN. Mine be that honor then. Now,
    sword, strike home;
For horns he gave, I'll have his head
    anon.

            Enter Faustus with the false head.

MART. See, see, he comes.
BEN.   No words; this blow ends all
Hell take his soul; his body thus must fall.
                        [*Strikes Faustus.*]
FAUST. O!   40
FRED. Groan you, master doctor?
BEN. Break may his heart with groans.
    Dear Frederick, see.
Thus will I end his griefs immediately.
                        [*Cuts off his head.*]
MART. Strike with a willing hand; his head
    is off.

---

[1] By this time.
[2] Present.

BEN. The devil's dead; the furies now may
    laugh.
FRED. Was this that stern aspect, that
    awful frown,
Made the grim monarch of infernal
    spirits.
Tremble and quake at his commanding
    charms?
MART. Was this that damnéd head, whose
    heart conspired
Benvolio's shame before the Em-
    peror?   50
BEN. Ay, that's the head, and here the
    body lies,
Justly rewarded for his villainies.
FRED. Come, let's devise how we may add
    more shame
To the black scandal of his hated name.
BEN. First, on his head, in quittance of
    my wrongs,
I'll nail huge forkéd horns, and let them
    hang
Within the window where he yoked me
    first,
That all the world may see my just
    revenge.
MART. What use shall we put his beard
    to?
BEN. We'll sell it to a chimney- [60
sweeper; it will wear out ten birchen
brooms, I warrant you.
FRED. What shall eyes do?
BEN. We'll put out his eyes, and they
shall serve for buttons to his lips, to keep
his tongue from catching cold.
MART. An excellent policy! And now,
sirs, having divided him, what shall the
body do?   [*Faustus stands up.*]
BEN. Zounds, the devil's alive again! [70
FRED. Give him his head, for God's sake.
FAUST. Nay, keep it! Faustus will have
    heads and hands,
Ay, all your hearts to recompense this
    deed.
Knew you not, traitors, I was limited
For four and twenty years to breathe
    on earth?
And had you cut my body with your
    swords,
Or hewed this flesh and bones as small
    as sand,
Yet in a minute had my spirit returned,
And I had breathed a man made free
    from harm.

But wherefore do I dally my re-
venge?   80
Asteroth, Belimoth, Mephostophilis!

Enter Mephostophilis and other Devils.

Go, horse these traitors on your fiery
backs,
And mount aloft with them as high as
heaven,
Thence pitch them headlong to the
lowest hell!
Yet stay, the world shall see their misery,
And hell shall after plague their treach-
ery.
Go, Belimoth, and take this caitiff hence,
And hurl him in some lake of mud and
dirt.
Take thou this other, drag him through
the woods,
Amongst the pricking thorns and sharp-
est briers,   90
Whilst with my gentle Mephostophilis
This traitor flies unto some steepy rock,
That, rolling down, may break the
villain's bones,
As he intended to dismember me.
Fly hence, dispatch my charge im-
mediately.
Fred. Pity us, gentle Faustus, save our
lives.
Faust. Away!
Fred.   He must needs go that the
devil drives.
          Exeunt Spirits with the Knights.

Enter the ambushed Soldiers.

1 Sold. Come, sirs, prepare yourselves in
readiness.
Make haste to help these noble gentlemen;   100
I heard them parley with the conjuror.
2 Sold. See where he comes. Dispatch,
and kill the slave!
Faust. What's here? An ambush to betray my life!
Then, Faustus, try thy skill. Base
peasants, stand!
For lo, these trees remove at my command,
And stand as bulwarks 'twixt yourselves
and me,
To shield me from your hated treachery.

Yet to encounter this your weak attempt,
Behold an army comes incontinent.[1]

*Faustus strikes the door, and enter a Devil
playing on a drum, after him another bearing
an ensign, and divers with weapons, Mephostophilis with fireworks; they set upon the
Soldiers and drive them out.*
                              [*Exit Faustus.*]

Act IV. Scene iv.

[*The same.*]

*Enter at several doors, Benvolio, Frederick,
and Martino, their heads and faces bloody,
and besmeared with mud and dirt; all having
horns on their heads.*

Mart. What ho, Benvolio!
Ben. Here, what, Frederick, ho!
Fred. O, help me, gentle friend! Where is
Martino?
Mart. Dear Frederick, here,
Half smothered in a lake of mud and dirt
Through which the furies dragged me by
the heels.
Fred. Martino, see, Benvolio's horns again!
Mart. O misery! How now, Benvolio?
Ben. Defend me, heaven! Shall I be
haunted still?
Mart. Nay, fear not, man. We have no
power to kill.   10
Ben. My friends transforméd thus! O
hellish spite,
Your heads are all set with horns.
Fred.   You hit it right.
It is your own you mean. Feel on your
head.
Ben. Zounds, horns again!
Mart.   Nay, chafe not, man; we
all are sped.
Ben. What devil attends this damned
magician,
That spite of spite, our wrongs are
doubléd?
Fred. What may we do, that we may hide
our shame?
Ben. If we should follow him to work
revenge,
He'd join long asses' ears to these huge
horns,
And make us laughing-stocks to all the
world.   20
Mart. What shall we do then, dear
Benvolio?

¹ Without delay.

BEN. I have a castle joining near these woods,
And thither we'll repair and live obscure
Till time shall alter these our brutish shapes.
Sith[1] black disgrace hath thus eclipsed our fame,
We'll rather die with grief than live with shame.   *Exeunt omnes.*

ACT IV. SCENE V.

[A room in Faustus' house.]

Enter Faustus and the Horse-Courser.

HORSE-C. I beseech your worship accept of these forty dollars.

FAUST. Friend, thou canst not buy so good a horse for so small a price. I have no great need to sell him, but if thou likest him for ten dollars more, take him, because I can see thou hast a good mind to him.

HORSE-C. I beseech you, sir, accept of this. I am a very poor man, and have lost very much of late by horse-flesh, and [10 this bargain will set me up again.

FAUST. Well, I will not stand with thee;[2] give me the money. Now, sirrah, I must tell you that you may ride him o'er hedge and ditch, and spare him not; but, do you hear, in any case ride him not into the water.

HORSE-C. How, sir, not into the water? Why, will he not drink of all waters?

FAUST. Yes, he will drink of all waters, but ride him not into the water; o'er [20 hedge and ditch, or where thou wilt, but not into the water. Go bid the ostler deliver him unto you, and remember what I say.

HORSE-C. I warrant you, sir. O joyful day! Now am I a made man forever.
      Exit.

FAUST. What art thou, Faustus, but a man condemned to die?
Thy fatal time draws to a final end;
Despair doth drive distrust into my thoughts.
Confound these passions with a quiet sleep.
Tush, Christ did call the thief upon the cross;   30
Then rest thee, Faustus, quiet in conceit.
      He sits to sleep.

Enter the Horse-Courser, wet.

HORSE-C. O, what a cozening doctor was this! I riding my horse into the water, thinking some hidden mystery had been in the horse, I had nothing under me but a little straw, and had much ado to escape drowning. Well, I'll go rouse him, and make him give me my forty dollars again. Ho, sirrah doctor, you cozening scab! Maister doctor, awake, and rise, and [40 give me my money again, for your horse is turned to a bottle[3] of hay. Maister doctor—
      He pulls off his leg.
Alas, I am undone! What shall I do? I have pulled off his leg!

FAUST. O, help, help! The villain hath murdered me!

HORSE-C. Murder or not murder, now[4] he has but one leg, I'll outrun him, and cast this leg into some ditch or other.
      [Exit.]

FAUST. Stop him, stop him, stop [50 him!—Ha, ha, ha, Faustus hath his leg again, and the horse-courser a bundle of hay for his forty dollars.

Enter Wagner.

How now, Wagner, what news with thee?

WAG. If it please you, the Duke of Vanholt doth earnestly entreat your company, and hath sent some of his men to attend you with provision fit for your journey.   60

FAUST. The Duke of Vanholt's an honorable gentleman, and one to whom I must be no niggard of my cunning. Come away.   *Exeunt.*

ACT IV. SCENE vi.

[The inn.]

Enter Clown [Robin], Dick, Horse-Courser, and a Carter.

CARTER. Come, my masters, I'll bring you to the best beer in Europe. What ho, hostess! Where be these whores?

Enter Hostess.

HOSTESS. How now, what lack you? What, my old guests, welcome.

[1] Since.   [2] Haggle over it.   [3] Bundle.   [4] Now that.

ROBIN. Sirrah Dick, dost thou know why I stand so mute?

DICK. No, Robin, why is't?

ROBIN. I am eighteenpence on the score; but say nothing, see if she have forgotten me.   10

HOSTESS. Who's this, that stands so solemnly by himself? What, my old guest!

ROBIN. O hostess, how do you? I hope my score stands still.

HOSTESS. Ay, there's no doubt of that, for methinks you make no haste to wipe it out.

DICK. Why, hostess, I say, fetch us some beer.

HOSTESS. You shall presently. Look [20 up into th'hall there, ho!   *Exit.*

DICK. Come, sirs, what shall we do now till mine hostess comes?

CARTER. Marry, sir, I'll tell you the bravest tale how a conjuror served me. You know Doctor Fauster?

HORSE-C. Ay, a plague take him. Here's some on's have cause to know him. Did he conjure thee too?

CARTER. I'll tell you how he served [30 me. As I was going to Wittenberg t'other day, with a load of hay, he met me, and asked me what he should give me for as much hay as he could eat. Now, sir, I, thinking that a little would serve his turn, bade him take as much as he would for three farthings. So he presently gave me my money, and fell to eating, and as I am a cursen[1] man, he never left eating, till he had eat up all my load of hay.   40

ALL. O, monstrous, eat a whole load of hay!

ROBIN. Yes, yes, that may be; for I have heard of one, that h'as eat a load of logs.

HORSE-C. Now, sirs, you shall hear how villainously he served me: I went to him yesterday to buy a horse of him, and he would by no means sell him under forty dollars; so, sir, because I knew him to be such a horse as would run over hedge [50 and ditch and never tire, I gave him his money. So when I had my horse, Doctor Fauster bade me ride him night and day, and spare him no time. "But," quoth he, "in any case ride him not into the water." Now, sir, I, thinking the horse had had some quality that he would not have me

[1] Christian.

know of, what did I but rid him into a great river, and when I came just in the midst, my horse vanished away, and I sat [60 straddling upon a bottle of hay.

ALL. O brave doctor!

HORSE-C. But you shall hear how bravely I served him for it. I went me home to his house, and there I found him asleep; I kept a-hallowing and whooping in his ears, but all could not wake him. I, seeing that, took him by the leg, and never rested pulling, till I had pulled me his leg quite off, and now 'tis at home [70 in mine host'ry.

ROBIN. And has the doctor but one leg then? That's excellent, for one of his devils turned me into the likeness of an ape's face.

CARTER. Some more drink, hostess!

ROBIN. Hark you, we'll into another room and drink awhile, and then we'll go seek out the doctor.   *Exeunt omnes.*

ACT IV. SCENE vii.

[*A room in the Duke of Vanholt's court.*]

Enter the Duke of Vanholt, his Duchess,
Faustus, and Mephostophilis.

DUKE. Thanks, master doctor, for these pleasant sights. Nor know I how sufficiently to recompense your great deserts in erecting that enchanted castle in the air, the sight whereof so delighted me, as nothing in the world could please me more.

FAUST. I do think myself, my good lord, highly recompensed, in that it pleaseth your grace to think but well of that which Faustus hath performed. But, gra- [10 cious lady, it may be that you have taken no pleasure in those sights; therefore, I pray you tell me, what is the thing you most desire to have? Be it in the world, it shall be yours. I have heard that great-bellied women do long for things are rare and dainty.

LADY. True, master doctor, and since I find you so kind, I will make known unto you what my heart desires to have; [20 and were it now summer, as it is January, a dead time of the winter, I would request no better meat than a dish of ripe grapes.

FAUST. This is but a small matter. Go, Mephostophilis, away!

Exit Mephostophilis.

Madam, I will do more than this for your content.

Enter Mephostophilis again with the grapes.

Here, now taste ye these; they should be good for they come from a far country, I can tell you. 30

DUKE. This makes me wonder more than all the rest, that at this time of the year, when every tree is barren of his fruits, from whence you had these ripe grapes.

FAUST. Please it your grace, the year is divided into two circles over the whole world, so that when it is winter with us, in the contrary circle it is likewise summer with them, as in India, Saba, and such countries that lie far east, where they [40 have fruit twice a year. From whence, by means of a swift spirit that I have, I had these grapes brought, as you see.

LADY. And, trust me, they are the sweetest grapes that e'er I tasted.

The Clowns bounce[1] at the gate, within.

DUKE. What rude disturbers have we at the gate?

Go pacify their fury, set it ope,

And then demand of them what they would have.

They knock again, and call out to talk with Faustus.

A SERV. Why, how now, masters? What a coil[2] is there! What is the reason you disturb the Duke? 50

DICK. We have no reason for it; therefore a fig for him.[3]

SERV. Why, saucy varlets, dare you be so bold?

HORSE-C. I hope, sir, we have wit enough to be more bold than welcome.

SERV. It appears so; pray be bold elsewhere, and trouble not the Duke.

DUKE. What would they have?

SERV. They all cry out to speak [60 with Doctor Faustus.

CARTER. Ay, and we will speak with him.

DUKE. Will you, sir? Commit[4] the rascals.

DICK. Commit[5] with us! He were as good commit with his father, as commit with us.

[1] Beat.
[2] Din.
[3] With a pun on reason-raisin.
[4] Imprison.   [5] Fornicate.

FAUST. I do beseech your grace let them come in.

They are good subject for a merriment.

DUKE. Do as thou wilt, Faustus; I give thee leave.

FAUST. I thank your grace. 70

Enter the Clown [Robin], Dick, Carter, and Horse-Courser.

Why, how now, my good friends? 'Faith, you are too outrageous, but come near.

I have procured your pardons. Welcome all.

ROBIN. Nay, sir, we will be welcome for our money, and we will pay for what we take. What ho! Give's half a dozen of beer here, and be hanged.

FAUST. Nay, hark you, can you tell me where you are?

CARTER. Ay, marry can I; we are [80 under heaven.

SERV. Ay, but, sir sauce-box, know you in what place?

HORSE-C. Ay, ay, the house is good enough to drink in. Zounds, fill us some beer, or we'll break all the barrels in the house, and dash out all your brains with your bottles.

FAUST. Be not so furious. Come, you shall have beer.

My lord, beseech you, give me leave awhile. 90

I'll gage[6] my credit, 'twill content your grace.

DUKE. With all my heart, kind doctor, please thyself.

Our servants and our court's at thy command.

FAUST. I humbly thank your grace. Then fetch some beer.

HORSE-C. Ay, marry, there spake a doctor indeed, and 'faith I'll drink a health to thy wooden leg for that word.

FAUST. My wooden leg? What dost thou mean by that?

CARTER. Ha, ha, ha, dost thou hear him, Dick? He has forgot his leg. 100

HORSE-C. Ay, ay, he does not stand much upon that.

FAUST. No, 'faith, not much upon a wooden leg.

[6] Engage, stake.

CARTER. Good Lord, that flesh and blood should be so frail with your worship! Do not you remember a horse-courser you sold a horse to?

FAUST. Yes, I remember one I sold a horse.

CARTER. And do you remember you bid he should not ride into the water?   110

FAUST. Yes, I do very well remember that.

CARTER. And do you remember nothing of your leg?

FAUST. No, in good sooth.

CARTER. Then I pray remember your curtsy.

FAUST. I thank you, sir.

[*He bows to the company.*]

CARTER. 'Tis not so much worth; I pray you tell me one thing.

FAUST. What's that?

CARTER. Be both your legs bed- [120 fellows every night together?

FAUST. Would'st thou make a colossus of me, that thou askest me such questions?

CARTER. No, truly, sir, I would make nothing of you, but I would fain know that.

Enter Hostess with drink.

FAUST. Then I assure thee certainly they are.

CARTER. I thank you, I am fully satisfied.

FAUST. But wherefore dost thou ask?

CARTER. For nothing, sir—but me- [130 thinks you should have a wooden bed-fellow of one of 'em.

HORSE-C. Why, do you hear, sir, did not I pull off one of your legs when you were asleep?

FAUST. But I have it again now I am awake. Look you here, sir.

ALL. O, horrible! Had the doctor three legs?

CARTER. Do you remember, sir, how [140 you cozened me and eat up my load of—

Faustus charms him dumb.

DICK. Do you remember how you made me wear an ape's—

HORSE-C. You whoreson conjuring scab, do you remember how you cozened me with a ho—

ROBIN. Ha' you forgotten me? You

think to carry it away with your hey-pass and re-pass?[1] Do you remember the dog's fa—   150

Exeunt Clowns.

HOSTESS. Who pays for the ale? Hear you, maister doctor! Now you have sent away my guests, I pray who shall pay me for my a—

Exit Hostess.

LADY. My lord,
We are much beholding to this learnéd man.

DUKE. So are we, madam, which we will recompense
With all the love and kindness that we may;
His artful sport drives all sad thoughts away.

Exeunt.

ACT V. SCENE i.

[*Faustus' house.*]

Thunder and lightning. Enter Devils with covered dishes. Mephostophilis leads them into Faustus' study. Then enter Wagner.

WAG. I think my master means to die shortly,
For he hath given to me all his goods;
And yet, methinks, if that death were near,
He would not banquet, and carouse, and swill
Amongst the students, as even now he doth,
Who are at supper with such belly-cheer
As Wagner ne'er beheld in all his life.
See where they come! Belike the feast is ended.   *Exit.*

Enter Faustus, Mephostophilis, and two or three Scholars.

1 SCH. Master Doctor Faustus, since our conference about fair ladies, which [10 was the beautifullest in all the world, we have determined with ourselves that Helen of Greece was the admirablest lady that ever lived; therefore, master doctor, if you will do us so much favor as to let us see that peerless dame of Greece, we should think ourselves much beholding unto you.

[1] Magical gestures.

FAUST. Gentlemen,
  For that I know your friendship is
    unfeigned,   20
  And Faustus' custom is not to deny
  The just requests of those that wish him
    well,
  You shall behold that peerless dame of
    Greece,
  No otherways for pomp and majesty
  Than when Sir Paris crossed the seas
    with her
  And brought the spoils to rich Dardania.
  Be silent then, for danger is in words.

*Music sounds. Mephostophilis brings in
Helen; she passeth over the stage.*

2 SCH. Too simple is my wit to tell her
    praise,
  Whom all the world admires for majesty.
3 SCH. No marvel though the angry Greeks
    pursued   30
  With ten years' war the rape of such a
    queen,
  Whose heavenly beauty passeth all
    compare.
1 SCH. Since we have seen the pride of
    Nature's works
  And only paragon of excellence,
  Let us depart, and for this glorious deed
  Happy and blest be Faustus evermore.
FAUST. Gentlemen, farewell; the same I
    wish to you.
                  Exeunt Scholars.

Enter an Old Man.

OLD MAN. O gentle Faustus, leave this
    damnéd art,
  This magic, that will charm thy soul to
    hell
  And quite bereave thee of salvation.   [40
  Though thou hast now offended like a
    man,
  Do not persever in it like a devil;
  Yet, yet, thou hast an amiable[1] soul
  If sin by custom grow not into nature.
  Then, Faustus, will repentance come too
    late,
  Then thou art banished from the sight
    of heaven.
  No mortal can express the pains of hell.
  It may be this my exhortation
  Seems harsh and all unpleasant; let it not,

[1] Lovable.

  For, gentle son, I speak it not in   [50
    wrath,
  Or envy of thee, but in tender love
  And pity of thy future misery;
  And so have hope that this, my kind
    rebuke,
  Checking[2] thy body, may amend thy soul.
FAUST. Where art thou, Faustus, wretch,
    what hast thou done?
  Damned art thou, Faustus, damned!
    Despair and die!
        Mephostophilis gives him a dagger.
  Hell claims his right, and with a roaring
    voice
  Says, "Faustus, come; thine hour is al-
    most come,"
  And Faustus now will come to do thee
    right.
        [Faustus prepares to use the dagger.]
OLD MAN. O, stay, good Faustus, stay thy
    desperate steps!   60
  I see an angel hover o'er thy head
  And with a vial full of precious grace
  Offers to pour the same into thy soul;
  Then call for mercy, and avoid despair.
FAUST. O friend, I feel
  Thy words to comfort my distresséd soul.
  Leave me awhile, to ponder on my sins.
OLD MAN. Faustus, I leave thee, but with
    grief of heart,
  Fearing the enemy of thy hapless soul.
                       Exit.
FAUST. Accurséd Faustus, where is mercy
    now?   70
  I do repent, and yet I do despair;
  Hell strives with grace for conquest in
    my breast.
  What shall I do to shun the snares of
    death?
MEPH. Thou traitor, Faustus, I arrest thy
    soul
  For disobedience to my sovereign lord.
  Revolt,[3] or I'll in piecemeal tear thy
    flesh.
FAUST. I do repent I e'er offended him;
  Sweet Mephostophilis, entreat thy lord
  To pardon my unjust presumption,
  And with my blood again I will   [80
    confirm
  The former vow I made to Lucifer.
MEPH. Do it then quickly with unfeignéd
    heart,

[2] Chiding.
[3] Return.

Lest greater dangers do attend thy drift.[1]

[Faustus pricks his arm and signs a paper with his blood.]

FAUST. Torment, sweet friend, that base and crookéd age,[2]
That durst dissuade me from thy Lucifer,
With greatest torment that our hell affords.
MEPH. His faith is great. I cannot touch his soul.
But what I may afflict his body with,
I will attempt, which is but little worth.
FAUST. One thing, good servant, let me crave of thee,   90
To glut the longing of my heart's desire,
That I may have unto my paramour,
That heavenly Helen, which I saw of late,
Whose sweet embracings may extinguish clear
Those thoughts that do dissuade me from my vow,
And keep mine oath I made to Lucifer.
MEPH. This, or what else my Faustus shall desire,
Shall be performed in twinkling of an eye.

Enter Helen again, passing over between two cupids.

FAUST. Was this the face that launched a thousand ships
And burnt the topless towers of   [100
Ilium?
Sweet Helen, make me immortal with a kiss!
Her lips suck forth my soul. See where it flies!
Come, Helen, come; give me my soul again.
Here will I dwell, for heaven is in these lips,
And all is dross that is not Helena.

Enter Old Man.

I will be Paris, and, for love of thee,
Instead of Troy shall Wittenberg be sacked;
And I will combat with weak Menelaus,
And wear thy colors on my pluméd crest;
Yea, I will wound Achilles in the heel,
          [110

And then return to Helen for a kiss.
O, thou art fairer than the evening's air,
Clad in the beauty of a thousand stars;
Brighter art thou than flaming Jupiter,
When he appeared to hapless Semele;
More lovely than the monarch of the sky
In wanton Arethusa's azured arms;
And none but thou shalt be my paramour.
          Exeunt [Faustus and Helen].
OLD MAN. Accurséd Faustus, miserable man,
That from thy soul exclud'st the grace of heaven,   120
And fliest the throne of His tribunal seat!

Enter the Devils.

Satan begins to sift[3] me with his pride,
As in this furnace God shall try my faith.
My faith, vile hell, shall triumph over thee!
Ambitious fiends, see how the heavens smiles
At your repulse, and laughs your state to scorn!
Hence, hell, for hence I fly unto my God.   *Exeunt.*

ACT V. SCENE ii.

[The Same.]

Thunder.   Enter Lucifer, Belzebub, and Mephostophilis.

LUC. Thus from infernal Dis do we ascend
To view the subjects of our monarchy,
Those souls which sin seals the black sons of hell,
'Mong which as chief, Faustus, we come to thee,
Bringing with us lasting damnation,
To wait upon thy soul; the time is come
Which makes it forfeit.
MEPH.   And this gloomy night
Here in this room will wretched Faustus be.
BELZ. And here we'll stay,
To mark him how he doth demean himself.   10
MEPH. How should he, but in desperate lunacy?
Fond[4] worldling, now his heart-blood dries with grief,

---

[1] Drifting; also purpose.
[2] *I.e.*, the old man.
[3] Sieve or screen out.   [4] Foolish.

His conscience kills it, and his laboring
   brain
Begets a world of idle fantasies,
To overreach the devil; but all in vain.
His store of pleasures must be sauced
   with pain.
He and his servant Wagner are at hand,
Both come from drawing Faustus'
   latest will.
See where they come.

                     [They stand apart.]

     Enter Faustus and Wagner.

FAUST. Say, Wagner, thou hast perused
   my will.   20
   How dost thou like it?
WAG.   Sir, so wondrous well
As, in all humble duty, I do yield
My life and lasting service for your love.
FAUST. Gramercies,[1] Wagner.

                     [Exit Wagner.]

     Enter the Scholars.

     Welcome, gentlemen.

1 SCH. Now, worthy Faustus, methinks
   your looks are changed.
   FAUST. Ah, gentlemen!
2 SCH. What ails Faustus?
   FAUST. Ah, my sweet chamber-fellow,
had I lived with thee, then had I lived still,
but now must die eternally. Look, [30
sirs, comes he not, comes he not?
1 SCH. O my dear Faustus, what imports
this fear?
2 SCH. Is all our pleasure turned to
   melancholy?
3 SCH. He is not well with being over-
   solitary.
2 SCH. If it be so, we'll have physicians,
   and Faustus shall be cured.
3 SCH. 'Tis but a surfeit, sir; fear nothing.
   FAUST. A surfeit of deadly sin, that hath
damned both body and soul.
2 SCH. Yet, Faustus, look up to [40
heaven, and remember God's mercy is
infinite.
   FAUST. But Faustus' offence can ne'er
be pardoned. The serpent that tempted
Eve may be saved, but not Faustus.
Ah, gentlemen, hear with patience, and
tremble not at my speeches; though
my heart pants and quivers to remember

   [1] Great thanks.

that I have been a student here these
thirty years—O, would I had never seen
Wittenberg, never read book—and [50
what wonders I have done, all Germany
can witness, yea, all the world—for which
Faustus hath lost both Germany and the
world—yea, heaven itself—heaven, the
seat of God, the throne of the blessed, the
Kingdom of joy; and must remain in hell
forever. Hell, ah hell, forever! Sweet
friends, what shall become of Faustus,
being in hell forever?
   2 SCH. Yet, Faustus, call on God.   60
   FAUST. On God, whom Faustus hath
abjured? On God, whom Faustus hath
blasphemed? Ah, my God—I would weep,
but the devil draws in my tears. Gush
forth blood instead of tears, yea, life and
soul. O, he stays my tongue! I would lift
up my hands, but see, they hold 'em, they
hold 'em.
   ALL. Who, Faustus?
   FAUST. Why, Lucifer and Mephosto- [70
philis! Ah, gentlemen, I gave them my soul
for my cunning.
   ALL. God forbid!
   FAUST. God forbade it indeed, but
Faustus hath done it. For the vain
pleasure of four and twenty years hath
Faustus lost eternal joy and felicity. I
writ them a bill with mine own blood.
The date is expired, this is the time, and
he will fetch me.   80
   1 SCH. Why did not Faustus tell us of
this before, that divines might have prayed
for thee?
   FAUST. Oft have I thought to have done
so, but the devil threatened to tear me in
pieces if I named God, to fetch me body
and soul if I once gave ear to divinity;
and now 'tis too late. Gentlemen, away,
lest you perish with me.
   2 SCH. O, what may we do to save [90
Faustus?
   FAUST. Talk not of me, but save yourselves and depart.
   3 SCH. God will strengthen me. I will
stay with Faustus.
   1 SCH. Tempt not God, sweet friend,
but let us into the next room, and there
pray for him.
   FAUST. Ay, pray for me, pray for me;
and what noise soever you hear, come [100
not unto me, for nothing can rescue me.

2 Sch. Pray thou, and we will pray, that
God may have mercy upon thee.

Faust. Gentlemen, farewell. If I live
till morning, I'll visit you. If not, Faustus
is gone to hell.

All. Faustus, farewell.
                                        Exeunt Scholars.

Meph. [*Advances.*] Ay, Faustus, now thou
    hast no hope of heaven,
Therefore despair, think only upon hell;
For that must be thy mansion, there to
    dwell.   110

Faust. O thou bewitching fiend, 'twas thy
    temptation
Hath robbed me of eternal happiness.

Meph. I do confess it, Faustus, and
    rejoice.
'Twas I that, when thou wert i'the way
    to heaven
Damned up thy passage; when thou
    took'st the book,
To view the Scriptures, then I turned the
    leaves
And led thine eye.
What, weep'st thou? 'Tis too late.
    Despair, farewell.
Fools that will laugh on earth, must
    weep in hell.   *Exit.*

*Enter the Good Angel and the Bad Angel
at several doors.*

Good A. O Faustus, if thou hadst given
    ear to me,   120
Innumerable joys had followed thee.
But thou didst love the world.

Bad A.   Gave ear to me,
And now must taste hell's pains
    perpetually.

Good A. O, what will all thy riches,
    pleasures, pomps,
Avail thee now?

Bad A.   Nothing but vex thee more,
To want in hell, that had on earth such
    store.
                Music while the throne descends.

Good A. O, thou hast lost celestial
    happiness,
Pleasures unspeakable, bliss without end.
Hadst thou affected sweet divinity,
Hell, or the devil, had had no power on
    thee.   130
Hadst thou kept on that way, Faustus,
    behold
In what resplendent glory thou hadst sat

In yonder throne, like those bright
    shining saints,
And triumphed over hell; that hast thou
    lost,
And now, poor soul, must thy good angel
    leave thee.
The jaws of hell are open to receive thee.
                                        Exit.[1]

Hell is discovered.

Bad A. Now, Faustus, let thine eyes with
    horror stare
Into that vast, perpetual torture-house.
There are the furies tossing damnéd souls
On burning forks; there bodies boil in
    lead;   140
There are live quarters broiling on the
    coals,
That ne'er can die; this ever-burning
    chair
Is for o'er-tortured souls to rest them
    in;
These, that are fed with sops of flaming
    fire,
Were gluttons, and loved only delicates,
And laughed to see the poor starve at
    their gates;
But yet all these are nothing: thou shalt
    see
Ten thousand tortures that more horrid
    be.

Faust. O, I have seen enough to torture me.

Bad A. Nay, thou must feel them, taste
    the smart of all.   150
He that loves pleasure, must for pleasure
    fall.
And so I leave thee, Faustus, till anon;[2]
Then wilt thou tumble in confusion.
                                        Exit.
                The clock strikes eleven.

Faust. Ah, Faustus,
Now hast thou but one bare hour to live,
And then thou must be damned
    perpetually.
Stand still, you ever-moving spheres of
    heaven,
That time may cease, and midnight
    never come.
Fair nature's eye, rise, rise again and
    make
Perpetual day; or let this hour be   [160
    but

[1] *I.e.*, the throne ascends.
[2] Soon.

A year, a month, a week, a natural day,
That Faustus may repent, and save his
soul.
O lente, lente currite noctis equi![1]
The stars move still, time runs, the clock
will strike,
The devil will come, and Faustus must
be damned.
O, I'll leap up to my God! Who pulls
me down?
See, see where Christ's blood streams in
the firmament!
One drop would save my soul, half a
drop. Ah, my Christ—
Rend not my heart for naming of my
Christ!
Yet will I call on him! O, spare me,
Lucifer!   170
Where is it now? 'Tis gone, and see
where God
Stretcheth out his arm and bends his
ireful brows.
Mountains and hills, come, come, and
fall on me,
And hide me from the heavy wrath of
God.
No, no!
Then will I headlong run into the earth.
Earth, gape! O, no, it will not harbor me.
You stars that reigned at my nativity,
Whose influence hath allotted death and
hell,
Now draw up Faustus like a foggy   [180
mist
Into the entrails of yon laboring cloud,
That, when you vomit forth into the air,
My limbs may issue from your smoky
mouths
So that my soul may but ascend to
heaven.
                    The watch strikes.
Ah, half the hour is past; 'twill all be
past anon!
O God,
If thou wilt not have mercy on my soul,
Yet for Christ's sake, whose blood hath
ransomed me,
Impose some end to my incessant pain.
Let Faustus live in hell a thousand   [190
years,
A hundred thousand, and at last be
saved.
O, no end is limited to damnéd souls!

[1] Run slowly, slowly, horses of night.

Why wert thou not a creature wanting
soul?
Or why is this immortal that thou hast?
Ah, Pythagoras' metempsychosis—were
that true
This soul should fly from me, and I be
changed
Unto some brutish beast.
All beasts are happy, for when they die,
Their souls are soon dissolved in
elements;
But mine must live still to be plagued
in hell.   200
Cursed be the parents that engendered
me!
No, Faustus, curse thyself, curse Lucifer,
That hath deprived thee of the joys of
heaven.
                    The clock striketh twelve.
It strikes, it strikes! Now body turn to
air,
Or Lucifer will bear thee quick to hell.
                    Thunder and lightning.
O soul, be changed into little water drops,
And fall into the ocean, ne'er be found.

                    Enter the Devils.

My God, my God! Look not so fierce
on me!
Adders and serpents, let me breathe
awhile!
Ugly hell, gape not! Come not, [210
Lucifer!
I'll burn my books—ah, Mephostophilis!
                    Exeunt with him.

Act V. Scene iii.

Enter the Scholars.

1 SCH. Come, gentlemen, let us go visit
Faustus,
For such a dreadful night was never seen
Since first the world's creation did begin;
Such fearful shrieks and cries were never
heard.
Pray heaven the doctor have escaped
the danger.
2 SCH. O, help us, heaven! See, here are
Faustus' limbs,
All torn asunder by the hand of death.
3 SCH. The devils whom Faustus served
have torn him thus,
For 'twixt the hours of twelve and one,
methought

I heard him shriek and call aloud for
help,   10
At which self time the house seemed all
on fire
With dreadful horror of these damnéd
fiends.
2 SCH. Well, gentlemen, though Faustus'
end be such
As every Christian heart laments to
think on,
Yet for he was a scholar, once admired
For wondrous knowledge in our German
schools,
We'll give his mangled limbs due
burial,
And all the students clothed in mourning
black
Shall wait upon his heavy funeral.

                     Exeunt.

EPILOGUE.

Enter Chorus.

CHORUS. Cut is the branch that might
have grown full straight,
And burnéd is Apollo's laurel bough
That sometime[1] grew within this learnéd
man.
Faustus is gone! Regard his hellish fall,
Whose fiendful fortune may exhort the
wise
Only to wonder at unlawful things,
Whose deepness doth entice such forward
wits
To practise more than heavenly power
permits.

                    [Exit.]

Terminat hora diem; terminat author opus.[2]

[1] Once.   [2] The hour ends the day; the
author ends his work.

FINIS.

CHRISTOPHER MARLOWE

EDWARD THE SECOND

In the opinion of many readers, *Edward the Second* is a greater play than either *Tamburlaine* or *Doctor Faustus* because it deals in a realistic and credible way with the lives, motives, and ambitions of historical Englishmen rather than with the aspirations of a far-off, bloody Oriental conqueror or an overreaching German magician. The characters, however, as in most of Marlowe's plays, are concerned with power—its attainment and its values. Although, as Ribner says, *Edward II* marks a new stage in the development of the history play, critics have fallen out over whether it should be classified primarily as a chronicle play or as a tragedy. Ribner attempted to solve the dilemma by saying that in it "we have the beginning of a type of historical tragedy not based upon the Senecan formula." In a new edition of his book in 1965 he urged still more strongly the historical and political aspects of the play, in opposition to other recent criticism.

In 1933, H. B. Charlton and R. D. Waller in their edition of *Edward II* for *The Works and Life of Christopher Marlowe* came to the conclusions that the play was composed in the autumn of 1591, that it was probably first produced in London in December 1592 by Pembroke's company (perhaps earlier in the provinces), that it was probably first printed in 1593 in an edition now lost, and that the earliest surviving editions came in 1594 and 1598. Marlowe may have been stimulated to write his play after having seen the productions of the second and third parts of Shakespeare's *Henry VI*, just as Shakespeare may have been reciprocally stimulated to write *Richard II* and *Richard III* after having seen *Edward II*. The main source of the material for Marlowe's play, however, was Raphael Holinshed's *Chronicle*, supplemented perhaps by ideas from two other historians, John Stow and Robert Fabyan, and by suggestions on the two Mortimers found in *A Mirror for Magistrates*.

With these historical facts Marlowe took the usual liberties, selecting only the characters and events which would give his story unity, placing many events out of chronological order, and telescoping almost thirty years into a very brief span without specifically mentioning time at all. Although the play still remains essentially episodic in construction, it has a clear and effective design, which traces the corrupting results of power and ambition on many characters—from Edward in a negative way to Gaveston, the younger Mortimer, and the younger Spencer in a positive way. Audience sympathy toward the pleasure-loving Edward grows as his sufferings increase, even though he never really shows penitence for his irresponsible actions. But early sympathies with Mortimer as a responsible, patriotic, and virtuous leader diminish as he becomes the victim of his own unscrupulous ambitions. (His career, as Ribner points out, is similar to that of the Duke of Guise in *The Massacre at Paris*.) Similarly the attitude of the audience toward Queen Isabella deteriorates as she changes from the loyal, loving wife of an utterly undeserving husband to the hardened, conniving mistress of Young Mortimer. These are all changing, moving characters, unlike the essentially static characters in most of *Tamburlaine*. Protagonists become antagonists, and antagonists protagonists, in a constantly shifting, but rhythmic pattern. (See, for instance, Charlton and Waller, as above, and R. Fricker, "The Dramatic Structure of *Edward II*," *ES*, 1953.) L. J. Mills, however, dissents from the view that Marlowe intended his play to be primarily a study of the effects of ambition and power, and decides that the theme lies in the Renaissance conception of the relative importance of male friendship vs. male-female love ("The Meaning of *Edward II*," *MP*, 1934). It is the "centrality of passion" which in this case causes tragedy because of the unworthiness of Gaveston and Young Spencer and the weakness and triviality of the King in his homosexual devotion to his "minions," or favorites, rather than to his love for his wife or the welfare of the state.

Once again, as in *Tamburlaine*, Marlowe is concerned with the problems and theories of government as another significant aspect of his theme. The major conflict in the play is between the two powers, the King and the barons, or, as Poirier puts it: "It is the story of a feudal monarch who attempts to govern as an absolute monarch, and fails." Edward himself is the chief spokesman for the idea of the kingdom and its citizens being his personal property, simply because he is "your lawful king." In this he is supported by the Spencers, who scheme to get advancement through flattering him, and by his brother Edmund, Earl of Kent, who vacillates in his convictions. Although he admits that it is treason to oppose the King, early in the play Mortimer, Jr., speaks for a greater distribution of power, not simply to include the nobility but even to extend to the commons. He argues that subjects have not only the lawful right but the positive duty to depose an unjust ruler—that "the realm and parliament" can elect a new king, as Edward himself concedes at the end. A third force at work in the play is the Church. In the first act the Archbishop of Canterbury reminds the King of his allegiance to Rome—an allegiance challenged by Edward in a very Protestant speech in scene iv, which must have gained him at least a temporary sympathy from the audience. Most of the play's critics (Ribner, in "Marlowe's 'Tragicke Glasse';" Wilson, in *Marlowe and the Early Shakespeare;* and Alfred Hart, in *Shakespeare and the Homilies*, Melbourne, 1934, for example) have maintained that there is not a single allusion in the play to the concept of the divine right of kings or of their responsibility to God, holding that man alone, by his virtue and strength, determines who deserves to rule. Some of the characters, nevertheless, clearly believe in the intervention of the power of heaven in human affairs, as does the Queen in scene xvi: "Successful battles gives the god of kings/To them that fight in right and fear his wrath." She then goes on to give thanks to "heaven's great Architect," who has awarded her forces the victory. Young Spencer and Edward himself in the next scene seem to recognize the possible intervention of a divine power when they refer to the "angry heavens" and the "gentle heavens." However, Mortimer Junior's political, moral, and religious philosophy in the last scenes of the play has nothing of Christian humanism left in it, for it is unabashedly that of the classical and stoical Wheel of Fortune, which has first exalted him to the top of its revolution and is then ready to carry him tumbling down, just as it has carried Edward in his gruesome torment and murder. Yet the implication of the whole play is not quite so pessimistic as Ribner says it is, since—as he himself admits—the final scene implies a better future for England through the person of the suddenly strong and resolute young new King, Edward III, who shows all the qualities of kingship his father lacked.

The basis of the present text is the 1594 edition as printed in Tucker Brooke's variorum *Works*, which has been checked against the Malone reprint prepared under the direction of W. W. Greg.

THE TROUBLESOME REIGN AND LAMENTABLE DEATH OF EDWARD THE SECOND[1]

BY

CHRISTOPHER MARLOWE

PERSONÆ

KING EDWARD THE SECOND.
PRINCE EDWARD, *his son, afterwards King Edward the Third.*
EDMUND, *Earl of Kent, brother to King Edward the Second.*
PIERS GAVESTON.
ARCHBISHOP OF CANTERBURY.
BISHOP OF COVENTRY.
BERKELEY, *Bishop of Winchester.*
EARL OF WARWICK.
EARL OF LANCASTER.
EARL OF PEMBROKE.[2]
EARL OF ARUNDEL.
EARL OF LEICESTER.
BEAUMONT.
SIR THOMAS BERKELEY.[3]
MORTIMER, SENIOR.
MORTIMER, JUNIOR, *his nephew.*
SPENCER, THE ELDER.
SPENCER, THE YOUNGER, *his son.*

BALDOCK, *a clerk.*
SIR WILLIAM TRUSSEL,[4] *Proctor of Parliament.*
GURNEY } *creatures of young*
MATREVIS[5] } *Mortimer.*
LIGHTBORN, *a murderer.*
SIR JOHN OF HAINAULT.
LEVUNE, *a Frenchman.*
RICE AP HOWELL.
JAMES, *servant to Pembroke.*
AN ABBOT, MONKS, A HERALD, LORDS, POOR MEN, A MOWER, THE KING'S CHAMPION, MESSENGERS, SOLDIERS, *and* ATTENDANTS.

QUEEN ISABELLA, *wife to King Edward the Second.*
A LADY, *niece to King Edward the Second and daughter to the Duke of Gloucester.*
OTHER LADIES.

SCENE: *England and Paris.*

TIME: *Early fourteenth century.*]

[SCENE i.

Near the court in London.]

Enter Gaveston, reading on a letter that was brought him from the King.

[GAV.] "My father is deceased! Come, Gaveston,
And share the kingdom with thy dearest friend."

Ah, words that make me surfeit with delight!
What greater bliss can hap to Gaveston
Than live and be the favorite of a king?
Sweet prince, I come. These, these thy amorous lines
Might have enforced me to have swum from France,

---

[1] The title continues: "King of England, with the Tragical Fall of Proud Mortimer, As It Was Sundry Times Publicly Acted in the Honorable City of London by the Right Honorable the Earl of Pembroke His Servants. Written by Chri. Marlowe, Gent."

[2] This name regularly appears as *Penbrook* in original.

[3] Consistent spelling of this name as *Bartley* indicates the pronunciation in this play.

[4] Dyce suggests that this character is represented in the speech head *Tru.* in Scene **xviii**.

[5] Dyce suggests Sir John Maltravers.

And, like Leander, gasped upon the sand,
So thou wouldst smile, and take me in
    thy arms.
The sight of London to my exiled eyes 10
Is as Elysium to a newcome soul;
Not that I love the city, or the men,
But that it harbors him I hold so dear—
The king, upon whose bosom let me die,
And with the world be still at enmity.
What need the ar[c]tic people love
    starlight,
To whom the sun shines both by day
    and night?
Farewell, base stooping to the lordly
    peers!
My knee shall bow to none but to the
    king.
As for the multitude, that are but
    sparks   20
Raked up in embers of their poverty,
Tanti! [1] I'll fawn [2] first on the wind
That glanceth at my lips, and flyeth
    away.
But how now, what are these?

Enter three Poor Men.

POOR MEN. Such as desire your worship's
    service.
GAV. What canst thou do?
1 POOR. I can ride.
GAV. But I have no horses.—What art
    thou?
2 POOR. A traveler.
GAV.   Let me see. Thou wouldst do well
    To wait at my trencher and tell me lies
    at dinner time;   30
    And, as I like your discoursing, I'll have
    you.—
    And what art thou?
3 POOR. A soldier that hath served
    against the Scot.
GAV. Why, there are hospitals for such as
    you.
I have no war, and therefore, sir, begone.
SOLDIER.[3] Farewell, and perish by a sol-
    dier's hand,
    That wouldst reward them with an hos-
    pital.
GAV. [*Aside.*] Ay, ay, these words of his
    move me as much
    As if a goose should play the porpen-
    tine,[4]

And dart her plumes, thinking to pierce
    my breast.   40
But yet it is no pain to speak men fair;
I'll flatter these, and make them live in
    hope.—
You know that I came lately out of
    France,
And yet I have not viewed my lord the
    king;
If I speed well, I'll entertain you all.
OMNES. We thank your worship.
GAV. I have some business; leave me to
    myself.
OMNES. We will wait here about the court.
    Exeunt.
GAV. Do.—These are not men for me.   49
I must have wanton poets, pleasant wits,
Musicians that with touching of a string
May draw the pliant king which way I
    please.
Music and poetry is his delight;
Therefore I'll have Italian masques by
    night,
Sweet speeches, comedies, and pleasing
    shows;
And in the day, when he shall walk
    abroad,
Like sylvan nymphs my pages shall be
    clad;
My men, like satyrs grazing on the lawns,
Shall with their goat feet dance an antic
    hay.[5]   59
Sometime a lovely boy in Dian's shape
With hair that gilds the water as it glides,
Crownets [6] of pearl about his naked arms,
And in his sportful hands an olive tree,
To hide those parts which men delight
    to see,
Shall bathe him in a spring; and there
    hard by,
One like Acteon peeping through the
    grove
Shall by the angry goddess be trans-
    formed,
And running in the likeness of an hart
By yelping hounds pulled down, and
    seem to die.
Such things as these best please his
    majesty,   70
My lord.—Here comes the king and the
    nobles
From the parliament. I'll stand aside.
    [*Retires.*]

[1] So much for them.   [3] *I.e., 3 Poor.*
[2] Original reads *fanne.*   [4] Porcupine.
[5] Country dance.   [6] Coronets, garlands.

Enter the King; Lancaster; Mortimer, Senior; Mortimer, Junior; Edmund, Earl of Kent; Guy, Earl of Warwick; etc.

EDW. Lancaster!

LAN. My lord.

GAV. [*Aside.*] That Earl of Lancaster do I abhor!

EDW. Will you not grant me this?—[*Aside.*] In spite of them
I'll have my will; and these two Mortimers,
That cross me thus, shall know I am displeased.

MOR. SEN. If you love us, my lord, hate Gaveston.

GAV. [*Aside.*] That villain Mortimer! I'll be his death.   80

MOR. JUN. Mine uncle here, this earl, and I myself
Were sworn to your father at his death
That he should ne'er return into the realm;
And know, my lord, ere I will break my oath,
This sword of mine, that should offend your foes,
Shall sleep within the scabbard at thy need,
And underneath thy banners march who will,
For Mortimer will hang his armor up.

GAV. [*Aside.*] *Mort Dieu!* [1]

EDW. Well, Mortimer, I'll make thee rue these words.   90
Beseems it thee to contradict thy king?
Frown'st thou thereat, aspiring Lancaster?
The sword shall plane the furrows of thy brows,
And hew these knees that now are grown so stiff.
I will have Gaveston; and you shall know
What danger 'tis to stand against your king.

GAV. [*Aside.*] Well done, Ned!

LAN. My lord, why do you thus incense your peers,
That naturally would love and honor you   99
But for that base and obscure Gaveston?
Four earldoms have I, besides Lancaster—

Derby, Salisbury, Lincoln, Leicester;
These will I sell, to give my soldiers pay,
Ere Gaveston shall stay within the realm.
Therefore, if he be come, expel him straight.

EDM. [2] Barons and earls, your pride hath made me mute;
But now I'll speak, and to the proof, I hope.
I do remember, in my father's days,
Lord Percy of the north, being highly moved,
Braved Mowbery [3] in presence of the king,   110
For which, had not his highness loved him well,
He should have lost his head; but with his look
The undaunted spirit of Percy was appeased,
And Mowbery and he were reconciled.
Yet dare you brave the king unto his face!—
Brother, revenge it, and let these their heads
Preach upon poles, for trespass of their tongues.

WAR. O, our heads!

EDW. Ay, yours; and therefore I would wish you grant—   119

WAR. Bridle thy anger, gentle Mortimer.

MOR. JUN. I cannot, nor I will not; I must speak.—
Cousin, our hands I hope shall fence our heads,
And strike off his that makes you threaten us.
Come, uncle, let us leave the brainsick king,
And henceforth parley with our naked swords.

MOR. SEN. Wiltshire hath men enough to save our heads.

WAR. [*Ironically.*] All Warwickshire will love him for my sake!

LAN. [*Ironically.*] And northward Gaveston hath many friends!—
Adieu, my lord; and either change your mind,
Or look to see the throne, where you should sit,   130

---

[1] God's death!

[2] The name of this character appears interchangeably as *Edmund* or *Kent* in speech heads throughout the play.   [3] Mowbray.

To float in blood, and at thy wanton head

The glozing [1] head of thy base minion thrown.

Exeunt Nobles [except Kent].

EDW. I cannot brook these haughty menaces.

Am I a king, and must be overruled?—

Brother, display my ensigns in the field;

I'll bandy [2] with the barons and the earls,

And either die or live with Gaveston.

GAV. I can no longer keep me from my lord. *[Comes forward.]*

EDW. What, Gaveston! Welcome! Kiss not my hand; 139

Embrace me, Gaveston, as I do thee.

Why shouldst thou kneel? Knowest thou not who I am? [3]

Thy friend, thyself, another Gaveston!

Not Hylas was more mourned of Hercules

Than thou hast been of me since thy exile.

GAV. And, since I went from hence, no soul in hell

Hath felt more torment than poor Gaveston.

EDW. I know it.—Brother, welcome home my friend.

Now let the treacherous Mortimers conspire,

And that high-minded [4] Earl of Lancaster. 149

I have my wish, in that I joy [5] thy sight;

And sooner shall the sea o'erwhelm my land

Than bear the ship that shall transport thee hence.

I here create thee lord high chamberlain,

Chief secretary to the state and me,

Earl of Cornwall, King and Lord of Man. [6]

GAV. My lord, these titles far exceed my worth.

KENT. Brother, the least of these may well suffice

For one of greater birth than Gaveston.

EDW. Cease, brother, for I cannot brook these words.

Thy worth, sweet friend, is far above my gifts. 160

Therefore, to equal it, receive my heart.

If for these dignities thou be envied,

I'll give thee more, for, but to honor thee,

Is Edward pleased with kingly regiment. [7]

Fear'st thou [8] thy person? Thou shalt have a guard!

Wants thou gold? Go to my treasury!

Wouldst thou be loved and feared? Receive my seal;

Save or condemn, and in our name command

Whatso thy mind affects, [9] or fancy likes.

GAV. It shall suffice me to enjoy your love, 170

Which, whiles I have, I think myself as great

As Cæsar riding in the Roman street,

With captive kings at his triumphant ear.

Enter the Bishop of Coventry.

EDW. Whither goes my Lord of Coventry so fast?

BISH. To celebrate your father's exequies. But is that wicked Gaveston returned?

EDW. Ay, priest, and lives to be revenged on thee,

That wert the only cause of his exile.

GAV. 'Tis true, and, but for reverence of these robes,

Thou shouldst not plod one foot beyond this place. 180

BISH. I did no more than I was bound to do;

And, Gaveston, unless thou be reclaimed,

As then I did incense the parliament,

So will I now, and thou shalt back to France.

GAV. Saving your reverence, you must pardon me.

EDW. Throw off his golden miter, rend his stole,

And in the channel [10] christen him anew.

KENT. Ah, brother, lay not violent hands on him,

For he'll complain unto the see of Rome!

GAV. Let him complain unto the see of hell; 190

I'll be revenged on him for my exile.

---

[1] Flattering.   [2] Fight.
[3] Here and in a few other passages the line division has been regularized.   [5] Enjoy.
[4] Arrogant.   [6] Isle of Man.
[7] Rule.   [9] Desires.
[8] Fear'st thou for.   [10] Gutter.

EDW. No, spare his life, but seize upon his goods.

Be thou lord bishop and receive his rents,
And make him serve thee as thy chaplain.
I give him thee—here, use him as thou wilt.

GAV. He shall to prison, and there die in bolts.

EDW. Ay, to the Tower, the Fleet, or where thou wilt.

BISH. For this offense, be thou accursed of God!

EDW. Who's there? Convey this priest to the Tower.

BISH. True, true.[1]   200

EDW. But in the meantime, Gaveston, away,

And take possession of his house and goods.

Come, follow me, and thou shalt have my guard

To see it done, and bring thee safe again.

GAV. What should a priest do with so fair a house?

A prison may best beseem his holiness.

[*Exeunt.*]

[SCENE ii.

Westminster.]

Enter [on one side] both the Mortimers; [on the other,] Warwick and Lancaster.

WAR. 'Tis true, the bishop is in the Tower,
And goods and body[2] given to Gaveston.

LAN. What, will they tyrannize upon the church?

Ah, wicked king! Accursèd Gaveston!
This ground, which is corrupted with their steps,
Shall be their timeless[3] sepulcher or mine.

MOR. JUN. Well, let that peevish Frenchman guard him sure;
Unless his breast be swordproof, he shall die.

MOR. SEN. How now! Why droops the Earl of Lancaster?

MOR. JUN. Wherefore is Guy of Warwick discontent?   10

LAN. That villain Gaveston is made an earl.

MOR. SEN. An earl!

WAR. Ay, and besides, lord chamberlain of the realm,
And secretary too, and Lord of Man.

MOR. SEN. We may not nor we will not suffer this.

MOR. JUN. Why post we not from hence to levy men?

LAN. "My Lord of Cornwall" now at every word!
And happy is the man whom he vouchsafes
For vailing[4] of his bonnet one good look.
Thus, arm in arm, the king and he doth march.   20
Nay, more, the guard upon his lordship waits,
And all the court begins to flatter him.

WAR. Thus leaning on the shoulder of the king,
He nods and scorns and smiles at those that pass.

MOR. SEN. Doth no man take exceptions at the slave?

LAN. All stomach[5] him, but none dare speak a word.

MOR. JUN. Ah, that bewrays[6] their baseness, Lancaster!
Were all the earls and barons of my mind,
We'll hale him from the bosom of the king,
And at the court gate hang the peasant up,   30
Who, swoln with venom of ambitious pride,
Will be the ruin of the realm and us.

Enter the [Arch]bishop of Canterbury [and an Attendant].

WAR. Here comes my Lord of Canterbury's grace.

LAN. His countenance bewrays he is displeased.

[ARCH]BISH. First were his sacred garments rent and torn;
Then laid they violent hands upon him; next,
Himself imprisoned, and his goods asseized.[7]
This certify the pope.—Away, take horse!   [*Exit Attendant.*]

---

[1] Alluding to euphemistic use of *convey*, taking the word in the sense of *steal, carry away feloniously.*   [2] Substance.   [3] Untimely.

[4] Lowering, doffing.   [6] Reveals.
[5] Resent.   [7] Seized upon.

LAN. My lord, will you take arms against
the king?

[ARCH]BISH. What need I? God himself is
up in arms,   40
When violence is offered to the church.

MOR. JUN. Then will you join with us that
be his peers,
To banish or behead that Gaveston?

[ARCH]BISH. What else, my lords? For it
concerns me near;
The bishopric of Coventry is his.

Enter the Queen.

MOR. JUN. Madam, whither walks your
majesty so fast?

QUEEN. Unto the forest, gentle Mortimer,
To live in grief and baleful discontent;
For now my lord the king regards me not,
But dotes upon the love of Gaveston.   50
He claps his cheeks, and hangs about his
neck,
Smiles in his face, and whispers in his
ears;
And, when I come, he frowns, as who
should say,
"Go whither thou wilt, seeing I have
Gaveston."

MOR. SEN. Is it not strange that he is thus
bewitched?

MOR. JUN. Madam, return unto the court
again.
That sly, inveigling Frenchman we'll exile
Or lose our lives; and yet, ere that day
come,
The king shall lose his crown, for we have
power,   59
And courage too, to be revenged at full.

[ARCH]BISH. But yet lift not your swords
against the king.

LAN. No, but we'll lift Gaveston from
hence.

WAR. And war must be the means, or he'll
stay still.

QUEEN. Then let him stay; for rather than
my lord
Shall be oppressed by civil mutinies,
I will endure a melancholy life,
And let him frolic with his minion.

[ARCH]BISH. My lords, to ease all this, but
hear me speak:
We and the rest, that are his counselors,
Will meet and with a general consent   70
Confirm his banishment with our hands
and seals.

LAN. What we confirm the king will frustrate.

MOR. JUN. Then may we lawfully revolt
from him.

WAR. But say, my lord, where shall this
meeting be?

[ARCH]BISH. At the New Temple.

MOR. JUN. Content.

[ARCH]BISH. And, in the meantime, I'll entreat you all
To cross to Lambeth, and there stay
with me.

LAN. Come then, let's away.

MOR. JUN. Madam, farewell!   80

QUEEN. Farewell, sweet Mortimer, and for
my sake
Forbear to levy arms against the king.

MOR. JUN. Ay, if words will serve; if not,
I must.   [*Exeunt.*]

[SCENE iii.

A street in London.]

Enter Gaveston and the Earl of Kent.

GAV. Edmund, the mighty Prince of Lancaster,
That hath more earldoms than an ass can
bear,
And both the Mortimers, two goodly
men,
With Guy of Warwick, that redoubted
knight,
Are gone towards Lambeth—there let
them remain!   *Exeunt.*

[SCENE iv.

The New Temple.]

Enter Nobles.

LAN. Here is the form of Gaveston's exile.
May it please your lordship to subscribe
your name.

[ARCH]BISH. Give me the paper!
[*He signs, followed by the others.*]

LAN. Quick, quick, my lord! I long to
write my name.

WAR. But I long more to see him banished
hence.

MOR. JUN. The name of Mortimer shall
fright the king,
Unless he be declined [1] from that base
peasant.

[1] Turned aside, parted.

Enter the King [, Kent,] and Gaveston.

EDW. What, are you moved that Gaveston
    sits here?
It is our pleasure; we will have it so.
LAN. Your grace doth well to place him by
    your side,   10
For nowhere else the new earl is so safe.
MOR. SEN. What man of noble birth can
    brook this sight?
Quam male conveniunt! [1]
See what a scornful look the peasant
    casts!
PEM. Can kingly lions fawn on creeping
    ants?
WAR. Ignoble vassal, that like Phaëton
Aspir'st unto the guidance of the sun!
MOR. JUN. Their downfall is at hand, their
    forces down;
We will not thus be faced and over-
    peered.[2]   19
EDW. Lay hands on that traitor Mortimer!
MOR. SEN. Lay hands on that traitor Gav-
    eston!
KENT. Is this the duty that you owe your
    king?
WAR. We know our duties—let him know
    his peers.
EDW. Whither will you bear him? Stay,
    or ye shall die.
MOR. SEN. We are no traitors; therefore
    threaten not.
GAV. No, threaten not, my lord, but pay
    them home!
Were I a king—
MOR. JUN. Thou villain, wherefore talks
    thou of a king,
That hardly art a gentleman by birth?
EDW. Were he a peasant, being my min-
    ion,   30
I'll make the proudest of you stoop to
    him.
LAN. My lord, you may not thus disparage
    us.—
Away, I say, with hateful Gaveston!
MOR. SEN. And with the Earl of Kent that
    favors him!
[Attendants remove Kent and Gaveston.]
EDW. Nay, then, lay violent hands upon
    your king.
Here, Mortimer, sit thou in Edward's
    throne;

[1] How ill they agree!
[2] Looked down upon, scorned. Actually he
was the son of a Gascon knight.

Warwick and Lancaster, wear you my
    crown.
Was ever king thus overruled as I?
LAN. Learn then to rule us better, and the
    realm.
MOR. JUN. What we have done, our heart
    blood shall maintain.   40
WAR. Think you that we can brook this
    upstart pride?
EDW. Anger and wrathful fury stops my
    speech.
[ARCH]BISH. Why are you moved? Be pa-
    tient, my lord,
And see what we your counselors have
    done.
MOR. JUN. My lords, now let us all be
    resolute,
And either have our wills or lose our
    lives.
EDW. Meet you for this, proud, overdaring
    peers?
Ere my sweet Gaveston shall part from
    me,
This isle shall fleet [3] upon the ocean,
And wander to the unfrequented Inde. 50
[ARCH]BISH. You know that I am legate to
    the pope!
On your allegiance to the see of Rome
Subscribe, as we have done, to his exile.
MOR. JUN. Curse him, if he refuse; and
    then may we
Depose him and elect another king.
EDW. Ay, there it goes! But yet I will
    not yield.
Curse me, depose me, do the worst you
    can.
LAN. Then linger not, my lord, but do it
    straight.
[ARCH]BISH. Remember how the bishop
    was abused!
Either banish him that was the cause
    thereof,   60
Or I will presently [4] discharge these lords
Of duty and allegiance due to thee.
EDW. *[Aside.]* It boots me not to threat; I
    must speak fair.—
The legate of the pope will be obeyed.
My lord, you shall be chancellor of the
    realm;
Thou, Lancaster, high admiral of our
    fleet;
Young Mortimer and his uncle shall be
    earls;

[3] Float, drift.   [4] Immediately.

And you, Lord Warwick, President of the
  North;
And thou, of Wales. If this content you
  not, 69
Make several kingdoms of this monarchy,
And share it equally amongst you all,
So I may have some nook or corner left
To frolic with my dearest Gaveston.

[ARCH]BISH. Nothing shall alter us; we are
  resolved.

LAN. Come, come, subscribe.

MOR. JUN. Why should you love him
  whom the world hates so?

EDW. Because he loves me more than all
  the world.
Ah, none but rude and savage-minded men
Would seek the ruin of my Gaveston. 79
You that be noble born should pity him.

WAR. You that are princely born should
  shake him off.
For shame, subscribe, and let the lown [1]
  depart.

MOR. SEN. Urge him, my lord.

[ARCH]BISH. Are you content to banish him
  the realm?

EDW. I see I must, and therefore am content.
Instead of ink, I'll write it with my tears.
                    [Signs.]

MOR. JUN. The king is lovesick for his
  minion.

EDW. 'Tis done; and now, accursèd hand,
  fall off!

LAN. Give it me; I'll have it published in
  the streets.

MOR. JUN. I'll see him presently despatched away. 90

[ARCH]BISH. Now is my heart at ease.

WAR.   And so is mine.

PEM. This will be good news to the common sort.

MOR. SEN. Be it or no, he shall not linger
  here.   *Exeunt Nobles.*

EDW. How fast they run to banish him I
  love!
They would not stir, were it to do me
  good.
Why should a king be subject to a priest?
Proud Rome, that hatchest such im-
  perial grooms,
For these thy superstitious taper lights,
Wherewith thy antichristian churches
  blaze, 99

[1] Worthless fellow.

I'll fire thy crazèd buildings, and enforce
The papal towers to kiss the lowly
  ground!
With slaughtered priests may Tiber's
  channel swell,
And banks raised higher with their sep-
  ulchers!
As for the peers that back the clergy thus,
If I be king, not one of them shall live.

Enter Gaveston.

GAV. My lord, I hear it whispered everywhere
That I am banished, and must fly the
  land.

EDW. 'Tis true, sweet Gaveston—O, were
  it false!
The legate of the pope will have it so,
And thou must hence, or I shall be de-
  posed. 110
But I will reign to be revenged of them,
And therefore, sweet friend, take it pa-
  tiently.
Live where thou wilt, I'll send thee gold
  enough;
And long thou shalt not stay, or, if thou
  dost,
I'll come to thee. My love shall ne'er
  decline.

GAV. Is all my hope turned to this hell of
  grief?

EDW. Rend not my heart with thy too
  piercing words.
Thou from this land, I from myself am
  banished.

GAV. To go from hence grieves not poor
  Gaveston,
But to forsake you, in whose gracious
  looks 120
The blessedness of Gaveston remains;
For nowhere else seeks he felicity.

EDW. And only this torments my wretched
  soul
That, whether I will or no, thou must
  depart.
Be governor of Ireland in my stead,
And there abide till fortune call thee
  home.
Here take my picture, and let me wear
  thine;   [They exchange pictures.]
O, might I keep thee here as I do this,
Happy were I, but now most miser-
  able!

GAV. 'Tis something to be pitied of a king.

EDW. Thou shalt not hence—I'll hide thee,
Gaveston.   131
GAV. I shall be found, and then 'twill
grieve me more.
EDW. Kind words and mutual talk makes
our grief greater;
Therefore, with dumb embracement, let
us part.—
Stay, Gaveston, I cannot leave thee thus!
GAV. For every look, my lord drops down
a tear.
Seeing I must go, do not renew my sor-
row.
EDW. The time is little that thou hast to
stay,
And, therefore, give me leave to look
my fill.
But come, sweet friend, I'll bear thee on
thy way.   140
GAV. The peers will frown.
EDW. I pass [1] not for their anger.—Come,
let's go;
O, that we might as well return as go.

Enter Edmund and Queen Isabel.

QUEEN. Whither goes my lord?
EDW. Fawn not on me, French strumpet!
Get thee gone!
QUEEN. On whom but on my husband
should I fawn?
GAV. On Mortimer, with whom, ungentle
queen—
I say no more. Judge you the rest, my
lord.
QUEEN. In saying this, thou wrong'st
me, Gaveston.
Is't not enough that thou corrupts my
lord,   150
And art a bawd to his affections,
But thou must call mine honor thus in
question?
GAV. I mean not so; your grace must
pardon me.
EDW. Thou art too familiar with that
Mortimer,
And by thy means is Gaveston exiled.
But I would wish thee reconcile the lords,
Or thou shalt ne'er be reconciled to me.
QUEEN. Your highness knows it lies not in
my power.
EDW. Away then! Touch me not.—Come,
Gaveston.

[1] Care.

QUEEN. Villain, 'tis thou that robb'st me
of my lord!   160
GAV. Madam, 'tis you that rob me of my
lord.
EDW. Speak not unto her; let her droop
and pine.
QUEEN. Wherein, my lord, have I deserved
these words?
Witness the tears that Isabella sheds,
Witness this heart, that, sighing for thee,
breaks,
How dear my lord is to poor Isabel!
EDW. And witness heaven how dear thou
art to me!
There weep, for till my Gaveston be re-
pealed,[2]
Assure thyself thou com'st not in my
sight.   *Exeunt Edward and Gaveston.*
QUEEN. O miserable and distresséd queen!
Would, when I left sweet France and
was embarked,   171
That charming Circes,[3] walking on the
waves,
Had changed my shape, or at the mar-
riage day
The cup of Hymen had been full of
poison,
Or with those arms that twined about
my neck
I had been stifled, and not lived to see
The king my lord thus to abandon me!
Like frantic Juno will I fill the earth
With ghastly murmur of my sighs and
cries;
For never doted Jove on Ganymede 180
So much as he on curséd Gaveston.
But that will more exasperate his wrath.
I must entreat him, I must speak him
fair,
And be a means to call home Gaveston.
And yet he'll ever dote on Gaveston,
And so am I forever miserable.

Enter the Nobles to the Queen.

LAN. Look where the sister of the King of
France
Sits wringing of her hands, and beats
her breast!
WAR. The king, I fear, hath ill entreated [4]
her.
PEM. Hard is the heart that injures such
a saint.   190

[2] Recalled from exile.   [4] Treated, used.
[3] Circe.

MOR. JUN. I know 'tis long [1] of Gaveston she weeps.

MOR. SEN. Why? He is gone.

MOR. JUN. Madam, how fares your grace?

QUEEN. Ah, Mortimer, now breaks the king's hate forth,
And he confesseth that he loves me not.

MOR. JUN. Cry quittance, madam, then, and love not him.

QUEEN. No, rather will I die a thousand deaths!
And yet I love in vain. He'll ne'er love me.

LAN. Fear ye not, madam; now his minion's gone,
His wanton humor will be quickly left.

QUEEN. O never, Lancaster! I am enjoined 200
To sue unto you all for his repeal.
This wills my lord, and this must I perform,
Or else be banished from his highness' presence.

LAN. For his repeal? Madam, he comes not back,
Unless the sea cast up his shipwrack [2] body.

WAR. And to behold so sweet a sight as that,
There's none here but would run his horse to death.

MOR. JUN. But, madam, would you have us call him home?

QUEEN. Ay, Mortimer, for till he be restored,
The angry king hath banished me the court; 210
And, therefore, as thou lovest and tend'rest [3] me,
Be thou my advocate unto these peers.

MOR. JUN. What! Would you have me plead for Gaveston?

MOR. SEN. Plead for him he that will, I am resolved.

LAN. And so am I, my lord. Dissuade the queen.

QUEEN. O Lancaster, let him dissuade the king,
For 'tis against my will he should return.

WAR. Then speak not for him; let the peasant go.

QUEEN. 'Tis for myself I speak, and not for him.

PEM. No speaking will prevail, and therefore cease. 220

MOR. JUN. Fair queen, forbear to angle for the fish
Which, being caught, strikes him that takes it dead;
I mean that vile torpedo, [4] Gaveston,
That now, I hope, floats on the Irish seas. [5]

QUEEN. Sweet Mortimer, sit down by me awhile,
And I will tell thee reasons of such weight
As thou wilt soon subscribe to his repeal.

MOR. JUN. It is impossible; but speak your mind.

QUEEN. Then thus—but none shall hear it but ourselves. [They stand aside.]

LAN. My lords, albeit the queen win Mortimer, 230
Will you be resolute, and hold with me?

MOR. SEN. Not I, against my nephew.

PEM. Fear not; the queen's words cannot alter him.

WAR. No? Do but mark how earnestly she pleads!

LAN. And see how coldly his looks make denial!

WAR. She smiles. Now for my life his mind is changed!

LAN. I'll rather lose his friendship, I, than grant.

MOR. JUN. Well, of necessity it must be so.
My lords, that I abhor base Gaveston,
I hope your honors make no question, 240
And therefore, though I plead for his repeal,
'Tis not for his sake, but for our avail;
Nay, for the realm's behoof, and for the king's.

LAN. Fie, Mortimer, dishonor not thyself!
Can this be true, 'twas good to banish him?
And is this true, to call him home again?
Such reasons make white black, and dark night day.

MOR. JUN. My Lord of Lancaster, mark the respect. [6]

LAN. In no respect can contraries be true.

QUEEN. Yet, good my lord, hear what he can allege. 250

[1] Because. [2] Shipwrecked. [3] Carest for.

[4] Electric ray (fish).
[5] A sample of Marlowe's telescoping of time.
[6] Reason.

WAR. All that he speaks is nothing; we are resolved.

MOR. JUN. Do you not wish that Gaveston were dead?

PEM. I would he were!

MOR. JUN. Why, then, my lord, give me but leave to speak.

MOR. SEN. But, nephew, do not play the sophister.

MOR. JUN. This which I urge is of a burning zeal

To mend the king, and do our country good.

Know you not Gaveston hath store of gold,

Which may in Ireland purchase him such friends 259

As he will front the mightiest of us all?

And whereas [1] he shall live and be beloved,

'Tis hard for us to work his overthrow.

WAR. Mark you but that, my Lord of Lancaster.

MOR. JUN. But were he here, detested as he is,

How easily might some base slave be suborned

To greet his lordship with a poniard,

And none so much as blame the murtherer,

But rather praise him for that brave attempt, [2]

And in the chronicle enroll his name

For purging of the realm of such a plague! 270

PEM. He saith true.

LAN. Ay, but how chance this was not done before?

MOR. JUN. Because, my lords, it was not thought upon.

Nay, more, when he shall know it lies in us

To banish him, and then to call him home,

'Twill make him vail the top flag of his pride,

And fear to offend the meanest nobleman.

MOR. SEN. But how if he do not, nephew?

MOR. JUN. Then may we with some color [3] rise in arms;

For, howsoever we have borne it out, 280

'Tis treason to be up against the king.

[1] Where. [2] Enterprise. [3] Excuse.

So shall we have the people of [4] our side,

Which for his father's sake lean to the king,

But cannot brook a night-grown mushrump, [5]

Such a one as my Lord of Cornwall is,

Should bear us down of [6] the nobility.

And when the commons and the nobles join,

'Tis not the king can buckler Gaveston;

We'll pull him from the strongest hold he hath.

My lords, if to perform this I be slack, 290

Think me as base a groom as Gaveston.

LAN. On that condition, Lancaster will grant.

WAR. And so will Pembroke and I.

MOR. SEN. And I.

MOR. JUN. In this I count me highly gratified,

And Mortimer will rest at your command.

QUEEN. And when this favor Isabel forgets,

Then let her live abandoned and forlorn.—

But see, in happy time, [7] my lord the king,

Having brought the Earl of Cornwall on his way, 300

Is new returned. This news will glad him much,

Yet not so much as me. I love him more

Than he can Gaveston. Would he loved me

But half so much, then were I trebleblessed.

Enter King Edward, mourning.

EDW. He's gone, and for his absence thus I mourn.

Did never sorrow go so near my heart

As doth the want of my sweet Gaveston;

And could my crown's revenue bring him back,

I would freely give it to his enemies,

And think I gained, having bought so dear a friend. 310

QUEEN. [*Aside.*] Hark, how he harps upon his minion!

[4] On. [6] *I.e.*, who would lower our standing as.
[5] Mushroom. [7] Opportunely.

Edw. My heart is as an anvil unto sorrow,
Which beats upon it like the Cyclops'
    hammers,
And with the noise turns up my giddy
    brain,
And makes me frantic for my Gaveston.
Ah, had some bloodless Fury rose from
    hell,
And with my kingly scepter stroke [1] me
    dead,
When I was forced to leave my Gaveston!
Lan. *Diablo!* [2] What passions call you
    these?
Queen. My gracious lord, I come to
    bring you news. 320
Edw. That you have parleyed with your
    Mortimer!
Queen. That Gaveston, my lord, shall be
    repealed.
Edw. Repealed! The news is too sweet to
    be true.
Queen. But will you love me, if you find
    it so?
Edw. If it be so, what will not Edward do?
Queen. For Gaveston, but not for Isabel.
Edw. For thee, fair queen, if thou lovest
    Gaveston.
I'll hang a golden tongue about thy neck,
Seeing thou hast pleaded with so good
    success.
Queen. No other jewels hang about my
    neck 330
Than these, my lord; nor let me have
    more wealth
Than I may fetch from this rich treasury.
O, how a kiss revives poor Isabel!
Edw. Once more receive my hand; and
    let this be
A second marriage twixt thyself and me.
Queen. And may it prove more happy
    than the first!
My gentle lord, bespeak these nobles
    fair,
That wait attendance for a gracious look,
And on their knees salute your majesty.
Edw. Courageous Lancaster, embrace thy
    king! 340
And, as gross vapors perish by the sun,
Even so let hatred with thy sovereign's [3]
    smile.
Live thou with me as my companion.
Lan. This salutation overjoys my heart.

Edw. Warwick shall be my chiefest coun-
    selor.
These silver hairs will more adorn my
    court
Than gaudy silks, or rich imbrothery. [4]
Chide me, sweet Warwick, if I go astray.
War. Slay me, my lord, when I offend
    your grace.
Edw. In solemn triumphs and in public
    shows, 350
Pembroke shall bear the sword before
    the king.
Pem. And with this sword Pembroke will
    fight for you.
Edw. But wherefore walks young Morti-
    mer aside?
Be thou commander of our royal fleet;
Or, if that lofty office like thee not,
I make thee here lord marshal of the
    realm.
Mor. Jun. My lord, I'll marshal so your
    enemies
As England shall be quiet, and you safe.
Edw. And as for you, Lord Mortimer of
    Chirke,
Whose great achievements in our foreign
    war 360
Deserves no common place nor mean
    reward,
Be you the general of the levied troops
That now are ready to assail the Scots.
Mor. Sen. In this your grace hath highly
    honored me,
For with my nature war doth best agree.
Queen. Now is the King of England rich
    and strong,
Having the love of his renownéd peers.
Edw. Ay, Isabel, ne'er was my heart so
    light.
Clerk of the crown, direct our warrant
    forth
For Gaveston to Ireland.—Beaumont,
    fly 370
As fast as Iris or Jove's Mercury.
Beau. It shall be done, my gracious lord.
Edw. Lord Mortimer, we leave you to
    your charge.
Now let us in, and feast it royally.
Against our friend the Earl of Corn-
    wall comes,
We'll have a general tilt and tournament; [5]

---

[1] Struck.   [2] The devil.
[3] From 1612 edn. Original reads *sovereign.*

[4] Embroidery.
[5] *I.e.*, in anticipation of his coming, we'll prepare for a general tilt, etc.

And then his marriage shall be solemnized.

For wot you not that I have made him sure [1]

Unto our cousin,[2] the Earl of Gloucester's heir?

LAN. Such news we hear, my lord.   380

EDW. That day, if not for him, yet for my sake,

Who [3] in the triumph [4] will be challenger,

Spare for no cost. We will requite your love.

WAR. In this, or aught, your highness shall command us.

EDW. Thanks, gentle Warwick. Come, let's in and revel.

Exeunt. Manent [5] Mortimers.

MOR. SEN. Nephew, I must to Scotland; thou stayest here.

Leave now to oppose thyself against the king.

Thou seest by nature he is mild and calm,

And, seeing his mind so dotes on Gaveston,

Let him without controlment have his will.   390

The mightiest kings have had their minions:

Great Alexander loved Ephestion;

The conquering Hercules [6] for Hylas wept;

And for Patroclus stern Achilles drooped;

And not kings only, but the wisest men:

The Roman Tully loved Octavius;

Grave Socrates, wild Alcibiades.

Then let his grace, whose youth is flexible,

And promiseth as much as we can wish,

Freely enjoy that vain, light-headed earl;

For riper years will wean him from such toys.   401

MOR. JUN. Uncle, his wanton humor grieves not me;

But this I scorn, that one so basely born

Should by his sovereign's favor grow so pert,

And riot it with the treasure of the realm.

While soldiers mutiny for want of pay,

He wears a lord's revenue on his back,

And Midas-like he jets [7] it in the court,

With base, outlandish cullions [8] at his heels,

Whose proud, fantastic liveries make such show   410

As if that Proteus, god of shapes, appeared.

I have not seen a dapper Jack [9] so brisk.

He wears a short Italian-hooded cloak

Larded with pearl, and in his Tuscan cap

A jewel of more value than the crown.

Whiles other walk below, the king and he

From out a window laugh at such as we,

And flout our train, and jest at our attire.

Uncle, 'tis this that makes me impatient.

MOR. SEN. But, nephew, now you see the king is changed.   420

MOR. JUN. Then so am I, and live to do him service.

But, whiles I have a sword, a hand, a heart,

I will not yield to any such upstart.

You know my mind; come, uncle, let's away.   *Exeunt.*

[SCENE v.

A room in Gloucester's castle.]

Enter Spencer [10] and Baldock.

BALD. Spencer, seeing that our lord th' Earl of Gloucester's dead,

Which of the nobles dost thou mean to serve?

SPEN. Not Mortimer, nor any of his side,

Because the king and he are enemies.

Baldock, learn this of me, a factious lord

Shall hardly do himself good, much less us;

But he that hath the favor of a king

May with one word advance us while we live.

The liberal Earl of Cornwall is the man

On whose good fortune Spencer's hope depends.   10

BALD. What, mean you then to be his follower?

SPEN. No, his companion, for he loves me well,

And would have once preferred [11] me to the king.

---

[1] Betrothed him.   [4] Tournament.
[2] Relative; here, niece.   [5] Remain.
[3] Whoever.   [6] Original reads *Hector*.

[7] Struts.   [10] *I.e.,* young Spencer.
[8] Rascals.   [11] Recommended.
[9] Knave.

BALD. But he is banished; there's small hope of him.

SPEN. Ay, for a while, but, Baldock, mark the end.
A friend of mine told me in secrecy
That he's repealed, and sent for back again;
And even now a post came from the court
With letters to our lady from the king,
And as she read she smiled, which makes me think　　20
It is about her lover Gaveston.

BALD. 'Tis like enough, for, since he was exiled,
She neither walks abroad, nor comes in sight.
But I had thought the match had been broke off,
And that his banishment had changed her mind.

SPEN. Our lady's first love is not wavering;
My life for thine, she will have Gaveston.

BALD. Then hope I by her means to be preferred,
Having read unto her since she was a child.

SPEN. Then, Baldock, you must cast the scholar off,　　30
And learn to court it like a gentleman.
'Tis not a black coat and a little band,
A velvet-caped coat, faced before with serge,
And smelling to a nosegay all the day,
Or holding of a napkin[1] in your hand,
Or saying a long grace at a table's end,
Or making low legs[2] to a nobleman,
Or looking downward with your eyelids close,
And saying, "Truly, an't[3] may please your honor,"
Can get you any favor with great men.　　40
You must be proud, bold, pleasant, resolute,
And now and then stab, as occasion serves.

BALD. Spencer, thou knowest I hate such formal toys,
And use them but of mere hypocrisy.
Mine old lord whiles he lived was so precise

That he would take exceptions at my buttons,
And, being like pin's heads, blame me for the bigness,
Which made me curatelike in mine attire,
Though inwardly licentious enough
And apt for any kind of villainy.　　50
I am none of these common pedants,[4] I,
That cannot speak without *propterea quod.*[5]

SPEN. But one of those that saith *quandoquidem,*[6]
And hath a special gift to form a verb.

BALD. Leave off this jesting; here my lady comes.

Enter the Lady [, Gloucester's daughter].

LADY. The grief for his exile was not so much
As is the joy of his returning home.
This letter came from my sweet Gaveston.
What need'st thou, love, thus to excuse thyself?
I know thou couldst not come and visit me.　　60
[*Reads.*] "I will not long be from thee, though I die."
This argues the entire love of my lord.
[*Reads.*] "When I forsake thee, death seize on my heart."
But rest thee here where Gaveston shall sleep.　　[*Puts the letter into her bosom.*]
Now to the letter of my lord the king.—
He wills me to repair unto the court,
And meet my Gaveston. Why do I stay,
Seeing that he talks thus of my marriage day?—
Who's there? Baldock!
See that my coach be ready; I must hence.　　70

BALD. It shall be done, madam.　　*Exit.*

LADY. And meet me at the park pale[7] presently.—
Spencer, stay you and bear me company,
For I have joyful news to tell thee of.
My Lord of Cornwall is a-coming over,
And will be at the court as soon as we.

SPEN. I knew the king would have him home again.

[1] Handkerchief.　　[2] Bows.　　[3] If it.
[4] From 1598 edn. Original reads *pendants.*
[5] On account of which.
[6] Seeing that.　　[7] Enclosure or gate.

LADY. If all things sort out [1] as I hope they
will,
Thy service, Spencer, shall be thought
upon.
SPEN. I humbly thank your ladyship. 80
LADY. Come, lead the way; I long till I am
there. [*Exeunt.*]

[SCENE vi.

Before Tynemouth Castle.]

*Enter Edward, the Queen, Lancaster, Mor-
timer [, Junior], Warwick, Pembroke,
Kent, Attendants.*

EDW. The wind is good—I wonder why he
stays;
I fear me he is wracked upon the sea.
QUEEN. Look, Lancaster, how passion-
ate [2] he is,
And still [3] his mind runs on his minion!
LAN. My lord—
EDW. How now! What news? Is Gaveston
arrived?
MOR. JUN. Nothing but Gaveston! What
means your grace?
You have matters of more weight to
think upon;
The King of France sets foot in Nor-
mandy.
EDW. A trifle! We'll expel him when we
please. 10
But tell me, Mortimer, what's thy device
Against the stately triumph we decreed?
MOR. JUN. A homely one, my lord, not
worth the telling.
EDW. Prithee, let me know it.
MOR. JUN. But, seeing you are so desirous,
thus it is:
A lofty cedar tree, fair flourishing,
On whose top branches kingly eagles
perch,
And by the bark a canker creeps me up,
And gets unto the highest bough of all.
The motto: *Æque tandem.*[4] 20
EDW. And what is yours, my Lord of Lan-
caster?
LAN. My lord, mine's more obscure than
Mortimer's.
Pliny reports there is a flying fish
Which all the other fishes deadly hate,
And therefore, being pursued, it takes
the air;

No sooner is it up, but there's a fowl
That seizeth it. This fish, my lord, I bear.
The motto this: *Undique mors est.*[5]
EDW. Proud Mortimer, ungentle Lancas-
ter,
Is this the love you bear your sov-
ereign? 30
Is this the fruit your reconcilement bears?
Can you in words make show of amity,
And in your shields display your ran-
corous minds?
What call you this but private libeling
Against the Earl of Cornwall and my
brother?
QUEEN. Sweet husband, be content; they
all love you.
EDW. They love me not that hate my
Gaveston.
I am that cedar; shake me not too much.
And you, the eagles, soar ye ne'er so high,
I have the jesses [6] that will pull you
down; 40
And *Æque tandem* shall that canker cry
Unto the proudest peer of Britainy.
Though thou compar'st him to a flying
fish,
And threatenest death whether he rise
or fall,
'Tis not the hugest monster of the sea
Nor foulest harpy that shall swallow him.
MOR. JUN. [*Aside.*] If in his absence thus
he favors him,
What will he do whenas [7] he shall be
present?
LAN. [*Aside.*] That shall we see; look
where his lordship comes.

Enter Gaveston.

EDW. My Gaveston! Welcome to Tyne-
mouth! Welcome to thy friend! 50
Thy absence made me droop and pine
away;
For, as the lovers of fair Danaë,
When she was locked up in a brazen
tower,
Desired her more, and waxed outrageous,
So did it sure with me; and now thy
sight
Is sweeter far than was thy parting
hence
Bitter and irksome to my sobbing heart.

[5] Death is everywhere.
[6] Legstraps fastening a hawk to his leash.
Original reads *gresses.*   [7] When.

[1] Chance, turn out.   [3] Always.
[2] Sorrowful.   [4] Justly at last.

GAV. Sweet lord and king, your speech preventeth [1] mine,

Yet have I words left to express my joy.

The shepherd, nipped with biting winter's rage, 60

Frolics not more to see the painted spring

Than I do to behold your majesty.

EDW. Will none of you salute my Gaveston?

LAN. Salute him? Yes. Welcome, lord chamberlain!

MOR. JUN. Welcome is the good Earl of Cornwall!

WAR. Welcome, Lord Governor of the Isle of Man!

PEM. Welcome, Master Secretary!

EDM. Brother, do you hear them?

EDW. Still will these earls and barons use me thus?

GAV. My lord, I cannot brook these injuries. 70

QUEEN. [Aside.] Ay me, poor soul, when these begin to jar.

EDW. Return it to their throats; I'll be thy warrant.

GAV. Base, leaden earls, that glory in your birth,

Go sit at home and eat your tenants' beef;

And come not here to scoff at Gaveston,

Whose mounting thoughts did never creep so low

As to bestow a look on such as you.

LAN. Yet I disdain not to do this for you!
[Offers to stab Gaveston.]

EDW. Treason! Treason! Where's the traitor?

PEM. Here! Here!

[EDW.] [2] Convey hence Gaveston; they'll murder him! 80

GAV. The life of thee shall salve this foul disgrace.

MOR. JUN. Villain, thy life, unless I miss mine aim. [Wounds Gaveston.]

QUEEN. Ah, furious Mortimer, what hast thou done?

MOR. JUN. No more than I would answer, were he slain.

EDW. Yes, more than thou canst answer, though he live.

[1] Anticipateth.
[2] Original has King printed as part of preceding speech.

Dear shall you both aby [3] this riotous deed.

Out of my presence! Come not near the court!

MOR. JUN. I'll not be barred the court for Gaveston.

LAN. We'll hale him by the ears unto the block.

EDW. Look to your own heads; his is sure enough. 90

WAR. Look to your own crown, if you back him thus.

EDM. Warwick, these words do ill beseem thy years.

EDW. Nay, all of them conspire to cross me thus;

But, if I live, I'll tread upon their heads

That think with high looks thus to tread me down.

Come, Edmund, let's away and levy men;

'Tis war that must abate these barons' pride.
Exit the King [with his Train].

WAR. Let's to our castles, for the king is moved.

MOR. JUN. Moved may he be, and perish in his wrath! 99

LAN. Cousin, it is no dealing with him now.

He means to make us stoop by force of arms,

And therefore let us jointly here protest

To prosecute that Gaveston to the death.

MOR. JUN. By heaven, the abject villain shall not live!

WAR. I'll have his blood, or die in seeking it.

PEM. The like oath Pembroke takes.

LAN. And so doth Lancaster.

Now send our heralds to defy the king;

And make the people swear to put him down.

Enter a Post.

MOR. JUN. Letters! From whence?

MESS. From Scotland, my lord. 110
[Gives letters to Mortimer.]

LAN. Why, how now, cousin, how fares all our friends?

[3] Pay for.

Mor. Jun. My uncle's taken prisoner
by the Scots.

Lan. We'll have him ransomed, man; be
of good cheer.

Mor. Jun. They rate his ransom at five
thousand pound.
Who should defray the money but the
king,
Seeing he is taken prisoner in his wars?
I'll to the king.

Lan. Do, cousin, and I'll bear thee company.

War. Meantime, my Lord of Pembroke
and myself
Will to Newcastle here, and gather
head.[1]   120

Mor. Jun. About it then, and we will
follow you.

Lan. Be resolute and full of secrecy.

War. I warrant you.

[*Exit with Pembroke.*]

Mor. Jun. Cousin, and if[2] he will not
ransom him,
I'll thunder such a peal into his ears
As never subject did unto his king.

Lan. Content, I'll bear my part.—Holla!
Who's there?

[*Enter Guard.*]

Mor. Jun. Ay, marry, such a guard as
this doth well.

Lan. Lead on the way.

Guard. Whither will your lordships? 129

Mor. Jun. Whither else but to the king?

Guard. His highness is disposed to be
alone.

Lan. Why, so he may, but we will speak
to him.

Guard. You may not in, my lord.

Mor. Jun. May we not?

[*Enter Edward and Kent.*]

Edw. How now! What noise is this?
Who have we there? Is't you?

Mor. Jun. Nay, stay, my lord; I come
to bring you news;
Mine uncle's taken prisoner by the
Scots.

Edw. Then ransom him.

Lan. 'Twas in your wars; you should
ransom him.   140

Mor. Jun. And you shall ransom him,
or else——

Edm. What, Mortimer, you will not
threaten him?

Edw. Quiet yourself; you shall have the
broad seal
To gather[3] for him throughout the
realm.

Lan. Your minion Gaveston hath taught
you this.

Mor. Jun. My lord, the family of the
Mortimers
Are not so poor but, would they sell
their land,
Would levy men enough to anger you.
We never beg, but use such prayers as
these.

Edw. Shall I still be haunted thus?   150

Mor. Jun. Nay, now you're here alone,
I'll speak my mind.

Lan. And so will I, and then, my lord,
farewell.

Mor. Jun. The idle triumphs, masques,
lascivious shows,
And prodigal gifts bestowed on Gaveston
Have drawn thy treasury dry, and made
thee weak,
The murmuring commons overstretchéd
hath.[4]

Lan. Look for rebellion; look to be de-
posed.
Thy garrisons are beaten out of France,
And, lame and poor, lie groaning at
the gates.
The wild O'Neill, with swarms of Irish
kerns,[5]   160
Lives uncontrolled within the English
pale.
Unto the walls of York the Scots made
road,
And unresisted drave away rich spoils.

Mor. Jun. The haughty Dane commands
the narrow seas,
While in the harbor ride thy ships un-
rigged.

Lan. What foreign prince sends thee ambassadors?

Mor. Jun. Who loves thee but a sort[6]
of flatterers?

Lan. Thy gentle queen, sole sister to Valois,
Complains that thou hast left her all
forlorn.

[1] Troops.   [2] Emphatic form of *if*.

[3] Collect alms.
[4] *I.e.*, the idle triumphs, etc., have over-
stretched the murmuring commons.
[5] Foot soldiers.   [6] Company.

MOR. JUN. Thy court is naked, being bereft of those   170
That makes a king seem glorious to the world—
I mean the peers, whom thou shouldst dearly love.
Libels are cast again [1] thee in the street;
Ballads and rimes made of thy overthrow.

LAN. The northern borderers, seeing the houses burnt,
Their wives and children slain, run up and down,
Cursing the name of thee and Gaveston.

MOR. JUN. When wert thou in the field with banner spread,
But once? And then thy soldiers marched like players,
With garish robes, not armor; and thyself,   180
Bedaubed with gold, rode laughing at the rest,
Nodding and shaking of thy spangled crest,
Where women's favors hung like labels down.

LAN. And therefore came it that the fleering Scots,
To England's high disgrace, have made this jig: [2]

Maids of England, sore may you mourn
For your lemans [3] you have lost at Bannocksbourn. [4]
   With a heave and a ho!
What, weeneth [5] the King of England
So soon to have won Scotland?   190
   With a rombelow!

MOR. JUN. Wigmore shall fly [6] to set my uncle free.

LAN. And, when 'tis gone, our swords shall purchase more.
If ye be moved, revenge it as you can;
Look next to see us with our ensigns spread.   *Exeunt Nobles.*

EDW. My swelling heart for very anger breaks!
How oft have I been baited by these peers,
And dare not be revenged, for their power is great!

[1] Against.   [2] Comic song.   [3] Lovers.
[4] Bannockburn was not actually fought until 1314.   [5] Imagineth.
[6] *I.e.*, Mortimer will sell his estate.

Yet shall the crowing of these cockerels
Affright a lion? Edward, unfold thy paws,   200
And let their lives' blood slake thy fury's hunger.
If I be cruel and grow tyrannous,
Now let them thank themselves, and rue too late.

KENT. My lord, I see your love to Gaveston
Will be the ruin of the realm and you,
For now the wrathful nobles threaten wars,
And therefore, brother, banish him forever.

EDW. Art thou an enemy to my Gaveston?

KENT. Ay, and it grieves me that I favored him.

EDW. Traitor, begone! Whine thou with Mortimer.   210

KENT. So will I, rather than with Gaveston.

EDW. Out of my sight, and trouble me no more!

KENT. No marvel though thou scorn thy noble peers,
When I thy brother am rejected thus.
             Exit.

EDW. Away!—Poor Gaveston, that hast no friend but me,
Do what they can, we'll live in Tynemouth here,
And, so I walk with him about the walls,
What care I though the earls begirt us round?—
Here comes she that's cause of all these jars.

Enter the Queen, Ladies three, [Gaveston,] Baldock, and Spencer.

QUEEN. My lord, 'tis thought the earls are up in arms.   220

EDW. Ay, and 'tis likewise thought you favor him. [7]

QUEEN. Thus do you still suspect me without cause.

LADY. [8] Sweet uncle, speak more kindly to the queen.

GAV. [*Aside.*] My lord, dissemble with her; speak her fair.

EDW. Pardon me, sweet, I forgot myself.

[7] *I.e.*, Mortimer.   [8] Gloucester's daughter.

QUEEN. Your pardon is quickly got of Isabel.

EDW. The younger Mortimer is grown so brave
That to my face he threatens civil wars.

GAV. Why do you not commit him to the Tower?

EDW. I dare not, for the people love him well.   230

GAV. Why, then we'll have him privily made away.

EDW. Would Lancaster and he had both caroused [1]
A bowl of poison to each other's health!
But let them go, and tell me what are these.

LADY. Two of my father's servants whilst he lived.
May't please your grace to entertain them now.

EDW. Tell me, where wast thou born? What is thine arms?

BALD. My name is Baldock, and my gentry
I fetched from Oxford, not from heraldry.

EDW. The fitter art thou, Baldock, for my turn.   240
Wait on me, and I'll see thou shalt not want.

BALD. I humbly thank your majesty.

EDW. Knowest thou him, Gaveston?

GAV.   Ay, my lord;
His name is Spencer; he is well allied.
For my sake, let him wait upon your grace;
Scarce shall you find a man of more desert.

EDW. Then, Spencer, wait upon me; for his sake
I'll grace thee with a higher style ere long.

SPEN. No greater titles happen unto me
Than to be favored of your majesty.

EDW. Cousin, this day shall be your marriage feast.   251
And, Gaveston, think that I love thee well
To wed thee to our niece, the only heir
Unto the Earl of Gloucester late deceased.

GAV. I know, my lord, many will stomach me,
But I respect neither their love nor hate.

[1] Drunk.

EDW. The headstrong barons shall not limit me;
He that I list to favor shall be great.
Come, let's away; and, when the marriage ends,   259
Have at the rebels, and their complices! [2]
                               Exeunt omnes.

[SCENE vii.

The rebels' camp near Tynemouth Castle.]

Enter Lancaster, Mortimer, Jun[ior,] Warwick, Pembroke, Kent.

KENT. My lords, of love to this our native land
I come to join with you and leave the king,
And in your quarrel and the realm's behoof
Will be the first that shall adventure life.

LAN. I fear me, you are sent of policy, [3]
To undermine us with a show of love.

WAR. He is your brother; therefore have we cause
To cast [4] the worst, and doubt of your revolt.

EDM. Mine honor shall be hostage of my truth;
If that will not suffice, farewell, my lords!   10

MOR. JUN. Stay, Edmund; never was Plantagenet
False to his word, and therefore trust we thee.

PEM. But what's the reason you should leave him now?

KENT. I have informed the Earl of Lancaster.

LAN. And it sufficeth. Now, my lords, know this,
That Gaveston is secretly arrived,
And here in Tynemouth frolics with the king,
Let us with these our followers scale the walls,
And suddenly surprise them unawares. 19

MOR. JUN. I'll give the onset.

WAR.   And I'll follow thee.

MOR. JUN. This tottered [5] ensign of my ancestors,

[2] Accomplices.   [4] Forecast, suspect
[3] In trickery.   [5] Tattered.

Which swept the desert shore of that
　　dead sea
Whereof we got the name of Mortimer,
Will I advance upon this castle walls.
Drums, strike alarum, raise them from
　　their sport,
And ring aloud the knell of Gaveston!
LAN. None be so hardy as to touch the
　　king;
But neither spare you Gaveston nor
　　his friends.　　　　　　　　*Exeunt.*

[SCENE viii.

In Tynemouth Castle.]

*Enter the King and Spencer; to them
　　　　　　　　　　　Gaveston, etc.*

EDW. O, tell me, Spencer, where is Gaves-
　　ton?
SPEN. I fear me he is slain, my gracious
　　lord.
EDW. No, here he comes; now let them
　　spoil and kill.—
Fly, fly, my lords; the earls have got
　　the hold!
Take shipping and away to Scarborough!
Spencer and I will post away by land.
GAV. O, stay, my lord; they will not in-
　　jure you.
EDW. I will not trust them; Gaveston,
　　away!
GAV. Farewell, my lord.
EDW. Lady, farewell.　　　　　　　　10
LADY. Farewell, sweet uncle, till we meet
　　again.
EDW. Farewell, sweet Gaveston, and fare-
　　well, niece.
QUEEN. No farewell to poor Isabel, thy
　　queen?
EDW. Yes, yes, for Mortimer, your lover's
　　sake.　　*Exeunt omnes; manet Isabella.*
QUEEN. Heavens can witness I love none
　　but you!
From my embracements thus he breaks
　　away.
O, that mine arms could close this isle
　　about,
That I might pull him to me where I
　　would,
Or that these tears that drizzle from mine
　　eyes
Had power to mollify his stony heart, 20
That when I had him we might never
　　part!

Enter the Barons. Alarums.

LAN. I wonder how he scaped!
MOR. JUN.　　　　Who's this? The queen!
QUEEN. Ay, Mortimer, the miserable
　　queen,
Whose pining heart her inward sighs have
　　blasted,
And body with continual mourning
　　wasted.
These hands are tired with haling of my
　　lord
From Gaveston, from wicked Gaveston;
And all in vain, for, when I speak him fair,
He turns away, and smiles upon his
　　minion.
MOR. JUN. Cease to lament, and tell us
　　where's the king.　　　　　　　　30
QUEEN. What would you with the king?
　　Is't him you seek?
LAN. No, madam, but that curséd Gaves-
　　ton.
Far be it from the thought of Lancaster
To offer violence to his sovereign.
We would but rid the realm of Gaveston.
Tell us where he remains, and he shall die.
QUEEN. He's gone by water unto Scar-
　　borough;
Pursue him quickly, and he cannot scape.
The king hath left him, and his train is
　　small.
WAR. Foreslow [1] no time, sweet Lancaster;
　　let's march.　　　　　　　　40
MOR. JUN. How comes it that the king and
　　he is parted?
QUEEN. That this your army, going several
　　ways,
Might be of lesser force, and, with the
　　power
That he intendeth presently to raise,
Be easily suppressed. And therefore be-
　　gone!
MOR. JUN. Here in the river rides a Flem-
　　ish hoy; [2]
Let's all aboard, and follow him amain.
LAN. The wind that bears him hence will
　　fill our sails.
Come, come aboard; 'tis but an hour's
　　sailing.
MOR. JUN. Madam, stay you within this
　　castle here.　　　　　　　　50
QUEEN. No, Mortimer, I'll to my lord the
　　king.

[1] Delay, lose.　　　　　　　　[2] Small ship.

Mor. Jun. Nay, rather sail with us to
Scarborough.

Queen. You know the king is so suspicious
As, if he hear I have but talked with you,
Mine honor will be called in question;
And therefore, gentle Mortimer, begone.

Mor. Jun. Madam, I cannot stay to answer you,
But think of Mortimer as he deserves.

Queen. [Aside.] So well hast thou de-
served, sweet Mortimer,
As Isabel could live with thee forever! 60
In vain I look for love at Edward's hand,
Whose eyes are fixed on none but Gaves-
ton;
Yet once more I'll importune him with
prayers.
If he be strange and not regard my
words,
My son and I will over into France,
And to the king my brother there com-
plain
How Gaveston hath robbed me of his
love.
But yet I hope my sorrows will have end,
And Gaveston this blessed day be slain.
                                        Exeunt.

[Scene ix.

A field near Pembroke's castle.]

Enter Gaveston, pursued.

Gav. Yet, lusty lords, I have escaped your
hands,
Your threats, your larums, and your hot
pursuits;
And, though divorcéd from King Edward's eyes,
Yet liveth Pierce of Gaveston unsur-
prised,[1]
Breathing, in hope (malgrado all your
beards,[2]
That muster revels thus against your
king)
To see his royal sovereign once again.

Enter the Nobles [with Attendants].

War. Upon him, soldiers; take away his
weapons!

Mor. Jun. Thou proud disturber of thy
country's peace,
Corrupter of thy king, cause of these
broils,   10

[1] Uncaptured.   [2] In spite of all your defiance.

Base flatterer, yield! And were it not for
shame,
Shame and dishonor to a soldier's name,
Upon my weapon's point here shouldst
thou fall,
And welter in thy gore.

Lan.   Monster of men,
That, like the Greekish strumpet,[3]
trained[4] to arms
And bloody wars so many valiant
knights,
Look for no other fortune, wretch, than
death!
King Edward is not here to buckler thee.

War. Lancaster, why talk'st thou to the
slave?
Go, soldiers, take him hence, for, by my
sword,   20
His head shall off. Gaveston, short warn-
ing
Shall serve thy turn; it is our country's
cause
That here severely we will execute
Upon thy person. Hang him at a bough.

Gav. My lord—!

War.   Soldiers, have him away!—
But, for[5] thou wert the favorite of a
king,
Thou shalt have so much honor at our
hands—[6]

Gav. I thank you all, my lords. Then I
perceive
That heading is one, and hanging is the
other,
And death is all.

Enter Earl of Arundel.

Lan.   How now, my Lord of Arundel?

Arun. My lords, King Edward greets you
all by me.   31

War. Arundel, say your message.

Arun.   His majesty,
Hearing that you had taken Gaveston,
Entreateth you by me, yet but he may
See him before he dies; forwhy,[7] he says,
And sends you word, he knows that die
he shall;
And, if you gratify his grace so far,
He will be mindful of the courtesy.

War. How now?

[3] Helen of Troy   [6] I.e., as to be beheaded.
[4] Lured.   [7] Because.
[5] Since.

Gav.　　　　　　Renownéd Edward, how
　thy name　　　　　　　　　　39
　Revives poor Gaveston!
War.　　　　　　No, it needeth not;
　Arundel, we will gratify the king
　In other matters; he must pardon us in
　this.
　Soldiers, away with him!
Gav.　　　　　　Why, my Lord of Warwick,
　Will not these delays beget my hopes?
　I know it, lords, it is this life you aim at;
　Yet grant King Edward this.
Mor. Jun.　　　　　　Shalt thou appoint
　What we shall grant?　Soldiers, away
　with him!
　Thus we'll gratify the king:
　We'll send his head by thee.　Let him be-
　stow　　　　　　　　　　49
　His tears on that, for that is all he gets
　Of Gaveston, or else his senseless trunk.
Lan.　Not so, my lord, lest he bestow more
　cost
　In burying him than he hath ever earned.
Arun.　My lords, it is his majesty's request,
　And in the honor of a king he swears,
　He will but talk with him, and send him
　back.
War.　When?　Can you tell?　Arundel, no!
　We wot
　He that the care of realm remits,
　And drives his nobles to these exigents [1]
　For Gaveston, will, if he sees him once,
　Violate any promise to possess him.　61
Arun.　Then if you will not trust his grace
　in keep, [2]
　My lords, I will be pledge for his return.
Mor. Jun.　It is honorable in thee to offer
　this;
　But, for we know thou art a noble gentle-
　man,
　We will not wrong thee so,
　To make away a true man for a thief.
Gav.　How mean'st thou, Mortimer?　That
　is overbase.
Mor. Jun.　Away, base groom, robber of
　king's renowm!
　Question with thy companions and thy
　mates.　　　　　　　　　　70
Pem.　My Lord Mortimer, and you, my
　lords, each one,
　To gratify the king's request therein,
　Touching the sending of this Gaveston,
　Because his majesty so earnestly

Desires to see the man before his death,
　I will upon mine honor undertake
　To carry him, and bring him back again;
　Provided this, that you, my Lord of
　Arundel,
　Will join with me.
War.　　　Pembroke, what wilt thou do?
　Cause yet more bloodshed?　Is it not
　enough　　　　　　　　　　80
　That we have taken him, but must we
　now
　Leave him on "had I wist," [3] and let
　him go?
Pem.　My lords, I will not overwoo your
　honors,
　But, if you dare trust Pembroke with the
　prisoner,
　Upon mine oath, I will return him back.
Arun.　My Lord of Lancaster, what say
　you in this?
Lan.　Why, I say, let him go on Pem-
　broke's word.
Pem.　And you, Lord Mortimer?
Mor. Jun.　How say you, my Lord of War-
　wick?
War.　Nay, do your pleasures; I know how
　'twill prove.　　　　　　　　　　90
Pem.　Then give him me.
Gav.　　　Sweet sovereign, yet I come
　To see thee ere I die.
War.　[Aside.]　　　　Yet not perhaps,
　If Warwick's wit and policy prevail.
Mor. Jun.　My Lord of Pembroke, we de-
　liver him you;
　Return him on your honor.　Sound away!
Exeunt.　　Manent　Pembroke,　Arundel, [4]
　　Gavest[on],　and　Pembroke's　Men for
　　　　　　　　　　　　　　soldiers.
Pem.　My lord, you shall go with me.
　My house is not far hence, out of the way
　A little; but our men shall go along.
　We that have pretty wenches to our
　wives,
　Sir, must not come so near and balk
　their lips.　　　　　　　　　　100
Arun. [4]　'Tis very kindly spoke, my Lord
　of Pembroke;
　Your honor hath an adamant [5] of power
　To draw a prince.

[3] "Had I known—the exclamation of those
who repent of what they have rashly done"
(Dyce).
[4] Original reads *Mat[revis]*, probably, as Dyce
suggests, because the parts of Arundel and Matrevis were taken by the same actor.　[5] Magnet.

[1] Straits.　　　　　　[2] Custody.

PEM.   So, my lord. Come
  hither, James.
I do commit this Gaveston to thee;
Be thou this night his keeper; in the
  morning
We will discharge thee of thy charge.
  Begone!
GAV. Unhappy Gaveston, whither goest
  thou now?   *Exit cum servis Pem.*[1]
HORSE BOY. My lord, we'll quickly be at
  Cobham.   *Exeunt ambo.*

[SCENE x.

A road to Boroughbridge, Yorkshire.]

*Enter Gaveston, mourning, and the Earl of
                    Pembroke's Men.*

GAV. O treacherous Warwick, thus to
  wrong thy friend!
JAMES. I see it is your life these arms pur-
  sue.
GAV. Weaponless must I fall, and die in
  bands?
O, must this day be period of my life?
Center of all my bliss! And ye be men,
Speed to the king!

Enter Warwick and his Company.

WAR.   My Lord of Pembroke's men,
Strive you no longer—I will have that
  Gaveston.
JAMES. Your lordship doth dishonor to
  yourself,
And wrong our lord, your honorable
  friend.
WAR. No, James, it is my country's cause
  I follow.   10
Go, take the villain; soldiers, come away.
We'll make quick work. Commend me
  to your master,
My friend, and tell him that I watched
  it well.
Come, let thy shadow [2] parley with King
  Edward.
GAV. Treacherous earl, shall I not see the
  king?
WAR. The King of Heaven, perhaps; no
  other king.
Away!
*Exeunt Warwick and his Men with Gavest[on].
          Manet James cum cæteris.*[3]

[1] With Pembroke's servants.   [3] With the rest.
[2] Ghost.

[JAMES.] Come, fellows, it booted not for
  us to strive.
We will in haste go certify our lord.
                    Exeunt.

[SCENE xi.

Near Boroughbridge.]

*Enter King Edward, [Baldock,] and Spencer,
                    with drums and fifes.*

EDW. I long to hear an answer from the
  barons
Touching my friend, my dearest Gaves-
  ton.
Ah, Spencer, not the riches of my realm
Can ransom him! Ah, he is marked to
  die!
I know the malice of the younger Mor-
  timer;
Warwick, I know, is rough; and Lan-
  caster
Inexorable; and I shall never see
My lovely Pierce, my Gaveston again!
The barons overbear me with their pride.
SPEN. Were I King Edward, England's
  sovereign,   10
Son to the lovely Eleanor of Spain,
Great Edward Longshanks' issue, would
  I bear
These braves, this rage, and suffer un-
  controlled
These barons thus to beard me in my
  land,
In mine own realm? My lord, pardon my
  speech:
Did you retain your father's magnanim-
  ity,
Did you regard the honor of your name,
You would not suffer thus your majesty
Be counterbuffed of [4] your nobility.
Strike off their heads, and let them
  preach on poles!   20
No doubt, such lessons they will teach
  the rest
As by their preachments they will profit
  much,
And learn obedience to their lawful king.
EDW. Yea, gentle Spencer, we have been
  too mild,
Too kind to them, but now have drawn
  our sword.
And, if they send me not my Gaveston,

[4] Curbed by.

We'll steel it [1] on their crest, and poll [2] their tops.

BALD. This haught [3] resolve becomes your majesty,
Not to be tied to their affection,
As though your highness were a school-boy still,   30
And must be awed and governed like a child.

Enter Hugh Spencer, an old man, father to the young Spencer, with his truncheon, and Soldiers.

SPEN. FA[THER.] Long live my sovereign, the noble Edward,
In peace triumphant, fortunate in wars!
EDW. Welcome, old man; com'st thou in Edward's aid?
Then tell thy prince of whence, and what thou art.
SPEN. FA. Lo, with a band of bowmen and of pikes,
Brown bills and targeteers, four hundred strong,
Sworn to defend King Edward's royal right,
I come in person to your majesty,
Spencer, the father of Hugh Spencer there,   40
Bound to your highness everlastingly,
For favors done, in him, unto us all.
EDW. Thy father, Spencer?
SPEN.   True, and it like your grace,
That pours, in lieu of all your goodness shown,
His life, my lord, before your princely feet.
EDW. Welcome ten thousand times, old man, again.
Spencer, this love, this kindness to thy king,
Argues thy noble mind and disposition.
Spencer, I here create thee Earl of Wiltshire,
And daily will enrich thee with our favor,   50
That, as the sunshine, shall reflect o'er thee.
Beside, the more to manifest our love,
Because we hear Lord Bruce doth sell his land,

And that the Mortimers are in hand [4] withal,
Thou shalt have crowns of us t' outbid the barons.
And, Spencer, spare them not, but lay it on.
Soldiers, a largess, and thrice welcome all!
SPEN. My lord, here comes the queen.

Enter the Queen and her Son, and Levune, a Frenchman.

EDW.   Madam, what news?
QUEEN. News of dishonor, lord, and discontent.
Our friend Levune, faithful and full of trust,   60
Informeth us, by letters and by words,
That Lord Valois, our brother, King of France,
Because your highness hath been slack in homage,
Hath seizéd Normandy into his hands.
These be the letters, this the messenger.
EDW. Welcome, Levune. Tush, Sib, [5] if this be all,
Valois and I will soon be friends again.—
But to my Gaveston! Shall I never see,
Never behold thee now?—Madam, in this matter   69
We will employ you and your little son;
You shall go parley with the King of France.—
Boy, see you bear you bravely to the king,
And do your message with a majesty.
PRINCE. Commit not to my youth things of more weight
Than fits a prince so young as I to bear,
And fear not, lord and father, heaven's great beams
On Atlas' shoulder shall not lie more safe
Than shall your charge committed to my trust.
QUEEN. Ah, boy, this towardness [6] makes thy mother fear
Thou art not marked to many days on earth.   80
EDW. Madam, we will that you with speed be shipped,
And this our son. Levune shall follow you

[1] Use steel(?).   [2] Crop.   [3] Haughty, bold.

[4] In negotiation (to sell their lands).
[5] Either *gossip, dear,* or an abbreviation for *Isabella.*   [6] Aptness.

With all the haste we can despatch him
hence.
Choose of our lords to bear you com-
pany,
And go in peace; leave us in wars at
home.
QUEEN. Unnatural wars, where subjects
brave their king.
God end them once! My lord, I take
my leave,
To make my preparation for France.
[*Exit with Prince Edward.*]

Enter Lord Arundel.[1]

EDW. What, Lord Arundel, dost thou
come alone?
ARUN. Yea, my good lord, for Gaveston is
dead.   90
EDW. Ah, traitors! Have they put my
friend to death?
Tell me, Arundel, died he ere thou
cam'st,
Or didst thou see my friend to take his
death?
ARUN. Neither, my lord; for, as he was
surprised,
Begirt with weapons and with enemies
round,
I did your highness' message to them all,
Demanding him of them, entreating
rather,
And said, upon the honor of my name,
That I would undertake to carry him
Unto your highness, and to bring him
back.   100
EDW. And tell me, would the rebels deny
me that?
SPEN. Proud recreants!
EDW.   Yea, Spencer, traitors all.
ARUN. I found them at the first inexorable.
The Earl of Warwick would not bide the
hearing;
Mortimer hardly; Pembroke and Lan-
caster
Spake least. And, when they flatly had
denied,
Refusing to receive me pledge for him,
The Earl of Pembroke mildly thus be-
spake:
"My lords, because our sovereign sends
for him,   109
And promiseth he shall be safe returned,

[1] Original gives Arundel's part to Matrevis
throughout the scene.

I will this undertake, to have him hence,
And see him redelivered to your hands."
EDW. Well, and how fortunes that he came
not?
SPEN. Some treason, or some villainy, was
cause.
ARUN. The Earl of Warwick seized him on
his way,
For, being delivered unto Pembroke's
men,
Their lord rode home, thinking his pris-
oner safe.
But, ere he came, Warwick in ambush
lay,
And bare him to his death, and in a
trench
Strake[2] off his head, and marched unto
the camp.   120
SPEN. A bloody part, flatly against law of
arms!
EDW. O, shall I speak, or shall I sigh and
die?
SPEN. My lord, refer your vengeance to
the sword
Upon these barons; hearten up your men;
Let them not unrevenged murther your
friends!
Advance your standard, Edward, in the
field,
And march to fire them from their start-
ing holes.[3]
EDWARD (*Kneels and saith:*)
By earth, the common mother of us all,
By heaven and all the moving orbs
thereof,
By this right hand, and by my father's
sword,   130
And all the honors longing[4] to my
crown,
I will have heads and lives for him, as
many
As I have manors, castles, towns, and
towers!—   [*Rises.*]
Treacherous Warwick! Traitorous Mor-
timer!
If I be England's king, in lakes of gore
Your headless trunks, your bodies will I
trail,
That you may drink your fill, and quaff
in blood,
And stain my royal standard with the
same,

[2] Struck.   [4] Belonging.
[3] Refuges taken by hunted animals.

That so my bloody colors may suggest 139
Remembrance of revenge immortally
On your accurséd traitorous progeny,
You villains, that have slain my Gaves-
ton!
And in this place of honor and of trust,
Spencer, sweet Spencer, I adopt thee
here;
And merely [1] of our love we do create
thee
Earl of Gloucester and lord chamber-
lain,
Despite of times, despite of enemies.
SPEN. My lord, here is a messenger from
the barons,
Desires access unto your majesty.
EDW. Admit him near. 150

*Enter the Herald from the Barons with his
coat-of-arms.*

MESS. Long live King Edward, England's
lawful lord!
EDW. So wish not they, iwis, [2] that sent
thee hither.
Thou com'st from Mortimer and his
complices;
A ranker rout of rebels never was.
Well, say thy message.
MESS. The barons, up in arms, by me
salute
Your highness with long life and happi-
ness,
And bid me say, as plainer [3] to your
grace,
That, if without effusion of blood
You will this grief have ease and rem-
edy, 160
That from your princely person you re-
move
This Spencer, as a putrefying branch,
That deads the royal vine, whose golden
leaves
Empale your princely head, your diadem,
Whose brightness such pernicious up-
starts dim,
Say they, and lovingly advise your
grace
To cherish virtue and nobility,
And have old servitors in high esteem,
And shake off smooth dissembling flat-
terers.

[1] Purely.
[2] Certainly.
[3] Complainer, petitioner.

This granted, they, their honors, and
their lives 170
Are to your highness vowed and conse-
crate.
SPEN. Ah, traitors, will they still display
their pride?
EDW. Away, tarry no answer, but begone!
Rebels, will they appoint their sover-
eign
His sports, his pleasures, and his com-
pany?
Yet, ere thou go, see how I do divorce
Embrace Spencer.
Spencer from me.—Now get thee to thy
lords,
And tell them I will come to chastise
them
For murthering Gaveston. Hie thee, get
thee gone!
Edward with fire and sword follows at
thy heels. 180
My lords, perceive you how these rebels
swell?
Soldiers, good hearts, defend your sov-
ereign's right,
For now, even now, we march to make
them stoop.
Away! *Exeunt.*
*Alarums, excursions, a great fight, and a
retreat.*

*Enter the King, Spencer the Father, Spencer
the Son, and the Noblemen of the King's
side.*

EDW. Why do we sound retreat? Upon
them, lords!
This day I shall pour vengeance with my
sword
On those proud rebels that are up in
arms
And do confront and countermand [4] their
king.
SPEN. I doubt it not, my lord, right will
prevail.
SPEN. FA. 'Tis not amiss, my liege, for
either part 190
To breathe awhile. Our men, with sweat
and dust
All choked well near, begin to faint for
heat;
And this retire refresheth horse and man.
SPEN. Here come the rebels.

[4] Oppose.

Enter the Barons, Mortimer, [Junior,] Lancaster, Warwick, Pembroke, cum cæteris.

MOR. JUN. Look, Lancaster; yonder is
Edward among his flatterers.

LAN. And there let him be
Till he pay dearly for their company.

WAR. And shall, or Warwick's sword shall
smite in vain.

EDW. What, rebels. do you shrink and
sound retreat?

MOR. JUN. No, Edward, no; thy flatterers
faint and fly.   200

LAN. Th'ad [1] best betimes forsake them [2]
and their trains, [3]
For they'll betray thee, traitors as they
are.

SPEN. Traitor on thy face, rebellious Lancaster!

PEM. Away, base upstart! Brav'st thou
nobles thus?

SPEN. FA. A noble attempt and honorable
deed
Is it not, trow ye, to assemble aid
And levy arms against your lawful king!

EDW. For which ere long their heads shall
satisfy,
T' appease the wrath of their offended
king.

MOR. JUN. Then, Edward, thou wilt fight
it to the last,   210
And rather bathe thy sword in subjects'
blood
Than banish that pernicious company?

EDW. Ay, traitors all, rather than thus be
braved,
Make England's civil towns huge heaps
of stones,
And plows to go about our palace gates.

WAR. A desperate and unnatural resolution!
Alarum! To the fight!
St. George for England, and the barons'
right!

EDW. Saint George for England, and King
Edward's right!   [*Alarums. Exeunt.*]

*Enter Edward [and his Followers,] with the
Barons captives.*

EDW. Now, lusty lords, now, not by chance
of war,   220
But justice of the quarrel and the cause,

Vailed is your pride. Methinks you hang
the heads;
But we'll advance [4] them, traitors.
Now 'tis time
To be avenged on you for all your
braves, [5]
And for the murther of my dearest friend,
To whom right well you knew our soul
was knit,
Good Pierce of Gaveston, my sweet
favorite.
Ah, rebels, recreants, you made him
away!

EDM. Brother, in regard of thee and of thy
land
Did they remove that flatterer from thy
throne.   230

EDW. So, sir, you have spoke; away, avoid
our presence!—   [*Exit Kent.*]
Accursèd wretches, was't in regard of us,
When we had sent our messenger to request
He might be spared to come to speak
with us,
And Pembroke undertook for his return,
That thou, proud Warwick, watched the
prisoner,
Poor Pierce, and headed [6] him against law
of arms?
For which thy head shall overlook the
rest,
As much as thou in rage outwent'st the
rest.

WAR. Tyrant, I scorn thy threats and
menaces;   240
'Tis but temporal [7] that thou canst inflict.

LAN. The worst is death, and better die to
live
Than live in infamy under such a king.

EDW. Away with them, my Lord of Winchester!
These lusty leaders, Warwick and Lancaster,
I charge you roundly, off with both their
heads!
Away!

WAR. Farewell, vain world!

LAN.   Sweet Mortimer, farewell.

MOR. JUN. England, unkind to thy nobility,
Groan for this grief; behold how thou art
maimed!   250

[1] Thou had.   [3] Plots.
[2] Original reads *thee.*

[4] Raise.   [6] Beheaded.
[5] Boasts.   [7] Supply *punisnment.*

EDW. Go take that haughty Mortimer to
the Tower;
There see him safe bestowed. And, for
the rest,
Do speedy execution on them all.
Begone!
MOR. JUN. What, Mortimer, can ragged,
stony walls
Immure thy virtue that aspires to
heaven?
No, Edward, England's scourge, it may
not be;
Mortimer's hope surmounts his fortune
far.   [*The Barons are led away.*]
EDW. Sound drums and trumpets! March
with me, my friends.
Edward this day hath crowned him king
anew.   260
Exit [*with his Train*]. *Manent Spencer*
filius,[1] *Levune, and Baldock.*
SPEN. Levune, the trust that we repose in
thee
Begets the quiet of King Edward's
land.
Therefore begone in haste, and with
advice
Bestow that treasure on the lords of
France,
That, therewith all enchanted, like the
guard
That suffered Jove to pass in showers of
gold
To Danaë, all aid may be denied
To Isabel, the queen, that now in France
Makes friends, to cross the seas with her
young son,
And step into his father's regiment. 270
LEVUNE. That's it these barons and the
subtle queen
Long levied [2] at.
BAL.   Yea, but, Levune, thou seest
These barons lay their heads on blocks
together.
What they intend, the hangman frus-
trates clean.
LEVUNE. Have you no doubts, my lords,
I'll clap s' close [3]
Among the lords of France with Eng-
land's gold
That Isabel shall make her plaints in
vain,

[1] Son.
[2] Frequently misused for *leveled* in this period.
[3] Contrive so secretly.

And France shall be obdurate with her
tears.
SPEN. Then make for France amain;
Levune, away!
Proclaim King Edward's wars and vic-
tories.   *Exeunt omnes.* 280

[SCENE xii.

Near the Tower of London.]

Enter Edmund.

EDM. Fair blows the wind for France.
Blow, gentle gale,
Till Edmund be arrived for England's
good!
Nature, yield to my country's cause in
this.
A brother? No, a butcher of thy friends!
Proud Edward, dost thou banish me thy
presence?
But I'll to France, and cheer the wrongéd
queen,
And certify what Edward's looseness is.
Unnatural king, to slaughter noble men
And cherish flatterers! Mortimer, I
stay [4]
Thy sweet escape; stand gracious, gloomy
night,   10
To his device.

Enter Mortimer, [*Junior,*] *disguised.*

MOR. JUN.   Holla! Who walketh there?
Is't you, my lord?
EDM.   Mortimer, 'tis I.
But hath thy potion wrought so happily?
MOR. JUN. It hath; my lord; the warders
all asleep,
I thank them, gave me leave to pass in
peace.
But hath your grace got shipping unto
France?
EDM. Fear it not.   *Exeunt.*

[SCENE xiii.

Paris.]

Enter the Queen and her Son.

QUEEN. Ah, boy, our friends do fail us all
in France.
The lords are cruel, and the king unkind.
What shall we do?

[4] Await.

PRINCE.   Madam, return to England,
And please my father well, and then a fig
For all my uncle's friendship here in
    France.
I warrant you, I'll win his highness
    quickly;
A [1] loves me better than a thousand
    Spencers.
QUEEN. Ah, boy, thou art deceived, at
    least in this,
To think that we can yet be tuned to-
    gether.
No, no, we jar too far. Unkind Valois! 10
Unhappy Isabel, when France rejects,
Whither, O, whither dost thou bend thy
    steps?

Enter Sir John of Hainault.

SIR J. Madam, what cheer?
QUEEN.   Ah, good Sir John of Hainault,
Never so cheerless, nor so far distressed.
SIR J. I hear, sweet lady, of the king's un-
    kindness.
But droop not, madam; noble minds
    contemn
Despair. Will your grace with me to
    Hainault,
And there stay time's advantage with
    your son?
How say you, my lord, will you go with
    your friends,   19
And shake off all our fortunes equally?
PRINCE. So pleaseth the queen, my mother,
    me it likes.
The King of England nor the court of
    France
Shall have me from my gracious mother's
    side,
Till I be strong enough to break a staff;
And then have at the proudest Spencer's
    head.
SIR J. Well said, my lord!
QUEEN. O, my sweet heart, how do I moan
    thy wrongs,
Yet triumph in the hope of thee, my joy!
Ah, sweet Sir John, even to the utmost
    verge
Of Europe, or the shore of Tanais,   30
Will we with thee to Hainault—so we will.
The marquis is a noble gentleman;
His grace, I dare presume, will welcome
    me.
But who are these?

[1] He.

Enter Edmund and Mortimer [, Junior].

EDM.   Madam, long may you live,
Much happier than your friends in
    England do!
QUEEN. Lord Edmund and Lord Morti-
    mer alive!
Welcome to France! The news was here,
    my lord,
That you were dead, or very near your
    death.
MOR. JUN. Lady, the last was truest of the
    twain;
But Mortimer, reserved for better hap, 40
Hath shaken off the thralldom of the
    Tower,
And lives t' advance your standard, good
    my lord.
PRINCE. How mean you, and [2] the king,
    my father, lives?
No, my Lord Mortimer, not I, I trow.
QUEEN. Not, son? Why not? I would it
    were no worse.
But, gentle lords, friendless we are in
    France.
MOR. JUN. Monsieur le Grand, a noble
    friend of yours,
Told us at our arrival all the news:
How hard the nobles, how unkind the
    king
Hath showed himself. But, madam, right
    makes room   50
Where weapons want; and, though a
    many friends
Are made away, as Warwick, Lancaster,
And others of our party and faction,
Yet have we friends—assure your grace—
    in England
Would cast up caps and clap their hands
    for joy
To see us there, appointed [3] for our foes.
EDM. Would all were well, and Edward
    well reclaimed,
For England's honor, peace, and quiet-
    ness.
MOR. JUN. But by the sword, my lord, it
    must be deserved; [4]
The king will ne'er forsake his flat-
    terers.   60
SIR J. My lords of England, sith [5] the
    ungentle king
Of France refuseth to give aid of arms
To this distressèd queen his sister here,

[2] If.   [4] Earned.
[3] Equipped.   [5] Since.

Go you with her to Hainault. Doubt ye
　　not,
We will find comfort, money, men, and
　　friends
Ere long, to bid the English king a base.[1]
How say, young prince? What think you
　　of the match?
PRINCE. I think King Edward will outrun
　　us all.
QUEEN. Nay, son, not so; and you must
　　not discourage
Your friends, that are so forward in your
　　aid.　　　　　　　　　　　　　　70
EDM. Sir John of Hainault, pardon us, I
　　pray;
These comforts that you give our woeful
　　queen
Bind us in kindness all at your command.
QUEEN. Yea, gentle brother; and the God
　　of heaven
Prosper your happy motion,[2] good Sir
　　John.
MOR. JUN. This noble gentleman, forward
　　in arms,
Was born, I see, to be our anchor-hold.
Sir John of Hainault, be it thy renown,
That England's queen and nobles in
　　distress
Have been by thee restored and com-
　　forted.　　　　　　　　　　　　80
SIR J. Madam, along, and you, my lord,
　　with me,
That England's peers may Hainault's
　　welcome see.　　　　　　[Exeunt.]

[SCENE xiv.

The King's palace in London.]

Enter the King, Arundel,[3] the two Spencers,
　　　　　　　　　　　　with Others.

EDW. Thus, after many threats of wrathful
　　war,
Triumpheth England's Edward with his
　　friends.
And triumph, Edward, with his friends
　　uncontrolled!
My Lord of Gloucester, do you hear the
　　news?
SPEN. What news, my lord?
EDW. Why, man, they say there is great
　　execution

[1] To challenge, as in the game of prisoner's
base.　　　　　　　　　　　　　[2] Proposal.
[3] As before, original reads Matr[evis].

Done through the realm. My Lord of
　　Arundel,
You have the note, have you not?
ARUN.[3] From the lieutenant of the Tower,
　　my lord.
EDW. I pray let us see it. What have we
　　there?　　　　　　　　　　　　10
Read it, Spencer.
　　　　　　　　Spencer reads their names.
Why, so; they barked apace a month
　　ago.
Now, on my life, they'll neither bark nor
　　bite.
Now, sirs, the news from France. Glou-
　　cester, I trow
The lords of France love England's gold
　　so well
As Isabel gets no aid from thence.
What now remains? Have you pro-
　　claimed, my lord,
Reward for them can bring in Morti-
　　mer?
SPEN. My lord, we have, and, if he be in
　　England,
A will be had ere long, I doubt it not.　20
EDW. "If," dost thou say? Spencer, as
　　true as death,
He is in England's ground. Our port
　　masters
Are not so careless of their king's com-
　　mand.

Enter a Post.

How now, what news with thee? From
　　whence come these?
POST. Letters, my lord, and tidings forth
　　of France—
To you, my Lord of Gloucester, from
　　Levune.　　　[Gives letters to Spencer.]
EDW. Read.
SPEN. (Reads the letter.)
　　"My duty to your honor premised,[4] etc.
I have, according to instructions in that
behalf, dealt with the King of France [30
his lords, and effected that the queen, all
discontented and discomforted, is gone.
Whither, if you ask: with Sir John of
Hainault, brother to the marquis, into
Flanders. With them are gone Lord Ed-
mund and the Lord Mortimer, having in
their company divers of your nation, and
others; and, as constant report goeth, they
intend to give King Edward battle in

[4] From 1598 edn. Original reads promised.

England sooner than he can look for   [40
them. This is all the news of import.

   Your honor's in all service,

                    LEVUNE."

EDW. Ah, villains, hath that Mortimer
   escaped?

With him is Edmund gone associate?

And will Sir John of Hainault lead the
   round? [1]

Welcome, a God's name, madam, and
   your son;

England shall welcome you and all your
   rout.

Gallop apace, bright Phœbus, through
   the sky,

And dusky Night, in rusty iron car;   50

Between you both shorten the time, I
   pray,

That I may see that most desiréd day

When we may meet these traitors in the
   field.

Ah, nothing grieves me but my little boy

Is thus misled to countenance their ills.

Come, friends, to Bristow,[2] there to make
   us strong;

And, winds, as equal be to bring them in

As you injurious were to bear them
   forth!   [*Exeunt.*]

[SCENE xv.

Near Harwich.]

*Enter the Queen, her Son, Edmund, Morti-
   mer, [Junior,] and Sir John.*

QUEEN. Now, lords, our loving friends and
   countrymen,

Welcome to England all, with prosperous
   winds!

Our kindest friends in Belgia have we
   left,

To cope with friends at home; a heavy
   case

When force to force is knit, and sword
   and glaive[3]

In civil broils makes kin and countrymen

Slaughter themselves in others, and their
   sides

With their own weapons gored! But
   what's the help?

Misgoverned kings are cause of all this
   wrack;

And, Edward, thou art one among them
   all,   10

[1] Dance.   [2] Bristol.   [3] Broadsword.

Whose looseness hath betrayed thy land
   to spoil,

And made the channels overflow with
   blood.

Of thine own people patron shouldst
   thou be,

But thou—

MOR. JUN.   Nay, madam, if you be a
   warrior,

Ye must not grow so passionate in
   speeches.

Lords,

Sith that we are by sufferance of heaven

Arrived and arméd in this prince's right,

Here for our country's cause swear we to
   him

All homage, fealty, and forwardness.   20

And, for the open wrongs and injuries

Edward hath done to us, his queen, and
   land,

We come in arms to wreak it with the
   swords,

That England's queen in peace may repossess

Her dignities and honors, and withal

We may remove these flatterers from
   the king,

That havocs England's wealth and
   treasury.

SIR J. Sound trumpets, my lord, and forward let us march.

Edward will think we come to flatter
   him.

EDM. I would he never had been flattered
   more.   [*Exeunt.*]   30

[SCENE xvi.

Near Bristol.]

*Enter the King, Baldock, and Spencer the
   Son, flying about the stage.*

SPEN. Fly, fly, my lord! The queen is
   overstrong;

Her friends do multiply, and yours do
   fail.

Shape we our course to Ireland, there to
   breathe.

EDW. What! Was I born to fly and run
   away,

And leave the Mortimers conquerors
   behind?

Give me my horse, and let's r'enforce our
   troops,

And in this bed of honors die with fame.

BALD. O, no, my lord, this princely resolution
Fits not the time. Away! We are pursued. [*Exeunt.*]

[*Enter*] *Edmund alone with a sword and target.*[1]

EDM. This way he fled, but I am come too late. 10
Edward, alas, my heart relents for thee!
Proud traitor, Mortimer, why dost thou chase
Thy lawful king, thy sovereign, with thy sword?
Vild [2] wretch, and why hast thou, of all unkind,[3]
Borne arms against thy brother and thy king?
Rain showers of vengeance on my cursed head,
Thou God, to whom in justice it belongs
To punish this unnatural revolt!
Edward, this Mortimer aims at thy life!
O, fly him, then! But, Edmund, calm this rage; 20
Dissemble, or thou diest, for Mortimer
And Isabel do kiss while they conspire,
And yet she bears a face of love forsooth.
Fie on that love that hatcheth death and hate!
Edmund, away! Bristow to Longshanks' blood
Is false. Be not found single for suspect. [4]
Proud Mortimer pries near into thy walks.

Enter the Queen, Mortimer, [*Junior,*] *the young Prince, and Sir John of Hainault.*

QUEEN. Successful battles gives the God of kings
To them that fight in right and fear his wrath.
Since then successfully we have prevailed, 30
Thanks be heaven's great Architect, and you.
Ere farther we proceed, my noble lords,

We here create our well-belovéd son,
Of love and care unto his royal person,
Lord warden of the realm, and, sith the fates
Have made his father so infortunate,
Deal you, my lords, in this, my loving lords,
As to your wisdoms fittest seems in all.
EDM. Madam, without offense, if I may ask,
How will you deal with Edward in his fall? 40
PRINCE. Tell me, good uncle, what Edward do you mean?
EDM. Nephew, your father; I dare not call him king.
MOR. JUN. My Lord of Kent, what needs these questions?
'Tis not in her controlment, nor in ours,
But as the realm and parliament shall please,
So shall your brother be disposéd of.—
[*Aside to the Queen.*] I like not this relenting mood in Edmund.
Madam, 'tis good to look to him betimes.
QUEEN. My lord, the Mayor of Bristow knows our mind.
MOR. JUN. Yea, madam, and they scape not easily 50
That fled the field.
QUEEN. Baldock is with the king.
A goodly chancellor, is he not, my lord?
SIR J. So are the Spencers, the father and the son.
EDM. This, Edward, is the ruin of the realm.

Enter Rice ap Howell and the Mayor of Bristow, with Spencer the Father [*, and Attendants*].

RICE. God save Queen Isabel and her princely son!
Madam, the mayor and citizens of Bristow,
In sign of love and duty to this presence,
Present by me this traitor to the state,
Spencer, the father to that wanton Spencer, 59
That, like the lawless Catiline of Rome,
Reveled in England's wealth and treasary.

---

[1] Shield.   [2] Vile.   [3] Most unnatural of all.
[4] Alone for fear of suspicion.

QUEEN. We thank you all.

MOR. JUN.　　　Your loving care in this
Deserveth princely favors and rewards.
But where's the king and the other
　　Spencer fled?

RICE. Spencer the son, created Earl of
　　Gloucester,
Is with that smooth-tongued scholar
　　Baldock gone
And shipped but late for Ireland with
　　the king.

MOR. JUN. Some whirlwind fetch them
　　back or sink them all!
They shall be started [1] thence, I doubt it
　　not.

PRINCE. Shall I not see the king my father
　　yet?　　　　　　　　　　　　　　70

EDM. [Aside.] Unhappy's Edward, chased
　　from England's bounds!

SIR J. Madam, what resteth? Why stand
　　ye in a muse?

QUEEN. I rue my lord's ill fortune. But,
　　alas,
Care of my country called me to this
　　war!

MOR. JUN. Madam, have done with care
　　and sad complaint;
Your king hath wronged your country
　　and himself,
And we must seek to right it as we
　　may.—
Meanwhile, have hence this rebel to the
　　block.—
Your lordship cannot privilege [2] your
　　head.

SPEN. FA. Rebel is he that fights against
　　his prince;　　　　　　　　　　80
So fought not they that fought in Ed-
　　ward's right.

MOR. JUN. Take him away; he prates.
　　[Exeunt Attendants with the Elder
　　Spencer.]—You, Rice ap Howell,
Shall do good service to her majesty,
Being of countenance [3] in your country
　　here,
to follow these rebellious runagates.[4]
We in meanwhile, madam, must take
　　advice
How Baldock, Spencer, and their com-
　　plices
May in their fall be followed to their end.
　　　　　　　　　　　　Exeunt omnes.

[1] Routed out.
[2] Exempt, free.
[3] In authority, favor.
[4] Renegades, traitors.

[SCENE xvii.

The Abbey of Neath.]

Enter the Abbot, Monks, Edward, Spencer,
　　and Baldock [, the last three disguised].

ABBOT. Have you no doubt, my lord; have
　　you no fear.
As silent and as careful will we be
To keep your royal person safe with us,
Free from suspect and fell invasion
Of such as have your majesty in chase,
Yourself, and those your chosen company,
As danger of this stormy time requires.

EDW. Father, thy face should harbor no
　　deceit.
O, hadst thou ever been a king, thy heart,
Piercéd deeply with sense of my dis-
　　tress,　　　　　　　　　　　　10
Could not but take compassion of my
　　state.
Stately and proud, in riches and in train,
Whilom [5] I was powerful and full of
　　pomp.
But what is he whom rule and empery [6]
Have not in life or death made miserable?
Come, Spencer; come, Baldock, come, sit
　　down by me.
Make trial now of that philosophy
That in our famous nurseries of arts
Thou suckedst from Plato and from
　　Aristotle.　　　　　　　　　　19
Father, this life contemplative is heaven.
O, that I might this life in quiet lead!
But we, alas, are chased; and you, my
　　friends,
Your lives, and my dishonor they pursue.
Yet, gentle monks, for treasure, gold,
　　nor fee,
Do you betray us and our company.

MONKS. Your grace may sit secure, if none
　　but we
Do wot of your abode.

SPEN. Not one alive; but shrewdly I sus-
　　pect
A gloomy fellow in a mead below.
A gave a long look after us, my lord,　30
And all the land, I know, is up in arms,
Arms that pursue our lives with deadly
　　hate.

BALD. We were embarked for Ireland,
　　wretched we!
With awkward winds and sore tempests
　　driven

[5] Formerly.
[6] Dominion.

To fall on shore, and here to pine in fear
Of Mortimer and his confederates.

EDW. Mortimer! Who talks of Mortimer?
Who wounds me with the name of
Mortimer,
That bloody man? Good father, on thy
lap   39
Lay I this head, laden with mickle care.
O, might I never open these eyes again,
Never again lift up this drooping head,
O, never more lift up this dying heart!

SPEN. Look up, my lord.—Baldock, this
drowsiness
Betides no good; here, even, we are
betrayed!

Enter, with Welsh hooks,[1] *Rice ap Howell, a
Mower, and the Earl of Leicester.*

MOW. Upon my life, those be the men ye
seek!

RICE. Fellow, enough!—My lord, I pray
be short;
A fair commission warrants what we do.

LEICES. [*Aside.*] The queen's commission,
urged by Mortimer.
What cannot gallant Mortimer with the
queen?   50
Alas, see where he sits, and hopes unseen
T' escape their hands that seek to reave[2]
his life.
Too true it is: "*Quem dies vidit veniens
superbum,
Hunc dies vidit fugiens jacentem.*"[3]
But, Leicester, leave to grow so passion-
ate.—
Spencer and Baldock, by no other names,
I arrest you of high treason here.
Stand not on titles, but obey th' arrest;
'Tis in the name of Isabel the queen.—
My lord, why droop you thus?   60

EDW. O day, the last of all my bliss on
earth!
Center of all misfortune! O my stars,
Why do you lour unkindly on a king?
Comes Leicester, then, in Isabella's name
To take my life, my company, from me?
Here, man, rip up this panting breast of
mine,
And take my heart in rescue of my
friends!

[1] A kind of weapon.   [2] Rob, take away.
[3] "Whom the dawning day sees proud, departing day sees prostrate" (Seneca, *Thyestes,*
l. 613).

RICE. Away with them!

SPEN.   It may become thee yet
To let us take our farewell of his grace.

ABBOT. [*Aside.*] My heart with pity earns[4]
to see this sight—   70
A king to bear these words and proud
commands!

EDW. Spencer, ah, sweet Spencer, thus
then must we part?

SPEN. We must, my lord; so will the angry
heavens.

EDW. Nay, so will hell and cruel Mortimer;
The gentle heavens have not to do in
this.

BALD. My lord, it is in vain to grieve or
storm.
Here humbly of your grace we take our
leaves;
Our lots are cast; I fear me, so is thine.

EDW. In heaven we may, in earth never
shall we meet—
And, Leicester, say, what shall become of
us?   80

LEICES. Your majesty must go to Killingworth.[5]

EDW. "Must!" 'Tis somewhat hard when
kings "must" go.

LEICES. Here is a litter ready for your
grace,
That waits your pleasure; and the day
grows old.

RICE. As good be gone as stay and be be-
nighted.

EDW. A litter hast thou? Lay me in a
hearse,
And to the gates of hell convey me
hence.
Let Pluto's bells ring out my fatal knell,
And hags howl for my death at Charon's
shore,
For friends hath Edward none but these
and these,   90
And these must die under a tyrant's
sword.

RICE. My lord, be going; care not for
these,
For we shall see them shorter by the
heads.

EDW. Well, that shall be, shall be! Part
we must!
Sweet Spencer, gentle Baldock, part we
must!

[4] Yearns, sorrows.   [5] Kenilworth.

Hence, feignéd weeds! [*Throws off his disguise.*] Unfeignéd are my woes!
Father, farewell! Leicester, thou stay'st for me,
And go I must. Life, farewell, with my friends.

     Exeunt Edward and Leicester.

SPEN. O, is he gone? Is noble Edward gone?
Parted from hence, never to see us more?   100
Rent,[1] sphere of heaven, and, fire, forsake thy orb!
Earth, melt to air! Gone is my sovereign,
Gone, gone, alas, never to make return!

BALD. Spencer, I see our souls are fleeted hence;
We are deprived the sunshine of our life.
Make for a new life, man; throw up thy eyes,
And heart, and hand to heaven's immortal throne;
Pay nature's debt with cheerful countenance.
Reduce we all our lessons unto this:
To die, sweet Spencer, therefor live we all;   110
Spencer, all live to die, and rise to fall.

RICE. Come, come, keep these preachments till you come to the place appointed. You, and such as you are, have made wise work in England. Will your lordships away?

MOW. Your lordship, I trust, will remember me?

RICE. Remember thee, fellow! What else? Follow me to the town.   [*Exeunt.*]

[SCENE xviii.

A room in Killingworth Castle.]

Enter the King, Leicester, with a Bishop [2] for the crown [, and Trussel].

LEICES. Be patient, good my lord; cease to lament.
Imagine Killingworth Castle were your court,
And that you lay for pleasure here a space,
Not of compulsion or necessity.

EDW. Leicester, if gentle words might comfort me,

 [1] Rend, split.
 [2] Berkeley, Bishop of Winchester.

Thy speeches long ago had eased my sorrows,
For kind and loving hast thou always been.
The griefs of private men are soon allayed,
But not of kings. The forest deer, being struck,
Runs to an herb that closeth up the wounds;   10
But, when the imperial lion's flesh is gored,
He rends and tears it with his wrathful paw,
[And,][3] highly scorning that the lowly earth
Should drink his blood, mounts up into the air.
And so it fares with me, whose dauntless mind
The ambitious Mortimer would seek to curb,
And that unnatural queen, false Isabel,
That thus hath pent and mewed me in a prison;
For such outrageous passions cloy my soul,
As with the wings of rancor and disdain   20
Full often am I soaring up to heaven,
To plain me [4] to the gods against them both.
But, when I call to mind I am a king,
Methinks I should revenge me of the wrongs
That Mortimer and Isabel have done.
But what are kings, when regiment is gone,
But perfect shadows in a sunshine day?
My nobles rule; I bear the name of king.
I wear the crown, but am controlled by them,   29
By Mortimer, and my unconstant queen,
Who spots my nuptial bed with infamy,
Whilst I am lodged within this cave of care,
Where sorrow at my elbow still attends,
To company my heart with sad laments,
That bleeds within me for this strange exchange.
But tell me, must I now resign my crown,
To make usurping Mortimer a king?

 [3] Supplied by Dodsley.   [4] Complain.

Bish. Your grace mistakes; it is for England's good
And princely Edward's right we crave the crown.

Edw. No, 'tis for Mortimer, not Edward's head;   40
For he's a lamb, encompasséd by wolves,
Which in a moment will abridge his life.
But, if proud Mortimer do wear this crown,
Heavens turn it to a blaze of quenchless fire,
Or, like the snaky wreath of Tisiphon,
Engirt the temples of his hateful head!
So shall not England's vines be perishéd,
But Edward's name survives, though Edward dies.

Leices. My lord, why waste you thus the time away?
They stay your answer. Will you yield your crown?   50

Edw. Ah, Leicester, weigh how hardly I can brook
To lose my crown and kingdom without cause;
To give ambitious Mortimer my right—
That like a mountain overwhelms my bliss,
In which extreme my mind here murthered is.
But what the heavens appoint, I must obey!
Here, take my crown—the life of Edward too;   [Takes off the crown.]
Two kings in England cannot reign at once.
But stay awhile; let me be king till night,
That I may gaze upon this glittering crown.   60
So shall my eyes receive their last content,
My head, the latest honor due to it,
And jointly both yield up their wishéd right.
Continue ever, thou celestial sun;
Let never silent night possess this clime.
Stand still, you watches of the element; [1]
All times and seasons, rest you at a stay,
That Edward may be still fair England's king!
But day's bright beams doth vanish fast away,

And needs I must resign my wishéd crown.   70
Inhuman creatures, nursed with tiger's milk,
Why gape you for your sovereign's overthrow—
My diadem, I mean, and guiltless life?
See, monsters, see, I'll wear my crown again!   [Puts on the crown.]
What, fear you not the fury of your king?
But, hapless Edward, thou art fondly [2] led;
They pass [3] not for thy frowns as late they did,
But seeks to make a new-elected king;
Which fills my mind with strange, despairing thoughts,
Which thoughts are martyréd with endless torments,   80
And, in this torment, comfort find I none,
But that I feel the crown upon my head;
And therefore let me wear it yet awhile.

Tru. My lord, the parliament must have present news,
And therefore say, will you resign or no?
                                        The King rageth.

Edw. I'll not resign, but whilst I live—
Traitors, be gone and join you with Mortimer!
Elect, conspire, install, do what you will—
Their blood and yours shall seal these treacheries!

Bish. This answer we'll return, and so farewell.   90

Leices. Call them again, my lord, and speak them fair;
For, if they go, the prince shall lose his right.

Edw. Call thou them back; I have no power to speak.

Leices. My lord, the king is willing to resign.

Bish. If he be not, let him choose.

Edw. O, would I might, but heavens and earth conspire
To make me miserable! Here receive my crown;
Receive it? No, these innocent hands of mine
Shall not be guilty of so foul a crime.
He of you all that most desires my blood,

---

[1] I.e., celestial bodies.

[2] Foolishly.   [3] Care.

And will be called the murtherer of a
    king,   101
Take it. What, are you moved? Pity
    you me?
Then send for unrelenting Mortimer,
And Isabel, whose eyes, being [1] turned
    to steel,
Will sooner sparkle fire than shed a tear.
Yet stay, for rather than I will look on
    them—
Here, here! [*Gives the crown.*] Now,
    sweet God of heaven,
Make me despise this transitory pomp,
And sit for aye enthronizéd in heaven!
Come, death, and with thy fingers close
    my eyes,   110
Or, if I live, let me forget myself.

Enter [Sir Thomas] Berkeley.

Bish. [2] My lord—
Edw. Call me not lord. Away—out of my
    sight!
Ah, pardon me. Grief makes me lunatic!
Let not that Mortimer protect my son;
More safety is there in a tiger's jaws
Than [3] his embracements. Bear this to
    the queen,
Wet with my tears, and dried again with
    sighs;   [*Gives a handkerchief.*]
If with the sight thereof she be not
    moved,   119
Return it back and dip it in my blood.
Commend me to my son, and bid him
    rule
Better than I. Yet how have I trans-
    gressed,
Unless it be with too much clemency?
Tru. And thus most humbly do we take
    our leave.
Edw. Farewell. [*Exeunt the Bishop of
    Winchester and Trussel.*] I know the
    next news that they bring
Will be my death, and welcome shall it
    be;
To wretched men, death is felicity.
Leices. [*Noticing Berkeley.*] Another post!
    What news brings he?
Edw. Such news as I expect.—Come,
    Berkeley, come,   129
And tell thy message to my naked breast.

---

[1] From 1598 edn. Original reads *been*.
[2] Original assigns this speech to Sir Thomas
Berkeley.
[3] From 1598 edn. Original reads *this*.

Berk. My lord, think not a thought so
    villainous
Can harbor in a man of noble birth.
To do your highness service and devoir,
And save you from your foes, Berkeley
    would die.
Leices. My lord, the council of the queen
    commands
That I resign my charge.
Edw. And who must keep me now? Must
    you, my lord?
Berk. Ay, my most gracious lord; so 'tis
    decreed.
Edw. [*Taking the paper.*] By Mortimer,
    whose name is written here!
Well may I rent his name that rends my
    heart!   [*Tears it.*]   140
This poor revenge hath something eased
    my mind.
So may his limbs be torn, as is this paper!
Hear me, immortal Jove, and grant it
    too!
Berk. Your grace must hence with me to
    Berkeley straight.
Edw. Whither you will; all places are
    alike,
And every earth is fit for burial.
Leices. Favor him, my lord, as much as
    lieth in you.
Berk. Even so betide my soul as I use
    him.
Edw. Mine enemy hath pitied my estate,
And that's the cause that I am now
    removed.   150
Berk. And thinks your grace that Berk-
    eley will be cruel?
Edw. I know not, but of this am I as-
    sured,
That death ends all, and I can die but
    once.
Leicester, farewell!
Leices. Not yet, my lord; I'll bear you on
    your way.   *Exeunt omnes.*

[Scene xix.

The King's palace in London.]

Enter Mortimer [, Junior,] and Queen Isabel.

Mor. Jun. Fair Isabel, now have we our
    desire;
The proud corrupters of the light-brained
    king
Have done their homage to the lofty
    gallows,

And he himself lies in captivity.
Be ruled by me, and we will rule the realm.
In any case take heed of childish fear,
For now we hold an old wolf by the ears,
That, if he slip, will seize upon us both,
And gripe the sorer, being gripped himself.
Think therefore, madam, that imports us [1] much 10
To erect [2] your son with all the speed we may,
And that I be protector over him;
For our behoof will bear the greater sway
Whenas a king's name shall be underwrit.
QUEEN. Sweet Mortimer, the life of Isabel,
Be thou persuaded that I love thee well,
And therefore, so the prince my son be safe,
Whom I esteem as dear as these mine eyes,
Conclude against his father what thou wilt,
And I myself will willingly subscribe. 20
MOR. JUN. First would I hear news that he were deposed,
And then let me alone to handle him.

Enter Messenger.

MOR. JUN. Letters! From whence?
MESS. From Killingworth, my lord.
QUEEN. How fares my lord the king?
MESS. In health, madam, but full of pensiveness.
QUEEN. Alas, poor soul, would I could ease his grief!

[*Enter the Bishop of Winchester with the crown.*]

Thanks, gentle Winchester.—[*To the Messenger.*] Sirrah, begone.
[*Exit Messenger.*]
WIN.[3] The king hath willingly resigned his crown.
QUEEN. O happy news! Send for the prince my son.
BISH. Further, or [4] this letter was sealed, Lord Berkeley came, 30

So that he now is gone from Killingworth;
And we have heard that Edmund laid a plot
To set his brother free; no more but so.
The Lord of Berkeley is so [5] pitiful
As Leicester, that had charge of him before.
QUEEN. Then let some other be his guardian.
MOR. JUN. Let me alone. Here is the privy seal.—
[*Exit the Bishop of Winchester.*]
[*To Attendants within.*] Who's there? –
Call hither Gurney and Matrevis.
To dash the heavy-headed Edmund's drift,[6]
Berkeley shall be discharged, the king removed, 40
And none but we shall know where he lieth.
QUEEN. But, Mortimer, as long as he survives,
What safety rests for us or for my son?
MOR. JUN. Speak, shall he presently be despatched and die?
QUEEN. I would he were, so 'twere not by my means.

Enter Matrevis and Gurney.

MOR. JUN. Enough.—Matrevis, write a letter presently
Unto the Lord of Berkeley from ourself
That he resign the king to thee and Gurney;
And, when 'tis done, we will subscribe our name.
MAT. It shall be done, my lord.
MOR. JUN. Gurney!
GUR. My lord. 50
MOR. JUN. As thou intendest to rise by Mortimer,
Who now makes Fortune's wheel turn as he please,
Seek all the means thou canst to make him droop,
And neither give him kind word nor good look.
GUR. I warrant you, my lord.
MOR. JUN. And this above the rest: because we hear
That Edmund casts [7] to work his liberty,
Remove him still from place to place by night,

---

[1] From 1612 edn. Original reads *as*.
[2] Crown.
[3] Regularly *Bish.* in speech heads.
[4] Ere.
[5] As.
[6] Plot.
[7] Plots.

Till at the last he come to Killingworth,
And then from thence to Berkeley back
    again.   60
And by the way, to make him fret the
    more,
Speak curstly [1] to him, and in any case
Let no man comfort him; if he chance
    to weep,
But amplify his grief with bitter words.
MAT. Fear not, my lord, we'll do as you
    command.
MOR. JUN. So now away; post thither-
    wards amain.
QUEEN. Whither goes this letter? To my
    lord the king?
Commend me humbly to his majesty,
And tell him that I labor all in vain
To ease his grief, and work his lib-
    erty;   70
And bear him this as witness of my love.
                                 [*Gives a ring.*]
MAT. I will, madam.
Exeunt Matrevis and Gurney. Manent
          Isabel and Mortimer.

Enter the young Prince, and the Earl of
          Kent talking with him.

MOR. JUN. [*Aside.*] Finely dissembled!
    Do so still, sweet queen.
Here comes the young prince with the
    Earl of Kent.
QUEEN. [*Aside.*] Something he whispers
    in his childish ears.
MOR. JUN. [*Aside.*] If he have such access
    unto the prince,
Our plots and stratagems will soon be
    dashed.
QUEEN. [*Aside.*] Use Edmund friendly, as
    if all were well.—
MOR. JUN. How fares my honorable
    Lord of Kent?
EDM. In health, sweet Mortimer.—How
    fares your grace?   80
QUEEN. Well, if my lord your brother were
    enlarged.[2]
EDM. I hear of late he hath deposed him-
    self.
QUEEN. The more my grief.
MOR. JUN.   And mine.
EDM. [*Aside.*]   Ah, they do dissemble!
QUEEN. Sweet son, come hither; I must
    talk with thee.

[1] Ill-temperedly.   [2] Freed.

MOR. JUN. Thou, being his uncle, and
    the next of blood,
Do look to be protector over the prince.
EDM. Not I, my lord. Who should protect
    the son
But she that gave him life? I mean the
    queen.
PRINCE. Mother, persuade me not to wear
    the crown.
Let him be king—I am too young to
    reign.   90
QUEEN. But be content, seeing it his
    highness' pleasure.
PRINCE. Let me but see him first, and then
    I will.
EDM. Ay, do, sweet nephew.
QUEEN. Brother, you know it is impos-
    sible.
PRINCE. Why, is he dead?
QUEEN. No, God forbid!
EDM. I would those words proceeded from
    your heart.
MOR. JUN. Inconstant Edmund, dost thou
    favor him,
That wast the cause of his imprisonment?
EDM. The more cause have I now to make
    amends.   100
MOR. JUN. [*Aside to queen.*] I tell thee,
    'tis not meet that one so false
Should come about the person of a
    prince.—
My lord, he hath betrayed the king his
    brother,
And therefore trust him not.
PRINCE. But he repents, and sorrows for
    it now.
QUEEN. Come, son, and go with this gentle
    lord and me.
PRINCE. With you I will, but not with
    Mortimer.
MOR. JUN. Why, youngling, 'sdain'st thou
    so of Mortimer?
Then I will carry thee by force away.
PRINCE. Help, uncle Kent! Mortimer will
    wrong me.   110
QUEEN. Brother Edmund, strive not; we
    are his friends;
Isabel is nearer than the Earl of Kent.
EDM. Sister, Edward is my charge; re-
    deem him.
QUEEN. Edward is my son, and I will keep
    him.
EDM. Mortimer shall know that he hath
    wronged me!—

[*Aside.*] Hence will I haste to Killing-
worth Castle,
And rescue aged Edward from his foes,
To be revenged on Mortimer and thee.
Exeunt omnes.

[SCENE xx.

An outbuilding at Killingworth Castle.]

*Enter Matrevis and Gurney [and Soldiers,]
with the King.*

MAT. My lord, be not pensive; we are your
friends.
Men are ordained to live in misery;
Therefore come—dalliance dangereth
our lives.
EDW. Friends, whither must unhappy Ed-
ward go?
Will hateful Mortimer appoint no rest?
Must I be vexéd like the nightly bird,
Whose sight is loathsome to all wingéd
fowls?
When will the fury of his mind assuage?
When will his heart be satisfied with
blood?
If mine will serve, unbowel straight this
breast,   10
And give my heart to Isabel and him.
It is the chiefest mark they level at.
GUR. Not so, my liege; the queen hath
given this charge
To keep your grace in safety.
Your passions make your dolors to in-
crease.
EDW. This usage makes my misery in-
crease.
But can my air of life continue long
When all my senses are annoyed with
stench?
Within a dungeon England's king is kept,
Where I am starved for want of suste-
nance.   20
My daily diet is heart-breaking sobs,
That almost rents the closet of my heart.
Thus lives old Edward, not relieved by
any,
And so must die, though pitiéd by many.
O, water, gentle friends, to cool my thirst,
And clear my body from foul excre-
ments!
MAT. Here's channel water, as our charge
is given.
Sit down, for we'll be barbers to your
grace.

EDW. Traitors, away! What, will you
murther me,
Or choke your sovereign with puddle
water?   30
GUR. No, but wash your face, and shave
away your beard,
Lest you be known and so be rescuéd.
MAT. Why strive you thus? Your labor
is in vain!
EDW. The wren may strive against the
lion's strength,
But all in vain; so vainly do I strive
To seek for mercy at a tyrant's hand.
*They wash him with puddle water, and shave
his beard away.*
Immortal powers, that knows the pain-
ful cares
That waits upon my poor distresséd
soul,
O, level all your looks upon these daring
men
That wrongs their liege and sovereign,
England's king!   40
O Gaveston, it is for thee that I am
wronged!
For me, both thou and both the Spencers
died,
And for your sakes a thousand wrongs
I'll take.
The Spencers' ghosts, wherever they
remain,
Wish well to mine; then tush—for them
I'll die!
MAT. Twixt theirs and yours shall be no
enmity.
Come, come away; now put the torches
out;
We'll enter in by darkness to Killing-
worth.

Enter Edmund.

GUR. How now, who comes there?
MAT. Guard the king sure; it is the Earl
of Kent.   50
EDW. O, gentle brother, help to rescue
me!
MAT. Keep them asunder; thrust in the
king.
EDM. Soldiers, let me but talk to him one
word.
GUR. Lay hands upon the earl for this
assault.
EDM. Lay down your weapons, traitors!
Yield the king!

MAT. Edmund, yield thou thyself, or thou shalt die!

EDM. Base villains, wherefore do you gripe me thus?

GUR. Bind him and so convey him to the court.

EDM. Where is the court but here? Here is the king.
And I will visit him; why stay you me? 60

MAT. The court is where Lord Mortimer remains.
Thither shall your honor go; and so farewell.

Exeunt Matr[evis] and Gurney, with the King. Manent Edmund and the Soldiers.

EDM. O, miserable is that commonweal
Where lords keep courts, and kings are locked in prison!

SOL. Wherefore stay we? On, sirs, to the court!

EDM. Ay, lead me whither you will, even to my death,
Seeing that my brother cannot be released.   *Exeunt omnes.*

[SCENE xxi.

The King's palace in London.]

Enter Mortimer alone.

MOR. JUN. The king must die or Mortimer goes down;
The commons now begin to pity him.
Yet he that is the cause of Edward's death
Is sure to pay for it when his son is of age,
And therefore will I do it cunningly.
This letter, written by a friend of ours,
Contains his death, yet bids them save his life.   [*Reads.*]
"*Edwardum occidere nolite timere bonum est:*"
"Fear not to kill the king; 'tis good he die."
But read it thus, and that's another sense: 10
"*Edwardum occidere nolite timere bonum est:*"
"Kill not the king; 'tis good to fear the worst."
Unpointed as it is, thus shall it go,
That, being dead, if it chance to be found,

Matrevis and the rest may bear the blame,
And we be quit that caused it to be done.
Within this room is locked the messenger
That shall convey it, and perform the rest;
And, by a secret token that he bears,
Shall he be murdered when the deed is done.—   20
Lightborn,
Come forth!

[*Enter Lightborn.*]

Art thou as resolute as thou wast?

LIGHT. What else, my lord? And far more resolute!

MOR. JUN. And hast thou cast how to accomplish it?

LIGHT. Ay, ay, and none shall know which way he died.

MOR. JUN. But at his looks, Lightborn, thou wilt relent.

LIGHT. Relent! Ha, ha! I use much to relent!

MOR. JUN. Well, do it bravely, and be secret.

LIGHT. You shall not need to give instructions;   29
'Tis not the first time I have killed a man.
I learned in Naples how to poison flowers;
To strangle with a lawn [1] thrust through [2] the throat;
To pierce the windpipe with a needle's point;
Or, whilst one is asleep, to take a quill
And blow a little powder in his ears;
Or open his mouth and pour quicksilver down.
But yet I have a braver way than these.

MOR. JUN. What's that?

LIGHT. Nay, you shall pardon me; none shall know my tricks.

MOR. JUN. I care not how it is, so it be not spied.   40
Deliver this to Gurney and Matrevis.
[*Gives letter.*]
At every ten miles' end thou hast a horse.
Take this. [*Gives money.*] Away, and never see me more!

[1] Handkerchief.   [2] Down.

LIGHT. No?

MOR. JUN. No;

Unless you bring me news of Edward's death.

LIGHT. That will I quickly do. Farewell, my lord.   [*Exit.*]

MOR. JUN. The prince I rule, the queen do I command,

And with a lowly congé to the ground   49

The proudest lords salute me as I pass.

I seal, I cancel, I do what I will.

Feared am I more than loved; let me be feared,

And, when I frown, make all the court look pale.

I view the prince with Aristarchus' eyes,

Whose looks were as a breeching [1] to a boy.

They thrust upon me the protectorship,

And sue to me for that that I desire.

While at the council table, grave enough,

And not unlike a bashful Puritan,

First I complain of imbecility,   60

Saying it is *onus quam gravissimum*,[2]

Till, being interrupted by my friends,

Suscepi that *provinciam*,[3] as they term it;

And, to conclude, I am protector now.

Now is all sure. The queen and Mortimer

Shall rule the realm, the king, and none rule us.

Mine enemies will I plague, my friends advance;

And what I list command who dare control?

"*Major sum quam cui possit fortuna nocere*." [4]   69

And that this be the coronation day,

It pleaseth me and Isabel the queen.

              [*Trumpets within.*]

The trumpets sound; I must go take my place.

Enter the young King, [Arch]bishop, Champion, Nobles, Queen.

[ARCH]BISH. Long live King Edward, by the grace of God

King of England and Lord of Ireland!

[1] Flogging.
[2] A very heavy burden.
[3] I have undertaken that office.
[4] "I am too great for fortune to harm me" (Ovid, *Metamorphoses*, vi, 195).

CHAM. If any Christian, heathen, Turk, or Jew

Dares but affirm that Edward's not true king,

And will avouch his saying with the sword,

I am the champion that will combat him!

MOR. JUN. None comes; sound trumpets.

             [*Trumpets sound.*]

KING.[5]   Champion, here's to thee!

             [*Gives a purse.*]

QUEEN. Lord Mortimer, now take him to your charge.   80

Enter Soldiers, with the Earl of Kent prisoner.

MOR. JUN. What traitor have we there with blades and bills?

SOL. Edmund, the Earl of Kent.

KING.   What hath he done?

SOL. A would have taken the king away perforce,

As we were bringing him to Killingworth.

MOR. JUN. Did you attempt his rescue, Edmund? Speak.

EDM. Mortimer, I did; he is our king,

And thou compell'st this prince to wear the crown.

MOR. JUN. Strike off his head! He shall have martial law.

EDM. Strike off my head? Base traitor, I defy thee!

KING. My lord, he is my uncle, and shall live.   90

MOR. JUN. My lord, he is your enemy, and shall die.

EDM. Stay, villains!

KING. Sweet mother, if I cannot pardon him,

Entreat my lord protector for his life.

QUEEN. Son, be content; I dare not speak a word.

KING. Nor I, and yet methinks I should command;

But, seeing I cannot, I'll entreat for him.—

My lord, if you will let my uncle live,

I will requite it when I come to age.

MOR. JUN. 'Tis for your highness' good, and for the realm's.—   100

How often shall I bid you bear him hence?

[5] Formerly the prince, now Edward the Third.

EDM. Art thou king? Must I die at thy command?

MOR. JUN. At our command.—Once more away with him!

EDM. Let me but stay and speak; I will not go.
Either my brother or his son is king,
And none of both [1] then thirst for Edmund's blood.
And, therefore, soldiers, whither will you hale me?

They hale Edmund away, and carry him to be beheaded.

KING. What safety may I look for at his hands,
If that my uncle shall be murthered thus?

QUEEN. Fear not, sweet boy; I'll guard thee from thy foes; 110
Had Edmund lived, he would have sought thy death.
Come, son, we'll ride a-hunting in the park.

KING. And shall my uncle Edmund ride with us?

QUEEN. He is a traitor; think not on him.
Come. *Exeunt omnes.*

[SCENE xxii.

A subterranean room in Berkeley Castle.]

Enter Matr[evis] and Gurney.

MAT. Gurney, I wonder the king dies not,
Being in a vault up to the knees in water,
To which the channels of the castle run,
From whence a damp continually ariseth,
That were enough to poison any man,
Much more a king brought up so tenderly.

GUR. And so do I, Matrevis. Yesternight
I opened but the door to throw him meat,
And I was almost stifled with the savor.

MAT. He hath a body able to endure 10
More than we can inflict; and therefore now
Let us assail his mind another while.

GUR. Send for him out thence, and I will anger him.

MAT. But stay, who's this?

[1] Neither.

Enter Lightborn.

LIGHT. My lord protector greets you.
[*Gives letter.*]

GUR. [*Reads.*] What's here? I know not how to conster [2] it.

MAT. Gurney, it was left unpointed for the nonce; [3]
"*Edwardum occidere nolite timere*"—
That's his meaning.

LIGHT. Know ye this token? I must have the king. [*Gives token.*]

MAT. Ay, stay awhile; thou shalt have answer straight.— 20
[*Aside.*] This villain's sent to make away the king.

GUR. [*Aside.*] I thought as much.

MAT. [*Aside.*] And, when the murder's done,
See how he must be handled for his labor.
Pereat iste! [4] Let him have the king.—
What else? Here is the keys; this is the lake. [5]
Do as you are commanded by my lord.

LIGHT. I know what I must do. Get you away.
Yet be not far off; I shall need your help.
See that in the next room I have a fire,
And get me a spit, and let it be red-hot. 30

MAT. Very well.

GUR. Need you anything besides

LIGHT. What else? A table and a feather bed.

GUR. That's all?

LIGHT. Ay, ay; so, when I call you, bring it in.

MAT. Fear not you that.

GUR. Here's a light, to go into the dungeon.

[*Gives a light, and then exit with Matrevis.*]

LIGHT. So now must I about this gear; [6] ne'er was there any
So finely handled as this king shall be.
[*Opens the door.*]
Foh! Here's a place indeed, with all my heart!

EDW. Who's there? What light is that? Wherefore comes thou? 40

---

[2] Construe. [5] Vault, dungeon.
[3] For the occasion, on purpose. [6] Affair.
[4] Let this man die.

LIGHT. To comfort you, and bring you joyful news.

EDW. Small comfort finds poor Edward in thy looks.

Villain, I know thou com'st to murther me.

LIGHT. To murther you, my most gracious lord?

Far is it from my heart to do you harm.

The queen sent me to see how you were used,

For she relents at this your misery.

And what eyes can refrain from shedding tears,

To see a king in this most piteous state?

EDW. Weep'st thou already? List awhile to me 50

And then thy heart, were it as Gurney's is,

Or as Matrevis', hewn from the Caucasus,

Yet will it melt, ere I have done my tale.

This dungeon where they keep me is the sink

Wherein the filth of all the castle falls.

LIGHT. O villains!

EDW. And there in mire and puddle have I stood

This ten days' space; and, lest that I should sleep,

One plays continually upon a drum.

They give me bread and water, being a king; 60

So that, for want of sleep and sustenance,

My mind's distempered, and my body's numbed,

And whether I have limbs or no I know not.

O, would my blood dropped out from every vein

As doth this water from my tattered robes.

Tell Isabel, the queen, I looked not thus

When for her sake I ran at tilt in France,

And there unhorsed the Duke of Cleremont.

LIGHT. O, speak no more, my lord! This breaks my heart.

Lie on this bed,[1] and rest yourself awhile. 70

EDW. These looks of thine can harbor naught but death.

I see my tragedy written in thy brows.

Yet stay awhile; forbear thy bloody hand,

And let me see the stroke before it comes,

That—and even then when I shall lose my life—

My mind may be more steadfast on my God.

LIGHT. What means your highness to mistrust me thus?

EDW. What means thou to dissemble with me thus?

LIGHT. These hands were never stained with innocent blood,

Nor shall they now be tainted with a king's. 80

EDW. Forgive my thought for having such a thought.

One jewel have I left; receive thou this. [Gives jewel.]

Still fear I, and I know not what's the cause,

But every joint shakes as I give it thee.

O, if thou harbor'st murther in thy heart,

Let this gift change thy mind, and save thy soul!

Know that I am a king! O, at that name

I feel a hell of grief! Where is my crown?

Gone, gone! And do I remain alive?

LIGHT. You're overwatched, my lord; lie down and rest. 90

EDW. But that grief keeps me waking, I should sleep,

For not these ten days have these eyelids closed.

Now as I speak, they fall, and yet with fear

Open again. O, wherefore sits thou here?

LIGHT. If you mistrust me, I'll be gone, my lord.

EDW. No, no, for if thou mean'st to murther me,

Thou wilt return again; and therefore stay. [Dozes.]

LIGHT. He sleeps.

EDW. O, let me not die yet! Stay, O, stay a while!

LIGHT. How now, my lord? 100

---

[1] Dyce suggests that the feather bed has been thrust in from the wing.

Edw. [*Waking.*] Something still buzzeth
     in mine ears,
     And tells me if I sleep I never wake;
     This fear is that which makes me tremble
     thus.
     And therefore tell me, wherefore art
     thou come?
Light. To rid thee of thy life.—Matre-
     vis, come!

[Enter Matrevis and Gurney.]

Edw. I am too weak and feeble to resist.—
     Assist me, sweet God, and receive my
     soul!
Light. Run for the table
Edw. O, spare me, or despatch me in a
     trice.   [*Matrevis brings in a table.*]
Light. So, lay the table down, and stamp
     on it,   110
     But not too hard, lest that you bruise
     his body.   [*They murder the King.*]
Mat. I fear me that this cry will raise
     the town,
     And therefore let us take horse and away.
Light. Tell me, sirs, was it not bravely
     done?
Gur. Excellent well; take this for thy
     reward!
             Then Gurney stabs Lightborn.
     Come, let us cast the body in the moat,
     And bear the king's to Mortimer our
     lord.
     Away!   *Exeunt omnes.*

[Scene xxiii.

The royal palace in London.]

Enter Mortimer and Matrevis.

Mor. Jun. Is't done, Matrevis, and the
     murtherer dead?
Mat. Ay, my good lord; I would it were
     undone!
Mor. Jun. Matrevis, if thou now growest
     penitent
     I'll be thy ghostly father;[1] therefore
     choose
     Whether thou wilt be secret in this,
     Or else die by the hand of Mortimer.
Mat. Gurney, my lord, is fled, and will, I
     fear,
     Betray us both; therefore let me fly.
Mor. Jun. Fly to the savages!   9
Mat. I humbly thank your honor. [*Exit.*]

[1] Father confessor.

Mor. Jun. As for myself, I stand as
     Jove's huge tree,
     And others are but shrubs compared to me.
     All tremble at my name, and I fear none.
     Let's see who dare impeach me for his
     death!

Enter the Queen.

Queen. Ah, Mortimer, the king my son
     hath news
     His father's dead, and we have murdered
     him!
Mor. Jun. What if he have? The king is
     yet a child.
Queen. Ay, ay, but he tears his hair, and
     wrings his hands,
     And vows to be revenged upon us both.
     Into the council chamber he is gone,   20
     To crave the aid and succor of his peers.
     Ay me! See where he comes, and they
     with him.
     Now, Mortimer, begins our tragedy.

Enter the King with the Lords.

Lords. Fear not, my lord; know that you
     are a king.—
King. Villain!
Mor. Jun. How now, my lord?
King. Think not that I am frighted with
     thy words!
     My father's murdered through thy
     treachery;
     And thou shalt die, and on his mournful
     hearse   29
     Thy hateful and accurséd head shall lie,
     To witness to the world that by thy means
     His kingly body was too soon interred.
Queen. Weep not, sweet son!
King. Forbid not me to weep; he was my
     father.
     And, had you loved him half so well as I,
     You could not bear his death thus
     patiently.
     But you, I fear, conspired with Mortimer.
Lords. Why speak you not unto my lord
     the king?
Mor. Jun. Because I think scorn to be
     accused.
     Who is the man dares say I murdered
     him?   40
King. Traitor, in me my loving father
     speaks,
     And plainly saith 'twas thou that mur-
     d'redst him

MOR. JUN. But hath your grace no other proof than this?

KING. Yes, if this be the hand of Mortimer.   [*Shows letter.*]

MOR. JUN. [*Aside.*] False Gurney hath betrayed me and himself.

QUEEN. [*Aside.*] I feared as much; murther cannot be hid.

MOR. JUN. 'Tis my hand. What gather you by this?

KING. That thither thou didst send a murtherer.

MOR. JUN. What murtherer? Bring forth the man I sent!

KING. Ah, Mortimer, thou knowest that he is slain,   50
And so shalt thou be too.—Why stays he here?
Bring him unto a hurdle; drag him forth;
Hang him, I say, and set his quarters up;
But bring his head back presently to me.

QUEEN. For my sake, sweet son, pity Mortimer!

MOR. JUN. Madam, entreat not; I will rather die
Than sue for life unto a paltry boy.

KING. Hence with the traitor, with the murderer!

MOR. JUN. Base Fortune, now I see that in thy wheel
There is a point to which when men aspire,   60
They tumble headlong down. That point I touched,
And, seeing there was no place to mount up higher,
Why should I grieve at my declining fall?—
Farewell, fair queen. Weep not for Mortimer,
That scorns the world, and, as a traveler,
Goes to discover countries yet unknown.

KING. What, suffer you the traitor to delay?   [*Mortimer is led away.*]

QUEEN. As thou receivedst thy life from me,
Spill not the blood of gentle Mortimer!

KING. This argues that you spilt my father's blood,   70
Else would you not entreat for Mortimer.

QUEEN. I spill his blood? No!

KING. Ay, madam, you, for so the rumor runs.

QUEEN. That rumor is untrue; for loving thee
Is this report raised on poor Isabel.

KING. I do not think her so unnatural.

LORDS. My Lord, I fear me it will prove too true.

KING. Mother, you are suspected for his death,
And therefore we commit you to the Tower
Till further trial may be made thereof.   80
If you be guilty, though I be your son,
Think not to find me slack or pitiful.

QUEEN. Nay, to my death, for too long have I lived
Whenas my son thinks to abridge my days.

KING. Away with her! Her words enforce these tears,
And I shall pity her if she speak again.

QUEEN. Shall I not mourn for my beloved lord,
And with the rest accompany him to his grave?

LORDS. Thus, madam, 'tis the king's will you shall hence.

QUEEN. He hath forgotten me. Stay, I am his mother.   90

LORDS. That boots not; therefore, gentle madam, go.

QUEEN. Then come, sweet death, and rid me of this grief.   [*Exit.*]

[*Enter Lords with the head of Mortimer.*]

LORDS. My lord, here is the head of Mortimer.

KING. Go fetch my father's hearse where it shall lie,
And bring my funeral robes. [*Exeunt Attendants.*]—Accursèd head,
Could I have ruled thee then, as I do now,
Thou hadst not hatched this monstrous treachery!—
Here comes the hearse; help me to mourn, my lords.

[*Enter Attendants with the hearse and funeral robes.*]

Sweet father, here unto thy murdered ghost
I offer up this wicked traitor's head; 100
And let these tears, distilling from mine eyes,
Be witness of my grief and innocency.
              [*Exeunt.*]

FINIS.

ATTOWELL'S JIG

Attowell's Jig is one of the most interesting specimens—though perhaps not the most typical—of a dramatic form that achieved a remarkable popularity with London audiences by the end of the sixteenth century. Many satiric allusions show that the masses were not satisfied without a jig at the end of every play. About the middle of the century the term jig begins to appear in literary allusions as applied to simple song or dance or to the two combined. During the Elizabethan period, song and dance entertainments under the name jig developed in complexity and were popularized on the stage among the various song and dance specialties of the players. These stage jigs apparently showed considerable variety, but the typical form was that of the ballad, which lent itself to the presentation of jest, tale, and satiric skit, with clowns, fools, vagabonds, and other figures traditional in farce and popular drama. The more formal stage jig was usually a brief ballad farce, sung and accompanied by dance. The chief rôles in the jigs, emphasizing the drollery or rascality of the clown, were taken by outstanding comedians of the various companies. Richard Tarlton, the great clown of the Queen's Company, who died in 1588, was the first to win fame for his jigs, both as author and as performer. In the last decade of the century the most famous exponent of the jig was William Kemp, the leading comedian of Shakespeare's company, whose feat of dancing from London to Norwich, a distance of about a hundred miles, to the accompaniment of his taborer Tom Sly's drum, became a nine days' wonder in England. In spite of the vogue of the jig until well into the seventeenth century, only six farce jigs are known to have survived in English. A larger number are extant in German, however, for English actors carried the formal jig to the Continent, where it remained popular for nearly a century, especially in Germany. *Rowland*, the most famous of the jigs, is lost in English, but preserved in several German texts. Another favorite was *Singing Simpkin*, almost certainly one of Kemp's successes, which survives in several languages.

Attowell's Jig was entered on the Stationers' Register on October 14, 1595, as "A Pretty New Jig between Francis the Gentleman, Richard the Farmer, and Their Wives." It was published as a broadside ballad in two parts, with the name George Attowell at the end. A manuscript form, published in *Shirburn Ballads*, has the title "Mr. Attowell's Jig between Francis," etc. There is also an early seventeenth century version in German, somewhat freely translated. Probably the name of Attowell is connected with the jig because he popularized it by his performances, not because he wrote it. Little is known of him beyond his connection with the jig. He was associated with Strange's men in 1590–91, and is mentioned, without reference to any company, in a business transaction of Henslowe's in 1595. One interesting feature of the jig is its early use of several scenes with different airs. Of the four tunes, "Walsingham" and "Go from My Window" had an extraordinary vogue. No exact source for the plot is known. Similar intrigue plots with a substitution motive are found in a German jest and in the story from the *Decameron* used by Shakespeare in *All's Well*, but the husband of the faithful wife does not appear. The coarse and farcical handling of characters usual in the dramatic jig is lacking. Instead of the droll, stupid, or crafty country clown and the light, tricky wife common in the jig, the farmer and his wife are presented

571

with sympathy and a measure of dignity. The style is characteristic of the ballad, and, while not distinguished, it is also not without occasional quaintness and charm.

The jig is almost unrepresented in anthologies, but in 1958 an Italian, Benevenuto Cellini, in a collection entitled *Drammi pre-Shakespeariani* (Naples), included "Mr. Attowell's Jig" along with seven other medieval and early Elizabethan plays, with the texts in modernized English, but the notes in Italian.

The present text is based on that of the only extant copy of the broadside, from the Pepys Collection, as printed by Baskervill in *The Elizabethan and Related Song Drama* (Chicago, 1929).

ATTOWELL'S JIG[1]

[*DRAMATIS PERSONÆ*

MASTER FRANCIS, *a gentleman.*   MISTRESS FRANCIS.
RICHARD, *a farmer.*   BESS, *Richard's wife.*

SCENE: *The farmer's home.*

TIME: *Contemporary.*]

BESS. [*Singing.*]

>   As I went to Walsingham,
>   To the shrine with speed,
>   Met I with a jolly palmer
>   In a pilgrim's weed.

[*Enter Francis.*]

>   Now God you save, you jolly palmer!

FRAN. Welcome, lady gay!
Oft have I sued to thee for love.
BESS.[2] Oft have I said you nay.

FRAN. My love is fixed. BESS. And so
    is mine,
But not on you;   10
For to my husband whilst I live
    I will ever be true.
FRAN. I'll give thee gold and rich array—
BESS. Which I shall buy too dear.
FRAN. Naught shalt thou want; then say
    not nay.
    BESS. "Naught" would you make me,
    I fear!

>   What though you be a gentleman,
>   And have lands great store?
>   I will be chaste, do what you can,
>   Though I live ne'er so poor.   20

FRAN. Thy beauty rare hath wounded
    me,
    And pierced my heart.

BESS. Your foolish love doth trouble me.
    Pray you, sir, depart.

FRAN. Then tell me, sweet, wilt thou con-
    sent
    Unto my desire?
BESS. And, if I should, then tell me, sir,
    What is it you require?
FRAN. For to enjoy thee as my love.
    BESS. Sir, you have a wife;   30
Therefore let your suit have an end.
    FRAN. First will I lose my life!

>   All that I have thou shalt command.
>   BESS. Then my love you have.
FRAN. Your meaning I well understand.
    BESS. I yield to what you crave.
FRAN. But tell me, sweet, when shall I
    enjoy
    My heart's delight?
I prithee, sweetheart, be not coy.
    BESS. Even soon, at night.   40

>   My husband is rid ten miles from home,
>   Money to receive.
>   In the evening see you come.
>   FRAN. Till then, I take my leave.   *Exit.*
BESS. Thus have I rid my hands full well
    Of my amorous love,
And my sweet husband will I tell
    How he doth me move.

Enter Richard, Bess's husband. To the tune
                    of the "Jewish Dance."

RICH. [*Not observing Bess.*] Hey, down a
    down,
    Hey, down a down, a down!   50
There is never a lusty farmer
    In all our town

That hath more cause
   To lead a merry life
Than I that am married
   To an honest,[1] faithful wife.
BESS. [*Coming forward.*] I thank you,
   gentle husband;
   You praise me to my face.
RICH. I cry thee mercy, Bessie;
   I knew thee not in place.   60

BESS. Believe me, gentle husband,
   If you knew as much as I,
The words that you have spoken
   You quickly would deny;
For, since you went from home,
   A suitor I have had,
Who is so far in love with me
   That he is almost mad.
He'll give me gold and silver store,
   And money for to spend,   70
And I have promised him therefore
   To be his loving friend.

RICH. Believe me, gentle wife,
   But this makes me to frown!
There is no gentleman nor knight
   Nor lord of high renown
That shall enjoy thy love, girl,
   Though he were ne'er so good!
Before he wrong my Bessie so,
   I'll spend on him my blood!   80
And therefore tell me who it is
   That doth desire thy love.
BESS. Our neighbor, Master Francis,
   That often did me move;

To whom I gave consent,
   His mind for to fulfill,
And promised him this night
   That he should have his will.
Nay, do not frown, good Dickie,
   But hear me speak my mind;   90
For thou shalt see, I'll warrant thee,
   I'll use him in his kind.
For unto thee I will be true
   So long as I do live;
I'll never change thee for a new,
   Nor once my mind so give.

Go you to Mistress Francis,
   And this to her declare,
And will her with all speed
   To my house to repair,   100

[1] Chaste.

Where she and I'll devise
   Some pretty knavish wile;
For I have laid the plot,
   Her husband to beguile.
Make haste, I pray, and tarry not,
   For long he will not stay.
RICH. Fear not; I'll tell her such a tale
   Shall make her come away!   [*Exit.*]

BESS. Now, Bess, bethink thee
   What thou hast to do.   110
Thy lover will come presently,
   And hardly will he woo.
I will teach my gentleman
   A trick that he may know
I am too crafty and too wise
   To be o'erreachéd so.
But here he comes now! Not a word,
   But fall to work again.
         She sews [*as Francis enters*].
FRAN. How now, sweetheart, at work so
   hard?
   BESS. Ay, sir, I must take pains.   120

FRAN. But say, my lovely sweeting,
   Thy promise wilt thou keep?
Shall I enjoy thy love,
   This night with me to sleep?
BESS. My husband rid[2] from home;
   Here safely may you stay.
FRAN. And I have made my wife believe
   I rid another way.
BESS. Go in, good sir, whate'er betide,
   This night and lodge with me.   130
FRAN. The happiest night that ever I
   had!
   Thy friend still will I be.   [*Exit.*]

Enter Mistress Francis with Richard. To
        the tune of "Bugle Bow."[3]

WIFE. I thank you, neighbor Richard,
   For bringing me this news.
RICH. Nay, thank my wife that loves me
   so,
   And will not you abuse.

WIFE. But see whereas[4] she stands
   And waiteth our return.

[2] Rode.
[3] The first sheet ends here with a separate colophon. The second is headed: "The Second Part of Attowell's New Jig. To the Tune of 'As I Went to Walsingham'." There is no division into stanzas marked in the section sung to the tune of "Bugle Bow."
[4] Where.

Rich. You must go cool your husband's
    heat,
    That so in love doth burn.   140

Bess. Now, Dickie, welcome home,
    And, mistress, welcome hither.
Grieve not, although you find
    Your husband and I together.

For you shall have your right,
    Nor will I wrong you so.
Then change apparel with me straight,
    And unto him do go.
                        [*They exchange clothes.*]

Wife. For this your kind good will
    A thousand thanks I give;   150
And make account I will requite
    This kindness, if I live.

Bess. I hope it shall not need;
    Dick will not serve me so.
I know he loves me not so ill
    A-ranging for to go.

Rich. No, faith, my lovely Bess;
    First will I lose my life
Before I'll break my wedlock bonds
    Or seek to wrong my wife.   160
                        [*Exit Mistress Francis.*]

Now thinks good Master Francis
    He hath thee in his bed,
And makes account he is grafting
    Of horns upon my head.

But softly! Stand aside!
    Now shall we know his mind,
And how he would have uséd thee,
    If thou hadst been so kind.
                        [*They stand aside.*]

Enter Master Francis with his own Wife,
    having a mask before her face, supposing
    her to be Bess. To the tune of "Go from
                    My Window."

Fran. Farewell, my joy and heart's de-
    light,
    Till next we meet again.   170
Thy kindness to requite
For lodging me all night,
    Here's ten pound for thy pain;

And more to show my love to thee
    Wear this ring for my sake.

Wife. Without your gold or fee
You shall have more of me.
    Fran. No doubt of that I make.

Wife. Then let your love continue still.
    Fran. It shall, till life doth end.   180
Wife. Your wife I greatly fear.
Fran. For her thou need'st not care
    So I remain thy friend.

Wife. But you'll suspect me, without
    cause,
    That I am false to you;
And then you'll cast me off
And make me but a scoff,
    Since that I prove untrue.

Fran. Then never trust man for my sake,
    If I prove so unkind!   190
[Wife.] So often have you sworn,
Sir, since that you were born,
    And soon have changed your mind.

[Fran.] Nor wife nor life, nor goods nor
    lands,
    Shall make me leave my love,
Nor any wordly treasure
Make me forgo my pleasure,
    Nor once my mind remove.

[*Richard and Bess, dressed as Mistress*
        Francis, come forward.]

Wife. But soft awhile! Who is yonder?
    Do you see
My husband? Out, alas!   200
Fran. And yonder is my wife!
Now shall we have a life!
    How cometh this to pass?

Rich. Come hither, gentle Bess! I charge
    thee, do confess
    What makes Master Francis here?
Wife.[1] Good husband, pardon me!
I'll tell the troth to thee.
    Rich. Then speak, and do not fear.

Fran. Nay, neighbor Richard, hark to
    me!
    I'll tell the troth to you.   210
Bess. Nay, tell it unto me,
Good sir, that I may see
    What you have here to do.

[1] In this stanza and the next, the names of
the women are reversed in the original, probably
because of the disguise.

But you can make no scuse [1] to color this
    abuse;
  This wrong is too-too great!
RICH. Good sir, I take great scorn
You should proffer me the horn.
    WIFE. Now must I cool this heat. [2]

Nay, neighbor Richard, be content;
  Thou hast no wrong at all.   220
                    [*Discloses herself.*]
Thy wife hath done thee right,
And pleasured me this night!
    FRAN. This frets me to the gall!

Good wife, forgive me this offense;
  I do repent mine ill.
WIFE. I thank you with mine heart
For playing this kind part,
    Though sore against your will.

Nay, gentle husband, frown not so,
  For you have made amends;   230
I think it is good gain
To have ten pound for my pain!
    Then let us both be friends.

FRAN. Ashamed I am, and know not what
    to say.
  Good wife, forgive this crime!
Alas, I do repent!
WIFE. Tut, I could be content
    To be served so many a time!

FRAN. Good neighbor Richard, be con-
    tent;
  I'll woo thy wife no more—   240

[1] Excuse.
[2] In the original, the rest of this speech is assigned to Francis.

I have enough of this.
WIFE. Then all forgiven is.—
  I thank thee, Dick, therefore,

And to thy wife I'll give this gold
  I hope you'll not say no.
Since I have had the pleasure,
Let her enjoy the treasure!
    FRAN. Good wife, let it be so.

BESS. I thank you, gentle mistress.
    RICH. Faith, and so do I.
Sir, learn your own wife to know,   250
And shoot not in the dark
For fear you miss the mark.
    BESS. He hath paid for this, I trow.

All women learn of me. FRAN. All men
    by me take heed
  How you a woman trust.
WIFE. Nay, women, trust no men.
FRAN. And, if they do, how then?
    WIFE. There's few of them prove just.

Farewell, neighbor Richard!   Farewell,
    honest Bess!
I hope we are all friends.   260
[*To Francis.*] [3] And, if you stay at home,
And use not thus to roam,
    Here all our quarrel ends.

FINIS.

GEORGE ATTOWELL.

[3] In the original, the speech head for "Wife" is repeated here.

MUCEDORUS

If the evidence of editions may be accepted, *Mucedorus* was the most popular play in all pre-Restoration drama, for after its initial publication in 1598 it went through at least sixteen new editions by 1668. The distribution of the parts suggests, however, that the unusual number of editions may have been called forth by a ready sale to small troupes of actors. The Citizen's Wife in Beaumont and Fletcher's *The Knight of the Burning Pestle* (printed in 1615) remarks of Ralph, the apprentice with histrionic ambitions, "Nay, gentlemen, he hath played before, my husband says—*Mucedorus* before the wardens of our company." In Cowley's *The Guardian* (1642) and in his Restoration revision of that play as *Cutter of Coleman Street* (1661), Jolly's servant Will disclaims having acted the Clown, but modestly admits to the Bear. *Mucedorus* was surreptitiously presented by strolling players while the theaters were closed during the Commonwealth, and was performed by village actors in the north of England as late as 1666. The reduction of the play to a ballad also emphasizes its popular character. The form printed here shows revision for acting before James I in 1610.

George F. Reynolds, in "*Mucedorus*, Most Popular Elizabethan Play?" (*Studies in English Renaissance Drama in Honor of Karl Holzknecht*), has offered several reasons for the sudden renewed popularity of the play after 1610: the prestige of a performance before the King and his court, a prestige which evidenced itself especially in the provinces, where audiences were less literate and more simpleminded than those in London; the possible use of a real, trained bear instead of a man in a bear's skin; and a production by the King's Men, who apparently had been under a cloud at this time and wanted to offer a simple, old-fashioned play to the King as a proof of their innocence and good intentions. As Holzknecht summed up the reasons for the play's long life: "*Mucedorus* has everything—several kinds of love, adventure, romance, melodrama, villainy, pathos, a little droll clownery; one cannot imagine greater audience appeal."

The bare outline of the play was derived from Sidney's *Arcadia:* the hero's name, his disguise as a shepherd, his rescue of the heroine from the bear, and the elopement, capture, and happy union of the two. With the action set in the forest, the author of the play has added the wild man, whose offer of rustic gifts to Amadine is an ancient convention of pastoral poetry. The wild man represents, however, the ogre of folk tale rather than the savage of the pastoral or of Spenser's *Fairy Queen*. As Robert H. Goldsmith put it in tracing the genealogy of "The Wild Man on the English Stage" (*RES*, 1958), Bremo not only combines hideous shape, cannibalism, and lechery, but also is the only representative of the type in any extant play who carries an active role in the plot. Shakespeare's Caliban (c. 1611) has only some of the characteristics, as has Silvanes in Jonson's masque of *Oberon* (1611); Bremo is the furthest developed in all respects. The constantly appearing Clown is of the droll and stupid type that popular taste seems to have demanded not only in farces and jigs but in the romantic plays of the University Wits and Shakespeare, and even in chronicle plays and tragedies. Thus the author of *Mucedorus* has shifted the treatment from Sidney's courtly mixture of pastoral and chivalric romance to make a play of the type that Sidney condemns in his *Apology for Poetry*, with its romantic absurdities and its inappropriate Clown crowding to the very throne of the King. The induction and the epilogue, which like those of several other sixteenth century plays show the continued interest in debates, or "fly-tings," are here used to emphasize the mixed nature of the play as a "tragicomedy." The appeal was to the taste of a public which had been enjoying plays about romantic heroes like the anonymous *Sir Clyomon and Sir Clamydes* for two or three decades (though the play was not printed until 1599), a play which belongs to the same dramatic genre as the old metrical romances about Guy of Warwick, Sir Bevis of Hampton, Amadis of Gaul, and Huon of Bordeaux. The mere fact that a prince disguised as a shepherd could win the unqualified love of a princess like Amadine illustrates the democratic yearnings of a public which was soon to enjoy plays like Thomas Heywood's *The Four Prentices of London*, in which seemingly mere apprentices are sent out on a series of knightly adventures, only to discover their noble births at the end.

The fact that, in spite of its vogue, the author of *Mucedorus* is unknown reveals a characteristic attitude of the sixteenth century. The cultured looked upon a play as mere entertainment rather than as literature, and printers were inclined to disregard the playwright unless he had achieved popularity with some class of readers. The author of *Mucedorus* was, however, a man of some literary as well as dramatic gifts, and from the characteristics of the play many attempts have been made to identify him as one of the better known dramatists. The older attribution in part or in whole to Shakespeare is now discarded by virtually all scholars. Claims have been made for Peele, Greene, and more especially Lodge. More likely, Tucker Brooke, who discussed the play in his *Shakespeare Apocrypha*, is right in his suggestion that it was written by "an obscure and only moderately gifted disciple" of the University Wits.

The present edition is based on the edition of 1610, with its added scenes showing the bear and the court of Mucedorus's father, the King of Valencia. Leo Kirschbaum, in "The Texts of *Mucedorus*" (*MLR*, 1955), has produced evidence to show that the editions of 1598 and 1606 were "memorial reconstructions," but that the edition of 1610, especially in its additions, was based on a transcription rather than on report. His further speculations on the copyright history of the play were challenged by Greg in a letter to *MLR* in 1955. The editors of the present text are indebted to the authorities of the Huntington Library for permission to use photostats of the 1610 quarto in the Library.

MUCEDORUS[1]

THE PROLOGUE[2]

Most sacred majesty, whose great deserts
Thy subject England, nay, the world ad-
 mires—
Which heaven grant still increase—O,
 may your praise,
Multiplying with your hours, your fame
 still raise;
Embrace your council; love, with faith,
 them guide,
That both, as one, bench by each other's
 side.
So may your life pass on and run so even

That your firm zeal plant you a throne
 in heaven,
Where smiling angels shall your guardians be
From blemished traitors, stained with per-
 jury.   10
And, as the night's inferior to the day,
So be all earthly regions to your sway.
Be as the sun to day, the day to night;
For, from your beams, Europe shall borrow
 light.
Mirth drown your bosom, fair delight
 your mind,
And may our pastime your contentment
 find.   *Exit.*

[DRAMATIS PERSONÆ]

Ten persons may easily play it.[3]

THE KING *and* RUMBELO } *for one.*

KING VALENCIA } *for one.*

MUCEDORUS, *the Prince of Valencia* } *for one.*

ANSELMO } *for one.*

AMADINE, *the king's daughter of Aragon* } *for one.*

SEGASTO, *a nobleman* } *for one.*

ENVY; TREMELIO, *a captain;* BREMO, *a wild man* } *for one.*

COMEDY; A BOY; AN OLD WOMAN; ARIENA, *Amadine's maid* } *for one.*

COLLEN, *a councilor;* A MESSENGER } *for one.*

MOUSE, *the clown* } *for one.*

[SCENE: *Valencia and Aragon.*

TIME: *Uncertain.*]

[INDUCTION]

Enter Comedy, joyfully, with a garland of bays on her head.

[COM.] Why, so! Thus do I hope to please.
 Music revives, and mirth is tolerable.
 Comedy, play thy part and please;

Make merry them that comes to joy
 with thee.
Joy, then, good gentles;[4] I hope to make
 you laugh.
Sound forth Bellona's[5] silver-tunéd
 strings.
Time fits us well; the day and place is ours.

Enter Envy, his arms naked, besmeared with blood.

ENV. Nay, stay, minion; there lies a block.
 What, all on mirth? I'll interrupt your
 tale
And mix your music with a tragic end. [10
COM. What monstrous, ugly hag is this,
 That dares control the pleasures of our
 will?

---

[1] The complete title of 1610 reads: "A Most
Pleasant Comedy of Mucedorus, the King's Son
of Valencia, and Amadine, the King's Daughter
of Aragon, with the Merry Conceits of Mouse.
Amplified with New Additions, As It Was Acted
before the King's Majesty at Whitehall on Shrove
Sunday Night. By His Highness' Servants, Usually Playing at the Globe. Very Delectable and
Full of Conceited Mirth."
[2] The prologue first appeared in the 1610 edn.
[3] In the following list no provision is made for
Roderigo, Borachius, and the Bear.

[4] Gentlefolk.   [5] Usually the Goddess of War,
more appropriate to Envy.

Vaunt,[1] churlish cur, besmeared with
gory blood,
That seem'st to check the blossom of
delight,
And stifle [2] the sound of sweet Bellona's
breath.
Blush, monster, blush, and post away
with shame,
That seekest disturbance of a goddess'
deeds.

ENV. Post hence thyself, thou counter-
checking trull!
I will possess this habit,[3] spite of thee,
And gain the glory of thy wishéd port.[4] 20
I'll thunder music shall appall the
nymphs,
And make them shiver their clattering
strings,
Flying for succor to their dankish [5]
caves.

Sound drums within and cry, "Stab! Stab!"
Hearken, thou shalt hear a noise
Shall fill the air with a shrilling sound,
And thunder music to [the] [6] gods above;
Mars shall himself breathe down
A peerless crown upon brave Envy's
head,
And raise his chivall [7] with a lasting
fame.   29
In this brave music Envy takes delight,
Where I may see them wallow in their
blood,
To spurn at arms and legs quite shivered
off,
And hear the cries of many thousand
slain.
How lik'st thou this, my trull?   This
sport alone for me!

COM. Vaunt, bloody cur, nursed up with
tiger's sap,
That so dost [seek to] [8] quail a woman's
mind.
Comedy is mild, gentle, willing for to
please,
And seeks to gain the love of all estates,
Delighting in mirth, mixed all with
lovely tales,

And bringeth things with treble joy
to pass.   40
Thou, bloody, envious disdainer of men's
joys,
Whose name is fraught with bloody
stratagems,
Delights in nothing but in spoil and
death,
Where thou mayst trample in their
lukewarm blood,
And grasp their hearts within thy curséd
paws.
Yet vail thy mind;[9] revenge thou not
on me—
A silly woman begs it at thy hands.
Give me the leave to utter out my play.
Forbear this place, I humbly crave thee:
hence,
And mix not death 'mongst pleasing
comedies,   50
That treats naught else but pleasure
and delight!
If any spark of human rests in thee,
Forbear, begone, tender [10] the suit of
me.

ENV. Why, so I will; forbearance [11] shall
be such
As treble death shall cross thee with
despite,
And make thee mourn where most thou
joyest,
Turning thy mirth into a deadly dole,
Whirling thy pleasures with a peal of
death,
And drench thy methods [12] in a sea of
blood.
This will I do; thus shall I bear with
thee;   60
And, more to vex thee with a deeper
spite,
I will with threats of blood begin thy
play,
Favoring thee with envy and with hate.

COM. Then, ugly monster, do thy worst;
I will defend them in despite of thee.
And, though thou think'st with tragic
fumes [13]
To prave [14] my play unto my deep dis-
grace,

---

[1] Avaunt, be off.
[2] From 1598 edn.   Original reads *stiffe*.
[3] Costume.
[4] Station.
[5] Emended by Collier.   Original reads *Danish*.
[6] Supplied from 1598 edn.
[7] 'Chieval, achieval, achievement (?).
[8] From 1598 edn.

[9] Modify thy intention.
[10] Regard favorably.
[11] From 1598 edn.   Original reads *forbear*.
[12] Designs, *i.e.*, the plot of her play.
[13] Fits of anger.
[14] Deprave, ruin.

I force it not;[1] I scorn what thou canst
   do;
I'll grace it so thyself shall it confess
From tragic stuff to be a pleasant
   comedy.   70
ENV. Why then, Comedy, send thy actors
   forth
And I will cross the first steps of their
   trade,
Making them fear the very dart of
   death.
COM. And I'll defend them mauger[2] all
   thy spite.
So, ugly fiend, farewell, till time shall
   serve
That we may meet to parley for the best.
ENV. Content, Comedy; I'll go spread
   my branch,
And scattered blossoms from mine en-
   vious tree
Shall prove to[3] monsters, spoiling of
   their joys.   *Exit* [*with Comedy*].

[SCENE i.[4]

The court of Valencia.]

Sound. Enter Mucedorus and Anselmo, his
                         friend.

MU. Anselmo!
ANS. My lord and friend!
MU. True, my Anselmo, both thy lord
   and friend
Whose dear affections bosom with my
   heart,
And keep their domination in one orb.
ANS. Whence ne'er disloyalty shall root
   it forth,
But faith plant firmer in your choice
   respect.
MU. Much blame were mine if I should
   other deem,
Nor can coy Fortune contrary allow.
But, my Anselmo, loath I am to say
I must estrange that friendship.   11
Misconster[5] not—'tis from the realm,
   not thee;
Though lands part bodies, hearts keep
   company.
Thou know'st that I imparted often
   have
Private relations with my royal sire,

Had as concerning beauteous Amadine,
Rich Aragon's bright jewel, whose face
   some say
That blooming lilies never shone so gay,
Excelling, not excelled. Yet, lest re-
   port
Does mangle verity, boasting of what is
   not,   20
Winged with desire, thither I'll straight
   repair,
And be my fortunes, as my thoughts
   are, fair.
ANS. Will you forsake Valencia, leave
   the court,
Absent you from the eye of sovereignty?
Do not, sweet prince, adventure on that
   task,
Since danger lurks each where. Be won
   from it.
MU. Desist dissuasion;
My resolution brooks no battery;
Therefore, if thou retain thy wonted
   form,
Assist what I intend.   30
ANS. Your miss[6] will breed a blemish in
   the court,
And throw a frosty dew upon that
   beard
Whose front Valencia stoops to.
MU. If thou my welfare tender, then no
   more;
Let love's strong magic charm thy
   trivial phrase,
Wasted as vainly as to gripe[7] the sun.
Augment not then more answers; lock
   thy lips,
Unless thy wisdom suit[8] me with dis-
   guise
According to my purpose.
ANS. That action craves no counsel,   40
Since what you rightly are will more
   command
Than best usurpéd shape.
MU. Thou still art opposite in disposi-
   tion.
A more obscure, servile habiliment
Beseems this enterprise.
ANS. Then like a Florentine or mounte-
   bank?
MU. 'Tis much too tedious; I dislike thy
   judgment.
My mind is grafted on an humbler
   stock.

---

[1] I care not for it.   [2] In spite of.   [3] Become.
[4] This scene appears first in the 1610 edn.
[5] Misconstrue.

[6] Absence.   [7] Seize.   [8] Clothe.

ANS. Within my closet does there hang
  a cassock;
  Though base the weed is, 't was a shep-
    herd's 50
  Which I presented in Lord Julio's
    masque.
MU. That, my Anselmo, and none else
    but that,
  Mask Mucedorus from the vulgar view!
  That habit suits my mind; fetch me
    that weed.   *Exit Anselmo.*
  Better than kings have not disdained
    that state,
  And much inferior, to obtain their mate!

Enter Anselmo with a shepherd's coat.

  So let our respect command thy secrecy.
  At once a brief farewell!
  Delay to lovers is a second hell!
                    Exit Mucedorus.
ANS. Prosperity forerun thee; awkward
    chance 60
  Never be neighbor to thy wish's ven-
    ture;
  Content and fame advance thee; ever
    thrive,
  And glory thy mortality survive. *Exit.*

[SCENE ii.[1]

A forest in Aragon.]

Enter Mouse with a bottle [2] of hay.

MOUSE. O, horrible, terrible! Was ever
poor gentleman so scared out of his seven
senses? A bear? Nay, sure it cannot be
a bear, but some devil in a bear's doublet,
for a bear could never have had that agility
to have frighted me. Well, I'll see my
father hanged before I'll serve his horse
any more. Well, I'll carry home my bottle
of hay, and for once make my father's
horse turn Puritan and observe fasting [10
days, for he gets not a bit. But soft! This
way she followed me; therefore I'll take
the other path; and, because I'll be sure
to have an eye on him, I will take hands
with some foolish creditor, and make
every step backward.
*As he goes backwards the bear comes in,
and he tumbles over her, and runs away and
        leaves his bottle of hay behind him.*

[1] This scene appeared first in the 1610 edn.
[2] Bundle.

[SCENE iii

The same.]

*Enter Segasto running and Amadine after
        him, being pursued with a bear.*

SEG. O, fly, madam, fly or else we are
    but dead!
AM. Help, Segasto, help! Help, sweet
    Segasto, or else I die!
SEG. Alas, madam, there is no way but
    flight;
  Then haste and save yourself!
                Segasto runs away.[3]
AM. Why, then I die; ah, help me in dis-
    tress!

*Enter Mucedorus like a shepherd, with a
  sword drawn and a bear's head in his
                          hand.*

MU. Stay, lady, stay, and be no more
    dismayed.
  That cruel beast most merciless and fell,
  Which hath bereavéd thousands of their
    lives,
  Affrighted many with his hard pursues,
  Prying from place to place to find his
    prey, 10
  Prolonging thus his life by others'
    death,
  His carcass now lies headless, void of
    breath.
AM. That foul, deforméd monster, is he
    dead?
MU. Assure yourself thereof; behold his
    head,
  Which, if it please you, lady, to accept,
  With willing heart I yield it to your
    majesty.
AM. Thanks, worthy shepherd, thanks
    a thousand times.
  This gift, assure thyself, contents me more
  Than greatest bounty of a mighty prince,
  Although he were the monarch of the
    world. 20
MU. Most gracious goddess, more than
    mortal wight—
  Your heavenly hue of right imports
    no less—
  Most glad am I in that it was my chance
  To undertake this enterprise in hand,
  Which doth so greatly glad your princely
    mind.

[3] All early edns. place this direction after l. 2.

Aᴍ. No goddess, shepherd, but a mortal
wight,
A mortal wight distresséd as thou seest.
My father here is king of Aragon.
I, Amadine, his only daughter am,   25
And after him sole heir unto the crown.
Now, whereas it is my father's will
To marry me unto Segasto, one [1]
Whose wealth through father's former
usury
Is known to be no less than wonderful,
We both of custom oftentimes did use,
Leaving the court, to walk within the
fields
For recreation, especially [in][2] the spring,
In that it yields great store of rare de-
lights,
And, passing further than our wonted
walks,
Scarce entered were within these luck-
less woods,   40
But right before us down a steep-fall
hill
A monstrous, ugly bear did hie him fast
To meet us both. I faint to tell the rest,
Good shepherd, but suppose the ghastly
looks,
The hideous fears, the thousand hun-
dred woes,
Which at this instant Amadine sustained.
Mᴜ. Yet, worthy princess, let thy sorrow
cease,
And let this sight your former joys re-
vive.
Aᴍ. Believe me, shepherd, so it doth no
less.
Mᴜ. Long may they last unto your heart's
content.   50
But tell me, lady, what is become of
him,
Segasto called, what is become of him?
Aᴍ. I know not, I; that know the powers
divine;
But God grant this, that sweet Segasto
live.
Mᴜ. Yet hard-hearted he in such a case,
So cowardly to save himself by flight,
And leave so brave a princess to the
spoil.
Aᴍ. Well, shepherd, for thy worthy valor
tried,

[1] Here and in a few other cases line divisions
have been regularized.
[2] Supplied by Hazlitt.

Endangering thyself to set me free,
Unrecompenséd sure thou shalt not be. 60
In court thy courage shall be plainly
known;
Throughout the kingdom will I spread
thy name,
To thy renown and never-dying fame.
And, that thy courage may be better
known,
Bear thou the head of this most mon-
strous beast
In open sight to every courtier's view.
So will the king my father thee reward.
Come, let's away, and guard me to
the court.
Mᴜ. With all my heart.   *Exeunt.*

[Scᴇɴᴇ iv.

The outskirts of the forest.]

Enter Segasto solus.

Sᴇɢ. When heaps of harms do hover over-
head,
'Tis time as then, some say, to look
about,
And of [3] ensuing harms to choose the
least.
But hard, yea, hapless, is that wretch's
chance,
Luckless his lot and caitiff-like accursed,
At whose proceedings fortune ever
frowns—
Myself I mean, most subject unto
thrall,
For I, the more I seek to shun the
worst,
The more by proof I find myself accursed.
Erewhiles assaulted with an ugly bear, 10
Fair Amadine in company all alone,
Forthwith by flight I thought to save
myself,
Leaving my Amadine unto her shifts;
For death it was for to resist the bear,
And death no less of Amadine's harms to
hear.
Accurséd I in ling'ring life thus long!
In living thus, each minute of an hour
Doth pierce my heart with darts of
thousand deaths.
If she by flight her fury do escape,
What will she think?   20
Will she not say—yea, flatly to my face,

[3] From 1613 edn. Original reads *so.*

Accusing me of mere [1] disloyalty—
A trusty friend is tried in time of need?
But I, when she in danger was of death
And needed me, and cried, "Segasto,
　help!"
I turned my back and quickly ran away.
Unworthy I to bear this vital breath!
But what! What needs these plaints?
If Amadine do live, then happy I;
She will in time forgive and so forget.　30
Amadine is merciful, not Juno-like,
In harmful heart to harbor hatred long.

Enter Mouse, the clown, running, crying,
　　　　　　　　　　　　　　"Clubs!"

Mouse. Clubs, prongs, pitchforks, bills! [2]
O, help! A bear, a bear, a bear! [3]
Seg. Still bears, and nothing else but
bears! Tell me, sirrah, where she is.
Clo. [4] O, sir, she is run down the woods!
I saw her white head and her white
belly.
Seg. Thou talkest of wonders, to tell me
　of white bears.　　　　　　　　　40
　But, sirrah, didst thou ever see any
　such?
Clo. No, faith, I never saw any such,
but I remember my father's words: he
bade me take heed I was not caught with
a white bear.
Seg. A lamentable tale, no doubt.
Clo. I tell you what, sir, as I was going
afield to serve my father's great horse, and
carried a bottle of hay upon my head—now
do you see, sir—I, fast hoodwinked [5] [50
that I could see nothing, I perceiving the
bear coming, I threw my hay into the hedge
and ran away.
Seg. What, from nothing?
Clo. I warrant you, yes, I saw something, for there was two load of thorns
besides my bottle of hay, and that made
three.
Seg. But tell me, sirrah, the bear that
　thou didst see,　　　　　　　　　59
Did she not bear a bucket on her arm?
Clo. Ha, ha, ha! I never saw bear go
a-milking in all my life. But hark you,

sir, I did not look so high as her arm; I
saw nothing but her white head and her
white belly.
Seg. But tell me, sirrah, where dost
thou dwell?
Clo. Why, do you not know me?
Seg. Why, no, how should I know thee?
Clo. Why, then, you know nobody,　[70
and [6] you know not me. I tell you, sir,
I am the Goodman Rat's son of the next
parish over the hill.
Seg. Goodman Rat's son? Why,
what's thy name?
Clo. Why, I am very near kin unto
him.
Seg. I think so, but what's thy name?
Clo. My name? I have a very pretty
name. I'll tell you what my name is; my
name is Mouse.　　　　　　　　　81
Seg. What, plain Mouse?
Clo. Ay, plain Mouse without either
welt or guard. [7] But do you hear, sir, I am
but a very young mouse, for my tail is
scarce grown out yet; look you here else.
Seg. But, I pray thee, who gave thee
that name?
Clo. Faith, sir, I know not that, but,
if you would fain know, ask my father's　[90
great horse, for he hath been half a year
longer with my father than I have.
Seg. [*Aside.*] This seems to be a merry
　fellow;
I care not if I take him home with me.
Mirth is a comfort to a troubled mind;
A merry man a merry master makes.—
How sayst thou, sirrah, wilt thou dwell
　with me?
Clo. Nay, soft, sir, two words to a bar-
gain! Pray you, what occupation are
you?　　　　　　　　　　　　　100
Seg. No occupation; I live upon my
lands.
Clo. Your lands! Away, you are no
master for me! Why, do you think that
I am so mad, to go seek my living in the
lands amongst the stones, briers, and
bushes, and tear my holiday apparel? Not
I, by your leave.
Seg. Why, I do not mean thou shalt.
Clo. How then?　　　　　　　　110
Seg. Why, thou shalt be my man, and
wait upon me at the court.

---

[1] Absolute.　　　　　[2] Pruning hooks.
[3] Ll. 33–45 and a number of other passages
printed as rough verse in the original are here
printed as prose.
[4] Clown, *i.e.,* Mouse.
[5] Completely blindfolded.
[6] If. The whole expression is proverbial.
[7] *I.e.,* undecorated.

CLO. What's that?

SEG. Where the king lies.

CLO. What's that same king, a man or a woman?

SEG. A man as thou art.

CLO. As I am? Hark you, sir; pray you, what kin is he to Goodman King of our parish, the churchwarden?   120

SEG. No kin to him; he is the king of the whole land.

CLO. King of the land! I never see him.

SEG. If thou wilt dwell with me, thou shalt see him every day.

CLO. Shall I go home again to be torn in pieces with bears? Nó, not I. I will go home and put on a clean shirt, and then go drown myself.   129

SEG. Thou shalt not need; if thou wilt dwell with me, thou shalt want nothing.

CLO. Shall I not? Then here's my hand; I'll dwell with you. And hark you, sir; now you have entertained me, I will tell you what I can do. I can keep my tongue from picking and stealing, and my hands from lying and slandering, I warrant you, as well as ever you had man in all your life.   140

SEG. Now will I to court with sorrowful heart, rounded [1] with doubts. If Amadine do live, then happy I; yea, happy I, if Amadine do live.   [*Exeunt.*]

[SCENE v.

The camp of the King of Aragon.]

Enter the King with a young Prince prisoner, Amadine, Tremelio,[2] with Collen and Councilors.

KING. Now, brave lords, our wars are brought to end,
Our foes, the foil,[3] and we in safety rest.
It us behooves to use such clemency in peace
As valor in the wars.
It is as great honor to be bountiful at home
As to be conquerors in the field.
Therefore, my lords, the more to my content,
Your liking, and your country's safeguard,

We are disposed in marriage for to give
Our daughter to Lord Segasto here,   10
Who shall succeed the diadem after me,
And reign hereafter as I tofore [4] have done,
Your sole and lawful King of Aragon.
What say you, lordings? Like you of my advice?

COL. An't [5] please your majesty, we do not only allow of your highness' pleasure, but also vow faithfully in what we may to further it.

KING. Thanks, good my lords; if long Adrostus live,
He will at full requite your courtesies.   20
Tremelio, in recompense of thy late valor done,
Take unto thee the Catalone,[6] a prince,
Lately our prisoner taken in the wars.
Be thou his keeper; his ransom shall be thine;
We'll think of it when leisure shall afford.
Meanwhile, do use him well; his father is a king.

TRE. Thanks to your majesty! His usage shall be such
As he thereat shall think no cause to grutch.[7]
     Exeunt [Tremelio and Prince].

KING. Then march we on to court, and rest our wearied limbs.
But, Collen, I have a tale in secret kept for thee: 30
When thou shalt hear a watchword from thy king,
Think then some weighty matter is at hand
That highly shall concern our state;
Then, Collen, look thou be not far from me.
And, for the service thou tofore hast done,
Thy truth and valor proved in every point,
I shall with bounties thee enlarge therefor.
So guard us to the court.

COL. Whatso my sovereign doth command me do,   39
With willing mind I gladly yield consent.
     Exeunt.

---

[1] Surrounded.   [3] *I.e.,* to defeat.
[2] Appears first in 1610 edn.

[4] Before.   [6] Man from Catalonia.
[5] If it.   [7] Grudge, murmur.

[SCENE vi.

The same.]

Enter Segasto and the Clown, with weapons about him.

SEG. Tell me, sirrah, how do you like your weapons?

CLO. O, very well, very well; they keep my sides warm.

SEG. They keep the dogs from your shins very well, do they not?

CLO. How, keep the dogs from my shins? I would scorn but my shins could keep the dogs from them.

SEG. Well, sirrah, leaving idle talk, [10 tell me dost thou know Captain Tremelio's chamber?

CLO. Ay, very well; it hath a door.

SEG. I think so, for so hath every chamber. But dost thou know the man?

CLO. Ay, forsooth; he hath a nose on his face.

SEG. Why, so hath everyone.

CLO. That's more than I know.

SEG. But dost thou remember the [20 captain that was here with the king even now, that brought the young prince prisoner?

CLO. O, very well.

SEG. Go unto him and bid him come unto me. Tell him I have a matter in secret to impart to him.

CLO. I will, Master.—Master, what's his name?

SEG. Why, Captain Tremelio. 30

CLO. O, the mealman! I know him very well. He brings meal every Saturday. But hark you, master, must I bid him come to you or must you come to him?

SEG. No, sirrah, he must come to me.

CLO. Hark you, master, how if he be not at home? What shall I do then?

SEG. Why, then leave word with some of his folks.

CLO. O, master, if there be nobody [40 within, I will leave word with his dog.

SEG. Why, can his dog speak?

CLO. I cannot tell; wherefore doth he keep his chamber else?

SEG. To keep out such knaves as thou art.

CLO. Nay, by Lady; then go yourself.

SEG. You will go, sir, will you not?

CLO. Yes, marry, will I. O, 'tis come to my head; and a [1] be not within, I'll [50 bring his chamber to you.

SEG. What, wilt thou pluck down the king's house?

CLO. Nay, by Lady, I'll know the price of it first. Master, it is such a hard name I have forgotten it again. I pray you, tell me his name.

SEG. I tell thee, Captain Tremelio.

CLO. O, Captain Treble-knave, Captain Treble-knave. 60

Enter Tremelio.

TRE. How now, sirrah, dost thou call me?

CLO. You must come to my master, Captain Treble-knave.

TRE. My Lord Segasto, did you send for me?

SEG. I did, Tremelio.—Sirrah, about your business.

CLO. Ay, marry, what's that? Can you tell? 70

SEG. No, not well.

CLO. Marry, then, I can; straight to the kitchen-dresser, to John the cook, and get me a good piece of beef and brewis,[2] and then to the buttery hatch to Thomas the butler for a jack [3] of beer, and there for an hour I'll so belabor myself! And therefore, I pray you, call me not till you think I have done, I pray you, good master.

Exit.

SEG. Well, sir, away.—Tremelio, this [80 it is: thou knowest the valor of Segasto spread through all the kingdom of Aragon, and such as have found triumph and favors, never daunted at any time; but now a shepherd [is][4] admired at in court for worthiness, and Segasto's honor laid aside. My will, therefore, is this: that thou dost find some means to work the shepherd's death. I know thy strength sufficient to perform my desire, and thy [90 love no otherwise than to revenge my injuries.

TRE. It is not the frowns of a shepherd that Tremelio fears. Therefore, account it accomplished, what I take in hand.

[1] He.
[2] Thickened broth.
[3] Leather pitcher.
[4] Added by Hazlitt.

Seg. Thanks, good Tremelio, and assure
thyself

What I promise that will I perform.

Tre. Thanks, my good lord, and in good
time see where

He cometh. Stand by a while, and you
shall see

Me put in practice your intended
drift.[1] 100

Enter Mucedorus.[2]

Have at thee, swain, if that I hit thee
right!

Mu. Vild [3] coward, so without cause to
strike a man!

Turn, coward, turn; now strike and do
thy worst! *Mucedorus killeth him.*

Seg. Hold, shepherd, hold; spare him,
kill him not!

Accursed villain, tell me, what hast
thou done?

Ah, Tremelio, trusty Tremelio!

I sorrow for thy death, and, since that thou,

Living, didst prove faithful to Segasto,

So Segasto now, living, will honor

The dead corpse of Tremelio with revenge. 110

Bloodthirsty villain, born and bred in
merciless murther,

Tell me, how durst thou be so bold as
once

To lay thy hands upon the least of
mine?

Assure thyself, thou shalt be used according to the law.

Mu. Segasto, cease; these threats are
needless.

Accuse not me of murther, that have
done nothing

But in mine own defense.

Seg. Nay, shepherd, reason not with me.

I'll manifest thy fact [4] unto the king,

Whose doom [5] will be thy death, as thou
deserv'st. 120

What ho, Mouse, come away!

Enter Mouse.

Clo. Why, how now, what's the matter? I thought you would be calling before
I had done.

Seg. Come, help; away with my friend!

Clo. Why, is he drunk? Cannot he
stand on his feet?

Seg. No, he is not drunk; he is slain.

Clo. Flain? [6] No, by Lady; he is not
flain. 130

Seg. He's killed, I tell thee.

Clo. What, do you use to kill your
friends? I will serve you no longer.

Seg. I tell thee, the shepherd killed
him.

Clo. O, did a so? But, master, I will
have all his apparel if I carry him away?

Seg. Why, so thou shalt.

Clo. Come, then, I will help. Mass,[7]
master, I think his mother sung [140
"looby"[8] to him, he is so heavy.

Exeunt [Segasto and Mouse].

Mu. Behold the fickle state of man, always mutable,

Never at one. Sometimes we feed on
fancies

With the sweet of our desires; sometimes again

We feel the heat of extreme miseries.

Now am I in favor about the court and
country;

Tomorrow those favors will turn to
frowns.

Today I live revengéd on my foe;

Tomorrow I die, my foe revenged on me.
Exit.

[Scene vii.

The forest.]

Enter Bremo, a wild man.

Bre. No passenger [9] this morning? What,
not one?

A chance that seldom doth befall.

What, not one? Then lie thou there,

And rest thyself till I have further need.
[*Puts down his club.*]

Now, Bremo, sith [10] thy leisure so affords—

An endless thing. Who knows not
Bremo's strength,

Who like a king commands [11] within
these woods?

The bear, the boar, dares not abide my
sight,

---

[1] Scheme.
[2] All early edns. have stage direction after next
line.
[3] Vile.
[4] Deed, crime.
[5] Judgment, sentence.
[6] Flayed.
[7] By the Mass.
[8] Lubber.
[9] Traveler.
[10] Since.
[11] Original reads *commander.*

But haste away to save themselves by flight.

The crystal waters in the bubbling brooks,   10

When I come by, doth swiftly slide away,

And claps themselves in closets under banks,

Afraid to look bold Bremo in the face.

The aged oaks at Bremo's breath doth bow,

And all things else are still at my command.

Else, what would I?

Rend them in pieces and pluck them from the earth,

And each way else I would revenge myself.

Why, who comes here with whom I dare not fight?

Who fights with me and doth not die the death? Not one.   20

What favor shows this sturdy stick to those

That here within these woods are combatants with me?

Why, death, and nothing else but present death.

With restless rage I wander through these woods;

No creature here but feareth Bremo's force;

Man, woman, child, beast, and bird,

And everything that doth approach my sight,

Are forced to fall if Bremo once do frown.

Come, cudgel, come, my partner in my spoils,

For here I see this day it will not be;   30

But, when it falls that I encounter any,

One pat sufficeth for to work my will.

What, comes not one? Then let's begone;

A time will serve when we shall better speed.   *Exit.*

[SCENE viii.

A room of state at the court of Aragon.]

Enter the King, Segasto, the Shepherd, and the Clown, with Others

KING. Shepherd, thou hast heard thine accusers;

Murther is laid to thy charge.

What canst thou say? Thou hast deservéd death.

MU. Dread sovereign, I must needs confess

I slew this captain in mine own defense,

Not of any malice, but by chance;

But mine accuser hath a further meaning.

SEG. Words will not here prevail;

I seek for justice, and justice craves his death.

KING. Shepherd, thine own confession hath condemned thee.   10

Sirrah, take him away, and do him to execution straight.

CLO. So he shall, I warrant him. But do you hear, master king, he is kin to a monkey; his neck is bigger than his head.

SEG. Come, sirrah, away with him, and hang him about the middle.

CLO. Yes, forsooth, I warrant you. Come on, sir. Ah, so like a sheepbiter a looks! [1]

Enter Amadine and a Boy with a bear's head.

AM. Dread sovereign and well-belovéd sire,   20

On bended knee I crave the life of this Condemnéd shepherd, which heretofore preserved

The life of thy sometime distresséd daughter.

KING. Preserved the life of my sometime distresséd daughter?

How can that be? I never knew the time

Wherein thou wast distressed; I never knew the day

But that I have maintainéd thy estate

As best beseemed the daughter of a king.

I never saw the shepherd until now.

How comes it, then, that he preserved thy life?   30

AM. Once walking with Segasto in the woods,

Further than our accustomed manner was,

Right before us, down a steep-fall hill,

A monstrous, ugly bear did hie him fast

To meet us both. Now whether this be true,

I refer it to the credit of Segasto.

SEG. Most true, an't like your majesty.

KING.   How then?

[1] *I.e.,* he has a hangdog look.

AM. The bear, being eager to obtain his
    prey,
  Made forward to us with an open mouth,
  As if he meant to swallow us both at
    once,   40
  The sight whereof did make us both to
    dread,
  But specially your daughter Amadine,
  Who, for I saw no succor incident
  But in Segasto's valor, I grew desperate,
  And he most cowardlike began to fly—
  Left me distressed to be devoured of him.
  How say you, Segasto, is it not true?
KING. His silence verifies it to be true.
    What then?   48
AM. Then I amazed, distresséd, all alone,
  Did hie me fast to scape that ugly bear;
  But all in vain, forwhy[1] he reachéd
    after me,
  And hardly I did oft escape his paws,
  Till at the length this shepherd came,
  And brought to me his head. Come
    hither, boy.
  Lo, here it is, which I present unto
    your majesty.
KING. The slaughter of this bear deserves
    great fame.
SEG. The slaughter of a man deserves
    great blame.
KING. Indeed, occasion oftentimes so falls
    out.
SEG. Tremelio in the wars, O king, pre-
    servéd thee.
AM. The shepherd in the woods, O king,
    preservéd me.   60
SEG. Tremelio fought when many men
    did yield.
AM. So would the shepherd, had he been
    in field.
CLO. [Aside.] So would my master, had
    he not run away.
SEG. Tremelio's force saved thousands
    from the foe.
AM. The shepherd's force hath[2] savéd
    thousands mo.[3]
CLO. [Aside.] Ay, shipsticks,[4] nothing
    else.
KING. Segasto, cease to accuse the shep-
    herd;
  His worthiness deserves a recompense;
  All we are bound to do the shepherd
    good.

Shepherd, whereas it was my sentence
    thou shouldst die,   70
So shall my sentence stand, for thou
    shalt die.
SEG. Thanks to your majesty.
KING. But soft, Segasto, not for this
    offense!—
Long mayst thou live, and, when the
    Sisters shall decree
To cut in twain the twisted thread of
    life,
Then let him die. For this I set him
    free.—
And for thy valor I will honor thee.
MU. Thanks to your majesty!
KING. Come, daughter, let us now de-
    part, to honor the worthy valor of the [80
shepherd with our rewards.
            Exeunt [all but Clown and Segasto].
CLO. O master, hear you. You have
made a fresh hand now. You would be
slow, you! What will you do now? You
have lost me a good occupation by the
means. Faith, master, now I cannot hang
the shepherd, I pray you, let me take the
pains to hang you—it is but half an hour's
exercise.   89
SEG. You are still in your knavery, but,
sith I cannot have his life, I will procure
his banishment forever. Come on, sirrah.
CLO. Yes, forsooth, I come.—[*To audience.*] Laugh at him, I pray you. *Exeunt.*

[SCENE ix.

A grove near the court.]

Enter Mucedorus solus.

MU. From Amadine and from her father's
    court,
With gold and silver and with rich re-
    wards,
Flowing from the banks of golden
    treasures [5]—
More may I boast and say; but I
Was never shepherd in such dignity.

Enter the Messenger and the Clown.

MESS. All hail, worthy shepherd!
CLO. All rain, lousy shepherd!
MU. Welcome, my friends. From
whence come you?   9
MESS. The king and Amadine greet

---

[1] Because.   [2] Brooke suggests *would have.*
[3] More.   [4] Sheep's ticks (?).   [5] Treasuries.

thee well, and, after greeting done, bids thee depart the court. Shepherd, begone!

CLO. Shepherd! Take law,[1] legs; fly away, shepherd!

MU. Whose words are these? Came these from Amadine?

MESS. Ay, from Amadine.

CLO. Ay, from Amladine.

MU. Ah, luckless fortune, worse than Phaëton's tale, 19
My former bliss is now become my bale.

CLO. What, wilt thou poison thyself?

MU. My former heaven is now become my hell.

CLO. The worst alehouse that ever I came in, in all my life.

MU. What shall I do?

CLO. Even go hang thyself half an hour.

MU. Can Amadine so churlishly command
To banish the shepherd from her father's court?

MESS. What should shepherds do in [30 the court?

CLO. What should shepherds do amongst us? Have we not lords enough on us in the court?

MU. Why, shepherds are men, and kings are no more.

MESS. Shepherds are men, and masters over their flock.

CLO. That's a lie. Who pays them their wages then? 40

MESS. Well, you are always interrupting of me, but you were best to look to him, lest you hang for him when he is gone. *Exit.*

The Clown sings.

CLO. And you shall hang for company,
For leaving me alone.

Shepherd, stand forth and hear my sentence: Shepherd, begone within three days in pain of my displeasure. Shepherd, begone; shepherd, begone; begone, begone, be- [50 gone, shepherd, shepherd, shepherd.

Exit.

MU. And must I go, and must I needs depart?
Ye goodly groves, partakers of my songs
In time tofore when fortune did not frown,

[1] Take a good lead (a hunting term).

Pour forth your plaints and wail awhile with me!
And thou, bright sun, my comfort in the cold,
Hide, hide thy face and leave me comfortless!
Ye wholesome herbs and sweet-smelling savors,
Yea, each thing else prolonging life of man,
Change, change your wonted course, that I, 60
Wanting your aid, in woeful sort may die.

Enter Amadine and Ariena, her maid.

AM. Ariena, if anybody ask for me,
Make some excuse till I return.

ARI. What and Segasto call?

AM. Do thou the like to him; I mean not to stay long. *Exit [Ariena].*[2]

MU. This voice so sweet my pining spirits revives.

AM. Shepherd, well met; ·tell me how thou doest.

MU. I linger life, yet wish for speedy death.

AM. Shepherd, although thy banishment already 70
Be decreed, and all against my will,
Yet Amadine—

MU. Ah, Amadine, to hear of banishment
Is death, ay, double death to me;
But, since I must depart, one thing I crave.

AM. Say on with all my heart.

MU. That in absence, either far or near,
You honor me, as servant, with your name.

AM. Not so.

MU. And why? 80

AM. I honor thee as sovereign of my heart.

MU. A shepherd and a sovereign? Nothing like.

AM. Yet like enough where there is no dislike.

MU. Yet great dislike, or else no banishment.

AM. Shepherd, it is only
Segasto that procures thy banishment.

[2] Stage direction appears after l. 63 in 1610 and later edns.

Mu. Unworthy wights are more in jealousy.

Am. Would God they would free thee from banishment,
Or likewise banish me.

Mu. Amen, say I, to have your company.   90

Am. Well, shepherd, sith thou suff'rest this for my sake,
With thee in exile also let me live—
On this condition, shepherd, thou canst love.

Mu. No longer love, no longer let me live!

Am. Of late I lovéd one indeed; now love
I none but only thee.

Mu.   Thanks, worthy princess.
I burn likewise, yet smother up the blast;
I dare not promise what I may perform.

Am. Well, shepherd, hark what I shall say:
I will return unto my father's court,   100
There for to provide me of such necessaries
As for my journey I shall think most fit;
This being done, I will return to thee.
Do thou, therefore, appoint the place
Where we may meet.

Mu. Down in the valley where I slew the bear.
And there doth grow a fair, broad-branchéd beech
That overshades a well; so who comes first
Let them abide the happy meeting of us both.
How like you this?

Am.   I like it very well.   110

Mu. Now, if you please, you may appoint the time.

Am. Full three hours hence, God willing, I will return.

Mu. The thanks that Paris gave the Grecian queen
The like doth Mucedorus yield.

Am. Then, Mucedorus, for three hours farewell.   *Exit.*

Mu. Your departure, lady, breeds a privy pain.   *Exit.*

[SCENE x.

The court of Aragon.]

Enter Segasto solus.

Seg. 'Tis well, Segasto, that thou hast thy will.
Should such a shepherd, such a simple swain
As he, eclipse thy credit famous through
The court? No, ply,[1] Segasto, ply!
Let it not in Aragon be said,
A shepherd hath Segasto's honor won.

Enter Mouse, the clown, calling his master.

Clo. What ho, master, will you come away?

Seg. Will you come hither? I pray you, what's the matter?   10

Clo. Why, is it not past eleven a-clock?

Seg. How then, sir?

Clo. I pray you, come away to dinner.

Seg. I pray you, come hither.

Clo. Here's such ado with you! Will you never come?

Seg. I pray you, sir, what news of the message I sent you about?

Clo. I tell you all the messes be on the table already. There wants not so [20 much as a mess of mustard half an hour ago.

Seg. Come, sir, your mind is all upon your belly;
You have forgotten what I bid you do.

Clo. Faith, I know nothing, but you bade me go to breakfast.

Seg. Was that all?

Clo. Faith, I have forgotten it; the very scent of the meat hath made me forget[2] it quite.   30

Seg. You have forgotten the errand I bid you do?

Clo. What arrant? An arrant knave, or an arrant whore?

Seg. Why, thou knave, did I not bid thee banish the shepherd?

Clo. O, the shepherd's bastard.

Seg. I tell thee, the shepherd's banishment.

Clo. I tell you, the shepherd's bas- [40 tard shall be well kept. I'll look to it myself. But, I pray you, come away to dinner.

[1] Apply, work.
[2] Original reads *made me hath forgot.*

Seg. Then you will not tell me whether you have banished him or no?

Clo. Why, I cannot say "banishment," and you would give me a thousand pounds to say so.

Seg. Why, you whoreson[1] slave, have you forgotten that I sent you and another to drive away the shepherd? 50

Clo. What an ass are you! Here's a stir indeed! Here's "message," "arrant," "banishment," and I cannot tell what.

Seg. I pray you, sir, shall I know whether you have drove him away?

Clo. Faith, I think I have; and you will not believe me, ask my staff.

Seg. Why, can thy staff tell?

Clo. Why, he was with me too.

Seg. Then happy I, that have [60 obtained my will.

Clo. And happier I, if you would go to dinner.

Seg. Come, sirrah, follow me.

Clo. I warrant you, I will not lose an inch of you, now you are going to dinner.— [To audience.] I promise you, I thought seven year before I could get him away.
　　　　　　　　　　　　　　　Exeunt.

[Scene xi.

The forest.]

Enter Amadine sola.[2]

Am. God grant my long delay procures no harm
Nor this my tarrying frustrate my pretense.[3]
My Mucedorus surely stays for me,
And thinks me overlong. At length I come,
My present promise to perform.
Ah, what a thing is firm, unfeignéd love!
What is it which true love dares not attempt?
My father he may make, but I must match;
Segasto loves, but Amadine must like
Where likes her best; compulsion is a thrall. 10
No, no, the hearty choice is all in all;
The shepherd's virtue Amadine esteems.
But what! Methinks my shepherd is not come.

[1] Rascally.
[2] Original reads solus.
[3] Intention.

I muse at that; the hour is at hand.
Well, here I'll rest till Mucedorus come.
　　　　　　　　　　　　　　She sits down.

Enter Bremo, looking about; hastily takes hold of her.

Bre. A happy prey! Now, Bremo, feed on flesh!
Dainties, Bremo, dainties, thy hungry panch[4] to fill!
Now glut thy greedy guts with lukewarm blood!
Come, fight with me; I long to see thee dead.

Am. How can she fight that weapons cannot wield? 20

Bre. What, canst not fight? Then lie thee down and die.

Am. What, must I die?

Bre. What need these words? I thirst to suck thy blood!

Am. Yet pity me and let me live awhile.

Bre. No pity I; I'll feed upon thy flesh;
I'll tear thy body piecemeal joint from joint.

Am. Ah, how I want my shepherd's company.

Bre. I'll crush thy bones betwixt two oaken trees.

Am. Haste, shepherd, haste, or else thou com'st too late!

Bre. I'll suck the sweetness from thy marrowbones. 30

Am. Ah, spare, ah, spare to shed my guiltless blood!

Bre. With this my bat will I beat out thy brains!
Down, down, I say; prostrate thyself upon the ground.

Am. Then, Mucedorus, farewell; my hopéd joys, farewell.
Yea, farewell, life, and welcome, present death! She kneels.
To thee, O God, I yield my dying ghost.

Bre. Now, Bremo, play thy part.—
How now, what sudden chance is this?
My limbs do tremble and my sinews shake;
My unweakened arms hath lost their former force. 40
Ah, Bremo, Bremo, what a foil[5] hast thou

[4] Paunch.
[5] Disgrace.

That yet at no time [ever][1] wast afraid
To dare the greatest gods to fight with
   thee,   *He strikes.*
And now wants strength for one down-
   driving blow!
Ah, how my courage fails when I should
   strike!
Some newcome spirit, abiding in my
   breast,
Saith, "Spare her," which never spared
   any.
Shall I spare her, Bremo? Spare her;
   do not kill.[2]
To it, Bremo, to it! Say [3] again.—
I cannot wield my weapons in my hand;
Methinks I should not strike so fair a
   one.   51
I think her beauty hath bewitched my
   force
Or else within me altered nature's course.
Ay, woman, wilt thou live in woods with
   me?
AM. Fain would I live, yet loath to live in
   woods.
BRE. Thou shalt not choose; it shall be
   as I say,
And, therefore, follow me.   *Exeunt.*

[SCENE xii.

The same.]

Enter Mucedorus solus.

MU. It was my will an hour ago and more,
As was my promise, for to make return,
But other business hindered my pre-
   tense.
It is a world [4] to see, when man appoints
And purposely one certain thing de-
   crees,
How many things may hinder his intent.
What one would wish, the same is
   farthest off.
But yet th'appointed time cannot be
   past,
Nor hath her presence yet prevented [5]
   me.
Well, here I'll stay, and expect [6] her com-
   ing.   10
They cry within, "Hold him, hold him!"
MU. Someone or other is pursued, no
   doubt;

[1] From 1598 edn.
[2] Ll. 47 and 48 are interchanged in the original.
[3] Essay.   [5] Preceded.
[4] It is wonderful.   [6] Await.

Perhaps some search for me. 'Tis good
   to doubt the worst;
Therefore I'll be gone.   *Exit.*

Cry within, "Hold him, hold him!" Enter
            Mouse, the clown, with a pot.

CLO. Hold him, hold him, hold him!
Here's a stir indeed. Here came hue after
the crier; and I was set close at Mother
Nip's house, and there I called for three
pots of ale, as 'tis the manner of us courtiers. Now, sirrah, I had taken the maidenhead of two of them. Now, as I was [20
lifting up the third to my mouth, there
came, "Hold him, hold him!" Now I could
not tell whom to catch hold on, but I am
sure I caught one—perchance a may be in
this pot. Well, I'll see! Mass, I cannot
see him yet. Well, I'll look a little further.
Mass, he is a little slave, if a be here. Why,
here's nobody. All this goes well yet; but
if the old trot should come for her pot—
ay, marry, there's the matter. But I [30
care not; I'll face her out, and call her old
rusty, dusty, musty, fusty, crusty firebrand, and worse than all that, and so
face her out of her pot. But soft, here
she comes!

Enter the Old Woman.

OLD W. Come, you knave! Where's
my pot, you knave?
CLO. Go, look your pot; come not to
me for your pot, 'twere good for you.
OLD W. Thou liest, thou knave; [40
thou hast my pot.
CLO. You lie, and you say it. I your
pot? I know what I'll say.
[OLD W.][7] Why, what wilt thou say?
CLO. But say I have him, and thou
dar'st.
OLD W. Why, thou knave, thou hast
not only my pot but my drink unpaid for.
CLO. You lie like an old—I will not
say whore.   50
OLD W. Dost thou call me whore? I'll
cap [8] thee for my pot.
CLO. Cap me and thou darest! Search
me whether I have it or no.
She searcheth him, and he drinketh over
   her head and casteth down the pot; she
   stumbleth at it; then they fall together by
   the ears; she takes up her pot and goes out.

[7] From 1598 edn.   [8] Arrest.

Enter Segasto.

SEG. How now, sirrah, what's the matter?

CLO. O, flies, master, flies.

SEG. Flies? Where are they?

CLO. O, here, master, all about your face. 60

SEG. Why, thou liest; I think thou art mad.

CLO. Why, master, I have killed a dungcartful at the least.

SEG. Go to, sirrah! Leaving this idle talk, give ear to me.

CLO. How? Give you one of my ears? Not and you were ten masters.

SEG. Why, sir, I bid you give ear to my words. 70

CLO. I tell you I will not be made a curtal [1] for no man's pleasure.

SEG. I tell thee, attend what I say. Go thy ways straight and rear the whole town.

CLO. How? Rear the whole town? Even go yourself; it is more than I can do. Why, do you think I can rear a town, that can scarce rear a pot of ale to my head? I should rear a town, should I not! [80

SEG. Go to the constable and make a privy search, for the shepherd is run away with the king's daughter.

CLO. How? Is the shepherd run away with the king's daughter, or is the king's daughter run away with the shepherd?

SEG. I cannot tell, but they are both gone together.

CLO. What a fool is she to run away with the shepherd! Why, I think I am [90 a little handsomer man than the shepherd myself. But tell me, master, must I make a privy search, or search in the privy?

SEG. Why, dost thou think they will be there?

CLO. I cannot tell.

SEG. Well, then, search everywhere; leave no place unsearched for them. *Exit.*

CLO. O, now am I in office; now will I to that old firebrand's house and [100 will not leave one place unsearched; nay, I'll to the alestand [2] and drink as long as I can stand, and, when I have done, I'll let out all the rest, to see if he be not hid in the barrel. And, if I find him not there, I'll to the cupboard; I'll not leave one

[1] Docked animal.   [2] Barrel.

corner of her house unsearched. I' faith, ye old crust, I will be with you now. *Exit.*

[SCENE xiii. [3]

The court of Valencia.]

Sound music.

Enter the King of Valencia, Anselmo, Roderigo, Lord Borachius, with Others.

KING [OF] VAL. Enough of music; it but adds to torment;
Delights to vexéd spirits are as dates
Set to a sickly man, which rather cloy than comfort.
Let me entreat you to entreat no more.

ROD. Let your strings sleep; have done there. *Let the music cease.*

KING [OF] VAL. Mirth to a soul disturbed are embers turned,
Which sudden gleam with molestation,
But sooner lose their sight for't;
'Tis gold bestowed upon a rioter,
Which not relieves, but murders him. 10
'Tis a drug given to the healthful,
Which infects, not cures.
How can a father that hath lost his son,
A prince both wise, virtuous, and valiant,
Take pleasure in the idle acts of time?
No, no; till Mucedorus I shall see again,
All joy is comfortless, all pleasure pain.

ANS. Your son, my lord, is well.

KING [OF] VAL. I prithee, speak that thrice.

ANS. The prince, your son, is safe. 20

KING [OF] VAL. O, where, Anselmo? Surfeit me with that.

ANS. In Aragon, my liege; and at his parture
Bound my secrecy
By his affectious love, not to disclose it.
But care of him and pity of your age
Makes my tongue blab what my breast vowed concealment.

KING [OF] VAL. Thou not deceiv'st me?
I ever thought thee what I find thee now,
An upright, loyal man. But what desire,
Or young-fed humor nursed within the brain, 30
Drew him so privately to Aragon?

[3] This scene appeared first in the 1610 edn.

Ans. A forcing adamant:[1]

Love, mixed with fear and doubtful jealousy,
Whether report gilded a worthless trunk,
Or Amadine deserved her high extolment.

King [of] Val. See our provision be in readiness;
Collect us followers of the comeliest hue
For our chief guardians; we will thither wend.
The crystal eye of heaven shall not thrice wink,
Nor the green flood six times his shoulders turn,   40
Till we salute the Aragonian king.
Music, speak loudly now; the season's apt,
For former dolors are in pleasure wrapped.   *Exeunt omnes.*

[Scene xiv.

The forest.]

Enter Mucedorus to disguise himself.

Mu. Now, Mucedorus, whither wilt thou go?
Home to thy father to thy native soil,
Or try some long abode within these woods?
Well, I will hence depart and hie me home.
What, hie me home, said I? That may not be;
In Amadine rests my felicity.
Then, Mucedorus, do as thou didst decree:
Attire thee hermit-like within these groves,
Walk often to the beech and view the well,
Make settles there and seat thyself thereon,   10
And, when thou feelest thyself to be athirst,
Then drink a hearty draught to Amadine.
No doubt she thinks on thee,
And will one day come pledge thee at this well.
Come, habit, thou art fit for me.
                         He disguiseth himself.

---

[1] Compelling magnet.   [2] Ant.

No shepherd now, a hermit must I be.
Methinks this fits me very well;
Now must I learn to bear a walking staff,
And exercise some gravity withal.

Enter the Clown.

Clo. Here's through the woods, and [20
through the woods, to look out a shepherd
and a stray king's daughter.—But soft,
who have we here? What art thou?

Mu. I am an hermit.

Clo. An emmet?[2] I never saw such a
big emmet in all my life before.

Mu. I tell you, sir, I am an hermit,
one that leads a solitary life within these
woods.

Clo. O, I know thee now; thou art [30
her that eats up all the hips and haws;
we could not have one piece of fat bacon
for thee all this year.

Mu. Thou dost mistake me. But, I
pray thee, tell me who dost thou seek in
these woods.

Clo. What do I seek? For a stray
king's daughter run away with a shepherd.

Mu. A stray king's daughter run away
with a shepherd! Wherefore, canst [40
thou tell?

Clo. Yes, that I can; 'tis this: my
master and Amadine, walking one day
abroad, nearer to these woods than they
were used—about what I cannot tell—but
towards them comes running a great
bear. Now my master, he played the man
and ran away, and Amadine crying after
him. Now, sir, comes me a shepherd and
he strikes off the bear's head. Now [50
whether the bear were dead before or no I
cannot tell, for bring twenty bears before
me and bind their hands and feet, and
I'll kill them all. Now, ever since, Amadine
hath been in love with the shepherd, and
for good will she's even run away with the
shepherd.

Mu. What manner of man was he?
Canst describe him unto me?

Clo. 'Scribe him? Ay, I warrant [60
you that I can. A was a little, low, broad,
tall, narrow, big, well-favored fellow—a
jerkin of white cloth, and buttons of the
same cloth.

Mu. Thou describest him well, but, if

I chance to see any such, pray you, where
shall I find you, or what's your name?

Clo. My name is called Master Mouse.

Mu. O, Master Mouse, I pray you,
what office might you bear in the [70
court?

Clo. Marry, sir, I am a rusher of the
stable.

Mu. O, usher of the table!

Clo. Nay, I say "rusher," and I'll
prove mine office good; for look, sir, when
any comes from under the sea or so, and
a dog chance to blow his nose backward,
then with a whip I give him the good time
of the day, and strow rushes presently.[1] [80
Therefore, I am a rusher, a high office,
I promise ye.

Mu. But where shall I find you in the
court?

Clo. Why, where it is best being, either
in the kitching a-eating or in the buttery
drinking. But, if you come, I will provide
for thee a piece of beef and brewis[2] knuckle-
deep in fat. Pray you, take pains; remember Master Mouse.   *Exit.* [90

Mu. Ay, sir, I warrant I will not forget
you.—
Ah, Amadine, what should become of
thee?
Whither shouldst thou go so long unknown?
With watch and ward each passage is
beset,
So that she cannot long escape unknown.
Doubtless she hath lost herself within
these woods
And, wand'ring to and fro, she seeks the
well,
Which yet she cannot find; therefore
will I seek her out.   *Exit.*

[Scene xv.

The same.]

Enter Bremo and Amadine.

Bre. Amadine, how like you Bremo and
his woods?

Am. As like the woods of Bremo's cruelty!
Though I were dumb and could not
answer him,
The beasts' themselves would with re-
lenting tears
Bewail thy savage and unhuman deeds.

[1] Strew rushes immediately.
[2] Thick broth.

Bre. My love, why dost thou murmur to
thyself?
Speak louder, for thy Bremo hears thee
not.

Am. My Bremo? No, the shepherd is my
love.

Bre. Have I not savéd thee from sudden
death,
Giving thee leave to live that thou
mightst love?   10
And dost thou whet me on to cruelty?
Come, kiss me, sweet, for all my favors
past.

Am. I may not, Bremo, and therefore
pardon me.

Bre. [*Aside.*] See how she flings away
from me; I will follow
And give attend to her.—Deny my
love!
Ah, worm of beauty, I will chastise thee!
Come, come, prepare thy head upon
the block.

Am. O, spare me, Bremo! Love should
limit life,
Not to be made a murderer of himself.
If thou wilt glut thy loving heart with
blood,   20
Encounter with the lion or the bear,
And like a wolf prey not upon a lamb.

Bre. Why then dost thou repine at me?
If thou wilt love me, thou shalt be my
queen;
I will crown thee with a chaplet[3] made
of ivory,
And make the rose and lily wait on thee.
I'll rend the burly branches from the
oak,[4]
To shadow thee from burning sun.
The trees shall spread themselves where
thou dost go,
And, as they spread, I'll trace[5] along
with thee.   30

Am. [*Aside.*] You may, for who but you?

Bre. Thou shalt be fed with quails and
partridges,
With blackbirds, larks, thrushes, and
nightingales.
Thy drink shall be goat's milk and crystal
water,
Distilled from the fountains and the
clearest springs.

[3] Original reads *complet.*
[4] From 1598 edn. Original reads *oxe.*
[5] Walk.

And all the dainties that the woods afford

I'll freely give thee to obtain thy love.

AM. [*Aside.*] You may, for who but you?

BRE. The day I'll spend to recreate my love   39

With all the pleasures that I can devise,

And in the night I'll be thy bedfellow,

And lovingly embrace thee in mine arms.

AM. [*Aside.*] One may; so may not you.

BRE. The satyrs and the wood-nymphs shall attend on thee

And lull thee asleep with music's sound,

And in the morning when thou dost awake,

The lark shall sing good morrow to my queen,

And, whilst he sings, I'll kiss my Ama-dine.

AM. [*Aside.*] You may, for who but you?

BRE. When thou art up, the wood lanes shall be strowed   50

With violets, cowslips, and sweet mari-golds

For thee to trample and to trace upon,

And I will teach thee how to kill the deer,

To chase the hart and how to rouse the roe,

If thou wilt live to love and honor me.

AM. [*Aside.*] You may, for who but you?

Enter Mucedorus.

BRE. Welcome, sir;

An hour ago I looked for such a guest.

Be merry, wench, we'll have a frolic feast.

Here's flesh enough for to suffice us both.   60

Say, sirrah, wilt thou fight or dost thou mean to die?

MU. I want a weapon; how can I fight?

BRE. Thou wants a weapon? Why then, thou yield'st to die.

MU. I say not so; I do not yield to die.

BRE. Thou shalt not choose. I long to see thee dead!

AM. Yet spare him, Bremo, spare him!

BRE. Away, I say; I will not spare him.

MU. Yet give me leave to speak.

BRE.   Thou shalt not speak.

AM. Yet give him leave to speak for my sake.

BRE. Speak on, but be not overlong.   70

MU. In time of yore, when men like brutish beasts

Did lead their lives in loathsome cells and woods

And wholly gave themselves to witless will,

A rude, unruly rout, then man to man

Became a present prey; then might prevailed;

The weakest went to walls.

Right was unknown, for wrong was all in all.

As men thus livéd in their great outrage,[1]

Behold, one Orpheus came, as poets tell,

And them from rudeness unto reason brought,   80

Who, led by reason, some forsook the woods.

Instead of caves they built them castles strong;

Cities and towns were founded by them then.

Glad were they, they found such ease, and in

The end they grew to perfect amity.

Weighing their former wickedness,

They termed the time wherein they livéd then

A golden age, a goodly golden age.

Now, Bremo, for so I hear thee called,

If men which lived tofore, as thou dost now,   90

Wild in wood, addicted all to spoil,

Returnéd were by worthy Orpheus' means,

Let me like Orpheus cause thee to return

From murther, bloodshed, and like cruelty.

What, should we fight before we have a cause?

No, let's live and love together faithfully.

I'll fight for thee.

BRE.   Fight for me or die!

Or fight, or else thou diest!

AM.   Hold, Bremo, hold!

BRE. Away, I say; thou troublest me.

AM. You promised me to make me your queen.   100

BRE. I did; I mean no less.

AM. You promised that I should hav my will.

BRE. I did; I mean no less.

[1] Violent conduct.

AM. Then save this hermit's life, for he may save us both.

BRE. At thy request I'll spare him, but never any after him. Say, hermit, what canst thou do?

MU. I'll wait on thee; sometime upon thy queen. Such service shalt thou shortly have as Bremo never had.   *Exeunt.* [110

[SCENE xvi.

The court of Aragon.]

Enter Segasto, the Clown, and Rumbelo.

SEG. Come, sirs; what, shall I never have you find out Amadine and the shepherd?

CLO. And I have been through the woods, and through the woods, and could see nothing but an emmet.

RU. Why, I see a thousand emmets. Thou mean'st a little one?

CLO. Nay, that emmet that I saw was bigger than thou art.   10

RU. Bigger than I?—What a fool have you to your man; I pray you, master, turn him away.

SEG. But dost thou hear? Was he not a man?

CLO. Think he was, for he said he did lead a saltseller's life about the woods.

SEG. Thou wouldest say a solitary life about the woods.

CLO. I think it was so, indeed.   20

RU. I thought what a fool thou art.

CLO. Thou art a wise man! Why, he did nothing but sleep since he went.

SEG. But tell me, Mouse, how did he go?

CLO. In a white gown, and a white hat on his head, and a staff in his hand.

SEG. I thought so; it was an hermit that walked a solitary life in the woods. Well, get you to dinner, and after, never leave seeking till you bring some news of [30 them, or I'll hang you both.   *Exit.*

CLO. How now, Rumbelo? What shall we do now?

RU. Faith, I'll home to dinner, and afterward to sleep.

CLO. Why, then, thou wilt be hanged.

RU. Faith, I care not, for I know I shall never find them. Well, I'll once more abroad, and, if I cannot find them, I'll never come home again.   40

CLO. I tell thee what, Rumbelo, thou

shalt go in at one end of the wood and I at the other, and we will meet both together in the midst.

RU. Content! Let's away to dinner.

                    Exeunt.

[SCENE xvii.

The forest.]

Enter Mucedorus solus.

MU. Unknown to any here within these woods,
With bloody Bremo do I lead my life.
The monster, he doth murder all he meets;
He spareth none, and none doth him escape.
Who would continue—who but only I—
In such a cruel cutthroat's company?
Yet Amadine is there. How can I choose?
Ah, silly soul, how oftentimes she sits
And sighs, and calls, "Come, shepherd, come;
Sweet Mucedorus, come and set me free,"   10
When Mucedorus present [1] stands her by!—
But here she comes!

Enter Amadine. [2]

What news, fair lady, as you walk these woods?

AM. Ah, hermit, none but bad and such as thou knowest.

MU. How do you like your Bremo and his woods?

AM. Not my Bremo nor Bremo his [3] woods.

MU. And why not yours? Methinks he loves you well.

AM. I like not him; his love to me is nothing worth.

MU. Lady, in this methinks you offer wrong,
To hate the man that ever loves you best.   20

AM. Ah, hermit, I take no pleasure in his love;
Neither doth Bremo like me best.

[1] Suggested by Hazlitt.   Original reads *peasant.*
[2] In the original this stage direction follows the next line.
[3] Original reads *his* Bremo.

Mu. Pardon my boldness, fair lady; sith we both
   May safely talk now out of Bremo's sight,
   Unfold to me, if so you please, the full discourse
   How, when, and why you came into these woods,
   And fell into this bloody butcher's hands.
Am. Hermit, I will.
   Of late a worthy shepherd I did love—
Mu. A shepherd, lady? Sure, a man un-fit   30
   To match with you.
Am. Hermit, this is true; and, when we had—
Mu. Stay there; the wild man comes!
   Refer [1] the rest until another time.

Enter Bremo.

Bre. What secret tale is this? What whisp'ring have we here?
   Villain, I charge thee tell thy tale again.
Mu. If needs I must, lo, here it is again:
   Whenas we both had lost the sight of thee,
   It grieved us both, but specially thy queen,   39
   Who in thy absence ever fears the worst,
   Lest some mischance befall your royal grace.
   "Shall my sweet Bremo wander through the woods?
   Toil to and fro for to redress my want,
   Hazard his life, and all to cherish me?
   I like not this," quoth she,
   And thereupon cravéd to know of me
   If I could teach her handle weapons well.
   My answer was I had small skill therein,
   But gladsome, mighty king, to learn of thee.
   And this was all.   50
Bre. Was't so? None can dislike of this. I'll teach
   You both to fight; but first, my queen, begin.
   Here, take this weapon; see how thou canst use it.
Am. This is too big; I cannot wield it in my arm.

[1] Postpone.

Bre. Is't so? We'll have a knotty crab-tree staff
   For thee.—But, sirrah, tell me, what sayest thou?
Mu. With all my heart I willing am to learn.
Bre. Then take my staff and see how thou canst wield it.
Mu. First teach me how to hold it in my hand.
Bre. Thou hold'st it well.   60
   Look how he doth; thou mayst the sooner learn.
Mu. Next tell me how and when 'tis best to strike.
Bre. 'Tis best to strike when time doth serve;
   'Tis best to lose no time.
Mu. [*Aside.*] Then now or never is my time to strike.
Bre. And, when thou strikest, be sure to hit the head.
Mu. The head?
Bre.   The very head.
Mu.   Then have at thine!
   He strikes him down dead.
   So, lie there and die,
   A death no doubt according to desert,
   Or else a worse as thou deserv'st a worse.   70
Am. It glads my heart this tyrant's death to see.
Mu. Now, lady, it remains in you
   To end the tale you lately had begun,
   Being interrupted by this wicked wight.
   You said you loved a shepherd?
Am. Ay, so I do, and none but only him,
   And will do still as long as life shall last.
Mu. But tell me, lady, sith I set you free,
   What course of life do you intend to take?
Am. I will disguiséd wander through the world,   80
   Till I have found him out.
Mu. How if you find your shepherd in these woods?
Am. Ah, none so happy then as Amadine.
   He discloseth [2] himself.
Mu. In tract of time a man may alter much.
   Say, lady, do you know your shepherd well?

[2] Early edns. read *disguiseth.*

AM. My Mucedorus! Hath he set me free?

MU. He hath set thee free.

AM. And lived so long unknown to Amadine?

MU. Ay, that's a question whereof you may not be resolved.
You know that I am banished from the court?　　90
I know likewise each passage is beset
So that we cannot long escape unknown;
Therefore my will is this: that we return
Right through the thickets to the wild man's cave,
And there awhile live on his provision,
Until the search and narrow watch be past.
This is my counsel, and I think it best.

AM. I think the very same.

MU.　　　　　　　　Come, let's begone.

The Clown [enters and] searcheth, and falls over the Wild Man, and so carries him away.

CLO. Nay, soft, sir; are you here? A bots [1] on you! I was like to be hanged [100 for not finding you. We would borrow a certain stray king's daughter of you—a wench, a wench, sir, we would have.

MU. A wench of me? I'll make thee eat my sword!

CLO. O Lord! Nay, and you are so lusty, I'll call a cooling card [2] for you. Ho, master, master, ay, come away quickly!

Enter Seg[asto].

SEG. What's the matter?　　109

CLO. Look, master, Amadine and the shepherd! O, brave!

SEG. What, minion, have I found you out?

CLO. Nay, that's a lie; I found her out myself.

SEG. Thou gadding huswife, what cause hadst thou to gad abroad,
Whenas thou knowest our wedding day so nigh?

AM. Not so, Segasto; no such thing in hand.
Show your assurance; [3] then I'll answer you.

SEG. Thy father's promise my assurance is.　　120

AM. But what he promised he hath not performed.

SEG. It rests in thee for to perform the same.

AM. Not I.

SEG. And why?

AM. So is my will, and therefore even so.

CLO. Master, with a nonny, nonny, no! [4]

SEG. Ah, wicked villain, art thou here?

MU. What needs these words? We weigh them not.

SEG. We weigh them not? Proud shepherd, I scorn thy company.

CLO. We'll not have a corner of thy company.　　130

MU. I scorn not thee, nor yet the least of thine.

CLO. That's a lie; a would have killed me with his pugsnando. [5]

SEG. This stoutness, Amadine, contents me not.

AM. Then seek another that may you better please.

MU. Well, Amadine, it only rests in thee
Without delay to make thy choice of three:
There stands Segasto; here a shepherd stands;
There stands the third. Now make thy choice.

CLO. A lord at the least I am.　　140

AM. My choice is made, for I will none but thee.

SEG. A worthy mate, no doubt, for such a wife.

MU. And, Amadine, why wilt thou none but me?
I cannot keep thee as thy father did;
I have no lands for to maintain thy state.
Moreover, if thou mean to be my wife,
Commonly this must be thy use:
To bed at midnight, up at four,
Drudge all day and trudge from place to place,　　149
Whereby our daily victual for to win;
And last of all, which is the worst of all,
No princess then, but plain a shepherd's wife.

CLO. Then, God gi' you good morrow, goody shepherd!

---

[1] *I.e.*, plague.

[2] A card that dashes the hopes of the adversary.　　[3] Pledge of betrothal.

[4] Refrain in popular songs.　　[5] Sword.

AM. It shall not need; if Amadine do
live,
Thou shalt be crownéd King of Aragon.
CLO. O, master, laugh! When he's
king, then I'll be a queen!
MU. Then know that which ne'er to-
fore was known:
I am no shepherd, no Aragonian I,
But born of royal blood—my father's
of   160
Valencia king, my mother, queen—
who for
Thy sacred sake took this hard task in
hand.
AM. Ah, how I joy my fortune is so good!
SEG. Well, now I see Segasto shall not
speed;
But, Mucedorus, I as much do joy
To see thee here within our court of
Aragon,
As if a kingdom had befall'n me this
time.
I with my heart surrender her to thee,
                    He gives her to him.
And loose[1] what right to Amadine I
have!   169
CLO. What barn's door, and born
where my father was constable! A bots
on thee! How dost thee?
MU. Thanks, Segasto; but yet you leveled
at the crown.
CLO. Master, bear this and bear all.
SEG. Why so, sir?
CLO. He sees you take a goose by the
crown.
SEG. Go to, sir! Away, post you to the
king,
Whose heart is fraught with careful
doubts,[2]
Glad him up and tell him these good
news,   179
And we will follow as fast as we may.
CLO. I go, master; I run, master!
                                Exeunt.

[SCENE xviii.

An open place near the court of Aragon.]

Enter the King and Collen.

KING. Break, heart, and end my pallid
woes!
My Amadine, the comfort of my life,

[1] Emended by Hazlitt. Original reads *looke.*
[2] Anxious fears.

How can I joy except she were in sight?
Her absence breeds sorrow to my soul
And with a thunder breaks my heart in
twain.
COL. Forbear those passions, gentle king,
And you shall see 'twill turn unto the
best,
And bring your soul to quiet and to joy.
KING. Such joy as death, I do assure me
that,
And naught but death, unless of her
I hear,   10
And that with speed; I cannot sigh thus
long—
But what a tumult do I hear within?
They cry within, "Joy and happiness!"
COL. I hear a noise of overpassing joy
Within the court; my lord, be of good
comfort.—
And here comes one in haste.

Enter the Clown running.

CLO. A king! a king! a king!
COL. Why, how now, sirrah? What's
the matter?
CLO. O, 'tis news for a king; 'tis worth
money.   20
KING. Why, sirrah, thou shalt have sil-
ver and gold if it be good.
CLO. O, 'tis good, 'tis good! Amadine—
KING. O, what of her? Tell me, and I
will make thee a knight.
CLO. How, a sprite? No, by Lady, I
will not be a sprite. Masters, get you
away; if I be a sprite, I shall be so lean I
shall make you all afraid.
COL. Thou sot, the king means to   [30
make thee a gentleman.
CLO. Why, I shall want parel.[3]
KING. Thou shalt want for nothing.
CLO. Then stand away; strike up thy-
self. Here they come.

Enter Segasto, Mucedorus, and Amadine.

AM. My gracious father, pardon thy disloyal daughter.
KING. What, do mine eyes behold my
daughter Amadine?
Rise up, dear daughter, and let these
my embracing arms
Show some token of thy father's joy,
Which ever since thy departure hath
languished in sorrow.   40

[3] Apparel.

Aᴍ. Dear father, never were your sorrows
Greater than my griefs,
Never you so desolate as I comfortless;
Yet, nevertheless, acknowledging myself
To be the cause of both, on bended knees
I humbly crave your pardon.

Kɪɴɢ. I'll pardon thee, dear daughter;
but, as for him—

Aᴍ. Ah, father, what of him?

Kɪɴɢ. As sure as I am king and wear the
crown,   49
I will revenge on that accursèd wretch.

Mᴜ. Yet, worthy prince, work not thy
will in wrath;
Show favor.

Kɪɴɢ.   Ay, such favor as thou
deservest.

Mᴜ. I do deserve the daughter of a king.

Kɪɴɢ. O, impudent! A shepherd and so
insolent?

Mᴜ. No shepherd I, but a worthy prince.

Kɪɴɢ. In fair conceit,[1] not princely born.

Mᴜ. Yes, princely born: my father is a
king,
My mother a queen, and of Valencia
both.

Kɪɴɢ. What, Mucedorus?   Welcome to
our court!
What cause hadst thou to come to me
disguised?   60

Mᴜ. No cause to fear; I causèd no of-
fense
But this: desiring thy daughter's virtues
for to see,
Disguised myself from out my father's
court,
Unknown to any. In secret I did rest,
And passèd many troubles near to death;
So hath your daughter my partaker been,
As you shall know hereafter more at
large,
Desiring you, you will give her to me,
Even as mine own and sovereign of
my life;
Then shall I think my travails are well
spent.   70

Kɪɴɢ. With all my heart, but this—
Segasto claims my promise made tofore,
That he should have her as his only
wife,
Before my council when we came from
war.

Segasto, may I crave thee let it pass,
And give Amadine as wife to Mucedorus?

Sᴇɢ. With all my heart, were it a far
greater thing;
And what I may to furnish up their rites
With pleasing sports and pastimes you
shall see.

Kɪɴɢ. Thanks, good Segasto, I will think
of this.   80

Mᴜ. Thanks, good my lord, and, while I
live,
Account of me in what I can or may.

Aᴍ. And, good Segasto, these great courtesies
Shall not be forgot.

Cʟᴏ. Why, hark you, master! Bones,[2]
what have you done? What, given away
the wench you made me take such pains
for? You are wise indeed! Mass, and I
had known of that, I would have had her
myself! Faith, master, now we may go   [90
to breakfast with a woodcock pie!

Sᴇɢ. Go, sir; you were best leave this
knavery.

Kɪɴɢ. Come on, my lords, let's now to
court,
Where we may finish up the joyfulest day
That ever happed to a distressèd king.[3]
Were but thy father, the Valencia lord,
Present in view of this combining knot!

A shout within. Enter a Messenger.

What shout was that?   98

Mᴇss. My lord, the great Valencia king,
Newly arrived, entreats your presence.

Mᴜ. My father?

Kɪɴɢ. Preparèd welcomes give him enter-
tainment.
A happier planet never reigned than that
Which governs at this hour.   *Sound.*[4]

*Enter the King of Valencia, Anselmo,
Roderigo, Borachius, with Others; the
King runs and embraces his Son.*

Kɪɴɢ [ᴏꜰ] Vᴀʟ. Rise, honor of my age,
food to my rest!
Condemn not, mighty King of Aragon,
My rude behavior, so compelled by
nature,
That manners stood unknowledged.

---

[1] Imagination.

[2] By God's bones.
[3] The rest of the scene is different in the 1598
edn., in which the King of Valencia does not
appear.   [4] *I.e.*, sound trumpets.

KING. What we have to recite would tedious prove   109
By declaration; therefore, in and feast.
Tomorrow the performance shall explain
What words conceal; till then, drums, speak; bells, ring.
Give plausive [1] welcomes to our brother king.
Sound drums and trumpets. Exeunt omnes.

[EPILOGUE]

Enter Comedy and Envy.

COM. How now, Envy? What, blushest thou already?
Peep forth; hide not thy head with shame,
But with a courage praise a woman's deeds.
Thy threats were vain; thou couldst do me no hurt.
Although thou seemest to cross me with despite,
I overwhelmed, and turnéd upside down thy blocks
And made thyself to stumble at the same.
ENV. Though stumbled, yet not overthrown!
Thou canst not draw my heart to mildness;
Yet must I needs confess thou hast done well,   10
And played thy part with mirth and pleasant glee.
Say all this, yet canst thou not conquer me;
Although this time thou hast got—yet not the conquest neither.
A double revenge another time I'll have.[2]
COM. Envy, spit thy gall;
Plot, work, contrive; create new fallacies;
Teem from thy womb each minute a black traitor,
Whose blood and thoughts have twins' conception;
Study to act deeds yet unchronicled;
Cast native monsters in the molds of men;   20

Case vicious devils under sancted rochets; [3]
Unhasp the wicket [4] where all perjureds roost,
And swarm this ball with treasons. Do thy worst,
Thou canst not, hellhound, cross my steer [5] tonight,
Nor blind that glory where I wish delight.
ENV. I can, I will.
COM.   Nefarious hag, begin,
And let us tug till one the mast'ry win.
ENV. Comedy, thou art a shallow goose;
I'll overthrow thee in thine own intent,   29
And make thy fall my comic merriment.
COM. Thy policy wants gravity; thou art Too weak. Speak, fiend! As how?
ENV. Why, thus:
From my foul study will I hoist a wretch,
A lean and hungry neger [6] cannibal,
Whose jaws swell to his eyes with chawing malice;
And him I'll make a poet!
COM.   What's that to th' purpose?
ENV. This scrambling raven, with his needy beard,
Will I whet on to write a comedy,
Wherein shall be composed dark sentences,   40
Pleasing to factious brains;
And every other where place me a jest,
Whose high abuse shall more torment than blows.
Then I myself, quicker than lightning,
Will fly me to a puissant magistrate,
And, waiting with a trencher at his back,
In midst of jollity, rehearse those galls,
With some additions,
So lately vented in your theater.
He, upon this, cannot but make complaint,   50
To your great danger, or at least restraint.
COM. Ha, ha, ha! I laugh to hear thy folly;
This is a trap for boys, not men, nor such,
Especially desertful in their doings,
Whose staid discretion rules their purposes.

[1] Applauding.
[2] In the 1598 edn. the remainder of the epilogue consists of nineteen lines in honor of Elizabeth.

[3] Holy surplices.   [5] Interfere with my rudder.
[4] Gate (in hell).   [6] Negro.

I and my faction do eschew those vices.
But see, O, see! The weary sun for rest
Hath lain his golden compass to the
west,
Where he perpetual bide and ever shine,
As David's offspring, in his happy
clime. 60
Stoop, Envy, stoop; bow to the earth
with me;
Let's beg our pardons on our bended
knee. *They kneel.*[1]
ENV. My power has lost her might;
Envy's date's expired.
Yon splendent majesty hath felled my
sting,
And I amazéd am. *Fall down and quake.*
COM. Glorious and wise Arch-Cæsar on
this earth,

[1] To King James, before whom one performance was given.

At whose appearance Envy's stroken
dumb,
And all bad things cease operation,
Vouchsafe to pardon our unwilling
error, 69
So late presented to your gracious view,
And we'll endeavor with excess of pain
To please your senses in a choicer strain.
Thus we commit you to the arms of
Night,
Whose spangled carcass would, for your
delight,
Strive to excel the Day; be blessed,
then.
Who other wishes, let him never speak.
ENV. Amen!
To Fame and Honor we commend your
rest;
Live still more happy, every hour more
blessed.

FINIS.

THOMAS DEKKER

Thomas Dekker is the first of the group of writers included in this anthology who represent the culmination of Elizabethan drama proper.   The literary decade extending from the first known publication of work by Lyly and Peele in 1584 to the death of Kyd shows dramatists utilizing a wide range of story and history and developing not only a variety of characters from both the real and the supernatural world, but also a variety of structural devices and styles.   For a period of a little over a decade from the middle of the nineties, the early literary drama continued with even greater imaginative fervor and range of style, as illustrated in the work of Shakespeare. Significant new forces, however, were producing a more searching and realistic interpretation of character and a more critical attitude to structure and style.   In these respects the drama of this decade prepares for the early Stuart drama or indeed merges with it, for the later work of most of the men represented here is at times more Jacobean than Elizabethan.   In Dekker the reaction is indicated not so much by the loss of the romantic or idealizing tendency of the age as by the centering of it on contemporary life, as a result no doubt of the growing wealth and splendor of courts and cities and of man's new adventures in travel, exploration, and war.   With old elements of romance Dekker blends new ones of commerce in the portrayal of the merchant class.   Primarily, however, he reflects the infinite Elizabethan zest for life—sometimes in ugly realistic scenes.

Appreciation for the plays of Dekker has grown steadily within the last century.   It progresses from the rather low estimation of Sir A. W. Ward in his *History of English Dramatic Literature to the Death of Queen Anne* (1875, 1899), to the much more admiring evaluation of the poet-critic Algernon Charles Swinburne in "Thomas Dekker" (*The Nineteenth Century*, 1887) and *The Age of Shakespeare* (1909), to the scholarly approval of W. Macneile Dixon in *The Cambridge History of English Literature* (1910), and on to the dictum of scholar Peter Ure in 1966 that *"The Shoemaker's Holiday* is still one of the few universally prescribed and tolerated Elizabethan plays" ("Patient Madman and Honest Whore: The Middleton-Dekker Oxymoron," *E & S*, 1966).   In spite of the considerable number of modern studies of Dekker's works, very few additional biographical facts have come to light since Mary Leland Hunt wrote her 1911 pioneer monograph entitled *Thomas Dekker, A Study* (Columbia University Press).   Even Mme. M. T. Jones-Davies's exhaustive two-volume examination of the subject, *Un Peintre de la Vie Londonienne: Thomas Dekker* (Paris, 1958), has been able to add little to the basic data and more or less permissible speculations previously known.

Thomas Dekker the dramatist—there are records of several other London contemporaries of this name—was born somewhere in London, probably about 1570, but nothing is known about his family relations or his education.   For some time the word "Merchantailor" scribbled opposite Dekker's name on the title page of a copy of his Lord Mayor's pageant, *Troja-Nova Triumphans.   London Triumphing* . . . (1612), now in the British Museum, was supposed to indicate his membership in that famous school. But since his name fails to appear in any of the school records and since the Lord Mayor whose installation this pageant was intended to immortalize was Sir John Swinerton, himself a merchant tailor, R. G. Howarth in a recent reexamination of the British Museum copy and all the other evidence has concluded that the note was either a mistake or was really intended to apply to Sir John ("Dekker Not a Merchant Taylor," *NQ*, 1954).   Dekker's works, however, indicate that he had at least a good grammar school education, based largely on the classics. Many of his commentators have suggested that the city of London itself was his only needful school. J. B. Steane in the introduction to his edition of *The Shoemaker's Holiday* (Cambridge University Press, 1965) quotes Dekker's pamphlet, *The Seven Deadly Sins of London* (1606), where he says that the city was his cradle: "from thy womb received I my beginning, from thy breasts my nourishment." Consequently it is not improbable that when a character in the poem "Dekker His Dream" (1620) refers to his "private readings," which "schooled" his soul more than any tutors, "when they sternliest did control/With frowns or rods," Dekker was thinking of himself. By assuming such private studies, augmented by a quick ear and a gregarious character which took him everywhere through London, it is possible to account for his fondness for introducing foreigners speaking a sort of bastard Dutch, French, or Welsh into his plays. There is no evidence that he either attended an important school or traveled abroad where he could pick up these languages. Although Miss Hunt raises the possibility that he might have campaigned in the Low Countries because of his military knowledge and his fondness for the Dutch, and although he sometimes placed his settings on the Continent, it was always the life of London that he drew.

Dekker's industry is attested to by the fact that twenty-four authenticated plays and thirteen prose works showing his hand have survived, and many more have no doubt not been recognized. The first record of his work is a payment to him in January 1598 as a member of Henslowe's stable of dramatists. Since he immediately took a very prominent place among them, it is safe to assume that he was not a mere tyro at that time, but had probably started writing professionally by at least 1593 or 1594. He seems never to have been an actor. His life, however, was unquestionably a precarious one, and for this reason many earlier critics concluded that it must also have been disreputable. He was always in Henslowe's books for having borrowed money, and he was imprisoned for debt it is hard to say how many times. Such an incident occurred in 1598 under peculiar circumstances (for some theorizing about this event see W. L. Halstead, "Dekker's Arrest by the Chamberlain's Men," *NQ*, 1939). In "Dekker His Dream" he reveals that he spent the seven years before 1619 in prison, and poignantly laments his unhappy life. As shown in letters printed by Hunt, his chief friend during this melancholy period was Henslowe's son-in-law, the great actor Edward Alleyn. Mark Eccles believes that the "Thomas Dekker, householder," who was buried at St. James's, Clerkenwell, on August 5, 1632, was in all probability the playwright. Since on September 4 of the same year his widow Elizabeth renounced the administration of his estate, he apparently was still in debt at the time of his death; but who this widow was or when he married her has not transpired ("Thomas Dekker's Burial Place," *NQ*, 1939). If this man, however, was another of the various London Thomas Dekkers, later references show that the dramatist was certainly dead by 1640 or 1641.

In his connection with Henslowe, Dekker had a hand in over forty plays, relatively few of which survive. *The Shoemakers' Holiday* and *Old Fortunatus* he wrote alone, but most of his work was done in collaboration with Henslowe's writers, small and great. These ranged from Henry Chettle, William Haughton, John Day, Anthony Munday, and William and Samuel Rowley to John Webster, John Marston, Thomas Middleton, Philip Massinger, Thomas Heywood, John Ford, and Ben Jonson. The group exploited many fields—the classics, romance of many periods, history (especially English chronicles), and, to a considerable extent, contemporary life. Of the individual extant plays, *Old Fortunatus*, printed in 1600, is Dekker's best romance. *Patient Grissel*, written with Chettle and Haughton in 1598 in the spirit of the domestic play, inaugurated a vogue for the patient wife character. In 1601 Dekker was drawn into one of the most famous quarrels in English literary history: the "Stage Quarrel" or "War of the Theaters," precipitated by Jonson's *The Poetaster*, to which Dekker successfully replied in his *Satiromastix*. John Marston and other playwrights were also involved, directly or indirectly, in the fray. *The Honest Whore*, with its two parts in 1604 and 1605, is the first of a series of dramatic studies which depict the contact of London gallants with the rising merchant classes. Toward the end of 1604 Dekker became implicated in a series of *"Ho"* plays: *Westward Ho*, which he and Webster wrote for the Paul's Boys, and which, in the opinion of Felix Schelling in his history, descended to "the depths of gross and vicious realism"; *Eastward Ho*, in which, as Ure puts it, Jonson, Marston, and Chapman "arose, strong in the righteousness of bourgeois morality, and delivered at the Blackfriars . . . a 'conscious protest' "; and *Northward Ho*, in which Dekker and Webster again used the boys of St. Paul's for their unmannerly satirical reply. Dekker collaborated with Middleton in *The Roaring Girl* about 1610. Among the later plays, *The Virgin Martyr*, written with Massinger about 1620, and *The Witch of Edmonton*, written with Ford and Samuel Rowley about 1621, are masterly tragedies. Appropriately, Dekker also made several contributions to the great civic pageants of London.

THE SHOEMAKERS' HOLIDAY

The plot of *The Shoemakers' Holiday* is derived from the three shoemaker stories that make up the first part of Thomas Deloney's *The Gentle Craft* (1598). The last story, "Simon Eyre," furnished most of Dekker's material, and is Deloney's romanticized account of a historical figure who rose from a position of upholsterer and draper (Deloney makes him a shoemaker) to become a wealthy Lord Mayor of London. Dekker is indebted to the other two stories for character suggestions. He may also have made use of popular ballads for the incident of Ralph, Jane, and Hammon. The three threads of the plot are neatly interwoven with one exception—at the end Dekker has carelessly left two Lord Mayors in office simultaneously. (Presumably, however, Oteley's term of two years has come to an end, and Eyre is unexpectedly succeeding him.) There is also some unreconciled confusion over Jane's marital status when her soldier-husband Rafe returns from the dead and finds her committed to the very amorous but eventually soft-hearted Master Hammon. James H. Conover has examined the entire structure of the play in his *Thomas Dekker: An Analysis of Dramatic Structure* (Monton Press, 1969).

The play shows the patriotism and many of the romantic conventions of *George a Greene*, transferred to London tradesmen of 1599. Although, as Arthur Brown concluded in his "Citizen Comedy and Domestic Drama" (*The Jacobean Theatre*, *Stratford-upon-Avon Studies*, 1960), Dekker was more interested in telling a good, jolly story than he was in preaching (in spite of his incorporation of examples of "personal, domestic, or national virtues"), the comedy does present an underlying democratic theme of class competition and the breaking down of social stratification. The pride and independence of the middle classes are voiced repeatedly by both Lord Mayors; and the Earl of Lincoln's aristocratic arrogance, which is well matched by Oteley's bourgeois snobbery, is shamed by the King himself at the end of the play. There is also some gentle satire at the expense of the newly "arrived" citizen's wife, Margery Eyre. Incidentally, the identity of the unidentified King has occasioned some controversy. Because of the King's democratic character, L. M. Manheim ("The King in Dekker's *The Shoemakers Holiday*," *NQ*, 1957) feels that the whole spirit of the play favors Henry V, although he admits that some anachronisms must be accepted. Steane, on the other hand, favors Henry VI, in spite of the fact that Leadenhall had been built many years before his reign. The theme of class pride and independence is also reinforced by the threat of Firk (who reminds us of the medieval Vice and whose name implies that he is a player of pranks and a jester of somewhat shady humor) and Hodge to walk off their jobs unless their demands are met. The idea of class distinction is further emphasized by the fact that, according to the principles of decorum, the upper-class characters generally speak in verse, whereas those of the lower classes use the racy, colloquial prose of which Dekker was such a master. Dekker achieves much comic effect, too, by his use of such constantly repeated catch-phrases as Margery's "but let that pass," her bluff, domineering husband's "Prince am I none, yet am I nobly born," and Sybil's lively slang and current proverbs.

The Shoemakers' Holiday is first mentioned by Henslowe under the date of July 15, 1599, evidently having been written during the preceding six weeks. (Incidentally, scholars have been unable to agree as to the proper placement of the apostrophe in the original word "Shomakers" in the title, which is unpunctuated. The present editors feel that the final scenes showing Simon Eyre's pancake party for the shoemaker apprentices at the great new building, Leadenhall, as well as Firk's reminder to these apprentices that on every Shrove Tuesday "we may shut up our shops, and make holiday," strengthen the plural implication.) A court performance was secured for the play on the night of January 1, 1600, and it was printed in the same year by Valentine Sims. Other quartos appeared in 1610, 1618, 1624, 1631, and 1657, each one being a reprint of its immediate predecessor. The present text is based on Alexis F. Lange's reprint of the 1600 quarto in C. M. Gayley's *Representative English Comedies, III* (New York 1914). Paul C. Davies has edited the play, for the Fountainwell Drama Texts old-spelling edition (University of California Press, 1969).

THE SHOEMAKERS' HOLIDAY[1]

BY

THOMAS DEKKER

[DRAMATIS PERSONÆ

THE KING.

THE EARL OF CORNWALL.

SIR HUGH LACY, *Earl of Lincoln.*

ROWLAND LACY,
otherwise HANS } *cousins and his*
ASKEW *nephews.*

SIR ROGER OTELEY, *Lord Mayor of London.*

MASTER HAMMON [2]
MASTER WARNER } *citizens of London.*
MASTER SCOTT

SIMON EYRE, *a shoemaker.*

ROGER, *commonly*
called HODGE
FIRK } *Eyre's journeymen.*
RAFE [3] DAMPORT

LOVELL, *a courtier.*

DODGER, *a servant to the Earl of Lincoln.*

A DUTCH SKIPPER.

A BOY.

COURTIERS, ATTENDANTS, OFFICERS, SOLDIERS, HUNTERS, SHOEMAKERS, APPRENTICES, SERVANTS.

ROSE, *daughter of Sir Roger.*

SYBIL, *her maid.*

MARGERY, *wife of Simon Eyre.*

JANE, *wife of Rafe.*

SCENE: *London and Old Ford.*

TIME: *Middle of the fifteenth century.*]

To ALL GOOD FELLOWS, PROFESSORS [4] OF THE GENTLE CRAFT,[5] OF WHAT DEGREE SOEVER.

Kind gentlemen and honest boon companions, I present you here with a merry-conceited [6] comedy, called *The Shoemakers' Holiday*, acted by my Lord Admiral's players this present Christmas before the queen's most excellent majesty, for the mirth and pleasant matter by her highness graciously accepted, being indeed no way offensive. The argument of the play I will set down in this epistle: Sir Hugh [10 Lacy, Earl of Lincoln, had a young gentleman of his own name, his near kinsman, that loved the lord mayor's daughter of London; to prevent and cross which love, the earl caused his kinsman to be sent coronel[7] of a company into France; who resigned his place to another gentleman, his friend, and came disguised like a Dutch shoemaker to the house of Simon Eyre in Tower Street, who served the mayor [20 and his household with shoes; the merriments that passed in Eyre's house, his coming to be mayor of London, Lacy's getting his love, and other accidents,[8] with two merry three-men's songs.[9] Take all in good

[1] The title continues: "Or the Gentle Craft. With the Humorous Life of Simon Eyre, Shoemaker and Lord Mayor of London. As It Was Acted before the Queen's Most Excellent Majesty on New Year's Day at Night Last by the Right Honorable the Earl of Nottingham, Lord High Admiral of England, his Servants." The running title is "A Pleasant Comedy of the Gentle Craft."

[2] Sometimes spelled *Hammond* in the play.

[3] Variant of *Ralph.*

[4] Followers, practitioners.

[5] According to Deloney, shoemakers were called "Gentlemen of the Gentle Craft" by Hugh, who became their patron saint.

[6] Amusing and fanciful.

[7] Colonel. [8] Occurrences.

[9] The two songs, which in the 1600 edn. follow this preface, have been removed to their probable places in the play.

worth that is well intended, for nothing is purposed but mirth; mirth length'neth long life, which, with all other blessings, I heartily wish you.

FAREWELL!

THE PROLOGUE

As it was pronounced before the queen's majesty

As wretches in a storm, expecting day,
With trembling hands and eyes cast up to heaven,
Make prayers the anchor of their conquered hopes,
So we, dear goddess, wonder of all eyes,
Your meanest vassals, through mistrust and fear
To sink into the bottom of disgrace
By our imperfit pastimes, prostrate thus
On bended knees, our sails of hope do strike,
Dreading the bitter storms of your dislike.
Since then, unhappy men, our hap is such
That to ourselves ourselves no help can bring,   11
But needs must perish, if your saintlike ears,
Locking the temple where all mercy sits,
Refuse the tribute of our begging tongues,
O, grant, bright mirror of true chastity,
From those life-breathing stars, your sun-like eyes,
One gracious smile, for your celestial breath
Must send us life, or sentence us to death.

[SCENE i.

A street in London.]

Enter Lord Mayor, Lincoln.

LINC. My lord mayor, you have sundry times
Feasted myself and many courtiers more;
Seldom or never can we be so kind
To make requital of your courtesy.
But, leaving this, I hear my cousin [1] Lacy
Is much affected to [2] your daughter Rose.
L. MAYOR. True, my good lord, and she loves him so well
That I mislike her boldness in the chase.
LINC. Why, my lord mayor, think you it then a shame
To join a Lacy with an Oteley's name? 10

[1] Applied to any collateral relative more distant than brother or sister.   [2] In love with.

L. MAYOR. Too mean is my poor girl for his high birth;
Poor citizens must not with courtiers wed,
Who will in silks and gay apparel spend
More in one year than I am worth, by far.
Therefore your honor need not doubt [3] my girl.
LINC. Take heed, my lord; advise you what you do!
A verier unthrift lives not in the world
Than is my cousin; for I'll tell you what:
'Tis now almost a year since he requested
To travel countries for experience;   20
I furnished him with coin, bills of exchange,
Letters of credit, men to wait on him,
Solicited my friends in Italy
Well to respect him. But, to see the end,
Scant had he journeyed through half Germany,
But all his coin was spent, his men cast off,
His bills embezzled,[4] and my jolly coz,[5]
Ashamed to show his bankrupt presence here,
Became a shoemaker in Wittenberg,
A goodly science for a gentleman   30
Of such descent! Now judge the rest by this:
Suppose your daughter have a thousand pound,
He did consume me more in one half year;
And, make him heir to all the wealth you have,
One twelvemonth's rioting will waste it all.
Then seek, my lord, some honest citizen
To wed your daughter to.
L. MAYOR.   I thank your lordship.
[*Aside.*] Well, fox, I understand your subtilty.—
As for your nephew, let your lordship's eye
But watch his actions, and you need not fear,   40
For I have [sent][6] my daughter far enough.

[3] Fear.   [5] Cousin.
[4] Wasted.   [6] Supplied from 1610 edn.

And yet your cousin Rowland might
do well,
Now he hath learned an occupation;
And yet I scorn to call him son-in-law.
LINC. Ay, but I have a better trade for
him.
I thank his grace, he hath appointed
him
Chief colonel of all those companies
Mustered in London and the shires
about,
To serve his highness in those wars of
France.
See where he comes!—Lovell, what news
with you?   50

Enter Lovell, Lacy, and Askew.

LOV. My Lord of Lincoln, 'tis his high-
ness' will
That presently [1] your cousin ship for
France
With all his powers; he would not for a
million
But they should land at Dieppe within
four days.
LINC. Go certify his grace it shall be done.
                Exit Lovell.
Now, cousin Lacy, in what forwardness
Are all your companies?
LACY.   All well prepared.
The men of Hertfordshire lie at Mile
End;
Suffolk and Essex train in Tothill [2]
Fields;
The Londoners and those of Middle-
sex,   60
All gallantly prepared in Finsbury,
With frolic spirits long for their parting
hour.
L. MAYOR. They have their imprest, [3]
coats, and furniture; [4]
And, if it please your cousin Lacy come
To the Guildhall, he shall receive his
pay;
And twenty pounds besides my brethren
Will freely give him, to approve [5] our
loves
We bear unto my lord, your uncle here.
LACY. I thank your honor.
LINC.   Thanks, my good lord mayor.

[1] At once.
[2] The spelling *Tuttle* in the original indicates
the pronunciation.   [4] Equipment.
[3] Advance pay.   [5] Prove.

L. MAYOR. At the Guildhall we will
expect [6] your coming.   *Exit.* 70
LINC. To approve your loves to me? No
subtilty!
Nephew, that twenty pound he doth
bestow
For joy to rid you from his daughter
Rose.
But, cousins both, now here are none
but friends,
I would not have you cast an amorous eye
Upon so mean a project as the love
Of a gay, wanton, painted citizen.
I know this churl even in the height of
scorn
Doth hate the mixture of his blood with
thine.
I pray thee, do thou so! Remember,
coz,   80
What honorable fortunes wait on thee.
Increase the king's love, which so
brightly shines,
And gilds thy hopes. I have no heir but
thee—
And yet not thee if with a wayward
spirit
Thou start from the true bias [7] of my
love.
LACY. My lord, I will for honor, not de-
sire
Of land or livings, or to be your heir,
So guide my actions in pursuit of
France
As shall add glory to the Lacys' name.
LINC. Coz, for those words here's thirty
Portuguese, [8]   90
And, nephew Askew, there's a few for
you.
Fair Honor, in her loftiest eminence,
Stays in France for you, till you fetch
her thence.
Then, nephews, clap swift wings on
your designs.
Begone, begone, make haste to the
Guildhall;
There presently I'll meet you. Do not
stay.
Where Honor beckons, [9] Shame at-
tends delay.   *Exit.*
ASKEW. How gladly would your uncle
have you gone!

[6] Await.   [8] Gold coins.
[7] Depart from the straight line (bowling).
[9] Malone's emendation of *becomes.*

LACY. True, coz, but I'll o'erreach his
policies.[1]

I have some serious business for three
days,   100
Which nothing but my presence can
despatch.
You, therefore, cousin, with the com-
panies
Shall haste to Dover; there I'll meet
with you.
Or, if I stay past my prefixéd time,
Away for France; we'll meet in Nor-
mandy.
The twenty pounds my lord mayor
gives to me
You shall receive, and these ten Portu-
guese,
Part of mine uncle's thirty. Gentle coz,
Have care to our great charge; I know
your wisdom   109
Hath tried itself in higher consequence.

ASKEW. Coz, all myself am yours; yet
have this care,
To lodge in London with all secrecy.
Our uncle Lincoln hath, besides his
own,
Many a jealous eye, that in your face
Stares only to watch means for your
disgrace.

LACY. Stay, cousin. Who be these?

*Enter Simon Eyre, his Wife, Hodge, Firk,
Jane, and Rafe with a piece.*[2]

EYRE. Leave whining, leave whining!
Away with this whimp'ring, this puling,
these blubbering tears, and these wet
eyes! I'll get thy husband discharged, [120
I warrant thee, sweet Jane; go to!

HODGE. Master, here be the captains.

EYRE. Peace, Hodge; husht, ye knave,
husht!

FIRK. Here be the cavaliers and the
coronels, master.

EYRE. Peace, Firk; peace, my fine Firk!
Stand by with your pishery-pashery.[3]
Away! I am a man of the best presence;
I'll speak to them, and[4] they were [130
popes.—Gentlemen, captains, colonels, commanders! Brave men, brave leaders, may
it please you to give me audience. I
am Simon Eyre, the mad shoemaker of
Tower Street; this wench with the mealy

mouth that will never tire, is my wife, I
can tell you; here's Hodge, my man and
my foreman; here's Firk, my fine firking[5]
journeyman; and this is blubbered Jane.
All we come to be suitors for this hon- [140
est Rafe. Keep him at home, and, as I am
a true shoemaker and a gentleman of the
gentle craft, buy spurs yourself, and I'll
find[6] ye boots these seven years.

WIFE. Seven years, husband?

EYRE. Peace, midriff, peace! I know
what I do. Peace!

FIRK. Truly, master cormorant,[7] you
shall do God good service to let Rafe and
his wife stay together. She's a young [150
new-married woman; if you take her husband away from her a-night, you undo
her; she may beg in the daytime; for he's
as good a workman at a prick and an awl
as any is in our trade.

JANE. O, let him stay; else I shall be
undone!

FIRK. Ay, truly, she shall be laid at
one side like a pair of old shoes else, and
be occupied for no use.   160

LACY. Truly, my friends, it lies not in
my power.
The Londoners are pressed,[8] paid, and
set forth
By the lord mayor; I cannot change a
man.

HODGE. Why, then you were as good
be a corporal as a colonel, if you cannot
discharge one good fellow; and, I tell you
true, I think you do more than you can
answer, to press a man within a year and
a day of his marriage.

EYRE. Well said, melancholy [170
Hodge; gramercy,[9] my fine foreman.

WIFE. Truly, gentlemen, it were ill
done for such as you to stand so stiffly
against a poor young wife, considering
her case, she is new-married; but let that
pass. I pray, deal not roughly with her;
her husband is a young man, and but
newly entered; but let that pass.

EYRE. Away with your pishery-pash-
ery, your pols and your edipols![10] [180
Peace, midriff;[11] silence, Cisly Bumtrinket!
Let your head speak.

[1] Tricks.   [2] Musket.   [3] Trifling talk.
[4] An, if.   [5] Frisking.   [6] Provide.
[7] His corruption of *coronel*.
[8] Impressed, drafted.
[9] Great thanks (French).
[10] Forms of *By Pollux*.   [11] Original has *midaffe*.

FIRK. Yea, and the horns too, master.

EYRE. Too soon, my fine Firk, too soon! Peace, scoundrels! See you this man? Captains, you will not release him? Well, let him go. He's a proper shot; let him vanish! Peace, Jane, dry up thy tears; they'll make his powder dankish. Take him, brave men. Hector of Troy was [190 an hackney to him; Hercules and Termagant, scoundrels; Prince Arthur's Round Table—by the Lord of Ludgate—ne'er fed such a tall,[1] such a dapper swordman; by the life of Pharaoh, a brave, resolute swordman! Peace, Jane! I say no more, mad knaves.

FIRK. See, see, Hodge, how my master raves in commendation of Rafe!

HODGE. Rafe, th'art a gull,[2] by this [200 hand, and thou goest.[3]

ASKEW. I am glad, good Master Eyre, it is my hap
To meet so resolute a soldier.
Trust me, for your report and love to him,
A common slight regard shall not respect him.

LACY. Is thy name Rafe?

RAFE.   Yes, sir.

LACY.   Give me thy hand.
Thou shalt not want, as I am a gentleman.
Woman, be patient. God, no doubt, will send
Thy husband safe again; but he must go—   209
His country's quarrel says it shall be so.

HODGE. Th'art a gull, by my stirrup,[4] if thou dost not go. I will not have thee strike thy gimlet into these weak vessels; prick thine enemies, Rafe.

Enter Dodger.

DODGER. My lord, your uncle on the Tower Hill
Stays with the lord mayor and the aldermen,
And doth request you, with all speed you may,
To hasten thither.

ASKEW.   Cousin, let's go.

LACY. Dodger, run you before; tell them we come.—   *Exit Dodger.*[5] 219
This Dodger is mine uncle's parasite,
The arrant'st varlet that e'er breathed on earth;
He sets more discord in a noble house
By one day's broaching of his pickthank[6] tales
Than can be salved again in twenty years,
And he, I fear, shall go with us to France
To pry into our actions.

ASKEW.   Therefore, coz,
It shall behoove you to be circumspect.

LACY. Fear not, good cousin.—Rafe, hie to your colors.
                    [*Exeunt Lacy and Askew.*]

RAFE. I must, because there's no remedy;   229
But, gentle master and my loving dame,
As you have always been a friend to me,
So in mine absence think upon my wife.

JANE. Alas, my Rafe!

WIFE.   She cannot speak for weeping.

EYRE. Peace, you cracked groats,[7] you mustard tokens,[8] disquiet not the brave soldier. Go thy ways, Rafe!

JANE. Ay, ay, you bid him go. What shall I do when he is gone?

FIRK. Why, be doing with me or my fellow Hodge; be not idle.   240

EYRE. Let me see thy hand, Jane. This fine hand, this white hand, these pretty fingers must spin, must card, must work; work, you bombast cotton-candle[9] quean;[10] work for your living, with a pox to you![11]— Hold thee, Rafe, here's five sixpences for thee. Fight for the honor of the gentle craft, for the gentlemen shoemakers, the courageous cordwainers, the flower of S[aint] Martin's, the mad knaves of Bedlam, [250 Fleet Street, Tower Street, and Whitechapel; crack me the crowns of the French knaves; a pox on them, crack them; fight, by the Lord of Ludgate; fight, my fine boy!

FIRK. Here, Rafe, here's three twopences. Two carry into France; the third

[1] Brave.   [2] Fool.
[3] Lange and other editors add *not*.
[4] A strap for steadying the shoemaker's last on his knee.
[5] This direction follows Dodger's speech in original.   [6] Talebearer's.   [7] Small coins.
[8] Yellow spots from the plague.
[9] "Bombast: cotton-wool; cotton-candle: a candle wfth a cotton wick. Jane's hands are as white as the wax of a candle, as soft as bombast" (Sutherland).   [10] Slut.   [11] A plague to you!

shall wash our souls at parting, for sorrow
is dry. For my sake, firk the *Basa mon
cues*.[1]   259

HODGE. Rafe, I am heavy at parting;
but here's a shilling for thee. God send thee
to cram thy slops [2] with French crowns,
and thy enemies' bellies with bullets.

RAFE. I thank you, master, and I thank
you all.

  Now, gentle wife, my loving, lovely
    Jane,
  Rich men, at parting, give their wives
    rich gifts,
  Jewels and rings, to grace their lily
    hands.
  Thou know'st our trade makes rings for
    women's heels.
  Here take this pair of shoes, cut out by
    Hodge,
  Stitched by my fellow Firk, seamed by
    myself,   270
  Made up and pinked [3] with letters for
    thy name.
  Wear them, my dear Jane, for thy hus-
    band's sake,
  And every morning when thou pull'st
    them on,
  Remember me, and pray for my return.
  Make much of them, for I have made
    them so
  That I can know them from a thousand
    mo.[4]

*Sound drum. Enter Lord Mayor, Lincoln,
Lacy, Askew, Dodger, and Soldiers.
They pass over the stage; Rafe falls in
amongst them; Firk and the rest cry
"Farewell," etc., and so exeunt.*

[SCENE ii.

A garden at Old Ford.]

Enter Rose, alone, making a garland.

[ROSE.] Here sit thou down upon this
    flow'ry bank
  And make a garland for thy Lacy's head.
  These pinks, these roses, and these
    violets,
  These blushing gilliflowers, these mari-
    golds,
  The fair embroidery [5] of his coronet,

  Carry not half such beauty in their
    cheeks
  As the sweet count'nance of my Lacy
    doth.
  O my most unkind father! O my stars,
  Why lowered you so at my nativity,
  To make me love, yet live robbed of my
    love?   10
  Here as a thief am I imprisonéd
  For my dear Lacy's sake within those
    walls
  Which by my father's cost were builded
    up
  For better purposes.   Here must I
    languish
  For him that doth as much lament, I
    know,
  Mine absence as for him I pine in woe.

Enter Sybil.

SYB. Good morrow, young mistress. I am
sure you make that garland for me, against [6]
I shall be Lady of the Harvest.

ROSE. Sybil, what news at London? [20

SYB. None but good. My lord mayor,
your father, and Master Philpot, your
uncle, and Master Scot, your cousin,
and Mistress Frigbottom by Doctors'
Commons do all, by my troth, send you
most hearty commendations.

ROSE. Did Lacy send kind greetings to
his love?

SYB. O, yes, out of cry,[7] by my troth.
I scant knew him. Here a [8] wore [a] [9] [30
scarf, and here a scarf; here a bunch
of feathers, and here precious stones and
jewels, and a pair of garters—O, monstrous!
—like one of our yellow silk curtains at home
here in Old Ford House, here in Master Bel-
lymount's chamber. I stood at our door in
Cornhill, looked at him, he at me indeed,
spake to him, but he not to me, not a
word. "Marry gup," [10] thought I, "with a
wanion!" [11] He passed by me as proud— [40
"Marry foh! Are you grown humorous?" [12]
thought I, and so shut the door, and in I
came.

ROSE. O Sybil, how dost thou my Lacy
    wrong!

---

[1] *I.e.*, the Frenchmen. *Cf.* vulgar French,
baisez mon queue.
  [2] Breeches.
  [3] Perforated.
  [4] More.
  [5] Embroidery.

[6] For the time when.   [8] He.
[7] Beyond all description. [9] From 1618 edn.
[10] Exclamation of impatience.
[11] With a vengeance.   [12] Capricious.

My Rowland is as gentle as a lamb;
No dove was ever half so mild as he.

Syb. Mild? Yea, as a bushel of stamped crabs.[1] He looked upon me as sour as verjuice. "Go thy ways," thought I; "thou mayst be much in my gaskins,[2] [50 but nothing in my netherstocks."[3] This is your fault, mistress, to love him that loves not you; he thinks scorn to do as he's done to; but, if I were as you, I'd cry, "Go by, Jeronimo, go by!"[4]

I'd set mine old debts against my new
    driblets,
And the hare's foot against the goose gib-
    lets,
For, if ever I sigh, when sleep I should take,
Pray God I may lose my maidenhead when
    I wake.[5]   60

Rose. Will my love leave me then, and
    go to France?

Syb. I know not that, but I am sure I see him stalk before the soldiers. By my troth, he is a proper[6] man; but he is proper that proper doth. Let him go snick-up,[7] young mistress.

Rose. Get thee to London, and learn
    perfectly
Whether my Lacy go to France, or no.
Do this, and I will give thee for thy
    pains
My cambric apron and my Romish
    gloves,   70
My purple stockings and a stomacher.
Say, wilt thou do this, Sybil, for my sake?

Syb. Will I, quotha? At whose suit? By my troth, yes, I'll go. A cambric apron, gloves, a pair of purple stockings, and a stomacher! I'll sweat in purple, mistress, for you; I'll take anything that comes a God's name. O, rich! A cambric apron! Faith, then have at "Up tails all."[8] I'll go jiggy-joggy to [80

[1] Crushed crab apples.   [2] Wide trousers.
[3] Stockings. "The meaning seems to be that, though we may be acquainted, we are not intimate friends" (Neilson).
[4] This tag from Kyd's Spanish Tragedy was a popular slang phrase.
[5] Lange suggests that these verses mean, "Off with the old love, on with the new." In these couplets and a few other passages the line division has been regularized.
[6] Handsome.   [7] Go and be hanged!
[8] I.e., make speed; the name of a dance tune.

London, and be here in a trice, young mistress.   Exit.

Rose. Do so, good Sybil.—Meantime wretched I
Will sit and sigh for his lost company.
                                        Exit.

[Scene iii.

Tower Street, London.]

Enter Rowland Lacy, like a Dutch shoe-
                                    maker.

Lacy. How many shapes have gods and
    kings devised
Thereby to compass their desired loves!
It is no shame for Rowland Lacy, then,
To clothe his cunning with the gentle
    craft,
That, thus disguised, I may unknown
    possess
The only happy presence of my Rose.
For her have I forsook my charge in
    France,
Incurred the king's displeasure, and
    stirred up
Rough hatred in mine uncle Lincoln's
    breast.
O love, how powerful art thou, that
    canst change   10
High birth to bareness,[9] and a noble
    mind
To the mean semblance of a shoemaker!
But thus it must be, for her cruel
    father,
Hating the single union of our souls,
Has secretly conveyed my Rose from
    London
To bar me of her presence; but I trust
Fortune and this disguise will furder
    me
Once more to view her beauty, gain her
    sight.
Here in Tower Street with Eyre the
    shoemaker
Mean I a while to work; I know the
    trade;   20
I learnt it when I was in Wittenberg.
Then cheer thy hoping sprites;[10] be not
    dismayed;
Thou canst not want. Do Fortune what
    she can,
The gentle craft is living for a man. Exit.

[9] 1631 edn. reads baseness.   [10] Spirits.

[SCENE iv.

n open yard before Eyre's house in Tower Street.]

Enter Eyre, making himself ready.

EYRE. Where be these boys, these girls, these drabs, these scoundrels? They wallow in the fat brewis[1] of my bounty, and lick up the crumbs of my table, yet will not rise to see my walks cleansed. Come out, you powder-beef[2] queans! What, Nan! What, Madge Mumblecrust! Come out, you fat midriff-swag-belly-whores, and sweep me these kennels[3] that the noisome stench offend not the nose of my neighbors. [10 What, Firk, I say! What, Hodge! Open my shop windows! What, Firk, I say!

Enter Firk.

FIRK. O master, is 't you that speak bandog and bedlam[4] this morning? I was in a dream, and mused what madman was got into the street so early. Have you drunk this morning that your throat is so clear?
EYRE. Ah, well said, Firk; well said, Firk. To work, my fine knave, to [20 work! Wash thy face, and thou 't be more blessed.
FIRK. Let them wash my face that will eat it. Good master, send for a souse-wife,[5] if you'll have my face cleaner.

Enter Hodge.

EYRE. Away, sloven! Avaunt, scoundrel! —Good morrow, Hodge; good morrow, my fine foreman.
HODGE. O master, good morrow; y'are an early stirrer. Here's a fair morning.— [30 Good morrow, Firk; I could have slept this hour. Here's a brave day towards.
EYRE. O, haste to work, my fine foreman, haste to work.
FIRK. Master, I am dry as dust to hear my fellow Roger talk of fair weather. Let us pray for good leather, and let clowns and plowboys and those that work in the fields pray for brave days. We work in a dry shop; what care I if it rain?   40

[1] Thickened broth.
[2] Salted beef.   [3] Channels, gutters.
[4] *I.e.*, like a watchdog and a madman.
[5] Pig-pickler.

Enter Eyre's Wife.

EYRE. How now, Dame Margery, can you see to rise? Trip and go; call up the drabs, your maids.
WIFE. See to rise? I hope 'tis time enough; 'tis early enough for any woman to be seen abroad. I marvel how many wives in Tower Street are up so soon. God's me,[6] 'tis not noon! Here's a yawling!
EYRE. Peace, Margery, peace! Where's Cisly Bumtrinket, your maid? She has a [50 privy fault—she farts in her sleep. Call the quean up; if my men want shoe thread, I'll swinge her in a stirrup.
FIRK. Yet that's but a dry beating; here's still a sign of drought.

Enter Lacy singing.

LACY. *Der was een bore van Gelderland*
    (Frolick si byen!);
    He was als dronck he cold nyet stand
    Upsolce se byen.
    Tap eens de canneken;   60
    Drincke, schone mannekin.[7]

FIRK. Master, for my life, yonder's a brother of the gentle craft; if he bear not Saint Hugh's bones,[8] I'll forfeit my bones; he's some uplandish[9] workman. Hire him, good master, that I may learn some gibble-gabble; 'twill make us work the faster.
EYRE. Peace, Firk! A hard world! Let him pass, let him vanish; we have journey-men enow. Peace, my fine Firk!   70
WIFE. Nay, nay, y'are best follow your man's counsel; you shall see what will come on 't. We have not men enow, but we must entertain every butterbox;[10] but let that pass.
HODGE. Dame, fore God, if my master follow your counsel, he'll consume little beef. He shall be glad of men and he can catch them.

[6] An exclamation of impatience.
[7] Adopting Baugh's emendation, "Op zulke zeebeenen," in line 4, we may translate the song thus:
    There was a boor from Gelderland
    (Jolly they be!);
    He was so drunk he could not stand
    On such sea legs.
    Tap once the cannikin;
    Drink, pretty mannikin.
[8] St. Hugh's bones were believed to have been made into shoemakers' tools.
[9] Up-country; perhaps an error for *outlandish*, foreign.   [10] Dutchman.

FIRK. Ay, that he shall. 80

HODGE. Fore God, a proper man and, I warrant, a fine workman. Master, farewell; dame, adieu. If such a man as he cannot find work, Hodge is not for you.

Offers to go.

EYRE. Stay, my fine Hodge.

FIRK. Faith, and your foreman go, dame, you must take a journey to seek a new journeyman; if Roger remove, Firk follows. If St. Hugh's bones shall not be set awork, I may prick mine awl in the walls, [90 and go play. Fare ye well, master; goodby, dame.

EYRE. Tarry, my fine Hodge, my brisk foreman! Stay, Firk! Peace, puddingbroth! By the Lord of Ludgate, I love my men as my life. Peace, you gallimaufry! [1] Hodge, if he want work, I'll hire him. One of you to him. Stay—he comes to us.

LACY. *Goeden dach, meester, ende u, vro, oak.*[2] 100

FIRK. Nails,[3] if I should speak after him without drinking, I should choke. And you, friend Oak, are you of the gentle craft?

LACY. *Yaw, yaw, ik bin den skomawker.*[4]

FIRK. "*Den skomaker,*" quotha! And hark you, *skomaker,* have you all your tools, a good rubbing pin, a good stopper, a good dresser, your four sorts of awls, and your two balls of wax, your paring knife, your hand-and-thumb-leathers, and [110 good St. Hugh's bones to smooth up your work?

LACY. *Yaw, yaw; be niet vorveard. Ik hab all de dingen voour mack skoes groot and cleane.*[5]

FIRK. Ha, ha! Good master, hire him; he'll make me laugh so that I shall work more in mirth than I can in earnest.

EYRE. Hear ye, friend, have ye any skill in the mystery[6] of cordwainers? 120

LACY. *Ik weet niet wat yow seg; ich verstaw you niet.*[7]

FIRK. Why, thus, man: [*Imitating a shoemaker at work.*] "*Ich verste u niet,*"[8] quotha.

LACY. *Yaw, yaw, yaw; ick can dat wel doen.*[9]

FIRK. "*Yaw, yaw!*" He speaks yawing like a jackdaw that gapes to be fed with cheese curds. O, he'll give a villainous [130 pull at a can of double beer; but Hodge and I have the vantage—we must drink first because we are the eldest journeymen.

EYRE. What is thy name?

LACY. Hans—Hans Meulter.

EYRE. Give me thy hand; th'art welcome.—Hodge, entertain him; Firk, bid him welcome; come, Hans. Run, wife, bid your maids, your trullibubs,[10] make ready my fine men's breakfasts. To him, Hodge! [140

HODGE. Hans, th'art welcome. Use thyself friendly, for we are good fellows; if not, thou shalt be fought with, wert thou bigger than a giant.

FIRK. Yea, and drunk with, wert thou Gargantua. My master keeps no cowards, I tell thee.—Ho, boy, bring him an heel block;[11] here's a new journeyman.

Enter Boy.

LACY. O, *ich wersto you; ich moet een halve dossen cans betaelen. Here, boy,* [150 *nempt dis skilling; tap eens freelicke.*[12]

Exit Boy.

EYRE. Quick, snippersnapper, away! Firk, scour thy throat; thou shalt wash it with Castilian liquor.

Enter Boy.

Come, my last of the fives,[13] give me a can. Have to thee, Hans; here, Hodge; here, Firk; drink, you mad Greeks, and work like true Trojans, and pray for Simon Eyre, the shoemaker.—Here, Hans, and th'art welcome. 160

FIRK. Lo, dame, you would have lost a good fellow that will teach us to laugh. This beer came hopping in well.

WIFE. Simon, it is almost seven.

EYRE. Is't so, Dame Clapperdudgeon?[14]

---

[1] Ragout of hashed meats.
[2] Good day, master, and you, wife, too.
[3] By God's nails.
[4] Yes, yes, I am the shoemaker.
[5] Yes, yes; be not afraid. I have everything to make shoes big and little. [6] Trade.
[7] I don't know what you say; I don't understand you. [8] "I don't understand you."
[9] Yes, yes, yes, I can do that well.
[10] Tripes, sluts.
[11] A last for making heels.
[12] O, I understand you; I must pay for a half dozen cans. Here, boy, take this shilling; tap one freely.
[13] My smallest last; my little one.
[14] Because her mouth rattles like a beggar's clapdish.

Is't seven a-clock, and my men's breakfast not ready? Trip and go, you soused cunger,[1] away! Come, you mad Hyperboreans. Follow me, Hodge; follow me, Hans; come after, my fine Firk; to work, to work [170 awhile, and then to breakfast! *Exit.*

FIRK. Soft! *Yaw, yaw,* good Hans, though my master have no more wit but to call you afore me, I am not so foolish to go behind you, I being the elder journeyman. *Exeunt.*

[SCENE v.

A field near Old Ford.]

Halloaing within.　　　Enter Warner and Hammon, like hunters.

HAM. Cousin, beat every brake; the game's not far.
　This way with wingéd feet he fled from death,
　Whilst the pursuing hounds, scenting his steps,
　Find out his highway to destruction.
　Besides, the miller's boy told me even now,
　He saw him take soil,[2] and he halloaed him,
　Affirming him so embossed [3]
　That long he could not hold.
WARN.　　　　　　　　　　If it be so,
　'Tis best we trace these meadows by Old Ford.

A noise of Hunters within. Enter a Boy.

HAM. How now, boy? Where's the deer?
　Speak! Saw'st thou him?　　　　　　10
BOY. O, yea; I saw him leap through a hedge, and then over a ditch; then, at my lord mayor's pale, over he skipped me, and in he went me, and "Holla" the hunters cried, and "There, boy; there, boy!" But there he is, a mine honesty.
HAM. Boy, God-a-mercy.[4]　Cousin, let's away;
　I hope we shall find better sport today.
　　　　　　　　　　　　　　Exeunt.

[1] Pickled cucumber, or perhaps a misspelling for *conger,* eel.
[2] Take to water. From 1610 edn. Original reads *saile.*
[3] Foaming at the mouth from exhaustion.
[4] Thanks.

Hunting within. Enter Rose and Sybil.

ROSE. Why, Sybil, wilt thou prove a forester?　　　　　　　　　　20
SYB. Upon some,[5] no. Forester? Go by; no, faith, mistress. The deer came running into the barn through the orchard and over the pale. I wot [6] well I looked as pale as a new cheese to see him. But whip, says Goodman Pinclose, up with his flail, and our Nick with a prong, and down he fell, and they upon him, and I upon them. By my troth, we had such sport; and in the end we ended him; his throat we cut, flayed [30 him, unhorned him, and my lord mayor shall eat of him anon, when he comes.
　　　　　　　　　　Horns sound within.
ROSE. Hark, hark, the hunters come.
　Y'are best take heed;
　They'll have a saying to you for this deed.

Enter Hammon, Warner, Huntsmen, and Boy.

HAM. God save you, fair ladies.
SYB.　　　　　　　　Ladies! O, gross! [7]
WARN. Came not a buck this way?
ROSE.　　　　　　　No, but two does.
HAM. And which way went they? Faith, we'll hunt at those.
SYB. At those? Upon some, no. When, can you tell?
WARN. Upon some, ay!
SYB.　　　　　Good Lord!
WARN.　　　　　Wounds! [8] Then farewell!
HAM. Boy, which way went he?
BOY.　　　　　This way, sir, he ran.　40
HAM. This way he ran indeed, fair Mistress Rose;
　Our game was lately in your orchard seen.
WARN. Can you advise which way he took his flight?
SYB. Follow your nose; his horns will guide you right.
WARN. Th' art a mad wench.
SYB.　　　　　O, rich!
ROSE.　　　　　Trust me, not I.
　It is not like [that] [9] the wild forest deer
　Would come so near to places of resort.
　You are deceived; he fled some other way.

[5] An intensive cant phrase of uncertain origin.
[6] Know.　　　　[8] God's wounds!
[7] Stupid.　　　[9] Supplied from 1610 edn.

WARN. Which way, my sugar candy, can you show? [*Puts his arm about Sybil.*]

SYB. Come up, good honeysops; upon some, no! 50

ROSE. Why do you stay, and not pursue your game?

SYB. I'll hold [1] my life, their hunting nags be lame.

HAM. A deer more dear is found within this place.

ROSE. But not the deer, sir, which you had in chase.

HAM. I chased the deer, but this dear chaseth me.

ROSE. The strangest hunting that ever I see.

But where's your park?
She offers to go away.

HAM. 'Tis here. O, stay!

ROSE. Impale me, and then I will not stray.

WARN. They wrangle, wench; we are more kind than they.

SYB. What kind of hart is that dear heart you seek? 60

WARN. A hart, dear heart!

SYB. Who ever saw the like?

ROSE. To lose your heart, is 't possible you can?

HAM. My heart is lost.

ROSE. Alack, good gentleman!

HAM. This poor lost heart would I wish you might find.

ROSE. You, by such luck, might prove your hart a hind.

HAM. Why, Luck had horns, so have I heard some say.

ROSE. Now, God, and 't be his will, send Luck into your way.

Enter L[ord] Mayor and Servants.

L. MAYOR. What, M[aster] Hammon? Welcome to Old Ford!

SYB. God's pitikins, hands off, sir! Here's my lord.

L. MAYOR. I hear you had ill luck, and lost your game. 70

HAM. 'Tis true, my lord.

L. MAYOR. I am sorry for the same. What gentleman is this?

HAM. My brother-in-law.

[1] Wager.

L. MAYOR. Y'are welcome both. Sith [2] Fortune offers you
Into my hands, you shall not part from hence
Until you have refreshed your wearied limbs.
Go, Sybil, cover the board! You shall be guest
To no good cheer, but even a hunter's feast.

HAM. I thank your lordship.—Cousin, on my life,
For our lost venison I shall find a wife.
Exeunt [all but Mayor].

L. MAYOR. In, gentlemen; I'll not be absent long.— 80
This Hammon is a proper gentleman,
A citizen by birth, fairly allied;
How fit an husband were he for my girl!
Well, I will in, and do the best I can
To match my daughter to this gentleman.
Exit.

[SCENE vi.

A room in Eyre's house.]

Enter Lacy, Skipper, Hodge, and Firk.

SKIP. *Ick sal yow wat seggen, Hans; dis skip dat comen from Candy, is al vol,[3] by Got's sacrament, van sugar, civet, almonds, cambrick, end alle dingen—towsand towsand ding. Nempt it, Hans, nempt it vor u meester. Daer be de bils van laden. Your meester Simon Eyre sal hae good copen. Wat seggen yow, Hans?* [4]

FIRK. *Wat seggen de reggen de copen, slopen*—Laugh, Hodge, laugh! 10

LACY. *Mine liever broder Firk, bringt Meester Eyre tot [5] det signe un Swannekin; daer sal yow finde dis skipper end me. Wat seggen yow, broder Firk? Doot it, Hodge.[6] Come, skipper.* *Exeunt.*

[2] Since.
[3] From 1610 edn. Original reads *wel.*
[4] I'll tell you what, Hans; this ship that is come from Candia is all full, by God's sacrament, of sugar, civet, almonds, cambric, and all things—a thousand thousand things. Take it, Hans, take it for your master. There are the bills of lading. Your master, Simon Eyre, shall have a good bargain. What say you, Hans?
[5] In early edns. *lot.*
[6] My dear brother Firk, bring Master Eyre to the sign of the Swan; there shall you find this skipper and me. What say you, brother Firk? Do it, Hodge.

FIRK. Bring him, quod you? Here's no knavery, to bring my master to buy a ship worth the lading of two or three hundred thousand pounds. Alas, that's nothing; a trifle, a bable,[1] Hodge.   20

HODGE. The truth is, Firk, that the merchant owner of the ship dares not show his head, and therefore this skipper that deals for him, for the love he bears to Hans, offers my master Eyre a bargain in the commodities. He shall have a reasonable day of payment; he may sell the wares by that time, and be an huge gainer himself.

FIRK. Yea, but can my fellow Hans lend my master twenty porpentines as an [30 earnest penny?

HODGE. Portuguese, thou wouldst say. Here they be, Firk; hark, they jingle in my pocket like St. Mary Overy's bells.

Enter Eyre and his Wife.

FIRK. Mum, here comes my dame and my master. She'll scold, on my life, for loitering this Monday; but all's one—let them all say what they can, Monday's our holiday.

WIFE. You sing, Sir Sauce, but I beshrew[2] your heart.   40
I fear for this your singing we shall smart.

FIRK. Smart for me, dame? Why, dame, why?

HODGE. Master, I hope you'll not suffer my dame to take down your journeymen.

FIRK. If she take me down, I'll take her up; yea, and take her down too, a button-hole lower.

EYRE. Peace, Firk; not I, Hodge; by the life of Pharaoh, by the Lord of Ludgate, [50 by this beard, every hair whereof I value at a king's ransom, she shall not meddle with you.—Peace, you bombast cotton-candle quean; away, queen of clubs! Quarrel not with me and my men, with me and my fine Firk; I'll firk you if you do!

WIFE. Yea, yea, man, you may use me as you please; but let that pass.

EYRE. Let it pass, let it vanish away! Peace! Am I not Simon Eyre? Are not [60 these my brave men, brave shoemakers, all gentlemen of the gentle craft? Prince am I none, yet am I nobly born, as being the sole son of a shoemaker. Away, rubbish! Vanish; melt, melt like kitchen stuff.

WIFE. Yea, yea, 'tis well; I must be called rubbish, kitchen stuff, for a sort[3] of knaves.

FIRK. Nay, dame, you shall not weep and wail in woe for me. Master, I'll stay [70 no longer; here's a venentory[4] of my shop tools. Adieu, master; Hodge, farewell.

HODGE. Nay, stay, Firk; thou shalt not go alone.

WIFE. I pray, let them go; there be mo maids than Mawkin, more men than Hodge, and more fools than Firk.

FIRK. Fools? Nails! If I tarry now, I would my guts might be turned to shoe thread.   80

HODGE. And, if I stay, I pray God I may be turned to a Turk, and set in Finsbury for boys to shoot at.—Come, Firk.

EYRE. Stay, my fine knaves, you arms of my trade, you pillars of my profession. What, shall a tittle-tattle's words make you forsake Simon Eyre?—Avaunt, kitchen stuff! Rip, you brown bread Tannikin;[5] out of my sight! Move me not! Have not I ta'en you from selling tripes in East- [90 cheap, and set you in my shop, and made you hail-fellow with Simon Eyre, the shoemaker? And now do you deal thus with my journeymen? Look, you powder-beef quean, on the face of Hodge; here's a face for a lord.

FIRK. And here's a face for any lady in Christendom.

EYRE. Rip, you chitterling, avaunt! Boy, bid the tapster of the Boar's Head [100 fill me a dozen cans of beer for my journeymen.

FIRK. A dozen cans? O, brave! Hodge, now I'll stay.

EYRE. [*Aside to the Boy.*] And the knave fills any more than two, he pays for them.—[*Exit Boy.—Aloud.*] A dozen cans of beer for my journeymen. [*Enter Boy.*] Heave,[6] you mad Mesopotamians; wash your livers with this liquor. Where be [110 the odd ten?—[*Aside.*] No more, Madge, no more.—Well said.[7] Drink and to work! —What work dost thou, Hodge? What work?

---

[1] Bauble.   [2] Curse.

[3] Pack.   [4] Firk's corruption of *inventory*.
[5] Dutch nickname for Anne.
[6] *I.e.*, lift your tankards.   [7] Well done.

HODGE. I am a-making a pair of shoes for my lord mayor's daughter, Mistress Rose.

FIRK. And I a pair of shoes for Sybil, my lord's maid. I deal with her.

EYRE. Sybil? Fie, defile not thy [120 fine workmanly fingers with the feet of kitchen stuff and basting ladles. Ladies of the court, fine ladies, my lads, commit their feet to our appareling; put gross work to Hans. Yark [1] and seam, yark and seam!

FIRK. For yarking and seaming let me alone, and I come to 't.

HODGE. Well, master, all this is from the bias. Do you remember the ship my fellow Hans told you of? The skipper and [130 he are both drinking at the Swan. Here be the Portuguese to give earnest. If you go through with it, you cannot choose but be a lord at least.

FIRK. Nay, dame, if my master prove not a lord, and you a lady, hang me.

WIFE. Yea, like enough, if you may loiter and tipple thus.

FIRK. Tipple, dame? No, we have been bargaining with Skellum Skanderbag [2] [140 Can-You-Dutch-Spreaken for a ship of silk Cyprus, [3] laden with sugar candy.

Enter the Boy with a velvet coat and an alderman's gown. Eyre puts it on.

EYRE. Peace, Firk; silence, Tittle-tattle! Hodge, I'll go through with it. Here's a seal ring, and I have sent for a garded [4] gown and a damask cassock. See where it comes. Look here, Maggy; help me, Firk; apparel me, Hodge; silk and satin, you mad Philistines, silk and satin!

FIRK. Ha, ha, my master will be as [150 proud as a dog in a doublet, all in beaten [5] damask and velvet.

EYRE. Softly, Firk, for rearing of the nap, and wearing threadbare my garments. How dost thou like me, Firk? How do I look, my fine Hodge?

HODGE. Why, now you look like yourself, master. I warrant you, there's few in the city but will give you the wall, [6] and

come upon you with the "right wor- [160 shipful."

FIRK. Nails, my master looks like a threadbare cloak new turned and dressed! Lord, Lord, to see what good raiment doth! Dame, dame, are you not enamored?

EYRE. How sayst thou, Maggy, am I not brisk? Am I not fine?

WIFE. Fine? By my troth, sweetheart, very fine! By my troth, I never liked thee so well in my life, sweetheart; but let [170 that pass. I warrant there be many women in the city have not such handsome husbands, but only for their apparel; but let that pass too.

Enter Hans and Skipper.

HANS. *Godden day, mester. Dis be de skipper dat heb de skip van marchandice. De commodity ben good; nempt it, master, nempt it.*[7]

EYRE. God-a-mercy, Hans; welcome, skipper. Where lies this ship of merchandise?

SKIP. *De skip ben in rouere; dor be* [181 *van sugar, cyvet, almonds, cambrick, and a towsand towsand tings. Gotz sacrament, nempt it, mester; yo sal heb good copen.*[8]

FIRK. To him, master! O sweet master! O sweet wares! Prunes, almonds, sugar candy, carrot roots, turnips! O brave, fatting meat! [9] Let not a man buy a nutmeg but yourself.

EYRE. Peace, Firk! Come, skipper, [190 I'll go aboard [10] with you.—Hans, have you made him drink?

SKIP. *Yaw, yaw, ic heb veale gedrunck.*[11]

EYRE. Come, Hans, follow me. Skipper, thou shalt have my countenance in the city.
Exeunt.

FIRK. "*Yaw, heb veale gedrunck,*" quoth 1. They may well be called butterboxes, when they drink fat veal and thick beer too. But come, dame, I hope you'll chide us no more.　200

WIFE. No, faith, Firk; no, perdy, [12]

[1] Pull stitches tight.
[2] An Albanian-Turkish hero, here equivalent to *rascal*.　[3] Black lawn.　[4] Edged with an ornamental band.　[5] Stamped.
[6] *I.e.*, yield him the favored position in walking the streets.

[7] Good day, master. This is the skipper that has the ship of merchandise. The commodity is good; take it, master, take it.
[8] The ship is in the river; there are sugar, civet, almonds, cambric, and a thousand thousand things. By God's sacrament, take it, master; you shall have a good bargain.
[9] Fattening food.
[10] First two edns. read *abroade*.
[11] Yes, yes, I have drunk rauch.
[12] *Par Dion*, truly.

Hodge. I do feel honor creep upon me, and, which is more, a certain rising in my flesh; but let that pass.

Firk. Rising in your flesh do you feel, say you? Ay, you may be with child, but why should not my master feel a rising in his flesh, having a gown and a gold ring on? But you are such a shrew, you'll soon pull him down. 210

Wife. Ha, ha! Prithee, peace! Thou mak'st my worship laugh; but let that pass. Come, I'll go in. Hodge, prithee, go before me; Firk, follow me.

Firk. Firk doth follow; Hodge, pass out in state. *Exeunt.*

[Scene vii.

A room in Lincoln's house at London.]

Enter Lincoln and Dodger.

Linc. How now, good Dodger, what's the news in France?

Dodger. My lord, upon the eighteen day of May
The French and English were prepared to fight;
Each side with eager fury gave the sign
Of a most hot encounter. Five long hours
Both armies fought together; at the length
The lot of victory fell on our sides.
Twelve thousand of the Frenchmen that day died,
Four thousand English, and no man of name
But Captain Hyam and young Ardington, 10
Two gallant gentlemen—I knew them well.

Linc. But, Dodger, prithee, tell me, in this fight
How did my cousin Lacy bear himself?

Dodger. My lord, your cousin Lacy was not there.

Linc. Not there?

Dodger. No, my good lord.

Linc. Sure, thou mistakest.
I saw him shipped, and a thousand eyes beside
Were witnesses of the farewells which he gave,
When I, with weeping eyes, bid him adieu.
Dodger, take heed.

Dodger. My lord, I am advised
That what I spake is true. To prove it so, 20
His cousin Askew, that supplied his place,
Sent me for him from France, that secretly
He might convey himself hither.

Linc. Is 't even so?
Dares he so carelessly venture his life
Upon the indignation of a king?
Hath he despised my love, and spurned those favors
Which I with prodigal hand poured on his head?
He shall repent his rashness with his soul;
Since of my love he makes no estimate,
I'll make him wish he had not known my hate. 30
Thou hast no other news?

Dodger. None else, my lord.

Linc. None worse I know thou hast.—
Procure the king
To crown his giddy brows with ample honors,
Send him chief colonel—and all my hope
Thus to be dashed! But 'tis in vain to grieve;
One evil cannot a worse relieve.
Upon my life, I have found out his plot;
That old dog, Love, that fawned upon him so,
Love to that puling girl, his fair-cheeked Rose,
The lord mayor's daughter, hath distracted him, 40
And in the fire of that love's lunacy
Hath he burnt up himself, consumed his credit,
Lost the king's love, yea, and, I fear, his life,
Only to get a wanton to his wife.
Dodger, it is so.

Dodger. I fear so, my good lord.

Linc. It is so—nay, sure it cannot be!
I am at my wits' end. Dodger!

Dodger. Yea, my lord.

Linc. Thou art acquainted with my nephew's haunts;
Spend this gold for thy pains; go seek him out.
Watch at my lord mayor's—there if he live, 50
Dodger, thou shalt be sure to meet with him.

Prithee, be diligent.—Lacy, thy name
Lived once in honor, now dead in
    shame!—
Be circumspect.   *Exit.*
DODGER.   I warrant you, my lord.   *Exit.*

[SCENE viii.

*A room in the Lord Mayor's house at
London.*]

Enter Lord Mayor and Master Scott.

L. MAYOR. Good Master Scott, I have
    been bold with you
To be a witness to a wedding knot
Betwixt young Master Hammon and my
    daughter.
O, stand aside; see where the lovers come.

Enter Hammon and Rose.

ROSE. Can it be possible you love me so?
No, no, within those eyeballs I espy
Apparent likelihoods of flattery.
Pray now, let go my hand.
HAM.   Sweet Mistress Rose,
Misconstrue not my words, nor miscon-
    ceive
Of my affection, whose devoted soul   10
Swears that I love thee dearer than my
    heart.
ROSE. As dear as your own heart? I judge
    it right,
Men love their hearts best when th' are
    out of sight.
HAM. I love you, by this hand.
ROSE.   Yet hands off now!
If flesh be frail, how weak and frail's
    your vow!
HAM. Then by my life I swear.
ROSE.   Then do not brawl;
One quarrel loseth wife and life and all.
Is not your meaning thus?
HAM.   In faith, you jest.
ROSE. Love loves to sport; therefore leave
    love, y' are best.
L. MAYOR. What? Square [1] they, Master
    Scott?
SCOTT.   Sir, never doubt,   20
Lovers are quickly in, and quickly out.
HAM. Sweet Rose, be not so strange in
    fancying me.
Nay, never turn aside, shun not my
    sight.

[1] Quarrel.

I am not grown so fond,[2] to fond [3] my
    love
On any that shall quit [4] it with disdain,
If you will love me, so—if not, farewell.
L. MAYOR. Why, how now, lovers, are you
    both agreed?
HAM. Yes, faith, my lord.
L. MAYOR.   'Tis well; give me your hand.
Give me yours, daughter.—How now,
    both pull back!
What means this, girl?
ROSE.   I mean to live a maid.   30
HAM. (*Aside.*) But not to die one; pause
    ere that be said.
L. MAYOR. Will you still cross me, still be
    obstinate?
HAM. Nay, chide her not, my lord, for
    doing well;
If she can live an happy virgin's life,
'Tis far more blessed than to be a wife.
ROSE. Say, sir, I cannot. I have made a
    vow.
Whoever be my husband, 'tis not you.
L. MAYOR. Your tongue is quick; but,
    Master Hammon, know,
I bade you welcome to another end.
HAM. What, would you have me pule and
    pine and pray,   40
With "lovely lady," "mistress of my
    heart,"
"Pardon your servant," and the rhymer
    play,
Railing on Cupid and his tyrant's dart?
Or shall I undertake some martial spoil,
Wearing your glove at tourney and at
    tilt,
And tell how many gallants I unhorsed?
Sweet, will this pleasure you?
ROSE.   Yea, when wilt begin?
What, love rhymes, man? Fie on that
    deadly sin!
L. MAYOR. If you will have her, I'll make
    her agree.
HAM. Enforcéd love is worse than hate
    to me.—   50
[*Aside.*] There is a wench keeps shop in
    the Old Change;
To her will I. It is not wealth I seek;
I have enough, and will prefer her love
Before the world.—My good lord mayor,
    adieu.
Old love for me; I have no luck with new.
                    Exit.

[2] Foolish.   [3] Found, set.   [4] Requite, return.

L. Mayor. Now, mammet,[1] you have well
behaved yourself,
But you shall curse your coyness if I
live.—
Who's within there?   See you convey
your mistress
Straight to th' Old Ford! I'll keep you
straight enough.
Fore God, I would have sworn the puling
girl   60
Would willingly accepted Hammon's
love;
But banish him, my thoughts!—Go,
minion, in!   *Exit Rose.*
Now tell me, Master Scott, would you
have thought
That Master Simon Eyre, the shoe-
maker,
Had been of wealth to buy such mer-
chandise?
Scott. 'Twas well, my lord, your honor
and myself
Grew partners with him, for your bills of
lading
Show that Eyre's gains in one commodity
Rise at the least to full three thousand
pound
Besides like gain in other merchandise. 70
L. Mayor. Well, he shall spend some of
his thousands now,
For I have sent for him to the Guildhall.

Enter Eyre.

See, where he comes.—Good morrow,
Master Eyre.
Eyre. Poor Simon Eyre, my lord, your
shoemaker.
L. Mayor. Well, well, it likes [2] yourself to
term you so.

Enter Dodger.[3]

Now, M[aster] Dodger, what's the news
with you?
Dodger. I'd gladly speak in private to
your honor.
L. Mayor. You shall, you shall.—Master
Eyre and M[aster] Scott,
I have some business with this gentle-
man;
I pray, let me entreat you to walk
before   80

To the Guildhall; I'll follow presently.
Master Eyre, I hope ere noon to call you
sheriff.
Eyre. I would not care, my lord, if you
might call me King of Spain.—Come, Mas-
ter Scott.   [*Exeunt Eyre and Scott.*]
L. Mayor. Now, Master Dodger, what's
the news you bring?
Dodger. The Earl of Lincoln by me greets
your lordship,
And earnestly requests you, if you can,
Inform him where his nephew Lacy keeps.
L. Mayor. Is not his nephew Lacy now in
France?   90
Dodger. No, I assure your lordship, but
disguised
Lurks here in London.
L. Mayor.   London? Is 't even so?
It may be; but, upon my faith and soul,
I know not where he lives, or whether
he lives;
So tell my Lord of Lincoln.—Lurk in
London?
Well, Master Dodger, you perhaps may
start him;
Be but the means to rid him into France,
I'll give you a dozen angels [4] for your
pains,
So much I love his honor, hate his
nephew.   99
And, prithee, so inform thy lord from me.
Dodger. I take my leave.   *Exit Dodger.*
L. Mayor.   Farewell, good Master
Dodger.—
Lacy in London? I dare pawn my life
My daughter knows thereof, and for that
cause
Denied young M[aster] Hammon in his
love.
Well, I am glad I sent her to Old Ford.
God's Lord, 'tis late! To Guildhall I must
hie;
I know my brethren stay [5] my company.
                                                             Exit.

[Scene ix.

A room in Eyre's house.]

Enter Firk, Eyre's Wife, Hans, and Roger.

Wife. Thou goest too fast for me,
Roger. [O, Firk!] [6]
Firk. Ay, forsooth.

---

[1] Puppet, doll.   [2] Pleases.
[3] Early edns. print this direction after the
following line.
[4] Gold coins.   [5] Await.
[6] Supplied from 1618 edn.

WIFE. I pray thee, run—do you hear?—run to Guildhall, and learn if my husband, Master Eyre, will take that worshipful vocation of m[aster] sheriff upon him. Hie thee, good Firk.

FIRK. Take it? Well, I go; and he should not take it, Firk swears to for- [10 swear him. Yes, forsooth, I go to Guildhall.

WIFE. Nay, when? Thou art too compendious and tedious.

FIRK. O, rare! Your excellence is full of eloquence; how like a new cart wheel my dame speaks, and she looks like an old musty ale bottle [1] going to scalding.

WIFE. Nay, when? Thou wilt make me melancholy.

FIRK. God forbid your worship [20 should fall into that humor. I run. *Exit.*

WIFE. Let me see now, Roger and Hans.

HODGE. Ay, forsooth, dame—mistress, I should say, but the old term so sticks to the roof of my mouth I can hardly lick it off.

WIFE. Even what thou wilt, good Roger; dame is a fair name for any honest Christian; but let that pass. How dost thou, Hans?

HANS. *Mee tanck you, vro.*   30

WIFE. Well, Hans and Roger, you see God hath blessed your master, and, perdy, if ever he comes to be m[aster] sheriff of London—as we are all mortal—you shall see, I will have some odd thing or other in a corner for you; I will not be your backfriend; [2] but let that pass. Hans, pray thee, tie my shoe.

HANS. *Yaw, ic sal, vro.*

WIFE. Roger, thou know'st the [40 length of my foot; as it is none of the biggest, so, I thank God, it is handsome enough. Prithee, let me have a pair of shoes made—cork, [3] good Roger, wooden heel too.

HODGE. You shall.

WIFE. Art thou acquainted with never a fardingale-maker nor a French hoodmaker? I must enlarge my bum—ha, ha! How shall I look in a hood, I wonder! [50 Perdy, oddly, I think.

HODGE. [4] [*Aside.*] As a cat out of a

pillory.—Very well, I warrant you, mistress.

WIFE. Indeed, all flesh is grass; and, Roger, canst thou tell where I may buy a good hair?

HODGE. Yes, forsooth, at the poulterer's in Gracious Street.

WIFE. Thou art an ungracious wag; [60 perdy, I mean a false hair for my periwig.

HODGE. Why, mistress, the next time I cut my beard, you shall have the shavings of it; but they are all true hairs.

WIFE. It is very hot; I must get me a fan or else a mask.

HODGE. [*Aside.*] So you had need, to hide your wicked face.

WIFE. Fie upon it, how costly this world's calling is; perdy, but that it is [70 one of the wonderful works of God, I would not deal with it.—Is not Firk come yet? Hans, be not so sad; let it pass and vanish, as my husband's worship says.

HANS. *Ick bin vrolicke; lot see yow soo.* [5]

HODGE. Mistress, will you drink [6] a pipe of tobacco?

WIFE. O, fie upon it, Roger, perdy! These filthy tobacco pipes are the most idle, slavering bables that ever I felt. [80 Out upon it! God bless us, men look not like men that use them.

Enter Rafe, being lame.

HODGE. What, fellow Rafe? Mistress, look here, Jane's husband! Why, how [now], [7] lame? Hans, make much of him; he's a brother of our trade, a good workman, and a tall soldier.

HANS. *You be welcome, broder.*

WIFE. Perdy, I knew him not. How dost thou, good Rafe? I am glad [to] see [90 thee well.

RAFE. I would to God you saw me; dame
     as well
As when I went from London into
     France.

WIFE. Trust me, I am sorry, Rafe, to see thee impotent. [8] Lord, how the wars have made him sunburnt! The left leg is not well; 'twas not a fair gift of God the infirmity took not hold a little higher, considering thou camest from France; but let that pass.   100

---

[1] Bottles made of leather.
[2] Reluctant friend.
[3] *I.e.*, with an inner pad of cork.
[4] The name now appears as Roger to the end of this scene.

[5] I am merry; let's see you so.
[6] Smoke.   [7] From 1610 edn.   [8] Injured.

Rafe. I am glad to see you well, and I rejoice

To hear that God hath blessed my master so

Since my departure.

Wife. Yea, truly, Rafe, I thank my Maker; but let that pass.

Hodge. And, sirrah Rafe, what news, what news in France?

Rafe. Tell me, good Roger, first, what news in England?

How does my Jane? When didst thou see my wife?

Where lives my poor heart? She'll be poor indeed,   110

Now I want limbs to get whereon to feed.

Hodge. Limbs? Hast thou not hands, man? Thou shalt never see a shoemaker want bread, though he have but three fingers on a hand.

Rafe. Yet all this while I hear not of my Jane.

Wife. O Rafe, your wife—perdy, we know not what's become of her. She was here awhile, and, because she was married, grew more stately than became her; I [120 checked [1] her, and so forth; away she flung, never returned, nor said bye nor bah; and, Rafe, you know, "ka me, ka thee." [2] And, so as I tell ye—Roger, is not Firk come yet?

Hodge. No, forsooth.

Wife. And so, indeed, we heard not of her, but I hear she lives in London; but let that pass. If she had wanted, she might have opened her case to me or my hus- [130 band, or to any of my men; I am sure, there's not any of them, perdy, but would have done her good to his power. Hans, look if Firk be come.

Hans. *Yaw, ik sal, vro.*   *Exit Hans.*

Wife. And so, as I said—but, Rafe, why dost thou weep? Thou knowest that naked we came out of our mother's womb, and naked we must return; and, therefore, thank God for all things.   140

Hodge. No, faith, Jane is a stranger here; but, Rafe, pull up a good heart—I know thou hast one. Thy wife, man, is in London; one told me he saw her a while ago very brave and neat; we'll ferret her out, and [3] London hold her.

[1] Scolded.
[2] "Scratch me and I'll scratch thee."   [3] If.

Wife. Alas, poor soul, he's overcome with sorrow; he does but as I do—weep for the loss of any good thing. But, Rafe, get thee in, call for some meat and drink; [150 thou shalt find me worshipful towards thee.

Rafe. I thank you, dame; since I want limbs and lands,

I'll trust to God, my good friends, and to my hands. [4]   *Exit.*

Enter Hans and Firk running.

Firk. Run, good Hans! O Hodge, O mistress! Hodge, heave up thine ears; mistress, smug up [5] your looks; on with your best apparel! My master is chosen, my master is called, nay, condemned by the cry of the country to be sheriff of the city for this famous year now to come. And, [160 time now being, a great many men in black gowns were asked for their voices and their hands, and my master had all their fists about his ears presently, and they cried, "Ay, ay, ay, ay,"—and so I came away.

Wherefore, without all other grieve, [6]

I do salute you, Mistress Shrieve. [7]

Hans. *Yaw, my mester is de groot man, de shrieve.*

Hodge. Did not I tell you, mistress? [170 Now I may boldly say, "Good morrow to your worship."

Wife. Good morrow, good Roger. I thank you, my good people all.—Firk, hold up thy hand; here's a threepenny piece for thy tidings.

Firk. 'Tis but three halfpence, I think. Yes, 'tis threepence; I smell the rose. [8]

Hodge. But, mistress, be ruled by me, and do not speak so pulingly.   180

Firk. 'Tis her worship speaks so, and not she. No, faith, mistress, speak me in the old key: "To it, Firk;" "There, good Firk;" "Ply your business, Hodge;" "Hodge, with a full mouth;" "I'll fill your bellies with good cheer, till they cry twang."

Enter Simon Eyre, wearing a gold chain.

Hans. *See, myn liever broder, heer compt my meester.* [9]

[4] From 1618 edn. Original reads *I'll to God, my good friends, and to these my hands.*
[5] Smarten up.   [6] Beyond every other sherif.
[7] Sheriff.   [8] This coin had a rose on it.
[9] See, my dear brothers, here comes my master.

WIFE. Welcome home, Master [190 Shrieve; I pray God continue you in health and wealth.

EYRE. See here, my Maggy, a chain, a gold chain for Simon Eyre! I shall make thee a lady; here's a French hood for thee; on with it, on with it! Dress thy brows with this flap of a shoulder of mutton,[1] to make thee look lovely. Where be my fine men? Roger, I'll make over my shop and tools to thee; Firk, thou shalt be the [200 foreman; Hans, thou shalt have an hundred for twenty.[2] Be as mad knaves as your master Sim Eyre hath been, and you shall live to be sheriffs of London.—How dost thou like me, Margery? Prince am I none, yet am I princely born. Firk, Hodge, and Hans!

ALL THREE. Ay, forsooth, what says your worship, Master [3] Sheriff?

EYRE. Worship and honor, you [210 Babylonian knaves, for the gentle craft. But I forgot myself; I am bidden by my lord mayor to dinner to Old Ford. He's gone before; I must after. Come, Madge, on with your trinkets! Now, my true Trojans, my fine Firk, my dapper Hodge, my honest Hans, some device, some odd crochets, some morris, or suchlike, for the honor of the gentle shoemakers. Meet me at Old Ford; you know my mind. [220 Come, Madge, away. Shut up the shop, knaves, and make holiday.   *Exeunt.*

FIRK. O, rare! O, brave! Come, Hodge; follow me, Hans;

We'll be with them for a morris dance.
                           Exeunt.

[SCENE x.

A room at Old Ford.]

Enter Lord Mayor, Eyre his Wife in a French hood,[4] [Rose,] Sybil, and other Servants.

L. MAYOR. Trust me, you are as welcome to Old Ford
As I myself.

WIFE.   Truly, I thank your lordship.

L. MAYOR. Would our bad cheer were worth the thanks you give.

EYRE. Good cheer, my lord mayor, fine cheer! A fine house, fine walls, all fine and neat.

L. MAYOR. Now, by my troth, I'll tell thee, Master Eyre,
It does me good, and all my brethren,
That such a madcap fellow as thyself
Is entered into our society.   10

WIFE. Ay, but, my lord, he must learn now to put on gravity.

EYRE. Peace, Maggy, a fig for gravity! When I go to Guildhall in my scarlet gown, I'll look as demurely as a saint, and speak as gravely as a justice of peace; but, now I am here at Old Ford, at my good lord mayor's house, let it go by, vanish, Maggy; I'll be merry. Away with flip-flap, these fooleries, these guller- [20 ies! What, honey? Prince am I none, yet am I princely born. What says my lord mayor?

L. MAYOR. Ha, ha, ha! I had rather than a thousand pound I had an heart but half so light as yours.

EYRE. Why, what should I do, my lord? A pound of care pays not a dram of debt. Hum, let's be merry whiles we are young; old age, sack, and sugar will steal upon us, ere we be aware.   31

THE FIRST THREE-MAN'S SONG [5]

O, the month of May, the merry month of May,
   So frolic, so gay, and so green, so green, so green!
O, and then did I unto my true love say:
   "Sweet Peg, thou shalt be my summer's queen!

"Now the nightingale, the pretty nightingale,
   The sweetest singer in all the forest's choir,
Entreats thee, sweet Peggy, to hear thy true love's tale;
   Lo, yonder she sitteth, her breast against a brier.

"But, O, I spy the cuckoo, the cuckoo, the cuckoo;   40
   See where she sitteth. Come away, my joy;
Come away, I prithee. I do not like the cuckoo[6]
   Should sing where my Peggy and I kiss and toy."

---

[1] "The flap of a hood trimmed with fur or sheep's wool" (Rhys).

[2] *I.e.*, the twenty Portuguese already lent.

[3] From 1657 edn. Earlier edns. read *Mistress.*

[4] First two edns. give Sybil the French hood.

[5] This seems the most appropriate place to insert this song.   [6] A reference to the cuckold.

O, the month of May, the merry month of
    May,
    So frolic, so gay, and so green, so green,
      so green!
And then did I unto my true love say:
    "Sweet Peg, thou shalt be my summer's
      queen!"

L. MAYOR. It's well done. Mistress
Eyre, pray give good counsel to my
daughter.   50
WIFE. I hope Mistress Rose will have
the grace to take nothing that's bad.
L. MAYOR. Pray God she do; for, i' faith,
    Mistress Eyre,
I would bestow upon that peevish
    girl
A thousand marks more than I mean
    to give her
Upon condition she'd be ruled by me.
The ape[1] still crosseth me. There came
    of late
A proper gentleman of fair revenues,
Whom gladly I would call son-in-law;
But my fine cockney[1] would have none
    of him.   60
You'll prove a coxcomb[2] for it, ere you
    die;
A courtier, or no man, must please
    your eye.
EYRE. Be ruled, sweet Rose; th' art
ripe for a man. Marry not with a boy
that has no more hair on his face than thou
hast on thy cheeks. A courtier! Wash,[3] go
by, stand not upon pishery-pashery.
Those silken fellows are but painted images, outsides, outsides, Rose; their inner
linings are torn. No, my fine mouse, [70
marry me with a gentleman grocer like my
lord mayor, your father. A grocer is a
sweet trade—plums, plums! Had I a son or
daughter should marry out of the generation and blood of the shoemakers, he should
pack. What! The gentle trade is a living
for a man through Europe, through the
world.
    A noise within of a tabor and a pipe.
MAYOR. What noise is this?
EYRE. O my lord mayor, a crew of [80
good fellows that for love to your honor are
come hither with a morris dance. Come
in, my Mesopotamians, cheerily.

*Enter Hodge, Hans, Rafe, Firk, and other
    Shoemakers in a morris; after a little
    dancing, the Lord Mayor speaks.*

MAYOR. Master Eyre, are all these shoe-
makers?
EYRE. All cordwainers, my good lord
mayor.
ROSE. [*Aside.*] How like my Lacy looks
    yond shoemaker!
HANS. [*Aside.*] O, that I durst but speak
    unto my love!   89
MAYOR. Sybil, go fetch some wine to
make these drink. You are all welcome.
ALL. We thank your lordship.
Rose takes a cup of wine and goes to Hans.
ROSE. For his sake whose fair shape thou
    represent'st,
Good friend, I drink to thee.
HANS. *Ic bedancke, good frister.*[4]
EYRE'S WIFE. I see, Mistress Rose,
you do not want judgment; you have drunk
to the properest man I keep.
FIRK. Here be some have done their
parts to be as proper as he.   100
MAYOR. Well, urgent business calls me
    back to London.
Good fellows, first go in and taste our
    cheer,
And, to make merry as you homeward go,
Spend these two angels in beer at Strat-
    ford Bow.
EYRE. To these two, my mad lads,
Sim Eyre adds another; then cheerily,
Firk; tickle it, Hans, and all for the honor
of shoemakers.   *All go dancing out.*
MAYOR. Come, Master Eyre, let's have
    your company.   *Exeunt.*
ROSE. Sybil, what shall I do?
SYB.   Why, what's the matter? 110
ROSE. That Hans the shoemaker is my
    love Lacy,
Disguised in that attire to find me out.
How should I find the means to speak
    with him?
SYB. What, mistress, never fear; I
dare venter[5] my maidenhead to nothing,
and that's great odds, that Hans the Dutchman, when we come to London, shall
not only see and speak with you, but in
spite of all your father's policies steal you
away and marry you. Will not this [120
please you?

---

[1] Pet.   [2] Fool.
[3] Stale urine, used in bleaching clothes.

[4] I thank you, good maid.   [5] Venture.

ROSE. Do this, and ever be assured of my love.

SYB. Away, then, and follow your father to London, lest your absence cause him to suspect something.

Tomorrow, if my counsel be obeyed, I'll bind you prentice to the gentle trade.   *Exeunt.*

[SCENE xi.

A street in London.]

Enter Jane in a semster's [1] shop, working; and Hammon, muffled, at another door. He stands aloof.

HAM. Yonder's the shop, and there my fair love sits.

She's fair and lovely, but she is not mine.

O, would she were!   Thrice have I courted her;

Thrice hath my hand been moistened with her hand,

Whilst my poor famished eyes do feed on that

Which made them famish.   I am infortunate:

I still love one, yet nobody loves me.

I muse [2] in other men what women see

That I so want!   Fine Mistress Rose was coy,

And this too curious! [3]   O, no, she is chaste, 10

And, for she thinks me wanton, she denies

To cheer my cold heart with her sunny eyes.

How prettily she works!   O pretty hand!

O happy work!   It doth me good to stand

Unseen to see her.   Thus I oft have stood

In frosty evenings, a light burning by her,

Enduring biting cold, only to eye her.

One only look hath seemed as rich to me

As a king's crown; such is love's lunacy.

Muffled I'll pass along, and by that try 20

Whether she know me.—

JANE.   Sir, what is 't you buy?

What is 't you lack, sir, calico, or lawn,

Fine cambric shirts, or bands?   What will you buy?

HAM. [*Aside.*]   That which thou wilt not sell.   Faith, yet I'll try.—

How do you sell this handkercher?

JANE.   Good cheap.[4]

HAM. And how these ruffs?

JANE.   Cheap too.

HAM.   And how this band?

JANE. Cheap too.

HAM.   All cheap!   How sell you then this hand?

JANE. My hands are not to be sold.

HAM.   To be given then!

Nay, faith, I come to buy.

JANE.   But none knows when.

HAM. Good sweet, leave work a little while; let's play.   30

JANE. I cannot live by keeping holiday.

HAM. I'll pay you for the time which shall be lost.

JANE. With me you shall not be at so much cost.

HAM. Look, how you wound this cloth, so you wound me.

JANE. It may be so.

HAM.   'Tis so.

JANE.   What remedy?

HAM. Nay, faith, you are too coy.

JANE.   Let go my hand.

HAM. I will do any task at your command;

I would let go this beauty, were I not

In mind to disobey you by a power

That controls kings.   I love you!

JANE.   So, now part. 40

HAM. With hands I may, but never with my heart.

In faith, I love you.

JANE.   I believe you do.

HAM. Shall a true love in me breed hate in you?

JANE. I hate you not.

HAM.   Then you must love?

JANE.   I do.

What, are you better now?   I love not you.

HAM. All this, I hope, is but a woman's fray,

That means, "Come to me," when she cries, "Away!"

In earnest, mistress, I do not jest;

---

[1] Seamstress'.   [2] Wonder.   [3] Scrupulous.   [4] At a bargain.

A true, chaste love hath entered in my
breast.
I love you dearly, as I love my life;   50
I love you as a husband loves a wife;
That, and no other love, my love re-
quires.
Thy wealth, I know, is little; my de-
sires
Thirst not for gold.   Sweet, beauteous
Jane, what's mine
Shall, if thou make myself thine, all be
thine.
Say, judge, what is thy sentence, life
or death?
Mercy or cruelty lies in thy breath.
JANE. Good sir, I do believe you love me
well;
For 'tis a silly conquest, silly pride,
For one like you—I mean a gentle-
man—   60
To boast that by his love tricks he hath
brought
Such and such women to his amorous
lure.
I think you do not so, yet many do,
And make it even a very trade to woo.
I could be coy, as many women be,
Feed you with sunshine smiles and
wanton looks,
But I detest witchcraft; say that I
Do constantly believe you, constant [1]
have—
HAM. Why dost thou not believe me?
JANE.   I believe you;
But yet, good sir, because I will not
grieve you   70
With hopes to taste fruit which will
never fall,
In simple truth this is the sum of all:
My husband lives—at least, I hope he
lives.
Pressed was he to these bitter wars in
France;
Bitter they are to me by wanting him.
I have but one heart, and that heart's
his due.
How can I then bestow the same on you?
Whilst he lives, his I live, be it ne'er
so poor,
And rather be his wife than a king's
whore.
HAM. Chaste and dear woman, I will not
abuse thee,   80

[1] Constantly.

Although it cost my life, if thou refuse
me.
Thy husband, pressed for France, what
was his name?
JANE. Rafe Damport.
HAM.   Damport?—Here's a letter sent
From France to me, from a dear friend
of mine,
A gentleman of place; here he doth
write
Their names that have been slain in
every fight.
JANE. I hope death's scroll contains not
my love's name.
HAM. Cannot you read?
JANE.   I can.
HAM.   Peruse the same.
To my remembrance such a name I read
Amongst the rest. See here!
JANE.   Ay me, he's dead!   90
He's dead! If this be true, my dear
heart's slain!
HAM. Have patience, dear love.
JANE.   Hence, hence!
HAM.   Nay, sweet Jane,
Make not poor sorrow proud with these
rich tears.
I mourn thy husband's death because
thou mourn'st.
JANE. That bill is forged; 'tis signed by
forgery.
HAM. I'll bring thee letters sent besides
to many,
Carrying the like report. Jane, 'tis too
true.
Come, weep not; mourning, though it
rise from love,
Helps not the mournéd, yet hurts them
that mourn.
JANE. For God's sake, leave me.
HAM.   Whither dost thou turn? 100
Forget the dead; love them that are
alive.
His love is faded; try how mine will
thrive.
JANE. 'Tis now no time for me to think
on love.
HAM. 'Tis now best time for you to think
on love,
Because your love lives not.
JANE.   Though he be dead,
My love to him shall not be buriéd.
For God's sake, leave me to myself
alone.

HAM. 'Twould kill my soul to leave thee drowned in moan.

Answer me to my suit, and I am gone;
Say to me yea or no.

JANE. No.

HAM. Then farewell!— 110
One farewell will not serve; I come again.

Come, dry these wet cheeks; tell me, faith, sweet Jane,

Yea or no, once more.

JANE. Once more I say no;
Once more be gone, I pray; else will I go.

HAM. Nay, then I will grow rude, by this white hand,

Until you change that cold "no"; here I'll stand

Till by your hard heart—

JANE. Nay, for God's love, peace!
My sorrows by your presence more increase.

Not that you thus are present, but all grief

Desires to be alone; therefore in brief 120
Thus much I say, and saying bid adieu:
If ever I wed man, it shall be you.

HAM. O blessed voice! Dear Jane, I'll urge no more;
Thy breath hath made me rich.

JANE. Death makes me poor.
Exeunt.

[SCENE xii.

The shop in Tower Street.]

Enter Hodge, at his shopboard, Rafe, Firk, Hans, and a Boy at work [, singing].

ALL. Hey, down a down, down derry!

HODGE. Well said, my hearts. Ply your work today; we loitered yesterday; to it pell-mell, that we may live to be lord mayors, or aldermen at least.

FIRK. Hey, down a down, derry!

HODGE. Well said, i' faith! How sayst thou, Hans, doth not Firk tickle it? [1]

HANS. *Yaw, mester.*

FIRK. Not so neither; my organ pipe [10 squeaks this morning for want of liquoring.

Hey, down a down, derry!

HANS. *Forward, Firk; tow best un jolly*

[1] "Go it."

yongster. Hort, I, mester, ic bid yo, cut me un pair vampres vor Mester Jeffre's bootes. [2]

HODGE. Thou shalt, Hans.

FIRK. Master!

HODGE. How now, boy?

FIRK. Pray, now you are in the cutting vein, cut me out a pair of counterfeits, [3] [20 or else my work will not pass current.

Hey, down a down!

HODGE. Tell me, sirs, are my cousin M[istress] Priscilla's shoes done?

FIRK. Your cousin? No, master; one of your aunts, [4] hang her; let them alone.

RAFE. I am in hand with them; she gave charge that none but I should do them for her.

FIRK. Thou do for her? Then 'twill [30 be a lame doing, and that she loves not. Rafe, thou mightst have sent her to me in faith; I would have yerked and firked your Priscilla.

Hey, down a down, derry.

This gear [5] will not hold.

HODGE. How sayst thou, Firk, were we not merry at Old Ford?

FIRK. How, merry? Why, our buttocks went jiggy-joggy like a quagmire. Well, [40 Sir Roger Oatmeal, [6] if I thought all meal of that nature, I would eat nothing but bagpuddings.

RAFE. Of all good fortunes my fellow Hans had the best.

FIRK. 'Tis true, because Mistress Rose drank to him.

HODGE. Well, well, work apace. They say seven of the aldermen be dead, or very sick. 50

FIRK. I care not; I'll be none.

RAFE. No, nor I; but then my M[aster] Eyre will come quickly to be l[ord] mayor.

Enter Sybil.

FIRK. Whoop, yonder comes Sybil.

HODGE. Sybil, welcome, i' faith; and how dost thou, mad wench?

FIRK. Sib [7]-whore, welcome to London.

[2] Go on, Firk, thou art a jolly youngster. Hark, ay, master, I pray you cut me a pair of vamps for Master Jeffrey's boots.
[3] With a pun on the sense of *anything made after a pattern.*
[4] Women. [5] Matter.
[6] Punning reference to Sir Roger Oteley.
[7] Punning on the sense of *friend.*

Syb. God-a-mercy, sweet Firk. Good Lord, Hodge, what a delicious shop you [60 have got! You tickle it, i' faith.

Rafe. God-a-mercy, Sybil, for our good cheer at Old Ford.

Syb. That you shall have, Rafe.

Firk. Nay, by the Mass, we had tickling cheer, Sybil. And how the plague dost thou and Mistress Rose and my l[ord] mayor? I put the women in first.

Syb. Well, God-a-mercy. But, God's me, I forget myself; where's Hans the Fleming?

Firk. Hark, butterbox, now you must yelp out some *spreken*.   72

Hans. *Vat begaie gou?   Vat vod gou, frister?* [1]

Syb. Marry, you must come to my young mistress, to pull on her shoes you made last.

Hans. *Vare ben your egle fro?* [2]   *Vare ben your mistris?*

Syb. Marry, here at our London [80 house in Cornhill. [3]

Firk. Will nobody serve her turn but Hans?

Syb. No, sir. Come, Hans, I stand upon needles.

Hodge. Why then, Sybil, take heed of pricking.

Syb. For that let me alone. I have a trick in my budget. [4] Come, Hans.   89

Hans. *Yaw, yaw, ic sall meete yo gane.* [5]
                    Exit Hans and Sybil.

Hodge. Go, Hans, make haste again. Come, who lacks work?

Firk. I, master, for I lack my breakfast; 'tis munching time, and past.

Hodge. Is't so? Why, then leave work, Rafe. To breakfast! Boy, look to the tools. Come, Rafe; come, Firk.   *Exeunt.*

[Scene xiii.

The same.]

Enter a Serving-man.

Serv. Let me see now, the sign of the Last in Tower Street. Mass, yonder's the house. What, haw! Who's within?

Enter Rafe.

Rafe. Who calls there? What want you, sir?

Serv. Marry, I would have a pair of shoes made for a gentlewoman against tomorrow morning. What, can you do them?

Rafe. Yes, sir, you shall have them. But what length's her foot?   10

Serv. [*Presenting a shoe.*] Why, you must make them in all parts like this shoe; but, at any hand, fail not to do them, for the gentlewoman is to be married very early in the morning.

Rafe. How? By this shoe must it be made? By this? Are you sure, sir, by this?

Serv. How, by this? Am I sure, by this? Art thou in thy wits? I tell thee, I must have a pair of shoes, dost thou [20 mark me? A pair of shoes, two shoes, made by this very shoe, this same shoe, against tomorrow morning by four a-clock. Dost understand me? Canst thou do 't?

Rafe. Yes, sir, yes—I—I—I can do 't. By this shoe, you say? I should know this shoe. Yes, sir, yes, by this shoe, I can do 't. Four a-clock, well. Whither shall I bring them?

Serv. To the sign of the Golden Ball [30 in Watling Street; inquire for one Master Hammon, a gentleman, my master.

Rafe. Yea, sir; by this shoe, you say?

Serv. I say, Master Hammon at the Golden Ball; he's the bridegroom, and those shoes are for his bride.

Rafe. They shall be done by this shoe. Well, well, Master Hammon at the Golden Shoe—I would say, the Golden Ball; very well, very well. But I pray you, sir, [40 where must Master Hammon be married?

Serv. At Saint Faith's Church, under Paul's. But what's that to thee? Prithee, despatch those shoes, and so farewell. *Exit.*

Rafe. "By this shoe," said he. How am I amazed
At this strange accident! Upon my life,
This was the very shoe I gave my wife,
When I was pressed for France—since when, alas!
I never could hear of her. It is the same,
And Hammon's bride no other but my Jane.   50

Enter Firk.

Firk. 'Snails, Rafe, thou hast lost thy part of three pots a countryman of mine gave me to breakfast.

---

[1] What do you want? What would you, girl?
[2] Where is your noble lady?
[3] First three edns. read *Cornwall.*
[4] Pouch, wallet.   [5] I shall go with you.

RAFE. I care not; I have found a better thing.

FIRK. A thing? Away! Is it a man's thing, or a woman's thing?

RAFE. Firk, dost thou know this shoe?

FIRK. No, by my troth; neither doth that know me! I have no acquaintance [60 with it; 'tis a mere stranger to me.

RAFE. Why, then I do; this shoe, I durst be sworn,
Once coveréd the instep of my Jane.
This is her size, her breadth; thus trod my love;
These truelove knots I pricked. I hold my life,
By this old shoe I shall find out my wife.

FIRK. Ha, ha! Old shoe, that wert new! How a murrain [1] came this ague fit of foolishness upon thee?

RAFE. Thus, Firk: even now here came a serving-man; 70
By this shoe would he have a new pair made
Against tomorrow morning for his mistress,
That's to be married to a gentleman.
And why may not this be my sweet Jane?

FIRK. And why mayst not thou be my sweet ass? Ha, ha!

RAFE. Well, laugh and spare not! But the truth is this:
Against tomorrow morning I'll provide
A lusty crew of honest shoemakers 78
To watch the going of the bride to church.
If she prove Jane, I'll take her in despite
From Hammon and the devil, were he by.
If it be not my Jane, what remedy?
Hereof am I sure, I shall live till I die,
Although I never with a woman lie. *Exit.*

FIRK. Thou lie with a woman to build nothing but Cripplegates! Well, God sends fools fortune, and it may be he may light upon his matrimony by such a device, for wedding and hanging goes by destiny. *Exit.*

[SCENE xiv.

A room in the Lord Mayor's house at London.]

Enter Hans and Rose, arm in arm.

HANS. How happy am I by embracing thee!
O, I did fear such cross mishaps did reign
That I should never see my Rose again.

[1] Plague.

ROSE. Sweet Lacy, since fair opportunity
Offers herself to furder our escape,
Let not too overfond esteem of me
Hinder that happy hour. Invent the means,
And Rose will follow thee through all the world.

HANS. O, how I surfeit with excess of joy,
Made happy by thy rich perfection! 10
But since thou pay'st sweet int'rest to my hopes,
Redoubling love on love, let me once more
Like to a bold-faced debtor crave of thee
This night to steal abroad, and at Eyre's house,
Who now by death of certain aldermen
Is mayor of London,[2] and my master once,
Meet thou thy Lacy, where in spite of change,
Your father's anger, and mine uncle's hate,
Our happy nuptials will we consummate.

Enter Sybil.

SYB. O God, what will you do, mis- [20 tress? Shift for yourself; your father is at hand! He's coming, he's coming! Master Lacy, hide yourself in my mistress! For God's sake, shift for yourselves!

HANS. Your father come! Sweet Rose, what shall I do?
Where shall I hide me? How shall I escape?

ROSE. A man, and want wit in extremity?
Come, come, be Hans still; play the shoemaker;
Pull on my shoe.

Enter Lord Mayor.

HANS. Mass, and that's well remembered.

SYB. Here comes your father. 30

HANS. *Forware, metresse, 'tis un good skow; it sal vel dute, or ye sal neit betallen.*[3]

ROSE. O God, it pincheth me. What will you do?

HANS. [*Aside.*] Your father's presence pincheth, not the shoe.

[2] Sir Roger Oteley, however, is called lord mayor in stage directions and speech heads throughout the play.

[3] Indeed, mistress, 'tis a good shoe; it shall well do it, or you shall not pay.

L. MAYOR. Well done; fit my daughter well, and she shall please thee well.

HANS. *Yaw, yaw, ick weit dat well; for ware, 'tis un good skoo; 'tis gimait van neits leither. Se ever, mine here.*[1]

Enter a Prentice.

L. MAYOR. I do believe it.—What's the news with you?　　　40

PREN. Please you, the Earl of Lincoln at the gate

Is newly lighted, and would speak with you.

L. MAYOR. The Earl of Lincoln come speak with me?

Well, well, I know his errand.—Daughter Rose,

Send hence your shoemaker, despatch, have done!—

Syb, make things handsome.—Sir boy, follow me.　　　*Exit [with Prentice].*

HANS. Mine uncle come! O, what may this portend?

Sweet Rose, this of our love threatens an end.

ROSE. Be not dismayed at this; whate'er befall,

Rose is thine own. To witness I speak truth,　　　50

Where thou appoints the place, I'll meet with thee,

I will not fix a day to follow thee,

But presently steal hence. Do not reply.

Love which gave strength to bear my father's hate

Shall now add wings to further our escape.　　　*Exeunt.*

Enter L[ord] Mayor and Lincoln.

L. MAYOR. Believe me, on my credit, I speak truth;

Since first your nephew Lacy went to France,

I have not seen him. It seemed strange to me,

When Dodger told me that he stayed behind,

Neglecting the high charge the king imposed.　　　60

LINC. Trust me, Sir Roger Oteley, I did think

Your counsel had given head to this attempt,

Drawn to it by the love he bears your child.

Here I did hope to find him in your house;

But now I see mine error, and confess

My judgment wronged you by conceiving so.

L. MAYOR. Lodge in my house, say you? Trust me, my lord,

I love your nephew Lacy too-too dearly,

So much to wrong his honor; and he hath done so,

That first gave him advice to stay from France.　　　70

To witness I speak truth, I let you know

How careful I have been to keep my daughter

Free from all conference or speech of him—

Not that I scorn your nephew, but in love

I bear your honor, lest your noble blood

Should by my mean worth be dishonoréd.

LINC. [*Aside.*] How far the churl's tongue wanders from his heart!—

Well, well, Sir Roger Oteley, I believe you,

With more than many thanks for the kind love

So much you seem to bear me. But, my lord,　　　80

Let me request your help to seek my nephew,

Whom if I find, I'll straight embark[2] for France.

So shall your Rose be free, my thoughts at rest,[3]

And much care die which now lies[4] in my breast.

Enter Sybil.

SYB. O Lord! Help, for God's sake! My mistress; O, my young mistress!

L. MAYOR. Where is thy mistress? What's become of her?

SYB. She's gone, she's fled!

L. MAYOR. Gone! Whither is she fled?

SYB. I know not, forsooth. She's fled

---

[1] Yes, yes, I know that well; indeed, 'tis a good shoe; 'tis made of neat's leather. See here, good sir!

[2] Ship him off.

[3] First two edns. have *my Rose . . . your thoughts.*

[4] From 1610 edn. Original reads *dies.*

out of doors with Hans the shoemaker; I saw them scud, scud, scud, apace, apace!

L. MAYOR. Which way? What, John! Where be my men? Which way? 92

SYB. I know not, and it please your worship.

L. MAYOR. Fled with a shoemaker? Can this be true?

SYB. O Lord, sir, as true as God's in heaven.

LINC. [*Aside.*] Her love turned shoemaker? I am glad of this.

L. MAYOR. A Fleming butterbox, a shoemaker!

Will she forget her birth, requite my care 100

With such ingratitude? Scorned she young Hammon

To love a honnikin,[1] a needy knave?

Well, let her fly; I'll not fly after her.

Let her starve, if she will; she's none of mine.

LINC. Be not so cruel, sir.

Enter Firk with shoes.

SYB. I am glad she's scaped.

L. MAYOR. I'll not account of her as of my child.

Was there no better object for her eyes But a foul drunken lubber, swill-belly, A shoemaker? That's brave! 109

FIRK. Yea, forsooth; 'tis a very brave shoe, and as fit as a pudding.

L. MAYOR. How now, what knave is this? From whence comest thou?

FIRK. No knave, sir. I am Firk the shoemaker, lusty Roger's chief lusty journeyman, and I come hither to take up the pretty leg of sweet Mistress Rose, and thus hoping your worship is in as good health as I was at the making hereof, I bid you farewell, yours—Firk.

L. MAYOR. Stay, stay, Sir Knave! 120

LINC. Come hither, shoemaker!

FIRK. 'Tis happy the knave is put before the shoemaker, or else I would not have vouchsafed to come back to you. I am moved, for I stir.

L. MAYOR. My lord, this villain calls us knaves by craft.

FIRK. Then 'tis by the gentle craft, and to call one knave gently, is no harm. [129

Sit your worship merry! Syb, your young mistress—I'll so bob[2] them,[3] now my master, M[aster] Eyre, is lord mayor of London.

L. MAYOR. Tell me, sirrah, whose man are you?

FIRK. I am glad to see your worship so merry. I have no maw[4] to this gear, no stomach as yet to a red petticoat.

Pointing to Sybil.

LINC. He means not, sir, to woo you to his maid,

But only doth demand whose man you are. 140

FIRK. I sing now to the tune of "Rogero." Roger, my fellow, is now my master.

LINC. Sirrah, know'st thou one Hans, a shoemaker?

FIRK. Hans, shoemaker? O, yes; stay, yes, I have him. I tell you what (I speak it in secret): Mistress Rose and he are by this time—no, not so, but shortly are to come over one another with "Can [149 you dance the shaking of the sheets?"[5] It is that Hans—[*Aside.*] I'll so gull these diggers![6]

L. MAYOR. Know'st thou, then, where he is?

FIRK. Yes, forsooth; yea, marry!

LINC. Canst thou, in sadness[7]—

FIRK. No, forsooth; no, marry!

L. MAYOR. Tell me, good honest fellow, where he is,

And thou shalt see what I'll bestow of thee.

FIRK. Honest fellow? No, sir; not so, sir; my profession is the gentle craft. I [160 care not for seeing; I love feeling. Let me feel it here; *aurium tenus*, ten pieces of gold; *genuum tenus*,[8] ten pieces of silver; and then Firk is your man—[*Aside.*] in a new pair of stretchers.[9]

L. MAYOR. Here is an angel, part of thy reward,

Which I will give thee; tell me where he is. 167

FIRK. No point![10] Shall I betray my brother? No! Shall I prove Judas to Hans?

---

[1] Low fellow.

[2] Fool. [3] From 1610 edn. Original reads *then.*
[4] Appetite. [6] *I.e.,* for information.
[5] An old dance song. [7] Seriousness.
[8] Firk's Latin phrases actually mean *up to the ears, up to the knees.*
[9] Shoe stretchers; also lies.
[10] Not at all.

No! Shall I cry treason to my corporation?
No, I shall be firked and yerked then. But
give me your angel; your angel shall tell you.

LINC. Do so, good fellow; 'tis no hurt to
thee.

FIRK. Send simpering Syb away.

L. MAYOR. Huswife, get you in.

Exit Syb[il].

FIRK. Pitchers have ears, and maids
have wide mouths; but for Hans Prans,
upon my word, tomorrow morning he and
young Mistress Rose go to this gear; they
shall be married together, by this rush, [180
or else turn Firk to a firkin of butter, to tan
leather withal.

L. MAYOR. But art thou sure of this?

FIRK. Am I sure that Paul's steeple is a
handful higher than London Stone, or that
the Pissing Conduit leaks nothing but
pure Mother Bunch? [1] Am I sure I am
lusty Firk? God's nails, do you think I
am so base to gull you?

LINC. Where are they married? Dost
thou know the church?   191

FIRK. I never go to church, but I know
the name of it; it is a swearing church—
stay awhile! 'Tis—ay, by the Mass! No,
no! 'Tis—ay, by my troth! No, nor that.
'Tis—ay, by my faith! That, that, 'tis,
ay, by my Faith's Church under Paul's
Cross. There they shall be knit like a pair
of stockings in matrimony; there they'll be
incony. [2]   200

LINC. Upon my life, my nephew Lacy
walks
In the disguise of this Dutch shoemaker.

FIRK. Yes, forsooth.

LINC.   Doth he not, honest fellow?

FIRK. No, forsooth; I think Hans is
nobody but Hans, no spirit.

L. MAYOR. My mind misgives me now,
'tis so, indeed.

LINC. My cousin speaks the language,
knows the trade.

L. MAYOR. Let me request your company,
my lord;
Your honorable presence may, no doubt,
Refrain their headstrong rashness, when
myself,   210
Going alone, perchance may be o'erborne.
Shall I request this favor?

LINC.   This, or what else.

FIRK. Then you must rise betimes, for

they mean to fall to their hey-pass and re-
pass, [3] pindy-pandy, [4] which hand will you
have, very early.

L. MAYOR. My care shall every way equal
their haste.
This night accept your lodging in my
house;
The earlier shall we stir, and at Saint
Faith's   219
Prevent this giddy hare-brained nuptial.
This traffic of hot love shall yield cold
gains;
They ban [5] our loves, and we'll forbid
their banes. [6]   *Exit.* [7]

LINC. At Saint Faith's Church, thou
say'st?

FIRK.   Yes, by their troth.

LINC. Be secret, on thy life.   *Exit.*

FIRK. Yes, when I kiss your wife! Ha,
ha, here's no craft in the gentle craft. I
came hither of purpose with shoes to Sir
Roger's worship, whilst Rose, his daughter,
be cony-catched [8] by Hans. Soft now; these
two gulls will be at Saint Faith's [230
Church tomorrow morning, to take Master
Bridegroom and Mistress Bride napping,
and they, in the meantime, shall chop up [9]
the matter at the Savoy. But the best
sport is, Sir Roger Oteley will find my fellow, lame Rafe's, wife going to marry a
gentleman, and then he'll stop her instead
of his daughter. O, brave! There will be fine
tickling sport. Soft now, what have I to
do? O, I know; now a mess of shoe- [240
makers meet at the Woolsack in Ivy Lane,
to cozen my gentleman of lame Rafe's
wife; that's true.

Alack, alack!
Girls, hold out tack! [10]
For now smocks for this jumbling
Shall go to wrack.

Exit.

[SCENE XV.

A room in Eyre's house.]

Enter Eyre, his Wife, Hans, and Rose.

EYRE. This is the morning, then; stay,
my bully, my honest Hans, is it not?

HANS. This is the morning that must

---

[3] Conjuring terms.   [5] Curse.
[4] Game of handy-dandy.   [6] Banns.
[7] From 1618 edn. First two edns. have *Exeunt.*
[8] Tricked. [10] *I.e.*, hold out against attack (?).
[9] Conclude.

[1] A well-known alewife.   [2] Fine.

make us two happy or miserable; therefore, if you—

EYRE. Away with these if's and and's, Hans, and these *et cetera's!* By mine honor, Rowland Lacy, none but the king shall wrong thee. Come, fear nothing. Am not I Sim Eyre? Is not Sim Eyre lord [10 mayor of London? Fear nothing, Rose. Let them all say what they can, "Dainty, come thou to me." [1] —Laughest thou?

WIFE. Good my lord, stand her friend in what thing you may.

EYRE. Why, my sweet Lady Madgy, think you Simon Eyre can forget his fine Dutch journeyman? No, vah! Fie, I scorn it; it shall never be cast in my teeth that I was unthankful. Lady Madgy, thou [20 hadst never covered thy Saracen's head with this French flap, nor loaden thy bum with this farthingale ('tis trash, trumpery, vanity); Simon Eyre had never walked in a red petticoat, nor wore a chain of gold, but for my fine journeyman's Portuguese. —And shall I leave him? No! Prince am I none, yet bear a princely mind.

HANS. My lord, 'tis time for us to part from hence. 30

EYRE. Lady Madgy, Lady Madgy, take two or three of my piecrust eaters, my buff jerkin varlets, that do walk in black gowns at Simon Eyre's heels; take them, good Lady Madgy; trip and go, my brown queen of periwigs, with my delicate Rose and my jolly Rowland to the Savoy; see them linked; countenance the marriage; and, when it is done, cling, cling together, you Hamborough turtledoves. I'll bear [40 you out; come to Simon Eyre. Come, dwell with me, Hans; thou shalt eat minced pies and marchpane. [2] Rose, away, cricket; trip and go, my Lady Madgy, to the Savoy; Hans, wed, and to bed; kiss, and away! Go, vanish!

WIFE. Farewell, my lord.

ROSE. Make haste, sweet love.

WIFE. She'd fain the deed were done.

HANS. Come, my sweet Rose; faster than deer we'll run. *They go out.*

EYRE. Go, vanish, vanish! Avaunt, [50 I say! By the Lord of Ludgate, it's a mad life to be a lord mayor; it's a stirring life, a fine life, a velvet life, a careful life. Well,

[1] The opening of a popular song.
[2] Marzipan.

Simon Eyre, yet set a good face on it, in the honor of Saint Hugh. Soft, the king this day comes to dine with me, to see my new buildings; his majesty is welcome; he shall have good cheer, delicate cheer, princely cheer. This day my fellow prentices of London come to dine with me too; [60 they shall have fine cheer, gentlemanlike cheer. I promised the mad Cappadocians, when we all served at the Conduit together, that, if ever I came to be mayor of London, I would feast them all, and I'll do 't, I 'll do 't, by the life of Pharaoh; by this beard, Sim Eyre will be no flincher. Besides, I have procured that upon every Shrove Tuesday, at the sound of the pancake bell, my fine dapper Assyrian lads [70 shall clap up their shop windows, and away. This is the day, and this day they shall do 't, they shall do 't.

Boys, that day are you free, let masters care,
And prentices shall pray for Simon Eyre. *Exit.*

[SCENE xvi.

A street near St. Faith's church.]

Enter Hodge, Firk, Rafe, and five or six Shoemakers, all with cudgels or such weapons.

HODGE. Come, Rafe; stand to it, Firk. My masters, as we are the brave bloods of the shoemakers, heirs apparent to Saint Hugh, and perpetual benefactors to all good fellows, thou shalt have no wrong. Were Hammon a king of spades, he should not delve in thy close [3] without thy sufferance. But tell me, Rafe, art thou sure 'tis thy wife?

RAFE. Am I sure this is Firk? This [10 morning, when I stroked on her shoes, I looked upon her, and she upon me, and sighed—asked me if ever I knew one Rafe. "Yes," said I. "For his sake," said she, tears standing in her eyes, "and for thou art somewhat like him, spend this piece of gold." I took it; my lame leg and my travel beyond sea made me unknown. All is one for that; I know she's mine.

FIRK. Did she give thee this gold? O [20 glorious, glittering gold! She's thine own,

[3] Field.

'tis thy wife, and she loves thee; for I'll stand to 't there's no woman will give gold to any man, but she thinks better of him than she thinks of them she gives silver to. And for Hammon, neither Hammon nor hangman shall wrong thee in London! Is not our old master Eyre lord mayor? Speak, my hearts.

ALL. Yes, and Hammon shall know it to his cost.				31

Enter Hammon, his Man, Jane, and Others.

HODGE. Peace, my bullies; yonder they come.

RAFE. Stand to 't, my hearts. Firk, let me speak first.

HODGE. No, Rafe, let me.—Hammon, whither away so early?

HAM. Unmannerly, rude slave, what's that to thee?

FIRK. To him, sir? Yes, sir, and to me, and others. Good morrow, Jane, how [40 dost thou? Good Lord, how the world is changed with you! God be thanked!

HAM. Villains, hands off! How dare you touch my love?

ALL. Villains? Down with them! Cry clubs [1] for prentices!

HODGE. Hold, my hearts! Touch her, Hammon? Yea, and, more than that, we'll carry her away with us. My masters and gentlemen, never draw your bird-spits; shoemakers are steel to the back, men every inch of them, all spirit.		51

ALL OF HAMMON'S SIDE. Well, and what of all this?

HODGE. I'll show you.—Jane, dost thou know this man? 'Tis Rafe, I can tell thee; nay, 'tis he in faith, though he be lamed by the wars. Yet look not strange, but run to him, fold him about the neck, and kiss him.

JANE. Lives then my husband? O God, let me go;				60
Let me embrace my Rafe.

HAM.			What means my Jane?

JANE. Nay what meant you, to tell me he was slain?

HAM. Pardon me, dear love, for being misled.—
[*To Rafe.*] 'Twas rumored here in London thou wert dead.

[1] The rallying cry of the London apprentices.

FIRK. Thou seest he lives. Lass, go, pack home with him.

Now, M[aster] Hammon, where's your mistress, your wife?

SERV. 'Swounds,[2] m[aster], fight for her! Will you thus lose her?

ALL. Down with that creature! Clubs! Down with him!				70

HODGE. Hold, hold!

HAM.			Hold, fool! Sirs, he shall do no wrong.
Will my Jane leave me thus, and break her faith?

FIRK. Yea, sir! She must, sir! She shall, sir! What then? Mend it!

HODGE. Hark, fellow Rafe, follow my counsel: set the wench in the midst, and let her choose her man, and let her be his woman.

JANE. Whom should I choose? Whom should my thoughts affect
But him whom heaven hath made to be my love?				80
Thou art my husband, and these humble weeds
Makes thee more beautiful than all his wealth.
Therefore, I will but put off his attire,
Returning it into the owner's hand,
And after ever be thy constant wife.

HODGE. Not a rag, Jane! The law's on our side; he that sows in another man's ground, forfeits his harvest. Get thee home, Rafe; follow him, Jane; he shall not have so much as a busk point[3] from thee. [90

FIRK. Stand to that, Rafe; the appurtenances are thine own. Hammon, look not at her!

SERV. O, 'swounds, no!

FIRK. Blue coat,[4] be quiet. We'll give you a new livery else; we'll make Shrove Tuesday Saint George's Day[5] for you. Look not, Hammon; leer not! I'll firk you! For thy head now, one glance, one sheep's eye, anything, at her! Touch [100 not a rag, lest I and my brethren beat you to clouts.

SERV. Come, Master Hammon, there's no striving here.

HAM. Good fellows, hear me speak; and, honest Rafe,

[2] God's wounds.			[3] Corset lace.
[4] Servants' livery.
[5] The day for renewing servants' contracts. Firk means, "We'll beat you black and blue."

Whom I have injured most by loving
Jane,
Mark what I offer thee. Here in fair gold
Is twenty pound; I'll give it for thy Jane;
If this content thee not, thou shalt have
more.
HODGE. Sell not thy wife, Rafe; make her
not a whore.
HAM. Say, wilt thou freely cease thy claim
in her,   110
And let her be my wife?
ALL.   No, do not, Rafe.
RAFE. Sirrah Hammon, Hammon, dost
thou think a shoemaker is so base to be a
bawd to his own wife for commodity?
Take thy gold; choke with it! Were I
not lame, I would make thee eat thy words.
FIRK. A shoemaker sell his flesh and
blood? O indignity!
HODGE. Sirrah, take up your pelf, and
be packing.   120
HAM. I will not touch one penny, but in
lieu
Of that great wrong I offeréd thy Jane,
To Jane and thee I give that twenty
pound.
Since I have failed of her, during my
life
I vow no woman else shall be my wife.
Farewell, good fellows of the gentle trade.
Your morning's mirth my mourning day
hath made.   *Exit.*
FIRK. [*To Serving-man.*] Touch the gold,
creature, if you dare! Y'are best be trudg-
ing. Here, Jane, take thou it. Now   [130
let's home, my hearts.
HODGE. Stay! Who comes here? Jane,
on again with thy mask!

Enter Lincoln, L[ord] Mayor, and Servants.

LINC. Yonder's the lying varlet mocked
us so.
L. MAYOR. Come hither, sirrah!
FIRK. I, sir? I am "sirrah"? You mean
me, do you not?
LINC. Where is my nephew married?
FIRK. Is he married? God give him joy,
I am glad of it. They have a fair   [140
day, and the sign is in a good planet,
Mars in Venus.
L. MAYOR. Villain, thou told'st me that
my daughter Rose
This morning should be married at Saint
Faith's;

We have watched there these three hours
at the least,
Yet see we no such thing.
FIRK. Truly, I am sorry for 't; a bride's
a pretty thing.
HODGE. Come to the purpose. Yonder's
the bride and bridegroom you look for, [150
I hope. Though you be lords, you are not
to bar by your authority men from women,
are you?
L. MAYOR. See, see, my daughter's masked.
LINC.   True, and my nephew,
To hide his guilt, counterfeits him lame.
FIRK. Yea, truly; God help the poor
couple, they are lame and blind.
L. MAYOR. I'll ease her blindness.
LINC.   I'll his lameness cure.
FIRK. [*Aside to his friends.*] Lie down,
sirs, and laugh! My fellow Rafe is   [160
taken for Rowland Lacy, and Jane for Mis-
tress Damask Rose. This is all my knavery.
L. MAYOR. What, have I found you,
minion?
LINC.   O base wretch!
Nay, hide thy face; the horror of thy
guilt
Can hardly be washed off. Where are
thy powers?
What battles have you made? O, yes,
I see,
Thou fought'st with Shame, and Shame
hath conquered thee.
This lameness will not serve.
L. MAYOR.   Unmask yourself.
LINC. Lead home your daughter.
L. MAYOR.   Take your nephew hence.
RAFE. Hence! 'Swounds, what mean   [170
you? Are you mad? I hope you cannot en-
force my wife from me. Where's Hammon?
L. MAYOR. Your wife?
LINC. What, Hammon?
RAFE. Yea, my wife; and, therefore, the
proudest of you that lays hands on her
first, I'll lay my crutch cross his pate.
FIRK. To him, lame Rafe! Here's brave
sport!
RAFE. Rose call you her? Why,   [180
her name is Jane. Look here else; do you
know her now?   [*Unmasks Jane.*]
LINC. Is this your daughter?
L. MAYOR. No, nor this your nephew.
My Lord of Lincoln, we are both abused
By this base, crafty varlet.
FIRK. Yea, forsooth, no varlet; forsooth,

no base; forsooth, I am but mean;[1] no crafty neither, but of the gentle craft.

L. MAYOR. Where is my daughter Rose? Where is my child?   189

LINC. Where is my nephew Lacy marriéd?

FIRK. Why, here is good laced mutton,[2] as I promised you.

LINC. Villain, I'll have thee punished for this wrong.

FIRK. Punish the journeyman villain, but not the journeyman shoemaker.

Enter Dodger.

DODGER. My lord, I come to bring unwelcome news.

Your nephew Lacy and your daughter Rose
Early this morning wedded at the Savoy,
None being present but the lady mayoress.   199
Besides, I learned among the officers
The lord mayor vows to stand in their defense
Gainst any that shall seek to cross the match.

LINC. Dares Eyre the shoemaker uphold the deed?

FIRK. Yes, sir, shoemakers dare stand in a woman's quarrel, I warrant you, as deep as another, and deeper too.

DODGER. Besides, his grace today dines with the mayor,
Who on his knees humbly intends to fall
And beg a pardon for your nephew's fault.

LINC. But I'll prevent him! Come, Sir Roger Oteley;   210
The king will do us justice in this cause.
Howe'er their hands have made them man and wife,
I will disioin the match, or lose my life.

Exeunt [*Lincoln, Mayor, Dodger, and Servants*].

FIRK. Adieu, Monsieur Dodger! Farewell, fools! Ha, ha! O, if they had stayed, I would have so lammed them with flouts! O heart, my codpiece point is ready to fly in pieces every time I think upon Mistress Rose. But let that pass, as my lady mayoress says.   220

HODGE. This matter is answered. Come, Rafe; home with thy wife. Come, my fine

shoemakers, let's to our master's, the new lord mayor, and there swagger this Shrove Tuesday. I'll promise you wine enough, for Madge keeps the cellar.

ALL. O, rare! Madge is a good wench.

FIRK. And I'll promise you meat enough, for simp'ring Susan keeps the larder. I'll lead you to victuals, my brave sol- [230 diers; follow your captain. O, brave! Hark, hark!   *Bell rings.*

ALL. The pancake bell rings, the pancake bell! Trilill, my hearts!

FIRK. O, brave! O sweet bell! O delicate pancakes! Open the doors, my hearts, and shut up the windows! Keep in the house; let out the pancakes! O, rare, my hearts! Let's march together for the honor of Saint Hugh to the great new hall [240 in Gracious Street corner, which our master, the new lord mayor, hath built.

RAFE. O, the crew of good fellows that will dine at my lord mayor's cost today!

HODGE. By the Lord, my lord mayor is a most brave man. How shall prentices be bound to pray for him and the honor of the gentlemen shoemakers! Let's feed and be fat with my lord's bounty.   249

FIRK. O musical bell, still! O Hodge, O my brethren! There's cheer for the heavens.[3] Ven'son pasties [4] walk up and down piping hot, like serjeants; beef and brewis comes marching in dryfats;[5] fritters and pancakes comes trolling in in wheelbarrows; hens and oranges hopping in porters' baskets, collops[6] and eggs in scuttles;[7] and tarts and custards comes quavering in in malt shovels.

Enter more Prentices.

ALL. Whoop, look here, look here!   259

HODGE. How now, mad lads, whither away so fast?

1 PREN. Whither? Why, to the great new hall, know you not why? The lord mayor hath bidden all the prentices in London to breakfast this morning.

ALL. O brave shoemaker, O brave lord of incomprehensible good-fellowship! Whoo! Hark you! The pancake bell rings.

    Cast up caps.

FIRK. Nay, more, my hearts! Every Shrove Tuesday is our year of jubilee; [270

---

1 *I.e.*, with a tenor, not "bass" voice.
2 Loose woman, with a pun on *Lacy*.
3 Food for the gods.
4 From 1610 edn. Original has *pastimes*.
5 Baskets.   6 Bacon.   7 Platters.

and, when the pancake bell rings, we are as free as my lord mayor; we may shut up our shops, and make holiday. I'll have it called Saint Hugh's Holiday.

ALL. Agreed, agreed! Saint Hugh's Holiday!

HODGE. And this shall continue forever!

ALL. O, brave! Come, come, my hearts. Away, away!

FIRK. O, eternal credit to us of the gentle craft! March fair, my hearts! O rare! [281

Exeunt.

[SCENE xvii.

A street in London.]

Enter King and his Train over the stage.

KING. Is our lord mayor of London such a gallant?

NOBLEMAN. One of the merriest madcaps in your land.

Your grace will think, when you behold the man,

He's rather a wild ruffian than a mayor.

Yet thus much I'll ensure your majesty,

In all his actions that concern his state

He is as serious, provident, and wise,

As full of gravity amongst the grave,

As any mayor hath been these many years.

KING. I am with child [1] till I behold this huffcap.[2] 10

But all my doubt is, when we come in presence,

His madness will be dashed clean out of countenance.

NOBLEMAN. It may be so, my liege.

KING. Which to prevent,

Let someone give him notice, 'tis our pleasure

That he put on his wonted merriment.

Set forward!

ALL. On afore! *Exeunt.*

[SCENE xviii.

A great hall.]

Enter Eyre, Hodge, Firk, Rafe, and other Shoemakers, all with napkins on their shoulders.

EYRE. Come, my fine Hodge, my jolly gentlemen shoemakers! Soft, where be these cannibals, these varlets, my officers?

Let them all walk and wait upon my brethren; for my meaning is that none but shoemakers, none but the livery of my company, shall in their satin hoods wait upon the trencher of my sovereign.

FIRK. O my lord, it will be rare!

EYRE. No more, Firk; come, lively! [10 Let your fellow prentices want no cheer; let wine be plentiful as beer, and beer as water. Hang these penny-pinching fathers, that cram wealth in innocent lambskins.[3] Rip, knaves, avaunt! Look to my guests!

HODGE. My lord, we are at our wits' end for room; those hundred tables will not feast the fourth part of them.

EYRE. Then cover me those hundred tables again, and again, till all my jolly [20 prentices be feasted. Avoid, Hodge! Run, Rafe! Frisk about, my nimble Firk! Carouse me fadom healths [4] to the honor of the shoemakers. Do they drink lively, Hodge? Do they tickle it, Firk?

FIRK. Tickle it? Some of them have taken their liquor standing so long that they can stand no longer; but, for meat, they would eat it and they had it.

EYRE. Want they meat? Where's [30 this swagbelly, this greasy kitchen stuff cook? Call the varlet to me! Want meat? Firk, Hodge, lame Rafe, run, my tall men, beleaguer the shambles,[5] beggar all Eastcheap, serve me whole oxen in chargers,[6] and let sheep whine upon the tables like pigs for want of good fellows to eat them. Want meat? Vanish, Firk! Avaunt, Hodge!

HODGE. Your lordship mistakes my man Firk; he means their bellies want meat, [40 not the boards, for they have drunk so much, they can eat nothing.

THE SECOND THREE-MAN'S SONG[7]

Cold's the wind, and wet's the rain—
Saint Hugh be our good speed.
Ill is the weather that bringeth no gain,
Nor helps good hearts in need.

Troll[8] the bowl, the jolly nut-brown bowl,
And here, kind mate, to thee.
Let's sing a dirge for Saint Hugh's soul,
and down it merrily, 50

[3] Purses.   [5] Slaughter houses.
[4] Fathom-deep healths.   [6] Large platters.
[7] A direction, "This is to be sung at the latter end," suggests the insertion of this song here.
[8] Pass.

[1] Impatient.   [2] Swaggerer.

Down a down, hey down a down,
        (Close with the tenor boy)
Hey derry derry, down a down!
Ho, well done; to me let come!
Ring compass,[1] gentle joy.

Troll the bowl, the nut-brown bowl,
  And here, kind, etc.
      As often as there be men to drink.

    At last, when all have drunk, this verse:

Cold's the wind, and wet's the rain—
  Saint Hugh be our good speed.
Ill is the weather that bringeth no gain,
  Nor helps good hearts in need.   60

    Enter Hans, Rose, and Wife.

WIFE. Where is my lord?

EYRE. How now, Lady Madgy?

WIFE. The king's most excellent majesty is new come; he sends me for thy honor. One of his most worshipful peers bade me tell thou must be merry, and so forth; but let that pass.

EYRE. Is my sovereign come? Vanish, my tall shoemakers, my nimble brethren; look to my guests, the prentices. Yet [70 stay a little! How now, Hans? How looks my little Rose?

HANS. Let me request you to remember me.

I know your honor easily may obtain
Free pardon of the king for me and Rose,
And reconcile me to my uncle's grace.

EYRE. Have done, my good Hans, my honest journeyman; look cheerily! I'll fall upon both my knees, till they be as hard as horn, but I'll get thy pardon.   80

WIFE. Good my lord, have a care what you speak to his grace.

EYRE. Away, you Islington whitepot![2] Hence, you hopper[3]-arse! Hence, you barley pudding, full of maggots! You broiled carbonado![4]   Avaunt, avaunt, avoid, Mephostophilus! Shall Sim Eyre learn to speak of you, Lady Madgy? Vanish, Mother Miniver-cap;[5] vanish, go, trip and go; meddle with your partlets[6] and [90 your pishery-pashery, your flews[7] and your whirligigs; go, rub,[8] out of mine alley!

---

[1] The fullest range of tones possible.
[2] Custard.
[3] Shaped like a hopper.
[4] Steak.
[5] Fur cap.
[6] Ruffs for the neck.
[7] Flaps.
[8] An obstruction in bowling.

Sim Eyre knows how to speak to a pope, to Sultan Soliman, to Tamburlaine, and he were here; and shall I melt, shall I droop before my sovereign? No, come, my Lady Madgy! Follow me, Hans! About your business, my frolic freebooters! Firk, frisk about, and about, and about, for the honor of mad Simon Eyre, lord mayor [100 of London.

FIRK. Hey, for the honor of the shoemakers!   *Exeunt.*

    [SCENE xix.

    An open yard before the hall.]

    A long flourish or two. Enter King, Nobles, Eyre, his Wife, Lacy, Rose. Lacy and Rose kneel.

KING. Well, Lacy, though the fact was very foul
Of your revolting from our kingly love
And your own duty, yet we pardon you.
Rise both, and, Mistress Lacy, thank my lord mayor
For your young bridegroom here.

EYRE. So, my dear liege, Sim Eyre and my brethren, the gentlemen shoemakers, shall set your sweet majesty's image cheek by jowl by Saint Hugh for this honor you have done poor Simon Eyre. I beseech [10 your grace, pardon my rude behavior; I am a handicraftsman, yet my heart is without craft; I would be sorry at my soul that my boldness should offend my king.

KING. Nay, I pray thee, good lord mayor, be even as merry
As if thou wert among thy shoemakers;
It does me good to see thee in this humor.

EYRE. Sayst thou me so, my sweet Dioclesian? Then, hump! Prince am I none, yet am I princely born. By the [20 Lord of Ludgate, my liege, I'll be as merry as a pie.[9]

KING. Tell me, in faith, mad Eyre, how old thou art.

EYRE. My liege, a very boy, a stripling, a younker; you see not a white hair on my head, not a gray in this beard. Every hair, I assure thy majesty, that sticks in this beard, Sim Eyre values at the King of Babylon's ransom; Tamar Cham's beard was a rubbing brush to 't. Yet I'll [30

---

[9] Magpie.

shave it off, and stuff tennis balls with it, to please my bully king.

KING. But all this while I do not know your age.

EYRE. My liege, I am six-and-fifty year old, yet I can cry "hump!" with a sound heart for the honor of Saint Hugh. Mark this old wench, my king; I danced the shaking of the sheets with her six-and-thirty years ago, and yet I hope to get two or three young lord mayors ere I die. [40 I am lusty still, Sim Eyre still. Care and cold lodging brings white hairs. My sweet majesty, let care vanish, cast it upon thy nobles; it will make thee look always young like Apollo, and cry "hump!" Prince am I none, yet am I princely born.

KING. Ha, ha!

Say, Cornwall, didst thou ever see his like?

NOBLEMAN. Not I, my lord.

Enter Lincoln and Lord Mayor.

KING.   Lincoln, what news with you?

LINC. My gracious lord, have care unto yourself,   50
For there are traitors here.

ALL.   Traitors? Where? Who?

EYRE. Traitors in my house? God forbid! Where be my officers? I'll spend my soul, ere my king feel harm.

KING. Where is the traitor, Lincoln?

LINC. [*Pointing to Lacy.*] Here he stands.

KING. Cornwall, lay hold on Lacy!— Lincoln, speak;
What canst thou lay unto thy nephew's charge?

LINC. This, my dear liege: your grace, to do me honor,
Heaped on the head of this degenerous [1] boy   59
Desertless favors; you made choice of him
To be commander over powers in France.
But he—

KING.   Good Lincoln, prithee, pause awhile!
Even in thine eyes I read what thou wouldst speak.
I know how Lacy did neglect our love,
Ran himself deeply, in the highest degree,
Into vile treason—

LINC.   Is he not a traitor?

---

[1] Degenerate.

KING. Lincoln, he was; now have we pardoned him.
'Twas not a base want of true valor's fire
That held him out of France, but love's desire.

LINC. I will not bear his shame upon my back.   70

KING. Nor shalt thou, Lincoln; I forgive you both.

LINC. Then, good my liege, forbid the boy to wed
One whose mean birth will much disgrace his bed.

KING. Are they not married?

LINC.   No, my liege.

BOTH.   We are.

KING. Shall I divorce them then? O, be it far
That any hand on earth should dare untie
The sacred knot, knit by God's majesty;
I would not for my crown disjoin their hands
That are conjoined in holy nuptial bands.
How say'st thou, Lacy, wouldst thou lose thy Rose?   80

HANS. Not for all Indians' wealth, my sovereign.

KING. But Rose, I am sure, her Lacy would forgo?

ROSE. If Rose were asked that question, she'd say no!

KING. You hear them, Lincoln?

LINC.   Yea, my liege, I do.

KING. Yet canst thou find i' th' heart to part these two?
Who seeks, besides you, to divorce these lovers?

L. MAYOR. I do, my gracious lord; I am her father.

KING. Sir Roger Oteley, our last mayor, I think?

NOBLEMAN. The same, my liege.

KING.   Would you offend Love's laws?
Well, you shall have your wills; you sue to me   90
To prohibit the match. Soft, let me see—
You both are married, Lacy, art thou not?

HANS. I am, dread sovereign.

KING.   Then, upon thy life,
I charge thee not to call this woman wife.

L. MAYOR. I thank your grace.

ROSE.   O my most gracious lord!
Kneel.

KING. Nay, Rose, never woo me; I tell you
  true,
  Although as yet I am a bachelor,
  Yet I believe I shall not marry you.

ROSE. Can you divide the body from the
  soul,   99
  Yet make the body live?

KING.   Yea, so profound?
  I cannot, Rose, but you I must divide.
  Fair maid, this bridegroom cannot be
  your bride.[1]—
  Are you pleased, Lincoln? Oteley, are
  you pleased?

BOTH. Yes, my lord.

KING.   Then must my heart be eased;
  For, credit me, my conscience lives in
  pain,
  Till these whom I divorced be joined
  again.
  Lacy, give me thy hand; Rose, lend me
  thine!
  Be what you would be! Kiss now! So,
  that's fine.   108
  At night, lovers, to bed!—Now let me see
  Which of you all mislikes this harmony.

L. MAYOR. Will you then take from me
  my child perforce?

KING. Why, tell me, Oteley, shines not
  Lacy's name
  As bright in the world's eye as the gay
  beams
  Of any citizen?

LINC.   Yea, but, my gracious lord,
  I do mislike the match far more than he;
  Her blood is too-too base.

KING.   Lincoln, no more.
  Dost thou not know that love respects
  no blood,
  Cares not for difference of birth or state?
  The maid is young, well born, fair, virtu-
  ous,
  A worthy bride for any gentleman.   120
  Besides, your nephew for her sake did
  stoop
  To bear necessity, and, as I hear,
  Forgetting honors and all courtly pleas-
  ures,
  To gain her love became a shoemaker.
  As for the honor which he lost in France,
  Thus I redeem it: Lacy, kneel thee
  down!—

[1] Used of both sexes.

Arise, Sir Rowland Lacy! Tell me now,
  Tell me in earnest, Oteley, canst thou
  chide,
  Seeing thy Rose a lady and a bride?

L. MAYOR. I am content with what your
  grace hath done.   130

LINC. And I, my liege, since there's no
  remedy.

KING. Come on, then, all shake hands.
  I'll have you friends;
  Where there is much love, all discord
  ends.
  What says my mad lord mayor to all
  this love?

EYRE. O my liege, this honor you have
  done to my fine journeyman here, Rowland
  Lacy, and all these favors which you have
  shown to me this day in my poor house
  will make Simon Eyre live longer by one
  dozen of warm summers more than he
  should.   141

KING. Nay, my mad lord mayor, that shall
  be thy name;
  If any grace of mine can length thy life,
  One honor more I'll do thee: that new
  building,
  Which at thy cost in Cornhill is erected,
  Shall take a name from us; we'll have it
  called
  The Leadenhall, because in digging it
  You found the lead that covereth the
  same.

EYRE. I thank your majesty.

WIFE.   God bless your grace!

KING. Lincoln, a word with you!   150

*Enter Hodge, Firk, Rafe, and more Shoe-
  makers.*

EYRE. How now, my mad knaves?
Peace, speak softly; yonder is the king.

KING. With the old troop which there we
  keep in pay,
  We will incorporate a new supply.
  Before one summer more pass o'er my
  head,
  France shall repent England was injuréd.
  What are all those?

HANS.   All shoemakers, my liege,
  Sometimes my fellows; in their com-
  panies
  I lived as merry as an emperor.

KING. My mad lord mayor, are all these
  shoemakers?   160

EYRE. All shoemakers, my liege; all

gentlemen of the gentle craft, true Trojans, courageous cordwainers; they all kneel to the shrine of holy Saint Hugh.

ALL. God save your majesty, all shoemaker[s]!

KING. Mad Simon, would they anything with us?

EYRE. Mum, mad knaves! Not a word! I'll do 't; I warrant you. They are all beggars, my liege; all for themselves, [170 and I for them all, on both my knees do entreat that, for the honor of poor Simon Eyre and the good of his brethren, these mad knaves, your grace would vouchsafe some privilege to my new Leadenhall, that it may be lawful for us to buy and sell leather there two days a week.

KING. Mad Sim, I grant your suit; you shall have patent
To hold two market days in Leadenhall, Mondays and Fridays—those shall be the times.   180
Will this content you?

ALL.   Jesus bless your grace!

EYRE. In the name of these my poor brethren shoemakers, I most humbly thank your grace. But, before I rise, seeing you are in the giving vein and we in the begging, grant Sim Eyre one boon more.

KING. What is it, my lord mayor?

EYRE. Vouchsafe to taste of a poor banquet that stands sweetly waiting for your sweet presence.   190

KING. I shall undo thee, Eyre, only with feasts;
Already have I been too troublesome.
Say, have I not?

EYRE. O my dear king, Sim Eyre was taken unawares upon a day of shroving [1] which I promised long ago to the prentices of London.

For, and 't please your highness, in time past,   198
I bare the water tankard,[2] and my coat Sits not a whit the worse upon my back; And then, upon a morning, some mad boys
(It was Shrove Tuesday, even as 'tis now) gave me my breakfast, and I swore then by the stopple of my tankard, if ever I came to be lord mayor of London, I would feast all the prentices. This day, my liege, I did it, and the slaves had an hundred tables five times covered. They are gone home and vanished.   209
Yet add more honor to the gentle trade; Taste of Eyre's banquet, Simon's happy made.

KING. Eyre, I will taste of thy banquet, and will say
I have not met more pleasure on a day. Friends of the gentle craft, thanks to you all;
Thanks, my kind lady mayoress, for our cheer.—
Come, lords, awhile let's revel it at home! When all our sports and banquetings are done,
Wars must right wrongs which Frenchmen have begun.   *Exeunt.*

FINIS.

[1] Merrymaking.   [2] As an apprentice.

THOMAS DEKKER

THE HONEST WHORE, PART I

Peter Ure regards *The Honest Whore* as one of the first signs of a new era in taste and morals in English drama, although Louis B. Wright in his *Middle-Class Culture in Elizabethan England* (London, 1958) has censured such works because they "sentimentalize vice and mock the virtues of respectable citizens," and L. C. Knights has objected to them because they are examples of "completely generalized conventionality" (*Drama and Society in the Age of Jonson*, London, 1937). The theme of the conversion and reform of a courtesan has always been a favorite one with dramatists, but Dekker has given it an original turn by having the beautiful but hardened fifteen-year-old prostitute Bellafront (which is of course a "humors" name meaning "beautiful face," just as Infelice means "unhappy" or "unfortunate" and Candido means "white," "innocent," or "sincere") rejected by the priggish Hippolito, the unwitting agent of her reform. The character of Candido, the meek but inflexible linen-draper, is a complex and paradoxical one. On the one hand, like most humors characters, he is expected to be laughed at because of his obsessive one-sidedness, but on the other there is a Christlike aspect to his turn-the-other-cheek behavior which actually brings about salutary reforms at the end of the play, even though, as Ure puts it, "The mirror of patience finds himself temporarily in Bedlam, the mirror of all impatience." There is also a vein of Puritanism in Candido's character, which is discussed by Mary J. M. Adkins in her *Puritanism in the Plays and Pamphlets of Thomas Dekker* (*UTSE*, 1939). The source of the plots and characters has never been discovered. It is probable that the plays are compounded of characters whom Dekker and Middleton had known on the London streets, along with imagination and the use of some conventional motifs, especially in the story of Hippolito. The distribution of prose and verse follows customary patterns, but the verse is marked by an unusual number of rhymed couplets.

Between the writing of the essentially fresh and good-natured plays like *The Shoemakers' Holiday*, *Old Fortunatus*, and *Patient Grissel*, and of the two parts of *The Honest Whore* and later works, a sudden change took place in Dekker's attitude toward life. Steane noticed the emergence in his plays of a more critical, complaining, and disillusioned attitude as disclosed in his treatment of the kindly relations between masters and employees in *The Shoemakers' Holiday* and his classification of the same relationship in *The Seven Deadly Sins* under the heading of "Cruelty." A clue to this change has been found by some scholars in Henslowe's entry in his diary of advances of £5 between January and March 1604 to Dekker and Middleton for their work on a play about "the pasyent man & the onest hore." In "Patient Madman and Honest Whore," Peter Ure discusses this new phase and Middleton's possible influence on it: "One version would seem to cast Middleton for a kind of villain of the piece. Before he came Dekker had written about the city in a kindly and wholesome manner; . . . then, under the malign influence of Middleton, Dekker developed what T. M. Parrott described as 'a partiality for questionable scenes and characters [i.e., brothels, bawds, and whores] and a general moral laxness, happily absent in the earlier plays'" (Ure quotes Parrott in *The Comedies of George Chapman*, London, 1914). Pointing out the difficulty of dating the various city plays by the two men between 1602 and 1606, Ure remarks that it is hard to say who infected whom, and suggests that if Dekker instead of Middleton was really the author of *Blurt, Master Constable*, as many now suppose, then it may well have been Dekker who started the vogue of courtesan scenes early in the seventeenth century (see D. B. Dodson, *"Blurt, Master Constable," NQ,* 1959). Nevertheless, in spite of Samuel Schoenbaum's rejection of any essential contribution by Middleton to *The Honest Whore* beyond a possible proposal of some ideas to Part I ("Middleton's Share in *The Honest Whore,* Parts I and II," *NQ,* 1952) and in spite of the absence of Middleton's name on the title page, Fredson T. Bowers in his edition of Dekker's plays in 1955 accepted Middleton as a secondary author of Part I, and his opinion represents the consensus of most scholars. Like many sequels written to take advantage of the success of the initial production, Part II of *The Honest Whore* introduced several unexpected reversals in situation and characters. Because of the reversals of the characters of Hippolito, who now becomes the tempter and potential seducer, and Candido, who at last loses his patience and threatens to strike his wife, Ure remarks that "it looks as though Dekker in the Second Part must have been botching the continuation of what was originally a Middleton idea." Nevertheless, this play—judged by itself and not in its relationship to its predecessor—represents a challenging attempt to deal with a significant social problem, which is voiced by most observers of the situation as "Once a whore, always a whore." Madeleine Doran in *Endeavors of Art* (University of Wisconsin Press, 1964) has suggested that the success of the patient prostitute (now reformed) has redeemed the play: "She has changed places, thematically, with the old Hippolito. Nothing illustrates more clearly the purely functional character of his role than the inability of her rhetoric to convert him. . . . By keeping alive the theme of Patience she partially saves the unity of the double-play." One of Dekker's favorite themes, as shown in this double-play and *Patient Grissel,* was patience as it affected and shaped both men and women.

Part I of *The Honest Whore* was printed by Valentine Sims in 1604 (other editions followed in 1605, 1615, 1616, and 1635), and was performed later in the year by the Henslowe-Alleyn company (known then as Prince Henry's Men rather than the earlier Admiral's Men), presumably at the Fortune playhouse. The present text is based on the John Pearson reprint of the quarto of 1605. Part II of *The Honest Whore* (not reprinted here) was not published by Elizabeth Allde until 1630 but was probably acted in 1605, shortly after Part I.

THE HONEST[1] WHORE[2]

[PART 1]

BY

THOMAS DEKKER

[*DRAMATIS PERSONÆ*

GASPARO TREBAZZI, *Duke of Milan.*
HIPPOLITO, *a count.*
CASTRUCHIO ⎫
SINEZI ⎪
PIORATTO ⎬ *gallants.*
FLUELLO ⎪
MATHEO ⎭
BENEDICT, *a doctor.*
ANSELMO, *a friar.*
FUSTIGO, *brother of Viola.*
CANDIDO, *a linen draper.*
GEORGE, *his servant.*
FIRST PRENTICE.

SECOND PRENTICE.
CRAMBO ⎫
POLI *or* POH ⎬ *ruffians.*
ROGER, *servant of Bellafront.*
PORTER.
SWEEPER.
MADMEN, SERVANTS, ETC.

INFELICE, *daughter of the Duke.*
BELLAFRONT, *a whore.*
VIOLA, *wife of Candido.*
MISTRESS FINGERLOCK, *a bawd.*

SCENE: *Milan and the neighborhood.*

TIME: *Contemporary.*]

SCENA i.[3]

[*A street in Milan.*]

*Enter at one door a funeral (a coronet lying on
the hearse, scutcheons and garlands hanging on the sides), attended by Gasparo
Trebazzi, Duke of Milan, Castruchio,
Sinezi, Pioratto, Fluello, and Others.
At another door enter Hippolito, in discontented appearance, Matheo, a gentleman, his friend, laboring to hold him
back.*

DUKE. Behold, yon comet shows his head
again!
  Twice hath he thus at cross turns[4]
  thrown on us

Prodigious[5] looks; twice hath he troubled
The waters of our eyes. See, he's turned
  wild!
Go on, in God's name.
ALL.   On afore there, ho!
DUKE. Kinsmen and friends, take from
  your manly sides
Your weapons to keep back the desperate
  boy
From doing violence to the innocent
  dead.
HIP. I prithee, dear Matheo—
MAT.   Come, y'are mad!
HIP. I do arrest thee, murderer! Set down,
  Villains, set down that sorrow; 'tis all
  mine.   11
DUKE. I do beseech you all, for my blood's
  sake
Send hence your milder spirits, and let
  wrath
Join in confederacy with your weapons'
  points;

---

[1] Chaste.
[2] The title of the first edn. continues: "With
the Humors of the Patient Man and the Longing Wife."
[3] Original reads *Actus Primus, Scena Prima,*
but from this point on, the play is not divided
into acts, although some scene divisions are indicated.
[4] Street crossings.
[5] Portentous.

If he proceed to vex us, let your swords
Seek out his bowels. Funeral grief loathes
　words.

ALL. Set on!

HIP. 　　　　　Set down the body!

MAT. 　　　　　　　　　　　O my lord!
Y'are wrong! I' th' open street? You see
　she's dead.

HIP. I know she is not dead.

DUKE. 　　　　　　　　Frantic young man,
Wilt thou believe these gentlemen? Pray
　speak. 　　　　　　　　　　　　20
Thou dost abuse my child, and mock'st
　the tears
That here are shed for her. If to behold
Those roses withered that set out her
　cheeks;
That pair of stars that gave her body light,
Darkened and dim forever; all those
　rivers
That fed her veins with warm and crim-
　son streams
Frozen and dried up—if these be signs of
　death,
Then is she dead. 　Thou unreligious
　youth,
Art not ashamed to empty all these eyes
Of funeral tears, a debt due to the
　dead, 　　　　　　　　　　　30
As mirth is to the living? Sham'st thou
　not
To have them stare on thee? Hark, thou
　art cursed
Even to thy face, by those that scarce
　can speak.

HIP. My lord—

DUKE. 　　　　　What wouldst thou have?
　Is she not dead?

HIP. O, you ha' killed her by your cruelty!

DUKE. Admit I had, thou kill'st her now
　again,
And art more savage than a barbarous
　Moor.

HIP. Let me but kiss her pale and bloodless
　lip.

DUKE. O fie, fie, fie!

HIP. Or, if not touch her, let me look on
　her. 　　　　　　　　　　　　40

MAT. As you regard your honor—

HIP. 　　　　　　　　Honor? Smoke!

MAT. Or, if you loved her living, spare her
　now.

DUKE. Ay, well done, sir; you play the
　gentleman.—

Steal hence.—'Tis nobly done.—Away!
　—I'll join
My force to yours to stop this violent
　torment.—
Pass on.

Exeunt with funeral [all except the Duke,
　　　　　　Hippolito, and Matheo].

HIP. 　　　　Matheo, thou dost wound me
　more.

MAT. I give you physic, noble friend, not
　wounds.

DUKE. O, well said, well done, a true
　gentleman!
Alack, I know the sea of lovers' rage
Comes rushing with so strong a tide, it
　beats 　　　　　　　　　　　50
And bears down all respects of life, of
　honor,
Of friends, of foes. Forget 'her, gallant
　youth.

HIP. Forget her?

DUKE. 　　　　Nay, nay, be but patient,
Forwhy [1] death's hand hath sued a strict
　divorce
Twixt her and thee. What's beauty but a
　corse?
What but fair sand-dust are earth's pur-
　est forms?
Queen's bodies are but trunks to put in
　worms.

MAT. Speak no more sentences,[2] my
good lord, but slip hence; you see they are
but fits. I'll rule him, I warrant ye. 　[60
Ay, so, tread gingerly; your grace is here
somewhat too long already. [*Exit Duke.*
Aside.] 'Sblood,[3] the jest were now, if
having ta'en some knocks o' th' pate already, he should get loose again, and, like
a mad ox, toss my new black cloaks into
the kennel.[4] I must humor his lordship.—
My Lord Hippolito, is it in your stomach
to go to dinner?

HIP. Where is the body? 　　　　70

MAT. The body, as the duke spake very
wisely, is gone to be wormed.

HIP. I cannot rest; I'll meet it at next
turn. I'll see how my love looks.

　　　　Matheo holds him in 's arms.

MAT. How your love looks? Worse than

---

[1] Because. 　　　　　　[2] Sententious sayings.
[3] God's blood. 　*Cf.* other mild oaths in this
play, such as '*Sfoot,* '*Swounds,* '*Snails, Ud's life,*
Godso.
[4] Channel, gutter.

a scarecrow. Wrastle not with me; the great fellow gives the fall for a ducat.

HIP. I shall forget myself.

MAT. Pray, do so; leave yourself behind yourself, and go whither you will. [80 'Sfoot, do you long to have base rogues that maintain a Saint Anthony's fire in their noses by nothing but twopenny ale, make ballads of you? If the duke had but so much mettle in him as is in a cobbler's awl, he would ha' been a vexed thing. He and his train had blown you up but that their powder has taken the wet of cowards. You'll bleed three pottles of Alicant,[1] by this light, if you follow 'em, and then [90 we shall have a hole made in a wrong place, to have surgeons roll thee up like a baby in swaddling clouts.

HIP. What day is today, Matheo?

MAT. Yea, marry, this is an easy question. Why, today is—let me see—Thursday.

HIP. O, Thursday!

MAT. Here's a coil [2] for a dead commodity. 'Sfoot, women when they are [100 alive are but dead commodities, for you shall have one woman lie upon many men's hands.

HIP. She died on Monday then.

MAT. And that's the most villainous day of all the week to die in. And she was well, and eat a mess of water gruel on Monday morning.

HIP. Ay? It cannot be
Such a bright taper should burn out so
soon.   110

MAT. O yes, my lord. So soon? Why, I ha' known them that at dinner have been as well, and had so much health that they were glad to pledge it, yet before three a-clock have been found dead—drunk.

HIP. On Thursday buried! And on Monday died!
Quick haste, by'r Lady. Sure her winding
sheet
Was laid out fore her body, and the
worms
That now must feast with her were even
bespoke,
And solemnly invited like strange
guests.   120

MAT. Strange feeders they are indeed,

my lord, and, like your jester or young courtier, will enter upon any man's trencher without bidding.

HIP. Cursed be that day forever that
robbed her
Of breath, and me of bliss! Henceforth
let it stand
Within the wizard's book (the calendar)
Marked with a marginal finger, to be
chosen
By thieves, by villains, and black mur-
derers,
As the best day for them to labor in. 130
If henceforth this adulterous, bawdy
world
Be got with child with treason, sacrilege,
Atheism, rapes, treacherous friendship,
perjury,
Slander (the beggar's sin), lies (sin of
fools),
Or any other damned impieties,
On Monday let 'em be deliveréd.
I swear to thee, Matheo, by my soul,
Hereafter weekly on that day I'll glue
Mine eyelids down, because they shall
not gaze
On any female cheek. And, being locked
up   140
In my close [3] chamber, there I'll meditate
On nothing but my Infelice's end,
Or on a dead man's skull draw out mine
own.

MAT. You'll do all these good works now every Monday, because it is so bad; but I hope upon Tuesday morning I shall take you with a wench.

HIP. If ever, whilst frail blood through
my veins run,
On woman's beams I throw affection,
Save her that's dead, or that I loosely
fly   150
To th' shore of any other wafting eye,
Let me not prosper, Heaven! I will be
true
Even to her dust and ashes. Could her
tomb
Stand whilst I lived, so long that it
might rot,
That should fall down, but she be ne'er
forgot.

MAT. If you have this strange monster, honesty,[4] in your belly, why, so jig- [5] makers and chroniclers shall pick something

[1] Six quarts of Spanish wine.
[2] Disturbance.
[3] Private.   [4] Chastity.   [5] Ballad.

out of you; but, and [1] I smell not you and a bawdyhouse out within these ten [160 days, let my nose be as big as an English bag pudding. I'll follow your lordship, though it be to the place aforenamed.

Exeunt.

[SCENA ii.

Another street.]

Enter Fustigo in some fantastic sea suit at one door; a Porter meets him at another.

FUS. How now, porter, will she come?

POR. If I may trust a woman, sir, she will come.

FUS. There's for thy ·pains. [*Gives money.*] God-a-mercy,[2] if I ever stand in need of a wench that will come with a wet finger,[3] porter, thou shalt earn my money before any clarissimo [4] in Milan; yet, so God sa' me, she's mine own sister, body and soul, as I am a Christian gentleman. Farewell; I'll ponder till she come. Thou [11 hast been no bawd in fetching this woman, I assure thee.

POR. No matter if I had, sir; better men than porters are bawds.

FUS. O God, sir, many that have borne offices. But, porter, art sure thou went'st into a true [5] house?

POR. I think so, for I met with no thieves.   20

FUS. Nay, but art sure it was my sister Viola?

POR. I am sure, by all superscriptions, it was the party you ciphered.[6]

FUS. Not very tall?

POR. Nor very low; a middling woman.

FUS. 'Twas she, faith, 'twas she. A pretty plump cheek, like mine?

POR. At a blush,[7] a little very much like you.   30

FUS. Godso, I would not for a ducat she had kicked up her heels, for I ha' spent an abomination this voyage; marry, I did it amongst sailors and gentlemen. There's a little modicum more, porter, for making thee stay. [*Gives money.*] Farewell, honest porter.

POR. I am in your debt, sir; God preserve you.   *Exit.*

[1] If.
[2] Thank you.
[3] Promptly.
[4] Grandee.
[5] Respectable.
[6] Described.
[7] Glance.

Enter Viola.

FUS. Not so neither, good porter. God's lid, yonder she comes.—Sister Viola, I [41 am glad to see you stirring. It's news to have me here, is't not, sister?

VIO. Yes, trust me. I wondered who should be so bold to send for me. You're welcome to Milan, brother.

FUS. Troth, sister, I heard you were married to a very rich chuff,[8] and I was very sorry for it that I had no better clothes, and that made me send; for you know we Milaners love to strut upon Span- [51 ish leather. And how does all our friends?

VIO. Very well. You ha' traveled enough now, I trow, to sow your wild oats.

FUS. A pox on 'em! Wild oats? I ha' not an oat to throw at a horse. Troth, sister, I ha' sowed my oats, and reaped two hundred ducats—if I had 'em here. Marry, I must entreat you to lend me some thirty or forty till the ship come. By this hand, I'll ˙discharge at my day, by [61 this hand.[9]

VIO. These are your old oaths.

FUS. Why, sister, do you think I'll forswear my hand?

VIO. Well, well, you shall have them. Put yourself into better fashion, because I must employ you in a serious matter.

FUS. I'll sweat like a horse if I like the matter.   [70

VIO. You ha' cast off all your old swaggering humors?

FUS. I had not sailed a league in that great fishpond, the sea, but I cast up my very gall.

VIO. I am the more sorry, for I must employ a true swaggerer.

FUS. Nay, by this iron, sister, they shall find I am powder and touch-box[10] if they put fire once into me.   80

VIO. Then lend me your ears.

FUS. Mine ears are yours, dear sister.

VIO. I am married to a man that has wealth enough, and wit enough.

FUS. A linen draper, I was told, sister.

VIO. Very true, a grave citizen; I want nothing that a wife can wish from a husband. But here's the spite[11]—he has not all things belonging to a man.

[8] Old miser.   [9] Violate my signature.
[10] A box containing powder for priming a fire-arm.
[11] Vexation.

Fus. God's my life, he's a very mandrake,[1] or else, God bless us, one a [2] [91 these whiblins,[3] and that's worse, and then all the children that he gets lawfully of your body, sister, are bastards by a statute.

Vio. O, you run over me too fast, brother. I have heard it often said that he who cannot be angry is no man. I am sure my husband is a man in print,[4] for all things else save only in this: no tempest can move him.   100

Fus. 'Slid, would he had been at sea with us! He should ha' been moved, and moved again, for I'll be sworn, la, our drunken ship reeled like a Dutchman.

Vio. No loss of goods can increase in him a wrinkle; no crabbed language make his countenance sour; the stubbornness of no servant shake him. He has no more gall in him than a dove, no more sting than an ant. Musician will he never be, yet I find much music in him; but he loves no [111 frets,[5] and is so free from anger that many times I am ready to bite off my tongue, because it wants that virtue which all women's tongues have, to anger their husbands. Brother, mine can by no thunder turn him into a sharpness.

Fus. Belike his blood, sister, is well brewed then.

Vio. I protest to thee, Fustigo, I love him most affectionately; but I know not— [121 I ha' such a tickling within me—such a strange longing; nay, verily I do long.

Fus. Then y'are with child, sister, by all signs and tokens; nay, I am partly a physician, and partly something else. I ha' read Albertus Magnus and Aristotle's Emblems.

Vio. Y'are wide a th' bow hand [6] still, brother; my longings are not wanton, but wayward. I long to have my patient [131 husband eat up a whole porcupine, to the intent the bristling quills may stick about his lips like a Flemish mustacho, and be shot at me. I shall be leaner than the new moon unless I can make him horn-mad.[7]

Fus. 'Sfoot, half a quarter of an hour does that: make him a cuckold.

Vio. Pooh, he would count such a cut no unkindness.

Fus. The honester citizen he. Then [141 make him drunk and cut off his beard.

Vio. Fie, fie, idle,[8] idle! He's no Frenchman, to fret at the loss of a little scald [9] hair. No, brother, thus it shall be—you must be secret.

Fus. As your midwife, I protest, sister, or a barber-surgeon.

Vio. Repair to the Tortoise here in St. Christopher's Street. I will send you money; turn yourself into a brave [10] [151 man. Instead of the arms of your mistress, let your sword and your military scarf hang about your neck.

Fus. I must have a great horseman's French feather too, sister.

Vio. O, by any means, to show your light head, else your hat will sit like a coxcomb. To be brief, you must be in all points a most terrible wide-mouthed swaggerer.   161

Fus. Nay, for swaggering points let me alone.

Vio. Resort then to our shop, and, in my husband's presence, kiss me, snatch rings, jewels, or anything, so you give it back again, brother, in secret.

Fus. By this hand, sister.

Vio. Swear as if you came but new from knighting.   170

Fus. Nay, I'll swear after [11] four hundred a year.

Vio. Swagger worse than a lievetenant [12] among freshwater soldiers; [13] call me your love, your ingle,[14] your cousin, or so—but sister at no hand.

Fus. No, no, it shall be cousin, or rather coz; that's the gulling word between the citizens' wives and their madcaps that man [15] 'em to the Garden.[16] To call you one a mine "aunts," sister, were as good [181 as call you arrant whore; no, no, let me alone to "cousin" you rarely.

Vio. H'as heard I have a brother, but

<hr/>

[1] The root of this plant was supposed to resemble the human figure.
  [2] Of.   [3] Weak, impotent creatures.
[4] To the letter, exactly; with a pun.
  [5] A common pun with reference to the frets of a stringed instrument.   [6] Wide of the mark.
  [7] Stark mad; with a pun on the "horns" of a cuckold.

[8] Foolish.   [11] According to an income of.
[9] Scurfy.   [12] Lieutenant.
[10] Richly dressed.
[13] Soldiers who had never crossed the sea.
[14] Darling.   [16] Presumably Paris Garden.
[15] Accompany.

never saw him; therefore put on a good face.

Fus. The best in Milan, I warrant.

Vio. Take up wares, but pay nothing; rifle my bosom, my pocket, my purse, the boxes for money to dice withal; but, brother, you must give all back again [191 in secret.

Fus. By this welkin that here roars I will, or else let me never know what a secret is. Why, sister, do you think I'll cunny-catch[1] you, when you are my cousin? God's my life, then I were a stark ass. If I fret not his guts, beg me for a fool.[2]

Vio. Be circumspect, and do so then. Farewell.   200

Fus. The Tortoise, sister? I'll stay there. Forty ducats!   *Exit.*

Vio. Thither I'll send.—This law can none deny:
Women must have their longings, or they die.   *Exit.*

[Scena iii.

A room in the Duke's palace.]

*Gasparo the Duke, Doctor Benedict, two
Servants.*

Duke. Give charge that none do enter; lock the doors.
And, fellows, what your eyes and ears receive,
Upon your lives trust not the gadding air
To carry the least part of it. The glass, The hourglass!

Doc.   Here, my lord.

Duke.   Ah, 'tis near[3] spent![4]
But, Doctor Benedict, does your art speak truth?
Art sure the soporiferous stream will ebb,
And leave the crystal banks of her white body
Pure as they were at first, just at the hour?

[1] Cheat.
[2] Beg the king for the custody of me as an idiot.
[3] Emended by Dyce. Original reads *meere*.
[4] The line division here and in a few later passages has been regularized. A few passages printed as prose in the original have also been changed to verse.

Doc. Just at the hour, my lord.

Duke.   Uncurtain her!   10

[*A curtain is drawn back, revealing Infelice
lying on a couch.*]

Softly!—See, doctor, what a coldish heat
Spreads over all her body!

Doc.   Now it works.
The vital spirits that by a sleepy charm
Were bound up fast, and threw an icy rust[5]
On her exterior parts, now gin[6] to break.
Trouble her not, my lord.

Duke.   Some stools! You called
For music, did you not? O ho, it speaks!
[*Music.*]
It speaks! Watch, sirs, her waking; note those sands.
Doctor, sit down. A dukedom that should weigh
Mine own down twice, being put into one scale,   20
And that fond[7] desperate boy, Hippolito,
Making the weight up, should not at my hands
Buy her i' th' tother[8] were her state more light
Than hers who makes a dowry up with alms.
Doctor, I'll starve her on the Apennine
Ere he shall marry her. I must confess
Hippolito is nobly born, a man—
Did not mine enemies' blood boil in his veins—
Whom I would court to be my son-in-law;
But princes, whose high spleens for empery[9] swell,   30
Are not with easy art made parallel.

2 Ser. She wakes, my lord.

Duke.   Look, Doctor Benedict.—
I charge you, on your lives, maintain for truth
Whate'er the doctor or myself aver,
For you shall bear her hence to Bergamo.

Inf. [*Waking.*] O God, what fearful dreams!

Doc.   Lady.

[5] Coating.
[6] Begin.
[7] Foolish.
[8] Other.
[9] Sovereignty.

INF.   Ha!

DUKE.   Girl.

Why, Infelice, how is't now, ha? Speak.

INF. I'm well. What makes[1] this doctor here? I'm well.

DUKE. Thou wert not so even now; sickness' pale hand

Laid hold on thee even in the midst of feasting;   40

And, when a cup crowned with thy lover's health

Had touched thy lips, a sensible, cold dew

Stood on thy cheeks, as if that death had wept

To see such beauty alter.

INF.   I remember

I sate at banquet, but felt no such change.

DUKE. Thou hast forgotten, then, how a messenger

Came wildly in, with this unsavory news,

That he was dead?

INF.   What messenger? Who's dead?

DUKE. Hippolito. Alack, wring not thy hands.

INF. I saw no messenger, heard no such news.   50

Doc. Trust me, you did, sweet lady.

DUKE.   La[2] you now!

2 SER. Yes, indeed, madam.

DUKE.   La you now!—[Aside.]

'Tis well, good knaves!

INF. You ha' slain him, and now you'll murder me.

DUKE. Good Infelice, vex not thus thyself.

Of this the bad report before did strike

So coldly to thy heart that the swift currents

Of life were all frozen up.

INF.   It is untrue,

'Tis most untrue, O most unnatural father!

DUKE. And we had much to do by art's best cunning

To fetch life back again.

Doc.   Most certain, lady.   60

DUKE. Why, la you now, you'll not believe me. Friends,

Sweat we not all? Had we not much to do?

1 Does.   2 Look.

2 SER. Yes, indeed, my lord, much.

DUKE. Death drew such fearful pictures in thy face

That, were Hippolito alive again,

I'd kneel and woo the noble gentleman

To be thy husband. Now I sore repent

My sharpness to him and his family.

Nay, do not weep for him; we all must die.—

Doctor, this place where she so oft hath seen   70

His lively presence, hurts her, does it not?

Doc. Doubtless, my lord, it does.

DUKE.   It does, it does!

Therefore, sweet girl, thou shalt to Bergamo.

INF. Even where you will; in any place there's woe.

DUKE. A coach is ready. Bergamo doth stand

In a most wholesome air—sweet walks—there's deer.

Ay, thou shalt hunt and send us venison,

Which, like some goddess in the Cyprian groves,

Thine own fair hand shall strike.—Sirs, you shall teach her

To stand, and how to shoot; ay, she shall hunt.   80

Cast off this sorrow. In, girl, and prepare

This night to ride away to Bergamo.

INF. O, most unhappy maid!   Exit.

DUKE.   Follow her close.

No words that she was buried, on your lives,

Or that her ghost walks now after she's dead.

I'll hang you if you name a funeral.

1 SER. I'll speak Greek, my lord, ere I speak that deadly word.

2 SER. And I'll speak Welsh, which [89 is harder than Greek.   Exeunt [Servants].

DUKE. Away, look to her.—Doctor Benedict,

Did you observe how her complexion altered

Upon his name and death? O, would 'twere true.

Doc. It may, my lord.

DUKE.   May! How? I wish his death.

Doc. And you may have your wish: say but the word,

And 'tis a strong spell to rip up his
grave.
I have good knowledge with Hippolito;
He calls me friend. I'll creep into his
bosom,
And sting him there to death; poison
can do 't.

DUKE. Perform it; I'll create thee half
mine heir. 100

DOC. It shall be done, although the fact [1]
be foul.

DUKE. Greatness hides sin; the guilt upon
my soul! *Exeunt.*

[SCENA iv.

A street.]

Enter Castruchio, Pioratto, and Fluello.

CAS. Signior Pioratto, Signior Fluello,
shall 's be merry? Shall 's play the wags
now?

FLU. Ay, anything that may beget the
child of laughter.

CAS. Truth, I have a pretty sportive
conceit [2] new crept into my brain, will
move excellent mirth.

PIO. Let's ha't, let's ha't. And where
shall the scene of mirth lie? 10

CAS. At Signior Candido's house, the
patient man, nay, the monstrous patient
man. They say his blood is immovable,
that he has taken all patience from a man,
and all constancy from a woman.

FLU. That makes so many whores nowadays.

CAS. Ay, and so many knaves too.

PIO. Well, sir.

CAS. To conclude, the report goes, [20
he's so mild, so affable, so suffering, that
nothing indeed can move him. Now do
but think what sport it will be to make
this fellow, the mirror of patience, as angry,
as vexed, and as mad as an English cuckold.

FLU. O, 'twere admirable mirth, that.
But how will 't be done, signior?

CAS. Let me alone; I have a trick, a
conceit, a thing, a device will sting [30
him, i' faith, if he have but a thimbleful of
blood in 's belly, or a spleen not so big as
a tavern token.[3]

PIO. Thou stir him? Thou move him?
Thou anger him? Alas, I know his approved [4] temper. Thou vex him? Why,
he has a patience above man's injuries.
Thou mayst sooner raise a spleen in an
angel than rough humor in him. Why,
I'll give you instance for it. This won- [40
derfully tempered Signior Candido upon a
time invited home to his house certain
Neapolitan lords, of curious [5] taste and
no mean palates, conjuring his wife, of all
loves,[6] to prepare cheer fitting for such
honorable trenchermen. She—just of a
woman's nature, covetous to try the uttermost of vexation, and thinking at last to
get the start of his humor—willingly neglected the preparation, and became [50
unfurnished not only of dainty but of ordinary dishes. He, according to the mildness of his breast, entertained the lords,
and with courtly discourse beguiled the
time, as much as a citizen might do. To
conclude, they were hungry lords, for
there came no meat in; their stomachs
were plainly gulled, and their teeth deluded, and, if anger could have seized a
man, there was matter enough, i' faith, [60
to vex any citizen in the world, if he were
not too much made a fool by his wife.

FLU. Ay, I'll swear for 't. 'Sfoot, had
it been my case, I should ha' played mad
tricks with my wife and family. First, I
would ha' spitted the men, stewed the
maids, and baked the mistress, and so
served them in.

PIO. Why, 't would ha' tempted any
blood but his.
And thou to vex him? Thou to anger
him 70
With some poor, shallow jest?

CAS. 'Sblood, Signior Pioratto, you that
disparage my conceit, I'll wage a hundred
ducats upon the head on 't that it moves
him, frets him, and galls him.

PIO. Done! 'Tis a lay;[7] join golls [8] on 't.
Witness, Signior Fluello.

CAS. Witness; 'tis done.
Come, follow me. The house is not far off.
I'll thrust him from his humor, vex his
breast, 80
And win a hundred ducats by one
jest. *Exeunt.*

---

[1] Deed.
[2] Idea.
[3] Small metal check.
[4] Proved.
[5] Fastidious.
[6] For love's sake.
[7] Bet.
[8] Hands.

[SCENA v.

Candido's shop.]

Enter Candido's Wife, George, and two Prentices in the shop.

WIFE.[1] Come, you put up your wares in good order here, do you not, think you? One piece cast this way, another that way! You had need have a patient master indeed.

GEO. [*Aside.*] Ay, I'll be sworn, for we have a curst [2] mistress.

WIFE. You mumble, do you? Mumble? I would your master or I could be a note more angry, for two patient folks in a [10 house spoil all the servants that ever shall come under them.

1 PREN. [*Aside.*] You patient! Ay, so is the devil when he is horn-mad.

Enter Castruchio, Fluello, and Pioratto.

ALL THREE.[3] Gentlemen, what do you lack? What is 't you buy? See, fine hollands, fine cambrics, fine lawns.

GEO. What is 't you lack?

2 PREN. What is 't you buy?

CAS. Where's Signior Candido, thy master?   20

GEO. Faith, signior, he's a little negotiated;[4] he'll appear presently.

CAS. Fellow, let's see a lawn, a choice one, sirrah.

GEO. The best in all Milan, gentlemen, and this is the piece. I can fit you gentlemen with fine calicoes too for doublets, the only sweet fashion now, most delicate and courtly, a meek gentle calico, cut upon two double affable taffetas—ah, most neat, [30 feat, and unmatchable!

FLU. A notable, voluble-tongued villain!

PIO. I warrant this fellow was never begot without much prating.

CAS. What, and is this she, say'st thou?

GEO. Ay, and the purest she that ever you fingered since you were a gentleman. Look how even she is, look how clean she is! Ha, as even as the brow of Cynthia, and as clean as your sons and heirs [40 when they ha' spent all!

[1] From this point Viola appears as *Wife* in speech heads.   [2] Ill-tempered.
[3] *I.e.*, George and the two prentices.
[4] Engaged, busy.

CAS. Pooh, thou talk'st! Pox on 't, 'tis rough.

GEO. How? Is she rough? But, if you bid pox on 't, sir, 'twill take away the roughness presently.[5]

FLU. Ha, signior! Has he fitted your French curse?[6]

GEO. Look you, gentleman, here's another. Compare them, I pray. *Compara* [50 *Virgilium cum Homero:* compare virgins with harlots.

CAS. Pooh, I ha' seen better, and, as you term them, evener and cleaner.

GEO. You may see further for your mind, but, trust me, you shall not find better for your body.

Enter Candido.

CAS. [*Aside.*] O, here he comes; let's make as though we pass.— Come, come, we'll try in some other shop.

CAND. How now? What's the matter? 60

GEO. The gentlemen find fault with this lawn, fall out with it, and without a cause too.

CAND. Without a cause? And that makes you to let 'em pass away. Ah, may I crave a word with you, gentlemen?

FLU. He calls us.

CAS.   Makes the better for the jest.

CAND. I pray come near; y'are very welcome, gallants. Pray gardon my man's rudeness, for I fear me H'as talked above a prentice with you. Lawns?   [*Shows lawns.*] 70 Look you, kind gentlemen, this—no— ay—this. Take this upon my honest-dealing faith To be a true weave, not too hard nor slack, But e'en as far from falsehood as from black.

CAS. Well, how do you rate it?

CAND. Very conscionably—eighteen shillings a yard.

CAS. That's too dear. How many yards does the whole piece contain, think you?

CAND. Why, some seventeen yards, I think, or thereabouts.   80

[5] Immediately.   [6] *I.e.*, the pox.

How much would serve your turn, I pray?

Cas. Why, let me see—would it were better too!

Cand. Truth, 'tis the best in Milan, at few words.

Cas. Well, let me have then—a whole pennyworth.

Cand. Ha, ha! Y'are a merry gentleman.

Cas. A penn'orth, I say.

Cand. Of lawn!

Cas. Of lawn? Ay, of lawn, a penn'orth. 'Sblood, dost not hear? A whole penn'orth! Are you deaf?   90

Cand. Deaf? No, sir; but I must tell you,
Our wares do seldom meet such customers.

Cas. Nay, and you and your lawns be so squeamish, fare you well.

Cand. Pray stay; a word, pray, signior. For what purpose is it, I beseech you?

Cas. 'Sblood, what's that to you? I'll have a pennyworth.

Cand. A pennyworth! Why, you shall. I'll serve you presently.   110   100

2 Pren. 'Sfoot, a pennyworth, mistress!

Wife.[1] A pennyworth! Call you these gentlemen?

Cas. [To Candido.] No, no. Not there.

Cand.   What then, kind gentleman?
What, at this corner here?

Cas.   No, nor there neither;
I'll have it just in the middle, or else not.

Cand. Just in the middle? Ha, you shall too. What?
Have you a single penny?

Cas.   Yes, here's one.

Cand. Lend it me, I pray.

Flu. An excellent-followed jest!   109

Wife. What, will he spoil the lawn now?

Cand. Patience, good wife.

Wife. Ay, that patience makes a fool of you.—Gentlemen, you might ha' found some other citizen to have made a kind gull on besides my husband.

Cand. Pray, gentlemen, take her to be a woman;
Do not regard her language.—O kind soul,

[1] Original has *Mist[ress]*.

Such words will drive away my customers.

Wife. Customers with a murrain![2] Call you these customers?   121

Cand. Patience, good wife.

Wife. Pox a your patience.

Geo. 'Sfoot, mistress, I warrant these are some cheating companions.[3]

Cand. Look you, gentleman, there's your ware. I thank you; I have your money here. Pray know my shop; pray let me have your custom.

Wife. Custom, quotha![4]   130

Cand. Let me take more of your money.

Wife. You had need so.

Pio. Hark in thine ear; th'ast lost an hundred ducats.

Cas. Well, well, I know 't. Is 't possible that *homo*
Should be nor man nor woman--not once moved—
No, not at such an injury, not at all!
Sure he's a pigeon, for he has no gall.

Flu. Come, come, y'are angry though you smother it.
Y'are vexed, i' faith; confess.

Cand.   Why, gentlemen,
Should you conceit[5] me to be vexed or moved?   140
He has my ware; I have his money for 't,
And that's no argument I'm angry. No,
The best logician cannot prove me so.

Flu. O, but the hateful name of a pennyworth of lawn,
And then cut out i' th' middle of the piece—
Pah, I guess it by myself—would move a lamb
Were he a linen draper; 'twould, i' faith.

Cand. Well, give me leave to answer you for that.
We're set here to please all customers,
Their humors and their fancies—offend none;   150
We get by many, if we leese[6] by one.
May be his mind stood to no more than that;
A pennyworth serves him, and, 'mongst trades 'tis found,
Deny a penn'orth, it may cross a pound.

[2] Plague.   [3] Fellows.   [4] Says he; indeed.
[5] Imagine.   [6] Lose.

O, he that means to thrive, with patient
  eye
Must please the devil if he come to
  buy!
FLU. O wondrous man, patient 'bove
  wrong or woe,
How blessed were men, if women could be
  so!
CAND. And to express how well my breast
  is pleased,
And satisfied in all—George, fill a beaker.
                              Exit George.
I'll drink unto that gentleman who
  lately   161
Bestowed his money with me.
WIFE.   God's my life,
We shall have all our gains drunk out in
  beakers
To make amends for pennyworths of
  lawn!

Enter Geor[ge with beaker].

CAND. Here, wife, begin you to the gentle-
  man.
WIFE. I begin to him!   [*Spills the wine.*]
CAND.   George, fill 't up again.
  'Twas my fault; my hand shook.
                              Exit George.
PIO.   How strangely this doth show!
A patient man linked with a waspish
  shrow.[1]
FLU. [*Aside.*] A silver and gilt beaker! I
  have a trick
To work upon that beaker. Sure 'twill
  fret him;   170
It cannot choose but vex him. Signior
  Castruchio,
In pity to thee I have a conceit
Will save thy hundred ducats yet. 'Twill
  do 't,
And work him to impatience.
CAS. [*Aside.*] Sweet Fluello, I should be
  bountiful to that conceit.
FLU. [*Aside.*] Well, 'tis enough.

Enter George [with beaker].

CAND.   Here, gentlemen, to you!
I wish your custom; y'are exceeding
  welcome.   [*Drinks.*]
CAS. I pledge you, Signior Candido!
                              [*Drinks.*]

Here, you that must receive a hundred
  ducats!
PIO. I'll pledge them deep, i' faith, Castru-
  chio.—   180
Signior Fluello.   [*Drinks.*]
FLU.   Come; play 't off to me;
I am your last man.
CAND.   George, supply the cup
FLU. So, so, good honest George.
Here, Signior Candido, all this to you.
CAND. O, you must pardon me; I use it
  not.
FLU. Will you not pledge me then?
CAND.   Yes, but not that;
Great love is shown in little.
FLU.   Blurt on [2] your sentences!
'Sfoot, you shall pledge me all.
CAND.   Indeed, I shall not.
FLU. Not pledge me? 'Sblood, I'll carry
  away the beaker then.
CAND. The beaker? O, that at your
  pleasure, sir.   190
FLU. Now by this drink I will. [*Drinks.*]
CAS.   Pledge him; he'll do 't else.
FLU. So; I ha' done you right on my thumb
  nail.[3]
What, will you pledge me now?
CAND.   You know me, sir!
I am not of that sin.
FLU.   Why, then, farewell!
I'll bear away the beaker, by this light.
CAND. That's as you please; 'tis very good.
FLU. Nay, it doth please me, and, as you
  say, 'tis a very good one.
Farewell, Signior Candido.
PIO.   Farewell, Candido.
CAND. Y'are welcome, gentlemen.
CAS.   Heart, not moved yet?
I think his patience is above our wit.
*Exeunt [Castruchio, Fluello with the beaker,
                            and Pioratto].*
GEO. I told you before, mistress,   [201
they were all cheaters.
WIFE. Why, fool! Why, husband! Why,
madman! I hope you will not let 'em
sneak away so with a silver and gilt beaker,
the best in the house too.—Go, fellows,
make hue and cry after them.
CAND. Pray let your tongue lie still; all
  will be well.—
Come hither, George; hie to the constable,

[1] Shrew.

[2] A fig for.
[3] So that only enough to stand on a thumb
nail is left.

And in calm order wish him to attach
   them.   210
Make no great stir, because they're
   gentlemen,
And a thing partly done in merri-
   ment.
'Tis but a size above a jest, thou
   know'st;
Therefore pursue it mildly. Go, begone;
The constable's hard by; bring him
   along.
Make haste again.

WIFE. O, y'are a goodly, patient woodcock,[1] are you not now? (*Exit George.*)
See what your patience comes to: everyone
saddles you, and rides you; you'll be shortly
the common stone-horse [2] of Milan. [221
A woman's well holped [3] up with such a
meacock.[4] I had rather have a husband
that would swaddle [5] me thrice a day than
such a one that will be gulled twice in half
an hour. O, I could burn all the wares in
my shop for anger.

CAND. Pray wear a peaceful temper; be
   my wife,
That is, be patient; for a wife and
   husband
Share but one soul between them. This
   being known,   230
Why should not one soul then agree in
   one?   *Exit.*

WIFE. Hang your agreements! But if
my beaker be gone!

Enter Castruchio, Fluello, Pioratto, and
                           George.

CAND. O, here they come.

GEO. The constable, sir, let 'em come
along with me, because [6] there should be
no wond'ring. He stays at door.

CAS. Constable, Goodman Abram! [7]

FLU. Now, Signior Candido, 'sblood,
why do you attach us?   240

CAS. 'Sheart! Attach us!

CAND.   Nay, swear not, gallants;
Your oaths may move your souls, but
   not move me;
You have a silver beaker of my wife's.

FLU. You say not true. 'Tis gilt.

CAND.   Then you say true;
And, being gilt, the guilt lies more on you.

CAS. I hope y'are not angry, sir.

CAND. Then you hope right; for I am
   not angry.

FLU. No, but a little moved.

CAND. I moved! 'Twas you were moved—
   you were brought hither.

CAS. But you, out of your anger and impatience,   250
Caused us to be attached.

CAND.   Nay, you misplace it.
Out of my quiet sufferance I did that,
And not of any wrath. Had I shown
   anger,
I should have then pursued you with the
   law,
And hunted you to shame, as many
   worldlings
Do build their anger upon feebler
   grounds,
The more's the pity. Many lose their lives
For scarce so much coin as will hide their
   palm—
Which is most cruel. Those have vexéd
   spirits
That pursue lives. In this opinion rest:
The loss of millions could not move my
   breast.   261

FLU. Thou art a blessed man, and with
   peace dost deal;
Such a meek spirit can bless a commonweal.

CAND. Gentlemen, now 'tis upon eating
   time.
Pray, part not hence, but dine with me
   today.

CAS. I never heard a carter yet say nay
To such a motion. I'll not be the first.

PIO. Nor I.

FLU. Nor I.

CAND. The constable shall bear you
   company.   270
George, call him in. Let the world say
   what it can,
Nothing can drive me from a patient
   man.   *Exeunt.*

[SCENA vi.
A room in Bellafront's house.]

Enter Roger with a stool, cushion, looking-
glass, and chafing dish; [8] *those being*
set down, he pulls out of his pocket a

---

[1] Simpleton.   [4] Milksop.
[2] Stallion.   [5] Beat.
[3] Helped.   [6] In order that.
[7] A man who shams madness to gain his ends.
[8] Used for heating the poker mentioned below.

*vial with white color in it, and two boxes,
one with white, another red painting.
He places all things in order, and a
candle by them, singing with the ends of
old ballads as he does it. At last Bellafront, as he rubs his cheek with the
colors, whistles within.*

Rog. Anon, forsooth.

Bell. [*Within.*] What are you playing
the rogue about?

Rog. About you, forsooth; I'm drawing
up a hole in your white silk stocking.

Bell. Is my glass there and my boxes
of complexion?

Rog. Yes, forsooth. Your boxes of
complexion are here, I think; yes, 'tis here.
Here's your two complexions—[*Aside.*]   10
and, if I had all the four complexions,[1]
I should ne'er set a good face upon 't.
Some men, I see, are born under hard-
favored planets as well as women. Zounds,
I look worse now than I did before, and it
makes her face glister most damnably.
There's knavery in daubing, I hold my
life; or else this is only female pomatum.

*Enter Bellafront not full ready,[2] without a
gown; she sits down; with her bodkin[3]
curls her hair; colors her lips.*

Bell. Where's my ruff and poker,[4]
you blockhead?   20

Rog. Your ruff, your poker, are en-
gend'ring together upon the cupboard of
the court, or the court-cupboard.[5]

Bell. Fetch 'em. Is the pox in your
hams, you can go no faster? [*Strikes him.*]

Rog. Would the pox were in your
fingers, unless you could leave flinging![6]
Catch—   *Exit.*

Bell. I'll catch you, you dog, by-and-
by. Do you grumble?   *She sings.*   30

Cupid is a God, as naked as my nail;
I'll whip him with a rod, if he my true love
     fail.

[*Enter Roger with ruff and poker.*]

Rog. There's your ruff. Shall I poke
it?

Bell. Yes, honest Ro[ger]—no, stay;
prithee, good boy, hold here.

[*Sings. Roger holds the glass and candle.*]

Down, down, down, down, I fall down and
     arise—down—
I never shall arise.

Rog. Troth, m[istress], then leave the
trade if you shall never rise.   40

Bell. What trade, Goodman Abram?

Rog. Why, that of down and arise, or
the falling trade.

Bell. I'll fall with you by-and-by.

Rog. If you do, I know who shall
smart for 't. Troth, mistress, what do I look
like now?

Bell. Like as you are, a panderly
sixpenny rascal.

Rog. I may thank you for that; in   [50
faith, I look like an old proverb, "Hold
the candle before the devil."

Bell. Ud's life, I'll stick my knife in
your guts and you prate to me so!—
What?   *She sings.*

"Well met, pug,[7] the pearl of beauty—
     umh, umh."
"How now, Sir Knave? You forget your
     duty—umh, umh.
Marry muff,[8] sir!" "Are you grown so
     dainty? Fa, la, la, etc."
"Is it you, sir?" "The worst of twenty!
     Fa, la, la, leera, la."

Pox on you, how dost thou hold my   [60
glass?

Rog. Why, as I hold your door—with
my fingers.

Bell. Nay, pray thee, sweet honey
Ro[ger], hold up handsomely.   [*Sings.*]

Sing, pretty wantons, warble, etc.

We shall ha' guests today, I lay my little
maidenhead; my nose itches so.

Rog. I said so too last night, when our
fleas twinged me.   70

Bell. So, poke my ruff now. My
gown, my gown! Have I my fall?[9] Where's
my fall, Roger?   *One knocks.*

Rog. Your fall, forsooth, is behind.

Bell. God's my pitikins! Some fool
or other knocks.

Rog. Shall I open to the fool, mistress?

Bell. And all these bables[10] lying
thus? Away with it quickly.—Ay, ay,

---

[1] Temperaments constituted by the four
humors.
[2] Dressed.
[3] Long hairpin.
[4] Rod for pleating ruffs.
[5] Movable sideboard.
[6] Smiting, striking.
[7] Darling; also harlot.
[8] An expression of contempt.
[9] A flat collar.
[10] Baubles.

knock, and be damned, whosoever you [80 be!—So; give the fresh salmon line now; let him come ashore. He shall serve for my breakfast, though he go against my stomach.

Roger fetch in Fluello, Castruchio, and Pioratto.

FLU. Morrow, coz.

CAS. How does my sweet acquaintance?

PIO. Save thee, little marmoset! How dost thou, good, pretty rogue?

BELL. Well, God-a-mercy, good, pretty rascal.　　　　　　　　　　　　90

FLU. Roger, some light, I pray thee.

ROG. You shall, signior, for we that live here in this vale of misery are as dark as hell.　　　　　　　*Exit for a candle.*

CAS. Good tobacco, Fluello?

FLU. Smell.

Enter Roger.

PIO. It may be tickling gear, for it plays with my nose already.

ROG. Here's another light angel,[1] si-gnior.　　　　　　　　　　　　100

BELL. What, you pied curtal,[2] what's that you are neighing?

ROG. I say God send us the light of heaven, or some more angels.

BELL. Go fetch some wine, and drink half of it.

ROG. I must fetch some wine, gentle-men, and drink half of it.

FLU. Here, Roger.

CAS. No, let me send, prithee.　　110

FLU. Hold, you cankerworm.

ROG. You shall send both, if you please, signiors.

PIO. Stay, what's best to drink a-morn-ings?

ROG. Hippocras, sir, for my mistress, if I fetch it, is most dear to her.

FLU. Hippocras? There then, here's a teston [3] for you, you snake.

ROG. Right, sir, here's three shil- [120 lings sixpence for a pottle and a manchet.[4]

　　　　　　　　　　　　Ex[it].

CAS. Here's most Herculanean tobacco; ha' some, acquaintance?

BELL. Faugh, not I—makes your breath stink like the piss of a fox. Acquaintance, where supped you last night?

CAS. At a place, sweet acquaintance, where your health danced the canaries,[5] i' faith. You should ha' been there.

BELL. I there among your punks![6] [130 Marry, faugh, hang 'em; I scorn 't! Will you never leave sucking of eggs in other folks' hens' nests?

CAS. Why, in good troth, if you'll trust me, acquaintance, there was not one hen at the board. Ask Fluello.

FLU. No, faith, coz, none but cocks. Signior Malavella drunk to thee.

BELL. O, a pure beagle; that horse-leech there?　　　　　　　　　　　　140

FLU. And the knight, Sir Oliver Lollio, swore he would bestow a taffeta petticoat on thee, but to break his fast with thee.

BELL. With me? I'll choke him then, hang him, molecatcher! It's the dream-ing'st snottynose.

PIO. Well, many took that Lollio for a fool, but he's a subtle fool.

BELL. Ay, and he has fellows. Of all filthy, dry-fisted knights, I cannot [150 abide that he should touch me.

CAS. Why, wench, is he scabbed?

BELL. Hang him, he'll not live to be so honest, nor to the credit to have scabs about him; his betters have 'em. But I hate to wear out any of his coarse knight-hood, because he's made like an alderman's nightgown, faced all with cony [7] before, and within nothing but fox. This sweet Oliver will eat mutton [8] till he be ready [160 to burst, but the lean-jawed slave will not pay for the scraping of his trencher.

PIO. Plague him! Set him beneath the salt, and let him not touch a bit till every-one has had his full cut.

FLU. Lord Ello, the gentleman usher, came in to us too. Marry, 'twas in our cheese,[9] for he had been to borrow money for his lord, of a citizen.

CAS. What an ass is that lord to [170 borrow money of a citizen!

BELL. Nay, God's my pity, what an ass is that citizen to lend money to a lord!

---

[1] Also a gold coin.　　[3] Sixpence.
[2] A docked horse.　　[4] Loaf of fine bread.
[5] A lively dance.　　[7] Rabbit skin.
[6] Prostitutes.　　[8] Strumpet.
[9] During the cheese course (?).

*Enter Matheo and Hippolito, who, saluting
the company as a stranger, walks off.
Roger comes in sadly behind them, with
a pottle[1] pot, and stands aloof off.*

MAT. Save you, gallants. Signior Fluello, exceedingly well met, as I may say.

FLU. Signior Matheo, exceedingly well
met too, as I may say.

MAT. And how fares my little pretty
mistress? 180

BELL. E'en as my little pretty servant—sees three court dishes before her,
and not one good bit in them.—How now?
Why the devil stand'st thou so? Art in
a trance?

ROG. Yes, forsooth.

BELL. Why dost not fill out their wine?

ROG. Forsooth, 'tis filled out already.
All the wine that the signior has bestowed
upon you is cast away; a porter ran [190
a little at me, and so faced me down that
I had not a drop.

BELL. I'm accursed to let such a withered, artichoke-faced rascal grow under
my nose. Now you look like an old hecat, going to the gallows. I'll be hanged if
he ha' not put up the money to cony-
catch us all.

ROG. No, truly, forsooth, 'tis not put
up yet. 200

BELL. How many gentlemen hast thou
served thus?

ROG. None but five hundred, besides
prentices and serving-men.

BELL. Dost think I'll pocket it up at
thy hands?

ROG. Yes, forsooth, I fear you will
pocket it up.

BELL. Fie, fie, cut my lace, good servant; I shall ha' the mother[2] presently, [210
I'm so vexed at this horse-plum.[3]

FLU. Plague, not for a scald[4] pottle
of wine!

MAT. Nay, sweet Bellafront, for a little
pig's wash!

CAS. Here, Roger, fetch more. [*Gives
money.*] A mischance, i' faith, acquaintance.

BELL. Out of my sight, thou ungodly,
puritanical creature. 220

ROG. For the tother pottle? Yes,
forsooth. *Exit.*

[1] Two-quart.
[2] Hysteria. [3] Wild plum. [4] Paltry.

BELL. Spill that too!—What gentleman
is that, servant? Your friend?

MAT. Godso; a stool, a stool! If you
love me, mistress, entertain this gentleman respectively,[5] and bid him welcome.

BELL. He's very welcome. Pray, sir,
sit.

HIP. Thanks, lady. 230
[*Matheo and Bellafront stand aside con-
versing.*]

FLU. Count Hippolito, is't not? Cry
you mercy, signior; you walk here all this
while, and we not heard you? Let me
bestow a stool upon you, beseech you.
You are a stranger here; we know the
fashions a th' house.

CAS. Please you, be here, my lord.
[*Offers] tobacco.*

HIP. No, good Castruchio.

FLU. You have abandoned the court, I
see, my lord, since the death of your [240
mistress. Well, she was a delicate piece.—
Beseech you, sweet, come let us serve
under the colors of your acquaintance still
for all that.—Please you to meet here at
my lodging of my coz, I shall bestow a banquet upon you.

HIP. I never can deserve this kindness,
sir. What may this lady be, whom you call
coz? 249

FLU. Faith, sir, a poor gentlewoman,
of passing good carriage; one that has
some suits in law, and lies here in an attorney's house.

HIP. Is she married?

FLU. Ha, as all your punks are, a captain's wife, or so. Never saw her before,
my lord?

HIP. Never, trust me! A goodly creature!

FLU. By gad, when you know her [260
as we do, you'll swear she is the prettiest,
kindest, sweetest, most bewitching, honest
ape under the pole. A skin, your satin is
not more soft, nor lawn whiter.

HIP. Belike, then, she's some sale
courtesan.

FLU. Troth, as all your best faces are.
A good wench!

HIP. Great pity that she's a good
wench. 270

MAT. [*To Bellafront.*] Thou shalt
ha', i' faith, mistress.—How how, signiors?

[5] Respectfully.

What, whispering? Did not I lay a wager I should take you within seven days in a house of vanity?

HIP. You did; and, I beshrew your heart, you have won.

MAT. How do you like my mistress?

HIP. Well, for such a mistress; better, if your mistress be not your mas- [280 ter.—I must break manners, gentlemen; fare you well.

MAT. 'Sfoot, you shall not leave us.

BELL. The gentleman likes not the taste of our company.

OMNES. Beseech you, stay.

HIP. Trust me, my affairs beckon for me; pardon me.

MAT. Will you call for me half an hour hence here?　　　　　　　　　　290

HIP. Perhaps I shall.

MAT. Perhaps? Faugh! I know you can swear to me you will.

HIP. Since you will press me, on my word, I will.　　　　　　　　　*Exit.*

BELL. What sullen picture is this, servant?

MAT. It's Count Hippolito, the brave count.

PIO. As gallant a spirit as any in [300 Milan, you sweet Jew.[1]

FLU. O, he's a most essential gentleman, coz!

CAS. Did you never hear of Count Hippolito, acquaintance?

BELL. Marry, muff a[2] your counts, and be no more life in 'em!

MAT. He's so malcontent, sirrah Bellafronta.—And you be honest gallants, let's sup together and have the count [310 with us.—Thou shalt sit at the upper end, punk.

BELL. Punk, you soused gurnet?[3]

MAT. King's truce! Come, I'll bestow the supper to have him but laugh.

CAS. He betrays his youth too grossly to that tyrant melancholy.

MAT. All this is for a woman.

BELL. A woman? Some whore! What sweet jewel is 't?　　　　　　　320

PIO. Would she heard you!

FLU. Troth, so would I.

CAS. And I, by heaven.

BELL. Nay, good servant, what woman?

MAT. Pah!

BELL. Prithee, tell me; a buss,[4] and tell me. I warrant he's an honest fellow, if he take on thus for a wench. Good rogue, who?

MAT. By th' Lord, I will not, must not, faith, mistress. Is 't a match, sirs? [330 This night, at th' Antelope. Ay, for there's best wine, and good boys.

OMNES. It's done; at th' Antelope.

BELL. I cannot be there tonight.

MAT. Cannot? By th' Lord, you shall.

BELL. By the Lady, I will not. Shall!

FLU. Why, then, put it off till Friday; woot[5] come then, coz?

BELL. Well.

Enter Roger.

MAT. Y'are the waspishest ape. [340 Roger, put your mistress in mind to sup with us on Friday next. Y'are best come like a madwoman, without a band, in your waistcoat,[6] and the linings of your kirtle outward, like every common hackney[7] that steals out at the back gate of her sweet knight's lodging.

BELL. Go, go, hang yourself!

CAS. It's dinner time, Matheo. Shall's hence?　　　　　　　　　　350

OMNES. Yes, yes.—Farewell, wench.

Exeunt [all but Bellafront and Roger].

BELL. Farewell, boys.—Roger, what wine sent they for?

ROG. Bastard wine,[8] for, if it had been truly begotten, it would not ha' been ashamed to come in. Here's six shillings to pay for nursing the bastard.

BELL. A company of rooks![9] O good sweet Roger, run to the poulter's, and buy me some fine larks!　　　　　　360

ROG. No woodcocks?

BELL. Yes, faith, a couple, if they be not dear.

ROG. I'll buy but one; there's one[10] already here.　　　　　　　　　　*Exit.*

Enter Hippolito.

HIP. Is the gentleman, my friend, departed, mistress?

BELL. His back is but new turned, sir.

HIP. Fare you well.

BELL. I can direct you to him.

---

[1] Term of endearment.　　[2] A curse on.

[3] Pickled fish.　　[4] Kiss.　　[5] Wilt thou.
[6] *I.e.*, without your upper dress.　[7] Harlot.
[8] Sweet Spanish wine.　　[9] Simpletons.
[10] *I.e.*, Hippolito, with a play on *woodcock* as simpleton.

HIP.   Can you, pray?

BELL. If you please stay, he'll not be absent long.

HIP. I care not much.

BELL.   Pray sit, forsooth.

HIP.   I'm hot.
   If I may use your room, I'll rather walk.

BELL. At your best pleasure.—Whew!
   Some rubbers [1] there!   370

HIP. Indeed, I'll none—indeed I will not; thanks.
   Pretty fine lodging.   I perceive my friend
   Is old in your acquaintance.

BELL.   Troth, sir, he comes,
   As other gentlemen, to spend spare hours.
   If yourself like our roof, such as it is,
   Your own acquaintance may be as old as his.

HIP. Say I did like, what welcome should I find?

BELL. Such as my present fortunes can afford.

HIP. But would you let me play Matheo's part?

BELL. What part?

HIP.   Why, embrace you,
   dally with you, kiss.   380
   Faith, tell me, will you leave him and love me?

BELL. I am in bonds to no man, sir.

HIP.   Why then,
   Y'are free for any man; if any, me.
   But I must tell you, lady, were you mine,
   You should be all mine. I could brook no sharers;
   I should be covetous, and sweep up all.
   I should be pleasure's usurer; faith, I should.

BELL. O fate!

HIP.   Why sigh you, lady? May I know?

BELL. 'T has never been my fortune yet to single
   Out that one man whose love could fellow mine,   390
   As I have ever wished it. O my stars!
   Had I but met with one kind gentleman,
   That would have purchased sin alone to himself,

[1] Towels.

For his own private use, although scarce proper[2]—
Indifferent handsome, meetly legged and thighed—
And my allowance reasonable, i' faith,
According to my body, by my troth,
I would have been as true unto his pleasures,
Yea, and as loyal to his afternoons,   399
As ever a poor gentlewoman could be.

HIP. This were well now to one but newly fledged,
And scarce a day old in this subtle world;
'Twere pretty art, good birdlime, cunning net.
But come, come, faith, confess. How many men
Have drunk this selfsame protestation,
From that red ticing [3] lip?

BELL.   Indeed, not any.

HIP. "Indeed," and blush not!

BELL.   No, in truth, not any.

HIP. "Indeed!" "In truth!"—how warily you swear!
'Tis well, if ill it be not; yet had I
The ruffian in me, and were drawn before you   410
But in light colors, I do know indeed
You could not swear "Indeed," but thunder oaths
That should shake heaven, drown the harmonious spheres,
And pierce a soul that loved her Maker's honor
With horror and amazement.

BELL.   Shall I swear?
Will you believe me then?

HIP.   Worst then of all;
   Our sins by custom seem at last but small.
   Were I but o'er your threshold, a next man,
   And after him a next, and then a fourth,
   Should have this golden hook and lascivious bait   420
   Thrown out to the full length. Why, let me tell you,
   I ha' seen letters sent from that white hand,
   Tuning such music to Matheo's ear.

BELL. Matheo! That's true, but, believe it, I

[2] Fine-looking.   [3] Enticing.

No sooner had laid hold upon your presence,
But straight mine eye conveyed you to my heart.

HIP. O, you cannot feign with me! Why, I know, lady,
This is the common passion of you all,
To hook in a kind gentleman, and then
Abuse his coin, conveying it to your lover,   430
And in the end you show him a French trick,
And so you leave him, that a coach may run
Between his legs for breadth.

BELL.   O, by my soul,
Not I! Therein I'll prove an honest whore,
In being true to one, and to no more.

HIP. If any be disposed to trust your oath,
Let him; I'll not be he. I know you feign
All that you speak; ay, for a mingled harlot
Is true in nothing but in being false.
What! shall I teach you how to loathe yourself?   440
And mildly too, not without sense or reason?

BELL. I am content; I would feign loathe myself
If you not love me.

HIP.   Then, if your gracious blood
Be not all wasted, I shall assay to do 't.
Lend me your silence and attention. You have no soul;
That makes you weigh so light. Heaven's treasure bought it,
And half a crown hath sold it. For your body
Is like the common shore, that still receives
All the town's filth. The sin of many men
Is within you; and thus much I suppose   450
That, if all your committers stood in rank,
They'd make a lane in which your shame might dwell,
And with their spaces reach from hence to hell.
Nay, shall I urge it more? There has been known

As many by one harlot maimed and dismembered
As would ha' stuffed an hospital. This I might
Apply to you, and perhaps do you right.
O, y'are as base as any beast that bears;
Your body is e'en hired, and so are theirs.
For gold and sparkling jewels, if he can,   460
You'll let a Jew get you with Christian—
Be he a Moor, a Tartar, though his face
Look uglier than a dead man's skull.
Could the devil put on a human shape,
If his purse shake out crowns, up then he gets;
Whores will be rid to hell with golden bits.
So that y'are crueler than Turks, for they
Sell Christians only; you sell yourselves away.
Why, those that love you, hate you, and will term you
Lickerish [1] damnation; wish themselves half-sunk   470
After the sin is laid out, and e'en curse
Their fruitless riot (for what one begets
Another poisons); lust and murder hit.
A tree being often shook, what fruit can knit?

BELL. O me unhappy!

HIP.   I can vex you more.
A harlot is like Dunkirk, true to none,
Swallows both English, Spanish, fulsome Dutch,
Back-doored [2] Italian, last of all, the French,
And he sticks to you, faith, gives you your diet,
Brings you acquainted, first, with Monsieur Doctor,   480
And then you know what follows.

BELL.   Misery!
Rank, stinking, and most loathsome misery!

HIP. Methinks a toad is happier than a whore.
That, with one poison, swells; with thousands more
The other stocks her veins. Harlot? Fie, fie!

[1] Lascivious.   [2] Sneaking.

You are the miserablest creatures breathing,
The very slaves of nature. Mark me
else.
You put on rich attires—others' eyes
wear them;
You eat, but to supply your blood with
sin.
And this strange curse e'en haunts you
to your graves. 490
From fools you get, and spend it upon
slaves.
Like bears and apes, y'are baited and
show tricks
For money; but your bawd the sweet-
ness licks.
Indeed, you are their journeywomen,
and do
All base and damned works they list
set you to,
So that you ne'er are rich; for do but
show me,
In present memory or in ages past,
The fairest and most famous courtesan,
Whose flesh was dear'st; that raised the
price of sin,
And held it up; to whose intemperate
bosom, 500
Princes, earls, lords, the worst has been
a knight,
The mean'st a gentleman, have offered
up
Whole hecatombs of sighs, and rained
in showers
Handfuls of gold; yet, for all this, at
last
Diseases sucked her marrow, then grew
so poor
That she has begged e'en at a beggar's
door.
And (wherein heaven has a finger) when
this idol,
From coast to coast, has leaped on foreign shores,
And had more worship than the outlandish whores;
When several nations have gone over
her; 510
When, for each several city she has
seen,
Her maidenhead has been new, and been
sold dear;
Did live well there, and might have
died unknown

And undefamed—back comes she to
her own,
And there both miserably lives and
dies,
Scorned even of those that once adored
her eyes,
As if her fatal, circled life thus ran:
Her pride should end there where it
first began.
What, do you weep to hear your story
read?
Nay, if you spoil your cheeks, I'll read
no more. 520
BELL. O yes, I pray, proceed.
Indeed, 'twill do me good to weep, in-
deed.
HIP. To give those tears a relish, this I
add—
Y'are like the Jews, scattered, in no
place certain;
Your days are tedious, your hours bur-
densome;
And, were 't not for full suppers, mid-
night revels,
Dancing, wine, riotous meetings, which
do drown
And bury quite in you all virtuous
thoughts,
And on your eyelids hang so heavily
They have no power to look so high as
heaven, 530
You'd sit and muse on nothing but
despair,
Curse that devil Lust, that so burns up
your blood,
And in ten thousand shivers break your
glass
For his temptation. Say you taste de-
light,
To have a golden gull from rise to set,
To mete [1] you in his hot, luxurious [2]
arms,
Yet your nights pay for all. I know you
dream
Of warrants, whips, and beadles, and
then start
At a door's windy creak; think every
weasel
To be a constable, and every rat 540
A long-tailed officer. Are you now not
slaves?
O, you have damnation without pleas-
ure for it!

[1] Measure, embrace.   [2] Lecherous.

Such is the state of harlots. To conclude:
When you are old and can well paint no more,
You turn bawd, and are then worse than before.
Make use of this. Farewell.

BELL. O, I pray, stay.

HIP. I see Matheo comes not; time hath barred me.
Would all the harlots in the town had heard me. *Exit.*

BELL. Stay yet a little longer! No? Quite gone!
Cursed be that minute—for it was no more, 550
So soon a maid is changed into a whore—
Wherein I first fell! Be it forever black!
Yet why should sweet Hippolito shun mine eyes,
For whose true love I would become pure-honest,
Hate the world's mixtures, and the smiles of gold?
Am I not fair? Why should he fly me then?
Fair creatures are desired, not scorned of men.
How many gallants have drunk healths to me,
Out of their daggered arms, and thought them blessed,
Enjoying but mine eyes at prodigal feasts! 560
And does Hippolito detest my love?
O, sure their heedless lusts but flattered me;
I am not pleasing, beautiful, nor young.
Hippolito hath spied some ugly blemish,
Eclipsing all my beauties. I am foul.
Harlot! Ay, that's the spot that taints my soul.
His weapon left here? O fit instrument
To let forth all the poison of my flesh!
Thy master hates me, cause my blood hath ranged;
But, when 'tis forth, then he'll believe I'm changed. 570

[*As she prepares to stab herself,*] enter Hipp[olito].

HIP. Mad woman, what art doing?

BELL. Either love me,
Or cleave my bosom on thy rapier's point.

Yet do not neither; for thou then destroy'st
That which I love thee for—thy virtues. Here, here;

[*Gives sword to Hippolito.*]

Th' art crueler, and kill'st me with disdain.
To die so, sheds no blood, yet 'tis worse pain. *Exit Hipp[olito].*
Not speak to me? Not look? Not bid farewell?
Hated! This must not be; some means I'll try.
Would all whores were as honest now as I! *Exit.*[1]

SCENA vii.

Enter Candido, his Wife, George, and two Prentices in the shop. Fustigo enters, walking by.

GEO. See, gentlemen, what you lack— a fine holland, a fine cambric! See what you buy.

1 PREN. Holland for shirts, cambric for bands! What is 't you lack?

FUS. [*Aside.*] 'Sfoot, I lack 'em all; nay, more, I lack money to buy 'em. Let me see, let me look again. Mass, this is the shop.—What, coz! Sweet coz! How dost, i' faith, since last night after candle- [10 light? We had good sport, i' faith, had we not? And when shall 's laugh again?

WIFE. When you will, cousin.

FUS. Spoke like a kind Lacedemonian. I see yonder's thy husband.

WIFE. Ay, there's the sweet youth, God bless him!

FUS. And how is 't, cousin? And how, how is 't, thou squall? [2]

WIFE. Well, cousin. How fare you? [20

FUS. How fare I? Troth, for sixpence a meal, wench, as well as heart can wish, with calves' chaldrons [3] and chitterlings; [4] besides, I have a punk after supper, as good as a roasted apple.

CAND. Are you my wife's cousin?

FUS. I am, sir. What hast thou to do with that?

CAND. O, nothing, but y'are welcome.

FUS. The devil's dung in thy teeth! [30

[1] Original reads *Exeunt.*
[2] Minx.
[3] Edible entrails.
[4] Tripe.

I'll be welcome whether thou wilt or no,
I.—What ring's this, coz? Very pretty and
fantastical, i' faith! Let's see it.

WIFE. Pooh! Nay, you wrench my
finger.

FUS. I ha' sworn I'll ha't, and I hope you
will not let my oaths be cracked in the
ring,[1] will you? [*Seizes the ring.*] I hope, sir,
you are not malicolly [2] at this, for all your
great looks. Are you angry? 40

CAND. Angry? Not I, sir; nay, if she
can part
So easily with her ring, 'tis with my
heart.

GEO. Suffer this, sir, and suffer all. A
whoreson [3] gull, to—

CAND. Peace, George! When she has
reaped what I have sown,
She'll say one grain tastes better of her
own
Than whole sheaves gathered from another's land.
Wit's never good till bought at a dear
hand.[4]

GEO. But in the meantime she makes an
ass of somebody. 50

2 PREN. See, see, see, sir; as you turn
your back, they do nothing but kiss.

CAND. No matter; let 'em. When I touch
her lip,
I shall not feel his kisses, no, nor miss
Any of her lip; no harm in kissing is.
Look to your business, pray; make up
your wares.

FUS. Troth, coz, and well remembered.
I would thou wouldst give me five yards of
lawn, to make my punk some falling bands
a the fashion—three falling one upon [60
another, for that's the new edition [5] now.
She's out of linen horribly, too; troth,
sh'as never a good smock to her back
neither, but one that has a great many
patches in 't, and that I'm fain to wear
myself for want of shift, too. Prithee, put
me into wholesome napery, and bestow
some clean commodities upon us.

WIFE. Reach me those cambrics, and the
lawns hither. 70

CAND. What to do, wife? To lavish out
my goods upon a fool?

FUS. Fool? 'Snails, eat the "fool," or

I'll so batter your crown that it shall
scarce go for five shillings.

2 PREN. Do you hear, sir? Y'are best
be quiet, and say a fool tells you so.

FUS. Nails, I think so, for thou tell'st
me.

CAND. Are you angry, sir, because I
named thee fool? 80
Trust me, you are not wise in my own
house
And to my face to play the antic [6] thus.
If you'll needs play the madman, choose
a stage
Of lesser compass, where few eyes may
note
Your action's error; but, if still you miss,
As here you do, for one clap, ten will
hiss.

FUS. 'Swounds, cousin, he talks to me
as if I were a scurvy tragedian.

2 PREN. [*Aside.*] Sirrah George, I ha'
thought upon a device how to break [90
his pate, beat him soundly, and ship him
away.

GEO. [*Aside.*] Do 't.

2 PREN. [*Aside.*] I'll go in, pass through
the house, give some of our fellow prentices
the watchword when they shall enter, then
come and fetch my master in by a wile, and
place one in the hall to hold him in conference, whilst we cudgel the gull out of his
coxcomb. 100

GEO. [*Aside.*] Do 't; away, do 't.
[*Exit 2 Prentice.*]

WIFE. Must I call twice for these cambrics and lawns?

CAND. Nay, see, you anger her, George;
prithee despatch.

1 PREN. Two of the choicest pieces are
in the warehouse, sir.

CAND. Go fetch them presently.
Exit 1 Prentice.

FUS. Ay, do, make haste, sirrah.

CAND. Why were you such a stran- [110
ger all this while, being my wife's cousin?

FUS. Stranger? No, sir, I'm a natural
Milaner born.

CAND. I perceive still it is your natural
guise to mistake me, but you are welcome,
sir; I much wish your acquaintance.

FUS. My acquaintance? I scorn that,
i' faith; I hope my acquaintance goes in
chains of gold three-and-fifty times double.

---

[1] Invalid, like a damaged coin.
[2] Corruption of *melancholy*.   [4] High price.
[3] Rascally.   [5] Kind, fashion.
[6] Buffoon.

You know who I mean, coz; the posts of his gate are a-painting too.[1] 121

Enter the 2 Prentice.

2 PREN. Signior Pandulfo, the merchant, desires conference with you.

CAND. Signior Pandulfo? I'll be with him straight.

Attend your mistress and the gentleman.
Exit.

WIFE. When do you show those pieces?

FUS. Ay, when do you show those pieces?

OMNES. [*Within.*] Presently, sir, presently; we are but charging them. 130

FUS. Come, sirrah. You flatcap,[2] where be these whites?

[*Enter 1 Prentice with cloth.*]

GEO. [*Whispering.*] Flatcap? Hark in your ear, sir; y'are a flat fool, an ass, a gull, and I'll thrum[3] you.—Do you see this cambric, sir?

FUS. 'Sfoot, coz, a good jest! Did you hear him? He told me in my ear, I was a "flat fool, an ass, a gull, and I'll thrum you.—Do you see this cambric, sir?" 140

WIFE. What, not my men, I hope?

FUS. No, not your men, but one of your men, i' faith.

1 PREN. I pray, sir, come hither. What say you to this? Here's an excellent good one.

FUS. Ay, marry, this likes[4] me well. Cut me off some half-score yards.

2 PREN. [*Whispering.*] Let your whores cut. Y'are an impudent coxcomb. [150 You get none, and yet I'll thrum you.—A very good cambric, sir.

FUS. Again, again, as God judge me! 'Sfoot, coz, they stand thrumming here with me all day, and yet I get nothing.

2 PREN. [*Whispering.*] A word, I pray, sir; you must not be angry. Prentices have hot bloods, young fellows.—What say you to this piece? Look you, 'tis so delicate, so soft, so even, so fine a thread, that [160 a lady may wear it.

FUS. 'Sfoot, I think so. If a knight

marry my punk, a lady shall wear it. Cut me off twenty yards. Th'art an honest lad.

1 PREN. Not without money, gull, and I'll thrum you too.

OMNES. Gull, we'll thrum you!

FUS. O Lord, sister, did you not hear something cry "thump"? Zounds, your men here make a plain ass of me. 170

WIFE. What, to my face so impudent?

GEO. Ay, in a cause so honest, we'll not suffer

Our master's goods to vanish moneyless.

WIFE. You will not suffer them?

2 PREN. No, and you may blush
In going about to vex so mild a breast
As is our master's.

WIFE. Take away those pieces!
Cousin, I give them freely.

FUS. Mass, and I'll take 'em as freely.
[*Other Prentices rush in.*]

OMNES. We'll make you lay 'em down again more freely.
[*They attack Fustigo with their clubs.*]

WIFE. Help, help! My brother will be murderéd. 180

Enter Can[dido].

CAND. How now, what coil is here? Forbear, I say.

[*Exeunt all the Prentices except the 1 and 2.*]

GEO. He calls us flatcaps, and abuses us.

CAND. Why, sirs, do such examples flow from me?

WIFE. They are of your keeping, sir. Alas, poor brother!

FUS. I' faith, they ha' peppered me, sister. Look, dost not spin? Call you these prentices? I'll ne'er play at cards more when clubs is trump. I have a goodly coxcomb, sister, have I not?

CAND. Sister and brother? Brother [190 to my wife?

FUS. If you have any skill in heraldry, you may soon know that; break but her pate, and you shall see her blood and mine is all one.

CAND. A surgeon! Run, a surgeon!
[*Exit 1 Prentice.*] Why then wore you that forged name of cousin?

FUS. Because it's a common thing to call coz and ningle[5] nowadays all the [200 world over.

---

[1] In reference to the painting of the sheriff's gateposts for displaying proclamations.
[2] Derisive name for apprentice.
[3] Beat.
[4] Pleases.
[5] Mine ingle, my intimate.

CAND. Cousin! A name of much deceit,
folly, and sin,
For under that common abuséd word
Many an honest-tempered citizen
Is made a monster, and his wife trained
out
To foul adulterous action, full of fraud.
I may well call that word a city's bawd.
FUS. Troth, brother, my sister would
needs ha' me take upon me to gull your
patience a little; but it has made [210
double gules [1] on my coxcomb.
WIFE. What, playing the woman? Blab-
bing now, you fool?
CAND. O, my wife did but exercise a jest
upon your wit.
FUS. 'Sfoot, my wit bleeds for 't, me-
thinks.
CAND. Then let this warning more of sense
afford;
The name of cousin is a bloody word.
FUS. I'll ne'er call coz again whilst [220
I live, to have such a coil about it. This
should be a coronation day, for my head
runs claret lustily. *Exit.*

Enter an Officer.

CAND. Go, wish the surgeon to have great
respect— *Exit 2 Prentice.*
How now, my friend? What, do they sit
today?
OFF. Yes, sir, they expect you at the senate
house.
CAND. I thank your pains; I'll not be last
man there.— *Exit Offi[cer].*
My gown, George, go, my gown.—A
happy land,
Where grave men meet each cause to
understand;
Whose consciences are not cut out in
bribes 230
To gull the poor man's right; but in even
scales,
Peise [2] rich and poor, without corrup-
tion's vails.[3]
Come, where's the gown?
GEO. I cannot find the key, sir.
CAND. Request it of your mistress.
WIFE. Come not to me for any key;
I'll not be troubled to deliver it.
CAND. Good wife, kind wife, it is a need-
ful trouble,
But for my gown!

[1] Heraldic term for red. [2] Weigh. [3] Bribes, tips.

WIFE. Moths swallow down your gown!
You set my teeth on edge with talking
on 't.
CAND. Nay, prithee, sweet, I cannot meet
without it. 240
I should have a great fine set on my
head.
WIFE. Set on your coxcomb; tush, fine
me no fines.
CAND. Believe me, sweet, none greets the
senate house
Without his robe of reverence—that's his
gown.
WIFE. Well, then, y'are like to cross that
custom once;
You get nor key nor gown. And so
depart.—
[*Aside.*] This trick will vex him sure, and
fret his heart. *Exit.*
CAND. Stay, let me see; I must have some
device.
My cloak's too short; fie, fie, no cloak
will do 't.
It must be something fashioned like a
gown, 250
With my arms out. O, George, come
hither, George!
I prithee, lend me thine advice.
GEO. Troth, sir, were it any but you,
they would break open chest.
CAND. O, no! Break open chest! That's a
thieves' office.
Therein you counsel me against my
blood;
'Twould show impatience, that. Any
meek means
I would be glad to embrace. Mass, I have
got it.
Go, step up, fetch me down one of the
carpets,[4]
The saddest [5]-colored carpet, honest
George; 260
Cut thou a hole i' th' middle for my
neck,
Two for mine arms. Nay, prithee, look
not strange.
GEO. I hope you do not think, sir, as you
mean.
CAND. Prithee, about it quickly; the hour
chides me.
Warily, George, softly, take heed of eyes.
Exit George.
Out of two evils he's accounted wise

[4] Table covers. [5] Quietest.

That can pick out the least. The fine
imposed

For an ungownéd senator is about

Forty crusadoes,[1] the carpet not 'bove
four.

Thus have I chosen the lesser evil yet,

Preserved my patience, foiled her desperate wit.   271

Enter George.

GEO. Here, sir, here's the carpet.

CAND. O, well done, George; we'll cut it
just i' th' midst. [*They cut the carpet.*]
'Tis very well; I thank thee. Help it on.

GEO. It must come over your head, sir,
like a wench's petticoat.

CAND. Th'art in the right, good George; it
must indeed.

Fetch me a nightcap, for I'll gird it close,

As if my health were queasy. 'Twill show
well

For a rude, careless nightgown,[2] will 't
not, think'st?   280

GEO. Indifferent well, sir, for a nightgown, being girt and pleated.

CAND. Ay, and a nightcap on my head.

GEO. That's true, sir; I'll run and fetch
one, and a staff.   *Ex[it] Ge[orge].*

CAND. For thus they cannot choose but
conster[3] it:

One that is out of health takes no delight,

Wears his apparel without appetite,

And puts on heedless raiment without
form.—

Enter Geo[rge with nightcap and staff].

So, so, kind George. [*Puts on nightcap.*]
Be secret now; and, prithee,   290
Do not laugh at me till I'm out of
sight.

GEO. I laugh? Not I, sir.

CAND.   Now to the senate house.
Methinks I'd rather wear, without a
frown,

A patient carpet than an angry gown.
      Exit.

GEO. Now looks my m[aster] just like
one of our carpet knights,[4] only he's somewhat the honester of the two.

---

[1] Portuguese coins.
[2] Dressing gown.   [3] Construe.
[4] A contemptuous term for a knight whose
achievements belong rather to the carpet (the
lady's boudoir) than to the field of battle.

Enter Candido's Wife.

WIFE. What, is your master gone?

GEO. Yes, forsooth, his back is but new
turned.

WIFE. And in his cloak? Did he not vex
and swear?   300

GEO. [*Aside.*] No, but he'll make you
swear anon.—No, indeed, he went away
like a lamb.

WIFE. Key, sink to hell! Still patient,
patient still?
I am with child[5] to vex him. Prithee,
George,
If e'er thou look'st for favor at my
hands,
Uphold one jest for me.

GEO.   Against my master?

WIFE. 'Tis a mere jest, in faith. Say, wilt
thou do 't?

GEO. Well, what is 't?

WIFE. Here, take this key; thou know'st
where all things lie.   310
Put on thy master's best apparel—gown,
Chain, cap, ruff, everything. Be like
himself,
And, gainst his coming home, walk in the
shop;
Feign the same carriage and his patient
look.
'Twill breed but a jest, thou know'st.
Speak, wilt thou?

GEO. 'Twill wrong my master's patience.

WIFE.   Prithee, George.

GEO. Well, if you'll save me harmless,
and put me under covert-barn,[6] I am content to please you, provided it may breed
no wrong against him.   320

WIFE. No wrong at all. Here, take the
key; begone.
If any vex him, this; if not this, none.
      Exeunt.

SCENA viii.

[*A room in Bellafront's house.*]

Enter a Bawd and Roger.

BAWD. O Roger, Roger, where's your
mistress, where's your mistress? There's
the finest, neatest gentleman at my house,
but newly come over. O, where is she,
where is she, where is she?

---

[5] Filled with longing.
[6] Covert-baron, *i.e.*, under protection.

Rog. My mistress is abroad, but not amongst 'em. My mistress is not the whore now that you take her for.

Bawd. How? Is she not a whore? Do you go about to take away her good [10 name, Roger? You are a fine pander indeed.

Rog. I tell you, Madonna Fingerlock, I am not sad for nothing; I ha' not eaten one good meal this three-and-thirty days. I had wont to get sixteenpence by fetching a pottle of hippocras, but now those days are past. We had as good doings, Madonna Fingerlock, she within doors, and I without, as any poor young couple [20 in Milan.

Bawd. God's my life, and is she changed now?

Rog. I ha' lost by her squeamishness more than would have builded twelve bawdyhouses.

Bawd. And had she no time to turn honest but now? What a vile woman is this! Twenty pound a night, I'll be sworn, Roger, in good gold and no silver. Why, [30 here was a time! If she should ha' picked out a time, it could not be better—gold enough stirring, choice of men, choice of hair, choice of beards, choice of legs, and choice of every, every, everything. It cannot sink into my head that she should be such an ass. Roger, I never believe it.

Rog. Here she comes now.

Enter Bellafront.

Bawd. O sweet madonna, on with your loose gown, your felt,[1] and your feather. [40 There's the sweetest, prop'rest, gallantest gentleman at my house; he smells all of musk and ambergris, his pocket full of crowns, flame-colored doublet, red satin hose, carnation silk stockings, and a leg, and a body—O!

Bell. Hence, thou, our sex's monster, poisonous bawd,

Lust's factor,[2] and damnation's orator! Gossip of hell! Were all the harlots' sins

Which the whole world contains, numbered together, 50

Thine far exceeds them all; of all the creatures

That ever were created, thou art basest.

What serpent would beguile thee of thy office?

It is destestable, for thou liv'st

Upon the dregs of harlots, guard'st the door

Whilst couples go to dancing. O coarse devil!

Thou art the bastard's curse—thou brand'st his birth;

The lecher's French disease, for thou dry-suck'st him;

The harlot's poison, and thine own confusion.

Bawd. Marry come up, with a pox! [60 Have you nobody to rail against but your bawd now?

Bell. And you, knave pander, kinsman to a bawd!

Rog. You and I, madonna, are cousins.

Bell. Of the same blood and making, near allied.

Thou, that slave to sixpence, base-metaled villain!

Rog. Sixpence? Nay, that's not so. I never took under two shillings fourpence; I hope I know my fee.

Bell. I know not against which most to inveigh, 70

For both of you are damned so equally.

Thou never spar'st for oaths, swear'st anything,

As if thy soul were made of shoe leather: "God damn me, gentlemen, if she be within!"—

When in the next room she's found dallying.

Rog. If it be my vocation to swear, every man in his vocation. I hope my betters swear and damn themselves, and why should not I?

Bell. Roger, you cheat kind gentle- [80 men.

Rog. The more gulls they.

Bell. Slave, I cashier[3] thee.

Bawd. And you do cashier him, he shall be entertained.

Rog. Shall I? Then blûrt a[4] your service!

Bell. As hell would have it, entertained by you! I dare the devil himself to match those two. *Exit.* [90

Bawd. Marry gup,[5] are you grown so holy, so pure, so honest, with a pox?

---

[1] Hat.   [2] Agent.   [3] Dismiss.   [4] A curse on.   [5] Go up, get along!

Rog. Scurvy, honest punk! But stay, madonna, how must our agreement be now? For you know I am to have all the comings-in at the hall door, and you at the chamber door.

Bawd. True, Roger, except my vails.

Rog. Vails? What vails?

Bawd. Why, as thus: if a couple [100 come in a coach, and light to lie down a little, then, Roger, that's my fee, and you may walk abroad, for the coachman himself is their pander.

Rog. Is a [1] so? In truth, I have almost forgot for want of exercise. But how if I fetch this citizen's wife to that gull, and that madonna to that gallant, how then?

Bawd. Why then, Roger, you are [110 to have sixpence a lain; [2] so many lains, so many sixpences.

Rog. Is't so? Then I see we two shall agree, and live together.

Bawd. Ay, Roger, so long as there be any taverns and bawdyhouses in Milan.
Exeunt.

Scena ix.

[*Another room in Bellafront's house.*]

Enter Bellafront with lute, pen, ink, and paper being placed before her.

Song

[Bell.] The courtier's flattering jewels,
    Temptation's only fuels;
The lawyer's ill-got moneys,
    That suck up poor bees' honeys;
The citizen's son's riot,
    The gallant, costly diet;
Silks and velvets, pearls and ambers—
    Shall not draw me to their chambers.
    Silks and velvets, etc.

She writes.
O, 'tis in vain to write! It will not
    please.   10
Ink on this paper would ha' but presented
The foul black spots that stick upon my
    soul,
And rather make me loathsomer than
    wrought
My love's impression in Hippolito's
    thought.

[1] He.   [2] Lying down (?).

No, I must turn the chaste leaves of
    my breast,
And pick out some sweet means to breed
    my rest.
Hippolito, believe me, I will be
As true unto thy heart as thy heart to
    thee,
And hate all men, their gifts and company!

Enter Matheo, Castruchio, Fluello, Pioratto.

Mat. You, goody punk—*subaudi*,[3] [20
cockatrice—O, y'are a sweet whore of
your promise, are you not, think you? How
well you came to supper to us last night!
Mew, a whore, and break her word! Nay,
you may blush, and hold down your head
at it well enough. 'Sfoot, ask these gallants if we stayed not till we were as
hungry as serjeants.[4]

Flu. Ay, and their yeomen [5] too.

Cas. Nay, faith, acquaintance, let [30
me tell you, you forgat yourself too much.
We had excellent cheer, rare vintage, and
were drunk after supper.

Pio. And, when we were in, our woodcocks, sweet rogue, a brace of gulls, dwelling
here in the city, came in, and paid all the
shot.[6]

Mat. Pox on her! Let her alone.

Bell. O, I pray do, if you be gentlemen;
    I pray, depart the house. Beshrew the
        door [7]   46
For being so easily entreated! Faith,
I lent but little ear unto your talk;
My mind was busied otherwise, in troth,
And so your words did unregarded pass.
Let this suffice—I am not as I was.

Flu. I am not what I was? No, I'll
be sworn thou art not, for thou wert honest at five, and now th'art a punk at fifteen.
Thou wert yesterday a simple whore, and
now th'art a cunning, cony-catching baggage today.   51

Bell. I'll say I'm worse; I pray, forsake
    me then.
I do desire you leave me, gentlemen,
And leave yourselves. O, be not what
    you are,
Spendthrifts of soul and body!

[3] Understand.   [6] Reckoning, bill.
[4] Sheriff's officers.   [7] Doorkeeper.
[5] Assistants.

Let me persuade you to forsake all
  harlots,
Worse than the deadliest poisons—they
  are worse,
For o'er their souls hangs an eternal
  curse.
In being slaves to slaves, their labors
  perish;
Th'are seldom blessed with fruit, for,
  ere it blossoms,   60
Many a worm confounds it.
They have no issue but foul, ugly ones,
That run along with them, e'en to their
  graves;
For, stead of children, they breed rank
  diseases,
And all you gallants can bestow on them
Is that French infant, which ne'er acts,
  but speaks.
What shallow son and heir then, foolish
  gallants,
Would waste all his inheritance to pur-
  chase
A filthy, loathed disease, and pawn his
  body
To a dry evil? That usury's worst of all,
When th' int'rest will eat out the princi-
  pal.   71
MAT. [*Aside.*] 'Sfoot, she gulls 'em the
best! This is always her fashion, when
she would be rid of any company that she
cares not for, to enjoy mine alone.
FLU. What's here? Instructions, ad-
monitions, and caveats? Come out, you
scabbard of vengeance.
MAT. Fluello, spurn your hounds when
they foist[1]— you shall not spurn my punk,
I can tell you; my blood is vexed.   81
FLU. Pox a your blood! Make it a
quarrel.
MAT. Y'are a slave! Will that serve
turn?
OMNES. 'Sblood, hold, hold!
CAS. Matheo, Fluello, for shame, put up!
BELL. O, how many, thus
  Moved with a little folly, have let out
  Their souls in brothel houses, fell down
    and died   90
  Just at their harlot's foot, as 'twere in
    pride!
FLU. Matheo, we shall meet.
MAT. Ay, ay; anywhere saving at church;
pray take heed we meet not there.

FLU. Adieu, damnation!
CAS.   Cockatrice, farewell!
PIO. There's more deceit in women than in
  hell.
Exeunt [Castruchio, Fluello, and Pioratto].
MAT. Ha, ha, thou dost gull 'em so
rarely, so naturally! If I did not think
thou hadst been in earnest! Thou art a
sweet rogue for 't, i' faith.   100
BELL. Why are not you gone too, Signior
  Matheo?
  I pray depart my house; you may be-
    lieve me,
  In troth, I have no part of harlot in
    me.
MAT. How is this?
BELL. Indeed, I love you not, but hate
  you worse
  Than any man, because you were the first
  Gave money for my soul. You brake the
    ice,
  Which after turned a puddle; I was led
  By your temptation to be miserable.
  I pray, seek out some other that will
    fall,   110
  Or rather, I pray, seek out none at all.
MAT. Is 't possible to be impossible! An
honest whore! I have heard many honest
wenches turn strumpets with a wet finger,[2]
but for a harlot to turn honest is one of
Hercules' labors. It was more easy for
him in one night to make fifty queans[3]
than to make one of them honest again in
fifty years. Come, I hope thou dost but
jest.   120
BELL. 'Tis time to leave off jesting; I
  had almost
  Jested away salvation. I shall love you
  If you will soon forsake me.
MAT.   God be with thee!
BELL. O, tempt no more women! Shun
  their weighty curse!
  Women at best are bad; make them not
    worse.
  You gladly seek our sex's overthrow,
  But not to raise our states. For all your
    wrongs,
  Will you vouchsafe me but due recom-
    pense,
  To marry with me?
MAT. How! Marry with a punk, a   [130
cockatrice, a harlot? Marry, foh, I'll be
burnt thorough the nose first.

---

[1] Break wind silently.

[2] Easily, quickly.   [3] Whores.

BELL. Why, la, these are your oaths!
 You love to undo us,
  To put heaven from us, whilst our best
   hours waste;
  You love to make us lewd, but never
   chaste.
MAT. I'll hear no more of this, this ground
 upon.
 Th'art damned for alt'ring thy religion.
           Exit.
BELL. Thy lust and sin speak so much.
 Go thou, my ruin,
  The first fall my soul took! By my ex-
   ample,
 I hope few maidens now will put their
  heads   140
 Under men's girdles; who least trusts is
  most wise.
 Men's oaths do cast a mist before our
  eyes.
 My best of wit, be ready! Now I go
 By some device to greet Hippolito.

SCENA x.

[An apartment in Hippolito's house.]

*Enter a Servant, setting out a table, on which
he places a skull, a picture [of Infelice],
a book, and a taper.*

SER. So, this is Monday morning, and
now must I to my huswif'ry. Would I
had been created a shoemaker, for all the
gentle craft are gentlemen every Monday
by their copy,[1] and scorn then to work one
true stitch. My master means sure to turn
me into a student, for here's my book,
here my desk, here my light, this my close
chamber, and here my punk—so that this
dull, drowsy first day of the week [10
makes me half a priest, half a chandler, half a
painter, half a sexton, ay, and half a bawd;
for all this day my office is to do nothing but
keep the door. To prove it, look you, this
good face and yonder gentleman, so soon as
ever my back is turned, will be naught together.

Enter Hippolito.

HIP. Are all the windows shut?
SER. Close, sir, as the fist of a courtier
that hath stood [2] in three reigns. 20

---

[1] Membership certificate.
[2] Waited without advancement (?).

HIP. Thou art a faithful servant, and ob-
 serv'st
 The calendar both of my solemn vows
 And ceremonious sorrow. Get thee gone;
 I charge thee on thy life, let not the
  sound
 Of any woman's voice pierce through
  that door.
SER. If they do, my lord, I'll pierce some
 of them.
 What will your lordship have to break-
  fast?
HIP. Sighs.
SER. What to dinner?
HIP. Tears.   30
SER. The one of them, my lord, will fill
you too full of wind, the other wet you too
much. What to supper?
HIP. That which now thou canst not
get me, the constancy of a woman.
SER. Indeed, that's harder to come by
than ever was Ostend.[3]
HIP. Prithee, away!
SER. I'll make away myself presently,
which few servants will do for their [40
lords, but rather help to make them away.
Now to my doorkeeping; I hope to pick
something out of it.   *Exit.*
HIP. *[Taking up the picture.]* My In-
 felice's face, her brow, her eye,
 The dimple on her cheek! And such
  sweet skill
 Hath from the cunning workman's
  pencil flown,
 These lips look fresh and lively as her
  own,
 Seeming to move and speak. 'Las, now
  I see
 The reason why fond women love to buy
 Adulterate complexion! Here 'tis
  read: 50
 False colors last after the true be dead.
 Of all the roses grafted on her cheeks,
 Of all the graces dancing in her eyes,
 Of all the music set upon her tongue,
 Of all that was past woman's excellence,
 In her white bosom—look!—a painted
  board
 Circumscribes all. Earth can no bliss
  afford.
 Nothing of her but this? This cannot
  speak,

---

[3] Taken Sept. 8, 1604, after holding out for
more than three years.

It has no lap for me to rest upon,
No lip worth tasting; here the worms
will feed,   60
As in her coffin. Hence, then, idle art!
True love's best pictured in a truelove's
heart.
Here art thou drawn, sweet maid, till
this be dead,
So that thou liv'st twice, twice art buriéd.
Thou figure of my friend, lie there.
What's here?   [*Takes up the skull.*]
Perhaps this shrewd[1] pate was mine
enemy's.
'Las, say it were! I need not fear him
now!
For all his braves,[2] his contumelious
breath,
His frowns, though dagger-pointed, all
his plot,
Though ne'er so mischievous, his Italian
pills,   70
His quarrels, and that common fence,
his law,
See, see, they're all eaten out! Here's
not left one!
How clean they're picked away to the
bare bone!
How mad are mortals, then, to rear
great names
On tops of swelling houses, or to wear out
Their fingers' ends in dirt, to scrape up
gold,
Not caring, so that sumpter horse, the
back,
Be hung with gaudy trappings! With
what coarse,
Yea, rags most beggarly, they clothe the
soul!
Yet, after all, their gayness looks thus
foul.   80
What fools are men to build a garish
tomb,
Only to save the carcass whilst it rots,
To maintain 't long in stinking, make
good carrion,
But leave no good deeds to preserve
them sound!
For good deeds keep men sweet, long
above ground.
And must all come to this? Fools, wise,
all hither?
Must all heads thus at last be laid together?

[1] Accursed.   [2] Boasts.

Draw me my picture then, thou grave
neat workman,
After this fashion, not like this. These
colors   89
In time, kissing but air, will be kissed off;
But here's a fellow—that which he lays
on
Till doomsday alters not complexion.
Death's the best painter then; they that
draw shapes
And live by wicked faces are but God's
apes.
They come but near the life, and there
they stay.
This fellow draws life too; his art is
fuller—
The pictures which he makes are with-
out color.

Enter his Servant.

SER. Here's a person would speak with
you, sir.
HIP. Hah!   100
SER. A parson,[3] sir, would speak with
you.
HIP. Vicar?
SER. Vicar? No, sir; h'as too good a
face to be a vicar yet; a youth, a very
youth.
HIP. What youth? Of man or woman?
Lock the doors.
SER. If it be a woman, maribones and
potato pies[4] keep me from meddling with
her, for the thing has got the breeches! [110
'Tis a male-varlet sure, my lord, for a
woman's tailor ne'er measured him.
HIP. Let him give thee his message and be
gone.
SER. He says he's Signior Matheo's
man, but I know he lies.
HIP. How dost thou know it?
SER. Cause h'as ne'er a beard. 'Tis
his boy, I think, sir, whosoe'er paid for his
nursing.
HIP. Send him and keep the door.   120
     [*Exit Servant.*]
(*Reads.*) "*Fata si liceat mihi,*
Fingere arbitrio meo,
Temperem zephyro levi vela."[5]

[3] Common pronunciation of *person.*
[4] Marrow bones and potato pies were regarded
as aphrodisiacs.
[5] "If I were permitted to determine my fate
according to my wish, I should regulate my sails
by a light breeze" (Seneca, *Œdipus,* l. 882).

I'd sail, were I to choose, not in the ocean;
Cedars are shaken when shrubs do feel no bruise.

Enter Bellafront, like a Page [, giving a letter].

How? From Matheo?
BELL.   Yes, my lord.
HIP.   Art sick?
BELL. Not all in health, my lord.
HIP.   Keep off!
BELL.   I do.—
  [Aside.] Hard fate when women are compelled to woo.
HIP. This paper does speak nothing.
BELL.   Yes, my lord,
Matter of life it speaks, and therefore writ   130
In hidden character; to me instruction
My master gives, and, less you please to stay
Till you both meet, I can the text display.
HIP. Do so; read out.
BELL.   I am already out.[1]
               [Discloses herself.]
Look on my face, and read the strangest story!
HIP. What, villain, ho!

Enter his Servant.

SER. Call you, my lord?
HIP. Thou slave, thou hast let in the devil!
SER. Lord bless us, where? He's [140 not cloven, my lord, that I can see; besides, the devil goes more like a gentleman than a page. Good my lord, *buon coraggio.*[2]
HIP. Thou hast let in a woman in man's shape. And thou art damned for 't.
SER. Not damned, I hope, for putting in a woman to a lord.
HIP. Fetch me my rapier!—Do not—I shall kill thee!
Purge this infected chamber of that plague
That runs upon me thus. Slave, thrust her hence!   150
SER. Alas, my lord, I shall never be able to thrust her hence without help. Come, mermaid, you must to sea again.

  [1] *I.e.*, out of words.   [2] Good courage.

BELL. Hear me but speak; my words shall be all music;
Hear me but speak.   *[Knocking within.]*
HIP.   Another beats the door;
Tother she-devil! Look!
SER. Why, then, hell's broke loose. *Exit.*
HIP. Hence; guard the chamber! Let no more come on!
One woman serves for man's damnation.
Beshrew thee, thou dost make me violate
The chastest and most sanctimonious vow   160
That e'er was entered in the court of heaven!
I was, on meditation's spotless wings,
Upon my journey thither; like a storm
Thou beat'st my ripened cogitations
Flat to the ground, and like a thief dost stand
To steal devotion from the holy land.
BELL. If woman were thy mother, if thy heart
Be not all marble, or, if 't marble be,
Let my tears soften it, to pity me.
I do beseech thee, do not thus with scorn   170
Destroy a woman!
HIP.   Woman, I beseech thee,
Get thee some other suit; this fits thee not.
I would not grant it to a kneeling queen;
I cannot love thee, nor I must not. See
       [Points to Infelice's picture.]
The copy of that obligation,
Where my soul's bound in heavy penalties.
BELL. She's dead, you told me; she'll let fall her suit.
HIP. My vows to her fled after her to heaven.
Were thine eyes clear as mine, thou mightst behold her,   179
Watching upon yon battlements of stars.
How I observe them! Should I break my bond,
This board would rive in twain, these wooden lips
Call me most perjured villain. Let it suffice,
I ha' set thee in the path; is 't not a sign
I love thee, when with one so most most dear
I'll have thee fellows? All are fellows there.

BELL. Be greater than a king; save not a
　　body,
But from eternal shipwrack keep a
　　soul.
If not, and that again sin's path I tread,
The grief be mine, the guilt fall on thy
　　head!　　　　　　　　　　　　190
HIP. Stay, and take physic for it. Read
　　this book;
Ask counsel of this head what's to be
　　done.
He'll strike it dead [1] that 'tis damnation
If you turn Turk again. O, do it not!
Though heaven cannot allure you to do
　　well,
From doing ill let hell fright you; and
　　learn this:
The soul whose bosom lust did never
　　touch
Is God's fair bride, and maidens' souls
　　are such;
The soul that, leaving chastity's white
　　shore,
Swims in hot sensual streams, is the
　　devil's whore.—　　　　　　　200
How now, who comes?

Enter his Servant [with a letter].

SER. No more knaves, my lord, that
wear smocks! Here's a letter from Doctor
Benedict. I would not enter his man,
though he had hairs at his mouth, for fear
he should be a woman, for some women
have beards; marry, they are half witches.
'Slid, you are a sweet youth to wear a
codpiece, and have no pins to stick upon 't.
HIP. I'll meet the doctor, tell him; yet
　　tonight　　　　　　　　　　　210
I cannot; but at morrow rising sun
I will not fail.—Go, woman; fare thee
　　well.
　　　　　Exeunt [Hippolito and Servant].
BELL. The lowest fall can be but into hell.
It does not move him. I must therefore
　　fly
From this undoing city, and with
　　tears
Wash off all anger from my father's
　　brow.
He cannot sure but joy, seeing me new
　　born.
A woman honest first, and then turn
　　whore,

[1] *I.e.*, state flatly.

Is, as with me, common to thousands
　　more;
But from a strumpet to turn chaste, that
　　sound　　　　　　　　　　　220
Has oft been heard, that woman hardly
　　found.　　　　　　　　　*Exit.*

SCENA xi.[2]

[A street near Candido's shop.]

Enter Fustigo, Crambo, and Poli.

FUS. Hold up your hands, gentlemen.
Here's one, two, three. [*Gives money.*] Nay,
I warrant they are sound pistoles, and
without flaws; I had them of my sister and
I know she uses to put [up] nothing that's
cracked—four, five, six, seven, eight, and
nine. By this hand, bring me but a piece of
his blood, and you shall have nine more.
I'll lurk in a tavern not far off, and provide supper to close up the end of the　[10
tragedy. The linen draper's, remember.
Stand to 't, I beseech you, and play your
parts perfectly.
CRAM. Look you, signior, 'tis not your
gold that we weigh.
FUS. Nay, nay, weigh it and spare not;
if it lack one grain of corn, I'll give you a
bushel of wheat to make it up.
CRAM. But by your favor, signior, which
of the servants is it? Because we'll　[20
punish justly.
FUS. Marry, 'tis the head man; you
shall taste him by his tongue; a pretty, tall,
prating fellow, with a Tuscalonian beard.
POLI. Tuscalonian? Very good.
FUS. God's life, I was ne'er so thrummed
since I was a gentleman. My coxcomb was
dry-beaten, as if my hair had been hemp.
CRAM. We'll dry-beat some of them.
FUS. Nay, it grew so high that my　[30
sister cried out murder, very manfully. I
have her consent, in a manner, to have him
peppered; else I'll not do 't, to win more
than ten cheaters do at a rifling.[3] Break
but his pate, or so, only his mazer,[4] because
I'll have his head in a cloth as well as mine.
He's a linen draper, and may take enough.
I could enter mine action of battery against
him, but we may perhaps be both dead and
rotten before the lawyers would end it.　[40
CRAM. No more to do, but ensconce

[2] Original reads *11.SCE.*　　[4] Mazzard, head.
[3] A game with dice.

yourself i' th' tavern. Provide no great cheer—a couple of capons, some pheasants, plovers, an orangeado [1] pie, or so. But how bloody soe'er the day be, sally you not forth.

Fus. No, no; nay, if I stir, somebody shall stink. I'll not budge; I'll lie like a dog in a manger.

Cram. Well, well, to the tavern; let [50 not our supper be raw, for you shall have blood enough, your belly full.

Fus. That's all (so God sa' me) I thirst after: blood for blood, bump for bump, nose for nose, head for head, plaster for plaster. And so farewell. What shall I call your names? Because I'll leave word, if any such come to the bar.

Cram. My name is Corporal Crambo.

Poh. And mine, Lieutenant Poh.　60
　　　　　　　　　　　　　　　Exit.[2]

Cram. Poli is as tall [3] a man as ever opened oyster; I would not be the devil to meet Poh. Farewell.

Fus. Nor I, by this light, if Poh be such a Poli.　　　　　　　　*Exeunt.*

[SCENA xii.]

Enter Candido's Wife in her shop, and the two Prentices.

Wife. What's a-clock now?

2 Pren.　　　　　'Tis almost twelve.

Wife.　　　　　　　　That's well.
The Senate will leave wording [4] presently.
But is George ready?

2 Pren.　　Yes, forsooth, he's furbushed.[5]

Wife. Now, as you ever hope to win my favor,
Throw both your duties and respects on him
With the like awe as if he were your master.
Let not your looks betray it with a smile
Or jeering glance to any customer;
Keep a true settled countenance, and beware
You laugh not, whatsoe'er you hear or see.　　10

2 Pren. I warrant you, mistress, let us alone for keeping our countenance; for, if I list, there's never a fool in all Milan shall

make me laugh, let him play the fool never so like an ass, whether it be the fat court fool or the lean city fool.

Wife. Enough then; call down George.

2 Pren.　　　　　I hear him coming.

Enter George [in Candido's dress].

Wife. Be ready with your legs [6] then; let me see
How court'sy would become him.—Gallantly!
Beshrew my blood, a proper, seemly man,　　20
Of a choice carriage, walks with a good port!

Geo. I thank you, mistress, my back's broad enough, now my master's gown's on.

Wife. Sure, I should think 'twere the least of sin
To mistake the master, and to let him in.

Geo. 'Twere a good *Comedy of Errors* that, i' faith.

2 Pren. Whist, whist! My master!

Enter Candido, and exit presently.

Wife. You all know your tasks.—God's my life,
What's that he has got on 's back? Who can tell?　　30

Geo. [*Aside.*] That can I, but I will not.

Wife. Girt about him like a madman! What, has he lost his cloak too? This is the maddest fashion that e'er I saw. What said he, George, when he passed by thee?

Geo. Troth, mistress, nothing! Not so much as a bee, he did not hum; not so much as a bawd, he did not hem; not so much as a cuckold, he did not ha; neither hum, [40 hem, nor ha; only stared me in the face, passed along, and made haste in, as if my looks had wrought with him to give him a stool.[7]

Wife. Sure he's vexed now; this trick has moved his spleen.
He's angered now, because he uttered nothing;
And wordless wrath breaks out more violent.
May be he'll strive for place when he comes down,
But, if thou lov'st me, George, afford him none.

---

[1] Candied orange peel.　　　　[4] Disputing.
[2] Original reads *Exeunt.*　　　[5] Furbished.
[3] Bold.

[6] Bows.　　　　　　　　[7] Defecation.

GEO. Nay, let me alone to play [50 my master's prize,[1] as long as my mistress warrants me. I'm sure I have his best clothes on, and I scorn to give place to any that is inferior in apparel to me; that's an axiom, a principle, and is observed as much as the fashion. Let that persuade you, then, that I'll shoulder with him for the upper hand in the shop as long as this chain [2] will maintain it.

WIFE. Spoke with the spirit of a [60 master, though with the tongue of a prentice.

Enter Candido like a prentice.

Why, how now, madman? What, in your tricksy coats?

CAND. O, peace, good mistress.—

Enter Crambo and Poli.

See, what you lack? What is 't you buy? Pure calicoes, fine hollands, choice cambrics, neat lawns! See what you buy! Pray come near; my master will use you well; he can afford you a pennyworth.

WIFE. Ay, that he can, out of a whole piece of lawn, i' faith.   70

CAND. Pray see your choice here, gentlemen.

WIFE. O fine fool! What a madman, a patient madman! Who ever heard of the like? Well, sir, I'll fit you and your humor presently. What, cross-points? [3] I'll untie 'em all in a trice; I'll vex you, i' faith. Boy, take your cloak; quick, come.
                    Exit [with 1 Prentice].
CAND. Be covered, George! This chain and welted gown
Bare to this coat? Then the world's upside down!   80
GEO. Umh, umh, hum.
CRAM. That's the shop, and there's the fellow.
POH. Ay, but the master is walking in there.
CRAM. No matter, we'll in.
POH. 'Sblood, dost long to lie in limbo?
CRAM. And limbo be in hell, I care not.
CAND. Look you, gentlemen, your choice. Cambrics?   90

[1] A public contest for a master's degree in fencing.
[2] Symbol of office.
[3] Crossed laces by which garments were fastened.

CRAM. No, sir, some shirting.
CAND. You shall.
CRAM. Have you none of this striped canvas for doublets?
CAND. None striped, sir, but plain.
2 PREN. I think there be one piece striped within.
GEO. Step, sirrah, and fetch it.—Hum, hum, hum.   99
[*Exit 2 Prentice and returns with the canvas.*]
CAND. Look you, gentlemen, I'll make but one spreading; here's a piece of cloth, fine yet shall wear like iron. 'Tis without fault; take this upon my word, 'tis without fault.
CRAM. Then 'tis better than you, sirrah.
CAND. Ay, and a number more? O, that each soul
Were but as spotless as this innocent white,
And had as few breaks in it!
CRAM.   'Twould have some then.
There was a fray here last day in this shop.
CAND. There was, indeed, a little flea-biting.   110
POLI. A gentleman had his pate broke; call you that but a flea-biting?
CAND. He had so.
CRAM. Zounds, do you stand to it?
                    He strikes him.
GEO. 'Sfoot, clubs, clubs! Prentices, down with 'em!

[*Enter Prentices, who disarm Crambo and Poli.*]

Ay, you rogues, strike a citizen in 's shop?
CAND. None of you stir, I pray. Forbear, good George.
CRAM. I beseech you, sir, we mistook our marks; deliver us our weapons.   120
GEO. Your head bleeds, sir; cry clubs!
CAND. I say you shall not; pray be patient;
Give them their weapons. Sirs, y'are best be gone;
I tell you here are boys more tough than bears.
Hence, lest more fists do walk about your ears.
BOTH. We thank you, sir.   *Exeunt.*
CAND.   You shall not follow them;
Let them alone, pray. This did me no harm;

Troth, I was cold, and the blow made
  me warm;
I thank 'em for 't.   Besides, I had
  decreed [1]
To have a vein pricked—I did mean to
  bleed,   130
So that there's money saved. They are
  honest men;
Pray use 'em well when they appear
  again.

GEO. Yes, sir, we'll use 'em like honest
men.

CAND. Ay, well said, George, like honest
men, though they be arrant knaves, for
that's the phrase of the city. Help to lay
up these wares.

[*He and the Prentices retire to the back of the
        shop.*] *Enter his Wife with Officers.*

WIFE. Yonder he stands.

[1] OFF.   What, in a prentice's coat?

WIFE. Ay, ay; mad, mad. Pray, take heed.

CAND.   How now,   140
What news with them? What make they
  with my wife?—
Officers, is she attached?[2]—Look to your
  wares.

WIFE. He talks to himself. O, he's much
  gone indeed.

[1] OFF. Pray, pluck up a good heart; be
  not so fearful.
Sirs, hark, we'll gather to him by degrees.

WIFE. Ay, ay, by degrees, I pray. O me!
What makes he with the lawn in his
  hand?
He'll tear all the ware in my shop.

[1] OFF. Fear not, we'll catch him on a
  sudden.

WIFE. You had need do so; pray take
  heed of your warrant.   150

[1] OFF. I warrant, mistress. Now, Signior
  Candido.

CAND. Now, sir, what news with you, sir?

WIFE. [*Aside to 1 Officer.*] "What news
  with you?" he says. O, he 's far gone!

[1] OFF. [*Aside to Wife.*] I pray, fear
  nothing; let's alone with him.—
Signior, you look not like yourself, methinks.—
Steal you a tother side.—Y'are changed,
  y'are altered.

CAND. Changed, sir? Why, true, sir. Is
  "changed" strange? 'Tis not
The fashion unless it alter. Monarchs
  turn
To beggars, beggars creep into the
  nests
Of princes, masters serve their prentices,
Ladies their serving-men, men turn to
  women.   161

[1] OFF. And women turn to men.

CAND. Ay, and women turn to men, you
say true. Ha, ha, a mad world, a mad
world.   [*Officers seize him.*]

[1] OFF. Have we caught you, sir?

CAND. Caught me? Well, well, you have
caught me.

WIFE. He laughs in your faces.

GEO. A rescue, prentices! My master's
  catchpolled.[3]   170

[1] OFF. I charge you, keep the peace, or
  have your legs
Gartered with irons! We have from the
  duke
A warrant strong enough for what we do.

CAND. I pray, rest quiet; I desire no rescue.

WIFE. La, he desires no rescue! 'Las, poor
  heart,
He talks against himself.

CAND.   Well, what's the matter?

[1] OFF. [*Binding Candido.*] Look to that
  arm.
Pray, make sure work; double the cord.

CAND.   Why, why?

WIFE. Look how his head goes. Should he
  get but loose,
O, 'twere as much as all our lives were
  worth!   180

[1] OFF. Fear not; we'll make all sure for
  our own safety.

CAND. Are you at leisure now?   Well,
  what's the matter?
Why do I enter into bonds thus, ha?

[1] OFF. Because y'are mad, put fear upon
  your wife.

WIFE. O, ay, I went in danger of my life
every minute.

CAND. What, am I mad, say you, and I
  not know it?

[1] OFF. That proves you mad, because
  you know it not.

WIFE. Pray talk to him as little as you
  can;
You see he's too far spent.

---

[1] Decided.   [2] Arrested.   [3] Caught by a bumbailiff.

CAND.   Bound with strong cord!
   A sister's[1] thread, i' faith, had been
     enough   191
   To lead me anywhere.—Wife, do you
     long?
   You are mad too, or else you do me
     wrong.
GEO. But are you mad indeed, master?
CAND.   My wife says so,
   And what she says, George, is all truth,
     you know.—
   And whither now, to Bethlem Mon-
     astery?
   Ha! whither?
[1] OFF.   Faith, e'en to the mad-
     men's pound.
CAND. A God's name! Still I feel my
     patience sound.   *Exit [with Officers].*
GEO. Come, we'll see whither he goes.
If the master be mad, we are his   [200
servants, and must follow his steps; we'll
be madcaps too. Farewell, mistress; you
shall have us all in Bedlam.
         Exeunt [George and Prentices].
WIFE. I think I have fitted you now, you
   and your clothes.
   If this move not his patience, nothing
     can;
   I'll swear then I have a saint, and not a
     man.   *[Exit.]*

SCENA·xiii.

[A street near an abbey.]

*Enter Duke, Doctor, Fluello, Castruchio,
                    Pioratto.*

DUKE. Give us a little leave.
[Exeunt Fluello, Castruchio, and Pioratto.]
          Doctor, your news.
DOC. I sent for him, my lord. At last he
   came,
   And did receive all speech that went
     from me
   As gilded pills made to prolong his health.
   My credit with him wrought it, for some
     men
   Swallow even empty hooks, like fools
     that fear
   No drowning where 'tis deepest, cause
     'tis clear.
   In th' end we sat and eat;[2] a health I
     drank
   To Infelice's sweet, departed soul.

This train[3] I knew would take.
DUKE.   'Twas excellent. 10
DOC. He fell with such devotion on his
   knees
   To pledge the same—
DUKE.   Fond, superstitious fool!
DOC. That had he been inflamed with zeal
   of prayer,
   He could not pour 't out with more
     reverence.
   About my neck he hung, wept on my
     cheek,
   Kissed it, and swore he would adore my
     lips,
   Because they brought forth Infelice's
     name.
DUKE. Ha, ha! Alack, alack!
DOC. The cup he lifts up high, and thus he
   said,
   "Here, noble maid!"—drinks, and was
     poisonéd.   20
DUKE. And died?
DOC.   And died, my lord.
DUKE.   Thou in that word
   Hast pieced mine aged hours out with
     more years
   Than thou hast taken from Hippolito.
   A noble youth he was, but lesser
     branches
   Hind'ring the greater's growth must be
     lopped off,
   And feed the fire. Doctor, we're now all
     thine,
   And use us so; be bold.
DOC.   Thanks, gracious lord.
   My honored lord—
DUKE. Hum.
DOC. I do beseech your grace to bury deep
   This bloody act of mine.
DUKE.   Nay, nay, for that, 31
   Doctor, look you to 't; me it shall not
     move.
   They're cursed that ill do, not that ill do
     love.
DOC. You throw an angry forehead on my
   face;
   But, be you pleased backward thus far
     to look,
   That, for your good, this evil I under-
     took—
DUKE. Ay, ay, we conster so.
DOC. And only for your love.
DUKE.   Confessed; 'tis true.

---

[1] Sewster's, seamstress'.   [2] Preterit.   [3] Device.

Doc. Nor let it stand against me as a bar
    To thrust me from your presence; nor
      believe,   40
    As princes have quick thoughts, that
      now, my finger
    Being dipped in blood, I will not spare
      the hand,
    But that for gold—as what can gold not
      do?—
    I may be hired to work the like on you.
Duke. Which to prevent—
Doc.   'Tis from my heart as far—
Duke. No matter, doctor; cause I'll
    fearless sleep,
    And that you shall stand clear of that
      suspicion,
    I banish thee forever from my court.
    This principle is old, but true as fate:
    Kings may love treason, but the traitor
      hate.   *Exit.*
Doc. Is 't so? Nay then, duke, your stale
    principle,   51
    With one as stale, the doctor thus shall
      quit: [1]
    He falls himself that digs another's
      pit.—
    How now! Where is he? Will he not
      meet me?

Enter the Doctor's Man.

Do. Man. Meet you, sir? He might
have met with three fencers in this time,
and have received less hurt than by meeting one doctor of physic. Why, sir, he has
walked under the old abbey wall yonder
this hour, till he's more cold than a   [60
citizen's country house in Janivere. You
may smell him behind, sir. La you, yonder he comes.
Doc. Leave me.

Enter Hippolito.

Do. Man. Ich lurch, [2] if you will.   *Exit.*
Doc. O my most noble friend!
Hip.   Few but yourself
    Could have enticed me thus to trust
      the air
    With my close sighs. You sent for me.
      What news?
Doc. Come, you must doff this black,
    dye that pale cheek

[1] Repay.
[2] Perhaps dialect for *I lurk* (*i.e.*, wait); or
perhaps a misprint for *i' th' lurch.*

Into his own color, go, attire yourself
Fresh as a bridegroom when he meets
    his bride.   71
The duke has done much treason to
    thy love,
'Tis now revealed; 'tis now to be re-
    venged.
Be merry, honored friend.   Thy lady
    lives.
Hip. What lady?
Doc.   Infelice; she's revived.
    Revived? Alack, Death never had the
      heart
    To take breath from her.
Hip.   Umh! I thank you, sir;
    Physic prolongs life when it cannot
      save.
    This helps not my hopes; mine are in
      their grave.
    You do some wrong to mock me.
Doc.   By that love
    Which I have ever borne you, what I
      speak   81
    Is truth. The maiden lives; that fun-
      eral,
    Duke's tears, the mourning, was all
      counterfeit.
    A sleepy draught cozened the world and
      you;
    I was his minister, and then chambered
      up
    To stop discovery.
Hip.   O treacherous duke!
Doc. He cannot hope so certainly for
    bliss
    As he believes that I have poisoned you.
    He wooed me to 't; I yielded, and con-
      firmed him
    In his most bloody thoughts.
Hip.   A very devil!
Doc. Her did he closely coach to Ber-
    gamo,   91
    And thither—
Hip.   Will I ride. Stood Bergamo
    In the Low Countries of black hell, I'll
      to her.
Doc. You shall to her, but not to Bergamo.
    How passion makes you fly beyond
      yourself!
    Much of that weary journey I ha' cut
      off,
    For she by letters hath intelligence
    Of your supposéd death, her own inter-
      ment,

And all those plots which that false
    duke, her father,
Has wrought against you; and she'll
    meet you—
HIP.   O, when? 100
DOC. Nay, see how covetous are your
    desires.
Early tomorrow morn.
HIP.   O where, good father?
DOC. At Bethlem Monastery. Are you
    pleased now?
HIP. At Bethlem Monastery! The place
    well fits;
It is the school where those that lose
    their wits
Practice again to get them. I am sick
Of that disease; all love is lunatic.
DOC. We'll steal away this night in some
    disguise.
Father Anselmo, a most reverend friar,
Expects our coming, before whom we'll
    lay   110
Reasons so strong that he shall yield
    in bands
Of holy wedlock to tie both your hands.
HIP. This is such happiness
    That, to believe it, 'tis impossible.
DOC. Let all your joys then die in mis-
    belief;
I will reveal no more.
HIP.   O, yes, good father,
I am so well acquainted with despair
I know not how to hope; I believe all.
DOC. We'll hence this night. Much must
    be done, much said;
But, if the doctor fail not in his
    charms,   120
Your lady shall ere morning fill these
    arms.
HIP. Heavenly physician! Far thy fame
    shall spread,
That mak'st two lovers speak when
    they be dead.   *Exeunt.*

[SCENA xiv.

A hall in the Duke's palace.]

Candido's Wife and George; Pioratto meets
                  them.

WIFE. O, watch, good George, watch
which way the duke comes.
GEO. Here comes one of the butter-
flies; ask him.

WIFE. Pray, sir, comes the duke this
way?
PIO. He's upon coming, mistress. *Exit.*
WIFE. I thank you, sir. George, are
there many mad folks where thy master
lies?   10
GEO. O, yes, of all countries some, but
especially mad Greeks—they swarm. Troth,
mistress, the world is altered with you;
you had not wont to stand thus with
a paper "humbly complaining."[1] But
you're well enough served; provender
pricked [2] you, as it does many of our city
wives besides.
WIFE. Dost think, George, we shall
get him forth?   20
GEO. Truly, mistress, I cannot tell;
I think you'll hardly [3] get him forth. Why,
'tis strange! 'Sfoot, I have known many
women that have had mad rascals to their
husbands, whom they would belabor by
all means possible to keep 'em in their
right wits; but of a woman to long to turn
a tame man into a madman, .why, the
devil himself was never used so by his
dam.   30
WIFE. How does he talk, George?
Ha! Good George, tell me.
GEO. Why, you're best go see.
WIFE. Alas, I am afraid!
GEO. Afraid! You had more need be
ashamed. He may rather be afraid of you.
WIFE. But, George, he's not stark mad,
is he? He does not rave; he is not horn-
mad, George, is he?
GEO. Nay, I know not that, but he [40
talks like a justice of peace, of a thousand
matters, and to no purpose.
WIFE. I'll to the monastery. I shall be
mad till I enjoy him; I shall be sick until
I see him; yet, when I do see him, I shall
weep out mine eyes.
GEO. Ay, I'd fain see a woman weep
out her eyes! That's as true as to say a
man's cloak burns, when it hangs in the
water. I know you'll weep, mistress, but [50
what says the painted cloth?[4]

Trust not a woman when she cries,
For she'll pump water from her eyes
With a wet finger, and in faster showers
Than April when he rains down flowers.

---

[1] The opening phrase of a petition.   [2] Urged.
[3] With difficulty.   [4] Hanging with mottoes on it.

WIFE. Ay, but, George, that painted cloth is worthy to be hanged up for lying. All women have not tears at will, unless they have good cause.

GEO. Ay, but, mistress, how easily [60 will they find a cause, and, as one of our cheese trenchers [1] says very learnedly:

As out of wormwood bees suck honey,
As from poor clients lawyers firk [2] money,
As parsley from a roasted cunny [3]—
So, though the day be ne'er so sunny,
If wives will have it rain, down then it drives;
The calmest husbands make the storm[i]est wives.

WIFE. Tame, George; but I ha' done storming now.   70

GEO. Why, that's well done. Good mistress, throw aside this fashion of your humor; be not so fantastical in wearing it; storm no more, long no more. This longing has made you come short of many a good thing that you might have had from my master. Here comes the duke.

Enter Duke, Fluello, Pioratto, Sinezi.

WIFE. O, I beseech you, pardon my offense,
    In that I durst abuse your grace's warrant;
    Deliver forth my husband, good my lord.   80

DUKE. Who is her husband?

FLU.   Candido, my lord.

DUKE. Where is he?

WIFE.   He's among the lunatics.
    He was a man made up without a gall;
    Nothing could move him, nothing could convert
    His meek blood into fury; yet, like a monster,
    I often beat at the most constant rock
    Of his unshaken patience, and did long
    To vex him.

DUKE.   Did you so?

WIFE.   And for that purpose
    Had warrant from your grace to carry him
    To Bethlem Monastery, whence they will not free him   90
    Without your grace's hand that sent him in.

[1] *I.e.*, inscriptions on cheese trenchers.
[2] Trick.   [3] Cony, rabbit.

DUKE. You have longed fair; 'tis you are mad, I fear.
    It's fit to fetch him thence, and keep you there.
    If he be mad, why would you have him forth?

GEO. And please your grace, he's not stark mad, but only talks like a young gentleman, somewhat fantastically, that's all. There's a thousand about your court, city, and country madder than he.

DUKE. Provide a warrant; you shall have our hand.   100

GEO. Here's a warrant ready drawn, my lord.

DUKE. Get pen and ink, get pen and ink.   [*Exit George.*]

Enter Castruchio.

CAS. Where is my lord the duke?

DUKE.   How now! More madmen?

CAS. I have strange news, my lord.

DUKE.   Of what? Of whom?

CAS. Of Infelice, and a marriage.

DUKE. Ha! Where? With whom?

CAS.   Hippolito.

[*Enter George, with pen and ink.*]

GEO.   Here, my lord.

DUKE. Hence with that woman! Void the room!

FLU.   Away!
    The duke's vexed.

GEO.   Whoop, come, mistress, the duke's mad too.

                    Exeunt [*Wife and George*].

DUKE. Who told me that Hippolito was dead?   109

CAS. He that can make any man dead, the doctor. But, my lord, he's as full of life as wildfire, and as quick. Hippolito, the doctor, and one more rid hence this evening; the inn at which they light is Bethlem Monastery; Infelice comes from Bergamo and meets them there. Hippolito is mad, for he means this day to be married. The afternoon is the hour, and Friar Anselmo is the knitter.

DUKE. From Bergamo? Is 't possible?
    It cannot be.   120
    It cannot be!

CAS.   I will not swear, my lord,
    But this intelligence I took from one
    Whose brains work in the plot.

DUKE.   What's he?

CAS.   Matheo.

FLU. Matheo knows all.

PIO.   He's Hippolito's bosom.[1]

DUKE. How far stands Bethlem hence?

OMNES.   Six or seven miles.

DUKE. Is 't so? Not married till the afternoon?

Stay, stay, let's work out some prevention. How?

This is most strange. Can none but
madmen serve

To dress their wedding dinner? All of
you

Get presently to horse, disguise your-
selves   130

Like country gentlemen,

Or riding citizens, or so; and take

Each man a several path, but let us
meet

At Bethlem Monastery, some space of
time

Being spent between the arrival each
of other,

As if we came to see the lunatics.

To horse, away! Be secret, on your
lives.

Love must be punished that unjustly
thrives.

Exeunt [all but Fluello].

FLU. Be secret, on your lives! Castruchio,
Y'are but a scurvy spaniel. Honest
lord,   140

Good lady! Zounds, their love is just,
'tis good,

And I'll prevent you, though I swim in
blood.   *Exit.*

[SCENE XV.

A room in Bethlem Monastery.]

*Enter Friar Anselmo, Hippolito, Matheo,
Infelice.*

HIP. Nay, nay, resolve,[2] good father, or
deny.

ANS. You press me to an act both full of
danger

And full of happiness; for I behold

Your father's frowns, his threats, nay,
perhaps death

To him that dare do this. Yet, noble
lord,

Such comfortable beams break through
these clouds

By this blessed marriage, that, your honored word

Being pawned in my defense, I will
tie fast

The holy wedding knot.

HIP.   Tush, fear not the duke.

ANS. O son, wisely to fear is to be free
from fear.   10

HIP. You have our words, and you shall
have our lives,

To guard you safe from all ensuing
danger.

MAT. Ay, ay, chop 'em up, and away.

ANS. Stay! When is 't fit for me, and
safest for you,

To entertain this business?

HIP.   Not till the evening.

ANS. Be it so. There is a chapel stands
hard by,

Upon the west end of the abbey wall;

Thither convey yourselves, and, when
the sun

Hath turned his back upon this upper
world,

I'll marry you; that done, no thund'ring
voice   20

Can break the sacred bond. Yet, lady,
here

You are most safe.

INF.   Father, your love's most dear.

MAT. Ay, well said; lock us into some
little room by ourselves, that we may be
mad for an hour or two.

HIP. O, good Matheo, no; let's make no
noise.

MAT. How! No noise! Do you know
where you are? 'Sfoot, amongst all the
madcaps in Milan; so that to throw the
house out at window will be the better,   [30
and no man will suspect that we lurk here
to steal mutton.[3] The more sober we are,
the more scurvy 'tis. And, though the
friar tell us that here we are safest, I am
not of his mind; for, if those lay here that
had lost their money, none would ever look
after them; but here are none but those
that have lost their wits, so that if hue
and cry be made, hither they'll come. And
my reason is, because none goes to be   [40
married till he be stark mad.

HIP. Muffle yourselves; yonder's Fluello.

---

[1] Bosom friend.   [2] Agree.   [3] *I.e.,* a wench.

Enter Fluello.

MAT. Zounds!

FLU. O my lord, these cloaks are not for this rain. The tempest is too great. I come sweating to tell you of it, that you may get out of it.

MAT. Why, what's the matter?

FLU. What's the matter? You have mattered it fair; the duke's at hand. 49

OMNES. The duke?

FLU. The very duke.

HIP. Then all our plots
Are turned upon our heads and we're blown up
With our own underminings. 'Sfoot, how comes he?
What villain durst betray our being here?

FLU. Castruchio told the duke, and Matheo here told Castruchio.

HIP. Would you betray me to Castruchio?

MAT. 'Sfoot, he damned himself to the pit of hell, if he spake on 't again.

HIP. So did you swear to me; so were you damned. 59

MAT. Pox on 'em, and there be no faith in men, if a man shall not believe oaths. He took bread and salt,[1] by this light, that he would never open his lips.

HIP. O God, O God!

ANS. Son, be not desperate;
Have patience. You shall trip your enemy
Down by his own sleights. How far is the duke hence?

FLU. He's but new set out. Castruchio, Pioratto, and Sinezi come along with him. You have time enough yet to prevent[2] them, if you have but courage. 70

ANS. Ye shall steal secretly into the chapel,
And presently be married. If the duke
Abide here still, spite of ten thousand eyes,
You shall scape hence like friars.

HIP. O blessed disguise! O happy man!

ANS. Talk not of Happiness till your closed hand
Have her by th' forehead, like the lock of Time.
Be nor too slow, nor hasty, now you climb

Up to the tower of bliss; only be wary
And patient, that's all. If you like my plot, 80
Build and despatch; if not, farewell; then not.

HIP. O, yes, we do applaud it! We'll dispute
No longer, but will hence and execute.
Fluello, you'll stay here; let us be gone.
The ground that frighted lovers tread upon
Is stuck with thorns.

ANS. Come, then away, 'tis meet,
Exeunt [Anselmo, Hippolito, and Infelice.]
To escape those thorns, to put on wingéd feet.

MAT. No words, I pray, Fluello, for it stands us upon.[3]

FLU. O, sir, let that be your lesson! 90
[Exit Matheo.]
Alas, poor lovers! On what hopes and fears
Men toss themselves for women! When she's got,
The best has in her that which pleaseth not.

Enter to Fluello, the Duke, Castruchio, Pioratto, and Sinezi from several doors, muffled.

DUKE. Who's there?

CAS. My lord—

DUKE. Peace;
send that "lord" away.
A lordship will spoil all; let's be all fellows.
What's he?

CAS. Fluello, or else Sinezi, by his little legs.

OMNES. All friends, all friends.

DUKE. What? Met upon the very point of time? 100
Is this the place?

PIO. This is the place, my lord.

DUKE. Dream you on lordships? Come no more "lords," I pray.
You have not seen these lovers yet?

OMNES. Not yet.

DUKE. Castruchio, art thou sure this wedding feat
Is not till afternoon?

CAS. So it is given out, my lord.

---

[1] To seal the oath.   [2] Anticipate.   [3] It is an important matter to us.

DUKE. Nay, nay, 'tis like. Thieves must
    observe their hours;
Lovers watch minutes like astrono-
    mers.
How shall the interim hours by us be
    spent?
FLU. Let's all go see the madmen.
OMNES.   Mass, content.   109

Enter Towne [1] *like a sweeper.*

DUKE. O, here comes one.   Question
him, question him.
FLU. Now, honest fellow, dost thou be-
long to the house?
TOWNE. Yes, forsooth, I am one of the
implements; I sweep the madmen's rooms,
and fetch straw for 'em, and buy chains to
tie 'em, and rods to whip 'em. I was a
mad wag myself here once, but, I thank
Father Anselmo, he lashed me into my
right mind again.   120
DUKE. Anselmo is the friar must marry
    them;
Question him where he is.
CAS. And where is Father Anselmo now?
TOWNE. Marry, he's gone but e'en now.
DUKE. Ay, well done. Tell me, whither
    is he gone?
TOWNE. Why, to God A'mighty.
FLU. Ha, ha! This fellow's a fool,
talks idly.
PIO. Sirrah, are all the mad folks in
Milan brought hither?   130
TOWNE. How, all? There's a question
indeed! Why, if all the mad folks in Milan
should come hither, there would not be
left ten men in the city.
DUKE. Few gentlemen or courtiers here,
ha?
TOWNE. O, yes, abundance, abundance.
Lands no sooner fall into their hands, but
straight they run out a their wits. Citizens' sons and heirs are free of the [140
house by their fathers' copy.[2] Farmers'
sons come hither like geese, in flocks, and,
when they ha' sold all their cornfields,
here they sit and pick the straws.
SIN. Methinks you should have women
here as well as men.
TOWNE. O, ay, a plague on 'em, there's
no "ho!"[3] with 'em; they're madder than
March hares.   149

FLU. Are there no lawyers amongst
you?
TOWNE. O, no, not one; never any lawyer. We dare not let a lawyer come in,
for he'll make 'em mad faster than we can
recover 'em.
DUKE. And how long is 't ere you recover any of these?
TOWNE. Why, according to the quantity of the moon[4] that's got into 'em. An
alderman's son will be made a great [160
while, a very great while, especially if his
friends left him well. A whore will hardly
come to her wits again. A Puritan, there's
no hope of him, unless he may pull down the
steeple, and hang himself i' th' bell ropes.
FLU. I perceive all sorts of fish come
to your net.
TOWNE. Yes, in truth, we have blocks
for all heads. We have good store of wild
oats here; for the courtier is mad [170
at the citizen, the citizen is mad at the
countryman; the shoemaker is mad at the
cobbler, the cobbler at the carman;[5] the
punk is mad that the merchant's wife is no
whore, the merchant's wife is mad that
the punk is so common a whore. Godso,
here's Father Anselmo; pray, say nothing
that I tell tales out of the school.   *Exit.*

Enter Anselmo[6] [*and Servants*].

OMNES. God bless you, father.
ANS.   I thank you, gentlemen.
CAS. Pray, may we see some of those
    wretched souls   180
That here are in your keeping?
ANS.   Yes, you shall;
But, gentlemen, I must disarm you
    then.
There are of mad men, as there are of
    tame,
All humored not alike. We have here
    some
So apish and fantastic, play with a
    feather,
And, though 'twould grieve a soul to
    see God's image
So blemished and defaced, yet do they
    act
Such antic and such pretty lunacies,

---

[1] Thomas Towne, the name of the actor who
took the part.   [2] Copyhold.

[3] A cry commanding to stop.
[4] Alluding to the superstition that the moon's
rays made lunatics.   [5] Carter.
[6] This direction appears after line 180 in the
original.

That spite of sorrow they will make
you smile;   189
Others again we have like hungry lions,
Fierce as wild bulls, untamable as flies,
And these have oftentimes from stran-
gers' sides
Snatched rapiers suddenly, and done
much harm,
Whom if you'll see, you must be weapon-
less.

OMNES. With all our hearts.
    [*They give Anselmo their weapons.*]
ANS.   Here, take these weapons in.—
    [*Exit Servant with weapons.*]
Stand off a little, pray; so, so, 'tis well.
I'll show you here a man that was some-
times
A very grave and wealthy citizen,
Has served a prenticeship to this mis-
fortune,
Been here seven years, and dwelt in
Bergamo.   200

DUKE. How fell he from his wits?
ANS.   By loss at sea.
I'll stand aside; question him you alone,
For, if he spy me, he'll not speak a word,
Unless he's throughly vexed.
   Discovers an Old Man, wrapped in a net.
FLU.   Alas, poor soul!
CAS. A very old man.
DUKE. God speed, father!
1 MAD. God speed the plow; thou
shalt not speed me.
PIO. We see you, old man, for all you
dance in a net.   210
1 MAD. True, but thou wilt dance in
a halter, and I shall not see thee.
ANS. O, do not vex him, pray.
CAS. Are you a fisherman, father?
1 MAD. No, I am neither fish nor flesh.
FLU. What do you with that net then?
1 MAD. Dost not see, fool? There's a
fresh salmon in 't. If you step one foot
furder, you'll be over shoes, for you see I'm
over head and ears in the salt water; [220
and, if you fall into this whirlpool where
I am, y'are drowned—y'are a drowned
rat. I am fishing here for five ships, but
I cannot have a good draught, for my net
breaks still,[1] and breaks; but I'll break
some of your necks and I catch you in my
clutches. Stay, stay, stay, stay, stay,
where's the wind? Where's the wind?

  [1] Always.

Where's the wind? Where's the wind? Out,
you gulls, you goosecaps,[2] you gud- [230
geon-eaters![3] Do you look for the wind in
the heavens? Ha, ha, ha, ha! No, no!
Look there, look there, look there! The
wind is always at that door; hark how it
blows, puff, puff, puff!
OMNES. Ha, ha, ha!
1 MAD. Do you laugh at God's creatures? Do you mock old age, you rogues?
Is this gray beard and head counterfeit
that you cry, "Ha, ha, ha"? Sirrah, [240
art not thou my eldest son?
PIO. Yes, indeed, father.
1 MAD. Then th'art a fool, for my eldest son had a polt foot,[4] crooked legs, a
verjuice face, and a pear-colored beard.
I made him a scholar, and he made himself a fool.—Sirrah, thou there, hold out
thy hand!
DUKE. My hand? Well, here 'tis.   249
1 MAD. Look, look, look, look! Has
he not long nails and short hair?
FLU. Yes, monstrous short hair, and
abominable long nails.
1 MAD. Tenpenny nails, are they not?
FLU. Yes, tenpenny nails.
1 MAD. Such nails had my second boy.
Kneel down, thou varlet, and ask thy father
blessing. Such nails had my middlemost
son, and I made him a promoter;[5] and
he scraped, and scraped, and scraped, [260
till he got the devil and all; but he scraped
thus, and thus, and thus, and it went
under his legs, till at length a company
of kites, taking him for carrion, swept up
all, all, all, all, all, all, all. If you love
your lives, look to yourselves! See, see, see,
see, the Turks' galleys are fighting with
my ships! "Bounce," goes the guns.
"Oooh!" cry the men. "Rumble, rumble,"
go the waters. Alas, there, 'tis sunk, [270
'tis sunk! I am undone, I am undone! You
are the damned pirates have undone me.
You are, by the Lord, you are, you are!
Stop 'em! You are!
ANS. Why, how now, sirrah! Must I fall
to tame you?
1 MAD. Tame me! No, I'll be madder
than a roasted cat. See, see, I am burnt
with gunpowder. These are our close
fights!   280

  [2] Boobies.   [4] Club foot.
  [3] Simpletons.   [5] Informer.

Ans. I'll whip you if you grow unruly thus.

1 Mad. Whip me? Out, you toad! Whip me? What justice is this, to whip me because I am a beggar? Alas, I am a poor man, a very poor man! I am starved, and have had no meat, by this light, ever since the great flood; I am a poor man.

Ans. Well, well, be quiet, and you shall have meat.   290

1 Mad. Ay, ay, pray do; for, look you, here be my guts. These are my ribs—you may look through my ribs—see how my guts come out! These are my red guts, my very guts, O, O!

Ans. Take him in there.

[*Servants take 1 Madman in.*]

Omnes. A very piteous sight.

Cas. Father, I see you have a busy charge.

Ans. They must be used like children, pleased with toys,   300
And anon whipped for their unruliness.
I'll show you now a pair quite different
From him that's gone. He was all words;
and these,
Unless you urge 'em, seldom spend their speech,
But save their tongues. [*Discovers 2 and 3 Madmen.*] La you, this hithermost
Fell from the happy quietness of mind
About a maiden that he loved, and died.
He followed her to church, being full of tears,
And, as her body went into the ground,
He fell stark mad. This is a married man   310
Was jealous of a fair, but, as some say,
A very virtuous wife; and that spoiled him.

2 Mad. All these are whoremongers, and lay with my wife! Whore, whore, whore, whore, whore!

Flu. Observe him.

2 Mad. Gaffer shoemaker, you pulled on my wife's pumps, and then crept into her pantofles.[1] Lie there, lie there!—This was her tailor. You cut out her loose- [320 bodied gown, and put in a yard more than I allowed her. Lie there by the shoemaker.—O Master Doctor, are you here? You gave me a purgation, and then crept

into my wife's chamber to feel her pulses, and you said, and she said, and her maid said, that they went pit-a-pat, pit-a-pat, pit-a-pat. Doctor, I'll put you anon [328 into my wife's urinal.—Heigh, come aloft, Jack![2] This was her schoolmaster, and taught her to play upon the virginals,[3] and still his jacks[4] leapt up, up. You pricked[5] her out nothing but bawdy lessons, but I'll prick you all, fiddler—doctor—tailor—shoemaker—shoemaker—fiddler—doctor—tailor! So, lie with my wife again, now!

Cas. See how he notes the other, now[6] he feeds.

2 Mad. Give me some porridge.   340

3 Mad. I'll give thee none.

2 Mad. Give me some porridge.

3 Mad. I'll not give thee a bit.

2 Mad. Give me that flapdragon.[7]

3 Mad. I'll not give thee a spoonful. Thou liest; it's no dragon—'tis a parrot that I bought for my sweetheart, and I'll keep it.

2 Mad. Here's an almond for parrot.[8]

3 Mad. Hang thyself!   350

2 Mad. Here's a rope for parrot.[8]

3 Mad. Eat it, for I'll eat this.

2 Mad. I'll shoot at thee, and thou't give me none.

3 Mad. Woot thou?

2 Mad. I'll run a tilt at thee, and thou't give me none.

3 Mad. Woot thou? Do, and thou dar'st.

2 Mad. Bounce!   [*Strikes him.*]   360

3 Mad. O, O! I am slain! Murder, murder, murder! I am slain; my brains are beaten out.

Ans. How now, you villains! Bring me whips; I'll whip you.

3 Mad. I am dead! I am slain! Ring out the bell, for I am dead.

Duke. How will you do now, sirrah? You ha' killed him.   368

2 Mad. I'll answer 't at sessions. He was eating of almond butter, and I longed

[1] Slippers.

[2] Command to a performing monkey.
[3] Musical instrument with keys.
[4] Devices which plucked the strings of the virginals.
[5] Wrote in musical notes.
[6] Now that.
[7] A tidbit in a flaming cup of liquor.
[8] Proverbial phrase of uncertain meaning.

for 't. The child had never been delivered out of my belly, if I had not killed him. I'll answer 't at sessions, so my wife may be burnt i' th' hand,[1] too.

ANS. Take 'em in both. Bury him, for he's dead.

3 MAD. Indeed, I am dead; put me, I pray, into a good pit-hole.

2 MAD. I'll answer 't at sessions.   379

Exeunt [Servants with 2 and 3 Madmen].

Enter Bellafront mad.

ANS. How now, huswife, whither gad you?

BELL. A-nutting, forsooth. How do you, gaffer? How do you, gaffer? There's a French curtsy for you, too.

FLU. 'Tis Bellafront!

PIO. 'Tis the punk, by th' Lord!

DUKE. Father, what's she, I pray?

ANS.   As yet I know not.
She came in but this day, talks little idly,
And therefore has the freedom of the house.   389

BELL. Do not you know me?—nor you?—nor you?—nor you?

OMNES. No, indeed.

BELL. Then you are an ass—and you an ass—and you are an ass—for I know you.

ANS. Why, what are they? Come, tell me, what are they?

BELL. They're fishwives. Will you buy any gudgeons? God's santy![2] Yonder come friars; I know them too.—How [400 do you, friar?

Enter Hippolito, Matheo, and Infelice disguised in the habits of friars.

ANS. Nay, nay, away, you must not trouble friars.—
[*Aside to Hippolito, etc.*] The duke is here; speak nothing.

BELL. Nay, indeed, you shall not go. We'll run at barleybreak first, and you shall be in hell.[3]

MAT. [*Aside.*] My punk turned mad whore, as all her fellows are?

[1] Punishment for adultery.
[2] Sanctity.
[3] Name of the middle compartment in the game of barleybreak.

HIP. [*Aside.*] Say nothing, but steal hence, when you spy time.   410

ANS. I'll lock you up, if y'are unruly. Fie!

BELL. Fie! Marry, so! They shall not go indeed, till I ha' told 'em their fortunes.

DUKE. Good father, give her leave.

BELL. Ay, pray, good father, and I'll give you my blessing.

ANS. Well then, be brief, but, if you are thus unruly,
I'll have you locked up fast.

PIO.   Come, to their fortunes.   419

BELL. Let me see: one, two, three, and four. I'll begin with the little friar[4] first. Here's a fine hand, indeed! I never saw friar have such a dainty hand. Here's a hand for a lady! Here's your fortune:—
You love a friar better than a nun;
Yet long you'll love no friar, nor no friar's son.
Bow a little; the line of life is out; yet I am afraid,
For all y'are holy, you'll not die a maid.
God give you joy!—Now to you, Friar Tuck.

MAT. God send me good luck!   430

BELL. You love one, and one loves you;
You are a false knave, and she's a Jew.
Here is a dial that false ever goes—

MAT. O, your wit drops!

BELL.   Troth, so does your nose.—
[*To Hippolito.*] Nay, let's shake hands with you too. Pray open. Here's a fine hand!
Ho, friar, ho! God be here!   438
So he had need. You'll keep good cheer,
Here's a free table,[5] but a frozen breast,
For you'll starve those that love you best;
Yet you have good fortune, for, if I am no liar,
Then you are no friar, nor you, nor you no friar!
Ha, ha, ha, ha!   *Discovers them.*

DUKE. Are holy habits cloaks for villainy?
Draw all your weapons!

HIP.   Do; draw all your weapons.

DUKE. Where are your weapons? Draw!

OMNES. The friar has gulled us of 'em.

[4] *I.e.*, Infelice.
[5] A quibble on a term in palmistry for a section of the hand.

MAT.   O rare trick!
    You ha' learned one mad point of arith-
      metic.
HIP. Why swells your spleen so high?
    Against what bosom   450
    Would you your weapons draw? Hers?
    'Tis your daughter's.
    Mine? 'Tis your son's.
DUKE.   Son?
MAT.   Son, by yonder sun.
HIP. You cannot shed blood here but 'tis
      your own;
    To spill your own blood were damnation.
    Lay smooth that wrinkled brow, and
      I will throw
    Myself beneath your feet.
    Let it be rugged still and flinted ore,
    What can come forth but sparkles, that
      will burn
    Yourself and us? She's mine; my claim's
      most good;
    She's mine by marriage, though she's
      yours by blood.   460
[ANS. (*Kneeling.*)] I have a hand, dear
      lord, deep in this act,
    For I foresaw this storm, yet willingly
    Put forth to meet it. Oft have I seen a
      father
    Washing the wounds of his dear son in
      tears,
    A son to curse the sword that struck his
      father,
    Both slain i' th' quarrel of your fami-
      lies.
    Those scars are now ta'en off, and I
      beseech you
    To seal our pardon! All was to this end,
    To turn the ancient hates of your two
      houses
    To fresh green friendship, that your
      loves might look   470
    Like the Spring's forehead, comfortably
      sweet,
    And your vexed souls in peaceful union
      meet.
    Their blood will now be yours, yours
      will be theirs,
    And happiness shall crown your silver
      hairs.
FLU. You see, my lord, there's now no
      remedy.
OMNES. Beseech your lordship!
DUKE. You beseech fair; you have me in
      place fit

To bridle me.—Rise, friar. You may be
    glad
You can make madmen tame, and tame
    men mad.
Since Fate hath conquered, I must rest
    content;   480
To strive now would but add new pun-
    ishment.
I yield unto your happiness; be blessed.
Our families shall henceforth breathe in
    rest.
OMNES. O, happy change!
DUKE.   Yours now is my content;
    I throw upon your joys my full consent.
BELL. Am not I a good girl, for find-
ing "the friar in the well"? [1] Godso, you
are a brave man! Will not you buy me some
sugarplums, because I am so good a fortune
teller?   490
DUKE. Would thou hadst wit, thou pretty
    soul, to ask,
    As I have will to give.
BELL. Pretty soul? A pretty soul is
better than a pretty body. Do not you
know my pretty soul? I know you. Is not
your name Matheo?
MAT. Yes, lamb.   497
BELL. Baa, lamb! There you lie, for
I am mutton.—Look, fine man! He was
mad for me once, and I was mad for him
once, and he was mad for her once, and
were you never mad? Yes, I warrant. I had
a fine jewel once, a very fine jewel, and
that naughty man stole it away from me—
a very fine and a rich jewel.
DUKE. What jewel, pretty maid?
BELL. Maid? Nay, that's a lie. O,
'twas a very rich jewel, called a maidenhead, and had not you it, leerer?   509
MAT. Out, you mad ass! Away!
DUKE.   Had he thy maidenhead?
    He shall make thee amends, and marry
    thee.
BELL. Shall he? O brave Arthur of
Bradley [2] then!
DUKE. And, if he bear the mind of a
gentleman, I know he will.
MAT. I think I rifled her of some such
paltry jewel.
DUKE. Did you? Then marry her; you
    see the wrong
    Has led her spirits into a lunacy.   519

[1] The name of a popular ballad.
[2] The opening of a well-known ballad.

MAT. How? Marry her, my lord? 'Sfoot, marry a madwoman? Let a man get the tamest wife he can come by, she'll be mad enough afterward, do what he can.

DUKE. Nay, then, Father Anselmo here shall do his best
  To bring her to her wits. And will you then?

MAT. I cannot tell; I may choose.

DUKE. Nay, then, law shall compel. I tell you, sir,
  So much her hard fate moves me, you should not breathe   529
Under this air unless you married her.

MAT. Well, then, when her wits stand in their right place,
  I'll marry her.

BELL. I thank your grace.—Matheo, thou art mine.—
  [To Hippolito.] I am not mad, but put on this disguise,
  Only for you, my lord; for you can tell
  Much wonder of me; but you are gone. Farewell.—
  Matheo, thou didst first turn my soul black;
  Now make it white again. I do protest,
  I'm pure as fire now, chaste as Cynthia's breast.

HIP. I durst be sworn, Matheo, she's indeed.   540

MAT. Cony-catched, gulled! Must I sail in your flyboat
  Because I helped to rear your mainmast first?
  Plague found [1] you for 't, 'tis well.
  The cuckold's stamp goes current in all nations.
  Some men ha' horns giv'n them at their creations;
  If I be one of those, why so. 'Tis better
  To take a common wench, and make her good,
  Than one that simpers, and at first will scarce
  Be tempted forth over the threshold door,
  Yet in one sennight, zounds, turns arrant whore.   550
  Come, wench, thou shalt be mine. Give me thy golls;

[1] Confound.

We'll talk of legs hereafter.—See, my lord,
  God give us joy!

OMNES. God give you joy!

Enter Candido's Wife and George.

GEO. Come, mistress, we are in Bedlam now. Mass, and see, we come in pudding time,[2] for here's the duke.

WIFE. My husband, good my lord!

DUKE. Have I thy husband?   559

CAS. It's Candido, my lord; he's here among the lunatics. Father Anselmo, pray fetch him forth. [Exit Anselmo.] This mad woman is his wife, and, though she were not with child, yet did she long most spitefully to have her husband mad; and, because she would be sure he should turn Jew, she placed him here in Bethlem. Yonder he comes.

Enter Candido with Anselmo.

DUKE. Come hither, signior. Are you mad?   570

CAND. You are not mad.

DUKE. Why, I know that.

CAND. Then may you know I am not mad, that know
  You are not mad, and that you are the duke.
  None is mad here but one.—How do you, wife?
  What do you long for now?—Pardon, my lord;
  She had lost her child's nose else. I did cut out
  Pennyworths of lawn; the lawn was yet mine own.
  A carpet was my gown, yet 'twas mine own.
  I wore my man's coat, yet the cloth mine own;   580
  Had a cracked crown, the crown was yet mine own.
  She says for this I'm mad. Were her words true,
  I should be mad indeed. O foolish skill![3]
  Is patience madness? I'll be a madman still.

WIFE. [Kneeling.] Forgive me, and I'll vex your spirit no more.

[2] In good time.
[3] Reason.

DUKE. Come, come, we'll have you
　　friends; join hearts, join hands.
CAND. See, my lord, we are even.—
　　Nay, rise, for ill deeds kneel unto none
　　but heaven.
DUKE. Signior, methinks patience has
　　laid on you
　　Such heavy weight that you should
　　loathe it—
CAND. 　　　　Loathe it?　　　590
DUKE. For he whose breast is tender,
　　blood so cool,
　　That no wrongs heat it, is a patient fool.
　　What comfort do you find in being so
　　calm?
CAND. That which green wounds receive
　　from sovereign balm.
　　Patience, my lord? Why, 'tis the soul
　　of peace;
　　Of all the virtues, 'tis near'st kin to
　　heaven;
　　It makes men look like gods. The best
　　of men
　　That e'er wore earth about him was a
　　sufferer,
　　A soft, meek, patient, humble, tranquil
　　spirit,
　　The first true gentleman that ever
　　breathed.　　　　　　　　　600
　　The stock of patience then cannot be
　　poor;
　　All it desires, it has; what monarch
　　more?
　　It is the greatest enemy to law
　　That can be, for it doth embrace all
　　wrongs,

And so chains up lawyers' and women's
　　tongues.
'Tis the perpetual prisoner's liberty,
His walks and orchards. 'Tis the bond-
　　slave's freedom,
And makes him seem proud of each iron
　　chain,
As though he wore it more for state
　　than pain.　　　　　　　　　609
It is the beggars' music, and thus sings,
Although their bodies beg, their souls
　　are kings.
O my dread liege, It is the sap of bliss
Rears us aloft, makes men and angels
　　kiss.
And last of all, to end a household
　　strife,
It is the honey gainst a waspish wife.
DUKE. Thou giv'st it lively colors. Who
　　dare say
　　He's mad, whose words march in so good
　　array?
　　'Twere sin all women should such hus-
　　bands have,
　　For every man must then be his wife's
　　slave.
　　Come, therefore, you shall teach our
　　court to shine;　　　　　　620
　　So calm a spirit is worth a golden
　　mine.
　　Wives with meek husbands that to vex
　　them long,
　　In Bedlam must they dwell, else dwell
　　they wrong.　　　　　　　*Exeunt.*

FINIS.

GEORGE CHAPMAN

George Chapman is probably best known today to the ordinary reader as the Elizabethan translator who inspired John Keats to write his famous sonnet, "On First Looking into Chapman's Homer." Although this was the work Chapman prized most (he called it "The Worke that I was borne to doe") and for which he was most noted in his own day, even his contemporaries somewhat churlishly pointed out that as a Greek scholar he was actually indebted to various Latin translations and glosses in transforming his Renaissance versions of the *Iliad* and the *Odyssey* into English (1598–1616). Moreover, they thought, anyone who could complete and successfully preserve the tone of Christopher Marlowe's passionate and romantic *Hero and Leander*, as Chapman did in 1598, could scarcely be regarded as a thoroughgoing classicist.

In addition to his translated and original poetry, Chapman also authored a substantial body of plays which in many respects placed him next to Ben Jonson in their reflection of learning and classical interests. Although these plays lived in print and on the stage until the end of the seventeenth century, difficult and often undramatic—even turgid—language accounted for their later disappearance from the theater. In recent times, however, there has been a considerable revival of interest in Chapman because of his portrayal of so many facets of Renaissance thought and speculation.

The most detailed study of Chapman's life and works is by a Frenchman, Jean Jacquot [*George Chapman (1559–1634). Sa Vie, Sa Poésie, Son Théâtre, Sa Pensée . . . , Annales de l'Université de Lyons*, Paris, 1951], but his account has been contributed to and supplemented by many English and American writers before and since. The running legend around the engraved portrait of the heavily bearded, mustached, curly-haired, and somewhat bald poet on the title page of *The Whole Works of Homer* in 1616 proclaims Chapman to have been fifty-seven years old. Thus he was evidently born about 1559, presumably in the town of Hitchin, Hertfordshire, where the family had lived for some generations. Mark Eccles has shown through the documents in a Chancery suit that Chapman's maternal grandfather was George Nodes, sergeant of the buckhounds to Henry VIII and his successors. Nodes's daughter Joan married Thomas Chapman of Hitchin, a small landholder, who willed his son George £100 and gave him the right to call himself "gentleman." On his mother's side the poet was also related to the Grimestone family, some of whose members were in the service of the English government in France as part of Francis Walsingham's secret service or as links between Queen Elizabeth and Henry of Navarre. After translating various French histories, Chapman's friend Edward Grimestone became the author of *A General Inventory of the History of France* in 1607, and it is very likely that Chapman's interest in France and his use of French history for almost all of his tragedies stemmed from this connection. (It is notable that he never selected events which might have represented France in an unfavorable light, although he did insert some fulsome passages of flattery of England.) According to Anthony à Wood's *Athenæ Oxonienses* (1691–2), Chapman studied at both universities, attending Oxford first ("where he was observed to be most excellent in the Latin and Greek tongues, but not in logic or philosophy"), but he took no degree.

Jean Robertson and Mark Eccles, in practically simultaneous and overlapping articles ("The Early Life of George Chapman," *MLR*, 1945, and "Chapman's Early Years,"

SP, 1946), discovered through various Chancery documents and certain inscriptions that about 1583 the young poet had borrowed money from a John Wofall to outfit himself for service with Sir Ralph Sadler, Chancellor of the Duchy of Lancaster and a member of the Privy Council, who had an estate in Hitchin.   Many years later, in February 1600, Wofall had Chapman arrested and imprisoned for nonpayment of the debt, though he lost the suit.   Wofall's son testified that his father had postponed taking action for so long a time because of Chapman's "absence . . . beyond the seas."   Miss Robertson concluded that this absence was due, at least in part, to Chapman's having volunteered for the wars in the Netherlands and felt that his description of Sir Francis Vere's strategic victory on the Waal River outside Nimeguen in "Hymnus in Cynthiam" was the work of an eye-witness.   He may also have lived in France for a time.   Miss Robertson believed that Chapman really owed the money, but Eccles was able to show from other sources that Wofall, acting with the Nicholas Skeres who had been present at Marlowe's murder, had victimized other young men devoted to what Wofall call "frutlesse and vayne Poetry," and had been pilloried twice.   The episode affords another example of the close relationship which existed between the underworld and many Elizabethan men of letters.   Other victims of the pair had been Thomas Lodge and Matthew Royden, a member of the circle of Sir Walter Raleigh.   Jacquot discusses at some length Chapman's close relations with this group, which included Marlowe and Harriot.   Chapman dedicated poems to Raleigh, Royden, and Harriot, as well as to his two patrons, Prince Henry and Robert, Earl of Somerset, none of whom helped him very much.   From Prince Henry, whom he had served as sewer, or server of meats at banquets, he had received promise of a large reward and a pension for his *Homer*, but after the death of the prince in 1612 the promise was not fulfilled.   Chapman wrote a poem on Henry's death and prepared a court masque the next year, but he did not continue in favor at court.   His money troubles continued.   Between November 1616, the year of his completion of *Homer*, and October 1619, he was involved in another Chancery suit concerning a loan from a friend, Henry Jones, his own brother Thomas, and the family estate at Hitchin (see C. J. Sisson, "George Chapman, 1612–1622," *MLR*, 1951).   In February 1622 the judge decided in favor of the Chapmans.   From the whole contretemps Robert Butman (*ibid.*) concluded that, except for a short visit to London in June 1617, from the fall of 1614 to the fall of 1619 Chapman was probably living in obscurity in the country in order to escape arrest.   This retirement halted his theater work and made him concentrate on translations, though nothing of importance resulted. Little is known about his last years.   He died in London in 1634, and was honored by a monument devised by his great friend, the architect and masque-designer, Inigo Jones.

As an author Chapman was first heard from upon the publication of his poem *The Shadow of Night* in 1594.   He was first mentioned as a dramatist in Henslowe's record of the performance of his comedy *The Blind Beggar of Alexandria* by the Admiral's Men in February 1596.   Henslowe always respectfully referred to him as "Master Chapman," whereas he referred familiarly to Dekker as "Dickers."   In 1598 Francis Meres in his *Palladis Tamia* placed Chapman among the best writers of both comedy and tragedy, though what tragedies he had in mind at this date remain unknown.   Not long after 1600 he seems to have been writing for the Children of the Chapel—called after 1604 the Children of the Queen's Revels—at the Blackfriars Theater.   His share in *Eastward Ho*, written for the Children in collaboration with Jonson and Marston, caused his imprisonment for a short while because James I was offended by its incidental satire on the Scots.   In *The Conspiracy and the Tragedy of Charles, Duke of Byron*, also written for the boy actors, Chapman offended again by his representation of French royalty on the stage.   His major activity as a playwright apparently ceased by 1614 or a little later.

In Chapman's plays the Elizabethan poetic and romantic treatment of life is united with the humanist's interest in classical learning.   Early in his career he experimented with elements of the comedy of humors, or manners, which Jonson, the dominant figure of the Stuart era, established in 1598 with his *Every Man in His Humor*.   After depicting characters warped by humors in *An Humorous Day's Mirth*, apparently written for Henslowe in 1597, Chapman made a still more searching study of follies in *All Fools* of 1599, based on two plays of Terence. But in his comic plots, drawn from various sources including the classics, he seems to be interested primarily in devices of romantic comedy—love story, intrigue, disguise, mistakes of identity, and other features of the complicated action developed under the influence chiefly of Italian comedy and novel. His later comedies are *The Gentleman Usher* (1606), *Monsieur D'Olive* (1606), *May Day* (1611), and *The Widow's Tears* (1612). *Sir Giles Goosecap*, printed in 1606, is often ascribed to Chapman. In tragedy Chapman also showed a kinship to Jonson in his combination of history, philosophic discourse drawn from classic writers, and Senecan technique; but he did not achieve the clarity and sustained tone that made Jonson a model for later writers. Chapman is distinctly Elizabethan in his style, which frequently rises to passionate intensity with passages lighted by felicitous figures as vivid and elaborate as his Homeric similes. But at times he becomes bombastic, strained, or "metaphysical." One of his tragedies, *Caesar and Pompey*, published in 1631 as written long before, deals with a theme of ancient history popular in drama. With the omission of some tragedies doubtfully ascribed to him, the rest are drawn from contemporary or recent French history: *Bussy D'Ambois* (printed in 1607), the two parts of *The Conspiracy and the Tragedy of Charles, Duke of Byron* (printed in 1608), *The Revenge of Bussy D'Ambois* (printed in 1613), and *The Tragedy of Chabot* (printed in 1639 as written by Chapman and Shirley). The main incidents of the Byron plays and some of *The Revenge of Bussy D'Ambois* were apparently drawn from Grimestone's *Inventory*. Seneca's influence on the tragedies is clear in such devices as the ghost and in Chapman's fondness for declamatory and sententious language. Ethical or metaphysical discourses were adapted from classical treatises (as F. L. Schoell has shown), often through Renaissance translations or through compilations like Erasmus's *Adagia* (*Études sur l'Humanisme Continental en Angleterre à la Fin de la Renaissance*, Paris, 1926). Plutarch's moral treatises furnished Chapman with numerous passages, and the Stoic philosophy of Clermont in *The Revenge of Bussy* is built up from passages in a Latin translation of Epictetus.

Although *Bussy D'Ambois* was not printed until 1607 (by William Aspley and without the author's name), it is believed to have been written some years earlier. E. E. Stoll concluded from an allusion to "Damboys" (which indicates the usual English pronunciation of the name) in Dekker's *Satiromastix* (1601) that the Chapman play was written in 1600 ("On the Dates of Some of Chapman's Plays," *MLN*, 1905). But the naming of certain *Bussy* characters in an inventory of costumes in Henslowe's diary seemed to F. S. Boas to take it back at least to 1598 (see his edition of *Bussy*, Boston, 1905). Elias Schwartz, at first arguing for 1597 ("The Dates and Order of Chapman's Tragedies," *MP*, 1959), later decided on about 1596 ("The Date of *Bussy D'Ambois*," *MP*, 1961). Ezra Lehman had previously argued that the success of Marlowe's *Massacre at Paris* (acted in January 1593) had encouraged his friend Chapman to write a tragedy about some of the same characters in 1595 or 1596 (see his edition of *Chabot*, Philadelphia, 1906). These opinions were disputed by Robert Ornstein (*MP*, 1961), who held that there is still insufficient evidence to "counterbalance the conservative scholarly arguments which support Parrott's dating of Chapman's plays" (in *MLR*, 1908). Irving Ribner, in *Jacobean Tragedy/The Quest for Moral Order* (London, 1962), took much the same view, saying that the earliest of Chapman's tragedies "could not have been written much later than 1603" and that "It would be fitting indeed if *Bussy D'Ambois* could be dated with certainty in that year." As Parrot summarized his own earlier conclusions in his introduction to the play in *Chapman's Tragedies* (London and New York, 1910):

Bussy was, I take it, composed for the Children of the Chapel shortly after the death of Elizabeth, and in 1603 or 1604 was carried over in MS.—perhaps before it had been acted—

to the rival company of boy actors, the Children of Paul's, by whom it was, as the title-page of the first edition tells us, "often presented." It was revised, probably for a new production at Whitefriars by Nat. Field, about 1610, and this revised form was transferred by him in MS. to the King's Men, Shakespeare's old company, by whom it was performed at Court so late as 1634, a month before Chapman's death.

Other companies performed it throughout the seventeenth century. Mrs. Samuel Pepys saw it on December 30, 1661; her husband made no diarial comment then, but on November 15, 1662, he bought a copy and pronounced it a good play. Dryden enjoyed the play on the stage, but after reading it he damned it in his dedication of *The Spanish Friar* (1681) as a "hideous mingle of false poetry and true nonsense." But Thomas D'Urfey, in the dedication of his distorted adaptation entitled *Bussy D'Ambois, or The Husband's Revenge* (1691), said the earlier performances in 1681 (as acted by Charles Hart) placed it "amongst the rank of the Topping Tragedies of that time."

No exact printed sources for the play have come to light, since the many historical accounts of Bussy were all published after the writing of the play. Claire-Elaine Engel suggested that Chapman knew the Huguenot Seigneur de Damportin's "Du Bonheur de la Cour," a dialogue between himself and Bussy, and perhaps also made use of some of the "tombeaux" or epitaphs written at the time of the murder ("Les Sources du *Bussy D'Ambois* de Chapman," *RLC*, 1932). But Miss Engel, like most other commentators, had to conclude finally that Chapman's information probably came mostly by word of mouth (perhaps Grimestone's), since all kinds of tales and rumors about Bussy and his assassination in 1579 were still floating about Europe many years later. Maurice Evans, in his edition of the play for the New Mermaids series in 1964, suggested that Chapman also made some allegorical and mythological use of Giordano Bruno's *Spaccio della Bestia Trionfante* ("The expulsion of the triumphant beast"), which was dedicated to Sir Philip Sidney in 1585 during Bruno's visit to England, where he became associated with Raleigh's discussion group. (See also Francis Yates, *Giordano Bruno and the Hermetic Tradition*, London, 1964. Johnstone Parr has also written about Chapman's interest in astrology in "The Duke of Byron's Malignant 'Caput Argol'," *SP*, 1946.) In many passages the tragedy is in the tradition of the old morality play, as well as that of Seneca—especially the *Hercules Oetœus*, which is echoed in many allusions and phrases. (See also Eugene M. Waith, *The Herculean Hero in Marlowe, Chapman, Shakespeare and Dryden*, London, 1962.) Marlowe's *Tamburlaine* and *Doctor Faustus* were also lurking somewhere in the wings.

In any case, as Jacquot has shown most fully, Chapman's portrait of Bussy D'Ambois gives a considerably truncated and contorted view of the actual man. The real Bussy was never poor or derelict; in fact, he was Louis de Clermont, Sieur de Bussy, and devoted himself so early to a military career that at the age of eighteen he was already commander of a company. Like the Duke of Guise in the play, he had helped to massacre the Huguenots on St. Bartholomew's Day in 1572, one of them being a cousin whose estate he then inherited. He had some scholarly and poetical pretensions, and the fascination of Neo-Platonism and hermetic magic drew him into the circle of Catherine de Medici and Henry III. His first court service was indeed with King Henry, but he later shifted to Monsieur, the King's brother—a time order which is reversed in the play. Monsieur, as the Duke of Anjou, appointed Bussy governor of the province of Anjou, but he made himself so hated because of his taxes and his arrogant, quarrelsome behavior that the Duke removed him. But in Flanders in 1578 Bussy participated in the futile negotiations of Monsieur for the hand of Elizabeth. He showed personel bravery on an expedition to the Low Countries in that year, but also proved himself no leader of men. He was involved in a famous duel at court, but not the triple one described in the play. His love affairs were notorious, one being with Marguerite de Valois, later to be the wife of Henry IV. According to one story his nemesis came when he boasted in a letter to Monsieur of his success in wooing the wife of the Count Montsoreau in

Anjou without realizing how greatly alienated Monsieur was by this time. The Duke gave the letter to the King, and the King sent it to the cuckolded Count, thereby implying his freedom to avenge his honor in any way he wished. While Anjou was in England, the Count, pistol in hand, forced his wife to arrange a rendezvous with her lover, and Bussy was ambushed and murdered after a brave fight against great odds.

Obviously Chapman took many liberties with these facts, suppressing many and reshaping others in the interest of turning Bussy into a worthy figure for tragic treatment. He explained his conception of the purpose of tragedy in his dedication to *The Revenge of Bussy*:

And for the authentical truth of either person or action, who (worth the respecting) will expect it in a poem, whose subject is not truth, but things like truth? Poor envious souls they are that cavil at truth's want in these natural fictions; material instruction, elegant and sententious excitation to virtue, and deflection from her contrary, being the soul, limbs, and limits of an authentical tragedy.

Chapman's results in applying these principles to his plays have baffled and perplexed many critics, while sending others onto flights of admiration; but all have had to agree that in *Bussy D'Ambois* he created one of the most provocative and controversial of Elizabethan tragedies. In its sequel, *The Revenge of Bussy D'Ambois* (probably 1610 or 1611), he produced a tragedy of considerable intellectual but no dramatic interest at all. From the ideational point of view, however, the two plays must be considered together, and within the context of the rest of Chapman's tragedies. So much has been written on the subject that it is impossible to do much more than cite the most important of these discussions and classify them as to discovered aspects of Chapman's thought. At the core of these investigations lies the idea of Stoicism—its nature and its degree—as focused chiefly in Seneca and Epictetus.

In "The Development of the 'Senecal Man'" (*RES*, 1947), Michael H. Higgins discussed the history of this type, examining many of Chapman's precursors, such as Kyd, but he culminated his study with Bussy rather than Clermont, Bussy's invented brother. (E. E. Wilson, in "The Genesis of Chapman's *The Revenge of Bussy D'Ambois*," *MLN*, 1956, believed that the original of Clermont might well have been the Count D'Auvergne, a friend of Byron included in the Byron plays.) To most critics Clermont is the real prototype of the complete "Senecal man." In Bussy, according to Higgins, Chapman has presented "the self-reliant hero pitting himself against a hostile world and adverse fates" and in the end facing death standing upright "like a Roman statue." In a later article (*RES*, 1945) Higgins discussed "Chapman's 'Senecal Man'" further as a "study in Jacobean psychology." He showed how the Stoic creed of Clermont and others allowed Chapman to illustrate his interest in the problems of fundamental justice, especially in the relations between the qualities of the just ruler and the character and duties of the upright subject. In 1939 Nancy von Pogrell, in *Die philosophisch-poetische Entwicklung George Chapmans* (Hamburg), had traced the development of Chapman's thought through his comedies, tragedies, and poems from a Platonic to a Stoic point of view, focusing her study on an analysis of *The Revenge* and showing how Chapman was both a man of the Renaissance and at the same time in revolt against it. Jacquot, too, in his 1951 analysis of the religious and philosophical background of Chapman's writings, stressed the early influence of Platonism, which then yielded to Stoicism, especially that of Epictetus. On the other hand, R. H. Parkinson, in "Nature and the Tragic Heir in Chapman's Bussy Plays" (*HLQ*, 1942), found that in *Bussy* Chapman, after taking over from Marlowe the idea of the superman as hero, had explained the still existent vulnerability of Bussy by throwing the blame on Nature, which works at random—first creating a "whole man," and then overthrowing him. This view, according to Parkinson, approximates Epicureanism; but by the time of *The Revenge* Chapman had absorbed Stoic doctrines and therefore Nature now became "the norm of right conduct" and the real protagonist became the world of corrupt mankind as represented in the court of Henry III.

Roy W. Battenhouse presented a somewhat different idea of Nature in "Chapman and the Nature of Man" (*ELH*, 1945), contending that "the religious concepts of Hellenistic philosophy rather than the definitions of Christian orthodoxy furnished Chapman the premises of his view of man." Thus Chapman, leaning toward the classical view that man's time on earth is one of struggle with his lower bodily nature, presents Bussy and Byron as following a course which makes them slaves of passion, whereas Clermont and Cato follow the way of self-control and reason. This non-Christian interpretation of Chapman was attacked by Ennis Rees in his monograph, *The Tragedies of George Chapman: Renaissance Ethics in Action* (Harvard University Press, 1954), which maintained that Chapman's tragedies had been consistently misunderstood and which aimed to build up a picture of Chapman's "Christian humanism." In this light Bussy and Byron represent everything that a truly virtuous man should avoid, and Clermont, Cato, and Chabot become truly virtuous heroes governed by self-control. Elias Schwartz refused to accept this Christian interpretation. In "Seneca, Homer, and Chapman's *Bussy D'Ambois*" (*JEGP*, 1957) he reiterated the Senecan approach to tragedy, in which the protagonist is blameless, but, because of the lack of order and justice in the world, suffers inescapable calamity. Schwartz also suggested that Chapman based the model for his Bussy on Homer's Achilles, who embodied the Greek concept of inborn *arete* or *virtus* in terms of valor, strength, and skill. In another article entitled "Chapman's Renaissance Man: Byron Reconsidered" (*SEGP*, 1959) Schwartz decided that the Byron of the two Byron plays actually stood between the "heroic" Bussy and the "apathetic" Clermont. C. L. Barker joined the argument in 1961 by asserting in "The Ambivalence of *Bussy D'Ambois*" (*REL*) that the play may be read in two ways: in terms of Christian morality or in terms of the code of honor, in the private rather than the public sense. The ambiguity of the play, he believed, is increased because it may also be interpreted as a representation of the triumph of passion (the tragic flaw) over reason. J. W. Wieler had already made the same point in his book, *George Chapman—The Effect of Stoicism upon His Tragedies* (New York, 1949), and Nicholas Brooke, too, in his edition of the play for the Revels series (London and Harvard, 1964), stressed the theme stated in the play itself: "Fortune, not Reason, rules the state of things."

In 1960 Peter Ure, in an essay on "Chapman's Tragedies" in *The Jacobean Theatre*, recognized and admitted the contradictions and inconsistencies of the play as far as the character of Bussy was concerned, although he still admired the play as a tragedy. Two years later Irving Ribner, in a chapter of his *Jacobean Tragedy*, offered an explanation for the major problem: "Chapman's first tragedy is a mirror of the pessimism which comes to dominate the vision of the Jacobean era, and his later plays reveal his attempt to resolve moral conflicts which are particularly a part of that era." Chapman's method was to attempt resolution in terms of the Stoic philosophy, as he did most deliberately in *The Revenge of Bussy* and *Caesar and Pompey*. The relative failure of these plays, asserted Ribner, "may stem in part from Chapman's own inability to embrace wholeheartedly the philosophy he proposed." Ribner regarded it as very significant that Chapman in *Chabot*, his last play, probably written in 1614 and revised years later with the young James Shirley, "seems to renounce the stoicism he had espoused in the intervening plays and to assert the moral vision of his early *Bussy D'Ambois*." Thus Chapman's search for a moral order led him to failure and resignation rather than to the affirmation found in the plays of Webster and Tourneur.

Nevertheless, Chapman must be recognized as "the most deliberate didactic tragedian of his age," working not towards "a more complete fusion of his talents as a poet to the exigencies of dramatic composition, but of an elimination as far as possible of those features of the drama which he wished his poetry to serve—the imaginative presentation of those somber ethical issues which are at the heart of all his acknowledged tragedies" (Prior, *The Language of Tragedy*). But despite his didacticism his plays must be considered as plays, and not as moral *exempla* or as pieces of Christian or non-Christian apologetics. Recognizing this, Ribner suggested that Bussy "is deliberately shaped as a dramatic symbol of humanity, faced with a problem which all mankind must face . . . the ancient question of how a man, endowed by his creator with reason, strength, and knowledge of virtue, can live in a world corrupted by evil." Chapman finds no answer to the question in this play except that virtue cannot survive the corruption of the world. Ribner believes that one reason the critics have fallen out so badly in interpreting and evaluating *Bussy* is that they have not realized that Chapman was not writing as a naturalistic dramatist, and that each of the characters "performs various thematic functions within the total design," which Ribner proceeds to analyze. In this manner he finds ways to defend the apparent inconsistency in the character of Tamyra, the sudden emergence of the Guise and Monsieur at the end of the play as "ministers of fate," and even the rather crude introduction of the devils Behemoth and Cartophylax in the fourth act. Thus Ribner unconsciously offered his answer to William Archer's earlier censure of these devices, as well as the ghost of the very unspiritual Friar, as "sheer unmitigated nonsense:" "The supernatural apparitions are dragged in to please the groundlings, avid of diablerie. It would be idle to pretend that they have any poetic or artistically dramatic value," (*The Old Drama and the New*, Boston, 1923). He also jeered at the ease with which Montsurry was able to pass himself off as the abruptly dead Friar by merely putting on some of his robes. Elizabethan playwrights, repeated Archer, were letting themselves work in too "soft" a medium. Alfred Harbage, too, in his discussion of "Intrigue in Elizabethan Tragedy" (*Essays on Shakespeare and Elizabethan Tragedy*), speaks of the frequent mixing of comic intrigue with tragedy, commenting: "Whether this Friar in *Bussy D'Ambois* is supposed to retain our approval is a moot point—his devices are certainly as catastrophic in their results as those of Friar Lawrence."

In 1951 Berta Sturman questioned the reliability of the statement on the title page of the 1641 edition of *Bussy* that the text was "much corrected and amended by the Author before his death," and concluded that "almost on linguistic and stylistic grounds alone one would be justified in rejecting the assertion . . . that the revision was by Chapman" ("The 1641 Edition of Chapman's *Bussy D'Ambois*," HLQ, 1951). In the next year Peter Ure challenged Miss Sturman's assertion ("The Date of the Revision of Chapman's *The Tragedy of Bussy D'Ambois*," NQ, 1952), and supported Parrott's view that Chapman himself made the revisions at about the same time he was writing *The Revenge*. In the following year, after making a detailed examination of the two texts, Ure modified his position slightly, and concluded that while he hesitated to identify the reviser positively with Chapman, this identification was still the easiest hypothesis to account for the features noted in his paper ("Chapman's *Tragedy of Bussy D'Ambois*: Problems of the Revised Quarto," MLR, 1953). When Nicholas Brooke edited the play in 1964, he offered the suggestion that there might have been a double revision, first by Chapman and later by Nat Field; and therefore a composite text was devised, using the 1607 edition as the base and adding three passages from 1641. When Maurice Evans published his edition in 1965, he decided that Brooke's evidence in favor of a double revision was "irrefutable," and followed him in using the 1607 text as his base, while including four passages from 1641 "for whose introduction the internal evidence seems specific and overwhelming." R. J. Lordi, however, in his edition of the play for the Regents Renaissance Drama Series (University of Nebraska Press, 1965), reexamined the evidence and the arguments, and decided to trust the 1641 text, thus following the examples of Parrott, Boas, Jacquot, and M. Pagnini.

The present text is based on Parrott's reprint of the 1641 quarto in *The Plays and Poems of George Chapman*. The edition of Boas in the Belles Lettres Series has also been consulted.

BUSSY D'AMBOIS[1]

BY

GEORGE CHAPMAN

[DRAMATIS PERSONÆ

HENRY III, *King of France.*
MONSIEUR, *his brother.*
MAFFÉ, *steward to Monsieur.*
THE DUKE OF GUISE.
MONTSURRY, *a count.*
BUSSY D'AMBOIS.
BARRISOR } *courtiers; enemies*
L'ANOU } *of D'Ambois.*
PYRRHOT }
BRISAC } *courtiers; friends*
MELYNELL } *of D'Ambois.*
FRIAR COMOLET.
NUNTIUS, *a messenger.*
MURDERERS.

BEHEMOTH } *spirits.*
CARTOPHYLAX }
UMBRA of FRIAR.

ELENOR, *Duchess of Guise.*
ANNABELLE, *English maid-in-waiting to Eleanor.*
BEAUPRÉ, *niece to Elenor.*
CHARLOTTE, *maid-in-waiting to Beaupré.*
TAMYRA, *Countess of Montsurry.*
PERO, *maid-in-waiting to Tamyra.*
PYRA, *a court lady.*
LORDS, LADIES, PAGES, *etc.*

SCENE: *Paris.*

TIME: *Late sixteenth century.*

PROLOGUE

NOT out of confidence that none but we[2]
Are able to present this tragedy,
Nor out of envy at the grace of late
It did receive, nor yet to derogate
From their deserts who[3] give out boldly
  that
They move with equal feet on the same
  flat;[4]
Neither for all nor any of such ends
We offer it, gracious and noble friends,
To your review. We, far from emulation
And (charitably judge) from imitation, [10
With this work entertain you, a piece
  known
And still believed in court to be our own.
To quit our claim, doubting our right or
  merit,

Would argue in us poverty of spirit
Which we must not subscribe to. Field[5]
  is gone,
Whose action first did give it name, and
  one
Who came the nearest to him,[6] is denied
By his gray beard to show the height and
  pride
Of D'Ambois' youth and bravery. Yet,
  to hold
Our title still afoot, and not grow cold [20
By giving it o'er, a third man[7] with his
  best
Of care and pains defends our interest;
As Richard he was liked, nor do we
  fear
In personating D'Ambois he'll appear
To faint, or go less, so[8] your free con-
  sent,
As heretofore, give him encouragement.

[1] The title continues: "A Tragedy, As It Hath Been Often Acted with Great Applause, Being Much Corrected and Amended by the Author before his Death."
[2] *I.e.*, the King's Men.
[3] A rival company which had given the play.
[4] Over the same ground.

[5] Nathan Field, one of the company when the play was acted about 1616.
[6] Unidentified, perhaps Joseph Taylor.
[7] Probably Elliard Swanston.
[8] If.

Actus Primi Scena Prima.[1]

[A forest near Paris.]

Enter Bussy D'Ambois, poor.

[Bus.] Fortune, not Reason, rules the state of things;
Reward goes backwards, Honor on his head;[2]
Who is not poor, is monstrous; only Need
Gives form and worth to every human seed.
As cedars beaten with continual storms,
So great men flourish, and do imitate
Unskillful statuaries,[3] who suppose,
In forming a colossus, if they make him
Straddle enough, strut, and look big, and gape,
Their work is goodly. So men merely great 10
In their affected gravity of voice,
Sourness of countenance, manners' cruelty,
Authority, wealth, and all the spawn of fortune,
Think they bear all the kingdom's worth before them,
Yet differ not from those colossic statues,
Which, with heroic forms without o'erspread,
Within are naught but mortar, flint, and lead.
Man is a torch borne in the wind; a dream
But of a shadow, summed[4] with all his substance;
And, as great seamen, using all their wealth 20
And skills in Neptune's deep invisible paths,
In tall ships richly built and ribbed with brass,
To put a girdle round about the world,
When they have done it, coming near their haven,
Are fain to give a warning-piece,[5] and call
A poor, staid fisherman, that never passed
His country's sight, to waft and guide them in;
So, when we wander furthest through the waves
Of glassy glory, and the gulfs of state,
Topped with all titles, spreading all our reaches, 30
As if each private arm would sphere the earth,
We must to Virtue for her guide resort,
Or we shall shipwrack in our safest port.
Procumbit.[6]

[Enter] Monsieur, with two Pages.

[Mon.] There is no second place in numerous state
That holds more than a cipher; in a king
All places are contained. His words and looks
Are like the flashes and the bolts of Jove;
His deeds inimitable, like the sea
That shuts still as it opes, and leaves no tracts
Nor prints of precedent for mean men's facts.[7] 40
There's but a thread betwixt me and a crown;
I would not wish it cut, unless by nature;
Yet to prepare me for that possible fortune,
'Tis good to get resolvéd spirits about me.
I followed D'Ambois to this green retreat,
A man of spirit beyond the reach of fear,
Who, discontent with his neglected worth,
Neglects the light, and loves obscure abodes;
But he is young and haughty, apt to take
Fire at advancement, to bear state, and flourish; 50
In his rise therefore shall my bounties shine.
None loathes the world so much, nor loves to scoff it,
But gold and grace will make him surfeit of it.—
What, D'Ambois?

Bus.   He, sir.

---

[1] The first scene of the first act. [3] Sculptors.
[2] *I.e.*, upside down. [4] Clothed.
[5] Signal shot. [6] He falls forward. [7] Deeds.

Mon.   Turned to earth, alive?
Up, man; the sun shines on thee.
Bus.   Let it shine.
I am no mote to play in 't, as great men
are.
Mon. Callest thou men great in state,
motes in the sun?
They say so that would have thee
freeze in shades,
That, like the gross Sicilian gourmandist,
Empty their noses in the cates they
love,   60
That none may eat but they. Do thou
but bring
Light to the banquet Fortune sets be-
fore thee,
And thou wilt loathe lean darkness like
thy death.
Who would believe thy mettle could
let sloth
Rust and consume it? If Themistocles
Had lived obscured thus in th' Athe-
nian state,
Xerxes had made both him and it his
slaves.
If brave Camillus had lurked so in
Rome,
He had not five times been dictator
there,
Nor four times triumphed. If Epami-
nondas,   70
Who lived twice twenty years obscured
in Thebes,
Had lived so still, he had been still un-
named,
And paid his country nor himself their
right;
But, putting forth his strength, he res-
cued both
From imminent ruin, and, like bur-
nished steel,
After long use he shined; for, as the
light
Not only serves to show, but renders us
Mutually profitable, so our lives
In acts exemplary not only win
Ourselves good names, but do to others
give   80
Matter for virtuous deeds, by which we
live.
Bus. What would you wish me?
Mon.   Leave the troubled streams,
And live, where thrivers do, at the well-
head.

Bus. At the wellhead? Alas, what should
I do
With that enchanted glass? See devils
there;
Or, like a strumpet, learn to set my
looks
In an eternal brake [1] or practice jug-
gling,
To keep my face still fast, my heart
still loose;
Or bear, like dame's schoolmistresses
their riddles,
Two tongues, and be good only for a
shift; [2]   90
Flatter great lords, to put them still in
mind
Why they were made lords; or please
humorous [3] ladies
With a good carriage, tell them idle
tales
To make their physic work; spend a
man's life
In sights and visitations that will make
His eyes as hollow as his mistress'
heart;
To do none good but those that have no
need;
To gain being forward, though you
break for haste
All the commandments ere you break
your fast;
But believe backwards, make your
period   100
And creed's last article, "I believe in
God;"
And, hearing villainies preached, t'un-
fold their art,
Learn to commit them? 'Tis a great
man's part.
Shall I learn this there?
Mon.   No, thou need'st not learn;
Thou hast the theory; now go there and
practice.
Bus. Ay, in a thridbare suit. When men
come there,
They must have high naps, [4] and go
from thence bare.
A man may drown the parts [5] of ten
rich men
In one poor suit. Brave barks [6] and out-
ward gloss

---

[1] Vise.   [4] Rich clothes.
[2] Deception.   [5] Abilities.
[3] Capricious.   [6] Fine coverings.

Attract court loves, be in-parts ne'er
 so gross.   110
MON. Thou shalt have gloss enough, and
 all things fit
 T'enchase in all show thy long-smothered
 spirit.
 Be ruled by me then. The old Scythians
 Painted blind Fortune's powerful hands
 with wings,
 To show her gifts come swift and sud-
 denly,
 Which, if her favorite be not swift to
 take,
 He loses them forever. Then be wise;
 Stay but awhile here, and I'll send to
 thee.
Exit Mon[sieur with Pages]. Manet [1]
                              Buss[y].
BUS. What will he send? Some crowns?
 It is to sow them
 Upon my spirit, and make them spring
 a crown   120
 Worth millions of the seed-crowns he
 will send.
 Like to disparking [2] noble husbandmen,
 He'll put his plow into me, plow me up.
 But his unsweating thrift is policy,
 And learning-hating policy is ignorant
 To fit his seed-land soil; a smooth plain
 ground
 Will never nourish any politic seed.
 I am for honest actions, not for great.
 If I may bring up a new fashion,
 And rise in court for virtue, speed his
 plow!   130
 The king hath known me long as well
 as he,
 Yet could my fortune never fit the
 length
 Of both their understandings till this
 hour.
 There is a deep nick in Time's restless
 wheel
 For each man's good; when which nick [3]
 comes, it strikes;
 As rhetoric yet works not persuasion,
 But only is a mean to make it work,
 So no man riseth by his real merit,
 But when it cries "Clink" [4] in his rais-
 er's spirit.
 Many will say, that cannot rise at all, [140

Man's first hour's rise is first step to his
 fall.
 I'll venture that; men that fall low must
 die,
 As well as men cast headlong from the sky.

                Ent[er] Maffé.

[MAF. (*Aside.*)] Humor of princes! Is this
 wretch indued
 With any merit worth a thousand
 crowns?
 Will my lord have me be so ill a steward
 Of his revenue, to dispose a sum
 So great with so small cause as shows in
 him?
 I must examine this.—Is your name
 D'Ambois?
BUS. Sir?
MAF.   Is your name D'Ambois?
BUS.   Who have we here?   150
 Serve you the Monsieur?
MAF. How?
BUS.   Serve you the Monsieur?
MAF. Sir, y'are very hot. I do serve the
 Monsieur,
 But in such place as gives me the com-
 mand [5]
 Of all his other servants. And, because
 His grace's pleasure is to give your good
 His pass [6] through my command, me-
 thinks you might
 Use me with more respect.
BUS.   Cry you mercy! [7]
 Now you have opened my dull eyes, I
 see you,
 And would be glad to see the good you
 speak of.
 What might I call your name?
MAF.   Monsieur Maffé. [160
BUS. Monsieur Maffé? Then, good Mon-
 sieur Maffé,
 Pray let me know you better.
MAF.   Pray do so,
 That you may use me better. For your-
 self,
 By your no better outside, I would judge
 you
 To be some poet. Have you given my
 lord
 Some pamphlet?

---

[1] Remains.   [4] "Now is the hour."
[2] Changing parks into open fields.
[3] Mechanism of a clock.

[5] At this point the original has the stage direction, "*Table, chessboard, and tapers behind the
arras,*" in preparation for the following scene.
 [6] Passage.   [7] I beg your pardon!

Bus.   Pamphlet?

Maf.   Pamphlet, sir, I say.

Bus. Did your great master's goodness
leave the good
That is to pass your charge to my poor
use,
To your discretion?

Maf.   Though he did not, sir,
I hope 'tis no rude office to ask reason 170
How that [1] his grace gives me in charge,
goes from me?

Bus. That's very perfect, sir.

Maf.   Why, very good, sir.
I pray then give me leave; if for no
pamphlet,
May I not know what other merit in you
Makes his compunction willing to re-
lieve you?

Bus. No merit in the world, sir.

Maf.   That is strange.
Y'are a poor soldier, are you?

Bus.   That I am, sir.

Maf. And have commanded?

Bus.   Ay, and gone without, sir.

Maf. [Aside.] I see the man; a hundred
crowns will make him
Swagger and drink healths to his grace's
bounty,   180
And swear he could not be more bounti-
ful;
So there's nine hundred crowns saved.—
Here, tall [2] soldier,
His grace hath sent you a whole hundred
crowns.

Bus. A hundred, sir? Nay, do his high-
ness right;
I know his hand is larger, and perhaps
I may deserve more than my outside shows.
I am a poet, as I am a soldier,
And I can poetize; and, being well en-
couraged,
May sing his fame for giving, yours for
delivering—
Like a most faithful steward—what he
gives.   190

Maf. What shall your subject be?

Bus.   I care not much,
If to his bounteous grace I sing the
praise
Of fair great noses, and to you of long
ones. [3]

<hr>

[1] That which.   [2] Brave.

[3] Monsieur's large nose was the object of much
satire.

What qualities have you, sir, beside
your chain
And velvet jacket? [4] Can your worship
dance?

Maf. [Aside.] A pleasant fellow, faith.
It seems my lord
Will have him for his jester, and, by'r
Lady,
Such men are now no fools; 'tis a knight's
place.
If I, to save his grace some crowns,
should urge him
T'abate his bounty, I should not be
heard;   200
I would to heaven I were an arrant
ass,
For then I should be sure to have the
ears
Of these great men, where now their
jesters have them.
'Tis good to please him, yet I'll take no
notice
Of his preferment, but in policy
Will still be grave and serious, lest he
think
I fear his wooden dagger. [5]—Here, Sir
Ambo!

Bus. How, Ambo, sir?

Maf.   Ay, is not your name Ambo?

Bus. You called me lately D'Ambois.
Has your worship
So short a head?

Maf.   I cry thee mercy, D'Ambois. 210
A thousand crowns I bring you from
my lord.
If you be thrifty and [6] play the good
husband, [7] you may make
This a good standing living. [8] 'Tis a
bounty
His highness might perhaps have bestowed better.

Bus. Go, y'are a rascal; hence, away, you
rogue!

Maf. What mean you, sir?

Bus.   Hence! Prate no more,

<hr>

[4] Emblems of a steward's office.

[5] Emblem of the jester.

[6] As Parrott points out, *If you be thrifty and*
has been substituted for the better reading *Serve
God* of the 1607 edn. "to avoid the penalty fixed
by the law of 1606 for the abuse of the name of
God in stage-plays." *Cf.* II, i, 207, for the
omission of *Mort Dieu*, and V, i, 41, 61, where
Heaven replaces *God* of the 1607 edn.

[7] *I.e.*, be economical.   [8] Regular income.

Or, by thy villain's blood, thou prat'st
  thy last!
A barbarous groom grudge at his master's bounty!
But, since I know he would as much abhor
His hind should argue what he gives his
  friend,   220
Take that, sir, [*Strikes him.*] for your
  aptness to dispute.   *Exit.*
MAF. These crowns are set in blood; blood
  be their fruit!   *Exit.*

[SCENA SECUNDA.

A room in the court.]

*Henry, Guise, Montsurry, Elenor, Tamyra,
  Beaupré, Pero, Charlotte, Pyra, Annabelle.* [*Henry and Guise are playing
                                    chess.*]

HEN. Duchess of Guise, your grace is much
  enriched
In the attendance of that English virgin,
That will initiate her prime of youth
(Disposed to court conditions) under the
  hand
Of your preferred instructions and com-
  mand,
Rather than any in the English court,
Whose ladies are not matched in Chris-
  tendom
For graceful and confirmed behaviors,
More than the court, where they are
  bred, is equaled.
GUISE. I like not their court fashion; it is
  too crestfallen   10
In all observance, making demigods
Of their great nobles, and of their old
  queen
An ever young and most immortal god-
  dess.
MONT. No question she's the rarest queen
  in Europe.
GUISE. But what's that to her immortal-
  ity?
HEN. Assure you, cousin Guise, so great a
  courtier,
So full of majesty and royal parts,
No queen in Christendom may vaunt
  herself.
Her court approves it, that's a court
  indeed,
Not mixed with clowneries used in com-
  mon houses,   20

But, as courts should be th' abstracts of
  their kingdoms
In all the beauty, state, and worth they
  hold,
So is hers, amply, and by her informed.[1]
The world is not contracted in a man
With more proportion and expression
Than in her court, her kingdom. Our
  French court
Is a mere mirror of confusion to it.
The king and subject, lord and every
  slave,
Dance a continual hay; [2] our rooms of
  state
Kept like our stables; no place more ob-
  served [3]   30
Than a rude market place; and, though
  our custom
Keep this assured confusion from our eyes,
'Tis ne'er the less essentially unsightly,
Which they would soon see, would they
  change their form
To this of ours, and then compare them
  both,
Which we must not affect, because in
  kingdoms
Where the king's change doth breed the
  subject's terror,
Pure innovation is more gross than error.
MONT. No question we shall see them im-
  itate,
Though afar off, the fashions of our
  courts,   40
As they have ever aped us in attire.
Never were men so weary of their skins,
And apt to leap out of themselves as
  they,
Who, when they travel [4] to bring forth
  rare men,
Come home, delivered of a fine French
  suit.
Their brains lie with their tailors, and
  get babies
For their most complete issue; he's sole
  heir
To all the moral virtues that first greets
The light with a new fashion, which be-
  comes them
Like apes, disfigured with the attires of
  men.   50
HEN. No question they much wrong their
  real worth

---

[1] Molded, fashioned.   [3] Respected.
[2] Country dance.   [4] With a pun on *travail.*

In affectation of outlandish scum;
But they have faults, and we more; they
  foolish-proud
To jet [1] in others' plumes so haughtily;
We proud that they are proud of foolery,
Holding our worths more complete for
  their vaunts.

Enter Monsieur, D'Ambois.

MON. Come, mine own sweetheart,[2] I will
  enter [3] thee.—
Sir, I have brought a gentleman to court,
And pray you would vouchsafe to do him
  grace.
HEN. D'Ambois, I think?
BUS.   That's still my name, my lord, 60
Though I be something altered in attire.
HEN. We like your alteration, and must
  tell you
We have expected th' offer of your serv-
  ice;
For we, in fear to make mild virtue
  proud,
Use not to seek her out in any man.
BUS. Nor doth she use to seek out any
  man.
They that will win must woo her [; she's
  not shameless].[4]
MON.[5] I urged her modesty in him, my
  lord,
And gave her those rites that he says
  she merits.
HEN. If you have wooed and won, then,
  brother, wear him. 70
MON. Th' art mine, sweetheart. See, here's
  the Guise's duchess,
The Countess of Montsurreau, Beaupré.
Come, I'll enseam [6] thee.—Ladies, y'are
  too many
To be in council; I have here a friend
That I would gladly enter in your graces.
BUS. Save you,[7] ladies.
DUCH. If you enter him in our graces,
my lord, methinks by his blunt behavior he
should come out of himself.
TAM. Has he never been courtier, [80
my lord?

MON. Never, my lady.
BEAU. And why did the toy [8] take him
in th' head now?
BUS. 'Tis leap year, lady, and therefore
very good to enter a courtier.
HEN. Mark, Duchess of Guise, there is
one is not bashful.
DUCH. No, my lord, he is much guilty of
the bold extremity. 90
TAM. The man's a courtier at first sight.
BUS. I can sing pricksong,[9] lady, at
first sight; and why not be a courtier as
suddenly?
BEAU. Here's a courtier rotten before
he be ripe.
BUS. Think me not impudent, lady. I
am yet no courtier; I desire to be one, and
would gladly take entrance, [*To the Duchess.*] madam, under your princely colors.

Enter Barrisor, L'Anou, Pyrrhot.

DUCH. Soft, sir, you must rise by [101
degrees, first being the servant [10] of some
common lady or knight's wife; then a little
higher to a lord's wife; next a little higher
to a countess; yet a little higher to a duchess, and then turn the ladder.[11]
BUS. Do you allow a man, then, four
mistresses when the greatest mistress is
allowed but three servants? 109
DUCH. Where find you that statute, sir?
BUS. Why, be judged by the groom
porters.[12]
DUCH. The groom porters?
BUS. Ay, madam; must not they judge
of all gamings i' th' court?
DUCH. You talk like a gamester.
GUISE. [*Rising from the chess table.*] Sir,
know you me?
BUS. My lord?
GUISE. I know not you. Whom do [120
you serve?
BUS. Serve, my lord!
GUISE. Go to, companion,[13] your court-
ship's too saucy.
BUS. [*Aside.*] Saucy! Companion! 'Tis
the Guise, but yet those terms might have

---

[1] Strut.
[2] Merely a term of affectionate address.
[3] Introduce, be sponsor for.
[4] From 1607 edn.
[5] The following eight lines are printed as prose
in the original.
[6] Introduce.   [7] God save you.

[8] Whim.
[9] Music pricked or noted down as distinguished from extemporaneous music, with an
obscene pun.
[10] Lover.   [11] *I.e.*, be hanged.
[12] Minor court officials in charge of gaming.
[13] Fellow.

been spared of the Guisard.[1] Companion! He's jealous, by this light. Are you blind of that side, duke? I'll to her again for that.—Forth, princely mistress, for [130 the honor of courtship. Another riddle!

GUISE. Cease your courtship, or by heaven I'll cut your throat.

BUS. Cut my throat? Cut a whetstone, young Accius Nævius! Do as much with your tongue as he did with a razor. Cut my throat!

BAR. [Aside.] What newcome gallant have we here, that dares mate [2] the Guise thus?   140

L'AN. [Aside.] 'Sfoot,[3] 'tis D'Ambois. The duke mistakes him, on my life, for some knight of the new edition.[4]

BUS. Cut my throat! I would the king feared thy cutting of his throat no more than I fear thy cutting of mine.

GUISE. I'll do 't, by this hand.

BUS.[5] That hand dares not do 't. Y'ave cut too many throats already, Guise, and robbed the realm of many thousand [150 souls, more precious than thine own.— Come, madam, talk on. 'Sfoot, can you not talk? Talk on, I say. Another riddle!

PYR. Here's some strange distemper.

BAR. Here's a sudden transmigration with D'Ambois—out of the Knights' Ward[6] into the duchess' bed.

L'AN. See what a metamorphosis a brave suit can work.

PYR. 'Slight, step to the Guise and [160 discover him.

BAR. By no means! Let the new suit work; we'll see the issue.

GUISE. Leave your courting!

BUS. I will not.—I say, mistress, and I will stand unto it, that, if a woman may have three servants, a man may have three score mistresses.

GUISE. Sirrah, I'll have you whipped out of the court for this insolence.   170

BUS. Whipped? Such another syllable

out o' th' presence,[7] if thou dar'st, for thy dukedom!

GUISE. Remember, poltroon!
            [He returns to his game.]

MON. Pray thee, forbear.

BUS. Passion of death! Were not the king here, he should strow the chamber like a rush.

MON. But leave courting his wife, then.

BUS. I will not. I'll court her in [180 despite of him. Not court her!—Come, madam, talk on, fear me nothing.—[To Guise.] Well mayst thou drive thy master from the court, but never D'Ambois.

MON. [Aside.] His great heart will not down. 'Tis like the sea,

That, partly by his own internal heat,

Partly the stars' daily and nightly motion,

Their heat and light, and partly of the place,

The divers frames,[8] but chiefly by the moon,

Bristled with surges, never will be won

(No, not when th' hearts of all those powers are burst)   191

To make retreat into his settled home,

Till he be crowned with his own quiet foam.

HEN. You have the mate. Another?

GUISE. No more.   *Flourish short.*[9]

Exit Guise, after him the King, Mons[ieur] whispering.

BAR. Why, here's the lion, scared with the throat of a dunghill cock, a fellow that has newly shaked off his shackles; now does he crow for that victory.

L'AN. 'Tis one of the best jigs that [200 ever was acted.

PYR. Whom does the Guise suppose him to be, trow?[10]

L'AN. Out of doubt, some new denizened[11] lord, and thinks that suit newly drawn out a[12] th' mercer's books.

BAR. I have heard of a fellow that, by a fixed imagination looking upon a bull-baiting, had a visible pair of horns grew out of his forehead; and I believe [210 this gallant, overjoyed with the conceit of

---

[1] Follower of the Guise, with a probable pun on guiser or masquerader.
[2] Checkmate, defy.
[3] God's foot.
[4] A reference to the recent creation of a number of knights by James I.
[5] Lines 148–53 and 241–44 are set as verse in the original.
[6] Part of the Counter, a London prison for debtors.

[7] Out of the king's presence.   [9] Trumpet call.
[8] Perhaps the bed of the sea.   [10] Think you.
[11] Naturalized, referring to James's new Scottish nobility.
[12] Of.

Monsieur's cast suit, imagines himself to be the Monsieur.

L'AN. And why not, as well as the ass, stalking in the lion's case,[1] bare himself like a lion, braying all the huger beasts out of the forest?

PYR. Peace, he looks this way.

BAR. Marry, let him look, sir. What will you say now if the Guise be gone to [220 fetch a blanket [2] for him?

L'AN. Faith, I believe it for his honor sake.

PYR. But, if D'Ambois carry it clean? [3]
                                        Exeunt Ladies.

BAR. True, when he curvets in the blanket.

PYR. Ay, marry, sir.

L'AN. 'Sfoot, see how he stares on 's.

BAR. Lord bless us, let's away.

BUS. Now, sir, take your full view. [230 How does the object please ye?

BAR. If you ask my opinion, sir, I think your suit sits as well as if 't had been made for you.

BUS. So, sir, and was that the subject of your ridiculous jollity?

L'AN. What's that to you, sir?

BUS. Sir, I have observed all your fleer-- ings, and resolve yourselves ye shall give a strict account for 't.   240

Enter Brisac, Melynell.

BAR. O, miraculous jealousy! [4] Do you think yourself such a singular subject for laughter that none can fall into the matter of our merriment but you?

L'AN. This jealousy of yours, sir, con- fesses some close defect in yourself that we never dreamed of.

PYR. We held discourse of a perfumed ass that, being disguised in a lion's case, im- agined himself a lion. I hope that [250 touched not you.

BUS. So, sir; your descants do mar- velous well fit this ground.[5] We shall meet where your buffoonly laughters will cost ye the best blood in your bodies.

BAR. For life's sake let's be gone; he'll kill 's outright else.

BUS. Go, at your pleasures. I'll be your

¹ Skin.   ³ *I.e.*, get the better of him.
² To toss him. ⁴ Suspicion.
⁵ With an additional reference to music, mean- ing variations on a theme.

ghost to haunt you; and ye sleep an 't,[6] hang me.   260

L'AN. Go, go, sir; court your mistress.

PYR. And, be advised, we shall have odds against you.

BUS. Tush! Valor stands not in num- ber; I'll maintain it that one man may beat three boys.

BRIS. Nay, you shall have no odds of him in number, sir; he's a gentleman as good as the proudest of you, and ye shall not wrong him.   270

BAR. Not, sir?

MEL. Not, sir. Though he be not so rich, he's a better man than the best of you, and I will not endure it.

L'AN. Not you, sir?

BRIS. No, sir, nor I.

BUS. I should thank you for this kind- ness, if I thought these perfumed musk cats, being out of this privilege,[7] durst but once mew at us.   280

BAR. Does your confident spirit doubt that, sir? Follow us and try.

L'AN. Come, sir, we'll lead you a dance.
                                        Exeunt.

FINIS ACTUS PRIMI.

ACTUS SECUND[I]   SCENA PRIMA.

[A room in the court.]

*Henry, Guise, Montsurry, [Beaumond,]
                          and Attendants.*

HEN. This desperate quarrel sprung out of their envies
      To D'Ambois' sudden bravery[8] and great spirit.

GUISE. Neither is worth their envy.

HEN.   Less than either
Will make the gall of Envy overflow.
She feeds on outcast entrails like a kite,
In which foul heap, if any ill lies hid,
She sticks her beak into it, shakes it up,
And hurls it all abroad, that all may view it.
Corruption is her nutriment; but touch her
With any precious ointment, and you kill her.   10
Where she finds any filth in men, she feasts,

⁶ If you sleep on it.
⁷ Area where no fighting is allowed.
⁸ In the double sense of *finery* and *daring*.

And with her black throat bruits it
   through the world,
Being sound and healthful; but, if she
   but taste
The slenderest pittance of commended
   virtue,
She surfeits of it, and is like a fly
That passes all the body's soundest parts,
And dwells upon the sores; or, if her
   squint eye
Have power to find none there, she forges
   some.
She makes that crooked ever which is
   straight;
Calls valor giddiness, justice tyranny. 20
A wise man may shun her, she not her-
   self;
Whithersoever she flies from her harms,
She bears her foes still clasped in her own
   arms.
And therefore, cousin Guise, let us avoid
   her.

Enter Nuntius.

NUN. What Atlas or Olympus lifts his
   head
So far past covert[1] that with air enough
My words may be informed, and from
   their height
I may be seen and heard through all the
   world?
A tale so worthy and so fraught with
   wonder   29
Sticks in my jaws, and labors with event.
HEN. Com'st thou from D'Ambois?
NUN.   From him, and the rest,
   His friends and enemies, whose stern
      fight I saw,
And heard their words before and in the
   fray.
HEN. Relate at large what thou hast seen
   and heard.
NUN. I saw fierce D'Ambois and his two
   brave friends
   Enter the field, and at their heels their
      foes,
Which were the famous soldiers, Bar-
   risor,
L'Anou, and Pyrrhot, great in deeds of
   arms;
All which arrived at the evenest piece of
   earth
The field afforded, the three challeng-
   ers   40

Turned head, drew all their rapiers, and
   stood ranked,
When face to face the three defendants
   met them,
Alike prepared, and resolute alike.
Like bonfires of contributory wood
Every man's look showed, fed with
   either's spirit,
As one had been a mirror to another,
Like forms of life and death, each took
   from other;
And so were life and death mixed at
   their heights
That you could see no fear of death, for
   life,
Nor love of life, for death; but in their
   brows   50
Pyrrho's opinion in great letters shone:
That life and death in all respects are one.
HEN. Passed there no sort of words at
   their encounter?
NUN. As Hector, twixt the hosts of Greece
   and Troy,
When Paris and the Spartan king should
   end
The nine years' war, held up his brazen
   lance
For signal that both hosts should cease
   from arms,
And hear him speak, so Barrisor, ad-
   vised,[2]
Advanced his naked rapier twixt both
   sides,
Ripped up[3] the quarrel, and compared
   six lives   60
Then laid in balance with six idle words;
Offered remission and contrition too;
Or else that he and D'Ambois might
   conclude
The others' dangers. D'Ambois liked the
   last;
But Barrisor's friends, being equally
   engaged
In the main quarrel, never would expose
His life alone to that they all deserved.
And, for the other offer of remission,
D'Ambois, that like a laurel put in fire
Sparkled and spit, did much, much more
   than scorn   70
That his wrong should incense him so like
   chaff
To go so soon out, and like lighted paper

---

[1] Wooded covering.   [3] Recalled the causes of.
[2] Cautious.

Approve [1] his spirit at once both fire and
  ashes.
So drew they lots and in them Fates
  appointed
That Barrisor should fight with fiery
  D'Ambois,
Pyrrhot with Melynell, with Brisac,
  L'Anou.
And then like flame and powder they
  commixed
So spritely that I wished they had been
  spirits,
That the ne'er-shutting wounds they
  needs must open
Might, as they opened, shut and never
  kill.   80
But D'Ambois' sword, that lightened as
  it flew,
Shot like a pointed comet at the face
Of manly Barrisor; and there it stuck.
Thrice plucked he at it, and thrice drew
  on thrusts
From him that of himself was free as fire;
Who thrust still as he plucked, yet, past
  belief,
He with his subtle eye, hand, body,
  scaped.
At last, the deadly-bitten point tugged
  off,
On fell his yet undaunted foe so fiercely
That, only made more horrid with his
  wound,   90
Great D'Ambois shrunk, and gave a little
  ground;
But soon returned, redoubled in [2] his
  danger,
And at the heart of Barrisor sealed his
  anger.
Then, as in Arden I have seen an oak
Long shook with tempests, and his lofty
  top
Bent to his root, which being at length
  made loose,
Even groaning with his weight, he gan to
  nod
This way and that, as loath his curléd
  brows,
Which he had oft wrapped in the sky with
  storms,
Should stoop; and yet, his radical fibers
  burst,   100
Stormlike he fell, and hid the fear-cold
  earth.

So fell stout Barrisor, that had stood the
  shocks
Of ten set battles in your highness' war
Gainst the sole soldier of the world,
  Navarre.
GUISE. O, piteous and horrid murther!
BEAUM.   Such a life
  Methinks had metal in it to survive
An age of men.
HEN.   Such often soonest end.—
  Thy felt report calls on; [3] we long to
  know
On what events the other have arrived.
NUN. Sorrow and fury, like two opposite
  fumes   110
Met in the upper region of a cloud,
At the report made by this worthy's fall,
Brake from the earth, and with them rose
  Revenge,
Ent'ring with fresh powers his two noble
  friends;
And under that odds fell surcharged [4]
  Brisac,
The friend of D'Ambois, before fierce
  L'Anou;
Which D'Ambois seeing, as I once did
  see
In my young travels through Armenia
An angry unicorn in his full career
Charge with too swift a foot a jew-
  eler   120
That watched him for the treasure of his
  brow, [5]
And, ere he could get shelter of a tree,
Nail him with his rich antler to the earth,
So D'Ambois ran upon revenged L'Anou,
Who, eying th' eager point borne in his
  face,
And giving back, fell back, and in his
  fall
His foe's uncurbéd sword stopped in his
  heart;
By which time all the lifestrings of the
  tw' other
Were cut, and both fell as their spirit[s]
  flew
Upwards, and still hunt honor at the
  view. [6]   130
And now, of all the six, sole D'Ambois
  stood

[3] Thy affecting report calls for more.
[4] Overpowered.
[5] I.e., his horn.
[6] Like dogs that have sighted the quarry.

[1] Prove.   [2] Coming a second time into.

Untouched, save only with the others'
  blood.
HEN. All slain outright but he?
NUN.   All slain outright but he,
  Who, kneeling in the warm life of his
  friends,
  All freckled with the blood his rapier
  rained,
  He kissed their pale lips, and bade both
  farewell—
  And see the bravest man the French
  earth bears!

Enter Monsieur, D'Amb[ois] bare[headed].

BUS. Now is the time. Y'are princely
  vowed my friend;
  Perform it princely, and obtain my
  pardon.
MON. Else heaven forgive not me! Come
  on, brave friend!— [*They kneel.*] 140
If ever nature held herself her own,
When the great trial of a king and sub-
  ject
Met in one blood, both from one belly
  springing,
Now prove her virtue and her greatness
  one,
Or make the t' one the greater with the
  tother,
As true kings should, and for your
  brother's love,
Which is a special species of true virtue,
Do that you could not do, not being a
  king.
HEN. Brother, I know your suit; these
  willful murthers
Are ever past our pardon.
MON.   Manly slaughter 150
Should never bear th' account of willful
  murther,
It being a spice ¹ of justice, where with life
Offending past law, equal life is laid
In equal balance, to scourge that offense
By law of reputation, which to men
Exceeds all positive law; and what that
  leaves
To true men's valors, not prefixing rights
Of satisfaction, suited to their wrongs,
A free man's eminence may supply and
  take.
HEN. This would make every man that
  thinks him wronged   160
Or is offended, or in wrong or right,

¹ Species, sort.

Lay on this violence, and all vaunt them-
  selves
Law-menders and suppliers, though mere
  butchers.
Should this fact, though of justice, be
  forgiven?
MON. O, no, my lord; it would make
  cowards fear
To touch the reputations of true men
When only they are left to imp ² the law.
Justice will soon distinguish murtherous
  minds
From just revengers. Had my friend
  been slain,
His enemy surviving, he should die,   170
Since he had added to a murthered
  fame,
Which was in his intent, a murthered
  man,
And this had worthily been willful mur-
  ther.
But my friend only saved his fame's dear
  life,
Which is above life, taking th' under
  value,
Which, in the wrong it did, was forfeit
  to him;
And in this fact only preserves a man
In his uprightness, worthy to survive
Millions of such as murther men alive.
HEN. Well, brother, rise, and raise your
  friend withal   180
From death to life. And, D'Ambois, let
  your life,
Refined by passing through this merited
  death,
Be purged from more such foul pollution,
Nor on your 'scape nor valor more pre-
  suming
To be again so daring.
BUS.   My lord,
I loathe as much a deed of unjust death
As law itself doth, and to tyrannize,
Because I have a little spirit to dare
And power to do, as to be tyrannized.
This is a grace that, on my knees re-
  doubled,³   190
I crave to double this, my short life's gift,
And shall your royal bounty centuple,
That I may so make good what law and
  nature
Have given me for my good; since I am
  free,

² Piece out.   ³ Rekneeling.

Offending no just law, let no law make,
By any wrong it does, my life her slave.
When I am wronged, and that law fails
    to right me,
Let me be king myself, as man was made,
And do a justice that exceeds the law;
If my wrong pass the power of single
    valor   200
To right and expiate, then be you my
    king,
And do a right, exceeding law and nature.
Who to himself is law, no law doth need,
Offends no law, and is a king indeed.
HEN. Enjoy what thou entreat'st; we give
    but ours.
BUS. What you have given, my lord, is
    ever yours.
Exit Rex [1] *cum Beau*[*mond, Attendants,
                Nuntius, and Montsurry*].
GUISE. [*Mort Dieu!*] [2]   Who would have
    pardoned such a murther?   *Exit.*
MON. Now vanish horrors into court at-
    tractions,
    For which let this balm make thee fresh
        and fair.
    And now forth with thy service to the
        duchess,   210
    As my long- love will to Montsurry's
        countess.   *Exit.*
BUS. To whom my love hath long been
    vowed in heart,
    Although in hand for show I held the
        duchess.
    And now through blood and vengeance,
        deeds of height
    And hard to be achieved, 'tis fit I make
    Attempt of her perfection. I need fear
    No check in his rivality,[3] since her virtues
    Are so renowned, and he of all dames
        hated.   *Exit.*

[SCENA SECUNDA.

A room in Montsurry's house.]

*Enter Monsieur, Tamyra, and Pero with a
                book.*

MON. Pray thee regard thine own good, if
    not mine,
    And cheer my love for that. You do not
        know

[1] King.
[2] God's death! From 1607 edn.; omitted in
the original.
[3] Rivalry.   [4] Concern.

What you may be by me, nor what with-
    out me;
I may have power t' advance and pull
    down any.
TAM. That's not my study.[4] One way I am
    sure
You shall not pull down me; my hus-
    band's height
Is crown to all my hopes, and his retiring
To any mean state shall be my aspiring.
Mine honor's in mine own hands, spite
    of kings.
MON. Honor, what's that? Your second
    maidenhead!   10
And what is that? A word. The word is
    gone;
The thing remains. The rose is plucked;
    the stalk
Abides. An easy loss where no lack's
    found!
Believe it, there's as small lack in the loss
As there is pain i' th' losing. Archers ever
Have two strings to a bow, and shall
    great Cupid,
Archer of archers both in men and
    women,
Be worse provided than a common
    archer?
A husband and a friend all wise wives
    have.
TAM. Wise wives they are that on such
    strings depend,   20
With a firm husband joining a loose
    friend!
MON. Still you stand on your husband; so
    do all
The common sex of you, when y'are
    encountered
With one ye cannot fancy. All men know
You live in court here by your own
    election,
Frequenting all our common sports and
    triumphs,
All the most youthful company of men.
And wherefore do you this? To please
    your husband?
'Tis gross and fulsome. If your husband's
    pleasure
Be all your object, and you aim at
    honor   30
In living close to him, get you from
    court;
You may have him at home. These
    common put-off.

For common women serve: "My honor!
  Husband!"
Dames maritorious [1] ne'er were meri-
  torious.
Speak plain and say, "I do not like you,
  sir;
Y'are an ill-favored fellow in my eye,"
And I am answered.

TAM.   Then, I pray, be answered;
For in good faith, my lord, I do not like
  you
In that sort you like.

MON.   Then have at you, here!
Take, with a politic hand, this rope
  of pearl,   40
And, though you be not amorous, yet be
  wise.
Take me for wisdom; he that you can love
Is ne'er the further from you.

TAM.   Now it comes
So ill prepared that I may take a poison
Under a medicine as good cheap [2] as it;
I will not have it were it worth the world.

MON. Horror of death! Could I but please
  your eye,
You would give me the like ere you
  would lose [3] me.
"Honor and husband!"

TAM.   By this light, my lord,
Y'are a vile fellow, and I'll tell the
  king   50
Your occupation of dishonoring ladies
And of his court. A lady cannot live
As she was born, and with that sort of
  pleasure
That fits her state, but she must be
  defamed
With an infamous lord's detraction.
Who would endure the court if these
  attempts
Of open and professed lust must be
  borne?—
Who's there? Come on, dame; you are
  at your book
When men are at your mistress. Have I
  taught you
Any such waiting-woman's quality?   60

MON. Farewell, good "husband."
                    Exit Mons[ieur].

TAM.   Farewell, wicked lord.

---

[1] Excessively fond of their husbands.
[2] Cheaply, readily.
[3] The original spelling *loose* carries a possible
meaning.

Enter Mont[surry].

MONT. Was not the Monsieur here?

TAM.   Yes, to good purpose;
And your cause is as good to seek him too,
And haunt his company.

MONT.   Why, what's the matter?

TAM. Matter of death, were I some hus-
  bands' wife.
I cannot live at quiet in my chamber
For opportunities [4] almost to rapes
Offered me by him.

MONT.   Pray thee bear with him.
Thou know'st he is a bachelor and a
  courtier,
Ay, and a prince; and their preroga-
  tives   70
Are to their laws as to their pardons are
Their reservations, after parliaments—
One quits another; form gives all their
  essence.
That prince doth high in virtue's reck-
  oning stand
That will entreat a vice, and not com
  mand.
So far bear with him; should another man
Trust to his privilege, he should trust
  to death.
Take comfort, then, my comfort; nay,
  triumph
And crown thyself; thou part'st [5] with
  victory.
My presence is so only dear to thee   80
That other men's appear worse than
  they be.
For this night yet, bear with my forcéd
  absence;
Thou know'st my business, and with
  how much weight
My vow hath charged it.

TAM.   True, my lord, and never
My fruitless love shall let [6] your serious
  honor;
Yet, sweet lord, do not stay; you know
  my soul
Is so long time without me, and I dead,
As you are absent.

MONT.   By this kiss, receive
My soul for hostage till I see my love.

TAM. The morn shall let me see you?

MONT.   With the sun   90
I'll visit thy more comfortable beauties.

---

[4] Importunities.   [6] Hinder.
[5] Depart'st, com'st off.

TAM. This is my comfort, that the sun hath left
The whole world's beauty ere my sun leaves me.

MONT. 'Tis late night now indeed; farewell, my light!   *Exit.*

TAM. Farewell, my light and life!—[*Aside.*]
But not in him,
In mine own dark love and light bent to another.
Alas, that in the wave [1] of our affections
We should supply it with a full dissembling,
In which each youngest maid is grown a mother.
Frailty is fruitful; one sin gets another.   100
Our loves like sparkles are that brightest shine
When they go out; most vice shows most divine.—
Go, maid, to bed; lend me your book, I pray—
Not, like yourself, for form; I'll this night trouble
None of your services. Make sure the doors,
And call your other fellows to their rest.

PER. I will.—[*Aside.*] Yet I will watch to know why you watch.   *Exit.*

TAM. Now all ye peaceful regents of the night,
Silently gliding exhalations,[2]
Languishing winds and murmuring falls of waters,   110
Sadness of heart and ominous secureness,
Enchantments, dead sleeps, all the friends of rest,
That ever wrought upon the life of man,
Extend your utmost strengths, and this charmed hour
Fix like the center.[3] Make the violent wheels
Of Time and Fortune stand, and great Existence,
The Maker's treasury, now not seem to be,
To all but my approaching friends and me!
They come, alas, they come! Fear, fear and hope

Of one thing, at one instant fight in me;   120
I love what most I loathe, and cannot live
Unless I compass that which holds my death;
For life's mere death, loving one that loathes me,
And he I love will loathe me, when he sees
I fly my sex, my virtue, my renown,
To run so madly on a man unknown.
                    The vault opens.[4]
See, see, a vault is opening that was never
Known to my lord and husband, nor to any
But him that brings the man I love, and me.
How shall I look on him? How shall I live,   130
And not consume in blushes? I will in,
And cast myself off, as I ne'er had been.[5]
                    Exit.

Ascendit Friar and D'Ambois.

FRI. Come, worthiest son, I am past measure glad
That you, whose worth I have approved so long,
Should be the object of her fearful love,
Since both your wit and spirit can adapt
Their full force to supply her utmost weakness.
You know her worths and virtues, for report
Of all that know is to a man a knowledge;
You know, besides, that our affections' storm,   140
Raised in our blood, no reason can reform.
Though she seek then their satisfaction,
Which she must needs, or rest unsatisfied,
Your judgment will esteem her peace thus wrought,
Nothing less dear than if yourself had sought;

---

[1] Wavering. Dilke suggests *wane.*
[2] Meteors.   [3] Center of the earth.
[4] This direction follows l.123 in the original.
[5] Undress as if I had never been here (?); completely cast off my old self (?).

And with another color,[1] which my art
Shall teach you to lay on, yourself must
    seem
The only agent, and the first orb [2] move
In this our set and cunning world of
    love.
Bus. Give me the color, my most hon-
    ored father,   150
And trust my cunning then to lay it on.
Fri. 'Tis this, good son. Lord Barrisor,
    whom you slew,
Did love her dearly, and with all fit
    means
Hath urged his acceptation, of all which
She keeps one letter written in his blood.
You must say thus, then, that you
    heard from me
How much herself was touched in con-
    science
With a report, which is in truth dis-
    persed,
That your main quarrel grew about her
    love,   159
Lord Barrisor imagining your courtship
Of the great Guise's duchess in the pres-
    ence
Was by you made to his elected mistress;
And so made me your mean now to re-
    solve her,[3]
Choosing, by my direction, this night's
    depth
For the more clear avoiding of all note
Of your presuméd presence; and with
    this,
To clear her hands of such a lover's blood,
She will so kindly thank and entertain
    you—
Methinks I see how—ay, and ten to one,
Show you the confirmation in his blood,
Lest you should think report and she
    did feign,   171
That you shall so have circumstantial
    means
To come to the direct, which must be
    used;
For the direct is crooked; love comes
    flying;
The height of love is still won with deny-
    ing.
Bus. Thanks, honored father.

[1] Pretense.
[2] *Primum mobile*, the sphere which, according
to the Ptolemaic system, set the other spheres
in motion.   [3] Explain to her.

Fri.   She must never know
That you know anything of any love
Sustained on her part; for, learn this of
    me,
In anything a woman does alone,
If she dissemble, she thinks 'tis not
    done;   180
If not dissemble, nor a little chide,
Give her her wish, she is not satisfied.
To have a man think that she never
    seeks,
Does her more good than to have all she
    likes.
This frailty sticks in them beyond their
    sex,
Which to reform, reason is too perplex.[4]
Urge reason to them, it will do no good;
Humor, that is the chariot of our food
In everybody, must in them be fed,
To carry their affections by it bred.   190
Stand close.   [*They withdraw.*]

Enter Tamyra with a book.

Tam. Alas, I fear my strangeness[5] will re-
    tire him.
If he go back, I die; I must prevent it,
And cheer his onset with my sight at
    least,
And that's the most. Though every step
    he takes
Goes to my heart, I'll rather die than
    seem
Not to be strange to that I most esteem.
Fri. [*Advancing.*] Madam!
Tam.   Ah!
Fri.   You will
    pardon me, I hope,
That so beyond your expectation,
And at a time for visitants so unfit,   200
I, with my noble friend here, visit you.
You know that my access at any time
Hath ever been admitted; and that friend
That my care will presume to bring with
    me
Shall have all circumstance of worth in
    him
To merit as free welcome as myself.
Tam. O father! But at this suspicious
    hour
You know how apt best men are to sus-
    pect us
In any cause that makes suspicious
    shadow

[4] Intricate.   [5] Distant behavior.

No greater than the shadow of a hair; 210
And y'are to blame.　What though my
　lord and husband
Lie forth tonight, and, since I cannot
　sleep
When he is absent, I sit up tonight;
Though all the doors are sure, and all
　our servants
As sure bound with their sleeps, yet
　there is One
That wakes above, whose eye no sleep
　can bind.
He sees through doors, and darkness, and
　our thoughts;
And therefore, as we should avoid with
　fear
To think amiss ourselves before his
　search,
So should we be as curious [1] to shun　220
All cause that other think not ill of us.
Bus. Madam, 'tis far from that, I only
　heard
By this my honored father that your
　conscience
Made some deep scruple with a false
　report
That Barrisor's blood should something
　touch your honor,
Since he imagined I was courting you
When I was bold to change words with
　the duchess,
And therefore made his quarrel, his long
　love
And service, as I hear, being deeply
　vowed
To your perfections, which my ready
　presence,　　　　　　　　　　230
Presumed on with my father at this
　season
For the more care of your so curious
　honor,
Can well resolve [2] your conscience is most
　false.
Tam. And is it therefore that you come,
　good sir?
Then crave I now your pardon and my
　father's,
And swear your presence does me so
　much good
That all I have it binds to your requital.
Indeed, sir, 'tis most true that a report
Is spread, alleging that his love to me
Was reason of your quarrel, and, because

[1] Careful.　　　　　　　　　[2] Assure.

You shall not think I feign it for my
　glory　　　　　　　　　　　　241
That he importuned me for his court
　service,[3]
I'll show you his own hand, set down in
　blood
To that vain purpose.　Good sir, then
　come in.
Father, I thank you now a thousandfold.
　　　　　　Exit Tamyra and D'Amb[ois].
Fri. May it be worth it to you, honored
　daughter.　　　　　Descendit Friar.

FINIS ACTUS SECUNDI.

ACTUS TERTII　SCENA PRIMA.

[A room in Montsurry's house.]

Enter D'Ambois, Tamyra, with a chain of
　　　　　　　　　　　　　　pearl.

Bus. Sweet mistress, cease!　Your con-
　science is too nice,[4]
And bites too hotly of the Puritan spice.
Tam. O, my dear servant, in thy close
　embraces
I have set open all the doors of danger
To my encompassed honor and my life.
Before, I was secure against death and
　hell,
But now am subject to the heartless fear
Of every shadow and of every breath,
And would change firmness with an as-
　pen leaf;
So confident a spotless conscience is,　10
So weak a guilty.　O, the dangerous siege
Sin lays about us, and the tyranny
He exercises when he hath expugned! [5]
Like to the horror of a winter's thunder,
Mixed with a gushing storm, that suffer
　nothing
To stir abroad on earth but their own
　rages,
Is Sin, when it hath gathered head above
　us.
No roof, no shelter can secure us so,
But he will drown our cheeks in fear or
　woe.　　　　　　　　　　　　19
Bus. Sin is a coward, madam, and insults
But on [6] our weakness, in his truest valor;

[3] I.e., to accept him as courtly lover.
[4] Scrupulous, squeamish.
[5] Attacked successfully, been victorious.
[6] Merely exults scornfully over.

And so our ignorance tames us, that we
let
His shadows fright us; and like empty
clouds,
In which our faulty apprehensions forge
The forms of dragons, lions, elephants,
When they hold no proportion,[1] the sly
charms
Of the witch, Policy, makes him like a
monster
Kept only to show men for servile money.
That false hag often paints him in her
cloth
Ten times more monstrous than he is in
troth.   30
In three of us, the secret of our meeting
Is only guarded, and three friends as one
Have ever been esteemed, as our three
powers
That in one soul are as one united.
Why should we fear then? For myself I
swear
Sooner shall torture be the sire to pleas-
ure,
And health be grievous to one long-time
sick,
Than the dear jewel of your fame in me
Be made an outcast to your infamy;
Nor shall my value (sacred to your vir-
tues)   40
Only give free course to it, from myself,
But make it fly out of the mouths of kings
In golden vapors and with awful wings.
TAM. It rests as all kings' seals were set in
thee.[2]
Now let us call my father, whom I swear
I could extremely chide, but that I fear
To make him so suspicious of my love,
Of which, sweet servant, do not let him
know
For all the world.
BUS.   Alas, he will not think it!
TAM. Come, then.—Ho, father, ope, and
take your friend.   50

Ascendit Friar.

FRI. Now, honored daughter, is your doubt
resolved?
TAM. Ay, father, but you went away too
soon.
FRI. Too soon?

[1] Resemblance.
[2] *I.e.*, it remains inviolable.

TAM.   Indeed you did; you should
have stayed.
Had not your worthy friend been of your
bringing—
And that contains all laws to temper
me—
Not all the fearful danger that besieged
us
Had awed my throat from exclamation.
FRI. I know your serious disposition well.
Come, son, the morn comes on.
BUS.   Now, honored mistress,
Till farther service call, all bliss supply
you!   60
TAM. And you this chain of pearl, and my
love only!
          Descendit Friar and D'Amb[ois].
It is not I, but urgent destiny,
That (as great statesmen for their gen-
eral end,
In politic justice, make poor men offend)
Enforceth my offense to make it just.
What shall weak dames do, when th'
whole work of nature
Hath a strong finger in each one of us?
Needs must that sweep away the silly
cobweb
Of our still undone labors, that lays still
Our powers to it; as to the line, the
stone,   70
Not to the stone, the line should be op-
posed.
We cannot keep our constant course in
virtue.
What is alike at all parts? Every day
Differs from other—every hour and min-
ute,
Ay, every thought in our false clock of
life
Ofttimes inverts the whole circumference.
We must be sometimes one, sometimes
another.
Our bodies are but thick clouds to our
souls,
Through which they cannot shine when
they desire.
When all the stars, and even the sun
himself,   80
Must stay the vapors' times that he ex-
hales
Before he can make good his beams to us,
O, how can we, that are but motes to
him,
Wand'ring at random in his ordered rays,

Disperse our passions' fumes, with our
    weak labors,
That are more thick and black than all
    earth's vapors?

Enter Mont[surry].

MONT. Good day, my love! What, up and
    ready [1] too?
TAM. Both, my dear lord; not all this
    night made I
Myself unready, or could sleep a wink.
MONT. Alas, what troubled my true love,
    my peace,   90
From being at peace within her better
    self?
Or how could sleep forbear to seize thine
    eyes
When he might challenge them as his just
    prize?
TAM. I am in no power earthly, but in
    yours.
To what end should I go to bed, my lord,
That wholly missed the comfort of my
    bed?
Or how should sleep possess my faculties,
Wanting the proper closer of mine eyes?
MONT. Then will I never more sleep night
    from thee.
All mine own business, all the king's
    affairs,   100
Shall take the day to serve them; every
    night
I'll ever dedicate to thy delight.
TAM. Nay, good my lord, esteem not my
    desires
Such doters on their humors that my
    judgment
Cannot subdue them to your worthier
    pleasure;
A wife's pleased husband must her object
    be
In all her acts, not her soothed fantasy.
MONT. Then come, my love, now pay
    those rites to sleep
Thy fair eyes owe him. Shall we now to
    bed?   109
TAM. O, no, my lord; your holy friar says
All couplings in the day that touch the
    bed
Adulterous are, even in the marriéd;
Whose grave and worthy doctrine, well
    I know,
Your faith in him will liberally allow.

MONT. He's a most learned and religious
    man.
Come to the presence then, and see great
    D'Ambois
(Fortune's proud mushroom shot up in
    a night)
Stand like an Atlas under our king's arm;
Which greatness with him Monsieur
    now envies
As bitterly and deadly as the Guise. 120
TAM. What, he that was but yesterday
    his maker,
His raiser and preserver?
MONT.   Even the same.
Each natural agent works but to this end,
To render that it works on like itself;
Which, since the Monsieur in his act
    on D'Ambois
Cannot to his ambitious end effect,
But that, quite opposite, the king hath
    power,
In his love borne to D'Ambois, to convert
The point of Monsieur's aim on his own
    breast,
He turns his outward love to inward
    hate.   130
A prince's love is like the lightning's
    fume,
Which no man can embrace, but must
    consume.   *Exeunt.*

[SCENA SECUNDA.

A room in the court.]

*Henry, D'Ambois, Monsieur, Guise, Duchess,
Annabelle, Charlotte, Attendants.*

HEN. Speak home, Bussy! Thy impartial
    words
Are like brave falcons that dare truss [2]
    a fowl
Much greater than themselves. Flatter-
    ers are kites
That check at [3] sparrows; thou shalt be
    my eagle,
And bear my thunder underneath thy
    wings.
Truth's words like jewels hang in th'
    ears of kings.
BUS. Would I might live to see no Jews
    hang there
Instead of jewels—sycophants, I mean,
Who use Truth like the devil, his true
    foe,

[1] Dressed.   [2] Seize.   [3] Pursue.

Cast by the angel to the pit of fears,   10
And bound in chains; Truth seldom decks
   kings' ears.
Slave Flattery (like a rippier's [1] legs
   rolled up
In boots of hay ropes) with kings' soothéd
   guts
Swaddled and strappled,[2] now lives only
   free.
O, 'tis a subtle knave; how like the
   plague
Unfelt he strikes into the brain of man,
And rageth in his entrails, when he can,
Worse than the poison of a red-haired
   man! [3]
HEN. Fly at him and his brood! I cast
   thee off,[4]
And once more give thee surname of
   mine eagle.   20
BUS. I'll make you sport enough, then;
   let me have
My lucerns [5] too, or dogs inured to hunt
Beasts of most rapine, but to put them
   up,[6]
And, if I truss not, let me not be trusted.
Show me a great man (by the people's
   voice,
Which is the voice of God) that by his
   greatness
Bombasts [7] his private roofs with public
   riches;
That affects royalty, rising from a clap-
   dish; [8]
That rules so much more by his suffering
   king [9]
That he makes kings of his subordinate
   slaves;   30
Himself and them graduate [10] (like wood-
   mongers,
Piling a stack of billets) from the earth,
Raising each other into steeples' heights;
Let him convey this on the turning
   props
Of Protean law, and, his own counsel
   keeping,[11]

[1] Fishmonger's.
[2] Strapped.
[3] Judas was supposed to have had red hair;
hence, a traitor.
[4] Release thee for flight.
[5] Properly lynxes; here, hunting dogs.
[6] Start them from cover.
[7] Stuffs out.   [9] By his king's sufferance.
[8] Beggar's dish.   [10] Rise by steps.
[11] Perhaps referring to the keeping of a private
lawyer.

Keep all upright—let me but hawk at
   him,
I'll play the vulture, and so thump his
   liver
That, like a huge, unlading argosy,
He shall confess all, and you then may
   hang him.
Show me a clergyman that is in voice   40
A lark of heaven, in heart a mole of
   earth;
That hath good living, and a wicked life;
A temperate look, and a luxurious gut;
Turning the rents of his superfluous
   cures [12]
Into your pheasants and your partridges;
Venting their quintessence as men read
   Hebrew[13]—
Let me but hawk at him, and, like the
   other,
He shall confess all, and you then may
   hang him.
Show me a lawyer that turns sacred law
(The equal rend'rer of each man his
   own,   50
The scourge of rapine and extortion,
The sanctuary and impregnable defense
Of retired learning and besiegéd virtue)
Into a harpy, that eats all but 's own,
Into the damnéd sins it punisheth,
Into the synagogue of thieves and athe-
   ists,
Blood into gold, and justice into lust—
Let me but hawk at him as at the rest,
He shall confess all, and you then may
   hang him.

Enter Montsurry, Tamyra, and Pero.

GUISE. Where will you find such game as
   you would hawk at?   60
BUS. I'll hawk about your house for one
   of them.
GUISE. Come, y'are a glorious [14] ruffian,
   and run proud
Of [15] the king's headlong graces. Hold
   your breath,
Or, by that poisoned vapor, not the king
Shall back your murtherous valor against
   me.
BUS. I would the king would make his
   presence free

[12] Income of his supplementary parishes.
[13] *I.e.*, backwards.
[14] Boastful.
[15] On account of.

But for one bout betwixt us; by the
  reverence
Due to the sacred space twixt kings
  and subjects,
Here would I make thee cast that
  popular purple,
In which thy proud soul sits and braves
  thy sovereign.   70
MON. Peace, peace, I pray thee, peace!
BUS.   Let him peace first
  That made the first war.
MON.   He's the better man.
BUS. And therefore may do worst?
MON.   He has more titles.
BUS. So Hydra had more heads.
MON.   He's greater known.
BUS. His greatness is the people's; mine's
  mine own.
MON. He's nobly [1] born.
BUS.   He is not; I am noble.
  And noblesse in his [2] blood hath no
  gradation
  But in his merit.
GUISE.   Th' art not nobly born,
  But bastard to the Cardinal of Ambois.
BUS. Thou liest, proud Guisard. Let me
  fly, my lord!   80
HEN. Not in my face, my eagle; violence
  flies
  The sanctuaries of a prince's eyes.
BUS. Still shall we chide and foam upon
  this bit?
  Is the Guise only great in faction?
  Stands he not by himself? Proves he
  th' opinion
  That men's souls are without them? Be
  a duke,
  And lead me to the field.
GUISE.   Come, follow me.
HEN. Stay them! Stay, D'Ambois! Cousin
  Guise, I wonder
  Your honored disposition brooks so ill
  A man so good, that only would uphold
  Man in his native noblesse, from whose
  fall   91
  All our dissensions rise; that in himself
  (Without the outward patches of our
  frailty,
  Riches and honor) knows he compre-
  hends
  Worth with the greatest. Kings had
  never borne
  Such boundless empire over other men,

Had all maintained the spirit and state
  of D'Ambois;
Nor had the full impartial hand of
  Nature,
That all things gave in her original [3]
Without these definite terms of "mine"
  and "thine,"   100
Been turned unjustly to the hand of
  Fortune,
Had all preserved her in her prime, like
  D'Ambois.
No envy, no disjunction had dissolved,
Or plucked one stick out of the golden
  faggot
In which the world of Saturn [4] bound
  our lives,
Had all been held together with the
  nerves,
The genius, and th' ingenious soul of
  D'Ambois.
Let my hand therefore be the Hermean
  rod [5]
To part and reconcile, and so conserve
  you,
As my combined embracers and sup-
  porters.   110
BUS. 'Tis our king's motion, [6] and we shall
  not seem
  To worst eyes womanish, though we
  change thus soon
  Never so great grudge for his greater
  pleasure.
GUISE. I seal to that; and, so the manly
  freedom
  That you so much profess, hereafter
  prove not
  A bold and glorious license to deprave, [7]
  To me his hand shall hold the Hermean
  virtue
  His grace affects, in which submissive
  sign
  On this his sacred right hand I lay mine.
BUS. 'Tis well, my lord, and, so your
  worthy greatness   120
  Decline not to the greater insolence,
  Nor make you think it a prerogative
  To rack men's freedoms with the ruder
  wrongs,
  My hand (stuck full of laurel, in true
  sign
  'Tis wholly dedicate to righteous peace)

[1] Boas emends to *noblier*.   [2] Its.
[3] In the beginning.   [6] Desire, proposal.
[4] The fabled Golden Age.   [7] Vilify.
[5] Caduceus, emblem of peace.

In all submission kisseth th' other side.

HEN. Thanks to ye both; and kindly I invite ye
Both to a banquet, where we'll sacrifice
Full cups to confirmation of your loves—
At which, fair ladies, I entreat your presence,   130
And hope you, madam, will take one carouse
For reconcilement of your lord and servant.

DUCH. If I should fail, my lord, some other lady
Would be found there to do that for my servant.

MON. Any of these here?

DUCH.   Nay, I know not that.

BUS. [To Tamyra.] Think your thoughts like my mistress', honored lady?

TAM. I think not on you, sir; y'are one I know not.

BUS. Cry you mercy, madam!

MONT.   O, sir, has she met you?
Exeunt Henry, D'Amb[ois], Ladies.

MON. What had my bounty drunk when it raised him?

GUISE. Y'ave stuck us up a very worthy flag,   140
That takes more wind than we with all our sails.

MON. O, so he spreads and flourishes.

GUISE.   He must down;
Upstarts should never perch too near a crown.

MON. 'Tis true, my lord; and as this doting hand,
Even out of earth, like Juno, struck this giant,
So Jove's great ordinance[1] shall be here implied
To strike him under th' Etna of his pride,
To which work lend your hands, and let us cast
Where we may set snares for his ranging greatness.
I think it best amongst our greatest women;   150
For there is no such trap to catch an upstart
As a loose downfall, for you know their falls
Are th' ends of all men's rising. If great men

[1] Ordnance, thunderbolt.

And wise make scapes to please advantage,[2]
'Tis with a woman. Women, that worst may,
Still hold men's candles:[3] they direct and know
All things amiss in all men; and their women,[4]
All things amiss in them, through whose charmed mouths
We may see all the close[5] scapes of the court.
When the most royal beast of chase, the hart,   160
Being old and cunning in his lairs and haunts,
Can never be discovered to the bow,
The piece,[6] or hound, yet where, behind some queach,[7]
He breaks his gall, and rutteth with his hind,
The place is marked, and by his venery[8]
He still is taken. Shall we then attempt
The chiefest mean to that discovery here,
And court our greatest ladies' chiefest women
With shows of love and liberal promises?
'Tis but our breath. If something given in hand   170
Sharpen their hopes of more, 'twill be well ventured.

GUISE. No doubt of that; and 'tis the cunning'st point
Of your devised investigation.

MON.   I have broken
The ice to it already with the woman
Of your chaste lady, and conceive good hope
I shall wade thorough to some wishéd shore
At our next meeting.

MONT.   Nay, there's small hope there.

GUISE. Take say of[9] her, my lord; she comes most fitly.

[2] "Commit escapades, and thereby give points against themselves" (Boas)..
[3] This passage is based on an old proverb. "Women, who hold the candles because of their inferiority to men, none the less know well how the game is going" (Parrott).
[4] Waiting-women.   [6] Gun.
[5] Secret.   [7] Thicket.
[8] Pun on *hunting* and *lust*.
[9] Assay, make trial of.

Enter Charlotte, Annabelle, Pero.

MON. Starting back?

GUISE. Y'are engaged, indeed.   180

ANN. Nay, pray, my lord, forbear.

MONT. What, skittish, servant?

ANN. No, my lord, I am not so fit for your service.

CHAR. Pray pardon me now, my lord; my lady expects me.

GUISE. I'll satisfy her expectation, as far as an uncle may.

MON. Well said; a spirit of courtship of all hands.   [*Takes Pero aside.*]
Now, mine own Pero, hast thou remembered me   190
For the discovery I entreated thee to make of thy mistress?
Speak boldly, and be sure of all things I have sworn to thee.

PER. Building on that assurance, my lord, I may speak, and much the rather because my lady hath not trusted me with that I can tell you, for now I cannot be said to betray her.

MON. That's all one, so we reach our objects. Forth, I beseech thee.

PER. To tell you truth, my lord, I   [200
have made a strange discovery.

MON. Excellent, Pero, thou reviv'st me. May I sink quick to perdition if my tongue discover it.

PER. 'Tis thus, then: this last night my lord lay forth, and I, watching my lady's sitting up, stole up at midnight from my pallet, and, having before made a hole both through the wall and arras to her inmost chamber, I saw D'Ambois and   [210 herself reading a letter.

MON. D'Ambois?

PER. Even he, my lord.

MON. Dost thou not dream, wench?

PER. I swear he is the man.

MON. The devil he is, and thy lady his dam! Why, this was the happiest shot that ever flew! The just plague of hypocrisy leveled it. O, the infinite regions betwixt a woman's tongue and her   [220 heart! Is this our goddess of chastity? I thought I could not be so slighted if she had not her fraught[1] besides, and therefore plotted this with her woman, never dreaming of D'Ambois. Dear Pero, I will advance thee forever. But tell me

now—God's precious, it transforms me with admiration[2]—sweet Pero, whom should she trust with this conveyance?[3] Or, all the doors being made sure, how   [230 should his conveyance be made?

PER. Nay, my lord, that amazes me; I cannot by any study so much as guess at it.

MON. Well, let's favor our apprehensions with forbearing that a little; for, if my heart were not hooped with adamant, the conceit[4] of this would have burst it. But hark thee!—   *Whispers.*

MONT. [*Aside to Annabelle.*] I pray   [240 thee, resolve me; the duke will never imagine that I am busy about 's wife. Hath D'Ambois any privy access to her?

ANN. No, my lord, D'Ambois neglects her, as she takes it, and is therefore suspicious that either your lady or the Lady Beaupré hath closely entertained him.

MONT. By'r Lady, a likely suspi-   [250 cion, and very near the life, especially of my wife.—

MON. [*Aside to Pero.*] Come, we'll disguise all with seeming only to have courted.—Away, dry palm![5] Sh'as a liver as hard as a biscuit; a man may go a whole voyage with her, and get nothing but tempests from her windpipe.

GUISE. Here's one, I think, has swallowed a porcupine, she casts pricks   [260 from her tongue so.

MONT. And here's a peacock seems to have devoured one of the Alps, she has so swelling a spirit, and is so cold of her kindness.

CHAR. We are no windfalls, my lord; ye must gather us with the ladder of matrimony, or we'll hang till we be rotten.

MON. Indeed, that's the way to make ye right openarses.[6] But, alas, ye have   [270 no portions fit for such husbands as we wish you.

PER. Portions, my lord? Yes, and such portions as your principality cannot purchase.

MON. What, woman! What are those portions?

---

[1] Freight.

[2] Wonder.
[3] *I.e.*, of Bussy to her room.
[4] Thought.

[5] Sign of chastity.
[6] Medlars, a fruit.

PER. Riddle my riddle, my lord.

MON. Ay, marry, wench, I think thy portion is a right riddle; a man shall [280 never find it out. But let's hear it.

PER. You shall, my lord.

What's that, that being most rare's most
* cheap?*
That when you sow, you never reap?
That when it grows most, most you in [1] *it?*
And still you lose it when you win it;
That, when 'tis commonest, 'tis dearest,
And, when 'tis farthest off, 'tis nearest?

MON. Is this your great portion?

PER. Even this, my lord.   290

MON. Believe me, I cannot riddle it.

PER. No, my lord; 'tis my chastity, which you shall neither riddle nor fiddle.

MON. Your chastity? Let me begin with the end of it; how is a woman's chastity nearest a man when 'tis furthest off?

PER. Why, my lord, when you cannot get it, it goes to th' heart on you; and that, I think, comes most near [300 you; and I am sure it shall be far enough off. And so we leave you to our mercies.

Exeunt Women.

MON. Farewell, riddle!

GUISE. Farewell, medlar!

MONT. Farewell, winter plum!

MON. Now, my lords, what fruit of our inquisition? Feel you nothing budding yet? Speak, good my Lord Montsurry.

MONT. Nothing but this: D'Ambois is thought negligent in observing the [310 duchess, and therefore she is suspicious that your niece or my wife closely entertains him.

MON. Your wife, my lord? Think you that possible?

MONT. Alas, I know she flies him like her last hour.

MON. Her last hour? Why, that comes upon her the more she flies it. Does D'Ambois so, think you?   320

MONT. That's not worth the answering. 'Tis miraculous to think with what monsters women's imaginations engross them when they are once enamored, and what wonders they will work for their satisfaction. They will make a sheep valiant, a lion fearful.

MON. [*Aside.*] And an ass confident.—

[1] Harvest, store.

Well, my lord, more will come forth shortly; get you to the banquet.   330

GUISE. Come, my lord; I have the blind side of one of them.

Exit Guise cum Mont[surry].

MON. O, the unsounded sea of women's bloods,
That, when 'tis calmest, is most dangerous;
Not any wrinkle creaming in their faces
When in their hearts are Scylla and Charybdis,
Which still are hid in dark and standing fogs,
Where never day shines, nothing never grows
But weeds and poisons that no statesman knows;
Not Cerberus ever saw the damnéd nooks   340
Hid with the veils of women's virtuous looks!
But what a cloud of sulphur have I drawn
Up to my bosom in this dangerous secret!
Which if my haste with any spark should light,
Ere D'Ambois were engaged in some sure plot,
I were blown up; he would be sure my death.
Would I had never known it, for before
I shall persuade th' importance to Montsurry,
And make him with some studied stratagem
Train D'Ambois to his wreak,[2] his maid may tell it,   350
Or I (out of my fiery thirst to play
With the fell tiger, up in darkness tied,
And give it some light) make it quite break loose.
I fear it, afore heaven, and will not see
D'Ambois again till I have told Montsurry
And set a snare with him to free my fears.
Who's there?

Enter Maffé.[3]

MAF.   My lord?

MON.   Go call the Count Montsurry,

[2] *I.e.,* to Montsurry's vengeance.
[3] The scene apparently shifts to Monsieur's chamber.

And make the doors fast; I will speak
  with none
Till he come to me.
Maf.   Well, my lord.   *Exiturus.*[1]
Mon.   Or else
  Send you some other, and see all the
    doors   360
  Made safe yourself, I pray; haste, fly
    about it.
Maf. You'll speak with none but with
  the Count Montsurry?
Mon. With none but he, except it be the
  Guise.
Maf. See even by this, there's one excep-
  tion more!
  Your grace must be more firm in the
    command,
  Or else shall I as weakly execute.
  The Guise shall speak with you?
Mon.   He shall, I say.
Maf. And Count Montsurry?
Mon.   Ay, and Count Montsurry.
Maf. Your grace must pardon me, that I
  am bold
  To urge the clear and full sense of your
    pleasure;   370
  Which whensoever I have known, I hope
  Your grace will say, I hit it to a hair.
Mon. You have.
Maf.   I hope so, or I would be glad—
Mon. I pray thee get thee gone; thou art
  so tedious
  In the strict form of all thy services
  That I had better have one negligent.
  You hit my pleasure well when D'Ambois
    hit you;
  Did you not, think you?
Maf.   D'Ambois? Why, my lord—
Mon. I pray thee talk no more, but shut
  the doors.
  Do what I charge thee.
Maf.   I will, my lord, and yet 380
  I would be glad the wrong I had of
    D'Ambois—
Mon. Precious! Then it is a fate that
  plagues me
  In this man's foolery! I may be mur-
    thered
  While he stands on protection of his folly.
  Avaunt about thy charge!
Maf.   I go, my lord.—
  [*Aside.*] I had my head broke in his
    faithful service;

[1] About to go out.

I had no suit the more, nor any thanks,
And yet my teeth must still be hit with
  D'Ambois.—
D'Ambois, my lord, shall know—
Mon.   The devil and D'Ambois!
                       Exit Maffé.
How am I tortured with this trusty fool!
Never was any curious [2] in his place 391
To do things justly, but he was an ass;
We cannot find one trusty that is witty,[3]
And therefore bear their disproportion.
Grant thou, great star and angel of my
  life,[4]
A sure lease of it but for some few days,
That I may clear my bosom of the snake
I cherished there, and I will then defy
All check to it but Nature's, and her
  altars
Shall crack with vessels crowned with
  every liquor   400
Drawn from her highest and most bloody
  humors.
I fear him strangely; his advancéd valor
Is like a spirit raised without a circle,
Endangering him that ignorantly raised
  him,
And for whose fury he hath learnt no
  limit.

Enter Maffé hastily.

Maf. I cannot help it; what should I do
  more?
  As I was gathering a fit guard to make
  My passage to the doors, and the doors
    sure,
  The man of blood is entered.
Mon.   Rage of death! 409
  If I had told the secret, and he knew it,
  Thus had I been endangered.

Enter D'Ambois.[5]

                         My sweetheart!
  How now, what leap'st thou at?
Bus.   O royal object!
Mon. Thou dream'st, awake; object in
  th' empty air?
Bus. Worthy the brows of Titan, worth
  his chair.[6]
Mon. Pray thee, what mean'st thou?
Bus.   See you not a crown

[2] Careful.   [3] Sensible.   [4] Guardian angel.
[5] In the original this direction comes at the end
of the speech.   [6] The sun-god's chariot.

Impale the forehead of the great King
    Monsieur?

MON. O, fie upon thee!

BUS.   Prince, that is the subject
    Of all these your retired and sole dis-
    courses.

MON. Wilt thou not leave that wrongful
    supposition?

BUS. Why wrongful, to suppose the doubt-
    less right   420
    To the succession worth the thinking
    on?

MON. Well, leave these jests. How I am
    overjoyed
    With thy wished presence, and how fit
    thou com'st,
    For, of mine honor, I was sending for thee.

BUS. To what end?

MON.   Only for thy company,
    Which I have still in thought; but that's
    no payment
    On thy part made with personal ap-
    pearance.
    Thy absence, so long suffered, often-
    times
    Put me in some little doubt thou dost
    not love me.
    Wilt thou do one thing therefore now
    sincerely?   430

BUS. Ay, anything but killing of the king.

MON. Still in that discord and ill-taken
    note?
    How most unseasonable thou playest
    the cuckoo,
    In this thy fall of friendship! [1]

BUS.   Then do not doubt
    That there is any act within my nerves [2]
    But killing of the king, that is not yours.

MON. I will not, then; to prove which
    by my love
    Shown to thy virtues, and by all fruits
    else
    Already sprung from that still flourish-
    ing tree,
    With whatsoever may hereafter spring,
    I charge thee utter (even with all the
    freedom   441
    Both of thy noble nature and thy friend-
    ship)
    The full and plain state of me in thy
    thoughts.

BUS. What, utter plainly what I think of
    you?

MON. Plain as truth!

BUS. Why, this swims quite against the
    stream of greatness;
    Great men would rather hear their flat-
    teries,
    And, if they be not made fools, are not
    wise.

MON. I am no such great fool, and there-
    fore charge thee,
    Even from the root of thy free heart,
    display me.   450

BUS. Since you affect [3] it in such serious
    terms,
    If yourself first will tell me what you think.
    As freely and as heartily of me,
    I'll be as open in my thoughts of you.

MON. A bargain, of mine honor! And
    make this,
    That, prove we in our full dissection
    Never so foul, live still the sounder
    friends.

BUS. What else, sir? Come, pay me home;
    I'll bide it bravely.

MON. I will, I swear. I think thee then
    a man
    That dares as much as a wild horse or
    tiger;   460
    As headstrong and as bloody; and to
    feed
    The ravenous wolf of thy most cannibal
    valor,
    Rather than not employ it, thou wouldst
    turn
    Hackster to any whore,[4] slave to a Jew
    Or English usurer, to force possessions
    (And cut men's throats) of mortgagéd
    estates;
    Or thou wouldst tire [5] thee like a tinker's
    strumpet,
    And murther market folks, quarrel with
    sheep,
    And run as mad as Ajax, serve a
    butcher—
    Do anything but killing of the king; 470
    That in thy valor th' art like other
    naturals [6]
    That have strange gifts in nature, but
    no soul
    Diffused quite through, to make them
    of a piece,

---

[1] The cuckoo, known for its monotonous song,
sings in spring rather than in autumn.
  [2] Strength, power.

[3] Desire.   [4] Ruffian serving her as bodyguard.
[5] Attire, dress.   [6] Idiots.

But stop at humors that are more absurd,
Childish, and villainous than that hackster, whore,
Slave, cutthroat, tinker's bitch, compared before;
And in those humors wouldst envy, betray,
Slander, blaspheme, change each hour
a religion—
Do anything but killing of the king;
That in thy valor (which is still the
dunghill,   480
To which hath reference all filth in thy
house)
Th' art more ridiculous and vainglorious
Than any mountebank, and impudent
Than any painted bawd; which, not to
soothe
And glorify thee like a Jupiter Hammon,
Thou eat'st thy heart in vinegar; and
thy gall
Turns all thy blood to poison, which is
cause
Of that toad pool that stands in thy
complexion,
And makes thee (with a cold and earthy
moisture,
Which is the dam of putrefaction,   490
As plague to thy damned pride) rot as
thou liv'st;
To study calumnies and treacheries;
To thy friends' slaughters like a screech
owl sing,
And to all mischiefs—but to kill the
king.
Bus. So! Have you said?
Mon.   How think'st thou? Do I
flatter?
Speak I not like a trusty friend to thee?
Bus. That ever any man was blessed
withal!
So here's for me! I think you are, at
worst,
No devil, since y'are like to be no king;
Of which, with any friend of yours, I'll
lay   500
This poor stillado [1] here gainst all the
stars,
Ay, and gainst all your treacheries, which
are more,
That you did never good, but to do ill;

[1] Stiletto.

But ill of all sorts, free and for itself,
That (like a murthering piece, making
lanes in armies,
The first man of a rank, the whole rank
falling),
If you have wronged one man, you are
so far
From making him amends that all his
race,
Friends, and associates fall into your
chase;   500
That y'are for perjuries the very prince
Of all intelligencers;[2] and your voice
Is like an eastern wind, that where it
flies
Knits nets of caterpillars, with which
you catch
The prime of all the fruits the kingdom
yields;
That your political head is the cursed
fount
Of all the violence, rapine, cruelty,
Tyranny, and atheism flowing through
the realm;
That y'ave a tongue so scandalous, 'twill
cut
The purest crystal, and a breath that
will
Kill to [3] that wall a spider; you will
jest   520
With God, and your soul to the devil
tender
For lust; kiss horror, and with death
engender;
That your foul body is a Lernean fen
Of all the maladies breeding in all men
That you are utterly without a soul;
And, for your life, the thread of that
was spun
When Clotho slept, and let her breathing rock [4]
Fall in the dirt; and Lachesis still draws
it,
Dipping her twisting fingers in a bowl
Defiled, and crowned with virtue's
forcéd soul;   530
And lastly, which I must for gratitude
Ever remember, that of all my height
And dearest life, you are the only spring,
Only in royal hope to kill the king.

[2] Spies.
[3] At the distance of.
[4] "The distaff from whence she draws the
breath of life" (Dilke).

Mon. Why, now I see thou lovest me.
Come to the banquet.   *Exeunt.*

FINIS ACTUS TERTII.

ACTUS QUARTI SCENA PRIMA.

[*A room in the court.*]

Henry, Monsieur with a letter, Guise,
Montsurry, Bussy, Elenor, Tamyra,
Beaupré, Pero, Charlotte, Annabelle,
Pyra, with four Pages.

HEN. Ladies, ye have not done our ban-
quet right,
  Nor looked upon it with those cheerful
    rays
  That lately turned your breaths to
    floods of gold.
  Your looks, methinks, are not drawn
    out with thoughts
  So clear and free as heretofore, but foul,
  As if the thick complexions [1] of men
  Governed within them.
Bus.   'Tis not like, my lord,
  That men in women rule, but contrary;
  For, as the moon, of all things God
    created,
  Not only is the most appropriate im-
    age   10
  Or glass to show them how they wax
    and wane,
  But in her height and motion likewise
    bears
  Imperial influences that command
  In all their powers, and make them wax
    and wane;
  So women, that, of all things made of
    nothing,
  Are the most perfect idols of the moon,
  Or still-unweaned, sweet mooncalves [2]
    with white faces,
  Not only are patterns of change to men,
  But, as the tender moonshine of their
    beauties
  Clears or is cloudy, make men glad or
    sad;   20
  So then they rule in men, not men in
    them.
Mon. But here the moons are changed,
  as the king notes,
  And either men rule in them, or some
    power

[1] Humors, bodily fluids.
[2] Deformed creatures, monstrosities.

Beyond their voluntary faculty,
For nothing can recover their lost faces.
MONT. None can be always one. Our
  griefs and joys
  Hold several scepters in us, and have
    times
  For their divided empires; which grief
    now in them
  Doth prove as proper to his diadem.
Bus. And grief's a natural sickness of
  the blood,   30
  That time to part asks, as his coming
    had;
  Only slight fools, grieved, suddenly are
    glad.
  A man may say t' a dead man, "Be re-
    vived,"
  As well as to one sorrowful, "Be not
    grieved."
  [*To the Duchess.*] And therefore, princely
    mistress, in all wars
  Against these base foes that insult on [3]
    weakness,
  And still fight housed behind the shield
    of nature,
  Of privilege, law, treachery, or beastly
    need,
  Your servant cannot help; authority
    here
  Goes with corruption, something like
    some states,   40
  That back worst men. Valor to them
    must creep
  That, to themselves left, would fear him
    asleep.
DUCH. Ye all take that for granted that
  doth rest
  Yet to be proved; we all are as we were,
  As merry and as free in thought as ever.
GUISE. And why then can ye not disclose
  your thoughts?
TAM. Methinks the man hath answered
  for us well.
MON. The man? Why, madam, d' ye
  not know his name?
TAM. Man is a name of honor for a king;
  Additions [4] take away from each chief
    thing.   50
  The school of modesty not to learn
    learns dames;
  They sit in high forms [5] there, that know
    men's names.

[3] Take advantage of.   [4] Titles.
[5] "On the stools of disgrace" (Boas).

Mon. [*To Bussy.*] Hark, sweetheart, here's
    a bar set to your valor!
It cannot enter here; no, not to notice
Of what your name is. Your great eagle's
    beak,
Should you fly at her, had as good en-
    counter
An Albion cliff as her more craggy liver.[1]
Bus. I'll not attempt her, sir; her sight
    and name,
By which I only know her, doth deter me.
Hen. So they do all men else.
Mon.   You would say so 60
    If you knew all.
Tam.   Knew all, my lord? What
    mean you?
Mon. All that I know, madam.
Tam.   That you know? Speak it.
Mon. No, 'tis enough I feel it.
Hen.   But, methinks
    Her courtship is more pure than here-
    tofore;
    True courtiers should be modest, and
    not nice;[2]
    Bold, but not impudent; pleasure love,
    not vice.
Mon. Sweetheart, come hither! What if
    one should make
    Horns at Montsurry? Would it not
    strike him jealous
    Through all the proofs of his chaste
    lady's virtues?
Bus. If he be wise, not.   70
Mon. What? Not if I should name the
    gardener
    That I would have him think hath
    grafted him?
Bus. So the large license that your great-
    ness uses
    To jest that all men may be taught in-
    deed
    To make a difference of the grounds you
    play on,
    Both in the men you scandal, and the
    matter.
Mon. As how? As how?
Bus.   Perhaps led with a train,[2]
    Where you may have your nose made
    less and slit,
    Your eyes thrust out.
Mon.   Peace, peace, I pray thee peace!
    Who dares do that? The brother of his
    king?

Bus. Were your king brother in you; all
    your powers,
Stretched in the arms of great men and
    their bawds,
Set close down by you; all your stormy
    laws
Spouted with lawyers' mouths and gush-
    ing blood
Like to so many torrents; all your glo-
    ries
(Making you terrible, like enchanted
    flames)
Fed with bare coxcombs and with crooked
    hams;[4]
All your prerogatives, your shames, and
    tortures;
All daring heaven, and opening hell
    about you—
Were I the man ye wronged so and pro-
    voked,   90
Though ne'er so much beneath you, like
    a box tree
I would, out of the roughness of my root,
Ram hardness in my lowness, and, like
    Death
Mounted on earthquakes, I would trot
    through all
Honors and horrors, thorough foul and
    fair,
And from your whole strength toss you
    into the air.
Mon. Go, th' art a devil! Such another
    spirit
Could not be stilled[5] from all th' Arme-
    nian dragons.
O my love's glory, heir to all I have
(That's all I can say, and that all I
    swear)   100
If thou outlive me, as I know thou must,
Or else hath Nature no proportioned
    end
To her great labors, she hath breathed
    a mind
Into thy entrails, of desert to swell
Into another great Augustus Cæsar,
Organs and faculties fitted to her great-
    ness;
And, should that perish like a common
    spirit,
Nature's a courtier and regards no merit.
Hen. Here's naught but whispering with
    us, like a calm

---

[1] Supposed to be the seat of love.   [2] Wanton.
[3] Trap.   [4] The bare heads and bent knees of
sycophants.   [5] Distilled.

Before a tempest, when the silent air 110
Lays her soft ear close to the earth to
hearken
For that she fears steals on to ravish
her,
Some fate doth join [1] our ears to hear
it coming.
Come, my brave eagle, let's to covert
fly;
I see almighty Æther in the smoke
Of all his clouds descending, and the
sky
Hid in the dim ostents [2] of tragedy.

Exit Henr[y] with D'Amb[ois] and Ladies.

GUISE. [*Aside to Monsieur.*] Now stir
the humor, and begin the brawl.

MONT. The king and D'Ambois now are
grown all one.

MON. [*Making horns at Montsurry.*] Nay,
they are two, my lord.

MONT. How's that?

MON. No more. 120

MONT. I must have more, my lord.

MON. What, more than two?

MONT. How monstrous is this!

MON. Why?

MONT. You make me horns!

MON. Not I; it is a work without my
power.
Married men's ensigns are not made
with fingers;
Of divine fabric they are, not men's
hands.
Your wife, you know, is a mere [3] Cynthia,
And she must fashion horns out of her
nature.

MONT. But doth she—dare you charge
her? Speak, false prince!

MON. I must not speak, my lord; but, if
you'll use
The learning of a nobleman and read, 130
Here's something to those points. Soft,
you must pawn [4]
Your honor, having read it, to return
it.

Enter Tamyra, Pero.

MONT. Not I! I pawn my honor for a
paper?

MON. You must not buy it under.

Exeunt Guise and Monsieur.

[1] Enjoin.
[2] Manifestations, omens.
[3] Absolute.
[4] Pledge.

MONT. Keep it then,
And keep fire in your bosom.

TAM. What says he?

MONT. You must make good the rest.

TAM. How fares my lord?
Takes my love anything to heart he
says?

MONT. Come, y'are a—

TAM. What, my lord?

MONT. The plague of Herod [5]
Feast in his rotten entrails.

TAM. Will you wreak
Your anger's just cause given by him,
on me? 140

MONT. By him?

TAM. By him, my lord. I have
admired [6]
You could all this time be at concord
with him,
That still hath played such discords on
your honor.

MONT. Perhaps 'tis with some proud
string of my wife's.

TAM. How's that, my lord?

MONT. Your tongue will still admire,
Till my head be the miracle of the world.

TAM. O, woe is me! *She seems to sound.* [7]

PER. What does your lordship
mean?—
Madam, be comforted; my lord but
tries you.
Madam!—Help, good my lord, are you
not moved?
Do your set looks print in your words
your thoughts? 150
Sweet lord, clear up those eyes, unbend
that masking forehead.
Whence is it you rush upon her with
these Irish wars,
More full of sound than hurt? But it
is enough.
You have shot home; your words are
in her heart.
She has not lived to bear a trial now.

MONT. Look up, my love, and by this
kiss receive
My soul amongst thy spirits for supply
To thine, chased with my fury.

TAM. O, my lord,
I have too long lived to hear this from
you.

MONT. 'Twas from my troubled blood,
and not from me.— 160

[5] Worms. [6] Wondered. [7] Swound, swoon.

[*Aside.*] I know not how I fare; a sudden night
Flows through my entrails, and a headlong chaos
Murmurs within me, which I must digest,
And not drown her in my confusions,
That was my life's joy, being best informed.—
Sweet, you must needs forgive me, that my love,
Like to a fire disdaining his suppression,
Raged, being discouraged; my whole heart is wounded
When any least thought in you is but touched,
And shall be till I know your former merits;   170
Your name and memory altogether crave
In just oblivion their eternal grave;
And then, you must hear from me, there's no mean
In any passion I shall feel for you.
Love is a razor, cleansing, being well used,
But fetcheth blood still, being the least abused.
To tell you briefly all, the man that left me
When you appeared, did turn me worse than woman,
And stabbed me to the heart thus, with his fingers.
Tam. O, happy woman! Comes my stain from him?   180
It is my beauty, and that innocence proves
That slew Chimera, rescued Peleus
From all the savage beasts in Pelion,
And raised the chaste Athenian prince from hell;
All suffering with me, they for women's lusts,
I for a man's, that the Augean stable
Of his foul sin would empty in my lap.
How his guilt shunned me! Sacred Innocence
That where thou fear'st, art dreadful, and his face
Turned in flight from thee, that had thee in chase!   190
Come, bring me to him; I will tell the serpent

Even to his venomed teeth, from whose cursed seed
A pitched field [1] starts up twixt my lord and me,
That his throat lies, and he shall curse his fingers
For being so governed by his filthy soul.
Mont. I know not if himself will vaunt t' have been
The princely author of the slavish sin,
Or any other; he would have resolved me,
Had you not come, not by his word, but writing,
Would I have sworn to give it him again,   200
And pawned mine honor to him for a paper.
Tam. See how he flies me still; 'tis a foul heart
That fears his own hand. Good my lord, make haste
To see the dangerous paper; papers hold
Ofttimes the forms and copies of our souls,
And, though the world despise them, are the prizes
Of all our honors. Make your honor then
A hostage for it, and with it confer [2]
My nearest woman here, in all she knows,
Who, if the sun or Cerberus could have seen   210
Any stain in me, might as well as they.
And, Pero, here I charge thee by my love,
And all proofs of it, which I might call bounties,
By all that thou hast seen seem good in me,
And all the ill which thou shouldst spit from thee,
By pity of the wound this touch hath given me,
Not as thy mistress now, but a poor woman,
To death given over, rid me of my pains;
Pour on thy powder; clear thy breast of me.
My lord is only here. Here speak thy worst;   220
Thy best will do me mischief. If thou spar'st me,

[1] Battle.   [2] Consult.

Never shine good thought on thy mem-
ory!
Resolve my lord, and leave me desper-
ate.
Per. My lord! My lord hath played a
prodigal's part,
To break his stock for nothing; and an
insolent,
To cut a Gordian [1] when he could not
loose it.
What violence is this, to put true fire
To a false train, [2] to blow up long-
crowned peace
With sudden outrage, and believe a
man
Sworn to the shame of women, gainst
a woman,   230
Born to their honors? But I will to him.
Tam. No, I will write (for I shall never
more
Meet with the fugitive) where I will
defy him,
Were he ten times the brother of my
king.
To him, my lord, and I'll to cursing
him.   _Exeunt._

[SCENA SECUNDA.

A room in Montsurry's house.]

Enter D'Ambois and Friar.

Bus. I am suspicious, my most honored
father,
By some of Monsieur's cunning passages,
That his still ranging and contentious
nostrils,
To scent the haunts of Mischief, have
so used
The vicious virtue of his busy sense
That he trails hotly of him, and will
rouse him,
Driving him all enraged and foaming on
us,
And therefore have entreated your deep
skill
In the command of good aërial spirits,
To assume these magic rites, and call
up one   10
To know if any have revealed unto him
Anything touching my dear love and me.
Fri. Good son, you have amazed me but
to make

[1] Gordian knot.   [2] Fuse.
[3] Original reads _and her maid._

The least doubt of it, it concerns so
nearly
The faith and reverence of my name and
order.
Yet will I justify, upon my soul,
All I have done; if any spirit i' th' earth
or air
Can give you the resolve, do not despair.

_Music; and Tamyra enters with Pero, her
maid,_ [3] _bearing a letter._

Tam. Away, deliver it! (_Exit Pero._) O,
may my lines
Filled with the poison of a woman's
hate,   20
When he shall open them, shrink up
his cursed eyes
With torturous darkness, such as stands
in hell,
Stuck full of inward horrors, never
lighted,
With which are all things to be feared,
affrighted.
Bus. [_Advancing._] How is it with my
honored mistress?
Tam. O servant, help, and save me from
the gripes
Of shame and infamy. Our love is known;
Your Monsieur hath a paper where is writ
Some secret tokens that decipher it.
Bus. What cold dull northern brain, what
fool but he   30
Durst take into his Epimethean breast
A box of such plagues as the danger
yields
Incurred in this discovery? He had
better
Ventured his breast in the consuming
reach
Of the hot surfeits [4] cast out of the clouds,
Or stood the bullets that, to wreak the
sky,
The Cyclops ram in Jove's artillery.
Fri. We soon will take the darkness from
his face
That did that deed of darkness; we will
know
What now the Monsieur and your hus-
band do,   40
What is contained within the secret
paper
Offered by Monsieur, and your love's
events;

[4] Lightning bolts.

To which ends, honored daughter, at
　your motion,
I have put on these exorcising rites,
And, by my power of learned holiness
Vouchsafed me from above, I will com-
　mand
Our resolution of [1] a raiséd spirit.

TAM. Good father, raise him in some
　beauteous form
That with least terror I may brook
　his sight.

FRI. Stand sure together, then, whate'er
　you see,　　　　　　　　　　　　50
And stir not, as ye tender all our lives.
　　　　　　　He puts on his robes.

*Occidentalium legionum spiritualium im-
perator, magnus ille Behemoth, veni, veni,
comitatus cum Astaroth locotenente invicto!
Adjuro te per Stygis inscrutabilia arcana,
per ipsos irremeabiles anfractus Averni:
Adesto, O Behemoth, tu cui pervia sunt
Magnatum scrinia; veni, per Noctis et tene-
brarum abdita profundissima; per labentia
sidera; per ipsos motus horarum furtivos,　[60
Hecatesque altum silentium!　Appare in
forma spiritali, lucente, splendida, et ama-
bili!* [2]

*Thunder.　Ascendit [Behemoth with Carto-
　　　　　phylax and other Spirits].*

BEH. What would the holy friar?
FRI.　　　　　　　　　　　I would see
What now the Monsieur and Montsurry
　do,
And see the secret paper that the Mon-
　sieur
Offered to Count Montsurry, longing
　much
To know on what events the secret loves
Of these two honored persons shall
　arrive.

BEH. Why calledst thou me to this ac-
　cursed light,　　　　　　　　　70

[1] From.
[2] O ruler of the legions of western spirits, that
mighty Behemoth, come, come, accompanied by
Astaroth, unconquered lieutenant! I command
thee by the hidden mysteries of the Styx, by the
unretraceable labyrinths of Avernus themselves:
Appear, O Behemoth, thou to whom the cab-
inets of the Mighty are accessible; come, by the
deepest caves of Night and the shades; by the
wandering stars; by the stealthy motions of the
hours themselves, and the deep silence of Hecate!
Appear in spirit form, shining, brilliant, and
lovely!

To these light purposes? I am emperor
Of that inscrutable darkness where are
　hid
All deepest truths and secrets never seen,
All which I know, and command legions
Of knowing spirits that can do more than
　these.
Any of this my guard that circle me
In these blue fires, and out of whose
　dim fumes
Vast murmurs use to break, and from
　their sounds
Articulate voices, can do ten parts
　more
Than open such slight truths as you
　require.　　　　　　　　　　　80

FRI. From the last night's black depth I
　called up one
Of the inferior ablest ministers,
And he could not resolve me. Send one
　then
Out of thine own command, to fetch the
　paper
That Monsieur hath to show to Count
　Montsurry.

BEH. I will. Cartophylax, thou that prop-
　erly
Hast in thy power all papers so inscribed,
Glide through all bars to it and fetch
　that paper.

CART. I will.　　　　*A torch [3] removes.*

FRI. Till he returns, great Prince of Dark-
　ness,　　　　　　　　　　　　90
Tell me if Monsieur and the Count Mont-
　surry
Are yet encountered?

BEH.　　　　　Both them and the Guise
Are now together.

FRI.　　　　Show us all their persons,
And represent the place, with all their
　actions.

BEH. The spirit will straight return, and
　then I'll show thee.

　　　　　[Enter Cartophylax.]

See, he is come; why brought'st thou
　not the paper?

CART. He hath prevented me, and got a
　spirit
Raised by another, great in our com-
　mand,
To take the guard of it before I came.

[3] *I.e.*, a torchbearer (Cartophylax).

BEH. This is your slackness, not t' invoke
    our powers   100
  When first your acts set forth to their
    effects;
  Yet shall you see it and themselves.
    Behold,
  They come here, and the earl now holds
    the paper.

Ent[er] Mons[ieur], Gui[se], Mont[surry]
                with a paper.

BUS. May we not hear them?
[FRI.][1]   No, be still and see.
BUS. I will go fetch the paper.
FRI.   Do not stir;
  There's too much distance and too many
    locks
  Twixt you and them, how near soe'er
    they seem,
  For any man to interrupt their secrets.
TAM. O honored spirit, fly into the fancy
  Of my offended lord, and do not let him
  Believe what there the wicked man
    hath written.   111
BEH.[2] Persuasion hath already entered
  him
  Beyond reflection.[3] Peace till their de-
    parture!—

MON. There is a glass of ink [4] where you
    may see
  How to make ready black-faced tragedy.
  You now discern, I hope, through all
    her paintings,
  Her gasping wrinkles and fame's sepul-
    chers.
GUISE. Think you he feigns, my lord?
    What hold you now?
  Do we malign your wife, or honor you?
MON. What, stricken dumb! Nay, fie,
    lord, be not daunted;   120
  Your case is common; were it ne'er so
    rare,
  Bear it as rarely. Now to laugh were
    manly.
  A worthy man should imitate the
    weather
  That sings in tempests, and, being clear,
    is silent.

GUISE. Go home, my lord, and force your
    wife to write
  Such loving lines to D'Ambois as she
    used
  When she desired his presence.
MON.   Do, my lord,
  And make her name her concealed mes-
    senger,
  That close and most inennerable [5]
    pander,   129
  That passeth all our studies to exquire; [6]
  By whom convey the letter to her love;
  And so you shall be sure to have him
    come
  Within the thirsty reach of your revenge;
  Before which, lodge an ambush in her
    chamber
  Behind the arras, of your stoutest men
  All close and soundly armed, and let
    them share
  A spirit amongst them that would serve
    a thousand.

Enter Pero with a letter.

GUISE. Yet stay a little; see, she sends
    for you.
MON. Poor, loving lady; she'll make all
    good yet.
  Think you not so, my lord?
      Exit Mont[surry] and stabs Pero.[7]
GUISE.   Alas, poor soul!   140
MON. This was cruelly done, i' faith.
PER.   'Twas nobly done.
  And I forgive his lordship from my soul.
MON. Then much good do 't thee, Pero!
    Hast a letter?
PER. I hope it rather be a bitter volume
  Of worthy curses for your perjury.
GUISE. To you, my lord.
MON.   To me? Now, out upon her.
GUISE. Let me see, my lord.
MON. You shall presently. How fares
    my Pero?
  Who's there?

Enter Servant.

           Take in this maid—sh'as
  caught a clap—
  And fetch my surgeon to her. Come,
    my lord,   150

---

[1] Original reads *Mon.*
[2] Original reads *Pre.*
[3] Turning back, return.
[4] *I.e.,* the letter is a mirror.

[5] Inenarrable, indescribable, unknown.
[6] Discover.
[7] Boas emends: *Mont[surry] stabs Pero, and*
exit.

We'll now peruse our letter.

Exeunt Mons[ieur], Guise. Lead her out.

PER.   Furies rise
  Out of the black lines, and torment his
    soul!—

TAM. Hath my lord slain my woman?

BEH.   No, she lives.

FRI. What shall become of us?

BEH.   All I can say,
  Being called thus late, is brief, and darkly
    this:
  If D'Ambois' mistress dye not her [1]
    white hand
  In her forced blood, he shall remain un-
    touched;
  So, father, shall yourself, but by your-
    self.
  To make this augury plainer, when the
    voice
  Of D'Ambois shall invoke me, I will
    rise,   160
  Shining in greater light, and show him
    all
  That will betide ye all. Meantime be
    wise,
  And curb his valor with your policies.
                Descendit cum suis. [2]

BUS. Will he appear to me when I invoke
  him?

FRI. He will, be sure.

BUS.   It must be shortly then;
  For his dark words have tied my
    thoughts on knots,
  Till he dissolve and free them.

TAM.   In meantime,
  Dear servant, till your powerful voice
    revoke him,
  Be sure to use the policy he advised;
  Lest fury in your too quick knowledge
    taken   170
  Of our abuse, and your defense of me,
  Accuse me more than any enemy.
  And, father, you must on my lord im-
    pose
  Your holiest charges and the church's
    power
  To temper his hot spirit and disperse
  The cruelty and the blood I know his
    hand
  Will shower upon our heads, if you put
    not

[1] Original has *his*.

[2] He descends with his attendants.

Your finger to the storm, and hold it up,
As my dear servant here must do with
  Monsieur.

BUS. I'll soothe his plots, and strow my
  hate with smiles,   180
  Till all at once the close mines of my
    heart
  Rise at full date, and rush into his
    blood.
  I'll bind his arm in silk, and rub his
    flesh,
  To make the vein swell, that his soul
    may gush
  Into some kennel, [3] where it longs to lie,
  And policy shall be flanked [4] with policy,
  Yet shall the feeling center [5] where we
    meet
  Groan with the weight of my approach-
    ing feet;
  I'll make th' inspired [6] thresholds of his
    court
  Sweat with the weather of my horrid
    steps,[7]   190
  Before I enter; yet will I appear
  Like calm security before a ruin.
  A politician must, like lightning, melt
  The very marrow, and not taint the
    skin;
  His ways must not be seen; the super-
    ficies
  Of the green center must not taste his
    feet,
  When hell is plowed up with his wound-
    ing tracts,[8]
  And all his harvest reaped by hellish
    facts.   *Exeunt.*

FINIS ACTUS QUARTI.

ACTUS QUINTI SCENA PRIMA.

[*A room in Montsurry's house.*]

*Montsurry, bare, unbraced,[9] pulling Ta-
  myra in by the hair; Friar; One bearing
  light, a standish,[10] and paper, which [11]
    sets a table [and exit]*

TAM. O, help me, father!

FRI.   Impious earl, forbear!

[3] Channel, gutter.   [4] Outflanked.

[5] The conscious earth, considered the center
of the universe.

[6] Blown upon. [7] Storm of my terrifying steps.

[8] Tracks.   [9] With his garments unfastened.

[10] Receptacle for pen and ink.   [11] Who.

Take violent hand from her, or by mine
　order
The king shall force thee.
MONT.　　　　　　　　　'Tis not violent.—
Come you not willingly?
TAM.　　　　　　　　Yes, good my lord.
FRI. My lord, remember that your soul
　must seek
　Her peace, as well as your revengeful
　　blood.
　You ever to this hour have proved your-
　　self
　A noble, zealous, and obedient son
　T' our Holy Mother; be not an apostate.
　Your wife's offense serves not, were it the
　　worst　　　　　　　　　　　　　10
　You can imagine, without greater proofs,
　To sever your eternal bonds and hearts,
　Much less to touch her with a bloody
　　hand;
　Nor is it manly, much less husbandly,
　To expiate any frailty in your wife
　With churlish strokes or beastly odds of
　　strength.
　The stony birth of clouds [1] will touch no
　　laurel,
　Nor any sleeper; your wife is your laurel,
　And sweetest sleeper. Do not touch her
　　then;
　Be not more rude than the wild seed of
　　vapor,　　　　　　　　　　　　20
　To her that is more gentle than that rude,
　In whom kind nature suffered one offense
　But to set off her other excellence.
MONT. Good father, leave us; interrupt no
　more
　The course I must run for mine honor
　　sake.
　Rely on my love to her, which her fault
　Cannot extinguish. Will she but disclose
　Who was the secret minister of her love,
　And through what maze he served it, we
　are friends.
FRI. It is a damned work to pursue those
　secrets　　　　　　　　　　　　30
　That would ope more sin, and prove
　　springs of slaughter;
　Nor is't a path for Christian feet to tread,
　But out of all way to the health of souls,
　A sin impossible to be forgiven;
　Which he that dares commit—
MONT. Good father, cease your terrors;
　Tempt not a man distracted; I am apt

To outrages that I shall ever rue!
I will not pass the verge that bounds a
　Christian,
Nor break the limits of a man nor hus-
　band.　　　　　　　　　　　　40
FRI. Then Heaven inspire you both with
　thoughts and deeds
　Worthy His high respect and your own
　　souls.
TAM. Father!
FRI.　　　　　　　I warrant thee, my dearest
　daughter,
　He will not touch thee. Think'st thou
　　him a pagan?
　His honor and his soul lies for thy safety.
　　　　　　　　　　　　　　　Exit.
MONT. Who shall remove the mountain
　from my breast,
　Stand the opening furnace of my
　　thoughts,
　And set fit outcries for a soul in hell?
　　　　　　　　Mont[surry] turns a key.
　For now it nothing fits my woes to speak
　But thunder, or to take into my throat 50
　The trump of heaven, with whose deter-
　　minate [2] blasts
　The winds shall burst, and the devouring
　　seas
　Be drunk up in his sounds; that my hot
　　woes,
　Vented enough, I might convert to vapor,
　Ascending from my infamy unseen,
　Shorten the world, preventing [3] the last
　　breath
　That kills the living and regenerates
　　death.
TAM. My lord, my fault (as you may cen-
　sure it
　With too strong arguments) is past your
　　pardon.
　But how the circumstances may excuse
　　me　　　　　　　　　　　　60
　Heaven knows, and your more temperate
　　mind hereafter
　May let my penitent miseries make you
　　know.
MONT. Hereafter? 'Tis a supposed infinite,
　That from this point will rise eternally.
　Fame grows in going; in the scapes of
　　virtue
　Excuses damn her: they be fires in cities
　Enraged with those winds that less lights
　　extinguish.

---

[1] I.e., the thunderbolt.　　　　[2] Final.　　　　[3] Anticipating.

Come, siren, sing, and dash against my rocks
Thy ruffian galley, rigged with quench for lust; [1]
Sing, and put all the nets into thy voice   70
With which thou drew'st into thy strumpet's lap
The spawn of Venus, and in which ye danced,
That, in thy lap's stead, I may dig his tomb,
And quit [2] his manhood with a woman's sleight,
Who never is deceived in her deceit.
Sing (that is, write), and then take from mine eyes
The mists that hide the most inscrutable pander
That ever lapped up an adulterous vomit,
That I may see the devil, and survive
To be a devil, and then learn to wive;   80
That I may hang him, and then cut him down,
Then cut him up, and with my soul's beams search
The cranks [3] and caverns of his brain, and study
The errant wilderness of a woman's face,
Where men cannot get out, for all the comets
That have been lighted at it. Though they know
That adders lie a-sunning in their smiles,
That basilisks drink their poison from their eyes,
And no way there to coast out to their hearts,
Yet still they wander there, and are not stayed   90
Till they be fettered, nor secure before
All cares devour them, nor in human consort
Till they embrace within their wife's two breasts
All Pelion and Cytheron with their beasts.
Why write you not?
TAM.   O, good my lord, forbear
In wreak of great faults to engender greater,

And make my love's corruption generate murther.
MONT. It follows needfully as child and parent;
The chain shot of thy lust is yet aloft,
And it must murther; 'tis thine own dear twin.   100
No man can add height to a woman's sin.
Vice never doth her just hate so provoke
As when she rageth under virtue's cloak.
Write! For it must be—by this ruthless steel,
By this impartial torture, and the death
Thy tyrannies have invented in my entrails,
To quicken life in dying, and hold up
The spirits in fainting, teaching to preserve
Torments in ashes, that will ever last.
Speak! Will you write?
TAM.   Sweet lord, enjoin my sin
Some other penance than what makes it worse.   111
Hide in some gloomy dungeon my loathed face,
And let condemnéd murtherers let me down
(Stopping their noses) my abhorréd food.
Hang me in chains, and let me eat these arms
That have offended; bind me face to face
To some dead woman, taken from the cart
Of execution, till death and time
In grains of dust dissolve me; I'll endure;
Or any torture that your wrath's invention   120
Can fright all pity from the world withal;
But to betray a friend with show of friendship,
That is too common for the rare revenge
Your rage affecteth. Here then are my breasts,
Last night your pillows; here my wretched arms,
As late the wishéd confines of your life;
Now break them as you please, and all the bounds
Of manhood, noblesse, and religion.
MONT. Where all these have been broken, they are kept,   129
In doing their justice there with any show
Of the like cruel cruelty; thine arms have lost

[1] I.e., D'Ambois is to be lured with the desire to quench his lust.   [2] Requite.   [3] Winding paths.

Their privilege in lust, and in their
    torture
Thus they must pay it.   *Stabs her.*
TAM.   O Lord!
MONT.   Till thou writ'st,
    I'll write in wounds (my wrong's fit
        characters)
    Thy right of sufferance. Write!
TAM.   O, kill me, kill me!
    Dear husband, be not crueler than death.
    You have beheld some Gorgon; feel, O,
        feel
    How you are turned to stone. With my
        heartblood
    Dissolve yourself again, or you will grow
    Into the image of all tyranny.   140
MONT. As thou art of adultery; I will ever
    Prove thee my parallel, being most a
        monster;
    Thus I express thee yet.[1] *Stabs her again.*
TAM.   And yet I live.
MONT. Ay, for thy monstrous idol is not
    done yet;
    This tool hath wrought enough; now,
        torture, use

Ent[er] Servants.

    This other engine[2] on th' habituate
        powers
    Of her thrice-damned and whorish forti-
        tude.
    Use the most madding pains in her that
        ever
    Thy venoms soaked through, making
        most of death,
    That she may weigh her wrongs with
        them, and then   150
    Stand Vengeance on thy steepest rock, a
        victor.
TAM. O, who is turned into my lord and
    husband?
    Husband! My lord! None but my lord
        and husband!
    Heaven, I ask thee remission of my sins,
    Not of my pains. Husband, O, help me,
        husband!

Ascendit Friar with a sword drawn.

FRI. What rape of honor and religion—
    O, wrack of nature!   *Falls and dies.*
TAM.   Poor man! O, my father!

---

[1] "Thus I give a further stroke to my delinea-
tion of thee" (Boas).   [2] Rack.   [3] Slant.

Father, look up; O, let me down, my lord,
    And I will write.
MONT.   Author of prodigies!
    What new flame breaks out of the fir-
        mament,   160
    That turns up counsels never known
        before?
    Now is it true earth moves, and heaven
        stands still;
    Even heaven itself must see and suffer
        ill.
    The too huge bias[3] of the world hath
        swayed
    Her backpart upwards, and with that
        she braves
    This hemisphere, that long her mouth
        hath mocked.
    The gravity of her religious face,
    Now grown too weighty with her sacri-
        lege,
    And here discerned sophisticate[4] enough,
    Turns to th' antipodes; and all the
        forms   170
    That her illusions have impressed in her
    Have eaten through her back; and now
        all see
    How she is riveted with hypocrisy.
    Was this the way? Was he the mean be-
        twixt you?
TAM. He was, he was; kind worthy man,
    he was!
MONT. Write, write a word or two.
TAM.   I will, I will.
    I'll write, but with my blood, that he may
        see
    These lines come from my wounds, and
        not from me.   *Writes.*
MONT. Well might he die for thought;[5]
    methinks the frame
    And shaken joints of the whole world
        should crack   180
    To see her parts so disproportionate,
    And that his general beauty cannot
        stand
    Without these stains in the particular
        man.
    Why wander I so far? Here, here was she
    That was a whole world without spot to
        me,
    Though now a world of spots. O, what a
        lightning
    Is man's delight in women! What a
        bubble

---

[4] Adulterated.   [5] From mental shock.

He builds his state, fame, life on, when
  he marries!
Since all earth's pleasures are so short
  and small,
The way t' enjoy it, is t' abjure it all. 190
Enough! I must be messenger myself,
Disguised like this strange creature. In!
  I'll after,
To see what guilty light gives this cave
  eyes,
And to the world sing new impieties.

*Exeunt [Servants]. He puts the Friar in the
vault and follows. She wraps herself in
              the arras.*

[SCENA SECUNDA.

Another room in Montsurry's house.]

Enter Monsieur and Guise.

MON. Now shall we see that Nature hath
  no end
In her great works responsive to their
  worths,
That she, that makes so many eyes and
  souls
To see and foresee, is stark blind herself;
And, as illiterate men say Latin prayers
By rote of heart and daily iteration,
Not knowing what they say, so Nature
  lays
A deal of stuff together, and by use,
Or by the mere necessity of matter,
Ends such a work, fills it, or leaves it
  empty   10
Of strength or virtue, error or clear
  truth,
Not knowing what she does; but usually
Gives that which she calls merit to a man,
And belief must arrive [1] him on huge
  riches,
Honor, and happiness, that effects his
  ruin,
Even as in ships of war, whole lasts [2] of
  powder
Are laid, methinks, to make them last
  and guard,[3]
When a disordered spark, that powder
  taking,

[1] Bring.
[2] Measures, in this case of twenty-four barrels.
[3] In ll. 13–17 the 1607 edition reads *wee call
for she calls, believe* for *beliefe, should* for *must,
Right* for *Even, men thinke* for *me thinks, gard
them* for *guard.* Parrott accepts all the readings
of 1607 as preferable.

Blows up with sudden violence and horror
Ships that, kept empty, had sailed long
  with terror.[4]   20
GUISE. He that observes but like a worldly
  man
That which doth oft succeed, and by th'
  events
Values the worth of things, will think it
  true
That Nature works at random, just with
  you;
But with as much proportion she may
  make
A thing that from the feet up to the
  throat
Hath all the wondrous fabric man should
  have,
And leave it headless, for a perfect man,
As give a full man valor, virtue, learning,
Without an end more excellent than
  those   30
On whom she no such worthy part be-
  stows.
MON. Yet shall you see it here; here will
  be one
Young, learned, valiant, virtuous, and
  full manned—
One on whom Nature spent so rich a
  hand
That with an ominous eye she wept to see
So much consumed her virtuous treas-
  ury.[5]
Yet, as the winds sing through a hollow
  tree
And (since it lets them pass through) lets
  it stand,
But a tree solid (since it gives no way
To their wild rage) they rend up by the
  root,   40
So this whole man
(That will not wind with every crooked
  way,
Trod by the servile world) shall reel and
  fall
Before the frantic puffs of blind-born
  chance,
That pipes through empty men, and
  makes them dance.[6]
Not so the sea raves on the Lybian
  sands,

[4] "Inspiring terror in their enemies" (Boas).
[5] Store of virtues.
[6] Lines 46–53 are adapted from Seneca's
Agamemnon.

Tumbling her billows in each other's
neck;
Not so the surges of the Euxine sea
(Near to the frosty pole, where free
Boötes
From those dark deep waves turns his
radiant team)   50
Swell, being enraged, even from their
inmost drop,
As Fortune swings about the restless
state
Of virtue, now thrown into all men's
hate.

*Enter Montsurry disguised [as the Friar,]
with the Murtherers.*

Away, my lord; you are perfectly dis-
guised;
Leave us to lodge your ambush.
MONT.   Speed me, vengeance! *Exit.*
MON. Resolve, my masters, you shall meet
with one
Will try what proofs your privy coats [1]
are made on.
When he is entered, and you hear us
stamp,
Approach, and make all sure.   59
MURTHERERS. We will, my lord. *Exeunt.*

[SCENA TERTIA.

A room in Bussy's house.]

D'Ambois with two Pages with tapers.

BUS. Sit up tonight, and watch; I'll speak
with none
But the old friar, who bring to me.
PAGES.   We will, sir. *Exeunt.*
BUS. What violent heat is this? Methinks
the fire
Of twenty lives doth on a sudden flash
Through all my faculties; the air goes
high
In this close chamber, and the frighted
earth   *Thunder.*
Trembles, and shrinks beneath me; the
whole house
Nods with his shaken burthen.

Enter Umb[ra] [2] Friar.

                    Bless me, heaven!
UMB. [FRI.] Note what I want, [3] dear son,
and be forewarned;

O, there are bloody deeds past and to
come.   10
I cannot stay; a fate doth ravish me;
I'll meet thee in the chamber of thy
love.   *Exit.*
BUS. What dismal change is here; the good
old friar
Is murthered, being made known to serve
my love;
And now his restless spirit would fore-
warn me
Of some plot dangerous and imminent.
Note what he wants? He wants his upper
weed;
He wants his life and body. Which of
these
Should be the want he means, and may
supply me
With any fit forewarning? This strange
vision   20
(Together with the dark prediction
Used by the Prince of Darkness that was
raised
By this embodied shadow) stir my
thoughts
With reminiscion [4] of the spirit's promise,
Who told me that by any invocation
I should have power to raise him, though
it wanted
The powerful words and decent rites of
art.
Never had my set brain such need of
spirit
T' instruct and cheer it; now, then, I will
claim   29
Performance of his free and gentle vow
T' appear in greater light, and make
more plain
His rugged [5] oracle. I long to know
How my dear mistress fares, and be
informed
What hand she now holds on the troubled
blood
Of her incenséd lord. Methought the
spirit,
When he had uttered his perplexed
presage,
Threw his changed countenance headlong
into clouds;
His forehead bent, as it would hide his
face,
He knocked his chin against his dark-
ened breast,

---

[1] Secret coats of mail.   [2] Shade, ghost.   [3] Lack.   [4] Remembrance.   [5] Unpolished, unfinished.

And struck a churlish silence through his
powers. 40
Terror of Darkness! O thou King of
Flames,
That with thy music-footed horse dost
strike
The clear light out of crystal on dark
earth,
And hurl'st instructive fire [1] about the
world,
Wake, wake the drowsy and enchanted
Night
That sleeps with dead eyes in this heavy
riddle!
Or, thou great Prince of Shades, where
never sun
Sticks his far-darted beams, whose eyes
are made
To shine in darkness, and see ever best
Where men are blindest, open now the
heart 50
Of thy abashéd oracle, that, for fear
Of some ill it includes, would fain lie hid,
And rise thou with it in thy greater light.

Thunders. Surgit spiritus cum suis. [2]

BEH. [3] Thus to observe my vow of appari-
tion
In greater light, and explicate thy fate,
I come, and tell thee that, if thou obey
The summons that thy mistress next will
send thee,
Her hand shall be thy death.
BUS. When will she send?
BEH. Soon as I set again, where late I rose.
BUS. Is the old friar slain?
BEH. No, and yet lives not. 60
BUS. Died he a natural death?
BEH. He did.
BUS. Who then
Will my dear mistress send?
BEH. I must not tell thee.
BUS. Who lets [4] thee?
BEH. Fate.
BUS. Who are Fate's ministers?
BEH. The Guise and Monsieur.
BUS. A fit pair of shears
To cut the threads of kings and kingly
spirits,

And consorts [5] fit to sound forth har-
mony,
Set to the falls of kingdoms! Shall the
hand
Of my kind mistress kill me?
BEH. If thou yield
To her next summons. Y'are fair-
warned. Farewell! *Thunders. Exit.*
BUS. I must fare well, however, though I
die, 70
My death consenting [6] with his augury.
Should not my powers obey when she
commands,
My motion must be rebel to my will,
My will to life. If, when I have obeyed,
Her hand should so reward me, they must
arm it,
Bind me, or force it; or, I lay my life,
She rather would convert it many times
On her own bosom, even to many deaths.
But, were there danger of such violence,
I know 'tis far from her intent to
send, 80
And who she should send is as far from
thought,
Since he is dead whose only mean she
used. *Knocks.*
Who's there? Look to the door, and let
him in,
Though politic Monsieur or the violent
Guise.

*Enter Montsurry, like the Friar, with a
letter written in blood.*

MONT. Hail to my worthy son!
BUS. O lying spirit,
To say the friar was dead! I'll now
believe
Nothing of all his forged predictions.
My kind and honored father, well re-
vived!
I have been frighted with your death and
mine,
And told my mistress' hand should be my
death 90
If I obeyed this summons.
MONT. I believed
Your love had been much clearer than
to give
Any such doubt a thought, for she is
clear,
And, having freed her husband's jealousy

---

[1] *I.e.*, the rays of the sun-god, Apollo.
[2] The spirit rises with his attendants.
[3] In the original this speaker is *Sp.* (for *Spirit*), clearly Behemoth, come to fulfill his promise of IV, ii, 159–62.
[4] Prevents.
[5] Companions, with a pun on the meaning *concerts*.
[6] Agreeing.

(Of which her much abused hand here is witness),

She prays, for urgent cause, your instant presence.

Bus. Why, then your Prince of Spirits may be called

The prince of liars.

Mont.   Holy Writ so calls him.

Bus. [*Opening the letter.*] What, writ in blood?

Mont.   Ay, 'tis the ink of lovers.

Bus. O, 'tis a sacred witness of her love.   100

So much elixir of her blood as this,

Dropped in the lightest dame, would make her firm

As heat to fire, and, like to all the signs,[1]

Commands the life confined in all my veins.

O, how it multiplies my blood with spirit,

And makes me apt t' encounter death and hell.

But come, kind father, you fetch me to heaven,

And to that end your holy weed was given.   *Exeunt.*

[Scena Quarta.

Same as Scena Prima.]

Thunder. Intrat[2] *Umbra Friar, and discovers*[3] *Tamyra.*

[Umb.] Fri. Up with these stupid thoughts, still lovéd daughter,

And strike away this heartless trance of anguish.

Be like the sun, and labor in eclipses;[4]

Look to the end of woes! O, can you sit

Mustering the horrors of your servant's slaughter

Before your contemplation, and not study

How to prevent it? Watch when he shall rise,

And, with a sudden outcry of his murther,

Blow[5] his retreat before he be revenged.[6]

Tam. O father, have my dumb woes waked your death?   10

When will our human griefs be at their height?

Man is a tree that hath no top in cares,

No root in comforts; all his power to live

Is given to no end, but t' have power to grieve.

Umb. Fri. It is the misery of our creation. Your true friend,

Led by your husband, shadowed in my weed,

Now enters the dark vault.

Tam.   But, my dearest father,

Why will not you appear to him yourself,

And see that none of these deceits annoy him?   20

Umb. Fri. My power is limited; alas! I cannot.

All that I can do—See, the cave opens!

                    Exit. D'Ambois at the gulf.[7]

Tam. Away, my love, away! Thou wilt be murthered!

Enter Monsieur and Guise above.

Bus. Murthered? I know not what that Hebrew means.

That word had ne'er been named had all been D'Ambois.

Murthered? By heaven, he is my murtherer

That shows me not a murtherer; what such bug[8]

Abhorreth not the very sleep of D'Ambois?

Murthered? Who dares give all the room I see

To D'Ambois' reach, or look with any odds   30

His fight i' th' face, upon whose hand sits death,

Whose sword hath wings, and every feather pierceth?

If I scape Monsieur's pothecary shops,

Foutre[9] for Guise's shambles! 'Twas ill plotted;

They should have mauled me here

When I was rising. I am up and ready.

Let in my politic visitants; let them in,

Though ent'ring like so many moving armors.

---

[1] Signs of the heavens, the stars.
[2] Enters.
[3] Reveals, unwraps from the arras.
[4] *I.e.*, to throw them off.
[5] Give a signal for.
[6] *I.e.*, before your husband's vengeance overtake him.
[7] Cave, vault.
[8] Object of terror, bogey.
[9] A fig (an expression of contempt).

Fate is more strong than arms and sly
    than treason,   39
And I at all parts buckled [1] in my fate.
Mon. ⎱ Why enter not the coward vil-
Guise. ⎰   lains?
Bus. Dare they not come?

Enter Murtherers with [Umbra] Friar at the
other door.

Tam.   They come!
First Mur.   Come all at once!
[Umb.] Fri. Back, coward murtherers,
    back!
Omnes.   Defend us, heaven!
    Exeunt all but the First [Murtherer].
First Mur. Come ye not on?
Bus.   No, slave, nor goest thou off!
    Stand you so firm? [*Strikes at him.*] Will
    it not enter there?
    You have a face yet. [*Kills him.*] So!
    In thy life's flame
I burn the first rites to my mistress' fame.
Umb. Fri. Breathe thee, brave son, against
    the other charge.
Bus. O, is it true then that my sense first
    told me?
Is my kind father dead?
Tam.   He is, my love.   50
    'Twas the earl, my husband, in his weed,
    that brought thee.
Bus. That was a speeding sleight,[2] and
    well resembled.
    Where is that angry earl? My lord, come
    forth
    And show your own face in your own
    affair;
    Take not into your noble veins the blood
    Of these base villains, nor the light re-
    ports
    Of blistered tongues for clear and weighty
    truth,
    But me against the world, in pure defense
    Of your rare lady, to whose spotless name
    I stand here as a bulwark, and project   60
    A life to her renown, that ever yet
    Hath been untainted, even in Envy's eye,
    And, where it would protect, a sanctuary.
    Brave earl, come forth, and keep your
    scandal in;
    'Tis not our fault if you enforce the spot,[3]
    Nor the wreak [4] yours, if you perform it
    not.

Enter Mont[surry], with all the Murtherers.

Mont. Cowards, a fiend or spirit beat ye
    off?
    They are your own faint spirits that have
    forged
    The fearful shadows that your eyes
    deluded.
    The fiend was in you; cast him out then,
    thus.   70
[*They fight.*]   *D'Ambois hath Montsurry*
down.
Tam. Favor my lord, my love, O, favor
    him!
Bus. I will not touch him; take your life,
    my lord,
And be appeased.
Pistols shot within.[5]   [*Bussy is wounded.*]
    O, then the coward Fates
    Have maimed themselves, and ever lost
    their honor.
Umb. Fri. What have ye done, slaves?
    Irreligious lord!
Bus. Forbear them, father; 'tis enough for
    me
    That Guise and Monsieur, death and
    destiny,
    Come behind D'Ambois. Is my body,
    then,
    But penetrable flesh? And must my
    mind   79
    Follow my blood? Can my divine part
    add
    No aid to th' earthly in extremity?
    Then these divines are but for form, not
    fact.
    Man is of two sweet courtly friends com-
    pact,
    A mistress and a servant; let my death
    Define life nothing but a courtier's
    breath.
    Nothing is made of naught, of all things
    made,
    Their abstract being a dream but of a
    shade.
    I'll not complain to earth yet, but to
    heaven,
    And, like a man, look upwards even in
    death.
    And, if Vespasian thought in majesty   90
    An emperor might die standing, why not
    I?   *She offers to help him.*[6]

---

[1] Armored.   [3] Emphasize the dishonor.
[2] Successful trick.   [4] Vengeance.

[5] In the original this direction follows l. 71.
[6] In the original this direction follows l. 93.

Nay, without help, in which I will exceed him;
For he died splinted with [1] his chamber grooms.
Prop me, true sword, as thou hast ever done!
The equal thought I bear of life and death
Shall make me faint on no side; I am up.
Here like a Roman statue I will stand
Till death hath made me marble. O my fame,
Live in despite of murther! Take thy wings
And haste thee where the gray-eyed Morn perfumes   100
Her rosy chariot with Sabean spices;
Fly where the Evening from th' Iberian vales
Takes on her swarthy shoulders Hecate,
Crowned with a grove of oaks; fly where men feel
The burning axletree, and those that suffer
Beneath the chariot of the snowy Bear; [2]
And tell them all that D'Ambois now is hasting
To the eternal dwellers; that a thunder
Of all their sighs together (for their frailties
Beheld in me) may quit my worthless [3] fall   110
With a fit volley for my funeral.
UMB. FRI. Forgive thy murtherers.
BUS.   I forgive them all,
And you, my lord, their fautor; [4] for true sign
Of which unfeigned remission, take my sword;
Take it, and only give it motion,
And it shall find the way to victory
By his own brightness, and th' inherent valor
My fight hath stilled [5] into 't, with charms of spirit.
Now let me pray you that my weighty blood,
Laid in one scale of your impartial spleen,   120
May sway the forfeit of my worthy love
Weighed in the other; and be reconciled

With all forgiveness to your matchless wife.
TAM. Forgive thou me, dear servant, and this hand
That led thy life to this unworthy end;
Forgive it, for the blood with which 'tis stained,
In which I writ the summons of thy death
(The forcéd summons) by this bleeding wound,
By this here in my bosom, and by this
That makes me hold up both my hands imbrued   130
For thy dear pardon.
BUS.   O, my heart is broken!
Fate nor these murtherers, Monsieur nor the Guise,
Have any glory in my death, but this,
This killing spectacle, this prodigy.
My sun is turned to blood, in whose red beams
Pindus and Ossa, hid in drifts of snow
Laid on my heart and liver, from their veins
Melt like two hungry torrents, eating rocks,
Into the ocean of all human life,
And make it bitter, only with my blood.   140
O frail condition of strength, valor, virtue,
In me (like warning fire upon the top
Of some steep beacon on a steeper hill)
Made to express it, like a falling star
Silently glanced [6] that like a thunderbolt
Looked to have stuck [7] and shook the firmament.   *Moritur.*[8]
UMB. FRI. Farewell, brave relics of a complete man!
Look up and see thy spirit made a star;
Join flames with Hercules,[9] and, when thou sett'st
Thy radiant forehead in the firmament,   150
Make the vast crystal [10] crack with thy receipt;
Spread to a world of fire, and the aged sky
Cheer with new sparks of old humanity.

---

[1] Supported by.
[2] *I.e.*, equatorial and arctic regions. This passage is adapted from Seneca, *Hercules Œtæus.*
[3] Unworthy.   [4] Patron.   [5] Instilled.

[6] Glimpsed.
[7] Pierced. Boas conjectures *struck.*
[8] He dies.
[9] From 1607 edn. 1641 edn. has *Jove flames with her rules.*   [10] Crystalline sphere.

[*To Montsurry.*] Son of the earth, whom my
  unrested soul
  Rues t' have begotten in the faith of
  heaven,
  Assay to gratulate [1] and pacify
  The soul fled from this worthy by per-
  forming
  The Christian reconcilement he besought
  Betwixt thee and thy lady. Let her
  wounds
  Manlessly [2] digged in her, be eased and
  cured   160
  With balm of thine own tears, or be
  assured
  Never to rest free from my haunt and
  horror.
MON. See how she merits this, still kneel-
  ing by,
  And mourning his fall more than her own
  fault.
UMB. FRI. Remove, dear daughter, and
  content thy husband;
  So piety wills thee, and thy servant's
  peace.
TAM. O wretched piety, that art so distract
  In thine own constancy, and in thy right
  Must be unrighteous! If I right my
  friend,
  I wrong my husband; if his wrong I
  shun,   170
  The duty of my friend I leave undone.
  Ill plays on both sides; here and there it
  riseth;
  No place, no good, so good but ill com-
  priseth.
  O, had I never married but for form,
  Never vowed faith but purposed to de-
  ceive,
  Never made conscience of any sin,
  But cloaked it privately and made it
  common,
  Nor never honored been in blood or
  mind,
  Happy had I been then, as others are
  Of the like license. I had then been
  honored;   180
  Lived without envy; custom had be-.
  numbed
  All sense of scruple, and all note of
  frailty;
  My fame had been untouched, my heart
  unbroken;
  But, shunning all, I strike on all offense.

O husband! Dear friend! O my con-
  science!
MON. Come, let's away; my senses are not
  proof
  Against those plaints.
*Exeunt Guise, Mon[sieur].   D'Ambois is
                              borne off.*
MONT. I must not yield to pity, nor to
  love
  So servile and so traitorous. Cease, my
  blood,
  To wrastle with my honor, fame, and
  judgment.—   190
  Away! Forsake my house; forbear com-
  plaints
  Where thou hast bred them. Here all
  things [are] [3] full
  Of their own shame and sorrow; leave my
  house.
TAM. Sweet lord, forgive me, and I will be
  gone,
  And till these wounds—that never balm
  shall close
  Till death hath entered at them, so I love
  them,
  Being opened by your hands—by death
  be cured,
  I never more will grieve you with my
  sight,
  Never endure that any roof shall part
  Mine eyes and heaven; but to the open
  deserts,   200
  Like to a hunted tigress, I will fly,
  Eating my heart, shunning the steps of
  men,
  And look on no side till I be arrived.
MONT. I do forgive thee, and upon my
  knees,
  With hands held up to heaven, wish that
  mine honor
  Would suffer reconcilement to my love;
  But, since it will not, honor never serve
  My love with flourishing object till it
  sterve! [4]
  And, as this taper, though it upwards
  look,
  Downwards must needs consume, so let
  our love!   210
  As, having lost his honey, the sweet taste
  Runs into savor, and will needs retain
  A spice of his first parents, till, like life,
  It sees and dies, so let our love! And
  lastly,

[1] Repay, please.   [2] In an unmanly fashion.
[3] Added by Dilke.   [4] Starve, die.

As, when the flame is suffered to look up,
It keeps his luster, but, being thus turned
    down,
His natural course of useful light in-
    verted,
His own stuff puts it out, so let our
    love!
Now turn from me, as here I turn from
    thee,
And may both points of heaven's straight
    axletree   220
Conjoin in one, before thyself and me.
               Exeunt severally.

FINIS ACTUS QUINTI ET ULTIMI.

EPILOGUE

WITH many hands you have seen D'Ambois
    slain,
Yet by your grace he may revive again,
And every day grow stronger in his skill
To please, as we presume he is in will.
The best deserving actors of the time
Had their ascents, and by degrees did climb
To their full height, a place to study due.
To make him tread in their path lies in you;
He'll not forget his makers, but still prove
His thankfulness as you increase your
    love.
               FINIS.

JOHN MARSTON

The career of John Marston can be succinctly summed up: from poet to playwright to priest. And these rather surprising changes all took place in roughly a decade. Marston is another Elizabethan writer about whom critical opinion has varied greatly. In the most complete study of Marston up to the present, Anthony Caputi says: "Although all critics have agreed that Marston was violent and unstable, some have charged him with obscurity, clumsiness, and insincerity, while others have admired his originality, skill, and moral fervor" (*John Marston, Satirist*, Cornell University Press, 1961).

Not as physically active and aggressive as many of his contemporaries, Marston had an intellectual pugnaciousness in his early years that challenged and angered many people. Most of the modern writers of major studies of Marston have emphasized his leading quality in their titles. Caputi labeled him "Satirist." Morse S. Allen entitled his dissertation *The Satire of John Marston* (Princeton University Ph.D. dissertation, Columbus, Ohio, 1920). A. José Axelrad called his thoroughgoing survey *Un Malcontent Élizabéthain: John Marston (1576–1634)* (Paris, 1955). Alvin Kernan discussed him in *The Cankered Muse/Satire of the English Renaissance* (Yale University Press, 1959). In his *Complaint and Satire in Early English Literature* (Oxford University Press, 1956), John Peter concluded that Marston would have been a much better dramatist if he had never heard of satire; but in "John Marston's Plays" (*S*, 1950), he had praised him for his "Protean performance" in various styles. Ford Elmore Curtis was more restrained, entitling his unpublished Ph.D. dissertation (Cornell, 1932) simply *John Marston, His Life and Works*. A. H. Bullen and A. B. Grosart laid the groundwork for his biography in their nineteenth century editions of Marston's works, and H. Harvey Wood, in his introduction to *The Plays of John Marston* (Edinburgh, 1934 ff.), added more material. Modern students have also profited from the biographical researches of R. E. Brettle (*MLR* and *RES*, 1927, 1928, and 1962).

John Marston was born in the early autumn of 1576 and was christened at Wardington parish church in Oxfordshire on October 7. His father, also named John Marston, was a prominent landowner in the area, who became a well-known lawyer in Coventry and London before entering the Middle Temple (in 1570) where he became a reader, or lecturer, and maintained residence for many years. He died in 1599. Marston's mother, Mary Guarsi, was the daughter of Andrew Guarsi, who was probably the son of Balthazar Guarsi. (Balthazar was an Italian who had been surgeon to Queen Katherine of Aragon before he was naturalized in England in 1522 and had a distinguished career as surgeon to Henry VIII.) Mary Marston survived her husband by twenty-two years, and bore him four sons and three daughters, John being the third son. The boy probably attended the free grammar school of Coventry, founded and endowed by John Hales, M. P., who was author of a text on grammar for use in the school; but the records are incomplete.

At any rate, young Marston matriculated at Brasenose College, Oxford, on February 4, 1592, and took his B.A. just two years later, at the age of eighteen. After taking an examination required of all B.A.'s who intended to proceed to the M.A., Marston changed his mind, and decided to follow his father in the law. In November 1595 he joined his father at the Middle Temple. To his father's reproachful regret, after only two years of exposure to the brilliant and inquisitive mixed society of the Inns of Court young Marston was persuaded that it was not law but literature that he wished to pursue as a profession.

Elizabethan students were challenging authority on all sides toward the turn of the century. They questioned Aristotle's logic; revolted against the rhetorical style of Cicero and Isocrates and preferred the plainer writing of Seneca, Tacitus, and Lucan; were interested in Platonism, Stoicism, and even occultism; and were stimulated by the skepticism of Montaigne and Roman satirists like Juvenal, Persius, and Horace. As Caputi says, it was this intellectual climate that led Marston to the publication of his first work, *The Metamorphosis of Pygmalion's Image and Certain Satires* in 1598, followed by *The Scourge of Villainy* later in the same year. The bitterness of the attack of some of these satires on society, coupled with what seemed to the puritanical to be the lasciviousness and immorality of others, led to an official order for their burning on June 4, 1599. The crabbed style of these poems (for a series of studies of Marston's highly original and inventive vocabulary and general use of language, see Gustav Cross, "Some Notes on the Vocabulary of John Marston," *NQ*, 1954–61), together with their crabbed attitude toward life (which some critics have thought to be only a pose), gave rise to the later remark that Marston was "a screech owl among the singing birds" of the more romantic school of poetry. His literary quarrel with another young rival satirist, Joseph Hall, recently a fellow of Emmanuel College, Cambridge, and the author of a collection of satires learnedly called *Virgidemiarum* (i.e., *A Harvest of Rods* or *Blows*), also brought him added publicity. (Hall later became the famous Bishop of Exeter and Norwich.)

Marston's work in verse satire was concentrated into a brief five or six months, but it served as a useful apprenticeship for his plays, to which he now turned. O. J. Campbell speculated that he made the change because the passage of the Act of Conflagration on June 1, 1599, made the publication of satiric and erotic works extremely risky (*Comicall Satyre and Shakespeare's Troilus and Cressida*, San Marino, California, 1938); but Caputi believes that Marston probably began revising the old "interlude-morality" play, *Histriomastix. Or, The Player Whipt* (acted in August or September 1599; printed in 1610), before this event. The evidence for assigning this rather crude allegorical satire to Marston is indirect, based only on style and external allusions; but Caputi thinks that the play may have been somehow connected with the entry in Henslowe's diary on September 28, 1599, that he had lent forty shillings "vnto mr. Maxton the new poete in earneste of a Booke called _____." If this "mr. Maxton" represented another case of Henslowe's usual ingenious and more or less phonetic spelling, here is the only instance of Marston's having written directly for a professional adult company of actors, except for his late expansion of *The Malcontent* for the King's Men. For all of Marston's known plays were done for the boy companies—first for the Children of Paul's from 1599 to 1604, and then (after he had acquired a sixth of a share in their company about 1603) for the Children of the Queen's Revels, formerly the Children of the Chapel, at the indoor private theater the Blackfriars, (E. K. Chambers, *The Elizabethan Stage*).

The new *Histriomastix* was largely a satire on one type of moral play being served up to adult audiences in the public theaters, and was performed by the Children of Paul's simultaneously with the revival of the children's companies, which had been discontinued in 1590. (For histories of these companies, see C. W. Wallace, *The Children of the Chapel at Blackfriars 1597–1603*, *University of Nebraska Studies*, 1908; H. N. Hillebrand, *The Child Actors*, *University of Illinois Studies*, 1926; and Chambers, *The Elizabethan Stage*.) In discussing why *Histriomastix* was particularly fitted for a performance by boys, Caputi makes a valuable and original analysis of the special assets and defects of child actors and their influence on the Elizabethan theater. First, a distinction must be made between the boys in the public theater, who were apprenticed in the ordinary way and enacted only women's and children's roles, and those in the private theater, who were "impressed into service and kept as long as they were useful" and played *all* the roles as well as specializing in singing and dancing. In spite of the pre-eminence of a few boy actors, they were still children between ten and fifteen years old, and were not really capable of serious adult parts; they were better in the "light, fanciful comedy and elaborate artifice" of John Lyly. Consequently, the list of the extant plays performed before the fashionable audiences at Paul's and Blackfriars after the revival reveals "a decisive movement toward instrumental music, song, dance, and satire." The popularity of satire encouraged an exaggerated burlesque acting style which went beyond the broad stylized methods of Elizabethan acting, and this was accentuated by the size, voices, and general immaturity of the boys, even though as time went on some of them were retained in the companies after their voices had changed. Therefore the directors exploited "the disparity between what the children pretended to be and what they obviously were, . . . relying heavily on inherent incongruity and exuberant gesticulation for comic and satiric effects." And even in the tragedies produced in the private houses, like Marston's and Chapman's, there was an avoidance of complex characterization and realistic action and an emphasis on stylization and artificiality. It is on these premises that Caputi analyzes *Histriomastix* and Marston's other plays.

Histriomastix involved Marston in the chief of the three so-called "Wars of the Theaters" (or "Stage Quarrels," or "poetomachias")—the one between the public and private theaters and the adult and child actors. (See Josiah H. Penniman, *The War of the Theaters*, Philadelphia, 1897; R. A. Small, *The Stage Quarrel between Ben Jonson and the So-Called Poetasters*, Breslau, 1899; Allen, *The Satire of John Marston;* etc.) According to Jonson, the quarrel arose from Marston's representing him unfavorably on the stage, but in spite of much study the early history of the affair remains obscure. It lasted from about 1599 until 1604. Very early in the century Marston apparently satirized Jonson in *What You Will*, and possibly aided Dekker in preparing the attack in the latter's *Satiromastix*. In his famous conversations with William Drummond of Hawthornden in 1618 Ben Jonson told his Scotch friend that he "had many quarrels with Marston, beat him, and took his pistol from him, wrote his Poetaster on him; the beginning of them were [*sic*] that Marston represented him on the stage." Marston's eulogistic dedication of *The Malcontent* to Jonson, however, indicates a renewal of friendly relations by 1604 and in the same year the two joined Chapman in writing *Eastward Ho*. As Jonson described the aftermath of this play to Drummond, he was accused by Sir James Murray to the King "for writting something against the Scots in a play Eastward Hoe, and voluntarily [*sic*] imprissonned himself with Chapman and Marston, who had written it amongst them. The report was, that they should then [have] had their ears cut and noses. After their delivery, he banqueted all his friends . . ." (*Ben Jonson's Conversations with Drummond of Hawthornden*, ed. R. F. Patterson, London, 1924). There is some evidence that Marston was released before the other two, though he had to leave the city; but in 1608 he was definitely committed to Newgate by the Privy Council—it has been conjectured for another satire on King James in a play now lost (Chambers, *Elizabethan Stage*).

Marston's plays after *Histriomastix* follow many of the romantic conventions of Elizabethan drama, but with a fundamental change in spirit. By the end of the sixteenth century, the growth of conservatism and nationalism in the middle classes had brought a sharp reaction against the Italianate elements in English life and literature. Marston and others, taking as their model the rugged style of the Roman satirists, made bitter attacks on the affected gallants of the day and on the artifices of romance and poetry. But their satire reflects also a reaction of Europe as a whole against the idealism of the earlier Renaissance, for many forces were tending to weaken man's faith in the glory of the world and in his own perfectibility. The mood of disillusion is reflected in the misanthropy and melancholy of many writers, who picture the follies of the age as inordinate, its crimes as monstrous. Marston's satire impressed even his contemporaries by its extravagance, its bitterness, and cynicism. As a vehicle for it, he developed—with an affectation equal to that he satirized—a style both blunt and tumid, which is the chief point of Jonson's ridicule of him in the character Crispinus in *The Poetaster*. Both mood and manner were carried over into Marston's plays, with a malcontent character used as a critic or an intriguer to set the tone. In keeping with the current conception of the evil of Italian life, he drew the material for his plots and his characters largely from Italy. Here libertinism and Machiavellian intrigue had indeed produced many sinister figures, which were vividly portrayed by Italian writers in both history and story, and which had already been utilized to some extent in Elizabethan novels and plays. But, where direct sources seem to be lacking, dramatists like Marston and the author of *The Revenger's Tragedy* were able to outdo their models in creating characters and situations of morbid lust and villainy.

Marston's first acknowledged play was *Antonio and Mellida*, an extravagant tragicomedy with disguises and other conventions of romance. The characters were quickly transformed and used as a basis for *Antonio's Revenge*, a form of revenge tragedy in which a malcontent revenger carried the type to new depths of gloom and terror. The double play was printed in 1602. *What You Will* (printed in 1607) soon followed. In *The Dutch Courtesan* (printed in 1605), with an English setting instead of the usual Italian scene, Marston has used a modification of the plot found in Bandello's famous story of the Countess of Celant, translated by Painter in *The Palace of Pleasure* and by Fenton in *Tragical Discourses*. The comic plot is drawn from a story of Masuccio translated by Painter. *Parasitaster, or The Fawn* (printed in 1606) is based on a story from Boccaccio's *Decameron*. Incidents from Roman history furnished the plot for *The Wonder of Women, or The Tragedy of Sophonisba* (printed in 1606). In *The Insatiate Countess* (published in 1613), which was apparently completed by William Barksted, Marston has used the story of the Countess of Celant for the main plot and another *novella* of Bandello for the subplot.

Caputi comments on the fact that before 1603 Marston's plays were filled with quotations and parallel passages from Seneca, whereas after that date they were filled with allusions to Florio's translation of Montaigne in that year. He feels, however, that Marston's debt to Epictetus and the new Stoicists like Justus Lipsius and Guillaume du Vair, while more elusive (Marston makes no direct allusions to them), was more profound, since their modifications of classical Stoicism were more in harmony with Christian doctrine. Not only in his emphasis on the rational faculty and its relation to the divine plan, but in his concept of "synteresis," or the doctrine of the "spark" (God "as a fire that was variously equated with spirit, soul, mind and reason"), did he come close to the ideas of the Neo-Stoics. Rather than advocating the classically Stoic attitude of apathy or passiveness, he believed that virtue must be achieved more actively. Paradoxically, in view of the superficial impressions made by his plays, Marston had a firm faith in human perfectibility. Nevertheless, he was not a deep or original thinker, and Jonson and others frequently ridiculed his philosophical pretensions.

Shortly after the middle of the first decade of the new century Marston apparently began to disengage himself from London society and the London theater, though by this time he seems to have reestablished himself temporarily in James's favor. In 1606 he wrote his *City Pageant* as part of the entertainments given for the visiting King of Denmark; in the following year he was asked to write the *Ashby Entertainment* to celebrate the visit of the Dowager Countess of Derby to her daughter and son-in-law, Lord and Lady Huntington, at Ashby-de-la-Zouch in Leicester; and his *Sophonisba* in 1606 struck a new note, which impressed T. S. Eliot with "its difference of tone, not only from that of Marston's other plays, but from that of any other English dramatist" (*Selected Essays*, New York, 1932). Nevertheless, in the summer of 1608 Marston sold his share in the Blackfriars, and in September 1609 he entered St. Mary's Hall, Oxford, to study for the Anglican priesthood. Within three months he was ordained. Early in December, when he made his routine "Supplicat" for library privileges at St. Mary's, he stated that he had spent more than three years in the study of philosophy. It seems fairly obvious that, like John Donne, he had undergone a conversion from the bitterness, eroticism, and excesses of his youth. But unlike Dean Donne he never became famous in his new profession. Early in 1610 Thomas Floyde, a member of the staff of Sir Thomas Edmondes in London, wrote to William Trumbull in Brussels that "Marston the poet is minister and hath preached at Oxon." (J. George, "John Marston and the Trumbull Correspondence," *NQ*, 1957), but there is no other record of his preaching prowess. He went first to the tiny parish of Barford St. Martin in Wiltshire, where he was apparently an assistant to its rector, Dr. John Wilkes, a former chaplain to King James. (R. E. Brettle speculates on his probable pastoral duties in this parish in "Notes on John Marston," *RES*, 1962.) On October 10, 1616, he was presented with a much better living, probably as a curate, at Christ Church, Hampshire.

Marston married Mary Wilkes, the daughter of his rector at Barford, but whether he married her after he settled there or settled there because he had already married her is not clear. The only clue is Ben Jonson's probably facetious remark to Drummond that "Marston wrott his Father-in-lawes preachings, and his Father-in-law his Comedies." Mary bore him one son, who died young. He resigned his Hampshire living on September 13, 1631, obviously because of ill-health, since when he made his will in Aldermanbury parish, London, on June 17, 1634, he was so ill he could make only a rough mark instead of signing his name. In 1633, when the publisher William Sheares issued a volume entitled *The Works of John Marston* (oddly enough, *The Malcontent* was not one of the six plays included), he wrote in his preface that Marston was "now in his autumn and declining years" and was "far distant from this place." How far distant Marston was from London at this time can only be guessed at. He died, however, at "Aldermanbury his house" on June 24, 1634, and was buried in the parish church, the regular burial place for many Middle Temple people. Although in the latter part of 1601 he had lost his rooms in the Temple because of his failure to pay his fees while absent from London, he was later restored to Fellowship. The Temple Church registry reads: "1634, June 26. Mr. John Marston, Minister, sometimes of the Middle Temple, who died in Aldermanbury Parish: buried below the communion table on the Middle Temple side." Anthony à Wood, in an entry on John Wilkes, wrote of Marston: "Dying 25 June, 1634, he was buried by his father (sometimes a counsellor of the Middle Temple), in the church belonging to the Temple in the suburb of London, under the stone which hath written on it *Oblivioni Sacrum*"—an inscription echoing the phrase in the dedication at the end of *The Scourge of Villainy:* "To everlasting oblivion." The phrase may still be read in the volume of poetry; the epitaph on the grave cannot, since the church was destroyed by the bombings in World War II. Marston's widow showed her affection for her dead husband by asking in her will that she be buried next to him. Most of her legatees were his friends, among whom was "his ancient friend Master Henry Walley of Stationer's Hall," to whom she bequeathed her "dear husband's picture." She also mentioned "a trunk full of books with lock and key, and a book of Martyrs not in the trunk"—which she perhaps had kept out to read by herself. Ben Jonson wrote his epitaph to his former foe and friend in his "Epigram No. 68":

> *Playwright*, convict of public wrongs to men,
> Takes private beatings and begins again;
> Two kinds of valour he doth show at once:
> Active in's brains, and passive in his bones.

The Malcontent, regarded by almost everyone but T. S. Eliot as Marston's best play, was probably first performed in its unaugmented form in 1603 by the Blackfriars' boys, though it was not printed until 1604. At least this is the orthodox view of Chambers and others, supported by Caputi. Still others, however, like Gustav Cross ("The Date of *The Malcontent* Once More," *PQ*, 1960), have produced new evidence to support E. E. Stoll's argument, first offered in 1905, that the play was written not later than

1600 (Stoll had repeated his position in "The Date of *The Malcontent:* A Rejoinder," *RES*, 1935). At the center of the controversy is the topical allusion in I, viii, to a "horn . . . growing in the woman's forehead, twelve years since." Three editions of the play were printed in the single year 1604, two of the shorter version for the boys and one of the longer for the adult actors at the Globe (W. W. Greg, *A Bibliography of English Drama to the Restoration*, London, 1939). In spite of the ambiguity of the extended title of the augmented version, Marston is now generally given credit for all the additions, and Webster only for the Induction (E. E. Stoll, *John Webster*, Boston, 1905). Caputi argues, on the basis of Sly's remark in the Induction that he had seen the play often, and from the fact that the plague had closed the theaters from May 1603 to April 1604, that the right to produce the play had been transferred from the Blackfriars to the Globe between those dates. He also argues that Marston made his additions, which Burbage in the Induction admits were not really "needful," in order to compensate for the loss of "the measure of satire and burlesque that proceeded normally from the children's acting style, but that the adults could not duplicate." Caputi likewise suggests that the obscure reference to the "not received custom of music in our theater" may simply mean that the entr'acte music in the private theaters was longer than in the public. Although Caputi finds it surprising that *The Malcontent* contains only four songs and one elaborate dance, Christian Kiefer discovered that there are more references to music, together with actual performances of it, in *The Malcontent* than in any other of Marston's plays, and that this music contributes more than is generally recognized to the depth and coherence of the play's satiric implications ("Music and Marston's *The Malcontent*," *SP*, 1954). J. S. Manifold, in his extensive study of *The Music in English Drama from Shakespeare to Purcell* (London, 1956), concluded that Marston seemed the most conscientious dramatist in this period about music for his plays.

When the play was entered on the Stationers' Register on July 5, 1604, it was described as a "tragiecomedia;" but Marston himself in his preface "To the Reader" described it as both a comedy and a satire, in spite of its melodramatic plot and its revenge-play features. As Caputi notes, in this case the revenge plot, though harking back to Marston's super-bloody *Antonio's Revenge*, "is marked by the important difference that none of the revenges is carried out successfully, save the protagonist's; and his is notably tame alongside those found in regular revenge plays." It is clear to the audience all along that the usurper-villain Mendoza, who, "in any other play, could well be a Machiavellian monster" (but whose every act has really been suggested by the deposed Duke Altofronto in his disguise role of Malevole), can never permanently succeed. The comic and even burlesque possibilities of this "top-heavy" villainy would naturally have been exploited by the child actors. The role of Malevole as the malcontent and railer, and its relation to other examples of the type—such as Kyd's Hamlet, Shakespeare's Jaques, Jonson's Macilente, and many others—have been well discussed by E. E. Stoll ("Shakespeare, Marston, and the Malcontent Type," *MP*, 1906) and Theodore Spencer ("The Elizabethan Malcontent, *J.Q. Adams Memorial Studies*, Washington, 1948). Because of Marston's adoption of the rather unusual and specialized situation of a duke in disguise (V. O. Freeburg, *Disguise Plots in Elizabethan Drama*, New York, 1915), Altofronto is enabled to act with the "multiple functions of protagonist, intriguer, critic, and judge," and Marston's development of these roles gives him the opportunity to fabricate a complex and original plot, for which no sources have been discovered.

The appropriateness—or in some cases the inappropriateness—of the humors names Marston gives to most of his characters may offer some clues to his knowledge of Italian, although some of these names appear in Florio's *A World of Words* (1598). They certainly offer helpful makeup and characterization hints to actors. The name of Mendoza, described by Malevole in I, iv, as "Impure Mendoza, that sharp-nosed lord," contains an echo of "mendoso," suggesting "faults that may be mended"—though his are not. "Malevole," of course, suggests "malevolent," or at least "cynical" or "malcontent," whereas his true name, Altofronto, means "high forehead" or "lofty face." Celso is properly described as "high," "bright," or "noble." "Maquerelle" derives from "macarello," a "bawd," as well as a "mackerel" or a "ravenous fowl." "Passarello" is the name of a clown, as well as "dried fish." Bilioso is described in the cast list as an "old choleric marshal" rather than a bilious one, though he does admit in III, i, that he is "horribly troubled with the gout." In I, i, Malevole insults him by calling him "half a man, half a goat, all a beast," and in I, iv, calls him "the father of Maypoles" with "a passing high forehead." Guerrino means "little war;" Biancha obviously means "white" or "innocent," though in reality her old husband ("Janivere" or January) married her with her "belly full of young bones"; Prepasso is obviously a courtier who "walks ahead;" Equato, a former philosophy scholar, is perhaps properly named since he has "equated" his former ideals with his material desires; and Ferrardo may be intended as an echo of "furetto," the Italian word for ferret. But names like Pietro, Aurelia, Ferneze, and Emilia seem to have no appropriate overtones, though Mendoza in I, vii, sums the first three up as "Honest fool duke, subtile lascivious duchess, silly novice Ferneze."

Two extremes in the evaluation of Marston's dramatic work as a whole are represented by Irving Ribner and William Archer. Archer, in *The Old Drama and the New*, announced that he would not spend much time on a playwright whose critics had almost all admitted that "his characteristics are mainly faults." Archer then went on to label him "a bad and barbarous playwright," with "a horribly coarse mind," no sense of humor, and the slightest of poetic gifts. As for *The Malcontent*: "When he tried to write comedy . . . , what he actually produced was a melodrama without murders, but full of lust and violence, and worked out by means of the most preposterous disguises." On the other hand, Ribner, in his *Jacobean Tragedy*, asserted that it could be argued that "next to Shakespeare Marston is the most influential dramatist of his age." Ribner admitted that Marston "wrote no play himself which is truly significant among the tragedies of his age," and excluded him from full examination in his book because in spite of his "indignant, crusading spirit" in attacking vice in its "most horrible and revolting forms," he was not really concerned with "the relation of good and evil to one another in the cosmos, or with the relation of human suffering to human joy." But Ribner makes a case for Marston's influence by asserting that he initiated devices which were later used with more artistry by Webster, Tourneur, Middleton, Ford, and even Shakespeare; created the pattern for the malcontent; developed the Machiavellian villain; was Kyd's great successor in revenge tragedy; was a master of dramatic irony; and "showed his followers how to end a play [*Antonio's Revenge*] in the bloody holocaust of a final masque scene." In fact, Ribner found that the technique of *The Malcontent*, "with its central omnipotent character manipulating the action," was later reflected in such diverse plays as *The Revenger's Tragedy*, *Measure for Measure*, and even *The Tempest*.

There are various modern editions of *The Malcontent*: G. B. Harrison's in the Temple Dramatists series in 1933; H. Harvey Wood's in the Blackfriars Dramatists in 1934; M. L. Wine's in the Regents Renaissance Drama series in 1964; and Bernard Harris's in The New Mermaids in 1967. The present text is based directly on a photostatic copy of the second, expanded edition (1604) in the possession of the Huntington Library, with the permission of the authorities of the Library. The editions of Bullen in *The Works of Marston* and of W. A. Neilson in *The Chief Elizabethan Dramatists* have also been consulted.

THE MALCONTENT[1]

BY

JOHN MARSTON

BENJAMINO [2] JONSONIO, POETÆ ELEGANTISSIMO, GRAVISSIMO, AMICO SUO, CANDIDO ET CORDATO, JOHANNES MARSTON, MUSARUM ALUMNUS, ASPERAM HANC SUAM THALIAM D.D.[3]

To the Reader

I am an ill orator, and, in truth, use to indite more honestly than eloquently, for it is my custom to speak as I think, and write as I speak.

In plainness, therefore, understand that in some things I have willingly erred, as in supposing a Duke of Genoa, and in taking names different from that city's families, for which some may wittily[4] accuse me; but my defense shall be as honest as many [10 reproofs unto me have been most malicious, since, I heartily protest, it was my care to write so far from reasonable offense that even strangers in whose state I laid my scene should not from thence draw any disgrace to any, dead or living. Yet, in despite of my endeavors, I understand some have been most unadvisedly overcunning in misinterpreting me, and with subtility as deep as hell have maliciously spread [20 ill rumors, which, springing from themselves, might to themselves have heavily returned. Surely I desire to satisfy every firm spirit, who, in all his actions, proposeth to himself no more ends than God and virtue do, whose intentions are always simple. To such I protest that, with my free understanding, I have not glanced at disgrace of any, but of those whose unquiet studies labor innovation,[5] contempt of holy [30 policy, reverent, comely superiority, and established unity. For the rest of my supposed tartness, I fear not but unto every worthy mind it will be approved so general and honest as may modestly pass with the freedom of a satire. I would fain leave the paper; only one thing afflicts me, to think that scenes invented merely to be spoken should be enforcively[6] published to be read, and that the least hurt I [40 can receive is to do myself the wrong. But, since others otherwise would do me more, the least inconvenience is to be accepted. I have myself, therefore, set forth this comedy, but so[7] that my enforced absence must much rely upon the printer's discretion; but I shall entreat slight errors in orthography may be as slightly overpassed, and that the unhandsome shape which this trifle in reading presents, may be par- [50 doned for the pleasure it once afforded you when it was presented with the soul of lively action.

Sine aliqua dementia nullus Phœbus.[8]

[1] The title continues: "Augmented by Marston. With the Additions Played by the King's Majesty's Servants. Written by John Webster."
[2] Original reads *Beniamini.*
[3] "To Benjamin Jonson, poet most accomplished and most eminent, his frank and judicious friend—John Marston, follower of the Muses—dedicates this his unpolished comedy."
[4] Learnedly.
[5] Work for revolution.
[6] Compulsorily.
[7] In such a manner.
[8] No poet is without some madness.

DRAMATIS PERSONÆ

GIOVANNI ALTOFRONTO,[1] *disguised Male-*
vole, sometime Duke of Genoa.
PIETRO JACOMO, *Duke of Genoa.*
MENDOZA, *a minion [2] to the duchess of Pietro*
Jacomo.
CELSO, *a friend to Altofront.*
BILIOSO, *an old choleric marshal.*
PREPASSO, *a gentleman usher.*
FERNEZE, *a young courtier, and enamored*
on the duchess.

FERRARDO, *a minion to Duke Pietro Jacomo.*
EQUATO } *two courtiers.*
GUERRINO }
AURELIA, *duchess to Duke Pietro Jacomo.*
MARIA, *duchess to Duke Altofront.*
EMILIA } *two ladies attending the*
BIANCHA } *duchess [, Aurelia].*
MAQUERELLE, *an old panderess.*
PASSARELLO, *fool to Bilioso.*
[CAPTAIN *of the citadel.*

SCENE: *Genoa.*

TIME: *Contemporary.*]

THE INDUCTION [3]

TO

THE MALCONTENT, AND THE ADDITIONS [4] ACTED BY THE KING'S MAJESTY'S
SERVANTS

WRITTEN BY JOHN WEBSTER

Enter W[illiam] Sly,[5] a Tireman[6] following
him with a stool.

TIRE. Sir, the gentlemen will be angry
if you sit here.
SLY. Why? We may sit upon the stage
at the private house.[7] Thou dost not take
me for a country gentleman, dost? Dost
think I fear hissing? I'll hold my life thou
took'st me for one of the players.
TIRE. No, sir.
SLY. By God's slid,[8] if you had, I would
have given you but sixpence for your [10
stool. Let them that have stale suits sit in
the galleries. Hiss at me! He that will be
laughed out of a tavern or an ordinary
shall seldom feed well, or be drunk in good
company.—Where's Harry Condell, D[ick]

Burbadge, and W[illiam] Sly? Let me speak
with some of them.
TIRE. An't [9] please you to go in, sir, you
may.
SLY. I tell you, no. I am one that [20.
hath seen this play often, and can give them
intelligence for their action. I have most
of the jests here in my table-book.[10]

Enter Sinklo.

SINK. Save you, coz! [11]
SLY. O, cousin, come, you shall sit between my legs here.
SINK. No, indeed, cousin; the audience
then will take me for a viol-de-gambo, and
think that you play upon me.
SLY. Nay, rather that I work upon [30
you, coz.
SINK. We stayed for you at supper last
night at my cousin Honeymoon's, the
woolen draper. After supper we drew cuts
for a score of apricocks,[12] the longest cut
still to draw an apricock. By this light,
'twas Mistress Frank Honeymoon's fortune
still to have the longest cut; I did measure
for the women.—What be these, coz?

[1] The significance of many of these names as
indicating "humors" or offices is obvious.
[2] Favorite, lover.
[3] The induction does not appear in the first
edn.
[4] The significant additions are indicated in
footnotes.
[5] William Sly, John Sinklo, Richard Burbadge,
etc., were prominent members of the King's
Company.
[6] Property man.
[7] The Blackfriars Theater.
[8] Eyelid.

[9] If it.
[10] Notebook.
[11] Cousin, friend.
[12] Apricots.

Enter D[ick] Burbadge, H[arry] Condell,
J[ohn] Lowin.

SLY. The players.—God save you!　40
BUR. You are very welcome.
SLY. I pray you, know this gentleman,
my cousin; 'tis Master Doomsday's son,
the usurer.
CON. I beseech you, sir, be covered.[1]
SLY. No, in good faith, for mine ease.
Look you, my hat's the handle to this fan.
God's so,[2] what a beast was I, I did not
leave my feather at home! Well, but I'll
take an order with you.　50
　　　　Puts his feather in his pocket.
BUR. Why do you conceal your feather,
sir?
SLY. Why? Do you think I'll have jests
broken upon me in the play, to be laughed
at? This play hath beaten all your gallants
out of the feathers. Blackfriars hath almost
spoiled Blackfriars for feathers.[3]
SINK. God's so, I thought 'twas for
somewhat our gentlewomen at home counseled me to wear my feather to the　[60
play; yet I am loath to spoil it.
SLY. Why, coz?
SINK. Because I got it in the tiltyard;
there was a herald broke my pate for taking
it up. But I have worn it up and down the
Strand, and met him forty times since, and
yet he dares not challenge it.
SLY. Do you hear, sir? This play is a
bitter play.
CON. Why, sir, 'tis neither satire nor　[70
moral, but the mean[4] passage of a history;
yet there are a sort of discontented creatures that bear a stingless envy to great
ones, and these will wrest the doings of any
man to their base, malicious applyment;
but, should their interpretation come to the
test, like your marmoset they presently
turn their teeth to their tail and eat it.
SLY. I will not go so far with you; but
I say any man that hath wit may cen-　[80
sure,[5] if he sit in the twelvepenny room;[6]
and I say again the play is bitter.
BUR. Sir, you are like a patron that,
presenting a poor scholar to a benefice,
enjoins him not to rail against anything

that stands within compass of his patron's
folly. Why should not we enjoy the ancient freedom of poesy? Shall we protest
to the ladies that their painting makes
them angels, or to my young gallant　[90
that his expense in the brothel shall gain
him reputation? No, sir, such vices as
stand not accountable to law should be
cured as men heal tetters, by casting ink
upon them. Would you be satisfied[7] in
anything else, sir?
SLY. Ay, marry, would I: I would know
how you came by this play.
CON. Faith, sir, the book was lost; and,
because 'twas pity so good a play　[100
should be lost, we found it, and play it.
SLY. I wonder you would play it, another company having interest in it.
CON. Why not Malevole in folio with us,
as Jeronimo in decimo-sexto with them?[8]
They taught us a name for our play; we
call it *One for Another*.
SLY. What are your additions?
BUR. Sooth, not greatly needful; only
as your sallet[9] to your great feast, to　[110
entertain a little more time, and to abridge
the not-received custom of music in our
theater.[10] I must leave you, sir.
　　　　　　　Exit Burbadge.
SINK. Doth he play the Malcontent?
CON. Yes, sir.
SINK. I durst lay four of mine ears the
play is not so well acted as it hath been.
CON. O, no, sir, nothing *ad Parmenonis*
suem.[11]

---

[1] Put your hat on.　　[2] A mild oath.
[3] This presumably refers to V, ii, 47–48, and
perhaps means that gallants wearing feathers
were so ridiculed that they quit the district.
[4] Common.　　[5] Judge, criticize.　　[6] Box.

[7] Answered.
[8] "*I.e.* Why should not the King's Company
of grown up (folio) actors play *The Malcontent*
(which was the property of the children's company playing at Blackfriars), since the children
(16mo actors) have appropriated *The Spanish
Tragedy*, in which the King's Company had
rights?" (Neilson).
[9] Salad.
[10] *I.e.*, fill in the interval ordinarily taken by
music in other theaters.
[11] "'Tis reported that Parmeno, being very
famous for imitating the grunting of a pig, some
endeavoured to rival and outdo him. And when
the hearers, being prejudiced, cried out, 'Very
well, indeed, but nothing comparable to Parmeno's sow,' one took a pig under his arm and
came upon the stage; and when, tho' they heard
the very pig, they still continued, 'This is nothing comparable to Parmeno's sow,' he threw the
pig among them to show that they judged according to opinion and not truth " (Plutarch's
Symposium, V, i, cited by "L. S." and Bullen).

Low. Have you lost your ears, sir, [120 that you are so prodigal of laying them?

Sink. Why did you ask that, friend?

Low. Marry, sir, because I have heard of a fellow would offer to lay a hundred pound wager, that was not worth five baubees;[1] and in this kind you might venter[2] four of your elbows; yet God defend[3] your coat should have so many!

Sink. Nay, truly, I am no great censurer; and yet I might have been one of [130 the College of Critics once. My cousin here hath an excellent memory, indeed, sir.

Sly. Who, I? I'll tell you a strange thing of myself; and I can tell you, for one that never studied the art of memory, 'tis very strange too.

Con. What's that, sir?

Sly. Why, I'll lay a hundred pound I'll walk but once down by the Goldsmiths' Row in Cheap, take notice of the signs, [140 and tell you them with a breath instantly.

Low. 'Tis very strange.

Sly. They begin as the world did, with Adam and Eve. There's in all just five-and-fifty. I do use to meditate much when I come to plays too. What do you think might come into a man's head now, seeing all this company?

Con. I know not, sir.

Sly. I have an excellent thought. [150 If some fifty of the Grecians that were crammed in the horse-belly had eaten garlic, do you not think the Trojans might have smelt out their knavery?

Con. Very likely.

Sly. By God, I would he had, for I love Hector horribly.

Sink. O, but, coz, coz!—
"Great Alexander, when he came to the tomb of Achilles,
Spake with a big loud voice, 'O thou thrice blessed and happy!'"[4]   [160

Sly. Alexander was an ass to speak so well of a filthy cullion.[5]

Low. Good sir, will you leave the stage? I'll help you to a private room.[6]

Sly. Come, coz, let's take some tobacco.—Have you never a prologue?

Low. Not any, sir.

---

[1] Halfpennies.   [2] Venture.   [3] Forbid.
[4] From John Harvey's translation of Petrarch's 153rd sonnet.
[5] Knave.   [6] Box.

Sly. Let me see, I will make one extempore.

*Come to them, and fencing of a congee[7] with
    arms and legs, be round[8] with them.[9]*

Gentlemen, I could wish for the [170 women's sakes you had all soft cushions; and, gentlewomen, I could wish that for the men's sakes you had all more easy standings.—What would they wish more but the play now? And that they shall have instantly.   [*Exeunt.*]

ACTUS PRIMUS.[10]   SCENA PRIMA.

[The palace of the Duke of Genoa.]

*The vilest out-of-tune music being heard,
    enter Bilioso and Prepasso.*

Bil. Why, how now! Are ye mad, or drunk, or both, or what?

Pre. Are ye building Babylon there?

Bil. Here's a noise in court! You think you are in a tavern, do you not?

Pre. You think you are in a brothel house, do you not?—This room is ill-scented.

Enter One with a perfume.

So, perfume, perfume; some upon me, I pray thee.—
The duke is upon instant entrance; so, make place there!   10

SCENA SECUNDA.

[The same.]

*Enter the Duke Pietro, Ferrardo, Count
    Equato, Count Celso before, and
                    Guerrino.[11]*

Piet. Where breathes that music?

Bil. The discord rather than the music is heard from the malcontent Malevole's chamber.

Fer. [*Calling.*] Malevole!

---

[7] Making a bow.
[8] Plain-spoken.
[9] This stage direction is printed as part of Sly's speech in the original.
[10] The title is repeated before this line, and in the margin appears Juvenal's phrase, *Vexat censura columbas,* "Censorship disturbs the doves" (*i.e.,* the peace).
[11] The characters from the preceding scene remain, as in general they do throughout the play.

Mal. (*Out of his chamber.*) Yaugh, God a [1] man, what dost thou there? Duke's Ganymede, Juno's jealous of thy long stockings. Shadow of a woman, what wouldst, weasel? Thou lamb a court, [10 what dost thou bleat for? Ah, you smooth-chinned catamite! [2]

Piet. Come down, thou ragged cur, and snarl here. I give thy dogged sullenness free liberty; trot about and bespurtle [3] whom thou pleasest.

Mal. I'll come among you, you goatish-blooded toderers,[4] as gum into taffeta, to fret, to fret.[5] I'll fall like a sponge into water, to suck up, to suck up. Howl [20 again! I'll go to church and come to you. 　　　　　　　　　　　　　　　[*Exit above.*]

Piet. This Malevole is one of the most prodigious affections [6] that ever conversed with nature; a man, or rather a monster, more discontent than Lucifer when he was thrust out of the presence. His appetite is unsatiable as the grave, as far from any content as from heaven. His highest delight is to procure others vexation, and therein he thinks he truly serves heaven; [30 for 'tis his position, whosoever in this earth can be contented is a slave and damned; therefore does he afflict all in that to which they are most affected.[7] Th' elements struggle within him; his own soul is at variance within herself; his speech is halterworthy at all hours. I like him; faith, he gives good intelligence to my spirit, makes me understand those weaknesses which others' flattery palliates.—Hark! They [40 sing.[8]

Scena Tertia.

[*The same.*]

Enter Malevole after the song.

[Piet.] See, he comes. Now shall you hear the extremity of a malcontent. He is as free as air; he blows over every man.— And, sir, whence come you now?

Mal. From the public place of much dissimulation, the church.[9]

Piet. What didst there?

---

[1] Of.　　　[2] Male prostitute.　　[3] Besprinkle.
[4] Perhaps dealers in sheep or mutton, *i.e.*, in prostitutes.　　[5] *I.e.*, to wear you out quickly.
[6] Passions.　[7] Inclined.　[8] The song is not given.
[9] *The church* does not appear in the first edn. and is erased in some copies of the second.

Mal. Talk with a usurer; take up at interest.

Piet. I wonder what religion thou [10 art of.

Mal. Of a soldier's religion.

Piet. And what dost think makes most infidels now?

Mal. Sects, sects. I have seen seeming Piety change her robe so oft that sure none but some arch-devil can shape her a petticoat.

Piet. O, a religious policy.

Mal. But damnation on a politic re- [20 ligion! I am weary. Would I were one of the duke's hounds now!

Piet. But what's the common news abroad, Malevole? Thou dogg'st rumor still.

Mal. Common news? Why, common words are, "God save ye," "Fare ye well;" common actions, flattery and cozenage; common things, women and cuckolds.— And how does my little Ferrard? Ah, ye [30 lecherous animal! My little ferret, he goes sucking up and down the palace into every hen's nest, like a weasel. And to what dost thou addict thy time to now more than to those antique painted drabs that are still affected of [10] young courtiers, Flattery, Pride, and Venery?

Fer. I study languages. Who dost think to be the best linguist of our age?

Mal. Phew, the devil! Let him pos- [40 sess thee; he'll teach thee to speak all languages most readily and strangely; and great reason, marry, he's traveled greatly in the world, and is everywhere.

Fer. Save i' th' court.

Mal. Ay, save i' th' court.—(*To Bilioso.*) And how does my old muckhill, overspread with fresh snow? Thou half a man, half a goat, all a beast! How does thy young wife, old huddle? [11]　　　　　50

Bil. Out, you improvident rascal!

Mal. Do, kick, thou hugely-horned old duke's ox, good Master Make-pleas.

Piet. How dost thou live nowadays, Malevole?

Mal. Why, like the knight, Sir Patrick Penlolians, with killing a spiders for my lady's monkey.

Piet. How dost spend the night? I hear thou never sleep'st.　　　　　60

---

[10] Liked by.　　　　　[11] Decrepit old man.

MAL. O, no, but dream the most fantastical! O heaven! O fubbery, fubbery![1]

PIET. Dream! What dream'st?

MAL. Why, methinks I see that signior pawn his footcloth,[2] that *metreza*[3] her plate; this madam takes physic that tother[4] *monsieur* may minister to her. Here is a pander jeweled; there's a fellow in shift of satin this day, that could not shift a shirt tother night. Here a Paris [70 supports that Helen; there's a Lady Guinevere bears up that Sir Lancelot. Dreams, dreams, visions, fantasies, chimeras, imaginations, tricks, conceits![5]—(*To Prepasso.*) Sir Tristram Trimtram, come aloft, Jackanapes,[6] with a whim-wham. Here's a knight of the land of Catito shall play at trap[7] with any page in Europe, do the sword dance with any morris dancer in Christendom, ride at the [80 ring[8] till the fin[9] of his eyes look as blue as the welkin, and run the wild goose chase even with Pompey the Huge.

PIET. You run!

MAL. To the devil. Now, Signior Guerrino, that thou from a most pitied prisoner shouldst grow a most loathed flatterer!— Alas, poor Celso, thy star's oppressed: thou art an honest lord. 'Tis pity.

EQU. Is 't pity?   90

MAL. Ay, marry is 't, philosophical Equato; and 'tis pity that thou, being so excellent a scholar by art, shouldst be so ridiculous a fool by nature.—I have a thing to tell you, duke; bid um avaunt, bid um avaunt.

PIET. Leave us, leave us.—Now, sir, what is 't?

Exeunt all saving Pietro and Malevole.

MAL. Duke, thou art a *becco*,[10] a *cornuto*.[11]

PIET. How?   100

MAL. Thou art a cuckold.

PIET. Speak; unshale[12] him quick.

MAL. With most tumblerlike nimbleness.

PIET. Who? By whom? I burst with desire.

MAL. Mendoza is the man makes thee a horned beast; duke, 'tis Mendoza cornutes thee.

PIET. What conformance?[13] Relate; [110 short, short!

MAL. As a lawyer's beard.
There is an old crone in the court-- her name is Maquerelle;
She is my mistress, sooth to say, and she doth ever tell me.
Blurt a rime,[14] blurt a rime! Maquerelle is a cunning bawd; I am an honest villain; thy wife is a close drab;[15] and thou art a notorious cuckold. Farewell, duke.

PIET. Stay, stay.

MAL. Dull, dull duke, can lazy pa- [120 tience make lame revenge? O God, for a woman to make a man that which God never created, never made!

PIET. What did God never make?

MAL. A cuckold! To be made a thing that's hoodwinked with kindness, whilst every rascal fillips his brows; to have a coxcomb with egregious horns pinned to a lord's back, every page sporting himself with delightful laughter, whilst he [130 must be the last must know it! Pistols and poniards! Pistols and poniards!

PIET. Death and damnation!

MAL. Lightning and thunder!

PIET. Vengeance and torture!

MAL. *Catzo!*[16]

PIET. O, revenge![17]

MAL. Nay, to select among ten thousand fairs
A lady far inferior to the most,
In fair proportion both of limb and soul;   140
To take her from austerer check of parents,
To make her his by most devoutful rites,
Make her commandress of a better essence
Than is the gorgeous world, even of a man;
To hug her with as raised an appetite
As usurers do their delved-up treasury[18]

[1] Deceit.
[2] The housings of a horse.
[3] Mistress.
[4] That other.
[5] Fancies.
[6] The ape-trainer's call to his monkey.
[7] A game played with a bat, a ball, and a trap.
[8] Tilt at a ring.
[9] Lid.
[10] Cuckold.
[11] A horned one.
[12] Unshell.
[13] Confirmance (?), proof.
[14] A fig for rhyme.
[15] Secret harlot.
[16] An obscure exclamation (It., *cazzo*, penis).
[17] Lines 138–85 are the first significant addition.
[18] Treasure.

(Thinking none tells [1] it but his private
    self);
To meet her spirit in a nimble kiss,
Distilling panting ardor to her heart;
True to her sheets, nay, diets strong his
    blood,   150
To give her height of hymeneal sweets—
PIET. O God!
MAL. Whilst she lisps, and gives him some
    court *quelquechose*,[2]
Made only to provoke, not satiate;
And yet, even then, the thaw of her de-
    light
Flows from lewd heat of apprehension,
Only from strange imagination's rank-
    ness,
That forms the adulterer's presence in
    her soul,
And makes her think she clips [3] the
    foul knave's loins.
PIET. Affliction to my blood's root! [160
MAL. Nay, think, but think what may
proceed of this; adultery is often the
mother of incest.
PIET. Incest?
MAL. Yes, incest. Mark! Mendoza of
his wife begets perchance a daughter;
Mendoza dies; his son marries this daugh-
ter. Say you? Nay, 'tis frequent, not
only probable, but no question often acted,
whilst ignorance, fearless ignorance, [170
clasps his own seed.
PIET. Hideous imagination!
MAL. Adultery! Why, next to the sin
of simony, 'tis the most horrid transgression under the cope of salvation.[4]
PIET. Next to simony?
MAL. Ay, next to simony, in which our
men in next age shall not sin.
PIET. Not sin? Why?
MAL. Because (thanks to some [180
churchmen) our age will leave them nothing to sin with. But adultery, O dullness, should show [5] exemplary punishment, that intemperate bloods may freeze
but to think it. I would dam [6] him and
all his generation; my own hands should
do it; ha, I would not trust heaven with
my vengeance anything.
PIET. Anything, anything, Malevole!
Thou shalt see instantly what temper [190

my spirit holds. Farewell; remember I
forget thee not; farewell.   *Exit Pietro.*
MAL.[7] Farewell.
Lean thoughtfulness, a sallow meditation,
Suck thy veins dry! Distemperance rob
    thy sleep!
The heart's disquiet is revenge most deep;
He that gets blood, the life of flesh but
    spills,[8]
But he that breaks heart's peace, the dear
    soul kills.[9]—
Well, this disguise doth yet afford me
    that
Which kings do seldom hear, or great
    men use,   200
Free speech; and, though my state's
    usurped,
Yet this affected strain gives me a
    tongue
As fetterless as is an emperor's.
I may speak foolishly, ay, knavishly,
Always carelessly, yet no one thinks it
    fashion
To poise [10] my breath, "for he that laughs
    and strikes
Is lightly felt, or seldom struck again."
Duke, I'll torment thee; now my just
    revenge
From thee than crown a richer gem
    shall part.
Beneath God, naught's so dear as a calm
    heart.   210

SCENA QUARTA.

[*The same.*]

Enter Celso.

CEL. My honored lord—
MAL. Peace, speak low; peace! O Celso,
    constant lord,
Thou to whose faith I only rest dis-
    covered,
Thou, one of full ten millions of men,
That lovest virtue only for itself,
Thou in whose hands old Ops [11] may put
    her soul,
Behold forever-banished Altofront,

---

[7] This speech is an addition.
[8] Destroys.
[9] Italics or quotation marks were often used
to mark sententious passages.
[10] Weigh seriously.
[11] The goddess of plenty.

[1] Counts.   [2] Kickshaws, delicacies.   [3] Embraces.
[4] Under the expanse of heaven.
[5] Original reads *show should.*   [6] Stop up, choke.

This Genoa's last year's duke. O truly
noble!
I wanted [1] those old instruments of
state—
Dissemblance and suspect.[2] I could not
time it, [3] Celso;			10
My throne stood like a point in middest
of a circle,
To all of equal nearness; bore with none;
Reined all alike; so slept in fearless virtue,
Suspectless, too suspectless; till the
crowd,
Still lickerous of [4] untried novelties,
Impatient with severer government,
Made strong with Florence, banished
Altofront.
CEL. Strong with Florence! Ay, thence
your mischief rose;
For, when the daughter of the Florentine
Was matched once with this [5] Pietro,
now duke,			20
No stratagem of state untried was left,
Till you of all— [6]
MAL.			Of all was quite bereft.
Alas, Maria too, close prisonéd,
My true-faithed duchess, i' the citadel!
CEL. I'll still adhere; let's mutiny and die.
MAL. O, no, climb not a falling tower,
Celso;
'Tis well held desperation, no zeal,
Hopeless to strive with fate. Peace!
Temporize!
Hope, hope, that never forsak'st the
wretched'st man,
Yet bidd'st me live, and lurk in this
disguise!			30
What, play I well the free-breathed
discontent?
Why, man, we are all philosophical
monarchs
Or natural fools. Celso, the court's afire;
The duchess' sheets will smoke for 't ere
it be long.
Impure Mendoza, that sharp-nosed lord,
that made
The curséd match linked Genoa with
Florence,

Now broad-horns the duke, which he now
knows.
Discord to malcontents is very manna;
When the ranks are burst, then scuffle,
Altofront.
CEL. Ay, but durst—			40
MAL. 'Tis gone; 'tis swallowed like a min-
eral. [7]
Some way 'twill work. Pheut, I'll not
shrink!
"He's resolute who can no lower sink."

[8] *Bilioso entering, Malevole shifteth his
speech.*

MAL. O, the father of Maypoles! Did
you never see a fellow whose strength consisted in his breath, respect in his office,
religion in [9] his lord, and love in himself?
Why, then, behold!
BIL. Signior—
MAL. My right worshipful lord, [50
your court nightcap makes you have a
passing high forehead.
BIL. I can tell you strange news, but I
am sure you know them already: the duke
speaks much good of you.
MAL. Go to, then; and shall you and I
now enter into a strict friendship?
BIL. Second one another?
MAL. Yes.
BIL. Do one another good offices?			60
MAL. Just. What though I called thee
old ox, egregious wittol, [10] broken-bellied
coward, rotten mummy? Yet, since I am
in favor—
BIL. Words, of course, terms of disport.
His grace presents you by me a chain, as
his grateful remembrance for—I am ignorant for what; marry, ye may impart. Yet
howsoever—come, dear friend. Dost know
my son?			70
MAL. Your son?
BIL. He shall eat woodcocks, dance jigs,
make possets, and play at shuttlecock with
any young lord about the court. He has
as sweet a lady, too. Dost know her little
bitch?
MAL. 'Tis a dog, man.
BIL. Believe me, a she-bitch. O, 'tis a

[1] Lacked.			[2] Suspicion.
[3] *I.e.*, could not force myself into time with
conditions.
[4] Craving.			[5] Original reads *his.*
[6] Here and in a few other passages the line
division has been regularized. Some later
passages printed in the original as prose have
been set as verse.

[7] Medicine.
[8] The passage from this point through the
stage direction in l. 103 is an addition.
[9] Original reads *on.*
[10] A man who winks at his own cuckoldry.

good creature! Thou shalt be her servant.
I'll make thee acquainted with my   [80
young wife too. What, I keep her not at
court for nothing! 'Tis grown to supper
time; come to my table; that—anything I
have—stands open to thee.

MAL. (*[Aside] to Cel[so].*) How smooth
    to him that is in state of grace,
  How servile is the rugged'st courtier's
    face!
*What profit, nay, what nature would keep
    down,*
Are heaved [1] *to them are minions to a crown.*
Envious ambition never sates his thirst,
Till, sucking all, he swells and swells,
    and bursts.   90

BIL. I shall now leave you with my
always-best wishes; only let's hold betwixt us a firm correspondence, a mutual
friendly-reciprocal kind of steady-unani-
mous-heartily-leagued—

MAL. Did your signiorship ne'er see
a pigeonhouse that was smooth, round,
and white without, and full of holes and
stink within? Ha' ye not, old courtier?

BIL. O, yes, 'tis the form, the fashion
of them all.   101

MAL. Adieu, my true court friend; farewell, my dear Castilio.[2]   *Exit Bilioso.*

CEL. Yonder's Mendoza.

MAL.   True, the privy-key.
                     Descries Mendoza.

CEL. I take my leave, sweet lord.
                       Exit Celso.

MAL.   'Tis fit; away!

SCENA QUINTA.

[The same.]

Enter Mendoza with three or four Suitors.

MEN. Leave your suits with me; I
can and will. Attend my secretary; leave
me.   *[Exeunt Suitors.]*

MAL. Mendoza, hark ye, hark ye. You
are a treacherous villain, God b' wi' ye!

MEN. Out, you baseborn rascal!

MAL. We are all the sons of heaven,
though a tripe-wife were our mother. Ah,
you whoreson,[3] hot-reined[4] he-marmoset!
Ægistus—didst ever hear of one Ægistus?

MEN. Gistus?   11

---

[1] Lifted.
[2] Alluding to Castiglione, author of *Il Cortegiano* (*The Courtier*).
[3] Rascally.   [4] Lecherous.

MAL. Ay, Ægistus; he was a filthy, incontinent fleshmonger, such a one as thou
art.

MEN. Out, grumbling rogue!

MAL. Orestes, beware Orestes!

MEN. Out, beggar!

MAL. I once shall rise!

MEN. Thou rise?

MAL. Ay, at the resurrection.   20
  "No vulgar seed but once may rise and
    shall;
  No king so huge but fore he die may
    fall."   *Exit.*

MEN. Now, good Elysium! What a
delicious heaven is it for a man to be in a
prince's favor! O sweet God! O pleasure!
O fortune! O all thou best of life! What
should I think, what say, what do, to be a
favorite, a minion? To have a general
timorous respect, observe [5] a man, a   [29
stateful silence in his presence, solitari-
ness in his absence, a confused hum and
busy murmur of obsequious suitors training [6] him, the cloth held up, and way
proclaimed before him, petitionary vassals
licking the pavement with their slavish
knees, whilst some odd palace-lampreels [7]
that engender with snakes, and are full
of eyes on both sides, with a kind of
insinuated humbleness, fix all their delights upon his brow! O blessed state! [40
What a ravishing prospect doth the Olympus of favor yield! Death, I cornute
the duke! Sweet women, most sweet
ladies, nay, angels! By heaven, he is more
accursed than a devil that hates you, or
is hated by you, and happier than a god
that loves you, or is beloved by you. You
preservers of mankind, lifeblood of society,
who would live, nay, who can live without you? O paradise, how majes-   [50
tical is your austerer presence! How
imperiously chaste is your more modest
face! But, O, how full of ravishing at-
traction is your pretty, petulant, languishing, lasciviously-composed countenance!
These amorous smiles, those soul-warming
sparkling glances, ardent as those flames
that singed the world by heedless Phaëton! In body how delicate, in soul how [59
witty, in discourse how pregnant, in life
how wary, in favors how judicious, in day
how sociable, and in night how—!   O

---

[5] Be obsequious to.   [6] Following.   [7] Lampreys.

pleasure unutterable! Indeed, it is most certain, one man cannot deserve only to enjoy a beauteous woman. But a duchess! In despite of Phœbus, I'll write a sonnet instantly in praise of her.   *Exit.*

Scena Sexta.

[*The same.*]

Enter Ferneze ushering Aurelia, Emilia and Maquerelle bearing up her train, Biancha attending; all go out but Aurelia, Maquerelle, and Ferneze.

Aur. And is 't possible? Mendoza slight me! Possible?

Fer. Possible! What can be strange in him that's drunk with favor,
    Grows insolent with grace?—Speak, Maquerelle, speak.

Maq. To speak feelingly, more, more richly in solid sense than worthless words, give me those jewels of your ears to receive my enforced duty. As for my part, 'tis well known. (*Ferneze privately feeds Maquerelle's hands with jewels during* [10 *this speech.*) I can put [1] anything, can bear patiently with any man. But, when I heard he wronged your precious sweetness, I was enforced to take deep offense. 'Tis most certain he loves Emilia with high appetite; and, as she told me (as you know we women impart our secrets one to another), when she repulsed his suit, in that he was possessed with your endeared grace, Mendoza most ingratefully renounced [20 all faith to you.

Fer. Nay, called you—speak, Maquerelle, speak.

Maq. By heaven, witch, dried bisque, [2] and contested blushlessly he loved you but for a spurt or so.

Fer. For maintenance.

Maq. Advancement and regard.

Aur. O villain! O impudent Mendoza!

Maq. Nay, he is the rustiest-[3] [30 jawed,[4] the foulest-mouthed knave in railing against our sex! He will rail against women—

Aur. How? How?

Maq. I am ashamed to speak 't, I.

Aur. I love to hate him. Speak.

Maq. Why, when Emilia scorned his base unsteadiness, the black-throated rascal scolded, and said—

Aur. What?

Maq. Troth, 'tis too shameless.   40

Aur. What said he?

Maq. Why, that, at four, women were fools; at fourteen, drabs; at forty, bawds; at fourscore, witches; and [at][5] a hundred, cats.

Aur. O unlimitable impudency!

Fer. But, as for poor Ferneze's fixéd heart,
    Was never shadeless meadow drier parched
    Under the scorching heat of heaven's Dog
    Than is my heart with your enforcing[6] eyes.   50

Maq. A hot simile!

Fer. Your smiles have been my heaven, your frowns my hell.
    O, pity, then! Grace should with beauty dwell.

Maq. Reasonable perfect, by 'r Lady.

Aur. I will love thee, be it but in despite
    Of that Mendoza. "Witch," Ferneze, "witch"!
    Ferneze, thou art the duchess' favorite;
    Be faithful, private; but 'tis dangerous.

Fer. "His love is liveless that for love fears breath;
    The worst that's due to sin, O, would 'twere death!"   60

Aur. Enjoy my favor. I will be sick instantly and take physic; therefore in depth of night visit—

Maq. Visit her chamber, but conditionally: you shall not offend her bed, by this diamond!

Fer. By this diamond.
                 Gives it to Maquerelle.

Maq. Nor tarry longer than you please, by this ruby!

Fer. By this ruby.   *Gives again.*   70

Maq. And that the door shall not creak.

Fer. And that the door shall not creak.

Maq. Nay, but swear.

Fer. By this purse.   *Gives her his purse.*

Maq. Go to, I'll keep your oaths for you. Remember, visit.

Enter Mendoza, reading a sonnet.

Aur. "Dried biscuit"!—Look where the base wretch comes.

Men. "Beauty's life, heaven's model, love's queen—"   80

---

[1] Endure.   [2] Biscuit.   [3] Filthiest.
[4] From Quartos. Original reads *Jade.*
[5] Supplied by Bullen.   [6] Ravishing.

MAQ. [*Aside.*] That's his Emilia.

MEN. "Nature's triumph, best on earth—"

MAQ. [*Aside.*] Meaning Emilia.

MEN. "Thou only wonder that the world hath seen—"

MAQ. [*Aside.*] That's Emilia.

AUR. [*Aside.*] Must I then hear her praised?—Mendoza!

MEN. Madam, your excellency is [90 graciously encountered; I have been writing passicnate flashes in honor of—

Exit Fer[neze].

AUR. Out, villain, villain! O judgment, where have been my eyes? What bewitched election made me dote on thee? What sorcery made me love thee? But be gone; bury thy head. O, that I could do more than loathe thee! Hence, worst of ill! No reason ask; our reason is our will.

Exit with Maquerelle.

MEN. Women! Nay, furies; nay, [100 worse, for they torment only the bad, but women good and bad. Damnation of mankind! Breath, hast thou praised them for this? And is't you, Ferneze, are wriggled into smock-grace? Sit sure. O, that I could rail against these monsters in nature, models of hell, curse of the earth, women that dare attempt anything, and what they attempt they care not how they accomplish; without all premeditation or prevention; [110 rash in asking, desperate in working, impatient in suffering, extreme in desiring, slaves unto appetite, mistresses in dissembling, only constant in unconstancy, only perfect in counterfeiting. Their words are feigned, their eyes forged, their sights [1] dissembled, their looks counterfeit, their hair false, their given hopes deceitful, their very breath artificial. *Their blood is their only god; bad clothes and old age are* [120 *only the devils they tremble at.* That I could rail now!

SCENA SEPTA.

[*The same.*]

Enter Pietro, his sword drawn.

PIET. A mischief fill thy throat, thou foul-jawed slave!

Say thy prayers.

MEN.   I ha' forgot um.

[1] Sighs.

PIET.   Thou shalt die!

MEN. So shalt thou. I am heart-mad.

PIET.   I am horn-mad.[2]

MEN. Extreme mad.

PIET.   Monstrously mad.

MEN.   Why?

PIET. Why? Thou, thou hast dishonoréd my bed.

MEN. I? Come, come, sit; here's my bare heart to thee,

As steady as is this center to the glorious world.

And yet, hark, thou art a cornuto—but by me?

PIET. Yes, slave, by thee.

MEN. Do not, do not with tart and spleenful breath   10

Lose him can lose thee. I offend my duke?

Bear record, O ye dumb and raw-aired nights,

How vigilant my sleepless eyes have been

To watch the traitor! Record, thou spirit of truth,

With what debasement I ha' thrown myself

To under offices, only to learn

The truth, the party, time, the means, the place,

By whom, and when, and where thou wert disgraced!

And am I paid with "slave"? Hath my intrusion

To places private and prohibited,   20

Only to observe the closer passages

(Heaven knows with vows of revelation),

Made me suspected, made me deemed a villain?

What rogue hath wronged us?

PIET.   Mendoza, I may err.

MEN. Err? 'Tis too mild a name; but err and err,

Run giddy with suspect fore through me thou know

That which most creatures, save thyself, do know.

Nay, since my service hath so loathed reject,[3]

Fore I'll reveal, shalt find them clipped together.

PIET. Mendoza, thou know'st I am [30 a most plain-breasted [4] man.

[2] Intensive, with a double meaning.
[3] Rejection.   [4] Plain-spoken.

MEN. The fitter to make a cuckold!
Would your brows were most plain too!
PIET. Tell me; indeed, I heard thee rail.
MEN. At women, true. Why, what cold
    fleam [1] could choose,
  Knowing a lord so honest, virtuous,
  So boundless-loving, bounteous, fair-
    shaped, sweet,
  To be contemned, abused, defamed,
    made cuckold?
Heart! I hate all women for 't—sweet
sheets, wax lights, antique bedposts, [40
cambric smocks, villainous curtains, arras
pictures, oiled hinges, and all the tongue-
tied lascivious witnesses of great creatures'
wantonness! What salvation can you
expect?
PIET. Wilt thou tell me?
MEN. Why, you may find it yourself;
observe, observe.
PIET. I ha' not the patience. Wilt thou
deserve [2] me? Tell, give it.   50
MEN. Take 't! Why, Ferneze is the
man, Ferneze. I'll prove 't; this night you
shall take him in your sheets. Will 't serve?
PIET. It will; my bosom's in some peace.
    Till night!
MEN. What?
PIET. Farewell.
MEN.   God! How weak a lord are you!
  Why, do you think there is no more but
    so?
PIET. Why?
MEN.   Nay, then will I presume to
    counsel you.
  It should be thus. You with some guard
    upon the sudden
  Break into the princess' chamber; I stay
    behind,
  Without the door through which he needs
    must pass.   60
  Ferneze flies—let him. To me he comes.
    He's killed
  By me—observe—by me. You follow; [3]
    I rail,
  And seem to save the body. Duchess
    comes,
  On whom (respecting her advancéd birth
  And your fair nature) I know, nay, I do
    know,
  No violence must be used. She comes; I
    storm;

I praise, excuse Ferneze, and still main-
    tain
  The duchess' honor; she for this loves me.
  I honor you, shall know her soul, you
    mine.
  Then naught shall she contrive in
    vengeance   70
  (As women are most thoughtful in re-
    venge)
  Of her Ferneze, but you shall sooner
    know' t
  Than she can think 't. Thus shall his
    death come sure;
  Your duchess brain-caught, so your life
    secure.
PIET. It is too well, my bosom and my
    heart!
  "When nothing helps, cut off the rotten
    part."   *Exit.*
MEN. "Who cannot feign friendship can
ne'er produce the effects of hatred." Hon-
est fool duke, subtile lascivious duchess, silly
novice Ferneze, I do laugh at ye. My [80
brain is in labor till it produce mischief,
and I feel sudden throes, proofs sensible the
issue is at hand.
  "As bears shape young, so I'll form my
    device,
  Which grown proves horrid. Vengeance
    makes men wise."   [*Exit.*] [4]

Enter Malevole and Passarello.

MAL. Fool, most happily encountered!
Canst sing, fool?
PASS. Yes, I can sing, fool, if you'll bear
the burden; [5] and I can play upon instruments, scurvily, as gentlemen do. O, [90
that I had been gelded! I should then have
been a fat fool for a chamber, a squeaking
fool for a tavern, and a private fool for all
the ladies.
MAL. You are in good case since you
came to court, fool. What, garded, [6]
garded!
PASS. Yes, faith, even as footmen and
bawds wear velvet, not for an ornament
of honor, but for a badge of drudgery; [100
for, now the duke is discontented, I am
fain to fool him asleep every night.
MAL. What are his griefs?
PASS. He hath sore eyes.
MAL. I never observed so much.

---

[1] Phlegm.   [3] Original reads *fellow.*
[2] Be serviceable to.

[4] The remainder of the scene is an addition.
[5] Sing the bass.   [6] Trimmed up.

Pass. Horrible sore eyes; and so hath every cuckold, for the roots of the horns spring in the eyeballs, and that's the reason the horn of a cuckold is as tender as his eye, or as that growing in the woman's [110 forehead, twelve years since, that could not endure to be touched.[1] The duke hangs down his head like a columbine.

Mal. Passarello, why do great men beg fools?[2]

Pass. As the Welshman stole rushes when there was nothing else to filch—only to keep begging in fashion.

Mal. Pooh, thou givest no good reason; thou speakest like a fool.   120

Pass. Faith, I utter small fragments, as your knight courts your city widow with jingling of his gilt spurs, advancing his bush-[3] beard, and taking tobacco. This is all the mirror of their knightly complements.[4] Nay, I shall talk when my tongue is a-going once; 'tis like a citizen on horseback, evermore in a false gallop.

Mal. And how doth Maquerelle fare nowadays?   130

Pass. Faith, I was wont to salute her as our English women are at their first landing in Flushing[5]—I would call her whore. But now that antiquity leaves her as an old piece of plastic[6] t' work by, I only ask her how her rotten teeth fare every morning, and so leave her. She was the first that ever invented perfumed smocks for the gentlewomen, and woolen shoes for fear of creaking for the visitant. She were [140 an excellent lady but that her face peeleth like Muscovy glass.[7]

Mal. And how doth thy old lord, that hath wit enough to be a flatterer, and conscience enough to be a knave?

Pass. O, excellent; he keeps beside me fifteen jesters to instruct him in the art of fooling, and utters their jests in private to the duke and duchess. He'll lie like to your Switzer or lawyer; he'll be of any side [150 for most money.

Mal. I am in haste; be brief.

Pass. As your fiddler when he is paid. He'll thrive, I warrant you, while your young courtier stands like Good Friday in Lent; men long to see it, because more fatting days come after it; else he's the leanest and pitifull'st actor in the whole pageant. Adieu, Malevole.

Mal. [Aside.] O world most vild,[8] when thy loose vanities,   160
Taught by this fool, do make the fool seem wise!

Pass. You'll know me again, Malevole.

Mal. O, ay, by that velvet.

Pass. Ay, as a pettifogger by his buckram bag. I am as common in the court as an hostess's lips in the country; knights, and clowns, and knaves, and all share me; the court cannot possibly be without me. Adieu, Malevole.   [Exeunt.]

ACTUS SECUNDUS. SCENA PRIMA.

[A hall outside the Duchess' chamber.]

Enter Mendoza with a sconce,[9] to observe Ferneze's entrance, who, whilst the act[10] is playing, enter unbraced,[11] two Pages before him with lights; is met by Maquerelle and conveyed in; the Pages are sent away.

Men. He's caught; the woodcock's head is i' th' noose.
Now treads Ferneze in dangerous path of lust,
Swearing his sense is merely[12] deified.
The fool grasps clouds, and shall beget centaurs;
And now, in strength of panting, faint delight,
The goat bids heaven envy him.—Good goose,
I can afford thee nothing but the poor comfort of calamity, pity.
"Lust's like the plummets hanging on clock lines,
Will ne'er ha' done till all is quite undone."
Such is the course salt[13] sallow lust doth run,   10
Which thou shalt try. I'll be revenged.
Duke, thy suspect,
Duchess, thy disgrace, Ferneze, thy rivalship

---

[1] A pamphlet describing this monstrosity was printed in 1588.   [4] Accomplishments.
[2] Seek the custody of idiots to enjoy their estates.   [6] Sculpture.   [7] Talc.
[3] Preceding seven words from corrected quarto.
[5] At this time controlled by the English.

[8] Vile.   [11] With garments unfastened.
[9] Lantern.   [12] Absolutely.
[10] Entr'acte music.   [13] Salacious.

Shall have swift vengeance. Nothing so
holy,
No band of nature so strong,
No law of friendship so sacred,
But I'll profane, burst, violate,
Fore I'll endure disgrace, contempt, and
poverty.
Shall I, whose very "Hum" strook all
heads bare,
Whose face made silence, creaking of
whose shoe
Forced the most private passages fly
ope,   20
Scrape like a servile dog at some latched
door;
Learn now to make a leg [1] and cry,
"Beseech ye,
Pray ye, is such a lord within?"; be
awed
At some odd usher's scoffed formality?
First sear [2] my brains! "*Unde cadis non
quo, refert.*" [3]
My heart cries, "Perish all!" How!
How! "What fate
Can once avoid revenge, that's desper-
ate?"
I'll to the duke. If all should ope—If?
Tush!
"Fortune still dotes on those who cannot
blush."   [*Exit.*]

SCENA SECUNDA.

[*The same.*]

*Enter Malevole at one door; Biancha,
Emilia, and Maquerelle at the other
door.*

MAL. Bless ye, cast [4] a ladies!—Ha,
dip-sauce! [5] How dost thou, old coal?
MAQ. Old coal?
MAL. Ay, old coal; methinks thou liest
like a brand under billets of green wood.
He that will inflame a young wench's
heart, let him lay close to her an old coal
that hath first been fired, a panderess, my
half-burnt lint, who, though thou canst
[not] flame thyself, yet art able to set a   [10

[1] Bow.
[2] Emended by Bullen. Original reads *seate*.
[3] "No matter whither, but from whence you
fall" (Seneca, *Thyestes*, l. 929. *Cf. Antonio and
Mellida*, Part I, III, ii, 115).
[4] Pair.
[5] With an allusion to *dipsas*, a fabulous snake,
and perhaps to Lyly's Dipsas.

thousand virgins' tapers afire.—[*Turns
to Biancha.*] And how doth Janivere thy
husband, my little periwinkle? Is he
troubled with the cough of th' lungs still?
Does he hawk a-nights still? He will not
bite.
BIAN. No, by my troth, I took him with
his mouth empty of old teeth.
MAL. And he took thee with thy belly
full of young bones. Marry, he took   [20
his maim by the stroke of his enemy.
BIAN. And I mine by the stroke of my
friend.
MAL. The close stock! [6]   O mortal
wench! Lady, ha' ye now no restoratives [7]
for your decayed Jasons? Look ye: crabs'
guts baked, distilled ox-pith, the pul-
verized hairs of a lion's upper lip, jelly of
cock sparrows, he-monkeys' marrow, or
pouldre [8] of fox-stones? And whither   [30
are you ambling now?
BIAN. To bed, to bed.
MAL. Do your husbands lie with ye?
BIAN. That were country fashion, i' faith.
MAL. Ha' ye no foregoers [9] about you?
Come, whither in good deed, la [10] now?
BIAN. In good indeed, la now, to eat
the most miraculously, admirably, astonish-
able-composed posset with three curds,   [39
without any drink. Will ye help me with
a he-fox?—Here's the duke.
                    The Ladies go out.
MAL. [11] (*To Bian[cha].*) Fried frogs are
very good, and Frenchlike too!

SCENA TERTIA.

[*The same.*]

*Enter Duke Pietro, Count Celso, Count
Equato, Bilioso, Ferrard, and Mendoza.*

PIET. The night grows deep and foul.
What hour is 't?
CEL. Upon the stroke of twelve.
MAL. Save ye, duke!
PIET. From thee! Begone, I do not love
thee! Let me see thee no more; we are
displeased.
MAL. Why, God be with thee! Heaven
hear my curse—may thy wife and thee
live long together!   10
PIET. Begone, sirrah!

[6] A thrust in fencing.   [9] Ushers.   [10] Lo, look.
[7] Aphrodisiacs.   [11] This speech is an addition.
[8] Powder.

MAL. "When Arthur first in court began"—Agamemnon—Menelaus—was ever
any duke a cornuto?

PIET. Begone hence!

MAL. What religion wilt thou be of
next?

MEN. Out with him!

MAL. With most servile patience time
will come

When wonder of thy error will strike
dumb   20

Thy bezzled [1] sense.—Slaves! Ay, favor!
Ay, marry, shall he rise?

"Good God! How subtile hell doth
flatter vice,

Mounts him aloft, and makes him seem
to fly,

As fowl the tortoise mocked, who to the
sky

Th' ambitious shellfish raised! Th' end
of all

Is only that from height he might dead
fall." [2]

BIL. Why, when? Out, ye rogue! Begone,
ye rascal!

MAL. I shall now leave ye with all my
best wishes.   30

BIL. Out, ye cur!

MAL. Only let's hold together a firm
correspondence.

BIL. Out!

MAL. A mutual-friendly-reciprocal-per-
petual kind of steady-unanimous-heartily-
leagued—

BIL. Hence, ye gross-jawed, peasantly
—out, go!

MAL. Adieu, pigeon house; thou burr,
that only stickest to nappy fortunes. [41
The sarpego,[3] the strangury,[4] an eternal,
uneffectual priapism seize thee!

BIL. Out, rogue!

MAL. Mayest thou be a notorious wit-
tolly pander to thine own wife, and yet
get no office, but live to be the utmost
misery of mankind, a beggarly cuckold!
                                    Exit.

PIET. It shall be so.

MEN. It must be so, for, where great states
revenge,   50

"'Tis requisite the parts with piety [5]

(And loft [6] respect forbears) be closely
dogged.

Lay one into his breast shall sleep with
him,

Feed in the same dish, run in self-
faction,

Who may discover any shape of danger;

For once disgraced, displayéd in offense,

It makes man blushless, and man is
(all confess)

More prone to vengeance than to grate-
fulness.

Favors are writ in dust; but stripes we feel
Depravéd nature stamps in lasting steel."

PIET. You shall be leagued with the [61
duchess.

EQU. The plot is very good.

MEN. You shall both kill, and seem the
corse to save.

FER. A most fine brain-trick.

CEL. (*Tacite.*) [7]   Of a most cunning
knave.

PIET. My lords, the heavy action we intend

Is death and shame, two of the ugliest
shapes

That can confound a soul. Think, think
of it.

I strike, but yet, like him that gainst
stone walls

Directs his shafts, rebounds in his own
face;   70

My lady's shame is mine, O God,
'tis mine!

Therefore I do conjure all secrecy.

Let it be as very little as may be, pray
ye, as may be.

Make frightless entrance, salute her with
soft eyes,

Strain [8] naught with blood.   Only
Ferneze dies,

But not before her brows. O gentlemen,

God knows I love her! Nothing else
but this.

I am not well. If grief, that sucks veins
dry,

Rivels [9] the skin, casts ashes in men's
faces,

Bedulls the eye, unstrengthens all the
blood,   80

---

[1] Drunken.   [5] Devotion.
[2] Lines 27–48 are an addition.
[3] Serpigo, a skin eruption.
[4] Disease of the bladder.

[6] Proud.   [7] Silently, aside.
[8] Do violence to; or perhaps a misprint for
stain.   [9] Wrinkles.

Chance to remove me to another
world,
As sure I once must die, let him succeed.
I have no child; all that my youth begot
Hath been your loves, which shall in-
herit [1] me;
Which as it ever shall, I do conjure it,
Mendoza may succeed; he's noble born,
With me of much desert.
CEL. (*Tacite.*) Much!
PIET. Your silence answers, "Ay."
I thank you. Come on now. O, that I
might die   90
Before her shame's displayed! Would
I were forced
To burn my father's tomb, unheal [2]
his bones,
And dash them in the dirt, rather than
this!
This both the living and the dead of-
fends:
"Sharp surgery where naught but death
amends."   *Exit with the others.*

SCENA QUARTA.

[*The same.*]

*Enter Maquerelle, Emilia, and Biancha
with the posset.*

MAQ. Even here it is, three curds in
three regions individually distinct, most
methodical according to art composed,
without any drink.
BIAN. Without any drink?
MAQ. Upon my honor. Will you sit
and eat?   [*They eat.*]
EM. Good! The composure, the receipt,
how is 't?
MAQ. 'Tis a pretty pearl; by this   [10
pearl (how does it with me?) [3] thus it is:
Seven-and-thirty yelks of Barbary hens'
eggs; eighteen spoonfuls and a half of
the juice of cock sparrow bones; one ounce,
three drams, four scruples, and one quarter
of the syrup of Ethiopian dates; sweetened
with three-quarters of a pound of pure
candied Indian eryngoes; [4] strewed over
with the powder of pearl of America, amber of Cataia, and lamb-stones of [20
Muscovia.
BIAN. Trust me, the ingredients are

very cordial, and, no question, good, and
most powerful in restoration.
MAQ. I know not what you mean by restoration, but this it doth—it purifieth the
blood, smootheth the skin, enliveneth the
eye, strengtheneth the veins, mundi-
fieth [5] the teeth, comforteth the stomach,
fortifieth the back, and quickeneth the [30
wit; that's all.
EM. By my troth, I have eaten but two
spoonfuls, and methinks I could discourse
most swiftly and wittily already.
MAQ. Have you the art to seem honest? [6]
BIAN. I thank advice and practice.
MAQ. Why, then, eat me of this posset,
quicken your blood, and preserve your
beauty. Do you know Doctor Plaster- [40
face? By this curd, he is the most exquisite
in forging of veins, sprightening [7] of eyes,
dyeing of hair, sleeking of skins, blushing
of cheeks, surphling [8] of breasts, blanch-
ing and bleaching of teeth, that ever
made an old lady gracious by torchlight;
by this curd, la!
BIAN. Well, we are resolved; what God
has given us we'll cherish.
MAQ. Cherish anything saving your [50
husband; keep him not too high, lest he
leap the pale. But, for your beauty, let
it be your saint; bequeath two hours to
it every morning in your closet. I ha'
been young, and yet, in my conscience,
I am not above five-and-twenty; but,
believe me, preserve and use your beauty;
for youth and beauty once gone, we are
like beehives without honey, out-a-fashion,
apparel that no man will wear; there- [60
fore use me your beauty.
EM. Ay, but men say—
MAQ. Men say! Let men say what they
will. Life a woman! They are ignorant
of your wants. The more in years, the
more in perfection they grow; if they lose
youth and beauty, they gain wisdom and
discretion. But when our beauty fades,
good night with us. There cannot be an
uglier thing to see than an old woman, [70
from which—O pruning, pinching, and
painting!—deliver all sweet beauties!
[*Music within.*]
BIAN. Hark! Music!

---

[1] Be heir to.
[2] Uncover.
[3] How does it become me?
[4] Candied sea-holly.
[5] Cleanseth.
[6] Virtuous.
[7] Brightening.
[8] Tinting.

MAQ. Peace, 'tis in the duchess' bed-chamber. Good rest, most prosperously-graced ladies.

EM. Good night, sentinel.

BIAN. Night, dear Maquerelle.

Exeunt all but Maq[uerelle].

MAQ. May my posset's operation send you my wit and honesty; and me, your   [80 youth and beauty. The pleasing'st rest!

Exit Maq[uerelle].

SCENA QUINTA.

[*The same.*]

A song [within].

Whilst the song is singing, enter Mendoza with his sword drawn, standing ready to murder Ferneze as he flies from the Duchess' chamber.

ALL. [*Within.*] Strike, strike!

AUR. [*Within.*] Save my Ferneze! O, save my Ferneze!

Enter Ferneze in his shirt, and is received upon Mendoza's sword.

ALL. [*Within.*] Follow, pursue!

AUR. [*Within.*] O, save Ferneze!

MEN. Pierce, pierce!—Thou shallow fool, drop there!

"He that attempts a princess' lawless love

Must have broad hands, close heart, with Argus' eyes,

And back of Hercules, or else he dies."

Thrusts his rapier in Fer[neze].

Enter Aurelia, Duke Pietro, Ferrard, Bilioso, Celso, and Equato.

ALL. Follow, follow!

MEN. Stand off, forbear, ye most uncivil lords!   10

PIET. Strike!

MEN.   Do not; tempt not a man re-solved.

Would you, inhuman murtherers, more than death?

AUR. O poor Ferneze!

MEN. Alas, now all defense too late!

AUR.   He's dead.

PIET. I am sorry for our shame.—Go to your bed;

Weep not too much, but leave some tears to shed

When I am dead.

AUR. What, weep for thee? My soul no tears shall find.

PIET. Alas, alas, that women's souls are blind!

MEN. Betray such beauty! Murther such youth! Contemn civility!   20

He loves him not that rails not at him.

PIET. Thou canst not move us; we have blood enough.—

And please you, lady, we have quite for-got

All your defects; if not, why, then—

AUR. Not.

PIET. Not. The best of rest; good night.

Exit Pietro with other Courtiers.

AUR. Despite go with thee!

MEN. Madam, you ha' done me foul disgrace; you have wronged him much, loves [1] you too much. Go to, your soul   [30 knows you have.

AUR. I think I have.

MEN. Do you but think so?

AUR. Nay, sure, I have; my eyes have witnessed thy love. Thou hast stood too firm for me.

MEN. Why, tell me, fair-cheeked lady, who even in tears

Art powerfully beauteous, what unad-vised passion

Strook ye into such a violent heat against me?

Speak, what mischief wronged us? What devil injured us?   40

Speak.

AUR. That thing ne'er worthy of the name of man, Ferneze;

Ferneze swore thou lov'st Emilia;

Which to advance, with most reproach-ful breath,

Thou both didst blemish and denounce my love.

MEN. Ignoble villain! Did I for this be-stride

Thy wounded limbs? For this? O God! For this

Sunk all my hopes, and with my hopes my life?

Ripped bare my throat unto the hang-man's ax?—   49

Thou most dishonored trunk!—Emilia!

[1] *I.e.*, who loves.

By life, I know her not—Emilia—!
Did you believe him?

Aur.   Pardon me, I did.

Men. Did you? And thereupon you gracéd him?

Aur. I did.

Men. Took him to favor, nay, even clasped with him?

Aur. Alas, I did!

Men.   This night?

Aur.   This night.

Men. And in your lustful twines the duke took you?

Aur. A most sad truth.

Men. O God, O God! How we dull honest souls,
Heavy-brained men, are swallowed in the bogs   60
Of a deceitful ground, whilst nimble bloods,
Light-jointed spirits, spent,[1] cut good men's throats,
And scape! Alas, I am too honest for this age,
Too full of fleam and heavy steadiness;
Stood still whilst this slave cast a noose about me;
Nay, then to stand in honor of him and her
Who had even sliced my heart!

Aur.   Come, I did err,
And am most sorry I did err.

Men. Why, we are both but dead; the duke hates us.
"And those whom princes do once groundly[2] hate,   70
Let them provide to die, as sure as fate.
Prevention is the heart of policy."

Aur. Shall we murder him?

Men. Instantly?

Aur. Instantly! Before he casts a plot,
Or further blaze my honor's much-known blot,
Let's murther him!

Men. I would do much for you; will ye marry me?

Aur. I'll make thee duke. We are of Medicis;   79
Florence our friend; in court my faction
Not meanly strengthful; the duke then dead;
We well prepared for change; the multitude

Irresolutely reeling; we in force;
Our party seconded; the kingdom mazed—
No doubt of swift success; all shall be graced.

Men. You do confirm me; we are resolute.
Tomorrow look for change; rest confident.
'Tis now about the immodest waist of night;
The mother of moist dew with pallid light
Spreads gloomy shades about the numbéd earth.   90
Sleep, sleep, whilst we contrive our mischief's birth.
This man I'll get inhumed. Farewell; to bed.
Ay, kiss the pillow; dream the duke is dead.   *Exit Aurelia.*
So, so, good night. How fortune dotes on impudence!
I am in private the adopted son of yon good prince.
I must be duke. Why, if I must, I must!
Most seely[3] lord, name me! O heaven!
I see God made honest fools to maintain crafty knaves.
The duchess is wholly mine too; must kill her husband
To quit her shame. Much![4] Then marry her! Ay.   100
O, I grow proud in prosperous treachery!
As wrastlers clip, so I'll embrace you all,
Not to support, but to procure your fall.

Enter Malevole.

Mal. God arrest thee!

Men. At whose suit?

Mal. At the devil's. Ah, you treacherous, damnable monster!
How dost? How dost, thou treacherous rogue?
Ah, ye rascal! I am banished the court, sirrah.

Men. Prithee, let's be acquainted; I do love thee, faith.   110

Mal. At your service, by the Lord, la! Shall's go to supper? Let's be once drunk together, and so unite a most virtuously strengthened friendship. Shall's, Huguenot?[5] Shall 's?

---

[1] Exhausted, dissolute.   [2] Completely.
[3] Silly, simple.   [4] Great! Excellent!
[5] Confederate (Ger., *Eidgenoss*).

MEN. Wilt fall upon my chamber to-morrow morn?

MAL. As a raven to a dunghill. They say there's one dead here—pricked for the pride of the flesh.   120

MEN. Ferneze. There he is; prithee, bury him.

MAL. O, most willingly; I mean to turn pure Rochelle [1] churchman, I.

MEN. Thou churchman! Why, why?

MAL. Because I'll live lazily, rail upon authority, deny kings' supremacy in things indifferent, and be a pope in mine own parish.   129

MEN. Wherefore dost thou think churches were made?

MAL. To scour plowshares; I have seen oxen plow up altars; "*et nunc seges ubi Sion fuit.*" [2]

MEN. Strange!

MAL. Nay, monstrous! I ha' seen a sumptuous steeple turned to a stinking privy; more beastly, the sacred'st place made a dogs' kennel; nay, most inhuman, the stoned coffins of long-dead Chris- [140 tians burst up, and made hogs' troughs: *Hic finis Priami.* [3] Shall I ha' some sack and cheese at thy chamber? Good night, good mischievous incarnate devil; good night, Mendoza; ah, you inhuman villain, good night! Night, fub. [4]

MEN. Good night; tomorrow morn.
           Exit Mendoza.

MAL. Ay, I will come, friendly damna-tion, I will come. I do descry crosspoints: [5] honesty and courtship straddle as far [150 asunder as a true Frenchman's legs.

FER. O!

MAL. Proclamations! More proclama-tions!

FER. O! A surgeon!

MAL. Hark! Lust cries for a surgeon. What news from Limbo? How doth the grand cuckold, Lucifer?

FER. O, help, help! Conceal and save me.   160
Ferneze stirs, and Malevole helps him up and conveys him away.

MAL. Thy shame more than thy wounds do grieve me far;

[1] Where persecuted Huguenots took refuge.
[2] Paraphrased from Ovid: "Now the corn grows where Sion stood."
[3] Here the end of Priam.
[4] Impostor.   [5] A step in dancing.

"Thy wounds but leave upon thy flesh some scar;
But fame ne'er heals, still rankles worse and worse;
Such is of uncontrolléd lust the curse.
Think what it is in lawless sheets to lie;
But, O, Ferneze, what in lust to die!
Then thou that shame respects, O, fly converse
With women's eyes and lisping wanton-ness!
Stick candles gainst a virgin wall's white back;
If they not burn, yet at the least they'll black."   170
Come, I'll convey thee to a private port,
Where thou shalt live (O happy man!) from court.
The beauty of the day begins to rise,
From whose bright form night's heavy shadow flies.
Now gins [6] close plots to work; the scene grows full,
And craves his eyes who hath a solid skull. [7]
          Exeunt.

ACTUS TERTIUS. SCENA PRIMA.

[*A room in the Duke's palace.*]

Enter Pietro the Duke, Mendoza, Count Equato, and Bilioso.

PIET. 'Tis grown to youth of day; how shall we waste this light?
My heart's more heavy than a tyrant's crown.
Shall we go hunt? Prepare for field.
          Exit Equato.

MEN. Would ye could be merry!

PIET. Would God I could! Mendoza, bid um haste.   *Exit Mendoza.*
I would fain shift place; O vain relief!
"Sad souls may well change place, but not change grief."
As deer, being struck, fly thorough many soils, [8]
Yet still the shaft sticks fast, so—

BIL. A good old simile, my honest lord.   10

PIET. I am not much unlike to some sick man
That long desired hurtful drink; at last

[6] Begins.   [7] Sound head.   [8] Streams.

Swills in and drinks his last, ending at
once
Both life and thirst. O, would I ne'er
had known
My own dishonor! Good God, that men
should
Desire to search out that which, being
found, kills all
Their joy of life! To taste the tree of
knowledge,
And then be driven from out paradise!
Canst give me some comfort?
BIL. My lord, I have some books [20
which have been dedicated to my honor,
and I ne'er read um, and yet they had
very fine names—*Physic for Fortune,
Lozenges of Sanctified Sincerity*, very pretty
works of curates, scriveners, and school-
masters. Marry, I remember one Seneca,
Lucius Annæus Seneca—
PIET. Out upon him! He writ of tem-
perance and fortitude, yet lived like a
voluptuous epicure, and died like an [30
effeminate coward.—
Haste thee to Florence.
Here, take our letters; see um sealed;
away!
Report in private to the honored duke
His daughter's forced disgrace; tell him
at length
We know too much; due compliments
advance.
"There's naught that's safe and sweet
but ignorance."   *Exit Duke*.[1]

Enter Bilioso [2] *and Bianc[h]a*.[4]

BIL. Madam, I am going ambassador
for Florence; 'twill be great charges to me.
BIAN. No matter, my lord, you [40
have the lease of two manors come out next
Christmas; you may lay your tenants on
the greater rack for it; and, when you come
home again, I'll teach you how you shall
get two hundred pounds a year by your
teeth.
BILL. How, madam?
BIAN. Cut off so much from housekeeping; that which is saved by the teeth,
you know, is got by the teeth.   50
BIL. Fore God, and so I may; I am in
wondrous credit, lady.

BIAN. See the use of flattery; I did
ever counsel you to flatter greatness, and
you have profited well. Any man that will
do so shall be sure to be like your Scotch
barnacle,[3] now a block, instantly a worm,
and presently a great goose. This it is to
rot and putrefy in the bosom of greatness.
BIL. Thou art ever my politician. [60
O, how happy is that old lord that hath a
politician to his young lady! I'll have
fifty gentlemen shall attend upon me.
Marry, the most of them shall be farmer's
sons, because they shall bear their own
charges; and they shall go appareled thus—
in sea-water-green suits, ash-color cloaks,
watchet [4] stockings, and popinjay-green
feathers. Will not the colors do excellent?
BIAN. Out upon 't! They'll look like [70
citizens riding to their friends at Whitsuntide, their apparel just so many several
parishes.[5]
BIL. I'll have it so; and Passarello, my
fool, shall go along with me; marry, he
shall be in velvet.
BIAN. A fool in velvet?
BIL. Ay, 'tis common for your fool to
wear satin; I'll have mine in velvet.   79
BIAN. What will you wear, then, my
lord?
BIL. Velvet too; marry, it shall be embroidered, because I'll differ from the fool
somewhat. I am horribly troubled with
the gout; nothing grieves me but that my
doctor hath forbidden me wine, and you
know your ambassador must drink. Didst
thou ask thy doctor what was good for
the gout?   89
BIAN. Yes; he said ease, wine, and
women were good for it.
BIL. Nay, thou hast such a wit! What
was good to cure it, said he?
BIAN. Why, the rack. All your em-
pirics[6] could never do the like cure upon
the gout the rack did in England, or your
Scotch boot.[7] The French harlequin[8] will
instruct you.
BIL. Surely, I do wonder how thou,
having for the most part of thy life- [100

---

[1] The rest of this scene is an addition.
[2] Apparently, however, he has really remained
on the stage.

[3] "It was formerly thought that this species of
shell-fish, which is found on timber exposed to
the action of the sea, became, when broken off,
a kind of geese" (Halliwell).   [4] Pale blue.
[5] *I.e.*, mismatched.   [6] Quacks.
[7] Instrument of torture.
[8] The wonder-working magician descended
from the commedia dell'arte.

time been a country body, shouldst have so good a wit.

BIAN. Who, I? Why, I have been a courtier thrice two months.

BIL. So have I this twenty year, and yet there was a gentleman usher called me coxcomb tother day, and to my face too. Was 't not a backbiting rascal? I would I were better traveled, that I might have been better acquainted [110 with the fashions of several countrymen; but my secretary, I think, he hath sufficiently instructed me.

BIAN. How, my lord?

BIL. "Marry, my good lord," quoth he, "your lordship shall ever find amongst a hundred Frenchmen forty hotshots;[1] amongst a hundred Spaniards, threescore braggarts; amongst a hundred Dutchmen, fourscore drunkards; [120 amongst an hundred Englishmen, fourscore and ten madmen; and amongst an hundred Welshmen"—

BIAN. What, my lord?

BIL. "Fourscore and nineteen gentlemen."

BIAN. But, since you go about a sad embassy, I would have you go in black, my lord.   129

BIL. Why, dost think I cannot mourn, unless I wear my hat in cypress,[2] like an alderman's heir? That's vile, very old, in faith.

BIAN. I'll learn of you shortly. O, we should have a fine gallant of you, should not I instruct you! How will you bear yourself when you come into the Duke of Florence' court?

BIL. Proud enough, and 'twill do well enough. As I walk up and down the [140 chamber, I'll spit frowns about me, have a strong perfume in my jerkin, let my beard grow to make me look terrible, salute no man beneath[3] the fourth button; and 'twill do excellent.

BIAN. But there is a very beautiful lady there; how will you entertain her?

BIL. I'll tell you that when the lady hath entertained me. But to satisfy thee, here comes the fool.—Fool, thou shalt [150 stand for the fair lady.

[1] Reckless persons.
[2] Crape.
[3] Bow no lower than.

Enter Passarello.

PASS. Your fool will stand for your lady most willingly and most uprightly.

BIL. I'll salute her in Latin.

PASS. O, your fool can understand no Latin.

BIL. Ay, but your lady can.

PASS. Why, then, if your lady take down your fool, your fool will stand no longer for your lady.   160

BIL. A pestilent fool! Fore God, I think the world be turned upside down too.

PASS. O, no, sir; for then your lady and all the ladies in the palace should go with their heels upward, and that were a strange sight, you know.

BIL. There be many will repine at my preferment.

PASS. O, ay, like the envy of an [170 elder sister, that hath her younger made a lady before her.

BIL. The duke is wondrous discontented.

PASS. Ay, and more melancholic than a usurer having all his money out at the death of a prince.

BIL. Didst thou see Madam Floria today?

PASS. Yes, I found her repairing her face today. The red upon the white [180 showed as if her cheeks should have been served in for two dishes of barberries in stewed broth, and the flesh to them a woodcock.

BIL. A bitter fowl![4] Come, madam, this night thou shalt enjoy me freely, and tomorrow for Florence.

[*Exeunt Bilioso and Biancha.*]

PASS. What a natural fool is he that would be a pair of bodies[5] to a woman's petticoat, to be trussed and pointed to them! Well, I'll dog my lord; and the [191 word is proper, for, when I fawn upon him, he feeds me; when I snap him by the fingers, he spits in my mouth. If a dog's death were not strangling, I had rather be one than a serving-man; for the corruption of coin is either the generation of a usurer or a lousy beggar.   *Exit.*[6]

[4] With a pun on *fool.*
[5] Bodice, pair of stays.
[6] In the original, this direction appears at the end of Passarello's preceding speech.

SCENA SECUNDA.

[*Another room in the Duke's palace.*]

*Enter Malevole in some frieze gown, whilst
Bilioso reads his patent.[1]*

MAL. I cannot sleep; my eyes' ill-neigh-
boring lids
Will hold no fellowship. O thou pale,
sober night,
Thou that in sluggish fumes all sense
dost steep;
Thou that gives all the world full leave
to play,
Unbend'st the feebled veins of sweaty
labor!
The galley slave, that all the toilsome
day
Tugs at his oar against the stubborn
wave,
Straining his rugged veins, snores fast;
The stooping scythe-man, that doth
barb [2] the field,
Thou makest wink [3] sure. In night all
creatures sleep;   10
Only the malcontent, that gainst his
fate
Repines and quarrels, alas, he's goodman tell-clock! [4]
His sallow jawbones sink with wasting
moan;
Whilst others' beds are down, his pillow's stone.
BIL. Malevole!
MAL. (*To Bilioso.*) Elder of Israel,
thou honest defect of wicked nature and
obstinate ignorance, when did thy wife let
thee lie with her?   19
BIL. I am going ambassador to Florence.
MAL. Ambassador?   Now, for thy
country's honor, prithee, do not put up
mutton and porridge in thy cloak bag.
Thy young lady wife goes to Florence with
thee too, does she not?
BIL. No, I leave her at the palace.
MAL. At the palace? Now, discretion
shield, man! For God's love, let's ha' no
more cuckolds! Hymen begins to put [30
off his saffron robe; keep thy wife i' the
state of grace. Heart a truth, I would
sooner leave my lady singled in a bordello [5]
than in the Genoa palace.

Sin, there appearing in her sluttish shape,
Would soon grow loathsome, even to
blushes' sense;
Surfeit would cloak [6] intemperate appe-
tite,
Make the soul scent the rotten breath of
lust.
When in an Italian lascivious palace, a
lady guardianless,
Left to the push of all allurement,   40
The strongest incitements to immodesty,
To have her bound, incensed with wan-
ton sweets,
Her veins filled high with heating deli-
cates,
Soft rest, sweet music, amorous mas-
querers,
Lascivious banquets, sin itself gilt o'er,
Strong fantasy tricking up strange de-
lights,
Presenting it dressed pleasingly to
sense,
Sense leading it unto the soul, con-
firmed
With potent example, impudent custom,
Enticed by that great bawd, Oppor-
tunity—   50
Thus being prepared, clap to her easy ear
Youth in good clothes, well-shaped, rich,
Fair-spoken, promising-noble, ardent,
blood-full,
Witty, flattering—Ulysses absent,
O Ithaca, can [7] chastest Penelope hold
out?
BIL. Mass, I'll think on't. Farewell.
                              Exit Bilioso.
MAL. Farewell. Take thy wife with thee.
Farewell.—
To Florence; umh! It may prove good,
it may!
And we may once unmask our brows.

SCENA TERTIA.

[*The same.*]

Enter Count Celso.

CEL. My honored lord—
MAL. Celso, peace! How is 't? Speak
low. Pale fears suspect that hedges, walls,
and trees have ears. Speak, how runs all?
CEL. I' faith, my lord, that beast with
many heads,

---

[1] Commission.   [2] Mow.   [3] Sleep.
[4] Counter of the clock; idler.   [5] Brothel.

[6] Bullen emends to *choke.*
[7] From first edn. Original has *Ithacan chastest.*

The staggering multitude, recoils apace.
Though thorough great men's envy, most
  men's malice,
Their much-intemperate heat hath ban-
  ished you,
Yet now they find envy and malice ne'er
Produce faint reformation.   10
The duke, the too soft duke, lies as a
  block,
For which two tugging factions seem to
  saw;
But still the iron through the ribs they
  draw.
MAL. I tell thee, Celso, I have ever found
  Thy breast most far from shifting cow-
    ardice
And fearful baseness; therefore I'll tell
  thee, Celso,
I find the wind begins to come about;
I'll shift my suit of fortune.
I know the Florentine, whose only force,[1]
By marrying his proud daughter to this
  prince,   20
Both banished me and made this weak
  lord duke,
Will now forsake them all; be sure he
  will.
I'll lie in ambush for conveniency,
Upon their severance to confirm myself.
CEL. Is Ferneze interred?
MAL. Of that at leisure; he lives.
CEL. But how stands Mendoza? How
is 't with him?
MAL. Faith, like a pair of snuffers—
snibs [2] filth in other men, and retains [30
it in itself.
CEL. He does fly from public notice,
methinks, as a hare does from hounds; the
feet whereon he flies betrays him.
MAL. I can track him, Celso.
O, my disguise fools him most power-
  fully!
For that I seem a desperate malcontent,
He fain would clasp with me; he is the
  true slave
That will put on the most affected grace
For some vild second cause.

Enter Mendoza.

CEL.   He's here.
MAL.   Give place.—   40
Illo, ho, ho, ho! Art there, old truepenny?
                    Exit Celso

[1] Whose force alone.   [2] Snubs, rebukes.

Where hast thou spent thyself this morn-
ing? I see flattery in thine eyes, and
damnation in thy soul. Ha, thou huge
rascal!
MEN. Thou art very merry.
MAL. As a scholar, *futuens*[3] *gratis.* How
doth the devil go with thee now?
MEN. Malevole, thou art an arrant
knave.   50
MAL. Who, I? I have been a sergeant,
man.
MEN. Thou art very poor.
MAL. As Job, an alchemist, or a poet.
MEN. The duke hates thee.
MAL. As Irishmen do bum-cracks.[4]
MEN. Thou hast lost his amity.
MAL. As pleasing as maids lose their
virginity.
MEN. Would thou wert of a lusty [60
spirit! Would thou wert noble!
MAL. Why, sure my blood gives me I
am noble, sure I am of noble kind; for I
find myself possessed with all their qualities: love dogs, dice, and drabs; scorn
wit in stuff-clothes; [5] have beat my shoemaker, knocked my semsters, [6] cuckold[ed] my potecary, and undone my
tailor. Noble, why not? Since the stoic
said, "*Neminem servum non ex regibus,* [70
*neminem regem non ex servis esse oriun-
dum,*"[7] only busy Fortune touses,[8] and
the provident Chances blends them together. I'll give you a simile. Did you
e'er see a well with two buckets—whilst
one comes up full to be emptied, another
goes down empty to be filled? Such is the
state of all humanity. Why, look you, I
may be the son of some duke; for, believe
me, intemperate lascivious bastardy [80
makes nobility doubtful. I have a lusty,
daring heart, Mendoza.
MEN. Let's grasp; I do like thee in-
finitely. Wilt enact one thing for me?
MAL. Shall I get by it?   (*[Mendoza]
gives him his purse.*) Command me; I am
thy slave, beyond death and hell.
MEN. Murther the duke.
MAL. My heart's wish, my soul's desire, my fantasy's dream, my blood's [90

[3] Fornicating.   [5] Persons coarsely dressed.
[4] Farts.   [6] Seamstresses.
[7] "There is no slave who has not sprung
from kings, and no king who has not sprung
from slaves" (Seneca, *Epist.*, xliv).
[8] Tears apart.

longing, the only height of my hopes! How,
O God, how? O, how my united spirits
throng together! So strengthen my resolve!

MEN. The duke is now a-hunting.

MAL. Excellent, admirable, as the devil
would have it! Lend me, lend me rapier,
pistol, crossbow. So, so, I'll do it.

MEN. Then we agree.

MAL. As Lent and fishmongers. Come,
à cap-a-pie.[1] How? Inform.   100

MEN. Know that this weak-brained duke,
        who only stands
    On Florence' stilts, hath out of witless
        zeal
    Made me his heir, and secretly confirmed
    The wreath to me after his life's full
        point.

MAL. Upon what merit?

MEN.   Merit! By heaven, I horn him.
    Only Ferneze's death gave me state's
        life.
    Tut, we are politic; he must not live now.

MAL. No reason, marry. But how must
        he die now?   108

MEN. My utmost project is to murder
the duke, that I might have his state, because he makes me his heir; to banish the
duchess, that I might be rid of a cunning
Lacedæmonian,[2] because I know Florence
will forsake her; and then to marry Maria,
the banished Duke Altofront's wife, that
her friends might strengthen me and my
faction. This is all, la.

MAL. Do you love Maria?   118

MEN. Faith, no great affection, but as
wise men do love great women, to ennoble
their blood and augment their revenue. To
accomplish this now, thus now: the duke
is in the forest, next the sea; single him,
kill him, hurl him in the main, and proclaim thou sawest wolves eat him.

MAL. Umh! Not so good. Methinks when
        he is slain,
    To get some hypocrite, some dangerous
        wretch
    That's muffled oe'r with feignéd holiness,
    To swear he heard the duke on some
        steep cliff
    Lament his wife's dishonor, and, in an
        agony   130
    Of his heart's torture, hurled his groan-
        ing sides
    Into the swoln sea. This circumstance,

[1] From head to foot.   [2] Strumpet.

Well made, sounds probable; and here-
        upon
    The duchess—

MEN. May well be banished.
    O unpeerable[3] invention! Rare!
    Thou god of policy, it honeys me.

MAL. Then fear not for the wife of Alto-
        front;
    I'll close to her.

MEN. Thou shalt, thou shalt. Our ex-
        cellency is pleased.   140
    Why wert not thou an emperor? When
        we
    Are duke, I'll make thee some great man,
        sure.

MAL. Nay, make me some rich knave, and
        I'll make myself
    Some great man.

MEN.   In thee be all my spirit.
    Retain ten souls; unite thy virtual
        powers.
    Resolve; ha, remember greatness! Heart,
        farewell.

Enter Celso.

"The fate of all my hopes in thee doth
        dwell."   [*Exit.*]

MAL. Celso, didst hear? O heaven, didst
        hear
    Such devilish mischief? Sufferest thou
        the world
    Carouse damnation even with greedy
        swallow,   150
    And still dost wink, still does thy ven-
        geance slumber?
    "If now thy brows are clear, when will
        they thunder?"   *Exit* [*with Celso*].

SCENA QUARTA.

[*A forest near the sea.*]

*Enter Pietro, Ferrard, Prepasso, and three
        Pages.*

FER. The dogs are at a fault.
                Cornets like horns.

PIET. Would God nothing but the dogs
were at it! Let the deer pursue safety,[4]
the dogs follow the game, and do you follow
the dogs. As for me, 'tis unfit one beast
should hunt another. I ha' one chaseth

[3] Peerless.
[4] Emended by Bullen. Original reads *safely.*

me; and 't [1] please you, I would be rid of you a little.

FER. Would your grief would as soon leave you, as we, to quietness. 10

Exeunt [Ferrardo and Prepasso].

PIET. I thank you.—Boy, what dost thou dream of now?

[1] PAGE. Of a dry summer, my lord; for here's a hot world towards.[2] But, my lord, I had a strange dream last night.

PIET. What strange dream?

[1] PAGE. Why, methought I pleased you with singing, and then I dreamt you gave me that short sword.

PIET. Prettily begged. Hold thee, [20 I'll prove thy dream true; take 't.

[Gives sword.]

[1] PAGE. My duty! But still I dreamt on, my lord; and methought, and 't shall please your excellency, you would needs out of your royal bounty give me that jewel in your hat.

PIET. O, thou didst but dream, boy; do not believe it. Dreams prove not always true; they may hold in a short sword, but not in a jewel. But now, sir, you dreamt [30 you had pleased me with singing; make that true, as I have made the other.

[1] PAGE. Faith, my lord, I did but dream, and dreams, you say, prove not always true; they may hold in a good sword, but not in a good song. The truth is, I ha' lost my voice.

PIET. Lost thy voice! How?

[1] PAGE. With dreaming, faith. But here's a couple of sirenical [3] rascals shall [40 enchant ye. What shall they sing, my good lord?

PIET. Sing of the nature of women, and then the song shall be surely full of variety, old crotchets,[4] and most sweet closes; it shall be humorous, grave, fantastic, amorous, melancholy, sprightly, one in all, and all in one.

[1] PAGE. All in one?

PIET. By 'r Lady, too many. Sing! [50 My speech grows culpable of unthrifty idleness.[5] Sing!

Song [by 2 and 3 Pages].

[1] If it.
[2] Approaching.
[3] Sirenlike.
[4] Quarter notes, with a pun.
[5] Triviality, folly.

SCENA QUINTA.

[The same.]

Enter Malevole, with crossbow and pistol.

[PIET.] Ah, so, so, sing. I am heavy. Walk off; I shall talk in my sleep. Walk off.

Exeunt Pages.

MAL. [*Aside.*] Brief,[6] brief, who? The duke? Good heaven, that fools
Should stumble upon greatness!—Do not sleep, duke;
Give ye good morrow. You must be brief, duke;
I am feed to murther thee. Start not! Mendoza,
Mendoza hired me; here's his gold, his pistol,
Crossbow, and sword. 'Tis all as firm as earth.
O fool, fool, choked with the common maze
Of easy idiots, credulity! 10
Make him thine heir! What, thy sworn murtherer!

PIET. O, can it be?

MAL. Can?

PIET. Discovered he not Ferneze?

MAL. Yes, but why? But why? For love to thee?
Much, much! To be revenged upon his rival,
Who had thrust his jaws awry;
Who being slain, supposed by thine own hands,
Defended by his sword, made thee most loathsome,
Him most gracious with thy loose princess;
Thou, closely [7] yielding egress and regress to her, 19
Madest him heir; whose hot unquiet lust
Straight toused [8] thy sheets, and now would seize thy state.
Politician! Wise man! Death! To be
Led to the stake like a bull by the horns;
To make even kindness cut a gentle throat!
Life, why art thou numbed? Thou foggy dullness, speak!
Lives not more faith in a home-thrusting tongue
Than in these fencing tip-tap [9] courtiers?

[6] In short.
[7] Privately.
[8] Disturbed.
[9] Light-thrusting.

Enter Celso, with a hermit's gown and beard.

PIET.[1] Lord Malevole, if this be true—
MAL. If? Come, shade thee with this
disguise. If? Thou shalt handle it; he [30
shall thank thee for killing thyself. Come,
follow my directions, and thou shalt see
strange sleights.
PIET. World, whither wilt thou?
MAL. Why, to the devil. Come, the morn
grows late.
A steady quickness is the soul of state.
Exeunt.

ACTUS QUÁRTUS. SCENA PRIMA.

[*A hall outside the chamber of Biancha and
Emilia.*]

*Enter Maquerelle, knocking at the Ladies'
door.*

MAQ. Medam, medam, are you stirring,
medam? If you be stirring, medam—if I
thought I should disturb ye—

[*Enter Page.*]

PAGE. My lady is up, forsooth.
MAQ. A pretty boy, faith. How old art
thou?
PAGE. I think fourteen.
MAQ. Nay, and ye be in the teens—Are
ye a gentleman born? Do you know me?
My name is Medam Maquerelle; I lie in [10
the old cunnycourt.[2]—See, here the ladies.

Enter Biancha and Emilia.

BIAN. A fair day to ye, Maquerelle.
EM. Is the duchess up yet, sentinel?
MAQ. O ladies, the most abominable
mischance! O dear ladies, the most piteous
disaster! Ferneze was taken last night in
the duchess' chamber. Alas, the duke
catched him and killed him!
BIAN. Was he found in bed?
MAQ. O, no; but the villainous cer- [20
tainty is, the door was not bolted; the
tongue-tied hatch[3] held his peace. So the
naked troth is, he was found in his shirt,
whilst I, like an arrand beast, lay in the
outward chamber, heard nothing; and yet
they came by me in the dark, and yet I felt
them not, like a senseless creature as I was.
O beauties, look to your busk-points,[4] if

not chastely, yet charily; be sure the door
be bolted.—Is your lord gone to Flor- [30
ence?
BIAN. Yes, Maquerelle.
MAQ. I hope you'll find the discretion
to purchase a fresh gown for his return.—
Now, by my troth, beauties, I would ha'
ye once wise. He loves ye; pish! He is
witty; bubble! Fair-proportioned; meaw!
Nobly-born; wind! Let this be still your
fixed position: esteem me every man according to his good gifts, and so ye shall [40
ever remain most dear and most worthy
to be most dear—ladies.
EM. Is the duke returned from hunting
yet?
MAQ. They say not yet.
BIAN. 'Tis now in midst of day.
EM. How bears the duchess with this
blemish now?
MAQ. Faith, boldly; strongly defies defame, as one that has a duke to her father.
And there's a note to you: be sure of a stout
friend in a corner, that may always awe
your husband. Mark the havior of the [50
duchess now. She dares defame; cries,
"Duke, do what thou canst, I'll quite[5]
mine honor." Nay, as one confirmed in her
own virtue against ten thousand mouths
that mutter her disgrace, she's presently for
dances.

Enter Ferrard.

BIAN. For dances?
MAQ. Most true.
EM. Most strange. [*Aside to Maque-* [59
relle.] See, here's my servant,[6] young Ferrard. How many servants think'st thou I
have, Maquerelle?[7]
MAQ. [*Aside to Emilia.*] The more, the
merrier. 'Twas well said, use your servants
as you do your smocks; have many, use
one, and change often, for that's most sweet
and courtlike.
FER. Save ye, fair ladies! Is the duke returned?
BIAN. Sweet sir, no voice of him as yet in
court.
FER. 'Tis very strange.   70
BIAN. [*Aside to Maquerelle.*] And how like
you my servant, Maquerelle?
MAQ. [*Aside to Biancha.*] I think he

[1] Original reads *Cel.*   [3] Half-door.   [4] Stay-laces.
[2] Rabbit-warren; women's quarters.
[5] Quit, acquit.   [6] Lover.
[7] Neilson suggests that this speech should
probably be given to Biancha.

could hardly draw Ulysses' bow; but, by my
fidelity, were his nose narrower, his eyes
broader, his hands thinner, his lips thicker,
his legs bigger, his feet lesser, his hair
blacker, and his teeth whiter, he were a
tolerable sweet youth, i' faith. And he will
come to my chamber, I will read him the
fortune of his beard. *Cornets sound.* [80
FER. Not yet returned! I fear—But the
duchess approacheth.

SCENA SECUNDA.[1]

[*The same.*]

*Enter Mendoza supporting the Duchess;
Guerrino. The Ladies that are on the
stage rise. Ferrard ushers in the
Duchess, and then takes a Lady to tread
a measure.*[2]

AUR. We will dance; music! We will
dance.
GUER. "*Les quanto,*" lady, "*Pensez
bien,*" "*Passa regis,*" or Biancha's brawl? [3]
AUR. We have forgot the brawl.
FER. So soon? 'Tis wonder.
GUER. Why, 'tis but two singles on the
left, two on the right, three doubles
forward, a traverse of six round; do this
twice, three singles side, galliard trick- [10
of-twenty, coranto-pace; a figure of eight,
three singles broken down, come up, meet,
two doubles, fall back, and then honor.[4]
AUR. O Dædalus, thy maze! I have
quite forgot it.
MAQ. Trust me, so have I, saving the
falling-back, and then honor.

Enter Prepasso.

AUR. Music, music!
PREP. Who saw the duke? The duke?

Enter Equato.

AUR. Music!
EQU.[5] The duke? Is the duke re-
turned?
AUR. Music!

Enter Celso.

CEL. The duke is either quite invisible
or else is not.

---

[1] Follows stage direction in the original.
[2] A grave or stately dance.
[3] Names of old dances.   [4] Curtsy.
[5] Original reads *Pre.*

AUR. We are not pleased with your
intrusion upon our private retirement;
we are not pleased. You have forgot
yourselves.

Enter a Page.

CEL. Boy, thy master? Where's the [30
duke?
PAGE. Alas, I left him burying the
earth with his spread, joyless limbs. He
told me he was heavy, would sleep; bid
me walk off, for that the strength of fantasy oft made him talk in his dreams. I
straight obeyed, nor ever saw him since;
but, wheresoe'er he is, he's sad.
AUR. Music, sound high, as is our
heart! Sound high!   40

SCENA TERTIA.

[*The same.*]

*Enter Malevole, and Pietro disguised like
an hermit.*

MAL. The duke—peace!—the duke is
dead.
AUR. Music!
MAL. Is 't music?
MEN. Give proof.
FER. How?
CEL. Where?
PRE. When?
MAL. Rest in peace, as the duke does;
quietly sit! For my own part, I beheld [10
him but dead; that's all. Marry, here's
one can give you a more particular ac-
count of him.
MEN. Speak, holy father, nor let any
brow
Within this presence fright thee from
the truth;
Speak confidently and freely.
AUR.   We attend.
PIET. Now had the mounting sun's all-
ripening wings
Swept the cold sweat of night from
earth's dank breast,
When I, whom men call Hermit of the
Rock,
Forsook my cell, and clambered up a
cliff,   20
Against whose base the heady Neptune
dashed
His high-curled brows; there 'twas I
eased my limbs,

When, lo, my entrails melted with the
  moan
Someone, who far 'bove me was climbed,
  did make—
I shall offend.
MEN. Not.
AUR. On.
PIET. Methinks I hear him yet: "O female
  faith!
*Go sow the ingrateful sand, and love a
  woman!*
And do I live to be the scoff of men?
To be the wittol-cuckold, even to hug
  my poison?   31
Thou knowest, O truth,
Sooner hard steel will melt with southern
  wind,
A seaman's whistle calm the ocean,
A town on fire be extinct with tears,
Than women, vowed to blushless im-
  pudence,
With sweet behavior and soft minioning
Will turn from that where appetite is
  fixed.
O powerful blood, how thou dost slave
  their soul!
I washed an Ethiope, who, for recom-
  pense,   40
Sullied my name. And must I, then, be
  forced
To walk, to live thus black? Must!
  Must! Fie!
*He that can bear with 'must,' he cannot
  die.*
With that he sighed so[1] passionately
  deep
That the dull air even groaned. At last
  he cries,
"Sink shame in seas, sink deep enough!"
  so dies,
For then I viewed his body fall and souse
Into the foamy main. O, then I saw
That which methinks I see: it was the
  duke
Whom straight the nicer-stomached sea
Belched up, but then—   51
MAL. Then came I in; but, 'las, all was
  too late,
For even straight he sunk!
PIET.   Such was the duke's sad fate.
CEL. A better fortune to our Duke Men-
  doza!
OMNES. Mendoza!

[1] From first edn. Original has *too*.

Cornets flourish. Enter a Guard.

MEN. A guard, a guard! We, full of
  hearty tears,
For our good father's loss—
For so we well may call him
Who did beseech your loves for our
  succession—   59
Cannot so lightly overjump his death
As leave his woes revengeless.—(*To
  Aurelia.*) Woman of shame,
We banish thee forever to the place
From whence this good man comes;
Nor permit, on death, unto the body any
  ornament;
But, base as was thy life, depart away!
AUR. Ungrateful!
MEN.   Away!
AUR.   Villain, hear me!
*Prepasso and Guerrino lead away the
  Duchess.*
MEN. Begone! My lords, address to [2]
  public council;
'Tis most fit
The train of Fortune is borne up by wit.
Away! Our presence shall be sudden;
  haste.   70
*All depart saving Mendoza, Malevole, and
  Pietro.*
MAL. Now, you egregious devil! Ha,
ye murthering politician! [3] How dost,
duke? How dost look now? Brave duke,
i' faith!
MEN. How did you kill him?
MAL. Slatted his brains out, then
soused him in the briny sea.
MEN. Brained him, and drowned him
too?
MAL. O, 'twas best, sure work; *for* [80
*he that strikes a great man, let him strike
home, or else ware he'll prove no man. Shoulder
not a huge fellow, unless you may be sure to
lay him in the kennel.* [4]
MEN. A most sound brainpan!
I'll make you both emperors.
MAL. Make us Christians, make us
Christians!
MEN. I'll hoist ye; ye shall mount.   89
MAL. To the gallows, say ye? Come!
"Præmium incertum petit certum scelus." [5]
How stands the progress? [6]

[2] Prepare for.   [3] Intriguer.   [4] Channel, gutter.
[5] "Uncertain is the reward sought, but certain
the crime" (adapted from Seneca's *Phœnissæ*,
l. 632).   [6] Plan of action.

Men. [*Gives ring.*] Here, take my ring
　　unto the citadel;
　Have entrance to Maria, the grave
　　duchess
　Of banished Altofront. Tell her we love
　　her;
　Omit no circumstance to grace our per-
　　son. Do 't.
Mal. I'll make an excellent pander.
Duke, farewell; 'dieu, adieu, duke.
　　　　　　　　　　　　Exit Malevole.
Men. Take Maquerelle with thee, for
　　'tis found　　　　　　　　　　99
　None cuts a diamond but a diamond.
　Hermit, thou art a man for me, my con-
　　fessor.
　O thou selected spirit, born for my good,
　Sure thou wouldst make
　An excellent elder in a deformed church.
　Come, we must be inward,[1] thou and I
　　all one.
Piet. I am glad I was ordained for ye.
　Men. Go to, then; thou must know
that Malevole is a strange villain; danger-
ous, very dangerous. You see how broad a[2]
speaks; a gross-jawed rogue. I would [110
have drawn poison him; he's like a corn upon
my great toe, I cannot go for him; he
must be cored out, he must. Wilt do 't, ha?
Piet. Anything, anything.
Men. Heart of my life! Thus, then, to
　　the citadel.
　Thou shalt consort with this Malevole;
　There being at supper, poison him.
　It shall be laid upon Maria, who yields
　　love or dies.
　Scud quick like lightning.
Piet. "Good deeds crawl, but mischief
　　flies."　　　　　　　　　　　120

Enter Malevole. Exit Pietro.

Mal. Your devilship's ring has no
virtue. The buff[3]-captain, the sallow
Westphalian gammon[4]-faced zaza,[5] cries,
"Stand out! Must have a stiffer warrant,
or no pass into the Castle of Comfort."
　Men. Command, our sudden letter.—
Not enter! Sha't![6] What place is there
in Genoa but thou shalt? Into my heart,
into my very heart! Come, let's love; we
must love, we two, soul and body.　130

Mal. How didst like the hermit? A
strange hermit, sirrah.
Men. A dangerous fellow, very peril-
ous. He must die.
Mal. Ay, he must die.
Men. Thou'st[7] kill him. We are wise;
we must be wise.
Mal. And provident.
Men. Yea, provident. Beware an hypo-
　　crite;　　　　　　　　　　139
　A churchman once corrupted, O, avoid!
　A fellow that makes religion his stalking-
　　horse,　　　　Shoots under his belly.
　He breeds a plague. Thou shalt poison
　　him.
Mal. Ho, 'tis wondrous necessary! How?
Men. You both go jointly to the citadel;
　There sup, there poison him; and Maria,
　Because she is our opposite,[8] shall
　　bear
　The sad suspect—on which she dies or
　　loves us.
Mal. I run.　　　　　　*Exit Malevole.*
Men. *We that are great, our sole self-good*
　　still moves us.
　They shall die both, for their deserts
　　craves more　　　　　　　　150
　Than we can recompense; their pres-
　　ence still
　Imbraids[9] our fortunes with beholding-
　　ness,
　Which we abhor; like deed, not doer.
　　Then conclude,
　They live not to cry out, "Ingratitude!"
　One stick burns tother; steel cuts steel
　　alone.
　'Tis good trust few; but, O, 'tis best trust
　　none!
　　　　　　　　　　　Exit Mendoza.

Scena Quarta.

[*The same.*]

Enter Malevole and Pietro still disguised, at
　　　　　　　　　　　several doors.

Mal. How do you? How dost, duke?
Piet. O, let the last day fall! Drop, drop
　on our cursed heads!

---

[1] Intimate.　　　　　　[4] Pig.
[2] He　　　　　　　　　　[5] Mercenary(?).
[3] Leather-jerkined.　　[6] Thou shalt.

[7] Thou must.
[8] Opponent.
[9] Upbraids.

Let heaven unclasp itself, vomit forth flames.

MAL. O, do not rand,[1] do not turn player. There's more of them than can well live one by another already. What, art an infidel still?

PIET. I am amazed, struck in a swown with wonder. I am commanded to poison thee. 10

MAL. I am commanded to poison thee at supper.

PIET. At supper?

MAL. In the citadel.

PIET. In the citadel?

MAL. Cross-capers! Tricks! Truth a heaven! He would discharge us as boys do eldern guns,[2] one pellet to strick[3] out another. Of what faith art now?

PIET. All is damnation, wickedness extreme. 20 There is no faith in man.

MAL. In none but usurers and brokers; they deceive no man. Men take um for bloodsuckers, and so they are. Now, God deliver me from my friends!

PIET. Thy friends?

MAL. Yes, from my friends, for from mine enemies I'll deliver myself. O, cutthroat friendship is the rankest villainy! Mark this Mendoza; mark him for a [30 villain; but heaven will send a plague upon him for a rogue.

PIET. O world!

MAL. World! 'Tis the only region of death, the greatest shop of the devil, the cruelest prison of men, out of the which none pass without paying their dearest breath for a fee. There's nothing perfect in it but extreme, extreme calamity, such as comes yonder. 40

SCENA QUINTA.

[The same.]

Enter Aurelia, two Halberts before and two after, supported by Celso and Ferrard; Aurelia in base mourning attire.

AUR. To banishment! Led on to banishment!

PIET. Lady, the blessedness of repentance to you!

AUR. Why? Why? I can desire nothing but death, Nor deserve anything but hell. If heaven should give sufficiency of grace To clear my soul, it would make heaven graceless; My sins would make the stock of mercy poor. O, they would tire heaven's goodness to reclaim them! Judgment is just, yet from that vast villain— But, sure, he shall not miss sad punishment 10 Fore he shall rule.—On to my cell of shame!

PIET. My cell 'tis, lady, where, instead of masques, Music, tilts, tourneys, and such court-like shows, The hollow murmur of the checkless winds Shall groan again, whilst the unquiet sea Shakes the whole rock with foamy battery. There usherless the air comes in and out; The rheumy vault will force your eyes to weep, Whilst you behold true desolation. 19 A rocky barrenness shall pain your eyes, Where all at once one reaches where he stands, With brows the roof, both walls with both his hands.

AUR. It is too good.—Blessed spirit of my lord, O, in what orb soe'er thy soul is throned, Behold me worthily most miserable! O, let the anguish of my contrite spirit Entreat some reconciliation! If not, O, joy, triumph in my just grief! *Death is the end of woes, and tears' relief.*

PIET. Belike your lord not loved you, was unkind. 30

AUR. O heaven! As the soul loved the body, so loved he. 'Twas death to him to part my presence, heaven To see me pleased. Yet I, like to a wretch given o'er to hell, Brake all the sacred rites of marriage To clip a base, ungentle, faithless villain. O God, a very pagan reprobate—

---

[1] Rant, storm.   [3] Strike.
[2] Elderwood guns, *i.e.*, popguns.

What should I say?—ungrateful, throws
me out,
For whom I lost soul, body, fame, and
honor. 40
But 'tis most fit. Why should a better fate
Attend on any who forsake chaste sheets,
Fly the embrace of a devoted heart,
Joined by a solemn vow fore God and
man,
To taste the brackish blood of beastly
lust
In an adulterous touch? O ravenous
immodesty!
Insatiate impudence of appetite!
*Look, here's your end; for mark, what sap
in dust,*
What sin in good, even so much love in lust.
Joy to thy ghost, sweet lord! Pardon to
me! 50
CEL. 'Tis the duke's pleasure this night
you rest in court.
AUR. Soul, lurk in shades; run, shame,
from brightsome skies;
*In night the blind man misseth not his
eyes.*
Exit [with Celso, Ferrardo, and Halberts].
MAL. Do not weep, kind cuckold; take
comfort, man; thy betters have been bec-
cos. Agamemnon, emperor of all the merry
Greeks, that tickled all the true Troyans,
was a cornuto; Prince Arthur, that cut off
twelve kings' beards, was a cornuto; Hercules, whose back bore up heaven, and [60
got forty wenches with child in one night—
PIET. Nay, 't was fifty.
MAL. Faith, forty's enow, a conscience
—yet was a cornuto. Patience; mischief
grows proud; be wise.
PIET. Thou pinchest too deep, art too
keen upon me.
MAL. Tut, a pitiful surgeon makes a
dangerous sore; I'll tent[1] thee to the
ground. Thinkest I'll sustain myself by [70
flattering thee, because thou art a prince?
I had rather follow a drunkard, and live by
licking up his vomit, than by servile
flattery.
PIET. Yet great men ha' done 't.
MAL. Great slaves fear better than love,
born naturally for a coal basket, though the
common usher of princes' presence, Fortune, hath blindly given them better place.
I am vowed to be thy affliction. 80

[1] Probe.

PIET. Prithee, be. I love much misery,
and be thou son to me.

Enter Bilioso.

MAL. Because you are an usurping
duke.—(*To Bilioso.*) Your lordship's well
returned from Florence.
BIL. Well returned, I praise my horse.
MAL. What news from the Floren-
tines? 88
BIL. I will conceal the great duke's
pleasure; only this was his charge. His
pleasure is that his daughter die; Duke
Pietro be banished for banishing his blood's
dishonor; and that Duke Altofront be re-
accepted. This is all. But I hear Duke
Pietro is dead.
MAL. Ay, and Mendoza is duke. What
will you do?
BIL. Is Mendoza strongest?
MAL. Yet he is.
BIL. Then yet I'll hold with him. 100
MAL. But if that Altofront should turn
straight again?[2]
BIL. Why, then, I would turn straight
again.
'Tis good run still with him that has most
might;
I had rather stand with wrong than fall
with right.
MAL. What religion will you be of
now?
BIL. Of the duke's religion, when I know
what it is. 110
MAL. O Hercules!
BIL. Hercules? Hercules was the son of
Jupiter and Alcmena.
MAL. Your lordship is a very wittol.
BIL. Wittol?
MAL. Ay, all-wit.
BIL. Amphitryo was a cuckold. 117
MAL. Your lordship sweats; your young
lady will get you a cloth for your old worship's brows. (*Exit Bilioso.*) Here's a
fellow to be damned! This is his inviolable
maxim—flatter the greatest and oppress
the least. A whoreson flesh-fly, that still
gnaws upon the lean, galled backs!
PIET. Why dost, then, salute him?
MAL. I' faith, as bawds go to church, for
fashion sake. Come, be not confounded;
thou art but in danger to lose a dukedom. Think this: this earth is the only grave

[2] Return straightway.

and Golgotha wherein all things that   [130
live must rot; 'tis but the draught[1] wherein
the heavenly bodies discharge their corruption; the very muck hill on which the
sublunary orbs cast their excrements.
Man is the slime of this dung pit, and
princes are the governors of these men, for,
for our souls, they are as free as emperors,
all of one piece. There goes but a pair of
shears betwixt an emperor and the son of a
bagpiper;[2] only the dyeing, dressing,   [140
pressing, glossing, makes the difference.

Now, what art thou like to lose?
A jailer's office to keep men in bonds,
Whilst toil and treason all life's good con-
   founds.

PIET. I here renounce forever regency.
O Altofront, I wrong thee to supplant
  thy right,
To trip thy heels up with a devilish
  sleight,
For which I now from throne am thrown,
  world-tricks abjure;
For vengeance, though 't comes slow, yet it
  comes sure.
O, I am changed! For here, fore the
  dread power,   150
In true contrition, I do dedicate
My breath to solitary holiness,
My lips to prayer, and my breast's care
  shall be
Restoring Altofront to regency.

MAL. Thy vows are heard, and we accept
  thy faith.   *Undisguiseth himself.*

Enter Ferneze and Celso.[3]

Banish amazement; come, we four must
  stand
Full shock of fortune. Be not so wonder-
  stricken.

PIET. Doth Ferneze live?

FER.   For your pardon.

PIET. Pardon and love. Give leave to
  recollect
My thoughts dispersed in wild astonishment.   160
My vows stand fixed in heaven, and from
  hence
I crave all love and pardon.

MAL.   Who doubts of providence,

That sees this change? A hearty faith to
  all!
He needs must rise [who][4] can no lower
  fall;
For still impetuous vicissitude
Touseth the world; then let no 'maze
  intrude
Upon your spirits. Wonder not I rise,
For who can sink that close can temporize?
The time grows ripe for action. I'll
  detect[5]
My privat'st plot, lest ignorance fear
  suspect.   170
Let's close to counsel, leave the rest to
  fate;
Mature discretion is the life of state.
                     Exeunt.

ACTUS QUINTUS. SCENA PRIMA.

[*Outside the citadel.*]

[6]*Enter Bilioso and Passarello.*

BIL. Fool, how dost thou like my calf in
a long stocking?

PASS. An excellent calf, my lord.

BIL. This calf hath been a reveler this
twenty year. When Monsieur Gundi lay
here ambassador, I could have carried a
lady up and down at arm's end in a platter;
and I can tell you, there were those at
that time who, to try the strength of a
man's back and his arm, would be   [10
coistered.[7] I have measured calves with
most of the palace, and they come nothing
near me; besides, I think there be not
many armors in the arsenal will fit me,
especially for the headpiece. I'll tell thee—

PASS. What, my lord?

BIL. I can eat stewed broth as it comes
seething off the fire, or a custard as it
comes reeking out of the oven, and I think
there are not many lords can do it.   [20
[*Displaying his pomander.*] A good pomander—a little decayed in the scent, but six
grains of musk, ground with rosewater and
tempered with a little civet, shall fetch her
again presently!

PASS. O, ay, as a bawd with aqua vitæ.

BIL. And, what, dost thou rail upon the
ladies as thou wert wont?

---

[1] Privy.

[2] *I.e.,* they are cut out of the same cloth.

[3] Here original adds, *Altofront, Ferneze, Celso, Pietro.*

[4] Supplied from first edn.

[5] Expose.

[6] The following lines to Bilioso's exit are an
addition.   [7] Coiled up (?).

PASS. I were better roast a live cat, and might do it with more safety. I am [30 as secret to [the] [1] thieves as their painting. There's Maquerelle, oldest bawd and a perpetual beggar. Did you never hear of her trick to be known in the city?

BIL. Never.

PASS. Why, she gets all the picter-[2] makers to draw her picture; when they have done, she most courtly finds fault with them one after another, and never fetcheth them. They, in revenge of this, [40 execute her in pictures as they do in Germany, and hang her in théir shops. By this means is she better known to the stinkards [3] than if she had been five times carted.[4]

BIL. Fore God, an excellent policy.

PASS. Are there any revels tonight, my lord?

BIL. Yes.

PASS. Good my lord, give me leave to break a fellow's pate that hath abused [50 me.

BIL. Whose pate?

PASS. Young Ferrard, my lord.

BIL. Take heed, he's very valiant; I have known him fight eight quarrels in five days, believe it.

PASS. O, is he so great a quarreler? Why, then, he's an arrant coward.

BIL. How prove you that?

PASS. Why, thus: he that quarrels [60 seeks to fight; and he that seeks to fight seeks to die; and he that seeks to die seeks never to fight more; and he that will quarrel, and seeks means never to answer a man more, I think he's a coward.

BIL. Thou canst prove anything.

PASS. Anything but a rich knave, for I can flatter no man.

BIL. Well, be not drunk, good fool. I shall see you anon[5] in the presence. [70

Exit [with Passarello].

Enter Malevole and Maquerelle, at several doors opposite, singing.

MAL. The Dutchman for a drunkard—

MAQ. The Dane for golden locks—

MAL. The Irishman for usquebath [6]—

MAQ. The Frenchman for the ( ).[7]

MAL. O, thou art a blessed creature! Had I a modest woman to conceal, I would put her to thy custody, for no reasonable creature would ever suspect her to be in thy company. Ha, thou art a melodious Maquerelle, thou picture of a woman, [80 and substance of a beast!

[8] *Enter Passarello.*

MAQ. O fool, will ye be ready anon to go with me to the revels? The hall will be so pestered [9] anon.

PASS. Ay, as the country is with attorneys.

MAL. What hast thou there, fool?

PASS. Wine; I have learned to drink since I went with my lord ambassador. I'll drink to the health of Madam [90 Maquerelle.

MAL. Why, thou wast wont to rail upon her.

PASS. Ay; but since I borrowed money of her, I'll drink to her health now, as gentlemen visit brokers, or as knights send venison to the city, either to take up more money, or to procure longer forbearance.

MAL. Give me the bowl. I drink a health to Altofront, our deposed duke. [100

[*Drinks.*]

PASS. I'll take it. [*Drinks.*] So? Now I'll begin a health to Madam Maquerelle.

[*Drinks.*]

MAL. Pugh! I will not pledge her.

PASS. Why, I pledged your lord.

MAL. I care not.

PASS. Not pledge Madam Maquerelle! Why, then will I spew up your lord again with this fool's finger.

MAL. Hold; I'll take it.   [*Drinks.*]

MAQ. Now thou hast drunk my health, fool, I am friends with thee.   111

PASS. Art? Art?

When Griffon saw the reconciléd quean
Offering about his neck her arms to cast,
He threw off sword and heart's malignant stream,
And lovely her below the loins embraced.—
Adieu, Madam Maquerelle.

Exit Passarello.

MAL. And how dost thou think a this transformation of state now?   119

---

[1] Supplied by Bullen.   [2] Picture.   [3] The mob.
[4] Bawds were punished by being carted through the streets.   [5] Immediately.
[6] Usquebaugh, whiskey.   [7] Pox.

[8] The passage from this point to the exit of Passarello is an addition.
[9] Crowded.

MAQ. Verily, very well; for we women always note, the falling of the one is the rising of the other. Some must be fat, some must be lean; some must be fools, and some must be lords; some must be knaves, and some must be officers; some must be beggars, some must be knights; some must be cuckolds, and some must be citizens. As for example, I have two court dogs, the most fawning curs, the one called Watch, th' other Catch. [130 Now I, like Lady Fortune, sometimes love this dog, sometimes raise that dog, sometimes favor Watch, most commonly fancy Catch. Now, that dog which I favor I feed; and he's so ravenous that what I give he never chaws it, gulps it down whole, without any relish of what he has, but with a greedy expectation of what he shall have. The other dog now—　　　　　　139

MAL. No more dog, sweet Maquerelle, no more dog. And what hope hast thou of the Duchess Maria? Will she stoop to the duke's lure? Will she cow, [1] think'st?

MAQ. Let me see, where's the sign now? Ha' ye e'er a calendar? Where's the sign, trow you?

MAL. Sign! Why, is there any moment in that?　　　　　　148

MAQ. O, believe me, a most secret power. Look ye, a Chaldean or an Assyrian, I am sure 'twas a most sweet Jew, told me, court any woman in the right sign, you shall not miss. But you must take her in the right vein then, as, when the sign is in Pisces, a fishmonger's wife is very sociable; in Cancer, a Precisian's [2] wife is very flexible; in Capricorn, a merchant's wife hardly holds out; in Libra, a lawyer's wife is very tractable, especially if her husband be at the term; [3] only in [160 Scorpio 'tis very dangerous meddling. Has the duke sent any jewel, any rich stones?

Enter Captain.

MAL. Ay, I think those are the best signs to take a lady in.—By your favor, signior, I must discourse with the Lady Maria, Altofront's duchess; I must enter for the duke.

CAP. She here shall give you interview. I received the guardship of this citadel

from the good Altofront, and for his [170 use I'll keep 't till I am of no use.

MAL. Wilt thou? O heavens, that a Christian should be found in a buff jerkin! Captain Conscience, I love thee, captain. (*Exit Captain.*) We attend. And what hope hast thou of this duchess' easiness?

MAQ. 'Twill go hard. She was a cold creature ever; she hated monkeys, fools, jesters, and gentlemen ushers ex- [179 tremely; she had the vile trick on 't, not only to be truly modestly honorable in her own conscience, but she would avoid the least wanton carriage that might incur suspect, as, God bless me, she had almost brought bed-pressing out of fashion. I could scarce get a fine [4] for the lease of a lady's favor once in a fortnight.

MAL. Now, in the name of immodesty, how many maidenheads hast thou brought to the block?　　　　　　190

MAQ. Let me see. Heaven forgive us our misdeeds!—Here's the duchess.

SCENA SECUNDA.

[The same.]

Enter Maria and Captain.

MAL. God bless thee, lady!

MAR. Out of thy company!

MAL. We have brought thee tender of a husband.

MAR. I hope I have one already.

MAQ. Nay, by mine honor, madam, as good ha' ne'er a husband as a banished husband; he's in another world now. I'll tell ye, lady, I have heard of a sect that maintained, when the husband was [10 asleep, the wife might lawfully entertain another man, for then her husband was as dead. Much more when he is banished!

MAR. Unhonest creature!

MAQ. Pish, honesty is but an art to seem so.

Pray ye, what's honesty, what's constancy,

But fables feigned, odd old fools' chat, devised

By jealous fools to wrong our liberty?

MAL. Mully,[5] he that loves thee is a duke, Mendoza. He will maintain thee [20 royally, love thee ardently, defend thee

[1] Submit.　　　　　　　　　　　　[3] Court.
[2] Puritan's.
[4] Fee.　　　　　　　　　　　　　　[5] Molly, lass.

powerfully, marry thee sumptuously, and
keep thee in despite of Rosicleer or Donzel
del Phebo.[1] There's jewels. [*Gives jewels.*]
If thou wilt, so; if not, so.

MAR. Captain, for God's sake, save poor
    wretchedness
    From tyranny of lustful insolence!
    Enforce me in the deepest dungeon dwell,
    Rather than here; here round about is
    hell.—
    O my dear'st Altofront, where'er thou
    breathe,   30
    Let my soul sink into the shades beneath
    Before I stain thine honor! This thou
    hast,
    And, long as I can die, I will live chaste.

MAL. Gainst him that can enforce, how
    vain is strife!

MAR. She that can be enforced has ne'er a
    knife;
    She that through force her limbs with lust
    enrolls,
    Wants Cleopatra's asps and Portia's coals.
    God amend you!   *Exit with Captain.*

MAL. Now, the fear of the devil forever
go with thee!—Maquerelle, I tell thee, [40
I have found an honest woman. Faith, I
perceive, when all is done, there is of
women, as of all other things, some good,
most bad; some saints, some sinners. For
as nowadays no courtier but has his mistress, no captain but has his cockatrice,[2]
no cuckold but has his horns, and no fool
but has his feather, even so, no woman but
has her weakness and feather too, no sex
but has his—I can hunt the letter no [50
farder.—[*Aside.*] O God, how loathsome
this toying is to me! That a duke should
be forced to fool it! Well, "*Stultorum plena*
sunt omnia."[3] Better play the fool lord
than be the fool lord.—Now, where's your
sleights, Madam Maquerelle?

MAQ. Why, are ye ignorant that 'tis said
a squeamish, affected niceness is natural to
women, and that the excuse of their yielding
is only, forsooth, the difficult obtaining? [60
You must put her to 't. Women are flax,
and will fire in a moment.

MAL. Why, was the flax put into thy
mouth, and yet thou—thou set fire, thou
inflame her?

MAQ. Marry, but I'll tell ye now, you
were too hot.

MAL. The fitter to have inflamed the
flax-woman.

MAQ. You were too boisterous, [70
spleeny, for, indeed—

MAL. Go, go, thou .art a weak pandress;
    now I see,
    Sooner earth's fire heaven itself shall waste
    Than all with heat can melt a mind that's
    chaste.
Go thou, the duke's lime-twig![4] I'll make
the duke turn thee out of thine office.
What, not get one touch of hope, and had
her at such advantage!

MAQ. Now, a my conscience, now I
think in my discretion, we did not take [80
her in the right sign; the blood was not in
the true vein, sure.   *Exit.*

[5] *Enter Bilioso.*

BIL. Make way there! The duke returns
from the enthronement.—Malevole—

MAL. Out, rogue!

BIL. Malevole—

MAL. "Hence, ye gross-jawed, peasantly—out, go!"

BIL. Nay, sweet Malevole, since my
return I hear you are become the thing [90
I always prophesied would be—an advanced virtue, a worthily-employed faithfulness, a man a grace, dear friend.

Come, what! *Si quoties peccant homines*—
if as often as courtiers play the knaves,
honest men should be angry—why, look
ye, we must collogue [6] sometimes, forswear
sometimes.

MAL. Be damned sometimes.

BIL. Right. *Nemo omnibus horis* [100
sapit: No man can be honest at all hours.
Necessity often depraves virtue.

MAL. I will commend thee to the duke.

BIL. Do let us be friends, man.

MAL. And knaves, man.

BIL. Right. Let us prosper and purchase;[7] our lordships shall live, and our
knavery be forgotten.

MAL. He that by any ways gets riches,
his means never shames him.   110

[4] Snare, trap.
[5] The remainder of the scene is another addition.
[6] Confer secretly.
[7] Acquire wealth (by illegitimate means).

[1] Heroes of the Spanish romance translated as
The Mirror of Knighthood.   [2] Courtesan.
[3] "All things are full of fools" (Cicero).

BIL. True.

MAL. For impudency and faithlessness are the main stays to greatness.

BIL. By the Lord, thou art a profound lad.

MAL. By the Lord, thou art a perfect knave. Out, ye ancient damnation!

BIL. Peace, peace! And thou wilt not be a friend to me as I am a knave, be not a knave to me as I am thy friend, and [120 disclose me. Peace! Cornets!

SCENA TERTIA.

[*The same.*]

Enter Prepasso and Ferrard, two Pages with lights, Celso and Equato, Mendoza in duke's robes, and Guerrino.[1] *Exeunt all saving Malevole [and Mendoza].*

MEN. On, on; leave us, leave us.— Stay, where is the hermit?

MAL. With Duke Pietro, with Duke Pietro.

MEN. Is he dead? Is he poisoned?

MAL. Dead as the duke is.

MEN. Good, excellent. He will not blab; secureness lives in secrecy. Come hither, come hither.

MAL. Thou hast a certain strong [10 villainous scent about thee my nature cannot endure.

MEN. Scent, man? What returns Maria—what answer to our suit?

MAL. Cold-frosty; she is obstinate.

MEN. Then she's but dead; 'tis resolute she dies.

Black deed only through black deed safely flees.

MAL. Pugh! "*Per scelera semper sceleribus tutum est iter.*"[2]   19

MEN. What, art a scholar? Art a politician? Sure, thou art an arrand knave.

MAL. Who, I? I have been twice an undersheriff, man.[3]

[1] Direction reads *Bilioso and Guerrino.*
[2] "The way to wickedness is always made safe by wickedness" (Seneca, *Agamemnon*, l. 115).
[3] Ll. 24–40 are an addition. In the original they are preceded by the passage:

"*Enter Malevole and Mendoza.*

MEN. Hast been with Maria?

MAL. As your scrivener to your usurer, I have dealt about taking of this commodity; but she's cold-frosty,"

The passage just quoted has been omitted here

Well, I will go rail upon some great man, that I may purchase the bastinado, or else go marry some rich Genoan lady, and instantly go travel.

MEN. Travel, when thou art married?

MAL. Ay, 'tis your young lord's fashion to do so, though he was so lazy, being a [30 bachelor, that he would never travel so far as the university; yet, when he married her, tales of—and, catso, for England!

MEN. And why for England?

MAL. Because there is no brothel houses there.

MEN. Nor courtesans?

MAL. Neither; your whore went down with the stews, and your punk came up with your Puritan.   40

MEN. Canst thou empoison? Canst thou empoison?

MAL. Excellently; no Jew, potecary, or politician better. Look ye, here's a box. Whom wouldst thou empoison? Here's a box (*Giving it.*) which, opened and the fume taken up in conduits thorough which the brain purges itself, doth instantly for twelve hours' space bind up all show of life in a deep senseless sleep. Here's an- [50 other (*Giving it.*) which, being opened under the sleeper's nose, chokes all the power of life, kills him suddenly.

MEN. I'll try experiments; 'tis good not to be deceived.—So, so; catso!

Seems to poison Malevole [, who falls].

Who would fear that may destroy?
    Death hath no teeth or tongue;
And he that's great, to him are slaves
    Shame, murder, fame, and wrong.—

Celso!   60

Enter Celso.[4]

CEL. My honored lord?

MEN. The good Malevole, that plain-tongued man, alas, is dead on sudden, wondrous strangely! He held in our esteem good place. Celso, see him buried, see him buried.

CEL. I shall observe ye.

MEN. And, Celso, prithee, let it be thy care tonight

because with its repetition of the earlier part of the scene it was apparently an alternate reading for all or part of the first twenty-three lines.
[4] In the original this direction follows l. 53.

To have some pretty show, to solem-
nize
Our high installment; some music,
masquery.   70
We'll give fair entertain unto Maria,
The duchess to the banished Altofront.
Thou shalt conduct her from the citadel
Unto the palace.   Think on some
masquery.

CEL. Of what shape, sweet lord?

MEN. Why, shape? Why, any quick-done
fiction,
As some brave spirits of the Genoan
dukes
To come out of Elysium, forsooth,
Led in by Mercury, to gratulate   79
Our happy fortune; some such anything,
Some far-fet [1] trick good for ladies, some
stale toy
Or other, no matter, so 't be of our de-
vising.
Do thou prepare 't; 'tis but for a fashion
sake.
Fear not; it shall be graced, man; it shall
take.

CEL. All service.

MEN. All thanks; our hand shall not be
close to thee; farewell.—
[*Aside.*] Now is my teachery secure, nor
can we fall.
Mischief that prospers, men do virtue call.
I'll trust no man; he that by tricks gets
wreaths
Keeps them with steel; no man securely
breathes   90
Out of deservéd ranks; the crowd will
mutter, "Fool!"
Who cannot bear with spite, he cannot rule.
The chiefest secret for a man of state
Is to live senseless of a strengthless hate.
                                               [*Exit.*]

MAL. (*Starts up and speaks.*) Death of
the damned thief! I'll make one i' the
masque; thou shalt ha' some brave spirits
of the antique dukes.   98

CEL. My lord, what strange delusion?

MAL. Most happy, dear Celso! Poisoned
with an empty box! I'll give thee all anon.
My lady comes to court; there is a whirl
of fate comes tumbling on; the castle's
captain stands for me, the people pray for
me, and the great leader of the just stands
for me. Then courage, Celso.

[1] Far-fetched.

For no disastrous chance can ever move him
That leaveth nothing but a God above him.
                                            [*Exeunt.*]

SCENA QUARTA.[2]

[*The presence chamber.*]

Enter Prepasso and Bilioso, two Pages before
them; Maquer[elle], Biancha, and
Emilia.

BIL. Make room there, room for the
ladies! Why, gentlemen, will not ye suffer
the ladies to be entered in the great chamber? Why, gallauts! And you, sir, to drop
your torch where the beauties must sit too!

PRE. And there's a great fellow plays
the knave. Why dost not strike him?

BIL. Let him play the knave, a God's
name; think'st thou I have no more wit
than to strike a great fellow?—The   [10
music! More lights! Reveling-scaffolds! Do
you hear? Let there be oaths enow ready
at the door; swear out the devil himself
Let's leave the ladies, and go see if the
lords be ready for them.
                        All save the Ladies depart.

MAQ. And, by my troth, beauties, why
do you not put you into the fashion? This
is a stale cut; you must come in fashion.
Look ye, you must be all felt, felt and
feather, a felt upon your bare hair.   [20
Look ye, these tiring things [3] are justly out of
request now. And, do ye hear, you must
wear falling bands,[4] you must come into
the falling fashion; there is such a deal a
pinning these ruffs, when the fine clean fall
is worth all; and again, if you should chance
to take a nap in the afternoon, your falling
band requires no poting stick [5] to recover
his form. Believe me, no fashion to the
falling, I say.   30

BIAN. And is not Signior St. Andrew a
gallant fellow now?

MAQ. By my maidenhead, la, honor and
he agrees as well together as a satin suit
and woolen stockings.

EM. But is not Marshal Make-room,
my servant in reversion,[6] a proper gentleman?

[2] In the original the new scene begins at the
entry of the duke's procession.
[3] Headdresses.
[4] Flat collars.   [5] Stick for plaiting ruffs.
[6] Upon the death or withdrawal of the present
owner.

MAQ. Yes, in reversion, as he had his office; as, in truth, he hath all things in [40 reversion. He has his mistress in reversion, his clothes in reversion, his wit in reversion, and, indeed, is a suitor to me for my dog in reversion. But, in good verity, la, he is as proper a gentleman in reversion as—and, indeed, as fine a man as may be, having a red beard and a pair of wrapped [1] legs.

BIAN. But, i' faith, I am most monstrously in love with Count Quidlibet-in-quodlibet. Is he not a pretty, dapper, [50 unidle gallant?

MAQ. He is even one of the most busy-fingered lords; he will put the beauties to the squeak most hideously.

Enter Bilioso.

BIL. Room! Make a lane there! The duke is entering. Stand handsomely, for beauty's sake; take up the ladies there! So, cornets, cornets!

Enter Prepasso; joins to Bilioso. Two Pages and lights; Ferrard; Mendoza. At the other door, two Pages with lights, and the Captain leading in Maria. The Duke meets Maria, and closeth with her. The rest fall back.

MEN. Madam, with gentle ear receive my suit;
A kingdom's safety should o'erpeise [2] slight rites; 60
Marriage is merely nature's policy.
Then since, unless our royal beds be joined,
Danger and civil tumult frights the state,
Be wise as you are fair, give way to fate.

MAR. What wouldst thou, thou affliction to our house?
Thou ever-devil, 'twas thou that banishedst
My truly noble lord!

MEN. I?

MAR. Ay, by thy plots, by thy black stratagems.
Twelve moons have suffered change since I beheld 70
The lovéd presence of my dearest lord.
O thou, far worse than Death! He parts but soul

From a weak body; but thou soul from soul
Disseverest, that which God's own hand did knit;
Thou, scant of honor, full of devilish wit!

MEN. We'll check your too-intemperate lavishness.
I can and will.

MAR. What canst?

MEN. Go to; in banishment thy husband dies. 79

MAR. *He ever is at home that's ever wise.*

MEN. You'st [3] never meet more; reason should love control.

MAR. Not meet?
She that dear loves, her love's still in her soul.

MEN. You are but a woman, lady; you must yield.

MAR. O, save me, thou innated [4] bashfulness,
Thou only ornament of woman's modesty!

MEN. Modesty? Death, I'll torment thee.

MAR. Do, urge all torments, all afflictions try;
I'll die my lord's as long as I can die.

MEN. Thou obstinate, thou shalt die.—
Captain, that lady's 90
Life is forfeited [5] to justice. We have examined her,
And we do find she hath empoisonéd
The reverend hermit; therefore we command
Severest custody.—Nay, if you'll do 's no good,
You 'st do 's no harm. A tyrant's peace is blood.

MAR. O, thou art merciful! O gracious devil,
Rather by much let me condemnéd be
For seeming murder than be damned for thee!
I'll mourn no more; come, girt my brows with flowers;
Revel and dance. Soul, now thy wish thou hast; 100
Die like a bride; poor heart, thou shalt die chaste.

Enter Aurelia in mourning habit.

AUR. *Life is a frost of cold felicity,*
And death the thaw of all our vanity.
Was't not an honest priest [6] that wrote so?

---

[1] Padded (or a misprint for *warped*). Perhaps a reference to Jonson's description of Marston in *Poetaster.* [2] Outweigh.

[3] You must. [4] Innate.
[5] From first edn. Original reads *forteified.*
[6] Thomas Bastard.

MEN. Who let her in?

BIL. Forbear!

PRE. Forbear!

AUR. *Alas, calamity is everywhere.*
Sad misery, despite your double doors,
Will enter even in court.

BIL. Peace!

AUR. I ha' done. One word—take
heed! I ha' done.

Enter Mercury with loud music.

MER. Cyllenian Mercury, the god of
ghosts, 110
From gloomy shades that spread the
lower coasts,
Calls four high-famed Genoan dukes to
come,
And make this presence their Elysium,
To pass away this high triumphal night
With song and dances, court's more soft
delight.

AUR. Are you god of ghosts? I have a
suit depending in hell betwixt me and my
conscience. I would fain have thee help
me to an advocate. 119

BIL. Mercury shall be your lawyer, lady.

AUR. Nay, faith, Mercury has too good
a face to be a right lawyer.

PRE. Peace, forbear! Mercury presents
the masque.

*Cornets. The song to the cornets, which play-
ing, the masque enters; Malevole,
Pietro, Ferneze, and Celso, in white
robes, with duke's crowns upon laurel
wreaths, pistolets and short swords under
their robes.*

MEN. Celso, Celso, court [1] Maria for our
love.—Lady, be gracious, yet grace—
Malevole takes his Wife to dance.

MAR. With me, sir?

MAL. Yes, more lovéd
than my breath;
With you I'll dance.

MAR. Why, then, you
dance with death.
But, come, sir, I was ne'er more apt to
mirth. 129
*Death gives eternity a glorious breath;
O, to die honored, who would fear to die?*

MAL. *They die in fear who live in villainy.*

[1] From first edn. Original reads *count.*

MEN. Yes, believe him, lady, and be ruled
by him.
Pietro takes his wife Aurelia to dance.

PIET. Madam, with me?

AUR. Wouldst then be miserable?

PIET. I need not wish.

AUR. O, yet forbear my hand! Away, fly,
fly!
O, seek not her that only seeks to die!

PIET. Poor lovéd soul!

AUR. What, wouldst court misery?

PIET. Yes.

AUR. She'll come too soon. O my
grieved heart!

PIET. Lady, ha' done, ha' done. 140
Come, let's dance; be once from sorrow
free.

AUR. Art a sad man?

PIET. Yes, sweet.

AUR. Then we'll agree.

*Ferneze takes Maquerelle, and Celso, Bi-
ancha; then the cornets sound the
measure, one change and rest.*

FER. (*To Biancha.*) Believe it, lady;
shall I swear? Let me enjoy you in private,
and I'll marry you, by my soul.

BIAN. I had rather you would swear by
your body; I think that would prove the
more regarded oath with you.

FER. I'll swear by them both, to please
you. 150

BIAN. O, damn them not both to please
me, for God's sake!

FER. Faith, sweet creature, let me enjoy
you tonight, and I'll marry you tomorrow
fortnight, by my troth, la.

MAQ. On his troth, la! Believe him not;
that kind of cunny-catching [2] is as stale as
Sir Oliver Anchovy's perfumed jerkin.
Promise of matrimony by a young gallant,
to bring a virgin lady into a fool's paradise;
make her a great woman, and then [161
cast her off—'tis as common, as natural, to a
courtier, as jealousy to a citizen, gluttony
to a Puritan, wisdom to an alderman, pride
to a tailor, or an empty hand basket to one
of these sixpenny damnations.[3] Of his
troth, la, believe him not; traps to catch
polecats!

MAL. (*To Maria.*) Keep your face constant; let no sudden passion
Speak in your eyes. [*Reveals himself.*]

MAR. O my Altofront!

[2] Cony-catching, deceiving. [3] Prostitutes.

Piet. [*To Aurelia.*] A tyrant's jealous-
ies   [*Reveals himself.*] 171
Are very nimble; you receive it all.

Aur.[1] My heart, though not my knees, doth
humbly fall
Low as the earth, to thee.

Piet. Peace! Next change; no words.

Mar. Speech to such, ay, O, what will
affords!

*Cornets sound the measure over again; which
danced, they unmask.*

Men. Malevole!

*They environ Mendoza, bending their pistols
on him.*

Mal. No!

Men. Altofront! Duke Pietro! Ferneze!
Ha!

All. Duke Altofront! Duke Altofront! 180

*Cornets, a flourish.—They seize upon
Mendoza.*

Men. Are we surprised? What strange de-
lusions mock
Our senses? Do I dream? Or have I
dreamt
This two days' space? Where am I?

Mal. Where an archvillain is.

Men. O, lend me breath till I am fit to die!
For peace with heaven, for your own
souls' sake,
Vouchsafe me life!

Piet. Ignoble villain, whom neither heaven
nor hell,
Goodness of God or man, could once
make good!

Mal. Base, treacherous wretch, what
grace canst thou expect,   190
That hast grown impudent in graceless-
ness?

Men. O, life!

Mal. Slave, take thy life.
Wert thou defenséd,[2] through blood and
wounds,
The sternest horror of a civil fight
Would I achieve thee; but, prostrate at
my feet,
I scorn to hurt thee. '*Tis the heart of slaves
That deigns to triumph over peasants'
graves;*
*For such thou art, since birth doth ne'er enroll
A man 'mong monarchs, but a glorious soul.*[3]
O, I have seen strange accidents of
state—   201

[1] Marginal note: *Aurelia to Pietro.*
[2] Defended.   [3] Lines 201–25 are an addition.

The flatterer, like the ivy, clip the oak,
And waste it to the heart; lust so con-
firmed
That the black act of sin itself not
shamed
To be termed courtship.
O, they that are as great as be their sins,
Let them remember that th' inconstant
people
Love many princes merely for their faces
And outward shows; and they do covet
more
To have a sight of these than of their
virtues.   210
Yet thus much let the great ones still
conceal.[4]
When they observe not heaven's imposed
conditions,
They are no kings, but forfeit their com-
missions.

Maq. O good my lord, I have lived in
the court this twenty year; they that have
been old courtiers, and come to live in the
city, they are spited at, and thrust to the
walls like apricocks, good my lord.   218

Bil. My lord, I did know your lordship
in this disguise; you heard me ever say, if
Altofront did return, I would stand for
him. Besides, 'twas your lordship's pleasure
to call me wittol and cuckold; you must not
think, but that I knew you, I would have
put it up so patiently.

[Mal.] (*To Pietro and Aurelia.*)   You
o'erjoyed spirits, wipe your long-wet
eyes.—
Hence with this man! (*Kicks out
Mendoza.*) An eagle takes not flies.—
(*To Pietro and Aurelia.*) You to your
vows—(*To Maquerelle.*) and thou
unto the suburbs.[5]
You to my worst friend I would hardly
give.—
(*To Bilioso.*) Thou art a perfect old
knave.—(*To Celso and the Captain.*)
All-pleased, live   230
You two unto my breast—(*To Maria.*)
thou to my heart.
The rest of idle actors idly part;
And as for me, I here assume my right,
To which I hope all's pleased. To all,
good night.
        Cornets, a flourish. Exeunt omnes.
                FINIS.

[4] Conceive (?).   [5] The disreputable district.

An Imperfect Ode, Being But One
Staff, Spoken by the Prologue

To wrest each hurtless thought to private
  sense
Is the foul use of ill-bred impudence.
    Immodest censure [1] now grows wild,
      All overrunning.
    Let Innocence be ne'er so chaste,
      Yet at the last
      She is defiled
    With too nice-brainéd cunning.
      O you of fairer soul,
        Control   10
    With an Herculean arm
      This harm;
And once teach all old freedom of a pen,
Which still must write of fools, whilst
  writes of men!

Epilogus

Your modest silence, full of heedy [2]
  stillness,
Makes me thus speak: a voluntary illness [3]

[1] Immoderate criticism.
[2] Heedful.
[3] Defect.

Is merely [4] senseless; but unwilling error,
Such as proceeds from too rash youthful
  fervor,
May well be called a fault, but not a sin.
*Rivers take names from founts where they
  begin.*
Then let not too severe an eye peruse
The slighter brakes [5] of our reforméd Muse,
Who could herself herself of faults detect,
But that she knows 'tis easy to correct,
Though [6] some men's labor. Troth, to err
  is fit,   11
As long as wisdom's not professed, but wit.
Then till another's [7] happier Muse appears,
Till his Thalia feast your learned ears,
To whose desertful lamps [8] pleased Fates
  impart
Art above Nature, Judgment above Art,
  Receive this piece, which hope nor fear
    yet daunteth:
  *He that knows most, knows most how
    much he wanteth.*

Finis.

[4] Wholly.
[5] Flaws.
[6] Supply *'tis.*
[7] Ben Jonson's.
[8] Nocturnal studies.

THOMAS HEYWOOD

After almost three and a half centuries few facts about the life of Thomas Heywood other than those having to do with his long association with the English theater during the reigns of three monarchs—Elizabeth I, James I, and Charles I—have emerged. The reason is simple and obvious: his whole career was focused on the London play-houses and the activities and interests of their occupants and patrons. It is true that Heywood also engaged in other forms of literary work, and therefore Arthur Melville Clark in his minutely detailed biography, *Thomas Heywood* (Oxford, 1931), was impelled to add the subtitle *Playwright and Miscellanist;* but it is always his theat-rical life that dominates. As a successful playwright, eminent actor, and something of a critic, there were almost no aspects of the Elizabethan theater that Heywood was not involved in. And perhaps no other playwright's life better reflects the struggles and problems of the professional and commercial stage writer, the tastes of audiences, and the fortunes and misfortunes of the period's various theatrical organizations and their members.

From this point of view the remark of T. S. Eliot in 1931 that in spite of Clark's labors the figure of Heywood remains one of the most indistinct among the Elizabethans is scarcely justified (*Elizabethan Essays*, London, 1934). Since Eliot wrote, however, Michel Grivelet has contributed notably to the picture in his *Thomas Heywood et le Drame Domestique Élizabéthain* (Paris, 1957), which actually affords a much wider view than its title indicates. Katherine Lee Bates had already laid a sound foundation for both Clark's and Grivelet's books in the introduction to her edition of *A Woman Killed with Kindness* and *The Fair Maid of the West* (New York, 1917). Three other significant studies of perhaps the most important type of Heywood's writings throw further light on his character, if not on his life: H. Mowbray Velte, *The Bourgeois Elements in the Dramas of Thomas Heywood* (Princeton Ph.D. dissertation, 1922); Otelia Cromwell, *Thomas Heywood/A Study in the Elizabethan Drama of Everyday Life* (*YSE*, 1928); and the section on Heywood in Henry H. Adams's *English Domestic or Homiletic Tragedy*. Clark also authored an annotated *Bibliography of Thomas Heywood* (*Oxford Bibliographical Society's Proceedings and Papers*, 1925).

The date of Heywood's birth was fairly well fixed by C. J. Sisson when he discovered a deposition signed, but not written, by Thomas Heywood on October 3, 1623, stating that he was then forty-nine or nearly fifty years old (see W. W. Greg, *Elizabethan Literary Autographs 1550–1650*, Oxford, 1925–32). Thus he was born toward the end of 1573, apparently somewhere in Lincolnshire, where he retained connections—some of them of considerable position and wealth, as shown in various dedications—until the end of his life. In a letter Heywood once referred to his uncle, Master Edmund Hey-wood, as "a good old gentleman," and he often signed "Gent." after his own name. Bates discovered and printed the uncle's will (proved on February 1, 1626) in which he left thirty shillings to Thomas Heywood and his wife, as well as another thirty to William Heywood (probably Thomas's brother) and his wife, along with some of his old clothes. The uncle stated that he came from "the ancient family of Heywood of Mottram in the county of Chester," but no clear genealogical evidence has been dis-covered. Grivelet rejects Clark's statement that he believed he had found the father in Robert Heywood, an Anglican priest ordained by the Bishop of Chester in 1562, who became rector of Rothwell in 1565, and, after an undistinguished and impoverished career, died there in 1593. As a matter of fact, Bates had already made this discovery and rejected it in favor of another theory ("A Conjecture as to Thomas Heywood's Family," *JEGP*, 1913). She traced the family back to a Richard Heywood—a Londoner, father of four sons, one named Edmund and another Christopher—who may have fathered Thomas. In spite of the fact that Christopher became a sort of prodigal son and Thomas was fond of writing about prodigal sons, Grivelet points out that there is no evidence that Christopher ever had a son, or even married. However, it would be especially pleasing to accept this speculation, since the Richard Heywood concerned was the brother of John Heywood (1497?–1580?), writer of interludes and epigrams, and often referred to as "the father of English comedy." (John W. Reed, in *John Heywood and His Friends*, 1917, accepted this genealogy as a fact.) Moreover, John Heywood became the father of Jasper Heywood, one of the translators of Seneca. But no conclusions can be drawn from these facts except that there were many Heywoods, or Heywards (as usual, there were many variations in spellings), in England, and that they repeated their good old solid English Christian names.

The next fact known about Thomas Heywood's life is somewhat more firm; he went to Cambridge University and there established his first contact with the drama. In his *An Apology for Actors*, published in 1612 but probably written five or six years earlier, he stated: "In the time of my residence in Cambridge, I have seen tragedies, comedies, histories, pastorals, and shows, publicly acted, in which graduates of good place and reputation have been specially parted." Without suggesting that he had taken any part in these activities, he went on to show his thorough acquaintance with the theories and procedures of academic life by explaining the practical and intellectual benefits to be derived by young college students from such exercises. But the college where he learned these things remains a mystery, since his name appears on none of the extant records. (William Cartwright, in reissuing the *Apology* under the new title of *The Actor's Vindication*, 1658, stated dogmatically that his author was "a Fellow of Peter House in Cambridge," but Cartwright was not trustworthy in various details. Clark, quoting J. A. Venn's *Alumni Cantabrigienses*, Cambridge, 1922, said that Heywood was a "pensioner" at Emmanuel in 1591, but there is no documentary verification. Allan Holaday in "Heywood's *Troia Britannica* and the *Ages*," *JEGP*, 1946, assigned him to Christ's College, again with no proof. Grivelet therefore seems justified in refusing to accept any of these identifications.)

After leaving Cambridge, probably without a degree, Heywood apparently went immediately to London. He seems from the start to have decided to devote his career to the theater, though in his "Funeral Elegy" on James I he wrote that he had once been a "servant" to Henry, Earl of Southampton. In spite of the fact that the Earl was never known to be the patron of any troupe of actors, Clark believes that it must have been in the capacity of actor that Heywood served him; but this conclusion is dubious. Some years later, in 1614, Heywood may have attended Southampton on a brief trip to the Netherlands to visit Prince Maurice of Orange-Nassau (Holaday, "Thomas Heywood and the Low Countries," *MLN*, 1951), but Grivelet discounts this possibility. Some students also believe that Heywood's handwriting can be identified with that in one of the passages in the fragmentary manuscript of *The Book of Sir Thomas More*, one of the very rare surviving play manuscripts of the time. This one is especially precious not only because it reveals how so many Elizabethan plays were the work of teams of collaborators ("play-patchers," in Dekker's phrase), but also because, in the opinion of some paleographical experts, one of the literary carpenters who worked over the basic plot by Anthony Munday was William Shakespeare. But if Thomas was really one of these "play-patchers," then he began his labors as a play-tinker fairly early in the last decade of the century. (For a summary and evaluation of scholarly research and opinions on the subject, see Samuel Schoenbaum, *Internal Evidence and Elizabethan Dramatic Authorship*, Northwestern University Press, 1966.)

In an interesting appendix on "Dramatic Collaboration" Schoenbaum discusses the various possible types and methods of such combinations of authors, and suggests that a distinction should be made between "collaboration" and "composite writing," since in some cases authors probably did work together, but in others they evidently worked separately, each contributing the kind of scene or passage he had been assigned or was best qualified to write. W. J. Lawrence, in an essay on "Early Dramatic Collaboration: A Theory" (*Pre-Restoration Stage Studies*, Harvard University Press, 1927), made a tabulation of the plays presented by the Admiral's Men at the Rose and the Fortune between 1597 and 1603, and found that of the 128 plays listed by Henslowe, seventy were composite, with sometimes as many as five dramatists working in association. This proportion, however, was considerably less in other companies.

After 1594 it is very probable, if not certain, that Heywood was a member of the Admiral's Company. Half a dozen anonymous plays between 1594 and 1596 might well be his work, in part or in whole, *Captain Thomas Stukeley* being the most likely. Speculation about his affiliations and activities ends on October 14, 1596, however, when Philip Henslowe entered in his diary that he had lent the sum of thirty shillings at various times to several of his men "for hawodes bocke"—otherwise unidentified. But on March 25, 1598, Henslowe also confirmed him as an actor: "Thomas hawoode came and hiered him seallfe with me as a covenante searvante for ij years . . . and not to playe any wher publicke a bout london not while these ij yeares be expired but in my howsse . . . ." This agreement was witnessed by seven men, beginning with Munday, all members of Henslowe's play factory. This situation probably meant that Heywood, already an actor of established reputation, had joined, or rejoined, the Admiral's Men on their reorganization, but that his status was that of a "hired man," or wage-earner, and not as a "sharer," or part owner sharing in the proceeds. And a "hireling" during this period earned about six shillings a week, although Heywood augmented this income with his writing, for which he received various sums according to the amount of his contribution. A complete independent play brought him at first only £5. By 1598, however, he had attained a recognized position in the drama; in that year the somewhat easily impressed Francis Meres named him as among the best writers of comedy in England.

The Admiral's Men acted at the Rose from April 1598 to July 1600. Being a sort of free lancer, Heywood stopped writing for them in the spring of 1599, but continued to act with them. He may have been at least part author of the chronicle play, *The First and Second Parts of King Edward the Fourth*, given by Derby's Men at the Curtain in 1599. If so, it was the first of his plays to be printed in that year. His juvenile romantic drama, *The Four Prentices of London. With the Conquest of Jerusalem* (when it was finally printed in 1615, he apologized for its "infancy") was probably given here, though Fleay wanted to take it back to 1592. Heywood was not directly involved in the "War of the Theaters," which broke out about this time. By Christmas 1601 he had become a sharer in the company of the Earl of Worcester (formerly Edward Somerset, Lord Herbert), and soon became their most valuable member, playing at both the inadequate Boar's Head innyard in Eastcheap and the better equipped Rose on the Bankside. (For a history of these companies see J. T. Murray, *English Dramatic Companies 1558–1642*, New York, 1910.) He made provincial tours from time to time, especially when the plague was rampant in London, and sometimes acted before the King and Queen. All this time he was also writing indefatigably, so that Webster praised him, along with Shakespeare and Dekker, for his "right happy and copious industry." During one period of about five months he helped in the assembly-line manufacture of at least nine plays. Toward the end of his life he confessed in his foreword to *The English Traveler* (1633) that he had had "either an entire hand or at least a main finger" in some two hundred and twenty plays, of which perhaps only thirty survive. In the playlist appended to his edition of John Dancer's *Nicomede* in 1671, Francis Kirkman wrote that Heywood "not only acted almost every day, but also obliged himself to write a sheet every day for several years together," and that many of his plays were "composed loosely in the taverns." As a result of these labors, Clark calculated that between September 1602 and March 1603, the date of the performance of his greatest success, *A Woman Killed with Kindness*, Heywood had increased his income to about £28—a very good sum in a time when the average worker was making about a shilling a day.

Before the end of the century Heywood apparently considered himself prosperous enough to marry, since the register of St. Savior's Church in Southwark, where he was obviously living near his theater, records the births of two sons and two daughters between October 1600 and September 1605 to Thomas "Heyward" and "Heywood," described as "a player" (G. E. Bentley, "Shakespeare's Fellows," *TLS*, November, 1928). Soon afterward he moved to the parish of St. James's, Clerkenwell, near the Red Bull, where he remained until his death. Clark, who went astray in his suppositions about Heywood's marriage, nevertheless discovered in this parish the recording of the births of five children who may have been Heywood's.

On the death of Elizabeth and the accession of James I in 1603, the Lord Chamberlain's Company (also Shakespeare's company) became the King's Men, and Worcester's (also Heywood's) became the Queen's. In the first list of the members of the new company the name of Thomas Heywood stands third, after the names of Thomas Greene and Christopher Beeston, the most important financial and managerial backers of the group. Heywood and the whole company marched in the official cortege in the ceremonies attending the entry of the King and his Queene Anne into London on March 15, 1604; and at Christmas time a new play by him, probably *The Wise Woman of Hogsdon*, was given at court.

As a possible result of the heavy incursions of the plague during the first decade of the new century, Heywood apparently decided to launch his career as a general man of letters. At this time he worked on his *Apology for Actors* (1612), a translation of two books of Sallust's Roman history (1608), and the tremendous narrative poem, *Troia Britannica* (1608), in which he versified many of the most popular myths and stories of the ancient world, stressing especially the pedigree of the British from Brutus, grandson of Æneas. Almost all of his nondramatic works were dedicated to his chief patron, the Earl of Worcester, or members of his family. Since the old theater at the Boar's Head no longer appealed to the public, the Queen's Men decided to erect the Red Bull in Clerkenwell. Although the building of this playhouse took two years (1605–1607), the job was badly done; this fact, combined with the popularity of the two children's companies, the Children of Paul's and the Children of the Revels, at the fashionable "private" theaters, resulted in the relegation of the company to an inferior rank in the eyes of the playgoing public. Audiences deteriorated in both quality and quantity and so did Heywood's dramatic productions. (See George F. Reynolds, *The Staging of Elizabethan Plays at the Red Bull Theater 1605–1625*, New York, 1940.) Grivelet suggests that perhaps Heywood was too much attached to the Elizabethan ideals and the spirit of a great national theater to be willing or able to accommodate himself to the new tastes and to Jacobean cynicism, violence, and atrocities. Nevertheless, this period brought forth the two parts of *If You Know Not Me, You Know Nobody*, his play about the early years of Elizabeth's reign; *Fortune by Land and Sea*, a collaboration with William Rowley; perhaps the first part of *The Fair Maid of the West*; and *The Rape of Lucrece*.

After this last exploitation of ancient Roman history followed a related group of plays on classical history and mythology which again focused the public's eye on him. This series on *The Golden Age*, *The Silver Age*, *The Bronze Age*, and *The Iron Age* not only allowed him to emphasize the spectacle, the machines, the costumes, etc., that the Red Bull was noted for, but also gave him an opportunity to introduce a bit of Greek culture into the homes of London's lower and middle classes. For some of these productions the Queen's and the King's Men accomplished an unprecedented amalgamation and acted together before the court. Nevertheless, these performances failed to bring Heywood all the profits he had hoped for, and in 1612 he published his *An Apology for Actors*, which showed him to be an eloquent advocate for the drama, well qualified by theatrical experience and knowledge of dramatic history to plead his cause.   In 1613 he became one of the defendants in a prolonged lawsuit brought against his company by Suzanne Baskervile, who was the remarried widow of both Edward Browne and Thomas Greene (the celebrated clown of the Boar's Head company).   This suit, combined with the devious behavior of their manager Beeston and other lawsuits, brought the company close to ruin.   In 1617 Beeston bought the Cockpit, built for cockfights, and turned it into a playhouse.   It was attacked on Shrove Tuesday by the apprentices on their annual holiday and by "the unruly people of the suburbs."   (To a Londoner the "suburbs" often meant the brothel district, or "stews.")   The players killed three of the rioters in defending themselves and while it is not known whether Heywood was actually involved in the fight, it is quite possible that some of his play manuscripts were destroyed.   The Queen's Company never fully recovered, and on March 2, 1619, it was disbanded.   When some of its members attempted to reorganize at the Red Bull as the Players of the Revels, they soon found themselves in difficulties, and in 1622 Heywood and six of his colleagues had to be enjoined to keep the roads in repair around their theater.   In fact, when Queen Anne died in 1619, he and his associates almost failed to walk in her funeral procession because the company had hesitated to provide each of its members with the requisite four yards of black cloth for official mourning clothing.   In his dedication of *Gunaikeion, or Nine Books of Various History concerning Women* to his old patron Worcester in 1624, he signed himself "Your poor, but faithful servant."   By this time he had formed an association with the Lady Elizabeth's Men, for whom he wrote *The Captives* in 1624.

When King Charles came to the throne in 1625, however, Heywood found his way into the favor of the new Queen, Henrietta Maria of France, and probably helped to form her new company from a nucleus of players from the Lady Elizabeth's Men.   In this changed environment he showed a new spurt of creative activity.   After the Plautine *The Captives* and the domestic *The English Traveler*, he perhaps collaborated with Webster and Rowley on *A Cure for a Cuckold*.   *The Rape of Lucrece* was revived at the Cockpit in 1628 before the dazzling Duke of Buckingham, and at Christmas 1630 *The Fair Maid of the West* was presented at Hampton Court before the King and Queen.   In 1634 he collaborated with Richard Brome on a topical play, *The Late Lancashire Witches*.   Three years earlier he had turned to the making of Lord Mayor's pageants (Dekker had retired from competition in this genre), and with his love for London and its greatness there was no one better qualified to celebrate these annual festivities.   Moreover, these duties, in the performance of which he was not expected to show any originality, brought him an annual £10 until his death.   The production which carried him closest to the Queen and the court, however, was that of his masque, *Love's Mistress*, in 1634 (printed in 1636).   Known also as the "Queen's Masque" because it was a birthday gift from Henrietta Maria to Charles, it represented Heywood's contribution to her new fad, the Platonic love cult, and offered direct competition to her favorite William D'avenant's masque on the same subject, *The Temple of Love*.   (See A. H. Nethercot, *Sir William D'avenant: Poet Laureate and Playwright-Manager*, University of Chicago Press, 1938.)   Aided by the staging of the great Inigo Jones, Heywood's piece was such a success that, as the printed text bragged, it was given three times in eight days before the King and Queen at Denmark House, in "the presence of sundry Foreign Ambassadors," and then "Publicly Acted by the Queen's Comedians at the Phoenix in Drury Lane."   Clark considers this occasion as "the apex of Heywood's career," at least for "one dizzy week."

Heywood's clown Midas, one of the characters in the masque, is regarded by Clark as standing for William Prynne, the brilliant young Puritan barrister of Lincoln's Inn, who in 1632, had published his famous *Histrio-Mastix, The Players' Scourge or Actors' Tragedy*.   In this piously polemical but savage volume Prynne had attacked not only

Heywood and his *Apology*, but had been so indiscreet as to reproach Henrietta Maria herself and her ladies for appearing publicly in another pastoral masque, *The Shepherd's Paradise*. For this bit of bad judgment the Star Chamber ordered the book to be burned by the public hangman and its author to lose one of his ears in the pillory at Westminster, to part with the other at Cheapside, to lose his academic degrees and be disbarred, and to be fined £5000 and suffer life imprisonment. From the Tower this zealot continued to write as valiantly as ever, and so he was hauled forth, deprived of the remnants of his ears (which had actually only been clipped by the sympathetic hangman), branded "S.L." for "Seditious Libeler" on his cheeks, and fined an additional £5000 (Ethel Williams Kirby, *William Prynne/A Study in Puritanism*, Harvard University Press, 1931). Such a punishment must have seemed a little severe to a man like Heywood who had finished another lengthy and pious poem just before the production of *Love's Mistress*—a poem entitled *The Hierarchy of the Blessed Angels. Their Names, Orders, and Offices. The Fall of Lucifer with His Angels*, which attempted to sum up, as Clark puts it, all the "medieval spiritistic beliefs when the great fabric of superstition was crumbling to its fall." At one point in this vast, dull, versified treatise Heywood showed that he was getting old by commenting indignantly on the insolence of the new young writers. But he was still alert enough to continue writing—plays like *A Challenge to Beauty*, acted by the "King's Majesty's Servants" at both the Blackfriars and the Globe, and various hack pieces and popular biographies. In 1635, however, he retired from the acting stage.

By the late 1630s and early 1640s the conflict between the authoritarian King Charles and his absolutist supporters on the one side and the Puritans and Parliamentarians on the other had erupted into what came to be known as the First and Second Bishops' Wars, which were preliminaries to the great Civil War and in which the royal forces were humiliated by defeat by the Scots. Heywood, like all Englishmen, had been much perturbed by these events, particularly because of his long-standing loyalty to the established government. At the same time his moral and philosophical position had inclined toward many Puritan principles. In 1641 a rash of dull, polemical Puritan pamphlets broke out, most of them anonymous but two signed "T. H." and one with a full "Thomas Heywood." This series has severely worried Heywood's biographers and divided them into two camps. Clark, in his chapter entitled "Politics and Puritanism," accepted them as authentic and as revealing a philosophical change in attitude on the part of Heywood. But Grivelet, following Bates, rejected them and tried to show not only how their writing would have controverted the fundamental forces behind Heywood's whole life but also how it would have been almost impossible for an old and busy man like him to have written them in the few remaining months of his life.

According to the register of St. James's, Clerkenwell, "Tho. Heywood, Poet," was buried in the church on August 16, 1641. Since the plague had been virulent in London that summer, Grivelet speculates that the kindly old playwright may have been one of its victims. Although various posthumous allusions to him for seven or eight years after his death suggest that many writers and other people were not aware that he was not still alive, he perhaps unwittingly had penned his own best epitaph in a well-known digression in the fourth book of the *Hierarchy*. Here he had called the roll of the great dramatists who had been his comrades—Greene, Marlowe, Kyd, Nashe, Beaumont, Fletcher, Jonson, Webster, Middleton, Dekker, Ford, and some lesser wits—giving each his personal nickname and ending with the request that he be treated like them: "I hold he loves me best that calls me Tom." Even though he was the most prolific playwright of the period, he had always been a modest man, doing his best to please the public tastes. In the prologue to *The English Traveler* he had admitted that he would be content if in his work the reader could find "Some mirth, some matter, and perhaps some wit."

Practically all critics are agreed that *A Woman Killed with Kindness* is not only Heywood's greatest play but also the best example of domestic tragedy in the Elizabethan age. It surpasses in impact and memorability its immediate progenitor, *Arden of Feversham*, and its corrivals, *A Yorkshire Tragedy* and *A Warning for Fair Women*, both of which have been attributed to Heywood by some scholars. Grivelet, however, has maintained that although Heywood is generally treated as the chief representative of the "drame bourgeois," he really specialized in a distinctively narrower genre and concerned himself especially with matrimonial and conjugal situations. According to Grivelet, who yields to no one in his admiration for *A Woman Killed with Kindness*, Heywood's two main themes were "le thème matrimonial" and "le thème national." He therefore refused to accept the conclusions of Adams, who treated the play as the leading example of "English Domestic or Homiletic Tragedy," believing that Adams put too much emphasis on its sermonistic and theological aspects. Irving Ribner, however, complained that in its deliberate didacticism "the morality this play preaches is that of the pulpit, and in its circumscribed domestic setting it fails to relate this morality to any larger cosmic design" (*Jacobean Tragedy*). T. S. Eliot had taken a somewhat similar position in his *Elizabethan Essays*, calling Heywood "a facile and sometimes felicitous purveyor of goods to the popular taste" and maintaining that his is "a drama of common life, not, in the highest sense, tragedy at all." Prior, too, in *The Language of Tragedy*, had called the play "sad and pathetic" rather than tragic, largely because the character of Frankford is "defined in terms which cannot embrace actions and feelings of great power, but his basic qualities remain in large part unthreatened by the action." L. C. Knights objected to what he regarded as the sentimentality of the play (*Drama and Society in the Age of Jonson*, London, 1937); but R. W. Van Fossen felt that this label was scarcely appropriate, except perhaps for some of the subplot (edition of the play for the Revels Plays, London, 1962). Most dramatic historians, however, have praised it as a domestic tragedy while admitting that it has some weaknesses.

The problem in large degree seems to be a matter of nomenclature, and when the play is taken on its own terms this difficulty almost disappears. From this point of view there is much to be said for the approach of Adams, who calls the drama "the earliest of the extant plays to deal with a situation of family life divorced from the extravagance and sensationalism of murder." He goes on to point out that to understand Heywood's treatment of the situation of the unfaithful wife it is necessary to realize the popular Renaissance conception of theological doctrine. This, rather than Elizabethan psychology, "directs the action of the characters." Since Frankford is obviously intended to epitomize the model Christian gentleman, he is most concerned with saving immortal souls—even of those who have wronged him. Knowing that adultery is not a civil offense but is punished only by the church with public penance in the pillory or the church porch, he designed his wife's punishment not as an act of kindness to her but as a way to save her soul. If he had immediately killed her, as popular tradition would seem to demand, she would not have had time to repent and thus would have been doomed to hell. There does, however, seem to be an element of subtle and refined revenge in the speech of Frankford which gives the play its title:

> . . .I'll not martyr thee,
> Nor mark thee for a strumpet, but with usage
> Of more humility torment thy soul,
> And kill thee even with kindness.

(For Heywood's variation on the handling of the revenge theme, see Fredson T. Bowers, *Elizabethan Revenge Tragedy*.) As a result of this "kindness," Anne soon realizes that everything she does must be to attain divine forgiveness. Paradoxically, her method, as many critics have failed to notice, is essentially suicide by starvation, and suicide was also a sin forbidden by the church. Although Frankford has carefully withheld forgiveness until Anne's penance and redemption are complete, he grants it before her death as "the duty of a merciful Christian," and kisses her as a token that they are now wedded "once again." Ribner even goes so far as to see a possible Biblical allegory in the three main characters, equating Anne with Eve, Wendoll with Satan, and Frankford with Christ.

There is no such religious indoctrination in the subplot, which contrasts with the main action in its happy and unblushingly sentimental ending. Heywood's purpose in entwining his main plot with this subplot has annoyed some critics, but has been praised by others. Freda L. Townsend, for instance, defended Heywood's method in her article, "The Artistry of Thomas Heywood's Double Plots" (*PQ*, 1946), insisting that the two plots illustrate the same central theme; and Ribner agreed with her. Peter Ure came to the same conclusion ("Marriage and the Domestic Drama in Heywood and Ford," *ES*, 1951), elaborating on her thesis concerning the virtue-honor relationship and the "surcharge" of kindness. (See also Patricia Spacks, "Honor and Perception in *The Woman Killed with Kindness*," *MLQ*, 1959.) Van Fossen and Grivelet have likewise accepted this analysis. Opposing critics like Eliot and Adams, however, have been severe in their criticisms of the play's structure from this point of view. But, after all, Heywood himself had planted a pretty obvious clue to his intentions when he had Sir Francis announce at the end of scene ix:

> Well, I will fasten such a kindness on her
> As shall o'ercome her hate and conquer it.

The subplot might therefore well be entitled "A Woman Won with Kindness." (Incidentally, the title itself echoed a proverbial phrase, well known when Heywood used it.) Praise of the structure of the play from another aspect was made by Lloyd E. Berry ("A Note on Heywood's *A Woman Killed with Kindness*," *MLR*, 1963) in his suggestion that the first and second scenes are really more closely related than has generally been realized, since the second is a sort of burlesque of the first and acts as a bridge between the comedy of the first and the tragedy of the third.

Criticism of the play's characterization centers on Anne and her too-quick fall before the eloquent tongue of Wendoll. (See Hallet D. Smith, "A Woman Killed with Kindness," *PMLA*, 1938, for a review of critical opinions.) But such suddenness was a convention in the Elizabethan theater, perhaps fostered by the ease with which many previously respectable women became royal mistresses, as in the frequently dramatized case of Jane Shore. Frankford has impressed most readers as a consistent and believable person, and not the "theological prig" that Adams surprisingly called him. Because of Wendoll's mixture of good and evil and the struggle with his conscience, he is both the most ambiguous and the most intriguing member of the major triangle. In the card scene, however, both he and Anne taunt Frankford callously and brazenly with their *double entendres;* and in the next to the last scene his resolve to wander in foreign countries, "like a Cain," until his trespasses have been forgotten at home and he may return, perhaps to be patronized by some great man, shows a resilient but superficial temperament. Louis B. Wright has pointed out that *A Woman Killed with Kindness* is only one of several plays by Heywood in which the ideal of unwavering friendship between men is exemplified, either positively or negatively ("The Male-Friendship Cult in Thomas Heywood's Plays," *MLN*, 1927); and certainly Frankford shows lack of good judgment in his loyalty to Wendoll. But Heywood treats all three with a considerable degree of sympathy and a desire to understand them.

The characters of the subplot, with the possible exception of Sir Francis, are less interesting because they are more sketchily drawn. To understand Sir Charles fully, Ribner reminds us, it is necessary to realize that in the eyes of Heywood, an old-fashioned conservative, Charles's determination to hold on to the meager piece of land he has left is not so much an indication that he values it more than his sister's life and chastity, as well as his own honor, as it is an attempt—at least in part—to call attention to "the gradual passing of the great country estates into the hands of the London merchant classes." Nevertheless, although all the leading characters are from the "gentleman" class, Heywood depicts them with a human intimacy that still justifies the term "domestic" for the play. As Adams remarks, the servants and the rustic characters are used to provide social contrast as well as comic relief, and they are skillfully handled, with considerable character differentiation. Nick, with his shrewdness, cleverness, and usual sympathy, is the best example in this play of Heywood's ability to create the clown who was so popular with Elizabethan audiences.

Arthur Brown, in his essay on "Thomas Heywood's Dramatic Art" (*Essays on Shakespeare and Elizabethan Drama*), reminds us that Heywood in "his prefaces, prologues, and addresses to readers made it clear beyond all possible doubt that for him the play lived on the stage and that its appearance in print was at best a poor substitute which the true dramatist should neither hope for nor fully approve." After all, Heywood was an actor as well as a practical playwright. It was the plot that counted first and it must be made to move from the outset. Grivelet also makes the point that, to judge from the carelessness of most playwrights concerning the printing of their own plays, and also to judge from the elements of a play which made the greatest appeal to the great majority of the audience, the general attitude in the theater was centered on the actor and on the scenic representations, the costumes, and such things. This peculiar imbalance is illustrated in five notorious entries in Henslowe's diary during February and March, 1602/3. This record shows that the manager made two payments of £3 apiece in those months to "thomas Hewwod" and "Thomas Hewode" for his play, but during the same period paid £8 5s. to the tailor for gowns of black velvet and black satin—presumably for the boy who acted Anne Frankford.

As for literary style, most of the play is written in verse, some of it rhymed, but few critics today would go as far as Charles Lamb did in calling Heywood a "prose Shakespeare." William Hazlitt went even further in describing the form as "beautiful prose put into heroic measure." But Heywood knew perfectly well what he was doing when in his prologue he referred to his "dull and earthy Muse," along with his "barren subject" and "bare theme." Even Eliot, although saying that Heywood's verse "is never on a very high poetic level," admitted that "verse that is only moderately poetical" can be "very highly dramatic." It is surprising, therefore, that William Archer in *The Old Drama and the New* did not praise Heywood's style but only analyzed a passage from scene vi as an example of the absurd unreality of the soliloquies and asides in the Elizabethan drama—"a sign of sheer artistic helplessness." Moody E. Prior in *The Language of Tragedy* made the most complete examination of the play linguistically, and came to the conclusion that Heywood would probably not have used verse at all except that it was a convention to do so: "The norm, therefore, for the dialogue is an easy conversational treatment of the verse, and clear, simple diction generally free of figurative suggestions. . . . He often used the resources of verse drama to momentary advantage, but they were not essential to what he was trying to do in the play."

In a play as thoroughly English in atmosphere as this, it is surprising to discover that the only fully recognized sources for even part of the plot are Italian, though undoubtedly known to Heywood in English translation. There seems to be no question that his immediate source for the subplot was a story in either William Painter's *The Palace of Pleasure* (1566) or Geoffrey Fenton's *Tragical Discourses* (1567), both of which went back to François de Belleforest's *Histoires Tragiques*, which itself went back to Matteo Bandello's *Tragical Discourses*, which was indebeted to a novella by Illicini about Angelica and a courteous Sienese gentleman named Salimbene. J. A. Symonds in 1884 and E. Koeppel in 1895 were responsible for this basic genealogy. Antecedents for the main plot have been more dubious. Robert Grant Martin and

McEvoy Patterson attempted to trace some of the situations and characters to other stories in Painter (who is preferred to Fenton as Heywood's main source by most scholars, since in other works Heywood shows a close familiarity with him), but their comparisons seem rather forced.   W. F. McNeir suggested an English source, feeling a rather remote resemblance between the main plot and Robert Greene's "The Conversion of an English Courtesan" (1592), itself adapted from a tale in George Gascoigne's *The Adventures of Master F.J.* (1573).   (See "Heywood's Sources for the Main Plot of *A Woman Killed with Kindness*," in Josephine W. Bennett, Oscar Cargill, and V. Hall, *Studies in the English Renaissance Drama*, New York University Press, 1959.)   A summary of these source studies can be found in the Revels edition of the play.   Heywood's knowledge of hawking, as demonstrated in scene iii, could have come from his own observation, but more likely was derived from *The Book of St. Albans*, first published in 1486.

The play presumably continued to be acted at the Curtain and the Red Bull for some years.   Then it disappeared as an acting, or even printed, play for some time, although in the eighteenth century unacted adaptations of it were made by Benjamin Victor and Joseph Moser.   On March 8, 1887, a somewhat bowdlerized version by Frank Marshall was staged by the Dramatic Students Society at the Olympic Theater, London.   The most famous modern performance was that given in Paris to open the renowned Vieux Colombier theater in 1913, but the text used was a translation into French prose by Jacques Coupeau, who omitted the subplot completely.   With its faithfully imitated Elizabethan stage settings by François Jourdain, it ran for twenty-nine performances, and was repeated in Switzerland in 1916.   In its original form it was revived by the Birmingham Repertory Theater in 1922 and by the Malvern Festival in 1931.   The BBC presented a radio version in 1947, and an adaptation was given at Oxford in 1959.   Thus *A Woman Killed with Kindness* is one of a relatively small number of Elizabethan plays, outside the Shakespearean repertoire, which are still alive on the modern stage.

A Woman Killed with Kindness was never entered on the Stationers' Register.   The earliest extant edition, of which the British Museum owns the unique copy, is dated 1607; but since the next extant edition, of which some twenty copies are known, described itself as "the third edition" when it appeared in 1617, there is no way to tell whether the 1607 edition was the first or the second.   The two extant editions are independent of each other, and may have gone back either to the missing text or even to a manuscript.   The basis of the present text is the reproduction of the 1617 edition by Bates in the Belles Lettres Series.

A WOMAN KILLED WITH KINDNESS[1]

BY

THOMAS HEYWOOD

[DRAMATIS PERSONÆ

SIR FRANCIS ACTON, *brother to Mistress Frankford.*

SIR CHARLES MOUNTFORD.

MASTER JOHN FRANKFORD.

MASTER MALBY, *friend to Sir Francis.*

MASTER WENDOLL, *friend to Frankford.*

MASTER CRANWELL.

MASTER SHAFTON, *false friend to Sir. Charles.*

OLD MOUNTFORD, *uncle to Sir Charles.*

MASTER SANDY, *former friend to Sir Charles.*

MASTER RODER, *former tenant to Sir Charles.*

MASTER TIDY, *cousin to Sir Charles.*

NICHOLAS ⎫
JENKIN ⎬ *household servants to Frankford.*
SPIGOT ⎭

ROGER BRICKBAT ⎫ *country fellows.*
JACK SLIME   ⎭

SHERIFF.

KEEPER OF PRISON.

SHERIFF'S OFFICERS, SERJEANT, HUNTSMEN, FALCONERS, COACHMEN, CARTERS, SERVANTS, MUSICIANS.

FRANKFORD'S CHILDREN.

MISTRESS ANNE FRANKFORD.

SUSAN, *sister to Sir Charles Mountford.*

SISLY,[2] *maid to Mistress Frankford.*

WOMEN SERVANTS *in Master Frankford's household.*

JOAN MINIVER ⎫
JANE TRUBKIN ⎬ *country wenches.*[3]
ISBEL MOTLEY ⎭

SCENE: *Yorkshire.*

TIME: *Contemporary.*]

PROLOGUE

I COME but as a harbinger, being sent
To tell you what these preparations mean.
Look for no glorious state; our Muse is bent
Upon a barren subject, a bare scene.
We could afford[4] this twig a timber tree,
Whose strength might boldly on your favors build;
Our russet, tissue;[5] drone, a honeybee;
Our barren plot, a large and spacious field;
Our coarse fare, banquets; our thin water, wine;
Our brook, a sea; our bat's eyes, eagle's sight;   10
Our poet's dull and earthy Muse, divine;
Our ravens, doves; our crow's black feathers, white.
But gentle thoughts, when they may give the foil[6]
Save them that yield, and spare where they may spoil.

[SCENE i.

A room in Frankford's house.]

Enter M[aster] John Frankford, Mistress Anne, Sir Francis Acton, Sir Charles Mountford, Master Malby, Master Wendoll, and M[aster] Cranwell.

FRAN. Some music there! None lead the bride a dance?

CHAR. Yes, would she dance "The Shaking of the Sheets";[7]
But that's the dance her husband means to lead her.

---

[1] The title continues: "As It Hath Been Oftentimes Acted by the Queen's Majest. Servants."

[2] Cicely.   [3] Their surnames mean a fur piece, a squat woman, and a coarse cloth.

[4] Wish.   [5] Fine cloth.

[6] A partial fall in wrestling.

[7] A popular ballad and dance tune, also known as "The Dance of Death."

811

WEN. That's not the dance that every man must dance,
According to the ballet.[1]
FRAN.   Music, ho!
By your leave, sister—by your husband's leave,
I should have said—the hand that but this day
Was given you in the church I'll borrow.—Sound!
This marriage music hoists me from the ground.
FRANK. Ay, you may caper; you are light and free!   10
Marriage hath yoked my heels; pray, pardon me.
FRAN. I'll have you dance too, brother!
CHAR.   Master Frankford,
Y'are a happy man, sir, and much joy
Succeed your marriage mirth, you have a wife
So qualified, and with such ornaments
Both of the mind and body. First, her birth
Is noble, and her education such
As might become the daughter of a prince;
Her own tongue speaks all tongues, and her own hand
Can teach all strings to speak in their best grace,   20
From the shrill'st treble to the hoarsest bass.
To end her many praises in one word,
She's Beauty and Perfection's eldest daughter,
Only found by yours, though many a heart hath sought her.
FRANK. But that I know your virtues and chaste thoughts,
I should be jealous of your praise, Sir Charles.
CRAN. He speaks no more than you approve.
MAL. Nor flatters he that gives to her her due.
ANNE. I would your praise could find a fitter theme
Than my imperfect beauty to speak on.   30
Such as they be, if they my husband please,
They suffice me now I am marriéd.

[1] Ballad.

His sweet content is like a flatt'ring glass,
To make my face seem fairer to mine eye;
But the least wrinkle from his stormy brow
Will blast the roses in my cheeks that grow.
FRAN. A perfect wife already, meek and patient!
How strangely the word husband fits your mouth,
Not married three hours since! Sister, 'tis good;
You that begin betimes thus, must needs prove   40
Pliant and duteous in your husband's love.—
Gramercies,[2] brother! Wrought her to 't already:
"Sweet husband," and a curtsy the first day!
Mark this, mark this, you that are bachelors,
And never took the grace of honest man,[3]
Mark this, against you marry,[4] this one phrase:
"In a good time that man both wins and woos
That takes his wife down in her wedding shoes."[5]
FRANK. Your sister takes not after you, Sir Francis.
All his wild blood your father spent on you;   50
He got her in his age, when he grew civil.
All his mad tricks were to his land entailed,
And you are heir to all; your sister, she
Hath to her dower her mother's modesty.
CHAR. Lord, sir, in what a happy state live you!
This morning, which to many seems a burthen
Too heavy to bear, is unto you a pleasure.
This lady is no clog, as many are;
She doth become you like a well-made suit,

[2] Many thanks.
[3] "Assumed the honorable estate of husband" (Bates).
[4] In preparation for your marriage.
[5] *I.e.*, tames her at once.

In which the tailor hath used all his
art,   60
Not like a thick coat of unseasoned
frieze,
Forced on your back in summer. She's
no chain
To tie your neck, and curb ye to the yoke;
But she's a chain of gold to adorn your
neck.
You both adorn each other, and your
hands,
Methinks, are matches. There's equality
In this fair combination; y'are both
Scholars, both young, both being de-
scended nobly.
There's music in this sympathy; it
carries
Consort [1] and expectation of much
joy,   70
Which God bestow on you from this
first day
Until your dissolution—that's for aye!
FRAN. We keep you here too long, good
brother Frankford.
Into the hall; away! Go cheer your
guests.
What! Bride and bridegroom both with-
drawn at once?
If you be missed, the guests will doubt
their welcome,
And charge you with unkindness.
FRANK.   To prevent it,
I'll leave you here, to see the dance
within.
ANNE. And so will I.
                Exeunt [Frankford and Anne].
FRAN.   To part you it were sin.—
Now, gallants, while the town musi-
cians   80
Finger their frets within, and the mad
lads
And country lasses, every mother's child,
With nosegays and bride-laces [2] in their
hats,
Dance all their country measures,
rounds, and jigs,
What shall we do? Hark! They're all
on the hoigh; [3]
They toil like mill horses, and turn as
round;

Marry, not on the toe! Ay, and they
caper,
Not without cutting; [4] you shall see to-
morrow
The hall floor pecked and dinted like a
millstone,
Made with their high shoes. Though
their skill be small,   90
Yet they tread heavy where their hob-
nails fall.
CHAR. Well, leave them to their sports!—
Sir Francis Acton,
I'll make a match with you. Meet to-
morrow
At Chevy Chase; I'll fly my hawk with
yours.
FRAN. For what? For what?
CHAR.   Why, for a hundred pound.
FRAN. Pawn [5] me some gold of that!
CHAR.   Here are ten angels;
I'll make them good a hundred pound
tomorrow
Upon my hawk's wing.
FRAN.   'Tis a match; 'tis done.
Another hundred pound upon your dogs,
Dare ye, Sir Charles?
CHAR.   I dare. Were I sure to lose, 100
I durst do more than that; here's my
hand,
The first course for a hundred pound!
FRAN.   A match!
WEN. Ten angels on Sir Francis Acton's
hawk;
As much upon his dogs!
CRAN. I'm for Sir Charles Mountford; I
have seen
His hawk and' dog both tried. What,
clap [6] ye hands,
Or is 't no bargain?
WEN.   Yes, and stake them down.
Were they five hundred, they were all
my own.
FRAN. Be stirring early with the lark to-
morrow;
I'll rise into my saddle ere the sun   110
Rise from his bed.
CHAR.   If there you miss me, say
I am no gentleman! I'll hold my day.
FRAN. It holds on all sides.—Come, to-
night let's dance;
Early tomorrow let's prepare to ride.
We had need be three hours up before
the bride.   *[Exeunt.]*

[SCENE ii.

The yard of Frankford's house.]

Enter Nick and Jenkin, Jack Slime, Roger Brickbat, with Country Wenches, and two or three Musicians.

JENK. Come, Nick, take you Joan Miniver, to trace [1] withal; Jack Slime, traverse [1] you with Sisly Milkpail; I will take Jane Trubkin, and Roger Brickbat shall have Isbel Motley. And now that they are busy in the parlor, come, strike up; we'll have a crash [2] here in the yard.

NICK. My humor is not compendious. Dancing I possess not, though I can foot it; yet, since I am fallen into the hands [10 of Sisly Milkpail, I consent.

SLIME.[3] Truly, Nick, though we were never brought up like serving courtiers, yet we have been brought up with serving creatures, ay, and God's creatures, too, for we have been brought up to serve sheep, oxen, horses, hogs, and suchlike; and, though we be but country fellows, it may be in the way of dancing we can do the horse-trick [4] as well as the serv- [20 ing-men.

ROGER. Ay, and the crosspoint [4] too.

JENK. O Slime! O Brickbat! Do not you know that comparisons are odious? Now we are odious ourselves, too; therefore there are no comparisons to be made betwixt us.

NICK. I am sudden, and not superfluous;
I am quarrelsome, and not seditious;
I am peaceable, and not contentious;   30
I am brief, and not compendious.

SLIME. Foot it quickly! If the music overcome not my melancholy, I shall quarrel; and, if they suddenly do not strike up, I shall presently strike thee down.

JENK. No quarreling, for God's sake! Truly, if you do, I shall set a knave between ye.

SLIME. I come to dance, not to quarrel. Come, what shall it be? "Rogero"? [40

JENK. "Rogero"? No; we will dance "The Beginning of the World."

SISLY. I love no dance so well as "John, come kiss me now."

NICK. I, that have ere now deserved a cushion, call for the "Cushion Dance."

[1] Dance.   [3] Original reads *Jack.*
[2] Revel.   [4] Vigorous movement of the dance.

ROGER. For my part, I like nothing so well as "Tom Tyler."

JENK. No; we'll have "The Hunting of the Fox."   50

SLIME. The hay,[5] the hay! There's nothing like the hay.

NICK. I have said, do say, and will say again—

JENK. Every man agree to have it as Nick says!

ALL. Content.

NICK. It hath been, it now is, and it shall be—   59

SISLY. What, Master Nich'las? What?

NICK. "Put on your Smock a Monday."

JENK. So the dance will come cleanly off! Come, for God's sake, agree of something; if you like not that, put it to the musicians; or let me speak for all, and we'll have "Sellenger's Round."

ALL. That, that, that!

NICK. No, I am resolved thus it shall be;
First take hands, then take ye to your heels.

JENK. Why, would ye have us run [70 away?

NICK. No; but I would have you shake your heels.—Music, strike up!

They dance; Nick, dancing, speaks stately and scurvily, the rest after the country fashion.

JENK. Hey! Lively, my lasses! Here's a turn for thee!   [*Exeunt.*]

[SCENE iii.

The open country.]

Wind horns. Enter Sir Charles, Sir Francis, Malby, Cranwell, Wendoll, Falconer, and Huntsmen.

CHAR. So; well cast off! Aloft, aloft! Well flown!
O, now she takes her at the souse,[6] and strikes her
Down to th' earth, like a swift thunderclap.[7]

WEN. She hath stroke ten angels out of my way.

FRAN. A hundred pound from me.

CHAR. What, falc'ner!

FALC. At hand, sir!

[5] A winding country dance.   [6] Swoop.
[7] Here and in a few other passages the line divisions have been regularized.

CHAR. Now she hath seized the fowl and
    gins to plume [1] her;
    Rebeck her not;[2] rather stand still and
    check her!   10
    So, seize her gets,[3] her jesses,[4] and her
    bells!
    Away!
FRAN. My hawk killed, too.
CHAR.   Ay, but 'twas at the querre,[5]
    Not at the mount like mine.
FRAN.   Judgment, my masters!
CRAN. Yours missed her at the ferre.[6]
WEN. Ay, but our merlin first had plumed
    the fowl,
    And twice renewed [7] her from the river
    too.
    Her bells, Sir Francis, had not both one
    weight,
    Nor was one semitune above the other.
    Methinks these Milan bells do sound
    too full,   20
    And spoil the mounting of your hawk.
CHAR.   'Tis lost.
FRAN. I grant it not.   Mine likewise
    seized a fowl
    Within her talents,[8] and you saw her
    paws
    Full of the feathers; both her petty
    singles [9]
    And her long singles griped her more
    than other;
    The terrials [10] of her [11] legs were stained
    with blood,
    Not of the fowl only; she did discomfit
    Some of her feathers, but she [12] brake
    away.
    Come, come; your hawk is but a rifler.[13]
CHAR.   How!
FRAN. Ay, and your dogs are trindle-
    tails [14] and curs.   30
CHAR. You stir my blood!
    You keep not one good hound in all
    your kennel,
    Nor one good hawk upon your perch.
FRAN.   How, knight!

[1] Begins to pluck.   [2] Do not call her off.
[3] Part of the hawk's harness.   [4] Leg straps.
[5] At the quarry, _i.e._, before the prey rose
from the ground.
  [6] At the far, _i.e._, at a higher point.   [8] Talons.
  [7] Driven again.   [9] Claws.
[10] Perhaps a misprint for _terrets_, a part of the
jesses.
  [11] Mountford's hawk's.   [13] Bungler.
  [12] The fowl.   [14] Curly-tailed dogs.

CHAR. So, knight! You will not swagger,
    sir?
FRAN. Why, say I did?
CHAR.   Why, sir,
    I say you would gain as much by swag-
    g'ring
    As you have got by wagers on your
    dogs.
    You will come short in all things.
FRAN.   Not in this!
    Now I'll strike home.
             [_Strikes Sir Charles._]
CHAR.   Thou shalt to thy long home,
    Or I will want my will.   40
FRAN. All they that love Sir Francis,
    follow me!
CHAR. All that affect Sir Charles, draw on
    my part!
CRAN. On this side heaves my hand.
WEN.   Here goes my heart.
They divide themselves. Sir Charles, Cran-
    _well, Falconer, and Huntsman fight
    against Sir Francis, Wendoll, his Fal-
    coner, and Huntsman; and Sir Charles
    hath the better, and beats them away,
    killing both of Sir Francis his men._
          [_Exeunt all but Sir Charles._]
CHAR. My God, what have I done! What
    have I done!
    My rage hath plunged into a sea of
    blood,
    In which my soul lies drowned. Poor
    innocents,
    For whom we are to answer! Well, 'tis
    done,
    And I remain the victor. A great con-
    quest,
    When I would give this right hand, nay,
    this head,
    To breathe in them new life whom I
    have slain!   50
    Forgive me, God! 'Twas in the heat of
    blood,
    And anger quite removes me from my-
    self.
    It was not I, but rage, did this vile
    murther;
    Yet I, and not my rage, must answer it.
    Sir Francis Acton, he is fled the field;
    With him all those that did partake his
    quarrel;
    And I am left alone with sorrow dumb,
    And in my heighth of conquest over-
    come.

Enter Susan.

Sus. O God! My brother wounded 'mong the dead!
Unhappy jests, that in such earnest ends! 60
The rumor of this fear stretched to my ears,
And I am come to know if you be wounded.

Char. O, sister, sister, wounded at the heart!

Sus. My God forbid!

Char. In doing that thing which he forbade,
I am wounded, sister.

Sus.   I hope, not at the heart.

Char. Yes, at the heart.

Sus.   O God! A surgeon, there!

Char. Call me a surgeon, sister, for my soul!
The sin of murther, it hath pierced my heart
And made a wide wound there; but for these scratches, 70
They are nothing, nothing.

Sus.   Charles, what have you done?
Sir Francis hath great friends, and will pursue you
Unto the utmost danger [1] of the law.

Char. My conscience is become mine enemy,
And will pursue me more than Acton can.

Sus. O, fly, sweet brother!

Char.   Shall I fly from thee?
Why, Sue, art weary of my company?

Sus. Fly from your foe!

Char.   You, sister, are my friend,
And, flying you, I shall pursue my end.

Sus. Your company is as my eyeball dear;
Being far from you, no comfort can be near. 81
Yet fly to save your life! What would I care
To spend my future age in black despair,
So you were safe? And yet to live one week
Without my brother Charles, through every cheek
My streaming tears would downwards run so rank,

Till they could set on either side a bank,
And in the midst a channel; so my face
For two saltwater brooks shall still find place.

Char. Thou shall not weep so much, for I will stay, 90
In spite of danger's teeth. I'll live with thee,
Or I'll not live at all. I will not sell
My country and my father's patrimony,
Nor [2] thy sweet sight, for a vain hope of life.

Enter Sheriff with Officers.

Sher. Sir Charles, I am made the unwilling instrument
Of your attach [3] and apprehension.
I'm sorry that the blood of innocent men
Should be of you exacted.[4] It was told me
That you were guarded with a troop of friends,
And therefore [I] came thus armed.

Char.   O, Master Sheriff, 100
I came into the field with many friends,
But see, they all have left me; only one
Clings to my sad misfortune, my dear sister.
I know you for an honest gentleman;
I yield my weapons, and submit to you.
Convey me where you please!

Sher.   To prison, then,
To answer for the lives of these dead men.

Sus. O God! O God!

Char.   Sweet sister, every strain
Of sorrow from your heart augments my pain;
Your grief abounds, and hits against my breast. 110

Sher. Sir, will you go?

Char. Even where it likes you best.
[Exeunt.]

[Scene iv.

A room in Frankford's house.]

Enter Master Frankford in a study.[5]

Frank. How happy am I amongst other men,
That in my mean [6] estate embrace content!

---

1 Penalty.

2 Original has *no*.   3 Arrest.
4 From 1607 edn. Original reads *enacted*.
5 Reverie.   6 Moderate.

I am a gentleman, and by my birth
Companion with a king; a king's no more.
I am possessed of many fair revenues,
Sufficient to maintain a gentleman;
Touching my mind, I am studied in all
   arts,
The riches of my thoughts; and of my
   time
Have been a good proficient; [1] but, the
   chief
Of all the sweet felicities on earth,   10
I have a fair, a chaste, and loving wife—
Perfection all, all truth, all ornament.
If man on earth may truly happy be,
Of these at once possessed, sure I am he.

Enter Nicholas.

NICK. Sir, there's a gentleman attends
   without
To speak with you.
FRANK.   On horseback?
NICK.   Yes, on horseback.
FRANK. Entreat him to alight, and I'll
   attend him.
Know'st thou him, Nick?
NICK.   Know him? Yes; his name's
   Wendoll.
It seems he comes in haste. His horse is
   booted [2]
Up to the flank in mire, himself all
   spotted   20
And stained with plashing. Sure, he rid
   in fear,
Or for a wager. Horse and man both
   sweat;
I ne'er saw two in such a smoking heat.
FRANK. Entreat him in. About it in-
   stantly!   [Exit Nick.]
This Wendoll I have noted, and his car-
   riage
Hath pleased me much; by observation
I have noted many good deserts in
   him.
He's affable, and seen [3] in many things;
Discourses well, a good companion,
And, though of small means, yet a gentle-
   man   30
Of a good house, somewhat pressed by
   want.
I have preferred him to a second place
In my opinion and my best regard.

[1] Have made good use.
[2] Covered.
[3] Skilled, accomplished.

Enter Wendoll, Mistress Frankford, and Nick.

ANNE. O, M[aster] Frankford, Master
   Wendoll here
Brings you the strangest news that e'er
   you heard.
FRANK. What news, sweet wife? What
   news, good M[aster] Wendoll?
WEN. You knew the match made twixt
   Sir Francis Acton
And Sir Charles Mountford?
FRANK.   True; with their hounds
   and hawks.
WEN. The matches were both played.
FRANK.   Ha? And which won?
WEN. Sir Francis, your wife's brother, had
   the worst,   40
And lost the wager.
FRANK.   Why, the worse his chance;
Perhaps the fortune of some other day
Will change his luck.
WEN.[4]   O, but you hear not all.
Sir Francis lost, and yet was loath to
   yield.
At length the two knights grew to dif-
   ference,
From words to blows, and so to banding
   sides,
Where valorous Sir Charles slew, in his
   spleen,
Two of your brother's men—his falc'ner
And his good huntsman whom he loved
   so well.
More men were wounded, no more slain
   outright.   50
FRANK. Now, trust me, I am sorry for the
   knight.
But is my brother safe?
WEN.   All whole and sound;
His body not being blemished with one
   wound.
But poor Sir Charles is to the prison led,
To answer at th' assize for them that's
   dead.
FRANK. I thank your pains, sir. Had the
   news been better,
Your will was to have brought it, M[as-
   ter] Wendoll.
Sir Charles will find hard friends; his case
   is heinous
And will be most severely censured on.[5]
I'm sorry for him. Sir, a word with you!

[4] Original reads Anne.   [5] Judged.

I know you, sir, to be a gentleman   61
In all things; your possibility [1] but mean.
Please you to use my table and my purse;
They are yours.

WEN.   O Lord, sir, I shall ne'er
    deserve it!

FRANK. O, sir, disparage not your worth
    too much;
You are full of quality and fair desert.
Choose of my men which shall attend
    you, sir,
And he is yours. I will allow you, sir,
Your man, your gelding, and your
    table,
All at my own charge. Be my compan-
    ion!   70

WEN. M[aster] Frankford, I have oft been
    bound to you
By many favors; this exceeds them all,
That I shall never merit your least favor;
But, when your last remembrance I for-
    get,
Heaven at my soul exact that weighty
    debt!

FRANK. There needs no protestation, for
    I know you
Virtuous, and therefore grateful.—
    Prithee, Nan,
Use him with all thy loving'st courtesy!

ANNE. As far as modesty may well ex-
    tend,
It is my duty to receive your friend. 80

FRANK. To dinner! Come, sir, from this
    present day,
Welcome to me forever! Come, away!
    [*Exeunt Frankford, Anne, and Wendoll.*]

NICK. I do not like this fellow by no
    means.
I never see him but my heart still earns.[2]
Zounds! I could fight with him, yet
    know not why;
The devil and he are all one, in mine eye.

Enter Jenkin.

JENK. O Nick, what gentleman is that
that comes to lie at our house? My master
allows him one to wait on him, and I believe it will fall to thy lot.   90

NICK. I love my master; by these hilts, I
    do;
But rather than I'll ever come to serve
    him,
I'll turn away my master.

[1] Possessions.   [2] Yearns, grieves.

Enter Sisly.

SISLY. Nich'las, where are you, Nich'-
las? You must come in, Nich'las, and
help the gentleman off with his boots.

NICK. If I pluck off his boots, I'll eat the
    spurs,
And they shall stick fast in my throat
    like burrs.

SISLY. Then, Jenkin, come you!   99

JENK. Nay, 'tis no boot [3] for me to
deny it. My master hath given me a coat
here, but he takes pains himself to brush it
once or twice a day with a holly wand.

SISLY. Come, come, make haste, that
you may wash your hands again, and help
to serve in dinner!

JENK. You may see, my masters, though
it be afternoon with you, 'tis but early days [4]
with us, for we have not dined yet. Stay
but a little; I'll but go in and help [110
to bear up the first course, and come to you
again presently.   *Exeunt.*

[SCENE V.

The jail.]

Enter Malby and Cranwell.

MAL. This is the sessions day. Pray, can
    you tell me
How young Sir Charles hath sped? Is he
    acquit,
Or must he try the law's strict penalty?

CRAN. He's cleared of all, spite of his
    enemies,
Whose earnest labor was to take his life.
But in this suit of pardon he hath spent
All the revenues that his father left him;
And he is now turned a plain country
    man,
Reformed [5] in all things. See, sir, here he
    comes.

Enter Sir Charles and his Keeper.

KEEP. Discharge your fees, and you are
    then at freedom.   10

CHAR. Here, M[aster] Keeper, take the
    poor remainder
Of all the wealth I have! My heavy foes

[3] Use.
[4] Jenkin addresses the audience, for whom the
time is afternoon, although on the stage it is
early morning.
[5] Transformed.

Have made my purse light, but, alas, to
  me
'Tis wealth enough that you have set me
  free.
MAL. God give you joy of your delivery!
  I am glad to see you abroad, Sir Charles.
CHAR. The poorest knight in England,
  M[aster] Malby.
My life hath cost me all my patrimony
My father left his son. Well, God forgive
  them
That are the authors of my penury!   20

Enter Shafton.

SHAFT. Sir Charles! A hand, a hand! At
  liberty?
Now, by the faith I owe, I am glad to see
  it.
What want you? Wherein may I pleas-
  ure you?
CHAR. O me, O, most unhappy gentleman!
I am not worthy to have friends stirred
  up,
Whose hands may help me in this plunge
  of want.
I would I were in heaven, to inherit there
Th' immortal birthright which my Savior
  keeps,
And by no unthrift [1] can be bought and
  sold;
For here on earth what pleasures should
  we trust?   30
SHAFT. To rid you from these contempla-
  tions,
Three hundred pounds you shall receive
  of me;
Nay, five for fail.[2] Come, sir, the sight
  of gold
Is the most sweet receipt for melancholy,
And will revive your spirits. You shall
  hold law
With your proud adversaries. Tush!
  Let Frank Acton
Wage[3] his knighthood-like expense[4]
  with me,
And a [5] will sink, he will. Nay, good Sir
  Charles,
Applaud your fortune and your fair
  escape
From all these perils.

[1] Spendthrift or unthriftiness.
[2] For fear of failure to give enough.
[3] Hazard.   [4] Expenditure.   [5] He.

CHAR.   O, sir, they have
  undone me!   40
Two thousand and five hundred pound
  a year
My father at his death possessed me of,
All which the envious [6] Acton made me
  spend;
And, notwithstanding all this large ex-
  pense,
I had much ado to gain my liberty;
And I have only now a house of pleasure,[7]
With some five hundred pounds, re-
  served
Both to maintain me and my loving
  sister.
SHAFT. [Aside.] That must I have; it lies
  convenient for me.
If I can fasten but one finger on him, 50
With my full hand I'll gripe him to the
  heart.
'Tis not for love I proffered him this coin,
But for my gain and pleasure.—Come,
  Sir Charles,
I know you have need of money; take
  my offer.
CHAR. Sir, I accept it, and remain in-
  debted
Even to the best of my unable power.
Come, gentlemen, and see it tendered
  down!   [Exeunt.]

[SCENE vi.

A room in Frankford's house.]

Enter Wendoll, melancholy.

WEN. I am a villain, if I apprehend
But such a thought! Then, to attempt the
  deed—
Slave, thou art damned without redemp-
  tion!
I'll drive away this passion with a song.
A song! Ha, Ha! A song! As if, fond[8]
  man,
Thy eyes could swim in laughter when
  thy soul
Lies drenched and drownéd in red tears
  of blood!
I'll pray, and see if God within my heart
Plant better thoughts. Why, prayers are
  meditations,
And when I meditate (O, God forgive
  me!)   10

[6] Malicious.   [7] Summer house.   [8] Foolish.

It is on her divine perfections.
I will forget her; I will arm myself
Not t' entertain a thought of love to her;
And, when I come by chance into her
    presence,
I'll hale [1] these balls until my eyestrings
    crack
From being pulled and drawn to look
    that way.

*Enter, over the stage, Frankford, his Wife,
        and Nick [, and exeunt].*

O God, O God! With what a violence
I'm hurried to mine own destruction!
There goest thou, the most perfect's[t]
    man
That ever England bred a gentleman,   20
And shall I wrong his bed?—Thou God
    of Thunder,
Stay, in thy thoughts of vengeance and
    of wrath,
Thy great, almighty, and all-judging
    hand
From speedy execution on a villain,
A villain and a traitor to his friend!

Enter Jenkin.

JENK. Did your worship call?
WEN. [*Not noticing Jenkin.*] He doth
    maintain me; he allows me largely
    Money to spend—
JENK. By my faith, so do not you me;
I cannot get a cross [2] of you.   30
WEN. My gelding, and my man—
JENK. That's Sorrel and I.
WEN. This kindness grows of no alliance [3]
    twixt us—
JENK. Nor is my service of any great ac-
quaintance. [4]
WEN. I never bound him to me by desert.
    Of a mere stranger, a poor gentleman,
    A man by whom in no kind he could
        gain,
    He hath placed me in the height of all
        his thoughts, [5]
    Made me companion with the best and
        chiefest   40
    In Yorkshire. He cannot eat without
        me,

---

[1] Draw away, turn away.   [3] Kinship.
[2] Coin.   [4] Close relationship.
[5] From 1607 edn. Original reads, *And he
hath placed me in his highest thoughts.*

Nor laugh without me; I am to his body
As necessary as his digestion,
And equally do make him whole or sick.
And shall I wrong this man? Base man!
    Ingrate!
Hast thou the power, straight with thy
    gory hands,
To rip thy image from his bleeding heart,
To scratch thy name from out the holy
    book
Of his remembrance, and to wound his
    name
That holds thy name so dear, or rend his
    heart   50
To whom thy heart was knit and joined
    together?
And yet I must. Then, Wendoll, be con-
    tent!
Thus villains, when they would, cannot
    repent.
JENK. What a strange humor is my new
master in! Pray God he be not mad; if he
should be so, I should never have any mind
to serve him in Bedlam. It may be he's
mad for missing of me.
WEN. [*Seeing Jenkin.*] What, Jenkin!
Where's your mistress?   60
JENK. Is your worship married?
WEN. Why dost thou ask?
JENK. Because you are my master; and,
if I have a mistress, I would be glad, like a
good servant, to do my duty to her.
WEN. I mean Mistress Frankford.
JENK. Marry, sir, her husband is riding
out of town, and she went very lovingly to
bring him on his way to horse. Do you
see, sir? Here she comes, and here I go.
WEN. Vanish!   [*Exit Jenkin.*] 71

Enter Mistress Frankford.

ANNE. Y'are well met, sir. Now, in troth,
    my husband,
Before he took horse, had a great desire
To speak with you; we sought about the
    house,
Hallooed into the fields, sent every way,
But could not meet you. Therefore he
    enjoined me
To do unto you his most kind commends.
Nay, more; he wills you, as you prize his
    love,
Or hold in estimation his kind friendship,
To make bold in his absence, and com-
    mand   80

Even as himself were present in the house;

For you must keep his table, use his servants,

And be a present Frankford in his absence.

WEN. I thank him for his love.—

[*Aside.*] Give me a name, you whose infectious tongues

Are tipped with gall and poison. As you would

Think on a man that had your father slain,

Murdered your children, made your wives base strumpets,

So call me, call me so; print in my face

The most stigmatic title of a villain, 90

For hatching treason to so true a friend!

ANNE. Sir, you are much beholding[1] to my husband;

You are a man most dear in his regard.

WEN. I am bound unto your husband, and you too.—

[*Aside.*] I will not speak to wrong a gentleman

Of that good estimation, my kind friend.

I will not, zounds! I will not. I may choose,

And I will choose. Shall I be so misled?

Or shall I purchase[2] to my father's crest

The motto of a villain? If I say 100

I will not do it, what thing can enforce me?

What can compel me? What sad destiny

Hath such command upon my yielding thoughts?

I will not. Ha! Some fury pricks me on;

The swift Fates drag me at their chariot wheel,

And hurry me to mischief. Speak I must;

Injure myself, wrong her, deceive his trust!—

ANNE. Are you not well, sir, that ye seem thus troubled?

There is sedition in your countenance.

WEN. And in my heart, fair angel, chaste and wise. 110

I love you! Start not, speak not, answer not.

I love you—nay, let me speak the rest.

Bid me to swear, and I will call to record

The host of heaven.

ANNE. The host of heaven forbid

Wendoll should hatch such a disloyal thought!

WEN. Such is my fate; to this suit I was born,

To wear rich pleasure's crown, or fortune's scorn.

ANNE. My husband loves you.

WEN. I know it.

ANNE. He esteems you

Even as his brain, his eyeball, or his heart.

WEN. I have tried it. 120

ANNE. His purse is your exchequer, and his table

Doth freely serve you.

WEN. So I have found it.

ANNE. O, with what face of brass, what brow of steel,

Can you, unblushing, speak this to the face

Of the espoused wife of so dear a friend?

It is my husband that maintains your state.

Will you dishonor him—I am his wife—

That in your power hath left his whole affairs?

It is to me you speak?

WEN. O, speak no more,

For more than this I know, and have recorded 130

Within the red-leaved table[3] of my heart.

Fair, and of all beloved, I was not fearful

Bluntly to give my life into your hand,

And at one hazard[4] all my earthly means.

Go, tell your husband; he will turn me off,

And I am then undone. I care not, I;

'Twas for your sake. Perchance in rage he'll kill me;

I care not, 'twas for you. Say I incur

The general name of villain through the world,

Of traitor to my friend; I care not, I.

Beggary, shame, death, scandal, and reproach— 141

For you I'll hazard all. Why, what care I?

For you I'll love, and in your love I'll die.

ANNE. You move me, sir, to passion and to pity.

---

[1] Beholden, indebted.   [2] Acquire, add.   [3] Tablet, notebook.   [4] At one throw.

The love I bear my husband is as pre-
cious
As my soul's health.
WEN.   I love your husband too,
And for his love I will engage my life.
Mistake me not; the augmentation
Of my sincere affection borne to you
Doth no whit lessen my regard of him.
I will be secret, lady, close as night; 151
And not the light of one small glorious
star
Shall shine here in my forehead, to be-
wray
That act of night.
ANNE.   What shall I say?
My soul is wand'ring, and hath lost her
way.
O, Master Wendoll! O!
WEN.   Sigh not, sweet saint,
For every sigh you breathe draws from
my heart
A drop of blood.
ANNE.   I ne'er offended yet.
My fault, I fear, will in my brow be writ.
Women that fall, not quite bereft of
grace,   160
Have their offenses noted in their
face.
I blush, and am ashamed. O, Master
Wendoll,
Pray God I be not born to curse your
tongue
That hath enchanted me! This maze I
am in
I fear will prove the labyrinth of sin.

Enter Nick [behind].

WEN. The path of pleasure and the gate
to bliss,
Which on your lips I knock at with a kiss!
NICK. [*Aside.*] I'll kill the rogue.
WEN. Your husband is from home; your
bed's no blab.
Nay, look not down and blush!
                    [*Exeunt Wendoll and Anne.*]
NICK.   Zounds! I'll stab!
Ay, Nick, was it thy chance to come just
in the nick?   171
I love my master, and I hate that slave;
I love my mistress, but these tricks I like
not.
My master shall not pocket up this
wrong;

I'll eat my fingers first. What sayst thou,
metal?   [*Draws his dagger.*]
Does not that rascal Wendoll go on legs
That thou must cut off? Hath he not
hamstrings
That thou must hock? [1] Nay, metal,
thou shalt stand
To all I say. I'll henceforth turn a spy,
And watch them in their close convey-
ances. [2]   180
I never looked for better of that ras-
cal,
Since he came miching [3] first into our
house.
It is that Sathan hath corrupted her,
For she was fair and chaste. I'll have an
eye
In all their gestures. Thus I think of
them,
If they proceed as they have done before:
Wendoll's a knave, my mistress is a ——.
                                        Exit.

[SCENE vii.

Near Mountford's house.]

Enter Charles and Susan.

CHAR. Sister, you see we are driven to hard
shift
To keep this poor house we have left
unsold.
I am now enforced to follow husbandry,
And you to milk. And do we not live
well?
Well, I thank God.
SUS.   O brother, here's a change
Since old Sir Charles died in our father's
house.
CHAR. All things on earth thus change,
some up, some down;
Content's a kingdom, and I wear that
crown.

Enter Shafton, with a Serjeant.

SHAFT. Good morrow, morrow, Sir Charles!
What, with your sister,
Plying your husbandry?—Serjeant, stand
off!—   10
You have a pretty house here, and a
garden,
And goodly ground about it. Since it lies
So near a lordship that I lately bought,

[1] Hack, cut.   [2] Secret trickery.   [3] Skulking.

I would fain buy it of you. I will give
  you—
CHAR. O, pardon me; this house succes-
  sively
Hath longed [1] to me and my progenitors
Three hundred years. My great-great-
  grandfather,
He in whom first our gentle style [2] began,
Dwelt here, and in this ground increased
  this molehill
Unto that mountain which my father
  left me.   20
Where he, the first of all our house, be-
  gun,
I now, the last, will end, and keep this
  house,
This virgin title never yet deflowered
By any unthrift of the Mountfords' line.
In brief, I will not sell it for more gold
Than you could hide or pave the ground
  withal.
SHAFT. Ha, ha! A proud mind and a
  beggar's purse!
Where's my three hundred pounds, be-
  sides the use? [3]
I have brought it to execution
By course of law. What, is my monies
  ready?   30
CHAR. An execution, sir, and never tell me
You put my bond in suit? You deal ex-
  tremely.
SHAFT. Sell me the land, and I'll acquit
  you straight.
CHAR. Alas, alas! 'Tis all trouble hath
  left me
To cherish me and my poor sister's life.
If this were sold, our names [4] should then
  be quite
Raced [5] from the beadroll of gentility.
You see what hard shift we have made
  to keep it
Allied still to our own name. This palm
  you see,
Labor hath glowed within; her silver
  brow,   40
That never tasted a rough winter's blast
Without a mask or fan, doth with a grace
Defy cold winter, and his storms outface.
SUS. Sir, we feed sparing, and we labor
  hard;
We lie uneasy, to reserve to us

And our succession this small spot of
  ground.
CHAR. I have so bent my thoughts to hus-
  bandry
That I protest I scarcely can remember
What a new fashion is, how silk or satin
Feels in my hand. Why, pride is grown
  to us   50
A mere, mere stranger. I have quite
  forgot
The names of all that ever waited on me.
I cannot name ye any of my hounds,
Once from whose echoing mouths I
  heard all music
That e'er my heart desired. What should
  I say?
To keep this place, I have changed my-
  self away.
SHAFT. [To the Serjeant.] Arrest him at my
  suit!—Actions and actions
Shall keep thee in continual bondage fast;
Nay, more, I'll sue thee by a late appeal,
And call thy former life in question.   60
The keeper is my friend; thou shalt have
  irons,
And usage such as I'll deny to dogs.—
Away with him!
CHAR. Ye are too timorous.[6] But trouble
  is my master,
And I will serve him truly.—My kind
  sister,
Thy tears are of no force to mollify
This flinty man. Go to my father's
  brother,
My kinsmen, and allies; entreat them for
  me,
To ransom me from this injurious man
That seeks my ruin.
SHAFT.   Come, irons, irons! Come away!
I'll see thee lodged far from the sight of
  day.   [Exeunt all except Susan.]   70
SUS. My heart's so hardened with the
  frost of grief,
Death cannot pierce it through.—Tyrant
  too fell![7]
So lead the fiends condemnéd souls to
  hell.

Enter Acton and Malby.

FRAN. Again to prison! Malby, hast thou
  seen
A poor slave better tortured? Shall we
  hear

---

[1] Belonged.   [4] Old edns. read *means.*
[2] Title of gentleman.   [5] Erased, scraped.
[3] Interest.
[6] Terrible.   [7] Cruel.

The music of his voice cry from the grate,[1]
"Meat, for the Lord's sake"? No, no; yet I am not
Throughly revenged. They say he hath a pretty wench
To his sister. Shall I, in my mercy sake   79
To him and to his kindred, bribe the fool
To shame herself by lewd, dishonest lust?
I'll proffer largely; but, the deed being done,
I'll smile to see her base confusion.

MAL. Methinks, Sir Francis, you are full revenged
For greater wrongs than he can proffer you.
See where the poor sad gentlewoman stands!

FRAN. Ha, ha! Now will I flout her poverty,
Deride her fortunes, scoff her base estate.
My very soul the name of Mountford hate.
But stay, my heart! O,[2] what a look did fly   90
To strike my soul through with thy piercing eye!
I am enchanted, all my spirits are fled,
And with one glance my envious spleen strook dead.

SUS. Acton, that seeks our blood!
                                        Runs away.
FRAN.   O chaste and fair!
MAL. Sir Francis, why, Sir Francis, in a trance?
Sir Francis, what cheer, man? Come, come, how is 't?

FRAN. Was she not fair? Or else this judging eye
Cannot distinguish beauty.
MAL.   She was fair.
FRAN. She was an angel in a mortal's shape,
And ne'er descended from old Mountford's line.   100
But soft, soft, let me call my wits together!
A poor, poor wench, to my great adversary
Sister, whose very souls denounce stern war

[1] Grating of prison.   [2] Original reads *Or.*

Each against other! How now, Frank? Turned fool
Or madman, whether?[3] But no! Master of
My perfect senses and directest wits.
Then why should I be in this violent humor
Of passion and of love? And with a person
So different every way, and so opposed
In all contractions[4] and still-warring actions?   110
Fie, fie! How I dispute against my soul!
Come, come; I'll gain her, or in her fair quest
Purchase my soul free and immortal rest.
                                        [Exeunt.]

[SCENE viii.

A room in Frankford's house.]

Enter three or four Serving-men, one with a voider [5] and a wooden knife, to take away; another the salt and bread; another the tablecloth and napkins; another the carpet;[6] Jenkin with two lights after them.

JENK. So; march in order, and retire in battle array! My master and the guests have supped already; all's taken away. Here, now spread for the serving-men in the hall!—Butler, it belongs to your office.

BUT. I know it, Jenkin. What d' ye call the gentleman that supped there tonight?

JENK. Who? My master?

BUT. No, no; Master Wendoll, he's a daily guest. I mean the gentleman that [10] came but this afternoon.

JENK. His name's M[aster] Cranwell. God's light! Hark, within there; my master calls to lay more billets upon the fire. Come, come! Lord, how we that are in office here in the house are troubled! One spread the carpet in the parlor, and stand ready to snuff the lights; the rest be ready to prepare their stomachs! More lights in the hall there! Come, Nich'las.   20
                                        [Exeunt all but Nick.]
NICK. I cannot eat, but, had I Wendoll's heart,

[3] Which one?
[4] Lawsuits.
[5] Tray for clearing the remains of the meal.
[6] Heavy covering for a table.

I would eat that. The rogue grows impudent!

O, I have seen such vild,[1] notorious tricks,

Ready to make my eyes dart from my head!

I'll tell my master; by this air, I will.

Fall what may fall, I'll tell him. Here he comes.

Enter Master Frankford, as it were brushing the crumbs from his clothes with a napkin, as newly risen from supper.

FRANK. Nich'las, what make [2] you here? Why are not you

At supper in the hall, among your fellows?

NICK. Master, I stayed [3] your rising from the board,   29

To speak with you.

FRANK.   Be brief then, gentle Nich'las;

My wife and guests attend [4] me in the parlor.

Why dost thou pause? Now, Nich'las, you want money,

And, unthriftlike, would eat into your wages

Ere you have earned it. Here, sir, 's half a crown;

Play the good husband.[5] And away to supper!

NICK. [*Aside.*] By this hand, an honorable gentleman! I will not see him wronged.—Sir, I have served you long; you entertained me seven years before your beard; you knew me, sir, before [40 you knew my mistress.

FRANK. What of this good Nich'las?

NICK. I never was a makebate [6] or a knave;

I have no fault but one—I'm given to quarrel,

But not with women. I will tell you, master,

That which will make your heart leap from your breast,

Your hair to startle from your head, your ears to tingle.

FRANK. What preparation's this to dismal news?

NICK. 'Sblood![7] Sir, I love you better than your wife.

I'll make it good.   50

FRANK. Y'are a knave, and I have much ado

With wonted patience to contain my rage,

And not to break thy pate. Th' art a knave.

I'll turn you, with your base comparisons, Out of my doors.

NICK.   Do, do!

There is not room for Wendoll and me too,

Both in one house. O master, master, That Wendoll is a villain!

FRANK. [*Striking him.*]   Ay, saucy!

NICK. Strike, strike, do strike; yet hear me! I am no fool;

I know a villain, when I see him act   60

Deeds of a villain. Master, master, that base slave

Enjoys my mistress, and dishonors you.

FRANK. Thou hast killed me with a weapon whose sharp point

Hath pricked quite through and through my shiv'ring heart.

Drops of cold sweat sit dangling on my hairs,

Like morning's dew upon the golden flowers,

And I am plunged into strange agonies.

What didst thou say? If any word that touched

His credit or her reputation,

It is as hard to enter my belief   70

As Dives into heaven.

NICK.   I can gain nothing.

They are two that never wronged me. I knew before

'Twas but a thankless office, and perhaps As much as is my service or my life is worth.

All this I know; but this, and more, More by a thousand dangers, could not hire me

To smother such a heinous wrong from you.

I saw, and I have said.

FRANK. [*Aside.*] 'Tis probable. Though blunt, yet he is honest.

Though I durst pawn my life, and on their faith   80

[1] Vile.
[2] Do.
[3] Awaited.
[4] Await.
[5] *I.e.*, be thrifty.
[6] Maker of debates, quarrels.
[7] God's blood.

Hazard the dear salvation of my soul,
Yet in my trust I may be too secure.
May this be true? O, may it? Can it be?
Is it by any wonder possible?
Man, woman, what thing mortal can we
  trust,
When friends and bosom wives prove so
  unjust?—
What instance [1] hast thou of this strange
  report?
NICK. Eyes, master, eyes.
FRANK. Thy eyes may be deceived, I tell
  thee;
For, should an angel from the heavens
  drop down,   90
And preach this to me that thyself hast
  told,
He should have much ado to win belief,
In both their loves I am so confident.
NICK. Shall I discourse the same by cir-
  cumstance?
FRANK. No more! To supper, and com-
  mand your fellows
To attend us and the strangers. Not a
  word,
I charge thee, on thy life! Be secret then,
For I know nothing.
NICK. I am dumb; and, now that I have
  eased my stomach, [2]
I will go fill my stomach.   *Exit.*
FRANK.   Away! Begone!—   100
She is well born, descended nobly;
Virtuous her education; her repute
Is in the general voice of all the country
Honest and fair; her carriage, her de-
  meanor,
In all her actions that concern the love
To me her husband, modest, chaste, and
  godly.
Is all this seeming gold plain copper?
But he, that Judas that hath borne my
  purse,
And sold me for a sin! O God! O God!
Shall I put up these wrongs? No! Shall
  I trust   110
The bare report of this suspicious groom
Before the double gilt, [3] the well-hatch [4]
  ore
Of their two hearts? No, I will loose [5]
  these thoughts;

---

[1] Evidence.   [2] Anger.
[3] Gold; with a pun on the meaning *guilt.*
[4] Well-hatched, nobly wrought.
[5] Possibly a spelling of *lose.*

Distraction I will banish from my brow,
And from my looks exile sad discontent.
Their wonted favors in my tongue shall
  flow;
Till I know all, I'll nothing seem to
  know.—
Lights and a table there! Wife, M[aster]
  Wendoll,
And gentle Master Cranwell!

Enter Mistress Frankford, Master Wendoll,
* Master Cranwell, Nick, and Jenkin*
* with cards, carpets, stools, and other*
*   necessaries.*

FRANK. O, Master Cranwell, you are a
  stranger here,   120
And often balk [6] my house; faith, y'are a
  churl!
Now we have supped, a table and to
  cards!
JENK. A pair [7] of cards, Nich'las, and a
carpet to cover the table! Where's Sisly,
with her counters and her box? Candles
and candlesticks there! Fie! We have
such a household of serving-creatures! Unless it be Nick and I, there's not one
amongst them all can say "bo" to a
goose!—Well said, [8] Nick!   130
They spread a carpet, set down lights and
*   cards.*
ANNE. Come, M[aster] Frankford, who
shall take my part? [9]
FRANK. Marry, that will I, sweet wife.
WEN. No, by my faith, when you are together, I sit out. It must be Mistress
Frankford and I, or else it is no match.
FRANK. I do not like that match.
NICK. [*Aside.*] You have no reason,
marry, knowing all.   139
FRANK. 'Tis no great matter, neither.—
Come, Master Cranwell, shall you and I
take them up?
CRAN. At your pleasure, sir.
FRANK. I must look to you, Master
Wendoll, for you'll be playing false. Nay,
so will my wife, too.
NICK. [*Aside.*] I will be sworn she will.
ANNE. Let them that are taken false,
forfeit the set!
FRANK. Content; it shall go hard but I'll
  take you.   150

---

[6] Avoid.   [8] Well done.
[7] Pack.   [9] Be my partner.

CRAN. Gentlemen, what shall our game be?

WEN. Master Frankford, you play best at noddy.[1]

FRANK. You shall not find it so; indeed, you shall not.

ANNE. I can play at nothing so well as double-ruff.[2]

FRANK. If Master Wendoll and my wife be together, there's no playing against them at double-hand.[3]

NICK. I can tell you, sir, the game that Master Wendoll is best at.

WEN. What game is that, Nick?   160

NICK. Marry, sir, knave-out-of-doors.

WEN. She and I will take you at loadum.

ANNE. Husband, shall we play at saint?

FRANK. [Aside.] My saint's turned devil.—No, we'll none of saint.

You are best at new-cut, wife; you'll play at that.

WEN. If you play at new-cut, I'm soonest[4] hitter of any here, for a wager.

FRANK. [Aside.] 'Tis me they play on.

Well, you may draw out;

For all your cunning, 'twill be to your shame;

I'll teach you, at your new-cut, a new game.—   170

Come, come!

CRAN. If you cannot agree upon the game, To post and pair!

WEN. We shall be soonest pairs, and my good host,

When he comes late home, he must kiss the post.[5]

FRANK. Whoever wins, it shall be to thy cost.

CRAN. Faith, let it be vide-ruff, and let's make honors!

FRANK. If you make honors, one thing let me crave:

Honor the king and queen; except[6] the knave.

WEN. Well, as you please for that.—Lift![7]

Who shall deal?   180

ANNE. The least in sight. What are you, Master Wendoll?

WEN. I am a knave.

NICK. [Aside.] I'll swear it.

ANNE.   I am queen.

FRANK. [Aside.] A quean, thou shouldst say.—Well, the cards are mine;

They are the grossest pair that e'er I felt.

ANNE. Shuffle; I'll cut. Would I had never dealt!

FRANK. [Misdealing]. I have lost my dealing.

WEN.   Sir, the fault's in me;

This queen I have more than mine own, you see.

Give me the stock![8]

FRANK.   My mind's not on my game.

Many a deal I've lost; the more's your shame.

You have served me a bad trick, Master Wendoll.   190

WEN. Sir, you must take your lot. To end this strife,

I know I have dealt better with your wife.

FRANK. Thou hast dealt falsely, then.

ANNE. What's trumps?

WEN. Hearts. Partner, I rub.[9]

FRANK. [Aside.] Thou robb'st me of my soul, of her chaste love;

In thy false dealing thou hast robbed my heart.—

Booty you play;[10] I, like a loser, stand,

Having no heart, or[11] here or in my hand.

I will give o'er the set; I am not well.

Come, who will hold my cards?   201

ANNE. Not well, sweet M[aster] Frankford?

Alas, what ail you? 'Tis some sudden qualm.

WEN. How long have you been so, Master Frankford?

FRANK. Sir, I was lusty, and I had my health,

But I grew ill when you began to deal.—

Take hence this table!—Gentle Master Cranwell,

Y'are welcome; see your chamber at your pleasure!

I am sorry that this megrim takes me so;

I cannot sit and bear you company.—

Jenkin, some lights, and show him to his chamber!   211

[Exeunt Cranwell and Jenkin.]

---

[1] A game like cribbage; also, a simpleton.
[2] Forerunner of whist; with a double meaning.
[3] The names of this and the following games, the nature of which is not known, are of course used with double meanings.
[4] Quickest, speediest.
[5] I.e., be shut out.
[6] Exclude.
[7] Cut.
[8] Remainder of the pack.   [9] Take the trick.
[10] Lose, by arrangement with a confederate, in order to draw the opponent on.
[11] Either.

ANNE. A nightgown [1] for my husband;
quickly there!
It is some rheum or cold.

WEN.   Now, in good faith,
This illness you have got by sitting late
Without your gown.

FRANK.   I know it, M[aster] Wendoll.
Go, go to bed, lest you complain like
me!—
Wife, prithee, wife, into my bedcham-
ber!
The night is raw and cold and rheumatic.
Leave me my gown and light; I'll walk
away my fit.

WEN. Sweet sir, good night!   220
FRANK. Myself, good night!
                         [Exit Wendoll.]
ANNE.   Shall I attend you, husband?
FRANK. No, gentle wife, thou't catch cold
in thy head.
Prithee, begone, sweet; I'll make haste to
bed.
ANNE. No sleep will fasten on mine eyes,
you know,
Until you come.   Exit.
FRANK.   Sweet Nan, I prithee, go!—
I have bethought me. Get me by degrees
The keys of all my doors, which I will
mold
In wax, and take their fair impression,
To have by them new keys. This being
compassed,   229
At a set hour a letter shall be brought me,
And, when they think they may securely
play,
They nearest are to danger. Nick, I must
rely
Upon thy trust and faithful secrecy.
NICK. Build on my faith!
FRANK.   To bed, then, not to rest!
Care lodges in my brain, grief in my
breast.   [Exeunt.]

[SCENE ix.

Near the home of Old Mountford.]

Enter Sir Charles his [2] *Sister, Old Mountford,
Sandy, Roder, and Tidy.*

MOUNT. You say my nephew is in great
distress.
Who brought it to him but his own
lewd[3] life?

[1] Dressing gown.   [2] *I.e.*, Charles's.
[3] Worthless.

I cannot spare a cross. I must confess
He was my brother's son; why, niece,
what then?
This is no world in which to pity men.

SUS. I was not born a beggar, though his
extremes
Enforce this language from me. I pro-
test
No fortune of mine own could lead my
tongue
To this base key. I do beseech you,
uncle,
For the name's sake, for Christianity, 10
Nay, for God's sake, to pity his dis-
tress.
He is denied the freedom of the prison,
And in the hole is laid with men con-
demned.
Plenty he hath of nothing but of irons,
And it remains in you to free him thence.

MOUNT. Money I cannot spare; men
should take heed.
He lost my kindred when he fell to need.
                              [Exit.]

SUS. Gold is but earth; thou earth enough
shalt have,
When thou hast once took measure of
thy grave.
You know me, Master Sandy, and my
suit.   20

SANDY. I knew you, lady, when the old
man lived;
I knew you ere your brother sold his
land.
Then you were Mistress Sue, tricked up
in jewels;
Then you sung well, played sweetly on
the lute.
But now I neither know you nor your
suit.   [Exit.]

SUS. You, Master Roder, was my brother's
tenant;
Rent-free he placed you in that wealthy
farm
Of which you are possessed.

RODER.   True, he did;
And have I not there dwelt still for his
sake?
I have some business now; but without
doubt   30
They that have hurled him in will help
him out.   Exit.

SUS. Cold comfort still. What say you,
cousin Tidy?

TIDY. I say this comes of roisting,[1] swag-
g'ring.
    Call me not cousin. Each man for him-
self!
    Some men are born to mirth, and some
to sorrow;
    I am no cousin unto them that borrow.
                      Exit.
SUS. O Charity, why art thou fled to
heaven,
    And left all things on this earth uneven?
    Their scoffing answers I will ne'er re-
turn,   39
    But to myself his grief in silence mourn.

Enter Sir Francis and Malby.

FRAN. She is poor; I'll therefore tempt
her with this gold.
    Go, Malby, in my name deliver it,
    And I will stay thy answer.
MAL. Fair mistress, as I understand your
grief
    Doth grow from want, so I have here
in store
    A means to furnish you, a bag of gold,
    Which to your hands I freely tender you.
SUS. I thank you, heavens! I thank you,
gentle sir;
    God make me able to requite this favor!
MAL. This gold Sir Francis Acton sends
by me,   50
    And prays you—
SUS. Acton? O God! That name I'm
born to curse.
    Hence, bawd; hence, broker![2] See, I
spurn his gold.
    My honor never shall for gain be sold.
FRAN. Stay, lady, stay!
SUS.   From you I'll posting hie,
    Even as the doves from feathered eagles
fly.   *Exit.*
FRAN. She hates my name, my face. How
should I woo?
    I am disgraced in everything I do.
    The more she hates me, and disdains my
love,
    The more I am rapt in admiration   60
    Of her divine and chaste perfections.
    Woo her with gifts I cannot, for all gifts
    Sent in my name she spurns; with looks
I cannot,
    For she abhors my sight; nor yet with
letters,

[1] Roistering, rioting.   [2] Go-between.

    For none she will receive. How then?
How then?
    Well, I will fasten such a kindness on
her
    As shall o'ercome her hate and conquer it.
    Sir Charles, her brother, lies in execu-
tion
    For a great sum of money; and, besides,
    The appeal is sued still for my hunts-
men's death,   70
    Which only I have power to reverse.
    In her I'll bury all my hate of him.—
    Go seek the keeper, Malby; bring him
to me!
    To save his body, I his debts will pay;
    To save his life, I his appeal will stay.
                      [Exeunt.]

[SCENE x.

A dungeon in York Castle.]

*Enter Sir Charles in prison, with irons, his
feet bare, his garments all ragged and
torn.*

CHAR. Of all on the earth's face most
miserable,
    Breathe in this hellish dungeon thy la-
ments,
    Thus like a slave ragg'd, like a felon
gyved!
    That hurls thee headlong to this base
estate!
    O unkind uncle! O my friends ingrate,
    Unthankful kinsmen, Mountfords all-
too [3] base,
    To let thy name be fettered in disgrace!
    A thousand deaths here in this grave I
die!
    Fear, hunger, sorrow, cold, all threat
my death,   9
    And join together to deprive my breath.
    But, that which most torments me, my
dear sister
    Hath left [4] to visit me, and from my
friends
    Hath brought no hopeful answer; there-
fore, I
    Divine they will not help my misery.
    If it be so, shame, scandal, and contempt
    Attend their covetous thoughts; need
make their graves!
    Usurers they live, and may they die
like slaves!

[3] Entirely.   [4] Ceased.

Enter Keeper.

KEEP. Knight, be of comfort, for I bring
thee freedom
From all thy troubles.
CHAR.   Then I am doomed to die:
Death is the end of all calamity.   20
KEEP. Live! Your appeal is stayed; the
execution
Of all your debts discharged; your
creditors
Even to the utmost penny satisfied;
In sign whereof your shackles I knock
off.
You are not left so much indebted to us
As for your fees; all is discharged, all
paid.
Go freely to your house, or where you
please;
After long miseries, embrace your ease.
CHAR. Thou grumblest out the sweetest
music to me
That ever organ played.—Is this a
dream?   30
Or do my waking senses apprehend
The pleasing taste of these applausive [1]
news?
Slave that I was, to wrong such honest
friends,
My loving kinsmen, and my near allies!
Tongue, I will bite thee for the scandal
breath [2]
Against such faithful kinsmen; they are
all
Composed of pity and compassion,
Of melting charity and of moving ruth. [3]
That which I spake before was in my
rage;
They are my friends, the mirrors [4] of
this age,   40
Bounteous and free. The noble Mount-
fords' race
Ne'er bred a covetous thought, or humor
base.

Enter Susan.

SUS. [*Aside.*] I can no longer stay from
visiting
My woeful brother. While I could, I
kept
My hapless tidings from his hopeful
ear.

CHAR. Sister, how much am I indebted
to thee
And to thy travail!
SUS.   What, at liberty?
CHAR. Thou seest I am, thanks to thy
industry.
O, unto which of all my courteous friends
Am I thus bound? My uncle Mount-
ford, he   50
Even of an infant loved me. Was it he?
So did my cousin Tidy. Was it he?
So Master Roder, Master Sandy, too.
Which of all these did this high kind-
ness do?
SUS. Charles, can you mock me in your
poverty,
Knowing your friends deride your
misery?
Now, I protest I stand so much amazed,
To see your bonds free, and your irons
knocked off,
That I am rapt into a maze of wonder;
The rather for I know not by what
means   60
This happiness hath chanced.
CHAR.   Why, by my uncle,
My cousins, and my friends. Who else,
I pray,
Would take upon them all my debts to
pay?
SUS. O brother, they are men all of flint,
Pictures of marble, and as void of pity
As chaséd bears. I begged, I sued, I
kneeled,
Laid open all your griefs and miseries,
Which they derided; more than that,
denied us
A part in their alliance, but, in pride,
Said that our kindred with our plenty
died.   70
CHAR. Drudges too much [5]—what did
they? O, known evil!
Rich fly the poor as good men shun the
devil.
Whence should my freedom come? Of
whom alive,
Saving of those, have I deserved so well?
Guess, sister, call to mind, remember me!
These I have raised, [6] they follow the
world's guise,
Whom, rich in honor, they in woe despise. [7]

---

[1] Worthy of applause, joyful.   [3] Pity.
[2] Scandalous talk.   [4] Paragons.
[5] Menials too base.   [6] Recalled, named.
[7] *I.e.*, those who are honorable but unfortunate they despise.

Sus. My wits have lost themselves; let's ask the keeper!

Char. Jailer!

Keep. At hand, sir. 80

Char. Of courtesy resolve me one demand![1]
What was he took the burthen of my debts
From off my back, stayed my appeal to death,
Discharged my fees, and brought me liberty?

Keep. A courteous knight, and called Sir Francis Acton.

Char. Ha! Acton! O me, more distressed in this
Than all my troubles! Hale me back,
Double my irons, and my sparing meals
Put into halves, and lodge me in a dungeon
More deep, more dark, more cold, more comfortless! 90
By Acton freed! Not all thy manacles
Could fetter so my heels as this one word
Hath thralled my heart, and it must now lie bound
In more strict prison than thy stony jail.
I am not free; I go but under bail.

Keep. My charge is done, sir, now I have my fees.
As we get little, we will nothing leese.[2]
Exit.

Char. By Acton freed, my dangerous opposite!
Why, to what end? Or what occasion? Ha!
Let me forget the name of enemy, 100
And with indifference balance[3] this high favor! Ha!

Sus. [*Aside.*] His love to me! Upon my soul, 'tis so!
That is the root from whence these strange things grow.

Char. Had this proceeded from my father, he
That by the law of nature is most bound
In offices of love, it had deserved
My best employment to requite that grace.
Had it proceeded from my friends, or him,

From them this action had deserved my life,
And from a stranger more, because from such 110
There is less execution of good deeds.
But he, nor father, nor ally, nor friend,
More than a stranger, both remote in blood,
And in his heart opposed my enemy,
That this high bounty should proceed from him—
O, there I lose myself! What should I say,
What think, what do, his bounty to repay?

Sus. You wonder, I am sure, whence this strange kindness
Proceeds in Acton; I will tell you, brother.
He dotes on me, and oft hath sent me gifts, 120
Letters, and tokens; I refused them all.

Char. I have enough, though poor; my heart is set
In one rich gift to pay back all my debt.
Exeunt.

[Scene xi.

A room in Frankford's house.]

Enter Frankford and Nick, with keys and a letter in his hand.

Frank. This is the night that I must play my part,
To try two seeming angels.—Where's my keys?

Nick. They are made according to your mold in wax.
I bade the smith be secret, gave him money,
And here they are. The letter, sir!

Frank. [*Giving letter.*] 'True, take it; there it is;
And, when thou seest me in my pleasant's[t] vein,
Ready to sit to supper, bring it me!

Nick. I'll do 't; make no more question but I'll do 't. *Exit.*

Enter Mistress Frankford, Cranwell, Wendoll, and Jenkin.

Anne. Sirrah, 'tis six a-clock already stroke; 10
Go bid them spread the cloth, and serve in supper.

---
[1] Answer me one question.
[2] Lose.   [3] Weigh with impartiality.

JENK. It shall be done, forsooth, mistress. Where's Spigot, the butler, to give us our salt and trenchers?   [*Exit.*]
WEN. We that have been a-hunting all the day
Come with preparéd stomachs.—Master Frankford,
We wished you at our sport.
FRANK. My heart was with you, and my mind was on you.—
Fie, Master Cranwell! You are still thus sad?—
A stool, a stool! Where's Jenkin, and where's Nick?   20
'Tis supper time at least an hour ago. What's the best news abroad?
WEN. I know none good.
FRANK. [*Aside.*]   But I know too much bad.

Enter Butler and Jenkin, with a tablecloth, bread, trenchers, and salt.

CRAN. Methinks, sir, you might have that interest
In [1] your wife's brother, to be more remiss [2]
In his hard dealing against poor Sir Charles,
Who, as I hear, lies in York Castle,
Needy and in great want.
    [*Exeunt Jenkin and Butler.*]
FRANK. Did not more weighty business of mine own
Hold me away, I would have labored peace   30
Betwixt them with all care; indeed I would, sir.
ANNE. I'll write unto my brother earnestly In that behalf.
WEN.   A charitable deed,
And will beget the good opinion
Of all your friends that love you, Mistress Frankford.
FRANK. That's you, for one; I know you love Sir Charles,
And my wife too, well.
WEN.   He deserves the love
Of all true gentlemen; be yourselves judge!
FRANK. But supper, ho!—Now, as thou lov'st me, Wendoll,
Which I am sure thou dost, be merry, pleasant,   40

And frolic it tonight! Sweet Master Cranwell,
Do you the like! Wife, I protest, my heart
Was ne'er more bent on sweet alacrity.
Where be those lazy knaves to serve in supper?

Enter Nick.

NICK. Here's a letter, sir.
FRANK. Whence comes it, and who brought it?
NICK. A stripling that below attends your answer,
And, as he tells me, it is sent from York.
FRANK. Have him into the cellar; let him taste
A cup of our March beer; go, make him drink!   [*Reads the letter.*]   50
NICK. I'll make him drunk, if he be a Trojan.[3]
FRANK. My boots and spurs! Where's Jenkin? God forgive me,
How I neglect my business! Wife, look here!
I have a matter to be tried tomorrow
By eight a-clock, and my attorney writes me
I must be there betimes with evidence,
Or it will go against me. Where's my boots?

Enter Jenkin, with boots and spurs.

ANNE. I hope your business craves no such despatch
That you must ride tonight?
WEN. [*Aside.*]   I hope it doth.
FRANK. God's me! No such despatch!   60
Jenkin, my boots! Where's Nick? Saddle my roan,
And the gray dapple for himself!—Content ye,
It much concerns me.—Gentle Master Cranwell,
And Master Wendoll, in my absence use
The very ripest pleasures of my house!
WEN. Lord, Master Frankford, will you ride tonight?
The ways are dangerous.
FRANK.   Therefore will I ride
Appointed [4] well; and so shall Nick, my man.

---

[1] Influence with.   [2] Lenient.
[3] Good fellow.   [4] Equipped, armed.

ANNE. I'll call you up by five a-clock to-
　　morrow.

FRANK. No, by my faith, wife, I'll not
　　trust to that.　　　　　　　　　　70
　'Tis not such easy rising in a morning
　From one I love so dearly. No, by my
　　faith,
　I shall not leave so sweet a bedfellow
　But with much pain. You have made
　　me a sluggard
　Since I first knew you.

ANNE.　　　　　Then, if you needs will go
　This dangerous evening, Master Wendoll,
　Let me entreat you bear him company.

WEN. With all my heart, sweet mistress.—
　My boots there!

FRANK. Fie, fie, that for my private busi-
　　ness　　　　　　　　　　　　　　79
　I should disease [1] a friend, and be a trouble
　To the whole house!—Nick!

NICK.　　　　　　　　　　Anon, sir!

FRANK. Bring forth my gelding! [Exit
　Nick.]—As you love me, sir,
　Use no more words. A hand, good Master
　　Cranwell!

CRAN. Sir, God be your good speed!

FRANK. Good night, sweet Nan; nay, nay,
　　a kiss, and part!—
　[Aside.] Dissembling lips, you suit not
　　with my heart.　　　　　　　Exit.

WEN. [Aside.] How business, time, and
　　hours all gracious prove,
　And are the furtherers to my new-born
　　love!
　I am husband now in Master Frankford's
　　place,
　And must command the house.—My
　　pleasure is　　　　　　　　　　90
　We will not sup abroad so publicly,
　But in your private chamber, Mistress
　　Frankford.

ANNE. [Aside to Wendoll.] O, sir, you are
　　too public in your love,
　And Master Frankford's wife—

CRAN.　　　　　　Might I crave favor,
　I would entreat you I might see my
　　chamber.
　I am on the sudden grown exceeding ill,
　And would be spared from supper.

WEN.　　　　　　　　Light there, ho!—
　See you want nothing, sir, for, if you do,
　You injure that good man, and wrong
　　me too.　　　　　　　　　　99

[1] Dis-ease, inconvenience.

CRAN. I will make bold. Good night!
　　　　　　　　　　　　　　　Exit.

WEN.　　　　　　　How all conspire
　To make our bosom [2] sweet, and full
　　entire! [3]
　Come, Nan, I prithee let us sup within!

ANNE. O, what a clog unto the soul is sin!
　We pale offenders are still full of fear;
　Every suspicious eye brings danger near,
　When they whose clear heart from offense
　　are free
　Despise report, base scandals do outface,
　And stand at mere [4] defiance with dis-
　　grace.

WEN. Fie, fie! You talk too like a Puritan.

ANNE. You have tempted me to mischief,
　　M[aster] Wendoll;　　　　　　　110
　I have done I know not what. Well, you
　　plead custom;
　That which for want of wit I granted
　　erst, [5]
　I now must yield through fear. Come,
　　come, let's in;
　Once o'er shoes, we are straight o'er
　　head in sin.

WEN. My jocund soul is joyful above
　　measure;
　I'll be profuse in Frankford's richest
　　treasure.　　　　　　　　Exeunt.

[SCENE xii.

Another room in the house.]

Enter Sisly, Jenkin, Butler.

JENK. My mistress and Master Wendoll,
my master, sup in her chamber tonight.
Sisly, you are preferred [6] from being the
cook to be chambermaid. Of all the loves
betwixt thee and me, tell me what thou
think'st of this.

SISLY. Mum; there's an old proverb,
"When the cat's away, the mouse may
play."

JENK. Now you talk of a cat, Sisly, I [10
smell a rat.

SISLY. Good words, Jenkin, lest you be
called to answer them!

JENK. Why, God make my mistress an
honest woman! Are not these good words?
Pray God my new master play not the
knave with my old master! Is there any

[2] Intimacy.　　　　　[5] Formerly.
[3] Very complete.　　　[6] Promoted.
[4] Absolute.

hurt in this? God send no villainy intended; and, if they do sup together, pray God they do not lie together! God make my mis- [20 tress chaste, and make us all His servants! What harm is there in all this? Nay, more; here is my hand; thou shalt never have my heart unless thou say amen.

SISLY. Amen, I pray God, I say.

Enter Serving-men.

SERVING-MAN. My mistress sends that you should make less noise, to lock up the doors, and see the household all got to bed. You, Jenkin, for this night are made the porter, to see the gates shut in.   30

JENK. Thus by little and little I creep into office. Come, to kennel, my masters, to kennel; 'tis eleven a-clock already.

SERV. When you have locked the gates in, you must send up the keys to my mistress.

SISLY. Quickly, for God's sake, Jenkin, for I must carry them. I am neither pillow nor bolster, but I know more than both.

JENK. To bed, good Spigot; to bed, [40 good honest serving-creatures; and let us sleep as snug as pigs in pea straw! *Exeunt.*

[SCENE xiii.

Outside Frankford's house.[1]]

Enter Frankford and Nick.

FRANK. Soft, soft! We have tied our [2] geldings to a tree,
Two flight-shot [3] off, lest by their thun-
    dering hoofs
They blab our coming. Hear'st thou no
    noise?

NICK. I hear nothing but the owl and you.

FRANK. So; now my watch's hand points upon twelve,
And it is just midnight. Where are my keys?

NICK. Here, sir.

FRANK. This is the key that opes my out-
    ward gate;
This, the hall door; this, the withdraw-
    ing-chamber;   10

[1] This scene shifts gradually to the hall of the house.
[2] From 1607 edn. Original reads *your.*
[3] Early edns. read *flight shoot;* long bow-shot.

But this, that door that's bawd unto my shame,
Fountain and spring of all my bleeding thoughts,
Where the most hallowed order and true knot
Of nuptial sanctity hath been profaned.
It leads to my polluted bedchamber,
Once my terrestrial heaven, now my earth's hell,
The place where sins in all their ripeness dwell.—
But I forget myself; now to my gate!

NICK. It must ope with far less noise than Cripplegate, or your plot's dashed. [20

FRANK. So, reach me my dark lanthorn to the rest! [4]
Tread softly, softly!

NICK.   I will walk on eggs this pace.
        [*They enter the house.*]

FRANK. A general silence hath surprised the house,
And this is the last door. Astonishment,
Fear, and amazement beat upon my heart,
Even as a madman beats upon a drum.
O, keep my eyes, you heavens, before 1 enter,
From any sight that may transfix my soul;
Or, if there be so black a spectacle,
O, strike mine eyes stark blind; or, if not so,   30
Lend me such patience to digest my grief,
That I may keep this white and virgin hand
From any violent outrage or red murther!
And with that prayer I enter.
        [*Exit.*]

NICK. [*Aside.*] Here's a circumstance, indeed! A man may be made cuckold in the time that he's about it. And [5] the case were mine, as 'tis my master's—'sblood, that he makes me swear!—I would have placed his action, [6] entered there! [40 I would, I would!

FRANK. [*Reenters.*] O! O!

NICK. Master! 'Sblood! Master, master!

FRANK. O me unhappy! I have found them lying

[4] *I.e.*, in addition to the other equipment.
[5] If.
[6] Established his case (Ward).

Close in each other arms, and fast asleep.
But that I would not damn two precious
souls,
Bought with my Savior's blood, and send
them laden
With all their scarlet sins upon their
backs
Unto a fearful judgment, their two lives
Had met upon my rapier.   50
NICK. Master, what, have you left them
sleeping still?
Let me go wake 'em!
FRANK.   Stay, let me pause awhile!—
O God! O God! That it were possible
To undo things done, to call back yester-
day;
That Time could turn up his swift sandy
glass,
To untell the days, and to redeem these
hours;
Or that the sun
Could, rising from the west, draw his
coach backward,
Take from th' account of time so many
minutes,   59
Till he had all these seasons called again,
Those minutes, and those actions done
in them,
Even from her first offense that I might
take her
As spotless as an angel in my arms!
But, O, I talk of things impossible,
And cast beyond the moon.[1] God give
me patience,
For I will in, and wake them.   *Exit.*
NICK.   Here's patience perforce!
He needs must trot afoot that tires his
horse.

Enter Wendoll, running over the stage in a
nightgown, he [Frankford] after him
with his sword drawn; the Maid in her
smock stays his hand, and clasps hold
on him. He pauses for a while.

FRANK. I thank thee, maid; thou, like an
angel's hand,
Hast stayed me from a bloody sacrifice.—
Go, villain, and my wrongs sit on thy
soul   70
As heavy as this grief doth upon mine!
When thou record'st my many courtesies,
And shall compare them with thy treach-
erous heart,

[1] *I.e.*, speak wildly.

Lay them together, weigh them equally,
'Twill be revenge enough.   Go, to thy
friend
A Judas; pray, pray, lest I live to see
Thee, Judas-like, hanged on an eldertree!

Enter Mistress Frankford in her smock,
nightgown, and night attire.

ANNE. O, by what word, what title, or
what name,
Shall I entreat your pardon? Pardon! O,
I am as far from hoping such sweet grace
As Lucifer from heaven.   To call you
husband—   81
O me, most wretched! I have lost that
name;
I am no more your wife.
NICK.   'Sblood, sir, she sounds.[2]
FRANK. Spare thou thy tears, for I will
weep for thee;
And keep thy count'nance, for I'll blush
for thee.
Now, I protest, I think 'tis I am tainted,
For I am most ashamed; and 'tis more
hard
For me to look upon thy guilty face
Than on the sun's clear brow.   What
wouldst thou speak?
ANNE. I would I had no tongue, no ears,
no eyes,   90
No apprehension, no capacity.
When do you spurn me like a dog? When
tread me
Under feet? When drag me by the hair?
Though I deserve a thousand thousand
fold
More than you can inflict, yet, once my
husband,
For womanhood—to which I am a
shame,[3]
Though once an ornament—even for His
sake
That hath redeemed our souls, mark not
my face,
Nor hack me with your sword, but let
me go   99
Perfect and undeforméd to my tomb!
I am not worthy that I should prevail
In the least suit; no, not to speak to you,
Nor look on you, nor to be in your
presence;
Yet, as an abject, this one suit I crave.
This granted, I am ready for my grave.

[2] Swoons.   [3] Early edns. read *ashamed*.

FRANK. My God, with patience arm me!—
Rise, nay, rise,
And I'll debate with thee. Was it for
want
Thou playedst the strumpet? Wast thou
not supplied
With every pleasure, fashion, and new
toy,
Nay, even beyond my calling? [1]
ANNE. I was. 110
FRANK. Was it, then, disability in me?
Or in thine eye seemed he a properer [2]
man?
ANNE. O, no!
FRANK. Did not I lodge thee in
my bosom?
Wear thee in my heart?
ANNE. You did.
FRANK. I did, indeed; witness my tears, I
did.—
Go, bring my infants hither!—
[*Exit Maid and returns with two Children.*]
O Nan! O Nan!
If neither fear of shame, regard of honor,
The blemish of my house, nor my dear love
Could have withheld thee from so lewd
a fact,[3]
Yet for these infants, these young, harm-
less souls, 120
On whose white brows thy shame is
charactered,
And grows in greatness as they wax in
years—
Look but on them, and melt away in
tears!—
Away with them, lest, as her spotted
body
Hath stained their names with stripe of
bastardy,
So her adulterous breath may blast their
spirits
With her infectious thoughts! Away with
them! [*Exeunt Maid and Children.*]
ANNE. In this one life, I die ten thousand
deaths.
FRANK. Stand up, stand up! I will do
nothing rashly.
I will retire awhile into my study, 130
And thou shalt hear thy sentence pres-
ently.[4] *Exit.*
ANNE. 'Tis welcome, be it death. O me,
base strumpet,

That, having such a husband, such sweet
children,
Must enjoy neither! O, to redeem mine
honor,
I would have this hand cut off, these my
breasts seared;
Be racked, strappadoed, put to any
torment;
Nay, to whip but this scandal out, I
would hazard
The rich and dear redemption of my soul!
He cannot be so base as to forgive me,
Nor I so shameless to accept his par-
don. 140
O women, women, you that yet have
kept
Your holy matrimonial vow unstained,
Make me your instance; when you tread
awry,
Your sins, like mine, will on your con-
science lie.

*Enter Sisly, Spigot, all the Serving-men, and
Jenkin, as newly come out of bed.*

ALL. O mistress, mistress! What have you
done, mistress?
NICK. What a caterwauling keep you here!
JENK. O Lord, mistress, how comes this
to pass? My master is run away in his
shirt, and never so much as called me to
bring his clothes after him. 150
ANNE. See what guilt is! Here stand I in
this place,
Ashamed to look my servants in the
face.

*Enter M[aster] Frankford and Cranwell,
whom seeing, she falls on her knees.*

FRANK. My words are registered in heaven
already.
With patience hear me. I'll not martyr
thee,
Nor mark thee for a strumpet, but with
usage
Of more humility torment thy soul,
And kill thee even with kindness.
CRAN. M[aster] Frankford—
FRANK. Good M[aster] Cranwell!—Wo-
man, hear thy judgment!
Go make thee ready in thy best attire,
Take with thee all thy gowns, all thy
apparel, 160
Leave nothing that did ever call thee
mistress,

---

[1] Estate, station.   [3] Act.
[2] Handsomer.   [4] Immediately.

Or by whose sight, being left here in the house,
I may remember such a woman by.
Choose thee a bed and hangings for thy chamber,
Take with thee everything which hath thy mark,
And get thee to my manor seven mile off,
Where live. 'Tis thine; I freely give it thee.
My tenants by [1] shall furnish thee with wains
To carry all thy stuff within two hours;
No longer will I limit [2] thee my sight.   170
Choose which of all my servants thou lik'st best,
And they are thine to attend thee.

ANNE.   A mild sentence.

FRANK. But, as thou hop'st for heaven, as thou believ'st
Thy name's recorded in the Book of Life,
I charge thee never after this sad day
To see me, or to meet me, or to send,
By word or writing, gift or otherwise,
To move me, by thyself or by thy friends,
Nor challenge any part in my two children.
So farewell, Nan; for we will henceforth be   180
As we had never seen, ne'er more shall see.

ANNE. How full my heart is, in mine eyes appears;
What wants in words, I will supply in tears.

FRANK. Come, take your coach, your stuff; all must along.
Servants and all make ready; all begone!
It was thy hand cut two hearts out of one.   *Exeunt.*

[SCENE xiv.

Before Sir Francis Acton's house.]

Enter Sir Charles, gentlemanlike, and his Sister, gentlewomanlike.

SUS. Brother, why have you tricked [3] me like a bride,
Bought me this gay attire, these ornaments?
Forget you our estate, our poverty?

¹ Near by.   ³ Tricked out, dressed.
² Allot, permit.

CHAR. Call me not brother, but imagine me
Some barbarous outlaw, or uncivil kern; [4]
For, if thou shutt'st thy eye, and only hear'st
The words that I shall utter, thou shalt judge me
Some staring ruffian, not thy brother Charles.
O sister!—

SUS. O brother, what doth this strange language mean?   10

CHAR. Dost love me, sister? Wouldst thou see me live
A bankrout [5] beggar in the world's disgrace,
And die indebted to mine enemies?
Wouldst thou behold me stand like a huge beam
In the world's eye, a byword and a scorn?
It lies in thee of these to acquit me free,
And all my debt I may outstrip by thee.

SUS. By me? Why, I have nothing, nothing left;
I owe even for the clothes upon my back;
I am not worth—

CHAR.   O sister, say not so!   20
It lies in you my downcast state to raise,
To make me stand on even points with the world.
Come, sister, you are rich; indeed you are,
And in your power you have, without delay,
Acton's five hundred pound back to repay.

SUS. Till now I had thought y' had loved me. By my honor,
Which I have kept as spotless as the moon,
I ne'er was mistress of that single doit [6]
Which I reserved not to supply your wants;
And d' ye think that I would hoard from you?   30
Now, by my hopes in heaven, knew I the means
To buy you from the slavery of your debts
(Especially from Acton, whom I hate),
I would redeem it with my life or blood!

CHAR. I challenge it, and, kindred set apart,

⁴ Peasant.   ⁵ Bankrupt.   ⁶ Half a farthing.

Thus, ruffianlike, I lay siege to thy heart.
What do I owe to Acton?

Sus. Why, some five hundred pounds,
towards which, I swear,
In all the world I have not one denier.[1]

Char. It will not prove so. Sister, now
resolve me: 40
What do you think (and speak your conscience)
Would Acton give, might he enjoy your
bed?

Sus. He would not shrink to spend a thousand pound
To give the Mountfords' name so deep a
wound.

Char. A thousand pound! I but five hundred owe;
Grant him your bed; he's paid with
int'rest so.

Sus. O brother!

Char.   O sister! Only this one way,
With that rich jewel you my debts may
pay.
In speaking this my cold heart shakes
with shame;
Nor do I woo you in a brother's name, 50
But in a stranger's. Shall I die in debt
To Acton, my grand foe, and you still wear
The precious jewel that he holds so dear?

Sus. My honor I esteem as dear and precious
As my redemption.

Char.   I esteem you, sister,
As dear, for so dear prizing it.

Sus.   Will Charles
Have me cut off my hands, and send
them Acton?
Rip up my breast, and with my bleeding
heart
Present him as a token?

Char.   Neither, sister;
But hear me in my strange assertion! 60
Thy honor and my soul are equal in my
regard;
Nor will thy brother Charles survive thy
shame.
His kindness, like a burthen, hath sur-
charged me,
And under his good deeds I stooping go,
Not with an upright soul. Had I re-
mained
In prison still, there doubtless I had died.
Then, unto him that freed me from that
prison,

Still do I owe this life. What moved my
foe
To enfranchise [2] me? 'Twas, sister, for
your love.
With full five hundred pounds he bought
your love,   70
And shall he not enjoy it? Shall the
weight
Of all this heavy burthen lean on me,
And will not you bear part? You did
partake
The joy of my release; will you not stand
In joint bond bound to satisfy the debt?
Shall I be only charged?

Sus.   But that I know
These arguments come from an honored
mind,
As in your most extremity of need
Scorning to stand in debt to one you
hate—
Nay, rather would engage your unstained
honor   80
Than to be held ingrate—I should con-
demn you.
I see your resolution, and assent.
So Charles will have me, and I am content.

Char. For this I tricked you up.

Sus.   But here's a knife,
To save mine honor, shall slice out my life.

Char. I know thou pleasest me a thousand
times
More in thy resolution than thy grant.—
[Aside.] Observe her love; to soothe it to
my suit,
Her honor she will hazard, though not
lose;
To bring me out of debt, her rigorous
hand   90
Will pierce her heart. O wonder, that
will choose,
Rather than stain her blood, her life to
lose.—
Come, you sad sister to a woeful brother,
This is the gate. I'll bear him such a
present,
Such an acquittance for the knight to seal,
As will amaze his senses, and surprise
With admiration [3] all his fantasies.

Enter Acton and Malby.

Sus. Before his unchaste thoughts shall
seize on me,
'Tis here shall my imprisoned soul set free.

FRAN. How! Mountford with his sister,
    hand in hand!   100
  What miracle's afoot?
MAL.   It is a sight
  Begets in me much admiration.
CHAR. Stand not amazed to see me thus
    attended!
  Acton, I owe thee money, and, being
    unable
  To bring thee the full sum in ready coin,
  Lo, for thy more assurance, here's a
    pawn—
  My sister, my dear sister, whose chaste
    honor
  I prize above a million. Here! Nay, take
    her;
  She's worth your money, man; do not
    forsake her.
FRAN. I would he were in earnest!   110
SUS. Impute it not to my immodesty.
  My brother, being rich in nothing else
  But in his interest that he hath in me,
  According to his poverty hath brought
    you
  Me, all his store, whom, howsoe'er you
    prize,
  As forfeit to your hand, he values highly,
  And would not sell, but to acquit your
    debt,
  For any emperor's ransom.
FRAN. [*Aside.*]   Stern heart, relent;
  Thy former cruelty at length repent!
  Was ever known, in any former age,   120
  Such honorable, wrested [1] courtesy?
  Lands, honors, life, and all the world forgo
  Rather than stand engaged to such a foe!
CHAR. Acton, she is too poor to be thy
    bride,
  And I too much opposed to be thy
    brother.
  There, take her to thee. If thou hast the
    heart
  To seize her as a rape or lustful prey,
  To blur our house, that never yet was
    stained,
  To murther her that never meant thee
    harm,
  To kill me now, whom once thou savedst
    from death,   130
  Do them at once; on her all these rely,
  And perish with her spotted chastity.
FRAN. You overcome me in your love, Sir
    Charles.

[1] Distorted.   [2] Lacks, deficiencies.

I cannot be so cruel to a lady
I love so dearly. Since you have not
  spared
To engage your reputation to the world,
Your sister's honor, which you prize so
  dear,
Nay, all the comfort which you hold on
  earth,
To grow out of my debt, being your foe,
Your honored thoughts, lo! thus I recom-
  pense.   140
Your metamorphosed foe receives your
  gift
In satisfaction of all former wrongs.
This jewel I will wear here in my heart;
And, where before I thought her, for her
  wants, [2]
Too base to be my bride, to end all strife
I seal you my dear brother, her my wife.
SUS. You still exceed us. I will yield to
  fate,
And learn to love, where I till now did
  hate.
CHAR. With that enchantment you have
  charmed my soul
And made me rich even in those very
  words!   150
I pay no debt, but am indebted more;
Rich in your love, I never can be poor.
FRAN. All's mine is yours; we are alike in
  state;
Let's knit in love what was opposed in
  hate!
Come, for our nuptials we will straight
  provide,
Blessed only in our brother and fair bride.
                            Exeunt.

[SCENE XV.

A room in Frankford's house.]

Enter Cranwell, Frankford, and Nick.

CRAN. Why do you search each room
  about your house,
Now that you have despatched your
  wife away?
FRANK. O, sir, to see that nothing may be
  left
That ever was my wife's. I loved her
  dearly,
And, when I do but think of her unkindness,
My thoughts are all in hell; to avoid
  which torment,

I would not have a bodkin or a cuff,
A bracelet, necklace, or rabato wire,[1]
Nor anything that ever was called hers
Left me, by which I might remember her.
Seek round about.   11
NICK. 'Sblood! Master, here's her lute
flung in a corner.
FRANK. Her lute! O God! Upon this in-
strument
Her fingers have rung quick division,[2]
Sweeter than that which now divides our
hearts.
These frets have made me pleasant, that
have now
Frets of my heartstrings made. O, Mas-
ter Cranwell,
Oft hath she made this melancholy wood
(Now mute and dumb for her disastrous
chance)[3]
Speak sweetly many a note, sound many
a strain   20
To her own ravishing voice, which being
well strung,
What pleasant strange airs have they
jointly rung!—
Post with it after her!—Now nothing's left;
Of her and hers I am at once bereft.
NICK. I'll ride and overtake her, do my
message,
And come back again.   [_Exit._]
CRAN.   Meantime, sir, if you please,
I'll to Sir Francis Acton, and inform him
Of what hath passed betwixt you and
his sister.
FRANK. Do as you please.—How ill am I
bestead,[4]
To be a widower ere my wife be dead!
     [_Exeunt._]

[SCENE xvi.

On the road to Frankford's manor.]

_Enter Mistress Frankford, with Jenkin, her
maid Sisly, her Coachmen, and three
Carters._

ANNE. Bid my coach stay! Why should I
ride in state,
Being hurled so low down by the hand
of fate?
A seat like to my fortunes let me have—
Earth for my chair, and for my bed a
grave!

[1] Wire to support a ruff.   [2] Variations.
[3] Because of her misfortune.   [4] Situated.

JEN. Comfort, good mistress; you have
watered your coach with tears already.
You have but two mile now to go to
your manor. A man cannot say by my
old master Frankford as he may say by
me, that he wants manors; for he hath [10
three or four, of which this is one that we
are going to now.
SISLY. Good mistress, be of good cheer!
Sorrow, you see, hurts you, but helps you
not; we all mourn to see you so sad.
CARTER. Mistress, I see some of my landlord's men
Come riding post;[5] 'tis like he brings
some news.
ANNE. Comes he from M[aster] Frankford,
he is welcome;
So is his news, because they come from
him.

Enter Nick.

NICK. [_Presents lute._] There!   20
ANNE. I know the lute. Oft have I sung
to thee;
We both are out of tune, both out of
time.
NICK. Would that had been the worst
instrument that e'er you played on! My
master commends him unto ye. There's
all he can find that was ever yours; he
hath nothing left that ever you could lay
claim to but his own heart—and he could
afford you that! All that I have to deliver you is this: he prays you to [30
forget him, and so he bids you farewell.
ANNE. I thank him; he is kind, and ever
was.
All you that have true feeling of my grief,
That know my loss, and have relenting
hearts,
Gird me about, and help me with your
tears
To wash my spotted sins! My lute shall
groan;
It cannot weep, but shall lament my
moan.   [_She plays._]

Enter Wendoll [behind].

WEN. Pursued with horror of a guilty soul,
And with the sharp scourge of repentance
lashed,   39
I fly from mine own shadow. O my stars!
[5] Posthaste.

What have my parents in their lives
    deserved,
That you should lay this penance on
    their son?
When I but think of Master Frankford's
    love,
And lay it to my treason, or compare
My murthering him for his relieving
    me,
It strikes a terror like a lightning's flash,
To scorch my blood up. Thus I, like
    the owl,
Ashamed of day, live in these shadowy
    woods,
Afraid of every leaf or murmuring blast,
Yet longing to receive some perfect
    knowledge   50
How he hath dealt with her.   [*Sees
    Anne.*] O my sad fate!
Here, and so far from home, and thus
    attended!
O God! I have divorced the truest
    turtles [1]
That ever lived together, and, being
    divided,
In several places make their several
    moan;
She in the fields laments, and he at home.
So poets write that Orpheus made the
    trees
And stones to dance to his melodious
    harp,
Meaning the rustic and the barbarous
    hinds,   59
That had no understanding part in them;
So she from these rude carters tears
    extracts,
Making their flinty hearts with grief to
    rise,
And draw down rivers from their rocky
    eyes.
ANNE. [*To Nick.*] If you return unto my
    master, say
(Though not from me, for I am all
    unworthy
To blast his name so with a strumpet's
    tongue)
That you have seen me weep, wish my-
    self dead!
Nay, you may say, too (for my vow is
    passed),
Last night you saw me eat and drink
    my last.

[1] Turtledoves.

This to your master you may say and
    swear,   70
For it is writ in heaven, and decreed here.
NICK. I'll say you wept; I'll swear you
    made me sad.
Why, how now, eyes? What now?
    What's here to do?
I'm gone, or I shall straight turn baby too.
WEN. [*Aside.*] I cannot weep; my heart is
    all on fire.
Cursed be the fruits of my unchaste
    desire!
ANNE. Go, break this lute upon my coach's
    wheel,
As the last music that I e'er shall make—
Not as my husband's gift, but my
    farewell
To all earth's joy; and so your master
    tell!   80
NICK. If I can for crying.
WEN. [*Aside.*]   Grief, have done,
Or, like a madman, I shall frantic run.
ANNE. You have beheld the woefull'st
    wretch on earth,
A woman made of tears. Would you
    had words
To express but what you see! My inward
    grief
No tongue can utter, yet unto your power
You may describe my sorrow, and disclose
To thy sad master my abundant woes.
NICK. I'll do your commendations.
ANNE.   O, no!
I dare not so presume; nor to my
    children!   90
I am disclaimed in both; alas, I am!
O, never teach them, when they come to
    speak,
To name the name of mother. Chide
    their tongue,
If they by chance light on that hated
    word;
Tell them 'tis naught, for, when that
    word they name,
Poor, pretty souls, they harp on their
    own shame.
WEN. [*Aside.*] To recompense her wrongs,
    what canst thou do?
Thou hast made her husbandless and
    childless too.
ANNE. I have no more to say.—Speak not
    for me;
Yet you may tell your master what you
    see.   100

NICK. I'll do 't.   *Exit.*
WEN. [*Aside.*] I'll speak to her, and com-
fort her in grief.
O, but her wound cannot be cured with
words!
No matter, though; I'll do my best good
will
To work a cure on her whom I did kill.
ANNE. So, now unto my coach, then to
my home,
So to my deathbed, for from this sad
hour
I never will nor eat, nor drink, nor taste
Of any cates ¹ that may preserve my life.
I never will nor smile, nor sleep, nor rest;
But, when my tears have washed my
black soul white,   111
Sweet Savior, to Thy hands I yield my
sprite.
WEN. [*Coming forward.*] O, Mistress
Frankford!
ANNE.   O, for God's sake, fly!
The devil doth come to tempt me, ere
I die.
My coach!—This sin, that with an
angel's face
Conjured ² mine honor, till he sought my
wrack,
In my repentant eye seems ugly black.
Exeunt all [except Wendoll and Jenkin], the
Carters whistling.
JENK. What, my young master, that fled
in his shirt! How come you by your
clothes again? You have made our [120
house in a sweet pickle, ha' ye not, think
you? What, shall I serve you still, or
cleave to the old house?
WEN. Hence, slave! Away with thy unseasoned mirth!
Unless thou canst shed tears, and sigh,
and howl,
Curse thy sad fortunes, and exclaim on
fate,
Thou art not for my turn.
JENK. Marry, and you will not, another
will; farewell, and be hanged! Would you
had never come to have kept this [130
quoil ³ within our doors! We shall ha'
you run away like a sprite again. [*Exit.*]
WEN. She's gone to death; I live to want
and woe,
Her life, her sins, and all upon my head.

¹ Food.   ³ Coil, disturbance.
² Enchanted, seduced.

And I must now go wander, like a Cain,
In foreign countries and remoted climes,
Where the report of my ingratitude
Cannot be heard.   I'll over first to
France,
And so to Germany and Italy,
Where, when I have recovered, and by
travel   140
Gotten those perfect tongues,⁴ and that
these rumors
May in their height abate, I will return;
And I divine (however now dejected),
My worth and parts being by some great
man praised,
At my return I may in court be raised.
                                      Exit.

[SCENE xvii.

*Before the manor house.*⁵]

Enter Sir Francis, Sir Charles, Cranwell,
[Malby,] and Susan.

FRAN. Brother, and now my wife, I think
these troubles
Fall on my head by justice of the heav-
ens,
For being so strict to you in your ex-
tremities;
But we are now atoned.⁶ I would my
sister
Could with like happiness o'ercome her
griefs
As we have ours.
SUS. You tell us, Master Cranwell, won-
drous things
Touching the patience of that gentle-
man,
With what strange virtue he demeans ⁷
his grief.
CRAN. I told you what I was witness of; 10
It was my fortune to lodge there that
night.
FRAN. O, that same villain, Wardoll! 'Twas his tongue
That did corrupt her; she was of her-
self
Chaste and devoted well.⁸ Is this the
house?

⁴ Learned those languages perfectly.
⁵ The scene shifts to the interior of the house
during the action.
⁶ Reconciled.
⁷ Manages.
⁸ *I.e.,* true to her marriage vow.

CRAN. Yes, sir; I take it, here your sister lies.

FRAN. My brother Frankford showed too mild a spirit
In the revenge of such a loathéd crime.
Less than he did, no man of spirit could do.
I am so far from blaming his revenge,
That I commend it. Had it been my case,   20
Their souls at once had from their breasts been freed;
Death to such deeds of shame is the due meed.

Enter Jenkin [and Sisly].

JEN. O my mistress, mistress! My poor mistress!

SISLY. Alas, that ever I was born! What shall I do for my poor mistress?

CHAR. Why, what of her?

JENK. O Lord, sir, she no sooner heard that her brother and her friends were come to see how she did, but she, for [30 very shame of her guilty conscience, fell into such a swound that we had much ado to get life in her.

SUS. Alas, that she should bear so hard a fate!
Pity it is repentance comes too late.

FRAN. Is she so weak in body?

JENK. O, sir, I can assure you there's no hope of life in her, for she will take no sust'nance. She hath plainly starved herself, and now she's as lean as a lath. She [40 ever looks for the good hour. Many gentlemen and gentlewomen of the country are come to comfort her.

Enter Mistress Frankford in her bed.[1]

MAL. How fare you, Mistress Frankford?

ANNE. Sick, sick, O, sick! Give me some air, I pray!
Tell me, O, tell me, where's Master Frankford?
Will not [he] deign to see me ere I die?

MAL. Yes, Mistress Frankford; divers gentlemen,
Your loving neighbors, with that just request

[1] Either the bed was pushed onto the stage or the curtains of the inner stage were drawn to disclose her.

Have moved and told him of your weak estate,   50
Who, though with much ado to get belief,
Examining of the general circumstance,
Seeing your sorrow and your penitence,
And hearing therewithal the great desire
You have to see him, ere you left the world,
He gave to us his faith to follow us,
And sure he will be here immediately.

ANNE. You have half revived me with the pleasing news.
Raise me a little higher in my bed.
Blush I not, brother Acton? Blush I not, Sir Charles?   60
Can you not read my fault writ in my cheek?
Is not my crime there? Tell me, gentlemen.

CHAR. Alas, good mistress, sickness hath not left you
Blood in your face enough to make you blush.

ANNE. Then sickness, like a friend, my fault would hide.
Is my husband come? My soul but tarries
His arrive; then I am fit for heaven.

FRAN. I came to chide you, but my words of hate
Are turned to pity and compassionate grief.
I came to rate you, but my brawls, you see,   70
Melt into tears, and I must weep by thee.—
Here's M[aster] Frankford now.

Enter Frankford.

FRANK. Good morrow, brother; morrow, gentlemen!
God, that hath laid this cross upon our heads,
Might, had He pleased, have made our cause of meeting
On a more fair and more contented ground;
But He that made us, made us to this woe.

ANNE. And is he come? Methinks that voice I know.

FRANK. How do you, woman?

ANNE. Well, M[aster] Frankford, well; but shall be better, 80
I hope, within this hour. Will you vouchsafe,
Out of your grace and your humanity,
To take a spotted strumpet by the hand?

FRANK. This hand once held my heart in faster bonds
Than now 'tis gripped by me. God pardon them
That made us first break hold!

ANNE. Amen, amen!
Out of my zeal to heaven, whither I'm now bound,
I was so impudent to wish you here,
And once more beg your pardon. O, good man, 89
And father to my children, pardon me.
Pardon, O, pardon me! My fault so heinous is
That, if you in this world forgive it not,
Heaven will not clear it in the world to come.
Faintness hath so usurped upon my knees,
That kneel I cannot; but on my heart's knees
My prostrate soul lies thrown down at your feet,
To beg your gracious pardon. Pardon, O, pardon me!

FRANK. As freely, from the low depth of my soul,
As my Redeemer hath forgiven His death,
I pardon thee. I will shed tears for thee, pray with thee, 100
And, in mere pity of thy weak estate,
I'll wish to die with thee.

ALL. So do we all.

NICK. So will not I;
I'll sigh and sob, but, by my faith, not die.

FRAN. O, Master Frankford, all the near alliance
I lose by her shall be supplied in thee.
You are my brother by the nearest way;
Her kindred hath fallen off, but yours doth stay.

FRANK. Even as I hope for pardon at that day
When the great Judge of Heaven in scarlet sits,

So be thóu pardoned! Though thy rash offense 110
Divorced our bodies, thy repentant tears
Unite our souls.

CHAR. Then comfort, Mistress Frankford!
You see your husband hath forgiven your fall;
Then rouse your spirits, and cheer your fainting soul!

SUS. How is it with you?

FRAN. How d' ye feel yourself?

ANNE. Not of this world.

FRANK. I see you are not, and I weep to see it.
My wife, the mother to my pretty babes!
Both those lost names I do restore thee back, 119
And with this kiss I wed thee once again.
Though thou art wounded in thy honored name,
And with that grief upon thy deathbed liest,
Honest in heart, upon my soul, thou diest.

ANNE. Pardoned on earth, soul, thou in heaven art free;
Once more thy wife dies, thus embracing thee. [Dies.]

FRANK. New-married, and new-widowed!— O! she's dead,
And a cold grave must be her nuptial bed.

CHAR. Sir, be of good comfort, and your heavy sorrow
Part equally amongst us. Storms divided
Abate their force, and with less rage are guided. 130

CRAN. Do, Master Frankford; he that hath least part
Will find enough to drown one troubled heart.

FRAN. Peace with thee, Nan!—Brothers and gentlemen,
All we that can plead interest in her grief,
Bestow upon her body funeral tears!
Brother, had you with threats and usage bad
Punished her sin, the grief of her offense

Had not with such true sorrow touched her heart.

FRANK. I see it had not; therefore, on her grave
Will I bestow this funeral epitaph,   140
Which on her marble tomb shall be engraved.
In golden letters shall these words be filled:
Here lies she whom her husband's kindness killed.

FINIS.

THE EPILOGUE

AN honest crew, disposéd to be merry,
  Came to a tavern by, and called for wine.
The drawer brought it, smiling like a cherry,
  And told them it was pleasant, neat,[1] and fine.
"Taste it," quoth one. He did so. "Fie!" quoth he,

[1] Pure.

"This wine was good; now 't runs too near the lee."[2]

Another sipped, to give the wine his due,
  And said unto the rest it drunk too flat;
The third said it was old; the fourth, too new;
  "Nay," quoth the fift, " the sharpness likes me not."   10
Thus, gentlemen, you see how, in one hour,
The wine was new, old, flat, sharp, sweet, and sour.

Unto this wine we do allude[3] our play,
  Which some will judge too trivial, some too grave.
You as our guests we entertain this day,
  And bid you welcome to the best we have.
Excuse us, then; good wine may be disgraced
When every several mouth hath sundry taste.

[2] Lees.   [3] Compare.